History of the NASUWT

National Association of Schoolmasters Union of Women Teachers

1919-2002

'The Story of a Battling Minority'

by Nigel de Gruchy

"Give us justice or we fight!" was the 1919 clarion call of the Union's founding leaders which echoed down the years. Whether it was outrageous denial of recognition, or low pay with negotiations conducted in secrecy, or voluntary 'duties' taken for granted, or controversial hikes in pension contributions (1956 and 1972 are being repeated today) or being expected to teach disruptive pupils in impossible circumstances, the NASUWT believed in the unique feature distinguishing a genuine trade union from other types of organisation – the willingness of employees to challenge by direct action gross injustice perpetrated by employers and government.

However, the NASUWT preferred compromise and consensus. National incomes policies and social contracts were supported, subject to fairness and even application to all. Third party intervention in salary negotiations proved more productive than the 'jungle of free collective bargaining'. The History of the NASUWT ends on an optimistic and positive note welcoming the Social Partnership with the Labour Government in the early 2000s. The wanton destruction of that productive relationship between government and all but one of the school teacher unions after the general election of 2010 by the Coalition Parties is in the words of the author "reckless and deplorable".

History of the NASUWT

Published 2013 by Abramis Academic Publishing

www.abramis.co.uk

ISBN 978 1 84549 578 7

© NASUWT 2013

Printed and bound in the United Kingdom

Typeset in Garamond 11/14

Abramis Academic Publishing
ASK House, Northgate Avenue
Bury St Edmunds, Suffolk IP32 6BB
t: (+44) 01284 700321

www.abramis.co.uk

I dedicate this book to my wife Judy and all other long-suffering spouses and partners of career teachers who 'get hooked' on the NASUWT.

Nigel de Gruchy

Acknowledgements

I would like to thank the NASUWT for all the co-operation and material help afforded me in writing this book. While I kept my own copies of many publications I have been granted free access to official NASUWT records and archives, the latter being housed at Warwick University.

I owe particular thanks to Patrick Roach, Deputy General Secretary, and Roger Darke, former Assistant General Secretary now retired, who read the first drafts, offering good advice and constructive criticism. They were joined in that exercise by Chris Wrigley, Professor of History at Nottingham University, who in addition offered invaluable help in setting the book in a wider and more accurate historical context. It also fell to Patrick to be my point of contact with the NASUWT and to deal on its behalf with all the business associated with the publisher.

Several other colleagues, staff and elected officers read parts of the original draft concerning events in which they had direct first-hand experience and were able to ensure factual accuracy as well as providing interesting insights. Fred Smithies (GS 1983-90) offered valuable comments on the first draft, and the (sadly) late John Scott (President, 1974) gave me great assistance in writing the chapter on Northern Ireland. Former Assistant Secretary Frank Howard and NE Regional Official Colin McInnes afforded me much help in relevant areas, and good friend and neighbour Neil Proudfoot, history specialist and former Bromley Secretary, read the first draft and offered detailed comments and corrections as befits a practising teacher. Sue Rogers, a Past-President and Honorary Treasurer, read the first draft and gave me encouragement to continue with the long exercise. Another Past-President and Honorary Treasurer, Mick Carney, also offered much support and made helpful comments especially in relation to disputes in Durham where he had also been the Negotiating Secretary. Solicitor David Haywood offered helpful comments on the Sacred Heart – Teesside Dispute. Last and by no means least colleagues at Rednal, particularly Paul Machlachlan and Angie Grant in the Union's services and records departments, assisted me greatly in securing relevant information and files.

Author's Note

Winston Churchill, preparing his memoirs, observed that: "History will be kind to me, for I intend to write it."

I bestow a lot of praise upon the National Association of Schoolmasters Union of Women Teachers (NASUWT). It is history as seen through NASUWT eyes and it would be idle to pretend otherwise. While unashamedly proud of the Union I also refer to mistakes and record some criticism. Readers can make their own judgements. I believe passionately that it is a story worth telling. The Union can lay claim to have become the most successful 'breakaway' union in British industrial relations history.

This book was never intended to be just a list of facts resembling nearly 90 'joined-up annual reports'. I offer the views and interpretations of events as expressed by NASUWT leaders over the years. I often allow my own views to encroach, especially from the 1970s onwards when the book also assumes an element of the autobiographical as I became personally involved.

The book begins with events leading up to the formation of the breakaway NAS in 1919 and finishes around the time of my retirement as General Secretary of the NASUWT in 2002. I extend the coverage a little mainly to incorporate the adoption of the National Agreement on Standards and Workload in 2003/04, which marked the birth of Social Partnership between (most of) the teacher and other staff unions and the New Labour Government. I believe this became a historically significant time in teacher union affairs, marking as it did the end of the 'battling minority' when, as the twenty-first century got under way, the NASUWT took over the majority role and assumed the leadership of the school teaching profession.

Some matters have inevitably been omitted to contain the story within reasonable limits. I dwell in detail on other events when I believe they are more interesting and illustrate the unique character of the NASUWT. I have tried to combine a chronological with a thematic approach.

History of the NASUWT is also in part intended to remind teachers and other employees of the need to insist upon fairness. Where that is absent the kind of courage and determination shown by NASUWT members in the past and described in this book is required. In 1920 addressing the inaugural Annual Conference A.E. Warren, our first President and General Secretary, established the tradition:

"These are days when to right the wrong you are compelled to adopt measures which may be distasteful to you."

Alas we had to fight militantly and this book makes no apology for that.

Hopefully the next 'historian' of the NASUWT, taking up the story from where I leave it at the opening of the twenty-first century, will be able to write about a more co-operative and productive time in the relationship between teachers and Government. Partnership is preferable to the traditional and confrontational ways of the past, but trade unions can only adopt such an approach in a context where employees are treated with dignity and justice.

Over 50 years ago in 1957 the Executive established a committee to write a history of the Union. The 'chapters' were readily divided up; the invitations to write were many, the volunteers few. The committee met periodically for the next three years but no book appeared. I hope I have met the committee's ambition, albeit too late for any of them to read it.

In conclusion I must emphasise that an authoritative NASUWT view on current issues is only available from the Union itself.

Nigel de Gruchy

PS These words were obviously drafted during a period of unparalleled and fruitful co-operation between teachers' unions and government which led to higher standards of pupil achievement and enhanced morale within the profession with improved pay and conditions of service. The speed with which these welcome developments have been dismantled by the Coalition Government post the general election of 2010 (not to mention the wider attacks upon public services) is as startling as it is reckless and disgraceful.

About the Author

Nigel de Gruchy was born in 1943 in the Channel Island of Jersey under the German Occupation during the Second World War. He was educated at De La Salle College in Jersey before attending Reading University from which he graduated in July 1965 with an Honours Degree in Economics and Social Philosophy. Nigel de Gruchy met his American wife Judy in Paris in 1966. They married in 1970 and have one son, Paul, born in 1975.

After graduation Nigel de Gruchy spent three years mainly teaching English as a foreign language in Spain and France where he witnessed at first hand the general strike and student riots of 1968 whilst also gaining a Diploma in French from the University of Paris. Coming over to London in the autumn of 1968 he secured a post as Head of the Economics Department at St. Joseph's Academy, a grammar school that went comprehensive in the Lewisham Division of the ILEA. He gained the Post Graduate Certificate of Education in July 1969 from the Institute of Education, London University, as an external student.

Nigel de Gruchy soon became active in the then NAS, rising through the ranks to become London Secretary and National Executive Member from 1975-78. In 1978 he joined the staff of NASUWT as an Assistant Secretary, becoming Deputy General Secretary in 1983. He assumed the office of General Secretary in April 1990, retiring from that position in 2002. He was a member of the TUC General Council from 1989 – 2003, becoming TUC President 2002-03. He was nominated by the TUC to be a UK union member of the Duke of Edinburgh Commonwealth Study Conference in 1974 and as a representative on the Accountancy Foundation from 1999-2004. From 1993 – 2004 he served on the Executive Board of Education International, a worldwide organisation of unions representing some 30 million teachers in over 300 unions from 164 countries.

When Nigel de Gruchy joined the then NAS early in 1969 it had some 41,000 members. On his retirement in 2002 the NASUWT membership exceeded 211,000.

Foreword
By Professor Chris Wrigley, University of Nottingham

One feature of twentieth century British history that is rarely commented on is the great growth of white collar trade unionism in Britain. In 1920, at the peak of trade union membership before the 1970s, white collar trade unionists were 13 % of all trade unionists. By 1979 they were 40% of trade unionists. The change in weight of union membership away from older to newer industrial sectors and then to service sectors was a feature of the nineteenth and twentieth centuries. In recent decades a range of white collar unions have been prominent in British trade unionism, and among these the teaching unions have been vocal and influential. The rise of NASUWT has been very impressive and has been a story very much needing to be told.

The NASUWT's origins lie in a small breakaway group, whose main issue was a highly inauspicious cause - opposing equal pay for women teachers. While breakaway unions were not uncommon in the first half of the twentieth century, they rarely thrived. NASUWT has been the biggest exception. It developed into a large and highly effective union, which has not been afraid to defend individual members in unreasonable predicaments as a result of upholding good standards in schools. It has much to be proud of, not least in the dark years of Thatcherism. From being a breakaway from the National Union of Teachers, it has gone on to be its major rival, and by the early twenty first century was very close to being its equal in size.

NASUWT has been very fortunate in having Nigel de Gruchy as its historian. He brings to this history his passionate belief in the union he has served so well, rare knowledge of its inner workings and the issues of recent decades as well as skills in writing interestingly yet analytically. He is writing at a time when many memories of union activists of the post Second World War period can still be tapped. He has also been assiduous in researching the union's archives.

The history of NASUWT is fascinating. It casts new light on education and society as well as on a major area of white collar trade unionism. It is a big book, but it could easily have been bigger, given the many important aspects of NASUWT's history. Although the union was initially Canute-like in resisting gender equality in teaching, this was a passing phase. Certainly, since those early days, the union can be very proud of its record in defending male and female teachers' interests while promoting the best interests of education for pupils, their parents and the country.

Sources

The NASUWT

Minutes and agendae of Annual Conferences, the National Executive and local associations.

Annual reports presented to Conference.

Correspondence.

Reports to schools, policy statements, booklets and press notices.

Publications including:

The New Schoolmaster, The New Schoolmaster & Career Teacher, London Schoolmaster and some local association newsletters.

Equal Pay, February 1921, published by the London Schoolmasters' Association, written by G.M. Graves, F.R.A. Jarvis and Alfred N. Pocock.

Schoolmasters' Salaries Since the Beginning of the 20th Century, September 1957, published by the NAS, written by H. Meigh BSc, President 1949-50.

Action 1919-1969 – A record of the growth of the NAS, published by the NAS, edited by Bernard Morton, President 1948-49.

"The Schoolmasters – A History of the NAS and of Education in its Time", September 1972, unpublished typescript with 200 copies circulated internally, written by R.A. Simons, President 1970-71.

"The Evolution of the NASUWT in Northern Ireland (1961-1985), A Dissertation leading to the Degree of Master of Education, Queen's University of Belfast", written by Jeffrey Hamilton, a member of the Union.

External

Government reports and official statistics, including *Hansard* and ONS.

Reports and publications from local education authorities (LEAs) and material from teachers' associations.

Reports of the Burnham Committee and other national bodies.

National and local newspapers and journals, especially the *Times Educational Supplement (TES)* and *Education*.

Frequently used acronyms in addition to NASUWT

Note: I often use 'the Association' when referring to the NAS and 'the Union' when referring to the NASUWT.

Unions

HMA: Head Masters' Association

AHM: Association of Head Mistresses

SHA Secondary Heads Association (formed by HMA and AHM)

ASCL: Association of School and College Leaders (SHA renamed)

AMA: Assistant Masters Association

AAM: Association of Assistant Mistresses

AMMA: Assistant Masters and Mistresses Association (formed by AMA and AAM)

The AMA, AAM, HMA and AHM were also known collectively as the Joint Four.

NUT: National Union of Teachers

PAT: Professional Association of Teachers

EIS: Educational Institute of Scotland

ATTI: Association of Teachers in Technical Institutions

NATFHE: National Association of Teachers in Further and Higher Education (ATTI combined with other education unions and renamed)

UCL: University and College Lecturers (formed from Association of University Teachers and NATFHE)

TUC: Trades Union Congress

Government

The State Department of Education has been officially entitled:

1870   Board of Education

1944   Ministry of Education

1964   DES – Department for Education and Science

1992   DFE – Department for Education

1995   DfEE – Department for Education and Employment

2001   DfES – Department for Education and Skills

2005 DfCSF – Department for Children, Schools and Families
2010 DfE   –   Department for Education

Local government and employers
LEA: Local Education Authority
AEC: Association of Education Committees
MBC: Metropolitan Borough Council
CC: County Council
AMA: Association of Metropolitan Authorities
ACC: Association of County Councils
LCC: London County Council
ILEA: Inner London Education Authority

Educational/governmental bodies
HMI: Her Majesty's Inspector (Inspectorate)
OFSTED: Office for Standards in Education (which incorporates HMI)
NCC: National Curriculum Council
SEAC: School Examinations and Assessment Council
SCAA: Schools Curriculum and Assessment Authority (which combined NCC and SEAC)
GTC: General Teaching Council
ACAS: Advisory, Conciliation and Arbitration Service

Miscellaneous
GS: General Secretary
DGS: Deputy GS
AGS: Assistant GS
NEM: National Executive Member
EP: Equal Pay
WP: Working Party
NC: National Curriculum
FE: Further Education
HE: Higher Education
School Rep: School Representative

Commendations for *History of the NASUWT*

Like the sound bites he delivered so pithily when I interviewed him for BBC News, Nigel de Gruchy's account moves at a blistering pace and plunges unhesitatingly to the heart of the key controversies in educational policy.

The chapter on arguably the union's greatest triumph – the legal victory to uphold teachers' rights to boycott the national curriculum tests in 1993 – is written with the verve, suspense and excitement of a political thriller. This is partisan history, but all the more fascinating for that.

The NASUWT has strongly divided opinion in education ever since it emerged as a breakaway group of male teachers unhappy with the National Union of Teachers' stance over equal pay. No doubt this book will cause further apoplexy amongst the union's opponents.

From its development as the champion of "the career teacher" to its determination to stand up to pupil indiscipline, this union's history provides a fascinating insight into past and current controversies. It's also a great read.

Mike Baker *(deceased, 21 September 2012)*
Education journalist and broadcaster, BBC and *The Guardian*.

No-one could deny that Nigel de Gruchy was a pivotal figure on the education scene in the two decades up to the early part of this century. His knack was to be able to sum up a complex educational argument in a pithy phrase or two – which stayed in the mind and often helped those involved to focus on solving the core of the problem. "Industrial action with a halo" comes to mind over the union's attempts to tackle discipline issues as does the "pupil friendly" great 'Test Boycott' of 1993. His insight into the history of his union is therefore a must read for all those connected with teacher trade unionism and the wider education issues the NASUWT has been involved with.

Richard Garner
Education Editor, *The Independent*

Contents

	Page
Acknowledgements	iv
Author's Note	v
About the Author	vii
Foreword	viii
Sources	ix
Frequently used acronyms in addition to NASUWT	x
Commendations for *History of the NASUWT*	xii

SECTION ONE
The Genesis of the NASUWT

Chapter 1	Introduction	1
Chapter 2	Not the Best Time for Equal Pay	4
Chapter 3	The Birth of the NAS	9
Chapter 4	Steps to Secession	18
Chapter 5	The Birth of the Union of Women Teachers	35
Chapter 6	The Divided Profession	44

SECTION TWO
THE LONG HARD SLOG

Chapter 7	The NAS in the 1920s	48
Chapter 8	Men Teachers for Boys	54
Chapter 9	The NAS in the 1930s	61
Chapter 10	Second World War Years	73
Chapter 11	The NAS and the 1944 Education Act	89
Chapter 12	The NAS Rebuilds after the War	93
Chapter 13	The School Meals Service	101

SECTION THREE
THE BATTLE OF BURNHAM
The 40 year campaign for recognition

Chapter 14	Moving the Goalposts	112

Chapter 15   Mood Moves to Militancy   128
Chapter 16   Saturday 25 February 1961   135
Chapter 17   And so to Action   143
Chapter 18   'No Co-operation without Representation'   156
Chapter 19   Burnham Cinders Smoulder   165

SECTION FOUR
TEACHERS' PAY 1900-1976

Chapter 20   Introduction to Teachers' Pay   178
Chapter 21   Cuts upon Cuts – The 1930s   188
Chapter 22   Salaries during the Second World War   199
Chapter 23   Pay after 1945   206
Chapter 24   "The Calamity of 1956" –   212
              Including the Sunderland Case
Chapter 25   Teachers' Salaries after Equal Pay   234
Chapter 26   The 1960s – The End of Servility   239
Chapter 27   The NASUWT Breaks Through in the 1970s   251
Chapter 28   The 1971 Arbitration   263
Chapter 29   One Step Forward, Two Steps Back   271
Chapter 30   The Houghton Heights   276

SECTION FIVE
TEACHERS' PENSIONS
The Notorious Notional Fund

Chapter 31   The Birth of the Teacher's Pension   289
Chapter 32   The NASUWT Sets the Agenda   294
Chapter 33   Defending Teachers' Pensions into   316
              the Twenty-First Century

SECTION SIX
THE RISE OF MILITANCY
The 1960s and after

Chapter 34   'Professional or Union'   323
Chapter 35   Reports on Education   327
Chapter 36   Northern Ireland   334
Chapter 37   '10/65' – The Comprehensive Revolution   343
Chapter 38   Battles over the Teacher's Contract   354

Chapter 39	Embracing the Wider Labour Movement	374
Chapter 40	The General Teaching Council	387
Chapter 41	The Durham Dispute 1969	397
Chapter 42	Sacred Heart School – Teesside Dispute	411
Chapter 43	The NAS and the UWT Merge	429
Chapter 44	The Merged NASUWT Becomes a Major Union	437
Chapter 45	The NASUWT Impacts on the Education Scene	450

SECTION 7
BATTLING ANTISOCIAL BEHAVIOUR IN SCHOOLS

Chapter 46	The Retreat from Authority	463
Chapter 47	The 'Grand Graffiti Dispute'	480
Chapter 48	The Elton Report	490
Chapter 49	The Bishop of Llandaff School Dispute	495
Chapter 50	Inappropriate Inclusion	497
Chapter 51	'Lots of Advice; Little Help'	504
Chapter 52	Glaisdale Refusal to Teach Hits Headlines	509
Chapter 53	Upheaval at Hebburn	517
Chapter 54	Madness at Manton	524
Chapter 55	Riot at The Ridings	542
Chapter 56	New Labour – Old Problems	565
Chapter 57	Refusal to Teach Challenged in the Courts	572
Chapter 58	The Big One – 'P' versus NASUWT	584
Chapter 59	High Noon in the House of Lords	595

SECTION 8
THE DESCENT INTO DEBACLE
Teachers' Negotiations 1977-1987

Chapter 60	Houghton Surrendered	604
Chapter 61	The Storms before the Tempest	614
Chapter 62	The Great Disaster of 1985	624
Chapter 63	Burnham begins to Topple	638
Chapter 64	Restructuring Resurrected	650
Chapter 65	Collapse at Coventry	663
Chapter 66	Government Passes the Death Sentence	675
Chapter 67	Nottingham in November	679
Chapter 68	The Execution	684

SECTION 9
THE NEW ERA
National Curriculum
The Great 'Test Boycott'
The New Pay Regime

Chapter 69	The Education Reform Act 1988	696
Chapter 70	The New Pay Regime	706
Chapter 71	A Pay Review Body for Teachers	726
Chapter 72	The Great 'Test Boycott'	730
Chapter 73	War Against Workload Continues	763
Chapter 74	Pay – Normal Service Resumed	773
Chapter 75	Life under New Labour	783
Chapter 76	"Let Teachers Teach"	788
Chapter 77	The Green Light for the Green Paper	800
Chapter 78	Crossing the Threshold	819
Chapter 79	Cover to Contract	825
Chapter 80	Social Partnership is Born	831

SECTION 10
CONCLUSION

Chapter 81	Conclusion	847

Appendices

Appendix A – Presidents of NAS, UWT and NASUWT	855
Appendix B – Honorary Treasurers	859
Appendix C – General Secretaries	860
Appendix D – NASUWT Membership 1923-2008	861
Appendix E - NASUWT Membership – 'Market Share'	862
Appendix F – Inflation	863
Appendix G – Average Salaries – England & Wales	864
Appendix H – Educational Policy Publications 1980s	866
Appendix J – Equality Publications Post 1988 – Education Reform Act	868

Notes to Appendices	870

Index	872

SECTION ONE
The Genesis of the NASUWT

Chapter 1 - Introduction

The history of the National Association of Schoolmasters Union of Women Teachers (NASUWT) is the account of 'a battling minority' willing to stand up, be counted and if necessary struggle against the odds and sometimes the prevailing views of the time.

The National Association of Schoolmasters (NAS) was born in 1919, the Union of Women Teachers (UWT) in 1965. They merged through a charmingly entitled technical legal procedure called a Transfer of Engagements on 1 January 1976.

It is wrong to allege that the breakaway of several thousand schoolmasters shortly after the end of the First World War from the largest established organisation, the National Union of Teachers (NUT), was _solely_ due to the then controversial issue of equal pay. 'Men teachers', as they first referred to themselves, were equally concerned with the failure of their colleagues in the NUT and other associations to stand up and fight for decent salaries for the whole profession.

They also believed passionately that the teaching profession should include a reasonable number of men to participate in the education of the nation's schoolboys. "Men teachers for boys" was a clarion call for many a year. How to secure an appropriate gender balance in the teaching profession remains an issue today.

The establishment of the UWT in 1965, initiated by a group of determined career-minded women teachers in a school in Brighton, also reflected their concerns with the lack of resolve on the part of other unions.

History of the NASUWT begins with an account of a relatively small band of determined men, some 5,000 in number, forming their own union against formidable odds. Many of them were ex-servicemen returning from the horrors of the First World War. They were accustomed to long, hard fights.

The courage and determination of our 'founding fathers' may partly explain why the NAS did not suffer the fate of most breakaway unions – mushrooming up followed by steady decline into history, if not oblivion. The fact that a significant element of breaking away from the NUT rested on the doomed principle of unequal pay makes the survival and subsequent growth of the Association all the more remarkable.

Apart from the founding dates, if there are only two 'defining years' in the history of the NASUWT they have to be 1961 and 1976. In 1961 the then NAS secured representation on the official body dealing with teachers' pay, the Burnham Committee. That was the year breakaway became breakthrough. Membership rose dramatically from 22,000 to 30,000. On 1 January 1976 the NAS and the UWT merged, giving both 'constituents' access to the entire career teacher 'market'. The ghost of unequal pay was well and truly laid to rest. Once again membership soared, within a couple of years passing the 'magic' 100,000 mark and placing the NASUWT in the 'first division' of trade unions.

Perhaps it was more than coincidence that in 1961 Shirley Lerner published her book *Breakaway Unions*. She wrote that breakaway unions were "manifestations of crises which occur when a section of the rank and file lose confidence in their union and develop different goals". The one-time powerful National Union of Miners (NUM) and its predecessor, the Miners' Federation of Great Britain, provided excellent examples of the fate of breakaways. Disputes in 1926 and in 1984/85 led to breakaways in Nottinghamshire, and internal conflicts led to schisms in Scotland in the 1930s. In 1929 there were notable breakaway unions formed amongst clothing workers and London bus drivers and in 1945 amongst post office engineers. None of those survived for very long.

The NAS proved the exception to the rule. One reason for the early NAS's ability 'to survive and prosper' must surely be that in the context of post-First World War Britain opposition to equal pay for women would not have cast the schoolmasters into the social pariahs they would undoubtedly and deservedly be regarded today.

Although the NAS was on the wrong side of history in relation to equal pay, on most of the other 'big issues' I believe the Association 'got it right', enabling it to defy the fate reserved for most 'breakaways'. The NASUWT's pragmatic philosophy, reflected in a cautious approach to reform based on experience and educational rather than social and political considerations, proved to be tellingly right over the long term. The Union's policies on teachers' salaries, conditions of service, pensions and negotiating machinery, combined with a willingness to make a stand at the right time on the right issue, better reflected the aspirations of those who intended to make teaching their lifelong career. In more recent times the need and willingness to tackle antisocial behaviour in schools set the NASUWT apart from and miles ahead of its rival organisations.

One NAS campaign, for official recognition by central and local Government, took nearly 40 years to be realised. Less determined people would surely have thrown in the towel years beforehand.

In the early years of the twenty-first century as the NASUWT approached its 90th birthday, in-service membership reached and surpassed 250,000. The NASUWT became firmly ensconced in the 'top ten' unions of both the British Trades Union Congress (TUC) and Education International, the worldwide body representing over 26 million teachers in 314 unions from 164 different countries. The NASUWT became every bit the equal of, if not more influential than, its great historical rival, the NUT. The welcome Social Partnership that finally developed with the New Labour Government around the same time saw the NASUWT emerge as the leading schoolteacher union participant.

Above all the NASUWT aspired to be the voice of the teacher in the classroom. NASUWT members over the years constantly expressed regret and frustration that education was frequently bedevilled by an endless parade of politicians, pundits and bureaucrats holding sway in the corridors of power. These people have on occasions plunged the service into ill-informed, badly implemented and contradictory reforms. Standards of achievement have risen sometimes in spite of, not because of, them.

My own 'thesis' of the history of education in Britain is that many mistakes could have been avoided and better decisions made had those in power heeded the voice of the teacher in the classroom. In turn classroom teachers could have made more strenuous efforts to ensure their views were being accurately articulated and then summoned more courage to stand up and fight for their beliefs.

History of the NASUWT is the story of how that voice often struggled to be heard but refused to go away.

Chapter 2 – Not the Best Time for Equal Pay

There were two major tensions producing serious divisions within the NUT by 1919. One was the equal pay policy; the other was the lack of determination on the part of the majority in the NUT to fight for the interests of all teachers, male and female. I deal with the former in this chapter, the latter being a constant theme that emerges throughout the history of the teaching profession and the NASUWT.

No purpose is served in being in denial or too defensive about the opposition to equal pay. It was wrong in principle but arguably understandable when set in the context of the time. Perhaps the biggest question over equal pay remains simply: Was it genuine? In tracing the history of teachers' pay I found much evidence that it was achieved by squeezing all teachers' salaries – men's severely, women's moderately – to achieve equality at a depressed level.

During the First World War women had contributed greatly to the national endeavour in a variety of employments that previously had been mostly or entirely for men. Notably they replaced enlisted men in the munitions factories. They had worked effectively and in so doing brought into greater question the wage gaps between men and women. Teaching had long been one of several areas where women were accepted as employees although they continued to suffer a perhaps greater injustice than unequal pay in so far as many were still forced to leave teaching upon marriage. That outrageous injustice was not finally and completely removed until outlawed under the 1944 Education Act.

During the course of the First World War, with many men teachers enlisted in the armed services, women became a majority in teaching. Their work and responsibilities burgeoned as they took over from the men and also covered for other schools closed for hospital or military purposes.

Male employees were often openly hostile to equal pay. The engineering industry experienced men sabotaging machinery which had come to be used by women employees during the First World War. The Government was forced to give guarantees that, after the end of the war, women would leave engineering factories. This was carried out under the Restoration of Pre-War Practices Act of 1919. There was a notable friction in other areas, not least in transport. Grading and job demarcation techniques were also used for this purpose. The entry of women into 'professional occupations' such as medicine, dentistry and accountancy was in practice severely restricted.

Schoolmasters protested they were not misogynists. They claimed their wives and families would be the biggest victims of equal pay. Men knew women were a natural majority in teaching and believed they would suffer financially if the gender gap in pay were closed. The two pay rates would meet 'somewhere in-between'.

Both sides failed to acknowledge the concerns of the other. The NUT offered no sympathy to the fears of the men. Indeed the NUT took a very proactive and hostile approach. Tom Smith was a young schoolmaster in the North East who joined the NAS in 1928. He was to become a very prominent figure in the Association's affairs and was President in 1955-56, a very eventful year for the NAS. My 'freshman' Annual Conference, Torquay 1971, was the last one in which Tom played an active part. We were both on the London delegation and I recall being very impressed with Tom's public speaking. He lived to the ripe old age of 97. I interviewed him with this book in mind a few years before he died. He told amusing but revealing stories of NUT representatives picketing recruitment meetings of the NAS to try to persuade young teachers to turn around and go home. If they did not take the advice offered they were threatened with all manner of things, including blighted career prospects, not to mention being cold shouldered by other teaching colleagues.

Such stories were corroborated in a series of articles in *The New Schoolmaster* in 1969 written by another great servant of the Association, Eric Arnott from Leeds, who joined the NAS in 1926 and rose to become President in 1958-59.

Therein lies an intriguing if unanswerable but huge historical question. Would NUT have better prevented the NAS's growth by a 'more in sorrow than anger approach' smothering 'misguided' people with kindness and regret rather than making martyrs of men already more militant and motivated than most?

Women through the suffragette movement had secured the right for those over 32 to vote in 1918. Full suffrage would come in 1929 following the 1928 Act. Women were naturally emboldened by their success. Equal pay, at least in principle was bound to come, even if it was going to take a long time.

Teachers seemed to be as civic minded as any occupational group and it was not surprising they were well to the forefront in campaigning for equal pay. The NAS pointed out that teaching had a majority of women. Granting equal pay in that context had different implications from other occupations where women were in a minority.

The economic circumstances could not have been worse. A time of expansion and prosperity with everyone's wages improving, even if women were benefiting at a faster rate, would undoubtedly have been a more propitious period for such a social revolution. Instead the 1920s and '30s turned out to be a period of deep depression and salary cuts.

The Geddes Committee on National Expenditure was established in 1922. The resulting report, known as the Geddes Axe, imposed savage cuts in educational (and other) expenditure, chiefly but not solely at the direct expense of teachers' salaries and pensions. A similar development took place at the beginning of the 1930s with the May Committee set up for the same purpose, producing a 10% cut in salaries.

In the event everybody in teaching seemed to lose out. The schoolmasters decided they had no alternative but to fight on their own. Equal pay was never going to be conceded by the Governments of the time. The only way of avoiding schism would have been for both sides to have adopted more consensual approaches. There were many problems demanding solutions, but not through pay discrimination.

Significantly the NUT Conferences of 1917 and 1918 rejected demands for equal pay. But in 1918, having lost the vote in Conference the supporters of equal pay successfully moved for a plebiscite of the membership. In the subsequent referendum a majority of over 2:1 voted in favour. But abstentions (intentional or otherwise due to the absence of many teachers, mostly men on military service) seemed to be the biggest winner. NUT membership for 1918 was just under 102,000 (65,000 women and nearly 37,000 men). But only a fraction over 50,000 voted, 35,000 in favour; 15,000 against.

Many men teachers complained bitterly that the women had taken the opportunity of their absence on military service to press for 'a quick fix'.

Some men retold emotional stories of receiving propaganda for equal pay whilst still under fire in the trenches. One such member who received a voting paper was Fred Adams. He finished his teaching days at the William Penn School, in Dulwich, south-east London. He was to be one of the band of 35 NAS members at that school who started the industrial action to secure representation on the Burnham Committee with a one-day strike on 1 May 1961.

Writing about him in *The London Schoolmaster* of October 1967, the William Penn School Representative, Bruce Given, said that Fred Adams was one of the two mentioned by the President as he welcomed them on to the stage at the evening mass rally at the Friends House, London, on that memorable day in NAS history. One member was in his first term as a schoolmaster; the other, Fred Adams, was in his last.

Bruce Given believed one reason for Fred Adams' unswerving support for the NAS "was a crumpled but carefully kept piece of paper which he used to produce, look at and sometimes show to others". It was his copy of a voting paper in the NUT referendum of equal pay which he had received whilst still in the trenches of the First World War.

In February 1921 the London Schoolmasters' Association (LSA) published a booklet entitled *Equal Pay* written by three of its members, G.M. Graves, F.R.A. Jarvis and Alfred N. Pocock. They reflected the view that the timing of the NUT plebiscite when "the fortunes of teachers – men and women alike – were at their lowest ebb, has reacted disastrously upon the profession". For men, they wrote, the results have been "calamitous, union has given way to disunion – peace to turmoil. Men and women teachers have ranged themselves in opposing camps, and as yet, no compromise is within sight."

The booklet revealed that the LSA had enrolled over 3,000 men teachers within a few months of the result of the plebiscite; that was a "decided majority" of schoolmasters in London.

The authors believed that separate consideration for men was essential if they were to be retained in teaching, albeit in a numerical minority. They quoted the example of teachers in New York and other parts of the USA. The February 1920 edition of *The Schoolmaster* had quoted figures from New York showing that of the city's 23,000 teachers only 2,000 were men.

The key philosophical difference seemed to centre upon whether people were paid 'qua labourers' or by other criteria which reflected broader social considerations. The ardent feminist, social campaigner and later an Independent Member of Parliament, Miss Eleanor Rathbone, had written in *The Common Cause* (1918) that: "The wages of women are, broadly speaking, based on the cost of individual subsistence; while the wages of men are, broadly speaking, based on the cost of subsistence of a family."

Eleanor Rathbone's realism drove her to point out the dilemma that granting equal pay at the men's rate "would mean in effect that seven-eighths of the teaching profession must be over-paid in order to meet the needs of one-eighth." The President of the National Union of Women Teachers (NUWT – founded to secure equal pay immediately) responded with brutal frankness to Rathbone's point: "The latest excuse . . . we can't get the right kind of men teachers . . . unless we offer them more money than women are paid was 'moonshine'. At least two thirds of teachers were women; let them ensure the right type for the greatest number, *and risk the rest.*" The NUWT President implied all the "risk" was with the men and paying the women's rate to everyone met their demand. There was little sympathy from either side for the other's predicament.

The NAS might have been on the wrong side of the argument historically but at the time they were in very distinguished company. The authors of the LSA's *Equal Pay* booklet paraded a long list of individuals and organisations sympathising with their case.

The most prominent was the Government's Departmental Committee on Teachers' Pay (the precursor to the Burnham Committee). Its last report published in 1918 had concluded: "Any scale of salaries, whether for men or women, should offer an adequate provision, and as schools cannot be efficiently staffed by teachers of one sex, the cases of men and women call for *'separate consideration'*" – the source of the NAS's second great clarion call of many years (running alongside "Men teachers for boys"). There were two NUT Representatives on the Departmental Committee and the report was unanimously agreed. H.A.L. Fisher, the legendary President of the Board of Education at the time, was later to concede in *Teacher's World*, January 1923, that equal pay at 'the men's level' would be prohibitively expensive and at the women's rate "would drive men from schools".

The leading LEA at the time, the London County Council (LCC), reported in July 1919 that "equal pay for equal work . . . would have the effect of making teaching wholly a woman's profession." In the charming if idealistic words of the LCC's Education Officer, Sir Robert Blair, "women must be sought in the women's market and paid generously; men must be sought in the men's market and paid generously." The War Cabinet Committee reporting on "Women in Industry" a few years before had come to the same conclusion as the LCC. The National Association of Head Teachers (NAHT) took the same view, whilst the Assistant Masters Association (AMA) said it could only support equal pay in the context of family allowances.

In one sense the NAS was content with equal pay if it meant women being paid the men's rate. 'Separate consideration' should first establish a men's rate which would then be paid to women. Terry Casey, General Secretary (GS) for 20 years from 1963 to 1983, rehearsed this argument as late as 1969 in the silver jubilee edition of the Association's journal, *The Schoolmaster*. Many would argue it was unrealistic, which if true is a revealing indication that equal pay was not going to be genuine in the sense of levelling women up.

Even the Royal Commission on Equal Pay, established in 1945 and reporting the following year, did not recommend in favour of the principle but limited itself to a very comprehensive review of all the 'pros' and 'cons'.

The great reforming Labour Government elected in 1945 decided to take no action on the Royal Commission report on equal pay. Ironically it took a Conservative Government in 1955 to concede the principle of equal pay in the civil service and teaching and implement it in stages from 1956 to 1961. Nevertheless, there are still continuing problems in securing genuine equal pay throughout society. While the gap has thankfully narrowed it is still proving very difficult completely to overcome the market and social forces that generally determine lower levels of pay for women.

Chapter 3 – The Birth of the NAS

The genesis of the NAS can be traced to the impoverished economic condition of the schoolmaster well before the outbreak of the First World War in 1914. Some schoolmasters, critical of the ineffectiveness of mere representation, began to think out loud in terms of direct action. Polite requests to Government would not deliver on their own. Furthermore some began openly to doubt the willingness or ability of the established unions, particularly the largest – the National Union of Teachers (NUT), to address the problem effectively.

The high percentage of women populating the teaching profession and thereby also the NUT, taken with their relatively lower outgoings compared to men with family responsibilities, fed the admittedly sexist belief that they were unlikely to be seriously interested in fighting for a better deal all round. According to Board of Education sources the proportion of men comprising the teacher force had declined steadily from 63% in 1854 to 22% in 1922. The developing feminist movement and the demand for equal pay in the teaching profession strengthened the belief of some that separate consideration was required for men teachers. There was also deep concern about the relentless increase in the number of unqualified or 'uncertificated' teachers, as they were known in those days.

In several cities impromptu and informal groupings of men teachers had already sprung up quite independently of one another before the outbreak of war in 1914. The earliest records available trace the first meeting to George Cording's organising activities in Cardiff in 1913. In fact it was a little earlier than that according to the writings of Cording himself.

George Cording was a teacher at Howard Gardens Secondary School in Cardiff and was also a well-known footballer and cricketer, later playing for Glamorgan County. He was active in the NUT Cardiff Branch.

George Cording wrote an account of the events for the Conference handbook produced by the host Association, Sunderland, in 1932. He also seems to have given a similar account to a meeting of some delegates to the 1935 Conference hosted by Swansea. A handwritten account of George Cording's talk was produced by Colin Mangham, a union stalwart who gave a lifetime of service to the Association, including many years as the Bolton Secretary.

Cording observed: "Once upon a time there was a happy NUT Association at Cardiff . . . with business carried out well and expeditiously." However, around 1910 business was taken over by "a powerful local National Union of Women Teachers" using the Cardiff Branch to rehearse their next moves within the NUT. The NUWT had been founded in 1906 (after beginning life as the Equal Pay League in 1904) by women who were seriously upset with the lack of support from their union for equal pay. It remained as a pressure group inside the NUT until 1920 when it broke away. It disbanded itself in 1961 when equal pay was finally conceded.

In response to those developments late in 1911 a well-attended meeting of Cardiff men teachers took place. The local NUT President took the Chair. After a long debate the meeting resolved that: "A Men's Association was advisable." It further empowered the Secretary to call another meeting, if instructed by the Chairman to do so.

Unfortunately, in George Cording's view, the Chairman never so authorised. Consequently towards the end of December 1913 Cording went ahead and called the meeting himself. This meeting of "men teachers", soon to call themselves "schoolmasters", took place at the Carlton Restaurant in Queen Street, Cardiff, on a Friday evening, 16 December 1913. It was the first known 'conception' of the NAS.

Some 30 men teachers attended and concluded an intense evening's debate by resolving to form an association of men teachers. Adjourning to the following evening and after further "prolonged discussion" the group resolved to name the organisation The Cardiff Men Teachers' Association. The object of the Association was "to promote and safeguard the interests of men certificated teachers".

Meeting again the following month on 7 January 1914 the group decided to rename itself The Cardiff Schoolmasters' Association. It also decided to send a deputation to the Cardiff Authority to complain about the poor level of schoolmasters' salaries.

That was it! All hell broke loose. Led by the National President, Mr Dakers, the entire NUT Executive descended on two hapless schoolmasters, the Cardiff NAS President, Alfred Burgess, and George Cording, the Secretary. They were arraigned before the NUT Executive. The two schoolmaster stalwarts threw the inquisitors a little by demanding to know why the Cardiff NUWT Representatives were not also on trial. Several weeks before the schoolmasters' deputation the NUWT Representatives had lobbied the LEA demanding equal pay, which was not then NUT policy. Cording merely records that "their contention was not received with the kindliness it merited but it held up the trial"!

Cording then speaks of much activity to get other associations of schoolmasters formed in different parts of the country: "Postal propaganda and the distribution of booklets were the chief means to this end." All conferences of teachers were lobbied and, as Cording recalls, "a memory of the distribution of Cardiff Schoolmasters' Association handbooks on Lowestoft Pier stands out amongst others".

With the outbreak of the First World War the trail goes cold, except that Cording refers to "The joy occasioned by a letter from Mr H. Parkinson of West Ham to Cardiff in 1915" reporting that a "Men-Teachers' organisation" had been formed. Cording adds: "By 1919 four such Associations had been formed; Walthamstow and East Ham having lined up with Cardiff and West Ham."

Many men teachers returning to the profession after all the horrors of war were not at all enamoured to find that very little had been done to protect their real salary levels. On top of that they found the NUT more strongly committed than ever to equal pay for women, a development that had gathered much pace in the absence of men in the trenches as it was often emotively put.

Returning to the 'Cardiff trail', although George Cording mentions Parkinson's letter of 1915, the Annual Report of the NAS for 1921 refers to the West Ham Association being formed in July 1917, making it possibly the second oldest to Cardiff. In 1919 East Ham and several others followed suit.

By 1919 there were cells of the men's movement in Cardiff, Gloucester, Leeds, Liverpool, London, Manchester, Newcastle, Nottingham and Sunderland. While correspondence between them was growing, they had arisen spontaneously and quite separately. Other commentators also mention Bristol, Southampton, Swansea and Tyneside.

To stretch the birth metaphor, after several acts of conception over the years in different parts of the country starting in Cardiff, the baby was finally induced by a decision taken by a group of men teachers attending the 1919 Conference of the NUT in Cheltenham to organise a meeting of their own.

Again it seems that George Cording was one of the organising forces behind the event. He writes: "The conspiring and arrangements for this meeting emanated from a small room half-way up the stairs in the Creamery Café on the promenade in Cheltenham." There were Representatives from five areas which already had local versions of the National Association of Men Teachers (NAMT), including Cardiff, London and Liverpool.

Frank Ordish from Walthamstow was another of the 'Creamery Café conspirators'. Writing several accounts in later years (in Conference handbooks and *The New Schoolmaster* in 1959), Ordish recalled the leading figures behind the events of 1919, the 'Cheltenham Seven'. Describing the birth of the NAMT at Cheltenham Ordish wrote: "We, Cording of Cardiff, Parkinson of West Ham, Metcalf of East Ham, Adams of Gloucester, Sprigge and Tasker of London and the writer of Walthamstow embarked on a venturesome voyage to be quickly joined by Warren of Willesden and Carter and Young of Liverpool and many more rebels and discontents."

Ordish, Cording and Parkinson set themselves the task of organising a meeting of 'Men Teachers'. Ordish refers to "a giant, with massive head and shaggy hair, a Londoner, named Tasker, [who] had rolled in to gather information", being conscripted to chair the planned meeting: "The smaller fry decided that his considerable presence qualified him to fill the chair and keep the peace!"

So on Easter Tuesday 22 April 1919, playing truant from the NUT Conference 'the men of Cheltenham' as they were to become known in the folklore, held a separate meeting at the Royal Well Hall starting at 3 p.m. According to George Cording "the large hall was packed".

Frank Ordish refers to "the oratory being of a high order throughout the meeting". He recalls three speakers – Arthur Warren, William Young and Charlie Carter – who, if the organisers had known who they were, "would have been given a very warm welcome as they took their seats in the body of the hall". Warren "was in rebellious mood" and Carter and Young spoke in favour of the Men's Guild, "well within the Union" (the NUT) which they already had in Liverpool.

The meeting decided to establish the NAMT and to set up a provisional executive to appoint officers and draft a constitution. Harold Parkinson became Honorary Secretary, George Cording Organising Secretary and Tasker Chairman. Frank Ordish of Walthamstow was elected 'Honorary Press Secretary', indicating the importance the founding fathers attached to publicity and campaigning.

In his *New Schoolmaster* article in 1959 Frank Ordish, describing himself as a "surviving founder member", wrote:

"But interestingly, the view amongst the NAMT was they should remain also as members of the NUT. They saw themselves very much as a pressure group to remain in the NUT. However, fierce debates were soon to emerge over whether they should secede from the NUT."

Cording speaks about the next few days at the Creamery "seeming like the centre of the universe. And how we argued! Ordish and I for secession; Samuel 'Sammy' Houldsworth [from Manchester who had joined the 'Creamery conspirators'] for folk pleasing themselves; Young and Carter [from Liverpool] stipulating we act inside the NUT or threatening to withdraw both themselves and their respectability. Sprigge [from London] said little but thought furiously. Houldsworth's policy, being a compromise won the day."

They planned their first Executive meeting in London at Anderton's Hotel in Fleet Street. However, Tasker of London who had been appointed Chairman failed to show up. It was rumoured he had decided "to eschew evil companions". So Cording took over the Chair for the first Executive meeting and shared that role with Herbert Sprigge and Arthur Warren for the rest of the year.

Frank Ordish writing on the early 'national' Executive meetings in 1919 refers to some suspicion falling on Sam Houldsworth that he was a spy. He had been sent to the Executive meetings by Manchester, whose spokesman at Cheltenham had opposed the establishment of the NAMT. But they were soon reassured as Sam's sincerity quickly became obvious as he was a strong supporter of Young and Carter from Liverpool who still at that time believed the NAMT should remain inside the NUT.

The first edition of the NAMT's official journal, then entitled *The Schoolmasters' Review* (September 1919), leads with the account of a very successful lobby of the National Association of Head Teachers' (NAHT) Annual Conference in Birmingham, June 1919. Two prominent NAHT members were recruited, F. Greaves, NAHT Ex-President, and A.L. Shires, current President. Both went on to assume the Presidency of the NAS respectively in 1924 and 1931.

The Schoolmasters' Review, distributed to members through local association secretaries, also called for action and organisation to fight against the emerging threat of equal pay being adopted by the NUT. Men were in "a permanent minority" and would inevitably suffer financially.

Frank Ordish refers to the "hectic months" of the first year of the 'National Executive' meetings in and around the hotel in Fleet Street. "It was literally trowel in hand and sword by side, drafting a constitution, recognising and encouraging new branches, preparing and circulating literature, getting in the National press, getting at our colleagues in the NUT and waiting 'for the progressive solution of the teachers' salaries problem' as promised by the President of the Board of Education, H.A.L. Fisher, in setting up the Burnham Committee."

Ordish says "the trowel went down and the sword came up" when, the Executive's statement on salary policy having been dispatched to H.A.L. Fisher and the Government, Parkinson and Sprigge went to the doors of the Board of Education and demanded admission. "This was of course refused; and one may say rightly, since we were still in the NUT."

Ordish simply records: "Then we went back to our building!"

By April the following year (1920) the NAMT had organised its own Conference, at Margate, running alongside the NUT event. Frank Ordish claims that "by the time we reached Margate at Easter 1920, we had increased our hazy five branches to thirty eight".

The minutes of those proceedings (on 6 April that year) reveal that a Mr A.E. Warren was appointed to the Chair and was soon to be referred to as the President. Arthur Warren was also destined to become the first General Secretary (GS) of the NAS.

The minutes refer to much work being done to build on "the five local associations that were present at Cheltenham" as an Executive Committee was elected of 12 representatives, one each from nine areas with three from London.

The name National Association of Schoolmasters (as opposed to 'Men Teachers') was adopted at the 1920 Margate Conference following the example set by Cardiff and four other local branches. I found no reasons given for the name change. Perhaps 'Schoolmasters' sounded more posh. If the meeting at Cheltenham had been the birth of the National Association, the adoption of the name NAS one year later at Margate must have marked the official 'christening'.

The first statement of the Association's objectives in 1920 included:

> to safeguard and promote the interests of schoolmasters;
>
> to secure men teachers for boys;
>
> to secure separate consideration for schoolmasters in recognition of their greater responsibilities;
>
> to secure educational progress;
>
> to provide Government, the Board of Education, and LEAs and others with the advice and experience of schoolmasters;
>
> to secure joint control of education.

Eligibility for membership was left to local discretion, something which was also to change over the years. The annual affiliation fee was set at two shillings and sixpence (twelve and a half pence in today's currency) per member. That was paid by branches to the National Association after collection locally of subscriptions. That was a practice which also changed, with today the national organisation collecting subscriptions from members and then rebating amounts to local associations.

The Annual Report for that first year states that the number of local associations had increased from five at Cheltenham to 39 'Provincial' ones in addition to London. Sources vary slightly but indicated in the round that membership was approximately 6,000, with about half coming from London. Thirty-seven local association secretaries were listed in the Annual Report.

The Annual Report spoke about intense activity despite the small size of the emerging union. Deputations went to the House of Commons and MPs were lobbied in their constituencies. LEAs were approached and some improvements in salaries secured. Much attention was focussed upon securing coverage for the schoolmasters' case in the local and national media and every occasion of publicity secured was duly monitored and recorded. Written advice on effective lobbying was provided to Local Secretaries.

The National Officers would travel anywhere at any time to address meetings of members and other schoolmasters, establishing a fine tradition of close contact between the leadership and the grass roots. The Report candidly concluded that the 'men's movement' had more support than members because teachers were hesitant about leaving the security of established organisations and taking the risk of joining the NAS. The Report stated that, despite intense activity, "our sphere of work is limited because our membership is limited".

The NAS thus began life as a federation of local associations. The constitution adopted at the 1920 Conference had a separate section entitled "Local Autonomy" which simply but boldly stated that: "Local Associations shall be afforded complete freedom of action in the conduct of their own local affairs." That did not last for long as the NAS soon became renowned for its strong centralist tendencies, although nothing stopped local associations from taking initiatives as their circumstances demanded.

At Margate six National Officers were elected. All positions were honorary and included Arthur Warren as President and Sam Houldsworth, Vice-President. The other four were Honorary GS, Treasurer, Organising Secretary and Press Secretary. The remaining ten members of the Executive were drawn from different Areas.

After the domestic business was completed the gathering in Margate on 6 April 1920 transposed itself into an open meeting, establishing the tradition of private and public sessions at Annual Conference. Immediately resolutions were carried on subjects which were to become 'hardy annuals'.

One such resolution called for no person to be "allowed to teach in any school who does not possess the minimum qualification recognised by organised teachers". One of the first of the highly centralising tendencies was a motion that called for: "The cost of teachers' salaries [to] be a National charge, and these salaries should provide for an equal and adequate standard of living for men teachers in all parts of the country."

The meeting called for a minimum salary for certificated male teachers of £500 per annum after not more than 12 years service to afford them the same "economic position as Women Teachers of equal Professional Status". The rate prevailing at the time was the November 1919 Burnham Provisional Minimum Scale. For men this represented a starting salary of £160 rising by 14 annual £10 increments to £300. The equivalent for women was £150 to £240.

Setting another tradition at the start of the public meeting Arthur Warren, who had been elected to the Chair and would soon be referred to as the President, delivered an opening speech.

He referred to the 'Fisher meeting' which had involved some kind of violent or rowdy demonstration. H.A.L. Fisher, President of the Board of Education and author of the 1918 Act of Parliament to which he gave his name, had set up a meeting through the LCC to discuss the deep discontent emerging in the teaching profession with representatives from LEAs together with some teachers carefully selected for the occasion. Attendance was by invitation and ticket only. The Chairman of the meeting was the Leader of the LCC, Sir Cyril Cobb, who had made some very disparaging and controversial remarks about teachers. Some 60 schoolmasters gatecrashed the meeting in London's Kingsway Hall and shouted Sir Cyril down, not even allowing him to introduce Fisher, an enlightened friend of the profession. The meeting broke up in chaos.

Warren said that: "The curious thing about the demonstration is that the President of the London Schoolmasters' Association [LSA] himself does not know who organised it." More revealingly Warren went on (the minutes are in bold print): "Mind you, I don't condemn the demonstration. These are days when to right the wrong you are compelled to adopt measures which may be distasteful to you."

Warren continued: "It does seem at present that forward movements can only attain success by violent measures." He noted how all other "possible means to secure economic conditions of comfort" had resulted in "endless interviews with the authorities" and they had "been fobbed off with vague promises". The minutes revert back to recording Warren in bold print concluding: "We are tired of all that, and if the authorities want schoolmasters to go back to methods of negotiation it is up to them to do something."

A.E. Warren, emerging as the first natural national 'leader' of the NAS, emphasised (as the bold print in the minutes illustrated) from the very beginning the need to take direct action if patient and rational representation for a just cause failed to secure progress. In so doing he established the militant and campaigning traditions that characterised the NAS and that led the membership to expect, indeed to demand, strong leadership from the top.

It was unfortunate that Fisher was caught in the crossfire between the teachers and Sir Cyril Cobb because he had been appointed President of the Board of Education by the Prime Minister, Lloyd George, to try to placate the profession. Lloyd George was on record saying: "Dissatisfaction in the teaching profession must be avoided at all costs. It was the disgruntled teachers of Glasgow who turned the Clyde red!" Prior to the outbreak of war in 1914 there had been serious industrial unrest in the coal-mining, transport and shipbuilding industries.

Besides the enlightened 1918 legislation, including secondary education for all, Fisher introduced a Teachers' Superannuation Act, giving the profession a non-contributory pension scheme. Then he set up a committee representative of LEAs and teachers "to secure an orderly and progressive solution of the salaries problem in Public Elementary Schools on a national basis and its correlation with the salary problem in Secondary Schools".

Fisher was forced to leave the platform in dignified silence. Another invited speaker and ally of teachers, the Bishop of London, showed less patience and berated the 'rioters' for being "disgracefully ill-mannered and a blot on the profession". Those who had shouted Sir Cyril Cobb down stressed they would have gladly listened to Fisher. However, the 'rioters' did not set a tradition for the NAS. The opposite occurred, with emphasis on listening to the opposing case politely with respect and then taking militant action if appropriate.

However, both these salary and superannuation developments, sponsored by Fisher and favourable to teachers in their creation, were soon to flounder in the economic depression and Government expenditure cuts of the 1920s. Better perhaps for them never to have been granted, but given and then taken back. The bitterness felt was exacerbated.

The committee on salaries eventually took its name from its first Chairman, Lord Burnham. The Burnham Committee was destined to remain in business, amidst much controversy for nearly 70 years.

Chapter 4 - Steps to Secession

Tensions surfaced immediately after the first Burnham Report on salaries. The inaugural meeting was held on 12 August 1919 and the Burnham Committee produced its first Report a few months later on 21 November. It established a Provisional National Minimum Scale to come into effect by March 1922 below which no qualified teacher would be paid. The men's scale was £160 rising by annual increments of £10 to a maximum of £300 per annum. For women it was £150 rising by £10 to £240.

The NUT called local meetings all over the country to parade their "successful negotiations". Instead of plaudits their Executive Members were faced with angry protests from two different sets of 'ungrateful' members. Women teachers demanded to know why equal pay had been ignored. Schoolmasters declared the settlement "insulting".

That also explains the heated protest against Sir Cyril Cobb at the 'Fisher meeting' in London. For many years a leading light on the LCC and then a controversial Conservative MP, Sir Cyril had assumed the crown of 'teachers' pet hate' by declaring they were "overestimating their importance" and "making extravagant salary claims". There was much criticism of the NUT leadership for tolerating the huge fall in real pay which had occurred since the beginning of the war in 1914. By 1919 pay had risen by only 124% against an inflation rate of 212%. The severe inflation had created massive industrial unrest elsewhere but it seemed to pass the NUT leadership by.

Many schoolmasters with families to support were literally on the breadline. They saw themselves as the victims of neglect. Many organisations agreed with the schoolmasters that the desirable aim of recruiting and retaining a sufficient number of men in the teaching profession was compromised by low salaries and would be exacerbated by equal pay.

Even the media showed some sympathy. An article appeared in the *The Daily Chronicle* on 31 March 1920 written by Harold Spender: "There are teachers who are scarcely able to feed their families. There are others who are unable to clothe them properly and there are many who cannot afford a decent house. Many of these men have fought throughout the war and have been assured that they would come back to better conditions."

The NAS complained from its earliest days about a fundamental fault in the constitution of the Burnham Committee. Central Government, already subsidising the cost of teachers' salaries to the tune of a 60% grant to LEAs, was bound to have a view on such expenditure. But it had established a committee on which it was not represented to determine such matters. Of course the inevitable happened. Central Government sought to control the business of Burnham behind the scenes. LEAs and the NUT pretended this did not happen, seriously compromising the interests of all teachers in protecting the real paymaster from direct negotiations.

The profoundly unsatisfactory settlement of 1919 played a very prominent role in the development of the 'men's movement' and the NAS. The NUT leadership seemed paralysed, apparently complacent over salary levels but torn in different directions by the anger of the feminists and the schoolmasters. The Board of Education itself was aware of the parlous pay position of men teachers. In its 1918-19 Report the Board expressed deep concern about the number of 'Student Men Teachers' in training which had fallen from 2,722 in 1908 to 809 in 1918. The figures for 'Student Women Teachers' were 6,892 and 5,279 respectively.

Consequently the Board urged action upon LEAs to deal with this "very critical" situation in which the "standard of efficiency in the public system of education is seriously threatened". The Board went on to "emphasise strongly that the shortage could only be met by substantial increases in the salaries of adult teachers and by general improvement in the prospects of the teaching profession".

Some of the local associations of the NAMT approached their LEAs pressing for improvements to the national minimum scale. Some LEAs were sympathetic but pointed out that the protesters' union, the NUT, had already spoken for them. Furthermore the NUT advised teachers to leave well alone. They had got the best deal possible in the circumstances and they should not risk national negotiations by pressing their case too hard locally.

The NUT's advice had already been shown to be false and supine. The first Annual Report of the NAS in March 1920 records the activities of the West Ham Branch, which had been formed in 1917. It had also been represented at the Cheltenham meeting through Harold Parkinson, himself briefly to be the first Honorary Secretary of the NAS.

In June 1919 the West Ham Men Teachers, still inside the NUT, secured a mass local meeting of the big union to press for an appeal to the LEA for a pay rise. In accordance with their national advice, local NUT officers refused to participate in any deputation. The men of West Ham decided to go it alone. A deputation was received. The result was an immediate increase of £50 backdated to 1 April and an interim scale for men starting at £200 and rising by £15 annual increments to £400, significantly besting the emerging Burnham (national minimum) scale of £160 rising by £10 increments to £300.

The LCC, faced with vigorous demonstrations by schoolmasters, anticipated the 1920 Burnham agreement. Having already conceded a bonus in 1919 of £30 to men teachers and £22 10s. for women, the LCC went ahead and implemented its own scales of £200 to £425 for men and £187 10s. to £340 for women, following pressure from the 'men teachers'.

In Liverpool a men teachers' guild had been formed as early as 1898 by W.H. Young around the time of the first Teachers' Superannuation Act. Another guild was still in existence at the end of the war in 1918 and it had a majority of local men teachers in membership. It naturally became the base for those critical of the NUT neglect of schoolmasters' interests. It was not therefore surprising that the Liverpool branch of the NAMT was formed on 6 May 1919.

Writing in *The Schoolmasters' Review* (No. 4 October 1920) Liverpool's Charlie Carter recorded the events surrounding the local implementation of the Second Burnham national agreement on pay in 1920. Liverpool, as a large city, was a Scale 3 Area. The men's maximum was recommended to be at £380 per annum, which was well below the level required to compensate for inflation since 1914. The men teachers, still inside the NUT, persuaded the Chairman of the Education Committee, Alderman Alsop, of the case to raise the men's maximum to £400. Alsop said he would so recommend to the Council subject to the women agreeing. They did not. The Chairman then abandoned the idea as it would treble the costs to give women the same proportionate increase. Carter believed that "separate consideration" took off in Liverpool at that moment. A "great meeting" was held at the Picton Hall in Liverpool on 21 June 1920 to decide on whether to accept the Burnham recommended scales. The men forecast rejection whilst the women indicated acceptance of the Burnham recommended scales. When the votes were taken 976 women voted to accept, with 123 rejecting the deal. On the men's side, 247 voted for rejection, 108 for acceptance.

Seen through the eyes of the Liverpool schoolmasters it was 'dog in the manger'. The women gained nothing financially by denying the men. They stood by the principle of equal pay but were not prepared to fight for it above the women's rate. The schoolmasters accused the women of "wilful ignorance as to the financial responsibilities of a married man teacher. The statement that his responsibilities were heavier was received by jeers by a crowded meeting of irresponsible women."

The result was that 96% of men teachers signed a petition of protest and membership of the previously "somnolent" Men's Guild surged and soon transferred en masse to the newly formed Men Teachers' Association which had been set up the previous year. By the end of 1920 membership of the Liverpool Branch of the NAMT stood at 506, some 75% of men teachers in the city.

Recalling these events some years later, John Kay, the third member along with Carter and Young of that great 'founding triumvirate' of the Liverpool Association of Schoolmasters (LAS), mused philosophically on how he had spent so much of his professional life building up that city's branch of the NUT into a strong and influential body. In the early days "general meetings were pitifully small and men in a pitiful minority . . . but by way of contrast the Committee was of men". He could not recall exactly when the 'feminist movement' – the "cloud no bigger than a man's hand" – first appeared but it was visible before the war. After it had "swelled and burst forth it was not easy to awake each morning to realise that after infinite toil we had created a machine that threatened our ruin. To those of us who had given a life of service to the great Union, building it brick by brick with missionary zeal came a bitter sense of bereavement and betrayal."

John Kay also reminisced about another meeting between the Liverpool schoolmasters and Alsop's committee on the issue of men's pay when the question of secession arose in sharp definition. Alsop: "We have just seen a deputation of the NUT. They have expressed directly opposite views. Do you belong to the NUT?" Kay observes: "We admitted the soft impeachment." Alsop: "Do you think it honest to address the Committee with two voices?" Kay: "We looked at each other . . . The answer seemed clear to us . . . To make it clearer came the voice of the great feminist, 'If you won't have Equal Pay, get out'."

Opinion in the LAS over secession, hitherto strongly in favour of remaining inside the NUT, began to shift over to the other side. They began to join the "whole-hoggers" as opposed to the "double barrellers" as the two camps became known.

At the Liverpool AGM in May 1920 a motion was moved from the floor that: "The time has now arrived when men should sever their connections with the NUT". Such was the gravity of the debate that the meeting had to adjourn to 22 May when the resolution was declared "largely carried".

Still showing signs of nerves of going it alone, the meeting then resolved to hold a plebiscite requiring a two-thirds turnout to show not less than one-half of the membership in favour for the secession policy to carry. In the event the result was 187 for, 143 against, with 189 failing to vote. Apparently many men were uncertain about the ability of a separate NAMT to provide all the services required of a union. Some were also concerned about centralisation, believing that local branches had to retain autonomy. Most local men teachers' associations were far too small for that.

The Bootle LEA was also disposed to increase the rate for men but was dissuaded by the NUT. These developments led to the formation of a

Merseyside Federation of Schoolmasters in 1920, comprising Liverpool, Bootle, Birkenhead and Wallasey.

The Leeds Men Teachers Association was formed on 5 March 1918. It was a very active Association. By January 1921, renamed the Leeds Schoolmasters' Association, it had affiliated to the NAS under the leadership of two future NAS Presidents, F.C. Greaves and A.L. Shires, recruited from the NAHT. It had often and openly discussed secession from the NUT. Walthamstow followed suit in October 1918, the moving spirit being Frank Ordish, one of the 'Cheltenham Seven'.

The founding of the London Schoolmasters' Association (LSA) in May 1919 at a meeting at St Anne's School in Wandsworth, provides an excellent example of the 'multiple but independent conceptions' of the NAS.

Writing possibly in response to the request from the National Executive Committee for a the history of the Association in the mid-1950s, the first Honorary General Secretary of the LSA, Henry Bolton Harris, recalled the events over 30 years previously. While still on active service at the Royal Naval Air Service in Felixstowe, he received a calling notice to a general meeting of the NUT at Farringdon Hall in the autumn of 1918. He was an NUT activist, having been an Executive Member of the West Lambeth Branch and a delegate to many Annual Conferences. He was keen to attend and went to great lengths to secure leave of absence from his unsympathetic commanding officer and thereafter to make sure none of his potentially jealous colleagues noticed his departure.

However, his attendance at the NUT meeting was a real "eye opener". For the first time he encountered the women's movement that left him in no doubt they would easily outvote the men and secure equal pay. "Amazed by what went on at the meeting" and back at his base he "meditated on what to do". Fortuitously, he was suddenly elevated to "the most popular personality on the Station" – demobilisation clerk. Coal miners were top of the pecking order but then came schoolmasters. Harris made sure he was one of the first!

Back at his LCC school, Merton Road in Wandsworth, and "vehemently opposed to equal pay", he was soon embroiled in staffroom discussion about his pet project – resigning from the NUT and forming a 'National Association of Schoolmasters'. He determined to carry out his plan. "This was a grave decision and a tremendous gamble. Here was I a puny freelance making a tilt at the massive, mighty and wealthy professional home of the Teaching Profession."

Harris and his staffroom colleagues heard about similar stirrings in other parts of the country but they had no idea of the personalities involved. One of his supporters, W.J. Berwick, knew the headmaster of St Anne's C. of E. School in Wandsworth, Mr Bagnall, and persuaded him to offer Harris the use of his premises for a meeting of schoolmasters. Harris claimed to be the first to coin the name "National Association of Schoolmasters" under which he advertised the inaugural meeting of the Wandsworth Branch on Friday 16 May 1919 at 5.15 p.m. at St Anne's School, "a few minutes from East Hill Tram Terminus".

As the day approached Henry Harris discovered that a Herbert Sprigge, one of the Cheltenham Seven, had heard of his meeting and was encouraging schoolmasters to attend. On learning that Mr Sprigge was an Executive Member of the NAMT Harris asked if he would chair the meeting. The rest is history. The well-attended meeting of some 80 men teachers decided to form the LSA, appoint an Executive and call an open general meeting of schoolmasters for a couple of weeks time.

The open meeting to which all schoolmasters in London were invited was planned for the Kingsway Hall on 31 May 1919. The NUT decided to organise a 'counter-meeting' one week before at the same venue on 24 May. The move backfired badly. Hundreds of men turned up to protest against the NUT, whose meeting turned out to be chaotic but an excellent advert for the schoolmasters' upcoming event. The 31 May meeting was packed out and the LSA well and truly launched. Soon it was to have over 2,500 members, around half of the entire NAS.

The affiliation of such a large block of members to the NAS may have been a crucial factor in ensuring its survival. The early days were full of uncertainty. Opinion on secession from the NUT was divided. 'Size' mattered in making a separate union viable. However, it was not just a question of 'quantity'. The men who formed these breakaway groups were determined and courageous, people of genuine calibre and quality, as they had to be to survive.

W. L. Marsland, who was to become NAS President in 1937-38, wrote about the early days of the Association in Manchester. He had resigned from the NUT early in 1919 when over half of the city's schoolmasters were in membership of the 'men's movement'. Most of the ex-servicemen and those who ran school sport were in membership. However, despite strong lobbying from Liverpool, who had learnt from bitter experience, Manchester, led by Sam Houldsworth who took over from Arthur Warren as National President in 1921, remained opposed to secession from the NUT. Houldsworth was well supported by the Manchester Executive in his view. They had tried to establish an effective Men's Guild inside the NUT to counterbalance a strong women's movement pressing vigorously for equal pay. When the LEA, in common with many others, refused to listen to their arguments for separate consideration for men's salaries, Manchester changed its policy and when the time came voted for secession. However, as predicted a very large number of Manchester men, around half, decided to remain within the 'Big Umbrella'.

The degree of personal hostility aroused was intense. When the Annual Conference arrived in Manchester in 1930 the city became unique in being the only one to refuse the NAS a civic welcome. The Director of Education refused to attend any part of the Conference. The great C.P. Scott, editor *of The Manchester Guardian* from 1872 to 1929, agreed to substitute and welcomed the Conference to the city.

The development of the 'men's movement' and the NAS took a little longer to get off the ground in the more isolated rural areas. Lincolnshire is a good example. William (Leo) Barford, who uniquely was NAS President for four years, serving between 1939 and 1943, sent in an account from his retirement home in St Leonards-on-Sea for the benefit of the "History of the Association Committee" in November 1956. He left Bede College for a post in Lincoln in April 1920. Despite many invitations he "stubbornly refused" to join the NUT. However, he "was accepted into the Men Teachers' Association, MTA, which was functioning inside the NUT". In March 1921 he moved to a country headship at Carlton Scroop, near Grantham, and found himself "in the wilderness as far as the MTA was concerned". He continued to spurn the NUT despite many invitations from his colleagues in the School Sports Association in which he was active.

Barford continues: "At some time in 1923 a fellow named Arthur Stone was appointed head of the Wesleyan School in Grantham. He came from Liverpool. He noticed my outcast state as regards the NUT and asked why I was not going to a meeting being held one Saturday afternoon after a football match. He wasn't going either so I asked him why. You can guess the rest: 'Let's form a Branch of the NAS'!"

They found another isolated soul in the shape of an old headmaster in Grantham and so became three. Then in February 1924 Jim Rice, a dynamic NAS leader from Hull and a future President (1926), came to address them and three other 'men teachers' and they formed the Grantham Association of Schoolmasters. There was no question of them 'seceding' from the NUT because they had never belonged. However, Barford notes that the MTA collapsed in Lincoln because no one would secede.

Barford's account also refers to "a Grantham lad [starting] the Scunthorpe Association in 1931". That must have been Tim Woodcock, a great leader of the NAS in Lincolnshire throughout his working life and one of those stalwarts who declined the chance of running for national office despite being eminently qualified to do so. Some 60 years later Tim was still attending meetings in Scunthorpe and Lincolnshire that I addressed as the General Secretary in the 1990s.

The development of the 'men's movement' across the country was stimulated by the unsatisfactory 1919 Burnham settlement which set an unfortunate precedent for future pay negotiations. The deteriorating economic situation post-First World War and the profoundly unwise deflationary policies pursued in the 1920s must surely have been contributing factors as well. How unions reacted to the great challenges presented was also crucial. While the NUT remained quiescent, the NAMT, soon to become the NAS, exhorted their members to protest.

On 30 March 1920 the London County Council (LCC) met with teachers' salaries on its agenda. LSA members were requested to leave school as early as possible and congregate at the Old County Hall in Spring Gardens at 4 p.m. The response was electric. Press reports indicated that between three and four thousand members turned up. It looks as if the LSA had not anticipated such a turnout, for neither a formal meeting nor rally appeared to have been organised. In the absence of a channel in which to the vent their anger, some 200 members stormed the main entrance and occupied the vestibule, demanding to see the LCC Chairman. It took all the persuasive powers of the LSA President, 'Cheltenham veteran' Harry Sprigge, to get them to disperse in return for leaving a written message.

The LSA Secretary, H.B. Harris, received a telegram that evening inviting a delegation to meet the LCC Chairman the following day. The outcome of that was an LCC decision to inform the next Burnham meeting of its intention to introduce a new Metropolitan Scale rising from £200 by £12 10s. increments to £425 for men coming into effect 1 April 1920.

Burnham was recalled. By 20 September that year the Provisional National Minimum Scale had disappeared. It was replaced by four separate area scales for elementary teachers: rural, small and large towns and the Metropolitan Police Area (London). The scales rose in the said ascending order from minima of £172 50s. men and £160 women to maxima of £425 men and £340 women per annum.

Teachers were to agree locally with their LEAs which area they entered. Apart from London, with implementation already locally agreed for 1 April 1920, the new scales were not to come into effect until April the following year.

However, those days were not ones of 'joined-up' Government. While H.A.L. Fisher was attempting to improve the pay and status of the teaching profession, the Government had set up a Select Committee on National Expenditure in 1920. This supposedly 'independent' Committee was to be chaired by Sir Eric Geddes, a businessman, Conservative MP and Government Minister. He had established a reputation for efficiency in getting things done organising the railways and ports in supplying the western front in the war. His

Committee was to attack the "atmosphere of financial laxity in which questions involving education are apt to be considered".

In a brutal reminder of the predominance of the Treasury in Whitehall, Fisher was informed that education expenditure had to be curtailed. The Board of Education had to send a circular to LEAs requesting them not to incur any new expenditure. On 24 December 1920 (a typically 'good day' to break bad news even in those times) Fisher wrote to Lord Burnham imposing a three-year staging (or 'carry over' as it was then called) of the settlement originally agreed for implementation on 1 April 1921.

That was not the end of the matter. Things got worse. On 4 February 1921 the NUT General Secretary, in his capacity as Leader of the Teachers' Panel of Burnham, was informed that while the Government stood by its commitment to pay a 60% grant to local authorities for their expenditure, it would be considered "wise and patriotic" if teachers were to forego £5m of the present award and also pay a 5% contribution towards their superannuation. Teacher numbers were also to be reduced by excluding pupils below the age of six from school.

Then things seemed to quieten for the rest of the year. On 10 February the following year, 1922, Geddes produced his first report. It achieved fame or infamy, depending on your view, and became a historical event, forever to be known as the 'Geddes Axe'. It recommended brutal reductions in public expenditure, including the armed services and health, with the severest cuts being reserved for education. In keeping with the previous year's 'softening up' Geddes recommended a 5% salary cut and a 5% contribution to superannuation. There were also to be savage cuts in secondary and higher education and the pupil-teacher ratio was to be trimmed back to 50:1. In short the Geddes Axe obliterated Fisher's 1918 Education Act and all the other positive measures he had introduced to improve the status, pay and conditions of the teaching profession.

Schoolmasters were predictably vehement in their reaction. Within hours of the announcement NAS members were raising fighting funds. In Leeds where the NAS Vice-President, G. Greaves, was addressing a meeting that evening, over £100 was raised within minutes.

The Prime Minister, Lloyd George, was quoted in the February 1922 edition of *The New Schoolmaster* saying that "apart from its injustice I cannot think of anything more dangerous to society than to starve the teachers". He could not "conceive anything more serious than that the nation should conclude that it cannot afford good education for its children". Lloyd George may have been 'in office' but not necessarily 'in power', his Liberal Party being in a minority of the (largely) Conservative Coalition Government.

H.A.L. Fisher as President of the Board of Education said that "an embittered teacher is a menace to the state". Lord Burnham said it would be "rank injustice if any attempt were made to take away from the teachers the benefit they received from the establishment and acceptance of the scales approved by the Board and the Treasury".

In the event the Government had decided by May 1922 to impose a 5% pension contribution and make other cuts in educational expenditure. In May a short (five clause) Teachers' Superannuation Bill was introduced into the House of Commons. Feigning 'honour' the Government said that since the pay award had been agreed between the LEAs and teachers it should be respected but the superannuation issue was different. It would have been better not to seek such 'justification'.

It provoked a massive reaction from all teachers, NAS and NUT alike. Teachers believed that their non-contributory pensions partly compensated for low salaries. Fisher had made reference to this when enacting the 1918 scheme, expressing the hope that it would offer some redress for the modest levels of pay.

The abatement of salary in recognition of a non-contributory pension was not just teacher folklore. It reflected a principle applied to the civil service which survived for the remainder of the 20th century. It was endorsed by many governments of different complexions and civil service unions made frequent reference to the fact.

Teachers responded with an unprecedented lobby and campaign, establishing another tradition which has been characteristic of many of their unions, not just the NAS. Every Member of Parliament was lobbied several times over, in their constituencies as well as in Westminster. Deputations, petitions, interviews in the media and public meetings took place. You name it and it was organised. The NUT even advertised in two national daily newspapers.

Huge meetings in Manchester and London had achieved much publicity. The defeat of two Government candidates in by-elections in Camberwell (London) and Clayton (Manchester) on the eve of the publication of the Geddes report in May 1922 was attributed to the teachers' campaign.

Recollecting events some years later in *The London Schoolmaster* in March 1965, Harry Meigh, NAS President in 1949-50, describes the Parliamentary Committee of the LSA, under the chairmanship of Dick Anderson, organising intensive canvassing in support of the Labour candidate with members descending on Camberwell from all parts of London. He was the only one of the three candidates interviewed who was committed to supporting education against the 'Geddess Axe'. The schoolmasters' canvass, based on "your children's education is in danger" was credited with securing victory for the Labour candidate, overturning a comfortable Government majority.

In Manchester Sam Houldsworth, President of the NAS at the time, led the same kind of successful operation on behalf of a candidate who was opposed to 'Geddes'.

The result of this massive campaign was a stunning Parliamentary defeat for the Government when the issue was debated during the Second Reading on 16 May 1922 in the House of Commons. Many Conservative MPs had rebelled against the Government. The Government knew when to beat a tactical retreat and how to live and fight another day. Lord Robert Cecil successfully moved the adjournment of the debate although that was only carried on the slender majority of 151-148.

The following day the Government set up a Select Committee. The terms of reference were to consider any evidence that the non-contributory pension depended upon the present salaries remaining in force and if teachers had accepted 'lower' pay in return for such a superannuation scheme. I cannot find any evidence of teachers denouncing this stitch-up in advance. Perhaps that was due to a naïve belief that evidence would be considered dispassionately and objectively.

Both Lord Burnham and H.A.L. Fisher testified that the teachers were correct in their belief. The Chairman of the Select Committee, F.D. Acland, in drafting his report conceded the point. But his drafting was challenged in the Committee. It was put to the vote and rejected on a 4-3 split. To make matters worse one of the four objectors, a Lt. Colonel Hughes, had not been present for the relevant hearings but nevertheless voted against. The draft was duly amended to conclude that "no undertaking expressed or implied" had been given that the 1918 Superannuation should not be altered whilst the salary scales remained in force.

Lt. Colonel Hughes was accused of caving in to the pressure generated by the anti-teacher campaign led by *The Daily Mail. The New Schoolmaster* of the time quoted an editorial from that newspaper which has often seemed to rejoice in the promulgation of robust right-wing views: "Public opinion is deeply aroused by the rapacity of elementary teachers, by their truculent and inflammatory methods of agitation, by their frequently unfortunate influence upon the young children committed to their care."

So on 3 July 1922 in the light of the 'findings' of the Select Committee the Second Reading was then carried by 210 votes to 54. The non-contributory pension scheme was killed off at the tender age of four years. The short Superannuation Act of 1922 made a 5% contribution compulsory, pending the report of a departmental inquiry, under the chairmanship of Lord Emmott.

With 5% of salary knocked off for pension contributions the Government moved to stage two. Under thinly veiled threats to reduce local authorities' grants (which Fisher had raised from 50% to 60%), towards the end of 1922 the Government got the management panel of Burnham to suggest a "voluntary reduction" of 5% in salary.

The NUT-dominated Teachers' Panel agreed to the 5% cut in the salary scales which were still being phased in from the agreement in 1920. Only London had implemented the new scales in full. The 5% cut ensured that apart from London no teacher received the full scales agreed in 1920.

As 1922 progressed PM Lloyd George was assailed on virtually all fronts: foreign policy, the Irish question, public expenditure and domestic scandal (including the sale of peerages), not to mention the economic slump. By November the Lloyd George Coalition had collapsed and the new Conservative Government was led by Bonar Law. H.A.L. Fisher had departed as President of the Board of Education.

As if the national cutbacks were not enough the NAS had to respond to some LEAs who were determined to 'out Geddes' the Government. Many local disputes flared up and played their part in expanding the number of branches and conditioning views on whether the NAS should secede from the NUT. Fighting funds were set up. Southampton was possibly the worst case. Even though it was a large town it had opted to pay its teachers on the lowest (rural) Scale 1 Area. Then it proposed a 20% cut in pay. The NAS and NUT objected and embarked upon strikes that were to last several weeks. The pay cut notification was withdrawn but both unions refused to return below the correct scale, obviously Scale 3 as a large town. Negotiations opened. The NAS expected to be included but the NUT refused to allow joint negotiations. So the NAS continued to take action and was charged with "interference". Addressing the Council the local NAS Treasurer claimed his membership to number 120. This caused uproar and was undoubtedly clouded by the fact of dual memberships.

A serious split in the NAS emerged. The local President, a Mr Knee, was also a member of the NUT, which was handling his case for sustentation. After some fierce internal arguments Knee and several other prominent NAS members in Southampton resigned. The episode strengthened the belief of the "whole-hoggers" that secession from the NUT was the way forward. After the dispute was over the Southampton Schoolmasters carried a resolution at their meeting on 15 July that all men teachers were eligible to join "provided they were not members of the NUT".

Schools in Southampton had been closed for three and a half months. The NAS Annual Report in 1923 said that all members had been "sustained magnificently" and were reinstated. The result of the dispute was that teachers were paid on a modified Scale 3. The NAS advised members to accept the compromise "under protest and without prejudice", presumably to facilitate their right to reopen the issue at a later stage if they wished and to make the point that it was not party to the agreement.

The NAS accounts for the year ended 31 December 1922 show that the Southampton Defence Fund raised just over £2,018, which except for a £100 contribution from the NAS, was provided by individual members and other local associations. Only around half that amount was actually needed to sustain the members and over £869 was refunded to local associations. Fifty pounds was advanced to Gateshead. It showed the solidarity that had quickly built up between the branches, a characteristic that was also to become part of the NAS tradition.

In Gateshead at the same time the schools were closed for two and a half months. Although correctly allocated to Scale 3, the Education Committee refused to accept the Council's decision to base its estimates on Scale 2 operating. The Council took teachers' salaries out of the hands of its Education Committee and gave notice of a 10% cut in salary. Teachers went on strike and were locked out. That dispute seemed to end with little progress having been made.

Despite all these expressions of anger with salary levels, in 1922 the NUT-controlled Teachers' Panel accepted a "temporary voluntary abatement" of 5% of salary. It was not surprising that opinion amongst schoolmasters in favour of secession from the NUT had hardened.

The tradition of active local associations vigorously pursuing members' interests was firmly established. The opening of more branches was seen by the National Association as a key ingredient for expansion and success. The tradition of militant action was also firmly set in place. It usually produced tangible and reasonably prompt dividends, although not always, as the case of Gateshead seemed to show. But even where success was not immediate, action contributed to the creation of the culture that if Government or LEAs were to treat schoolmasters badly, the Association would react and not accept injustice lying down.

In the context of savage cutbacks the young and small NAS had to gain its feet. It was a baptism of fire. The context played a huge part in determining the character of the Association. It was born to fight and campaign. It had to struggle not just against the Government and the employing LEAs on one side but also deal with the hostility of the NUT and the reluctance of many teachers to stand up and be counted. The NAS had no option but to be 'a battling minority".

Although not mentioned in the minutes of the 1920 NAS Margate Conference, secession from the NUT must have been an issue lurking in the background that dare not speak its name. As Frank Ordish has revealed, some openly favoured it, others were against and possibly many wished it in their hearts but remained nervous of the practical consequences. However, it seemed not to surface openly at the 1920 Conference.

The Second Annual Conference of the NAS was held at the Municipal Secondary School in Cardiff on Friday and Saturday 13/14 May 1921. No doubt the venue reflected the election at the previous year's Conference of George Cording from Cardiff as Organising Secretary. A 16-man Executive, including six Officers, joined 56 other Representatives from 28 out of the 38 different local associations, with Bristol, Cardiff, Liverpool, Leeds and London featuring strongly. Samuel Houldsworth from Manchester succeeded Arthur Warren as President. In the elections later on in the meeting Warren was returned unopposed as Honorary Secretary.

The public sessions dealt with debates on policies but it was in the private session on the Saturday that the more significant historical development of the NAS took place. That was on the issue of secession from the NUT. Stretching the childbirth and growth metaphor, that was perhaps the day on which the NAS took its first unaided steps.

Two delegates from Liverpool, J. Kay and R. Tetley, proposed a motion declaring that membership of "an organisation that has adopted the principle of equal pay is entirely inconsistent with the objects for which we are contending and that consequently all members of NAS should resign from the NUT".

It was not surprising that the first formal open move to secede from the NUT came from the Liverpool delegation. They had one of the most potent and bitter experiences of the NUT thwarting potentially promising opportunities to increase men's salaries locally without adverse effect upon women teachers' pay. Unless the NAS were separate its Representatives could not be received in deputation by LEAs.

But there was obviously still much apprehension of going it alone. Rather than putting the issue to a straight vote on its merits, Arthur Warren moved the formal amendment, "The previous question". That was carried on a card vote, 3,917 votes for, 1,460 against. A motion from Sunderland declaring "That after 31 December, 1921, no member of NUT be eligible for membership of NAS" was then ruled out of order. There was obviously a division of opinion on the issue. Whilst a formal vote had been sidelined the secession genie was out of the bottle and would return to dominate the 1922 Conference.

A motion demanding representation on the pay negotiating body, the Burnham Committee, was lost. That may surprise some, bearing in mind the issue was to become one of the great 'causes célèbres' of the first four decades of the Association's existence. It was lost in 1921 because the Conference had effectively decided to remain in the NUT and separate recognition of the NAS on Burnham would amount to double representation.

1922 proved to be the year of the momentous decision with events beginning to unfold at the third Annual Conference held at the Central Technical School in Liverpool over a long weekend, 2–5 June 1922. This time the 17- strong Executive, including six Officers, was joined by 95 delegates from 29 local associations from all over England and Wales.

George Cording from Cardiff assumed the Presidency. If there is one person who could claim the greatest single credit for forming the NAS it was probably this man from Cardiff. He had been a consistently strong supporter of secession from the NUT for many years.

The drama of the Liverpool Conference centred upon the proposed revision to the Association's Rules. Rule 2 dealt with eligibility for membership. After some discussion F.C. Greaves and J.W. Selby (both from Leeds and the former also an Executive member) moved an amendment stating: "That in the interests of the NAS, and of education generally, it is desirable that members of this association should secede from any organisation of teachers which advocates 'equal pay'." Many delegates reported the same 'Liverpool experience' when approaching their LEAs on the salary question. The schoolmasters felt stymied. Their voice could not even be heard so long as they remained inside the NUT. On a show of hands the amendment was lost. A card vote was demanded and the result reversed with 3,197 in favour, 1,649 against.

Executive members W.H. Young (Liverpool) and H. Sprigge (London) moved a further amendment: "That this question be referred to a special conference." This was a sound suggestion since the crunch issue of secession had been forced to a vote on an amendment. It had not been notified in advance to the membership by way of a proposal to change the Rules. Further discussion led to the President successfully proposing that: "An adjourned Conference be held in October to debate the question of secession on Rule 2."

T. Jacques from Manchester had delivered the most potent speech against secession, reinforcing the indecision which clearly lingered on making the final break. He had quite rightly outlined all the problems that would have to be faced, none the least of which being that if a choice had to be made, many might decide to stay with the NUT.

Significantly other important domestic business was deferred, obviously subject to the outcome of the adjourned Conference. This included the subscription and the status of the General Secretary (GS). A motion was moved stipulating that the GS be a full-time paid official but it was amended to express the desirability of such and authorising the Executive to act accordingly subject to the decision on secession.

The Swansea Association probably provides a good example of where opinion lay on secession. It invited Arthur Warren to address a special public meeting on the issue which took place on 29 September at Dynemor Place School with the Swansea President, Mr Beanland, in the Chair. The minutes record Mr Warren "addressed the meeting dealing with the aims of the NAS . . . and put the case for 'Secession' very fairly and made great impression on the minds of his hearers".

On 6 October 1922 the Swansea Association called a general meeting for all members to discuss the motion on secession, down for debate at the forthcoming Special Conference. The minutes record "a very keen discussion in which the pros. and cons. were exhaustively dealt with". A secret ballot was then conducted on whether the Swansea Association supported the Special Conference motion. The result was 30 in favour and 18 against. Perhaps reflecting the hard economic circumstances of the time, the meeting then decided "to forward this result by post and thus save the expense of sending delegates to Nottingham".

Saturday 21 October 1922 turned out to be one of those defining moments in the history of the NAS as the Special Conference being held at University College, Shakespeare Street, in Nottingham, convened.

The 18-strong Executive was joined by 72 delegates from 27 local associations. Amongst the names of the delegates, I noticed the first appearance of a Mr R. Anderson from London who was to play a very prominent role in the Association's affairs, becoming President in 1927 and General Secretary in 1941.

As the card vote at Liverpool might have suggested, those for secession were more convinced of their case than those opposed. They seemed to have been more active in lobbying for their cause than those in favour of the status quo.

On the evening of 20 October, as the trains arrived at Nottingham Station, delegates were greeted with the cry "Manchester is for secession". According to Ron Simons (NAS President 1970-71 and author of an unpublished book on the history of the NAS), one delegate wrote: "I could not help but notice the glow of unbounded satisfaction on the faces of Young, Kay and Carter, leaders of the Liverpool detachment. To them belonged the honours of converting Manchester."

The motion was framed in terms declaring that no one could be eligible for membership of the NAS if they belonged to an association of teachers that had adopted the principle of equal pay or one that was opposed to separate consideration for men. This time the motion carried on a show of hands. A card vote was demanded. This time the decision was not reversed. The card vote resulted in 4,047 for, 699 against.

It was entirely fitting and appropriate that George Cording was the President in the Chair at the time. According to Ron Simons he said after the vote: "I preached secession in 1913 at Cardiff, and they talked of putting me in a home. I was a voice crying in the wilderness. However you have not won your fight. It is only just beginning. It will be harder than ever. You are going to be in a big fight with the NUT. That will cause friction. We hope in time that will wear away and we may be able to work in contact. As Mr Kay has said, there are points of contact."

The NUT dismissed the venture as a "cock-boat – a little cockleshell which would founder on the first rocks". That prediction proved horribly wrong, completely underestimating the determination and courage of the founding generation of the NAS.

The same Special Conference resolved to appoint a full-time paid GS with effect 1 January 1923. The Executive appointed Arthur Warren who gave up a secure and promising teaching career to take on the post and stake his own future on that of the NAS. A number of members mortgaged their houses to provide the backing for the first year's GS salary and the Association's running expenses. Such was the degree of commitment by activists which was to ensure the survival of the NAS.

The affiliation fee was set at 10 shillings. In addition there was a legal aid subscription of two shillings. That was a significant increase on the subscription of two shillings and six pence payable whilst dual membership with the NUT existed.

Time was also found at the Special Conference to receive a report from Gateshead where a bitter salary dispute was raging and to organise financial support for members who had been suspended.

The NAS was set upon an independent and separate existence from the NUT. A great inter-union rivalry would develop for the remainder of the twentieth century.

Chapter 5 – The Birth of the Union of Women Teachers

To do justice to the UWT and acknowledge the crucial part it played in the development of the combined union I fast-forward to the mid-sixties and describe the circumstances surrounding its quite remarkable birth and rapid development. The birth of the UWT in 1965 was truly symptomatic of a fighting spirit and a strong dissatisfaction with other unions. In that sense its birth was similar to that of the NAS.

However, the genesis of the UWT was single and easily identifiable, unlike the 'multiple conceptions' of the NAS ongoing independently if contemporaneously around the time of the First World War. The UWT was founded quite independently of the NAS, but being born to campaign, militantly if need be, on behalf of the career woman teacher, it quickly became a sister and natural ally of the NAS.

The only recorded harbinger of the UWT occurred in December 1961. The Executive minutes record correspondence with a Mrs I. Hughes from a 'National Association of Schoolmistresses' who had requested advice and the names and addresses of NAS Local Secretaries. Nothing materialised despite a friendly and co-operative reply to the request.

The UWT was born in a 'slum' school in Brighton during the Spring Term of 1965. I say 'slum' school because of the disgraceful state of the buildings. It was no 'slum' in respect of its educational, social and sporting achievements which were quite magnificent, especially when set in the context of its catchment area and resources.

The school was Queens Park Secondary in Brighton. It served a tough working-class area in the town's north-eastern suburbs composed mostly of relocated overspill population from the East End of London. The area was rarely seen by the many visitors, day trippers and conference-goers who over the years have descended on the seaside resort in their hundreds of thousands along the A23, which travels through some lush green suburbs and parks as it winds its way to the seafront.

The photographs of the dilapidated school tell their own story. But they do not tell the story of five courageous and determined young women teachers who taught at Queens Park Secondary.

One day in February 1965 after classes were finished these five women teachers stayed behind to discuss what they might do about the appalling physical conditions of the buildings in which they worked. They thought the decaying disrepair of the buildings was also symptomatic of the state of their profession. The 'Brighton Five' were Sally Rodgers, Pam Goodridge, Carole Cuthbertson, Molly Pates and Mavis Wright.

In Mavis Wright's opinion Sally Rodgers was the leading light and the real driving force behind the initiative. Sally was an impressive figure, commanding natural authority and already had much organising and political experience, having been very active in the Worthing Liberal Party. Sally was to become the first Honorary General Secretary of the UWT. As Mavis Wright was the oldest of the five, having attained in her own words "the ripe old age of 32", she was appointed Chairman of the group. Let me hand over to Mavis:

'Five young women teaching in extremely difficult conditions at Queens Park Secondary School, Brighton, met to discuss ways of bringing pressure to bear to improve things. I, as the oldest was asked to chair this gathering.

"From this humble meeting in a classroom and fired by youthful enthusiasm, we decided to contact other schools checking if there was interest in setting up a union of women teachers committed to teaching as a career, to improving conditions in schools and furthermore a union prepared to take positive action if necessary to achieve these goals.

"Ten pounds each was put into a kitty to cover postage and with the assistance of a delightful school secretary we sent letters addressed to 'Women Members of Staff' to schools in London, Liverpool, Birmingham and Bristol.

"We were surprised by the immediate response. Marie Smyth (from Liverpool) was among the first to reply. And so it all began! The five of us became a very inexperienced and naïve set of 'Officers'. I remained in the Chair in those early, stumbling days, until 1970 when I handed over to Sidella Morten.

"All these first 'Officers' meetings' were held in my home – a very supportive and patient husband (AMA member to boot) making coffee for us when requested.

"Our first union meeting was held in 1966 at Friends Meeting House, Euston. A meeting of about 30 people, all enthusiasts, agreed to recruit locally. Sally Rodgers was appointed Honorary General Secretary. In 1967 the first UWT Conference was held at the Royal Hotel, Woburn Place, London."

As well as circulating other women teachers around the country, the founding Brighton Five at Queens Park Secondary decided upon another course of action in February 1965 that had quite dramatic results in their locality. They decided to pass the photographs of the disgraceful state of their school buildings they had taken to *The Brighton Evening Argus*.

The Argus, never a newspaper to shy away from campaigning, published the photographs. All hell broke loose. It provoked a controversy that ran for several months in Brighton. The Conservative- run LEA was not amused and defended their expenditure on education, quoting the fine achievements of the school. Others said those were achieved in spite of, not because of, the resources provided to the school.

The newly elected Labour MP for the area (Kemp Town), Dennis Hobden, was very vocal and played a leading role in campaigning for repairs to the school, raising the matter in the House of Commons as well. Some parents became very active on the issue and formed a group to campaign against "the scandalous state of the school buildings".

Articles and letters appeared in *The Argus* complaining of serious overcrowding, poor resources (only one radio for the whole school), dark dank rooms, unsafe gas and electrical systems, exposed pipes, classes with no blackboards, old and broken furniture, unsanitary toilets and cracked masonry. Pupils often had to traipse long distances between various buildings on the site in all sorts of weather.

Eventually in May 1965 the headmaster, Mr R.B. Tibble, in a prominent feature article in *The Argus*, was forced to break his diplomatic silence and defend the reputation of the school. Mavis Wright remembers Mr Tibble as a very good headmaster, a man of great personal integrity, who ran a fine school despite the circumstances. Alas, he was totally unprepared for the publicity. He defended 'his school' saying that despite the conditions it was very successful. Perhaps understandably he felt isolated, unable publicly to support the teachers' view that the disadvantaged pupils and the hard-working staff deserved decent conditions.

Groups of parents in other Brighton schools also began complaining of the poor state of their buildings, adding to the pressure on the Council. Brighton Education Committee was forced to take some action and began (in March 1965) with a decision to spend £18,000 on a new heating system.

To cut a long story short the Brighton Five had succeeded in raising a very effective campaign. In so doing they had exposed themselves to the risk of disciplinary action by their employers, the LEA. They were 'reluctantly arraigned' by their headmaster, privately sympathetic to their cause but traumatised by their 'revolutionary methods'.

Now retired, Mavis Wright freely admits they did not appreciate the risks they took. She quickly concedes they should have operated through a union. But they had no "real union". They had no confidence in the NUT to take the action required. Being women they could not join the NAS, the only union consistently willing to take action.

Quickly appreciating their kindred spirits, the NAS was happy to despatch a national official, Deputy Secretary Don Jarmin, to the town to defend one of the

Brighton Five, the Press Secretary Carole Cuthbertson, charged with unacceptable conduct in making public comment.

Although there was absolutely no NAS input into the Brighton Five's original decision to circulate other schools and campaign for decent buildings, many of the respondents were the wives and friends of NAS members, the most notable being Marie Smyth whose husband Arthur was NAS President and a future Honorary Treasurer. By the end of the year in December 1965 the UWT wrote to the NAS disclosing a membership of 235.

An early document giving information on the UWT succinctly summed up the rationale for the new union's existence: "Its formation arose out of the increasing dissatisfaction experienced by many women teachers at the way in which their interests were being represented, both to employers and the general public. The UWT was formed to combat inertia. The two main objectives were 'to improve standards in school buildings and equipment and teachers' pay and status'."

The document went on:

"Many members of the profession appear to believe that working in conditions of squalor and overcrowding shows an admirable dedication to duty. They forget that by doing this, they are not only accepting these things for themselves, but they are also condemning whole generations of children to a school life of poverty and unequal opportunity. Headlines such as 'Lessons held in the Lavatory' (*Daily Mirror* 19 February 1965) are met with comments of 'Yes, but we are a happy school' (letter to Editor 20 February). Apathy such as this is commonplace."

The document, signed by the entire UWT Executive, went even further:

"The Union believes that when bad conditions exist it is the teachers who are at fault. We believe that a union of teachers, pledged to fight against such conditions, will receive the overwhelming support of the general public and that this support will, in turn, help us to attain our correct pay and status."

The UWT Executive asserted that "every teacher has the right to teach in a classroom and not in a place which is a poor substitute" and they would if necessary "seek to enforce recommendations of the Ministry on class size by refusing to take extra children". Successful action had already been taken and the UWT would "not be afraid to take [it] again".

On salaries the UWT declared unequivocally that its "main concern must be the career teacher. We believe that teachers should receive a salary commensurate with their worth to society: to this end we support the introduction of long service increments, as these will make career-teaching more attractive."

The declaration on action at the conclusion of the document ran:

"For too long the teaching profession has talked without acting. The UWT offers you the chance for action." These words reminded me of the recorded comments of Arthur Warren in the minutes of the first NAS Conference at Margate in 1920.

Despite some 'male caution' on the Executive, the UWT's appeal and daring quickly led to a close liaison being established with the NAS. The NAS provided a room to facilitate meetings of the UWT Executive at its HQ, 59 Gordon Square in London, WC2. A few years later the first 'proper' offices occupied by the UWT were to be at Bank Court, adjacent to Swan Court, Hemel Hempstead, where in 1971 the NAS transferred its HQ, having outgrown the facilities available at Gordon Square.

During the course of 1966 detailed exchanges took place between the UWT and NAS Officers with a view to establishing a 'Joint Two' working agreement. The December 1966 NAS Executive meeting considered the proposed agreement with the UWT. There must have been some fears that the 'liaison' was headed in a certain direction and naturally there were some in the NAS who were nervous if not opposed to establishing too close a relationship. G. Lloyd Williams, a fiery Welsh NAS 'legend', recently retired Honorary Treasurer, a Past-President and obviously opposed to a 'Joint Two' arrangement, had somehow secured permission to come along to London and address the meeting. Rank and file folk would have been told to operate through their Executive Member. Lloyd Williams also wanted to stay behind and listen to the debate but the Executive drew a line at that. After Lloyd Williams had addressed the Executive it appears that two of his supporters then moved the adoption of a different agreement. That proposal was rejected by the Executive.

Instead the Officers successfully moved the adoption of a draft eight-point agreement to create "a special relationship" to pursue mutual interests and to provide efficient professional services. The UWT retained full autonomy in matters of policy and organisation, with the two GSs exchanging information on proposed changes in either case. The NAS would provide the UWT with advice and assistance for development. The NAS also agreed to provide the UWT with facilities at Bank Court, Hemel Hempstead for membership and subscription record keeping and for paying such monies received into the UWT account at the Westminster Bank.

The NAS would also provide its legal services and insurance benefits to the UWT in return for which the Association would be paid 50 shillings per capita per annum, or such other sum as might be agreed from time to time. The agreement did not confer membership of one union upon the other. The agreement would come into effect on 1 January 1967 and could be terminated by either party giving the other 12 months notice.

The UWT Executive agreed to these proposals establishing the Joint Two. Although formal separation between the two organisations was embodied in the agreement the potential for the 'partnership' to develop into 'marriage' was clearly apparent.

The UWT quickly lived up to the courageous campaigning promised in their literature. Despite their small numbers UWT colleagues joined in the NAS protest action against the deplorable salary situation in 1967. *The Birmingham Evening Mail* reported: "A lonely 15 women teachers are working to rule in Birmingham schools this week in support of 1,100 schoolmasters in the city who are refusing to undertake out-of-school activities."

Sadly within a few months of attending the 1967 NAS Conference as a sororial delegate, the Honorary GS of the UWT, Sally Rodgers, suffered an untimely and tragic death in October 1967. Mrs Beryl Gandy was appointed to succeed her.

In 1968 the UWT held its second AGM and first Annual Conference at the Hotel Russell in London, WC1. Three fraternal Representatives from the NAS were present, including the President, Joe Pretty, who addressed the Conference. The resolution carried on salary policy declared that a scale rewarding long-serving teachers was "the only way to ensure a just and economically sound distribution of the resources available". The UWT was unequivocal in its support for the career teacher and sided strongly with the NAS in opposition to the NUT's emphasis on the first few steps of the salary scale. Other motions carried referred to school buildings, cuts in educational spending and social education.

By 1968 the UWT had 21 recognised Executive Areas with a further one for Northern Ireland in the pipeline. A Scottish Branch had also been formed. The UWT had also secured representation on some local bodies in Havering, Oxford and Nuneaton.

During the 1960s as the UWT was rising, the resistance of the NAS to equal pay was fading away. By the end of the decade it had disappeared into history for all but a few diehards and of course our critics. Yet the fear the NAS had harboured that equal pay was not genuine was extremely well illustrated by none other than the UWT President, Mavis Wright. As the 1969 Interim Pay Campaign was beginning to take off, Mavis gave an interview to Bruce Kemble, the doyen in his day of education correspondents who worked on *The Daily Express,* which was published on 17 February 1969:

"Blonde Mavis Wright, leader of an all-female teachers' union, spoke out yesterday in support of the 'better pay fight' of the all-male NAS. She said: 'We are backing the NAS in their fight for a better deal for career teachers. People think they are anti-women; but they are not. They are only opposed to women preventing the profession getting better, proper salaries.'

"Mrs Wright, the 36 year old president of the UWT added at her Brighton home: 'We recognise that when teachers got equal pay it was at the expense of the men. They had to accept being paid at the women's rate.'

She says that the largest union, the NUT, has not managed to get a proper salary scale because there are too many women in it.

"Her union and the NAS recognise that these women are less militant about salaries. These 'fly-by-night teachers' stop the career masters and mistresses getting well paid for long service. Said Mrs Wright: 'I have been teaching for 15 years. I left to have a baby but returned to work after two years.'"

Bruce Kemble concluded his article by referring to the 42,000-strong NAS continuing their nationwide go-slow in their campaign to get an independent inquiry into teachers' pay.

I checked with Mavis. Did she still stand by those words all of (then) 36 years ago?

"Of course I do," she snapped back quickly. "I saw it with my own eyes. [My teacher husband] John's salary stood still for five years whilst mine caught his up." (Equal pay was implemented in five stages between 1956 and '61.)

The UWT's 1969 Annual Conference was held at the Metropole Hotel in Leeds. Gaps in the constitution were filled, including definition of the Officer posts, and Mavis Wright formally became the first UWT President. The arrangements reflected the NAS structure, except that the UWT was still too small to employ a full-time paid GS. An Organising Secretary had been appointed to deal with the increasing amount of office work.

The first motion debated at the 1969 Conference was to offer full support to the interim salary claim. The UWT joined with the NAS in putting aside the preferred policy on career structured salaries to promote unity with the NUT in pursuing a flat-rate claim. Other subjects debated included the inadequate preparation of student teachers in educational methods, class sizes, expenditure cuts and promotion procedures.

By 1970 the UWT was emerging as a significant development in the world of education trade union affairs. Although the expansion of the UWT from 235 members at the end of 1965 to over 7,000 by 1970 was quite spectacular, it remained in comparative terms still quite small. The significance lay in the partnership with the NAS. The 'Joint Two' had opened up their 'combined market' to all teachers, men and women.

At its 1970 Conference the UWT took a strong line opposing the raising of the school leaving age (ROSLA) from 15 to 16, due later that year. The UWT feared the totally inadequate resources available for the education service would be stretched even more thinly. Some members in Manchester boycotted ROSLA preparation meetings in protest.

In the October 1970 UWT's broadsheet the new President, Sidella Morten, hailed with obvious pride and satisfaction the attendance at the TUC Congress of two of its Officers with the NAS delegation through the Joint Two arrangements. Sidella, referring to the all-male NUT delegation, asked: "What are the women of the NUT doing? Do they really want to abdicate responsibility for themselves and their careers to the 25% of the NUT who are men? When are they going to wake up and realise they are a very silent majority?"

The press picked up on the appearance at the TUC Congress of the UWT and its phenomenal threefold growth over the previous year, going from just under 3,000 to 7,000 members. *The Daily Telegraph*, 10 September 1970, carried an article entitled "Misogyny Astray":

"Delegates have been somewhat puzzled by the sight of two young women among the NAS delegation of eight. This union of 48,000 is not only all male but has a reputation for misogyny. They are in fact . . . Sidella Morten and Margaret Bugg, Acting GS. The UWT it seems quietly affiliated to the NAS last January. Oddly enough, the rival NUT seated alongside has no women among the 22 delegates although its female members outnumber the male by 212,000 to 78,000."

A few days previously *The Financial Times* had run a somewhat similar tongue-in-cheek article on the same theme, "Don't Forget the Ladies":

"The Schoolmasters have a secret weapon in its perennial inter-union battle with the NUT. This secret weapon is women – to be exact the UWT . . . the NAS's sister organisation."

When the UWT held its fourth Annual Conference in Birmingham in October 1970 it became the first union to welcome the new Secretary of State for Education, Margaret Thatcher, to a public platform. The NAS observed that it was "appropriate that a career woman in politics should show more than an ordinary interest in the affairs of career women in teaching". Mrs Thatcher's attendance at the 1970 UWT Conference generated much press coverage for herself as well as for the Union. It was the first public speech of the new Secretary of State for Education, appointed as she had been by Ted Heath following his surprise victory in the October 1970 General Election.

As well as the now customary motion on career structured salaries, the UWT Conference developed further policies on minimum standards for entry to teacher training, equality of opportunity, contracts and conditions. Like the NAS, the UWT was based on pragmatism and not ideology.

The UWT had expanded its membership to such a level that it became both possible and desirable to appoint a full-time paid General Secretary. Pennie Yaffe became the first UWT GS, being appointed in 1970.

The UWT played a prominent role with the NAS during the protracted salary negotiations of 1970-71 which eventually led to a very significant arbitration. The 'A' Day is 'D' Day march and rally in London, successfully aimed at influencing the Burnham Arbitration in favour of a career structured salary award, was extremely well supported by UWT members. Pennie Yaffe addressed the rally in Hyde Park along with the NAS speakers, GS Terry Casey and President Ron Cocking.

The June 1971 issue of the UWT's journal *Career Teacher* contained a very eloquent, clear and coherent article (entitled "Seeking a voice") on the philosophy of career structured salaries written by its Honorary Treasurer, Mary Lewis. She conceded starting salaries were reasonable but the gap widens with experience until a career teacher is unable to look forward to the financial rewards of other professions:

"The only way in which a teacher can progress above the maximum of the basic scale is to scramble after posts of responsibility . . . which involves instability . . . and extra money for administrative work rather than teaching. Teachers who wish to remain in the classroom, because they feel their best work is done there, have to decide if they can afford to. Skill and experience no longer receive the rewards to which they are entitled."

Mary Lewis placed the blame for this "sorry state of affairs" squarely on the shoulders of the NUT's "dominance . . . and concentration on the first steps of the basic scale".

I will return to the history of the UWT and its relationship with the NAS in later chapters, when the general narrative reaches the mid-1970s in the lead-up to the effective full merger of the two unions through the Transfer of Engagements, negotiated in 1975, coming into effect on 1 January 1976.

There is much to tell of the 50 years between the mid-twenties and the mid-seventies during which the NAS battled on against the odds but never gave up, slowly but surely increasing in membership until, united fully with the UWT, the platform had been created to launch the combined NASUWT into the predominance it enjoys today, in the first decade of the twenty-first century.

Although the junior partner at the time, reversed of course in time as women were to comprise a majority of the combined Union, the role played by the UWT should never be underestimated. Without its founding, fighting spirit and clear understanding of the needs of the career woman teacher, the history of trade unionism in the British teaching profession would have been very different.

Chapter 6 – The Divided Profession

Fragmentation seemed to be the natural state of the teaching profession from the earliest times.

The 1870 Education Act, generally regarded as the beginning of the nationwide state education service, had established a dual system based on local authority (council) and voluntary (mostly church) schools. In the same year, the NUT was born, starting life as the National Union of Elementary Teachers. It became the NUT in 1889. Around the same time the National Association of Voluntary Teachers had been set up to apply pressure inside the NUT.

At the start of the period covered by this book, membership of the NUT was just over 100,000. It rose above 200,000 but in the 1970s the NUT was reported to have lost a significant number of members and appeared to slip back to between 170,000 and 180,000. At the end of 2003 the NUT declared a membership of 232,280 to the TUC and 324,284 to the Certification Officer, the latter figure including all categories of membership such as supply, part-time and student teachers, together with associate and retired members.

Membership of teachers' unions is 'not an exact science'. The number of members affiliated to the TUC (not a cheap option) is probably the best guide to realistic fully-paid-up in-service membership.

In 1906 the National Union of Women Teachers was formed to lobby for equal pay as they were disillusioned with the NUT's efforts on their behalf. It remained in existence until equal pay in teaching was achieved.

When a National Federation of Class Teachers was founded the heads responded with an organisation of their own. In 1897 the National Federation of Head Teacher Associations was established. The organisation survives to the present day under a slightly different name, the National Association of Head Teachers (NAHT) and declared a membership of 40,233 to the Certification Officer in 2003. It is not affiliated to the TUC.

Towards the end of the 19th century four organisations of heads and assistants 'masters and mistresses' were founded and in time formed a loose federation known as the Joint Four.

The first was the Association of Head Mistresses (AHM), founded in 1874 by Miss Buss and Miss Beale. The major reason for the founding of the AHM was to campaign for the extension of education for girls. It seemed reluctant to focus on pay and conditions issues.

In 1884 180 women teachers met to inaugurate the Association of Assistant Mistresses (AAM). Their primary concern was with work in schools founded for the higher education of girls and they shared their headmistress colleagues' reluctance to engage in conditions of service matters. Indeed some of its members resigned when the AAM decided to give evidence at a salaries enquiry. Respectable ladies did not engage in such vulgar matters. Nevertheless, in 1921 the AAM appointed representatives to the newly formed Burnham Committee on Salaries in Secondary Schools.

In 1891 the Assistant Masters Association in Secondary Schools (AMA) was formed. Its purpose was to protect and improve the conditions of service of secondary men teachers, mostly in grammar and independent schools. The AMA originally opposed equal pay unless it was accompanied by family allowances.

In 1978 the AAM and AMA merged to form the Assistant Masters and Mistresses Association (AMMA) with approximately 75,000 members. Membership rose rapidly in the 1980s following 'fall-out' from the more militant unions (the NASUWT and NUT) and it reached well over 100,000.

In 1993, after the AMMA had out of the blue been afforded recognition in Further Education by employers eager to break the established union's (NATFHE) monopoly, it changed its name to the Association of Teachers and Lecturers (ATL). In 2003 it affiliated a membership of 110,083 to the TUC and declared 201,845 to the Certification Officer.

The Head Masters' Association (HMA) was established in 1890 to serve grammar school headmasters. Heads of independent schools in the HMC (Headmasters' Conference) were all incorporated into membership and the two associations worked closely together, sharing a secretariat. Membership was always open to all relevant headmasters, including those of secondary modern schools created after the 1944 Act and of comprehensive schools that followed in later times.

The Secondary Heads Association (SHA) was formed in 1977 by the amalgamation of the AHM and the HMA. In 1983 the SHA took a further significant step when its members overwhelmingly voted in favour of the admission of deputy heads as full members, thus recognising the specific role of the senior management team in secondary education. Membership also included members of the HMC, GSA (Girls Grammar School Association) and HAS (Headteachers' Association of Scotland).

The SHA changed its name to the Association of School and College Leaders (ASCL) on 1 January 2006 to reflect its membership drawn from the full leadership teams of secondary schools and colleges. By that time the organisation claimed a membership of 12,000 but is not affiliated to the TUC.

The NAS was formed as a nationally based organisation in 1919, the UWT in 1965. On 1 January 1976 the NASUWT came into being. Membership rose above 200,000 in 2001. In 2003 the NASUWT declared a membership of 211,779 to the TUC and 304,762 to the Certification Officer.

The Professional Association of Teachers (PAT) was formed in 1970 directly in opposition to industrial action by the NAS, UWT and NUT over the Interim Award campaign which opened in 1969. Its guiding principle was never to take industrial action, no matter the circumstances. Perhaps it was an extremist position to say "never ever" regardless of the situation. It was a kind of 'militant pacifism'. NASUWT GS Terry Casey, in his own inimitable style, declared: "Every one had the right to join a union of their choice, even if it wasn't one."

PAT was quickly recognised in the early 1970s for Burnham purposes by a Conservative Government 'keen to teach militant unions a lesson'. At maximum it claimed a membership of 40,000 but soon slipped backwards in quieter times. To maintain membership it spread its wings beyond teaching, absorbing an organisation known as PANN – the Professional Association of Nursery Nurses – which also included nannies and childcarers. Lately it has recruited education support staff and changed its name to 'Voice', which is surely an occupationally neutral description of its business. Although the organisation is registered as a listed union with the Certification Officer it has appeared neither to declare membership numbers for 2003 nor indeed for other recent years.

In addition there were many other kinds of teachers' associations most of which were specific to subjects taught in schools; some types of institutions, e.g. residential and 'approved' establishments; certain religions; and particular circumstances such as teaching children with special learning needs. Very few if any claimed to be unions representing teachers' interests across the whole range of education, pay and conditions of service. Some from time to time made special pleas for their members in certain respects. Practically all the members of such organisations also belonged to the main unions, a few having formal links with the NUT for some periods of time.

It should also be remembered that the founding fathers of the NAS had all been very active stalwarts of the NUT. The NUT faced huge internal pressures, with the women pressing for an equal pay policy and a significant number of men threatening to break away if such a policy were to be adopted.

In addition many other teachers had already joined different associations, particularly in the secondary sector, not seeing their interests being protected or promoted by the NUT. Apart from pious pleadings for unity the NUT failed completely to propose any practical and realistic measures designed to achieve it. The NUT only ever proposed one 'solution' – dissolution all round and re-establishment as one. But that was the equivalent of take-over, or as one NAS commentator put it many years ago, "the unity typified by the cat after it has eaten the canary".

Given the deep divisions of views and perceived interests, the only way forward lay in a power-sharing formula. The NUT always sought the very opposite, preferably monopoly, but failing that overall majority. The NAS put forward at various times proposals for a federal approach or a 'Common Council' to deal with those issues upon which agreement had been identified.

From time to time motions calling for unity and merger with the NUT would be put forward for the agenda of Annual Conferences. They rarely attracted sufficient votes to get to the debating stage except on one or two occasions, such as in 1988, when they were deliberately voted up for debate in order to get knocked down.

The famous disunity of the British teaching profession is as old as the hills..

SECTION TWO
THE LONG HARD SLOG

Chapter 7 – The NAS in the 1920s

As well as fighting the attacks on teachers' pay and pensions and settling the issue of secession, the 1920s saw the NAS developing a wide range of policies on educational and other issues as well as putting in place the fundamentals required for a union to survive and prosper.

By the time of the second Annual Conference (Cardiff, 1921) 'hardy annual' motions were already making their appearance. One of the 'founding principles' of the NAS, 'men teachers for boys', was to find regular expression for many years. The Conference "viewed with alarm" the Government reneging on its "great progressive Education Act of 1918 thus endangering the national wellbeing at a time when it was more than ever necessary to develop the latent power of the nation's children". The NAS regretted "the two services most essential for social reconstruction, health and education, have been specially selected for attack by a section of the Press and certain reactionary bodies".

Another motion protested strongly against "the appointment of a teacher to any post being made conditional on the promise to perform extraneous duties voluntarily outside school hours". A reminder supporting the cynic's view that there is not much new in education was to be found in a motion calling for Her Majesty's Inspectors to cease "examining and setting written tests" in favour of them becoming "Educational Advisers".

The Cardiff Conference requested the Executive to establish a fighting or sustentation fund to reflect the importance of campaigning, militantly if need be.

The 1921 Conference instructed the Executive to set up a Benevolent Fund, reflecting the dire financial circumstances of many schoolmasters. It remained voluntary for many years and was the subject of constant and sometimes heated debate at Conferences. Whilst contributions were voluntary every member was entitled to benefit. Eventually the conflict was resolved by incorporating an identifiable element for benevolence into the national subscription.

A motion calling for local autonomy based on the Executive Districts, with the National Association reconstituted as a federation of such, was defeated.

The dye was set for the highly centralised character of the NAS to evolve over the years.

The accounts for the year ended 31 March 1921 revealed 5,381 members had paid the full subscription of two shillings and six pence, with around 300 others paying reduced rates, to provide an income of £747 17s. 2d. The operations of the Executive and its committees, together with publications, advertising and propaganda, took up most of the expenditure. Four guineas were spent on press cuttings, reflecting the importance attached to campaigning and publicity. One of the 'men of Cheltenham', Frank Ordish, had been elected Press and Propaganda Secretary at the Margate Conference in 1920.

The 1922 Conference in Liverpool instructed the Executive to establish a Legal Aid Fund after two years of debate over whether it should be optional or mandatory. It was decided to incorporate a legal aid element in the national affiliation fee such was the importance of the issue in the debate over secession from the NUT. Many who supported the NAS cause stayed with the NUT after secession through fear of losing entitlement to legal aid.

Besides the familiar themes there were some interesting variations. A Captain J.R. Beckett from Liverpool moved the Government should make grants to LEAs conditional upon them providing adequate playing fields for elementary school children.

Another motion criticised the dual and duplicating system of inspection by LEAs and HMI as "unnecessary, expensive and conducive to friction". A call for all inspectors to have continued experience teaching in schools reflected schoolmasters' concerns to ensure practice prevailed over theory in the determination of education policy.

The Association's concern with social issues surfaced for the first time in 1922. A motion moved by Arthur Warren condemned the press reporting of "the sordid details of crimes to be inimical to the interests of youth" and called for those responsible to exercise some self-censorship.

In 1922 the objects of the NAS were defined:

> to safeguard and promote the interests of schoolmasters;
> to facilitate communication and to give collective expression of views;
> to enable action to be taken when necessary;
> to secure separate consideration of schoolmasters' claims;
> to secure educational progress locally and nationally;
> to secure official recognition on relevant bodies;
> to afford Government, LEAs and others the advice and experience of schoolmasters;
> to secure joint control of education;
> to promote friendly relations between schoolmasters;

to recruit every schoolmaster into membership.

In 1923, the first full year as an independent association, the Conference came to London, opening on Easter Monday and establishing the tradition of holding the annual event during Easter week. Arthur Warren had been appointed General Secretary (GS) by the Executive. Some 28 local associations were represented at the Conference of over 150 delegates.

Conference declared that as a consequence of "broken promises" it could not recommend to parents that their sons should enter training for the profession. Against the background of rising economic gloom and depression, not to mention serious social and industrial unrest, Conference deplored the rise in juvenile unemployment.

On the educational front the Conference opposed the suggestions that practical work be curtailed in schools. The 'vocational v academic' curriculum remains an issue, largely unresolved in British schools, to this very day. Pressure was building on the facilities of the education service whilst resources were being savagely cut.

F.C. Greaves from Leeds was elected Vice-President for 1923-24 and in the first contested election for Honorary Treasurer W.H. Thoday (London) beat W.H. Young (Liverpool) by 1,862 votes to 1,372. Whilst ballot turnouts are not authoritative statements of membership numbers, they can be indicative. The difference between the turnout for the Treasurer election (3,234) and the card vote (of 4,700) on secession from the NUT seemed to confirm the general belief that some 1,500 members had decided to stay within the safer 'large tent'. The loss had been predictable but regarded by the "whole-hoggers" as a price worth paying.

In 1924 the Annual Conference moved to Leeds, with 49 local associations represented by 181 delegates. Three resolutions were carried on the iniquities of the Burnham Committee and the lack of NAS representation. A motion on the failure to implement the 1918 'Fisher' Education Act deplored the "surrender of the late Governments to the irrelevant clamours of reactionary panic-mongers" despite the "self-sacrificing exertions" of the war.

The 1924 Conference embraced a more international concern. A motion on the League of Nations was proposed by Richard Anderson, a future President and GS, which called for the speedy establishment of a fully representative League of Nations as the best way of reducing international tension and avoiding "such devastating conflicts as the one from which the world had just emerged". The resolution committed the NAS "to use every means at its disposal, in and out of school, to further the cause of world peace".

A motion opposed "mere mechanical tests" on pupils, declaring that it retarded true educational progress and was inimical to the welfare of children.

The Conference declared the present structure of education to be based on class prejudice and social custom and called for fundamental reform dividing schools on genuine educational principles, namely primary for 7-to-11 and secondary for the adolescent.

Hopelessly inadequate and unsanitary school buildings were deplored. In addition to pay, pensions had become a deep source of grievance with the imposition of a 5% contribution from salaries which had also been cut by 5%. The Conference deplored the failure of Lord Emmot and his Committee to mitigate this "glaring injustice" and arbitrary levy upon a relatively "pliant section of the community".

On the domestic front the General Fund income exceeded £2,000 for the first time at £2,419 17s. 10d. The Legal Aid Fund took in £2,323 16s. 10d. An Emergency Fighting Fund stood at just over £455, having taken in surpluses from the Southampton and Gateshead appeals.

The financial statements showed that the loss of membership at the time of secession in 1922 had been recovered by the end of the following year with membership restored to over 5,000 (5,113 at least paying the full subscription). The subscription, then collected locally, was raised to 15s. and included an NAS affiliation fee and a Legal Aid Fund contribution.

Within five years of its birth much of the character and traditions of the Association had been set. The tradition of resolution-based Conferences was firmly established. There was a strong belief that was the correct way to formulate policy. Amendments were even permitted during the course of Conference debates, something unheard of in other organisations. Debates were well conducted with speakers listened to. Decisions were readily accepted by those defeated in debate because the process was so open and transparent.

This way of going about business generated good publicity. Journalists did not have to search behind the scenes for stories of plots, scandals or divisions. The best stories could be found by listening to the speakers drawing on their experiences and expressing their views from the podium.

The Association developed a reputation for strong internal discipline, loyalty and cohesion. With the NAS regarded by some as a pariah, one had to be made of sterner stuff than average to be a member and to possess significant moral courage to be an activist.

The NAS gave strong support to the most renowned of the Hadow Reports, *The Education of the Adolescent* (1926). Sir Henry Hadow, Vice-Chancellor of the University of Sheffield, had been appointed Chairman of the Consultative Committee of the Board of Education established during the brief period of the first Labour Government in 1924. The Committee also included Dr R. H.

Tawney, a great historian, economist and social philosopher, whose writings influenced the Labour Party.

It was possibly the single most important event which sustained the aim of secondary education for all in the 1920s despite the broken promises surrounding the "land fit for heroes" after the First World War. The 1926 Hadow Report redefined education along the now familiar lines of primary and secondary with transfer at 11 plus. Perhaps its most important recommendation was free secondary education for all children. In 1926 only 8.3% of pupils went on to secondary education. Hadow envisaged selective grammar, 'modern' and 'continuation' schools, an enhanced role for vocational education and also recommended the leaving age be raised to 15. The recommendations were to prove a long time in being implemented.

The NAS, whilst acknowledging the desirability of raising the school leaving age, stressed that the length of time in the secondary school was less important than ensuring that boys came under the influence of men teachers.

Full-scale school reorganisation along a clear primary-secondary divide at 11 plus was not to arrive until the 1944 Act. The National Executive took a hostile line against Circular 1350 from the Board of Education which recommended senior schools for the education of pupils aged over 11 years. The Executive thought this to be a cheap option. The idea was more favourably received by the NAS President of 1927, Richard Anderson. In his Presidential speech he saw the positive side in so far as "it is possible to see in the senior schools of today the secondary schools of tomorrow".

Debates on the school-leaving examination raged in the NAS. For example, the Newcastle Association of Schoolmasters produced a widely read booklet expressing concern that the new examination might be too limiting and restrictive, squeezing out those aspects of education dealing with the development of the whole child. The debate culminated in a motion put to the 1927 Conference which acknowledged the right of LEAs to assess the work of schools and teachers but asserted that a standardised examination would not achieve the desired aim and would "seriously prejudice the work of education".

Throughout the 1920s NAS members joined in the condemnation of Sir Eric Geddes who had dismissed education as a "one-eyed policy of educating people for jobs that aren't there". The NAS expressed deep concern about the devastating effects of widespread youth unemployment as an estimated 60,000 14-year-olds left school every year immediately to join the dole queues and of whom 80% would never experience any form of education again.

In the wake of Hadow the NAS stipulated that the work of junior and senior schools had to be recognised as of equal importance and that there should be no differentiation in regard to status, professional prospects or salary or in any other way.

I noted with interest that the Yorkshire Federation of the NAS invited Sir Henry Hadow to debate his 1926 report at its Annual Conference in November 1929. The Annual 'Yorks Fed' Conference survives to present times and I was pleased to be invited to address it on a number of occasions during my time as GS.

Chapter 8 – Men Teachers for Boys

No history of the NAS would be complete without a chapter on the issue of 'men teachers for boys'. Our founding fathers also stressed the equally important corollary of 'women teachers for girls' although that required no campaign for it was already guaranteed. One of the reasons for retaining the titles of both organisations in the new 'NASUWT' after the Transfer of Engagements on 1 January 1976 was to symbolise the importance of retaining a good number of both men and women career teachers in schools.

The second NAS Annual Conference at Cardiff in 1921 had set the tone for the policy. G. Bain and A.H. Russell from Bristol successfully moved and seconded an uncompromising motion: "That this Conference demands in the National interests, on moral, physical and psychological grounds, that boys, 7 to 17 years, shall be taught by men teachers." The resolution was softened over the following three years as the lower age was raised from 7 to 8 years and some ambiguity removed by referring to the desirability of boys coming *predominantly* under the influence of men teachers.

The NAS naturally had its critics. The NUT, which led much of the criticism, at times appeared to accept the principle of 'complete interchangeability'. It mattered not if teaching became entirely a female or male occupation. To be fair to the NUT, it did not always proclaim the extremist line of complete interchangeability. The NUT Conference of 1908 had deplored "the growing practice of substituting women for men teachers in schools" and resolved to take "every legitimate means" to prevent it. The following year the NUT declared its "opinion that the employment of women teachers in boys' departments is undesirable on educational grounds". In 1925 the NUT stated: "Wherever possible the older boys in public elementary schools should be taught by men teachers."

According to Ron Simons (NAS President 1970-71) some schoolmasters believed that deteriorating promotion prospects after the Hadow reorganisations of the 1920s drove more men away from teaching. Prior to Hadow most schools had been single sex dealing with pupils 8-14 often staffed entirely by teachers of the same gender. Reorganisation produced mixed junior and senior schools, the former mostly with headmistresses, the latter with headmasters. More men were reluctant to serve in junior schools under a headmistress than women were to work under a headmaster in the senior sector. As a consequence men lost out on employment opportunities as well as on the possibility of promotion to headship, virtually ruling themselves out in the junior schools.

Some 'hardliners' in the NAS argued that mixed schools should be abolished in order to secure the position of men teachers to be exclusively in charge of boys and the corollary for women and girls.

Board of Education figures for 1929 showed that headships in single sex junior schools achieved a fairly even gender balance. But in the case of mixed junior schools there were just over 1,900 headmistresses compared to around 350 male heads. In mixed un-reorganised schools men outnumbered women heads, 8,550 to 5,600 in round figures.

Thus to take the case of Leicester, after reorganisation in 1930, of the 16 headships available 13 passed to women and only three to men. In protesting about the situation the local NAS was joined by some NUT members, unable to do so through their own union.

In 1927 the NAS position on 'men teachers for boys' was afforded a high media profile by the trenchant and colourful articulation of the case by the incoming President, Richard Anderson, delivering his inaugural speech to the Annual Conference in Bristol. Headlines the following day included "Wild West Women not wanted as Teachers", "Can Women Teachers Teach Boys Manliness?" "Schoolmaster Says He Would not use a Powder Puff to Tar a Garden Fence!"

Richard Anderson proclaimed that since the business of education was preparing children to live in the community, boys as men and girls as women, teachers had to posses the qualities they were seeking to impart. "One of the essential qualities in the adult male is 'manliness', and in the adult woman, 'womanliness'. Does Nature produce anything more abhorrent than a 'female man' or a 'male woman'?

"No woman can train a boy in the habits of manliness. It is true that one occasionally meets a woman who can 'manage boys as well as any man'. Well, such a one might be an admirable proprietress of a Wild West saloon, but we have no room for her in our boys' schools."

In today's context such views would be derided but they were typical of the times. Anderson had seen active service in the First World War, where physical courage was required. He was no red-necked right-winger but quite the opposite. He was a distinguished and highly regarded member of his community in Deptford, both as a headmaster and a civic leader, a Justice of the Peace, and a Labour Party councillor who later became Leader (1936), Mayor (1946) and an honorary freeman of the borough (1960). He was a passionate supporter of education, attacking the Government for "the great calamity" in ditching the

1918 Act and surrendering "to the blatant clamouring of those who from various motives regard education as an extravagance which we cannot afford".

Another twist of the 'men teachers for boys' policy was the parallel demand for 'headmasters for men teachers'. The 1925 NAS Conference had carried a resolution expressing opposition to an assistant master serving under a headmistress. The Conference went further, "pledging itself to afford full financial support to any member . . . who may be called upon to serve under a headmistress and, acting on the advice and instruction of the Executive, refuses to do so".

The 'Tottenham Case' of spring 1931 was one of several celebrated instances of men refusing to serve under headmistresses. A woman was recommended for appointment as acting head during the absence through illness of the headmaster. Her name had been submitted to the Director of Education by the headmaster himself. All the male teachers, including NAS and NUT members, sent a letter of protest to the School Management Committee. The school management then decided to recommend to the Education Committee that a male assistant head be appointed. The Education Committee heard conflicting representations from both the NAS and the NUWT. It then appointed a man, the first senior assistant who did have a claim under 'seniority', as acting head on a ten votes to five decision.

Around the same time in 1931 a controversy blew up in Peckham, South London, at the LCC Friern (mixed) School, over the appointment of a woman head. The LCC stood firm and maintained the appointment despite a large protest meeting organised by the NAS and its London Branch, the LSA, at the Dulwich Swimming Baths, attended by over 300 parents, schoolmasters and sportsmen including players from the Dulwich Hamlet Football Club (in those days a famous amateur sporting institution).

The 'sex war' as it was dubbed seemed to bubble on into the 1930s. Later in 1931 the London schoolmasters protested against "this flood of feminism" which was robbing boys of men teachers and diminishing the latter's promotion prospects. An editorial in *The Times* in April 1931 declared that: "After a certain age boys are most efficiently taught by men teachers."

Speakers at the 1933 NAS Conference in Southampton were in full flow over the issue. A resolution was carried asserting that it was against the best interests of education for men to have to serve under women. A. J. Taylor, also from Liverpool, claimed: "It is impossible for a man to serve under a woman and retain his self-respect and manhood."

Today one can only sympathise with the editorial which appeared in the *News Chronicle* attacking A. J. Taylor's speech. It said he was doing the cause of the proper place for men and women "the worst kind of disservice", observing that it was "rather depressing to find Victorian sex prejudice in this crude and extravagant form still surviving in the teaching profession of all others".

The same culture led schoolmasters to resent being inspected by women. According to Simons most LEAs and heads arranged sensible compromises which avoided confrontation. In single sex schools it was usually possible to arrange for an inspector of the same gender to visit. In mixed schools it was accepted that men and women inspectors would visit, and in many cases care was taken to avoid the problem while recognising that PE presented particular problems.

The NAS issued a circular in 1934 declaring it was strongly opposed to the inspection or supervision of boys' PE by women. The language and reasoning reflect a bygone age:

"The NAS is confident that it expresses a normal view of both sexes when it states that it is neither desirable nor natural that a woman should be placed in charge of the physical training of a boy. Such a position entails dealing with intimate matters concerning the pupil's person. It is not usually accepted as fit or proper for women to undertake duties involving such dealings with boys, except in the cases of nurses or mothers of the boys concerned." The circular applied the same principle to the inspection of PE, arguing that "a competent inspector must be an expert demonstrator."

In 1935 an NAS member, Harold Lomas, provided the most celebrated case of men teachers refusing to serve under women. Lomas taught PE at the Fareham Senior Boys School in Hampshire. The case came to a climax in April 1935, coinciding with the Annual Conference being held in Swansea where the incoming President, F.C. Arkless from Sunderland, had highlighted the issue in his address, claiming: "A man is not a fitting person to develop the character of a girl for the simple reason that he has never trod the path she is to tread" and vice versa.

The Lomas case had first surfaced nearly two years previously in June 1933. On that occasion Lomas politely refused to parade his class for the woman inspector. Later the Director of Education for the authority visited the school to warn Lomas he had orders to suspend him unless he relented. Under protest Lomas complied and reported the matter to the NAS who requested the Education Committee to receive a deputation. The authority ignored that request, which was to prove a costly mistake.

When the woman inspector returned to the school on 26 February 1935 Harold Lomas again refused and this time stood his ground despite the threats of suspension and dismissal. No pressure was applied on him to place his job on the line. He acted entirely voluntarily while knowing that the Association would support him.

Harold Lomas was a strong character and a committed member of the NAS. He had served in the Royal Navy as a physical training instructor, where he had also become a boxing champion. The ages of the boys in the class concerned ranged from 12 to over 14. The Director told Lomas that he would accompany the inspector when she returned to his school the following week to ensure he complied. When the time arrived, Lomas, acting with the full support of the NAS, again declined. He was then dismissed with effect from 13 May.

The case received widespread publicity. Public opinion was strongly on the schoolmaster's side. The Authority was condemned for refusing to meet the NAS, for many such potentially explosive cases had been resolved through discussion.

These events raised a storm at the Swansea Conference. The Ex-President, Harold Gordon, deployed his great powers of oratory to the full in moving a resolution applauding the member and condemning the Hampshire Education Committee. Conference pledged itself to support any action taken by the Executive of behalf of the member and to oppose such decisions "which can only bring ridicule on a great national service and is entirely out of harmony with social conditions". Richard Anderson, Honorary Treasurer, in seconding the motion pledged the Association would sell its (unique, built in situ) boardroom table and pawn the (massive gold) Presidential chain before abandoning Lomas.

The National Executive Member for Southampton and Hampshire, Harold Judd, together with a recently retired Past-President, W. Woodward, lobbied the LEA hard and continuously. GS Warren raised the case with Ministers and MPs at Westminster. Eventually Harold Lomas was offered another job in Southampton with a higher salary, which he was pleased to accept. The NAS covered all his salary and pension loss for the relevant time. Lomas was very content with the support he had received.

It had taken to the spring of 1938 to resolve the Lomas case. Neither the Hampshire County Authority nor any other LEA ever again forced the issue. There was a rapid increase in the number of PT inspectors appointed, with small LEAs agreeing to share staff when necessary to avoid such confrontations occurring again. Lomas was seen as a martyr who won his case for everyone else if not completely for himself.

In 1935 the NAS claimed success in the Rhondda where headships of all single sex boys' and mixed schools were reserved for men teachers.

In 1938 the NAS conducted a series of public opinion polls through its local associations on the issue of men teachers for boys over the age of eight. The results were overwhelming as I am sure the schoolmasters expected. Percentages in favour ranged from 96.5 to 99!

The NAS also resorted to conducting opinion polls amongst parents when the headships of some mixed schools became vacant and controversial. In West Derby, Middlesbrough, West Hartlepool, Preston and Birtley (County Durham) polls showed huge majorities of around two-thirds in favour of men heads in mixed schools. In 1938 there was a huge row in Lancashire following the appointment of a woman head to an all-boys' school in Huyton which was resolved by the Director writing to the local NAS Secretary informing him that the practice would not be repeated.

The last controversy before the Second World War which broke out on the issue of men teachers for boys occurred at the Berkshire Road School, Hackney Wick, in the Autumn Term of 1938. The LCC Education Committee appointed Miss M.B. Spender, MBE, as headteacher in the newly reorganised mixed senior school. She was previously head of Wordsworth Road School in Stoke Newington. It was the first time the LCC had appointed a woman as head of such a school.

The LSA predictably was vehement in its condemnation of the appointment, although its GS Frank Gibbs was careful to emphasise there was nothing personal in the matter as he and Miss Spender were on friendly terms. Gibbs spoke very highly of her qualifications. Miss Spender was very dignified over the affair, merely saying she was "surprised by the storm" and "did not wish to do anything to add to it".

The LSA formally presented objections to Herbert Morrison, leader of the LCC. The LCC stood by its decision, insisting that Miss Spender had applied in the normal way "and she was accepted as the most capable and best qualified applicant".

On 14 October *The Hackney Gazette* reported strong public opinion against the appointment. Some men were quoted but "Mothers were particularly vehement against the proposal, but, having children at the school, they preferred to remain anonymous". As a last throw of the dice the LSA conducted its customary plebiscite amongst residents, the result of which was 2,957 in favour of a headmaster, 198 for a headmistress. However, that also failed to persuade the LCC Chairman to reconsider. In its editorial of 14 October *The Hackney Gazette* described the LSA as "Ungallant Schoolmasters", dismissed their views as "Victorian" and deplored the LSA's tactics, which "smacked of coercion rather than persuasion".

As secondary education spread NAS policy focussed more on securing a higher percentage of men teachers for boys in this sector. This aspect had assumed a greater importance by the end of the 1920s with increased pressure to raise the school leaving age to 15 by 1931. Already all infants' schools were entirely staffed by women, as were a large proportion of junior ones. Women were well represented in the senior schools and thus it was possible for some boys never to have had a male teacher throughout their education.

The NAS claimed to have achieved some success in its campaign for men teachers. In 1932 Board of Education statistics revealed that women teachers were in charge of 6,479 boys' classes. By 1938 that figure had declined to 3,248. The number of headships held by women in all-boys' schools had fallen from 26 to 7. In mixed schools the number had declined from 5,617 to 4,043. But the number in charge of senior mixed schools had risen from 2 to 19.

From 1922 to 1937 the number of men teachers rose from 38,500 to 46,000, representing an increase from 22% to 29%. For a number of years the NAS defined the ideal gender balance in the teaching profession to be 60%-40% women and men respectively. The issue has passed into history although there remains much concern amongst educationalists about the declining number of men in the teaching profession, especially in the primary sector.

Chapter 9 – The NAS in the 1930s

The external challenges facing the NAS in the 1930s were dominated by the depression, exacerbating the divisions within society which saw mass unemployment and extensive child poverty, pay cuts rather than increases and on the international front the rise of fascism and the slide towards the Second World War.

From the domestic viewpoint the development of the NAS had been slow but steady. Membership stood at over 7,000 according to the 1930 Annual Report. A very large proportion of that membership was to be found in the London Schoolmasters' Association (LSA), some 2,500. That meant that apart from some other strong areas in large cities and towns, such as Bristol, Cardiff, Birmingham, Liverpool, Manchester, Leeds, Newcastle, Southampton and Sunderland, membership was often spread very thinly on the ground.

Nonetheless the Schoolmasters were never the ones to give up whatever the odds. Great attention was paid to recruitment and the 1930 Annual Report compliments the Sunderland, Salford, Birmingham, Chester-le-Street, Nottingham, Leicester and Sheffield local associations for their above-average success. Many new schoolmasters were approached individually, sometimes in their homes, by NAS activists. This personal approach, illustrating dedication and conviction, often proved the key point in persuading schoolmasters to join the Association.

The implementation of the recommendations of the Hadow Report of the previous decade still dominated the education debates of the times. The school leaving age was supposed to be raised to 15 in 1931 but the cuts put paid to that. Many LEAs were in the throes of reorganising their schools and questions of accommodation, staffing and curriculum took up much of the Schoolmasters' concerns.

The early days taught self-reliance. Local associations had to deal with their issues largely on their own. The full-time help available consisted of no more than one official, the incredibly hard-working and dedicated Arthur Warren, operating originally from his home in Willesden and only after 1926 with secretarial help and an office at 59 Gordon Square in London, WC1. In 1928 an extremely competent administrative assistant in the person of C.S. (Sidney) Hines was appointed. A full-time Organiser was not appointed until 1937, in the person of Tom Smith, an activist from the North East who later became a very distinguished President of the NAS in 1956, having returned to teaching after war service in the RAF with the Meteorological Office.

It was not until October 1932 that the number of local associations reached 100. The National Executive consisted of 22 members, comprising four Officers – President, Vice-President, Ex-President, Honorary Treasurer – six representatives from London, two from Liverpool and one each from ten districts covering the rest of England and Wales.

The National Executive Member (NEM) became the vital link between the grass roots and the leadership. The tradition sprung up of an NEM attending virtually every meeting called by a local association. Activists appreciated the efforts of their NEMs fostering loyalty and genuine friendships. The leadership was kept abreast of the feelings and views of the classroom practitioners. Issues were debated on their merits and factionalism was rare.

This philosophy of self-reliance meant that the NAS never favoured collecting union subscriptions through the employer, the practice known as debiting at source. Subscriptions were paid to local associations, often having been collected by the NAS school 'secretary', today known as the 'school rep'. The national element was subsequently passed on and an amount retained which could vary according to local discretion within limits set by the NAS. Eventually subscriptions were to be collected nationally with moneys being rebated to the local associations. As national aspects became stronger and modern banking practices arrived the NAS was the first union (in the 1960s) to develop standing orders and direct debiting as the most effective and independent method of collecting 'subs'.

Throughout the whole of the period from 1922 (the year of secession from the NUT) to the outbreak of war in 1939 the national affiliation fee (including the Legal Aid Fund) remained at 18 shillings per member – 90 pence in today's currency. It was mostly a period of intense depression. Indeed in the 1930s prices fell by around a third overall, thereby increasing the purchasing power of any given sum of money.

Fifteen shillings was taken for the running expenses of the Association and three were allocated to the Legal Aid Fund. In addition the Rules stated that a minimum local subscription of six shillings had also to be raised. The overall 'sub' was thus a minimum of 24 shillings, which was applied by the majority of local associations. Some, however, charged more.

The Benevolent Fund and its administration was the subject of keen debate at Annual Conference. In the early days there was much genuine hardship amongst schoolmasters and their families. The welfare state was some time away and benevolence was consequently a very important element in the work of most trade unions – and the NAS was no exception.

The strong traditions of Liverpool in this area explains why the Association's voluntary sickness insurance scheme, originally known as the Schoolmasters' Provident Society (now as the Schoolteachers' Friendly Society) was run from that city.

When benevolence contributions were voluntary about half the members chipped in. For many years the Rules stipulated that benefits had to be available to all. The two were mutually inconsistent. It took until the 1960s for a sensible resolution to be found. As the subscription was raised to £5 for all it included 10 shillings to be paid to benevolence.

The Legal Aid Fund, launched at the very first Conference at Margate in 1920, continued to be the source of a vitally important service to members. Denied official recognition, the law courts provided a forum in which the NAS could act on behalf of individuals as well as establishing helpful precedents for others. The Legal Aid Fund had grown to £3,300 by 1930 and £4,600 by 1937.

The 1938 accounts showed that the NAS's 'turnover' was in the region of £7,000 per annum. Expenditure at £7,317 slightly exceeded income at £7,177, leaving a small deficit, which was uncharacteristic of the NAS.

The challenges facing the national and local leaders of the NAS were awesome. The resources they had at their disposal were limited to say the least. Overall membership remained small. Simons speculates that without the calibre of national leaders like Warren and Anderson it is doubtful if the NAS would have survived beyond the start of the Second World War in 1939.

By rule the Honorary Treasurer was subject to annual election, whereas anyone elected Vice-President was guaranteed (other things being equal) a three-year term of national office, proceeding automatically to become President and then Ex-President. In the 1960s a four-year term was provided by the creation of Junior and Senior Vice-Presidents. An unofficial 'culture' developed that the position of Treasurer should only be subject to a contested vote upon retirement or resignation. There was a belief that the Treasurer should provide a degree of continuity in office to provide a balance between elected officers (all serving teachers) and the more 'permanent' appointed staff position of General Secretary (GS). In recent times that 'culture' has waned and the situation is more fluid – and many might say more open and democratic.

At the time of writing (2008), every GS appointed has been both a practising teacher and a member of the National Executive, although there is no rule governing 'previous experience' for any post, except of course full membership of the NASUWT for elected positions. The situation has been complicated by the industrial relations legislation of the 1980s requiring certain positions to be subject to membership-wide ballots even where officials do not exercise a vote within their unions' democratic structures.

The relationship between the two 'permanent' post holders, the Honorary Treasurer and the GS, has been seen as the most critical for the Association. This 'special relationship' began with the first GS, Arthur Warren, and Richard (Dick) Anderson who had been President in 1927, become Honorary Treasurer in 1929 and was destined to succeed to the position of GS upon the death of the former in 1941.

The 'golden oldies' from that era with whom I had conversations on the subject all spoke in glowing terms of the Warren-Anderson relationship. They described the two as strong, level headed, dedicated, courageous, principled and for ever prepared to travel the length and breadth of the country to meet with members in groups however large or small. They did not always start out agreeing with one another on an issue but always managed to find a sensible way forward. They were able to learn from one another.

Inevitably in such a small organisation the leaders knew their men and the men knew their leaders. Most delegates to Conference attended at their own expense. There was much respect and trust for such leaders amongst the membership generally.

Arthur Warren became GS in January 1923, giving up the security of his post as headmaster of a large elementary school to risk his career for the purpose of building up a new and controversial union in incredibly difficult circumstances. A few years later Warren mortgaged his own home in Clifford Gardens, Willesden, to provide collateral for the lease of 59 Gordon Square, the elegant Bloomsbury house in London, WC1 which became the first 'proper' office and HQ of the Association.

Arthur Warren was a workaholic, with only a small number of staff to assist in providing advice and support to Officers and the Executive as well as individual members. He had a good appreciation of the law, saving much money that otherwise would have been spent on legal advice. He knew and understood the professional and union aspects of the teaching job. He became well respected by Government Ministers, civil servants and their local equivalents – LEA committee members and Directors of Education. Warren was a man of sacrifice and integrity who set a wonderful example and was responsible in my view for the start of the tradition in which members afforded great respect, trust, support and even affection for the GS.

Approaching his own retirement in 1983, one of Warren's successors, Terry Casey, wrote of his "personal regret" at never having met him. Warren had died five years before Terry's delayed entry into teaching caused by the Second World War. Terry wrote about Warren's influence "continuing to imbue the reinvigorated NAS and his memory was cherished by my mentors – Gibbs, Gordon, Meigh and John Evans. They all had a dedicated sincerity and charismatic qualities of leadership. But they themselves were inspired by Warren."

Simons believes Anderson's greatest contribution to the development of the NAS came in the 1930s when he was one-half of the GS-Honorary Treasurer partnership. Although a Liverpudlian by birth he had embarked on a teaching career in London. Coming out of the army after the First World War he became embroiled in the new 'men's movement' along with other ex-soldiers and servicemen. His talents were quickly recognised and he was elected from London on to the National Executive and became President in 1927, taking over as Honorary Treasurer from Woodward in 1929. As I have already observed, Richard Anderson, affectionately known as Dick or simply 'Andy', was also very active in civic affairs and in 1946 was elected Mayor of Deptford.

Simons describes Anderson as "a big man, occasionally ponderous but never dull". Apparently he did not often intervene in debates at Executive and Conference but when he did it was to telling effect. He commanded great respect, possibly due to "his very manner which bred confidence". He was the epitome of stability and reliability.

From the external viewpoint salaries remained a potent source of grievance, particularly in the early 1930s as more cuts were imposed. Naturally the country became more concerned with other international developments as the 1930s progressed. Education had to take a back seat and there were relatively few initiatives to provide spark and debate which might have aided recruitment. Equal pay seemed more remote as both the LEA employers and the Westminster governments were unresponsive to the NUT's demands.

By 1930 more perceptive commentators were already expressing fears that humanity was beginning to lose the battle between war and peace. Education was seen as pivotal in this struggle. A Lord Mayor of London had said: "Education is engaged in a race with catastrophe unless education is sufficiently powerful to retain control."

The first motion debated at the 1932 Conference of the NAS recognised "the immeasurable value of the League of Nations as the world's greatest power for peace" and it pledged its members "to embody the aims of its work in emphatic and continuous teaching in the schools". A second resolution called for the establishment of "Junior Branches of the League of Nations Union" in the senior classes of schools.

From time to time two broad divisions of opinion, or perhaps emphasis, appeared in the NAS: the 'broad-fronters' and 'narrow-fronters'. 'My generation' of young activists had been brought up in the 'narrow-front' tradition, which held that broad issues, such as war or peace, should be left to the political parties. That view, common in the '60s and '70s, possibly reflected a reaction against the political agitation that surfaced in the NUT. The 1930s were different. Schoolmasters were right to see how the general economic and political situation spelt trouble for the education service and for their living standards.

Some of the more cynically minded believed the instability had been generated deliberately to rein in social advance and restore the old class-ridden system that had briefly been threatened by the First World War. Schoolmasters could see at first-hand the effects of grinding child poverty in many cities and regions of the UK. The unsuccessful General Strike of 1926 had been followed by the Wall Street Crash in 1929 and the deepening of the worldwide economic depression.

In 1931 the Prime Minister proclaimed that mechanisation of production would condemn more workers to unemployment. Young workers were particularly at risk. It seemed that Sir Eric Geddes' callous judgement 'that education was training pupils for jobs that were not there' was a self-fulfilling prophecy. It must also have represented one of the few occasions in history when business people did not complain of the inability of schools properly to prepare pupils for work.

The clouds having gathered, the storm began to break in 1931 when the Chancellor of the Exchequer, Philip Snowden, called for a "restriction of national expenditure". The outcome was a decision by Parliament to establish 'another Geddes' Committee, this time under the chairmanship of Sir Eric May. The resultant decision to cut teachers' salaries yet again provoked unprecedented levels of anger and bitterness which I write about in Chapter 21: "Cuts upon Cuts".

The May Report contains an astonishing example of the rich and powerful rationalising naked self-interest:

"Since the standard of education, elementary and secondary, that is being given to the child of poor parents is already in many cases superior to that which the middle class parent is providing for his own child, we feel that it is time to pause in this policy of expansion, to consolidate the ground gained, to endeavour to reduce the cost of holding it, and to reorganise the existing machine before making a fresh general advance."

On 23 August 1931 the Ramsay MacDonald Government fell. It was replaced by a coalition consisting mainly of Conservatives but still led by the same MacDonald. That proved extremely controversial in the Labour Party, vividly remembered by those involved for many a year thereafter.

Student teachers suffered gravely as a result of all these cuts. From 1929 to 1931 student intake to teacher training had been increased in anticipation of the raising of the school leaving age to 15. On 18 July 1929 the President of the

Board of Education, Sir Charles Trevelyan, defiantly declared the determination of a Labour Government to press on regardless of resources to raise the leaving age with effect from 1 April 1931.

With the fall of the Labour Government in 1931 the forward-looking policies of Trevelyan had been replaced by the strictures of May. The NAS quoted evidence to counteract the prejudiced view of May that state school children were getting a better deal than middle-class children. Some 43,000 classes contained between 40 and 50 pupils each. Classes numbering between 50 and 60 pupils stood at nearly 20,000. Only 9.5% of elementary school children transferred to secondary education.

The 1927 Conference of the NAS had carried a resolution pointing out the "disappointing and foreboding" facts disclosed by the Annual Report of the Chief Medical Officer to the Board of Education. Disease and poverty were rife. Child mortality remained high with nearly 70,000 deaths below the age of five.

A future President of the NAS, William Barford, summed up members' feelings when he said: "We must have patience; the misery in our coalfields, continual depression due to bad trade; low wages; unsanitary housing and the inevitable physical, mental and moral deterioration associated with such conditions are enough to appal."

In December of 1928 the President of the Board of Education, Lord Eustace Percy, had conceded in Parliament that there were 2,827 schools on a 'blacklist' for unsanitary conditions and buildings in desperate need of repair.

The schools themselves often reflected the same impoverished environment the children experienced at home. Many schools had limited, if any, play areas. The street was often the only play area for children. 'Gutter cricket' and 'pavement football' were common sights in the streets even though such games were apparently a police court offence.

In 1927 the National Playing Fields Association, supporting the Duke of York's Appeal, had published research revealing that there was only one public football ground for every 8,100 people, one cricket field for every 11,550 and one playground for every 11,263. Research conducted by the Association revealed that there were over 4 million children attending elementary schools without the proper facilities of any kind to play sport.

Many NAS members were keen on sport and did their best to develop it in their schools and districts. The best example was to be found in Liverpool where virtually the whole of boys' sport was run by the LAS. In 1930 the NAS published a textbook, *Swimming for Schoolboys*, written by the President at the time, W.R. Shimmin, another member from Liverpool who was very active in school sports. It was a best- seller. Over 160,000 copies were sold. It was widely recognised as the most helpful and authoritative book on the subject of its time.

In February 1931 the House of Lords rejected the proposal to raise the school leaving age, perhaps 'conditioned' by the May Report and fearful of those who had argued for a much higher level of additional resource. The Government made no effort to reinstate the proposal in the Commons. As a result there were over 1,000 newly qualified teachers unemployed by December 1932. The Board of Education then imposed a limit on the number of entrants to teacher training establishments.

The 1931 Conference saw, appropriately, the Jarrow and Hebburn Association moving a resolution calling for the Treasury to pay for the provision of boots for necessitous children because local voluntary effort could not cope. A few years later in October 1936 Jarrow saw the start of the famous 'hunger march' of some 200 unemployed miners to London to protest against the impoverished economic and social conditions of the time.

NAS members, displaying a deep concern for educational issues and the general social well-being of the children in their schools, were appalled at the prejudice and ignorance found in the May Committee. They saw no conflict in also standing up to fight for their own interests as any good trade union should. They established the tradition in the NAS that there is no fundamental conflict between the 'union' and the 'professional' sides of their work.

Reflecting serious salary discontent north of the border the Scottish Schoolmasters Association (SSA) was formed in 1934. It seemed initially to have constituted a fairly loose association of men teachers to present the case for schoolmasters but who had no intention of leaving the dominant Educational Institute of Scotland (EIS).

In the view of W.L. Marsland, President of the NAS in 1938, who visited the AGM of the SSA, schoolmasters were not being firm enough in their demands to compel the EIS to take their concerns seriously. In contrast to the denial of representation of the NAS on the Burnham Committee for England and Wales, the SSA was represented on the Scottish Council dealing with teachers' pay negotiations.

The older members seemed content to stay inside the EIS but Marsland said he detected more discontent amongst the younger element. One delegate attacked the SSA President's complacent report and threatened secession of 4,000 schoolmasters from the EIS if nothing more were done. The Glasgow Branch produced a report in favour of separation. However, there were still strong views in favour of remaining in the EIS, especially for services such as benevolence and legal aid, reflecting the same NAS experience of resignation threats in 1922. The President felt that secession was nearer than the leaders thought.

Eventually the SSA did secede from the EIS and formed a partnership with the NAS. In 1975/76 the SSA integrated fully into the merging NAS and UWT.

The divisions in British society, sharpened by the privations of the Great Depression, were reflected most vividly in the Annual Conferences of the early and mid-1930s. The NAS President of 1934, A. H. Russell from Bristol, who had also gained some national renown as a 'mathemagician', having written books and broadcast on the subject, hit the headlines with his warning that schools could become the "forcing beds of revolutionaries" in the wake of all the cuts imposed by 'May'. In his Presidential address Russell said he was "appalled by the fact that hundreds of men teachers are coming to the conclusion that the present economic system is tottering to its fall, and that they are instilling into the children of the nation the notion that social revolution is inevitable".

A.H. Russell blamed the Government and called for the "restitution of the ten percent so callously deducted by force a year and a half ago" when "legal contracts were forcibly broken at the Government's command and Orders in Council had to be specially passed, so that no action for breach of contract could be tried in the Courts". That was "without parallel in the history of England".

The 1934 Conference carried the most politically charged resolution in the history of the Association. With only three delegates dissenting, the resolution regretted that the teaching profession had been forced into the political arena, but it contended that "professional integrity demands that the schoolmaster should do his utmost against the sinister, reactionary policy revealed in the recent activities of the Government," being persuaded that "such policy is dictated by class prejudice and has a definite anti-social tendency".

Richard Anderson, then Honorary Treasurer, in moving the motion compared the 5.4% of national income spent on education in Britain with Holland, 22.5%; Denmark 20.6%; Switzerland 24%; Norway 14.9%; and France 6.6%. He suggested the cuts in education had a more permanent and sinister motive: "Whilst it is the duty of Government to safeguard the well being of the nation, the policy of the 'National Government' would appear to be to safeguard the interests of the bankers".

The 'class war' continued with Vice-President Harold Gordon seconding the motion with accusations of "class conscious, anti-social, sinister and reactionary policies of the 'Dictatorship Government' installed in 1931".

The News Chronicle of 3 April 1934 credited Haydn Davies, the fiery young leader of the LSA, with "the most revolutionary speech" of the gathering when he said: "The golden road to university via the private and public schools has not been touched. The attack has been made on the secondary and elementary schools." Davies called for the nationalisation of the public schools, which were riven with class prejudices. In due course that became NAS policy. Haydn Davies had fought the 1929 General Election as the Liberal candidate for St Pancras SW.

Many other speakers on various motions throughout the Conference continued to rail against the cuts in teachers' salaries and other educational spending. Responding to the attacks, Lord Irwin, Minister of State for Education, said the schoolmasters were becoming too political. Mr W. Craven-Ellis, the local MP for Southampton, the venue for the 1934 Conference, who was present for the debate, criticised the teaching profession for becoming "too closely allied with politics . . . and endeavouring to put into the minds of young people political ideas". His comments were greeted with loud protests from the floor.

Throughout the 1930s the NAS became more and more concerned with the international situation. It was not a question of party politics but a belief that governments around the world should pay much more regard to social and economic circumstances, the deterioration of which were all combining to rekindle the threats of war.

The NAS was closely involved in the activities of the National Peace Council. The Association supported the national petition for a new peace conference. NAS Conferences had consistently called upon all governments to promote a sense of respect and authority for the League of Nations, for without that developing public support, the slide back into force and violence to determine international disputes would be inevitable.

The Association was very active in the Workers' Educational Association (WEA), a far more important body in those times with little other means of providing adult learning. The WEA was a champion of world peace. Local associations were encouraged to purchase copies of *Ploughshare*, the publication of the 'swords into scythes' movement.

In his Presidential address to the 1935 Conference, F. C. Arkless from Sunderland joined many of his immediate predecessors in calling for higher spending on education. He denounced the increased expenditure on armaments "since it stimulates the arms race which leads to war". The Conference called for an International Peace Day for national observation. Mr Arkless also spoke about his direct witness of the appalling effects of unemployment upon children: "The life of children cannot be lived apart from the life outside. The children are ill-housed, ill clothed and ill-fed, ready victims of illness and disease."

The 1935 Conference in Swansea received a telegram of good wishes from former Prime Minister Lloyd George: "As the loyal son of a Welsh schoolmaster I would like to associate myself with the welcome extended by my fellow countrymen to the Conference of NAS. Schoolmasters should feel at home in Wales, for it is a land where for a long time education has been held in high and general regard . . ."

In 1938 the NAS sent four representatives to the League of Nations Union Young Teachers Conference in Geneva. In the same year the Executive supported the appeal on behalf of stricken children in Czechoslovakia, recently occupied by Nazi forces.

By October 1938 with the prospect of war increasing, the Officers reported to the Executive that they were making preparations in the event of a state of emergency being declared. The GS was to arrange for a cellar at headquarters to be rendered waterproof and fitted with a steel door. Arrangements were to be made for the immediate transfer in suitable containers of all books, papers, important documents and effects relating to the affairs of the NAS. Local associations were to be urged to adopt similar plans.

If necessary the GS would have authority to deal with all matters, financial or otherwise, necessary for the conduct of the affairs of the Association. The GS would consult with available Officers. In the event of the GS being not available the Honorary Treasurer would act in lieu of him, and failing that the powers would be passed respectively to the President, Vice-President, Ex-President and Past-Presidents. All Members of the Executive would continue in office until circumstances permitted the calling of elections.

The GS would make enquiries about the temporary removal of headquarters to some suitable locality outside the London area and arrange for staff to follow if possible. Members of staff if called up for military duty would be treated in the same way as teachers. Plans were made to deal with air raids. Schoolmasters were to be allowed to retain their membership without subscription if on national or military service and not receiving their normal salary.

In the event these plans were not totally successful. Many of the NAS records were lost as a result of enemy action in the war. My understanding is that 59 Gordon Square did not receive a direct hit in the Blitz but was badly damaged through the effects of blasts from bombs falling nearby and resulting fires.

The problem of juvenile delinquency was raising its head before the Second World War. Late in 1938 the Executive formed a special committee to consider the subject. The committee decided to conduct surveys. The results showed public concern with declining standards of discipline, poor parenting, ineffective probationary services and lenient sentencing in the courts. A Memorandum on Juvenile Delinquency reflecting such concerns was approved by the Executive in November 1938.

The Memorandum quoted the official criminal statistics for 1900-34 and compared the average for that period with 1936. Offences had risen from approximately 58,000 to over 80,000. The number of offences per million people rose from 2,700 to 6,000.

The Memorandum also noted the greater involvement of boys and blamed the increased indiscipline on "the much misunderstood or misapplied modern psychology" which left young adults to find their own self-discipline. The Committee did not think much of self-expression. "Time enough for 'self-expression' when there is a 'self' worth expressing – and that came later", proclaimed the Memorandum. It was too often "but a fanning of the inchoate and anti-social elements of its nature, the very things that need discipline and control."

By the end of 1938, the year before the outbreak of the Second World War, NAS membership had increased to 10,923. That was more than double the number who had some 16 years earlier seceded from the NUT. The 1920s and '30s had been tough times for everyone but I suspect the NAS leaders of the day must have been a little disappointed with the slow if steady rate of growth. The NAS was still a small organisation but it punched way above its weight. The NAS could take some credit for the restoration of the 10% salary cut as members never stopped protesting whilst other organisations, larger and better resourced, seemed to stand idly by. The NAS was able to maintain its self-respect. Key issues such as men teachers for boys were kept vigorously alive.

On the domestic side, important benevolent and legal work occupied much of the time and effort of the small numbers of staff and many local Officers. As the Second World War approached Arthur Warren had to make provision for some office functions to be moved out of central London for safety reasons. He was about to lose his two key members of staff, Sidney Hines and Tom Smith, who were soon to be conscripted into the armed forces.

Before the end of 1939, with war having broken out in September, membership slipped back to 10,103, dipped to 8,801 in 1944 and was not to rise again above 10,000 until 1947. However, the NAS had to operate on a shoestring as only about 4,000 members were able to pay their subscriptions during the war.

And as for being put to the test, greater challenges were to follow during the course of the Second World War.

Chapter 10 – Second World War Years

There were many events in the twentieth century which shaped the nature of the NAS. But the way schoolmasters were treated during the Second World War despite their patriotism and flexibility in meeting challenge after challenge probably explains better than anything else why militancy grew more pronounced in the years following 1945.

With Hitler having invaded Poland in August 1939 war was about to be declared. On 23 August the Government announced over the radio that teachers were to return to their schools, which would be reassembled in two days time to await instructions. On 31 August the order to evacuate school children from the major towns and cities was issued. It was to start the next day, for some as early as 6 a.m. Contingency plans had been prepared.

The largest operation was obviously in London. There were 1,589 assembly points identified. School parties, including teachers and children, departed from 168 different stations. By the end of the day some 287,000 children and adults had been evacuated, transported to 271 places and thereafter dispersed mostly by bus and coach to towns, villages, hamlets and homes in eastern England, the South West and the Midlands.

The same exercise was repeated in many other large towns and cities of the nation. The teachers and the Women's Voluntary Service worked long and hard. That virtually every child got from A to B must count as a miracle. It does not require much imagination to comprehend the many and manifest problems that inevitably were experienced in such a massive and almost instantaneous rendition of so many thousands of children into totally strange domestic and social environments. Teachers became social workers overnight.

Whilst reasonable arrangements had been made for evacuated children from grammar schools to attend the local equivalents, there had been much less provision made for the education of the majority from elementary schools. Teachers on the ground had to make it up as they went along. Evacuated elementary pupils had to share accommodation with the local village school or make do and move into the parish hall, working men's clubs or even the Scouts' or Girl Guides' huts.

A Board of Education survey carried out in January 1940, some four months after the evacuation, revealed that a quarter of all 'elementary' children were not in school. For 'grammar' youngsters the problem was around half the size.

Some were receiving part-time education. Nature rambles, field work and games were often the order of the day for many.

NAS headquarters and local association secretaries were inundated with requests for advice and support. In the chaotic situation Directors of Education had to make instant decisions with little time for the 'niceties' of consultation. Inevitably many seemed arbitrary and personal disappointments and inconsistencies abounded.

An NAS deputation to the LCC took place in October 1940 in which GS Arthur Warren, accompanied by his LSA counterpart Frank Gibbs, acquainted the Director of Education with the multifarious problems being encountered on the ground.

In addition to the logistical and practical problems faced, evacuated NAS members were incensed with the poor financial support they received. Once again the class system reared its ugly head. The well- paid mandarins in Whitehall had looked after their own kind and arranged for evacuated civil servants to receive a billeting allowance of 21 shillings per week. Teachers were fobbed off with five shillings and were expected to make up the difference with the charge for board and lodging imposed by the billeter for which no standard rate was set but had to be reached by "mutual" agreement between the schoolmaster and his host. Charges varied considerably. Simons quotes a case of three guineas per week at a time when the average industrial wage was at £185 per annum, roughly equal on a weekly basis to that amount.

Naturally the NAS set about lobbying and targeted MPs, Directors of Education, civil servants and Government Ministers. The official answer given in the House by the Minister of Health, Mr Elliot, was intriguing: "The householder on whom a teacher who *voluntarily* [my emphasis] accompanies his school is billeted is only called upon to provide lodging. The teacher may remain so billeted during his stay . . . The payment to a householder of 21 shillings per week for a billeted civil servant *compulsorily* [my emphasis] evacuated with his department covers the cost of certain meals and lodging."

One might be tempted to joke that teachers were not expected to eat but the double standards stuck in their gullets. The pretence that their involvement was voluntary amounted to cheap and nasty cynicism. One can imagine the opprobrium that would have been heaped upon schoolmasters if they had treated the whole business as genuinely voluntary and decided to keep out of it. Such treatment soured the concepts of professionalism and extraneous 'voluntary duties' amongst schoolmasters and led to many disputes in later times.

On 9 October 1939 the Labour MP for West Willesden, Samuel Viant, put down a question to the Financial Secretary to the Treasury asking on what grounds billeting allowances to civil servants were assumed to cover food and lodging, but only the latter for teachers. The appropriately named Minister, Captain Crookshank, replied with bland patrimony, claiming "the position of the Civil Servant and that of the school teacher are not comparable", whilst conceding "the matter is being investigated".

The NAS protest and lobby succeeded. After investigation the Government said it was prepared to change its mind and apply the civil service scheme to teachers. However, the NAS had not reckoned on the NUT who rejected the offer because few of its women members were householders. The NUT insisted on a revised scheme which disadvantaged the schoolmasters, the overwhelming majority of whom were householders incurring 'double costs' of maintaining two residencies. The NUT treated the issue as one of salary, not of compensation for genuine additional costs. One cannot blame schoolmasters for concluding with ever-greater conviction that their interests lay outside the NUT.

The Local Government Staffs War Service Act of 1939 empowered (but did not force) LEAs to make up the salaries of their employees, including teachers, to their 'normal' civil levels had they not enlisted for active service. The NAS had many members who were in the reserve forces or the Territorial Army and who had naturally been called up at the beginning of the war. By the end of 1940 younger schoolmasters were also being conscripted. Some LEAs exercised their discretion under the 1939 Act, others did not.

The NAS had joined forces with branches of the local government employees union, NALGO, to conduct vigorous campaigns in the 'reluctant' local authorities. NALGO won a case against Bolton in the House of Lords establishing the right of the National Arbitration Tribunal (NAT) to make binding decisions where employers and employees could not agree. The NAS immediately took up a similar case in Penge where the authority had declined to exercise its discretion. A somewhat repentant LEA offered the 'Bolton' deal, to be effective from 1 March 1943. The NUT accepted that. The NAS objected, arguing it should be retrospective to 1 August 1940, and took its case to the NAT. The Tribunal ruled in the NAS's favour. NAS men in Penge were triumphant, but it has to be said such success was not achieved in every area of the country concerned.

Agitation over voluntary 'duties' surfaced again in 1942. Schoolmasters were concerned their goodwill, freely offered in times of crisis, was being taken for granted and voluntary 'duties' were becoming expected and then demanded as a permanent contractual obligation. Circular 1596 issued by the Board of Education shortly before the summer vacation of 1942 proposed that schools should remain open during the holidays. Furthermore holiday duties should be imposed upon teachers.

It was incredibly ill-timed and unnecessary. In the middle of wartime there was no question that teachers were suddenly going to abandon the children, still evacuated in large numbers. But the NAS rightly saw the long-term implications that they were to lose their holiday entitlement and be compelled to become social workers and carers during school vacations. The NAS also objected strongly to the lack of consultation over the Circular. The only other organisation that protested was the very pro-equal-pay NUWT.

By this time Richard Anderson had succeeded Arthur Warren as General Secretary. He lobbied a friendly MP, Sir Ernest Graham Little – the Independent MP who represented the University of London from 1924 until the constituency was abolished in 1950 – asking him to pursue the matter in the House of Commons and with the Government. Sir Ernest did this with great skill and enthusiasm, so much so that the Government soon produced an amending circular, 1615. It reflected a significant change of heart, conceding that on past experience "most needs were likely to be adequately met by the opening of a limited number of schools as holiday play centres or holiday clubs".

The NAS's concerns had already surfaced publicly at the 1941 Conference when a resolution had been adopted declaring "all extraneous duties be regarded as voluntary" and without prejudice to future consideration of the issue, "the Executive should take immediate action to secure remuneration for members who voluntarily undertake such duties".

GS Richard Anderson had a letter published in the *TES* on 29 November 1941, a day on which *The Times* also devoted much coverage to the issue of "the multitude of extraneous duties which particularly in these days [the schoolmaster] finds himself at least morally compelled to undertake".

Anderson wondered whether "these days the last thing that matters in school is education". "Bewildered" teachers were being swamped by 'duties' associated with meals, milk, clothing, rationing and massive amounts of social work. Being patriotic, schoolmasters had not protested hitherto but something had to be done. The schoolmaster was "well aware of the fate of the willing horse and realizes that docile acquiescence in this matter does not necessarily increase the respect in which he is held by the public at large".

Calling upon the Board of Education and LEAs to face these issues Anderson added: "If the schoolmaster is called upon for extra work, the claim for extra pay is not merely vexatious . . . [If] his leisure time is now devoted to supervisory duties, this period is no longer his leisure, it is his duty, and extra duty at that." The *TES* in its editorial comment was moved to observe that the NAS claim was "a reasonable request and should receive sympathetic consideration".

The NAS President at the time, William Barford, captured the feelings of members in his message carried in *The New Schoolmaster*. No preparation for the possible emergency could have "visualised such a violent and sudden disruption of the even tenor of our way. The call to the teaching service was answered unanimously. Despite all the difficulties and injustices . . . we have fought them ceaselessly and are seeking from the Government those adjustments so necessary if professional embitterment is to be avoided."

Barford drew an interesting comparison with the Fisher Act of 1918 "having concluded that wartime presented possibly the only opportunity for laying the legislative foundations for educational and social progress. The exigencies of national struggle exposed the glaring inequalities in society and the degrading conditions in which millions of the less fortunate people lived. War has deepened our loyalty to the children."

Problems also remained in the cities. By the end of 1939 the LCC had concluded that some 120,000 children had not been evacuated, 72,000 had returned and 71,000 were not accounted for on school rolls. Accordingly about 230,000 children were 'roaming the streets' receiving no education. Emergency schools began to open on a voluntary basis.

Responding to a call from the LCC in December 1940, volunteer 'truancy officers' uniformed with LCC armlets were enlisted 'to round up' the children, some of whom were still 'running wild' as it decided to enforce school attendance.

Slowly a wartime 'normality' of schooling developed which was characterised by much disruption, especially during periods of heavy enemy bombing. In London 290 schools were destroyed or seriously damaged and 310 extensively affected. Important ports and industrial cities such as Liverpool and Coventry suffered similarly. Many schools were commandeered as emergency rest centres and children had to be diverted to other schools.

Like many others, teachers and pupils were traumatised by their experiences of the bombing. During the period when the Germans deployed incendiary bombs, teaching staff often took turns to spend the night on school roofs watching for fires. In this context teachers were heavily involved in extensive social work to help children cope with the wartime traumas of shattered lives and homes. But schoolmasters were soon to be embittered with the poor financial support they received.

Like many organisations the work of the NAS was seriously disrupted by the war. More than half the NAS membership had been displaced, either through call-up for military service or evacuation from the large cities with their pupils. The conscientious Arthur Warren, with poor eyesight failing even more, was under enormous pressure as he struggled to maintain the high standard of service he wished to provide as the GS. His health, already poor, deteriorated quickly and on 4 March 1941 he died. He had not reported to the admittedly intermittent meetings of the Executive since 24 February of the previous year. Those who knew Warren were convinced the outbreak of war had hastened his death.

Arthur Warren had been greatly assisted by 'his last President', William Barford of Leeds. Barford was described by his contemporaries as one of the greatest orators ever to serve the Association. He had been elected to the Presidency in 1939 and served, in the absence of Annual Conferences, until 1943 when once again they were resumed, starting in Nottingham. During those early war years Barford travelled thousands of miles on NAS business all over the country in darkened and unheated trains, on occasions at risk to his life and safety.

At the request of Terry Casey, Bernard Morton from Sheffield, another very distinguished President (1948-49), wrote a confidential account (in 1979) of the events surrounding the appointment of Warren's successor.

Bernard Morton drew on accounts he had from William Barford, who chaired the proceedings, Harold Gordon, President 1934-35 and a very persuasive operator, and some comments from other Executive Members, as well as conversations with Dick Anderson.

Warren had been the uncontested 'natural' choice in 1922 as the first full-time GS. In 1941 the outstanding and perhaps 'obvious' person for the position, the Honorary Treasurer Dick Anderson, did not apply. He held the post of the 'permanent officer' and that, coupled with his ability and presence, afforded him much influence. He was a successful headmaster of a large boys' elementary school in London, was a Labour councillor in Deptford (becoming Leader in due course) and had a promising political career ahead if he so chose. Furthermore, according to Morton, "Executive and Conference insisted on keeping the GS in his place as a servant and not as a master – not even a leader" thereby putting Anderson off. (Given the leadership role the Executive has invariably expected, if not demanded, of the GS, I believe Morton considerably exaggerates the relevance of this point.)

The Executive had drawn up a shortlist of three candidates for interview. They were F.C. Arkless of Sunderland, Jim Rice of Hull and Frank Gibbs of London. Arkless and Rice were Past-Presidents, respectively 1935 and 1926, Gibbs a future President, 1947.

Morton believed the division of opinion between the 'broad-fronters' and 'narrow-fronters' complicated matters although the purpose of each group was "obscure and the definition depended upon who was defining". The narrow-fronters believed the Association should restrict its activities to its fundamental aims, particularly securing 'men teachers for boys' and separate consideration for pay. The broad-fronters believed the NAS had also to concern itself with the wider issues of the day in addition to education. (It appeared there had been some controversy over the telegram which the NAS sent to Mussolini, supporting the campaign seeking to persuade the Italian dictator to stop bombing Abyssinia.)

On the morning of the interviews the Executive learned that Arkless, a broad-fronter, had withdrawn. Apparently he had second thoughts and concluded the job would be too much of a gamble and the remuneration insufficient to justify the move from the North East to London. That left only two candidates, Rice and Gibbs, both narrow-fronters.

Quoting "one of those present", Morton said that neither candidate produced any ideas to show he was the man for the job. "They rehashed the points of view associated with them and with which the Executive was familiar – and bored!"

After the interviews the Executive discussed the candidates but adjourned for lunch without having made any progress. This is where a few conspiracy theories surfaced. Members went their separate ways, William Barford to a small café he frequented on Executive days. Morton says it was unlikely that Harold Gordon went with him, but he could have. Barford said not. Morton believed Barford and thought collusion had been unlikely, although it was alleged.

Immediately after lunch Harold Gordon was first on his feet. He told the Executive that it was clear they were satisfied with neither candidate. "They all knew who they wanted," claimed Gordon. Morton speculates whether that was really true but "who better to persuade them that it was than Harold"! Gordon then moved that the Executive discharge the original reference and proceed to appoint by invitation. That was carried. Gordon then moved that Anderson be invited to become GS. Morton says he was told the proposal was carried "unanimously". Anderson agreed to consider the matter.

Anderson later confided to Morton that he had not wanted the job for the reasons already stated. However, when he consulted his wife Mary about the offer, apparently she was not at all surprised, smiled at him and said: "It was obvious all along that you were the only man for the job." Anderson accepted the job on condition that he would not be required to give up his political work and would be allowed time off to do it, his estimate being half a day each week.

Morton says Rice and Gibbs were "infuriated". Rice was appointed Honorary Treasurer (in succession to Anderson), causing a by-election in his own Executive District, Hull and surrounding areas. He promptly resigned as Honorary Treasurer but stood for re-election. Unfortunately for Rice, he was then defeated by Charlie Carter, described by Morton as "the old fox from

Liverpool". Thereupon Jim Rice walked away from the NAS and took no further part in the work of the Association, nationally or locally.

It is possible (this my speculation) that Jim Rice had made himself unpopular with his criticism of some Presidential rulings at Conferences which had gone against the Hull delegations, including one made in 1928 when Carter was in the Chair.

Frank Gibbs left the Executive immediately but stayed active in the NAS by becoming the Honorary GS of the LSA. Frank was held in very high regard by the LSA and had shown outstanding leadership in the 1930s, leading the fight against the 10% salary cut. It is pleasing to note that Frank Gibbs was elected President of the NAS for the year 1947-48.

In order to deal with War Bonuses a Joint Sub-Committee of Burnham was formed from its three constituent parts, Primary, Secondary and Further Education. In July 1940 it issued proposals for the teachers' first war bonus. The NAS was still unrecognised officially and therefore denied a say in the determination of the proposals.

The proposals were, firstly, to pay a war allowance of 6% of salary to teachers whose remuneration was £260 p.a. or less. Secondly, those earning between £261 and £275 15s. were to receive an amount that would bring their pay to the same level as the first group.

Examination of the effects quickly revealed that the exercise had been distorted away from a war bonus and become a redistributive exercise towards equal pay for women. The details meant that a large proportion of women would receive a bonus whilst the vast majority of schoolmasters, who believed they bore heavier financial and family responsibilities, would get nothing.

Even men in the NUT were deeply dissatisfied with the outcome. Responding to their criticism at the NUT Special Salaries Conference, GS Sir Frederick Mander declared that: "If there is any feeling today that the war bonus operates unfairly against men, the remedy is not to criticise the Executive but to alter the policy of the Union which you yourselves have made." Clever if slightly disingenuous stuff, for it was sharp practice to treat a war bonus as a normal pay increase. Schoolmasters' belief in the need for a separate NAS strengthened even more.

Some LEAs were sympathetic to the NAS concerns. In Liverpool, where the NAS was strong, the LEA introduced its own scheme, granting war bonuses on the basis of 5% for salaries up to £300 p.a. and 2½% on the next £200.

In the spring of 1941 the age at which teaching was defined as a reserved occupation was further raised from 30 to 35, having been 25 at the start of the war. The NAS opposed the move. The lesson from the First World War was that a society capable of winning the peace had to be built. The survival of men in the teaching profession to maintain good standards of behaviour in school and elsewhere was essential for that purpose. The recruitment of men into teacher training had fallen by nearly 50%, down from 2,311 in 1938 to 1,125 in 1941. (It had also fallen for women, but 'only' by 12% from 4,846 to 4,284.)

The NAS drew a parallel with the coal miners. The reduction in coal output according to some commentators was threatening the war effort and miners would be better employed back home. The social and educational cost of withdrawing men teachers at the height of their powers between the ages of 30 and 35 was out of all proportion to the marginal benefit it would afford the military effort.

The *TES* supported the NAS and on several occasions devoted editorials to the issue:

"What does the country stand to lose if these men are withdrawn? Much of the very cream of the teaching profession . . . These men are the backbone of a school staff . . . To take them out of the educational system is equivalent to taking the lynch-pin out of a wheel.

"The lessons of the last War cannot with impunity be ignored. Already the shadow of a rising wave of juvenile delinquency – a boys' disease – falls darkly over the country: certain signs of loosening of that firm and wise control yet a little more and it is lost altogether; take from the schools just those men who on the whole can and do exercise it most wisely and a deadly blow is dealt."

One of the first duties of the newly installed NAS GS, Richard Anderson, was to congratulate R. A. (Rab) Butler on his appointment as the new President of the Board of Education which hopefully was to usher in a new dawn. In his press statement welcoming Butler to his new position Anderson said: "Dare one hope that, at this critical time, the new President [of the Education Board] may be permitted to remain at the helm sufficiently long to make that effective contribution to the nation's educational well-being which has been denied so many of his predecessors?"

The answer to Anderson's perhaps rhetorical question was, surprisingly, 'yes'. Within a few months of taking office Butler started informal soundings on a new education act. He commissioned reports and established consultative machinery. Naturally the NAS requested representation on consultative committees which were to include officials from the Board, the LEAs, teachers' organisations and indeed "other interested bodies".

At first the NAS was denied representation, not even gaining admission through the 'other interested bodies' door. Once again it seemed the NUT had blocked the NAS and the Minister and others capitulated to its pressure. No Minister had ever called the NUT's bluff, allowing it to continue exercising this outrageous veto. That was rather surprising in the light of its weak stand on other issues.

Undeterred the NAS had proceeded internally to set up its own arrangements to formulate new policy to respond to the emerging challenge of a new education act. That was no mean feat with the members dispersed; over 3,000 NAS men were on active service and many others displaced. Union organisation, meetings and travel were difficult enough under wartime conditions, not to mention the depleted financial resources.

The NAS was blessed by having another leader of great calibre and foresight in 1941, namely Ernest Martin from Nottingham, then Vice-President, who finally succeeded to the Presidency when Annual Conferences and elections resumed in 1943. Ernest Martin led the NAS contribution to the developing call for post-war educational reconstruction. Martin wrote in the NAS Bulletin No. 14 in June 1941:

"Can we afford to sit back and let matters go from bad to worse. Schools have been destroyed and others will be . . . [The President of the Board] has spoken about the place of Education in the Reconstruction as the basis of the great democracy we intend to build. How are we to realise that glorious future? . . . We must start now."

One can only admire the determination and far-sighted idealism of such people in times when they had every excuse to do nothing of the kind. As a result of Martin's initiative the June 1941 meeting of the Executive set up the NAS Research Committee on Post-War Reconstruction in Education under the chairmanship of F.C. Arkless from Sunderland, another leader of great calibre who had been a very renowned President in 1935-36.

The Committee produced many papers on Post-War Educational Reconstruction which were published in two booklets of the same name. They provided the basis for the representations made by the Association to the Government during the planning stages of the Education Bill leading to the Act of 1944.

After the initial uncertainties of the war and the fear of immediate bombing, which did not materialise for some time, the Executive began to function again in 1941. However, to save on time and travel the Committee structure was altered. Members from the north formed the salaries and education committees and those from the south dealt with legal aid, propaganda and general purposes. The NAS retained its Gordon Square HQ but moved its administration out to Chesham in Buckinghamshire.

As part of the policy development process the Association organised a one-day Conference at the Bonnington Hotel in London on 15 November 1941. The Conference said it was "deeply disturbed and amazed at this incomprehensible policy" denying the NAS representation and condemned "the attitude of the Board which seriously handicaps the efforts of the Association to safeguard the interests of its members of whom nearly 3,000 are now serving in HM Forces, and represents an unwarrantable violation of the British standards of liberty which the nation is fighting to maintain".

The NAS continued to campaign for representation and eventually a compromise was reached. The President of the Board called for the views of the NAS on educational planning. NAS "educationists of proved capacity" were then co-opted on to the Reconstruction Committee. Whilst none of the leading figures such as President and GS were on the Committee, the NAS was indirectly present through individuals probably deemed to be acting in personal rather than representative capacities. Whilst less than completely satisfactory it amounted to a step forward and the NAS in its pragmatic nature accepted the compromise and got on with the important business in hand, ready to fight another day on the principle of full representation.

The NAS Research Committee first reported to the Executive in September 1942. It called for the raising of the school leaving age from 14 to 15 and subsequently at an unspecified date to 16. Thereafter continuation schools (later termed 'County Colleges' in the 1944 Act) should be established for boys and girls up to the age of 18.

When the NAS policy was published shortly afterwards it proved quite controversial in the media, attracting headlines such as: "Public Schools Must Go, say Masters; Citizenship by Merit".

The NAS Memorandum, sent to Rab Butler, was blunt in its social and political message. It said that public schools, "the most exclusive employment agency in the world", must disappear if there is to be equality of opportunity. "Schools which cater for only one caste cannot be included in a national system...

"Products of these schools hold positions in the Services, the Church, politics and colonial administration out of all proportion to their numbers, their potentialities or their service to the community. A large proportion of our rulers are educated in these schools where they are segregated from the ordinary people. What can they know of their lives, needs and aspirations?"

Revolutionary stuff perhaps, but it was still impossible to pigeonhole the NAS into preconceived political 'boxes' of right or left wing. At the same time the NAS Memorandum put forward a very traditional proposal that "during adolescence there must be some training in citizenship, part of which should be National Service of some kind . . .

"In a true democracy we should have proof of the worthiness of adolescents to pass into adult life. There must be some training in citizenship . . . to fit the boy or girl to become a practical citizen, trained to consider service as of primary importance."

The Memorandum suggested psychological testing of children in their last year at school to help provide good career advice. Mindful of recent high unemployment, the NAS recommended the establishment of pools of young workers for the provision of full-time study courses to alleviate the pressure on jobs.

The NAS was on relatively safe ground recommending the extension of school life from nursery to 18 years and the provision of adult education, but on the more sensitive subject of religious teaching it came down firmly against the presentation of the Gospel as a call to faith. The NAS has traditionally been opposed to religious indoctrination but supportive of the study of theistic and other beliefs.

The Research Committee also advocated free university education open to all who could profit from it. Teacher training should be reformed with colleges integrated into universities with professional courses following the normal three-year degree courses. After a trial period in which students would decide if they wished to teach, a two-year training course would follow, ending with a professional examination conducted by a body such as the Royal Society of Teachers as a first step towards a self-governing profession.

The 1943 Conference, the first since 1939 and appropriately presided over by Ernest Martin, a native of Nottingham the host city, also adopted a report on all the extraneous duties schoolmasters had accumulated during the war. They included the supervision of meals, the sale and distribution of milk, medical and dental inspections, service in connection with youth movements, war savings, clothes coupons, respirator and shelter duties, formation of clubs and help with concerts and employment advice, to name but a few.

The schoolmasters protested that they were now expected to do "almost everything for children except teach them" as one newspaper headline ran! Whilst prepared to help with the war effort the schoolmasters rightly reiterated their warnings over 'contractual drift' into peacetime and they were determined to prevent that happening.

The Government produced a White Paper, *Educational Reconstruction*, which was to prove a precursor to the 1944 Act of Parliament. Stating that the future of the nation depended upon the education service, the White Paper envisaged:

the introduction of nursery schools for children under 5;

the raising of the school leaving age to 15 and later to 16;

the division of compulsory education between primary (5-11) and secondary schooling for all of diversified types but equal standing;

the elimination of large classes and poor conditions in primary schools and the standard of accommodation in the secondary sector to rise to the level of the best examples;

the provision of school meals and milk to be obligatory;

the provision of education beyond the compulsory age.

The White Paper also commented that there was "nothing to be said in favour of a system which subjects children at the age of 11 to the strain of a competitive examination" on which their school and future careers depended. It further claimed that the curriculum was "too often cramped and distorted by over-emphasis on examination subjects" and that consequentially the curiosity and wider potential of young children were being stifled.

These two reflections did not achieve fulfilment in the 1944 Act but remained issues of considerable contention, neither one of which is resolved to this day. The White Paper was more heavily influenced by 'educationalists', the eventual Act by politicians responding to wider lobbies and interest groups.

In the secondary field the White Paper promised more than the Act was to deliver. It suggested three main types of such schools: grammar, modern and technical. They were not necessarily to remain separate and apart, with different types possibly combined on one site with free interchange of pupils between one and another.

In addition the 1944 Act was to make very specific provision for the future of the Burnham Committee and the 'negotiation' of teachers' salaries.

Responding to the White Paper in its Memorandum on Post-War Reconstruction in Education the NAS began by commenting on the general social and economic background:

"True democracy will not come overnight, but the time is favourable for making a start towards it. 'Laissez-faire' has had a long innings and has outlived its usefulness. The problem of two million unemployed was everybody's business, so nobody did anything about it, and that tragedy was only one symptom. Undirected groping must give way to conscious planning." The NAS rejected the idea that 'planning' was inconsistent with 'liberty'. Indeed the nation had been caught unprepared for war in 1939 because it had failed to face realities and plan accordingly. It must not be unprepared for peace and democracy because of the same failing.

The NAS pointed to the influence the older universities, public and grammar schools had had upon the education service, distorting its growth and relevance in attempting to meet the new needs of the emerging 'masses'. The 'classical tradition', while modified in part, still held sway.

The majority of pupils were to be found in elementary schools which had been established to remove illiteracy and so make a more efficient and manageable workforce. The NAS claimed that while there had been a "tremendous liberalising of the work of these schools, they have not reached that state of freedom that will allow them to fulfil their proper function in a democracy".

The NAS called for a much closer link and co-operation between the school and the community to create a system of education which was free enough to enable the whole child to develop and participate in a true democracy where there would be an end to privilege on the one side and handicap on the other by accident of birth.

There was much idealism in the Association's collective view, reflecting a social concern with and reaction against the deprivation and poverty of the slump-ridden 1920s and '30s. That was to be reflected in the outcome of the 1945 General Election and the subsequent establishment of the welfare state. The Association was certainly in tune with the majority view of the time on the fundamental direction a nation should take.

In 1944 under the Reconstruction plan a committee was set up under Arnold McNair, Vice-Chancellor of Liverpool University, to consider and offer advice on the supply, recruitment and training of teachers and youth leaders. McNair somewhat surprisingly recommended that teachers should receive a substantial increase in their salaries, the Burnham Primary and Secondary Committees be combined and a three-year training period introduced.

All this work continued despite the ravages of war. In 1943 children in the towns along the south coast had to be evacuated as Hitler began using the towns as convenient 'target practice' in 'hit and run' operations. In 1944, the year of the great Education Act, London suffered its utmost threat with the attack by pilot-less planes and then the V-2 flying bombs against which the only defence available was to take out the launch sites. June 1944 saw the D-Day landings of the Allied Forces in Normandy and the start of the long march to Berlin and the eventual defeat of Hitler and his Nazi Germany.

Despite the dislocation of the war the NAS had managed to mount its 'Annual' Conference in 1943. Members took the opportunity of raising the vexed issue of extraneous duties. A resolution demanded "that all such duties imposed upon schoolmasters during holiday periods should be adequately remunerated to bring men teachers in line with civil servants and members of trade unions".

Besides laying down markers for the future there was a more immediate justification for the resolution as a statement was issued following a conference organised by the NUT, the LEAs and the Board of Education in response to the NAS demands. The main points of that statement were twofold:

"1 The position therefore is that all these bodies withhold recognition from the small minority of teachers who seek to impose a salary condition upon services they are rendering in connection with the outside activities of the school.

"2 The parties to the conference have agreed that it would be reasonable to expect that there should be a general recognition by teachers and authorities alike that the school holidays of all teachers may properly be reduced from nine weeks to seven weeks in the year."

It seems unbelievable by today's standards that a union should be so supine and badly ignore the interests of its own members. That it should combine with Government and employers to attack the position of "the small minority of teachers" (i.e. the NAS) who believed their interests should be defended is incomprehensible. It fuelled the determination of the NAS to fight on and explained the intense rivalry that continued with the NUT.

The NAS was not alone in its concern about the volume of these additional duties. An Administrative Memorandum issued by the Board of Education had conceded there were problems:

"The war has inevitably involved teachers in a number of extraneous duties, and the participation in these duties has been of the greatest help in forwarding the war effort. The incidence of these duties is naturally uneven, but there is evidence that in some cases they have reached a volume which seriously interferes with the teachers' primary duty of teaching."

Throughout the war the NAS Bulletin published a list of those members killed or missing in action or taken prisoner. That, coupled with deep concern over the decline in the number of male recruits to teacher training, led the NAS in 1943 to consider measures to restore the number of men in the profession to more desirable levels as it responded to the White Paper.

Perhaps the most controversial NAS recommendation was for an emergency recruitment scheme of personnel who would be required. The obvious source would be the people being demobbed from the armed services. After much heart searching the Executive, by no means unanimously, backed an emergency training scheme. It was not easy. The NAS would be open to the charge of dilution with relaxed entry requirements. An opportunity to exploit a shortage to increase salaries would be lost. However, there would be an opportunity to boost the recruitment of men. Recognising there was no other viable or realistic alternative the 1943 Conference backed the Executive in declaring that in order to secure educational progress after the war "it will be necessary to recruit schoolmasters from other sources than the normal ones".

Conference also instructed the Executive to request the Board of Education to administer such a scheme (in preference to LEAs and colleges of education) and approach the Army, Navy and Air Force with a view to identifying and enlisting suitable recruits and setting up the necessary training.

So the Emergency Training Scheme concept was launched and would be taken up by the Government in 1945. The NAS had showed itself willing to be constructive, accept compromise and risk the wrath of other unions for sensible progress to be made. Through the Scheme many excellent ex-servicemen and women were recruited into the teaching profession. Many Emergency Trained Teachers joined the NAS and became active and indeed prominent in its affairs. None more so than Terry Casey, who joined the Scheme after demobilisation from the Royal Army Education Corps, became a teacher and then a headmaster and quickly established himself as an outstanding union leader, becoming NAS President in 1962 and GS one year later.

Rab Butler was acting with speed and skill in lining up a huge consensus to support the passage of his Education Bill through Parliament. He seemed to have learnt the lesson from Fisher in 1918 that war, for all its appalling aspects, nevertheless afforded the best opportunity for laying the ground for future progress. The country was now ready for the 1944 Education Act.

Chapter 11 - The NAS and the 1944 Education Act

The most significant change introduced by the 1944 Act was the open and decisive shift in power from LEAs to the Westminster Government in the person of the 'Minister of Education', a post created by the legislation itself.

Under the famous and oft-quoted Clause One of the Act it became the "duty" of the Minister "to promote the education of the people of England and Wales and the progressive development of institutions devoted to that purpose and *to secure the effective execution by local authorities, under his control and direction, of the national policy for providing a varied and comprehensive educational service in every area*" (my emphasis).

The NAS welcomed the acknowledgement in the Act that central government was the major partner in education. Only government had the necessary resources to deliver on the ambitious promises inherent in the Act. However, in day-to-day practice governments seemed content to nurture the myth that local authorities were 'equal partners' in this "national service locally delivered". The NAS was sceptical because it often suited Westminster to wield the power but not to carry the visible responsibility.

Although the 1944 Act was regarded as extremely beneficial in principle to the cause of education, in practice it led to a long and sometimes acrimonious debate about the merits of grammar schools, selection at 11 plus and comprehensive schools, which is still not completely resolved to the present day.

Under the 1944 Act the Westminster Government was able to enforce its will over LEAs in fairly straightforward, even crude, ways. Section 112 allowed Government grants to be withheld if an LEA failed to abide by Ministerial regulations or to comply with "such other requirements as may be determined".

Section 99 gave the Minister power to declare that an LEA, or indeed 'anyone' such as a governing body, was acting unreasonably and to issue 'remedial instructions' accordingly, although the courts were on occasions to interpret those powers very restrictively. The Minister at Westminster also had the final say in approving LEAs' development plans, including decisions over building new schools and closing existing ones.

The most important part of the 1944 Act that affected teachers was undoubtedly Section 89, which placed the Burnham Committee on a statutory basis, compelling all LEAs to pay the rates that emerged from negotiations to all teachers in their schools. Arguably the real difference in practice was less, since by the mid-1920s all LEAs had with occasional exceptions voluntarily followed

Burnham. Nevertheless the formality was important. The Act also made it plain that the LEAs and teacher unions made recommendations to the Minister who retained final power of decision making. The Primary (formerly Elementary) and Secondary Burnham Committees were merged and henceforth the pay scales of primary and secondary teachers were to be the same. The Minister of Education was required to recognise organisations representing teachers and employers for the purpose of negotiating salaries by granting them membership of the Burnham Committee.

The NAS shared the public mood as the Second World War drew to a close demanding more centralisation, indeed in some cases literally nationalisation. It was idle to pretend that uniformly high standards of education could be available to all the nation's children from a patchwork quilt of LEAs that varied so much in their revenue base (the rates, based on property values) and their commitment to and ability to provide such quality.

There was a strong sense during and after the war that everyone had made sacrifices, endured dangers and hardships and that consequently all should benefit from the peace and prosperity that hopefully would follow. Equality of opportunity, which became a universally proclaimed mantra, was impossible to achieve in practice unless Government was actively pursuing such a goal from the centre and providing the necessary resources from a tax base that had some chance of meeting the people's needs.

The place of religious schools in the education service was the subject of a settlement in the 1944 Act which stood the test of time for many years until disturbed by the 1988 Education Reform Act and subsequent legislation. From the moment Government published a booklet in September 1941, *Education after the War* (known as the Green Book), outlining its plans for reform, the churches became very active to ensure their privileged positions were protected. The Archbishop of Canterbury led a powerful deputation to Rab Butler. The churches wanted their schools to remain in being (mostly as voluntary aided (VA) institutions), to receive state aid and also ensure that 'Christian teaching' would be given in all schools.

The 1944 Act required all schools to commence the day with a collective act of worship and also to provide religious instruction. Until the 1988 Act introducing the National Curriculum, it was the only subject laid down by statute. Parents were given the right to opt their children out of the act of worship and religious instruction. The principle was seen as crucial and a vital part of the balancing compromises so important to the 1944 Act, even though few were to exercise such rights over the years.

Teachers had a variety of views on church schools and religious instruction. Naturally teachers in church schools tended to support them whilst those in the county sector were more sceptical. Many teachers were certainly hostile to enforced religious instruction. Teachers were also given the right to opt out of religious assemblies, although the practical situation was more subtle for members in church schools who also professed the same faith.

Roman Catholic VA schools developed a model contract which required their teachers not to behave in a way which might be contrary to the beliefs of that church. Over the years after 1944 there was a small but steady stream of cases of teachers who were dismissed or 'edged out' for divorce or 'living in sin' with their spouses or partners. The NAS made many representations to the Catholic Education Council to modify the terms of its model contract but it remains a bone of contention to the present day.

The NAS generally took a 'relaxed' attitude on VA schools. Many of its members worked in them and some held religious beliefs. The Association welcomed the fact that teachers' salaries were paid by the state in VA schools under the national system and the same conditions of service applied in both the voluntary and county sectors.

This even-handed approach by the NAS did not prevent it from pointing out some of the educational arguments over VA schools. In his Presidential address to the 1943 Conference, referring to the "vexed problem of dual control", Ernest Martin suggested that church schools were impeding progress because many, still un-reorganised despite the Hadow Report of 1926, were 'all-age', retaining their senior sections against the perceived wisdom of the day favouring the clear primary-secondary divide. He called for "the churches to surrender some of their entrenched positions and for compromise on all sides".

The 1944 Act set stiff 'tests' for voluntary bodies wishing to participate in the state maintained sector of education in requiring them to carry a certain proportion of their capital costs. The 1988 Education Reform Act and the 1998 Education and Standards Framework Act, together with associated legislation, disturbed this useful 'test of serious intent and support' by allowing and encouraging a variety of bodies and individuals of unproven record and uncertain future to assume responsibility for running state schools.

The emerging tensions in the early years of the twenty-first century over faith schools and the potential they had to cause divisions in society finally led the NASUWT to come down in favour of a secular state maintained system.

The generally cautious and tolerant attitude taken by the Union in the area of religious education has been in my view well judged. The delicate compromises of 1944 survived the test of time over a long period. To disturb such consensus by actively promoting the development of schools funded by all taxpayers but based on religious beliefs cherished by some but condemned by others carries some risk. Such risk is surely heightened in times which promise to be more complex and dangerous than the relatively peaceful second half of the twentieth century.

Chapter 12 - The NAS Rebuilds after the War

The immediate post-war Britain was characterised by shortages and rationing. Repairing damaged school buildings and developing new ones had to take second place to the more urgent need to reconstruct homes destroyed and ruined in the enemy bombing or providing 'temporary' alternatives in the form of 'prefabs'.

The NAS faced huge internal problems. Besides the dislocation caused by the war, the Association had lost about 2,000 members. Membership by the end of 1938 had reached a fraction below 11,000. At the end of 1945 it stood at just below 9,000. Repeating the practice adopted in the 1920s during "The Long Hard Slog", post-war NAS leaders rolled up their sleeves and got on with the vital work of recruitment to rebuild.

There was no finer example of the devotion to recruitment than that provided by Harry Gardner, an outstanding servant of the Association from the North East throughout his student and working life. Harry had served in the Royal Navy during the war, returning briefly to his first teaching post in Sheffield before going back to his native North East. Harry laid the foundations of a nationwide and very personalised system of recruitment. He spearheaded the visit to potential members' homes and told amusing stories of enlisting the help of the few activists who could afford a car to transport him around and wait patiently outside as he went in to recruit. Once on the National Executive, he soon became known as 'Mr Recruitment' and he was the obvious choice to be the Chairman of the Committee of the same name.

With some of his comrades-in-arms, notably George Limburn, an Executive Member from Kent who later joined the staff as an Assistant Secretary, John Scott from Northern Ireland, President 1974-75, and Len Cooper, President in 1976-77, Harry Gardner's emphasis on bread-and-butter organisation necessary for successful recruitment eventually led to the establishment of a Training Committee in the mid 1970s. The NAS was one of the first unions into the business of training workplace representatives, in our case the School Reps. It proved highly effective in ensuring good organisation on the ground, so essential if sound policies pursued at national level were to be translated into effective implementation. In short, the work of these individuals and many other unsung heroes played a crucial role in rescuing the NAS from the ravages of war and slowly but surely building it up to become an effective and influential fighting force by the start of the 1960s.

According to Bernard Morton, President in 1948-49 and editor of the booklet *Action 1919-1969: a record of the growth of the National Association of Schoolmasters,* the end of the Second World War marked a limited breakthrough by the NAS in respect of 'recognition'. Although still denied representation on Burnham, there was a marked change in the attitude of Ministers of Education. Whereas before the war it had been extremely difficult to secure meetings with Ministers, now requests for such were readily agreed.

However, a readiness to discuss was not matched by a willingness to agree with the NAS! The disposition of Government to treat teachers as a soft option remained strong. As the NAS grew in strength the opposition of at least some teachers to the second-class treatment reserved for the profession hardened in tandem. The ability of the NAS to make itself felt in the lobbies of Parliament became almost legendary as the 40-year fight for official recognition refused to go away and gradually gained more Parliamentary support.

Things might have been easier for teachers to tolerate had the Government been more realistic and sympathetic to the profession's manifest problems. Instead the Government went ahead and raised the school leaving age to 15 in 1947, a proposal first put forward in the Hadow Report of 1926 and subject to 'perpetual delay', the latest being in 1939.

That seriously exacerbated the overcrowding problem, already severe enough. It also put additional and very direct pressure on the supply of teachers and particularly schoolmasters, already long-running problems. The NAS had voiced concerns in 1938 when it published a Memorandum, The Extra School Year.

The NAS Conference of 1949 deplored the fact that so little progress had been made in the repair and construction of school buildings. It took until the 1950s for the plans to improve buildings to begin to be realised.

By the early 1950s additional pressure arrived in the primary sector, thanks to the post-war 'bulge' in the birth rate. The secondary sector had also been marked out for some priority, given the decision to raise the leaving age. There were also problems left over from previous reforms. Despite the great achievement of the 1944 Act in promulgating 'secondary education for all', some ten years later in 1954 there were still over 200,000 pupils of that age in the senior sections of 'all age' schools. To the buildings and staff problems were added those of low salaries.

The 'statistical shortage' of teachers had been exacerbated by the otherwise welcome decision of the Ministry of Education in 1945 to introduce new regulations stipulating maximum class sizes of 40 children in the primary sector and 30 for secondary. These were eventually to be revoked in controversial circumstances by the Education Minister Ted Short in 1970 as he responded to moves by teacher unions to take action based on such limits. In any event they were as much honoured in the breach as the observance due to financial pressures.

In 1945 the Government set about implementing the Emergency Training Scheme. It began with six 'Emergency Training Colleges' being set up in London with more planned around the country. However, many LEAs were reluctant to follow. Under the Scheme recruits were to be given one year's intensive training before being awarded qualified teacher status. At the time uncertificated teachers gaining 20 years experience were offered qualified status. Those with less experience had to attend training college to become qualified.

The Scheme, designed to appeal to personnel being demobbed from the forces, attracted 124,000 applications. Some 54,000 applicants were taken on and 35,000 completed the training successfully. Of the 35,000 new teachers produced, 23,000 were men. Setting that ratio against the prevailing gender balance in the profession, it could be seen that the NAS-inspired Scheme had produced a remarkable step forward in attracting men teachers into the profession.

It was always accepted that the Emergency Training Scheme was a temporary palliative. It helped in the elimination of unqualified entry and the uncertificated teacher. Whilst dilution of entry standards inevitably occurred the Scheme introduced capable people with a wider experience than that possessed by the 'typical' entrant. The Scheme was certainly better than employing unqualified staff but it ended in 1951 with few if any arguing that it should be continued.

Despite their commitment Emergency Trained Teachers were not treated particularly well. The training establishments tended to be in very poor buildings and many recruits waited a long time before admission. Many taught as uncertificated teachers whilst waiting and were only granted one year's recognition for every three of pre-teaching experience for purposes of salary increments. They were denied recognition of such experience for pensionable service.

The supply of teachers continued to be problematic in following decades. In July 1951 the National Advisory Council on the Training and Supply of Teachers published its first report. The NAS was severely critical, saying the Report was "completely barren of ideas" to tackle the problem of the post-war 'bulge' in the child population. It totally ignored the need to make the profession attractive to men. Anticipating future events the NAS warned against any lowering of the standards of entry as the Report itself predicted a growing shortage of teachers.

Throughout the remainder of the 1940s and until the late 1950s men aged 18 were conscripted into (military) national service of two years. Those who subsequently entered teaching were granted two salary increments but unfortunately governments resolutely refused to recognise such service for pension purposes. National service was also disruptive of plans to enter university or training college. Obviously it was an issue that only affected men and was pursued with vigour by NAS but largely ignored by others.

With the election of the reforming Labour Government in 1945 and under the Beveridge plans for the welfare state, the National Insurance Act of 1948 applied to everyone in work. Efforts by the NAS to have teachers included in earlier national insurance schemes (especially to benefit widows) had been defeated by the feminist-dominated NUT who would probably not want to be reminded of such hostility today.

Many schoolmasters still maintained a very strong belief in the need for a separate union. When the NUT approached the NAS in 1949 with plans to secure unity – mainly, it appeared, to eliminate competitive recruitment – the schoolmasters' answer was not a straight 'no' but a willingness to explore a Common Council to identify issues on which there was agreement and the possibility of joint campaigning. This did not meet the NUT's aspiration to end competitive recruitment and so the initiative lapsed.

An opportunity to make common cause occurred in 1950 during the first of several disputes between the NAS and the Durham Authority. Durham was 'solid Labour', heavily influenced by members of the National Union of Miners (NUM). In those days the NUM was one of several very powerful unions affiliated to the Labour Party. Durham decided that it would require every candidate for a teaching post to declare which union he or she belonged to, effectively establishing a 'closed shop'.

The closed shop was never supported by any of the teachers' unions. The NAS has always believed in persuading people to join unions voluntarily. It was outlawed by the Thatcher legislation of the 1980s. In 1950 the NAS offered full support to any of its members in Durham who refused to comply with the intrusive demand from the employer. The NUT was also opposed to Durham's move. The prospect of a joint representation was scotched when the NUT General Secretary, Ronald Gould, flatly refused to talk to the Authority whilst "that man" was in the same room. "That man" was Harold Gordon, a Past-President and Honorary Treasurer of the NAS. He happened also to be a legendary figure in the annals of the NAS, described by many of his contemporaries as the greatest platform orator they had ever heard. He had travelled up to Durham to represent NAS members in the dispute. The Durham Authority was forced to back down. However, an opportunity to work together in their mutual interests was lost to both the unions.

As the 1950s progressed, more and more concern was expressed about the class divide in education. Children of the poorer parents were less likely to pass the 11 plus and gain entry to the grammar schools, complete school leaving examinations and secure places at university.

Recruitment, especially of men, to the teaching profession proved problematic as the post-war baby bulge entered the school system. By the end of the 1950s plans were afoot to extend the period of teacher training to three years, placing further pressure on numbers. Class sizes inevitably rose. To add to the pressure the Crowther Report recommended that the school leaving age be raised from 15 to 16 between 1966 and 1968.

The 1950s saw the start of the process of examination reform which was to last for the remainder of the twentieth century and beyond. It had a dramatic impact upon the professional lives of NAS members, particularly in the secondary sector. In 1951 the Government decided to trial a new examination for school leavers, the General Certificate of Education (GCE) at Ordinary ('O') and Advanced ('A') Levels, intended respectively for 15/16- and 18-year-olds. These GCE exams were aimed at the top 30% or thereabouts of the ability range, typically but not wholly exclusively at those who had passed the 11 plus and gone to grammar schools.

In 1953 the GCE replaced the General and Higher Schools Certificate, which was based on a group of subjects all of which had to be passed. The 'group' consisted of English, Maths, a modern foreign language, a science and one optional subject. The GCE O and A Levels were all single-subject examinations where failure in one subject did not prevent gaining passes and certificates in others.

More and sometimes incessant reform to the examination system was to follow in the final quarter of the twentieth century. That was prompted by the development of the comprehensive school which, dealing with pupils of all abilities, required public examinations to cover the same range. The Certificate of Secondary Education (CSE) developed and after much hesitation was eventually (and controversially) merged with the GCE O Level in the 1980s. A national testing system was also to follow in the wake of the abolition of the 11 plus and the lack of accountability which many politicians believed had accompanied it.

Teacher union membership remained very high at over 90% of the profession. Most unions had members in different kinds of schools. However, each union had a type of school in which it featured strongly. For NAS that was the secondary modern. The Joint Four (assistant and headmasters and mistresses) were prominent in the grammar schools. The NUT drew the majority of its members from the primary schools but as the largest union also had considerable numbers in the secondary sector.

This pattern of union memberships remained fairly constant from 1945 until the middle of the 1960s. As the battle to end selection at 11 was won secondary schools began to be reorganised along comprehensive lines. The old distinctions between grammar and secondary modern fell away and union memberships became increasingly fluid. By the mid-sixties the issue of militant action began to play a role in determining union membership.

One observer of the UK trade union scene once described an organisation as being "a bunch of Tories run by a bunch of Trots"! That description reminded me somewhat of the NUT, which had many left-wing radical activists but a largely inactive and placid primary teacher majority. The assistant masters and mistresses tried to pretend the genteel poverty of the profession did not apply to them with their graduate allowances and promotion prospects. Terry Casey once described such associations as "organised timidity".

The NAS represented a breed of teacher which increasingly became distinctly unwelcome to the cosy gentility of the existing educational establishment. This was the awkward, perhaps truculent schoolmaster, no longer prepared to accept the second-class treatment handed out to the teaching profession.

In the immediate aftermath of the war and during the 1950s the NAS remained too small to achieve major progress for the teaching profession on its own. But its willingness to speak its mind and to take protest action began to have an increasing influence on events and particularly upon the NUT.

Two developments in the mid-1950s spurred the NAS into a significantly higher gear of activity. First, in 1955 the NUT finally succeeded in securing equal pay. On 4 March that year the Minister of Education, Sir David Eccles, received a deputation from the NUT and agreed its demand for equal pay. It was to be implemented by stages, full equality coming by 1961. Second, in 1956 the Government decided to implement its proposal to raise teachers' superannuation contributions from five to six per cent.

The NAS was alone in taking serious action to oppose the increase in teacher contributions. Whilst that issue was lost, through no fault of the NAS who fought it to the bitter end, a massive victory was achieved by the Association over the Sunderland LEA which had tried to establish a legal right to enforce various duties connected with school meals upon schoolteachers. The precedent-setting victory in the High Court finally signalled that the NAS had not just arrived on the national scene but could not longer be ignored. I write about these events in Chapter 24: "The Calamity of 1956".

In addition to the supply problems over men teachers, an overall shortage was also developing even though the number of teachers in-service in England

and Wales had risen to 315,000. The birth rate had continued to increase and in 1956 the decision had been taken to lengthen the training period to three years.

A sign of Burnham's inability to provide adequate salaries was the shortage of graduate teachers particularly for science, mathematics and technical subjects. The Government offered indefinite deferment from national service to graduate students of certain subjects if they had been appointed to teaching posts. That 'carrot' turned out to be short-lived with the abolition of national service with effect from 1 January 1960.

With equal pay conceded the NAS set about finding alternatives to protect the interests of its members. The 1955 Conference adopted a Report on Family Allowances and the Schoolmaster. The economy was beginning to expand and get out of the post-war blues but inflation started to rise as well. For the schoolmaster with family responsibilities the increased cost of living was keenly felt. This was followed up in 1958 when a further Report on Salaries, examining the subject of Marriage and Child Allowances, was presented to Conference.

The NAS continued with its long-running demand for representation on the Burnham Committee. The Teachers' Panel was under pressure during negotiations to make a quick settlement because retrospective payments were not permissible under the statute. The NAS demanded retrospection should be allowed. The Association was surprised to discover in a reply from the Minister that it was the first time such a suggestion had been made.

By 1959 pressure on teacher supply had built up so much that the NAS feared the inevitable – more professional dilution. Conference in 1959 called upon the Executive to produce a report on the issue for the following year. The Association's concern was soon justified. Before 1959 was out the Ministry of Education had produced Circular 6/59 stating that it was impractical to set a date from which all aspiring teachers had to complete a training course. Just over 14% of teachers were unqualified in the sense of not having completed a specified training course. Many other qualifications, particularly university degrees, were recognised as granting fully qualified teacher status. Temporary staff and instructors could also be engaged if the employer were unable to find a qualified teacher for the post.

Despite all those 'temporary measures' the Government still found it necessary to insist upon a quota system based on a formula whereby each LEA had a limit on the number of qualified teachers it could employ. By the end of the 1950s the provision of suitable school buildings had improved but the teacher supply problem remained critical. The NAS made strong representations to the Minister that unqualified and untrained teachers should be a thing of the past by 1965.

The constant and relevant campaigning on a wide variety of issues by the NAS in the post-war period yielded slow but steady membership increases. By 1947 membership had recovered to pre-war levels, around 10,300. By 1950 membership had reached 13,500 and by the end of the fifties it stood at just under 22,000. It was approaching the 'critical mass' level which would lead to much more rapid advances in the years ahead.

Chapter 13 - The School Meals Service

More by accident than design the school meals service played a special role in the history of the NASUWT. The service was also very typical of the twentieth century. It exemplified the increased 'socialisation' of education in which schools and teachers were 'expected' to fulfil roles previously ascribed to the family. Like the education service itself, it developed in response to severe social need, often most dramatically exposed during times of great national crisis such as war.

For teachers the school meals service was to become the prime example of being taken for granted. Teachers often drew comparisons with other 'professional occupations'. No one ever demanded that doctors should supervise hospital meals! Events were to illustrate the principle that the employee had to be careful before offering free services to the employer. 'Gratefully accepted' at first, they easily became 'expected' and then 'demanded'.

There was no better example of the 'arrival of the NAS' and its rising influence than that provided by the action taken in relation to the school meals service, which often became a battleground where several issues crucial to the history of the NASUWT and teacher trade unionism were fought out. The Union implemented sanctions banning school meals 'duties' to protest about other injustices on representation, salaries and pensions.

In short, no history of the NASUWT and of industrial relations in education in the twentieth century would be complete without a special mention of the school meals service.

Many of the problems faced by Britain in the twentieth century had their origins in the appalling social conditions endured by large sections of the population in the wake of the Industrial Revolution. Typically these problems were largely ignored by governments until war broke out. Enlistment and conscription for the Boer and the First World Wars revealed that many people were in an appalling state of personal health. It seemed not to trouble Government that many people were unfit to live. But if they were unfit to die for their country that was another matter.

After many volunteers for the Boer War had been rejected on medical grounds the engagingly entitled Physical Deterioration Committee was established. It reported in 1904 and, setting a precedent that was often to be followed in the twentieth century, its two main recommendations were school based. First, much 'unfitness' could be avoided by closer attention to the health of children by the introduction of the School Medical Service. Second, malnutrition could best be overcome by systematic and proper feeding. This led to the 1906 Education (Provision of Meals) Act.

The Act empowered (although it did not compel) LEAs to form School Canteen Committees to provide meals for children who could not profit from education because they were so badly underfed. Thus canteens were established, mostly in town centres, not – interestingly – at first in the schools themselves.

After the 1906 Act local authorities could charge for meals or offer them free, with the right to raise up to a halfpenny for this purpose from the rates. In general the practice was to offer free meals in the canteens but, significantly in the light of later developments, the schools distributed the necessary tokens or tickets. Grammar schools did not participate, providing their own meals at a cost on the premises.

The 1918 Act established central schools, drawing in children some distance away from their homes. Like the grammar schools they were encouraged to provide and charge for a midday meal. The schemes were relatively small scale, without posing big problems for staff. But this represented another step towards the provision of meals on site rather than at centrally located canteens.

The First World War produced its own pressures for the development of the school meals service. The inevitable shortages of war coupled with the vulnerability to naval attack and blockade of a densely populated island like Great Britain (relying on food imported from the old empire), heightened awareness of the importance of good nutrition. So did the ravages of the 1918 Spanish flu epidemic, which killed more people than the war itself had done. The employment of women to work in the factories left a midday gap in the care of children which 'naturally' fell to the schools and canteens to cover.

With the onset of the Second World War the decision was taken in 1939 to evacuate children en masse from large towns and cities to protect them from the obvious dangers of aerial bombardment. This was the single event that most precipitated the development of the school meals service as known in modern times.

With so many children relocated and with fears of widespread privation, if not starvation, Government decided that school feeding had to be developed on a large scale. LEAs were asked to install more school kitchens. Those already in possession of canteen facilities were asked also to provide for neighbouring schools.

Teachers willingly gave of their own time and effort to assist in the expansion of the school meals service. They saw it as their patriotic and humanitarian duty. At the same time the NAS, whilst not dissuading its members from so acting, saw the dangers of 'contractual drift' and warned that such participation in a non-teaching activity should not be permanently expected of teachers.

The NAS reacted to the Soulbury Award of 1942, which appeared to link the parsimonious war allowance awarded to teachers to the performance of extraneous duties, of which school meals represented the most common. Lord Soulbury stated:

"In making my Award I have had some regard to the fact that the many extraneous duties undertaken by teachers in wartime in connection with their professional work are not reflected in their normal remuneration."

Thanks to the Soulbury Award, Bristol withdrew a token payment that had been made to teachers for meals' supervision. In Liverpool the LEA had agreed to pay teachers four shillings a time for meal supervision, subject to a maximum of two per week for each participant; however, the Board of Education refused to approve such expenditure.

The NAS, together with its Liverpool Association, naturally took strong exception to this withdrawal. Both argued that overtime payments should not be part of a cost of living salary increase. The NAS Executive set up a special committee which recommended the Association should support the principle of overtime payments for all such extraneous duties. That committee rightly forewarned that duties voluntarily undertaken in wartime without remuneration would prejudice teachers' bargaining position when peace and normality returned.

Unfortunately, but once again typically, the NAS found itself on its own. Opposition was only to be expected from Government and LEAs but it was galling to find all the other associations represented on the Burnham Committee were not prepared to defend the teacher interest. Burnham issued the following statement in February 1943:

"All [our constituent members] withheld recognition from the small minority of teachers who seek to impose a salary condition upon the services they are rendering in connection with the outside activities of the school."

The NAS expected the Government and employers to act out of their own financial self-interest but could not understand why teachers should deny themselves the same privilege. They seemed to hide a lack of resolve and courage behind a mask of so-called professionalism. Somehow the myth had been created in education that it would be 'unprofessional' for teachers to charge extra for extraneous services despite most other professions doing precisely that. Arguably, the very word 'professional' means doing something for money, indeed 'pro fees', and performing it well. 'Amateurish' is an antonym. The NAS was not prepared to capitulate to management threats that such payments would simply come off the global sum available for teachers' salaries.

The refusal of most teacher associations to insist on payment for extra duties had the seriously detrimental effect of making them literally 'cheap'. Over the course of the second half of the twentieth century a plethora of duties and responsibilities was heaped upon the teaching profession that never had to be costed and seriously evaluated. Some were of dubious value in their own right and subjugated the teaching role, which should have been paramount.

Nobody can justifiably accuse the NAS of not issuing warnings at the time when the problems first surfaced. The White Paper presaging the 1944 Education Act with all its laudable ambitions was published in 1943. The NAS, whilst welcoming the principles, warned about the growing pressure on teachers:

"It has for a long time been clear that teachers cannot cope with the multifarious duties which have been pressed upon them with constantly growing weight . . . It must be the duty of the Board [of Education] to provide such staffing as will enable the work to be carried on without interference with teaching duties."

Delivering his Presidential speech to Conference in 1944 a future General Secretary, Bert Rushworth, warned about the demise of the 'home': "We thought of dinner and home. Nowadays it is dinner and school!" He acknowledged the better balanced diet but spoke of the tendency for the state to take over the functions of the family and "for the home to become a thing of the past. Before we agree to travel too far along that path let us see clearly what the end is to be". He did not want "those grand words 'mother' and 'home' to lose too much of their richness of connotation which has been theirs down the ages".

The NAS 1945 Conference adopted a resolution calling for the ancillary services envisaged in the 1944 Act, particularly those relating to the provision of meals and milk, to be carried out by non-teaching staff appointed for the purpose. It also regretted the conditions under which the services were being provided, describing them as "deplorable". Another motion at the same Conference specifically stated: "The supervision of children during school meals and in the midday interval should not be part of a schoolmaster's duty in peace time."

Section 49 of the 1944 Act required that: "Regulations made by the Minister shall impose upon LEAs the duty of providing milk, meals and other refreshment for pupils in attendance at schools and colleges maintained by them." The discretionary power created in the 1906 Act became compulsory.

The Minister took the power to impose this requirement; the LEAs were left to implement it. NAS members, whilst having willingly borne such extra demands during the war years, became more and more exasperated with the requirement to continue that work, which was clearly outwith the teaching function.

As part of the Beveridge Plan for social and family welfare, born towards the end of the Second World War, the Government saw the provision of a free school meal to needy youngsters as an essential ingredient. The Government's declared intention was in the fullness of time to provide the meals free and to cater for around 75% of all children.

After the introduction of Family Allowances in August 1946 it was decided that milk was to be provided free of charge, but the question of meals was complicated by their uneven provision over many parts of the country, itself partly due to lack of appropriate resources and space. Free meals were provided for the poorest children but charges remained in place for others.

That meant teachers were 'required' to collect dinner moneys and supervise the meals in a range of accommodation, varying from purpose-built dining halls in the newer buildings to makeshift and often unsuitable rooms and corridor spaces in others.

Since the birth of the meals service in 1906 most of the administrative work had been carried on by heads and other teachers. As the service expanded so did the administrative burden, increasingly distracting staff away from their core teaching activities. However, the 1921 Education Act protected teachers against being required, as part of their duties, to "assist in any way in the handling of or supervising the handling of food or in the collection of the cost thereof". The regulations imposed on teachers under the 1944 Act did not disturb this legal protection. This was to prove a very significant factor in the 1956 court case when the NAS won a spectacular victory upholding the rights of teachers to decline to perform such 'duties'. Teachers could take some comfort from Section 49 of the 1944 Act which explicitly stated that "no duties should be imposed in respect of meals other than the supervision of pupils".

'Beveridge' and the 1944 Act also combined to produce a sea change in the scale and rationale for the school meals service. Hitherto the service had been provided to meet direct and basic nutritional need. The expansion envisaged, clearly going beyond that basic need, required an enhanced justification. The rationale alighted upon was 'social training', which made the provision of the meal so important that it should be regarded as *"an integral part of the school day"*.

This easy ploy for Government and employers to justify the impositions on staff was embellished a couple of years later in Circular 97 (April 1946), which stated explicitly:

"Under proper conditions the school dinner affords an outstanding opportunity for social training, without which education is incomplete, for teaching good manners and for the establishment of sound dietetic habits." It is

105

difficult to find a more explicit example of the state taking over a role previously expected of the family. A later circular added that it "requires the active participation of the teachers as well as suitable dining conditions".

The NAS warnings on the subject, explicitly stated in its response to the White Paper in 1943, went ignored. Significant commercial interests were now involved, particularly kitchen furniture and equipment, and they would lobby for continued expansion of their industry. Thus the school meals service was set on the road to expansion. However, so was the NAS and in the fullness of time the action taken by the Association could not be ignored.

The first target of banning dinner duties was the imposition of an increase in teachers' pension contributions from five to six per cent in 1956. I write fully about those dramatic events in chapter 24: "The Calamity of 1956".

By 1961 NAS anger at the continued refusal to be granted recognition on Burnham reached boiling point and led to the school meals service again being placed in the front line. After the initial strikes starting at the William Penn School in Dulwich more plans were announced to involve every member in banning extraneous duties, including lunchtime supervision. The LEAs and Government could see that the NAS was prepared to use such sanctions against a variety of many grievances. They decided the best thing to do was to make other arrangements for lunchtime to avoid difficulties in the future.

By March 1962 another Working Party had to be convened. A series of meetings between representatives of teachers associations and officials at the Ministry of Education was opened on the 27th of that month by the Minister, Sir David Eccles. It was to result in a circular (5/63) issued the following year.

Now officially recognised, the NAS was at last included and a whole new chapter opened up in which the voice of the teacher in classroom was no longer to be ignored but heard loud and clear. Hard negotiations at last began.

The agenda opened up every aspect of the school meals service for discussion. Sir David Eccles immediately announced he was open to suggestions on how the present burdens on teachers could be lightened. The Government was embarking upon a building programme to improve the conditions under which the meals were served.

For the NAS GS Bert Rushworth welcomed parts of the Minister's statement but firmly rejected the notion that the school meal "was an integral part of the school day" and that teachers should be compelled to supervise. The presence of the NAS had a great impact on the NUT and other associations. The NUT GS, Sir Ronald Gould, supported the statement made by Bert Rushworth as did the Joint Four.

The 1962 Easter Conferences followed soon after these developments with the NAS meeting in Plymouth. Terry Casey took over the Presidency and with

Bert Rushworth's health beginning to decline he moved imperceptibly into the role of GS. The major item on the agenda was a special report on the school meals issue. The NAS's 'bottom lines' were twofold: withdrawal of the legal requirement to supervise children during mealtimes and, leading up to that, some immediate relief from the duty. If progress were not made the Executive was "empowered to take such militant action as it may decide to bring this long-standing dispute to a successful conclusion". Full support was offered to any member declining to participate in voluntary duties such as the collection of meals moneys.

The talks continued for nearly a year before a new circular (5/63) was issued in April 1963. Much progress had been made, although some areas were left a little unclear. The circular suggested the school meals service should be under the general direction of the head; that LEAs should appoint additional supervisory staff as required in consultation with unions locally, based on some voluntary assistance from teachers.

The main principle had been won by teachers but there was a slight ambiguity left in the reliance upon some volunteering. All the unions expressed their belief that where the head enjoyed the confidence of teachers a sufficient number would volunteer. However, doubts soon resurfaced with the NAHT expressing concerns that secondary schools in particular experienced problems, leaving their members in some difficult positions.

Heads and LEAs pestered the Government to do something about it. Arguably there was some 'collective responsibility' left to teachers to volunteer but it was unenforceable against any individual. Headteachers naturally asked: what do they do if no teacher volunteers? In July 1964 someone persuaded the Ministry of Education to issue a statement answering that very question. The answer was that if the "understanding" in the agreement was reflected locally the problem "did not arise". However, if it was not, "the authority is bound to take steps to see that appropriate supervision is provided by exercising powers vested in it under the 1944 Act".

The Government and LEAs were 'trying it on' once more! The Ministry was resurrecting Section 49 of the Act, which had been put into operation by the 1945 Provision of Milk and Meals Regulations, No. 14. It had not been officially repealed despite the agreement of 1963, which clearly ran counter to it.

Once again all the other associations capitulated at the first sign of pressure. Only the NAS refused to accept the statement, which was intended as the prelude to a further circular from the Ministry. The NAS remained adamant, determined to support a statement in a previous circular that "a direction under regulation 14 should not be given to an individual teacher, because the terms of the agreement allow an individual to withhold his services". Action would be taken if need be.

That seemed to put some backbone into the NUT, who eventually accepted the NAS position. In any event the new circular had little to no impact upon the situation. The answer to 'that question' was once again turned back on headteachers. They were expected to exercise their 'leadership skills' in 'persuading' others to 'volunteer'.

Some schools got around the problem by providing 'free' meals to staff who in return agreed to do one week's lunchtime supervision per term. It was a payment in kind of a sort which many teachers found convenient. Some unhelpful 'pedants' questioned the legality of such arrangements.

Many schools were gradually to increase the number of support staff to supervise meals and indeed lunchtime breaks as well. Still many headteachers found it necessary to conduct lunchtime supervision themselves, particularly in the more challenging schools with serious discipline problems. Classroom teachers were generally content with the status quo but some were still very conscious of the fact that poor behaviour at lunchtime easily led to difficulties in the classrooms in the afternoons. Many schools began to shorten the lunch break and arrange a shift system to contain disciplinary problems.

The 'stand-off' after the 1963 circular continued until December 1967 when the Secretary of State, at the request of the teachers' and the local authority associations, agreed to set up a Working Party. The remit was to "consider and make recommendations on the position of teachers in relation to all aspects of the School Meals Service".

The Report of the Working Party was contained in the DES Circular 16/68, issued on 15 August 1968. It began with the good news that in the light of all parties' support for the principles set out in the Report the Secretary of State was formally revoking numbers 13 and 14 of the provisions of the Milk and Meals Regulations of 1945. The Report referred to the background of a common desire to remove the burden on teachers without impairing the service or adding unreasonably to its cost whilst at the same time providing adequately for the safety and welfare of the children. In addition to the NAS 'union' pressure a key moment in shifting the Government/Employers' position came when GS Terry Casey almost casually lobbed a grenade into the discussions. As the law required education to be provided free of charge, a contractual requirement on teachers to supervise school meals implied they had likewise to be provided free to all children. According to NAS sources the faces of the trained lawyers among the LEA representatives, notably Sir Ashley Bramall from the ILEA, froze with fear.

The Report noted the history and developments that had taken place, including the increased use of supervisory and clerical assistance. There were no longer specific Government moneys for the service; it was all wrapped up in the rate support grant. Other social and educational developments had also taken place, including increased extra-curricular activities; the greater tendency for children to spend the midday break in school; and the growing number of cases where both parents of a child went out to work. Added to these was the closure of small village schools and the introduction of larger comprehensives requiring longer distances to be travelled from home to school by many pupils. Along with developments of canteen facilities at many workplaces, there was a general expectation amongst parents that their children should be provided with a midday meal at school.

The Report recognised the pressure generated by these social changes on top of the fundamental reforms to school organisation and the nature of the curriculum. The expansion of extra-curricular activities during the midday break and after school hours was valued but their voluntary nature contrasted with the compulsory requirements to provide meals and milk. All played a part in the overall success of a school which clearly depended upon "the extent and quality of the voluntary efforts of individual teachers under the leadership of the head".

The Report continued: "The head teacher must retain overall responsibility for the conduct of the school meal, just as he does for all that takes place in and about the school and there is a professional responsibility on the teaching staff as a whole to support the head teacher in fulfilling these responsibilities.

"It is also important to the teacher, whether head or assistant, that he should be able to enjoy a proper and satisfactory break in which he can relax and rest and, if he wishes, leave the school premises."

In the light of these considerations the Working Party recommended:

"Regulation 14 should be amended so as to remove the power given to authorities to require teachers to supervise pupils taking dinners;

That teachers supervising pupils be entitled to a free meal;

That Authorities should in consultation with their teachers locally review the arrangements for supervisory and clerical assistance in accordance with the principles set out and ensure that teachers are not expected to undertake unreasonable burdens;

That all bodies represented on the Working Party give full support to these recommendations."

An appendix then set some guidance on the precise levels of supervisory assistance in relation to the numbers of pupils. The appendix also contained a 'no detriment' clause indicating that previous provision in the light of Circular

5/63 should not be worsened if it were more generous than the guidance now offered.

The Report of the Working Party formed the basis of the 1968 School Meals Agreement (also known as the Rosetti Agreement) between the LEAs and the teacher associations. With the formal revocation of the infamous Regulation 14 the Agreement effectively sewed up the position from the classroom teacher's point of view. Nevertheless an area of fudge had been left behind, as is often the case in difficult areas of negotiation. Whilst no individual could be compelled, there was a 'collective responsibility' which was implied but unenforceable.

While opinion over the 1968 Agreement remained divided there was no doubt that in times of disputes many problems would arise. Unfortunately the 1970s and '80s saw many disputes erupt and led by the NASUWT the 'withdrawal of goodwill', in effect banning voluntary activities and working to rule, placed lunchtime 'duties' in the front line. Headteachers and LEAs found themselves in great difficulties running schools. The NASUWT held that 'withdrawal of goodwill' was not a 'breach of contract'. LEAs and headteachers generally took a different view but were unable to enforce it.

Various attempts were made to deal with the situation, such as providing pay flexibilities by way of second contracts to enable teachers to be paid for supervision as well as additional support staff. Many in management still believed the presence of a fully qualified teacher was essential to maintain good order. But by then it was all too late. Teachers were angry over their poor pay and exhausted by many other developments and in no mood to add to their workload, even if paid for the privilege. The fundamental problems of a fair salary and decent working conditions lay unresolved. And teachers, with the NASUWT increasing its influence on the union scene all the time, were less prepared to put up with unsatisfactory arrangements than ever before. The NASUWT had grown big and strong enough to ensure the classroom teacher interest was not to be ignored, and indeed on such a matter had to prevail. Other organisations had to adopt the NASUWT position as well.

The school meals service had a more chequered history with the arrival of the Thatcher period of retrenchment in public expenditure in the 1980s. By then the worthy thoughts had evaporated as the time arrived for Government to cut back on milk and meals provision in order to reduce public expenditure. An interesting harbinger of what might happen had taken place in the early 1970s when Margaret Thatcher, as Education Secretary, had presided over the demise of the free milk provision and earned her first distinctive right-wing spurs as "Thatcher milk snatcher".

School meals were then the subject of much economising in the 1980s. Requirements were changed to providing a space where pupils could bring their own food for consumption at lunchtime. Vending machines made their appearance in schools, often selling fizzy, sugary and unhealthy products. Many school kitchens were closed down. Food began to be delivered from a central point for schools to warm up and serve to children.

By the 1990s people began to notice adverse effects of the decline in the balance and quality of some pupils' diets, not to mention the increasing problem of child obesity. Some research pointed to poor diets leading to disruptive behaviour. The New Labour Government began to turn back in the opposite direction, laying down basic nutritional standards which school meals had to meet.

The return of the nutritional school meal received a huge boost in 2005 in the run-up to the General Election. A TV celebrity chef, Jamie Oliver, famously showed how school meals could be made interesting and healthy at or below the same costs incurred by the old-fashioned and often unpopular 'school dinner'. That was enough to produce an instant and favourable reaction from Prime Minister Tony Blair on the campaign trail. Overnight the provision of a healthy school dinner à la Jamie Oliver became Government policy!

SECTION THREE
THE BATTLE OF BURNHAM
The 40-year campaign for recognition

Chapter 14 - Moving the Goalposts

The reader may recall that the President of the Board of Education, H.A.L. Fisher, well disposed as he was to teachers and the education service, had established the Burnham Committee in 1919 with the admirable intentions of improving the pay and status of the profession.

All the existing teacher associations of any size and reputation were recognised and given seats on the various committees. The NUT took a complete monopoly of all the 25 union seats on the Elementary Committee, in which schools it had an overwhelming majority of the teachers in its membership.

The secondary sector was much smaller in those days, when the school leaving age was 14. Membership of the Secondary Committee was more evenly divided between several associations. Representation was shared, with the NUT and three of the Joint Four having five seats apiece whilst the Assistant Masters, in recognition of its slightly larger membership, was awarded six places.

In 1919 the NAS was in the process of being born. It began life as a pressure group inside the NUT. The first call for representation on the Burnham Committee was a motion put down on the 1921 Conference agenda in Cardiff by the Gloucester Association. Ironically perhaps, that motion was lost. But it was rightly lost because with members still in the NUT it would have amounted to double representation.

I say 'ironically' because the sense of fair play and logic inherent in the correct decision not to seek double representation was to be conspicuous by its absence over the course of the following 40 years. Indeed, the refusal of many LEAs to receive deputations from NAS members "because we have already heard from your union" was one of the key reasons for secession from the NUT.

Soon after its establishment as a separate independent association the NAS made its first formal application for membership of the Burnham Committee in 1923. NAS membership itself had recovered from the temporary losses predictably suffered as a result of secession from the NUT and stood at slightly over 5,000.

Responding to the first request from the NAS, the new Conservative President of the Board of Education, E.F.L. Wood (who later became Lord Halifax), wrote that if Burnham itself did not agree and if he was "faced with the alternative of a continuance of the work of the Committee or its discontinuance through the withdrawal of the largest and most widely representative association of teachers [i.e. the NUT] [he] would feel bound in the interests of the public service of education and the teaching profession to choose the former".

That was the only straightforward and honest rejection the NAS was ever to receive. One may not admire the supine surrender to the NUT threat but it reflected the real reason for rejection.

Shut out from Burnham the NAS was never going to be silenced. Indeed the exclusion from Burnham, an injustice that grew in size along with NAS membership, served only to heighten the Association's sense of purpose, militancy and determination to fight on, whatever the odds.

The next request for representation from the NAS came in 1930 when, under Labour, Sir Charles Trevelyan had become the President of the Board. His reply floated the fiction that the composition of Burnham was "not a matter for the Board of Education". So began the descent into deceit and doublespeak which characterised Ministerial responses for the following 30 years. In reality, from day one Ministers could, and when they wished did, enforce their will on any Burnham matter even in its pre-statutory days before the 1944 Education Act. The threat to withdraw government grant from any area of expenditure was always there in the background to ensure compliance with Ministerial wishes.

Twice in 1931, with membership standing at fractionally under 8,600, the NAS was rejected. On the first occasion Hastings Lees-Smith (then a Labour MP) did acknowledge that as the President of the Board of Education he was responsible for the composition of Burnham. In so doing at least he destroyed the myth that Trevelyan had tried to create.

The October 1931 General Election campaign was used by the NAS to lobby all Parliamentary candidates on salaries, the dangers of equal pay and representation on Burnham. Appropriate briefing documents were produced, a practice which remains in place to the present day at times of General Elections. The national Government secured a huge majority and Ramsay MacDonald continued as Prime Minister.

The NAS took advantage of the change of Minister once again to claim representation, only to be rejected by the new Liberal President of the Board of Education, Sir Donald MacLean. On this occasion the Minister found a new 'line' saying he could "see no reason to alter the decisions of my predecessors".

That formula for rejection was to be used many times in the future, reflecting a good filing system on the part of civil servants.

In 1934, with membership approaching 9,000, Lord Halifax (back in his old job with his new name), after the usual polite reference to "careful consideration" cited his predecessors' decisions to maintain the status quo.

In 1936, with membership just over 9,500, the Conservative Oliver Stanley "after carefully reviewing the information" found "no reason to modify the attitude adopted by my predecessors".

For most of the Second World War the desire to secure representation obviously took a back seat whilst every effort was made by the NAS merely to survive. However, there is reference in NAS records to a request for recognition in 1941, but no details seem to have survived.

As plans unfolded for post-war reconstruction and development, the NAS took the opportunity provided by the 1944 Education Bill to promote an amendment designed to secure representation on Burnham, which under the proposed legislation was due to become a statutory committee. Samuel Storey, Conservative MP for Sunderland where NAS membership was strong, moved an amendment to the Bill to this effect. Responding to Mr Storey, the Conservative Minister of Education, R. A. Butler, proffered the asinine reason that "no request had been made by the Burnham Committee for a change".

In other occasions in 1944, R.A. Butler, sometimes responding directly to the NAS, other times speaking in Parliamentary debates, repeated the well-known reasons for the previous rejections and added a few new ones. Butler claimed: "The fact is that the Burnham machinery has worked well." Far from 'fact', that was of course a judgement, a view, which was certainly not shared by the NAS. Butler went on: "The present arrangements take the teachers' point of view fully into account. I am satisfied, after examination over a long period of time, that if we altered the system of representation, the Burnham machinery would not work as well as it does." On another occasion in 1944 Butler conceded that exclusion of the NAS "was not entirely logical and had elements which could be unjust".

Mr Storey could only contrast the weakness of Butler hiding behind the old prejudices and succumbing to the NUT threat of boycott with the reforming zeal he brought to other aspects of the 1944 Education Bill. He went on: "The rich man's chances of achieving eternal salvation are bright compared with the NAS's chances of persuading the NUT to abandon its monopolistic claims and to loosen the stranglehold it has on the [Education] Board's representatives."

Another MP, Mr W.G. Cove, who was a former teacher, member and indeed President of the NUT, claimed that admitting the NAS would break up the good working of the Burnham Committee. Within a few minutes he went on to lament the low salaries of teachers, against which as a young NUT activist in the Rhondda, he had fought courageously in 1917, bringing members out on an unofficial but successful strike in protest against low pay in his LEA.

The Burnham Committee certainly worked well for Government and LEAs. Whether it did the same for teachers was another matter. NAS members believed passionately that it did not and pointed to the lack of resolve to fight for decent salaries coming from the NUT and other weak unions granted representation.

Rab Butler claimed: "Unless you get teachers speaking with one voice you will not get satisfactory machinery." He suggested the NAS and NUT should get together to sort out their differences. The NAS responded that it had tried to work together on issues of agreement but the NUT simply refused to be in the same room. The NAS was only claiming a minority voice, not minority rule.

Ever since the start of state education in 1870, in which the elementary sector had been the dominant part, the NUT had constituted the one 'united' voice for teachers. Yet pay had always remained pitifully low, a view confirmed by the independent Lord McNair and his committee in 1944. The NUT had predominated in the elementary field for many years, affording it opportunity galore to deliver the benefits of unity.

The Joint Four, representing mostly secondary grammar school teachers, were equally quiescent and with a separate committee for their sector maintained a differential with elementary school teachers. Whilst that was all to change in 1944, those associations had been content to let the NUT put an effective veto on NAS applications for representation.

In another debate on the 1944 Education Bill Rab Butler added new reasons for rejection to the old: "I agree the minority have a case, but if I depart from the principle of working with the largest of the organisations . . . it will be very difficult to know where to stop. The number of different teachers' organisations is very considerable, and if I concede one I shall have to concede another."

This 'floodgates' argument was extremely thin. Apart from the NAS, only the National Association of Head Teachers (NAHT) purported to be a genuine union representing their members across the whole field of pay, conditions and education although its case was weakened by dual membership with the NUT, which would produce double representation. In contrast NAS rules prohibited membership of the NUT.

The National Union of Women Teachers was composed of militant pro-equal pay campaigners. It never seemed to publish detailed membership figures but was thought to have no more than 3,000 at most. The degree of dual membership with the NUT was another unknown. It appeared to be a single-issue union and duly carried out its promise to disband itself when equal pay was conceded. Another 'NUT MP', Mr R. Morgan, had claimed therefore that the NAS and NUWT cancelled one another out!

Despite the golden opportunity afforded by the reform of the Burnham machinery under the great 1944 Act the response from the Minister of Education had once again been 'no' despite intensive lobbying by the NAS.

It has to be a matter of speculation that governmental deference to the NUT 'veto' was prompted by the threat of a Burnham boycott or a fear of NAS militancy over pay, or a combination of both. All the sophistry of refusal could not hide the stark fact that other minority organisations (the Joint Four and Technical Teachers) were already recognised, which seemed to cause the NUT no problems. The difference with the NAS was that we would pose problems through our militancy and determination to fight for better salaries.

Under the 1944 Act reforms the Primary (former Elementary) and Secondary elements merged to form one Main Committee for Schools, with FE remaining separate. The NUT was granted an overall majority on the Teachers' Side with 16 out of the 26 seats. The alliance of the Joint Four 'Masters and Mistresses' remained represented, with two seats each for 'Assistants' and one each for the 'Heads'.

Outrageously, the Association of Teachers in Technical Institutions (ATTI), with barely any members in primary or secondary schools, was given four seats on the Main Committee while retaining its separate arrangements in Burnham FE. ATTI was institutionally linked to the NUT through reciprocal representation on their Executives. They also shared the same premises. Effectively the NUT had 20 seats. The four reciprocal places granted to the NUT on the FE Committee completed another circular argument, and its other justification, the need for liaison, remained decidedly unconvincing.

It is difficult to understand how and why the Joint Four watched the disappearance of their separate secondary committee without a whimper. Effectively they ceded control of the representation of their members' interests to the NUT with its large primary membership. I know the educational arguments in favour of equal treatment for primary and secondary. But from a self-interested point of view and the inevitable workings of the labour market, it was obvious that the pay of their members in the secondary field would be held down by being merged with the primary sector.

The debate over the Thelma Cazalet 'equal pay' amendment to Clause 82 of the 1944 Bill wrecked another opportunity for the NAS to present its case. On 29 March Thelma Cazalet, a Conservative MP, had surprised Government whips, managing to insert an 'equal pay' amendment into the Bill on a one-vote majority late in the evening only to see it overturned the following night as Winston Churchill, incandescent with rage, brought 36 Tory 'rebels' back into line. The Association had mounted yet another lobby and secured the support of hundreds of MPs, but in the wake of the consternation produced by Thelma Cazalet's activities the 'NAS amendment' on recognition was withdrawn before it was even debated.

While Burnham was reformed in 1944, the ability or willingness of the Teachers' Panel to fight for decent salary settlements remained as it had always been, very weak. The Independent MP who had helped the NAS in 1941 over billeting allowances, Sir Graham Little, referring to the McNair Report's description of teachers' pay and conditions as unsatisfactory, added in a House of Commons debate in 1945: "I could not understand how the scales which the Burnham Committee had adjudicated had become possible except that the teachers were not adequately represented."

In 1946, with NAS membership recovering after the dislocation of the war at 8,800, the new Labour Minister of Education, Ellen Wilkinson, "did not see her way to suggest any change" following another NAS application.

In 1947 and again in 1950 the Minister, George Tomlinson, refused recognition to the NAS. He was "unwilling to change" on the first occasion and denying on the second that "the conditions existed in which it would be possible for him to proceed against the wishes of the Teachers' Panel". By 1950 NAS membership had reached over 13,500, making it as large as each of the Assistant Masters and Mistresses Associations. Interestingly, on another occasion, in conversation with NAS Representatives, George Tomlinson conceded that it would be difficult to resist the Association's demands if the membership reached 20,000.

In 1952 the new Conservative Education Minister, Florence Horsburgh, saw "no reason to dissent from her predecessor's decision in 1950". However, during a deputation from the NAS she might have opened a little chink of light by agreeing to give serious consideration to the "consequential exclusions" of the NAS from many other bodies at national and local levels. Such exclusion had always been a very sore point for the NAS and another big motivating factor behind the determination to secure representation on Burnham.

The County of Durham was to feature strongly for various reasons in the history of the NASUWT. The year of 1954 provided an example of the strong feelings that often characterised the conduct of affairs in that county. The LEA co-opted a well-respected headteacher, Bill Gladstone, who was also a prominent NAS member, on to its consultative committee. The NUT objected and carried out its threat to walk out and boycott the committee. For three years everyone managed to get on quite well without the NUT who eventually returned, tails between their legs.

On 21 April 1955 George Thomas MP, a former teacher, NUT Executive Member and a future Speaker of the House of Commons, put the matter quite bluntly to the Conservative Minister David Eccles in Parliamentary exchanges: "Is the honourable gentleman aware that if he interferes with the present constitution of the Burnham Committee he will be asking for trouble?" Eccles' somewhat defensive reaction reflected the constant lobbying by NAS members putting him under pressure via some of his critical Conservative colleague MPs. The NAS had by this time nearly 16,700 members.

The year 1957 started with a sharp reminder to the NAS of the uphill battle it faced in securing recognition and the degree of hostility perpetrated by the NUT. The Liverpool Association of Schoolmasters (LAS) was one of the NAS's strongholds and the LEA consulted openly and officially with it. In January 1957 the Liverpool NUT persuaded the City Council's Finance and General Purposes (FGP) Committee to bring a recommendation to Education calling for the Authority to consult only with unions represented on Burnham when requesting views from teachers. The LAS naturally counter-lobbied vigorously and to its great credit the Education Committee rejected the recommendation, referring it back to FGP where it was rescinded.

The NAS lobbying for Burnham representation moved into a higher gear in 1957. The reactions of an equally combative Minister of Education, Lord Hailsham, moved in the same direction. Addressing the Annual Conference of the Midland Federation of Schoolmasters in October 1957, the then NAS Chairman of Salaries, Terry Casey, caused quite a furore in describing Lord Hailsham as "the Conservative's Khrushchev".

Writing to the NAS, Hailsham propounded the extraordinary view that he did not accept that "any particular body had a right to representation or that any particular criteria is conclusive in favour of any particular body". His responsibility, now a statutory one under the 1944 Education Act, was to ensure both employers and teachers were represented. "The precise constitution is a matter for the Minister to decide on general grounds taking into account the different bodies representing sometimes conflicting aims," wrote the Minister.

Hailsham went on to say that: "It must be the aim of the Minister to reconcile and take into account the widest possible set of considerations with a view *to making the Committee as effective an advisory body as possible* [my emphasis]; it is utterly wrong in my view to attempt to codify at any given moment what these should be." Therefore after "giving your arguments the most careful consideration . . . I cannot conscientiously see my way to alter my predecessors' decisions".

Leaving the recognition issue to one side for the moment, it is interesting to note how the Minister saw the Burnham Committee as "an advisory body" – not the high-powered independent negotiating machine dreamt of by the employers and the NUT.

Hailsham's description of an 'advisory' body might have reflected the reality on the face of the statute (which did indeed require the Burnham Committee to present recommended salary scales for the Minister's consideration). However, under the same statute (Section 89 of the 1944 Act) the Minister's sole duty regarding membership of the Burnham Committee "*was to appoint organisations representing teachers and employers*" (my emphasis).

Hailsham's views denying "any particular body had a right", or "any particular criteria is conclusive", or that such matters should not be 'codified', were astonishing. They could have been used to deny NUT representation! They seemed to imply that he did not have to act on rational and consistent grounds.

In November 1957 the NAS produced a comprehensive Memorandum in Support of Claim for Representation on the Burnham Committee. It was circulated to "All Members of Parliament, Commoners and Lords". By this time Geoffrey Lloyd had replaced Hailsham as Minister of Education and a future holder of this office, Sir Edward Boyle, was Parliamentary Under Secretary.

The Memorandum set out the facts on current membership of Burnham. Five of the six unions represented were now smaller than the NAS. The Head Masters/Mistresses had around 1,000 members each (with one seat apiece on Burnham). The Assistant Masters had 15,000; Assistant Mistresses 13,000 (with two seats apiece). ATTI, with no members in schools, had four seats and was institutionally linked to the NUT, reflecting double representation, and had only 5,000 members.

The NUT had around 200,000 members, with 16 seats. (Precise membership figures for the NUT were a little difficult to ascertain.) The NAS, established for 34 years, now had a membership over 18,000 strong. Size was the determining factor in granting the NUT its overall majority; it counted for nothing in respect of the NAS.

As size became a more difficult ground on which to reject the NAS, the 'goalposts were moved'. According to the Minister other smaller organisations were on Burnham because they represented "distinctive kinds of teachers", namely those from grammar schools. The NAS represented mostly secondary modern and elementary teachers and those were already covered by the NUT. The fact that the NUT also represented grammar school teachers was ignored.

The rationale was risible and nothing more than a cynical excuse to keep the NAS out and avoid the 'risk' of upsetting the NUT. Conservative backbench MPs sympathetic to the NAS case hinted that their Ministers should not give way to NUT threats, forcing them on to the defensive.

The Memorandum argued that the NAS did represent a distinctive kind of teacher, the schoolmaster, whose interests were not spoken for in Burnham but who were vital for the well-being of the education service. However, the main justification for the NAS claim lay in simple but fundamental rights to freedom of association and the right to have a voice, granted to many others. As the NAS grew in size, so did the strength of these arguments. The NAS also pointed out it was not for the Government or employers to dictate which unions anybody should join if they wished to have representation. This was a matter for teachers to decide for themselves.

On 17 June 1957 Hailsham had written to the NAS stating, inter alia, that he "would be very slow to allow the Burnham Committee to be used as a vehicle for undermining the [equal pay] policy of the Government". At the NAS deputation to Hailsham a few weeks earlier on 1 May, the Minister had gone even further in declaring that it would be "immoral" to do so. The NAS rejected the sinister implication that only those who supported government policy should be recognised. After all, the NUT had used Burnham from 1919 to 1956 to undermine the then policies of successive governments opposing equal pay! The opposition of the Assistant Masters to equal pay in the absence of family allowances was also conveniently ignored.

The Memorandum concluded by reminding members of both Houses of Parliament that denial of representation on Burnham led to the doors of many other national and local consultative and negotiating committees remaining shut to the NAS. The increasing injustice, the incoherent, inconsistent and ever-changing rationale for rejecting the NAS case served only to intensify the NAS lobbying of MPs.

It is also worth noting that 1957 saw the first recorded correspondence from grass roots members demanding militant action for Burnham recognition. A letter dated 16 October that year from a Mr Dunhill, Secretary of the South West Branch, to the LSA Honorary GS, Dan Newbery, quoted a resolution carried unanimously at a recent meeting. It stated that members "although agreeing to the continued lobbying of MPs strongly urge action at the national level, either by way of petition or by other means, preferably of a spectacular nature". The motion had been proposed by a well-known London activist, Bob Holloway.

No MP, however exalted, escaped the NAS lobby. Peter Addison, Secretary of the East London Branch, engaged the Prime Minister in correspondence. Harold Macmillan responded to Peter Addison, one of his constituents, in a letter dated 13 October 1957. The language used was identical in many parts to the reasons for rejection given by Lord Hailsham around the same time.

Several MPs, mostly it has to be said Conservatives, became very sympathetic to the NAS cause. The Labour Party, populated quite significantly with many NUT activists, was opposed. Its General Secretary, Morgan Phillips, was later to write to the NAS in 1960 saying that Labour was "unlikely to offer support" and the Parliamentary Party supported Eccles' decision on continued exclusion. However, individual Labour MPs were in support, although some, like Harold Wilson, did not broadcast their views. Fred Willey, a future Labour spokesman on Education, was supportive of the NAS case. Another was the Labour MP for Burnley, Daniel Jones, who was also an official with the engineering union, AEU. He took a dim view of the NUT, which he believed to be ineffective. He was loud in praising the subsequent NAS decision in 1961 to take militant action.

One of the sympathetic Conservatives was Fergus Montgomery, a former member of the NAS during his schoolmaster days. Three other Conservative MPs, Sir Robert Jenkins, Sir Charles Fletcher-Cooke and Sir Wavell Wakefield, were also strong supporters of the NAS case for recognition. The last named had been introduced to Terry Casey by a mutual friend and the two became very close, even described by some journalists at the time as "co-conspirators" for the NAS cause. Some observers believe Sir Wavell badgered Sir David Eccles almost on a daily basis to "stop upsetting all those schoolmasters" and grant recognition to the NAS.

These four MPs along with many others organised much Parliamentary activity on behalf of the NAS. Questions were put down to Ministers and the PM. Early day motions (EDMs) and adjournment debates were set up. They led several deputations of Parliamentary colleagues, sometimes of a cross-party composition, to Ministers. They became very familiar with the customary grounds for refusal. They had received so many that eventually the Ministerial replies were simply that they had read and heard all the arguments before and that "regrettably" they could not see "any reason to change their previous decisions and those of all their predecessors".

Sir Robert Jenkins was a prominent member of the Conservative Parliamentary Education Committee. Along with a number of his colleagues he pressed the NAS to abandon its opposition to equal pay (EP) to assist its case for recognition. Jenkins asked at a meeting between his Committee and the NAS on 18 November 1957: "Seeing that the policy of EP was not confined to the Conservative Party, might not [the NAS] be wise to think again about their present 'die-hard' attitude towards it?"

Bert Rushworth responded: "The findings of the Royal Commission supported our contention that the labour market would work against schoolmasters under equal pay. In spite of this however, we were quite prepared to face realities. NAS now proposed the introduction of a child allowance, such as operated in the field of university remuneration." That was as close as the GS could go in abandoning the NAS's opposition to EP policy without a decision of the Executive and Conference. Without stirring up the 'die-hards', opposition to EP was diplomatically ditched for all practical purposes step by step in quiet admissions as typified by Rushworth's response.

The NAS developed new policies which effectively subsumed the question of EP without even mentioning it. This focussed upon better financial prospects for all career teachers for genuine EP at decent levels of remuneration.

The NAS was very meticulous in its lobbying, keeping details of the results of such activity at national and local levels. By the end of 1957 the list of MPs recorded as favourable to NAS representation came to 231. The total number of MPs was around 630.

The 182 'favourable' Conservative MPs included some young backbenchers who were to rise to positions of great prominence, the most famous of whom was Margaret Thatcher. Others included Jim Prior, Willie Whitelaw, Reginald Maudling, Robert Carr, Ian Macleod, Tony Barber and Peter Thorneycroft, several of whom were to become Chancellors of the Exchequer. The list also included the famous Olympic athlete and one-time 5,000 metre world-record holder, Christopher Chataway.

Some MPs declared they supported the NAS case but did not wish to go as far as signing a Commons motion. Of these 182 MPs, 79 had signed the relevant motion in support of NAS recognition, including Margaret Thatcher. A total of 45 Labour MPs were recorded as favourable, including (in addition to Harold Wilson) a future Cabinet member, Harold Lever, and chief whip Bob Mellish, along with veteran MP Manny Shinwell. Three of the four Liberal MPs recorded as favourable had signed the motion.

The NAS produced a detailed briefing for its deputation to the Minister, Geoffrey Lloyd, on 13 July 1959. As well as the usual well-rehearsed arguments there were some references to recent developments. The claim that Burnham "worked well" and had no need to change was being challenged by the ATTI and Assistant Masters who were openly critical of the recent settlement. The NUT itself had initially rejected the 1959 award, only to accept a slightly revised one later, but had then been ordered by its own Conference to conduct an examination of the workings of the Burnham machinery.

The briefing also nailed the lie about the 'floodgates' argument. Most of the relevant organisations were small subject associations, devoted to their specialist fields, whose members already belonged to the mainstream unions and who harboured no ambitions to represent teachers more generally. Only the NUWT and NAHT entertained such aims and in addition to double representation their small size rendered their cases weak. Such associations were rarely named for fear of exposing the weakness of the case. However, in a letter dated 3 April 1956 to Donald Johnson, MP, who had obviously been lobbied by the NAS, the floodgates argument had been pleaded by Sir David Eccles, citing "the NUWT and the various associations of domestic science and physical education teachers who would have an equal claim to admission". The domestic science teachers' claim was manifest nonsense, being in the NUT's own words "a centrally attached association" of that union. The PE teachers belonged to a variety of 'mainstream' unions.

Confidential correspondence between Robert Jenkins MP and the Minister, Geoffrey Lloyd, in 1959 indicated considerable backbench concerns about the continued denial of the NAS. The case of the failed boycott by the Durham NUT in 1954 was cited to argue against the assumption that the NUT would walk out of Burnham if the NAS were to be recognised. Robert Jenkins organised another joint party deputation of MPs, consisting of five Conservatives, four Labour and one Liberal in July 1959. Bert Rushworth's previous assurances on taking a realistic attitude on EP and of a willingness to work responsibly inside the Burnham Committee were repeated in December 1959.

A letter from T.L. Ironmonger, a Conservative MP, to Bert Rushworth, 22 December 1959, said that the matter "has very nearly reached a satisfactory conclusion and that too many inquiries for the present stage might upset the applecart". It seemed that the NAS might have been close to achieving recognition that year. The high profile of the NAS, the determination to go on lobbying and the fiasco surrounding the 1959 Burnham pay negotiations had all contributed to a very healthy recruitment of over 4,000 new members in the year.

January and February 1960 saw the conflict between the NAS and NUT laid bare before all Members of Parliament. Lengthy briefings were sent to MPs by both the NAS and NUT, each one responding further to the other. The exchanges were blunt but not vitriolic. The NUT produced a response to the NAS lobbying in a circular to all MPs dated 26 January repeating the asinine argument that no one currently on the Burnham Committee had requested any change. There was the usual warning that any decision to admit the NAS risked "serious difficulties and the fragmentation of the teachers' side". The circular repeated the Ministerial 'post hoc rationalisation' claim that representation was designed to reflect "different types of schools", not simply size.

The NUT claimed increased membership, like the NAS. But the NAS was distinct only through pursuing a different policy on EP. The NAS counterclaimed that it did represent a special group, namely schoolmasters whose interests were buried under the overwhelming majority of women members of the NUT. The NUT accused the NAS of unscrupulously exploiting the dissatisfaction of men teachers over salary settlements which it claimed had been the best in the circumstances.

The NUT circular admitted "the Burnham Committee can only make recommendations to the Minister if it comes to an agreement". Recognising the NAS would show divisions on the Teachers' Panel and signal a retreat by the Government on EP, the NUT repeated its offer of disbanding itself in order for all unions to unite under one banner.

The NAS sent two lengthy briefings reviewing all the well-known arguments but also accepting the fact that Parliament has legislated for EP. Whilst retaining the right to speak freely it would not act irresponsibly in the Burnham Committee. The NAS also reminded MPs of the disingenuous NUT point that LEAs were free to recognise the NAS if they wished, bearing in mind the events in Durham in 1954 and Liverpool in 1957. In 1958 the Newport NUT had also threatened boycott if the NAS were to be recognised by the LEA. Some MPs found the implied threat by the NUT of "serious consequences" if the NAS were granted representation to be 'unfortunate'.

The NAS kept up its running total of MPs supportive of recognition. Again the list was over 200 with a good number having signed the latest Parliamentary motion.

On 29 January 1960, Sir David Eccles, back at his old job as Minister of Education, received yet another deputation from the NAS for the start of some interesting times. Contrary pressure was also coming from the NUT, which had circulated a document on the same morning vigorously opposing the NAS case. The NUT letter repeated the obvious and silly point that there had been no demand from either side of Burnham for any change. Of course not! The employers were happy with a weak and quiescent Teachers' Panel who in turn wished no disturbance of the cosy status quo. The NUT letter again threatened that any change "could lead to serious difficulties and to the enforced fragmentation of the teachers' side". Sir David seemed to make sure the NAS delegation saw that the NUT document was already in his hands.

On 15 February the NAS met the Conservative Backbench Parliamentary Education Committee. The number attending was significant, some 70 MPs being registered as present, with minutes taken. There was some feeling in the air that the answer this time might be positive.

Even the *TES* was moved to a sympathetic editorial on 4 March 1960:

"It is important first to remember that it is for the Minister to decide . . . It is not for one union to keep another out. It is difficult to see that the Minister can much longer ignore the claims of the NAS. The arguments against it on size, sectional interest and so on could each hold good against the organisations that already have a place. On the grounds of equity alone the NAS deserves to be considered."

In the correspondence that flowed between NAS members, MPs and Ministers, as well as in records of meetings between the same people, there is more evidence of the NAS again being pressed to drop its opposition to EP to smooth the path towards recognition. Bert Rushworth and others responded, repeating the assurances already given that the NAS would not use opposition to EP to obstruct the workings of the Burnham Committee. How could it possibly win a vote on the issue anyway?

Alas, when Sir David Eccles made his decision in March it was the same. The only differences were the way it was delivered and in some of the reasons given, the latter only making matters worse. In a bid to sweeten the bitter pill the NAS was given a day's notice (on 23 March 1960) that the decision was on its way. The letter duly arrived on 24 March repeating the same old reasons, including rejection of the NAS's claim that its members were a distinct group. In addition the Minister wrote he wished "to reach his decision on positive grounds . . . and what I consider would be in the best interests of the profession as a whole". He had concluded that: "Unity is at the present time most important to the professional status of the teachers, and that this cause would not be best served by the grant to [the NAS] of representation . . . on the Burnham Committee." The NAS learned later that Eccles' decision had been considered and approved by a Cabinet subcommittee.

Naturally the NAS condemned the patronising attitude of the Minister. The claim that unity would enhance professional status while the quiescent Teachers' Panel ensured genteel poverty was regarded as risible by the NAS. Who was he to lecture schoolmasters on how they should organise themselves? What were the implications for the continued recognition of other non-NUT organisations?

The NAS had taken a positive but realistic attitude to unity, having suggested a British Council of Teachers and later a Common Council to progress those matters on which there was agreement and joint endeavour possible. Along with all the other associations, the NAS had rejected the NUT notion of unity, which was to be swallowed up in one union dominated by the largest.

The NAS spent 25 March preparing literature to be sent out to every member and all MPs vigorously protesting against the decision and the new 'reasons'. It was difficult not to be cynical. Besides the outrageous denial of simple justice and the effective right to join the union of your choice (if you wished to have recognition), nowhere in the statute was there reference to 'types of school'. The statute merely required the Minister to recognise "organisations representing teachers". This and the new-found urge to have "unity and solidarity" were merely excuses to deny simple justice and to cloak the Government's cowardice in the face of the threat of NUT boycott.

The NUT was jubilant. A circular to its members merely copied the Minister's letter to the NAS with the only comment: "In view of the Minister's reply, its bare reproduction would seem to serve our purposes admirably."

But it was one rejection too many. The NAS Special Committee 'K' (which had been established to secure recognition) met in emergency session on 26 March. It resolved to redouble lobbying activity. Far from going away the NAS was intent on returning with more force than ever before. Friendly MPs would be asked to become even more active.

Committee 'K' also took the first step on the road to militant action – carefully as always. The members were to be fully briefed and a campaign launched to expose the weaknesses of the Burnham Committee. A suitable urgency resolution was to be framed for Annual Conference (1960), due within two weeks. Local associations were asked to organise protest meetings in school time.

GS Bert Rushworth, together with the President and Honorary Treasurer, called a press conference on 30 March. The GS began by expressing the NAS's bitter disappointment with the Minister's decision and the reasons given. The NAS would press for it to be reconsidered, if necessary approach the Prime Minister and call for a Royal Commission on the negotiating machinery.

Rushworth was pressed: "What would the NAS do if these measures failed?" He responded quite explicitly: "If these constitutional approaches are not successful the NAS will certainly consider militant action." The newspaper headlines the following day duly reflected that threat. The die was being cast, not yet 'in concrete' – to mix the metaphors – but carefully to allow the members to be properly prepared.

Press and public opinion appeared to be on the side of the NAS. Again the *TES* in its editorial, 1 April, stated:

"The Minister's refusal . . . simply will not do. He declares that representation . . . should be by type of school. This is a quite arbitrary amplification of the duty laid upon him by the 1944 Act. Forcing the NAS to stay outside will always be a rallying call for discontented teachers . . . and will be a hindrance to unity."

In the early days there might have been some justification for opponents pointing to our relatively small numbers. But as numbers increased to 22,000 by the beginning of 1960, with Burnham now a statutory body and with representation long afforded to other organisations of smaller size, it was outrageous that it should be denied to the NAS. The injustice was rank, gross and blatant. The 'reasons' deployed by successive Ministers of Education were a disgraceful bunch of self-contradictory excuses, trotted out as occasions demanded in stock departmental answers. At best it was naked expediency, at worst downright cowardice, hiding behind threats from the NUT which when eventually put to the test were found to be empty.

Chapter 15 - Mood Moves to Militancy

Although the NAS had constantly demanded representation on the Burnham Committee from 1923 onwards it was not until the rebuttal of 1960 that a really determined high-profile campaign envisaging militant action got under way. There was a certain irony in the NAS demanding representation on Burnham. The NAS was its severest critic. But it was necessary to get on Burnham to further the cause of its much-needed reform. It was not a good show, but it was the only one in town.

The NAS Annual Conference in April 1960 at Blackpool was an angry affair. It was another turning point in the campaign. It was also the largest in the Association's history. Conference decided that enough was enough. The urgency motion on representation declared that constitutional approaches might not be sufficient to secure recognition and instructed the Executive that, whilst not abandoning them, it "must initiate such other activity as is necessary to impress upon the Government the determination of the Association to secure the rights of its members. Conference pledges the full support of the Association to every member who takes such action as the Executive may request."

The Immediate Past-President, A. L. Jones, proposing the urgency motion, brought the Conference, in the words of the *TES*, "cheering to its feet". "It is clear", ALJ said, "we are not going to get justice by presenting a reasoned case. I do not think that a just claim can ever have been received with such callous denial. There comes a time when any man of principle must be prepared to fight... This time has now come for the Association."

Seconding the motion, the newly elected Vice-President, Terry Casey, spoke of the "scandal that such a body of men should be denied an elementary right". Terry Casey claimed Ministers feared "losing the co-operation if not the servility of the NUT" for continuing to refuse recognition to the NAS. On another occasion Sir David Eccles had let slip to one of his correspondents that "the NAS had been the Association which had caused [him] so much trouble at the time of the superannuation bill". In response to correspondence from an MP, Donald Johnson, David Eccles had observed in a letter dated 3 April 1956, " . . . but you will have noticed that it [the NAS] took a leading part in the more extreme forms of agitation against the Teachers' Superannuation Bill". What did the NAS 'extremism' amount to? In Eccles' own words the NAS was "almost wholly concerned with the propagation of particular views, especially on salary matters". That was a gross exaggeration, but even if true, so what!

In its report on the salaries debate when Terry Casey proposed the motion seeking a ten-year basic scale of £800-£1,500 the *TES* described him as an "Irishman whose militant eloquence held the attention of the delegates more closely than that of any one else and smoothed the path of the Executive throughout the three days".

Commenting on the Easter 1961 teacher union Conferences, the *TES*, drawing on a boxing analogy – "a midget flooring a giant" – wrote in an editorial on 14 April:

" . . . in last week's contest for public attention . . . the NAS for all its minority in numbers belted the NUT out of the ring.

" . . . exasperated at its continued exclusion from Burnham . . . angry at the Government's refusal to permit an independent review of the negotiating machinery . . . enraged at what it considers to be a gross under-payment of schoolmasters . . . no one can doubt for one moment the resolution of the NAS. You only have to look at the sense of purpose it has shown in the past.

"Can the NUT count on keeping its members aloof? Many of its individual members will wish their colleagues in the other union good luck.

"The rank and file of the NUT are always badgering their executive to be more militant. With the NAS the executive are as militant as the rest.

"But strikes surely are not the way. Professional people do not withhold their services. And the NAS knows it. Instinctively it has not been able to abandon its sense of responsibility. It is going to give one week's notice of any plans. So, on the brink of unprofessional behaviour the NAS is behaving most professionally. The situation is ludicrous. It must not be allowed to come true.

"When everything is said against it, the NAS remains a free and vigorous association of teachers. And it is going from strength to strength. Cannot the Minister and the NUT recognize this? They will have to do so sooner or later."

The first fruits of even more intensive NAS Parliamentary lobbying in the wake of the 23 March 1960 rejection appeared soon afterwards. Charles Fletcher-Cooke, Conservative MP for Darwen, secured an adjournment debate in the House of Commons for 14 April. Opening the debate Mr Fletcher-Cooke articulated the NAS case eloquently, speaking not as an "educationalist" but as someone interested in labour relations and concerned that the Government should show "a good example".

Mr Fletcher-Cooke conceded that 'break-away' unions posed problems but the principle of free choice had been agreed in international charters. Not every 'break-away' group could be instantly recognised for obvious reasons; they had to stand the test of time and retain a substantial number of members, in other words have "a high survival rate" in a harsh world to show they were meeting a genuine need.

One of the Minister's reasons for refusal was "to promote unity and solidarity in the profession". Tongue in cheek Fletcher-Cooke asked if refusing the NAS recognition had promoted more "unity and solidarity"! Denying "elementary rights to a substantial minority" would not in the future achieve that which it has failed in the past.

Charles Fletcher-Cooke concluded the reasons for refusal were so unconvincing that "we are bound to ask if there were other unexpressed reasons". Referring to a "very violent and inflammatory circular from the NUT, which cannot have done its cause very much good", Fletcher-Cooke commented: "If that is not something in the nature of a threat, I do not know what is." He appealed to the Minister: "How many members does the NAS require to secure recognition, 30,000, 40,000? Is the Burnham constitution, now old, never to be amended whatever changes there might be in the structure of education or the sentiments of teachers?"

The first Labour MP called to speak was Dr Horace King, who declared his membership of the NUT. He was gracious enough to acknowledge the "fairness and moderation" of the Honorary Member for Darwen, which he hoped to emulate. He welcomed the conversion of the Conservatives not to create breakaway unionism and to 'solidarity' of the workers. He agreed with professional unity and deplored the NAS policy on EP. Dr King claimed the Burnham Committee was "built on functionality" and representation was "never on a proportional basis", totally ignoring the very basis for the NUT's overall majority.

In the same breath as Dr King shared the belief of the Minister and employers that the Burnham Committee "worked well" he acknowledged that over 100,000 primary teachers were "profoundly disappointed at the recent Burnham decisions which gave them unequal treatment as compared to their secondary colleagues".

The Minister, Sir David Eccles, replied to the debate, emphasising the difficulty of the decision, acknowledging the sincerity of both sides but raising no new reasons and rebutting some of the criticisms. In accordance with Parliamentary procedure the adjournment debate lapsed after one hour without a vote. It had been a useful exercise, with the arguments on both sides fully and fairly aired.

The debate and the lobbying continued throughout the rest of 1960. Perhaps they went on for too long, for the patience of NAS activists was being tested to breaking point. The context was one in which EP had been conceded despite the dire warnings of the NAS of the economic implications for the schoolmaster with family responsibilities. Teachers' superannuation contributions had been unnecessarily and unfairly increased in 1956, with only the NAS fighting a rearguard action against that injustice. To crown all that, teachers' pay settlements had been held down to disastrously low levels. In the view of the NAS, this had been done deliberately to facilitate EP on the cheap.

Older members were still conscious of the disastrous history of teachers' pay during the 1920s and 1930s and the thoroughly miserable awards that followed in the 1940s and 1950s. The same pattern was being repeated in 1959 to which there was added the 'constitutional' complication of direction intervention by the Minister, exposing the charade long complained about by the NAS. Significantly, some prominent NUT people began to speak publicly about the failings of Burnham as a pay negotiating machine. The 1959 settlement had been so poor as to cause much anger and bitterness in the NUT as well as plundering greater depths of anger in the NAS. And there was worse to come in 1961.

In his book *The Schoolmasters* Ron Simons, President 1970-71, wrote about "a new spirit" coming over the Association. It was one of "determination born out of aggravation and bitterness". He believed that within a short period of time the 'average' NAS schoolmaster had changed from being somewhat passive "into an active, crusading member". He went on: "Members in the staff rooms were talking about the NAS, arguing about the NAS and convincing men who had been hesitant for years that their proper place was in the NAS. The ordinary member was proud of his Association."

Around the same time one of the greatest figures in NAS history, Terry Casey, was rising through the ranks: LSA President, Member of the National Executive, Chairman of Salaries and in 1961 National Vice-President. He was soon to assume a leading role in the world of teacher union politics, becoming GS in 1963 in succession to Bert Rushworth. He was the architect of the modern NASUWT. Terry had entered the profession as an Emergency Trained Teacher in 1945 upon demobilisation from war service in the Royal Army Education Corps. He was of 'London Irish stock' and, as he used to observe himself, was "begot" at the same time and in the same way as the NAS: by soldiers returning from the First World War. He was a charismatic figure, a great platform orator, who, in the words of one his great friends and partners in NAS battles, Tom Smith, "could argue the paint off the wall".

In typical Terry fashion he had inveigled himself into the chairmanship of Special Committee 'K', whose membership consisted simply of the National Officers and himself. Committee 'K' was charged with overseeing the campaign to secure recognition. Terry was a long-standing critic of the Burnham structure. He was a consummate dialectician and argued the case for Burnham to reflect the realities of government's fiscal and constitutional responsibilities in a way few could emulate.

There were also other outstanding national leaders. Bert Rushworth, a quiet but determined Yorkshireman commanded much respect as the GS. The Honorary Treasurer, G. Lloyd Williams, was a fiery Welshman and another great platform orator and Past-President. Presidents around the same time, A.L. Jones (1960) from Liverpool and Harry Bell (1961) from Croydon, were renowned for their own great oratory and fighting spirits. Tom Smith, President during 1956 and headmaster of a large secondary school in south-east London, commanded huge respect and was regarded as a man of the highest calibre. Terry Casey confided to me many years later that if Tom had allowed his name to go forward for GS in 1963 he "would not have bothered to apply".

There were many outstanding and courageous local leaders, too numerous to mention by name. But one deserves a special mention in this context. He is Bruce Given, a great driving force for several years behind the demand for militant action. He told me he had to galvanise the leadership into action.

Ron Simons writes about a crucial telephone call he took during the course of the December 1960 National Executive meeting, being held at the Cora Hotel close to Euston Station and the NAS HQ at 59 Gordon Square. The call was from Bruce Given, an LSA activist and Rep at William Penn School in Dulwich, south-east London. Ron writes about taking the call in the "narrow confines of an unlit telephone booth" and struggling to get the text written down accurately.

Bruce Given wanted his NEC member to convey the resolution which had just been carried by a specially convened meeting of his school's members. This direct and immediate access to the Executive was very much in the NAS tradition of close contact between the leadership and the grass roots. Ron Simons managed to note down the text which represented a very significant move in unlocking the deadlock over the NAS's claim for recognition:

"We, the members of the NAS at William Penn School, . . . feeling insulted, embittered and angry at the continued refusal of the Ministry of Education to grant representation . . . and having come to the conclusion that the redress of this situation is not likely to come about by constitutional means only, invite the National Executive to use this and similar schools where membership is sufficiently strong to make the functioning of the school impossible without our members, as a means of focussing attention on the injustice of the present situation . . . We say this in the full knowledge that such action as may be decided by the National Executive might entail some sacrifice by ourselves and other members."

It was in every sense a fine motion in the best traditions of the NAS. It asked not what the Association could do for 'us' but, realising that the members were the Association, boldly stated what 'we' wanted to do for our association. Ron

Simons says he took it back into the meeting and at the first available opportunity read it out. It was received with acclamation.

The William Penn members took their resolution to the Southwark Branch of the LSA and a few days later HQ received a letter from 20 members at Samuel Pepys School in New Cross, south-east London demanding the same action, pledging their full support, acknowledging the risks which they were prepared to carry.

So the scene was set, the leaders in place, for the climax of the greatest campaign to be run in the history of the Association. The campaign for official recognition through representation on the Burnham Committee, already nearly 40 years in duration, had to be waged against the unrelenting hostility of our biggest rival, the NUT, matched by that of the LEA employers represented by the AEC, with the Government indifferent if not antagonistic.

In November 1960 the Conservative Party's Parliamentary Education Committee had elected officers who were all favourable to the NAS case. In the same month NAS branches were alerted to another Commons early day motion on NAS representation put down by MPs Fergus Montgomery and Robert Jenkins. Members all over the country had been asked to approach their MPs to persuade them to sign the motion. By the beginning of the year the number of signatories had reached an impressive 235.

The signatories again included the future Prime Minister, Margaret Thatcher. Supporters recorded as privately sympathetic again included another future PM, Harold Wilson. Local lobbying in Wilson's Huyton constituency had yielded results, but he wrote that as a member of the Shadow Cabinet (he was the 'Opposition' Chancellor) he could not invade the territory of the Labour Education equivalent, Anthony Greenwood. In correspondence he declined an invitation to meet with the NAS GS on the grounds that he would also have to meet with Gould of the NUT. Harold Wilson recalled that local NAS lobbyists had taken up much of his time on the eve of the previous General Election so he was very familiar with the case!

Possibly it had become too late for lobbying to succeed. It was the emerging determination to take action rather than a belief in diplomacy and sound argument winning the day that led to the feverish lobbying that produced so many signatories so quickly.

Following the December 1960 Executive Bert Rushworth and Terry Casey met members from William Penn and Samuel Pepys Schools. They persuaded the members to withhold action until after a national mass meeting being planned for February the following year.

The GS was also able to report to the January 1961 Executive that the spirit of these members was excellent but it had not been easy persuading them to wait. Bert Rushworth noted that such members would have to be satisfied and if the national mass meeting failed to produce recognition it would have to be followed by a series of strikes.

Responding to such pressure the Executive announced a national mass meeting in London for Saturday 25 February 1961 to promote three demands: representation on Burnham, an independent inquiry into the negotiating machinery and a new pay structure.

I have already observed that if there were one 'defining' year in the Association's history it was 1961. If there were one defining event it must surely be that meeting in the Central Hall Westminster on 25 February.

Chapter 16 - Saturday 25 February 1961
'A Defining Day in the History of the Association'

From time to time in the affairs of organisations a seminal event occurs. Saturday 25 February 1961 was one such day for the NAS.

For nearly 40 years the Association had been demanding representation on the Burnham Committee dealing with teachers' pay. The Government set all the rules including membership and thereby determined whether a union was officially recognised. Notwithstanding Burnham's serious defects official recognition was crucial for the future of the NAS.

Despite strong, vigorous representations to Government Ministers which grew in strength as the NAS membership expanded, when it came to decision time the NUT had been allowed an effective veto. As the economic position of the career schoolmaster got worse and worse the anger and frustration of members finally reached breaking point by the beginning of the 1960s. More militant voices were demanding strike action if the Government continued to refuse recognition.

In response to this pressure the National Executive called a mass meeting in the Central Hall Westminster for Saturday 25 February 1961. It was seen as a prelude to the forthcoming Annual Conference at Easter carrying a motion committing the Association to strikes if recognition were not granted. Few, if any, of the Executive could have foreseen how successful the mass meeting was to be.

Over 6,000 schoolmasters out of a total membership of 22,000 turned out for the meeting. A special edition of *The New Schoolmaster,* in March 1961, carried a full and moving report of the proceedings, much better capturing the oratory and the atmosphere that electrified the audience than I can, reporting second-hand nearly 50 years after the event. Some of the Association's 'golden oldies' I knew vividly remembered the day; their eyes lit up when I asked them about it.

The New Schoolmaster claimed it was the largest meeting of teachers ever to be held. Over a quarter of the Association's entire membership had gathered together to express their anger in the heart of Westminster under the shadow of Big Ben. If the same percentage of the membership attended such a meeting after the turn of the twenty-first century, a stadium with a 50,000-plus capacity would be required.

The meeting was scheduled to start at 11.00, but by 9.30 a.m. there was already a queue. The LSA was stewarding the meeting under the "efficient control of veteran Harry Meigh, a seasoned campaigner and organiser of many large meetings in the Capital, for whom this was the largest of all".

Soon the Great Hall holding 3,000 seats filled up. Two overflow halls, each holding around a thousand, connected to the main hall by loudspeakers, had quickly to be set up. After that the last thousand to arrive were packed in and around the rooms and corridors of Central Hall. The President of the day was the renowned Arthur L. Jones (known as 'ALJ') from Liverpool. To illustrate the emphasis placed upon the individual he had positioned himself at the entrance to Central Hall, personally welcoming as many of the delegates as possible.

At 11.00 sharp, with the press table filled, the television cameras rolling and the photographers' bulbs flashing, ALJ led the National Officers onto the platform to a rousing standing ovation. An individual roll call was obviously impossible so the President called for members from the regions to indicate their presence. They had come from every part of the United Kingdom. When it came to Wales, the whole contingent stood and struck up "Land of My Fathers" in which they were joined by the entire assembly. There is nothing quite like setting the right emotional atmosphere. It reminds me of Samuel Goldwyn's philosophy of film-making: "Start with a climax and build it from there."

Union leaders and veterans of countless conferences know only too well how morale and a determination to fight your cause can be uplifted by such moving and emotional occasions. The trick is of course to ensure that the emotion is not simply stirred up and then left to die away. A union has to make sure that it is transformed through action into real results. Delivering on militant motions passed in the admittedly hothouse of Conference has always been a hallmark of the NAS. There is no need for me here to make any comparisons with others.

After a few more formalities the General Secretary, Bert Rushworth, was called to address the meeting. His address was delayed for a further few minutes while once again the meeting rose to greet him with a standing ovation.

Bert Rushworth first reminded his listeners that they "had gathered together to show the country and especially the Government that there are matters giving serious concern in the education service and to demonstrate their determination to bring to an end injustices which have become intolerable".

Referring to "this, the largest demonstration in the history of education in this country – probably in the world," Rushworth said it was "a gathering of serious responsible men". He dismissed the NAS detractors as "ministerial lackeys bearing a heavy responsibility for the schoolmaster's present plight". He expressed the confidence the Association had in its case by saying it was content to place it before the public, before any committee or inquiry and even before a Royal Commission.

He deplored the denial of basic democratic rights to over 22,000 men in the second largest teachers' union to have a say in the determination of their salary and a voice in the educational councils of the land. The nation could not afford to neglect the talents and knowledge of so many.

He condemned the message conveyed by governments that if schoolmasters sought professional rights they had to join a union of the Minister's choice. "If we have left even a modicum of honour we who fought to make sure that Hitler failed must not allow Sir David Eccles to succeed." The many ex-servicemen in the audience led loud and prolonged applause.

The Burnham Committee "ensured continued humility of schoolmasters as was planned nearly a century ago". A 20% cut in their pay before the war and continued poor treatment thereafter led to the schoolmaster having a social status lower than most of the parents of the pupils he taught.

As a former teacher Bert Rushworth was able to speak from experience and the heart: "I taught for over 30 years. I was a less good teacher than I ought to have been because too much of my mind was occupied with the need to keep my humble expenditure within the limits of my low salary. Never has the schoolmaster expected wealth. Scarcely has he expected comfort. Now he is sick and tired of depressing poverty which prevents him from giving of his best in the service of education."

Deploring the employment of unqualified staff "and even adolescent childminders", not to mention 3 million children in overcrowded classes, Rushworth asked "if the taxpayers realise that they are paying for the present expensive advertising campaign of the Minister of Education, whose main purpose seems to be to keep the schools open irrespective of the means employed and without regard to the future of the teaching profession."

Bert Rushworth pointed to the low level of spending on education in Britain, which remained at 3% of Government expenditure, the same as in 1939. Other countries such as Russia, Japan and the USA spent much more, having learned the lesson of the war so they could make the necessary social and economic progress in a competitive world. To more prolonged applause Bert Rushworth claimed "we needed a Minister of Education who would fight for education and not allow it to be starved".

Bert Rushworth then posed a list of rhetorical questions, asking why members were denied representation across the board, to which the audience responded with ever-increasing crescendo: "Because we are NAS".

Bert Rushworth declared the aims of the schoolmaster to be:

to seek improvement of the education service;

to ensure an adequate supply of the best possible men and women respectively to educate the nation's 'boyhood' and 'girlhood';

to earn a salary to provide a reasonable standard of living for his wife and family.

These "were hardly the aims of fanatics".

Rushworth declared this day to mark the end of patient acquiescence in frustrating exclusion and injustice for what should be a noble profession. To more prolonged and vociferous applause Rushworth proclaimed in conclusion:

"There is a limit at which forbearance ceases to be a virtue. In the belief of the Executive that limit has now been reached. Forty years have been too long. Now let the pride of men assert itself. Claim your rights, say to the Minister – Give us justice or we fight."

The *New Schoolmaster* report continued:

"The scene which followed can hardly be conveyed in print. All three thousand men rose to their feet as one clapping and cheering demonstrating their unity and it seemed to go on and on until the strains of 'for he's a jolly good fellow' were taken up from all sides even in the overflow meetings".

"Thank you gentlemen", from the General Secretary ended what must have been the most stirring speech in the history of the Association to the largest meeting ever held. Bert Rushworth was not renowned as a great orator. Indeed some who knew him told me he was naturally a rather quiet if persuasive speaker given to becoming very nervous before big public speeches. He died soon after leaving office. If these comments are true it serves only to illustrate the magnificent manner in which he rose to the occasion on 25 February 1961.

The Association's wealth of oratorical talent was underlined as Terry Casey rose to propose the motion being considered by the mass meeting. I recognised in the account of his speech the persuasive logic backed up with the killer emotive point that was his mark.

Terry Casey reminded the meeting that the Association had grown over 40 years in spite of the strong opposition from rival unions, the LEAs and the Government. But it was now clearly a travesty of democracy to deny a substantial minority the right to have a say in the matters concerning their employment. But, sad as it was to attack another union, he had to say that the reason for exclusion stemmed from the NUT.

Referring to the meeting with Sir David Eccles in which the Minister had openly relied upon the NUT briefing on his desk, Terry Casey claimed the advice given to the Minister was: "Leave the Teachers' Panel as it is and you will get compliance and stability. Bring in the NAS and you will get a bit of backbone." In his covering letter to the Minister the NUT GS, Sir Ronald

Gould, had said: "May I impress upon you the gravity of this matter and the serious consequence which might follow from any decision to alter the composition of the Teachers' Panel . . ."

With characteristic mocking humour reflecting the NAS's long-standing criticisms of Burnham, Terry referred to the latest meeting of the Committee on Wednesday 15 February 1961 – Ash Wednesday and the occasion of an eclipse of the sun – provoking much laughter.

Lampooning the vacillations of the NUT Terry referred to its Executive recently rejecting its own salaries' committee recommendation to lodge a claim for a scale from £700 to £1,300 only to reinstate it following the Royal Commission reports on the pay of doctors, dentists and the police force, which had produced good results for the personnel concerned.

Terry Casey quoted Article 5 of the Charter unanimously adopted by the then International Federation of Teachers' Associations at its meeting in Moscow in August 1954: "Teachers should have the right freely to join professional bodies, and such bodies should be entitled to represent them on all occasions." "Who was the President?" Terry asked. "Sir Ronald Gould of course, refusing to practise in London that which he preached in Moscow!" Like Bert Rushworth, Terry Casey received a standing ovation.

The motion was seconded by Ex-President J.A.C. Thomson from Scotland, who well complemented the previous contributions from Bert Rushworth and Terry Casey. He was expert in and a fierce critic of Burnham's constitutional arrangements, revealing that Scottish teachers had discovered the Treasury-predetermined sum through the obscure Goschen formula, which gave Scotland a proportion of the central government rate support payments made to England and Wales. The largest teachers' union in Scotland, the EIS, took a similar blinkered attitude as its close ally south of the border, the NUT.

Needless to say, there was hardly any requirement for the motion to be put formally. As soon as the President raised the issue there were roars around the entire building, loud applause and shouts of "all". The motion demanding recognition of the 22,000-strong NAS, the establishment of an independent review of the negotiating machinery and a ten-year incremental scale of not less than £800-£1,500 was declared unanimously carried by the President.

The President then declared that he proposed to march up Whitehall and deliver a letter containing the resolution to the Prime Minister's official residence. He wanted everybody to follow him. When the cheering and applause had once again died down, the General Secretary very fittingly called upon Bruce Given of the William Penn School, London, to give a vote of thanks to the President.

The New Schoolmaster records:

"In a few well chosen words Mr Given expressed his pleasure in being given the opportunity to thank the President. He indicated that the staff of his school had been critical of the Leadership in the past, but they were now together and at one with the Executive and indeed the whole NAS. He welcomed the resurgent militancy and pledged that the men of Penn were ready and they wished to be in the vanguard of the fight. He was confident of the great support that would be forthcoming and confident of the ultimate result."

D.J. Harterre, from the Gelli-Dawel Secondary Modern School in Glamorgan, seconded the vote of thanks to the President.

Typically the Honorary Treasurer from Wales, G. Lloyd Williams, made one of his characteristic flamboyant and forceful interventions to put the vote of thanks. He asked members to carry back the fighting spirit shown here to their staffrooms and prepare to support some important motions which would be put to the forthcoming Annual Conference at Easter in Blackpool. He concluded: "Today's meeting marks the beginning of the real fight for justice for schoolmasters."

So ended a great historic meeting. But the story was not quite over.

Outside the morning rain had stopped. A small body of police efficiently and unobtrusively marshalled the eager and determined schoolmasters five abreast to be led by the President to march up Whitehall to deliver the letter to the Prime Minister containing the terms of the motion unanimously carried.

It took 35 minutes to pass the cenotaph. When the head of the procession reached Admiralty House the President and the Officers left to deliver the letter to the Prime Minister at his temporary official residence. (10 Downing Street was being renovated.) The rest of the marchers went on to disperse around Trafalgar Square. There were more press interviews in the courtyard of Admiralty House and then it was all over.

Reflecting on the great success of the demonstration *The New Schoolmaster* recorded: "It was interesting to see the reports and reactions of the press, radio and television on Saturday evening, Sunday and Monday. There is no doubt that much favourable publicity was obtained. This must have had its effect in our favour."

The Sunday Post said: "This was the largest demonstration in the history of education in Britain, and probably in the world."

The Sunday Times: "The ominous word 'action' tolled like a bell through both meeting and march. They roared with approval when their Secretary announced that the schoolmaster is sick and tired of depressing poverty."

The Times headlined: "6,000 Men Teachers in Pay Protest Letter Delivered to Prime Minister".

The Guardian reported " . . . in case it be thought that the NAS is a middle-class apology for a trade union, let any industrial trade unionist recall when more than a quarter of his national membership turned out for a mass meeting".

The Evening News: "Wild cheering broke out as the General Secretary of the Association made a biting attack on the Education Minister . . . "

The Observer: "The schoolmasters received an hour and a half of fighting speeches with embattled unanimity."

The Daily Express in its editorial: "A sight to shame the Government . . . thousands of schoolmasters march in pay protest through Whitehall . . . The nation entrusts them with its future, but most of them can never earn more than £1,000 a year."

"Over the passage of time," *The New Schoolmaster* recorded, "it is not without significance that the importance and value of the meeting and all that went with it seemed to increase. Saturday, 25 February 1961 will rank as one of the greatest days in the history of the Association."

The special edition of *The New Schoolmaster* also recorded some reflections on the meeting by several members. They are identifiable only by their initials. Probably the most eloquent of all was one signed 'M.A.L.' – Maurice Langdell, at the time of writing the most senior Past-President of the Association, well into his nineties and until recently in regular attendance at Annual Conference as all Past-Presidents are entitled to be. Maurice wrote:

"History as far as the NAS is concerned spans but four decades, but those four decades embrace a succession of magnificent occasions. The leadership has never been lacking, the sense of direction has always been highly developed and indeed prophetic.

"Recall, if you will, annual conferences; the mass meetings; the London march in November fog; Sunderland and the special gathering at the Friends Meeting House. Remember the depression years and the protest march along the River Thames Embankment. Then there was the 10% salary cut imposed deliberately by the Government as a gesture to the country in difficult days. Teachers were readily available for unwilling subjects for the act of sacrifice. That 10% was eventually restored but since 1938 successive Governments through the machinations of the Burnham Committee have contrived to administer a cut in real salary of 20%. Has no-one but the schoolmaster noticed?

"Thus, with these thoughts in mind, I walked again the route along the embankment, finally joining the throng entering Westminster Central Hall. Never before has any teachers' organisation convened such a mighty gathering. This was a pinnacle of achievement. The reporters, photographers, television, the thrill of the roll call, the oratory; the enthusiasm and solidarity which stirred the emotions, the pride, the dignity of the march; the challenge, the impatience, the promise of it all.

"Where will it end? Why Gentlemen, it is just the beginning. The march is still on, ahead stretches the road in one direction to the one end, then will all men of worth be marching with us. Hamilton House will be truly the headquarters of a re-incarnated National Union of Women Teachers and the National Association of Schoolmasters will negotiate from a position of strength for the rights so long denied."

Maurice Langdell's prophecy regarding the 'permanent separation of the sexes' proved wrong; but his belief that one day the Association would "negotiate from a position of strength" was to be fulfilled.

Footnote to the National Mass Meeting

Checking through the archives relating to these events I was intrigued to discover the source of much of the culture I imbibed from my monitors who included some of the National Officers and officials of the time. Little was left to chance. Risks, while sometimes unavoidable, had to be minimised. Great attention was paid to detail by Committee 'K' in planning the mass meeting:

the option of the overflow hall to be retained;

the roll call to be by area;

no speakers to the motion be allowed other than the mover and seconder; (This might appear dictatorial and undemocratic but the real purpose was not another debate but a staged public demonstration of our determination. Once moved and seconded by inspiring speakers, the motion needed to be put and carried with acclamation. One had to avoid mavericks, self-promoters, pedants, publicity seekers, hobby-horse riders or plain simple bores deflating the 'climax' by introducing dissent or distraction.)

Mr B. Given of the William Penn School be asked to move the vote of thanks to the President, at the same time pledging the support of NAS members in his school for whatever action Conference decided to take;

the Honorary Treasurer (G. Lloyd Williams) be asked to make a parallel arrangement for a seconder (from Wales);

the GS to make arrangement with the police for the ('spontaneous') march at the end of the meeting to the Prime Minister's official residence;

that no publicity be given to the march until the President announces it at the end of the meeting and invites all members to follow him.

Even the 'spontaneity' was well planned!

There were further recommendations from Committee 'K' for Conference. The ground was being laid for militant action, carefully and meticulously in the best traditions of the Association, as the situation required.

Chapter 17 – And so to Action

Despite the intensified lobbying and the mass meeting on 25 February with all the attendant publicity, the Minister remained unmoved and the NAS was still denied recognition. The NAS and supporters, especially some Conservative MPs, were genuinely disappointed. Some had believed that a positive reply was coming.

When the Conservative MP Fergus Montgomery became aware of plans for strike action he wrote a 'panic letter' to the GS threatening resignation and begging the Association to reconsider. He warned about other MPs abandoning support for the NAS. Terry Casey lobbied Fergus Montgomery very hard and eventually succeeded in calming him down and persuading him to stay with the NAS. To his credit he did 'stick with us' even though it might have been uncomfortable for him inside the Tory Party.

Conference 1961, just a couple of months beyond the great mass meeting on 25 February, duly gave the National Executive full power to embark upon a campaign of militant action to achieve the three great ambitions of the Association. They were all important aims. But *the* most crucial was undoubtedly the first, Burnham representation. That would provide a vital tool to tackle the others as time went on.

However, it was unusual for the NAS to be lining up militant action for three different albeit interlocking aims at the same time. An agenda demanding recognition, a Royal Commission or independent inquiry into negotiating machinery and a salary claim for a basic scale of £800-£1,500 was a lot to be achieved in one go! I was 'taught' that one aim, clearly defined and achievable, was enough. As it turned out, when the time came for action other events also occurred which led to more militancy.

The meticulous preparation and planning, as well as risk management carried out by Committee 'K' and the Executive, continued into and beyond Conference. The mass meeting on 25 February had been a 'softening up process' and in media terms the first of two bites of the cherry. The urgency Conference motion carried in public session on 6 April was very similar to the one passed at the national mass meeting on 25 February. That had been preceded the day before in private session at Conference with another motion which dealt with action having to pay regard to "prevailing local and national conditions" as judged by the Executive. The discussion around this motion prepared members for various eventualities which might follow and for obvious reasons was better conducted in private. The Special Meeting of the National Executive immediately following Conference got down to further 'nitty-gritty'.

Appropriately as Bruce Given had offered, the Executive decided to start the action on 1 May 1961 when members at the William Penn School in Dulwich, south London, would be called out on a one-day strike. The LSA was asked to organise a mass meeting for the evening of 1 May.

The next decision by the Executive is revealing. It decided: "That should members at William Penn be suspended by the LCC, all members of the LSA be asked to join a one-day strike." The NAS had enough experience and foresight to prepare for such retaliatory action. If it occurred it would be necessary to regroup and focus the entire Association's strength on the one 'offending' school or authority. The disadvantage is of course that the issue changes from the one originally in contention to the 'right' to take action without dismissal. But the latter had to be defended at all costs.

The next decision was that should William Penn members not be suspended then members at Edge Hill Secondary Modern in Liverpool and the Gelli-Dawel School in Glamorgan would be brought out on 1 June with a similar pattern of supporting activity. Should those members not be suspended Committee 'K' was to prepare further action.

Meanwhile the NUT had been galvanised into 'doing something' on salaries by the NAS agitation. The NUT's official journal was still rather surprisingly named *The Schoolmaster*, with the subtitle *and Woman Teacher's Chronicle – SWTC*. The 21 April edition carried a front-page headline proclaiming: "Wrong Tactics, Wrong Timing". It went on to launch a scathing attack on the NAS and its plans "in some as yet unknown town for some few men teachers [to be] absent from one school for one day". The NUT declared strikes only to be justified as a very last resort on matters "of supreme professional importance" and had to go back ten years (to Durham 1951) to find an example of it taking such action.

"For purely selfish reasons", claimed the NUT, "the NAS are throwing our negotiations for better salaries into jeopardy". These were "far more important than tactical manoeuvres to resolve the membership problem of a minority movement". The magnificent public relations work the NUT had conducted building up support for the teacher's case on salaries, allegedly already producing dividends, was being placed in jeopardy. The NUT was soon to be disabused of such romantic notions by a brutal Government intervention in Burnham.

And so to 1 May 1961. The 35 NAS members at William Penn went on strike with the main purpose to secure representation on Burnham. The NAS had half the teaching staff at William Penn, including the headmaster, George Dennis, in membership. The LCC decided to close the school completely to the pupils rather than risk uncertainty and inter-union complications over 'scabbing'. Other staff were to report for work to the divisional education office.

The headmaster had been summoned to County Hall. Courageously he informed the Chief Education Officer of the LCC, his boss Sir William Houghton, that he would be on strike that day. He would happily report to the CEO on another occasion.

George Dennis had made a special request for the school not to be picketed, which the NAS respected. Instead the members on strike congregated at the nearby St Barnabas Parish Church Hall where they were joined by national leaders in giving a packed press conference to over 20 journalists from TV, radio and newspapers.

The effect in public relations terms was out of all proportion to the size of the action. After all, only 35 schoolmasters were out on strike for one day, but the publicity generated via TV, radio and newspapers was massive. Strike action by teachers had been very rare. The leadership of Bruce Given and the courage of "the men of Penn", as he liked to describe them, could not be overestimated.

In September 1981, after I had joined the staff of the NASUWT, Bruce passed me a few papers he had saved from the day for safe keeping, including the original petition addressed to the Executive demanding action signed by his 35 members. (He had retrieved it from HQ and there were ticks alongside every name – checked to make sure they were bona fide paid-up members!) The paper that took my fancy was a cutting from 1 May 1961 of an interview given by Bruce to a journalist working on *The Daily Express*, one Michael Parkinson who was later to achieve much fame and fortune as a national TV personality. Although the angle Michael Parkinson took focussed more on Bruce's disgracefully low salary than Burnham recognition, an issue perhaps too arcane for a tabloid, it said it all!

The article was headlined: "Full stop at 49! That – and a £50 Jalopy – is why a teacher is angry enough to strike".

Looking for a reason to understand this militancy, Parkinson found it "embodied in a car parked at the William Penn School. It is an old car, made in 1938. The sort of car you get a giggle out of nowadays. It cost fifty quid and it wasn't cheap at that. But it is lovingly cared for by someone who obviously had a hard job getting that fifty quid."

"I taught nearly 20 years before I could afford that car", Parkinson quoted Bruce Given. "It is the first I have ever owned and I had to earn thirty bob a night, three nights a week, teaching at evening class to buy it . . . Every time I look at it I realise that this strike is right."

Parkinson described Bruce Given as "a tall, friendly humorous man of 49. He wears soft suede shoes, hand knitted socks, a well worn grey pin-stripe, that looks something like a demob suit . . . the red tie is dusted with chalk . . . he smokes his cigarettes down past the trade mark – he can't afford the luxury of throwing away half smoked cigarettes . . .

"With his wife and three children to support, he only earned just over £1,000 per year and at 49 had come 'to a financial full stop'."

One has to admire the journalistic qualities of Michael Parkinson, exploiting to the full the typical image of the poor schoolmaster! But he concluded on deadly serious note: "The warning will have been given by sensible dedicated men like Bruce Given, and if the country and the Minister of Education ignore it, they do so at their peril."

On the other side of the coin the unctuous *Daily Mail* published an article quoting a schoolboy at William Penn which implied that Mr Dennis had used his position as headmaster to influence the pupils to side with the NAS. This was strongly denied by Mr Dennis, and the NAS solicitors, Craigen Wilders & Sorrell, wrote to the *Mail* demanding a retraction and an apology. (I found no evidence of it being received.)

Reviewing the situation a few days later, Committee 'K', whilst delighted with the "wonderfully successful" coverage, noted how the quality newspapers had rightly focussed on the claim for recognition, whereas the popular press had played up the pay issue. The Executive subsequently decided to try to keep the major focus on the claim for recognition, although other events were to intervene. 'K' also noted that recruitment was up by 1,683, compared to 67 for the same period the year before. Six letters of resignation had been received. By the time the Executive next met on 23 June, recruitment of new members was 2,450, compared to 75 for the same period the previous year.

Correspondence from the CEO of the LCC was reported in which the authority expressed regret at the strike and the fact that the boys' education had been disrupted. In the view of the LCC the members had committed "a very serious breach of their contracts with the Council".

Strikes at Edge Hill in Liverpool and Gelli-Dawel in Glamorgan duly followed on 1 June. Again the publicity was massive and on the whole extremely supportive. The mass meetings that followed were, like London, incredibly well attended with thousands of schoolmasters attending and cheering the speeches to the hilt.

More strikes followed in July in carefully chosen areas around the country. The action was planned on the basis of a long-distance race, not a sprint, with pressure built up gradually but relentlessly. With no members suspended, more action took place on:

3 July	Handsworth New Road Senior Boys School	Birmingham;
5 July	Prudhoe Secondary Modern School	Northumberland;

| 12 July | Lancastrian Secondary Boys School | Chichester; |
| 19 July | Cheam County Secondary Boys School | Surrey; |

all with appropriate supporting events, such as mass meetings, around the relevant dates.

On my retirement from the post of GS at Easter 2002 members got to know about my intention to write a history of the Association. A retired member, Paul Groves, wrote to me out of the blue enclosing his account of the day his school was called out in 1961. The NAS was better represented in the industrial towns of the North and Midlands where understandably the tradition of trade unionism was both more prevalent and better understood. It makes the case of the Lancastrian Boys School in Chichester at which Paul Groves taught all the more poignant and symbolic of the strength of feeling amongst all NAS members. It is also a bit critical of the NAS for failing in one or two areas, notably training local representatives to deal with the media.

Let me hand over to Paul Groves:

"THE NAS STRIKE – CHICHESTER 1961

"I was a teacher at the Lancastrian Boys School, Chichester. I was a mature entrant of 31. I had been in teaching just four years. I had entered in 1957 and this was my first job.

"It was soon obvious that teaching was going to be a tremendous financial strain. My first child had been born and my wife had had to give up work. So I was attracted to the NAS which promised to fight for a fair wage for men teachers. It was never an anti-female organization but one which saw that the teaching profession needed a balance of male and females. At the time it was felt that men were being paid the rate that women had been historically forced to accept.

"To have any influence on this we needed to be on the Burnham Committee, the wage deciding body at the time controlled by the NUT and the employers, to wit, the Government. To do this, despite constant approaches to the Minister it was felt we had no option but to strike. The public was not unused to strikes but for a professional body of men to do this was, at that time, unthinkable to many. At home my wife had to plan out every penny. What if things went wrong and I was sacked? We had faith that our brothers would support us and there was enough feeling up and down the country for us to take the risk.

"We had over thirty members at the school which is why we were chosen as part of the third wave of strikes. It began with the Men of the William Penn – perhaps the real heroes – to put their toe in the water – and it was now our turn.

"I was the representative. I collected the weekly subs – in itself a sign of the financial times. I had also been promoted to a Head of Department job in Grantham – the only way to get a living wage was the promotion route open only to a few of us. I loved Chichester but it was a very affluent town which made me feel doubly poor. I had to move. Derek Boreham, our executive member, came over from Bognor where he taught to see us. To this day I can picture him talking to us in the staff-room. I agreed to organize and lead the strike as I was going and we did not know what could happen if an organiser had stayed on in the school.

"As the day of the strike came nearer, the headmaster called me in. He pleaded with me to call it off. I told him I had no power to; it was an NAS decision. The general feeling in the town was against us. Professional people just did not strike, certainly not in Chichester. I remember we had some difficulty in hiring a hall for the evening rally, but eventually were accommodated in the Donnington Church Hall.

"Looking back I should have been briefed more by the NAS, but it was new ground. On the morning of the strike *The Brighton Evening Argus* reporter was at my front gate. To each of his questions, mainly about destroying children's education and setting a bad example to them, I replied 'No Comment'. The paper printed a string of these 'No Comments' on the front page and it looked bad. The national TV coverage we got the same day was more balanced.

"The evening rally was a great success. I made a speech. Terry Casey came down and also made a speech. Those members who have never heard Terry speak have missed an atmosphere and a wit that inspired us in those times. I rated him second only to Churchill as a speaker. There were constant cheers echoing through the speeches.

"We knew we had done the right thing through striking. As I remember it the union had made its point. There were no more strikes and eventually we began to get represented on the Burnham Committee. Afterwards Terry took us all to a local pub. Probably his influence on the Government played as big a part as the strike.

"Looking back I did not suffer in my career as a striker. Pay remained very poor until the Wilson era. I see teaching as a wonderful and interesting career. Why is it that the Government does not realise that a happy teacher force is an efficient teacher force? The NASUWT and its members have had to spend so much time and energy looking after their welfare when all this energy could have gone into teaching the children.

"I am still in touch with colleagues who were with me on that strike. It made us life-long friends. We have a lot of respect for each other. Four of us worked each summer as deck-chair men at Bognor. It was a sign of the times that we were dependent on this extra income. Pat Mitchell, Pete Simmonds and W. O'Hara got a tan in this way.

"I did not become financially comfortable until I became an educational writer. I just hope future governments do not treat their teachers with such contempt."

Thank you Paul for such an eloquent testimony to the NAS case!

By the end of the Summer Term 1961 the number of schools volunteering for action had risen to 205, coming from all parts of the country. Further strikes were planned for the Autumn Term with seven schools in Brighton and one in Rochdale during September. A similar pattern of action in October would follow, based on one school in an area and several more in another LEA all coming out on single-day strikes. But these carefully laid plans were soon to be overtaken by another dramatic event of great relevance to the issues in contention.

While all this action was continuing the Burnham Committee was going through another of its tortuous triennial tribulations and had reached another unsatisfactory settlement based on an overall increase of 16.25%, costing £47.5m. Of course in today's (2006) context 16.25% sounds enormous, but it had to cover three years and still left teachers lagging behind. However, on 25 July 1961 it was thrown into complete turmoil as dramatic events about which I have hinted erupted. The Chancellor of the Exchequer, Selwyn Lloyd, announced a 'mini budget' to deal with another financial crisis. Introducing a policy of public sector wage restraint, the Chancellor singled out the teachers' settlement, saying it would have to be cut back to £42m (14%). Burnham was thrown into turmoil, exposed beyond peradventure as a subordinate body.

In subsequent correspondence the Government explained that it had rejected the 18% settlement reached in the Scottish National Joint Council in April; proposed 12.5% instead; but agreed a final 14%. The NUT Special Conference in Margate had rejected the 16.25% provisional agreement of 30 May (coming into effect 1 January 1962) and since Burnham was to meet two days after the Chancellor's statement the Government thought it only "honourable" to make its position publicly well known.

The NAS reacted immediately. A strong press statement said: "The whole profession was deeply shocked and the Association has been inundated with demands for immediate protest action. For the time being members were being advised not to act hastily but the position is so serious that it is imperative that the Government should take immediate ameliorative action if it is to avoid a catastrophic breakdown in the education service."

On 27 July the NAS sent a letter to the Prime Minister urging him to set up an independent inquiry. On 28 July the NAS Action Committee 'K' met in emergency session. It called for a national one-day strike on 20 September to protest against "the invidious attack on the education service made by the Chancellor of the Exchequer".

However, one of the consequences was that the plans for action in support of the claim for representation in September, for Brighton and Rochdale, had to be put to one side. The October plans would proceed.

The day after the Chancellor's bombshell, the Minister of Education declared he would reject the Burnham provisional 'agreement', stipulating another one would have to be worked out within the £42m 'envelope'.

As Burnham reconvened early in August the NUT quickly ditched its own Special Salaries Conference decision at Margate to reject the 16.25% provisional agreement. It united with the Management Panel 'to stand firm' (at least for a couple of weeks – as events proved). Acting jointly, both Panels of the Committee formally objected to the Minister's dictat. The Teachers' Panel declared its refusal to accept anything less than the provisional agreement.

The NUT was extremely sensitive on the Burnham negotiating issue. In the 11 August edition of its journal *SWTC* it launched a thinly veiled attack on the NAS, although on this occasion not naming us. Mindful obviously of the fact that its own Conference had rejected the deal as inadequate, the NUT argued that the problem had to be "simplified": namely, Burnham had reached agreement and no government should cast it aside. Conveniently it ignored its own Conference mandate to do just that.

The leading article in the *SWTC* dismissed "the machinations of those outside this battle" as of "no importance", quoting a saying "that comes from the East: 'When two elephants are fighting, the ant should stand aside'!"

With 'elephantine' subtlety the NUT had criticised the NAS reaction in calling a one-day strike. It boasted a "degree of unparalleled unity which teachers can consolidate if they act wisely. Those who were privileged to be present at the meeting of the Teachers' Panel on August 2 saw an outstanding demonstration of solidarity between the Joint Four, the ATTI and the NUT."

"Privileged to be present", indeed! That must have caused some wry amusement to the NAS, having been quite outrageously denied that 'privilege' by government turpitude and NUT veto for some 40 years!

The NUT argued that teachers' best interests were served by the two Panels uniting against the Government. The issue was between the Minister and the Burnham Committee and it had to have "absolute priority".

The Government reacted in its usual bullying fashion. On 5 September the Minister threatened legislation to get his way. Of course he was only acting 'in the teachers' best interests' to ensure they received their pay award in time for 1 January 1962.

The Minister also threatened more fundamental reform of Burnham to enable Government to make its intentions openly known at an early stage in the negotiating process. This was a curious mixture of the logical and the disingenuous. It already occurred informally and did not require legislation. However, giving it formal legal expression would expose the reality, which would please the NAS and place the Government in the front line but destroy the fiction so beloved by the LEA employers and the NUT that Burnham was an independent negotiating machine.

On 6 September *The Times* produced an editorial which could have been lifted from innumerable NAS statements:

"The Burnham system of negotiating teachers' salaries, which has lasted forty years, is finished. There is no great harm in that. Over recent years the pretence that teachers' salaries were settled between them and the local authorities has worn very thin. It was, on the face of it, ridiculous that the Government, which has to find the greater part of the money, should be expected to keep out of the negotiations. In fact, the Minister of Education has been increasing his influence over the Burnham Committee in recent years and his action now brings in to the open what has for sometime been confusingly hidden."

On 11 September 1961 Sir Ronald Gould and Sir William Alexander wrote a joint letter to *The Times* proclaiming the sanctity and independence of Burnham and deploring the Government's gross interference. It is difficult to believe the two, especially the latter, did not understand the reality behind the Burnham façade, although the former was generally regarded as a very honourable man.

In a pamphlet around the same time entitled *The NAS and Equal Pay*, the NUT had stated boldly that: "The Union has never subscribed to the theory that there is a sum of money fixed by the Authorities' Panel for teachers' salaries." Perhaps that was a 'clever' statement or merely confused because nobody ever alleged the 'fixing' was done by the LEAs; it was the work of Government.

In *The Sunday Telegraph* of 26 February 1961, reporting on the historic NAS mass meeting the previous day, Fred Jarvis, a future GS but then an Assistant Secretary of the NUT, had been quoted firmly denying the existence of a global sum. The reporter Nicholas Bagnall wrote: "Mr Fred Jarvis . . . told me that the Treasury does not give the Burnham Committee a salaries figure. He said 'there is no truth' in the allegation." However, despite the events of July 1961, in a letter to *The Times* of March 1963 Sir Ronald Gould was still protesting: "Now we teachers thought that we were freely negotiating with our employers uninfluenced by the Ministry."

A little later in a letter to the *TES* Sir Ronald confessed: "My latest error, for which I apologise, is to have said something which at the time I believed to be true, but which is now shown to be untrue. From the experience of 16 years as leader of the Teachers' Panel, and because earlier Ministers have accepted this view I genuinely thought the Minister exerted no influence on the authority's side before or during negotiations, and that it was improper to do so, but the Minister now admits he discussed salaries informally with LEA representatives."

It was noble of Sir Ronald to admit and apologise for his error. But it raised a massive question over the competence of the NUT to conduct the affairs of the teaching profession. Everyone else seemed to know.

Back to September 1961, it was natural for the NUT to play the unity card. It enabled those who wished to believe that if all teachers were in one union they would be strong and better able to resist the heavy hand of government. In reality a monolithic NUT would have made negligible impact on the weak majority in the profession unwilling to fight. It would merely have prevented the minority in the NAS who were prepared to take action from so doing. True, with all teachers in one union government would not be able to divide and rule. It would simply rule.

With action over representation on hold in September, the NAS went ahead with plans for the strike over pay on the 20th. As a matter of courtesy and for operational reasons the NAS always kept the employers and the other teacher associations informed of its plans for action. The normal understanding was that no union would undertake the work of teachers on strike, i.e. no 'scabbing' (or no 'blacklegging' as it was rather inappropriately referred to in those days).

The first few weeks of September 1961 saw some acerbic correspondence exchanged between Bert Rushworth and Sir Ronald Gould. The NUT hinted that the normal convention could not be guaranteed on this occasion since the NAS was acting against the interests of teachers. It was a bad time to strike with all the other unions and the Management united against the Government's intervention. This was the worst possible time to call for an independent inquiry into negotiating machinery. The NUT regarded the maintenance of an independent negotiating machine as "vital to the future economic position of teachers". The NUT fervently believed a Treasury-determined salary "would be less satisfactory than would be achieved in free negotiation". Both Rushworth and Gould accused the other of 'un-brotherly and un-sisterly' intentions. The NAS was allegedly seeking to recruit. The NUT had done the NAS down on Burnham recognition by its threats of boycott. The correspondence led nowhere.

In my research I discovered a most unlikely supporter of the NAS analysis of Burnham: none other than a former NUT GS, Sir Edward (Ted) Britton. Ted was commissioned by the *TES* to write an obituary about Terry Casey after he died on 18 March 1987. Published in the *TES* of 27 March, it has to be said that Ted's tribute to Terry was very generous, all the more so for they had been arch opponents in the teacher union political world. Describing how Terry Casey had treated Burnham "as his main area of opposition", Ted Britton conceded that the Committee, "especially as it developed after the Remuneration of Teachers Act, was seriously flawed as a negotiating machine. It was never likely to produce satisfactory salaries, but it was the best we had." Revealingly, Britton concluded: "Terry Casey's appointment as NAS GS coincided with the Association's first appearance on Burnham. And Burnham was never the same again!"

The 20 September 1961 turned out to be another momentous day in the history of the NAS. Support for the strike was solid. Eight mass meetings were held in different parts of the country. The Royal Albert Hall, with its capacity of 8,000 seats, was packed out for the mass rally of London and South East members.

Other huge rallies took place in Birmingham, Bristol, Cardiff, Leeds, Manchester, Newcastle and Plymouth. Over 20,000 members attended the rallies that day. The media coverage was enormous. New members kept pouring into the ranks of the NAS.

The massive support for the NAS strike from its members had dramatic effects upon the NUT. The NUT's weak words were no match for the action of the NAS. The NUT called a press conference a few days before the NAS strike. It announced it was calling a Special Conference on 7 October when plans for 'strike action' would be put forward. I use the term 'strike action' advisedly. The reader will see why.

In calling for a strike the NUT Executive had to eat all their pious words condemning the NAS. Sir Ronald Gould had written to the NAS on 6 September arguing against strike action in favour of concerted lobbying by a wide coalition of "professional classes" caught up in the same government squeeze, which the NUT (self-appointed) would be leading.

Bert Rushworth must have enjoyed the ironic opening of his response on 19 September to Gould, stating he was "sure you would appreciate the difficulty of replying to your letter in which you ask the NAS not to strike". In the event the NAS was not even invited to the meeting setting up the "coalition of professional classes", about which nothing more was heard.

But when was a strike not a strike? Answer: when it was organised by the NUT. All the NUT members would be doing is giving up their pay. It was unbelievable! Explaining the curious NUT version of strike action Sir Ronald Gould said that: "In order to cause the least possible harm, the NUT will give adequate notice of its intentions to parents and authorities in the areas concerned, at the same time asking the authorities on the one hand to put their buildings and equipment at the disposal of the teachers so they could carry on with their professional duties and the parents, on the other, to continue to send their children to the union run schools which will be pledged to maintain the highest educational standards. Thus the striking teachers would in no way be abandoning their professional duties but would be in a position to refuse to cooperate in any other way with the government or its officials."

The *TES* (13 October 1961) described the NUT plans as "working strikes". The NUT members were to be balloted on raising a levy of 5% of their salaries to support the 'working strikers'.

Worse was to follow for the beleaguered NUT. Whilst its Special Conference on 7 October endorsed the actions taken by the Executive, other doubts were raised and the union did not secure the necessary majorities in the areas selected for 'working strikes', and only one-third of the members voted in favour of being levied 5% of salary to finance this curious form of action.

Instead the Conference narrowly voted for an amendment from its Crawley Branch to urge members, according to their conscience, to adopt one of two alternatives. Either join an opposition political party to call for support for genuine free negotiations as distinct from arbitrary imposition by Ministers, or sign up for the Conservative Party to protest from within. The Executive was left with the possibility of a one-day strike and a temporary refusal to undertake duties at lunchtime. Neither one materialised.

The *TES* commented that the results of all the fuss were to expose a divided Executive and "to make the NUT look pretty silly after all the bravado in Margate in June". The contrast with the effective and united day of action by the NAS could not have been starker. As the *TES* observed, the NAS was a "well tried opponent with the advantage of a united chain of command and a better view of the whole terrain".

Agreement with the NAS's view of the NUT 'action' later came from an unexpected quarter. Max Morris, possibly the most prominent President of the NUT, reviewing a recently published book, *Teacher Militancy: A History of Teacher Strikes 1896-1987*, by Roger Seifert in *Education*, 22 April 1988, wrote:

"The key change for that body [the NAS] was the recruitment of thousands of members following the tragic betrayal of the NUT leadership of conference decisions in what seemed to so many of us the annus mirabilis, 1961."

A few years later Sir Ronald Gould was to caricature the NAS facility to act when he was reported to have complained in exasperation to an NUT meeting that: "It was all very well for Terry Casey. He just has to blow a whistle and all his members are out!"

In fact it was much more complicated than that. Over the years every GS and Executive of the NAS had earned the trust of the membership. Many people had tried to break the NAS, testing us to the ultimate. The Association had lived through earlier campaigns when powerful figures like Sir William Alexander had openly urged LEA employers to suspend and then sack striking NAS members. A few LEAs had taken his advice seriously, especially in the North East. The NAS had stood firm and taken action, sometimes in the most challenging of situations.

The *TES* also observed that "the NUT action was now aimed at restoring Burnham to its former 'independence'" rather than protesting about salaries directly. In the view of the NAS this was to pursue a damaging fiction which had cost teachers dear for over 40 years.

Noting that the NAS strike had secured a meeting with the Minister to discuss the negotiating machinery, the *TES* further opined that the "success of the NAS may have been due to its straightforward militancy during the crisis, [but] it has now been wise enough not to commit itself to a timetable for further militant action until it has talked to the Minister".

Chapter 18 - 'No Co-operation without Representation'

Although the immediate reason for the NAS's strike on 20 September had been the cut in the salary award, the solid support it received was possibly the final scene of the penultimate act in the 40-year struggle for representation.

The following day was probably the opening scene of the final act, although the NAS leadership may not have realised it at the time. On 21 September a telephone call was received from the Conservative Party's Central Office making an "unofficial enquiry as to the future intentions of NAS regarding militant action in support of its claim for representation". The caller was left in no doubt that unless the claim was met more action would certainly follow.

Decisions were soon to be formalised to involve all the membership in various forms of continuous action banning supervision at lunchtime and other extraneous activities, which was a significant escalation to the action of one-day strikes.

One week later on 28 September the NAS issued a press statement echoing the famous dictum that heralded the American War of Independence, saying that: "Unless representation is granted the NAS will continue its campaign on the principle of 'NO CO-OPERATION WITHOUT REPRESENTATION'. On dates to be announced NAS members will be asked to cease co-operation on school savings, the collection of dinner money and all forms of recording and accounting in that service and also to stop performing any tasks in the midday break."

On Tuesday 3 October one of the civil servants at the DES, Mr H. Weber, Head of Salaries Branch, telephoned Bert Rushworth asking if he would like a meeting with the Minister to give the NAS views on a review of the negotiating machinery, ostensibly "in the light of the economic and financial circumstances of today". A confirming letter arrived a couple of days later from the Permanent Secretary, Dame Mary Smieton, explaining the Minister was contemplating the "nature of the legislation to introduce in the next session of Parliament" to push through the (reduced) salary settlement ordered by the Chancellor.

Committee 'K' and the Executive readily agreed at their meetings over the following weekend. Meanwhile the plans for "No Co-Operation without Representation" would continue, but the implementation dates would be withheld pending the outcome of the meeting with the Minister. The meeting was fixed for 16 October. The starting time of 3 p.m. was brought forward to

2.30 as the Minister was to meet the Teachers' Panel of Burnham at 4 o'clock, which the NAS thought was "interesting".

In my judgement the meeting was to prove to be the most significant one between a Minister of Education and the Association in the entire history of the NAS and NASUWT. This was not just due to the decision that eventually flowed from it but also because of the relevance and bluntness of the views expressed on the fundamental issues the NASUWT has grappled with throughout its history. Accordingly, I recount the exchanges and events surrounding them in some detail.

The NAS went armed with its intended post-meeting press statement. Led by the President and GS, the six-man delegation intended to deplore the cut in the salary award and call for the reform of the Burnham machinery to facilitate genuine free voluntary negotiations with recourse to arbitration, in which the Minister and the NAS would be directly represented along with others.

However, the Minister had his own agenda, opening the meeting with a half-hour lecture on the evils of the world. These included a reduced public image of the teaching profession, inflation and a universal fall in standards of conduct in a society steadily growing more materialistic. "Our people must be led to a less materialistic position, and in this connection all of us have our responsibilities since children learn from adults", declared Sir David. The Minister did concede "there were natural strains [in the profession], for example between primary and secondary, graduates and non-graduates and men and women".

In talking about the country's economic problems, Sir David declared that "too much expenditure and too little exporting" were the results of *"the occupational disease of full employment"* (my emphasis.) He accused the NUT and the NAS of "not doing their sums". The real cost of the NUT's claim was £110m; that of the NAS added up to £137m. He said such claims, if met, would set off an inflationary trend in which teachers' money "would go to Hell".

Sir David said that Burnham was outdated and ineffective. He was determined to keep the Government veto and the new statute would have to reflect that. He did not want to impose salary scales but if he had to "every time Burnham came out with an award unacceptable to Government he would apply a brutal axe".

In spite of the extraordinary social views the Minister expounded and his failure to grasp that inflation was as much the result of the Government's own election-inspired 'stop go' policies as due to wage costs, there was some common ground with the NAS, although it was not immediately apparent from the discussion.

The Minister had stressed that teachers' pay could only be improved in a context of "planning" where groups would have to take their turn and not try to leapfrog each other. I cannot find any evidence that the NAS had discussed such an issue before these times, but later on the Association was to favour an effective and fair incomes policy applied to all. As Terry Casey observed in the 1970s, "teachers would be better off in the well run zoo than in the jungle of free collective bargaining".

The Minister had declared that the crucial point was the minimum of the basic scale as that set off the inflationary comparisons and leapfrogging. The NAS had long complained that the short-term interests of the high numbers of young people, despite their rapid turnover, had always been given priority by the NUT over the needs of those who were in teaching for a lifelong career. Soon that consideration was to form the principle underpinning NAS policy, which the NASUWT upheld for the succeeding 25 years; namely, career-structured salary scales.

Sir David Eccles was obviously in a bad mood that day. Perhaps the NAHT had contributed to this, for they had visited the Minister in the morning and told him of the sad conditions of strife in the staffrooms and the jeopardy in which the school meals service was being placed.

The Minister finished his lecture complaining about the media which was distorting his valiant efforts to improve the standing of the profession. He was a misrepresented man. In any event, in a mood of exasperation he declared: "I am not going to have the educational system messed about for salaries!"

Despite the angst raised by the Minister, Bert Rushworth in typically calm and unflustered fashion told the Minister that the poor standing of the teaching profession was due to their low salaries. As regards standards of conduct the GS reminded the Minister of the concern the NAS had raised on this subject and emphasised the importance of men teachers being available to deal with badly behaved boys. The NAS also had a great deal to contribute on educational policy, which would be of benefit to the country if only it were given a place to express its views in the councils of the land.

According to the NAS report of the encounter, unsigned but probably written by the Deputy Secretary, Don Jarmin, the GS and the whole delegation then raised their demands for a genuine voluntary negotiating machine with the open involvement of the Government, reflecting the situation for civil servants. However, the Government should not be a party to the negotiations and also retain a veto, which it did under Section 89 of the 1944 Act.

The Minister flatly refused to countenance an end to the Government veto. Arbitration procedures had "gone near to breaking the back of the economy". There were two crucial points: the global sum and its distribution. There could be give and take on the latter but the veto had always to be available on arbitration and the global sum.

For the NAS that crystallised the crucial issue for teachers' pay negotiations: how to prise open some flexibility on the global sum. After the long and bitter strikes of the mid-1980s it led the NASUWT to argue that a pay review body was the best means of doing that.

The Minister readily conceded that the veto on the global sum was nothing new. He also freely admitted that a pre-known global sum had always existed. The Association always believed events had virtually proved the point but it was the first time the NAS had heard it "straight from the horse's mouth". So much for Alexander and Gould's joint letter to *The Times* a few weeks before!

The most productive part of the meeting followed. In response to the NAS repeating its claim for representation the Minister insisted Burnham would remain in being, but reformed. He said: "I cannot make you any offer but I do not rule out a change." He continued: "I am very anxious to make a sound job. I cannot make you an offer this afternoon but I suggest that you write a letter to me defining your position in regard to equal pay (EP), assuming that you were given representation on this body." The door was definitely ajar, if not completely open.

The meeting concluded with the NAS advising the Minister of the plans for militant action and that a decision on representation could not be delayed. Both sides spoke of the respective pressures they were each under. The Minister said he intended to meet again with the NAS in a few days time.

GS Bert Rushworth composed the crucial letter from the NAS the following day. The text of this letter, and other correspondence, is important because of the inter-union controversy that subsequently developed. In addition to the formalities and the repeated request for representation, Bert Rushworth's letter referred to the enclosed pamphlet 75, which set out the NAS's basic policies on education and salaries, including a section on EP. The GS's letter also emphasised the NAS's "hope to be given the opportunity of working responsibly inside the negotiating machinery".

Having despatched the letter to the Minister, Bert Rushworth telephoned Mr P.R. Odgers, a civil servant in Teaching Staff Branch at the DES, to arrange the next meeting. Instead of the expected formality, Bert Rushworth found himself being fobbed off by Mr Odgers. It was obvious that something must have happened at the meeting with the Teachers' Panel which had taken place immediately after the one with the NAS on 16 October. "The Minister had to review the situation and await the outcome of a meeting with the Burnham Committee" planned for the next day.

Odgers advised Rushworth to be patient. Rushworth reminded Odgers of the Minister's promise of another meeting "in a few days" and that the NAS plans for action could not be held in abeyance beyond 23 October (the following Monday).

On the evening of Wednesday 18 October, perhaps smelling a rat, the NAS approached one of its chief Parliamentary allies, Fergus Montgomery MP, and must have asked him to organise more pressure on the Minister. That may have appeared necessary to the NAS in the circumstances. It might also have set the alarm bells ringing in other quarters, for the inevitable leak to the media and associated rumours were soon to start flowing.

On Thursday 19 October the GS was asked to go to the Ministry for a meeting with Mr Weber (Head of Teaching Staff Branch) and Odgers the next day to discuss "matters relevant to the claim for representation" and provide "further enlightenment for the Minister". That evening the Minister met Conservative backbenchers.

So on Friday afternoon 20 October Bert Rushworth, accompanied by the President, Harry Bell, went off to the DES for a meeting that was to last four hours. During that meeting the NAS was told that the Minister, with Government support, was prepared to concede the principle of representation but wanted some assurances. (It was later confirmed that the Minister was under pressure "to keep the NUT quiet".)

As often on such occasions time was pressing in on events. The NAS had to have a decision by Monday or further action would be announced. The Minister was "in the country", possibly, one is tempted to speculate, enjoying the material things of life he would deny to others. The NAS needed some assurance for Committee 'K' on Monday. It would be best coming from the Minister himself, but the GS and President agreed that a letter from the Head of Teaching Staff Branch giving the Government's assurance of intention to concede representation would suffice. It had to arrive by Monday or Tuesday at the very latest. Committee 'K' was meeting on Monday and could receive an oral report of developments, but something in writing was essential for the full Executive, gathering on Tuesday morning.

The letter had to be agreed immediately. So in the presence of the GS and President, Weber dictated a letter setting out (in remarkable detail) the 'flesh on the bones' of how the NAS would "work responsibly" inside the Burnham Committee. It was a detailed statement of the obvious, conceding the right of the NAS to advocate its salary policy (including its position on EP) inside Burnham as well as more publicly, but if it failed to carry a majority on any issue it would not use that as a pretext for obstructing the work of the Committee. Furthermore the NAS representatives would be free to report back to their Executive and Conference who would likewise be free to accept or reject any agreement or proposal emanating from Burnham.

The NAS had no problem agreeing to such a statement. The reader might well ask, 'Why all this fuss over the obvious?', but this would be to underestimate the importance of words in human affairs. Words were needed to placate the NUT, allowing it to allege the NAS had dropped opposition to EP in return for representation.

Even if the NAS had done as the NUT alleged, so what! It was not a bad bargain to recognise reality and to get recognition in return. Common sense dictated that if the NAS pressed its view on EP to a vote it would be destined to defeat, and it was extremely difficult to see how this could 'disrupt' the work of Burnham in any significant way.

It was not surprising that such a detailed treatise of the obvious, perhaps considered important in the pressurised circumstances of the Friday, was not to see the light of day as other events unfolded. However, copies were sent over the weekend in triplicate to the home addresses of the GS and President and to the NAS HQ office.

Discussion took place on the size of NAS representation. The GS indicated that one seat would be insulting, four would be proportionate, two ungenerous and three the only acceptable compromise figure likely.

Odgers agreed to telephone the Minister in the country to ascertain his availability for a meeting on the Monday. The GS and President left, indicating that a decision could be made by the Executive on Tuesday hopefully accepting representation and withdrawing militant action. But action would resume if the principle of recognition had not been conceded. They would meet with the Minister or his officers on Monday at 6 p.m. Rushworth and Bell left the meeting believing that victory was in sight.

On the Saturday evening Odgers telephoned Bert Rushworth at home saying he had reported to Sir David Eccles who in turn had consulted the Prime Minister. There was a difficulty with the proposed meeting on Monday at 6 p.m. There was to be a major debate on the country's economic situation and the PM was anxious that as one of the sponsors of the Government's motion, Sir David's presence was required on the front bench to avoid any misunderstanding.

Odgers added that the Minister was trying to make himself available at 9.15 on the Tuesday morning in order for the Executive, congregating at 9.30, to be informed. The timing of this meeting indicated that it would be a mere formality.

Committee 'K' met on Monday morning and duly supported the actions of the President and GS. The civil servants were informed accordingly. However, Odgers said "a new point had arisen about which the Minister needed to consult the Association" but "he did not think it would be found difficult". Beware such words. They can often mean the opposite! And they did.

Accordingly Committee 'K' trooped across to Curzon St, W1 to the DES to meet the Permanent Secretary, Dame Mary Smieton. The NAS letter giving assurances on 'non-obstruction' was handed over. The relevant part read:

"The NAS agrees that if it were accorded representation on the Burnham Committee it would, in and in regard to the Committee, accept the fact that equal pay is now accepted national policy and that it would not allow opposition to that policy to obstruct the working of the Committee. The Association retains its democratic rights . . . "

But Dame Mary had other matters on her mind. Over the weekend new difficulties had arisen. There had been a leak, apparently from a Parliamentary source. The Minister had consulted "certain other bodies" and had been asked to require the NAS to agree to the Burnham settlement (the one reduced on the insistence of the Chancellor). The Minister's position had become "very difficult". The NAS would have a favourable recruitment position, representation without responsibility for the award.

The NAS responded immediately, saying in effect "no way!" "We could not accept any responsibility for decisions to which we had not been party." The NAS had already given undertakings to work responsibly in the Burnham Committee. Dame Mary professed herself unable to understand our problem, a likely sign that she did! She thought it was "a trifle", prompting the NAS to ask why therefore raise it.

The NAS agreed to withdraw for a separate discussion as it seemed the point could lead to breakdown. The deputation was agreed that "we could not whitewash the past. We had not fought for all these years to replicate the usual surrender of the NUT." But it was agreed the NAS could participate in the administration of the agreement, like every other organisation represented on the Burnham Committee.

Dame Mary was not too pleased and could only agree to report to the Minister, asking to be reminded of the timetable for action. She said the leak from the Parliamentary meeting the previous Thursday (19 October) had embarrassed the Minister and stirred up those opposed to NAS recognition. The Minister desperately needed a few more days to sort things out. The NAS remained adamant. The leak was not its responsibility. The timetable for action would not be altered. The deputation was promised a telephone call by 11 a.m. the next day.

The 'day of recognition' finally arrived on Tuesday 24 October 1961. The NAS Executive assembled at 9.30 a.m. in one of its customary meeting places, Dr Williams's Library in Gordon Square. The President and others gave reports of the previous day's events. The GS and Honorary Treasurer waited at 59 Gordon Square for the promised call from the DES.

That was the famous occasion in NAS folklore when the telephone rang at 10.35 a.m. As Bert Rushworth went to answer it, a restraining hand from the Honorary Treasurer, G. Lloyd Williams, obstructed him: "Let it ring for a while. We don't want to give them the impression we are anxiously waiting for a call!"

When Bert Rushworth was eventually allowed to answer the call it turned out to be a bit of an anticlimax. It was not the Minister with the expected decision. It was just a civil servant asking if the Association could call on the Minister, who was at Curzon St, at its earliest convenience. The Executive agreed to adjourn whilst Committee 'K' once again went off to the Ministry.

The Minister began the meeting by announcing up front that he had decided to enlarge the Committee, without saying exactly how. He had difficulties on several fronts but wished to develop a major campaign to better the education service. He wanted the NAS "to be welcomed, not merely received" on the Burnham Committee. This could only happen if he succeeded in "keeping the NUT quiet". That merely confirmed NAS suspicions that the NUT was behind all the conditions the Minister was trying to impose upon the NAS.

The Minister then read a proposed letter he intended to send to the GS of the NAS. It was quite different from the one the GS and President had agreed with Weber and Odgers the previous week. The first paragraph was not controversial, accepting the NAS assurances already given that it would "not allow its policy on equal pay to obstruct the working of the Committee".

The second paragraph was likewise uncontroversial, conceding the principle of representation in the light of the new situation opened up by discussions on the negotiating machinery, on the understanding that the Association would cancel its campaign of militant action.

The third caused a huge problem. It repeated the demand for the NAS formally to accept the recent (reduced) settlement (to operate from 1 January 1962).

The fourth paragraph, apart from referring to further consultation required on the number of seats, unacceptably lectured the Association on the 'expectation' of "all those interested in education" for it to make "a constructive contribution towards ending the present disharmony in the teaching profession and promoting that greater unity we all desire".

The Minister and his officials stood their ground. Breakdown seemed possible. The NAS withdrew for private discussion. The NAS delegation insisted that it could not accept the salary settlement. It was prepared to give an assurance it would carry out its share of responsibility to administer it, in line with all other members of the Committee. On return the NAS restated its position and for a time the Minister appeared to stand his ground and breakdown seemed "imminent". Suddenly Sir David relented and agreed a revised third paragraph as the NAS had suggested. The Minister further agreed to delete all the offending parts of the fourth and concluding paragraph. There only remained the one sentence: "The number of seats to be allotted to the Association will need further consideration and consultation."

Then suddenly it was all over. The final negotiations had lasted from 11.30 a.m. until 1.15 p.m. Agreement had been reached. The NAS had secured representation on Burnham. The record of the meeting does not refer to any concluding 'niceties'. Perhaps there were none! I should imagine the NAS side was relieved and the Minister probably glad to get rid of the issue – and let the NUT do its damnedest!

Committee 'K' returned to the reconvened Executive at 2.30 p.m. GS Bert Rushworth reported on the afternoon's dramatic denouement. He concluded his report: "The struggle of 40 years has ended in victory. Gentlemen of the NAS, the fight for the future can now begin." The Executive meeting was over by 3.45 p.m.

The letter dated 24 October 1961 duly arrived from Sir David Eccles. The crucial third paragraph now read: "These are welcome assurances, and imply recognition by your Association's representatives on the Committee that they will share the duty of administering the current Burnham agreement from which basis future negotiations will have to start." Whilst the NAS remained free to promulgate and pursue all its policies the three assurances were all freely given as part of the deal: no obstruction on EP, participation in the administration of the pay award and an end to the militant action.

In subsequent bitter exchanges the NUT was to allege the NAS secured representation on Burnham in return for agreeing EP and accepting the (reduced) Burnham settlement. I have tried to set out all the relevant facts and given the NAS view. The readers may judge for themselves.

There is no mention of any formal celebrations by the NAS on its historic victory although local association officers were brought together in a London hotel for what must have been a 'celebratory debriefing' on 11 November, appropriately Armistice Day!

Chapter 19 - Burnham Cinders Smoulder

While the NAS had secured representation other developments were taking place. The Government, at the Conservative Party Conference at Brighton, 9-14 October 1961, made further threats about collective bargaining and courts of arbitration. The Government believed that such courts disregarded the interests of the national economy, either through design or lack of competence to do so.

After further consultations with teacher associations on 3 November, the Minister announced "constructive" legislative proposals. He would only intervene to prescribe salary scales if there were deadlock. In which case the Minister would first refer matters back to Burnham, giving his reasons. Failing acceptable alternative proposals he would prescribe. These "reserve powers" would only be exercised as a last resort, in return for which he would leave the Burnham Committee in existence.

At a further meeting on 2 January 1962 the NAS told the Minister that the crucial test of his proposals was their likely effects upon teachers' salaries and the education service. They could only lead to further deterioration. Whilst fully accepting the right of all parties to be represented openly in negotiations, the NAS could not accept the Government being advocate, judge and jury in its own case.

The NAS had reluctantly accepted the compromise of only two seats on Burnham to assist in the ongoing discussions about salaries and reform of the machinery. The Government promised to return to the issue at a later date. The NAS continued lobbying in line with its policy favouring an open, transparent and non-statutory negotiating machine with full rights to arbitration and the retrospective payment of salary awards where relevant.

In a surprise move announced on 9 March 1962 to LEAs and teacher associations the Minister said he had decided (against the advice of his colleagues) to postpone legislation. Section 89 (of the 1944 Act) still needed change, but the Government was working on a wages and incomes policy and the National Economic Development Council had been established. It is open to interpretation but possibly the Government saw these alternative avenues as better options for general wage control without targeting teachers too specifically.

From the NAS perspective an uneasy truce had developed over Burnham reform, including the issue of confidentiality, which could not continue indefinitely. In 1963 the Government found it necessary to introduce a temporary Remuneration of Teachers Act (RTA) to deal with a specific problem. The Minister was not prepared to sanction the 1963 Burnham Agreement, objecting to the method of distribution. This time the Burnham Panels were not prepared to give way. So the Secretary of State legislated to give himself the power to impose his own settlement.

The draconian nature of the Government's intervention in 1963 resurrected the need to find a more permanent and acceptable reform of the Burnham machine. From mid-1964 a series of meetings began, involving central and local government and the teacher unions, which eventually led to the RTA of 1965.

Reforms such as arbitration and retrospection had to await agreement from Government but on the issue of confidentiality the NAS had taken matters into its own hands. The Teachers' Panel seemed to have trapped itself into a belief that Management would not negotiate unless the proceedings were conducted in secrecy. The unions denied themselves the opportunity of exerting pressure which could flow from membership reactions to poor Management Panel offers.

After the first Burnham meeting the NAS representatives attended, reports were sent out to Executive Members and Local Secretaries and press comment was made where relevant. All hell broke loose. It was if the NAS had violated the Official Secrets Act and betrayed the national interest. But the NAS always appreciated that recognition marked not the end but the beginning of the real struggle for a just wage. And central to that struggle was a more open and effective negotiating machinery, not one stacked in the Government's/employers' favour.

According to an authoritative report dating from 1961 seen by the NAS, the Minister, Sir David Eccles, was also – in private, at least – an advocate of reform. Apparently he wished to replace Burnham with a concordat or convention. This would start with the Government giving detailed statistics on the supply of teachers and identifying problems. Multilateral consultations would follow, ending up with the Government openly setting a global sum for the Committee to divide up. The results would be delivered to the Minister, hopefully for acceptance but, failing that, he would have the power to impose his own settlement.

Although somewhat tortuous this was a much more open system, reflecting the realities of Section 89. The LEAs predictably objected, complaining that they would be left "with the façade of collective bargaining to cloak a reality of direct control". They were absolutely right. The big problem in the view of the NAS was that the LEAs' perceptive and articulate judgement, intended to reflect their fears of the future, deftly defined the current reality.

Sir David Eccles' successor, Sir Edward Boyle who became Minister of Education in July 1962, was later to write, correctly in the view of the NAS, that his own "starting point" was that "each of the responsible parties in the education service, including the Minister, should be assured of an appropriate place in any revised machinery and procedures".

Sir Edward had laid out similar views at a meeting with the NAS in 1962 in the wake of all the controversy over the Association blowing the lid on Burnham secrecy. Having finally gained admission in 1961 the NAS, always suspicious of the secrecy surrounding Burnham – until it was all over – had lost patience with the unduly protracted negotiations, often extending for over a year. Mindful of the distorted leaks from some inside 'the four walls', the NAS decided to issue its Local Secretaries with brief reports on how the negotiations had proceeded.

It may seem extraordinary in the context of the twenty-first century, but the NUT and Management objected fiercely to this 'breach of confidence and the rules' by the NAS. As a result of the furore the entire NAS Executive was called in to see the Minister. Far from apologetic the GS Bert Rushworth gave a spirited justification for the NAS's action. I suspect Sir Edward Boyle must have privately had sympathy for the NAS position. In any event the meeting ended with Sir Edward agreeing to review the Burnham machinery in respect of provision for backdating awards, arbitration procedures and the Ministry's role in the negotiating process. In return for the potential progress of the Minister's concessions the NAS accepted a compromise and agreed to issue no further press statements in the current round of negotiations.

The NAS did not get all it wanted out of the meeting with Sir Edward Boyle. The Minister would do nothing about the one-voice procedure on both sides which for the teachers meant that only the NUT view would be presented.

The NAS always accepted that on occasions confidentiality could be helpful when for example potential breakthroughs might have to be checked out with other parties. But the practice of keeping the members you supposedly represented in total darkness for months on end was disgraceful and unacceptable.

Furthermore, it seemed the NUT leadership was content for the Burnham machinery to continue without the desirable reforms. Perhaps the lack of arbitration and retrospection was a useful 'arm twist' for the NUT's Special Salary Conferences to be persuaded to vote in favour of the meagre awards normally recommended by the leadership. In 1962 there was some suspicion that the NUT was content to allow the lack of retrospection to teach an uncharacteristically independent ATTI a lesson for initially rejecting but later accepting for FE teachers the same low award granted to primary and secondary.

The long series of meetings in the Autumn Term of 1964 which led up to the RTA of the following year did not get off to an easy start. The employers had secured an early meeting with the Minister and apparently reached some accommodations. The NAS tried to secure a bilateral Minister-Teacher Unions meeting but was outmanoeuvred by the NUT and other associations who curiously favoured having the employers present.

The resultant row and acerbic exchange of detailed correspondence between the new NAS GS, Terry Casey, and his NUT counterpart, Sir Ronald Gould, although ostensibly concerned with short-term issues dealing with proper consultation, really reflected the fundamental differences between the two organisations. The NAS wanted serious reforms; the NUT wished to preserve the status quo, which included an 'unbelievable belief' that despite all that had happened in 1961 and 1962 the LEA employers' position of 'independence' should be protected.

However, the early bilateral Government-LEA employers meeting had concluded a deal which recognised the inevitability of the Treasury setting a global sum from the beginning of negotiations. This became known as the 'Concordat' and was supposed to be confidential between the Government and LEA employers. Besides the global sum, the question of distribution was also crucial. To recognise the Minister's interest in distribution he was to be given a weighted vote of 20 in the Management Panel, alongside the LEA employers' 26 seats.

The NUT did not like these developments one bit. At the first tripartite unions-employers-Government meeting on 25 September 1964 (the arrangements for which were regarded as controversial by the NAS) the NUT took up these issues. Recognising the embarrassing situation he was embracing, Sir Ronald Gould 'apologised' for apparently fighting the employers' corner (which explained why the NUT sidelined the NAS efforts to have a bilateral Government-unions meeting). The Government immediately, if brutally, let it be known that it was not impressed with the LEA's apparent acquiescence in the NUT's efforts to reopen issues that had been the subject of a done deal on 'Ministers' and employers' business' into which the Teachers' Panel should not poke its nose. Gould reduced himself to pleading that at least negotiations should start without the global sum being set.

The NUT fought against compulsory arbitration but had no convincing argument on how to make progress in the event of deadlock. Significantly, the NAS began to gain support from other members of the Teachers' Panel on this and other issues such as the open involvement of the Minister in setting the global sum. However, the NUT vote, combined with ATTI, was always enough to ensure its policies prevailed in the Teachers' Panel.

Naturally the Government was not impressed and in autumn 1964 pushed on, intent on serious reform of Burnham. The continuation of supposedly 'free negotiations' in Burnham would only be tolerated if there were clear arrangements for resolving difficulties. Government was willing to use Parliamentary procedures to assist in the process and would concede provision for retrospection but insist upon arbitration when necessary and the role of the Minister in setting the global sum. On arbitration the Government intended to ensure the Chairman of Burnham would decide on the issue of referral if the two Panels could not agree between themselves. Retrospection had been such a glaring omission from previous arrangements that not even the NUT could maintain its opposition to reform.

The setting of a global sum could either be on the face of legislation or left to other arrangements. Bearing in mind Ministers made this absolutely plain during the course of the autumn 1964 meetings, it was extraordinary to behold the apparent outrage and surprise expressed by some members of the Teachers' Panel when the 'secret' Concordat to this very effect was 'revealed' some years later.

The NAS was winning the day on retrospection, arbitration and the open involvement of Government, but remained isolated on the questions of the one-voice procedure, an independent secretariat for the Teachers' Panel and, more importantly, on confidentiality. Despite membership having risen to 35,000 by 1964, prospects for securing a fairer representation than the two seats the NAS possessed seemed remote.

In October 1964 came a change of Government, with Labour being returned to power. Harold Wilson appointed Michael Stewart, a former teacher and an NUT-sponsored MP, to the newly entitled position of Secretary of State for Education. Although I found no evidence of immediate complaint of possible conflict of interest coming from any quarter, the appointment soon proved to be very controversial.

The NUT moved quickly. Under the plausible guise of getting on with the negotiations for 1965, the NUT tried to get Burnham reform put on to the back-burner with the possibility of indefinite (perhaps even 'permanent') postponement. The NAS supported the prompt progress of negotiations, even if it were under 'Burnham in suspense', since the Labour Party in opposition had recently made commitments to give teachers a "substantial award".

At the same time, the NAS continued to lobby the new Minister hard to continue with reform. At a meeting between Michael Stewart and the Teachers' Panel on 9 November 1964, the NUT was disappointed to hear him say he intended to continue with the previous Government's plans for reform.

Revealingly, Michael Stewart said the Government had to be involved from the start, otherwise "I have to get in obliquely, and this causes offence".

The NAS pressed hard on the proposed power of government to set aside an arbitration award. In the view of the NAS this should only happen for national economic reasons, applied generally to all employees, and therefore should be subject to decision of Parliament. Following a meeting with Stewart early in December 1964, the NAS was reasonably content with the way discussions appeared to be going save for the issues of confidentiality and level of NAS representation, which remained unresolved.

The NAS was disappointed to hear Michael Stewart express his view that confidentiality helped negotiations. The NAS reminded Stewart that his predecessor, Sir Edward Boyle, had promised a thorough review of Burnham procedures and conventions (which were not on the face of legislation) and any decision on such matters should await that consideration.

The 'smouldering cinders' of 'The Battle of Burnham' reignited towards the end of 1964. The NAS position was under serious fire. Resentment was still deep inside the NUT against the recognition granted to the NAS in 1961. The Management was having great difficulty coming to terms with the truculence of the NAS which stood in sharp contrast to the quiescent majority on the Teachers' Panel.

The NUT boasted it was the most democratic of the teacher unions in giving members a final say over salary settlements through the Special Conference required by their rules for ratification. After the first year's truce over confidentiality the NAS resumed reporting freely to its members and exposed the damaging effects of secrecy, which made teachers aware of the situation when it was too late. Without provision for retrospection delay only cost more money. 'Accept now or get nothing' or 'this is the best deal in the circumstances' (which secrecy had conspired to fix against the teachers) were typical of the alternatives offered to their 'democratic' Special Conferences by the NUT leadership.

Some in the NAS suspected that the NUT leadership, having recently secured full implementation of equal pay, and mindful of its 'soft underbelly' of quiescent members, was anxious neither to rock the boat nor stir up 'unrealistic' expectations.

Government and LEA employers found themselves inconvenienced. Burnham was no longer 'working quite so well' holding teachers' salaries down. The NAS could not quickly break the NUT's dominance of the Teachers' Panel but did inject some element of protest and greater resolve better to fight the teacher's corner.

The NAS also continued to press the case for arbitration, retrospection and open acknowledgement of the Minister's role in setting the global sum. The inherent logic of the NAS case was difficult to deny and eventually late in 1964 a Bill finally came before Parliament to reform Burnham.

Outside of the legislation two other issues had to be settled: the number of seats for the NAS and Burnham secrecy. The NAS accepted that delicate stages in negotiations could be helped by limited confidentiality, but the blanket secrecy destroyed accountability and was totally unacceptable. The case for representation to be based on certified membership numbers was undeniable.

Of the 28 seats on the Teachers' Panel the NUT had 16, ATTI 4, the Joint Four 6 and the NAS 2. The NUT GS had conceded the need to discuss matters by suggesting a meeting of unions during the course of 1964. The meeting had finally taken place on 27 November but it was not serious. The NUT, the Joint Four and ATTI (the last named still with four seats but with no members in schools) denied the existence of any principles to inform representation on an objective basis – a risible at best, downright dishonest attempt at worst, to justify the status quo.

Terry Casey had also written to Stewart immediately after the abortive attempt to reach agreement in the Teachers' Panel on 27 November, requesting a meeting to present the NAS case. The NAS had been patient in allowing negotiations to proceed without the complications of representational issues. With the Parliamentary Bill due to receive its second reading by Christmas 1964 and come into effect for 1 April 1965, the issue could no longer be avoided. The NAS was informed that the tight timetable for the Bill and other business made a meeting impossible. However, the Secretary of State would consider written representations before making a decision.

Before the NAS could submit its case in writing, Terry Casey's breakfast the following Friday morning was disturbed by several telephone calls. Irate and surprised Executive Members told him that the NUT journal, *The Teacher*, was carrying the contents of a letter from Stewart to the unions informing them of his decision to leave the Teachers' Panel pattern of representation unchanged. The logistics of posting letters and printing journals soon proved that the NUT had advance notification and that the Minister had reached his decision despite the assurances to consider further representations.

The decision, which defied rationality and elementary fairness, had also been reached in very controversial circumstances. It left the NAS seriously under-represented with only two seats. Since recognition in 1961 the NAS had increased its in-service membership by 70% to over 35,000. It was clearly the second-largest union.

In the furore that followed Stewart agreed to meet with the NAS. At the meeting on 15 December the Minister stood accused of deceit. Terry Casey lectured the Secretary of State on his responsibility to act impartially and objectively. Terry referred to the appalling lack of information and checks on claimed union memberships, with some unions absurdly claiming audits were impossible. Alluding to the 'friendly relations' between the NUT and the Minister boasted about in *The Teacher*, Terry Casey told Stewart he was in need of advice from an independent body to which he should look for some adjudication. Terry Casey was brutally frank with the Minister, telling him to his face that NAS members thought he was acting with favouritism to the NUT. Terry concluded by saying the NAS would be renewing the struggle of 1961 if it were not recognised as the second-largest union. The NAS regarded his decision to maintain the status quo as "patently unjust and frankly irrational".

In his defence Stewart claimed his decision to maintain the status quo on representation was only for the short term to allow negotiations to start under the new arrangements. But no reference had been made to the temporary nature of the decision.

The situation deteriorated to new depths the day after the meeting on 15 December. While representation obviously remained fraught, there had been no hint of any change in the Bill. However, on the morning of 16 December there were press reports of last-minute changes. One of these was to give the Minister the power unilaterally to expel any organisation from the proposed new Burnham Committee. It was described as "the power to revoke" membership of the Committee. Every commentator and others 'in the know' seemed to have been briefed that this was aimed at the NAS who would be "kicked off Burnham unless it observed confidentiality".

The NAS was flabbergasted, if for no other reason than the Minister had given no hint of any such move only the day before in the face-to-face meeting. Naturally accusations of bad faith began to flow. The NAS was well aware of Mr Stewart's previous history as a teacher and member of the NUT. The NAS was already suspicious of recent events, and the double-dealing, favouritism and disgraceful lack of objective criteria in Ministerial decisions. The NUT expressed surprise at the move; but the NAS suspected that was feigned. Sir William Alexander and the management were obviously content.

Furthermore a letter from Stewart to the NAS on 21 December seeking to clarify his decisions and reassure the NAS, was studiously non-committal on doing anything, not even acknowledging the strength of the NAS concerns. Denial of the reported target of 'the power to revoke membership' had taken a long time to emerge against a background in which the Scottish Schoolmasters Association (SSA) had already been expelled from their Joint Negotiating

Committee for refusing to accept confidentiality. The SSA had to engage in strike action in three different schools on 4 March 1964 before regaining access to their SJNC.

That was the signal for another letter from Terry Casey to Michael Stewart (30 December) deploring "the lack of frankness" and lamenting the failure of the Minister to take any notice of the exchanges on 21 December. Terry Casey concluded: "The 'power to revoke membership' was widely interpreted as a threat to NAS and it contained an obnoxious principle which is hostile to the spirit of free trade unionism."

The NAS swung into immediate action. A special one-day Conference was called for Saturday 9 January 1965 in Brighton. The mood was militant. Introducing his Report GS Terry Casey said the Association faced the greatest crisis in its history. Within a few weeks of the Minister announcing that Burnham was going to be replaced with negotiating machinery more in line with NAS principles, we were being told that unless we agreed to silence we would be expelled. There was no way the NAS would agree to be muzzled.

By this stage it was not just a question of Burnham representation. By 1964 the NAS was represented on a variety of important national bodies. These included the Advisory Council on the Supply and Training of Teachers, the Secondary Schools Examination Council and the Working Party on the Proposed Schools Council for the Curriculum and Examinations. Representation at local level on many diverse LEA consultative and negotiating committees could no longer be denied after the breakthrough in 1961. Such committees were often of considerable importance, dealing with local application and interpretation of national agreements on conditions of service.

The Special Conference carried a comprehensive and determined resolution. It declared that as a "free association of schoolmasters it would continue to respect and defend the inherent right of members to be informed about all matters of substance affecting their interests". The resolution went on to demand the NAS be recognised as the second-largest body of teachers. It expressed concern at the power to revoke membership of any organisation being incompatible with the UK's international obligations under the International Labour Organisation (ILO). The resolution instructed the Executive "to resist all threats or blandishments which would weaken or destroy the NAS as a free association, especially any attempt to impose a ban of secrecy". And last but by no means least the resolution instructed the Executive "to take protest action in defence of the integrity of the Association", pledging "full support for such measures, including militant action".

The Executive did not hang around. Immediately after the Conference a national one-day strike was called for 21 January 1965. Plans were under way for the usual rally at a venue in central London. Then other dramatic events of national importance took over.

Sir Winston Churchill, already of advanced years in his nineties, fell into a coma in what were obviously going to be his final days. The NAS took the right decision to cancel the arrangements for the strike. It was called off two days beforehand on 19 January. It was unthinkable that a strike could take place, together with the usual lobby of Parliament, in such a time of national mourning. It had been a courageous decision to hold the strike and a statesmanlike one to call it off.

A little later came some more surprising but good news (for some). The Prime Minister seemed to turn adversity to advantage. Patrick Gordon Walker, appointed Foreign Secretary despite a surprising defeat in the 'safe' Labour seat of Smethwick at the recent General Election, suffered the same fate at a subsequent by-election at Leyton, in East London, designed to secure him a seat in the House of Commons. His defeats were largely due to some unsavoury use of the race card by opponents.

The Prime Minister, Harold Wilson, took the opportunity to switch Michael Stewart to the Foreign Office and install a new Secretary of State for Education, Anthony Crosland. This had the potential to relieve some of the tension created personally by Michael Stewart.

Then more good, if surprising, news came on 28 January. At the Burnham Committee meeting both Sir William Alexander and Sir Ronald Gould suddenly and surprisingly announced significant departures from their position on confidentiality. From now on it would be proper for representatives to report back in full to their association executives. However, a general release of information, including press statements, would be subject to agreement between the two sides. For the Management Panel Sir William Alexander insisted that the release of information during negotiations had to assist and not hinder the process.

Terry Casey acknowledged that some movement had been made towards the NAS position. Early in February the NAS Executive endorsed a proposal to give this 'limited publicity' a fair trial, subject to experience. The NAS's hostility to blanket secrecy was well justified by the negotiations that took place leading up to the (arbitrated) settlement for 1 April 1965. As I relate in chapter 26, the months of February and March 1965 were dominated by an elaborate charade of negotiations in which the Management insisted on distinguishing between 'open' and 'closed' offers. It would only increase its (rejected) open offer which had been publicised if the Teachers' Panel would agree to receive a closed offer. Such a closed offer could not be publicised until the whole process, including arbitration if used, had been completed.

In the view of the NAS the whole purpose of confidentiality stood revealed. Management did not want any improved offers to be considered by the arbiters. It explained why the NUT was so nervous of publicity and reluctant to accept reform which included provision for arbitration. It showed the NUT lacked confidence in negotiations, fearing the only way to secure a better deal was through this debilitating process of closed offers.

Management was insisting that teachers could either have negotiation or arbitration, but not both. The NAS objected to the Management being allowed to set the rules. On 27 March a special meeting of the NAS Executive gave notice that if there were no satisfactory release of information agreed by the two sides, the Association would withdraw from the undertaking it had given on 11 February to give 'limited publicity' a fair trial.

Eventually the NUT votes ensured the Teachers' Panel would listen to a closed offer, which in the event was also rejected. The extended exchanges had inevitably leaked to the press, which in its own way helped to collapse much of the nonsense associated with confidentiality. The NUT and some Joint Four representatives were keen to report breaches of confidentiality by local NAS Officers and School Reps to the Teachers' Panel in the forlorn hope of embarrassing us. How on earth they expected Executives to receive information and not pass it on to activists beggars belief.

As all the drama associated with confidentiality had been unfolding, two other demands by the NAS remained outstanding. The 'power to revoke membership of the Burnham Committee' was still on the face of the Bill and the question of serious under-representation of NAS seats remained.

The 'power to revoke' was sufficiently amended for the NAS to be able to accept a compromise. NAS representatives in Exeter, lobbying some of their local members of the Upper House, persuaded Lords Colyton and Bowles to seek an amendment to the Bill. On 25 February the Bill was amended during its third reading in the Lords to take the power away from the Minister. In its place was inserted the requirement to lay an Order before the Commons if a Minister wished to remove an organisation from membership. That would enable full discussion and a vote to occur should the circumstances arise. The pernicious power sought by the individual Minister was removed.

Responding to Lord Bowles, the Earl of Iddesleigh observed that their Lordships had taken part in "a piece of industrial conciliation" and noted that the "NAS had not found it necessary to have recourse to a one-day strike or a mass lobby of Parliament in order to obtain the substance of what they justly desire". He also took the opportunity of getting in a plug for the Upper Chamber, expressing the "hope that some schoolmaster in instructing his class in civics may find a good word to say of your Lordships' House as a body which is at least occasionally useful"!

On 15 March Minister of State Reg Prentice announced the Government would accept the Lords' amendment. Responding for the Opposition, Christopher Chataway complimented the Minister in fairly accepting the amendment, "though he made only discreet and glancing references to the causes of the Government's change of mind. In fact of course the NAS felt so strongly about the matter that it threatened to strike, and it was a strike which almost took place". Mr Chataway echoed Lord Iddesleigh's hope that the schoolmaster would use his class on civics to good effect for the standing of the House of Lords.

The Remuneration of Teachers Act 1965 was then passed into law, receiving the royal assent on 23 March. Within a few days, on 2 April, the teachers' pay claim was referred to arbitration. Three significant improvements were secured, all of them thanks to NAS lobbying. Provision was made for arbitration and retrospection and the Government was openly represented on the Management Panel of Burnham in the persons of two senior officials from the DES. Somewhere along the way the Government had agreed to reduce its weighted vote on the Management Panel from 20 to 13. An alternate Chairman was introduced in the person of John Wordie who was destined to preside over the Burnham Committee during some very troubled times in the 1970s and 1980s and who was also knighted for his commendably patient endeavours and good-natured disposition.

Recognising the feelings of the NUT and the LEA employers, the Government had left the global sum question off the face of the legislation but insisted on a clear written agreement. The 'Concordat' was reached and it suited the convenience of some for it to remain 'secret'. When it was later 'revealed' some Burnham Committee members feigned shocked surprise.

On the issue of adequate and fair representation the NAS accepted compromise by settling for a promise to return to the matter at a later time. There was an element of risk but, I believe to its credit, the NAS accepted the compromise in the interest of not delaying negotiations which were supposed to be proceeding for 1 April (1965). The NAS was soon to be accorded one more seat on Burnham, taking the number to three.

Much later in October 1978 the Secretary of State reviewed representation on the Teachers' Panel of Burnham. The NASUWT, with a membership now in excess of 110,000, was granted 6 seats. However, the NUT retained its overall majority with 16 seats, with AMMA being granted 4, NAHT 2 and SHA 1. NATFHE was allowed to retain one seat despite having no members in schools. The NASUWT welcomed its fairer level of representation but still complained about proportionality. The NUT claimed 220,000 members and retained 16 seats, whereas the NASUWT was only granted 6 seats despite having half the level of NUT membership.

It was not until 1986 that the NASUWT was accorded something approaching equity with seven seats. NATFHE (formerly ATTI) was removed and the NUT overall majority dismantled. But it was all too late. As I describe in chapters 61-63, the NUT used its overall majority to block an early resolution of the 1985 pay claim, thereby disastrously prolonging and embittering the dispute, which landed us all in an unholy mess and led directly to the abolition of Burnham and teachers' negotiating rights, such as they were, in 1987. All battles, as well as 'The Battle of Burnham', were well and truly over.

SECTION FOUR
TEACHERS' PAY 1900-1976

Chapter 20 - Introduction to Teachers' Pay

The subject of teachers' pay provides an intriguing study of economics, 'education' politics and industrial relations. The Association made a unique and often controversial contribution to the subject, on one issue very wrong, on others very right, but often in a minority of one.

One of the policies espoused originally by the NAS, opposition to equal pay (EP) for men and women, was doomed by the progress of history. But, arguably, genuinely EP has only recently begun to be addressed in a significant and perhaps permanent way.

Other policies which the Association advocated – for example, career structured salary scales recognising the value of continuity of service and, in more recent decades, 'collegiality' emphasising the central importance of the teacher in the classroom – have a universal truth and relevance which should stand the test of time.

Underlying the seemingly eternal problem of teachers' pay have been the adverse effects of fundamental economic laws and Government policies. They relate to supply and demand, the forces determining the price for goods and services in the marketplace. Unless you are in a position like that of a Government it is difficult to exert much control over such forces.

And Government is Government is Government. More particularly the Treasury is the Treasury is the Treasury. Whatever party is in power the desire to purchase the goods and services required to run the country at a low, if not the lowest possible, price is always there.

On the demand side the state enjoys much of the power of a monopsonist, being by far the largest employer of teachers (over 90%), with the private sector claiming to cater for around 7% of school-age children. In the strict legal sense LEAs and school governing bodies are the employers of teachers, appointing them to particular posts. But for purposes of pay, pensions, regulations governing the profession and since 1987 the main conditions of service, the Government acts as the de facto employer of teachers.

The NASUWT has never had any problems recognising that reality. Paying an ever-increasing proportion of the teachers' salary bill over the years it is both inevitable politically, and indeed correct constitutionally, for the Government to assume the predominant employer role. The NASUWT believed one of the unnecessary handicaps self-imposed on the profession was the reluctance by some unions to recognise that reality, aided and abetted as they were in that unfortunate endeavour by LEAs, anxious to perpetuate illusions of independence over their 'empires'.

If the power of the monopsonist were not enough, Government was also a monopolist in the sense of determining the rules over supply. While nobody can force people to become teachers, Government decides how many training places are to be on offer as well as regulating entry requirements and final qualifications for licence to practise.

Teachers generally made it more difficult for themselves by continuously pressing for more and more of their number. This was justified on educational grounds but ruinous in respect of teachers' financial interests. Some other professions, more in control of their destinies, made sure they kept their numbers low, sometimes through clever and professionally acceptable means such as artificially high standards of entry and unnecessarily long periods of training. Teachers were such a large group that even a small percentage increase in salaries cost a huge amount of money, with implications for the macro economic policy of governments.

Teaching has largely been an occupation in which women have predominated in numerical terms. It seems to have been an unfortunate fact of life (which hopefully is now changing for the better) that the market rate for the employment of women is lower than it is for men.

The Association believed through bitter experience that polite representation had little or no influence upon governments on matters which had financial implications. Unlike other professions, often self-governing and selling their services in the marketplace, teachers had either to accept penury or fight against it with the only 'real' weapon available, industrial action with all its 'blue collar' connotations. Even then there was little real muscle to flex, for unlike profit-eroding private-sector strikes those conducted by teachers saved Government and LEA employers money. That was one reason why the NASUWT tended to favour 'action short of strike', such as working to rule or boycotting certain activities, as a means of applying pressure.

Teachers only had the power to embarrass Government and employers and to inconvenience parents, albeit a potentially large section of the populace. Set against that teachers taking action faced the inevitable emotional and moral blackmail: allegations they were damaging children's education and setting a bad example. The media, mostly in the hands of employers (apart from the BBC), were only too keen to jump on the bandwagon of such charges.

Comparison was the key concept applied by unions in pay negotiations, while employers were mostly guided by the market conditions of supply, with the 'over-arching employer' – the Government – determining demand through public expenditure decisions on education. The NASUWT always attached great importance to two comparisons. The first related to the cost of living, one of the yardsticks for measuring inflation. If a pay award fell below the percentage rise in the cost of living or retail price index, then teachers were suffering a cut in their living standards. The second concerned comparison with other occupations. If the teachers' award fell below the average gained elsewhere, the profession was declared by the NASUWT to have become less attractive through comparative erosion.

There were many indices for measuring and comparing pay between occupations: white and blue collar, manual and non-manual, male and female. Teachers on the whole preferred the male white-collar salaries index, itself perhaps an interesting comment on EP. The base year and periods chosen for comparison obviously could produce interesting variations.

Teachers' salaries were low in 1914 when the First World War broke out. The President of the Board of Education, Herbert Fisher, conceded the case for substantial increases when he established the Burnham Committee in 1919. The proposed increases, apart from those payable in London, never materialised, the victim of the Geddes Axe to cut public expenditure. The story of teachers' salaries for the entire inter-war period from 1919 to the outbreak of the Second World War in 1939 was a disaster of one cut after another, only some of which were restored. The result, almost unbelievable in today's context, was that teachers' salaries were virtually the same in 1939 as they had been 20 years earlier. Meanwhile the cost of living had risen and income tax had soared.

The McNair Report of 1944, part of the exercise on post-war reconstruction, conceded that teachers were seriously underpaid. Never was there a better context in which to press for substantial increases. The golden opportunity provided by the 1944 Act was squandered by the NUT accepting a meagre award, setting a pattern which was not to be challenged until the arrival of the NAS (soon to be accompanied by the UWT) on the Burnham Committee in the 1960s. During this period the NUT seemed rarely to lift its sight above securing EP, literally at any price.

That was the context in which the NAS, joined by the UWT in the 1960s, set out on 'mission impossible' – to secure decent salaries firstly for men and subsequently for all 'career teachers' who would devote a substantial amount of their working lives to the profession.

Teachers' pay featured prominently in the great Education Acts of Britain's history, particularly 1902, 1918 and 1944, all in times of war.

The 1902 Act set up a system for paying teachers that was to last over 40 years until the legislation of 1944. In 1902 some 2,500 School Boards were replaced by much larger Local Education Authorities (LEAs) divided into four different kinds or 'Parts'. An additional Act in 1903 established the London County Council (LCC), taking over from the School Board and becoming a Part IV Authority.

According to Ministry of Education Reports there was no standard scale for teachers' pay. There was a great disparity in pay between voluntary (mostly church) and Board (state) schools. More than half of certificated men teachers were paid less than £100 a year, with headmasters generally receiving under £150. The equivalents for women teachers and heads were £75 and £100 respectively.

The McNair Report of 1944 judged that the structural changes of 1902 had little impact upon the salary situation, although some LEAs made slight efforts at improvement. Small wonder McNair observed that an "atmosphere of the Poor Law and a trail of cheapness lay across the elementary schools right up to the end of the Nineteenth Century".

However, in 1905 the LCC introduced a new scale, applying it to all teachers in county and voluntary schools. The scale for the two-year trained schoolmaster became £100 rising to £200 over 14 years.

In a booklet published by the NAS in 1957 and written by one of its most distinguished Past-Presidents, Harry Meigh, some anecdotal evidence is supplied by reference to a Charles Nathan. This latter gentleman wrote a book, *A Schoolmaster looks back,* in which he recounts being appointed an assistant master under the Liverpool Education Committee in 1907 at an annual salary of £70. Mr Nathan was able to top up his salary with some educational qualifications, for example Stage III Maths or Science adding £1 10s.

From 1861 teachers' salaries were subject to the infamous 'payment by results' regime. Individual salaries were not linked directly to pupil results but the Government grant which helped to finance the system was dependent upon them. School Board Inspectors conducted tests in 'the three Rs'. Their establishment by Robert Lowe, a prominent Liberal politician and Cabinet member who was also Vice-President of the Committee of the Council on Education (as the Government department was originally named), afforded him a special place in Britain's educational history, with one of its most famous quotes: "If the new system is not cheap it will be efficient, and if it is not efficient it will be cheap."

The system was phased out between 1897 and 1902 although school managers were able to withhold increments in salary for poor performance by teachers. In its early days many teachers believed withholding took place for financial rather than genuine reasons. Apart from minor alterations these scales and rates of pay remained unchanged until the establishment of the Burnham Committee by H.A.L. Fisher in 1919, following the Education Act of the previous year.

The May Report of the Committee on National Expenditure in 1931 quoted the following table of average annual salaries as at 31 March 1914:

TEACHERS

	£
Certificated men	147
Certificated women	103
All certificated	118
All uncertificated	58
All supplementary	40
Total men	139
Total women	82
All teachers	97

One can see that broadly there had been very little improvement in salaries in the pre-First World War period (possibly from the time of the major 1870 Education Act). By 1914 income tax had been levied and had risen to 1s. 8d. in the £ (about 7% in today's terms). The cost of living had also risen, although the Government's official retail price index did not come into being until 1914.

To its credit the NUT early in 1914 (enjoying as it then did an unchallenged monopoly in elementary school teacher representation) embarked upon an intensive campaign to get salaries raised. There was much support and interest from the press, some MPs and even the general public despite the high levels of unemployment. Recruitment to teaching remained difficult despite the profession being the only avenue for poor and lower-middle-class children to secure secondary education.

Some sections of the press even called teaching "a sweated occupation", reflecting national concern about "sweated industries". Although equal pay was then only a distant prospect, there seemed to be a particular concern over the inability to attract enough men into the teaching profession.

With the outbreak of war in August 1914 teachers, like everyone else, responded patriotically and the campaign died a natural death, although the merits of the case strengthened. Income tax continued to rise, reaching five shillings in the pound by the end of the war in 1918.

Many other groups secured pay rises together with generous cost of living adjustments and war bonuses as often occurred during such inflationary times. Teachers were at the mercy of a variety of LEAs, only a few of whom awarded bonuses coming anywhere near generous. Some LEAs refused any bonuses to men on active service. The NUT was lukewarm at best on this issue, reflecting the predominance of women members in its ranks, heightened by the high number of men away on active service.

Harry Meigh describes the war bonuses for teachers as "miserly". The best were probably in London where the pay of teachers had been increased by around 25% by the end of the war. But that was based on low and outdated salary levels dating from 1902 and widely acknowledged to be deplorable. Furthermore inflation had soared during the course of the First World War, at least by 100%.

The desire for EP amongst women teachers naturally grew as the war drew on. Women generally were rightly emboldened by their great contribution to the war effort. With many men teachers away on military service women replaced them in boys' schools. The profession soon became identified as the first major battleground for EP.

The enlightened Liberal President of the Board of Education, H.A.L. Fisher, was setting about his agenda to improve the prospects of teaching following his declaration to the House of Commons on 17 February 1917:

"There is, I believe, a consensus of opinion that the only way in which the supply of teachers can be placed on a permanently satisfactory footing will be by substantial improvement in the emoluments and prospects of the teaching profession."

In 1918 Fisher set up the Burnham Committee in pursuit of this aim, also establishing a non-contributory pension scheme, as well as raising Government grant for teachers' salaries from 50% to 60% of the relevant expenditure.

In November 1917 a report to Parliament in response to an MP's question showed that as of 31 March that year there were approximately 36,800 certificated schoolmasters in England and Wales. Nearly 5,700 of those were employed by the LCC, the most 'generous' paymaster. Only 3,300 earned salaries above £200 per annum. Fisher's concerns were well grounded in fact.

Burnham got off to a bad start with its first Report, published on 21 November 1919, producing the Provisional Minimum Scale:

Two-year trained certificated teachers:

Men: £160 x 10 increments to £300;
Women: £150 x 10 increments to £240.

It also established the 4:5 ratio of women's to men's pay at the maximum.

Under the 'inducement' of the increased grant to 60%, by 1920 every LEA had adopted the minimum scale or something superior. However, the NUT agreed in return not to apply further pressure locally pending more negotiations to construct the four 'scale areas' salary structure.

There was much criticism by schoolmasters of the NUT leadership for tolerating the huge fall in real pay which had occurred since pre-war times. By 1919 pay had risen by only 124% against an inflation rate of 212%. The NUT claimed it had to strike a balance between sacrificing EP and retaining national negotiations. Naturally that cut little ice with men teachers.

Following very vocal, almost violent demonstrations in London led by irate schoolmasters, the LCC decided in July 1919 to make a special 'bonus' payment of £30 to its men and £22 10s. to its women teachers. That failed to quieten the rebellious men.

London teachers and the LCC employers themselves pressed for an early decision on the Scale 4 Area. The LCC anticipated the emerging Scale 4 Area payment, putting it into effect by 1 April 1920, thereby escaping the misfortune that was to overtake the other Scale Areas.

The Second Burnham Report emerged on 20 September 1920, containing Scale Areas 2, 3 and 4. In December the exercise was completed when Scale 1 replaced the National Provisional Minimum and was applied to rural areas. Scales 2 and 3 were reserved respectively for small and large towns. However, LEAs were given the discretion to choose which scale they adopted whatever their real character, except that Scale 4 was reserved exclusively for LEAs in the MPD (Metropolitan Police District) of London.

The Burnham Report of 1920 recommended, however, that the new scales should be implemented from 1 April 1921 in three equal and annual instalments (or 'carry-overs' as they were termed). London had already fully implemented Scale 4 on its own decision. The original Burnham Scales were thus:

Certificated two-year trained teachers' annual salaries

	Men		Women	
	£		£	
Areas	Min	Max	Min	Max
Scale 1	172½	325	160	260
Scale 2	172½	340	160	272
Scale 3	182½	380	170	304
Scale 4	200	425	187½	340

All scales consisted of ten annual increments of £12½.

However, the 'instalments' were overtaken by events. The Geddes Committee on Public Expenditure was set up in May 1921 by the Chancellor of the Exchequer, Sir Robert Horne. He demanded restrictions on public expenditure and the first suggested figure of £75m was not enough. A sum of £180m was required. A Government Minister with a background in business, Sir Eric Geddes, was appointed to carry out the job, under the pretext of an independent inquiry.

The Geddes Committee reported in December 1921. Sir Eric duly recommended swingeing cuts including £18m from education. The Bank of England vote for education had grown from £19m to £50m since 1918-19. Geddes also recommended teachers should pay a 5% superannuation contribution, having just a few years previously been granted a non-contributory scheme like that for civil servants. Geddes recommended that Government should keep out of teachers' salaries, merely telling LEAs how much money was available for the purpose and leaving it up to them. In effect Geddes recommended the abolition of the Burnham Committee. The 'Geddes Axe' resulted in no teacher outside London receiving the new scales in full.

In stark contrast to governments' willingness to enforce cuts in teachers' existing salaries the NUT-dominated Teachers' Panel had agreed that the period of 'abstention of pressure on LEAs' should be extended until 31 March 1925, a standstill of four years.

This agreement 'to abstain from pressure' also exempted the LEAs from any requirement to carry out their side of the bargain. Some LEAs failed to adopt any higher scale and continued on the old National Provisional Minimum. Others adopted clearly inappropriate scales, for example Southampton deeming itself a 'rural area' (Scale 1).

In October 1922 the tottering Lloyd George Coalition Government finally fell. By the end of 1922 the NUT was in a state of panic and capitulated to threats in 'agreeing' to a "temporary voluntary abatement of salaries" of 5% for 1923-24, coming into effect 1 April 1923.

Harry Meigh cites examples of some LEAs responding to schoolmasters' pressure by offering different Area Scale payments for men and women. Whilst perhaps a neat solution to one problem it was an inappropriate use of the Scale Area concept. Liverpool, Bootle, Birkenhead, Swansea and Croydon offered to adopt one scale for men and another for women but were prevented from doing so by NUT opposition. They adopted the lower scale for both.

The new scales did not enjoy universal implementation by the LEAs for some time. As late as 1925 there were still 40 LEAs not fully accepting them. It was not until 1925 that Burnham recommended which of the scales each LEA should adopt, thereby bringing all of them into line. By that time the scales had been butchered by the Geddes Axe.

The First Burnham Report completed in 1920 was due for a four-year duration. Despite all the (successful) pressure from Government and LEAs for the teachers to accept cuts, there was not the slightest hint of moves in the other direction from the NUT. Indeed the 'temporary abatement' continued by agreement for 1924-25. In 1925, after more skulduggery on the part of Government, the 'temporary' teachers' 5% pension contribution was made permanent by legislation.

According to Harry Meigh men teachers were "dissatisfied and disillusioned" with the results of national bargaining. He also believed that whilst some women teachers were "quite pleased", others "deplored the failure to obtain equal pay" despite the NUT claiming some progress had been made in diminishing the gender differential.

The employers conceded the scales and increases had little to do with the cost of living. During the period of negotiation the cost of living (based on 1914 being 100) had risen from 250 to 266 in the continuing post-war inflation. However, the average increase in (all teachers') salaries was 138% over 1914.

In any event the base salary in 1914 was over ten years old and then already regarded as disgracefully low. Figures quoted by Fisher in November 1920 claimed that teachers' salaries should have been raised by 164% to keep pace with the cost of living, whereas they had only risen by 138%. "The teachers complain, therefore, and not without justice, that even with these great additions . . . they are no better off, and, in fact, some degrees worse off, than . . . before the war; [when], as I think everybody recognises, the teaching profession was underpaid."

The employers gave teachers two choices: first, high current salaries but falling when and if prices fell; second, scales based on normal prices, which would not be altered at least for a number of years. The teachers chose the second. Provision was made to reconsider salaries if the cost of living index were to rise to 270 and remain there for at least six months. There was no provision made for a fall in prices because the scales were designed for an index of 150. Lord Burnham, the independent Chairman of the Committee, said in 1922: "The scales were undoubtedly fixed as standards with the knowledge that they would be of greater value with falling prices". That was confirmed by F.J. Leslie, Secretary to the Management Panel, who said at the same time: "What we had in our minds was to base our scales on an amount 50% above pre-war prices."

At no time within the next ten years did the index fall as low as 150. However, to the disgust of schoolmasters, that did not stop Government and LEAs from demanding cuts from the time of the Geddes Axe and afterwards.

So in 1925 the time arrived to review the First Burnham Scales. There was no question of an increase. Quite the reverse. The LEAs and Government were determined to see a reduction in teachers' salaries. The LEAs' 'bidding' started at a 15% reduction, coming down firstly to 12½% and then to 10%. To its credit the NUT refused to accept any reduction. However, it was agreed to refer the matter for arbitration to Lord Burnham, Chairman of the Committee to which he gave his name.

Lord Burnham's decision was to impose a cut of 4%. To give a couple of examples, Scale 3 maximum came down from £380 to £366 and Scale 4 from £425 to £408 for men. The women's increment was reduced to £9 per annum.

The NAS was disgusted with the entire outcome and called for a vigorous campaign of action against the cuts. The NUT, showing no interest in taking action, seemed more preoccupied with equality for its own sake as its 1925 Conference deplored "the lowering of the status of women teachers by the change of increment to £9". NUT GS F.W. Goldstone identified that issue as the Union's main preoccupation.

The new scales were to last for six years, until 1931. They were also now subject to 5% deduction for pension contributions. The cost of living index for December 1924 was 180, still significantly above the 150 level upon which the First Burnham Scales had been based.

The period 1925-31 seemed to be one of inactivity on teachers' salaries. It appeared nothing could be done to improve the situation. The country was in the middle of an economic slump amidst a worldwide recession made doubly worse by the disastrously deflationary decision to revert to the gold standard in 1925 taken by Winston Churchill, Chancellor of the Exchequer from 1924 to 1929. The decision was reversed in 1931, but not before it had inflicted huge damage on the British economy.

However, more cuts in public expenditure surfaced in 1931 following the pattern set ten years earlier. The Chancellor of the Exchequer, Philip Snowden, called for a restriction in national expenditure. The economic depression was spreading, markets were falling, unemployment was rising and a financial crisis seemed inevitable. Such cuts only made the depression worse as they were another deflationary device, whereas the very opposite was required, as pointed out by the famous economist John Maynard, later Lord, Keynes.

Chapter 21 - Cuts Upon Cuts
The 1930s

Negotiations were due to have started in 1930 to implement revised scales to be effective from 1 April 1931. Rather than the Teachers' Panel claiming pay increases, the Management put in for a reduction in salaries, citing declining markets and falling prices. To its credit the NUT-dominated Teachers' Panel refused to accept a reduction, and, no doubt in the light of experience six years before, also declined to accept arbitration. Deadlock ensued. The Burnham Committee ceased to function, once again establishing that it was a body subservient to central government and the Treasury.

However, that did not stop the Government in its tracks. On 11 February 1931 the House of Commons passed a resolution (by a staggering majority of 468 votes against only 21) demanding that "a small and independent committee should be appointed to recommend all practicable and legitimate reductions of national expenditure consistent with the efficiency of the services". It had all the hallmarks of a stitch-up, probably originated by the Government itself. A committee was duly set up. As for 'independent', the Chairman appointed was a businessman, none other than the Chairman of the Prudential Insurance Company, Sir George May. It was Geddes Mark 2.

Although the May Report was known to the Government by mid-July it was not published until the middle of the school holidays on 12 August. Teachers allegedly were shaken out of their deckchairs on the seafronts of Britain as they were confronted with newspaper headlines: "Teachers' Salaries Should Be Cut by 30%".

The 30%-cut headline was part of a softening-up process. Despite having been denied the principle of salary increases to compensate for previous inflation, teachers were soon to find May and the Government embracing the other side of the coin by justifying reductions on the basis of deflation. The May Report went on to acknowledge the difficulty of imposing so big a cut, that it graciously concluded that taking everything into account and balancing the interests of the teachers, tax- and ratepayers a 20% minimum reduction should be made.

May's main justification lay in the claim that falling prices had doubled the pre-war (i.e. 1913) purchasing power. That was untrue. The index of prices had fallen back to 119.5 in 1930, still above the 1914 base of 100. The reader may recall the pre-war average salary was a miserable £97 p.a. That was regarded as a suitable reference point for May some 17 years later despite Fisher having conceded the levels of 1914 were already ten years out of date and the first Burnham settlement should have been substantially higher. Furthermore, since 1920, teachers' salaries had subsequently been cut twice by amounts of 5% each time, not to mention the compulsory 5% contribution levied for pensions. Income tax had also been levied and increased since the First World War, depressing take-home pay even more.

May strayed from his terms of reference as a "Committee on National Expenditure" into pay comparability. Besides the "sacrifices necessitated by national financial stringency", salary cuts were also a way "to re-establish fair relativities over the field of Government and local service and with wage earners generally". Support for the principle of comparability was absent from Government and employers when the logic pointed in the opposite direction.

The NAS treated Government soothing talk of 'temporary' cuts with derision in the light of recent experience in the 1920s. Even more infuriating for the NAS was the Government's slogan of Equality of Sacrifice, for no other group was singled out for such savage cuts in pay. Teachers' nearest 'comparator', local Government administrative and clerical grades, were being subjected to cuts of between 4% and 5%.

'May' and all that followed poisoned relationships between teachers, their employers and Governments for years to come, arguably perhaps for the rest of the twentieth century. The generation of young NAS activists of the 1930s who were to become the mentors of my cohort inevitably passed on that culture of suspicion together with the need to stand and fight militantly for the teacher's cause.

May also recommended that Government grant to LEAs in respect of teachers' salaries should be reduced from 60% to 50%, banging in the final nail in the coffin of H.A.L. Fisher's heroic attempts to improve the status and conditions of the profession.

Within a few days of publication of the May Report (12 August) the Labour Government was in the throes of collapse. Prominent members of the Government and backbenchers had repudiated the Report. It was unlikely to secure majority support amongst Labour MPs. On 23 August Labour fell from power and was replaced by a Coalition National Government, predominantly composed of Conservatives, but still led by Ramsay MacDonald, inflicting a wound on the Labour Party which is still felt to the present day.

The first task of the new Government was to introduce the National Economy Bill, scheduled for its first reading on 11 September. The NAS was already preparing to fight, the 11 September Parliamentary event serving as an obvious focus. Earlier in 1931 in response to the LEA employers' demand for a

10% reduction, the NAS had published its pamphlet *Memorandum on Schoolmasters' Salaries*. This was widely circulated and served as the rationale for members to set about yet another massive lobby. Ministers, MPs, local councillors and their representatives on the Burnham Committee were all approached by the relevant NAS leaders and members. As well as the President of the Board of Education, the Chancellor of the Exchequer and the Chairman of Burnham were both interviewed.

If there were ever any doubt that 'May' was 'Geddes Mark 2', it was surely removed by the former quoting the latter to remind everyone that most teachers had "acquired their qualifications at the expense of the public at an average cost to the State of £70 a year for either two or four years". Teachers had seen it all before: cuts, 'voluntary' abatement of salaries and promises broken over enforced pension contributions.

As the day approached for the first reading in the House of Commons of the National Economy Bill, on 11 September, many MPs had already repudiated the 20% proposed cut. By 9 September the Government had reduced the proposed cut to 15%, faced with the outrage of the entire teaching profession.

Whilst also protesting against the reduced Government grant for teachers' salaries, the Association of Education Committees (AEC) wrote to the Prime Minister disowning any responsibility for the cut, which in the opinion of its Executive was "unduly severe". The cut should be of the shortest possible duration and should be reviewed no later than 31 March 1933. The AEC also argued for the preservation of teachers' pension rights in a similar manner to that being applied to the police.

NAS members demanded action from their Executive, with the strongest stirrings coming from London. LSA members were led by their NEM and Honorary GS Frank Gibbs, a man held in huge regard by his contemporaries. Two of my predecessors as LSA GS, Ron Simons and Eddie Chandler, always spoke in glowing terms of Frank. In his book *Schoolmasters' Salaries* Harry Meigh describes Frank Gibbs "taking occasion by the hand" in 1931 and whose leadership "shone through as a beacon". Frank called a meeting in London for Tuesday 8 September, a few days before the second reading of the National Economy Bill.

Over 2,000 members showed up at Kingsway Hall. In public session they declared their bitter opposition to the Bill. In private session they were "electrified", as Ron Simons describes it, by a fiery speech from Frank Gibbs. He proposed a march and mass meeting of all schoolmasters, irrespective of union affiliation, on Friday of the same week, 11 September, the day chosen for the second reading of the Bill. Furthermore, Frank proposed a ban on all extraneous, out-of-school, voluntary activities for the period 1 October to 31 December. Frank Gibbs' proposals were unanimously adopted by the meeting.

Newspaper headlines the following day (Wednesday 9 September) reflected the anger felt in the profession. "Teachers in an 'Ugly' Mood", "Working to Rule", "Refusal to take Part in Boys' Sport and Games" and "Schoolmasters to Resist" were typical.

The Daily Herald, championing the teacher's cause, reported that letters to the editor on the proposed cuts "dominated the huge protest postbag". Figures were bandied about, showing that minimum annual pay for teachers would fall below that paid to road repairers, £154 14s., and road sweepers, £140 8s.

The urbane President of the Board of Education, the Liberal Sir Donald Maclean, stated to the House of Commons that the position on teachers' salaries should be reviewed "on its merits when the financial position improved". He drew laughter from the House when, responding to a question from a Labour MP on whether the Government would make the first move, he said: "Any Government may safely rely on the initiative being taken by the teacher organisations."

Despite the incredibly short notice some 5,000 schoolmasters from London and the extra-metropolitan areas turned up on the Friday. Many were obviously not NAS members. They assembled at the Blackfriars end of the Embankment. Office workers leaving their work lined the streets to watch this curious but impressive demonstration.

The Daily Herald reported on 12 September:

"Three quarters of a mile long, four deep, 5,000 strong, a procession of teachers marched through London last night to a Kingsway Hall meeting of protest against the proposed 15 per cent cut in their salaries.

"Traffic was held up for twenty minutes while they crossed the Strand. Unable to gain admission to the hall, 3,000 of the demonstrators, escorted by police, marched to an overflow meeting at the Conway Hall, Bloomsbury, thereby dislocating more traffic." Police had to be called to bar entry to both halls after they had filled up.

"It was the most remarkable demonstration of its kind that London has seen for some years. The disorganisation of traffic was as complete as at a Lord Mayor's Show."

The NAS President, A. L. Shires from Leeds, shuttled by taxi between the meetings to address the demonstrators. NAS GS Arthur Warren declared that: "The confidence of 200,000 teachers throughout the country in their national leaders was gone." He pledged the NAS "to use every legitimate means to combat this grave injustice".

Another 5,000 teachers attended a protest meeting organised by the NUT, at Central Hall Westminster. Instead of pulling together, the NUT President, Angus Roberts, sanctimoniously criticised the LSA's decision to ban extraneous duties. Mr Roberts believed that "as a profession we should put the children first and guard their development", adding "we should not declare war on the children". Another NUT spokesman was quoted: "The march by London Schoolmasters was not organised by the LTA [whose] leaders were busy with other and more effective work." The NAS march had raised the public profile of the teachers' case like nothing before.

Predictably parts of the media turned on the LSA and criticised its "drastic step" to cut all sports and other voluntary activities outside school hours. Many London school sports associations were run by NAS members in their own time and at their own financial cost. They came to an abrupt halt as many activities and events were cancelled.

The Daily Express condemned the LSA action, even though it was only planned to last from 1 October until the end of the year. The newspaper declared it "foolish and misguided", calling upon other teachers to force the LSA to withdraw "from a position of such little dignity and public spirit". Frank Gibbs wrote a stinging rebuke to the editor which was published the following day (19 September). Describing the 15% cut as "a rank, gross injustice and a complete violation of the principle of equal sacrifice for all", Frank pointed to the voluntary nature of the work for which schoolmasters received neither pay nor expenses. "Schoolmasters would not dream of telling the editor of a newspaper how he must spend his leisure time. They certainly will not accept such dictation from an editor."

The Express might have been encouraged by Angus Roberts of the NUT returning to the fray and declaring the schoolmasters "totally out of harmony with [and] not in any way connected to the NUT". Mr Roberts seemed in no doubt that the NUT was an educational lobby first and foremost and not a union: "It has always been the boast of the NUT that we have put the child first, and have cared for its development."

That was a crucial statement, delineating a fundamental difference from the NAS. The implication was never lost on Governments. As many NAS spokesmen said at the time, the teachers were being treated in this outrageous way "because their salaries were easily accessible". The NUT President had by implication declared they would always succumb to the moral blackmail. NAS members believed the lack of effective action damaged children even more in the longer run but we never denied we were acting out of self-interest. The patronising and sanctimonious attitude of the NUT leadership, aiding and abetting the impoverishment of the teaching profession, was despised by the NAS membership.

The political pressure generated paid some dividend as ten days later on 21 September the Prime Minister informed the House of Commons that the cut in teachers' salaries would not be more than 10%. That was enough to placate the NUT, which gave it a "guarded welcome". The NAS remained adamantly opposed to any cut. Frank Gibbs declared that despite the "less penally drastic cut", the LSA would still "bitterly resent and resist their selection as a class to bear special burdens".

The cut was duly imposed by Order in Council as from 1 October 1931 and persisted in full until 30 June 1934 and did not completely disappear until one year later. The reductions were applied to the 1925 arbitrated salaries, themselves twice reduced by cuts of 5%. The Burnham Committee was simply swept aside by the Order in Council, although it met on 20 November 1931 to go through the formality apparently required to endorse the reduced salaries for another period of time, to 31 March 1933.

Schoolmasters' salaries for Scales 4, 3 and 2 had thus moved as follows from 1919/20 to 1934:

	£ s.	£ s.	
Scale 4	Min	Max	
First Burnham 1919	200	425	(18 yrs)
1925 Arbitral Award	192	408	(19 yrs)
1931-34 10% cut	172	367-4	(19 yrs)
Scale 3			
Second Burnham 1920	182-10	380	(17 yrs)
1925 Arbitral Award	180	366	(18 yrs)
1931-34 10% cut	162	329-8	(18 yrs)
Scale 2			
Second Burnham 1920	172	340	(17 yrs)
1925 Arbitral Award	168	330	(18 yrs)
1931-34 10% cut	151-4	297	(18 yrs)

1925- and 1931-determined salaries were subject also to 5% contribution to pension. Although the rampant inflation immediately after the First World War had abated, prices in 1934 were still above those of 1919.

NAS members continued to object to the 10% cut and organised more mass protest meetings. The NAS, unlike the NUT, never 'accepted' the cuts of 1931 and never gave up trying to get them restored. Whilst no breakthrough was achieved before 1934, every effort was made on all possible occasions to right this gross injustice. That included the LSA promoting petitions and trying to secure joint campaigns with other unions in London, which were always boycotted by the NUT. A strong and successful campaign was launched against two more cost-cutting committees set up in 1932 by the Chancellor and chaired by two Conservative politicians, MP Sir William Ray and LCC Leader Sir Gervais Rentoul, whose predictable recommendations were left not implemented.

The Burnham Committee met on 10 March 1933 and obeyed Government dictat, by 'agreeing' – if that is the right word – to freeze teachers' salaries for another two years. The NAS local associations all over the country lobbied their LEAs asking them to pass resolutions calling for the restoration of the cuts. The campaign was quite successful in so far as by the middle of the Autumn Term 36 LEAs had complied.

Unfortunately the premier education authority in the country, the LCC, under the control of the 'Progressives' and 'Municipal Reformers', declined to offer support to the teachers' cause in very provocative circumstances. Soon after the Burnham decision to maintain the cut, the LCC seemed to add insult to injury when at the same meeting it accepted the continuing freeze on teachers' salaries but decided to terminate the 3½% cut that had been imposed upon its administrators, inspectors, clerical staffs, school keepers and cleaners.

The LSA reacted immediately, organising a mass letter-writing campaign to every member of the LCC. In September it was the turn of the LTA (the London NUT) to organise a Memorial on Salaries, as the LSA had previously done. In stark contrast to the LTA, the LSA advised members to sign the Memorial in a good spirit of co-operation. Nearly 20,000 teachers signed that petition.

In October the London Headteachers' Association took the initiative in seeking united action but again the NUT refused to co-operate. Separate deputations were received by the LCC which again refused to call for the restoration of the cuts.

Early in November the Middlesex County Council had decided to restore half of the 10% pay cut, representing the amount it would have to find from its own rates. In those days Burnham was not a statutory binding system on all LEAs. The LSA called upon the LCC to do likewise.

On 28 November (1933) the agenda for the full Council contained in Harry Meigh's estimation a "wishy washy" report from its Teaching Staffs Sub-Committee. Again led by the dynamic Frank Gibbs the LSA called for an 'occupation' of County Hall to coincide with the LCC meeting. The precise nature of the intended occupation remains a mystery. According to some reports the LCC had been warned to expect "a deputation of about 100" to protest against the continuation of their 10% pay cut. In the event thousands of schoolmasters descended upon County Hall.

Acting on last-minute instructions, by 4.45 p.m. thousands of teachers, including many LTA colleagues of the LSA members, had crowded out the vestibule and corridors of County Hall. Press reports variously estimated the crowd to be between "over 2,000" and "more than 4,000". The place was so full to overflowing that reserve police had to be called in to bar the door to hundreds of late arrivals.

The headlines the following day were dramatic:

The Daily Express:

"2,000 Schoolmasters Raid LCC Meeting

Surging Crowd at Locked Gates

Police Called to Pay-Cut Debate

Amazing Scenes at the County Hall"

The Daily Sketch:

"Teachers Raid County Hall

Police Guard Entrances After 'Let's Jump the Gates!' Cry"

The Daily Herald:

"Teachers Demanding 'Justice' Invade LCC"

The Daily Mirror:

"Teachers in Uproar

4,000 Demonstrate at LCC Meeting"

The Daily Telegraph:

"Teachers' Pay Cut Protest

3,000 Invade County Hall

Doors Locked and Guarded"

The Evening Chronicle:

"LCC Besieged by Teachers"

Only *The Times* exercised any restraint:

"Teachers and the Cuts

Give us back our Ten Per Cent

Noisy Protest to LCC"

The prize for writing up the event in the most colourful and dramatic fashion must go to Gordon Beckles of *The Daily Express*:

Referring to the "expected 100" Beckles described how: "The authorities became alarmed as the first hundred grew to the first thousand – each man or woman saying 'I want to see my member please'.

"Police whistles blew, constables appeared from nowhere, and the great metal gates at the foot of the grand staircase were hurriedly closed.

"There were two thousand people crowding the corridors and struggling against the gates.

"Anything less like schoolmasters and mistresses I have never seen: it might have been an incident out of the French Revolution, modernised. A storming of the Bastille, by men in bowler hats and women with umbrellas."

To their credit the National Union of Women Teachers had also been demonstrating. According to Beckles, its deputation had been turned away and its members were "gripping the grilled gates of the grand staircase and shrieking at the four policemen behind them".

Beckles continued referring to slogans being shouted and the songs being sung, which included "Tipperary"! "Their yells and singing easily penetrated the council chamber":

"We want Cobb!" (the Chairman of the Education Committee).

"Justice".

"Break down the gates".

"The mob hysteria was at its height when the little Welsh leader [the LSA President Haydn Davies] sprang before the gates and spread his arms dramatically apart, for all the world like a shock-headed Danton."

To refrains of "soft soap" Haydn Davies appealed for calm whilst a meeting was hurriedly arranged. The Chairman refused to receive a deputation in full Council, arguing that was unprecedented, but he did agree to leave the Chair to meet the leaders of the LSA. But the 'no action report' from the Teaching Staffs Sub-Committee was carried. Opposition leaders, including Labour's Herbert Morrison – then rising to prominence – unsuccessfully moved a motion calling for the LCC "to welcome the return of the 'cuts' in teachers' salaries".

The LCC was not to join the 36 LEAs, including some of the largest in the country, which had already carried similar motions.

When the thousands of teachers at County Hall heard of the LCC decision they bayed, "We want [Sir William] Ray!" Somehow Haydn Davies, LSA President, persuaded his members to disperse in orderly fashion and return home.

The Daily Express – whose reporter was in the middle of the occupation and ended up being very well briefed by LSA members whether he liked it or not – in its editorial condemned the LCC Municipal Reformers "for holding back the hands of the clock". But, the editorial continued: "You cannot hold back the municipal elections next spring. You will have to face the charge that you restored the pay of the cleaners of your schools but not of the teachers, that you took pity on the sweepers of your streets but refused it to the instructors of your children."

Again in sanctimonious mode, if also somewhat sour, Walter Bentcliffe, a former Treasurer of the NUT, described the demonstration as "futile and undignified" and "he was glad that neither the LTA nor the NUT had anything to do with it".

How wrong he was. On 8 March the following year in the LCC elections the Municipal Reformers and Progressives suffered heavy losses and Labour gained control of the LCC. On 23 March the Education Committee, followed by the full Council on the 27th of the same month, carried strongly worded resolutions calling for restoration of the cuts.

At its 1934 Conference early in April the NAS again strongly condemned the 10% cut, accused the Government of "leading the profession into the wilderness" and demanded restoration. A couple of weeks later in the Budget of 17 April, the Government announced a restoration of 5% as from 1 July. That was good news but the fight for full restoration continued.

The 1 February 1935 meeting of the Burnham Committee decided to peg teachers' salaries at existing levels for a further year. The NAS continued to lobby at local and national levels to persuade LEAs to restore the second half of the cut. In April 1935 the Government finally conceded the restoration of the second half of the cut. It would be included in the May Budget although implementation would be delayed until 1 July.

'Hostilities' seemed then to abate but much bitterness had been sown. Speaking at the NAS Swansea Conference of 1935 Frank Gibbs, who had played such a prominent role in the protests over the previous few years, summed up the mood of the NAS when he said that he felt "as grateful as a man who has suffered three and half years punishment for a crime he did not commit and is graciously given a free pardon".

The NAS was acutely aware that the campaign for restoration of the cuts had finally been won but such 'success' merely restored salaries fixed in 1925 on an outdated base.

Furthermore, Government grants had been reduced (to 50% of relevant expenditure). The threats of 'Ray and Rentoul' were still in the background. The Burnham Committee was due to resume negotiations in the autumn and the NUT would press hard for equal pay.

There was bad news on the pensions front. The first report of the Government's Actuary on the Teachers' Superannuation Account (for the period up to 31 March 1934) was published on 18 April 1935 and recommended that teachers' contributions should be raised to 6%. Newspaper headlines screamed: "Teachers' Pensions Ten Millions in the Red".

Strangely a kind of exhausted peace seemed to develop over the teaching profession. Perhaps the looming crisis over Nazi Germany focussed minds elsewhere. Perhaps politicians were wary of imposing more sacrifices upon teachers and provoking them yet again into protest. Teachers seemed placated by the 'hostile' pensions report of the Government Actuary, together with those by Ray and Rentoul, being quietly pigeonholed.

Although public and press opinion showed widespread and strong belief that teachers were seriously underpaid, they did not appear ready to press a vigorous campaign forward in the fraught economic circumstances of the 1930s. The Conferences of the NAS for the second half of the 1930s did not focus on hard, specific salary claims but merely reiterated its policy of separate consideration for men teachers.

Unemployment was approaching its height, around the 2 million mark. Young teachers bore the brunt of unemployment in the profession, with many LEAs cutting back on recruitment even though there was clearly a shortage of teachers when compared to the number of large classes above 40 pupils, let alone the number exceeding 30.

After the restoration of the cuts the Burnham round of negotiations for April 1936 only produced one significant change, the elimination of Scale 1. Although the 1936 scales were due for revision on 1 April 1939, no one dared to submit a claim in the fraught circumstances prevailing. Harry Meigh describes an "apathy seizing the profession" even though "the majority of men did not know how good a case they had, and could not bother to find out". He added: "It is easy enough to show that conditions were not favourable for a salary campaign – but they never are!"

By the outbreak of war in September 1939 teachers' salaries bore a marked resemblance to those of 1919. Taken in the round, teachers had been paid salaries based on half their purchasing power in 1914, twice reduced by amounts of 5% in the 1920s, subjected to a 5% deduction for pensions and subject to another 10% cut in 1931 (the last mentioned only restored in stages in 1934 and 1935). Income tax was also levied post-1914. The only alleviation of this incredible state of affairs was an overall 30% drop in the cost of living during the Great Depression.

Chapter 22 - Salaries during the Second World War

Enlistment for military service and the evacuation of children and some of their teachers from large towns and cities at the beginning of the war resulted in over 60% of NAS members being displaced.

The NAS tried to raise concerns over the extra costs of running two places of abode for the married schoolmaster with a family. Their treatment was appalling in its discrimination and nature. They received a billeting allowance of only five shillings per week. Civil servants were awarded 21 shillings. Government tried to justify this discrimination on the grounds that for teachers evacuation was voluntarily; for civil servants it was compulsory. Some teachers were charged much more than the five shillings for their board, on occasions as much as £2 or £3 per week.

Teachers were finally offered better billeting expenses similar to the civil service scheme but the NUT rejected the proposal in favour of war allowances. Those favoured unmarried women teachers who constituted the majority of the profession. The NAS saw it as outrageous that billeting allowances should be treated as salary and therefore susceptible to NUT manipulation towards EP by the back door. The NAS belief in the need for separate unions, already strong, was further strengthened.

Teachers proved reluctant 'to stir the salaries pot' after the restoration of the cuts in 1935. War broke out in 1939 and by the end of 1940 it was rapidly becoming obvious that many other occupational groups harboured no such reluctance to protect their financial interests, notwithstanding the war.

By the end of 1940 wages were rising rapidly, and the cost of living had risen by 20% since the declaration of war. In February 1940 the NAS, still denied membership of Burnham, went in deputation directly to the President of the Board of Education to argue the case for schoolmasters' salaries to be increased. Much sympathy and understanding were forthcoming but nothing else.

Burnham did not meet until July of 1940. The NUT pressed for a flat-rate war bonus, the NAS believing that was done to achieve a further step towards EP. The LEAs refused to concede the case. The result was a compromise on the principles at an extremely low overall level.

A cap was effectively put on the award. It was 6% of salary up to £260 p.a., with that sum being the maximum payable to anyone. Teachers who already earned £260 plus 6% or more received nothing, despite the 20% rise in the cost of living. The result was that very few schoolmasters received anything at all whilst most women teachers benefited. The Board of Education took until October 1940 to approve the deal, which was backdated to 1 April. The award compared very unfavourably with other war bonuses, particularly in the civil service.

By March 1941 the cost of living stood at 127 based on 100 at the start of the war. The NUT pressed again for a flat-rate increase, which the employers refused to concede. The result was a new bonus of £26 for men and £19 10s. for women on salaries exceeding £262 10s. but below £370, with a tapering at the two limits. From 1 September that year the ceiling was raised to £525. Once again the Board of Education seemed to have reservations, for approval was not forthcoming until February 1942, although the award was backdated to 1 April 1941.

In June 1942 Burnham met again to consider a third war bonus. The NUT claimed a flat-rate bonus of £52, representing a round figure of £1 per week. The employers rejected the claim and this time negotiations broke down. The matter was referred to the Chairman of Burnham, Lord Soulbury (who also gave his name to another local authority negotiating committee). Soulbury awarded £45 for men and £36 for women teachers over the age of 21 in receipt of salaries up to £262 10s. Teachers with salaries between £262 10s. and £525 received £35 for men and £36 for women. This award became effective on the day it was published, 1 July 1942.

The fourth and final war bonus negotiations began in October 1943. Predictably the NUT claimed a flat-rate increase, 30 shillings per week for all teachers, irrespective of gender and basic salary. The LEA's customary refusal led to another breakdown with a second reference to arbitration. Lord Soulbury awarded teachers under 21 years of age £32 (men) and £26 (women), while those older received £52 (men) and £42 (women) irrespective of basic salary, and the £525 ceiling was abolished.

The NAS felt embittered with the war bonuses. At no time did they compensate for the increased cost of living. The men's final war bonus brought the increase overall to 14.2% at the maximum of Scale 3. The March 1945 cost of living index (1939 100) had reached 154. The schoolmaster's war bonus compared unfavourably with other public sector awards.

The NUT had used war bonuses to pursue its goal of EP pay. This reaffirmed the belief of NAS members that EP, if it were secured, would be on the basis of reducing men's salaries to those paid to the women. Women would win the principle, but not the money.

Significant changes were soon to take place. Two years before war ended the Teachers' Panel (in April 1943) served the required one year's notice to terminate the current Burnham agreement with effect from 1 April 1944.

Putting EP to the forefront the NUT declared: "The salaries of teachers should depend on qualifications, length of service and special responsibility and not on the sex of the teacher or the type of school or the area in which the service is rendered." However, in practice the NUT usually ditched length of service as a guiding principle in favour of flat-rate claims. A permanent role for 'qualifications' beyond the entry point was questionable and the 'responsibilities' were often not very 'special', to put it mildly. The LEAs remained opposed to EP.

Consideration of new scales was deferred pending the outcome of the Government's plans for post-war educational reconstruction. In March 1942 Rab Butler, then President of the Board of Education, set up a departmental committee under the chairmanship of Sir Arnold McNair, Vice-Chancellor of the University of Liverpool. Its terms of reference were to consider the 'recruitment and training of teachers and youth leaders'.

The Report that emerged bearing the name of its Chairman was supposed to be read as part of the Government's plans in its 1943 White Paper on educational reconstruction. Unfortunately the four criteria the Report espoused for the determination of teachers' salaries were largely ignored in practice. There were four 'tests' put forward: personal need; the market; the professional; and educational.

The McNair Report stated bluntly that teachers' salaries were "demonstrably inadequate" and should be "substantially increased". The four helpful criteria laid down by McNair were ignored by the NUT in favour of EP. Unfortunately the NUT lacked the resolve to ensure teachers' pay kept pace with inflation, let alone to summon the courage needed to challenge the market forces and secure EP at reasonable levels for all.

A storm blew up in Parliament over the initial success but subsequent failure of the Conservative MP Thelma Cazalet-Keir's 'equal pay' amendment to the 1944 Education Bill in March of that year. Soon afterwards, however, a Royal Commission on Equal Pay was established. It first met on 17 October 1944 and published its report two years later in November 1946.

The Royal Commission's terms of reference had been cast in wide-ranging mode, asking it to report on all aspects, including the social, economic and financial implications, of EP. Unlike the Burnham arrangements, the NAS had a voice and presented oral and written evidence to the Commission. The Commission had not been asked to make specific recommendations but the general tenor of the Report in the view of the NAS did not come down in favour of EP.

At its 1944 NAS Conference at Blackpool the Association adopted a comprehensive report on salary policy, proposing two scales, one for the

Metropolitan Area and another for the Provinces. The 1938 Burnham Secondary Scales were taken as the base from which to argue for a radical new assessment of teachers' pay requirements.

By the time of the next Burnham Award in 1945 the Committee had been placed on a statutory basis by the 1944 Education Act. Section 89 of the Act clearly required the Committee "to submit such scales of remuneration as they consider suitable" to the Minister. The Minister had the ultimate power, subject to some Parliamentary checks. In addition to the power as described in law, the Government also wielded considerable influence through holding the major part of the purse strings. Once again the NAS seemed to be alone in criticising the constitutional aspects of Burnham, which clearly belied the damaging pretence that it was a genuine free-standing negotiating body.

One of the most significant structural changes introduced by the 1944 Act (under Section 89) was the merging of the Burnham Primary and Secondary Committees. The educational arguments in favour won over the economic forces which inevitably depressed secondary teachers' pay and hugely influenced the shape of the salary structure. Various devices became necessary to circumvent the obvious difficulties in seeking to treat the primary and secondary labour market forces as if they were one and the same. Despite the opportunities presented by the radical reforming 1944 Act the NAS was again denied representation on Burnham.

Section 89 of the 1944 Act turned Burnham into a compulsory statutory system forcing LEAs to pay their teachers the rates determined   nationally. Although Burnham pre-1944 had been 'voluntary' few LEAs ignored national agreements for fear of losing Government grant. Those were the days of specific, as opposed to the block, grants of later times when 'doing your own thing' would have been very visible.

Both the pre- and post-war systems, despite being national in their different ways, nevertheless embodied certain flexibilities. The pre-war system provided for four different Areas which reflected to some degree the varying 'market conditions', namely rural, small and large towns and the MPD of London. Post-war the Scale Areas were abolished. Within the new, more unified system the LEA employers were given discretion to operate within certain bands of minima and maxima, particularly in respect of promoted posts above the basic scale.

The new Burnham Primary and Secondary Committee met after the passing of the 1944 Act to revise the pay scales. The proposals were published in November. A new basic scale was introduced and was destined to become a shibboleth for the NUT. 'The primacy of the basic scale' was a slogan that rang out from the NUT for at least another 30 years. The separate scale for secondary grammar schools disappeared. The basic scale (combined in time with a system of promoted posts) replaced the old Scales 2, 3 and 4 Area payments and was the same for primary and secondary.

NEW BASIC SCALE FOR TWO-YEAR TRAINED TEACHERS 1945

Men	Women
£300 x £15 £525	£270 x £12 £420

To compensate for the obvious differences in the cost of living in the Metropolitan Area, a London Allowance of £36 at the minimum and £48 after 16 years of service or at age 37, the same for men and women, was introduced.

The award took a long time to be approved by the Government, perhaps reflecting once again some reluctance to accept the shape of the new salary structure. The Minister did not sign the new Statutory Order until October 1945, although payment was backdated to 1 April of the same year by special provision of the Order.

As a concept to reflect the 'central importance of the teacher in the classroom' the basic scale possessed enormous potential for good. Unfortunately the fine concept was ruined by the distorted way the NUT sought to implement it. In practice the 'primacy' was never to be attached to the *whole* basic scale but only to the first three or four steps, where the NUT found most of its members. In practice the interests of young short-term teachers, the majority of whom had left the profession within five years of entry, were placed ahead of those who made teaching their lifelong career.

In the words of Harry Meigh who became NAS President 1949-50, the post-war story on salaries is one "of grotesquely inadequate demands by the Teachers' Panel, submitted in a spirit of defeatism, and the acceptance, time after time, of even lower figures than those demanded". For the NAS it was a "story of continuous effort . . . to make MPs, members of LEAs, the Press and the Public aware of the soundness of the case for a considerable improvement in salaries".

For the NAS the key comparator related to the typical salary of the schoolmaster. For this purpose the pre-war Scale 3 (the one for large towns) was the equivalent of the new basic scale. The figures showed an alarming picture. Despite the pay rise in 1945 the salary of the schoolmaster had declined in real (i.e. purchasing power) terms since the start of the war in 1939.

The NAS, along with many other observers, was sceptical about the reliability of the official cost of living index. The official Government figures showed the 1945 index to be 131 based on 100 for 1939. The index was, however, still based on the 1914 expenditure pattern of a manual worker. It was totally out of date, even for the manual worker, in 1945, let alone the salaried 'white collar' workers. *The Economist*, never a bedrock of pro-union opinion, researched the matter and concluded the 1945 index should have been 154. Taking that figure the NAS argued that if Scale 3, previously condemned as "grossly inadequate" by McNair, had been increased by 54% it would have produced a basic scale of:

£277 x £18 £564.

Instead the new basic scale was:

£300 x £15 £525.

It was significant that the minimum had been enhanced by a little more than that required to compensate for inflation. But the maximum had not; indeed it had fallen in real terms.

The Ministry of Labour changed the cost of living index in 1947, introducing a retail price index, RPI. This RPI rose 55% between 1947 and 1956 when it was again renewed and a new baseline set. *The Economist* continued to express doubts and quoted much higher figures it believed reflected the true picture.

Although the LEA employers had resisted the NUT's claim for EP, the practical effect of the 1945 settlement was to be redistributive in favour of the younger teacher, where the 'natural feminine majority' of the teaching profession was even further pronounced. The 1945 settlement took no account of McNair's recommendations that salaries should be substantially increased. Furthermore, income tax had risen from 5½s. in the £ in 1938-39 to 10s. in 1941, staying at that rate for the rest of the war. Schoolmasters' disposable real income had been savaged. The prospect of full EP in such a context positively scared the schoolmasters.

The Joint Four accepted the merger of the Primary and Secondary Burnham Committees without a murmur of protest. They lost their majority voice in the secondary sector. The determining voice on the Teachers' Panel was gifted to the NUT, based on its overall majority which stemmed largely from its predominance in the primary sector.

Ironically the Joint Four, according to the Minister, were represented on Burnham whilst the NAS was denied, precisely because they spoke for a "distinct kind of teacher" – from the grammar schools. Yet these were the teachers who suffered the most serious salary erosion during the war. Eventually the Management set about introducing a system of 'allowances' or 'special responsibility' payments which favoured secondary over primary. The number of such allowances a school was permitted to pay was to be based upon a pupil age weighting system. The older the pupil, the more points gained. Sixth-form students were the most 'valuable'; primary pupils the least. Thereby grammar schools benefited most.

The interests of headteachers, never short of representatives on the NUT Executive and indeed on the Teachers' Panel, were looked after by the provision of their own separate scales.

The basic scale, supposedly the rock upon which teachers' salaries were to be built, soon proved manifestly incapable of serving the needs of the whole profession. It could only be afforded its 'primacy' at the expense of being depressed.

In the view of the NAS a largely inappropriate superstructure of promoted posts was to be developed to compensate for the inadequacy of the basic scale. It exploited the goodwill of staff by effectively 'buying' extra commitment from teachers for relatively little reward. It also served to distort the focus away from the core function of schools, teaching in the classroom, by bestowing 'status' and a little extra pay on those who took on the performance of additional tasks. Only some of those were concerned with teaching and learning, whilst many were purely administrative at best and mundane clerical at worst.

In 'The Battle of Burnham' (section 3) I referred to the Independent MP Sir Graham Little's comments during a debate in the House of Commons in 1945. He could "not understand how the scale which the Burnham Committee have adjudicated can have become possible except that the teachers were not properly represented".

Some key facts spoke for themselves:

Taking 1938 as the base 100:

by 1945, average earnings had risen to 175, the RPI to 149;

the old Scale 3 Area minimum schoolmaster salary had risen to 167 (£180 to £300);

the maximum basic scale for schoolmasters had risen to 143 (£366 to £525).

One can see that only the minimum salary at 167 had 'beaten' the RPI at 149. The maximum for schoolmasters at 143 had lost out to RPI. Both minimum and maximum salaries had fallen badly behind average earnings at 175.

Chapter 23 – Pay after 1945

In the years after the Second World War the scene was set for the great teacher salary debates of the second half of the twentieth century. Equal pay (EP) was settled in principle in 1956. As the fifties gave way to the sixties the NAS and UWT became convinced the answer to the seemingly eternal problem of low pay in the profession lay in the concept of career structured salary scales. Applied equally to men and women the salary structure should better reward the longer contribution and greater experience of those who remained in teaching for a considerable period of time. Over a lifetime of teaching, overall earnings would far outstrip the awards being made to teachers which concentrated the largest percentage increases on the first few steps of the salary scale.

In the opinion of the NAS the NUT-dominated Teachers' Panel had failed lamentably to take advantage of the favourable negotiating context of 1945. The McNair Report was a gift in terms of justification. The cost of living, general wage levels and the salaries of comparable occupational groups had risen significantly during the war. And if those were not enough by way of 'ammunition', there was a substantial shortage of teachers.

After the war the NAS continued the lonely fight for fair salaries and recognition on Burnham. Denied official representation, the NAS was never going to go away but would carry its campaign directly to Ministers, MPs, local councillors, the media, the public and indeed 'onto the streets'.

The post-war decade (1945-55) saw teachers' salaries left in the doldrums. The 1948 Burnham Agreement resulted in an increase of only £30 at the maximum of the scale. The minimum was unchanged. In 1951 (the agreements ran for three years) a flat-rate increase of £75 was secured. Discontent with this meagre settlement produced an interim flat-rate increase of £40 early in 1954, taking the basic scale from £375 (minimum) to £630 (maximum). The 'main' 1954 settlement produced an extra £35 at the minimum and £55 at the maximum. With a profession seething with anger over an unjustified increase in pension contributions, the settlement in 1956 resulted in some compensatory award to restore differentials with an increase of only £35 at the minimum but £175 at the maximum.

The NAS believed the 1948 basic scale should have run from £400 to £800 and campaigned for rejection or arbitration, but at the NUT Special Salaries Conference a defeatist leadership saw off the minority band of 'militants'. The settlement extended the system of allowances (based on pupil age weightings), which would also be used in determining the headteachers' scales. Only headteachers and the 15% of the profession (mostly in the grammar schools) earmarked to receive special allowances ranging from £50 to £150 p.a. were satisfied to some degree.

The graduate secondary schoolmasters suffered the most. Taking 1938 as a base of 100, the minimum salary at £249 moved to 145 by 1948, reaching £360. The maximum salary at £480 moved to 128 at £615. Meanwhile the cost of living had risen to 180 and average earnings to 200. Teachers' salaries were pegged for yet another three years at miserably low levels.

Dissatisfaction with the 1948 award was intense in NAS circles. The 1949 NAS Conference in Bournemouth unanimously decided to claim an immediate bonus of £250 and launched a vigorous campaign in support. The Executive established an Action Committee chaired by the Welsh firebrand and later President and Honorary Treasurer of the NAS, G. Lloyd Williams. The response from the membership was magnificent, resulting in a massive two-year campaign during which the public, press, Parliament and the employers (nationally and locally) were lobbied by the schoolmasters. Many mass meetings were held in 1949 including Liverpool (twice), Bristol, Birmingham, Leeds, Sheffield, Cardiff, Brighton, Newcastle, Sunderland and London (three times), with attendance on all occasions exceeding 1,000 members.

The reaction of the press was generally favourable. Indeed the harshest critic had been the NUT, which described the £250 claim as extravagant. The NUT was galvanised into calling a Burnham meeting, which resulted in the Management agreeing to consult its constituents on offering an extra £75 for men and £60 for women.

Sadly in September 1949, after several years of economic difficulties and whilst LEAs were still deciding their attitude to the Management Panel's suggestions, the Chancellor of the Exchequer, Sir Stafford Cripps, carried out his shattering devaluation of the pound from $4.08 to a new parity of $2.80. The devaluation was also accompanied by a call for a wage freeze in the public and private sectors.

The NAS immediately declared that there was no justification for freezing teachers' pay, which had been given enough of the cold shoulder for far too many years. However, one by one the LEA employers backed off and the NUT soon collapsed, claiming "That no further action could be taken through the machinery of the Burnham Committee". The NUT placed the survival of the Burnham machinery above everything else, even when it failed completely to deliver anything for teachers.

The NAS determined to fight on and approached the Minister of Education, arguing for his intervention under Section 89 of the 1944 Act which entitled him to require the LEAs to recommend "suitable scales". The Minister declined to do so, conveniently hiding behind the customary smokescreen: "Teachers' pay is a matter for the Burnham Committee".

The General Election of 1950 provided another opportunity for the NAS to ensure every Parliamentary candidate was lobbied hard, producing a document on salaries entitled *The Men's Case* in support. The NUT remained cool at best and was sometimes even critical of the NAS campaign. It engaged a Dr Corlett to visit meetings of NUT members to discredit the activities of the NAS. In May 1950 the NAS updated its briefing material with a new Memorandum on Schoolmasters' Salaries for extensive lobbying of employers and politicians following yet another refusal by the Minister to grant the NAS recognition.

Burnham continued to meet in its usual secrecy. The NUT pursued flat-rate claims with mixed success. The NUT demands for EP were constantly rebuffed by Management and Government, including on occasions the Prime Minister and Chancellor of the Exchequer. Burnham agreements continued to have a three-year currency despite rising levels of inflation. The NAS Conference condemned the new scales in strident terms and called for a third-party intervention to circumvent the inadequacy of the Burnham machinery.

In October 1951 Parliament was dissolved and a General Election called. The NAS produced its customary briefing material for members to lobby as many candidates as possible. A new leaflet, *Schoolmasters' Salaries: The case for an immediate revision,* was based on the four criteria so strongly recommended by McNair in 1944 but ignored thereafter. The NAS called for a basic minimum of £550 rising to a maximum of £850. The NAS pressure led to Burnham being recalled but no movement taking place. By 1951, taking the 1938 base of 100, the cost of living had risen to 208%; average earnings to 241%; but schoolmasters' maximum only to 172%. Salary erosion was further ensconced.

The NAS responded promptly with yet another new pamphlet, *The Story of a Raw Deal – during the war and since,* which was published in January 1952 and widely circulated to Parliament, the press, LEAs and of course to members. The lobby was interrupted and suspended on Monday 6 February when the news arrived of the sudden death of King George VI.

In February 1952 the NAS took an innovative step, engaging an outside expert, R.G. Allen, Professor of Statistics at London University. He had become well known for his work in connection with the successful doctors' campaign for improved remuneration. Professor Allen advised the NAS to argue the case from the comparability point of view as well as the cost of living.

The NUT must have been feeling the pressure constantly generated by the ongoing NAS campaign and our refusal 'to go away'. In February 1952 negotiations were reopened and a very modest increase accepted by the NUT despite protests and lobbying by the NAS to fight for a better deal. The settlement did not even compensate for inflation from 1950.

Professor Allen surveyed the longer-term scene going back to 1938. If men teachers' salaries were to be uprated in line with inflation, a ten-point incremental scale would produce a minimum of £600 rising to a maximum of £950. The June 1952 adjustment resulted in a scale of £415-£670.

On 16 May 1952 the Equal Pay Campaign Committee of the civil service organisations and the NUT managed to secure the tabling of a motion in the House of Commons calling for immediate implementation of equality for these two occupational groups.

Apart from the "temporary additions" of £40 and £32, the 1951 Burnham Agreement was on course to run its full three-year term to 1954.

In the lead-up to the 1954 negotiations the NUT Conference made a firm statement on EP but its resolution on salaries was vague. Delegates tried to write in firm commitments to a basic scale of £500-£900. The platform resisted and when one of the Officers suggested they did not want their hands tied "in case we might ask for more" the hall collapsed in derisory laughter!

In contrast the NAS Report on Salaries adopted at its 1953 Conference in Margate was a closely argued and clear-cut statement of aims, with figures to match based on the departmental report of 1918. The NAS became the first teachers' union to call for a basic scale maximum to be at least £1,000 p.a., using Professor Allen's recommended approach. Further updating for inflation and average earnings in the autumn produced a claim for a basic scale to rise from £630 to £1,050. The Association repeated its claim for representation on the Burnham Committee and also called for an annual review of salaries as well as the full subvention of the cost of teachers' pay by the central government.

The negotiations for 1954, beginning the previous summer, still conducted in secrecy, proved to be more of the same. The standstill on London Allowance was particularly infuriating for LSA members who, having suffered more than most through inflation, lobbied and picketed the NUT meetings and Special Conference urging rejection of the offer.

Again the threat of stalemate with no increase at all (given the alleged unavailability of retrospection) served to focus the minds of the 'timid majority' which populated the NUT. The decision went to a card vote but the offer was still accepted by 140,589 to 48,188 votes. Even the normally quiescent Assistant Masters' Association, claiming to represent some 15,000 members, rejected the proposed new scales.

The new scale was therefore to be £450 rising to £725. To the NAS it was crystal clear that the Teachers' Panel did not share the objective of at least restoring teachers' salaries in real terms to the already low levels of 1938.

The LEA employers were making good progress in their strategy of depressing the basic scale but enhancing the allowances or responsibility payments despite the division and discord the 'promotion' system fostered. Furthermore the graduate allowances (£60 per annum and £90 for a good honours degree) were around five times greater than the equivalents in 1939. The basic scale had not been uprated in such a way. By offering a little bit more to relatively few the Management got away with impoverishing the many. Once again the NAS, disgusted at the latest sell-out, resolved to fight on.

The experience of the ATTI in the FE Committee, initially rejecting the same offer made to schoolteachers, but later deciding to accept it, highlighted the lack of provision for retrospection. The NAS supported the ATTI, quoting the precedent of the Order in Council in October 1945 backdating an award to 1 April that year. Pressed in Parliament, the Minister explained that the precedent quoted by the NAS had been implemented without the legal advice of the Crown's law officers.

Some other parts of the public services suffered from the same disadvantage and in 1956 a Bill was to be rushed through Parliament to remove this injustice for police, firefighters and probation officers. The NAS continued to press for backdating to be allowed for teachers, but it was to take until 1965 for this to be achieved.

Despite (in the words of Harry Meigh) the "rampant dissatisfaction" amongst many teachers with the 1954 award, the NUT's principal objective remained securing EP. It targeted the Chancellor, Rab Butler, a very 'liberal' Conservative, who had been Minister of Education at the time of the 1944 Act. On 19 May 1954 he informed the House of Commons that he was discussing the matter with the civil service unions with a view to a phased introduction.

On 25 January 1955 Rab Butler announced in the Commons that he was prepared to accept the recommendation of the Whitley Council on EP in the non-industrial civil service, implementing it in seven equal instalments, for good measure applying the first with a little retrospection to 1 January that year.

The Chancellor of the Exchequer seemed to have been persuaded to drop all his previous stated objections together with those of his predecessors. With the door wide open the NUT made a direct approach to the Chancellor to secure agreement on EP in principle. The opposition of the employers melted away quickly even though the Leader of the Management Panel, Alderman Jackson, had stated as recently as 1954 that the introduction of EP in the civil service would not be followed in the teaching profession. On 4 March 1955 the Burnham Committee met and took very little time to reach agreement to follow the civil service model.

In a last throw of the dice the NAS promptly produced a two-page Memorandum, Equal Pay and the Teaching Profession. It drew on widespread evidence given to, and the conclusions reached by, the Royal Commission on EP in 1946 pointing out the dangers. Referring to the Ministry's own evidence the Commission had concluded: "that a material drop in the number of male teachers is a possibility which cannot be ignored".

The NAS's appeal to history fell on deaf ears. After allowing one month for members to consult their 'constituencies', Burnham reassembled on 4 April to confirm the agreement. There was very little discussion. The first instalment was agreed for 1 May, with the remaining six coming on 1 April in each succeeding year.

The NUT had wisely from its own position sidestepped the opposition of the Management Panel and taken its case directly to the Chancellor and won! In so doing the NUT implicitly endorsed the long-standing criticism of the NAS that Government was the key player and that Burnham was a charade. Burnham was the 'monkey', central Government the 'organ-grinder'!

THE LONDON ALLOWANCE

From 1919 to 1945 the extra cost of living and working in London had been recognised by the exclusive payment of the old Scale 4 Area to teachers serving in LEAs which were either wholly or in part contained within the MPD (Metropolitan Police District).

By 1944 the effective London differential (at the maximum of Scale 4) was £78 higher. Following the abolition of these Area payments in 1945 and the introduction of the basic scale, the new London Allowance was pitched in 1945 at a very low level, only £36 at the minimum, rising to £48 for those on the maximum point or aged 37 or over. Incomprehensibly the London Allowance remained frozen at its 1945 level despite inflation reducing its real value by 30%. Burnham did set up a small tribunal of inquiry in 1951 but it recommended no increase. The London Allowance was not to be increased until 1959.

Chapter 24 - "The Calamity of 1956"
Including the Sunderland Case

The 'Calamity of 1956' remarkably brought together many issues of historical significance for the Association. The Calamity sprung mainly from the Government's proposal to increase teachers' pension contributions from 5% to 6% of salary and the bitter anger this decision provoked throughout the teaching profession. Some pride was salvaged by the successful stand of the NAS against the Sunderland LEA, establishing the right of teachers to decline to perform voluntary 'duties'. They both had implications for teachers' pay, their contract under the law and other conditions of service, the methods of militant action, the school meals service and last and by no means least the reputations of the unions. The NUT's humiliation was self-inflicted. In stark contrast the NAS greatly enhanced its reputation as 'a battling minority', courageously continuing the good fight against the full force of the Government and some hard-nosed employers, notably the Sunderland LEA.

The first sign of the Calamity that was to engulf the teaching profession in 1956 appeared at Easter time 1951 with the publication of the Government Actuary's (GA) Second Report on the Teachers' Superannuation Scheme (TSS) covering the period 1935-48. The Report concluded there was an actuarial deficit of £102m. It recommended that teachers' and employers' contributions be raised to 6%.

There was an eerie silence after the publication of the Report. Nothing was said in Parliament. However, there were fundamental political changes afoot. By autumn of 1951 the Labour Prime Minister Clement Atlee had requested the King to dissolve Parliament and in the subsequent General Election the Conservatives returned to power, albeit on a slender majority of 16 seats, with Winston Churchill again Prime Minister.

Churchill took a long time to appoint his Minister of Education. For the first time since 1931 Education had been relegated to non-Cabinet status, perhaps dissuading more prominent 'candidates' from accepting the portfolio. Eventually the surprise choice was Florence Horsburgh, who was to experience a torrid time as Minister of Education. Teachers feared that perhaps a repetition of 1931 was on the cards, with severe cutbacks in educational expenditure. The Tories had been returned to power amid fears of inflation.

The NAS Executive presented a Report on Pensions to its 1952 Conference which acknowledged the need to take cognisance of the GA's findings that the

TSS was "not paying its way". Even in those early times the Executive realised that something was amiss. The Report observed "that the Actuary had to deal with a set of circumstances which might have obtained if a Pensions Fund had been created. Though advocated, a [real] Fund was never established . . . and the Scheme has run on an annual cash basis. It is also a fact than many more millions of pounds have been paid in by teachers as contributions than have been drawn out as benefits. This state of affairs, so profitable to the Government, will continue, though on a progressively diminishing scale. . ." It did not diminish quickly but continued, getting better and better, until circumstances changed towards the end of the twentieth century.

The Report noted that in 1949 contributions of £10.5m had exceeded benefits paid out by over £1m. The net profit to Government from 1922 to 1948 had been £167m, a staggering sum for those times. The Report ruefully concluded that teachers "were certainly ill advised" to accept a contributory scheme in 1925.

The NAS Report called for improvements including the pension to be based on the average salary for the final five years of service, the introduction of widows and orphans benefits along the same lines as those provided to civil servants and some protection against inflation, such principle having been conceded in limited degree through the 1947 Pensions (Increase) Act.

Shortly before the start of the summer holidays the following year (1952) the teacher associations received a letter from Florence Horsburgh announcing her intention to take very serious note of the GA's Report and conclusions.

The ridiculously low return of 3.5% (albeit notional) interest was becoming more and more acute as rates were improving in the post-war period. The 'rules of the actuarial game' somehow produced deficits despite the 'surplus' of income over expenditure of £167m for the period up to 1948.

To soften these blows some limited improvements were offered, but the NAS reacted swiftly with customary vigour. Following meetings of the Officers in August 1952 and the Executive in September, the issues were taken up with the chief officials at the Ministry together with the GA on 10 October. The NAS deputation pointed out the original intention of the Government for a non-contributory scheme. The civil service scheme remained non-contributory.

Once again the NAS pointed out that the Notional Fund was being treated selectively as a real one and expected to cover not only current expenditure (which it did easily) but future liabilities. It was assumed that the scheme had to be capable of meeting all current liabilities from the day of the valuation without any further contributions. Under questioning from the NAS, the GA admitted that the current combined contribution of 10% of teachers and employers was sufficient to cover all the liabilities for new entrants from 1948.

NAS members regarded it as particularly outrageous that the teachers were being singled out for 'special' treatment. Despite the civil service, the armed services, the police, the nationalised industries and the health service all being run on roughly the same lines as the teachers' scheme, there was no proposal to raise their contributions to meet similarly increasing liabilities for the future. Even the LEA employers were strongly opposed to the legislation despite the subvention they would receive from the rate support grant to help cover the extra costs.

The entire teaching force was seething with anger over the issue. A long and bitter campaign followed in which MPs were lobbied like never before. There was much coverage in the media. The complexities of notional funds and actuarial deficits were difficult to argue for teachers, whereas the 'deficit' of £107m hit home with the general public even if it were not truly understood for the artifice that it was.

Nevertheless, teachers scored well on the Treasury having benefited from the £167m 'profit' and the fact that an increased contribution meant a cut in salaries which were already lagging seriously behind comparable occupations and national average earnings. Many MPs and even some sections of the press were on the teachers' side. *Teachers' World* was particularly forthright in its support of our case.

The strong lobby by the NAS and, it must be said, by other teachers on this occasion, led to the Government back-pedalling. Many Labour MPs were very supportive together with a number of Conservatives who disapproved of the way teachers were being treated. That was telling in the circumstances of the Government's small majority of 16 seats.

Florence Horsburgh retreated and the planned date of 1 April 1953 for the new legislation had to be abandoned. But true to form, the Minister set up a Burnham-style Working Party on which the NAS, despite its strong objections, would be denied representation in the usual way. This brazen sidelining of the NAS fuelled the schoolmasters' anger even more.

Somehow the Government must have found a way to browbeat the LEAs into submission. Thankfully, for a few months at least, the Teachers' Side of the Working Party refused to accept any increase in contributions. But the LEAs capitulated, saying they now regarded the proposal as "reasonable". Their earlier call had been "Not one farthing" more.

One 'detail' is worth noting. The Working Party considered a proposal from the Minister for a scheme for widows and dependants. The LEAs immediately declared themselves uninterested, stating they had no objections but they would pay nothing towards it themselves. The other unions were at best ambivalent about such a scheme. The NAS supported the principle of a scheme for widows and dependants, similar to the civil service.

Meanwhile Burnham was conducting salary negotiations of a particularly difficult nature. Comparative salary levels for teachers had slipped badly behind. The Teachers' Panel was claiming a substantial rise with the NUT also demanding equal pay (EP).

Around the same time as the Superannuation Working Party reported (early 1954), the Burnham Committee reached an appalling settlement (only £35 per annum at the minimum and £55 at the maximum). This poured petrol on the pension flames.

At the end of January 1954 the Minister made a statement to the House and to the press that she intended to implement the Burnham settlement and then introduce a Superannuation Bill giving effect to most of the Working Party's recommendations. Contributions were to rise to 6%. The Bill would also include a widows and dependants scheme, but the cost would be borne by reducing the lump sum and death gratuities, in the case of the former by two-thirds. Once again teachers' resentment was deep. Even the NUT representatives who had sold out on the meagre salary increase rallied against the superannuation proposals.

Again a massive lobby developed of MPs, at Westminster as well as in their constituencies. The NAS was anxious to push for amendment rather than outright opposition to the entire Bill, for if the contribution rate rise could be dropped and the widows scheme amended the Government might be left with something rather than no bill at all. This was the position adopted at the NAS Conference at Porthcawl in 1954.

The teachers' lobby succeeded in turning much opinion, including many Conservatives, against the Government's proposals generally and against Florence Horsburgh in particular. The Bill's date for a second reading had to be postponed until after Easter, the time of the unions' Conferences.

Conservative backbenchers were telling the Minister that they had faced the heaviest lobby and biggest postbag on this issue for years. Florence Horsburgh faced an angry meeting of the 1922 Backbenchers Committee having to resort to making it a vote of confidence. Even so many Tories indicated they would vote against. The Minister was left with no option but to bury the Bill. The postponed second reading never took place. During the summer term rumours of Florence Horsburgh's 'position' were circulating freely. By the end of the summer holidays she had been sacked.

In her place came Sir David Eccles, with a post in the Cabinet as well. Teachers may have rid themselves of a Minister, but not of a Government determined to use them as a soft option in the battle against inflation. Sir David

Eccles was a more accomplished, suave and skilled politician than Florence Horsburgh. Both were very determined but Sir David masked his real intentions better. He did not go directly ahead but bided his time and cultivated support amongst Conservative backbenchers more assiduously than his predecessor Minister had done.

In a carefully planned strategy Sir David was unusually given the job of winding up for the Government on the debate on the Queen's Speech in October 1954. During his speech he 'led the teachers and LEAs on' by indicating he was prepared to scrap the existing superannuation scheme and start again from scratch, ensuring in the process that deficiencies would not recur time and time again. He would invite teachers and LEAs in for consultation. On 15 January the following year Sir David Eccles duly invited the recognised associations of Burnham in for a meeting to start the process. True to form the NAS was again excluded despite all the work it had done on pensions, a subject crucial to its members' interests. However, conceding some ground Sir David agreed to meet with the NAS once concrete proposals had emerged from the consultation.

Early in 1955 came the two cataclysmic announcements on EP for the civil service and teaching. The NUT was naturally ecstatic. The NAS was suspicious. Time soon hinted, albeit without definitive proof, that the EP development may have been linked to other events.

There may have been a wider political 'vote gathering' motive in the Government's moves on EP. Parliament was dissolved for a May General Election. The ageing Sir Winston Churchill had finally been persuaded to resign and Sir Anthony Eden had replaced him as Prime Minister. With the opinion polls favourable, Eden had decided to seek a new mandate and an enhanced Parliamentary majority over and above the rather precarious 16 he had inherited. He succeeded as the Conservative Party was returned to power with a comfortable overall majority of 62.

Teachers were hoping for a new Education Minister but were disappointed to find Sir David Eccles reappointed. Ron Simons wrote in his unpublished book that teachers found Sir David had "an airy blandness that failed to inspire confidence. His method of dealing with problems seemed to be to apply local anaesthetics . . ." rather than seeking fundamental solutions.

Many complain about teachers' long summer holidays but they often proved to be a good time to release bad news. In late July 1955 the Working Group on Teachers' Superannuation for England and Wales issued its Report. Sir David was even courteous enough to send the NAS a copy directly. It was a clever operation. There were no clear recommendations, just factual statements. But the 'facts' were carefully presented to reveal the Government's intentions. The existing actuarial deficiency would be wiped out providing a new self-supporting scheme was evolved.

The 'information' from the GA was highly significant. Previous GA Reports (1935 and 1951) had stated that a combined contribution rate of 10% was sufficient to cover all new entrants' benefits (post-1948). The new Report observed that 11.5% would be required. This was due to increased longevity, some improvements envisaged including changes to the retirement age and higher salary scales.

The NAS could see the writing was on the wall. Furthermore, the Report suggested that more periodic valuations might be appropriate. Eventually quinquennial valuations became the practice. The NAS believed that would merely provide more occasions on which governments could raise contribution rates.

The NAS was intrigued to notice in the appendix to the Report that the main features of nine other public sector superannuation schemes were summarised. In five of those any deficiency was to be met by the employer. No account at all was kept in two other cases. In the remaining two no party was named as being responsible for remedying deficiencies. The Report's silence on this issue was deafening for the NAS. The omens were not good.

On 20 October 1955 the Minister finally showed his hand in publicising a new Superannuation Bill. In essence the proposals were the same as Florence Horsburgh's. Nothing could disguise the proposal to increase contributions to 6%. The minor improvements envisaged paled into insignificance against the higher costs.

The NAS was incensed. Disbelief that the Government could return with such proposals which had led to the downfall of the previous Minister soon gave way to intense anger and a determination to fight against any increase in the contribution rate. The NUT felt embittered, having hailed Sir David as their champion over EP a few months earlier. Now the NUT accused him of betrayal.

The NAS appealed for co-operation amongst all teacher associations to fight against the increased contributions. The NAS met with the Assistant Masters on 12 November and was extremely disappointed to find their colleagues in resigned, defeatist mode, unwilling to contemplate militant action. They would simply register a formal protest, living up to Terry Casey's description of them as "organised timidity".

The NAS again visited the Ministry of Education on 15 November to restate its total opposition to increased contributions but willingness to consider a widows, orphans and dependants scheme.

A few days later on 19 November teachers' prospects brightened, albeit only briefly, with the news that the NUT was going to stage a protest against the contribution increase.

On Friday 25 November the Bill was published and given its first reading. The following Monday and Tuesday the LSA swung into action supported by hundreds of colleagues from the Extra Metropolitan area. The lobbies were packed with teachers arguing intensely with MPs. However, there was a noticeable change in attitude, with many Tory MPs listening sympathetically (unable or unwilling to counter the teachers' case) but declining to give commitments to vote against the Government. The larger Commons majority of the new Government and the better groundwork undertaken by Sir David Eccles knocking the Tory MPs into line were telling.

The NAS also sensed that Sir David felt confident of getting his Bill through the House. He was even a bit over-cocky in declaring to a meeting at Leamington in Warwickshire that the teachers' protests were a bit of "a song and dance". That infuriated teachers even more. As if that were not enough Sir David added on another occasion: "Professional dignity and an insolvent pensions account go ill together." He was waving the red flag to the bull!

The meeting of the National Executive on Friday/Saturday 2/3 December 1955 reviewed the situation and concluded that mere representation would not be enough. Militant action would be required. A press statement was issued, embargoed until the following Monday morning.

The press statement expressed "profound regret at the Minister's determination to inflict a salary cut on the profession by increasing the superannuation contribution from 5% to 6%". The NAS pointed out that this had never been inflicted on any existing body of public servants. Consequently the NAS had decided "to take a ballot of the Association on the question of the cessation of extraneous duties". Three main targets of the ban were:

all duties connected with the school meals service;

all out-of-school activities, including school sport;

all duties connected with school savings.

Other forms of direct action were discussed, including strikes. These were not immediately pressed in the hope of resolving the issue and of keeping something in reserve, a tactic often deployed by the NAS when resorting to militant action.

The NAS statement was not enough to deflect the Government from its chosen path. On Tuesday 6 December the second reading took place and was voted through. The Labour Opposition voted against but they were joined by only one Tory MP, an ex-schoolmaster, who had the courage of his convictions and had not forgotten his 'origins'.

The following Saturday the NUT Executive met and decided to follow suit with the NAS and take action. It announced its members would be called upon to suspend the collection of school savings during the Spring Term of 1956. Later on that same evening the NUT President seemed to extend the intended action by announcing to the press that his members would take action "parallel to that of the NAS".

Back in Parliament the Committee stage of the Bill was accelerated with double sessions. The Opposition pressed the Ministers hard but there was no hint of concession whatsoever. In the run-up to Christmas, rumours of Ministerial reshuffles surfaced again, as if the Government were toying with the teachers, raising expectations that Sir David Eccles might follow Florence Horsburgh to a similar fate. The rumours were right and a Cabinet reshuffle followed, but not for Sir David. He remained at Education. It was a statement from Government of firm intent to proceed.

By the end of the year the NAS had the results of its ballot showing:

92% in support of banning the collection of school savings;

89% for banning duties connected to the school meals service;

82% for banning extraneous duties, including sport.

The NAS Executive immediately announced a go-ahead on the school savings ban as that seemed to be supported by others in the NUT. It decided to consult and hopefully co-ordinate with the NUT before announcing further action.

GS Bert Rushworth wrote to the other unions suggesting a meeting to see if action could be co-ordinated. Despite the militant words of several of the unions, none was willing to have talks with the NAS. This was extremely disappointing. The NAS was willing to put aside differences to fight for the cause in which all teachers seemed united. However, the NAS took some crumb of comfort in assurances received from other unions that they would not instruct their members to undertake work banned by NAS members – 'no scabbing', to use the plainer term.

The depth of feeling amongst 'grass roots' teachers was vividly illustrated on 27 January 1956 when over 3,000 turned up at a meeting at Central Hall Westminster. It was addressed by representatives from different unions and by MPs, including a few brave Conservatives who at least displayed some guts in turning up to argue their case against an extremely hostile audience.

Similar meetings took place in many other parts of the country. It was clear that whatever the positions adopted by union leaders, there was massive anger amongst their respective memberships. Furthermore, although joint action had been declined at national level, there was obviously no attempt to dissuade different union people from coming together to hold local rallies and lobbies.

Despite Sir David Eccles' smooth but steely determination to do teachers down, he showed some signs of yielding a little to the intense pressure put upon Conservative MPs by the lobby. The Government was particularly exposed on the 'cut in salary' argument. Teachers' salaries were generally regarded as extremely poor and almost alone they had received no increase for two years, and that last one had been pitifully low.

The Minister conceded that a salary increase was overdue and he hinted, with a curious circularity, that teachers could plead the superannuation contribution increase in their claim. At the end of January salary negotiations were commenced somewhat earlier than anticipated and the Minister let it be known that he would consider delaying the Superannuation Bill until 1 October that year, the date on which a salary increase was due to operate.

The 10 February meeting of the NAS Executive marked a decisive step in the emerging dispute. The Executive decided to send a circular letter to all its local associations outlining the details of its plans to cease the collection of school meals money. Volunteer local associations to start the action were also asked to identify themselves.

In addition the NAS asked for the promised meeting with the Minister and also wrote directly to the Chairman of Burnham requesting that the salary increase should operate from 1 April.

The planned NAS action generated much coverage in the media and also provoked a public debate about the legality of the proposed ban on meals money collection. The first opinion NAS received from counsel confirmed its view that whilst the 1944 Act clearly required the supervision of children during mealtimes, that was all. Other duties were ultra vires and beyond the power of an LEA to enforce. However, NUT legal advisers cast doubt on the ban's validity, arguing the principle of 'usage', or custom and practice. The length of time these 'duties' had been provided placed an obligation upon teachers to continue.

It is difficult to understand the disgraceful folly of the NUT people in making such observations public. Some may have wished to engineer a defeat for the NAS, a bitter rival. But the statements undermined its own plans for action as banning the collection of school savings was subject to the same custom and practice argument. The statements also undermined the teachers' position, foisting additional contractual obligations upon their own members as well as everyone else.

The NAS sought a second legal opinion, this time consulting an eminent QC, Gerald (later Lord) Gardiner. His opinion supported the NAS view. Fortified with this second opinion the NAS continued with its plans for action. The third reading of the Bill had proceeded on 7 December the previous year and the time had come when the NAS had to deliver.

One last opportunity to put the NAS 'on the spot' was lost on 18 February 1956. The Bill was in the House of Lords and in response to NAS lobbying an amendment had been introduced to secure widows and orphans allowances in return for the proposed increase in contributions to 6%. The failure of that amendment served only to raise the level of schoolmasters' disgust.

Following the invitation issued to local associations in February 1956 six volunteers were selected to start the first wave of action, with another ten standing by to come in at the second stage. Each one deserves a mention in the history of the NAS. They were:

first wave: Cardiff, Leicester, Newport, Sheffield, Sunderland and Swansea;

second wave: Birmingham, Bristol, Halifax, Hull, Leeds, Liverpool, London, Manchester, Rhondda and Southend.

The first six were to inform their LEAs that members would cease the collection and recording of all moneys connected with school meals from the beginning of the Summer Term 1956.

Our Swansea Association had jumped the gun and already written to their LEA and imposed the ban a week before the letter from NAS HQ arrived. In later years I described such events as "good problems to have". But this was no time for constitutional niceties. On with the fight! Swansea members received the full backing of the Executive. We would have to insist on stricter discipline in later times.

The news that the NAS was to take this action broke in the media on Friday 2 March although the identities of the areas to be involved were not divulged until the following Monday in order that local Officers could be first informed. "All hell broke loose" at NAS HQ at 59 Gordon Square in London and in the homes of Executive Members and local Officers as they were besieged by the media.

The level of publicity generated by the somewhat modest action proposed was out of all proportion. After all, teachers were not proposing to bring the education service to its knees with an all-out indefinite strike. It was simply that 'professional' people did not engage in 'blue collar' militant action of any kind. A stereotypical class attitude lay only an inch below the surface and the media loved to exploit that.

Meanwhile the NUT Executive had met on 18 February and carried an interesting resolution by 21 votes to 9. It stated that in the event of the Superannuation Bill going forward with the increase in contributions, then "from the beginning of the Summer Term members of the NUT be instructed to take no part in school meals accounting and other non-statutory ancillary tasks connected with the school meals service." This was to be in addition to the continuation of the School Savings ban.

It was an interesting resolution on several counts, being militant action and an apparent contradiction of the legal opinion previously promulgated to the media. The NUT solicitor in a subsequent statement to the Executive was reported as saying: "There has been a lot of nonsense talked about non-statutory duties . . . Under the Education Act 1944 and the Regulations (1945) the LEAs cannot force and cannot require teachers to perform duties in connection with the School Meals Service other than supervision. That was the position in 1945. But 11 years have gone by and I would say that every teacher in this room, probably every teacher in the country has altered that position to some extent either voluntarily or contractually."

The NAS had tried to secure a co-ordinated approach on action but the NUT showed great hesitation. At first the NUT conceded the case for an increase in the contributions required. Then, responding to the pressure generated by NAS activity, the NUT Executive passed this motion on 18 February in favour of similar moves, including the controversial refusal to collect and account for school dinner moneys.

However, the most intriguing aspect of the NUT Executive's resolution was the astonishing decision to keep it confidential for the time being. The reason was never fully explained at the time nor indeed later. The sheer impracticability of maintaining confidentiality seemed also to have been ignored. The decision to keep it secret must rank as one of the worst ever made by a union executive.

Then disaster befell the teaching profession. On 25 February the NUT Executive's great secret leaked out, as inevitably it would, with *The News Chronicle* carrying the story. This was to unleash a chain of events that had a profound effect upon the fortunes of teachers as well as upon the history of the unions that aspired to represent the profession.

The Burnham Committee was in session over the salary increase for the following October. As the story broke the Burnham management in the persons of Sir Harold Jackson (Leader) and Sir William Alexander (Secretary), high on righteous indignation, 'carpeted' the NUT GS Sir Ronald Gould and his President. They must have smelled an easy killing. The attempt to keep it secret played into the hands of the employers and Government. They must have realised the NUT was extremely nervous about the whole matter. Alexander demanded to know if the press story were true. Inevitably the NUT GS and President, like guilty schoolboys caught red-handed in the middle of a naughty act, had to acknowledge it was.

The forlorn NUT leaders were threatened with the indefinite suspension of all salary negotiations. And by the way, Jackson and Alexander had cleared their position with the Government who, surprise surprise, would not intervene. Sir David Eccles could hardly have believed his luck! The hapless NUT caved in. The climbdown was humiliating.

NAS leaders at the time described these events as "calamitous", possibly an understatement. Not only was the pension contribution rendered a lost cause, but the opportunity in the Minister's own words for a "thorough review of salaries" was likewise ruined. Inevitably yet another poor salary award was to result from the negotiations in 1956.

At the 3 March meeting of the NUT Executive their Officers presented a motion to rescind the 18 February decision on action. The President made a statement full of the defeatist language of capitulation. The Superannuation Bill was scheduled to receive its third reading on 7 March. Its passage was a certainty, with the key provision to increase contributions unchanged. The President thought it his "constitutional duty" to afford the Executive an opportunity to consider the "changing situation".

The President spoke of the meeting with Alexander and Jackson and the LEAs' "grave concern" with the proposed action. The management leaders claimed they were not in the business of interfering in the internal affairs of the NUT. (Of course not!) But they had to point out that LEAs might find themselves unable to carry out their statutory duties and therefore having to close schools. The deployment of such a weak argument was surely to treat the NUT with contempt.

A motion was then tabled to rescind the resolution on action. After an apparently rancorous debate it was carried by 26 votes to 14. The only crumb of comfort was the 14 brave souls on the NUT Executive. To their credit some of them withdrew from the meeting in protest.

One could only speculate why on earth the NUT Executive had passed the resolution in the first place. Threats of this kind are inevitable. Employers were bound to receive the support of the Government. Minister after Minister in Government after Government has supported the right to take action, so long as it is never exercised.

On Monday 5 March the dismal news from the NUT was published. The passage of the Superannuation Bill was guaranteed. Pension contributions would be raised. One of the most critical points in the history of teacher trade unionism had come and gone. Despite widespread membership support for action the leaders of the then largest-by-far teachers' union had capitulated in humiliating circumstances. Government and employers could treat teachers as easy meat. Teachers' interests could be largely ignored.

Fortunately for the teaching profession the fightback was to begin immediately. On the very same day, the NAS published the names of its local associations which were to operate the ban on the collection of meals moneys. One can only admire the courage of those NAS stalwarts in holding firm against all the odds in such difficult circumstances.

In London there was pandemonium at two meetings at Central Hall Westminster, which had been organised by local branches of various teachers' unions. The London NUT Chairman was presiding over one of them and had to refuse to accept motions calling for militant action that flowed freely from the body of the hall. It was quite evident that they were as embarrassed as the delegates were furious. There were scenes of near riot as irate teachers grabbed the microphone and refused to accept the rulings of the Chairman. The meeting collapsed in chaos.

But it was all too late; the damage had been done. There was little NUT members could do about it except join the NAS. But many were reluctant to do that for other reasons. The obvious anger of many NUT members only made the situation more tragic. Membership support and fighting spirit were present in abundance. The leadership had let the members down through sheer cowardice.

The NAS continued lobbying to the end. On 20 February Association representatives met with a group of 20 Conservative MPs. But there was no breaking of ranks despite the NAS emphasising its flexibility over paying for a widows scheme.

The Bill was given its third reading on 22 March 1956, having first appeared in July 1952. Many Labour MPs made bitter attacks upon the Bill. Michael Stewart, a future Labour Minister of Education, perhaps best summed up the teachers' feelings. He described the manner in which the Bill had been trailed through as "an affront to Parliament and the matter it contained . . . an affront to education".

The NAS Conference at Southsea a few weeks later at Easter was a sombre affair but there was unstinting praise for the brave and steadfast stand of the leadership. There was deep and genuine regret at the weakness of other associations and above all for the abject surrender of the largest union, the NUT, which with all its size and resources was best placed to lead a campaign. In stark contrast to the NAS, the NUT Conference of 1955 castigated its leaders severely.

A week or two before Conference the Secretary to the Management Panel of Burnham (and the teachers' pet hate figure), Sir William Alexander, publicly castigated the Association for its plans to refuse to undertake certain 'duties' connected with school meals in protest against the increased pension contributions.

Lunchtime 'duties' naturally featured prominently in Richard Anderson's last address as GS to the 1956 NAS Conference before his retirement. It had been an issue dear to his heart, having taken over as GS from Arthur Warren in 1941 as the school meals service was in the throes of a vast expansion with implications for teachers' contracts, about which he had repeatedly warned. In fine fighting spirit he said that NAS members would not be intimidated as others had been by Sir William's threats. Conference proved true to his word and offered complete support to the local associations taking the action. The Executive was empowered to raise a levy on all members if this proved necessary to sustain those taking action. The wisdom and foresight of this move became evident very quickly.

Thus from (14 April) the beginning of the Summer Term 1956, members in the six local associations already mentioned, including Sunderland, were told to cease the collection of school meals money and any clerical work in connection with the service. Neither for the first nor the last time was NAS action to be carefully prepared and crafted. The Officers and Executive had studied the legislation carefully and concluded the law was on their side.

Section 49 of the Act defined the duties that the Minister could impose upon staff in respect of the provision of milk and meals. They could not be required when schools were closed during holiday times, "Nor should duties be imposed in respect of meals other than the supervision of pupils." These words were to prove crucial in the High Court case. The regulations left the collection of the moneys, a time-consuming, inappropriate and educationally wasteful activity, outside the duties that could be required of teachers. At least this was the view of the NAS.

The Sunderland Authority immediately decided to challenge the NAS's right to take such action and in hard-nosed, high-handed retaliatory mode gave notice of dismissal to nearly 200 NAS members within a couple of days of the action starting. The NAS responded promptly and decided to fight the matter in the courts. The NAS wrote to Sunderland indicating that it expected the dismissal notices to be stayed whilst the matter was decided in the High Court.

It was to prove a wise move. The Sunderland LEA initiative had shifted the issue from the increased pension contributions, now probably 'unwinnable', to the question of whether teachers had the right to decline voluntary duties. It might have unwittingly done the NAS a favour. It was a crucial issue in its own right and, in the view of the NAS legal opinion, winnable.

The NAS decided to take six cases of the dismissal notices to the High Court. Supported by the NAS the 'Sunderland Six' would claim they had the right to withdraw from such 'duties' — or 'tasks', as they should more properly be described. So the High Court case *Price and Others v Sunderland Metropolitan*

Borough Council was set down. The courage of the Sunderland Six who laid their jobs on the line cannot be overestimated. If the action failed the members faced inevitable dismissal. All volunteers, they deserve a special mention. They were:

A.G. James Cowen, the founder of the Sunderland Association and the man who in 1919 had met Arthur Warren off the train and taken him to address a gathering of schoolmasters;

Philip Price, the man who gave his name to the case;

together with James Robson, George Stafford, Ralph Forster and Frederick Carr.

The case started in the High Court on 23 April and the hearings lasted four days. The case was heard by Mr Justice Barry. The NAS engaged a leading counsel, Gerald Gardiner, later to become Lord Chancellor. Confident of victory, on 27 April Sunderland promised that no individual notices of dismissal would be served until the NAS had had time to think again. Mr Justice Barry reserved judgment.

Meanwhile the NAS still fought on politically to the bitter end. When the Superannuation Bill came to the House of Lords in June 1956 every member of the Upper House was lobbied by letter and many in person. Amendments were drafted to provide a widows and orphans scheme but in accordance with protocol on financial matters were not pressed to a vote. In the debates the Government spokesman made it plain it opposed such a scheme along with the LEA employers.

The reserved judgment was delivered on Wednesday 11 July in the Queen's Bench Division of the Royal Courts of Justice. The Sunderland Six were all present to hear Mr Justice Barry declare: "I have come to the conclusion that the Plaintiffs' contention as regards Section 49 [of the 1944 Act] is the correct one."

In his landmark judgment Mr Justice Barry declared that any service rendered by a teacher other than the supervision of pupils in connection with the school meals service was voluntary. LEAs could neither require such duties nor still less dismiss teachers for declining to perform them. The NAS victory on the voluntary duty issue was complete.

Justice Barry also specifically ruled that the collection and recording of moneys was clearly not supervision of pupils and that the resolution of the Council terminating the employment of the six plaintiffs was ultra vires and a breach of the defendants' statutory duty. The NAS was awarded full costs. Justice Barry added there was nothing to stop teachers continuing to carry out the tasks, but they were voluntary and could not be required of them. He hoped teachers would continue.

The Barry judgment reverberated around the education service. Government and LEAs were stunned. The NAS had struck a decisive blow in defence of teachers' rights. The superannuation contribution issue was lost but a glorious victory won on the right to decline voluntary duties. Not only was some pride restored to the teaching profession but a valuable weapon to defend and promote the interests of teachers had been secured. Banning voluntary 'duties' was to prove a very effective weapon for the Association to employ in future years.

The money collected by the NAS to sustain its members in case of need became known as the Sunderland Reserve Fund. It survives to the present day and is the official 'fighting fund' for the NASUWT supporting members in many forms of direct action. It stood at over £12m in the accounts for 2005.

The victory in the High Court was a defining moment in the history of the Association. It had fought a lone fight and won.

Unfortunately the NUT's calamitous failure to resist the increase in pension contributions had another dramatic and depressing ramification upon the salary negotiations that were ongoing at the same time. Talks began early in 1956 to produce a badly needed interim increase pending a full review scheduled for 1957. That was against the background of the 1954 Burnham Award, which had left the schoolmaster, in the view of the NAS, some £200 worse off than he would have been with the mere restoration of 1939 salaries purchasing power.

Even the NUT Easter Conference of 1954 showed signs of rebellion, which had to be met by a decision to launch a long-term campaign to educate the public on the need for a decent rise in 1957. However, that NUT campaign was itself so modest as to be out of date before it had barely begun. The NUT demand was for a scale running from £500 to £900 at a time when a cost of living adjustment would already produce a maximum of at least £915, and there were still three years to run, with inflation rising steeply.

This modest, hesitant, even pusillanimous approach was soon too much even for the NUT to stomach. Its Conference the following year in 1955 demanded there should be an interim increase to compensate for the rising cost of living. A clause in the 1954 settlement allowed for the reopening of negotiations in the event of rising inflation.

The NAS wrote to the Chairman of Burnham, Lord Percy, on 1 November 1955 asking him to reconvene the Committee to order an upward revision of schoolmasters' salaries. Another NAS Memorandum was sent to LEAs and MPs. On 24 November Burnham met to consider a request by the Teachers' Panel for an interim adjustment "in view of economic changes since the 1954 scales were negotiated".

On 5 January 1956 the Minister, Sir David Eccles, made an intriguing intervention in the Burnham pay talks whilst he was in the throes of resurrecting the Superannuation Bill. Keen to avoid a repeat of Florence Horsburgh's mistakes and determined to neutralise the effectiveness of the NAS lobby on the 'pay cut issue', Sir David cleverly offered a thorough review of salaries rather than an interim increase. He managed to persuade the NUT to withdraw the interim claim lodged on the previous 21 December. The Minister said he would have been prepared to concede a "reasonable interim increase" as from 1 April but he agreed a thorough revision of salaries was needed and would welcome a start to negotiations. If they were completed expeditiously he would give "sympathetic consideration" to approving an earlier starting date than 1 April 1957. The Minister's tactics were obviously to ensure that any increase in salaries should not come later than the rise in pension contributions and he tabled an amendment to his Superannuation Bill postponing its coming into operation until October 1956.

The Teachers' Panel duly met on 31 January 1956, abandoned the proposal for an interim increase from 1 April and submitted a request to Management to open negotiations for new scales to come into effect on or before 1 October that year. Burnham commenced its round of meetings on 8 February. The NAS still had no confidence in Burnham and repeated its request early in February 1956 for the appointment of a Royal Commission or other independent tribunal on Teachers' Pay.

Then came the disastrous and bungled NUT attempt to mount action on the increased pension contributions.

By Easter time the NUT was unable to report any progress on the salary negotiations. The NUT Conference was sceptical and despite heavy pressure from the Executive decided that the claim had to be a scale rising from £500 to £1,050. The NAS had submitted its 'own claim' directly to the management for a scale rising from £675 to £1,125 (based on the cost of living index 31 July 1955).

After the Easter Conferences Burnham meetings restarted and the NUT put forward the claim as dictated by Conference. The management offered only £475-£850, hardly the 'substantial increase' suggested by the Minister as being necessary. Deadlock resulted.

But having succeeded in blackmail over the NUT's aborted attempts to take action against the increased pension contributions a few weeks previously, the Management Panel Leaders tried it on again. The Teachers were told that a final offer could be made of £475-£875 but if they refused to accept it negotiations would come to an end and the Management would blame them for it.

My subsequent experience of Burnham negotiations leads me to suspect that this might have been a set-up between the leaders of both sides. It took only a few minutes for the Teachers' Panel to respond, suggesting that if the 'final' offer could be increased by another £25 at the maximum (to £900), it would be accepted. The management readily agreed, probably delighted at such an easy victory and a 'thorough review' so cheaply concluded.

The report in *The Teacher* – the new name for the official newspaper of the NUT – of the subsequent Executive meeting was informative. Various Teachers' Panel members were reported saying "that there was no case for a maximum of £1,050"; "the limit had been reached at £900"; "the very last penny had been obtained"; and the pièce de résistance: "If anyone thought that there had ever been a possibility of even approaching £1,050 they had been living in cloud cuckoo land."

To their credit some members of the NUT Executive urged rejection of the agreement. But they were soon outmanoeuvred by threats of resignation from members of the Teachers' Panel and even by some of the National Officers. The Executive decided to recommend acceptance to the Special Conference. The Conference, which had a few months before been so resolute, meekly accepted the defeatist language of the NUT leadership. It was a done deal.

The new system of graded posts was firmly established, there was increased differentiation between primary and secondary and the restoration of the major part of teachers' salaries, as represented by the basic scale, to 1939 purchasing power was postponed indefinitely.

The Government and management gave their usual polished performance to the media, focussing on "increases ranging from 10s. to £10 per week", which glossed over the fact that the £10 was for the few, the 10s. for the many. For most teachers the rise came nowhere near restoring real salaries to 1939 levels. In addition they would have to pay more for their pensions, and income tax was much higher than it had been before the war.

The Economist had published an article on the so-called 'black-coated workers' a month earlier. Examining the common range of salaries between £200 and £700 p.a., *The Economist* calculated that present-day salaries should be three times as high to compensate for inflation and three and a half times greater to keep pace with the rise in average earnings.

Those figures corresponded closely to the analysis provided by Professor Allen to the NAS. If the multipliers of 3 and 3.5 had been applied to the 1939 Scale 3 for men teachers (£180-£366), they would have respectively produced:

£540-£1,098 and £630-£1,281;

as opposed to the Burnham:

£475-£900.

The Report of the Royal Commission on Equal Pay in 1944 stated that EP would tend to stabilise the common rate at the standard satisfactory to women. If the pre-war women's salaries are multiplied by 3 they approximate closely to the 1956 Burnham scales. All had suffered comparative erosion with average earnings. Schoolmasters were still below 1939 in terms of real pay (i.e. adjusted for inflation).

The agreement of 1956 unusually did not stipulate the normal three-year period. The Minister 'put that right' when he indicated acceptance of the Report on the condition that it ran its normal three-year period, barring exceptional circumstances. The overall £35m cost of the increase amounted to 15% over the three years

The events of 1955-56 took place as EP was conceded and the first instalment paid. Whilst I found no direct evidence to link the two, NAS members were naturally suspicious, for in their eyes nothing else could rationally explain the "calamitous" behaviour of the NUT leadership.

One of the features of the history of the NASUWT has been the disproportionately large number of bitter battles fought with some very hard-nosed employers in the North East of England. NASUWT members in that region seem to be made of particularly stern stuff. So were the employers, proving that the private sector did not enjoy a monopoly of such people. The names of Sunderland, Durham (twice) and Teesside (Sacred Heart School) spring to the minds of a couple of generations of NASUWT activists. They all arose due to action being taken in the respective localities following national developments.

The first of these disputes which became causes célèbres was the Sunderland Case in 1956. Besides its unique place in the history of teachers' superannuation, the case also had a heavy impact upon the definition of the teachers' contract and of course the school meals service itself. The Sunderland Case also played its part in the establishment of the NAS as an association to be reckoned with and not ignored.

To a large extent the Sunderland LEA set itself up by such a belligerent response to the NAS action against the increased pension contributions. On 23 March 1956 a well-attended meeting of the Sunderland Association agreed that the LEA should be informed of NAS intentions to ban meals money collection as from 9 April, the beginning of the Summer Term. The letter written by the Secretary, Ray Hannington, was extremely polite, referring to the activities that would not be affected, emphasising that special schools would be exempt and generally regretting the need for such a protest in the light of the pension contribution rise.

The Director of Education, W. Thompson, immediately contacted his Chairman who ordered him to convene a special subcommittee at the earliest opportunity. The Education Sub-Committee (School Health and Welfare)

reacted in bellicose fashion. Instead of suggesting a meeting to explore the issues they demanded the action be cancelled immediately.

The Director's letter to Ray Hannington said the action was "quite unwarranted" and claimed that teachers had a contractual obligation to carry out the duties because they were done "in school hours" and had been the custom and practice of many years. Furthermore the Director demanded an answer by Thursday morning, 29 March, his letter having been delivered by hand to Ray Hannington's home on the evening of the 26th. It seemed the LEA was deliberately engineering a negative response to its request.

It is a great tribute to Ray Hannington's organisational abilities and desire not to raise the temperature unnecessarily that he managed to convene a general meeting of the Branch within two days (despite the constitutionally required notice of seven).

Virtually the entire Sunderland membership turned up for the meeting on 28 March. The members were in more militant mood than ever, spurred on by the crass 'timetable' demands of their employer. Nevertheless the reply from Ray Hannington was anything but inflammatory. He drafted his reply the same evening, stating the Director's communication had been considered and he had been instructed to say that the action proposed was in accordance with a request from the NAS and therefore "we must abide by the terms of our letter of 23 March". The Easter holidays intervened and the NAS leadership and activists went off to Southsea for their Annual Conference.

On 11 April, just two days into the action, the Education Committee recommended to the full Council to terminate the employment of NAS members taking action, with effect 31 August. That was the notice due under the standard teacher's contract. All members were so informed on 13 April.

Members were also pressurised to answer two questions in the LEA's 13 April letter: (1) Do you normally collect dinner money and (2) Are you prepared to collect . . .? A stamped addressed envelope was enclosed for their replies, demanded by the 18th of the month. Some 14 members found the pressure too great and they did the honourable thing and resigned from the NAS.

However, the LEA's attempts at divide and rule failed miserably. Whilst it claimed that only 198 members were taking the action, a packed meeting of the Sunderland NAS showed on a count that 263 were operating the ban. This meeting of the NAS on 14 April was attended by virtually 100% of the membership.

The ban had been put into effect as planned on 9 April. The LEA had to import other people to collect the money, mostly welfare officers and clerks as there was no clerical assistance in Sunderland schools.

There was much coverage in the national media, and of course locally the debates raged. There was speculation on whether the LEA could sack so many teachers at the same time and keep its service going.

On 14 April the NAS, condemning the response of Sunderland who alone amongst the LEAs affected had reacted in such a way, announced in a press statement that it was going to challenge in the High Court the right of the Authority to sack teachers for the reasons given.

GS Bert Rushworth wrote to Sunderland saying the NAS had taken leading counsel's opinion on the legal claims set out by the LEA in its letter of 13 April. The NAS opinion received was that the notice to dismiss was directly contrary to Section 49 of the 1944 Education Act. The NAS intended to apply to the Court without further notice to the LEA. The NAS would loyally accept the judgment of the Court, whichever way it went, and he expected the LEA to take no further action whilst the matter was sub judice.

Sunderland responded repeating their assertion of legal right to insist upon the 'duty' and accusing the NAS of evading the issue. Now that the NAS had achieved the "fullest possible publicity" for its protest it was time to stop damaging the children and the LEA. The NAS said it could not possibly concede on the principle that to volunteer for a task implied after some (unspecified) time an obligation to continue to perform it. The LEA continued to go through the procedures for dismissal, writing to the Association reminding teachers of their right to appear, accompanied by a friend, before the relevant committee considering dismissal.

At this time the NUT intervened in its customary confusing way. Both GS Sir Ronald Gould and the NUT Sunderland Branch Secretary wrote to the LEA expressing the very same legal opinion regarding Section 49 and voluntary duties as the NAS, although without mentioning us by name. If the LEA attempted to enforce the 'duty', "the NUT would be bound to resist". One could only speculate what that meant in the light of the fiasco in February/March over the NUT's disastrous decision to rescind its resolution on action.

The Barry judgment settled all such matters. The NAS won a sensational victory against an aggressive and dictatorial employer. The NAS had shown teachers that a little courage could go a long way. It was a victory that had many repercussions, none the least of which was establishing the principle that voluntary 'duties' are just that – voluntary!

The original cause, the increase in superannuation contributions, had been lost, although the NAS was satisfied it had fought as hard as it could. The Sunderland LEA, in taking such an aggressive stance, had unwittingly raised another issue, voluntary duties, which turned a defeat for all teachers into a great victory for the NAS.

The Association was on many occasions over the course of the next half-century to employ the tactic of 'withdrawing goodwill' and refusing to undertake such voluntary activities as a means of exerting pressure on the Government and employers in numerous disputes over pay and conditions. The NAS was prepared to go on strike but appreciated that such action saved employers money.

The Sunderland Case led directly to the LEAs establishing a working party to review the midday break. Incredibly the NAS was kept excluded although it was the organisation that had caused everything to happen. After more goings-on which I relate in chapter 13 on the school meals service, during which the NUT once again compromised itself, the working party did hasten the arrival of far more systematic clerical and administrative help for schools in the midday break, especially after the official recognition finally granted to the NAS in 1961. A more formal School Meals Agreement was to arrive in 1968. The NAS believed such work did not require professionally qualified teachers to carry it out. Indeed teachers were likely to be much better placed to perform well in the afternoon classes if they arrived after lunch properly refreshed after a decent break.

Chapter 25 - Teachers' Salaries after Equal Pay

With Equal Pay (EP) adopted in 1956 the NAS had turned its attention to family allowances, despite the difficulties, as the best means of tackling the problem of inadequate salaries on which to raise a family. The agendas of the Annual Conferences for 1957, 1959 and 1960 all contained motions calling for family allowances. The NAS came to favour the scheme operated by the universities which was specifically funded and identified through Government grant. The NAS was joined by the Assistant Masters in calling for family allowances.

The NAS drew attention to the interests of a neglected minority, the long-serving teachers, who were not just the schoolmasters but also many women who devoted a lifetime to teaching. The 'career teacher' provided the continuity of service so valuable in the running of schools and essential for the development of an effective education service. Establishing salaries to make teaching an attractive long-term career able to compete successfully with other professions was becoming more and more of a pipe dream as one inadequate award followed another.

Financing teachers' salaries, never absent from NAS thought, returned to prominence in the late 1950s. The NAS recognised the 'dual' factor in pay negotiations and openly recognised that both Government and LEA employers should be involved. However, each hid behind the other when 'buck passing' was convenient, especially if the party in power at Westminster differed from the majority one in local Government from which the Burnham Management Panel was drawn.

Central government revenue (including income tax, purchase tax and corporation tax) was progressive and buoyant, in contrast to the property tax, better known as the rates. The rating system was the only significant independent source of local authority finance. It was deeply unpopular and largely regressive and had long ago lost the ability to finance the education service independently. A pay rise for teachers was readily and easily identifiable in its effect on the rates.

The NAS had spotted the problem from its earliest days. At the first Annual Conference in Margate in 1920, before secession from the NUT, the NAS adopted a resolution calling for hundred per cent funding of teachers' salaries from the central exchequer. The motion was proposed by the Leeds local association and seconded by Bristol.

From Harrogate in 1952 practically every Annual Conference of the NAS for the rest of the twentieth century carried a resolution calling for the central payment of salaries. The 1952 resolution said simply: "This Conference believes that the grants to LEAs should fully cover the cost of teachers' salaries." The Burnham scales were mandatory under Act of Parliament and consequently the NAS believed the Westminster Government should openly play the dominant role in Burnham instead of exercising control surreptitiously behind the scene.

LEAs naturally opposed any change in the status quo, despite their often-quoted financial difficulties. 'Control' – such as it was – of teachers' salaries and the education service was a vital and indispensable part of local democracy. The NAS considered this to be 'empire protection' for its own sake, with little consideration of fitness for purpose.

A few years later in 1974 the NAS was to argue before the Layfield Inquiry into Local Government Finance "that authorities should be responsible for what they pay for and pay for what they are responsible for". They were no longer responsible for teachers' salaries. Westminster had assumed the key powers in that area and should accordingly pay the bill entirely.

On top of such fundamental constitutional problems the NUT brought a very egalitarian approach which defied labour market economics. No Government was ever going to pay the top market rates to everyone. The NUT lacked the resolve to apply real pressure. A plethora of additional payments was introduced to circumvent the theoretical 'primacy of the basic scale'. In the decade following the Second World War every Burnham agreement had introduced some kind of new differential:

- 1945: posts of responsibility;
- 1948: 22 new levels for determining headteachers' salaries (against five previously);
- 1951: new scheme of special allowances;
- 1954: good honours graduate allowance was introduced;
- 1956: heads of department (HoDs) in secondary and deputy headships and graded posts in all but the smallest of schools; higher levels for heads of large schools.

By 1956 the Management Panel itself began to have doubts on where its own policies were leading. The AEC Secretary of the Management Panel, the domineering Sir William Alexander, normally produced commentaries on Burnham Reports, exhorting LEAs to exercise their discretion at the minima, perhaps undermining their own case for local democracy.

One such commentary issued in 1956 observed that the new salary structure was becoming too "cumbersome". There were "unduly wide variations of practice between schools and LEAs" and this was also "permitting even encouraging financial competition between authorities". The suggested remedy was to create more designated posts "so far as practicable" and to adopt "agreed formulae for other assistant teachers' grades of salary or fixed allowances". The NAS believed that codifying a basically flawed system was the wrong way forward.

Schools developed an unbelievably complex superstructure of promoted posts when their main function was (or should have been) to teach children, a very singular activity entirely devoid of the need for complex management and administrative systems. Graded posts I, II and III, and HoDs A, B, C, D and E had been established, together with second master or mistress posts below deputy and headship.

A seemingly endless chain of promotions, each one creating a domino effect of vacancies, increased staff turnover. Suspicion, rivalry and dissatisfaction reigned in some staffrooms, stirred up by sometimes surprising if not capricious decision making in this over-elaborate promotion system. The most inappropriate decision I came across a few years later in my early days as a local representative of the NAS in Inner London was a Scale II awarded to a teacher to assume responsibility for the tuck shop!

A formidable figure from Scotland and the NAS President 1959-60, J.A.C. Thompson was also a self-made expert in constitutional and salary matters. Writing in the *Scottish Schoolmaster* in 1961 he quoted figures from *Occupation and Pay in Great Britain 1906-1960* written by Guy Routh (published by Cambridge University Press). Ron Simons followed suit in the *London Schoolmaster*.

Comparing rises in money incomes for men and taking account of inflation for the period 1913-60 Guy Routh found that "lower professional workers: teachers and librarians" had experienced the smallest increase in living standards of only 20%. Top of the 'league table' came managers and administrators with 104%, and thereafter in descending order foremen 98%, unskilled workers 88%, semi-skilled workers 87%, skilled workers 78%, clerks 52% and then higher professionals: doctors, lawyers, scientists and journalists 37%.

The post-war Burnham settlements had been mediocre at best, insulting at worst, in the view of the NAS. Inflation had risen rapidly. By 1959 EP was on its way with four of the six introductory steps completed. In December 1958 *Teachers' World*, a paper generally well disposed to the profession, had commented that EP had "created many problems" and "teachers should not blind themselves" to them "for LEAs surely will not". In January 1959 *The Daily Telegraph* observed that a "straight increase does not solve the staffing difficulties of schools. The basic scale is inadequate for men with families." The NUT had to "put a stop to such business".

Before the currency of the 1956 settlement had run its course, a special addition of 5% was granted for 1 February 1959 to run until 30 September. From 1 October 1959 the men's basic scale was increased to £520 at the minimum and to £1,000 at the maximum. The women's equivalent was raised to £468 and £800.

The NAS press statement "deplored the proposed salary award" on 4 July. At age 21 after completing training, men teachers would earn £8 per week net and take 17 years to reach the maximum of £1,000 p.a., which represented a cut in real terms of 20% compared to the 1939 position, itself regarded (by McNair and others) as inadequate.

Open criticism of the Burnham system and the Teachers' Panel 'performance' surfaced in the media and in the ranks of the NUT itself. To its credit *The Teacher* published correspondence from members hostile to the 1959 settlement. One spoke of many feeling "betrayed by our negotiators and who will leave the Union in the belief that our only hope lies in the strengthening of a more outspoken Association. The Authorities would be very simple minded if they did not conclude that they can do just as they like with teachers. Our future is very dark."

The leader in the *Teachers' World* of 19 June was entitled "Burnham Bungle". The Committee had "failed to produce a reasonable basic scale and to rationalise or improve the special payments", the awards of which were "capricious". The leader concluded: "A lamentable situation is made worse."

The NUT Ex-President, Peter Quince, revealed in *The Teacher* 10 July 1959 that deadlock in May was only broken by the direct intervention of the Minister, Geoffrey Lloyd, who "forced the Management's final offer down teachers' throats. Clearly the Burnham machinery is creaking badly."

J.A.C. Thompson, writing in the September 1959 *New Schoolmaster,* referred to the Minister becoming "the arbiter between his own views and those of the teachers. The result was a foregone conclusion." The Treasury's predetermination of the global sum "has been well known for many years" in Scotland thanks to their discovery of the Goschen formula, which determined the level of grant from Westminster and also disclosed the amount being allocated for teachers' salaries, among other things. To refuse a say over the global sum, to withhold provision for arbitration, denied effective negotiations. The Educational Institute of Scotland, "a sister body to the NUT", refused to recognise this reality "and so enchained Scottish teachers to the system".

Teachers' World, 17 July, commented: "The silly season is here with the sad, inevitable attempts of the NUT to blame the Minister. Of course a suitable version of the Burnham story must be added to the myth of invincible martyrdom . . . It is perfectly proper for NUT members to incorporate the myth into their belief. Only they must not expect outside observers to agree."

Without naming the NAS the *TES* on 24 July articulated its case: "It should open the teachers' eyes once and for all . . . to the fiction, long upheld, that teachers and employers negotiate a settlement and take it for approval to the Minister, who has carefully stood aloof. The truth is that the Minister is vitally concerned throughout, because his Government have to provide most of the money. Furthermore this is known quite early in the proceedings."

In September 1959 the *TES* printed a very succinct summary of the NAS case on salaries submitted in a letter from GS Bert Rushworth. The letter began by referring to the "growing realisation of the difficulties concerning the adequate remuneration of schoolmasters in a profession which ought always to be composed of some 60 per cent women and 40 per cent men".

The NAS case was predicated upon some basic principles:
> schoolmasters are needed in the education service;
> they should be of good quality;
> both these statements apply also to schoolmistresses;
> equal pay in a mixed occupation will be at a rate sufficient to satisfy the majority; in teaching it will be women;
> if this common rate is unsatisfactory to men, it will become impossible to recruit sufficient men of the required ability.
> Three broad options were left to the nation:
> it could decide men were not needed;
> it could recognise the existence of two problems and provide separate consideration;
> it could mitigate the difficulties by superimposing on the common scale systems of ameliorative allowances, in effect undoing equal pay.

The NAS plumped decisively for the second of the alternatives. If this were rejected then the third alternative had to be followed, as had increasingly been the case over the last ten years, despite its deficiencies. These allowances caused much "irritation and discontent", the basis for their award often hard to define and understand. The NAS believed they should be severely pruned, awarded only to heads, deputies and heads of department. They were particularly unhelpful to schoolmasters with family responsibilities whose financial position was "difficult in the extreme".

The letter concluded, in order "that all these weighty matters can have full and independent consideration the NAS recommends the establishment of a Royal Commission on the Recruitment and Remuneration of Teachers."

Chapter 26 - The 1960s – The End of Servility

The 1960s marked the dividing line between supine acceptance of poor pay deals by the NUT-dominated Teachers' Panel and some backbone being injected into the negotiations, such as they were. However, the particularly sad fiasco of the 1961 pay 'negotiations' had to play itself out before things began to change.

Three hugely significant events occurred in 1961 although there was no pay increase to operate until the 1959 settlement had run its three-year course through to 1962. Firstly, 1961 saw the final instalment of equal pay, which naturally was hailed as a great success by the NUT. Secondly, in October the same year the NAS achieved its own historic breakthrough in securing representation on the Burnham Committee. Thirdly, during the course of 1961 a shambolic process of Burnham 'negotiation' took place over the award to operate from 1962.

As I have already related in "The Battle of Burnham" section, in the middle of the NAS's campaign of militant action for recognition the Government intervened dramatically in the negotiations to overturn an agreement between the Teachers' and Management Panels and reduce the award.

The effect was to leave a basic scale running from £570 to £1,170, the Teachers' Panel having originally claimed £700 to £1,300. The reader may also recall the vacillating and bewildering tactics of the NUT in firstly criticising NAS militancy, followed subsequently by organising and then cancelling its own plans for 'industrial action' – the 'working strikes'.

The negotiations in and after 1962 were enlivened by the refusal of the NAS to observe the Burnham convention on secrecy. Teachers could be told of the pay claim submitted on their behalf but they were not acquainted with management offers unless and until a provisional agreement had been concluded. The NAS could see no advantage for teachers but only huge benefit for management (and Government) in such outrageous secrecy. A huge row broke out as the two first NAS representatives on Burnham, GS Bert Rushworth and Honorary Treasurer G. Lloyd Williams, reported back fully and freely to their Executive and members.

Rushworth and Lloyd Williams received a frigid and hostile 'reception' in the Teachers' Panel. They were cold shouldered with many refusing even to pass the time of day with them. Whilst there was little angst directed towards the Management, you could cut the atmosphere between the two NAS representatives and the rest. Far from hard bargaining between the Sides the

NAS found a situation "resembling a ritual mating dance. It was dignified and formal, but it was not real. It was only an exercise in sharing out the sum of money predetermined by the Treasury – the 'global sum'."

The Burnham Award for 1962 came into effect on 1 January, again reflecting agitation during the three-year currency of the previous agreement. Booster increments were introduced for study and training qualifications.

Conference 1962 held in Plymouth called for a campaign to secure a review of salary negotiating machinery to ensure a truly voluntary and genuine system. The Conference also received another hard-hitting and illuminating Report on Salaries. The year 1962 was also the year that saw Terry Casey installed as President. One year later he was to become GS. Much of Terry's drive was behind the Report on Salaries.

The Report began in forthright style, declaring that the introduction of equal pay (EP) "has set the profession new and as yet unresolved problems". It reiterated policy calling for an "adequate separately considered salary scale for schoolmasters" and accepted women being levelled up to the same rate as the men. However, the Report concluded firmly: "Up to 1961 the 'EP' scales have been approximately at the pre-war woman's rate." Perhaps it is of interest to note that I had come to that view through my own research quite independently before reading this Report.

The Report quoted the Ministry of Labour's statistics, revealing that average male earnings had risen by a factor of 4.3 between 1939 and 1961 (from 69s. per week to £3 1s. 3d.). Multiplying the old Scale 3 Area salary of £180-£366 by that factor would produce a basic scale (in 1961) of £774 to £1,573 16s. The claim for 1962 by the NUT-dominated Teachers' Panel was only for £755 to £1,375. The NAS Report stated that an element for "betterment" should be included "to enable schoolmasters to share in the increased wealth of the nation". The NAS believed a factor of 5 was justified, based on the research by *The Economist*. It produced the NAS claim for the basic scale to run from £875 to £1,650 in ten equal increments.

Applying these factors to compensate for inflation and allow for comparability revealed that EP was indeed "at the woman's pre-war rate". And furthermore, only the first few points of the scale kept pace with the woman's 1939 pay level uprated for inflation. In terms of comparative earnings, all teachers, men and women, lost out badly.

The Report reproduced figures published by the Royal Commission for Doctors' and Dentists' Remuneration on comparative career 'lifetime' earnings of professional men between 30 and 65. They were interesting, to say the least.

	£
Consultants	117,000
NHS doctors	84,000
Dentists	79,000
Accountants	71,000
Graduates in industry	84,000
Solicitors	88,000
Surveyors	63,000
Graduates in teaching	40,000
Honours graduates	42,000
Certificated teachers	35,000

In its 1962 Report the NAS repeated the call it had made at its Conference in 1958 for the abolition of the points score system for all but heads, deputies and departmental heads, and for an adequate professional salary to subsume the basic scale and graded posts. This was perhaps the first step towards the NASUWT's career-structured 'collegiate' salary policy, which finally found some favour with management in the 1980s and with Government towards the end of the 1990s.

In 1962 teachers claimed a basic scale minimum of £755 rising to a maximum of £1,375. The Burnham Award that resulted gave £630 to £1,250 respectively and came into effect on 1 April 1963.

The NAS began a more active campaign on relativities and again highlighting *The Economist* research *(Salaries – Are you better off?)*, which showed that by 1963 an employee required a fivefold increase in salary to maintain comparable values with pre-war 1938-39. Applying a fivefold increase in 1963 would have produced £1,830 based on 1939 Scale 3 (large town) male maximum of £366. The shortfall on the actual 1963 salary of £1,250 resulted in a deficit of £580, approximately 40%. If the same exercise were applied to the women's maximum rate without EP, a fivefold increase based on £288 would have produced £1,440, leaving a deficit of £190 compared to the actual salary of £1,250, i.e. of 20%. Both those sums were above the £1,250 settlement figure with full EP in operation. And McNair had described the 1939 salaries as demonstrably inadequate in its 1944 Report. Even the Teachers' claim for 1963, £1,375, was below the £1,440 that women should have received without EP.

In 1963 the Minister of Education, Sir Edward Boyle, had intervened in the Burnham negotiations because he disagreed strongly with some of the provisions of the agreement. A quick and short Remuneration of Teachers Act (1963) was passed by Parliament to ensure the Minister had the legal powers to impose his own provisions without necessarily having a Burnham agreement to that effect. A more fundamental reform of Burnham would follow in the shape of the 1965 Act.

The Burnham negotiations in 1965 took place against a background of 'constitutional crisis' within the Committee. There was a lingering dispute over confidentiality, the NAS continued to object to its under-representation and it had fierce rows with the Minister over threats of expulsion. The procedures still failed to make provision for arbitration and retrospection. After many crises the Remuneration of Teachers' Act (RTA) of 1965 finally emerged which dealt with these grievances in part, if not in a wholly satisfactory fashion.

In addition the newly elected Labour Government faced severe economic difficulties. On 16 December 1964 the *Joint Statement of Intent on Productivity, Prices and Incomes* was published. It was the first genuine attempt at Social Partnership, involving Government, employers and unions through their national representative bodies. In our case that meant the TUC, although the NAS was three years away from a decision to affiliate to that body.

The Government's basic objectives were "to achieve and maintain a rapid increase in output and real incomes combined with full employment" and to ensure the benefits of faster growth were distributed in a way that satisfied "the claims of social need and justice".

The Government undertook to invest in and to promote economic development, whilst employers and unions would work to end restrictive practices and raise productivity. Employers and unions were "to keep increases in wages, salaries and other forms of income in line" with rises in real output.

The National Economic Development Council was established. The Government would also establish machinery (the Prices and Incomes Board) to keep matters under review and which could allow exceptions to the general rules implied in the *Joint Statement*.

It was a tall order, to say the least. Few doubted the good intentions but many believed it was 'pie in a socialist sky'. Furthermore, many unions were hostile to the very notion of Social Partnership, reluctant to get involved in 'management's problems'. Wildcat strikes were spreading, undermining the 'official leadership' of unions and rendering the prospect of Social Partnership even more remote.

The Government was later to produce a White Paper on pay which envisaged setting a norm of 3.5% increases, unless productivity were improved or "it is generally recognised that the existing pay levels are too low to maintain a reasonable standard of living". Given the comments of McNair as far back as 1944 and the succession of low awards ever since, the NAS believed teachers had a good case to go above the norm but little confidence the Government would recognise it.

Teachers had a huge problem in formulating pay claims since erosion had been so massive that restoration to virtually any 'previous position' either in relation to the RPI or average earnings entailed very high percentage demands.

For 1965 the Teachers' Panel claimed a basic scale running from £900 to £1,700. The management offered £700 to £1,360. That was rejected. Management raised the offer to £710 to £1,400, which was also turned down by the Teachers' Panel. The increased offer amounted to 12.6% over two years. The Teachers had claimed 44% increase. NAS policy was for a basic scale of £900-£1,800.

With the second management offer rejected the claim ended up at arbitration, the first under the new provisions afforded by the new RTA passed a few weeks before. The arbitration turned out to be very unsatisfactory for the teachers. The basic scale was only raised by £100 at the minimum and £150 at the maximum to run from £730 by 14 increments to £1,400, representing 16% at the minimum, tapering off to 12% at incremental step six and above.

Management, in welcoming the arbitral award, argued that it set a new benchmark, a "new datum line for future settlements". The NAS argued that having agreed to go to arbitration the award had to be accepted as a fact but not as just and fair.

However, pouring petrol on the flames of teacher discontent, Sir William Alexander had argued before the arbitrators that 'teachers were well paid once their short hours and long holidays were taken into account'. Teachers only had 40 working five-day weeks per year, making "teachers' conditions of service unique and direct comparison with most other occupations the less relevant . . . The short hours and long holidays, even allowing for preparation and out-of-school activities, allow teachers to undertake work . . . which brings in payments additional to salary earned as a full-time teacher."

Rubbing salt into the NAS wound Alexander reminded everyone of EP "benefiting nearly 60% of all teachers . . . raising the salary levels in the profession as a whole". The NAS reminded Alexander of his previous concerns over EP. He had asked in *Education*: "Is it not true that the single woman and the married man with family responsibilities do not even live on the same social plane? Is this good for education?"

The NAS reacted immediately by instigating a campaign to get LEAs to disown Sir William's document. No LEA did so but many tried to deny the NAS interpretation and issued pious assertions about teachers' professionalism and commitment whilst also condemning the protest action that the NAS was about to embark upon.

At the post-arbitral meeting of the Teachers' Panel on 23 July 1965 the NAS moved a motion condemning the award and called upon the Government to honour its election promise to secure a satisfactory salary structure for teachers. It failed by 12 votes to 10 but it was unique for the NAS to attract 8 votes in addition to its own 2.

The NAS also decided to call a rally of all its members at Central Hall, Westminster on Saturday 11 September to protest against the award and demand an independent and thorough inquiry into the deficiencies of teachers' pay. The magnificent turnout for the rally (estimated at around 10,000, which required two separate sessions in the main hall), together with various demands from some 200 local associations, prompted the Executive to call for a limited two-week protest action. From 4 to 16 October members were instructed to operate Alexander's 'short working day'.

All work outside normal school hours was banned, including:

marking of books at home;

formal preparation of lessons at home;

voluntary activities such as those concerned with sports, clubs, drama groups and others (but national and international events were exempted);

staff meetings;

parent-teacher meetings, open-day activities arranged in the evenings, prize-giving functions;

school journeys or other activities involving groups of pupils at weekends.

There was much genuine regret amongst members on the need for such action but the NAS believed that some formal protest action was essential. That was why it was limited to two weeks. The demand for a Royal Commission on Teachers' Pay had to be kept alive.

The war of words between Alexander and the NAS heated up. Accustomed to dealing with a quiescent Teachers' Panel, Sir William had a problem with 'truculent' people. Alexander was goaded into trying publicly to justify his 'short working day long holiday' jibe. He denied alleging that teachers did not have full-time jobs: "The management side based their evidence wholly on facts and figures. It would be pleasant to think that once exposed this canard could be relied upon to go to ground. Unfortunately, mendacious propaganda of this kind has been meat and drink to the NAS." The overbearing Alexander believed his views were "fact", those of the NAS "mendacious propaganda"!

Alexander accused the NAS of "personal abuse of those of us responsible for running the Burnham Committee". He said the NAS action "was not the best way to present an acceptable public image of the education service" nor for us "to achieve status as a body". Sir William even suggested the NAS should learn the refrain from Marlene Dietrich's hit song "Where Have All The Flowers Gone": "When will they ever learn?" The NAS quickly retorted that Alexander should learn another line of the same song: "Where have all the young men gone?"!

NAS unrest did not die down after the two-week action in October. Local associations continuously demanded action from the Executive. A 'go slow' along the lines of Alexander's 'short working day' was widely implemented all over the country following another refusal by the Minister on 18 November to institute a Royal Commission into the state of education and the teaching profession.

The Executive resolved to instruct members in selected schools to refuse to work with unqualified staff and in others not to teach classes containing over 30 pupils, in accordance with the 1959 Schools Regulations. Although many schools volunteered for action, it was decided by the Executive to proceed carefully and Birmingham was chosen to start the action on 6 December 1965 for a limited duration.

A survey in Birmingham had revealed:

over 200 primary classes taught by unqualified teachers;

many subjects and classes in secondary schools taught by unqualified staff;

in 34 schools 33 were found to have oversized classes of between 3 and 13 pupils;

together with great shortages in subjects such as mathematics, science and domestic science many schools had buildings which were substandard.

The NAS believed that a Royal Commission on the state of the education service was essential to draw up a comprehensive plan to secure sufficient funds to provide the teachers, buildings and equipment for a proper education service. The quota system whereby LEAs were allotted the number of qualified teachers they could employ was insufficient to meet the needs of the country. It merely shared out a shortage. NAS members were no longer prepared to paper over the cracks.

At a meeting well-remembered by NAS activists of the Burnham Committee on 4 November 1966 the Association managed to break the one-voice rule – but only for a few minutes. Against a background of a government pay freeze Sir Ronald Gould spent 90 minutes setting out the Teachers' Panel claim for 1967 which anyway had already been in the possession of the Management for several months. Management took just five minutes to say they could say nothing ahead of the Government's expected White Paper. Incensed by the unreality of Burnham, Terry Casey demanded to be heard. The Chairman overruled Gould's protests and allowed Terry to speak on the grounds that the one-voice procedure applied to "normal" circumstances, which these were clearly not. Terry voiced the customary criticism of Burnham being a poodle which needed reform to place the Government in the front line as the decider of the global sum. However, when Sir William Alexander protested, the Chairman backed off and ruled "that Mr. Casey's comments be expunged from the record!"

In 1967 another deadlock occurred after management made a final offer of a basic scale running from £800 by 14 steps to £1,470 in response to the Teachers' claim for £900-£1,700. At the arbitration teachers secured an additional £70 at the minimum and £100 at the maximum to produce a Basic Scale of £800-£1,500 p.a. Limited backdating was awarded to 1 July but the currency of the settlement (to 31 March 1969) consolidated the move from triennial to biennial settlements.

The NAS commented that the award was totally inadequate, although it went some way to meeting its case on structure. The Association believed the arbitral body was influenced by the report it had commissioned from the Economist Intelligence Unit (EIU) which had shown that teaching lacked good career prospects.

The arbitral body also awarded safeguarding of salaries upon closure or reorganisation following the famous 'comprehensive circular' 10/65, subject to the teacher not unreasonably refusing an alternative offer. The NAS welcomed this decision, which it felt had been brought about by the determined stand of its members at the Down School in Bexhill-on-Sea in Sussex refusing to accept posts in the reorganised school without full salary safeguarding for other teachers who had lost promoted positions.

The Durham Dispute erupted as the negotiations for 1969 got under way. Locally it gave rise to long and bitter exchanges between the NAS and the LEA. Its origins lay in the widespread discontent felt by the NAS over pay, and the fighting spirit shown by Durham members had an impact on the national salary situation.

Throughout and beyond the negotiations and settlement of 1967 the NAS remained profoundly dissatisfied. After the Birmingham-led action (end of 1965 into 1966) grass roots members continued to call for action. The career teacher was being called upon to shoulder the major part of the burden in running an ever more demanding education service in the familiar context of a high wastage rate of young teachers. The report of the EIU had strengthened these beliefs of the NAS membership. No other union seemed at all concerned about the situation.

The NAS called a Special Conference in London on 7 December 1968. Recognising that a forthcoming 'D Day' meeting of Burnham would either be 'deadlock or defeat' the Conference decided to call for protest action in various parts of the country in support of the Association's salary demands. The action would start in February 1969. It was originally intended to be of limited duration. The form of the action was to be a refusal to teach oversized classes. The regulations dating from 1944 laid down maxima of 40 pupils per class for primary (with 30 for senior pupils) and 30 for nursery and secondary children. They were more honoured in the breach than the observance.

There was an escape clause which allowed the regulations to be breached: if there were a "shortage of teachers or other unavoidable circumstances the number of pupils on a register of any class shall be such as is reasonable in all the circumstances". The NAS thought that after 24 years 'these circumstances were avoidable'!

The Executive decided to limit the action to secondary schools since some pupils might have to be sent home at short notice when NAS members implemented the action. By the end of January 1969 HQ had some 100 volunteering schools, a number that increased several times over as the starting date for the action approached. The week beginning 3 February was to see the Bertram Ramsay School in Teesside start, followed by two in Durham, Milton Hall in Newton Aycliffe and Acre Rigg in Peterlee. More schools in Birmingham, Bradford, Brighton, Bristol, Bromley, County Durham, Coventry, Leeds, London, Liverpool, Plymouth, Rochdale, Teesside, Warwickshire and West Sussex were to join in successive waves.

The NAS defined the action as a work to rule. The normal timetable would be rigidly adhered to and in addition to refusing to take oversized classes members would decline to cover for staff absences. Voluntary activities, including those over the lunchtime, were on this occasion excluded from the ban. Members were instructed not to take any action which might endanger the safety of pupils.

The LEAs met in London on 30 January and under the active encouragement of their national leader, AEC Secretary Sir William Alexander, decided to take a common and hostile line against the NAS members. In short the AEC's strong advice was for LEAs to give warnings of serious breaches of contract. If action persisted after five days the offending teachers should be disciplined, suspended and regarded as having terminated their contracts. The NAS believed that Alexander was determined "to teach us a good lesson" in return for all the trouble we were causing in Burnham. Alexander declared: "The NAS would have to take what's coming to them."

However, as the action unfolded most LEAs viewing the situation at close quarters chose to ride events as NAS members implemented their protest action for the planned limited time. Some reacted in accordance with the Alexander line but found that NAS members extended the duration of their protest action as a consequence. Most of those LEAs soon relented, wisely appreciating that it was not worth the candle, except Durham. The Council took a hard line and although they were soon looking over their shoulders and complaining that no other LEA was following the 'Alexander line', nevertheless persisted.

The result was a prolonged and bitter battle, the like of which was rarely seen in teacher trade union affairs. The NAS gained the support of the parents and the councillors lost out badly. Eventually over £90,000 of lost salary was returned to the NAS who had subsidised its suspended and 'sacked' members throughout the dispute, all of whom were reinstated. I write more about the remarkable detail of the dispute in chapter 41.

1969 proved to be a pivotal year in the hitherto sad history of teachers' pay negotiations. It was to mark the end of a 50-year period when the majority of teachers meekly accepted whatever fate was determined for them by governments and employers hell-bent on securing their services at the lowest possible price. The determined fight put up by NAS members in Durham was another sign that times were changing.

The 1969 settlement, whilst yet again profoundly unsatisfactory, was nevertheless to set in motion a chain of events that led to nearly 20 years of repeated industrial action, mainly by NASUWT and NUT. The main reason for the change was the increasing influence and size of the NAS and thereafter the NASUWT.

The developments post-1969 also have to be seen in the context of an ideological struggle between the 'flat raters', represented by the NUT, and the 'careerists' identified with the NAS and UWT. The NUT's doctrinaire adherence to the 'primacy of the basic scale' meant that if it were conceded in practice the salary of teachers would largely reflect the price of young, short-term albeit professional employees just out of college. One could partly staff the teaching service on that basis but it was impossible to run a high-quality education system without the continuity, experience and skills accumulated by a sufficient number of career teachers, men and women.

Governments and employers tried to balance the conflicting pressures, paying some respect to egalitarian principles, but having at the same time to invent a whole series of ploys to recognise the realities of the marketplace, especially in respect of graduates. The result was a very hierarchical salary structure that was depressed by 'the primacy of the basic scale' and which diminished the status of the classroom teacher by awarding money and promotion to those who moved away from the 'chalk face'.

Arguably it took until the Green Paper on the *Future of the Teaching Profession*, published late in 1998, and followed up by some fundamental salary structural and workforce reforms at the beginning of the twenty-first century, for these issues to be properly addressed. Serious attempts to resolve these fundamental problems during the great battles of the mid-1980s came to grief.

The story of how we got there really begins in 1969. The NAS was not alone in identifying the need for fundamental reforms to the salary structure. Governments and employers were often with us. The LEAs published a booklet, *The Burnham Story*, in April 1963 thinking that the Committee was about to be abolished. Writing about the development of salary differentials and career opportunities between 1948 and 1961 the booklet claimed that "they had been extended and strengthened more than for any other comparable group". It went on revealingly to say: "Had it lived, the Burnham Committee was pledged to carry this process a stage further in 1965."

The LEAs stated candidly that: "The superstructure of above basic scale posts erected in the 1950s has served to maximise the opportunities of those who make long-term careers in education. Investigation of how they work has shown clearly that they have gone to men more than women, to graduates more than non-graduates, to those with the best qualifications and those possessing the scarcest skills."

So much for equal pay! That which the Government and Management conceded in 1955 they at least partly took away by stealth through the salary superstructure. The Ministry's statistical information showed that the percentage of teachers with promoted posts had risen from 30% in 1947 to 43% in 1961 (respectively around 56,500 out of 188,400 and 115,300 out of 266,500).

The NAS shared the employers' desire to reward the career teacher but disagreed strongly that the elaborate superstructure was the way to do it. As well as protesting against pay levels the NAS had been greatly concerned with the salary structure (not to mention the negotiating machine itself), which prevented any sensible review. The NAS engaged the EIU, which produced reports vindicating its view that the system of responsibility payments was not flexible enough to reward individual merit and did not necessarily reflect the benefits of continuity of service. Starting salaries compared reasonably well with other occupations but career prospects had worsened appreciably after some eight to ten years.

Following the devaluation of the pound sterling in 1967, another traumatic experience for the Labour Party in Government, Prime Minister Harold Wilson had decided to impose wage restraint, establishing at the same time the Prices and Incomes Board (PIB), which was also charged with controlling prices. The norm was set at 3.5% p.a. for all wage settlements over the following two years. Trade union discipline was falling apart, with many workers taking unofficial action across the country. The 3.5% 'norm' was largely ignored but the Teachers' Panel accepted it.

Thus Burnham 1969 was yet another profoundly unsatisfactory experience for the NAS. The Teachers' Panel claimed a basic scale of £900-£1,700. This was the same claim as for the previous five years despite the rapidly rising rates of inflation.

Faced with the usual management refusal to make an acceptable offer, the Teachers' Panel reduced its claim for the basic scale, to run from £860 to £1,615. In what may have been a stitch-up 'behind the chair' (to secure an improved offer at the price of foregoing arbitration) the Teachers' Panel was then offered £860 to £1,600 which it accepted by majority vote. In effect the NUT and the Joint Four, almost entirely alone in national negotiating fora, were accepting Wilson's 3.5% annual norm for wage rises. The NAS walked out in disgust, formally dissociating itself from the agreement. I appreciate the irony of the NAS, having fought for 40 years to be included, then walking out to emphasise its opposition to the deal. It was becoming increasingly clear that Burnham produced either deadlock or surrender for the teachers.

This was one sell-out too many even for the NUT. This time there was a genuine revolt. The NUT Conference just a few weeks after the settlement, whilst accepting the money, refused to accept the two-year currency of the deal and sent their leaders back to demand an interim award for 1970. The NAS was delighted to see some backbone injected into the NUT negotiators and fully supported the call for an interim award.

Chapter 27 - The NASUWT Breaks Through in the 1970s

Towards the end of 1969 the NAS and UWT quite deliberately set aside their policies in favour of restructuring to unite with the NUT in the demand for a flat-rate £135 claim for an interim rise for 1 April 1970. This was done on the understanding that when the interim business was settled the issue of restructuring would be addressed in a Working Party (WP). Thus the Interim Pay Campaign opened on a more harmonious note in the relationships between teachers' unions.

The Management initially refused to make any offer at all but then relented a little, suggesting a £50 (per annum!) interim increase. The NAS was quick to publicise this sum, amounting precisely to 19s. 2¾d. per week, setting it against a background of widespread industrial unrest in which there were offers of £3 for shipbuilders, £4 10s. for firemen (14-17%), £1 10s. for transport workers, £2 10s. for London dustmen and £85 for BOAC captains on the new jumbo jets!

Following up earlier informal exchanges Terry Casey wrote to Ron Gould on 9 October 1969 suggesting joint action to pursue the Interim Claim. The NAS and NUT decided to embark upon co-ordinated strike action for maximum impact. By November 1969 the NAS was inviting areas to volunteer for a series of rolling strikes of between three and five days together with half-day walkouts.

By 25 November the NAS had chosen 21 LEAs to launch its first wave of strikes in the period 1 to 12 December. Most of the schools selected were in rural areas and medium-sized 'country' towns in East Anglia, the East and West Midlands and the Home Counties. The traditionally more militant large cities were held back to later to illustrate the depth of anger and widespread support for action. The NAS Report to Schools was headed "Avalanche" and went on to say:

"Reservations and inhibitions about strikes have been swept away in an avalanche of teacher militancy. Concern for a pseudo-professional image, fears about 'breach of contract' and even genuine conscientious scruples have been brushed aside by tens of thousands of men and women teachers incensed at last by Burnham's futility."

A detailed joint statement on co-ordinated action was signed by the two GSs, Casey and Gould, and circulated to schools in January 1970. "The principle is that no teacher in a strike affected school will undertake any task, whether rostered or not, which would normally have been done by a striking colleague.

No re-arranged time-tables will be worked. Classes affected by the strike will have to be sent home," explained the NAS Report to Schools.

Nearly 500 members in Wales started the second rota of strikes in January 1970. The *Financial Times (FT)* quoted Terry Casey on 6 January explaining the tactics behind the strikes. The *FT* credited Casey with taking the NAS into the TUC and creating the militant mood which had now spread to the NUT.

On 21 January the LEA employers circulated advice to their members which was generally well balanced and non-inflammatory. They recognised their duty to provide education but at the same time advised against "exercising this duty in such a way as to exacerbate relations with teachers in the delicate situation". However, in March the Birmingham LEA had to be threatened with a 'Durham-style reaction' if it persisted with its 'Durham-style salary deductions' for members who had been excluded for refusing to scab on teachers out on strike. The LEA quickly relented.

There were soon signs of the Secretary of State, Ted Short, making noises designed to placate the NAS and possibly divide and rule the Teachers' Panel. He suggested the Burnham machinery was unsatisfactory, he would be willing to open talks on the whole structure and that he was not sure statutory machinery was needed. That was music to NAS ears but not to the NUT's. However, that was not going to distract the NAS from securing a good settlement of the interim pay claim.

By the end of January strike action spread to many areas and towns in Yorkshire. The NAS held a one-day strike in London. That was the first time I heard Terry Casey speak – to a mass rally at Friends House in Euston. To this day I recall his apt metaphor when, concluding his address, he likened the NAS to a "powerful tug-boat which is pulling the big NUT liner away from its 'sleepy berth' in safe harbour out onto the adventurous high seas!"

On a personal note I might add that these events were the reason I became involved in teacher union affairs. Aware of the row about teachers' salaries I had enquired about the matter of the three unions' representatives at my school, St Joseph's Academy in Blackheath, south-east London, where in November 1968 I had taken a temporary job filling in for a teacher who had left unexpectedly for maternity reasons.

Listening to the NAS, AMA and NUT Reps explain their union positions I had no hesitation in joining the Schoolmasters. My next move was to attend a meeting of the Lewisham Branch of the LSA, being held after school one day in a public house (The Albion I recall) on the High Street in the Summer Term of 1969 as the interim campaign was emerging. I made the mistake of opening my mouth and within a few months I was the Local Secretary. My intended temporary sojourn in London was to last for over 30 years and these events were to transform my life, turning me into a teacher trade union representative, something I had never contemplated hitherto.

The interim claim, backed up by an impressive and high-profile series of rolling strikes by NAS, UWT and NUT members, was finally settled on 3 March 1970. Significantly it was settled in direct talks with the Education Secretary, Ted Short, who had to get the approval of the Treasury to offer £120 which the Teachers' Panel unanimously agreed as acceptable. Once again the subsidiary nature of Burnham had been fully (and indeed helpfully) exposed.

During the talks that led up to the settlement Ted Short also stipulated that as soon as convenient Burnham should re-examine the salary structure with the aim of making it more attractive to the career teacher. The NAS understood this to have been part of the deal from the start and supported the Management when it formally put the proposal forward after the interim claim had been settled.

However, the NUT began to backslide, disputing the existence of such an agreement; but the record was clear. At the Burnham meeting 15 December 1969 Management offered a full re-examination of the structure of teachers' salaries "within the Burnham Committee or independently by reference to the National Board for Prices and Incomes", which could allow rises above the Government's 'norm' on special grounds such as pay and productivity deals.

Mrs Lena Townsend, Management Panel Leader, again raised the salary structure WP at the Burnham meeting 5 January 1970, to which the Teachers' Panel Leader and NUT GS Sir Ronald Gould (who was on the point of retirement) responded, saying it was unwise to press the issue until the interim claim was settled.

At the next Burnham meeting on 6 February 1970 in response to the same pressure, Mr Clarke, who as Chairman of the NUT Salaries Committee had been appointed to the same position on the Teachers' Panel, formally moved: "That this Panel reaffirms that they are prepared to discuss a new structure when there is a satisfactory settlement on the present interim claim." Terry Casey on behalf of the NAS immediately seconded the motion, which was then carried unanimously.

The question of members who did not comply with Executive instructions and who declined to do the honourable thing and resign came to the boil at Conference 1970. There was a strong philosophical belief in the NAS that once decisions had been made to strike, everyone should accept the majority verdict and participate. That was a fundamental tenet of trade unionism. If unable to participate, through conscience or other consideration, then resignation was the only honourable alternative.

Besides the action instructions over the Interim Pay claim, the Executive had also decided to levy all members £2 to build up the Sunderland Reserve Fund to meet contingencies such as members being victimised for participating in the strikes. The levy was also seen as a way for all members to participate in the struggle, as not everyone could be summoned to strike – members in special schools, for example, generally being exempt.

The NAS prided itself on issuing instructions when all members were to be involved in national action. There was a widespread belief that instructions issued by the National Executive afforded members some degree of protection from headteachers and employers who might pressurise members not to comply. They could deflect such pressure by referring management to the National Executive, under whose instructions they were acting.

The rules of the Association stipulated that members could be expelled for "refusing to carry out a competent instruction of the Executive". Some might say that echoed a military-style discipline. They would be right!

However, there was inevitably controversy over consistency of reporting and the granting of dispensations, some official, others not so. Conference insisted the rules be rigorously applied, but of course no one was in a position to police and enforce the rules comprehensively.

Over the succeeding few years several hundred non-strikers and levy-defaulters were expelled and many others left of their own accord when challenged under the rules. Some took up the offer of a hearing and making representations to the Executive. There was a minority view that we should not be too rigorous in enforcement, for that reduced membership. Others scorned such views, believing in 'quality' rather than 'quantity'. When the TUC got to know about our practices they expressed surprise that a union would expel some 500 members. The TUC believed we held the record for the most expulsions!

The issue remained live for many more years. It enabled the NASUWT to claim to be a disciplined union that would not tolerate 'free riders', although implementation on the ground was not always so clear-cut and easy. One of the first so-called 'employment' acts of Parliament under Mrs Thatcher in the 1980s effectively buried the issue as it made expulsion of members for such reasons illegal.

After the unions' Easter Conference season was over Burnham reassembled on 17 April. The new Management Leader, Alderman (later Sir Fred) Hutty, restated their desire to establish the WP which everyone (outside the NUT at least) believed had been agreed. He suggested both sides prepare papers.

By this time the NUT had a new GS, Ted Britton, who had previously been an official with its partner organisation, the ATTI. His predecessor Sir Ronald Gould had established a reputation amongst a large section of the educational world as a statesman. As far as I could judge, NAS members viewed Sir Ronald as a distinguished leader of an undistinguished organisation.

Ted Britton seemed to have come from nowhere, 'to have risen without a trace', and he possessed neither the charisma nor the reputation of Sir Ronald. He was never to be a match for the energetic, articulate and charismatic Terry Casey, leading the militant band of schoolmasters into one battle after another. Ted Britton replied to Mr Hutty, saying that while the Teachers' Panel was in agreement in principle to have a WP, it did not wish to table a paper at this stage. Procrastination, the father of volte-face, had raised its ugly head.

At the next Burnham meeting on 3 July Ted Britton spent a lot of time presenting the Teachers' Panel claim for another pay rise. But it was simply the NUT's policy. No account was taken of other views despite the real prospects of advance occasioned by the expressed wish of the Secretary of State for restructuring. The NUT-cum-Teachers' Panel claim was heavily 'basic scale weighted', demanding it run from £1,250 to £2,375, representing a 37½% rise. Once again Sir Ronald Gould's maxim, "Either all teachers get it or no one gets it", was alive and doing well despite the sad history of the latter prevailing over the former.

Sir William Alexander for the Management said, "let us reach agreement on structure"; values could be discussed afterwards. When pressed on the WP issue Ted Britton came a little 'cleaner' on the NUT's real intentions. He said he doubted the usefulness of a WP in which we could not "discuss structure with figures because this becomes negotiation and we do not want negotiation in a small committee".

That was of course palpable nonsense since 'progress' was often only possible in the small 'behind the chair group' regularly and willingly operated by the NUT and Management leaders. Burnham, with over 50 representatives together with supporting staff and officials, was far too large a group. The NUT's real intention was to stifle the freer exchange of views in a WP where other unions would be able to have a voice.

The NAS, and indeed the emerging UWT, felt betrayed. We had compromised our interests by uniting with the NUT to fight for the flat-rate interim award. Now the time had come to consider the prospects for the career teacher. The NUT reneged. It preached unity but was never prepared to compromise to make it work in practice.

It was almost like going back to the pre-recognition days. Unable to get any genuine hearing inside the Burnham arrangements for the 50,000 plus members it now represented, the NAS had no option but to take its case into the public arena. In September 1970 the NAS Executive publicised the policy it intended to present to a Special Salaries Conference in Birmingham the following month.

The Executive updated the Economist Intelligence Unit (EIU) report it had commissioned on teachers' pay a few years previously. The new version, entitled *The Teacher Shortage and the Economic Status of the Schoolmaster*, concluded: "There is no financial incentive for the really able to enter teaching."

The report identified two major reasons for this: poor career prospects, and in comparison with other occupations the range of teachers' salaries was too narrow, with the maximum being too low. Starting salaries compared reasonably well but by their late twenties and thirties teachers were falling seriously behind their contemporaries with broadly similar qualifications.

The NAS salary policy advocated four new and overlapping scales:

Scale 1 covering ten years from £1,100-£1,800, with entry points of two and four increments respectively for ordinary and good honours graduates;

after four continuous years service the teacher would automatically be transferred to Scale 2, allowing the unpromoted classroom teacher to reach a maximum of £2,600 after ten years;

Scales 3 and 4 would cover the promoted and head of department posts whilst heads' and deputies' salaries would have their own scales all suitably enhanced in salary terms.

While the NUT predictably tried to silence the NAS 'minority' in Burnham, public opinion seemed more sympathetic. The popular tabloid, *The Daily Mirror*, in an editorial on 4 September 1970 said that both unions wanted more money, "But the NAS want a special rate for the long serving career teacher. On this issue *The Daily Mirror* is firmly on the side of the NAS. It is not enough to make teaching attractive for young men and women entering the profession. The prospects must be good enough to prevent the best talent walking out after a few years to better paid jobs elsewhere."

In the 11 September 1970 edition of *Education* the NAS's 'arch enemy', Sir William Alexander, wrote strongly in support of career structured salaries and the EIU report. It must be doubtful that such enthusiasm would have extended to the level of pay the NAS envisaged, as opposed to the shape of the salary structure.

The NAS found another unlikely ally in *The Daily Telegraph*, which believed that a united teacher voice would betray common sense: "The NUT has undoubtedly made an ass of itself. The NAS claim, which is still much more than the employers will concede, is more sensibly argued and more likely to win public approval than the NUT's wild demands."

A couple of days later the Sunday newspaper, *The Observer*, opined:

"The schoolmasters' plan is of course based on self interest . . . but in this case self interest coincides with the public interest. The problem is how to avoid the waste of the country's resources involved in training teachers who stay only a relatively short time in the profession. The schoolmasters' plan would be a welcome step in the right direction."

On 16 September the *FT* observed that: "The truly gloomy prospect facing the NUT is the probability of its being outflanked on salary policy by the NAS."

The NAS salary policy, already ambitious enough, would at an extra £152m cost much less but represent better value for money than the massive NUT claim of 37½%, amounting to a stratospheric £225m, of which £160m would go on the basic scale. At the same time those who stayed in teaching for 25 years and remained on the 'NAS Scale 1' would earn £10,000 more than they would under the NUT's proposals with the emphasis on the first few steps of its basic scale.

The NUT, having followed the NAS into membership of the Trades Union Congress, lodged an official complaint with the TUC General Secretary, Vic Feather, that we were undercutting the Teachers' Panel claim. The NAS responded insisting it had the right, like the NUT, to pursue its members' best interests.

The Special Conference on Saturday 3 October 1970 at the Digbeth Hall in central Birmingham duly adopted the Executive's Report on Salary Restructuring. A second session in the afternoon was devoted to policy on pensions, in which several important issues were coming to the boil. It was the first NAS Conference I attended and I recall being very impressed once again with Terry Casey who, in summing up the debate on salaries, had been at his electrifying best. It was also the first occasion on which I heard the NAS pensions consultant Dryden Gilling-Smith speak. He was also very impressive, combining much humour with technical wizardry, making the hugely complicated business of pensions easily understandable to the lay person.

Back to Burnham on 6 October; the NAS pressed inside the Teachers' Panel for the WP to go ahead. It was the best way to unlock the door for more money, have a meaningful discussion on a new structure and avoid the danger of delay with the economic situation deteriorating.

Management tabled an "illustrative" restructuring offer but it only amounted to a meagre 7½%, was insufficient for a genuine restructuring and produced serious anomalies. The NAS dismissed this as a "dummy offer" but said it illustrated the potential of a WP if only the Teachers' Panel would "Come and get it".

At first the NUT reacted with some warmth. *The Guardian* summarised Ted Britton's comments: "Although Management had not paid sufficient attention to the basic scale, they were clearly moving towards the structural proposals made by his own union, in being based on the grading of posts rather than the grading of teachers."

The other major spokesman for the NUT, soon to be its President and for many years the unofficial leader of the communist block on the Executive, Max Morris, took a very different line. He dismissed the offer, saying "restructuring is totally unacceptable. It is an impertinence. The money they have offered is peanuts. We are not interested in restructuring, it is a ruse."

The *FT* on 8 October supported the NAS case, stating the profession needed "to attract and retain enough teachers of the right calibre" by a better salary structure rather than higher basic pay. The *FT* believed the situation was changing. The NUT, much larger and with a high proportion of young teachers, was losing influence with the Management, which "was not slow to show which approach it preferred. Yesterday it submitted proposals for a new five-tier pay structure – not quite what the NAS is after but much closer to its objectives than to that of the NUT".

At the same time as pressing the case for salary restructuring the NAS secured sensational coverage, starting in *The Daily Express* in mid-October 1970 for the fraudulent nature of the notorious Notional Fund for teachers' pensions which I write about in section 5, Teachers' Pensions. Banner headlines in *The Express claimed that the Treasury owed teachers £1 billion* for mismanagement of their pension contributions.

Before the next meeting of the Teachers' Panel there were some signs through correspondence between Casey and Britton of rapprochement between the NAS and NUT although both made statements 'safeguarding' their respective positions. Again the 'alternative' NUT spokesman, Max Morris, took his own line in public, declaring the "olive branch" from the NAS to be a "stinging nettle"!

Perhaps the rapprochement had been occasioned by another event of great importance which occurred in October 1970. Harold Wilson had called a snap General Election, the opinion polls having recently moved in his Labour Government's favour. But to much surprise Ted Heath's Conservative Party was elected to power. The "dangerous delay" the NAS had complained about many months ago was materialising more quickly than we had feared. The Conservative Government would be taking a harder line on pay than its Labour predecessor.

The Teachers' Panel meeting on 5 November ended on a more consensual note with agreement to expose the weaknesses of the Management's offer and to press for improvements in the quantum and the shape. The differences between the unions were to be put to one side for the time being at least. However, on 10 November Management replied they were not prepared to drop restructuring and repeated their demand for the WP to be established. The NUT again refused, claiming that a WP would weaken its "primacy in the Teachers' Panel".

Management declared that "the one voice rule" was nonsense in present circumstances. Writing in *Education* on 20 November 1970, Sir William Alexander observed wryly how 'times had changed' in respect of the secrecy surrounding Burnham negotiations when he surveyed all the press comment over recent meetings of that Committee. He went on to say that "it is surely reasonable to suggest that such detailed discussion [on restructuring] can only take place in a WP in which all concerned have an opportunity to make their contribution".

The year was to end in deadlock. The NAS again deplored the "dangerous delay" as the economy deteriorated and there was much talk of wage restraint in the public sector to counter the rapidly rising rate of inflation.

On 4 December 1970 the NUT finally agreed to a WP, nearly 12 months late. Management had laid it on the line. The Teachers' Panel could choose between a WP now or a "straight" offer in January. Ted Britton said the NUT would agree providing Management "did not rule out the possibility of reaching a settlement which included the concept of the basic scale".

The NUT then wrecked the rationale behind a WP by insisting on ten seats with two for the NAS and one each for all the other unions. The sheer size of the WP would ensure progress was slow and render completion of its work, supposedly planned for the end of January 1971, completely impossible.

The *FT* described the development as a "climb-down by the NUT". *The Guardian* reported "strong rumours . . . that hard talking in the Working Party could produce £83m for teachers' pay, although it might come in stages".

Burnham next met on 14 February 1971 when the Management tabled a marginally improved offer amounting to 8% on the same structure as previously proposed. The offer was unanimously rejected on the grounds that the money was too low, with the NUT adding that it also objected to the new structure. An NUT spokesman was quoted the following day in the press: "We are not going to be saddled with a structure it would take us 20 years to get rid of."

Burnham adjourned to the following Friday, 19 February, when Management made a conditional or "reserved" offer. This was a process whereby 'behind the chair' Management indicated it would make a formal offer in full Committee if the Teachers indicated they would accept it.

That offer was for 9.7% on the new structure. The Teachers' Panel rejected it. Management said it was not prepared to make any offer based on the present structure or the Teachers' Panel proposals. In an apparently desperate attempt to conserve the old structure and in typical defeatist fashion the NUT dropped its claim to 15% (from 37½%).

The NAS quickly exposed the absurd position the NUT had got the teaching profession into. The NAS rejected the Management offer because it was too low. But the NAS was even more opposed to the NUT revised claim, for that produced less money for the career teacher than the Management offer. Adding 15% to the present basic scale for those entering teaching after 1 April 1971 produced more money in the first three years but less for every one thereafter in comparison with the Management offer. Young teachers commencing service on or after 1 April 1971 would gain £110 during the first three years but thereafter lose £3,100 for the rest of their careers. Those reaching the maximum on the same date would gain £83 in the first year and subsequently lose £2,400.

There was no better example of the willingness of the NUT to sacrifice the interests of the career teacher in favour of those who would be in teaching for just a few years.

Burnham resumed on 22 February. With no further movement from either Panel, deadlock loomed and arbitration beckoned. The NAS opposed arbitration in the circumstances of the one-voice procedure and the chaotic situation in the Teachers' Panel in which "the NUT had torpedoed its own claim" and reduced it below the amount Management was prepared to offer to career teachers.

The NUT's procrastination could well have been extremely expensive. Tom Driver, GS of the NUT's partner the ATTI, speaking in the Teachers' Panel on 19 February, said he believed that if negotiations had been conducted three months previously, they could have been offered 15% and secured 20%. The National Association of Head Teachers' (NAHT) GS, M.J. Camish, was quoted in *The Daily Telegraph* on 20 February saying that: "We could have got £87m last April but for the NUT left wingers."

When Burnham gathered again on 5 March the NUT still resisted all the available alternatives: arbitration or a WP or an independent inquiry. The NAS was scathing in its criticism of the NUT. In its Report to Schools in March 1971 the NAS reminded teachers that under deadlock and arbitration both sides reverted to their original positions. "The Management now stand on their miserly 8% offer. The Teachers' Panel, having slid to 15% must now climb back to their original 37½% claim. Having abandoned their pinnacle in the clouds to come down to earth with a bump, they must now pretend that they never left their exalted position. How can they persuade outsiders to take seriously the claim they so readily dropped inside Burnham?"

In Burnham on 31 March the NUT indicated it would boycott arbitration by refusing to nominate the teachers' representative.

The NAS was clear and united in its approach. It demanded an independent inquiry to achieve the fullest implementation of the proposed five new scales to secure the best deal for career teachers in the rapidly deteriorating economic situation.

The NUT was a house divided. Its militant left wing was in open rebellion against the vacillating antics of the leadership. The Inner London Teachers' Association (ILTA) was threatening to stage a one-day strike before the NUT Annual Conference, due to open in Scarborough on 10 April.

April 1971 in Torquay was the first Annual Conference of the Association that I attended. Like most first timers it still strikes me as one of the best of the 37 I have attended to date as I draft these words. Two debates were particularly memorable: one on ROSLA (Raising of the School Leaving Age); the other on the salaries situation.

That was the occasion of one of the finest fighting speeches on salaries ever heard at the Association's Annual Conferences. It was delivered by "the bruising speaker from Liverpool", as the *TES* described our Honorary Treasurer, Arthur Smyth.

The emergency motion Arthur Smyth proposed on behalf of the Executive dissociated the NAS "from the unrealistic attitude of the Teachers' Panel during the past 12 months" and "deplored" its failure to negotiate on structure. The motion recognised the structural proposals went some way to meet NAS demands but it declared "the global sum inadequate especially in view of recent settlements in the private sector".

The motion called for an independent inquiry to be set up by the Government "to resolve the deadlock and to ensure the interests of the career teacher can be effectively represented". The motion concluded by empowering the Executive "to take whatever action is necessary to meet the changing circumstances".

Arthur Smyth rehearsed all the events and broken promises of the previous 12 months and asked: "What have the NUT to fear? Is it the voice of the career teacher? Or the logic of career structure?"

Arthur Smyth reserved his most blistering comments for the issue of Government restraint for the public services but free rein for the private sector. Referring to the generous settlements in the car industry, Arthur Smyth said the NAS could respect "the smack of firm Government administered to a chaotic economy, but Mr Heath [the Prime Minister and a master yachtsman] who runs away from Ford and is terrified of Leyland doesn't frighten us very much.

"Restraint is for everybody or it is not for us. To Mr Heath and his crew we say, 'Listen sailor, if you can't ride the squalls, get out of the boat'.

"If we are being asked not to rock the boat what assurances have we of a satisfactory landfall and safe harbourage in the shape of career salaries? Is Ted

Health the salty strongman? Is Ted Heath the lugubrious landlubber? Will the real Ted Heath stand up?

"If Ted Heath can't stand up for the public sector, will he lie down and let us face the elements alone. If this is one nation let's have one set of rules for putting us back on the road to stability. In a free-for-all we'll fight for fair shares. Will the Government defend us or do we defend ourselves?" Arthur Smyth's speech received a rousing standing ovation.

At the NAS Conference dinner the guest of honour and Secretary of State for Education, Margaret Thatcher, supported the proposed restructuring. She said that "allowances encourage staff mobility, make schools less stable institutions and damage the continuity of class work".

At the May Executive meeting the NAS decided enough was enough after 13 months of procrastination and deadlock. The NAS blamed both the NUT and Government, the latter now operating an unofficial incomes policy in the public sector, whilst tolerating a free-for-all elsewhere. Furthermore the Government had put a block upon an independent inquiry, insisting that Burnham arbitration would have to be the only way out of deadlock. The NUT feared arbitration would rule in favour of restructuring; the NAS was scared it might not!

The Executive resolved that "Failing tangible movement towards a satisfactory salaries settlement by 24 May the NAS embarks on a work to contract policy which shall continue indefinitely". Strike action was specifically ruled out as it would save money for the Government and employers. Another very significant if little noticed event also occurred at this meeting of the Executive. For the first time the Union of Women Teachers (UWT) were present in the capacity as observers. Immediately after the meeting they declared they would fully support and implement the work to contract adopted by the NAS.

The NAS secured more support in the court of public opinion when *The Sunday Times* on 25 April savaged the NUT's approach:

"Teachers and pupils pay a high price for the NUT's romantic insistence that all teachers shall, nominally and basically, be equal. There is insufficient discrimination between the long-serving teacher and the short-term entrant to the profession. Only by taking administrative work can most teachers rise above the basic rate. Altogether the system is managerially antiquated, and perhaps its salient feature is the lamentably slow increase in teachers' salaries it has encompassed." *The Sunday Times* agreed with the NAS that the only way out of this impasse was an independent inquiry.

Chapter 28 - The 1971 Arbitration
A Pivotal Event in the History of Teachers' Pay

At the Burnham meeting on 18 May 1971 the NUT finally accepted defeat. After hours of internal wrangling the NUT Executive had voted by a narrow majority of three votes to accept arbitration. The NAS declared the issue facing the arbitrators would be: Do the teachers want the extra 5% or do they want the going rate without structure?

The issue was so stark that even the Joint Four abandoned their traditional tolerance of the NUT line to join with the NAS and NAHT in voting against the doctrinaire proposal seeking to delete restructuring from the terms of reference for the arbitration. That was carried by 18 (NUT and ATTI) votes to 10 (all the other unions). It was a proposition inevitably doomed to rejection by the Chairman of Burnham, who under the procedures was called upon to rule on contested terms of reference. Inevitably the positions of both Panels had to be included. To pretend they could rule out reference to such a bitterly contested issue once again reflected the triumph of futility over sanity that characterised so much of the NUT's approach.

The NUT had also lost its fight to nominate an independent chairman for the arbitration panel, having to accept Terry Casey's description of the Minister of Employment Robert Carr's "boy scout promise" of Government impartiality.

The newspapers on 19 May quoted Terry Casey saying he expected the public sector pay norm of about 10-11% to be applied to the arbitral award "if we are lucky, just enough to keep our noses above inflation". Terry added: "There was a smell of defeat about the meeting."

At the Burnham meeting on 24 May the NUT duly failed in its attempt to exclude restructuring from the terms of reference for arbitration. After the Burnham meeting the NAS held an emergency Executive and decided to boycott the arbitration hearing "since our presence might be mistaken for silent support whereas our absence would be noted". Instead the NAS would take militant action on the day, the details of which would be released later. Members were put on standby for action.

The NAS viewed the arbitration as crucial and asked why would the arbitrators force money down teachers' throats if the NUT-dominated Panel could convince them they preferred the going rate without restructuring. If the NUT won, Management would not contemplate restructuring for years to come.

The case for the career teacher, suppressed under the current one-voice procedure, would also be sidelined for a long time.

Officers of the UWT met immediately after the NAS Executive and decided to give full support to the action proposed. The 'Joint Two', as we became known, now had a combined membership of 67,000. The NAS had 55,000 members and the UWT 12,000, with both recruiting well.

The war of words between the NAS and NUT heated up with the announcement that we intended to take action. Whilst the NUT claimed most teachers were "heartily sick of disunity", the NAS asked: "Unity for what; to secure less money for the career teacher than that offered by the Management?"

The Teacher, 11 June, quoted Max Morris, then a future NUT President (1973-74), encouraging his members to 'blackleg' the NAS action on the pretext that it was unprecedented for a body of workers to take strike action in support of the employers' case. He was supported by the normally moderate Alf Wilshire, Chairman of the NUT Action Committee, not the most demanding role in British trade unionism.

The NAS retorted it was unprecedented for a union to seek less than the employer was prepared to offer. At the Teachers' Panel meeting, 16 June, the NAS recorded its strong objection to the lack of any reference to its views in the submission to the arbitration.

The NAS then continued its tradition of making its voice heard by the only other alternative – a protest march past the venue for the arbitration. On 30 June 1971 under the banner *'A' Day is 'D' Day*, some 30,000 NAS members, for the first time accompanied by many UWT colleagues, were transported to London on a one-day strike. They were assembled at various termini and then marched past the arbitral hearing in Carey Street, central London. They literally chanted their demands for 'career structure' for the arbiters to hear. In the afternoon members congregated in Hyde Park for a rally which was addressed by the NAS President, Ron Cocking, and the GS Terry Casey, together with Pennie Yaffe, GS UWT. Later on and into the evening many NAS and UWT strikers went on to lobby their MPs at Westminster.

It was an extremely orderly and effective protest which received massive media coverage. Over half the Association's members had attended. It was another first for me, on strike and on duty for the LSA, where we had the special task of 'picketing' the arbitral hearing as thousands of our colleagues marched past. Nor did we forget our local problems, carrying placards demanding a London Allowance of £200.

The arbitral award was announced a few weeks later on 20 July. The award was for a 10% increase plus structure. The 10% was above the Management's last formal offer but within the Government's norm unofficially laid down for the public sector. The arbitral body ruled there would be a new structure of five overlapping scales. They would replace the basic scale, posts 1, 2 and 3 and the special allowances, A to E. The money was inadequate; the structure far from perfect, but nevertheless an improvement on the old and a significant step towards the NAS policy.

Scale 1 to run from	£1,055 by	12 increments to	£2,090
Scale 2	£1,195	13	£2,206
Scale 3	£1,460	10	£2,320
Scale 4	£1,850	10	£2,710
Scale 5	£2,229	8	£3,005

(The former basic scale became Scale 1;
former Scale 1 became Scale 2;
Scale 2 posts and HoD A became Scale 3;
Scale 3 posts and HoDs B and C became Scale 4;
HoDs D and E became Scale 5.)

The graduate allowances were absorbed into the new scales. The graduate 'premium' was applied by way of additional increments at the point of entry. The Inner London Allowance was raised to £118, backdated to 1 November 1970.

The effective differentiation between primary and secondary was maintained by the number of Scale 2,3,4 and 5 posts available to a school continuing to be based on the pupil age weightings system. If a school were below a certain size it could not appoint above a Scale 3 post.

This system was also used to determine the salaries of heads. Schools were divided into 14 different groups, with the smallest paying heads on a scale ranging from £2,030 to £2,334, the largest from £5,135 to £5,480. The same system was used for deputies, and a differential of approximately 80% of the heads' salaries was maintained.

The system favoured the larger schools, overwhelmingly secondary, as intended by the Management with the tacit acquiescence of the teacher organisations.

The new structure was therefore much simpler, better reflecting the basic function of schools which was supposed to be about teaching children. The less than generous assimilation arrangements meant that the full consequences of the restructuring were not immediately available to teachers. But the benefit to the career teacher was illustrated by the new maximum of Scale 1 (for those 'unpromoted') rising from £1,720 to £2,090. That represented an eventual increase of 21½% as the scales then stood.

The historical significance of the 1971 arbitral award lay in the fact that it was the first time the NAS, now working openly with the UWT, had secured the adoption of a significant element of its policy against the majority NUT-dominated Teachers' Panel. Given the circumstances, that was no mean achievement.

The arrival of the annual round of pay negotiations was another historical development. The new scales were to operate from 1 April 1971 until 31 March 1972. That was long overdue. But it also meant that disputes were to become more frequent, given the fraught political and economic circumstances and the increasing influence of the NAS injecting more "backbone", to use Terry Casey's term, into the Teachers' Panel.

The 1970s were to prove to be a tumultuous time in teacher pay negotiations. Domestic problems and an unstable international situation added to intrinsic difficulties long associated with teachers' pay negotiations in the UK. Inflation soared, prompted by national and international events such as the US war in Vietnam and the space race with Russia, as well as the ambitious domestic reforms of President Johnson after the assassination of his predecessor, John F. Kennedy.

By the early 1970s the Middle East was again in turmoil with almost constant conflict, if not outright war, between Israel and its Arab neighbours. The fuel embargo placed by the Arab oil-producing countries generally against 'the West' led to a massive rise in price which in turn sparked more inflation and then led to some depression. Economists were faced with a new problem, 'stagflation'.

The 1960s, whilst generally regarded as a 'good time' for Britain, had been storing up economic problems which were not solved by temporary palliatives such as the devaluation of the pound sterling in 1967.

Edward Heath's Government of 1970-74, whilst well intentioned as perhaps the last Tory 'one nation' attempt to rule Britain in the twentieth century, failed in its economic policies. An attempt to expand out of economic difficulties led to stagflation, providing a new experience which defied traditional Keynesian analysis in that rising prices were accompanied by a downturn in output and an increase in unemployment.

Powerful unions, such as the miners' (NUM) and those in the car industry, were able to protect their members in the short term by securing high pay awards, taking industrial action when necessary. Unofficial industrial action became widespread, complicating matters even further. However, large increases in 'money' but not in 'real wages', whilst successful in the short term, was another factor stoking the fires of inflation and eroding the UK's competitive position.

The differences between the 'successful' and powerful industrial trade unions and the generally meek and mild teacher organisations became very stark. The situation played into the hands of the NAS as the most, relatively speaking, 'militant' teacher union. The NUT was forced to become more militant by the example of the NAS and the general 'industrial relations' climate in the UK.

The Teachers' Panel as a whole also became more aware of the movements in earnings across the economy and between comparable occupational groups. It became more vociferous in arguing the case for decent pay rises, given the escalation in general pay levels prompted by the inflationary pressures. The arguments that were made virtually every year in support of teachers' pay claims for the rest of the twentieth century became very familiar, with only the figures changing.

The case presented by the Teachers' Panel to the arbitral body of 1971 was a good example. Characteristically the submission began with a reference to the four principles or tests advocated by the McNair Committee way back in 1944, underlining both the 'eternal' nature of the problem and union negotiators' long memories. Many references were then made to comparative and absolute erosion going back to 1938, the like of which I have already quoted.

More recent erosion was also quoted since 1965. For example, the overall increase of approximately 7% for the two-year period 1967-69 had to be set against the RPI rise of 9% and an average earnings hike of over 13%. Hence the need for the Interim Pay Campaign of 1969-70 and the £120 flat-rate settlement of February 1970.

The Central Statistical Office Index of Purchasing Power indicated that the net annual salary required to provide the same purchasing power in 1971 as in 1938 for the equivalent of a Scale 3 Area teacher would be £1,548.28. The comparable 1971 teacher received less than that, with a take-home pay of only £1,264.75. Worst of all was the graduate secondary teacher whose loss in purchasing power was 33.5%. The average male earner had seen his purchasing power in relation to 1938 increase by 39.7%. The equivalent salaried or white-collar employee had seen a rise of 53.9%.

In a perhaps unintended stark admission of failure, the NUT dominated Teachers' Panel submission confessed all this was "the effect of 30 years' hard-hitting Burnham negotiations!" The NAS agreed completely, except for the description of 'hard-hitting'!

Using such data the Teachers' Panel claimed a minimum of £1,250 for the basic scale. Doing the same to the maximum of the basic scale produced a claim for £2,200 although compared with 1938 a figure of £2,950 would be justified. That was viewed as a bit too much in percentage terms. Instead the Panel took the 1967 base, increased by the 38% rise in average earnings and a "betterment factor" of £130 added to produce the £2,200 figure.

Proportionately similar increases were claimed for all the other allowances, scale posts and heads' and deputies' scales. Graduate allowances of £175 and £300 were claimed.

On the London Allowance the Teachers' Panel claimed a flat-rate £200 although the Management had offered a two-tier Inner and Outer Allowances of £138 and £90 respectively. The Arbitrators awarded £118.

The Teachers' Panel evidence also made much of the increased complexity and demands of the job of teaching, the longer hours worked and the widened social role now performed by schools.

Wastage rates were high and large classes in excess of 30 pupils, some with over 40, were quite common. In relation to demand, including the forthcoming raising of the school leaving age to 16 in 1972, there was a serious shortage of teachers.

The NAS, as was the case for all the unions on the Teachers' Panel, had no problems (apart from one or two details here and there) agreeing with the analysis and statistics on salary erosion. There was no disagreement that teaching had become a more onerous job, although many in the NAS believed some teachers had brought those problems upon themselves to some degree by arrogating social functions unto themselves.

When it came to strategy and salary structure there were quite fundamental differences, mostly with the NAS on one side and the 'others' strongly opposed to, or somewhat sceptical of, our philosophy on the other.

However, the 1970s were to mark a period in which the Joint Four were to begin breaking with their tradition of silent acquiescence to NUT policy as they increasingly realised the career structured approach of the NASUWT much better reflected the interests of their own members. The NAHT, recognised in Burnham thanks to the NAS's breakthrough, also saw far more merit in the career structured approach.

The NUT and NAS were the two major players: the NUT through its sheer size and established position; the NAS through its militant challenge to the status quo. The NAS was always more pragmatic in its approach. The NUT brought a 'fundamentalist' and egalitarian approach. The NUT argued that all teachers should be paid the same for the basic role of teaching. Extra payments could only be justified by qualifications or assuming additional responsibilities. There was a strong 'moral' tone in the arguments. The NUT believed it was "unacceptable" to pay one teacher more than another because one taught older children, or a special subject, or had to be attracted to a post from another school.

According to individual philosophies that may have been 'right' in purely ethical terms. However, it ignored market forces and the potential to secure higher increases for some if not all teachers. But the NUT took the argument one dangerous stage further, claiming it was also "unacceptable" that a 'good' teacher should be paid more than a 'bad' one. Recognising that this argument was more difficult to justify on ethical grounds, the NUT said this was so because "the criteria for judging 'goodness and badness' were largely subjective and had never been agreed within the profession, even in quite general terms".

Thus the Teachers' Panel submission in 1971 argued: "The nature of the teachers' work in the classroom was such that no one was in a position to make a sound judgement upon the relative merits of teachers, even if the criteria for the judgement could be agreed." The argument got worse: "Certainly the people who would make the judgement – school governors, members of education committees and the like – had neither the knowledge nor the qualification to make assessments of this nature." That was patronising and prejudged the experience and qualifications of such people, some of whom might even have been teachers. It also ignored the role the very same people already played in deciding who got promotion. This argumentation was 'keep out of my secret garden' of the worst kind, which ultimately caused much grief to be visited upon teachers.

The NAS became very wary of the two arguments: that there were no criteria for distinguishing a good teacher and that no one was in a position to make such a judgement. If teachers could not identify good practice, what claim could there be to professionalism? To claim there were no criteria to judge good teaching also seemed to fly in the face of common sense. Everyone familiar with a school knew who the good and weak teachers were.

It seemed to the NAS that criteria did exist for judging a teacher to be good or otherwise. The ability to command the respect and attention of pupils, to explain clearly, to motivate children, sound knowledge of the subject being taught, effective organisation and good working relationships with colleagues are but a few that immediately and easily spring to mind. The NAS soon got round to drawing up such criteria. What was the use of references if such judgements were impossible? The NAS believed that whilst overly fine distinctions could not sensibly be made, judgements of some kind were possible and indeed desirable if promotion were to be soundly based.

The submission to arbitration in 1971 also showed signs that even the NUT was at least subconsciously becoming aware of inconsistencies in their arguments. It conceded that: "The quality of education depended primarily upon the work that was done in the classroom. It had long been a complaint that financial advancement was dependent upon getting further and further away from the classroom. A premium was put upon duties other than teaching. If education was to be good, it was essential that classroom teaching should be a worthwhile career in itself. Teachers should not be forced by financial necessity to take on responsibilities outside the classroom for which they had no desire and, possibly, no particular aptitude" – a stunning condemnation of the promotion system being proposed!

Having already ruled out reliable criteria for judging good teachers, the submission tellingly went on to state with admirable if unintentional candour that: "Promotion in the teaching profession had long been a sore point with teachers, and, even where committees of laymen conscientiously tried to reach wise decisions, promotions could be an extraordinarily chancy business." As if realising the submission was arguing against itself it went on in apologetic fashion to claim (in this obviously flawed system) that "at least the person promoted would carry the responsibility and do the work"! That was (supposedly) infinitely better than having 'good' teachers paid more than 'bad' ones on dodgy criteria interpreted by suspect people.

This was an astonishing admission that the very structure the NUT and others in the Teachers' Panel were seeking to justify and maintain was fundamentally flawed. This problem was exacerbated by the inability of the basic scale to offer the financial rewards necessary. Whilst it could be justified on ethical or equality grounds, those considerations flew in the face of market forces and the ability/willingness of governments to pay up. As Sir Ronald Gould had often said, "Either all teachers get it; or no one gets it." The problem was that largely no one got it.

The argumentation was rich in setting up false antitheses. The suspicions of the NAS were soon to be justified. During the 1970s a series of surveys by LEAs themselves, not to mention the work of the NAS, began to reveal that the promotion system was flawed. Payment for additional responsibilities can indeed be justified if they are genuine, important and relevant to the task in hand. But schools were using promoted posts in vastly different ways and often for quite spurious reasons. Indeed, promotion for 'additional responsibility' was only half the story. The other half was being used for exactly the reasons supposedly rejected by the Teachers' Panel 1971 submission – rewarding 'good' teachers.

By the end of the 1970s the NASUWT had developed criteria by which teachers could be sensibly judged. The Union had also become acutely aware of the vagaries of the promotion system and had developed detailed policy on how the system needed to be radically overhauled. I return to those issues later as they became more and more 'live' as the influence of the NASUWT grew and Government and LEAs saw sense in our policies on collegiality and "the central importance of the teacher in the classroom".

Chapter 29 - One Step Forward, Two Steps Back

Whilst advantageous for teachers, annual negotiations brought their own problems. The tortuous Burnham procedures were often to lead to negotiations flowing continuously from one year into the next.

Two weeks after the 1971 arbitrated settlement was completed, business commenced for 1972. Most unions favoured percentage increases and building on the structure recently arbitrated. However, in November the NUT forced through the Teachers' Panel a flat-rate claim for £250, even rejecting the Joint Four compromise of 15% subject to £200 minimum.

A serious credibility problem was emerging. Most unions had gained members whilst the NUT had suffered losses, casting doubt on its claim to represent more than 50% of teachers. It was possible for 9 NUT votes to commit all its 16 on the 28-member Panel, so determining policy. One understood unions voting as one. The problem lay in the NUT policy being unrepresentative and totally ignoring other views. Consequently the one-voice procedure was also under increasing strain.

The global sums claimed by the NAS, NUT and AMA were broadly the same. However, the different proposals on distribution meant that during the course of a 40-year teaching career, with no promotion, a teacher would earn £95,600 under the NAS proposals, £87,180 under those of the AMA and £85,896 under the NUT's. The £685 which would be gained for the first five years of teaching under the NUT's proposals were at the expense of nearly £10,000 lost over a lifetime career achievable by those of the NAS.

The post-1971 arbitration period became dominated by flat-rate v career structure in a context of a deteriorating economy and (eventually) a Government-imposed incomes policy following its humiliation by a very successful miners' strike in 1972. With Management adamantly refusing to countenance flat rate, the 1972 claim ended up at arbitration before the unions' Conference season in April. Lord Pearson, Chairman of the Arbitral Panel, awarded between 9% and 11%, thereby slightly eroding the 1971 differentials. After the 1972 Pearson Arbitration, Scale 1 started at £1,179, rising to £2,279. Scale 2 ran from £1,319 to £2,406.

In March Management's impatience over the futility of Burnham "as at present constituted" had been reflected in Sir William Alexander's public comments about deadlock leading inevitably to arbitration: "If this is what the future holds it might be better to establish a permanent review body to which the teachers and management could make their submissions and which would then resolve the differences which might exist." Little did Sir William realise how canny and prescient his comments were eventually to prove.

By 1972 I had become Secretary of the Lewisham Branch of the LSA. I was angry that the London Allowance had not been increased despite its low level. With my colleague Officers in Lewisham we persuaded the LSA Executive and then the NAS leadership to sanction a ban on ghosting – refusing to cover for posts left vacant – as a serious teacher shortage developed in London. Twenty large secondary schools in ILEA were put on part-time education.

The NAS Special Salaries Conference called in Nottingham, October 1972, concentrated as much upon the need to reform Burnham as it did upon maintaining the career structure introduced in 1971. The Conference was in no mood to rely upon pious hopes, and the floor instructed the Executive to prepare plans for militant action and pledged its unconditional support to enable the Association's objectives to be achieved.

By November 1972 in the face of economic crises, the Government had introduced a statutory wage policy, beginning with Phase One – a complete freeze, or "standstill", to use the official softer language. Three more 'phases' were to follow, allowing for limited rises.

Despite Management offers to increase the London Allowance from 1 November it was caught up in the freeze and the Government resolutely refused to countenance any exceptions. In October 1972 the Management Panel was prevented from making an offer which the ILEA and other London authorities believed would have been for £220, but the Government's Phase One curtain came down. Around 250 NAS members demonstrated outside the Burnham Committee meeting. I recall the occasion well. It was the first time I had participated in a 'spontaneous strike', having the previous night used our quick telephone chain communication system 'to get the members out'. In November 1972 and January 1973 several derisory offers of £13 and £15 were made but rejected as "risible". Deadlock ensued.

The Government's Phase Two allowed for £1.00 per week plus 4% for all workers. In February 1973 the Management offered a flat-rate amount yielding 9% for teachers at the bottom end of the scales and 3.8% for the heads of the larger schools at the top end. It was obvious that a weak-kneed Management was ready to abandon the 1971 structure in the belief that this would avoid another arbitration and so save the Burnham Committee.

Terry Casey tried to intervene to put the case of the career teacher. The Chairman, Sir John Wordie, adjourned Burnham for over an hour for consultations in a forlorn attempt to find a way around the one-voice procedure but the NUT would not relent. The NAS claimed that under Phase Two of the incomes policy when the Government had legislated for a set level increase for all employees, other bodies such as Burnham should not be allowed to redistribute that amount. The NAS also stated it could support a just incomes policy fairly applied to all.

After several long withdrawals by the NUT contingent from the Teachers' Panel, early in April 1973 the Burnham Committee reached agreement on a flat-rate £127.00 increase subject to minor variations. It was rumoured that the NUT members of the Teachers' Panel had withdrawn because they were deeply divided amongst themselves. It was believed that they split nine to seven in favour of the £127.00 offer.

The NAS expected nothing else from the NUT but was disgusted with the Management's capitulation, reneging on its support for the 1971 structure. It seemed absurd that an unfair and illogical settlement was reached to maintain an equally unfair and illogical negotiating machine.

Undeterred, the NAS carried on with promoting the interests of the career teacher and commissioned an independent report dealing with pay, pensions and conditions of service in the EEC countries. Entitled *The Schoolmaster in the EEC* it was researched by the Foreign Business Advisory Service (FOBAS), which was linked to Manchester University Institute of Science and Technology. It showed that taking the average salary of an unpromoted teacher aged 45, the British schoolmaster earned £1,670 net after deductions, the German equivalent received £3,700, the Belgian £3,330, the Dutchman £3,050 and the Frenchman £3,760. Furthermore, in EEC countries many extra-curricular activities attracted additional payments.

In November 1973 the NAS made submissions to the Government's Pay Board. The latter was now engaged in reporting some anomalies and disparities so that the Government could, if the Pay Board reported favourably, allow modifications to its pay code. The NAS made a strong case to restore the differentials introduced by the 1971 arbitral settlement on the new structure. The two settlements of 1972 and 1973 had produced salary increases of 10.8% at the start of the scales but only of half that amount for a teacher on the maximum of Scale 2. Management had reneged on assurances in 1972 that the inadequate funds would be available for proper restructuring and would not count against increases to cover inflation.

Meanwhile local councils were in the throes of Government-imposed reorganisation. The Association of County Councils (ACC) and AMA took the opportunity to sideline the AEC, viewing it as a special interest lobby on behalf of education, and seized direct control of the Management Panel of Burnham. A few months later (in May 1974) a new Secretary of State implemented the necessary Parliamentary action to remove the AEC from Burnham in line with the demands of the AMA and ACC. This signalled the end of Sir William Alexander's reign as the effective boss of the Management Panel of Burnham. The NAS observed it was poetic justice that statutory provision used to chop the AEC was devised to threaten the NAS during the row over Burnham secrecy after the Association had secured representation in 1961. Few teachers lamented the demise of Sir William Alexander and 'his' AEC, but education was not well served by the change of regime.

By 1974 NAS protests about the inadequate flat-rate salary settlements of recent years had produced pressure to secure overtime payments for the many additional duties carried out by career teachers. Bans on unpaid overtime started to spread around the country with the full support of the Executive. The 'southern bias' at the start of the action was unusual for the NAS. I was very active in getting the ban implemented in Lewisham, described by *The Evening Standard* as "a militant branch", which supplemented our existing action of 'no ghosting' which had already forced many schools onto part-time education. I recall having to overcome resistance from some PE teachers anxious to continue with their school sports teams.

January 1974 saw the unusual but welcome practice adopted by the Management Panel of making an offer by post. It was in line with the Government's incomes policy Phase Three allowing 7% plus 1% for flexibility.

In a meeting with the Pay Board the NAS deputation claimed that the 1971 arbitration differentials had been eroded and should be re-established. The NAS also pointed out that average earnings, despite the Government's incomes policy, had nevertheless risen by 13.1%. Teachers, not being paid overtime, had only received a 6% increase on average.

In February 1974 the Management Panel again betrayed career teachers in another desperate attempt to secure agreement rather than risk another deadlock and possible arbitration. Despite the Government's incomes policy under Phase Three stipulating 7% plus 1% for flexibility (with an escalator or 'Threshold' clause if inflation rose above 7%), Management offered increases of 11% at the start of the scales, tapering to 6% for those in the middle and upper parts. Agreement was soon reached on that basis early in March 1974.

The negotiations had taken place in the middle of a miners' strike and a General Election called by Prime Minister Edward Heath to determine who governs Britain (Parliament or the NUM). It produced a perhaps surprisingly close result in which the Labour Party was returned to power. Reg Prentice was appointed Secretary of State for Education.

The NAS pointed out that the employers had stated last year that "differentials had been now diminished to such an extent that any similar approach to last year would be inappropriate". The NAS said their actions belied their words and they had forfeited the goodwill of the career teacher. The ban on unpaid overtime spread further, notably into the Merseyside region, as the NAS saw payment for extra duties as the only way around the problems posed by the restrictive Government incomes policy and the 'flat rate' policies of the NUT, aided and abetted by the Management Panel.

Progress was made in Ealing where the Council had agreed a scheme for additional payments for teachers undertaking extra duties at the request of the Chief Education Officer either within their own school after normal hours or at another outside such time under a separate contract. Following submissions from the LSA, the ILEA put out positive proposals for overtime payments. However, the initiative stalled as all the other unions, led by the London NUT, strongly opposed the proposals. The ILEA was already paying for second contracts outside 'normal' schooling, which the other unions ignored.

At Conference April 1974 the Senior Vice-President, John Chalk, condemned the Management's "wet, weak and waiving policy" which had damaged career teachers' living standards. Conference demanded a reversal of Management's policy and declared that the working hours of teachers shall be on the basis of a maximum of 40 working weeks a year of not more than 25 hours per week. All work undertaken outside these working hours shall be defined as overtime and paid for at appropriate rates. The motion strongly urged the Executive to instruct the membership to ban all unpaid overtime. The motion was overwhelmingly carried with only 14 votes against. Speaking to the press after the Conference debate Terry Casey said that after 4 o'clock: "If there is no pay, there is no stay."

Addressing Conference, the new Secretary of State for Education, Reg Prentice, said he favoured higher pay for teachers but held out little hope as there were other more important priorities. He regretted the conference decision to ban unpaid overtime, angering members by declaring that had he been a delegate the number voting against would have been increased by one, to 15.

Chapter 30 - The Houghton Heights

As May 1974 arrived the future looked bleak. The NAS was expanding its ban on unpaid overtime, which appeared to hold out little prospect of success at least in the short term. But events were soon to happen which dramatically illustrated the benefits of never giving up the good fight; of demonstrating that you were not prepared to accept a thoroughly unjust situation without some response.

A meeting was called of Burnham for 24 May after the Secretary of State had suddenly announced that there was an extra £10.8m available for schools in areas of social deprivation. The LEAs were somewhat surprised by the announcement and expressed resentment against Government interference in the Burnham machinery. Some interference!

Meanwhile the nurses had also been expressing great concern about the level of their salaries. At a Cabinet meeting held on the morning of 24 May 1974 the Secretary of State for Health secured an independent inquiry into the pay of nurses. It seemed that Reg Prentice, aware of the depth of resentment manifested by the unpaid overtime ban, suddenly decided that if the nurses could have it, so could the teachers. Apparently he immediately made a similar request for an inquiry into teachers' pay which was quickly if surprisingly agreed in the Cabinet.

One hour after the end of the Cabinet meeting Reg Prentice told Parliament: "The Government are well aware of the depths of feeling among teachers that the relative position of their pay in recent years has suffered a particularly serious decline." He emphasised "the need to give more adequate rewards to career teachers". He announced an independent inquiry into teachers' pay with increases backdated to the present day, 24 May. On the day there was no other information provided. The DES was as surprised as anyone else.

Incredibly the NUT declared that it "resented this interference". The NAS representatives on Burnham immediately welcomed this long-sought inquiry. Terry Casey declared: "Reg Prentice lobbed a political bombshell into Burnham. The NAS wanted all salaries to be increased both for the young entrants and the career teachers but one group should not have to pay for the other." He warned that these two objectives could not be achieved cheaply.

Terry Casey said the Executive would reconsider the ban on unpaid overtime. I recall hearing the news of the independent inquiry as I arrived for a meeting of the Lewisham Branch after school to prepare for an LSA demonstration due on 4 June. The LSA was calling for members to attend a meeting for that afternoon to lobby ILEA leaders. The ILEA had tabled proposals to pay teachers for work after school organised as 'third sessions' but all the other unions were refusing to discuss them.

Instead of preparing for the lobby I had to listen to one of my National Executive Members, Gerry Lee, normally a very militant person, argue that we should accept the view of the National Officers and cancel the demonstration since the NAS had suddenly achieved an ambition it had pursued against the views of the entire Management Panel and the NUT for many years.

I had to accept the logic of the National Executive and again found myself learning something new but important. Recognise when you have achieved something. Accept and build on it. It was an important principle to the pragmatic NAS.

The newspapers' comments the following day were revealing. *The Guardian* on 25 May reported teacher unions welcoming the announcement "but the largest, the NUT, reacted fiercely against the idea of an independent body interfering with the teachers' pay structure".

The weekly *TES* deadline had just missed the Houghton news but on 31 May it reported: "The Education Secretary announced an independent review of teachers' salaries and pay structure last week to the delight of the NAS, the chagrin of the NUT and a cautious welcome from the local authorities. The only organisation that has consistently campaigned for a better deal for 'career teachers' is the NAS/UWT."

A few years later on, after big pay rises for teachers had been secured, an inter-union dispute broke out on the issue of "Who got Houghton?" Unbelievably the NUT claimed the credit. In addition to the newspaper reports referred to above the NASUWT reminded those with conveniently short memories of the official record of the Burnham Committee of 24 May 1974:

Minutes:

"3. The Teachers' Panel placed on record their concern that the activities of the Committee were being circumscribed by announcements made by the Secretary of State without prior consultation with the Committee."

Verbatim:

Mr Britton (NUT General Secretary):

"We are further disturbed that we now have had announced to us that there will be an independent inquiry, which is going to deal with structure and presumably the internal relativities within the teaching profession".

It was entirely typical that, given the chance, the NUT would have quashed the establishment of such an inquiry, seeing it as an invasion of its empire, the crumbling Burnham edifice it wanted to protect above all other considerations.

The NUT had consistently opposed independent inquiries in the past and indeed any 'invasion' of its 'monopoly position' such as working parties even when they offered potential to secure more money for teachers' pay. In total contrast the NAS greeted the inquiry with its full support, indeed with undisguised elation. The inquiry became the most famous and significant event in the history of teachers' pay in the twentieth century, producing the largest pay rises ever experienced by the profession.

In June the Secretary of State announced that the Independent Inquiry into Teachers' Pay would be chaired by the Rt Hon Douglas Houghton, CH, who had been in his time a long-serving GS of the Inland Revenue Staff Federation union, an MP and Cabinet member. Lord Houghton had also been Chairman of the Staff Side of the Civil Service National Whitley Council. He was extremely well qualified to conduct an inquiry of this kind. The membership included people with trade union, industrial and educational interests with none having any specific teacher union or LEA allegiance.

The Houghton Inquiry was charged with reviewing the salaries of all non-university teachers, thereby including all schoolteachers in England, Wales and Scotland as well as lecturers in FE and Colleges of Education. 'Houghton' would also eventually apply to Northern Ireland, subject to negotiations between the unions and the Department for Education in the Province.

The terms of reference were to examine the pay of non-university teachers in Great Britain and to make recommendations. In addition the Education Secretary wrote in a letter to the Chairman amplifying the terms of reference: "Although the Committee is entirely free to deal with whatever aspects of pay are considered by it to be relevant, . . . I would be glad if you and your colleagues would consider evidence relating to pay structure as well as levels of remuneration."

The NAS strongly welcomed the emphasis placed on structure by Reg Prentice. Predictably the NUT tried to get the Management Panel of Burnham to do the opposite. At the meeting on 24 June the Teachers' Panel at the insistence of the NUT sought the approval of Management to make a joint statement to the Houghton Committee urging it not to consider details of structure. Ted Britton said they had the experience of arbitration (in 1971) to reveal what could be done to structure.

Management replied it was impossible to stop reference to structure now that the Secretary of State had specifically requested it. In any event the report would have to come back to the Burnham Committee. Ted Britton protested that seemed only to be a technicality. His Panel regarded it as a legality rather than a reality. The new Management Leader, Sir Ashley Bramall, quickly and perceptively retorted: "The legality reveals the reality."

The NAS said that Houghton had not only to consider structure but ensure that teaching became a worthwhile career, able to attract and retain people of the right calibre.

Naturally the NAS quickly got down to the business of drawing up its own submission to the Houghton Committee. The Association had immediately upon the announcement of the membership of the Inquiry forwarded a copy of its recent publication *The Schoolmaster in the EEC*, which concluded that teaching had to offer better career prospects.

The 24 June Burnham meeting agreed to allocate the £10.8m 'forcibly injected' into teachers' pay by decision of the Secretary of State through salary supplements in Educational Priority Areas (EPAs) on a two-tier basis. Teachers in schools designated EPA would receive allowances of £200 p.a. for those with fewer than three years service in such establishments; those with more than three would be paid £275 p.a.

The NUT had tried to secure a flat-rate payment. But the Management Panel spokesman, Sir Ashley Bramall who was also the Leader of the ILEA where EPA schools abounded, was adamant that an additional incentive was required to encourage teachers to serve longer in such places.

By the time Burnham next met, in December 1974, it decided that a rose by any other name would not smell as sweet and EPA was changed to Socially Deprived Area and then again to Social Priority School (SPS). Teachers of Special Classes in 'ordinary' schools designated SPS would be paid either the SPS or the Special Schools Allowance, but not both. LEAs had to submit lists of schools to be designated SPS by the Burnham Committee, which would determine the criteria and 'cut-off' points after local consultation.

The NAS evidence to the Houghton Inquiry was an extremely important statement of salary policy and philosophy. Essentially the Association took the structure and the relativities established by the arbitration of 1971 and uprated the salary levels based on a return to the comparative position of the schoolmaster in 1938.

In 1938 the schoolmaster started on a salary equal to the average national wage. He could expect to attain a salary equal to twice that average. In the previous 36 years the status and pay of the career teacher had been seriously eroded as the Secretary of State had conceded in establishing the Inquiry.

To re-establish the 1971 relativities at a commencing salary equal to the average national wage would give the existing scales the following values:

Scale 1	£2,200 x	13 increments of	£154 to £4,202	
Scale 2	£2,400	13	£154 to £4,402	
Scale 3	£3,000	10	£160 to £4,600	
Scale 4	£3,800	10	£160 to £5,400	

Scale 5 £4,400   10   £200 to £6,000
Senior
Teacher £4,800   8   £200 to £6,400

The NAS also proposed a reduction in the number of scales by automatic progression from 1 to 2, effectively combining the two. The effect would be to ensure that every career teacher could earn twice the national average wage without promotion away from the classroom. Career prospects would be enhanced in the interests of teachers and education.

The NAS also suggested a change in the points system, which was based on the age weightings of pupil numbers and determined the number of promoted posts available. In the future the number of promoted posts should depend upon the level of staffing. This would help eliminate the injustice felt by primary teachers.

Towards the end of the year speculation began to grow in the press about 'when' and 'how much' Houghton would report and recommend. By early December the Burnham Management, with the express permission of the Secretary of State, authorised LEAs to pay their full-time teachers £100 "on account" as soon as possible and hopefully in time for Christmas. This welcome development had the intriguing description of "extra statutory authority". Management emphasised the sum had no implications for the recommendations Houghton might make.

The *TES* speculated on 6 December that Houghton could be recommending 30% pay rises judging by DES evidence to the Inquiry. The *TES* also pointed to the "rocketing cost of living" which could be of relevance to the 1975 negotiations, Houghton being based on salaries as at 24 May 1974, the date the Inquiry was established.

The *TES* speculated that the teachers' unions had pitched their 'claims' too low: "The NUT told the Committee in their evidence that starting salaries should be £2,000 p.a. The NAS pitched it a little higher at £2,200. But both claims seem rather low of the mark." That was not the usual kind of comment made by the press!

Lord Houghton published his report a few days before Christmas on 20 December 1974. He recommended rises varying between 25% and 32%. The overall long-term increase in the total pay bill was estimated at 29%. This time all the teachers' unions welcomed the report. Those that had opposed the establishment of the Inquiry were now claiming the credit!

The recommended new scales were as follows:

Scale 1   £1,677 to £3,069;
Scale 2   £2,103 to £3,474 (old Scales 2 and 3 merged);
Scale 3   £2,727 to £4,068;

Scale 4   £3,339 to £4,611;

Senior Teacher   £3,609 to £4,977;

Deputy Heads   £2,307 to £6,234;

Head Teachers   £3,381 to £8,523.

(Cost of living 'Threshold Payments' had to be added to the scales.)

Lord Houghton also recommended "periodic reviews of the pay of teachers independently of the separate negotiating bodies every seven years". The NAS, commenting on this "seven year itch", said it belied Houghton's confidence in the Burnham negotiating machinery.

The recommended increases for teachers in Scotland were primary 31% and secondary 30% (in the long term). In the short term they were respectively 28% and 26%. Interestingly, Houghton made no recommendation to alter the Scottish practice of separate scales for primary and secondary.

The increases recommended for other groups were:

England & Wales:

Further Education	29%
Farm Institutes	27%
Colleges of Education	36%

Scotland:

Further Education	29%
Colleges of Education	35%
Central Institutions	32%

Houghton estimated the total annual pay bill for full-time teachers in regular service in primary, nursery, secondary and special schools in England and Wales would reach £1019.6 millions for the year 1974-75. The equivalent figure for Scotland was £129.3 millions. These included employers' on-costs of national insurance and pension contributions (about 15% of the totals).

Houghton did not 'formally' cover teachers in Northern Ireland, which was then in the middle of the worst sectarian violence of the 'current troubles'. Negotiations between the local unions and the Northern Ireland Department for Education (DENI) would follow. The rising importance and influence of the NASUWT in Northern Ireland would ensure that parity with the rest of the UK was to be maintained. Significantly the first NAS President from Northern Ireland, John Scott, had been installed earlier in 1974 at the Easter Annual Conference.

In his letter to the Secretary of State Lord Houghton indicated his Committee had rejected the possibility of an interim report because the 'Royal Commission' aspect of the exercise was far more important than the 'arbitration' element. He wrote: "It became impossible to contemplate making an interim report in the face of all the evidence put to us for structural change."

Houghton also hoped that: "Attention will be given to the absence of any place for joint negotiation on matters of pay and conditions of service." Burnham only dealt with pay, which Houghton thought was 'unusual and inconsistent'.

Houghton noted that: "The teaching profession is a large and important group within the public sector which lacks any agreed doctrine of comparability or a reliable estimate of public esteem."

Perhaps suspecting there would be those wanting to cherry-pick, Lord Houghton concluded his letter: "We emphasise that our recommendations stand as a whole and represent the Committee's considered judgement of what is needed comprehensively to bring salaries and structures more into line with current needs and expectations. We hope no time will be lost in implementing the improvements and reforms which we unanimously recommend."

The NAS and UWT found much satisfaction in the Houghton Committee's commentary on the general issues surrounding teachers' pay. Houghton noted the decline in the number of graduates entering the profession and agreed with the unions' submissions that teacher supply was as much an issue of quality as quantity.

Houghton decided to base his recommendations on the salaries index for men rather than average male manual earnings. Making the comparison based on 1965-66, primary teachers' pay had fallen by 17.4% and those in secondary by 16.6%. The pay of those in FE and Colleges of Education had fallen more, by around 20%.

Houghton observed that direct job comparators with teaching were difficult to establish. However, some civil service and local government grades seemed to recruit from the same 'market' as teaching. Executive Officer (EO) grades in civil service for classroom teachers and Higher EO grades for heads appeared reasonably close comparators as far as one could establish.

Houghton agreed completely with the views of the NAS, UWT and EIU, that starting salaries compared favourably but career prospects were poor in teaching.

Once again the NUT failed completely to understand how such an inquiry reporting directly to the real paymaster, central government, was the best and probably the only realistic way in which *both* starting and career salaries could receive the decent consideration required. The NUT was perhaps the biggest prisoner in its own 'empire' – the Burnham Committee. Burnham was sinking, but the NUT was the captain and could not bring itself to abandon ship in favour of better ways forward dealing directly with Government.

All the unions noted with satisfaction that in its commentary the Houghton Committee accepted the teachers' case that the job had become more complex and demanding. The Committee particularly acknowledged the greater diversity of the curriculum, involving much increased preparation. The trends towards more individualised as well as mixed-ability teaching involving harder work during classes; increased pastoral work; the enhanced activity outside normal school hours; and contact with parents and external agencies were all acknowledged. Last, but by no means least, Houghton freely conceded the escalating difficulties of keeping good discipline, particularly in the secondary sector following the raising of the school leaving age in 1972.

Houghton also accepted the NAS and UWT arguments that the salary structure had become bloated out of proportion and with its proliferation of allowances and extra scales, involving "fine differences between tasks and levels of responsibility" was increasingly inappropriate for schools. Houghton believed that the promotion system was too geared towards administrative responsibility, "leaving no scope for recognition of teaching ability alone".

The Committee did not have sufficient time to sort out the structure as much as it would have liked but nevertheless made recommendation for simplification despite the risks of creating further anomalies. Houghton also urged the negotiating bodies to continue "working towards structures as simple and straightforward as possible". That was music to the ears of the NAS and UWT.

Houghton believed the correct differential between heads and deputies should be in the region of 73-83%.

In short Houghton accepted the principles of the 1971 arbitration. The Committee fully accepted that starting salaries had much better kept pace with comparable occupations and more needed to be done to reward the career teacher. The importance the NAS and UWT had attached to the 1971 arbitration and the long struggle to secure it was well justified. The campaign to secure a Royal Commission or some other form of independent inquiry into teachers' pay, advocated for so many years by the NAS, was also fully vindicated.

The NAS declared in its first Report to Schools early in January 1975: "Houghton Strengthens Structure".

Predictably the NUT, inside the first meeting of the Teachers' Panel in 1975, quickly got into the business of tinkering to favour the early points on Scale 1. The NUT even suggested the implementation date of 24 May (1974) be delayed until 1 June to find money for this purpose. The NUT also tried reducing the salaries of all those in receipt of £2,001 or more to facilitate higher pay at the entry points.

Management was adamant in firmly rejecting all these ploys, being determined to stand by Houghton: "Doctor Houghton has made his prescription: we are not prepared to call in another Doctor." The Secretary of

State also let it be known he was not prepared to contemplate departures from Houghton.

After six hours the NUT gave in. However, the Management, possibly wanting to get home that night, did concede an assurance that "significant attention" would be given to the minimum of Scale 1 in the next round of negotiations. Before Houghton was formally implemented the NUT had begun the process of undermining the finest report on teachers' pay that has ever existed in the UK.

It took another eight hours of talks at another Burnham meeting later in January to tie up all the formalities. These included complicated arrangements for special schools and changes to the points score system for determining the group size of schools as recommended by Houghton.

The Burnham meeting on 10 February (1975) agreed the 1974 statutory salaries document and the Secretary of State indicated he would make an Order on the 28th of the month bringing the Houghton scales into operation w.e.f. 24 May the previous year.

Houghton recommended that his scales be uprated by the increase in the RPI for 1975. That indicated increases of around 20% would be required. Naturally the Threshold increases would have to be subsumed in the 20% figure, having already been paid to compensate for inflation covering the same period. As Burnham 1975 got under way the NUT predictably began to undermine the Houghton structure by proposing complicated arrangements to pay only 10% across the board. The Threshold Payments of £231 would be incorporated into the scales with the addition of a flat-rate £363 or 10%, whichever was the greater. The figures were deliberately calculated to favour the first four points of Scale 1 where the majority of NUT members were to be found.

The NAS protested vigorously, insisting on Houghton and the Social Contract for everyone. All employees were entitled under the terms of the Social Contract to the 20% required to compensate for inflation. If Management wished to honour its commitment to give "significant attention " to the minimum of Scale 1 it should do so by putting up more money, not by robbing Peter to pay Paul. The customary Joint Four compromise halfway between NAS and NUT was also rejected by the NUT.

However when Burnham next met in March the Management Panel was back in the two-faced business. Despite warning that Houghton differentials and career patterns should not be endangered by substantial enhancements of the lower points, it nevertheless offered to increase them by more than the 10% proposed for other teachers above point 4 of Scale 1. Nevertheless, the Teachers' Panel rejected the offer.

At the NAS Conference, April 1975, GS Terry Casey reflected on the irony that Houghton had given teachers a measure of justice in the present hard economic times which had not been apparent in the years when the country had, in the words of a Prime Minister (Harold MacMillan): "Never had it so good." Despite Houghton's efforts the Teachers' Panel was playing about with the structure to enhance starting salaries at the direct expense of the career teacher.

Reg Prentice received a warm welcome when he visited the NAS Conference. Despite his great achievement in securing the finest inquiry into teachers' pay, he had been barracked at the NUT Conference.

The Secretary of State pointed out that, during his tenure, spending on education had increased from £4.5 billion to £6 billion, reflecting the Houghton rise, amongst other things. Reg Prentice claimed he had been labelled the principal saboteur of the Social Contract because of Houghton. Whilst he claimed that the special treatment was necessary, the Minister also pointed out that teachers and other public sector employees needed a Social Contract to protect their interests in the longer term. He noted a periodic review had been recommended by Houghton but the profession should not fall behind and need to be jacked up from time to time. The NAS came to support this view quite strongly and argued for it in the TUC and elsewhere. The problem lay in securing an effective Social Contract applicable to all.

Lord Houghton was also at Conference. He was the guest of honour at the Association's Annual Dinner which took place in those days. It was a humorous and enjoyable evening. Terry Casey introduced him as "Lord save-us-from-Burnham Houghton"!

As Lord Houghton stood up to respond he was greeted with rapturous refrains of "More", to which he said he wished he had a supplementary report to read. He said he "had drifted into our lives when the job of establishing salaries could not be done by normal procedure. He came, reported and faded away." It was not the job of his Committee to make political decisions on major changes in public sector salaries, "but when he had listened to the NAS evidence it was not alien to his own way of thinking". In the civil service he "had lived by a policy of career prospects and had come to the conclusion that he had to do a major conversion job". He added that his Committee had not been restrained by the usual Treasury-imposed predetermined limits.

Every word Lord Houghton uttered seemed to be a justification for the NAS's career structured salary policies and its criticism of the Burnham negotiating machinery.

The next morning it was back to normal business. The salaries motion at Conference welcomed the Houghton report, whilst calling for more improvements through automatic transfer from Scale 1 to 2 and better promotion prospects based on the number of staff employed in a school rather than the ages of the children.

Conference, however, took issue with Houghton over the famous paragraph 294. That was the only major point on which there was serious disagreement between the NAS and Houghton. Paragraph 294, the conclusion of the main part of the report, defined the teachers' contract in vague terms. In it the Houghton Committee called for teachers to accept an obligation to use their professional power and expertise in the community's service. The salary levels they were recommending "justify expectations of professional standards of performance in return. As in other professions, these salary levels are in part recognition of the fact that the job cannot be compressed within a rigid structure of prescribed duties, hours or days. The majority of teachers, we believe, approach their task in this spirit."

The NAS believed that the contract could be so defined. However, if salary levels typified by Houghton had been maintained the issue would become academic, for teachers would indeed continue to give generously of their time and commitment. The NAS did not believe the Houghton analysis of "other professions" was correct. In many of them account was taken of "prescribed duties" and time. The problem of an ill-defined contract lay in the ever-increasing demands being laid upon the profession which had already become exploitative and indeed detrimental to the efficient performance of teachers' duties.

That is why the NAS insisted on the need for a well-defined contract whilst at the same time conceding that teachers would continue performing voluntary activities but that they had to be recognised as such. Teachers had already experienced the quite inappropriate tasks that their employers would gladly heap upon their shoulders in connection with the school meals service if the NAS had let them.

The NAS might have been better disposed to a vague definition of the contract if Government guaranteed (allowing for special circumstances) salary levels in real and comparative terms. The problem with paragraph 294 was that it allowed contractual demands to be increased whilst real salary levels could be eroded through inflation. And that, alas, is what happened. Inflation once again took off.

Soon after the Conference season it was unfortunately back to reality and to Burnham business as usual. Management got short shrift from the NUT as it rejected an offer which went some way towards favouring the first few steps on the salary scales. The NUT introduced an entirely new claim (in May 1975) for an overall 26% rise in the light of an award made to the civil service. The distribution would range from 37.5% at the bottom to 20.6% at the top of the scales.

Management dismissed the NUT-Teachers' Panel claim out of hand. With inevitable deadlock the claim was referred to arbitration. Once again the NUT refused to include 'minority views' in the Teachers' Panel arbitral submission. The NAS believed all teachers were entitled to compensation for inflation in accordance with Houghton's recommendations and the Social Contract, implying straight 21.2% increases for all. Redistribution of income should be a matter for the tax system.

Arbitration recommended a median increase of 22.3% with a distribution range between 34.3% at the bottom of Scale 1 and 17.3% at the top of the headteacher range.

The new pay scales became:

Scale 1 £2,252-£3,744
Scale 2 £2,655-£4,212
Scale 3 £3,357-£4,917
Scale 4 £4,056-£5,520
Senior
Teacher £4,368-£5,940

By this time the NAS was in open support for the Social Contract and an effective incomes policy. The NUT attacked the NAS position. But the Association was quick to point out that teachers had suffered badly in the catch-as-catch-can free collective bargaining decades. Houghton was set up to give teachers special treatment under the terms of the Social Contract. With great foresight the NAS warned in a Report to Schools in June 1975:

"Teachers must realise, even if some other trades unions will not, that the collapse of the Social Contract can lead only to the destruction of the Houghton advances by raging inflation or a statutory pay policy which will probably, as in the past, clobber the public sector."

That is what precisely happened. Within a few years (by 1978-79) teachers' pay was referred amidst much controversy to a Standing Commission, presided over by Hugh Clegg, previously Professor of Industrial Relations at Warwick University. And before the end of 1979 the Labour Government was forced to go to the country and lose a General Election to the Conservative Party. Margaret Thatcher became Prime Minister and set out about applying free market 'remedies' to the problems which the Social Contract had tried to solve. Teachers and the public sector suffered as never before.

The next phase of the Social Contract for pay increases for 1976, agreed between the Government and the TUC, amongst others, was very simple. It was a £6 per week increase for everyone. The NAS did not favour such a brutal flat-rate approach but accepted the situation and appreciated the longer-term benefit of a successful incomes policy. The NAS expressed the hope that differentials would be restored in due course. Naturally the NUT became a sudden convert to the Incomes Policy. At least it led to a very simple Burnham round of negotiations.

By 1976 the NAS and UWT had transferred engagements and become one. The fourth quarter of the twentieth century was to see even more dramatic developments in the determination of teachers' pay, including the longest and most bitter series of strikes in the mid-eighties.

SECTION FIVE
TEACHERS' PENSIONS
'The Notorious Notional Fund'

Chapter 31 - The Birth of the Teacher's Pension

Throughout its history the NASUWT has been the leading teachers' union on the vexed issue of pensions, often fighting lone battles to secure justice. The result today is a scheme which is comparatively good and certainly superior to many. But it could have been so much better had it been run properly, as the Union consistently argued, in the interests of all – teachers, employers, Government and taxpayers. By the beginning of the twenty-first century the amounts of money involved were so gargantuan that it is difficult to conceive of a plan that would put matters on a proper and sound financial footing. But the NASUWT could never be rightly accused of failing to try its best.

The fundamental problem lay in the Government acting as banker to the Teachers' Superannuation Scheme (TSS). Throughout most of the twentieth century governments pocketed the surpluses of teacher and employer contributions over expenditure, giving nothing more than paper 'IOUs' in return. This constituted the notorious Notional Fund, which benefited Government and subsidised the taxpayer to the tune of billions of pounds. A proper or real fund should have been established to invest these surpluses to assist in the payment of future pensions.

These facts fly in the face of the normal media stereotype which portrays public sector pensions as feather-bedded privilege, a one-way street in which Government carries massive liabilities to pay out billions of pounds. The fact that teachers and their employers have contributed massive sums of money over the years to pay for the pensions is largely ignored.

Despite pressure from the fledgling NAS at the time, the Government refused to set up an independent fund back in the 1920s as the Lord Emmott Committee recommended. It was to lead some 50 years later to the NASUWT pension consultant Dryden Gilling-Smith writing in the *TES* (December 1970): "The real scandal of teachers' pensions is that since 1925 successive governments have run a mock funding operation. It has always astonished me that such a learned profession could be taken for such a long ride."

The benefits of acting as banker explain why governments also refused to set up a 'proper' fund in the 1950s, 1960s and 1970s when the NAS was again demanding they should do so.

After some 50 years of uneven, intermittent, grace-and-favour selective provision, a proper teachers' pension scheme was born in 1898. The Elementary Teachers' (Superannuation) Act of that year set up the scheme, into which men paid £3 annually. An amending Act of 1912 increased the contribution for men to £3 12s. and for women to £2 8s. A very limited money-purchase scheme was introduced. Participation in the scheme was compulsory. Unfortunately the money was unwisely invested entirely in one 'basket', namely government consols just before the outbreak of the (Second) Boer War in 1899, when the value of the stock collapsed.

The commendable efforts of H.A.L. Fisher, President of the Board of Education, to improve the status and condition of the profession included the Teachers' Superannuation Act of 1918, the next major milestone in the history of our pensions.

Fisher enacted a non-contributory scheme, very similar to the one for the civil service. But it was short lived, chopped by the Geddes Axe in 1922. The Teachers' Superannuation Act of 1922 made teachers pay a compulsory contribution of 5% of salary for the time being. There was deep bitterness, for teachers believed, and there is much evidence to support their contention from Fisher and other public figures, they had accepted lower salaries in recognition of the non-contributory pension. An identical understanding underpinned civil service pensions, which in the main were non-contributory until changes were introduced in recent times.

To circumvent this inconvenient 'understanding' a fairly cynical exercise was conducted. A Committee under Lord Emmott was set up to consider the nature of this alleged 'understanding', and a review of the 5% contribution was promised pending its report.

Emmott 'found' amidst much controversy that there was no such understanding, flying in the face of the evidence presented by some of the major players involved. The relevant parts of Emmott's report were altered by narrow votes on the Committee to fit in with the Government's predetermined outcome.

Other less convenient recommendations by Emmott were not enacted. They included the establishment of a central superannuation fund from which all benefits would be paid and into which LEAs and Government would each pay 2.5% of salary, matching the teachers' 5% contribution.

The Teachers' Superannuation Act of 1924 continued the previous two years' arrangements until 1926. In 1925 a Bill was presented to Parliament which ended up as the Teachers' Superannuation Act of the same year, laying down the definitive arrangements for many years to come. Not surprisingly it made the teachers' 5% contribution permanent. Ignoring Emmott's recommendation for a government contribution it exacted 5% from the LEA employers, although the implementation was delayed until 1 April 1928. However, it should be stated that the LEA contribution was grant aided. The Government also undertook full responsibility for all pre-1922 service, effectively closing down the independent fund established to run the scheme from 1898.

It was significant that the Act did not take up Emmott's recommendation for an independent real fund. This calculated decision, illustrating that the Government had a sharp eye as to where its own financial interest lay, created a considerable controversy in the House of Commons, but the 'fundists', which included the NAS, lost the day. Lord Emmott, speaking in the Upper House, attacked the Notional Fund as a fraud and a swindle. Ministers stated: " . . . neither teachers nor their employers will be allowed to suffer financial loss as a result of this unconventional method of financing teachers' pensions . . ." That turned out to be the most hollow, if often repeated, assurance in the history of teachers' pensions.

The 1925 Act provided for an actuarial review every seven years, based upon the operation of the scheme as if it were a real fund. Government administered the scheme, paid out the pensions due and kept an account of the surpluses even though the money was actually spent on revenue expenditure, thereby keeping taxation down.

This 'paper account' was the 'notorious' Notional Fund. It was tantamount to borrowing from teachers and LEAs. From day one it should have been included in the national debt as it was clearly a liability to meet future payment. Today 'off balance sheet debt' is condemned and governments demand pension liabilities be fully exposed on company balance sheets while they have consistently refused to do the equivalent for the public sector schemes for which they act as banker.

Of course there are notions and notions. Another problem with 'our' Notional Fund was that for many years it was deemed to be invested in First World War stock attracting only 3.5% annual interest. Notional interest was paid in to the Notional Fund. It was another paper exercise, a glorified IOU operation. The 'fund' never had the opportunity of spreading investments and taking advantage of changing circumstances by buying and selling stocks and shares and perhaps other assets. The Government-recommended model pension fund for the private sector provides for an investment spread of one-third gilts, two-thirds equities. The NASUWT produced figures to show such models would have outperformed the teachers' Notional Fund many times over. In later times the NASUWT's constant campaigning for a real fund led to improvements in the notional interest arrangements although that was regarded by the Union as second best.

For most of the twentieth century contributions vastly exceeded pension payments, adding cash to Government coffers. Now that the boot is on the other foot there is clamour to charge teachers more. Yet over the years governments said they would guarantee the pensions in return for 'looking after' the cash so that teachers would not lose out. However, on two famous occasions (in 1956 and 1973) major disputes blew up as governments tried to increase teachers' contributions to cover actuarial deficits in large measure caused by the scandalously low interest deemed to be paid into the Notional Fund.

In this respect the fund operated as a real one, demanding more contributions from teachers and employers to remain 'solvent' and able to meet all its obligations in the long term. But it was far from 'real' in having its annual cash surpluses pocketed by the Exchequer and deemed to be invested in 'make-believe' Government War Loan Stock at 3.5%. Actuarial accounting is far from an exact science. Results can vary enormously depending on the assumptions made. Assuming the 3.5% return helped produce a long-term 'deficit' – the value of the fund on one given day being less than all the accumulated liabilities for the future.

The first actuarial report for the TSS appeared in 1935, covering the years 1922-33. It produced a deficit of £10m and the Government Actuary (GA) recommended an additional 2% contribution, shared equally between teachers and employers. Fortunately that recommendation was not implemented, probably due to the hostility of schoolmasters to the cuts in salaries.

The year 1925 witnessed an interesting development over the provision of state pensions. A Bill was presented to Parliament entitled "Widows', Orphans' and Old Age Contributory Pensions". In the original Bill teachers were included. The NAS judged that while the benefits were not generous, the Bill represented a good step forward and was an economic proposition for the schoolmaster.

In a move which greatly reaffirmed the conviction of NAS members that their interests demanded a separate union, an MP, Charles Crook, acting in close liaison with the NUT, successfully moved an amendment to exclude teachers. Mr Crook claimed the majority of teachers were women, and single at that. Amidst much laughter he joked they were therefore unlikely to leave widowers and orphans! NAS members were incensed and asserted they were not the misogynists. There was nothing of benefit to them personally. They were just trying to provide for their wives and children who would be left in dire financial straits in the event of their early death.

Another opportunity arose in 1929 when a new Widows' Pensions Bill came before Parliament. The NAS persuaded some friendly MPs to sponsor an amendment to include teachers, but it failed with no support coming from elsewhere.

As the world stumbled from depression to political crises in the lead-up to the Second World War pensions receded from public attention. The issues surrounding the TSS remained dormant until they exploded back on to the national scene in the 1950s. They came to a head in 1956 and drew together many other issues concerning teachers' pay, pensions, contracts, the law and the way in which the unions conducted themselves. The vacillations of the NUT produced 'The Calamity of 1956', which I write about in chapter 24.

Chapter 32 - The NASUWT Sets the Agenda
Teachers' Pensions in the 1960s and '70s

Despite 'The Calamity of 1956' the NAS did not give up the campaign for a widows and orphans scheme. That was not surprising, given the nature of the membership – predominantly married men. In 1961, '62 and '63 the Association sent deputations to the Ministry of Education and the Association of Education Committees (AEC) representing the employers, arguing for the amendment of the 1956 Act to facilitate such a change. The AEC opposed our plans, and other teacher unions appeared lukewarm at best, if not indifferent. Once again it fortified the fierce belief in the NAS of the need for a separate union to represent the interests of men.

By 1963 the NAS (now officially recognised) had succeeded in getting a tripartite Government-unions-employers Working Party (WP) established to consider the matter. The Executive's Salaries Committee immediately set to work gathering evidence on the provision for widows and orphans from a great many public and private sector schemes which, after analysis and collation, was presented to the WP.

In carrying out this volume of work many NAS activists became quite expert in the complex area of pension provision. This expertise and interest was passed down to grass roots members and established a tradition of informed lobbying. Many MPs also became well informed whether they wanted to or not, thanks to the activities of their NAS constituents.

In February 1965 the Report of the Working Party on Widows' and Orphans' Pensions was published. The NAS had very mixed feelings, welcoming the acceptance of the scheme in principle but deploring the terms under which it would be implemented.

First, the cost was to be borne entirely by the teacher at an additional 2% contribution of salary. The AEC, adamantly refusing to bear any contribution, agreed only to cover the costs of administration. Second, to rub salt in the wound, buying in past service was to be at 2% of current salary and not of the relevant earnings for the years (plus interest at the 'notional' rate) in question. The NAS demanded an ex gratia credit for past service.

With only the NAS dissenting on the terms, the Secretary of State for Education was able to steer the enabling legislation through Parliament before the end of 1965. However, one of the little noticed but interesting details was the decision to establish a real fund for the widows scheme in stark contrast to the notorious notional arrangements for the main TSS. When this new fund was wound up under the reforms of 1971 and integrated into the main scheme, it revealed a very healthy 'real' surplus despite only having received contributions from teachers.

A minor breakthrough was achieved by the NAS in 1966, after five years of lobbying, in securing free medical examinations which were required for the TSS. The NAS also secured the right for teachers to see the reports.

The NAS remained deeply concerned with the plight of the schoolmaster pensioner throughout the sixties. Men had a life expectancy some four years shorter than women. With national service (only abolished in 1958 with effect from 1 January 1960) men retirees had their pensionable service reduced by two years. Women drew their National Insurance (state) pension from age 60, men from 65. The schoolmaster generally had a wife to support. If he died his pension went with him unless from 1966 onwards he had opted in to the Widows and Orphans Scheme and paid the entire cost himself.

Many Conference motions in the 1960s called for much more generous and fair treatment for the retired schoolmaster. Pension Increases legislation was already on the statute book but the practice ungenerous, especially at a time of significantly rising prices. For example, the Pensions (Increase) Act of 1956 updating payments since 1952, only amounted to the equivalent of 3% per annum. Inflation had averaged 4.7% a year during that period. Improvements to inflation proofing were promised by the Labour Government in 1968 and eventually delivered by the Conservatives after their General Election victory in 1970.

The NAS continued to expose the 'fraudulent' nature of the notorious Notional Fund 'underpinning' the TSS. The NAS stated as long ago as the 1960s that it was willing to have a real fund for teachers where we would manage our own risks. Other unions argued we were safer and better off with the notional arrangements, with Government ultimately guaranteeing the pensions. However, in 1956 the Government reneged on the earlier assurances that teachers would not suffer from the notional arrangements and exacted increased contributions, precisely what would have been required with a real fund in genuine deficit.

The question of teachers' pensions returned to the front line in 1970 almost by accident. It all started with the Labour Government's attempts to introduce an earnings related national state pension scheme. In January 1969 Richard Crossman, Secretary of State for Social Security, published a White Paper, *National Superannuation and Social Insurance.*

To cut a long and complex story short, the plans involved contributions on salaries up to the level of one and a half times national average earnings. Taken with their occupational scheme, teachers would have been subjected to 'over-contributing', leaving them with pensions possibly up to 80% of salary. In effect teachers would be 'underpaid' but 'over-pensioned'. One alternative was for a large part of the money from the Teachers' Scheme to be diverted into the new state earnings related one. Consequently the Teachers' Scheme had to be re-examined.

When the DES pension branch officials visited the NAS HQ at 59 Gordon Square in London, they argued "very complacently" that with the teachers' occupational scheme, investment income from the lump sum, National Insurance and earnings related state pension, they could hardly expect to be 'left alone' receiving 85% of salary in retirement.

The NAS did not accept that logic for one moment. If teachers were to be 'over-pensioned' they had certainly been 'over-contributing'. Teachers paid 6% of salary plus 2% if opting in to the family benefits scheme, while the employers handed over 6% together with supplementary contributions. Taking these contributions and National Insurance payments together, something approaching 25% of salary was being paid in for all these benefits. The NAS representatives wondered where all the money was going.

Following 'The Calamity of 1956' and Burnham recognition in 1961 the NAS could no longer be excluded from membership of official working parties. That made a difference as NAS influence increased. Salaries and pensions were the bread and butter of NAS concerns but they were afforded a lower priority by other teacher unions. Many NAS activists had made themselves knowledgeable about pensions, enough to appreciate that 'real experts' in this notoriously complex area were needed. Terry Casey often used to joke that as a general secretary he could only be expected to possess general knowledge! On Terry's suggestion the Executive agreed to engage a pensions expert, Dryden Gilling-Smith, a consulting actuary who also ran his own company, Employee Benefits Services (EBS), accumulating an unrivalled knowledge of private sector schemes. Social Security Secretary of State, Sir Keith Joseph, was later to describe Dryden as "the best un-hanged pensions' expert"!

Dryden immediately developed an intense interest in the public sector schemes. He saw straight through the ruses employed by the Government experts which had bamboozled us. We suspected something was wrong, but we could not always prove it. Dryden explained that Government concern with our 'over-contributing' and 'over-pensioning' was a smokescreen to hide its real anxiety. As the 'de facto' employer the State would have to match teachers' contributions to the emerging national earnings related scheme under the Crossman proposals. The Government's dilemma was that schemes such as the Teachers' would have to be revised to reduce benefits by more than the cut in contributions for the Government to break even on its employee costs.

Following a series of bilateral exchanges with individual unions, the Department set up a Working Party on National Superannuation and Teachers' Occupational Schemes. It met first at the DES HQ in Curzon St, London, W1 and subsequently at the offices of the Schools Council in Great Portland Street. It was later to be known as the Teachers' Superannuation Working Party (TSWP), with Government and LEA employers forming the Official Side, effectively to negotiate with the teacher unions.

At the beginning some interesting discussions took place on emerging issues such as transferability, preservation of benefits, qualifying periods and family benefits. They were interrupted by the General Election of June 1970, which returned the Conservative Party to power.

Naturally the Crossman proposals were shelved, but the issues they were designed to address did not disappear. The NAS had a strong desire to reopen some neglected issues such as the Widows and Orphans Scheme where, despite a healthy real fund, benefits lagged behind many improvements that had been secured elsewhere.

At the Special One Day NAS Conference held at the Digbeth Hall, Birmingham, on 3 October 1970, whilst the morning had been devoted to the question of a new career structured salary system, the afternoon was given over to reform of the Teachers' Superannuation Scheme (TSS).

Being my 'maiden' NAS Special Conference it was also the first time I and a large number of activists heard Dryden Gilling-Smith in person. I recall everyone being impressed with his technical knowledge and his ability to explain complicated detail in simple language we could all understand, with some humour to boot. Over the years to come Annual Conference would eagerly look forward to another of Dryden's lively, entertaining and informative briefings on pensions.

The NAS Special Conference in October 1970 adopted a Report on Pensions which included six main demands:

1) a pension based on two-thirds of salary 'dynamised' to keep pace with increased average earnings;
2) a qualifying period of 35 years for full pension at 60 in recognition of longer education and training periods;
3) a widow's pension equal to half that which was received by her husband;
4) a 6% contribution rate for all, regardless of sex or marital status, to include a widows and dependants scheme;
5) recognition of war and national service;
6) a totally new scheme with contributions put into a real fund under the control of trustees, half of whom who should be teachers' representatives.

Shortly after the Conference the NAS secured an outstanding public relations coup to which I referred in Chapter 27. Despite the technical complexities of pensions, Terry Casey had managed to persuade Bruce Kemble, the education correspondent of *The Express*, a major national newspaper, to run a story on the 'one billion pound scandal' – the difference between the value of the Notional Fund and a real one with the annual surpluses properly invested in accordance with the Government's recommended model (one-third gilts; two-thirds equities). *The Express* decided to make it their page one splash:

> "Teacher
> I.O.U.
> £1,000,000,000
> Her Majesty's Treasury"

Other reports in the media followed. The NAS argued that had the surpluses over the years been properly invested in a real fund, teachers could be receiving 50% improvements in benefits at no extra cost.

Immediately after the Conference Terry Casey wrote to the new Secretary of State for Education, none other than Margaret Thatcher, requesting that the pensions Working Party be reconvened. She replied that recall of the WP should be delayed, pending the publication of the new Government's plans for national superannuation.

Terry Casey also took the initiative in suggesting the recall of the Teachers' Side of the WP. Led by the NAS, the earlier discussions had revealed many areas in which the Teachers' Scheme had fallen behind others in respect of benefits. Dryden Gilling-Smith wrote extensively in the national press to emphasise that the NAS claims could be at nil extra cost if a real fund were established. He wrote in the *TES* at the end of December 1970:

"The issues raised in the NAS policy statement go far beyond an Oliver Twist type request for more." A real fund properly invested would provide better benefits with 6% contribution from teachers and employers. He continued, "Where other pension funds have been earning around 10% on their reserves and chalking up substantial tax free financial gains, the teachers' fund, which is imaginary because the Government has pocketed any surplus, has only been credited with interest of 3.5%. Since 1961 a higher rate has been credited on new money but the fact remains that over 1,000 million pounds of teachers' money was still only earning 3.5% interest. It is as if teachers have been forced to put all their retirement savings into a war loan."

Writing in the *Financial Times* (*FT*), 25 February 1971, Dryden Gilling-Smith observed: "That a major overhaul of public sector schemes was expected. Many of those schemes have been little more than copies of the service prototype dating back to 1839. Public sector pension schemes had been overtaken by more vigorous and imaginative developments in the private sector."

The *FT* superannuation correspondent John Williams, writing on the same day, reported that the BMA had adopted the same position as the NAS in calling for a proper fund for doctors' pensions. He also wrote that: "Surprisingly enough the NUT, seems judging by a recent article in its official organ *The Teacher* to have adopted a lukewarm attitude to the question of a properly invested fund. This attitude is difficult to comprehend because although the NAS had always been a union primarily concerned with the wellbeing of the career teacher one expected NUT members to be interested in pensions as well."

After some toing and froing the Teachers' Side finally got together in February 1971. The TSWP provided a good example of the benefit of a more flexible approach which allowed all unions represented to have a say. Furthermore, central government was openly represented at the table.

Contrary to the predictions of some, that did not produce chaos. On the contrary; everyone recognised the benefit of a common approach if possible, and accordingly worked in a much better spirit of co-operation and compromise to achieve it. The coverage of the TSWP was wider than the Burnham Primary and Secondary Committee. Significant other groups of teachers, such as those in Scotland and Further Education (FE), were also included in the TSWP negotiations as they had parallel pension schemes.

There was some residual inter-union politics. The NUT de facto claimed the right to act as the Teachers' Side Secretariat but this was never officially agreed. The NUT did, however, make a small gesture in the direction of sharing jobs and responsibilities in so far as the Assistant Masters' GS, Andrew Hutchings, was placed in the Chair. After Hutchings retired, ATTI (later NATFHE) provided the Chair.

At the meeting in February 1971 the NUT famously objected to the presence of Dryden Gilling-Smith, whom Terry Casey had brought along as one of the NAS representatives to provide the expertise to counterbalance the actuaries who were present for the DES. It was a silly move by the NUT. In terms of autonomy, each union was entitled to decide who should represent it. In 'political' terms it allowed Terry Casey to make fun of the fact that the NUT objected to the presence of an expert who could be of great help to teachers. The NUT objections were otherwise ignored and it was not very long before it was engaging its own expert.

At the 1971 Conference held in Southport, the then Ex-President Ron Simons moved a motion on the TSS calling for the Association "to pursue a vigorous campaign for improvement" as agreed at the Special Conference in October 1970. Ron had made himself an 'amateur expert' on pensions, reflecting the tradition of self-reliance in the early days of the NAS in the absence of sufficient resources to employ a large staff. Ron quoted some shameful cases where schoolmasters had died within a few months of retirement at 65 and left widows penniless despite the fact that together with the employers some 14.5% of salary had been paid in contributions over many years.

By September 1971 after several meetings of the Teachers' Side of the TSWP had been held in London and Edinburgh, widespread agreement had been reached to pursue a range of improvements. They represented a combined effort, with input from different associations, including much from the NAS document adopted in October 1970. 'Breakdown pensions' for those forced to leave teaching through ill health or accident were also added to the shopping list.

On 14 September 1971 the Conservative Government published its *Strategy for Pensions*. The White Paper envisaged the state reserve scheme requiring a widows pension of 50%. That was only available to men teachers from 1965 if they opted in and paid an additional 2% over and above the 6%. The 1971 reforms made the widows scheme compulsory.

With Dryden Gilling-Smith's expertise the NAS was also able to argue that other schemes with a 6% contribution already provided many of the improvements such as widows' and family benefits, together with the payment of pension guaranteed for five years.

The Conservative Government's plans for pensions were far more modest than those envisaged under Labour's Crossman. They proposed the same basic National Insurance state pension which would be supplemented either by occupational schemes (required therefore to meet certain standards), or by a new reserve and additional state pension with earnings related contributions and benefits.

When the TSWP met in January 1972 it had become obvious that the wholesale revision of the Teachers' Scheme envisaged under Crossman would no longer be necessary. However, it would require examination to ensure it met the standards to enable teachers and their employers to opt out of the state earnings related scheme. The Teachers' Side also wished to keep the agenda open to secure improvements.

Inevitably the Management Side (including the Treasury) argued that such improvements would cost money. The NAS was able to counter those arguments with all the information supplied by Dryden Gilling-Smith on the Notional Fund arrangements and the comparisons with other schemes. The NAS also quoted the proposal in the state earnings related scheme for it to be properly funded, unlike the 'pay as you go' state flat-rate pension, not to mention the teachers' notorious Notional Fund.

The more flexible approach to negotiations as opposed to the rigidities of Burnham (the stifling NUT overall majority and one-voice procedure) proved immensely valuable to teachers. Dryden often confided to me in later years how Terry Casey had dominated proceedings in the 1970s and secured improvements which in a Burnham context would have proved impossible.

The simplest aspect of the fraudulent nature of the Notional Fund was the level of interest deemed to be earned. This was set by the Government at the 3.5% earned by its own stock of consols from the First World War. This state of affairs was only partly rectified in 1956. Trustees of a private sector fund are under a legal duty to act in the best interests of the beneficiaries when better investments are available at no additional risk. The trouble was that the 'trustee' was the Government.

Even after 1956 all subsequent investments also had to be deemed to be placed in Government 'Gilt' Edged Securities, so called because they were guaranteed by the State. There was only a minor improvement with some earning more than 3.5% annual interest. The huge disadvantages were that no capital appreciation could be secured as was the case for shares and other kinds of assets such as property, and no trading could take place to take advantage of changing circumstances. As the stocks were only notional and did not exist in reality, one could hardly sell them and keep out of jail! Unfortunately the NAS and its Scottish 'partner', the SSA, were the only organisations to favour the establishment of an independent real fund.

When the TSWP reassembled in January 1972 the Official Side argued that the cost of the Pensions (Increase) Act of 1971 had to be taken on board in determining the level of contributions. The Teachers contended that the Act applied generally across the whole of the public sector and they should not be selectively charged higher contributions for the 'inflation proofing'. The cost at this time (of high inflation) was estimated to amount to the equivalent of a 2.2% contribution.

Nevertheless, by January 1972 some progress had been made. The Official Side had indicated that from 1 April teachers' pensions would be based on final salary so that inflation would not erode them before the first payments arrived. The qualifying period for pensions was to be reduced to five years. Preservation of conserved pension rights of over five years would also be implemented. It appeared likely that a 50% widows' scheme would be incorporated in the main one, although the Official Side was not yet prepared to accept that all the benefits should be included in the 6% contribution.

More support for the NAS from the press was noted in February 1972 when *The Daily Telegraph's* pension correspondent, Geoffrey Van Dyke, wrote: "Terry Casey, GS of NAS, says teachers have been robbed and he is perfectly right. Apart from the obvious loss of interest earnings these notional funds have missed out on the capital growth bonanza that most pension funds were able to obtain in the 1950s and 1960s."

By March 1972, however, the WP had run into serious difficulties. The *TES* reported on 10 March that the Government had set its face against any change to the present notional funding of the scheme. The LEAs were also reported to be equally concerned about the financial basis of the bogus fund. They feared having to bear bigger burdens than at present.

The *TES* reported that the teachers, now "wised up by the NAS", were refusing to pay more when it was clear that the total overall contributions of 14.5% would be plenty for a decent scheme if it were properly invested; adding: "The Government White Paper *Strategy for Pensions* declares that pension funds must be properly invested if they are to command confidence."

The NAS observed that: "Teachers had long lost confidence in the Government's manipulation of their pension scheme. It's time we demanded that the Government disgorged the ill-gotten gains from teachers otherwise we must ask the fraud squad to step in."

Conference 1972 at Southport held a major debate on the pension situation. The NAS Report to Schools refers to "another masterly and lucid statement" from Dryden Gilling-Smith. He said that the NAS was the only teacher association with a strategy for pensions. It had taken a whole year to get an agreed statement with the other teacher organisations. Despite the NAS having highlighted Government mismanagement of the scheme for nearly 50 years there were rumours that the NUT might scuttle the boat before negotiations had even started. Teachers must look for restitution, not retribution. Teachers had been done; they should fight the injustices and not bite the dust with a 7% contribution which was being rumoured by the Government.

Moving the motion, the Honorary Treasurer, Arthur Smyth, emphasised that whilst the interests of those about to retire were important, an early settlement must not compromise the interests of the majority and the key principle of the contribution rate. Conference unanimously passed the resolution deploring the Government's refusal to fund the superannuation scheme properly and instructed the Executive to sustain the necessary action to secure improved benefits for the present 6% contribution.

Amid signs that the other organisations were not standing firm the NAS produced a succinct but hard-hitting 'flyer' pointing out why teachers had to insist upon improvements within the 6% contribution. It included four key reasons.

First, all public schemes had to conform to the Government's new principles of a pension based on the last year's earnings and the build- up to 50% widows' pension.

Second, local authorities had given these new benefits to their employees at no additional cost. Yet the Government demanded additional contributions from teachers for the same benefits.

Third, the key to better pensions, without additional contributions (including the LEAs deficiency payments of 2.5%), was to ensure the funds were properly invested.

Fourth, the NAS had shown that Government acting as the banker for teachers' pensions had benefited enormously, gaining more than £1,000 million over the past 47 years.

At the TSWP gathering on 17 May 1972 the fateful decision was taken by the majority on the Teachers' Side of the WP to agree to a higher contribution rate. In order to save face the NUT and the other unions had agreed to a withdrawal of some of the fringe benefits proposed in the 7% package in return for a 6¾% contribution rate. In the view of the NAS that represented even worse value for money.

The NAS did its best to try to persuade other unions to stand firm at 6%. Besides Dryden Gilling-Smith, another actuary was present, having been engaged by the Teachers' Side. He was questioned by the NUT. When asked what would be the effect of a real fund properly invested he replied that a 1% increase in investment income would reduce the cost of the scheme by between 15% and 20%.

But the fear factor, so prevalent in salary negotiations, returned. Many doubted the willingness of the Government to make available the surplus of £1,037m previously identified. Fear of losing the 1 April start date echoed the old Burnham bogeys. Dryden Gilling-Smith stressed there was a common package deal available across the whole of the public sector for a contribution rate of 6%. Terry Casey emphasised that the NAS had already begun a Parliamentary campaign to keep the rate at 6% and a supportive Labour MP, Fred Willey, had put down a question for the Secretary of State. Why could not all the teacher associations use the political influence they had?

ATTI questioned Terry Casey: Would he be prepared to wait another year or two to secure a better deal? Terry replied without hesitation: "Yes! We are legislating for the future generations of teachers. It was selfish for teachers who were about to retire to bring pressure for an early acceptance."

A source of embarrassment during the negotiations had been the 2% family benefits scheme. Whilst wanting such a scheme in principle the NAS alone had opposed the required 2% contribution rate when it was introduced in 1966. The Government and employers had been able to argue that members of that scheme who had been paying a total of 8% would have their contributions reduced.

On 6 June 1972 the DES announced that the TSWP had reached agreement to implement improvements, taking effect from 1 April that year. Three main areas of improvement were identified:

1) benefits would be based on the best 365 days in the final three years of service;
2) the family benefits would be integrated into the main scheme on a shared cost basis. For future service the widow's pension would be half that of the husband's and there would be provision to buy in and uprate past service;
3) the existing contribution rate of 6%, plus 2% for family benefits, would be replaced by a single rate of 6.75% for all teachers and the employers would make similar payments.

The press statement also referred to the NAS and SSA dissenting from the agreement. It did not refer to the basic reasons for this, namely the contribution rate was too high and the notional funding arrangements were to continue.

The exercise had been the most comprehensive review since the early 1920s. There were undoubtedly long-overdue improvements, although many had been signalled by a combination of Crossman and the Conservative Government's *Strategy for Pensions* before the TSWP got down to its business. Besides the advances mentioned above, the new proposals allowed for:

1) a five-year qualifying period;
2) an ill-health (breakdown) pension with enhancement;
3) no repayment of contributions after five years service (it was regarded as beneficial to compel people to make proper provision for their retirement);
4) transferability of pensions where possible between public and private sector employments;
5) abatement of pension to cease where beneficiaries were re-employed outside teaching;
6) abolition of the five-year qualifying period for death gratuity;
7) the facility to buy in previous experience.

Major disappointments for the NAS still continued, in addition to the funding arrangements and the higher contribution rate. In particular the NAS objected to the failure:

1) to offer a full pension based on 35 years service;
2) to award pension enhancement to those who continued to teach after 60;
3) to recognise war service of teachers who joined the profession after the event.

The NAS decided to continue its campaign and produced a Minority Report. It said the NAS was broadly in agreement with the improvements on offer but totally opposed the section on Contributions and Finance. The NAS agreed with the observation of Geoffrey Haywood, President of the Institute of Actuaries, that a 7% contribution seemed "rather high for the proposed scale of benefits".

The Minority Report examined other schemes. The Government Actuary's own survey of private sector schemes showed normally the employer paid twice as much as the employee. In the university world employers paid 10%; employees 5%. The local government employees' contributions were to remain at 6% notwithstanding improvements. Other public sector pensions had seen family benefits incorporated from inception into their main schemes. A survey conducted by the British Institute of Management showed that over two-thirds of pension schemes had employee contribution rates of 5.5% or less.

As recently as 22 May 1972 the Lord President of the Council and Leader of the House of Commons, introducing the Parliamentary and Other Pensions Bill, stated that MPs were to pay three-eighths of the new entrant cost (14.2%) of their pension, with the Exchequer paying the remainder. He went on: "This is in line with normal modern practice where the contribution of the employer is usually greater than that of the employee." MPs would thus pay 5.3%. The NAS was prepared to stick at 6%!

In the TSS the large deficiency payments (met mostly by the employers) brought the total cost to 17.5%. That was largely due to the inadequate funding arrangements. The NAS actuary advised that proper investment should reduce that cost by at least 2% (to 15.5%) bringing the employers' share down to 9.5%, which was 1% less than the 10.5% they had agreed to pay.

Finally, the NAS emphasised that if the Government were sincere in offering further talks on the funding of the scheme, there was no immediate need to raise contributions given the current cash flow surpluses, the latest one being £26m for 1969/70.

The NAS determined to fight on, convinced that the rise to a 6.75% contribution, itself a sharp reminder of the increase from 5% to 6% in 1956, would set an unfortunate precedent for the future. At a meeting of the TSWP in October 1972 Terry Casey made another attempt to retrieve the situation and rehearsed the arguments over the Notional Fund. After his address the Government spokesman conceded that, "shorn of adjectives", Terry's statement was "factually accurate".

However, disagreement with the NUT burst out into the open when its GS, Ted Britton, declared that Terry Casey only spoke for the NAS, not the rest of the profession. Interestingly, the ATTI representative said he agreed with Terry Casey as did the Scottish Secondary Teachers' Association and the Association of Teachers in Colleges and Departments of Education (ATCDE). The Joint Four remained silent. Later on some of the NUT representatives appeared to disown Ted Britton's position. The local authorities were on record as having expressed disquiet with the basis of the Notional Fund.

Although the immediate task of the TSWP was completed, Mrs Thatcher had agreed that it could continue to meet to discuss the financial basis of the scheme. Teachers naturally wanted the TSWP to remain in being permanently. It had de facto gained negotiating status. Strictly speaking it was a consultative body since the Government through Parliament had to legislate or draw up statutory orders to implement relevant changes and therefore had the final power of decision.

Meanwhile the Government was being hammered by the well-informed NAS and UWT lobby of MPs on the Notional Fund scandal and the discriminatory high contribution rate demanded. Many MPs recognised that it was inconsistent with the Government's policy in respect of the state reserve scheme which required strict adherence to normal funding principles. A former Labour Secretary of State for Education and Science, Ted Short, had agreed to move the annulment of the $6\frac{3}{4}\%$ regulation imposing the increase on teachers' contributions.

The Association's lobby, conducted vigorously at local constituency and national levels, was strengthened by the modest demand for a Parliamentary select committee to investigate the financial mismanagement of the scheme. The NAS also called on members to remind MPs that they only had to pay 5% of salary for their pensions.

Faced with the intense lobbying the Minister of State, William Van Straubenzee, was kept very busy responding to many MPs, justifying the Notional Fund on the basis that Government would guarantee the payment of teachers' pensions. Van Straubenzee claimed that if there were to be a deficit when expenditure exceeded income, Government would cover the cost. That was not a difficult point for the NAS and UWT lobbyists to rebut, bearing in mind the history of 1925 and 1956, not to mention the Widows and Orphans Scheme of 1966 and current events.

Obviously, with the incorporation of family benefits into the main scheme in 1972, it became necessary to integrate the two. In September that year the Board of Management began a series of meetings to investigate how this could be achieved. By 30 March 1974 the Board was able to publish a very interesting report. The GA had valued the Fund as at 31 March 1972 at £30.77m. Furthermore there was a surplus of assets over liabilities of £11.10m. The Board of Management had a legal duty to distribute the surplus to the members of the Fund, some 90,500 teachers of whom just over 2,000 were retired. The Government still pocketed nearly £20m of 'real' money as the 'paper' in the Notional Fund was increased by an equivalent amount.

The final paragraph of the March 1974 report, signed by E. Homer, Chairman of the Board of Management, was extremely interesting. Commenting upon the "very complicated task and satisfactory outcome", the report went on: "The financial advisers throughout adopted a far-seeing policy of investment; the Treasurer of the GLC [who was the investment manager] and his staff were most efficient in the day-to-day work of investment, covering fixed interest stocks, equities and properties." The contrast with the notorious Notional Fund could not have been starker! According to the NAS, the Fund over its six years of existence had grown by 25%, achieved in part by securing a compound interest of 8% p.a. on its assets, substantially more than that deemed to be credited to the main scheme's Notional Fund.

At the request of the NAS the Teachers' Side also consulted Geoffrey Haywood, President of the Institute of Actuaries. He responded saying: "The contribution rates proposed for teachers are reasonable and in line with market rates. However, the overall cost of the TSS is very much greater than it would be if the scheme were invested in a more normal way."

The question of funding was to be a major source of disagreement between the NAS and Government. Within the Teachers' Side the NAS, together with the UWT and SSA, were opposed by all the other unions. Papers and 'counter-papers' were produced by the Government and the NAS.

After the agreement of June 1972 the first paper considered by the TSWP on funding was produced by the Government and set out three alternatives:

1) continue on the present Notional Fund basis;
2) change to an unfunded pay-as-you-go scheme (current contributions would have to match the cost of current benefits);
3) restructure as a properly invested fund.

Not surprisingly the Government stuck to its desire to maintain the status quo, the real reason appearing in one of the papers referred to above:

"The Government Actuary's latest valuation report indicated that the account balance [of the TSS] as on 31 March 1966 amounted to some £1,037 million. Apart from the obvious impossibility of producing a cash sum of this magnitude at one point in time, it would be impossible to introduce such a sum into the investment market without serious disturbance." That figure of £1,037m was remarkable. Besides being massive for its time, it also represented the amount of financial benefit gained by successive governments. As borrowed money against a future 'guarantee' it should have been declared as part of the national debt.

Once again Dryden Gilling-Smith came into his own drafting the NAS response to the paper (TS1/72) from the Government. The NAS paper (TS7/72) began with the figures quoted by the Education Secretary, Margaret Thatcher, on 8 February 1971, that for the year 1969-70 teachers contributed £38m, employers £54m, whilst the scheme paid out £66m in benefits. This meant that there was a £26m surplus of contributions over expenditure, which could by itself pay for many improvements. Furthermore, that did not take into account the interest the 'fund' should have received. Even a modest rate of return of 8% on the accumulated surplus of £1,037m would generate over £80m of additional money.

If the Government were to live up to the 1925 promise that 'teachers would not suffer from the adoption of the funding arrangements' the accumulated surplus would be over £2,000m. That was the figure which would have accrued had the Notional Fund been real and achieved average growth since 1956. The NAS based its calculations on the *FT* Ordinary Share Index and the Government's own 'model fund', which recommended the 'one-third gilts, two-thirds equities' spread.

Although receipts into the Notional Fund had exceeded expenditure, low returns had produced inevitable actuarial deficits when future liabilities were matched against the notional assets. In 1951 the GA had identified a £102m deficit; in 1956 it had risen to £247m; in 1961 it was £148m; in 1966 it was £307m; and by 1971 it was £334m. The higher contributions often demanded of LEAs and teachers were controversial and provoked the NASUWT into intense Parliamentary lobbying and, on occasions, into industrial action.

Between 1956 and 1961 the *FT* Index had risen from 200 to 300. The balance in the teachers' scheme in 1956 stood at £536m. Had it been subject to the same rate of growth it would have added £268m to the 1961 balance, increasing it from £722m to £990m.

By 1971 the *FT* Index stood at around 500 and the £990m for 1961 would have increased by approximately two-thirds, adding another £660m of capital growth.

The additional growth of £268m and £660m (totalling £928m) for the two periods added to the 31 March 1966 balance of £1,037m and a total fund value of over £2,000m could have resulted, to which one should also add the surpluses each year from 1966.

As time went on the figures became more mind-boggling in their size. Of course stock markets also suffer falls and at any one time a very different picture might be presented. But the long-term trend is upwards, reflecting the advances generally available to Western-style democracies which today also have vastly improved techniques for better management of economies.

Doing the same 'real v notional' fund exercise the NAS showed that by the beginning of 1976 the value of a real fund would have stood at £6.4 billion. That compared to the Government Actuary's Quinquennial Report on the Notional Fund in the Teachers' Superannuation Account showing a value of £3.7 billion.

By the 1980s the figures became even more 'stratospheric' as time went on. When the NASUWT repeated this exercise in 1982 it revealed a 'real' fund standing at £20.9 billion, the Government's notional one at £9.3 billion.

To return to 1972, it was obvious that a properly invested real fund could have financed all the improvements teachers sought in the paper put forward in December 1971, plus indeed a lot more!

Responding to the NAS paper, the DES produced TS16/72. It conceded that a real fund "would have fared significantly better" than the notional one. However, it claimed the Exchequer deficit payment of 1956 and the bearing of the cost of inflation proofing (IP) would at least "offset the disadvantage".

Despite the 1972 increase in contributions the NAS was determined to fight on. Another welcome development of the pensions lobby was the active involvement of UWT members. Many MPs remarked that they were pleased and impressed to see so many members of the UWT lobbying with their NAS colleagues and showing the same degree of professionalism and grasp of the complexities. Pensions had hitherto been considered to be a male issue.

The Autumn Term of 1972 saw the NAS and UWT campaign roll on. Once again intense local lobbying of MPs was combined with national moves which were led by Terry Casey and Dryden Gilling-Smith, both very active at Westminster. A friendly Labour MP, Brian O'Malley, was persuaded to move a prayer of annulment in the House of Commons, a device to secure the rejection of amendments to statutory regulations placed before Parliament.

Shortly after 10 p.m. on 6 November 1972 Brian O'Malley rose to move in the House of Commons:

"That a humble Address be presented to Her Majesty praying that the Teachers' Superannuation . . . (Amendment) Regulations 1972 . . . a copy of which was laid before this House on 2 August, in the last session of Parliament, be annulled."

Brian O'Malley spoke admirably to the NAS and UWT briefings. He also quoted the views of the employers agreeing with the NAS that the balances in the scheme were not attracting a fair return. Many MPs wished to speak but time was limited under the procedures in force. A Conservative MP, Mr J.C. Jennings from Burton, railed against the financial arrangements, calling upon the Government to "get rid of all ideas of notional funding".

The NAS and UWT lobby had been remarkable. When the vote was called the Government's majority slumped from 60 to a mere 5. The 'ayes' in favour of the prayer of annulment numbered 178, the 'noes' 183.

I remember the occasion well, having travelled up to the House of Commons to listen to the debate despite the late hour. By chance I met Terry Casey and Dryden Gilling-Smith in the Central Lobby. While I had to climb the many stairs up to the Strangers' Gallery, Terry and Dryden were escorted to a special box, raised just above the floor of the Commons and reserved for 'guests' with a special interest in the business being conducted. Terry enjoyed telling the story of how, after the debate and within earshot of MPs lining up to go through the lobbies, they could see the vote was close and overheard conversations that "the Secretary of State [Margaret Thatcher] had been caught unawares with her pants down" in the words of one fellow member of the Cabinet. However, I also recall her very combative defence of the Government's position that night and being impressed with her ability to argue a brief even if I disagreed with it.

Spurred on by the closeness of the vote the NAS decided to continue the fight. Parliamentary lobbying intensified as there was obviously much support for the NAS and UWT position.

In December 1972 the NAS went in deputation to the Secretary of State. Possibly at the insistence of the Treasury, Mrs Thatcher was forced into a corner, repeatedly saying "no" to NAS requests at least for a start to be made on a proper fund, even if it were just to use the surplus accumulated by the family benefits scheme.

One of the reasons put forward by the Government in response to MPs' enquiries prompted by the lobbying was that the annual surplus "had become an established means of exchequer finance", a sure indication that teachers were subsidising the taxpayer. Government also pleaded the 'guarantee to pay' factor.

Responding to Margaret Thatcher, Terry Casey reminded her that all the promises of the past and assurances that teachers would not suffer from the Notional Fund arrangements had been broken. And shortly after the 1956 increase the GA had conceded that the overall contribution of teachers and employers could be reduced to 10.9%. When Terry Casey pressed Margaret Thatcher on a Parliamentary or other enquiry on the notional funding, she repeatedly said "no, no and no".

Another anomaly and injustice of great concern to the NAS was the question of war service. The NAS was determined to secure the right to buy in past (especially war) service at cost – that is, 10% of 'deemed' salary (applicable at the time) plus 3.5% compound interest. However, the Treasury demanded the purchase of past service at a cost based on current salaries. This meant that while the Government was denying the benefits of real funding it charged rates based on the assumption that it existed. The difference in cost could be £2,226 as against £407 for seven years war service.

Once again the teachers' pension scheme was a big issue for the 1973 Conference held in Eastbourne. In the customary post-Conference deputation to the Secretary of State, the NAS pursued two issues. The first was war and national service, which the NAS believed ought to be available at special rates. Many NAS members who had served in the Second World War were approaching retirement. Civil servants with service of this kind before entering public employment were credited with half of the period for pension purposes. The NAS also pointed out that the UK was alone in the EEC in denying this right to teachers who served in the respective armed forces.

The deputation also renewed the NAS demand for contributions to be put back to 6%. The case had grown even more compelling as a repeat of the 1956 overcharge seemed likely to be revealed in the TSS valuation due soon. The same applied to other schemes that had exacted higher contributions. Phase Two of the Government's programme for better pensions also specifically allowed for improvements or reductions in employees' contributions.

On 12 June 1973 another deputation from the NAS met the Secretary of State, Margaret Thatcher, to seek her support for war service to count for pension entitlement for all the teachers concerned, even if they had not entered the profession (or training) before enlisting. The Minister and her civil servants appeared unimpressed that teachers in other European countries enjoyed that right.

Giving up on 'technical' arguments Terry Casey believed that two 'emotive' points finally won the day. First he cited the example that members of Hitler's Gestapo 'got it'. That point seemed to strike home with Mrs Thatcher. Then as the civil servants accompanying 'Mrs T' were entering the argument against the NAS deputation with some gusto, Terry Casey quoted their own case, pointing out that their war service counted for pension purposes. At that moment, Terry often recalled, Mrs T turned to the Permanent Secretary, Sir William Pile, seated at her side, demanding to know if he "got it"! Sheepishly, Sir 'Bill' had to reply "yes". That was the moment, Terry believed, the NAS won the argument. Mrs T observed "that was interesting" and she would "review the situation".

A few weeks later in July 1973 the GA's report on the TSS was published. It showed a surplus and proved the NAS point that the other unions had been conned into accepting the increased contribution in 1972. It also emerged that the DES was trying to do a deal with the LEAs to reduce their contributions by nearly 2%. Employees in the National Health Service whose contributions had also been raised to 6¾% were to have them cut back to 6% as a result of their actuarial valuation.

It was not until an 'emergency meeting' of the TSWP on 8 October 1973 that other unions apart from the NAS, UWT and SSA were finally angered enough to protest against the shabby treatment meted out to teachers.

The Government was trying to buy off the employers by deeming that the £263m standing in the account in 1956 earning only 3.5% notional interest had been spent on benefits and replaced by new money which would be given a higher rate of notional interest. This meant that as the regulations stood the LEAs would benefit from this ploy.

As it had turned out, the LEAs were not being required to increase their supplementary contributions from 2.5% to over 3% because this was no longer required. Instead they were to have the supplementary contribution reduced to 1.5%. The GA had also found that the new entrant cost of 14.2% was higher than that required, which was only 13.9%. Overall, therefore, total costs were to be reduced by nearly 2%, with the Government and LEAs sharing virtually all the benefit.

Teachers were only to be offered a 0.15% reduction in their contributions as their 'share' of the 2% overall saving. A further meeting of the Working Party was called for 5 November 1973. The NAS was outraged and declared itself in dispute with the Government and the LEA employers. Some authorities such as ILEA, Sheffield and Wolverhampton responded by declaring themselves in favour of going back to 6%. The Government pleaded it was still considering the issue of teachers' war service.

Following the Parliamentary reply earlier in the year on 8 February, the NAS had challenged the figures given by the DES that contributions exceeded the pension costs by £26m in 1969/70. The DES was forced to admit that the figures were inaccurate. The surplus should have been declared as £36m. But the GA's report revealed that the true surplus taking (albeit notional) interest into account was £116m. The next year showed a running surplus of £137m.

The NAS continued to pile on the Parliamentary pressure. Half war service for those entering teaching after 1945 had to be granted. The contribution rate had to be put back to 6%; nothing else would suffice.

A final meeting of the TSWP took place early on 5 November 1973. The teacher organisations were unanimous in their determination to seek a return to the 6% contribution. The Official Side stood by its original offer of a reduction of only 0.15% (to 6.6%), which was unanimously rejected and the meeting ended in complete deadlock. All the other teacher organisations (some 14) joined the NAS and SSA in declaring themselves in dispute with the Government and LEAs. (The UWT remained unrecognised on the TSWP.) The NAS suggested joint action on 12 November, the day of an adjournment debate in Parliament. The NUT was not prepared to act despite its GS having said "speed is of the essence".

The NAS and UWT went ahead with action plans. With a Parliamentary debate announced for the evening of Monday 12 November the NAS and UWT decided to organise a mass lobby at Westminster, with members taking strike action if 'leave' were not agreed. Members in London and surrounding areas were told to leave school early and report for briefing sessions prior to lobbying between 3.30 and 5.30 p.m. Members from more distant areas were asked to organise local representative deputations and demonstrations.

Despite only having four days notice over 10,000 NAS and UWT members came to London while local demonstrations were held in all parts of the country on 12 November. The LSA naturally played a large part in the domestic arrangements in the Methodist Central Hall, Westminster, where a rolling series of briefings were held for members before they went across Parliament Square to lobby their MPs. I had a job inside the Central Hall and became well briefed, listening to the same speeches three times, knowing exactly when the jokes were coming!

Dryden Gilling-Smith updated the figures in the 'notional v real fund' exercise. The present notional surplus stood at £1,567m. If those balances had been invested in a Government model real fund, representing a mixture of equities and gilts over the past 17 years since the 1956 Act, then it would now stand at a staggering £6,500m. To the timid who say that markets can go down as well as up Dryden Gilling-Smith pointed out that the higher market of three years previously would have produced a balance of over £7,500m. Thus the relative loss of £1,000m since that time could have been borne without any wincing and still leave the teachers five times better off.

The pressure of over 10,000 lobbyists hammered home to hundreds of MPs the seething discontent of NAS and UWT members with their shabby treatment on pensions. Coupled with dozens of demonstrations around the country, the lobby produced a remarkable transformation on the pension scene.

The 'number two' in the hierarchy, the Minister of State for Education, Norman St John Stevas, replied to the debate. He made sympathetic and optimistic noises about some progress on war service. MPs of all parties began to support an early day motion (EDM) demanding a return to 6% and recognition of war service.

Some other big cities, such as Birmingham, Leeds, Liverpool and Southampton, joined those breaking ranks with their national representatives and supporting a return to a 6% contribution. However, some LEAs, such as Lancashire, decided to deduct pay from members who took part in lobbies and deputations. Worse still, teachers in Devon were threatened with the sack for participating in the protest in school time.

Two more supportive EDMs on teachers' superannuation were tabled in the House of Commons and subsequently signed by some 250 MPs. As a result of this the Labour Opposition tabled the following motion for debate on 28 November:

"That this House noting the reductions in the cost of the teachers' superannuation scheme revealed by the 1971 valuation calls upon Her Majesty's Government to reduce the contributions paid by teachers to their superannuation scheme to 6% thus bringing their scheme into line with practice in most other public services . . . and to allow half of all teachers' war service to be credited for pension entitlement as is the practice of the civil service."

In a very effective and highly informed speech introducing the EDM on 28 November Roy Hattersley, a future deputy leader of the Labour Party, referred to the NAS brief and to its minority report.

Secretary of State Mrs Thatcher immediately accepted the motion. She had obviously won her battle with the Treasury, having hinted to this effect in another meeting with the NAS. Undoubtedly she was assisted in her fight by the many MPs who had been fully appraised of the situation by NAS and UWT members. Formalities remaining, it seemed that the NAS and UWT had won an outstanding and famous victory on the pensions front.

Provided that the proposals were accepted by the Pay Board, teachers' contributions would be returned to 6% and half war service would count for pension purposes. In her speech to the House, Mrs Thatcher said that on this matter the NAS had taken the lead among teachers' organisations. Since they had lobbied her in June she had given the matter her consideration.

In winding up the debate the Minister of State, Norman St John Stevas, said: "Credit for this happy outcome has been claimed by many. Whenever there is a victory there are many claimants for the credit but when there are disasters the flight from responsibility is equally rapid. We have claims made by the NUT. I would say about the NAS that it took a leading part in this campaign and individual members on both sides of the House also have claims to a certain amount of credit."

There was no requirement to vote that night, the Government having accepted the motion. Listening to the radio news on BBC the next morning before going off to school, I was delighted to hear the headlines: "Teachers win concession from the Government over their pensions".

Yes! We had won. Mrs Thatcher had formally announced overnight that our contribution rate was going to be put back to 6%. The NAS had not just persuaded the Government. Together with the UWT and our Scottish partner SSA, we had overcome the torpidity of the other unions, all of whom had originally agreed to accept the higher contribution rate despite the strong pleadings of the NAS not to do so. Another 'old' lesson had also been repeated. Despite the powerful lobby over a long period it was not until the half-day strike by the NAS and UWT on 12 November that success was finally achieved.

I still remember the following morning going into school. Fellow members were full of congratulations for the NAS. Our critics were subdued. Those who had taken the trouble to join in the lobbying felt particularly satisfied.

Apart from a further controversy that blew up in January 1974 on the basis on which teachers would be credited half their war service, which was eventually resolved, the Teachers Superannuation Scheme was then placed on a much-improved basis with significantly improved benefits although the fundamental problem of the Notional Fund remained unaddressed. As time went on it became increasingly difficult to maintain this question as a live issue.

Chapter 33 - Defending Teachers' Pensions into the Twenty-First Century

After the intensity and success of the NASUWT lobbying in the early 1970s, the remaining quarter of the twentieth century proved to be a somewhat quieter period for teachers' pensions. The provisions secured in 1972/73 have remained substantially the same. More general matters have come to the fore such as the vexed issue of inflation proofing and in very recent times the affordability of public sector pensions in the context of increased longevity and diminishing investment returns. The main concern of the NASUWT became 'holding fast to what ye hath'. Probably the most significant area of progress was driven by the increasing equalities legislation which granted widowers' benefits. In time teachers were also allowed to nominate partners as dependants entitled to receive the equivalent of widows and widowers benefits.

Against a background of financial pressure and falling rolls, premature retirement became an issue in 1976. Local government had recently undergone significant reorganisation where redundancy or retirement "in the interests of the efficiency of the service" was used as a means of reducing the workforce.

After clarifying that 'efficiency of the service' did not relate to individual performance, the NASUWT argued for pension to be available at age 50 with entitlement based on length of service augmented by premature retirement compensation (PRC). The NASUWT held that the Notional Fund rightly should bear the costs of enhancement because teacher unemployment and redundancy were national problems and should be solved by national measures.

In 1980 after the high inflation of the previous decade, indexation of public sector pensions became very controversial. With the tacit support of Mrs Thatcher's Conservative Government, sections of the media campaigned mercilessly against index linking. Although the examples quoted were invariably of top civil servants drawing generous benefits, the average public sector pension was extremely modest. The NASUWT counter-lobbied vigorously.

Mrs Thatcher set up the Scott Inquiry to examine the differences between the public and private sectors vis-à-vis inflation proofing and job security. Giving evidence to Sir Bernard Scott, the NASUWT cited all the 'old' arguments connected to the Notional Fund which, if properly invested, could have carried the cost of inflation proofing for teachers. Furthermore, the new Index Linked Government Bonds afforded public and private pension funds the opportunity of protection against inflation. The NASUWT also reminded the committee that the Clegg Commission had reduced its award to teachers in 1979 by an amount of 1½% in recognition of "generally superior pension benefits".

Remarkably Sir Bernard Scott recommended inflation proofing be preserved, referring at the same time to the availability of the new Index Linked Bonds. In February 1981 a letter from Baroness Young, Minister of State, to an MP, acknowledged the intensity of the NASUWT lobby. By this time the estimated surplus gained by the Treasury (the difference between the Notional and a real fund) was £7 billion.

By the end of 1981 the Government Actuary (GA) disclosed to the TSWP that the 1980/81 surplus of receipts over payments was £1 billion. At the same time the cost of inflation proofing was £232m, which could comfortably be met by interest on a real fund. The same information led the NASUWT to continue its campaign to have the Fund meet the costs of enhanced PRC rather than leaving the LEA employers to pick up the bill.

Eventually the arrangements for the Notional Fund 'investments' were improved, in return for which it would have to bear the cost of index linking. Any future deficit in the Fund would then have to be met by increased contributions from the employers.

The problems of 1956 and 1972 resurfaced in January 1984 with another GA report on the TSS revealing the 'customary deficit' and recommending increased overall contributions to 15.45% of salary (up from 14.4%). The GA made no recommendation on how cost should be shared between teachers and employers. The NASUWT quickly responded, leaving no one in doubt about the consequences of trying to raise teachers' contributions in the context of the controversial Notional Fund, itself standing at £10 billion, and the surplus of income over expenditure for 1981/82 alone at £720m.

Soon after these events the Government established an Inquiry into Pensions by Norman Fowler, Secretary of State for Social Services. The NASUWT renewed the pressure, revealing the Notional Fund could have stood at nearly £22 billion, £11.7 billion above the £10 billion level recorded by the GA. The Union mounted yet another lobby of MPs and also tried to engage the LEA employers in the exercise, pointing out their interests were also seriously affected.

Further research in November 1984 showed that the Government was benefiting to the tune of £1.2 billion per year. With a real fund the overall contribution rate could be reduced by 3.5% rather than being increased by 1.05%. However, thanks to the vigilance of the NASUWT, alone amongst the teacher unions in maintaining a high-profile refusal to countenance increased teacher contributions, the extra burden fell upon the hapless LEA employers.

One of the most destructive measures taken by the Thatcher Governments of the 1980s was the Social Security Act of 1987. It enabled employees in hitherto compulsory occupational pension schemes to opt out. Ironically it was done in the name of freedom. It resulted in fundamentally unsound decisions to forego significant amounts of contributions from one's employer to set up your own personal pension. Rank malpractice was rampant by unscrupulous salespeople selling inferior financial products which could never compensate for the loss of a large slice of employer contributions.

The NASUWT strongly advised its members to remain in the Teachers' Scheme. Although capable of being vastly superior through a real fund it was nevertheless a final salary scheme into which the teacher paid 6% and the employer varying amounts between 8% and 9%. Employers were only required to pay 3% of salary into a personal pension. In time several 'reputable' insurance companies were forced to repay millions of pounds worth of compensation for the mis-selling that occurred. By 1998 the NASUWT had secured the reinstatement in the TSS of 111 members with compensation. Furthermore, 285 members were awaiting reinstatement.

Today the principle of compulsory participation in occupational schemes is restored to legality. The NASUWT fully supported the principle of compulsion for employees and employers to make provision for retirement.

In the 1980s PRC and the 'breakdown' (Infirmity) pension rules were freely and some might say loosely applied by employers with the tacit support of the Government as a means of managing the contraction of the teaching force. By 1992/93 premature retirements had reached 12,214. In addition demographic factors and massive additional workload and stress inflicted upon the profession by non-stop Government reforms led to a deepening teacher supply crisis. Furthermore, the costs of pension provision were rising through lower interest rates and returns on capital, not to mention longer life expectancy.

In October 1996 the "pensions chickens came home to roost", as I put it in a press statement. The National Audit Office had identified a shortfall in the Teachers' Superannuation Account at March 1996 exceeding £1½ billion for England and Wales, with Scotland's deficit being £207m. In the year to September 1996, 13,055 teachers and lecturers in England and Wales had retired early, at a cost of £480m. Early retirements (excluding ill health) had numbered a mere 500 in 1978/79.

Whilst the quinquennial valuation for 1991-96 had still to be completed we already knew that the number of early retirements had risen by 21% and ill-health ones by 60%. The overall numbers in the workforce had declined, men by 13% (women had risen by 2%). The GA report of 31 March 1991 had revealed an £18.9 billion write up into the Notional Fund to pay for past inflation proofing. Whilst only a paper exercise, it had the implication of reducing the call on teachers' and employers' contributions.

The Government announced that the application of the early retirement and infirmity (or 'breakdown') pension rules would be rigorously tightened and the element of enhancement under PRC would pass to the LEA employers from 1 April 1997, thereby ensuring it would all but disappear. The Government also decreed that from 1997 the number of teachers granted premature or infirmity retirement would be cut by 45% over three years. Naturally that set off a panic for the exit. The prejudgement implied in setting such a precise figure was astonishing, as cases were supposed to be decided on their merits.

The table below shows how premature and infirmity retirements rose to a peak in 1997/98 and then fell sharply:

Teacher retirements	95/96	96/97	97/98	98/99	01/02
Premature	13,055	15,799	19,061	2,917	2,561
Infirmity	5,980	6,336	4,115	2,718	2,113
Normal age	4,497	4,450	4,862	5,266	6,291

(By 2000/01 the newly introduced actuarial reduced pensions numbered 861, increasing to 2,113 in 2001/02.)

In my press statements I accused the Government "of building a Berlin-style wall to keep teachers in the profession".

The NASUWT continued to oppose the Government's proposals to restrict PRC for teachers until the notorious Notional Fund was afforded a realistic valuation. The GA put the book value of the Fund at £21.6 billion, the market value at £26.9 billion as on 31 March 1991 (to which the £18.9 billion write up could be added). The outstanding liability to teacher pensioners then stood at £75.9 billion.

Once again the NASUWT lobbied MPs about the disgraceful mismanagement of the pension fund, which lay at the heart of the financial problems. Now Government was denying teachers, forced out of employment, access to the pension fund which, properly invested, could have cushioned the costs of early retirement. At the same time the NASUWT pointed to the Government's evidence to the School Teachers' Review Body (STRB) that recruitment and retention were fine, despite the panic measures to halt early retirement.

The DfEE, in attempting to halt the 'exodus' before the 1 April 1997 changes, overstepped its lawful powers. After the Manchester LEA withdrew two early retirements it had granted to NASUWT members as a consequence of DfEE 'instructions', the NASUWT sought legal advice and decided to apply for a judicial review of the LEA decision and the DfEE's actions.

The DfEE and Manchester soon relented, respectively reviewing their 'instructions' and reinstating the early retirements. Similar problems were resolved in Leicester and Sefton. The judicial review hearing, set for 30 January, was no longer necessary. In my press statement I said the NASUWT action against the ill-conceived DfEE measures had protected the early retirement of some 11,250 teachers. The DfEE's misjudgement had sown panic.

A march and rally in central London to take place on 1 February 1997 was called by all the unions represented on the TSWP at a meeting on 17 January to protest against the Government's proposals. The initiative had come from NATFHE. At the same time, news began to leak that the Government was thinking of postponing the implementation date from 1 April to 1 September, i.e. until after the General Election. The turnout for the march and rally on 1 February (a Saturday) only proved to be 'respectable' thanks to the NASUWT contingent which outnumbered all the other unions combined. Supported by a marching band, banners, and other paraphernalia of demonstrations, as well as back-up staff and vehicles, it was a small but revealing indication of the health and strength of the NASUWT and its ability 'to deliver on the ground'.

Later in February the Government confirmed the postponed implementation date of 1 September to allow other alternatives to be considered and permitting those teachers whose applications had been lodged but not yet processed to remain until the end of the Summer Term without prejudicing their claims.

The Government also announced a fundamental review of the Teachers' Scheme, which I described as "a mixed blessing", bearing history in mind. The NASUWT emphasised it would fight any proposal to increase teachers' contributions given the continued mismanagement of the Notional Fund. The latest valuation by the GA put the Notional Fund at a 'mere' £36 billion.

In a hastily convened meeting with teacher unions on 19 February, Secretary of State Gillian Shephard conceded that a review would not lead to any detriment in existing pension entitlement. I suggested the Minister might do well to examine the reasons why so many teachers wanted "to reach 50 and run": ill-financed and non-stop reforms, relentless denigration of the profession, excessive workload and pupil indiscipline.

In a report to Conference 1997, "Financial Mismanagement and Future Pension Benefits for Teachers", the NASUWT updated the figures since 1956 in the 'real v Notional Fund' exercise to show that by 1991 the former would have produced a fund worth £68 billion and an incredible £117.5 billion by 1996. However, it also pointed out that the TSS account had gone into annual deficit in 1995/96, with expenditure exceeding income, significant factors in that being the cost of PRC at £480m, rising costs of indexation and the below-par returns credited to the Notional Fund.

The 1991 GA report had projected a £75.9 billion actuarial deficit and the 91-96 review was awaited. A credit of £18.9 billion had been awarded to the Fund on 14 December 1990 for poor past performance in return for it carrying the costs of indexation. The NASUWT report argued that the write up should have been at least double that amount. The Union could not understand the proposal from the GA to reduce the employers' contribution from 8.05% to 7.2% w.e.f. 1 April 1997 when he was projecting a need in the long-term for a rate of 14.2%. However, the NASUWT was pleased to note there was no proposal to increase teachers' contributions.

In 1997 the new Education Secretary, David Blunkett, set up an inquiry into the long-term affordability of the TSS to report by the following year. In the event, the exercise was to take much longer and a working group was established. In 1998 the NASUWT Conference mandated the Executive to produce another report on teachers' pensions. The 1999 report, entitled – appropriately – "Teachers' Pensions: A Bleak Future", followed in the same vein as the one of 1997. It pointed out that net expenditure on teachers' pensions was £1.8 billion in 1997. However, the value a real fund would have reached was estimated at £176.3 billion, while the report from the GA was awaited on the Notional Fund.

In the summer of 2003 the Department for Work and Pensions published the results of its consultation exercise on its Green Paper on pensions. The Labour Government confirmed it intended to consult further on a proposal to make the normal pension age 65 rather than 60. The change would apply to new entrants from 2006 and from 2010 for existing staff. The NASUWT opposed the move, believing that a full pension should be available after 40 years service.

Fortunately, in 2005/06 the Government behaved better than on previous occasions. Teachers were not singled out for special treatment. The whole public sector was taken into account and genuine dialogue took place with the unions through the TUC. Constructive negotiations then took place with the various occupational groups. Teacher unions were better prepared and more determined than most had been in 1956 and, for that matter, in the early 1970s. Furthermore, most of the teacher unions, led by the NASUWT, were in a good Social Partnership with the New Labour Government. The genuine negotiation that resulted facilitated an agreement to retain current entitlements of existing staff in respect of retirement at 60 but changes were accepted for future entrants whilst the all-important final-year salary pension was retained. That undoubtedly represented a reasonable compromise, which when seen in the context of many private sector final salary pension schemes disappearing, not to mention the unrelenting media hostility, was no mean achievement.

Whilst the usual suspects in the media and elsewhere condemned the Government for 'selling out to the unions', the truth was that current benefits for existing teachers were preserved in return for an increase of 0.4% in contributions. The Government expected to make some savings in the long-term, compared with previous arrangements. However, the fact remained that the 'Government guarantee' to pay the pension, dating from the 1920s, once again came at a price – exactly what would have occurred if a 'real fund' had existed and found itself in genuine long-term actuarial deficit.

The final irony was that many commentators began to argue that the liabilities on teachers' and other public sector pension schemes should be properly declared as part of the national debt – a transparency that had been advocated by the NASUWT for nigh on 50 years!

Postscript

I raise the issue debated in depth over the years of whether a real pension fund would have better served the teacher interest. Could it have coped with recent developments including volatile stock markets, lower investment yields and demographic changes? An authoritative answer would require extensive research beyond the scope of this book and my resources.

However, the massive public debt incurred in the bank bail-outs of 2007/08 make the prospects for a real fund even more academic and problematical than they were previously. In any event the NASUWT always argued that retrospective compensation for all the lost opportunities of the good years would be a prerequisite before teachers could contemplate assuming their own risks with a real fund. The sums often appeared too massive to cope with, but as decade followed decade retrospectively they assumed more manageable proportions. Furthermore, such gargantuan amounts of money have become almost 'commonplace' in the wake of the big bail-out of the banks to save the financial system from meltdown and the economy from collapse.

Whatever view one takes, the brutal fact remains that governments, despite profiting for 70 years as banker to the Superannuation Scheme, have charged teachers and the LEA employers for guaranteeing the pensions by exacting higher contributions – exactly what would be required with a real fund in genuine deficit.

SECTION SIX
THE RISE OF MILITANCY
The 1960s and after

Chapter 34 - 'Professional or Union'

The turmoil the NAS had to cause to gain official recognition on the Burnham Committee in 1961 naturally led to a great debate to emerge on the 'professional or union' issue. As the '60s progressed teacher and indeed general 'industrial' militancy increased, so raising the question to an even higher profile in public debate. It was not surprising that by the early 1970s an association of teachers dedicated to never taking militant action at any time on any issue, indeed naming itself the Professional Association of Teachers (PAT), had been born.

Critics of the NAS philosophy believed the 'professional' and the 'union' were mutually exclusive. Were we a professional organisation, which by popular definition (if not in reality) put the clients – the children – first, ahead of any consideration of self-interest? Or were we a trade union which put its members' interests first and 'to hell with the kids'?

If forced to answer the question in terms of such simplistic and brutal alternatives we came down on the side of being a trade union. We had a very clear belief that our first duty was to serve our members' interests. After all, they paid for our existence. That did not mean we ignored the interests of pupils. The NAS view was someone had to look after the teachers, and if their unions were not going to do it, no one would.

In reality the issues are not so starkly opposed as I have portrayed in order to highlight them. Anyone truly concerned for the children must have some regard for the welfare of teachers, for the interests of the youngsters are not served by riding roughshod over those of staff. On the other side of the same coin, there would be little job satisfaction for teachers if they had no regard for the educational progress and general welfare of their pupils.

Many teachers felt the poor and sometimes cynical treatment they received exposed the cant of some who professed to put the children first. Ethics should be indivisible, and high-minded concern for the children sat ill with shabby treatment of teachers. I often wondered why so many of our critics had not become teachers themselves if they believed that education was the most important thing in the world and the interests of children always had to predominate regardless of all other circumstances. As the legendary President of the American Federation of Teachers, the late Al Shanker, observed in an address to the 1982 NASUWT Conference when referring to the 'pushy parent': "I could show those teachers how to do their job, if only I wasn't so busy making three times as much as they did!"

In practice most of the time the interests of pupils and teachers ran parallel. The key divergence of interest usually surfaced over the vexed issue of militant action. The NAS always took the view that ultimately, while in the short term there would be disruption to children's education, in the longer period everyone's interests would be served by resolving disputes and grievances that otherwise would fester.

The low pay and relatively easy entry to teaching were the two main reasons why it was regarded as the profession of last resort. A common attitude among young adults was: 'I'll try this and that; but if all else fails I can always go into teaching'. Low pay curtailed the ability of teaching to attract its fair share of high-calibre people, to the detriment of the pupils' interests. Hard experience taught the NASUWT that Government only gave teachers some measure of justice when put under pressure by unions, without which the situation would have been worse.

The claims of other professions to put their clients first are not always justified. The real difference between many other professions and teaching was that for historical and accidental reasons they had greater control over their own affairs and thus were better able to protect their interests by discreet restrictive practices. They could claim to be 'professional' without having to resort to the 'blue collar' tactics of trade unions whose members were not so fortunate. Even then disputes over their remuneration led occasionally to militant action. In more recent consumerist and litigious times, not mention a more militant media, the perception has grown that professional bodies are conspiracies against the laity.

The NAS and UWT always believed from their very beginnings that militant action could be justified. Indeed their births were largely motivated by a conviction that the teachers' interests were being cynically ignored because they were a soft touch for cost cutting by parsimonious governments and employers. But at the same time NAS and UWT activities over many years displayed a deep concern with matters educational and professional.

The controversy surrounding 'professional people' taking trade union action was brought into sharp focus in blunt exchanges at the NAS Golden Jubilee Conference Dinner in 1969. The Labour Secretary of State, Edward Short (later Lord Glenamara), also a former secondary school head in Blyth, took the opportunity to criticise recent militant action. The response from the NAS was equally blunt.

Ted Short had not endeared himself to members at the dinner by expressing regret that the NAS and NUT had not got together to form the 'NAT'. Whilst he conceded that some demands upon teachers "had increased to an unreasonable degree" and that "the temptation to follow the methods of other workers in their demands for their rights was strong", he claimed "the real dilemma facing an honoured profession is how far it should go along this line in order to establish its position".

The background at the time was the NAS protest action against the unsatisfactory 1968 salary settlement in Burnham, the bitter dispute developing in the light of the gross overreaction of the Durham LEA, which was a close neighbour of Ted Short's Newcastle Central Constituency, and the Interim Pay Claim that was just getting off the ground.

The Minister went on: "Phrases such as 'industrial action' had an odd ring against the background of the teachers' past record of service and their claim to professional status." Ted Short claimed the NAS was setting a bad example for the pupils who would draw their own conclusions about "what constitutes responsible behaviour". He questioned whether teachers really wanted "a rule book instead of a contract of service". What would happen to "a once dedicated profession marked by its intense pastoral concern for its children"?

With GS Terry Casey present at Conference but 'off duty' due to illness, a very distinguished and lifelong servant of the Association and member of the Executive about to retire, A.C.E. 'Tubby' Weston, had been asked to reply to the Secretary of State. Tubby was an extremely good choice in the circumstances, for he needed no lecture on professional commitment, having had an impressive record of 40 years service to education at county (Herefordshire) and national levels, including the presidency of the English Schools Swimming Association.

Expressing surprise he had to respond to the toast to "education" in terms as proposed by the Secretary of State, Tubby Weston picked up on Ted Short's comments that "we were teachers, psychologists, counsellors, social workers, supervisors and friends". "Yes," said Tubby, "six jobs for which all we wanted was one decent salary", bringing the house down with thunderous applause.

Tubby Weston went on to say, "for fifty years the NAS had sought professional status, but the denial of economic justice made a mockery of this". He conceded that "restrictionist practices would impair the education service" and, if the Minister wished to ensure that did not happen, "the moral was obvious: give teachers economic justice".

Proposing the toast to the guests the Ex-President, Bernard Wakefield, soon to become the first Assistant GS of the Association to relieve the pressure on Terry Casey, while politely complimenting the Minister for his sincerity and courage, in good NAS tradition firmly rejected his proposal "that we should all belong to a 'National Association of Teachers' as analogous to suggesting all politicians should belong to one party. That was nothing but a device to ensure that what were considered to be right decisions were reached without due consideration being paid to minority views."

The NAS had made great efforts to get a suitable General Teaching Council (GTC) established, which was designed to enhance the professional standing of teachers. At the same time the Association made the obvious point that salary was the most important ingredient of status.

The 'Retreat from Authority' in the face of rising levels of disruptive and violent behaviour on the part of some pupils, aided and abetted by their parents, which began in the 1960s, also highlighted the 'professional or union' debate. The Association made strenuous efforts to convince Government and LEAs that a serious problem was developing and required urgent attention. Such behaviour was causing immense damage to children's education and was not being acknowledged, let alone dealt with. Unfortunately those 'in authority' retreated from it and we were left to our own devices, taking militant action refusing to teach certain pupils and going on strike if instructed to do otherwise by management.

Such militant action was not centred upon serving self-interest, legitimate though that can be. Members were taking risks with their jobs to ensure decent standards of behaviour prevailed to facilitate education and learning and to ensure the safety of pupils and teachers alike. It was a unique example of the 'professional' and the 'union' marching hand in hand. To coin a phrase I was later to use, it was "industrial action with a halo".

Chapter 35 – Reports on Education

The sixties also saw a good number of major reports on education. The three most important from the teacher's point of view were probably Robbins, *Higher Education*, 1960; Newsom, *Half our Future*, 1963; and Plowden, *Children and their Primary School*, 1966.

Robbins recommended a virtual doubling of the university student population from just over 200,000 at the start of the sixties to nearly 400,000 by '73-74 and to 560,000 by the opening of the eighties.

The NAS gave evidence to the Robbins Committee in 1961 that it wished teacher training institutions to become integral parts of universities as an important step towards raising the quality and status of the profession. The NAS began to press for a more practical and school-based approach to teacher training.

Whilst Robbins recommended that teacher training institutions be renamed Colleges of Education, it took many more years for all of them to be incorporated into the HE sector.

The Newsom report was charged with inquiring into the long-standing problem of the education of youngsters between ages 13 and 16 of average-or-below ability. The partly 'predetermining' terms of reference given to the Newsom Inquiry stipulated that education be understood to include extra-curricular activities.

That was a sensitive area for the NAS. We held to the principle that such activities were voluntary and objected when management took teachers' participation in them for granted. The NAS argued that if teachers were paid for volunteering to engage in these activities their continuation would be guaranteed. The NUT always opposed teachers being paid for undertaking these extra-curricular activities.

Newsom duly recommended a longer school day, proposing a third session to include 'voluntary' activities in the normal curriculum. In its publication *The Longer School Day* the NAS warned against the dangers of pressurising teachers down the road of offering more 'social services'. The Association supported other appropriately qualified personnel providing such services but saw the danger of teachers being diverted from their core task.

A follow-up document entitled *Ancillary Assistance in Schools* was published setting out the precise conditions under which such staff should be employed.

The NAS emphasised they should not be used as teacher substitutes but they could provide vital support to the work of schools.

Newson also reiterated the call that the school leaving age be raised to 16. It was another attempt, largely unresourced, to discover ways of motivating the 'other half' of low-achieving youngsters, the Achilles heel of the education service, who were so put off by school.

The Plowden report, delivered to the Secretary of State for Education on 26 October 1966, was probably the one which impacted most significantly upon teachers and society generally in the 1960s. It became generally credited (or blamed, depending on your opinion) for introducing 'progressive' or 'child-centred' teaching methods. The references to teaching methods were more limited in the report than folklore was later to have us believe.

Lady Bridget Horatia Plowden, the daughter of an admiral, was well connected, and a chance encounter seated at a dinner next to Sir Edward Boyle, a very 'liberal' Conservative Minister of Education, led to the invitation to give up being a lay magistrate in London and assume the Chair of the Central Advisory Council on Education. She was asked to chair a committee "to consider primary education in all its aspects". The massive report which followed, published in two volumes, ran to over 1,000 pages.

Lady Plowden's advocacy of new teaching methods was aimed principally at the needs of newly arrived immigrant groups. While the 'typical' NAS member would take a sceptical approach to new learning methods, believing that they must be shown in practice to produce better results before widespread adoption, he would certainly have agreed with Plowden's analysis that much educational failure and bad behaviour was due to adverse social conditions, particularly poor housing and unemployment.

Whatever the controversy over child-centred learning, the Plowden report was received with almost universal approval when it recommended systematic nursery education and the provision of additional funds and staff to schools in socially deprived areas. Specific measures were proposed including improved pupil-teacher ratios, and salary additions for teachers willing to work in those deprived areas.

The NAS supported all the recommendations and in 1974 SPS (Social Priority School) payments were introduced in controversial circumstances connected to the sensitivities surrounding the age-old problems of the Burnham Committee.

At the time of Plowden in the mid-'60s the NAS campaigned for improved buildings in the primary sector, but expressed deep concern with some of the new designs which appeared to forget that children would be the main inhabitants.

The Plowden report, published shortly after 'Newsom', raised the same issue of ancillary help in schools but lacked precision on the matter. The NAS published a further document, *Teacher Aides – Help or Substitutes?* The year 1965 saw the publication by the NAS of a report on "Ancillary Assistance for Teachers". The NAS took a forward-looking view, accepting the valuable role ancillary staff could play and believing teachers were already too deeply distracted from the core role of teaching. The NAS insisted that qualified teachers had always to be responsible for the teaching of pupils in 'normal' classroom circumstances.

The issue was left to drift for many years, resulting in a wide variety of doubtful practices with many schools 'doing their own thing' in respect of voluntary and, especially, parental help. In 1974 the NAS published a booklet entitled *The Staffing of Schools: A Discussion Paper on Class Sizes and their Professional Implications.* I recall the document being regarded as somewhat 'courageous' at the time, dealing with a very sensitive issue for teachers.

However, rereading the booklet for this history I was stunned by the uncanny, even enlightened but positively prophetic relevance it had in respect of the National Agreement on Standards and Workload, reached in 2003 under a Social Partnership between the New Labour Government and most of the staff unions, the teachers led by the NASUWT.

The booklet raised the possibility that "the wider use of support staff would free teachers for greater teaching involvement". In non-teaching situations it would be uncontroversial, but in teaching situations it would have to be under "close professional supervision". Examples of the former included the preparation, distribution, repairing and reordering of materials, the supervision of pupils during breaks and whilst travelling to locations outside school, administration, projecting films and running some extra-curricular activities such as school newspapers, magazines and clubs.

In the second and more sensitive area of "teaching situations", ancillary staff could assist in "the supervision of pupils engaged in routine work and preparation". The discussion document conceded that "this would lead to support staff being engaged in a low-level teaching operation because such supervision would inevitably involve them in responding to queries made by pupils". Inevitably "nice judgement" would be required and defining the limits "could only be solved by continuing experiment".

These issues became vital ingredients (although not to everyone's liking) under the 2003 National Agreement referred to above.

Perhaps Plowden, like many other reports, 'failed' in the sense that the Committee was unable to enforce the conditions upon which the success of their otherwise good ideas depended. However, for all the opprobrium heaped upon Plowden by the 'traditional right' over teaching methods, her critics tended to forget she was ahead of her time in expressing concerns over 'school failure' and the need for a broad and balanced curriculum.

Throughout the 1960s and '70s the NAS and UWT became increasingly concerned about teacher training. Policy statements were submitted to the Committee of Enquiry on Teacher Training and to the James Committee, which were established in the early 1970s.

The 1960s saw the final and successful assault upon allowing unqualified staff to teach in the state maintained sector. In 1960 the NAS presented a report on "Dilution in the Teaching Profession" to its Annual Conference taking place in Hastings. The report revealed that there were nearly 36,500 unqualified teachers. This figure included 11,300 'untrained graduates', i.e. degree holders who had not undergone teacher training. This implied that 'professional dilution' amounted to just over 14% of the teacher workforce of nearly 256,000.

The NAS participated in the long struggle to establish an adequate force of fully qualified teachers. It opposed many of the short-term palliatives, put forward by many governments to plug the gaps in the staffing needs of schools. The NAS welcomed the phasing out of unqualified teachers announced by the DES in 1968 and a later decision taken in 1969 to introduce compulsory training for graduates, although it regretted the delay in implementation in secondary schools until 1 January 1972.

There was some ambiguity in the NAS approach which insisted on professional training but was deeply critical of its current quality and relevance to the practicalities of the classroom. That was resolved by calling for a much more school-based system. In particular, behaviour management training needed to be in the hands of successful practising teachers, not theorists in College of Education 'ivory towers'. Although school-based training was more expensive, aspiring teachers had to be prepared to work in schools and classrooms as they existed, not in the promised land of adequate resources, good teacher-pupil ratios and angelic children.

A very pertinent statement on teacher training in all its aspects, initial and in-service, came in January 1972 with the publication of the James Report. Many of the recommendations reflected the evidence the NAS had submitted to the James Committee which included:

1) higher standards of entry to teacher training (two A Level GCE passes parallel to university requirements);

2) an all-graduate profession;

3) a flexible and consecutive pattern of 2 + 2 years of academic study and professional training.

James recommended three cycles of initial, induction and in-service training for teachers. Although not expressly charged to do so James recommended the radical step to give all practising teachers the contractual right to a sabbatical term once every seven years for in-service training. That turned out to be hopelessly ambitious, never coming remotely close to implementation.

Whilst the NAS and UWT harboured reservations about some recommendations of James relating to the status and validation of the new Bachelor of Education Degree and some other diplomas, the overall thrust of James was for more school-based training of an all-graduate profession, which reflected the approaches of the 'Joint Two'.

In publishing its White Paper, *Education: A Framework for Expansion*, at the end of 1972 (constituting Education Secretary Margaret Thatcher's major policy statement), the Government expressed agreement with many of James' recommendations including higher entry standards, moves towards an all-graduate profession, induction, teacher tutors and in-service education.

The NAS, while welcoming some aspects, particularly the proposals for nursery education, nevertheless criticised the plans for expanding the teacher force as being inadequate. The estimated 510,000 workforce for 1981 would still leave a 20,000 shortfall compared to the recommendations put forward in 1965 by the National Advisory Council on Teacher Supply. While welcoming the proposal to establish the Advisory Committee on the Supply and Training of Teachers (ACSTT), the NAS was critical of the limited terms of reference granted to it and opposed plans to reduce the numbers in teacher training following the decline in the birth rate.

However, a critical motion put down by the Executive for the 1973 Conference reflecting these concerns was lost; probably due, I have to confess, to my warning we had to be wary of demands to increase teacher supply: "Imagine, another 100,000 to share our miserable little global sums!" In the real world demands to increase teacher supply were mutually incompatible with the vastly improved career structured salaries we sought. More ancillary staff were required to carry out the many non-teaching tasks currently undertaken by fully qualified teachers.

By 1974, amidst much financial instability and an economy wobbling through international tensions and serious industrial unrest in the UK, GS Terry Casey, in representing the NAS on ACSTT, argued that supply had to be related to realistic future demand if serious unemployment amongst teachers were to be avoided.

There were many other committees of enquiry and reports concerning education, all covering important matters but simply too numerous to comment upon in detail. The NAS submitted evidence to the Bullock Inquiry into Reading and the Use of English and to the Select Committee on Race Relations and Immigration in 1972. The NAS published booklets on *The Education of Immigrant Children and Problems of Social Deprivation*. A report on the 1973 NAS Christmas Education Conference theme *Unwilling to (more) School*, dealing with provision for ROSLA, was also published. Many publications were produced in response to the Schools Council agenda for reform and development of the curriculum and examinations.

By 1971 Westminster's insatiable appetite to reform local government was surfacing once again and an inquiry was established for the purpose. The NAS argued for education to be administered by local authorities large enough to cope with the challenges. That meant county and metropolitan authorities. The NAS also said teachers should be allowed to stand for election to the LEA in which they served.

In January 1975 the NAS presented evidence to the Layfield Committee of Inquiry into Local Government Finance. The Association based its arguments on the principle that LEAs "should be responsible for what they pay for and pay for what they are responsible for". Thus central government should bear the full costs of teachers' salaries, pensions, training, supply and distribution. LEAs should be given more control over the provision of buildings, equipment, school transport and other ancillary services.

The NAS evidence to Layfield had been timely, for very soon afterwards an era of serious cuts in educational expenditure was to follow. The position adopted by the NAS and UWT was to accept some inevitability of reduced public expenditure in the wake of all the domestic and international economic crises of the early '70s, but to respond to and actively resist any worsening of staffing ratios.

Reflecting its belief in a common council of teacher unions to deal with matters which commanded general agreement, the NAS welcomed the establishment of the Schools Council in 1963. It brought together the leading 'players' in the education service to study how the curriculum and public examinations could be improved. Unfortunately the NUT insisted on dominating teacher representation on the Council's committee structure. With many civil servants and employers' representatives fearful of upsetting the NUT, the Council became a mouthpiece for so-called progressive and left-wing policies on education which were highly partisan and not based on consensus. After initial good work the NUT-dominated Council squandered the wider support such a body needed to survive in the longer term. The NAS was not at all surprised that one of the first things the Conservative Government under Margaret Thatcher did after attaining power in 1979 was to abolish the Schools

Council. Arguably, a more consensual Council might have prevented the intense party politicisation of the education service that subsequently developed.

Chapter 36 - Northern Ireland

The achievement of NASUWT Northern Ireland has a special quality of its own. At the start of 1961 the NAS had eight centrally attached members from Northern Ireland, mostly returnees from other parts of the UK where they had joined the Association. By the end of that year there were 161 members. The 'founding meeting' took place at the Kensington Hotel Belfast in May 1961. The meeting took a crucial decision to recruit teachers irrespective of religion, political affinity or school type. The meeting also decided to request the NAS Executive to establish a Northern Ireland Local Association. The Executive readily agreed, attaching the new Local Association to District 6, Merseyside and Isle of Man.

In 1965 Northern Ireland NAS became an Executive District in its own right. Membership had increased to 813, not large enough to justify a new District on its own; but taken on the basis of its unique position and characteristics, it was a wise decision. It was also an act of faith by the National Executive, a declaration that the NAS had a great future in the Province. That was soon to be well repaid. At this stage Northern Ireland began to be divided into several local associations, starting with Belfast, followed by Derry & Antrim and then North Down. In those times 200 was considered the ideal size of membership for a Local Secretary (also a full-time schoolmaster) to manage.

Thereafter the NASUWT soon rose to become the largest teacher organisation in Northern Ireland, achieving a membership of 3,200 in 1975 and 7,700 in 1980. As a percentage of the school teaching force NASUWT membership rose from 1.5% in 1961 to 17.6% in 1975. By 1980 over one-third of teachers in Northern Ireland were in membership of the NASUWT. By 1984 14 local associations had been established.

Membership continued to grow, reaching in excess of 10,000 in 1990. The year 2000 saw in-service membership rise above 12,000. Official DENI statistics state the total full-time equivalent teacher numbers to have been 20,642. Even making allowances for numbers of part-time and supply teachers in membership, the NASUWT was able to claim to represent an overall majority of schoolteachers in Northern Ireland.

The NASUWT offered many distinctive features to teachers in Northern Ireland but the greatest was undoubtedly its strictly non-sectarian approach, recruiting members from both sides of the sad divide. Before the arrival of the NAS and UWT in Northern Ireland, teachers joined the 'cross-border' Irish

National Teachers Organisation (INTO) if they came from the Catholic community or the Ulster Teachers' Union (UTU) if they belonged to the Protestant section. ATL, then AMMA, also established a small presence in Northern Ireland, recruiting primarily from the voluntary sector but otherwise displaying the same differences from the NASUWT that existed elsewhere in the UK.

Great personal qualities of leadership and courage, both moral and physical, often had to be displayed by NAS representatives in Northern Ireland as they resolutely refused to be drawn into the sectarian conflict. Instead they insisted upon members remaining united and focussed upon the many issues that arose from their employment as teachers. In so doing, and in company with several other trade unions such as the then Post Office Workers, the NASUWT made a huge but unsung contribution to the peace process that slowly but thankfully has grown in Northern Ireland.

If there is one single 'founding' leader in Northern Ireland who displayed these qualities and deserves to be recognised for his contribution towards the success of the Union it is John Scott. In 1965 John was elected to the National Executive to represent the new District of Northern Ireland. He was elected to national office and became President for 1974-75.

Later other leaders emerged in Northern Ireland who went on to assume high office in the NASUWT. The most prominent was Eamonn O'Kane, President in 1987-88, who became Deputy GS in 1990 and succeeded me as the GS in 2002 only to suffer a tragic and premature death from cancer in 2004. Another prominent leader was Bill Herron, the first full-time Regional Official in Northern Ireland (1974-78) who went on to become the NASUWT Assistant GS from 1983 to 2000.

One other candidate for the NASUWT's Northern Ireland 'Hall of Fame' has to be Tom McKee who was the Regional Official from 1978 to his retirement in 2003. As a widely known and respected figure and spokesman for the largest education union in Northern Ireland, Tom was regarded as 'Mr Teacher' in the Province.

The aforementioned leaders from Northern Ireland recognised the invaluable support and advice they received from GS Terry Casey during his period in that office, 1963-83. Terry, a man of 'London Irish stock', was a frequent visitor to Northern Ireland and often played a direct personal role in dealing with the many diverse and sometimes volatile situations that arose.

Going back to the early days, it is evident that the invitation to the NAS from Northern Ireland was also sparked by the successful campaign on Burnham recognition in 1961. Besides the non-sectarian approach the appeal of the NAS was basically the same as was found in other parts of the UK. The mood of the teaching profession was changing. As the old 'professional' reliance upon rational argument through representation was increasingly exposed as ineffectual, teachers turned more towards the NAS as a dynamic union no longer prepared to accept 'genteel poverty'.

There were also some high-profile and outstandingly successful examples of individual casework conducted by the NAS which impressed teachers in Northern Ireland. Probably the most significant one involved none other than John Scott himself in the "Ballymoney Affair", which began in 1964 and concluded with an official inquiry in 1967. It was not a financial scandal as its title might suggest, but that was the name of the secondary school at which John taught.

A serious dispute arose between the NAS members and some individuals involved in the management and governance of the school. The dispute concerned aspects of running the school, lack of consultation and the role of a certain individual on the Management Committee in respect of the award of graded allowances and 'tampering' with the minutes of meetings. An exchange of letters in the press led to ten NAS members being suspended from duty.

John Scott was personally involved through claims that he had been treated unfairly in his application for a post in Ballycastle High School due to the activities of an individual on the Management Committee. The case was raised by the Hon. Phelin O'Neill in the Stormont Parliament, who said the case had given him "the greatest anxiety". The Minister of Education, on the same day in March 1966 stated, "I have decided that the candidate concerned should be appointed to the post."

The furore led to the Director of Education for Antrim establishing a public inquiry presided over by a QC (and future Lord Chief Justice in Northern Ireland), J.C. MacDermott. Whilst MacDermott's findings did little for any of the parties to the dispute, he was scathing in his comments on the NAS tactics, which suggested "an aggressively militant approach which was alien to the traditions of the members of this profession in this country". MacDermott advised the NAS "to desist".

MacDermott had not realised how much teacher opinion was changing. Teachers were not impressed with his failure to reach conclusions. They were impressed by the courage of the NAS and its refusal to bow the knee in front of flagrant injustice and the reluctance of those in authority to deal fairly. Teachers were also impressed by the fact that John Scott was eventually appointed to Ballycastle High School, later becoming its vice-principal. A few years later John was appointed principal of Ballee HS.

The NAS was gaining 'street credibility'. The days of servility in the face of injustice masquerading as 'professionalism' were coming to an end in Northern Ireland, as they were in other parts of the UK.

By the end of 1966 NAS membership stood at over 1,000 and formal recognition was accorded by the Minister of Education in the following year. After the prorogation of the Stormont Parliament and the introduction of direct rule in 1972, the NAS (together with the UWT after the merger in 1976) was fully recognised by the Department of Education Northern Ireland (DENI).

The Northern Ireland Labour Relations Agency (LRA) was a statutory body charged, amongst other matters, with dealing objectively on some inter-union issues. In stark contradistinction with the 40 years of government – NUT – and other union shenanigans over NAS claims for recognition on the Burnham Committee, the LRA was also able to decree that Northern Ireland NAS be recognised on the Further Education Negotiating Body since its membership in that field had reached 300.

In 1966 following 'UK' developments the NAS in Northern Ireland declared itself "opposed to selection for secondary education on academic and social grounds", neatly in effect supporting the comprehensive school but avoiding the minefield of the almost total separation of youngsters between 'Controlled' (Protestant) and 'Maintained' (Roman Catholic) schools.

Again following UK developments the Northern Ireland Representative Council of the NAS in 1967 demanded the withdrawal of the requirement for teachers to supervise school meals. This was successfully secured in 1968, the year of the School Meals Agreement across the water in England and Wales.

In 1969 the first Northern Ireland Conference of the NAS was held. The big 'teacher political' issues had to be debated against the background of rising sectarian tensions.

In 1969 controversy blew up as the NAS identified the number of members it had in Roman Catholic (RC) schools. This was done to secure recognition by the Maintained Schools' Authority (the RC sector), for which it was also necessary to convince the All Ireland Primate, Cardinal Conway. Some Protestant elements in the membership, particularly in Belfast, misinterpreted the motivation behind the move, and the issue was resolved by giving assurances that it was a one-off exercise for good purpose which would not be repeated.

October 1969 saw the first of many challenges for the NAS generated directly by the 'troubles'. Serious rioting broke out in Belfast and 'London/Derry' – if I might so name the latter in a neutral way. With the immediate aim of restoring order on the streets, British troops were deployed. The NAS came under criticism for greeting these events with silence. Challenged to respond, GS Terry Casey said our "silence was not cowardice if by making any statement you destroyed your ability to reconcile opposing views". The NAS was not in the business of political and religious beliefs but of representing members as teachers. If local Officers of the NAS expressed views they did so as individuals, not as representatives.

The next challenge came in August 1971 with the decision by the Northern Ireland Home Secretary, Brian (later Lord) Faulkner, to introduce internment without trial. That was generally applauded by the Protestants and condemned by the Catholics. At 4 a.m. on 9 August some 350 people were arrested and detained out of 452 wanted suspects. Five of the internees were NAS members and both sides of the divide were represented in the group.

There were calls from one side to applaud and, with equal predictability from the other, to condemn the move, all of which were resisted by the local and national leaderships. A Belfast Teachers' Action Group was formed to fight internment and invited the NAS to send a delegate to a meeting which was intended to organise a strike demanding the internees' release and the protection of their employment rights. The NAS Northern Ireland replied to the Belfast Group stating that the objects of the Association were about representing schoolmasters in respect of employment and educational issues.

The Armagh and W. Down Association had been particularly vociferous on internment, taking a 'Catholic' line in calling upon the NAS publicly to condemn it. In what became a much-quoted letter, Terry Casey wrote on 16 September 1971 to Paul Hoben, Secretary of the Northern Ireland Federation, setting out the NAS rationale with consummate clarity, his dialectical skills equally at home in the written word as on the public platform. Terry began by attributing "the almost miraculous survival" of the NAS in the Province to its determination "to defend the professional interests of schoolmasters, irrespective of any political, religious or other difference". Internment without trial, although "abhorrent" in itself, could not be considered in isolation from the anarchy of civil strife which occasioned the loss of other fundamental rights. "The Rules of the Association charged the Executive with defending the interests of members as schoolmasters, not as citizens." The professional interests of members interned would be protected, "their position being analogous to a schoolmaster suspended, a move which was preventative, not punitive". He would ask John Scott to make representations for interned members to receive full salary. Any obligation under our Benevolence Rules to relieve distress to the families concerned would be discharged.

Terry Casey concluded his letter asking that the camaraderie established by the NAS being "one of the few hopeful indications that people of differing political and religious views can work in harmony for their professional advancement", should be supported as "an instrument of reconciliation even while all around you polarization and increased bitterness is the order of the day". Terry Casey's letter was widely and frequently copied to explain the NAS's position as similar events recurred.

The Northern Ireland Federation published a quality journal, originally entitled *Sir* and later named *Platform*, which was widely read and respected throughout the NASUWT. Writing in *Sir* in November 1971 John Scott encapsulated the Association's approach to controversial developments and various atrocities committed by both sides of the divide, explaining that "the NAS would neither condone nor condemn".

Thus whilst remaining resolutely silent on the issue of internment without trial which otherwise would have torn the Association apart, the NAS took up the interests of the internee members as teachers employed by the State. Shortly before Christmas 1971 John Scott and Terry Casey personally visited interned members in Long Kesh, later known as the Maze prison. The NAS sought to have the Northern Ireland Government treat them as suspended employees and therefore entitled to receive full pay.

That was a decision so politically charged and full of financial implications if a precedent were set for all 350, that it had to be referred to London. After much deliberation the Government turned down the request of the NAS. Nevertheless the NAS continued to support its interned members and Terry Casey made representations directly to Reginald Maudling, British Home Secretary, alas without success.

The Association responded to requests for benevolence assistance for the families of the internees in accordance with its rules. That proved controversial and some members objected. The Executive overruled the objectors, laying down quite firmly that all members and their families were entitled to benevolence if they met the criteria laid down, which they clearly did. Threats of resignation were received as they usually were on such matters but very few materialised.

In September 1971 the INTO union sprung a trap for the NAS in respect of the Oath of Allegiance. Undoubtedly a repressive measure on its own merits, it was relic of the events surrounding the establishment of the Irish Free State and the partition of the North, having been enacted by the Stormont Government in 1923. The Act required all teachers in publicly funded schools to take the Oath of Allegiance to the British monarch. Over 100 teachers had met in County Derry and invited the NAS and INTO to call for its abolition. When in 1969 INTO had called for the Act's repeal no such invitation to the NAS 'to join in' had been received. INTO was trying to portray the NAS as a 'lackey British union'. The Association again refused to participate in a partisan-motivated move but declared that no teacher anywhere should be subject to political or religious tests. The Oath was removed in 1979.

Operation Motorman, an intensive search and occupation of schools by the British Army to counter 'terrorist activity', was the next crisis that tested the determination of the NAS to remain non-partisan. It was launched in August 1972 and all but three schools had been vacated by the Army in time for the start of the Autumn Term. One of those three schools was St Genevieve's, which had many NAS and UWT members. The situation was tense and shots were fired in one of the schools, St Peter's Secondary. INTO campaigned for the Army to vacate the schools. The NAS authorised its members not to attend school on grounds of safety. Once again INTO accused the NAS of being a British union fearful of a Protestant reaction. Again NAS found a way of protecting members as employees without entering the partisan debate about the presence of British troops and 'counter-terrorist activity'.

On occasions too numerous to mention, the NAS constantly came under pressure from the victims' section of the community to condemn the latest atrocity committed by the other side. The NAS simply pointed out its previously publicised position, totally abhorring all acts of violence. It was vital to avoid the controversy that would follow if a competitive league of denunciation developed. John Scott's articulation of the policy 'neither to condone nor to condemn' proved invaluable in keeping the NAS above the sectarian fray, a policy which ironically but helpfully assisted in diminishing the divide.

The visits of the Queen in 1977 and the Pope in 1979 provided ample opportunity for the partisan mischief makers on both sides. Some aspects were so complicated that the reader would not thank me for attempting a summary even within reasonable bounds of brevity, which I doubt I could do. Suffice it to say that normally welcome decisions to grant an extra school holiday were opposed by the 'other side' on both occasions.

The presence of the Association also afforded Northern Ireland members the opportunity of participating in the 'big UK-wide issues' facing teachers and other professional public sector employees. None the least of these was the amount of money being made available for their salaries. Even before the prorogation of the Stormont Parliament at the height of the troubles in 1972, bringing direct governance and Ministers from London, Northern Ireland members of the NAS and UWT had taken sympathy action with their English and Welsh colleagues in some of the pay disputes of the sixties and early seventies, especially in 1969, 1970 and 1971. Indeed in December 1969 when NAS and UWT members in Northern Ireland went on a one-day strike to support the interim claim being conducted 'over the water', the UTU, while sanctimoniously observing "nobody wants to strike", nevertheless invited its members "to let English and Welsh teachers fight for us!"

In 1970 John Scott led the demand for formal 'de jure' pay parity with teachers in England and Wales. In effect this meant simply applying the Burnham agreements directly in the Province without having to go through the formality of 'negotiations' between the Northern Ireland Teachers' Council (NITC) and Stormont-cum-DENI. This has not been achieved to the present day but the NASUWT has been the key player in securing 'de facto' parity, even if it had to be maintained on several occasions after frank exchanges giving clear indications that action would follow its severance. It remains an issue to the present day and may be heightened with the restoration of devolved government following the eventual implementation of the 1997 Peace Agreement.

In the meantime the NAS had to deal with some extraordinary and petty-minded attempts by other unions on the NITC to ostracise it through various ruses including a stipulation that 'Burnham style' secrecy had to prevail. Attempts were made to keep NAS representation well below that justified by its ever-increasing size. To this day the purely locally based unions put extraneous considerations ahead of achieving the best financial deal for schoolteachers in Northern Ireland.

Whilst mentioning the special circumstances surrounding the development of the NASUWT in Northern Ireland, tribute should also be paid to the distinctive contributions made by the two other 'devolved nations' in the UK, Wales and Scotland.

Wales was always more closely linked with England in terms of its education system and the NASUWT than Scotland. The Burnham Committee covered England and Wales, as did much educational legislation. Other important committees such as CLEA/ST, dealing with conditions of service, applied equally to England and Wales. That may be in the process of changing as devolution develops in Wales.

Wales played a very full and active part in the development of the NAS. Indeed, the most prominent single founding father of the Association was George Cording from Cardiff, who most strongly advocated and presided over the 'secession' in 1922. Wales also produced one of the Association's most renowned National Officers and orators in the person of George Lloyd Williams, President 1952-53, who went on to serve as Honorary Treasurer from 1956 to 1965.

A Wales Committee was formed mainly to represent NAS interests to the Welsh Office as there had long been some devolution in respect of educational affairs. In 1972 the first annual NAS Wales Conference took place, a practice also replicated in Northern Ireland and Scotland.

Wales has provided two other National Presidents, Hywel Thomas, 1973, and Eric Powell, 1982-83. Furthermore Wales has exported many thousands of teachers to England to play vital roles in the education service. Many joined the NASUWT and brought fine traditions of trade unionism with them, especially those who were the children of coal miners. Wales has hosted six Annual Conferences of the Union to date (2008).

For Scotland the NASUWT 'story' has been a lower-key affair. Despite forming itself in 1934 the original Scottish Schoolmasters' Association (SSA) never really matched the expansion of the NAS in England, Wales and Northern Ireland. Membership hovered between 1,000 in the early days to around 2,000 by the 1970s. The SSA merged fully into the National Association at the same time (1 January 1976) as the Transfer of Engagements between the NAS and UWT. NASUWT Scotland has played a very valuable role in ensuring every part of the UK is represented in the Association, providing comparative information and experience mutually beneficial to all the constituent parts of the Union. Scotland has hosted three Annual Conferences and provided a renowned President in the person of J.A.C. Thompson in 1959-60, who played a valuable role in the campaign for Burnham representation, which came to fruition in 1961. The early part of the twenty-first century has witnessed a considerable expansion of the NASUWT in Scotland.

Chapter 37 - '10/65' – The Comprehensive Revolution

Circular 10/65, issued in July 1965, is still regarded as the most famous in British educational history. It demanded English and Welsh LEAs abolish their grammar and secondary modern schools and introduce a comprehensive system of secondary education, thereby ending selection through the 11 plus examination. Many people believed the 11 plus inflicted great injustices upon the majority of children, declaring between 70% and 80% 'failures' at such a tender age by virtue of their inability to pass the exam and gain entry to a grammar school. Circular 10/65 was the main education plank of the Labour Party's manifesto in the October 1964 General Election which returned it to power after 13 years in opposition.

The circular impacted dramatically upon the lives of secondary teachers, including the majority of NAS and UWT members who were to be found in that sector. It also had great repercussions in the primary field, for it led to the abolition of the 11 plus exam, affording much freedom to the primary schools. At the same time huge social changes were taking place. Relatively small secondary schools were soon to be merged into large comprehensives. Teachers were woefully underprepared for the massive challenges that followed. The NAS together with the UWT were soon to be embroiled in many bitter and long disputes over 'management' and conditions of service issues. It was to be a time of great unhappiness and upheaval.

10/65 marked a sea change in the politicisation of the education service. Opinions on comprehensive reorganisation differed sharply. Given the waxing and waning fortunes of political parties, the inevitable result was a continuous period of fundamental reforms pushing and pulling the education system in different directions, which arguably continues to the present day.

A strong supporter of comprehensive schooling, Tony Crosland had been appointed to succeed Michael Stewart as Minister of Education early in 1965. The main thrust of 10/65 was to advocate the 'orthodox' 11-18 comprehensive. However, other alternatives were acceptable, including a variety of middle school arrangements and 11-16 comprehensives with sixth-form colleges dealing with the 16-18-year-olds. LEAs were given one year, until July 1966, to submit their plans.

Naturally the circular provoked a wide public debate with the 'class war' lying just below the surface. The 'conservative' middle classes feared the loss of 'their' grammar schools, which incidentally also provided some working-class children with an 'escape route' up the social and 'occupational' ladder. The left-wing media sided with the underdogs, the bulk of working-class parents who were glad their children would not be prematurely condemned to a (supposedly) inferior secondary modern education.

The NAS, along with most other teacher organisations, took a cautious approach. Only the NUT, run by heads and socialist activists, was strongly in favour. While recognising the injustice of the 11 plus exam, NAS members were cognisant of the practical effects of secondary reorganisation. They believed one had to be certain that the new would in practice be better than the old. In 1964 the Association published a book, *The Comprehensive School – An Appraisal from within*, which rehearsed all the arguments but also considered the experiments that were already in existence. It was generally favourable to the comprehensive but warned that a final judgement could not be made until much later, by which time, if we had 'got it wrong', it would be too late to put right.

A little later the London Schoolmasters Association (LSA) published a booklet, *Problems of the Comprehensive School*. The London County Council (LCC) had been ahead of 10/65, already having comprehensive schools in operation. The LCC was committed to a fully comprehensive system across the whole of the capital. Written by practising schoolmasters the booklet was full of the operational problems, many of which were generated by the huge increase in the size of schools.

Much more emphasis had to be placed on administrative systems, risking considerable bureaucracy, to deal with the day-to-day problems in large schools, where every teacher no longer knew every pupil. Major issues of streaming or setting or mixed ability teaching arose which had not been necessary to address in the grammar-secondary modern divide. Homework, transport, noise and movement within the building were identified as greater problems in the comprehensive school. Timetabling and the curriculum became more complicated. Pupil indiscipline, always a problem with some, became doubly difficult to deal with in the large and impersonal comprehensive schools in spite of valiant attempts to establish house, year and form groups to regain the more friendly informality lost with the demise of the smaller grammar and secondary modern schools.

The new schools had to deal with a fast-changing society where immigrant children had arrived in considerable numbers, bringing with them different cultures and attitudes. Management of large institutions was a much more complex business and headteachers had little training for this new demand placed on their shoulders.

The LSA was "not convinced that the ambitious claims of the advocates of the comprehensive school would be completely justified" and so called upon the

LCC Education Committee "to slow down" and allow time for the 'experiments' to be properly evaluated. The LSA quoted a former Conservative Minister of Education, Florence Horsburgh, who "saw no educational advantage in the comprehensive school that could outweigh the enormous disadvantage of size". She wanted to see "diversity and not uniformity in education – independent and maintained schools, church, county, town and village schools".

The views held by Miss Horsburgh, and indeed the very words she used to express them, have a remarkable resonance with the slide away from the traditional comprehensive by both Labour and Conservative Governments in recent times. It seems that Miss Horsburgh was in favour of "modernisation" over 50 years ago!

Representing those who had to implement the reforms day in and day out, the NAS based its judgement on outcomes in practice. Indeed it was the practice, rather than the theory, which was later to be often found wanting, giving rise to many disputes and other problems. While well conceived and motivated in the opinion of the majority of NAS members, comprehensive reorganisation was inadequately planned and resourced.

10/65 also led to increased political interference in the internal organisation of schools. Hitherto politics had not invaded the space for purely educational issues, such as teaching methods, streaming and setting. It opened up the great danger of educational issues being settled on social and political grounds. The LSA was convinced the LCC was acting mainly out of social and political motives. When the LSA raised practical problems they were constantly fobbed off with remarks that made it clear those were for the headteachers and administrators to sort out.

Naturally most Labour-controlled LEAs were reasonably content to draw up plans for comprehensive schools. It was their party's policy. Not so for the Conservative LEAs. Some quietly complied, more or less accepting their fate; others sought delay whilst some actively opposed and began to defy the circular. Some cases ended up in the courts.

There were serious practical problems of planning for the LEAs. There was little if any additional finance guaranteed at the time. Whilst mergers could be produced on paper, in reality many LEAs had schools which were too small to house comprehensives. Split-site comprehensives were to prove particularly troublesome to establish on a satisfactory basis, but they were often deemed the only way of going comprehensive on the basis of limited finance. There was to be no capital grant for comprehensive reorganisation until 1969.

With the return to power of the Conservatives in October 1970 Prime Minister Ted Heath appointed Margaret Thatcher, the only woman in his

Cabinet, as Secretary of State for Education. One of her first acts was to issue Circular 10/70, which revoked 10/65.

LEAs remained free to continue with their plans for reorganisation if they wished, but there was no obligation to do so. Most LEAs continued with schemes that the previous Minister had approved whilst some did not. The pace of reform certainly slowed down. Nevertheless the future Prime Minister was destined to approve more comprehensive reorganisations than any other Secretary of State for Education, much to her later embarrassment as a right-wing Premier.

The NAS, reflecting its strictly non-party political approach, was highly critical of the vacillating uncertainties into which politicians of both the main parties had plunged the education service.

The refusal to allocate sufficient resources to match political ambition was again well illustrated as Margaret Thatcher decided to concentrate on rebuilding primary schools, seeking to rectify previous neglect. Inevitably the claims of secondary comprehensive reorganisation upon the education budget suffered. As the hopes for a fair secondary system were being raised, so the seeds of future difficulties were being sown.

The Conservative Government's desire to have it 'both ways', grammar and comprehensive, led to further confusion and division. Supporters of comprehensive reform complained that the continued existence of grammar (and direct grant) schools in their areas compromised the very principle on which the new system was to be based, i.e. no selection, no 11 plus examination and a genuine all-ability pupil intake.

In 1970 the Secretary of State ordered Surrey CC to reinstate the 11 plus exam (which it had abolished) to enable pupils in the new Rydens School's catchment area to seek entry to grammar schools elsewhere in the Council area. Some parents took exception to such exercise of powers by the Minister but despite threats were unable to mount a full legal challenge.

To the confusion generated by a mixed bag of grammar and comprehensive schools, the nature of the reorganisations added further complexity. Instead of a streamlined common system, secondary reorganisation produced a patchwork quilt of middle schools (some deemed primary, others secondary) together with 11-16 and 11-18 comprehensives. Sixth-form colleges also appeared.

The NAS had argued in the 1960s for a Royal Commission on Education. Many different and often worthy reports had been commissioned and published, each one advocating specific causes. A review of the whole had become necessary to examine the overall distribution of resources and priorities that should be established. Despite extreme differences with Sir William Alexander over Burnham and salary-related matters, the NAS found an ally in him in calling for this overview when he wrote in support of the movement, *Towards a New Education Act*. Her Majesty's Chief Inspector of Schools, W.R. Elliot, writing in 1971, called for a limit to be placed upon experimentation: "I believe some hard decisions need to be taken about the limits within which experimentation with organisation variants can be accepted."

By the end of the 1960s a considerable number of immigrant children had arrived in British schools. They raised social and educational issues of some magnitude. As a consequence the NAS published a major piece of work, *Education and the Immigrants*, which was very well received.

In 1969, giving evidence to the Royal Commission on Public Schools, the NAS argued that it was inconsistent for an LEA, having decided on comprehensive education, to continue to select pupils for places at direct grant schools and to pay the necessary fees. The Association advocated a gradual withdrawal to allow for an orderly run down of places and for the schools concerned to make the necessary adjustments.

As fierce debate continued over comprehensive reform, the Labour Government commissioned the National Foundation on Educational Research (NFER) to conduct a number of inquiries. All the reports were generally favourable to comprehensive schooling but this conflicted with other evidence that observers could also see. Members reported widespread problems particularly, but not exclusively, in urban areas in the late sixties and early seventies. The overall picture appeared to be mixed. My experience as a young Branch Secretary in the Inner London Borough of Lewisham was typical in hearing of first-hand accounts from members of serious problems of indiscipline and even chaos. Equally, I also heard accounts of other comprehensive schools doing well, with the typical comment from members: "We are lucky, we teach in a nice area and the kids are generally pretty good and fairly well behaved."

Starting in 1969 a group of scholars led by Brian Cox, Professor of English Literature at Manchester University, published several 'Black Papers' extremely critical of the abolition by the Labour Government of grammar schools and attacking the records of comprehensives. They painted a very bleak picture of life in some comprehensives, citing deplorable behaviour and low standards of learning prompted by too excessive reliance upon 'progressive' teaching methods.

Steering an independent non-dogmatic line, the NAS was neither in the Black Paper nor the (self-proclaimed) 'progressive' camp. In some areas we recognised that comprehensive education was a necessity, for example in large remote rural areas such as Anglesey where the first example was pioneered in the country. We saw good sense in localities having a significant say in deciding their own system, knowing their circumstances best.

From 1950 to 1965 the number of comprehensive schools in England and Wales rose from 10 to 262. From the time of 10/65 to 1970 when Labour lost power the number rose to 1,145. From 1950 to 1970 the percentage of secondary pupils educated in comprehensives rose from 0.3% to 31%. Today around 90% of secondary school children are educated in comprehensive schools. The economy has expanded; living standards have risen for most people. But there is still much controversy, and discontent remains with politicians from both the major parties who have formed governments constantly seeking to change the system.

Increased international competition, the desire to raise living standards, the Cold War and the final demise of 'empire' were among the pressures that led politicians to demand more from the education service to produce citizens of the future who could cope with these diverse challenges. These economic and political pressures, according to some, generated a need to move away from exam-cramming 'convergent thinking' education to a more 'creative' one. Teaching should become less didactic and more child centred, allowing pupils to discover things for themselves to genuinely understand, rather than by having knowledge and 'thinking' drummed in to them by the 'authority figure' of the traditional teacher.

Seating arrangements in classrooms were changed. Children were grouped around tables rather than seated at the traditional rows of desks. School design changed with more open-plan spaces to facilitate developments such as team teaching. Emphasis was placed on individual work; projects constructed by teachers were given to pupils to work on themselves or in groups. With the gradual if not total demise of the 11 plus exam, primary schools were set free to adopt new methods without much checking of the results.

Secondary schools, increasingly comprehensive, were caught up in debates about methods and organisation. Debates over mixed-ability teaching, streaming or setting arose. In London local politicians argued and sometimes insisted that mixed-ability teaching was the natural corollary of the comprehensive school, reflecting their belief in equality of opportunity. The NAS believed that such decisions should be left to the schools and teachers to determine themselves in the light of their professional judgement.

Unfortunately the voice of the teacher in the classroom struggled to be heard. The agenda was set by politicians, education management and a variety of so-called experts outside the classroom who could pontificate without being required to prove their theories worked in practice. The typical NAS member was a traditionalist by instinct who was nevertheless prepared to consider new ideas and methods so long as the process was well managed. Often it was not and many members became lost and overwhelmed as the new regime took over with very mixed results.

The NAS never took up firm positions on teaching methods for the simple reason that views varied so much between members. The Association argued for as much teacher professional independence in the classroom as possible but recognised that such autonomy had to be circumscribed in respect of 'whole school' policy matters such as behaviour management where applying different standards and rules could lead to more difficulties. As the NASUWT's collegiate philosophy was later to emphasise, classroom teachers needed to be fully consulted in the determination of school policies. After the 'comprehensive revolution' the NAS came to the very firm view that the organisation and management of schools was a vital matter in which many people involved were singularly unprepared and undertrained. Indeed the NAS Christmas Education Conference of 1972 was devoted to that theme.

Giving evidence to the Royal Commission on Local Government in 1966, the NAS accepted the widely shared basic premise that "education was a national service locally administered". However, if that were to be sensibly carried forward into practice it required large, single-purpose education authorities with the resources and range of personnel and support services capable of delivering a high-quality service.

The Association acknowledged the constitutional propriety of the Westminster Government making fundamental political decisions on the nature of the 'national service of education', but called for less politicisation of LEAs, which should be more concerned with 'administration' than politics. In a state system government had the right to determine the basic nature of the education service, but dictating teaching methods was a step too far down the road of micro-management. Government should determine the 'what' but not the 'how' of education.

As these great comprehensive reforms were being visited upon schools, attitudes to authority and behaviour were also changing rapidly, in line with the social revolution of the sixties to which I refer in "The Retreat from Authority" (Chapter 46). Massive differences of opinion blew up between the teacher in the classroom having to deal first-hand with behavioural problems and those charged with managing and governing the system.

NAS members experienced for themselves the lack of management skills exhibited in too many schools. Systems of promotion were amateurish, even susceptible to political influence. It was no coincidence that as early as the 1970s the NAS was advocating open promotion procedures based on identifiable and agreed criteria and indeed experiencing difficulties in getting LEAs to engage in serious discussion on the issue.

Major disputes were to erupt over the way comprehensive reform was managed locally. Once again the NAS and UWT were in the thick of it, fighting for teachers' rights against sometimes arbitrary and macho management. Disputes broke out in different parts of the country, sometimes assuming major proportions as in the North East and on the south coast at Bexhill-on-Sea.

The NAS continued to steer a cautious approach based on members' evidence as reflected in its 1964 booklet. It accepted the sound principle of abolishing the unjust 11 plus whilst reserving judgement on final outcomes in practice. It was entirely within the Association's pragmatic traditions. It was not until the mid-1980s that the NASUWT accepted that the comprehensive system is what we (largely) had and we had to make it work. We could not be in the business of constant fundamental change.

Many of the secondary reorganisation schemes were achieved by the 'technical' closure of two or more schools, typically one grammar and one secondary modern, and the creation of a 'new' comprehensive, invariably on two or more sites. The 'split-site' comprehensive was to produce many problems and was one of the worst examples of reform on the cheap.

Together with the growth of the over-elaborate salary superstructure of special allowances, the new schools were faced with a great deal of duplication of post holders. There could only be one head of department, so some were bound to lose out.

Consequently Burnham Reports had incorporated a clause giving LEAs the discretion to pay an allowance to mitigate or prevent hardship to a teacher whose post was lost or whose salary was diminished as a result of the reorganisation or closure of a school. This was known as safeguarding. True to form few LEAs exercised their discretion generously. Some conceded a year's protection or safeguarding after which, if the teacher had not secured another promoted post, led to a return to the basic scale. A few more-enlightened LEAs conceded complete safeguarding to teachers over 50, obviously with their pensions in mind.

The question of safeguarding became the subject of much anger and debate as more and more teachers were affected. There was much suspicion of victimisation and 'settling old scores', particularly amongst strong union representatives and 'difficult' headteachers. The demand grew for complete safeguarding.

The first breakthrough came in Oldham, with Liverpool following soon afterwards. These examples are quoted elsewhere and London and Birmingham 'came into line', the capital conceding the safeguarding with retrospection.

It seemed as if the battle would have to be fought LEA by LEA, until a development occurred in perhaps an unlikely place for union militancy – Bexhill-on-Sea, a town on the coast of East Sussex, a very 'conservative' part of the country.

In 1967 the Down County Boys' and Girls' Secondary Schools in Bexhill-on-Sea were closed and then amalgamated to form a new mixed establishment of the combined names. In March 1967 the two staffs received notice terminating their appointments at the end of the school year, 31 August, and offering new posts from 1 September. The 16 NAS members of the school refused to accept the new appointments because complete safeguarding was only afforded to those over 50, with five years for those below that age.

Leslie Smith was the NAS Executive Member for the area and rose to the occasion to meet the unexpected challenge. With the backing of the NAS Executive he invited all the teachers of the two staffs to join in the action. They were reluctant to do so and, without the support of their unions, declined. The NAS 16 decided to go it alone, displaying enormous personal courage bearing in mind they constituted a rather small minority of the staffs.

Over the course of the next four months Leslie Smith made many representations to the East Sussex LEA. Two NAS deputations visited the Education Committee. A mass meeting, attended by over 500 NAS members, was organised in the Corn Exchange of the old market town of Lewes but deadlock persisted. The LEA refused complete safeguarding; the NAS members declined to accept their new posts.

The NAS 'blacklisted' the school and instructed all members not to apply for any post advertised by it. To give credit where it is due, the NUT acted as a good trade union in doing the same. The school broke up for the summer holidays with the LEA not knowing whether it would be able to open its new establishment in September and the NAS members not knowing if they were to have jobs.

The Bexhill dispute had become a national educational *cause célèbre* and the courage shown on the south coast spread to many other areas, with more members standing firm to demand full safeguarding.

The issue was raised in the Burnham Committee where the Management Panel refused full safeguarding. The matter was referred to arbitration. The arbitral report was published in the summer holidays and found in favour of full safeguarding for all teachers. However, that was subsequently to be diluted when the Teachers' Panel accepted some limitations, for example when the post had been held for less than two years.

The courage of the 'men of Bexhill' (as they became known in NAS folklore) had been directly responsible for the breakthrough. Thousands of teachers for the rest of the twentieth century were to benefit from their stand. However, there was one particular hero amongst heroes. NAS member Jim Thomas was offered the deputy headship. He declined the offer in line with the NAS action. He was called to account by the LEA and put under intense pressure to accept: "We have plenty of people who would be only too glad to accept this appointment." To his enormous credit Jim stood his ground, saying he had given his word to his colleagues and the NAS and he would not break it.

In 1969 the 'old stalwart from Oldham', Harry Stott, supported by the NASUWT, won a Court of Appeal judgment that his temporary appointment pending the reorganisation of his school entitled him to have his salary safeguarded.

Another serious dispute developed with the reorganisation and merger of the Pelton and Roseberry Schools in the County of Durham on 1 September 1971. All the 'promoted' posts went to Roseberry staff, none to Pelton. It took until December the following year for the dispute to be resolved after threats of action by the NAS and UWT and the intervention of Department of Employment conciliation officers.

In the autumn of 1971 the NAS won a significant victory in *J.K. Case v the County Borough of Rochdale*. On behalf of the member the NAS argued successfully that a teacher enjoying a safeguarded salary as a result of reorganisation was entitled, in addition, to receive the special schools allowance if he became employed in such a school. The AEC reacted angrily against the court judgment, denouncing the NAS's decision to go to law.

A serious dispute over reorganisation broke out in Huddersfield in the Autumn Term 1972. As the long-serving NAS stalwart and Secretary of the Huddersfield Association, Ernest Lambe, observed, previous school reorganisations had been well conducted. Suddenly the LEA changed tack. After all headteachers were confirmed in their posts deputies and then heads of departments were informed they would have to apply for their own jobs (which would also be advertised nationally) and be subject to searching interviews to reassess their capabilities. The NAS and UWT commenced a work to contract on 6 November. Action escalated to a half-day strike on 29 November accompanied by a mass meeting which was addressed by GS Terry Casey. LEA attempts to turn parents against the teachers backfired badly and in January the employers relented, confirming all deputies in their posts and giving satisfactory assurances for heads of departments.

The Sacred Heart School – Teesside Dispute was undoubtedly the most intensely bitter local dispute of all time in the history of the NASUWT. It began as a dispute over secondary comprehensive reorganisation. It surpassed the bitterness of the neighbouring Durham dispute over pay and the right to take action which had occurred a few years earlier. The Sacred Heart – Teesside dispute endured for nearly three years, from 1972 to 1975, and I write about it in chapter 42.

Chapter 38 - Battles over the Teacher's Contract

As one dispute followed another, the 1960s saw the emergence of informal meetings between unions and the LEA employers to discuss the teacher's contract, which became increasingly controversial. The problems over school meals provided perhaps the greatest impetus towards this development. Controversy continued after the war, through the 1950s, and the 1962 NAS Conference reaffirmed policy that no teacher should be required by law to take part in the supervision of school children eating their lunches.

Discussions were held with the LEAs and the Ministry and by 1963 a new circular was issued (5/63) stating there was no requirement for teachers to supervise the meals themselves.   However, the status of the circular seemed to be questioned by some LEAs.   A woman teacher in Southampton was threatened with dismissal for asserting her rights under the new circular in 1966. The NAS Annual Report for that year refers to action by members in support of their woman colleague and to the successful outcome. The issue was never wholly resolved to everyone's satisfaction but the NAS believed the School Meals Agreement of 1968 resolved the matter for all 'assistant teachers' – the rather patronising misnomer for all non-heads and non-deputies who carried out the lion's share of teaching.

As other issues also arose the ad hoc discussions gradually became more formalised, transforming themselves into gatherings known successively as the Employer/Employee Relations Working Party by 1972, and a body known as CLEA/ST (Council of LEAs/School Teachers' Committee) by 1974.

Many different agreements were reached covering important areas such as sick leave entitlement, notice periods and leave of absence rights. Minimum standards were established, an example being entitlement to sick leave, typically six months on full pay and a further six months on half pay, built up over six years of service. Some LEAs, including Birmingham and Inner London, improved on these national minimum standards.

Sometimes the impetus for agreements stemmed from events. Early in the 1960s a schoolmaster in the North East of England was killed by a javelin thrown by a boy at an inter-school athletics meeting. The NAS Conference called for a special committee to examine the legal position of teachers killed or injured in the course of their duties or when engaging in voluntary activities. Whilst employer liability remained a problematic area, LEAs were persuaded to draw up a memorandum detailing the amounts of compensation which should be paid for various injuries and losses. It took several more years to secure a more formal national agreement.

The teacher's typical contract was not very specific, with a letter of appointment to a particular post paid on the appropriate scale determined under the statutory Burnham arrangements. The letter also normally referred to a requirement to carry out other 'reasonable duties' under the direction of the head. Most significantly, hours of work and holiday entitlement were not specified. This led the NAS to assert that teachers could only be contractually required to perform duties during normal school hours.

Other aspects of the contract were covered by LEA regulations and national legislation governing qualifications to teach, period of probation, and maximum class sizes – only for a time and largely theoretical, as well as some basic medical requirements, among others. Such legislation included the 1959 Standards for School Premises Regulations drawn up under Section 10 of the 1944 Act as amended by further legislation in 1948. The standards were mainly concerned with the size of sites, playing fields, fire prevention, lighting, heating and ventilation, together with teaching, staff, toilet, changing and meals accommodation. They were minimum requirements; the 'standards' were vague in definition, subject to much ministerial discretion and in the view of the NAS lacked any means of effective enforcement.

The Contracts of Employment Act 1963, the (admittedly controversial) 1971 Industrial Relations Act and Labour's amending 1974 Trade Union and Labour Relations Act required conditions of service for all employees to be more explicitly defined.

The NAS examined the scope of the Factory Acts and of the Shops, Offices and Railway Premises Act (1963) to see if they should be applicable to schools. The Association concluded that the School Premises Regulations of 1959 would be of greater help, if only they were implemented in practice on the ground. The NAS believed that finance for repairs and new premises would be far preferable to largely ineffectual regulations. However, the Association conceded that the cost of bringing all school premises up to standard immediately would be "quite impractical", not to mention the unavailability of the labour and materials required. The 1964 booklet concluded by calling upon members to combine with parents, other bodies and the media to campaign against obvious safety hazards where they occurred.

The tragedy of Aberfan in Wales, where on 21 October 1966 the Pantglas Junior School was engulfed by an avalanche of coal waste from an adjacent pit which killed 144 people including 116 children, prompted a new level of concern for health and safety in schools.

In 1969 the NAS produced a 14-page booklet, *Safety and Health in Schools*. It was a very helpful and informative document setting out in layman's terms the 1959 Regulations and also explaining the relevance of the Shops, Offices and Railway Premises Act of 1963 which had some bearing on schools. Besides covering locational issues, such as schools placed next to major roads and industrial premises, it also dealt with recently completed buildings which placed pupils and staff at risk through slippery floors and dangerous staircases and windows. The NAS called for much closer consultation with teachers by architects drawing up plans for new schools. Inappropriate design which assumed pupils were angels moving quietly about their school business greatly exacerbated safety risks.

The Robens Report of 1972 provided another impetus to raising the profile of health and safety in schools through its recommendation that educational establishments should be brought within the scope of forthcoming legislation. The NAS welcomed this development, at the same time expressing reservations on the weakness of the proposed means of enforcement.

The resultant Health and Safety and Welfare at Work Act (HASAWA) introduced by the Labour Government in 1974 was to prove a decisive step forward. Schools were defined to be "new entrants" into this important area. The Act established the Health and Safety Commission together with an Executive to implement and oversee the provisions. The Act itself was mainly enabling, leaving the Commission and the Executive charged with the task of detailed implementation over the years. They were tripartite institutions, with membership drawn from representatives of government, employers (CBI) and trade unions (TUC). The NAS was represented on a CLEA/ST Working Party established in 1974 to consider the implications of the Act for schools.

A whole new era of enhanced activity – health and safety at work – was to open up and prove to be one in which the Association assumed a leading role in the education sector. Health and safety became a vast and complicated area. The NAS and UWT immediately saw the implications for union organisation. Whilst the legislation (primary and subsidiary) was national, the enforcement was an extremely local affair. The Association began a massive programme of appointing Health and Safety Representatives at school and LEA levels and then training them in the complex business of how to set about enforcing the new standards. The Executive's Training Committee undertook the main responsibility for this task under the chairmanship, notably, of Barrie Ferguson (who became National President in 1997-98), having established himself as an expert in the field.

The question of promoted posts in teaching assumed great importance for the NAS in the 1960s and 1970s as the employers developed over-elaborate staffing structures in attempts to compensate for the inadequacies of the basic scale. The NAS challenged employers to ensure fair procedures applied in deciding who was going to be appointed to such posts. The NAS first formally turned its attention to promotion procedures when mandated to consider the subject by the 1960 Hastings Conference. A report on "Promotion in the Teaching Profession" was presented to the 1961 Conference held in Blackpool.

While the framework set by the 1944 Act in which local politicians, officials and headteachers selected and appointed teachers to various posts in schools was considered fair, the NAS report in 1961 identified two "valid criticisms". First, it was believed that in some areas there was too much 'canvassing'. That should be barred as unprofessional, with a British Teachers' Council given the role of enforcement. Second, practice varied too much between LEAs on the question of 'open' posts. Some 'opened' every post to all applicants within and without the LEA; others did not. In some 'open areas' too many posts were filled by external candidates. The Executive's report seemed content to let this issue alone, a small price to pay for the welcome flexibility provided by the 'locally administered' service of education.

The first report by the Executive was probably too complacent. There was no mention made of assessment methods, or lack thereof, which are essential for proper promotion procedures. The report failed to mention the issue of secret reports, oral or written. By the time the 1970s arrived these issues forced themselves on to the agendas of Annual Conferences and the National Executive.

One of the most interesting examples of the need for proper professional procedures for promotion was provided by the 'Tea Cosy Case' at the West Stanley Front Primary School in Durham in July 1970. The contest for a post of special responsibility was settled by putting the names of the contenders into a tea cosy and drawing out the winner! The Chair of Governors who drew the winner happened to be the grandmother of the 'successful' (or lucky) candidate. The NAS protested vigorously and when no remedial action was taken by the governors and the LEA the Association complained to the Secretary of State for Education. In January 1971 the Secretary of State informed the NAS that the appointment was "null and void".

At the TUC Congress in September 1970 GS Terry Casey successfully moved a resolution asserting the rights of all employees to know what assessment is made of them, particularly when promotion is dependent upon it. The motion was seconded by the Medical Practitioners Association.

The incoming President at Conference 1971 was Ron Cocking, a very active and ambitious NAS campaigner of many years. He used his presidential speech to advocate a greater concern with professionalism, including open, consistent and rational systems for assessment and promotion. How else could efficiency and justice be assured? He condemned the confidential "over-a-drink" assessments.

In November 1971 the NAS produced a discussion paper calling for an end to confidential reports and a national system of annual assessments together with professionally dominated promotion boards. Commenting on the paper the *TES*, in an editorial on 26 November, said that:

"If one had to choose the area which produces the most horror stories in the teaching profession, appointments and promotions would be the safe bet. No one will ever succeed in abolishing some kind of confidential references – but official filed reports should be open to the people concerned."

Ironically the NAS found it difficult in the early 1970s to get LEAs seriously interested in proper promotion procedures and assessment systems. Although a paper on promotion procedures was tabled in the Employer/Employee Relations Working Party no progress was made.

The Executive presented a Report on Promotion Procedures to Conference 1975 in Brighton. Despite a vastly increased workforce and a more complex staffing structure, appointment procedures had changed little since pre-war. Promotion was a game of chance with private invitation, nepotism, confidential telephone calls, preferment and appointment by non-quorate bodies rife. Advertising of posts and shortlisting techniques varied from the punctilious to the non-existent. Furthermore, teachers were left in a vacuum. Once through their probationary year there was no official feedback to teachers, neither on their teaching skills, nor ability, nor suitability for promotion.

The Report proposed a national system to establish clear and comparable criteria to assess teachers for promotion. The Report outlined some criteria that readily came to mind: personality, teaching skills, ability to control pupils and organise work, length and variety of experience and administrative ability. Other recommendations included: annual assessment at the start of a career and thereafter at longer intervals; the involvement of other teachers as well as the head; and the prohibition of confidential (secret) reports.

The Executive was authorised to conclude a national agreement with CLEA. When the NAS took its Report together with recommendations to CLEA/ST it was met with opposition from other unions led by the NUT. The NUT declared it was not satisfied that such was either desirable or necessary, declaring that 'good' teachers could not be identified and that the NAS was doing the management's "dirty work". Remarkably, the LEA employers said little, failing to realise the constructive aspects of NAS (and UWT) policy which afforded management the opportunity of securing improved motivation and performance by teachers of their own volition. Today most of the proposals put forward by the Association in the 1970s are taken as given.

The CLEA/ST agreements were voluntary with 'enforcement' left to decisions by LEAs and voluntary schools to incorporate their terms into teachers' contracts. Most LEAs signed up fairly promptly. Voluntary schools, being the legal employers of their teachers, were content to follow suit since LEAs bore the costs and they had no reason to place themselves in a disadvantageous recruiting position.

CLEA/ST contained none of the rigidities of the Burnham structure, with no 'single voice' procedure. The Committee was smaller and everyone present had the right to speak. Agreements did not have to be expressed in statutory language and instruments. Naturally they had to be written and formal agreement registered. Unions had the right to dissent but in practice consensus was more common than in the Burnham Committee.

One of the first measures enacted by the Labour Government returned to power in the February General Election of 1974 was to repeal the hated Industrial Relations Act of 1971. New legislation was introduced known as TULRA – the Trade Union and Labour Relations Act of 1974. It was sympathetic to the problems faced by unions but also imposed new duties on them to organise properly and accept responsibility for all that happened inside their organisations. Responsibility was given to employers and unions to negotiate time off for properly accredited representatives to carry out their work. A distinction was drawn between 'duties' for which time off with pay was obligatory and 'activities' where it was not.

After much discussion a CLEA/ST agreement was finally secured in 1975. The NASUWT had already prepared itself and was quickly into the business of organising a comprehensive training programme for local Officers and School Representatives. The newly established Training Committee of the National Executive organised and participated actively in the conduct of courses nationally and locally. In 1971 the NAS had purchased a 26-acre property, Hillscourt, attractively located at Rednal in the Lickey Hills just south of Birmingham, for £50,000. This became the Association's residential training centre and was also used for many educational/professional courses, all of which continue to the present day. They contributed enormously to increasing the NAS's effectiveness 'on the ground' at school and LEA levels. In due course the Executive transferred its meetings to Hillscourt, which also became the registered HQ of the Association.

By the 1970s the teacher's contract was a compound of personal service agreement, education statutes, statutory instruments, High Court cases, national and local agreements on the conditions side, and of course Burnham on the pay front. In the view of the NASUWT, teachers had two main 'de jure' employers, LEAs and voluntary aided school governing bodies. In addition there was the 'de facto' employer in the shape of the Government of the day who determined training, entry and qualification requirements and pensions, as well as exercising control over salaries as the chief paymaster.

Pay remained a matter for the statutory Burnham Committee and the rigid separation from conditions of service became controversial. The NAS and UWT, along with the other unions, could see some advantages for teachers in this separation. But we also saw some disadvantages and believed it was ultimately an illogical and therefore untenable position.

Extremely important aspects of conditions of service, namely the definition of the teacher's day, duties and holidays, proved to be extremely contentious and agreement impossible. The NAS work to contract sanction, increasingly deployed in one dispute after another, propelled the issue into prominence. The NAS claimed that custom and practice had in effect defined teachers' contractual obligations to be limited to the normal school day. Everything outside that was voluntary. This was in truth nothing more than assertion on the part of the NAS, put forward to establish a position to protect the interests of the teacher.

Employers and Government naturally took a different position, claiming that the teacher's job could not be defined in precise terms and was inevitably open ended, limited only by the flexible notion of what was "reasonable".

Discussions opened up on these issues in 1974 in CLEA/ST. While the unions were interested in defining matters such as contact hours with pupils in the classroom, the employers were concerned to introduce a wider, more demanding requirement upon teachers during the school day, including the midday break, together with commitments outside normal hours such as attendance at evening (especially parents') functions.

The NAS Annual Report of 1974 records: "The Association's representatives . . . continue to resist attempts by the LEAs to extend teachers' contractual obligations beyond the normal school day, and to impose upon teachers pseudo-contractual obligations. The worsening of the contracts of Scottish teachers in this respect has encouraged CLEA to increase their pressure and not all teachers' organisations are as resolute as the NAS and UWT."

A Working Party of CLEA/ST had been set up in 1975 to codify existing collective agreements and recommendations on conditions of service. In March 1977 the WP completed its task and reached agreement. The Code, which was to become known as the Burgundy Book, was then subject to ratification by both sides.

Discussions on the contract dragged on intermittently over four years with no progress. However, the issue assumed a sharper perspective with the employers having to meet the Houghton pay awards of the mid-1970s and the efforts by the teachers to maintain their value against a background of rampant inflation.

In his GS Monday evening 'state of the union' address to Conference 1978, Terry Casey accused the employers of not coming clean on their intentions. If teachers continued to give extra to their employers it became accepted, then expected and then demanded by implied terms of contract. CLEA was out to ensnare teachers and Conference had to be alert to the dangers. Later in the week a motion demanding an undertaking from employers that parent consultation, staff and departmental meetings and other activities after school hours were voluntary was carried, together with an amendment from the floor that members be instructed not to undertake them if such assurances were not given.

Before the end of April the NASUWT had announced the start of the ban on voluntary activities from 8 May, with exemptions only granted on National Executive authority in those LEAs which had provided satisfactory assurances. The ACC and AMA strongly advised their constituents against giving such assurances, claiming the 'duties' were part of the teacher's implied contract. The NASUWT claimed the employers had been smoked out. However, several LEAs, including Liverpool and Nottingham, quickly conceded the NASUWT demand.

The ACC was more aggressive on the issue than the AMA and quoted the famous paragraph 294 of the Houghton Report claiming it implied teachers had contractual obligations beyond the school day. Terry Casey reminded the ACC that 294 had not been the subject of negotiations, but if employers wanted a 'Houghton contract' they would have to start by uprating Houghton salaries for inflation as had been strongly recommended in the Report.

By the end of May (1978) 24 LEAs had offered assurances to the NAS. That included the large LEA of Hampshire giving a very explicit statement that it "had not changed its position regarding teacher activity outside normal school hours, namely that teachers are not open to disciplinary action for non-attendance at meetings or other school functions held outside the normal working hours of their school".

To circumvent the separation of pay from conditions of service negotiations the employers suggested end-on Burnham – CLEA/ST meetings. The NASUWT objected furiously to the prospect of 'Burnhamising' more of teachers' affairs whilst emphasising on the positive side it was prepared to accept joint pay/conditions negotiations in a rational non-statutory machine without

Government veto and monopoly/single-voice procedure rights for one union. Management was seeking to divide the unions, appealing to the NUT by offering (by implication) a Burnham-style overall majority. While the Labour Secretary of State for Education, Shirley Williams, had reformed the composition of the Teachers' Panel, doubling NASUWT representation to six, she had preserved the NUT overall majority.

In March 1979 the NUT succumbed to temptation and the danger materialised. A meeting of CLEA/ST was 'urgently' (and in the view of the NASUWT suspiciously) convened with only three days clear notice. The meeting duly agreed to establish a Working Party (WP) to discuss the contract "to consider the feasibility of a precise definition of the teacher's day and duties and of a job description and to give consideration to guaranteed non-teaching time".

The Conditions of Service WP, quickly assuming the acronym COSWOP, (and inevitably corrupted in NASUWT circles to 'CODSWALLOP') was intended to report within six months but NASUWT objected fiercely to the arrangement. CLEA had yet to complete the process of binding all its constituents, thus making 'guarantees' about contractual improvements problematical. The NASUWT had little confidence in the NUT and even less in the LEAs who were still in a parlous financial position, unable in their own words to honour their commitments to Houghton salary standards. The time was entirely ill chosen to open negotiations on the contentious contract. Terry Casey repeatedly asked: "Why are the employers going to market when they have no money?" The NASUWT Executive at its next meeting decided it would boycott COSWOP.

It was to prove a long and messy affair but COSWOP was soon overshadowed by the 1979 pay dispute as the NASUWT took its Five Hour Day Action in protest against Management reneging on its Houghton commitment and attempts to refer teachers' pay to the Clegg Commission.

After a further period of hibernation COSWOP re-emerged with a series of meetings in the Autumn Term. Again the droplets leaking out of the meetings were not good for the teachers. The employers wanted a 205-day working year (as against the current 190-195) and a 37½-hour working week. The NUT 'claim' was for a 190-day year and a 32½-hour week.

However, in a hard-hitting poster the NASUWT revealed that the NUT had conceded that "teachers would continue to undertake professional activities beyond these new limits, an agreement in no way seeking to restrict them". In other words teachers would still be expected to perform voluntary duties beyond the new extended contractual limits. The NASUWT poster also revealed that 'Other Professional Duties' were to be added to teaching timetables, including midday supervision, attendance at meetings outside school hours and various extra-curricular sporting and 'artistic performances'.

While the employers openly insisted "there has to be a way of building mid-day supervision into teachers' professional obligations", the unions' responses were a mixture of the weak and dangerous. The NUT meekly commented: "Lunch time supervision has become a bone of contention between the two sides." The NAHT "would refuse to ratify any agreement that did not contain a mid-day supervision clause". The AMMA "demanded that the lunch hour should be taken out of the talks and studied under a separate WP".

The business led to one of Terry Casey's renowned articles in the Association's magazine headed "The Spider's Parlour", also released as a separate flyer. Terry likened the spider's invitation to the fly, "Will you walk into my parlour", to the LEAs' proposal for COSWOP and a Burnham-style negotiating body for conditions of service which would favour the NUT. "The little lady fly at first displayed prudent suspicion but was ultimately undone when the spider appealed to her vanity."

More soothing statements from Doug McAvoy, who as DGS led for the NUT in CLEA/ST, about the employers making "a significant move towards teachers' demands on a professional contract of employment", were contradicted by press reports. The *TES* headline ran: "Proposed contract covers meal duties" and *Education* led with: "Teachers offered free periods in their own time". To add insult to injury the employers emphasised the new offer comprised only "a minimum contractual responsibility".

By January 1981 COSWOP had collapsed. Doug McAvoy was quoted in *The Guardian* stating: "The NUT said all along that these talks were impractical given the climate of education cuts". The NASUWT observed it had taken the NUT and others 18 months to discover the obvious. The talks had broken down on the LEAs' insistence on lunch supervision and their refusal to contemplate limits on class sizes.

However, more significantly, it was reported that the LEAs were "not too dismayed at the breakdown". They would now press for the repeal of the 1965 Remuneration of Teachers Act (RTA) and for the establishment of a single negotiating body for pay and conditions. The NASUWT warned members that the danger to the contract was far from over with the collapse of COSWOP.

Within a matter of days the Secretary of State announced "a review of present arrangements for negotiating pay and conditions with a view to establishing new unified machinery". Mark Carlisle was also proposing to change the arrangements for arbitration, making it more difficult for teachers to access.

In a Report to Schools (January 1981) the NASUWT identified the beginnings of a trend that was to dominate the 1980s and beyond: the emergence of excessive workload for teachers resulting from the non-stop reforms to education. The NASUWT also took the lead in fighting against the ever-growing tendency of central and local government to require teachers to solve social as well as educational problems through an unending series of bureaucracy-laden initiatives. Those who bucked the trend were labelled as 'unprofessional'. The NASUWT refused to be cowed and strongly rejected the false antithesis between the 'professional' and the 'trade union'. The Union carried out an enormous amount of work analysing educational reforms and advising Government of the serious workload implications which would jeopardise their success if not accompanied by a fair and reasonable contract for teachers.

The Report focussed on Terry Casey's message to Conference delegates to "Hold fast what ye hath". The NASUWT had successfully torpedoed COSWOP through its boycott but Management and Government were returning to the attack. Education Secretary Mark Carlisle, in open alliance with the Conservative-dominated ACC, claimed his planned reform of the 1965 RTA to insert conditions of service into Burnham negotiations was "normal practice elsewhere". The NASUWT accepted normality so long as it applied throughout. Normality also demanded non-statutory free collective bargaining, and no Government veto.

Early in 1981 Terry Casey had produced another of his celebrated pamphlets, *Goodwill Garrotted*, the very title an excellent aphorism encapsulating the danger of providing voluntary 'duties' to an employer.

Conference duly carried motions reasserting its policy on negotiating machinery and pledging to resist any attempts to worsen teachers' conditions of service.

In July 1981 Mark Carlisle announced a delay in amending the 1965 RTA. According to *The Daily Telegraph* this was "due to the pressure from teacher unions". The NASUWT had been lobbying hard. The ACC Leader, Councillor Philip Merridale from Hampshire, expressed "surprise and disappointment", claiming that "legislation was the only avenue after conditions of service negotiations again failed in COSWOP after one union boycotted the exercise". The NASUWT reiterated its willingness to accept reform, subject to it being comprehensive, fair and fit for purpose.

The economic slump of the early 1980s occasioned by the Thatcher Government's disastrous experiment with monetarism placed LEAs in dire financial straits and pushed the contract dispute into abeyance.

The NASUWT position on the contract was strengthened in July 1982 with a handsome High Court victory. In May 1979 an NASUWT member, Paul Evans, had applied for seven days unpaid leave of absence to go on a rugby tour of the

USA. The seven days straddled the half-term holiday. The Gwent LEA granted the request but then proceeded to deduct salary for 16 days, including two weekends and the five days of the half-term holiday. Strong representations by the NASUWT failed to change the incredibly mean-minded attitude of Gwent.

Accordingly the NASUWT instructed solicitors to proceed against Gwent in the High Court. Judgment was delivered by Mr Justice Foster in July 1982. He ruled in favour of Paul Evans, declaring that the LEA did not have the discretion to grant leave of absence at the weekends or during holiday periods and its decision was therefore a "nullity". Paul Evans was awarded his lost salary in full with interest at 12% for three years and four days. The NASUWT was awarded its costs, which together with Gwent's were estimated at £10,000.

Meanwhile another dispute in Wales with Mid Glamorgan had been raging since February 1981 over the LEA's unilateral cancellation of the half-term break to compensate for loss of school days due to snow. NASUWT members took their break and the LEA deducted pay. A local disputes panel found fault with both sides but recommended no penalties be imposed and the matter be closed. Mid Glamorgan refused to accept the findings and repeatedly declined further attempts at conciliation and arbitration. It took the NASUWT 15 months of action before the LEA finally agreed a compromise, effectively reinstating some pay.

In May 1983 the London NASUWT was forced to take strike action and mount a lobby of the ILEA to kill off a 'mini-COSWOP' exercise with the leadership of the local NUT. Proposals were on the table to surrender the voluntary principle of lunchtime supervision and activities outside the normal school day in return for guaranteed non-contact time (which turned out upon examination to be after present school hours). Members of the NUT were not best pleased when the NASUWT action exposed what was being done in their name. The ILEA quickly closed the talks down.

The turn of 1983/84 marked a decisive time in the determination of teachers' conditions although few recognised it at the time. The hard-line the NASUWT had taken on the contract and the voluntary principle reflected the unpropitious financial times and our determination to have sensible negotiating machinery.

The Burnham Committee had established a Joint Working Party on Salary Structure (JWPSS) on 2 March 1981. For the first couple of years of its existence Management proved reluctant to tackle the issue of salary restructuring for fear of the cost implications in very difficult financial times. The Teachers' Side were united in their concern about the effect falling pupil numbers would have on promotion prospects in a forthcoming review in 1982 but only the NASUWT was prepared to develop radical and relevant new policies on salary restructuring to deal with the situation.

In 1983 after the collapse of COSWOP, the employers began looking towards the JWPSS as a means by which they could continue to pursue their concerns over the contract. The NASUWT believed the JWPSS provided a sensible forum and the potential to tackle the problems of pay and the contract in a constructive fashion, as unlike COSWOP both unions and employers agreed that more central government money would be a precondition for progress. All three 'partners' were openly represented and everyone had full speaking rights. Because it dealt with salary structure as well as levels, it inevitably dragged conditions of service into the arena.

The NASUWT response was to embrace restructuring and develop policies on the contract that protected the teacher interest and reflected the needs of the time. However, the NUT's positions on two matters were illogical and ultimately untenable. It insisted on a rigid separation of pay and conditions and when the time came refused again (repeating the mistakes of history) to discuss salary restructuring in the sensible forum of a WP.

Progress in the JWPPS and within the Teachers' Side had therefore been painfully slow. It was obvious the NUT had no desire for reform. On the initiative of Management a residential three-day meeting was arranged for 12-14 December (1983) at the Piccadilly Hotel in Manchester. With the employers conceding "the central importance of the teacher in the classroom", the NASUWT responded positively with policies on a new main professional grade (MPG) which raised the status and pay of the classroom teacher and developed a more collegiate approach to the running of schools. Teachers would have a more clearly defined contract but with an overall limit. In addition teacher assessment had to be grounded in acceptable procedures and criteria. Most importantly, substantial extra cash had to be forthcoming to produce a successful outcome. The Manchester meeting was a reasonably positive, although only a preliminary, canter through potentially difficult territory. The NASUWT was intrigued to pick up comments from management participants that it was "the only union well prepared whose representatives all sang from the same hymn sheet".

The JWPSS was sidelined during the pay dispute and industrial action of 1984. When it resumed, progress was again stymied by the NUT for the reasons already stated above. The other unions seemed indifferent and only the NASUWT, having developed its collegiate policies for the purpose, was keen to enter discussion. At a meeting of the JWPSS on 15 November 1984 the Management pressed a little too hard, producing a more detailed paper on its restructuring proposals and in the response it drew from the NUT exposed the filibuster for what it was. The NUT decided that enough was enough, walked out and in due course collapsed the WP. I was deputising for Fred Smithies and

I recall trying to persuade the Management at the fatal meeting to continue without the NUT, but they did not have the bottle to do so.

The decision of the NUT to collapse the restructuring talks was to have the most serious repercussions, leading to unnecessarily protracted and bitter negotiations in the strike-laden year of 1985. The NUT timing was poor. We could not continue for ever to boycott difficult talks. Pay and conditions had ultimately to be taken together, and with the desperate need to address salaries the JWPSS provided a suitable forum in which to do so. From the turn of 1984/85 onwards the separation of pay and conditions effectively ceased. Accordingly I deal with them together when I return to the narrative on pay.

The roaring inflation and other economic problems of the early 1970s produced inevitable pressures on public expenditure. During the 1974 General Election campaign the Government signalled cuts in public expenditure, including £80m from education.

Two fundamental principles dear to the NAS heart were raised – specific grants and 100% central government payment of teachers' salaries. The NAS strongly opposed the block grants which enabled local authorities to vire RSG monies away from education although they had been allocated on service needs. I joked at the time that 'RSG' was supposed to stand for Revenue Support Grant, not receiving stolen goods!

In 1974 the NAS and UWT Executives took decisions in principle that stood the test of time over a period of some 25 years before the New Labour Government in 1999, after adhering controversially for two years to Conservative spending limits, began to invest seriously in public services, including education. The NAS and UWT accepted that given the parlous financial position of the UK and the fact of falling pupil numbers, cuts were inevitable. However, industrial action would be taken against cuts in staffing standards and compulsory redundancies. Terry Casey even argued unions had a "constitutional duty" to expose the effects of government cuts and not to paper over them.

The first manifestation seems to have been in Salford in May 1974 where Ex-President Ray Holden addressed an NAS and UWT strike/protest meeting against proposed cuts by the LEA in its £18m education budget. The unions were particularly concerned that Salford had benefited from the redistribution of rate relief away from the counties (mostly Conservative) to the metropolitan areas (mostly Labour) following the recent General Election result.

Following Salford, action involving strikes, working to contract and refusal to cover for absent and 'unappointed' teachers was to follow in 48 LEAs over the next two decades. During this period the NASUWT combined realism with determination in plotting its path along the difficult public expenditure route.

We accepted that redeployment was preferable to unemployment. A move in Conference 1977 by some more militantly minded members to fight *all* cuts with industrial action was defeated on the grounds of being unrealistic and a breach of faith following assurances given to LEAs that maintained staffing standards and avoided compulsory redundancies. In 1979 the NASUWT accepted the principle of LIFO (last in, first out) as the only 'acceptable' method of selection for redundancy, failing all other alternatives.

Over the 20 years of crisis, some of the proposed cuts threatened hundreds of teachers' jobs. Among the most significant early threats were Buckinghamshire, Derbyshire, Cleveland, Stockport (1975), and Bromley and Lincolnshire in 1976.

In June 1977 the question of diverting RSG monies intended for education to other purposes was brought into sharp focus by the failure of many LEAs to use the £7m allocated by the new Labour Education Secretary, Shirley Williams, for induction and in-service teacher training. The Secretary of State professed her deep concern.

The transition from 1978 to '79 marked the 'Winter of Discontent', with widespread industrial action by unions in the public sector. The failure of unions and Government to reach some accommodation was all the more tragic as the economy was recovering from the crisis of 1976 and the bail out by the IMF with the tight public expenditure controls being eased by Chancellor Denis Healey. It led to the Labour Government losing a confidence motion in the Commons by one vote and a subsequent General Election which saw a right-wing Tory Party under Margaret Thatcher's leadership gain power, which was to have devastating consequences for the public sector.

By October 1980 the implications of the Conservative election victory began to unfold in more horrifying detail. Secretary of State for the Environment, Michael Heseltine, announced swingeing cuts in local authorities' budgets in which of course education was the largest component. The NASUWT referred to the "RSG lunacy" and called for education to have its own clearly identified budget. The "smokescreen of RSG" enabled the Government, just like the Burnham set-up, to make the decisions but the LEAs to carry the can for cutbacks.

This time massive cuts were threatened, with Hampshire estimating 1,000 teachers' jobs at risk, Northamptonshire 300, East Sussex 380 and Manchester 767, all of which threatened serious deterioration in staffing standards.

At the 1981 Conference held in Brighton incoming President Alan Poole highlighted the disparities in education provision between LEAs. He accused LEAs who spent taxpayers' money intended for education on other purposes of behaving "as immorally as parents who spend their weekly child allowances on bingo and cigarettes". Alan called for the staffing establishment of schools to be determined by the needs of the curriculum to be taught, which would guarantee a minimum entitlement to all children.

Conference 1982 duly accepted a report from the Executive entitled *Curriculum Related Staffing Levels*. Staffing based on a given pupil-teacher ratio should be abolished in favour of the number of teachers in any given school required to deliver the curriculum. This policy was to assume even greater relevance, resonating strongly with the demands of a national curriculum to be introduced by the 1988 Education Reform Act.

About 12,000 teachers had taken early retirement, which relieved the pressure for redundancies although LEAs were being "stingy" in the view of the NASUWT over applying the enhancement provisions, the costs of which they had to carry themselves.

Action over staffing standards commenced in Durham in 1982 using the customary no-cover action for 'vacant posts'. In keeping with its unfortunate traditions the Durham LEA insisted on deducting pay despite the teachers continuing to deliver their full week's work. This dispute within a dispute continued long after the staffing issue was resolved. Despite the existence of a joint campaign committee with the NUT, again in keeping with an unfortunate tradition, it broke ranks and secretly reached a unilateral settlement (previously rejected by both unions) with the LEA which conceded salary deductions for no-cover action. Inter-union hostilities broke out into the public domain. The NASUWT fought on, fighting a bitter battle alone, and it was not until 1983 that full repayment of moneys deducted for 'no cover' was secured. In 1986 the NUT, against the strong advice of the NASUWT, was to pursue this issue with disastrous consequences in the High Court.

Following action starting in May 1980 in Trafford, the NASUWT won a High Court case in November 1983 against the LEA on behalf of a member, Peter Royle, who had followed union instructions not to accept larger classes caused by the cuts. Accordingly, Peter Royle refused to accept an additional five pupils over and above the normal 31 the headteacher had allocated to his class. The Union challenged the LEA's docking all of Royle's pay over several months. Mr Justice Park ruled that Trafford was only entitled to deduct 5/36ths of Royle's pay since it had accepted the imperfect delivery of his contract. Peter Royle was awarded compensation of £3,060 plus interest at 13.5% (£814). In January 1985 Trafford again claimed the right to deduct moneys for no-cover action against unfilled vacancies but this time a deal was struck. Trafford and the NASUWT agreed on a statement acknowledging the parties had different views but the LEA would deduct 1p per occasion.

In October 1983 the NASUWT famously went in delegation to the new Education Secretary Sir Keith Joseph to discuss fundamental issues of the day, including resources for the education service. As the chief intellectual architect of Thatcher's disastrous experiment with hard-line monetarism, Sir Keith was the last person who could be convinced to increase public expenditure on anything. The blunt, even blistering, exchanges were kept within the bounds of civility by Sir Keith's stark honesty, unusual in experienced Ministers, in fully accepting the brutal implications of the cuts made necessary by the overriding need to tame inflation.

During 1985 the staffing standards issue was totally swamped by the widespread action in the bitter dispute over pay. At the same time a massive crisis erupted in Liverpool where the City Council had been taken over by Militant Tendency members who had infiltrated the majority Labour Party. Led by a colourful and articulate character, Derek Hatton, the Council refused to accept the Government's rate capping and spent on, eventually bringing the city to the brink of bankruptcy. Dismissal notices were issued to thousands of local government workers in Liverpool, including teachers. General Secretaries of the relevant unions, under the auspices of the TUC, met in crisis talks with the Council which led eventually to the withdrawal of the notices. To cut a long story short, the crisis was eventually averted with the Militant Tendency leaders backing down.

As 1986 got under way the continuing dispute over pay kept the issue of staffing standards in the background. However, in March the NASUWT issued a statement in a Report to Schools ("Cover in Court") warning of the great danger of the NUT's decision to take the matter of pay deductions for no-cover action to court. The NASUWT's stated belief that the matter was best settled through negotiation was to prove tellingly correct.

More action on pay in 1987/88 again kept staffing standards in the background. However, in March 1988 revealing statistics were published by the DES showing that between 1981/82 and 1985/86 the proportion of GDP spent on education fell by 12.7% whilst pupil numbers dropped by only 8.5%.

As measures enacted in the 1988 Education Reform Act came into effect, in the following year another source of threat to teacher employment arrived in the form of Local Management of Schools (LMS). The NASUWT conducted extensive research and calculated school budgets according to LEA formulae. The exercise revealed that many schools would have reduced budgets compared to their historic ones, revealing a risk to some 10,000 teachers' jobs in the context of an overall teacher shortage.

In 1989 the admittedly unpopular domestic rates were being replaced by the detested poll tax. It was a regressive form of per capita tax which at Mrs

Thatcher's insistence was foisted on the nation against overwhelming public opinion. Eventually her own Cabinet rebelled against it, forcing her out of office in October 1990. The setting of the poll tax, accompanied by capping, posed yet more serious threats to the funding of the education service and the employment of teachers.

In 1990 further threats to jobs had appeared as the Government insisted upon LEAs delegating average rather than actual costs of teachers' salaries to schools. That penalised good schools that had retained staff as they became more expensive through the incremental pay system. 'Winning' schools were faced with bonuses, 'losing' ones with having to make teachers redundant. Urgent meetings took place in LEAs up and down the country to try to find "humane" ways of shedding teachers through premature retirement packages, severance pay schemes and voluntary redeployment arrangements between governing bodies. The NASUWT was still standing by its active opposition to compulsory redundancy and worsened staffing standards.

In 1990 LMS caused more problems over redundancies in Nottingham, Surrey and Gateshead. In 1991 at a school in Gateshead, for the second successive year, appeals against redundancy involving the same four NASUWT members were upheld. The NASUWT had taken strike action in July and subsequently put forward constructive proposals to deal with the situation. Those were turned down and the school management ploughed on regardless. In October the NASUWT Local Secretary, Bill Gardiner, was again identified for redundancy but won his appeal. Of the three other NASUWT members involved, one had his appeal upheld, another took early retirement with maximum pension enhancement of ten years and the third agreed to be redeployed within the LEA. Changes were then made to the management of the school.

With Thatcher gone the Government began to soften its hard line on public expenditure as it remained intensely unpopular, with the next General Election appearing on the horizon. Action was limited mostly to Brent and Warwickshire in 1991 and Staffordshire in 1992.

One of the first tasks of John Major's Government had been to abolish the poll tax and find a replacement. Around this time after skilful and discreet lobbying by the NASUWT the Government was in the process of establishing the School Teachers' Review Body. The Government also decided to take on a greater share of the total cost of the teachers' salary bill, thereby relieving the pressure on the new Council Tax system and teacher employment prospects.

The excesses of the national curriculum and the flood of paperwork were beginning to make their presence felt as Conference 1991 opened with the incoming President, Sue Rogers from Sheffield, one of the most dynamic and popular national representatives ever produced by the Union, declaring in her speech "that it was time for teachers to learn to say 'no'. Too many are prepared to make the system work by putting their health and wellbeing at risk." Calling for equality of opportunity Sue went on: "The overall reduction of resources combined with LMS and grant maintained schools opting out of LEA control have put education at the mercy of market forces in which there are few winners and lots of losers. Schools, strapped for cash, have been reduced to begging bowl status, while Government wastes public money on expensive city technology colleges for the favoured few."

By March 1992 the next General Election was looming close as PM John Major stayed the full five-year term, desperately hoping for a change in fortune to facilitate a Conservative victory. An NASUWT-commissioned poll by Gallup early in March showed 48% of teachers intending to vote Labour. A later *TES/ICN*-sponsored poll showed Labour having 51% of teachers in support, Liberal Democrats with 24% and Conservative 20%. However, public opinion did not fully reflect teachers' views and despite predictions of a hung Parliament John Major managed to pull off a surprise Conservative victory.

After Conference 1992 the NASUWT returned to the business of defending jobs and staffing standards. Reviewing events over the past year I commented that whilst there had been 4,000 job losses and several hundred redundancies, very few had been compulsory. Our campaign had achieved far more successes than failures. Nevertheless the problem could become more acute if we failed to change the Standard Spending Assessments for LEAs and the allocation of funds to schools under LMS. Many teachers had taken the opportunity to retire early with enhanced pensions, which relieved the pressure on compulsory redundancies as well as providing welcome escape routes for older teachers having serious difficulties coming to terms with the 'totalitarian' regime of the new national curriculum, testing and assessment. However, the pool of over-50s qualifying for enhanced early retirement was now much diminished.

By January 1993 the developing NASUWT campaign against excessive workload was well under way. At the same time the NASUWT was becoming increasingly concerned about schools' unspent balances under LMS. Many headteachers and governing bodies approved plans to cut back on revenue expenditure to save up for capital projects. NASUWT research covering over 20,000 school budgets revealed £750m in unspent balances. One LEA which had allocated an additional £9m to its schools over and above the Government's SSA level discovered £7.5m remained unspent. The same research showed that 1993 unspent balances amounted to between 4.3% and 7.3% of school budgets.

Official statistics on class sizes published by the DES in November 1995 showed a rise to more than 1.5 million primary school pupils being taught in classes exceeding 30.

The Conservatives held a special 'brainstorming' session for the Cabinet at Chequers one weekend in October 1995. Instead of producing positive results the event was dominated by a leaked memorandum from Education Secretary Gillian Shephard conceding that "insufficient resources threatened the provision of education in the LEA sector as well as in the grant maintained schools".

By 1996 pensions were coming under intense pressure as costs mounted for a variety of reasons and the numbers seeking early retirement escalated. The Government began to make early retirement more difficult, applying long-standing rules in more stringent fashion. Enhanced premature retirement compensation (paid for by LEAs) came to a virtual standstill.

It was not until the end of 1998 with the publication of the New Labour Government's Green Paper, *Teachers – Meeting the Challenge of Change*, that clear indications emerged that significant extra funding would be available for the education service. It was to mark the end of some 25 years of struggle on the staffing front for the NASUWT which, while not always completely successful, nevertheless saved many thousands of teachers' posts.

Chapter 39 - Embracing the Wider Labour Movement

The cautious but sensible and pragmatic approach of the NAS to new ideas was again in evidence as the Association considered affiliation to the Trades Union Congress (TUC) during the course of the 1960s. Affiliation was finally agreed at the 1968 Conference, held at Llandudno in North Wales.

A few years prior to affiliation to the TUC the NAS had joined the National Federation of Professional Workers (NFPW). Terry Casey probably used this as a first step towards the TUC, for it was a kind of 'white collar' trade union centre. The NFPW relied very heavily on its well-respected General Secretary, John Fryd. It was very active in the pensions field. Terry Casey was elected President of the NFPW in April 1971.

The NFPW maintained cordial relations with the TUC, to which it actively recommended its member organisations to affiliate, a policy that was possibly calculated to anticipate its own demise. In any event the NFPW was soon to disappear with John Fryd's impending retirement and as more white-collar unions saw their way to TUC affiliation.

Soon after becoming GS in 1963 Terry Casey initiated a discussion within the NAS on the merits of joining the TUC. After two hesitant debates within the Executive and at Annual Conferences which led to decisions being postponed, a decisive move came towards the end of 1967. The October National Executive meeting that year resolved "to take steps to seek affiliation to the TUC subject to the prior approval of Conference".

A discussion document, "TUC Affiliation – For or Against?", was widely circulated throughout the Association. However, the balance of the document reflected the leadership's view in favour. The TUC was the authoritative voice of all organised employees in every field, with direct access to the Prime Minister (at that time Labour's Harold Wilson). The 1960s had witnessed the development of national prices and incomes policies, a process that was to be continued in the 1970s. By definition such national policies transcended traditional occupational negotiating boundaries. The TUC naturally constituted the 'union side' and it was important for the NAS to be able to influence the debate from within. Membership of the TUC would also bring greater respect for the NAS from other trade unions and employers as well.

The discussion document anticipated two major reservations: one, affiliation would compromise the non-party political stance of the NAS; two, it would be inappropriate for professional people to identify too closely with 'blue collar' workers. Those arguments were countered by reference to the fact that more than half the unions in membership of the TUC were not affiliated to the Labour Party. Furthermore the huge local government 'white collar' employees' union, NALGO, had recently joined the TUC, declaring at the same time it would maintain its political neutrality, which was also a decision welcomed by the Conservative Party.

A very good and healthy debate developed in the correspondence columns of the Association's journal, *The New Schoolmaster.* Opponents claimed the arguments put forward in favour relied heavily upon assumption and assertion rather than hard fact. There was no mention of the costs involved. Membership of the TUC might constrain action on the part of the NAS. And the more traditionally inclined were quick to point out that the TUC supported equal pay!

Other opponents of affiliation had some more esoteric reasons. One alleged that "The Red Flag" was sung at the TUC Congress, confusing it with the Labour Party practice. (The TUC sang "Auld Lang Syne"!) Others pointed to the prominence of communists in some TUC unions. The block voting system was wrong; the objectors on that ground not apparently realising that the NAS had a provision for the card vote in its own standing orders for Annual Conference. The closed shop operated by many TUC affiliates was a controversial issue and there was some sympathy amongst significant sections of the community for its 'victims'.

Tom Smith confided to me that he believed that "the master tactician, Terry Casey, was the only NAS leader at the time capable of persuading the NAS to affiliate. Terry pretended to be changing the wallpaper in the NAS house when in reality he was digging up the foundations." Terry Casey persuaded even the most hesitant union-minded member that it had become crystal clear that in order to achieve decent salaries teachers would have to emulate other organised employees and take protest or direct action.

Terry Casey argued that teachers were 'workers' of a kind, professional employees of the state, with the same problems of representation to government and employers in the public sector. Many teachers came from families where the father was a blue-collar worker.

The vigorous debate continued at the 1968 Llandudno Conference. Opponents of affiliation such as Past President Eric Arnott, warned of membership losses, others called for a 75% majority in favour to secure approval. Some such as Harry Stott and Past President Harry Bell warned respectively of dire consequences that "the NAS would lose its identity" and that affiliation would mean "the end of the Association". However, the Executive Report recommending affiliation won the day, 423 votes in favour, 205 against.

A card vote was then demanded which resulted in a similar 2:1 majority of 20,092 in favour, 10,698 against.

The NUT quickly followed the NAS into the TUC the following year, with many alleging the former's decision to do so was determined by the latter's.

The Joint Four remained uncomfortable with the notion of affiliation to the TUC. In Terry Casey's inevitable aphorism they preferred to tolerate their "genteel poverty" rather than adopt militant blue-collar tactics. It was not until after the New Labour victory of 1997 that the freshly renamed ATL affiliated to the TUC under the general secretaryship of Peter Smith. The exclusively head, deputy and 'leadership' organisations to this day remain outside the TUC despite the affiliation of unions such as the First Division Association, representing the top civil servants of the country.

The benefits of TUC membership quickly became apparent. Soon after affiliation in 1969 the NAS secured the support of the TUC in several bitter disputes in the North East, with picketing and 'blacking' made far more effective as a consequence. Over the years the Association assembled wider support through the TUC for policies which had implications beyond the education sector, starting with the right of employees to see assessments of their work, particularly when they were linked to promotion.

The affiliation to the TUC also marked a definitive and more permanent answer to the question of the NAS's sphere of activity. Those who favoured a narrow approach, limiting involvement to teachers' pay, conditions of service, purely union affairs and education, were put on the defensive. The reader may recall that under the pressures generated by the events of the 1930s and the continued difficulties the NAS experienced in securing official recognition, the 'narrow-fronters' v 'broad-fronters' had emerged as a significant undercurrent in the selection of a General Secretary to replace Arthur Warren in 1941.

Nevertheless for the first decade or so of TUC membership the delegation to the Annual Congress abstained from voting on a wide range of more general, social and (some would say) political issues. Conference retained a keen interest in the matter, insisting that local associations be informed of the NAS delegation's voting record at TUC Congress.

However, developments in the 1980s, particularly the onslaught of Thatcherism and the ever-expanding size and influence of the NASUWT, including representation on the TUC's General Council, gradually led to the Union's delegations to Congress taking a line and voting on most of the issues debated.

The early 1970s saw much debate over the state of industrial relations in the country. In 1968/69 Labour's Barbara Castle, then Secretary of State for Employment, had famously been forced to retreat from her White Paper *In Place of Strife*, which had sought the co-operation of trade unions in establishing better industrial relations in more of a 'partnership' and less of a confrontational approach. Unofficial action by unions had become quite common. The NAS had been a strong supporter of the Donovan Commission's recommendations for trade union reform which, whilst representing a more common sense way forward, relied upon voluntary implementation from within the organisations themselves.

In later times it became a moot point as to whether the failure of unions 'to put their own house in order' opened up the opportunity for Margaret Thatcher to embark upon a series of so-called 'employment' legislation reforms of the 1980s which so weakened the labour movement. Arguably one of the casualties of this failure was Prime Minister James Callaghan whose 1979 defeat at the hands of Thatcher was largely attributed to the unions' Winter of Discontent that preceded the General Election of the same year. Callaghan had been one of the leading members of the Labour Cabinet who had conspired to scupper Barbara Castle's proposals, which had been backed by Premier Harold Wilson.

Becoming Prime Minister in 1970, Ted Heath tried to reform unions through his 1971 Industrial Relations Act, which outlawed wildcat strikes. In the event open revolt by trade union members, most notably the support for the unofficial strike in the Port of London, led to chaos in which the Official Solicitor, whom nobody had heard about, was plucked from obscurity to order the release from jail of the dockers' leaders who had been imprisoned for their activities. Many observers believed Heath's 1971 Act had been mortally wounded.

But in the meantime TUC policy was to oppose the 1971 Act and all its affiliates were enjoined to de-register as unions under the legislation. The NAS duly de-registered but openly asserted its right to do otherwise if its interests so dictated. Those opposed to TUC affiliation claimed de-registration implied a party political bias. At the 1972 Conference a motion was moved by the old stalwart from Oldham, Harry Stott who opposed affiliation to the TUC, instructing the Executive to register the Association as a Trade Union under the Act. The motion was kicked into the long grass with amendments which added "if and when the time becomes appropriate subject to a report being presented by the Executive to a Conference convened for the purpose". Conference 1973 saw a rerun of a similar motion and amendments, but by 1974 Labour had been returned to power and promptly repealed the 1971 Act.

Compared with the 'big boys' such as the huge TGWU (general workers), with over a million members, the (engineers) AUEW, the then large NUM (miners) and some powerful groups such as the electricians' union, ETU, the NAS (combined later with the UWT) was very much a junior affiliate to the TUC. Nevertheless the NAS played its part conscientiously. The NAS gave financial and practical support to the National Union of Public Employees in its famous 'dirty jobs dispute' in 1970. In February 1971 the NAS donated £1,000 to the postal workers hardship fund to help POWU members and their families during the course of a long and bitter strike.

The NASUWT in the now devolved nations of Scotland and Wales affiliated to their respective TUCs and participated actively in their affairs. The situation in Wales was marred for a certain time as the NASUWT was unwisely and unjustifiably denied a seat on the Executive Committee despite constituting a quite large block of overall union membership in the Principality. Pressure had to be applied via the UK TUC to put matters right.

One of the most active Regional Councils of the TUC was to be found in the North West, based on Manchester. The NAS and UWT members in the Region were very supportive of its activities, none more so than two distinguished Presidents, Ray Holden (1971) and Maurice Littlewood (1992). Maurice was later to receive the TUC Gold Badge in recognition for a lifetime of contribution towards its work at local, regional and national levels.

Debates on some internal TUC reforms led to the principle of 'automaticity' being adopted at the Congress in September 1981. Unions with 100,000 members or more were automatically granted representation on the General Council (GC). Out went the supposedly more democratic elections at the annual Congress (in reality dominated by the big union slates) and in came a more representative GC, reflecting the growing importance of the medium-sized white-collar unions of which the NASUWT was a typical example. The NUT argued against the change in the name of democracy, no doubt glad to have found some reason to try to keep the NASUWT out and retain its 'monopoly' position as the sole school teacher union on the GC. 'Automaticity' won the day by 6.4 million votes to 5.1 million. The NASUWT influence in TUC affairs increased as a consequence.

The implementation of the new system was left till the following year (1982/83) ironically when Terry Casey would be retiring. Thus it fell to Fred Smithies to become the first NASUWT Representative to serve on the GC. Fred Smithies experienced a baptism of fire as the TUC was plunged into crisis and division over the bitter miners' strike of 1984. The NASUWT was also itself divided over support for the NUM. While the then NAS had contributed financially to the miners' strike in 1972, the majority view came down on the side of withholding support in 1984. There were complications over the NUM leadership breaking its own balloting rules. Furthermore the NUM President, Arthur Scargill, also a self-declared Marxist, had spoken openly about using the strike (originally sparked by job cuts) to bring down the elected government of Mrs Thatcher. The debate raged intensively within the NASUWT delegation to

Congress 1984 but the decision taken received very clear majority support from the National Executive.

The NASUWT contingents were always prominent in TUC demonstrations in London and around the country, including the annual Tolpuddle March which took place in July every year to commemorate the transportation to Australia in 1834 of six agricultural workers found 'guilty' of forming a trade union to oppose more cuts in their wages.

The NASUWT contingent was similarly very prominent in the protest marches organised in January every year by the TUC to mark the anniversaries of Mrs Thatcher's ban in 1984 on trade unions at the GCHQ intelligence gathering centre after an industrial dispute over pay. Fourteen civil servants had been dismissed for refusing to give up their union membership despite the 'bribe' of £1,000 offered by the Government. As the New Labour Government quickly restored the right to belong to a union after the 1997 General Election, following one final 'celebration' march, they came to a natural and successful end.

I became the second NASUWT representative on the GC, serving from 1989 to 1993, just long enough to take my 'Buggins's turn' of seniority and become TUC President in 1992. Much of my work inside the GC was devoted to promoting Social Partnership with the expected change of Government (delayed until 1997), defending the establishment of the School Teachers' Review Body from NUT attacks and seeking appropriate reforms to the anti-trade union legislation of the Thatcher administrations. Reflecting the broad-fronters approach the Union put forward several motions to Congress in the 1990s on partnership and the need for socially enlightened economic policies considered essential properly to finance the education service.

The TUC experienced difficulties persuading Tony Blair's New Labour Government to amend some of the harsh anti-trade union legislation of its predecessor Tory administrations. By June 1998 the Government produced a White Paper, *Fairness at Work*, which went some way towards this but not far enough in the opinion of the more traditional 'Old Labour' elements in the 'movement'. There was much argument inside the TUC on whether the cup was half full or half empty but it was difficult to agree with those who held there was no difference between New Labour (with its admittedly modest reforms) and the Conservatives' policy for more draconian anti-union employment legislation as contained in their 1997 General Election manifesto.

The NASUWT welcomed the proposed new rights, including improved protection against and compensation for unfair dismissal together with enhanced provision for union recognition and representation. There was also much-improved provision for 'family' rights including maternity leave and time off for parental duties. The NASUWT welcomed these measures but regretted the lack of reform on the rights of unions to determine their own internal democratic procedures such as the method of choosing their general secretaries.

The attacks on the twin towers in New York on '9/11' 2001 took place while Prime Minister Tony Blair was backstage about to address the TUC Congress in Brighton. My TUC presidential year (September 2002/03) was dominated by the Fire Workers' dispute and strike and the UK Government's decision to support the US invasion of Iraq in 2003. After Blair's second election victory in 2001 he became more relaxed about government–union relations and regular tri-monthly meetings took place between the TUC and the Prime Minister at 10 Downing Street. On two occasions the TUC deputation tried to persuade Tony Blair not to participate with the USA in the invasion of Iraq, a position fully supported by the NASUWT. The TUC believed an invasion would further destabilise a volatile region, there was no evidence that Iraq was behind the 9/11 attacks, the UN Inspectors had found scant evidence of weapons of mass destruction and no threat to the UK's national interest had been identified.

The TUC, being founded in 1868, was inevitably a 'cross-border' organisation in the island of Ireland as several 'British' unions retained members in both the UK and the Irish Free State after independence in 1922. For many years the question of the NASUWT affiliating its membership in 'The North' to the Irish Congress of Trade Unions (ICTU) was a 'hot political potato'. However, after the Good Friday Agreement and the development of more cross-border co-operation the atmosphere had become sufficiently relaxed for the NASUWT to affiliate relevant members to the ICTU in 1998, in the words of the Annual Report, "after extensive debate".

On the initiative of Terry Casey, who had attended the annual ILO Conference in Geneva, the NASUWT Executive was persuaded in 1976 to affiliate to the International Federation of Free Teachers' Unions (IFFTU). In 1976 the NASUWT became the first British teachers' union to join the European Teachers' Trade Union Committee (ETTUC), which had been established to relate to the then European Economic Community.

In 1975 the UK had confirmed its entry into the EEC in a national referendum which cut across traditional party political affiliations. Whilst the Treaty of Rome did not envisage much EEC intervention in matters educational, there were two areas, namely training and qualification equivalence, which could have direct bearing upon teachers' interests. However, as time went by the EEC expanded its sphere of influence as it transformed itself into the European Union of today with an ever-increasing role in social, employment and legal affairs, which had direct implications for all unions and employees.

The GS of IFFTU, Andre Braconnier, a fiery Belgian with a platform rhetoric matching the British image of 'continentals', addressed the 1976 Conference of the NASUWT and was very well received. He was sadly soon to collapse and die of a heart attack.

The teacher unions were again divided in their international affiliations. The NUT, AMMA, EIS, INTO and UTU were affiliated to an organisation rejoicing in the acronym WCOTP – World Confederation of Organisations of the Teaching Profession – much bigger and better resourced than IFFTU. However, WCOTP included in its membership many organisations that were not free and independent unions, especially those coming from the Communist Block where they were organs of the state. IFFTU was more trade union orientated and belonged to the ICFTU – International Confederation of Free Trade Unions, the 'worldwide trade union centre', to which the British TUC was also affiliated.

Terry Casey served on the Executive of IFFTU and became Treasurer of ETTUC and its successor body, the European Trade Union Committee for Education (ETUCE), established in 1981 and officially recognised as one of the 'social partners' of the EU. Fred Smithies, who succeeded Terry in 1983 as GS, also became Treasurer of IFFTU and the ETUCE. Within the ETUCE there were some regional groupings including one for the Nordic countries. In time a British–Irish Group, popularly known as BIG, developed, in which the NASUWT participated.

The NASUWT involvement in international union affairs was an enriching experience. Those of us who began to travel more widely in connection with this international work, besides meeting some wonderful characters and making fine friends, also became more aware of abuses of human and civil rights in various countries where democracy was lacking.

We found that our practical and member-orientated views on the role of a trade union contrasted somewhat with some of our newly found comrades' more philosophical approaches sometimes based on political and even religious groupings. We learnt a lot from each other.

The NASUWT hosted the leaders of the main European teachers' unions, representing 1.5 million employees, at its Rednal HQ in October 1979. The AGM of the ETTUC reviewed its domestic business but also developed plans to assist in training their colleagues in 'emerging' democracies such as Spain, Portugal and Greece.

With much goodwill and compromise the divisions between the 'teacher internationals' were eventually overcome, possibly also helped by historical developments in Eastern Europe. In January 1993 in Stockholm, after several years of long discussions and negotiations, IFFTU and WCOTP merged to form

Education International (EI) after initially meeting in separate 'winding up' conferences followed immediately by a joint gathering of the new body.

EI assumed the major worldwide representational role for over 300 teacher unions from around 160 different countries with some 30 million members. I was elected to the Interim Executive Board that was established and held a seat at successive triennial World Conferences held in Harare, Zimbabwe, 1995; Washington, DC, 1998; Thailand, 2001; and Porto Alegre, Brazil, 2004. Deputy GS Jerry Bartlett was elected to the EI Executive Board in 2004 and again in 2007 at the Congress held in Berlin.

The European divisions of the various teacher internationals managed to come together in a united forum to establish the ETUCE – European Trade Union Committee for Education – mainly to relate to the European Union.

After a shaky start in the 1970s, the NASUWT built up good relations with the National Union of Students (NUS). At the beginning of the 1975 academic year at Goldsmiths College in south-east London (which contained an important teacher-training establishment) the NUS informed the NAS that it was withdrawing the facilities previously provided to the Association to make its case to the student teachers and to have a display stand at the Freshers' Fair. The NAS and UWT attached great importance to student teacher recruitment for obvious reasons. I had recently become the Honorary GS of the LSA and a member of the National Executive. I immediately wrote to the College, to its NUS branch and to the CEO of the ILEA informing them that NAS members in London would not be accepting Goldsmiths' students on teaching practice in their classes.

All hell broke loose and within a matter of a day or two assurances were received that the NAS and UWT would never be excluded again. I even caused a little stir with the National Officers who informed me politely they should have been consulted first. Not that it would have made any difference to the action taken!

In March 1977 a similar situation developed at Trent Park College in north-west London where the local NUS refused to allow an NASUWT speaker to address a meeting to take place in the Union building. Members in Greater London, fully supported by the National Officers and Executive, threatened to withdraw teaching practice facilities for Trent Park students who very promptly forced their local leadership to reverse their ban.

The pro-NUT element in the NUS remained sceptical of the NASUWT but their rank-and-file members were impressed with our no-nonsense approach which also seemed more relevant to the problems young student teachers encountered on the pupil behaviour front when they found themselves on teaching practice. The Union's Assistant Secretary in charge of recruitment,

George Limburn, reported sharp increases in the recruitment of student teachers following these two incidents. Consequently, the Recruitment Committee resolved to approach the NUS nationally and seek to establish and maintain a proper dialogue. As time went on relationships improved greatly as the NASUWT explained its position on all the educational and union issues of the times. Regular meetings took place between NEC Members from our Recruitment Committee and NUS Officers, and fraternal/sororal guests were exchanged at our respective conferences. By 1982 more than 10,000 student teachers in training had joined the NASUWT. The figure climbed steadily, reaching over 31,500 in 1992.

The NAS tried valiantly but unsuccessfully to secure recognition on the Burnham FE Committee over a long period of time, led by Terry Casey and the Association's President in 1971-72, Ray Holden. Ray was among the finest of NAS leaders and had a lifetime's record of distinguished service not only to the NAS but also to the wider trade union movement. In retirement he became the Chair of Governors of one of the largest FE colleges in the country, Stretford, where he had previously been a lecturer.

Many of the schoolmasters transferring to the FE sector, better paid in those days, wished to retain their NAS membership. The NAS had some 2,000 NAS members who worked full-time in this sector, with another 12,000 part-timers mostly in adult education (evening classes), all coming under the Burnham FE Committee. Schoolteachers 'moonlighting' in adult education has disappeared today, reflecting higher pay and the near impossibility of fitting in more work.

Terry Casey and Ray Holden came close to securing recognition in the early 1970s but never quite made it. Some Education Secretaries such as Margaret Thatcher and Mark Carlisle were reportedly favourable but 'it never happened'. I suspect the 'departmental' (DES) view was against and perhaps the civil servants talked them out of any sympathy they might have entertained towards the Association.

At the same time, after prolonged negotiations inside the TUC an agreement was finally worked out between the NAS and ATTI which in effect recognised the right of the Association to retain existing members in, or transferring to, FE but denied us the right actively to recruit. Individuals could take their own initiative and join us if they wished. The NAS could continue to represent members in the various colleges where they taught but would not have collective negotiating rights at LEA and national levels.

The penalty in those days for any union found guilty after a hearing before the TUC Disputes Committee of poaching members outside their recognised sphere of influence from a fellow affiliate was expulsion if it defied a direction to return the members concerned. Oldham's Harry Stott alleged TUC affiliation had cost the NAS its sovereignty and ability to recruit freely in FE. He proposed various amendments to motions and Annual Reports at several Conferences to restore our 'independence' which would have the effect of placing the NAS at risk of complaint and possible ejection from the TUC. At the 1972 Conference Ray Holden vigorously defended the actions taken by the Executive in endorsing the limited achievements of the draft agreement with ATTI which at least recognised the existence of the NAS in FE. Conference consistently denied Harry Stott and backed the affiliation to the TUC. During the course of 1973 the NAS and ATTI endorsed the Joint Agreement on Membership brokered by the TUC.

The last 'serious' chance the Association had of securing recognition in the FE field ebbed away early in 1975. A delegation had met the Secretary of State, Reg Prentice, on 20 January to press the case. Giving his decision, Reg Prentice wrote to Terry Casey in polite but decisive terms explaining that "none of the arguments you or your colleagues made have persuaded me to reconsider my decision not to give the NAS/UWT a seat on the Burnham FE Committee".

Although the NASUWT repeated the exercise claiming representation and produced several statements in support over the course of the remainder of the seventies and into the eighties, the case was neither compelling enough nor supported by sufficient numbers of militant members to wage the kind of campaign that would have been necessary to shift a government, either of Labour or Conservative complexion.

With the exception of Northern Ireland where recognition was gained in 1981 as the issue was determined by a government-set criterion based simply on membership numbers, the issue was slowly (and painfully for our FE activists) to die away during the eighties and nineties. That happened despite some spirited demands from members in a few colleges, such as Bury and Peterlee in County Durham where effectively the NASUWT was involved in 1995 negotiations producing a new contract. In the same year at Truro College in Cornwall the NASUWT secured formal recognition. These cases showed that where Union members were to be found in some number and prepared to act, they could secure de facto negotiations with their employers.

The FE sector was greatly challenged by the strictures of the Thatcher administrations, the abolition of LEA control and the move to the 'incorporation' of colleges. FE teachers lost national bargaining along with their school colleagues in 1987. The Purple Book, featuring their national (and very favourable) conditions of service, was also whittled away. ATTI had become NATFHE and it was torn between its different political factions and failed to bite the bullet and commit itself to supporting effective college-based bargaining, the only viable option it had left.

By the 1990s FE teachers found themselves worse paid than their school colleagues. With the demise of statutory Burnham and the incorporation of FE colleges, any question of recognition had passed from Government to the employers who were even less likely to cede the NASUWT claim. Nevertheless the light on the candle flickered back briefly into life in the early 1990s when out of the blue the FE employers suddenly recognised AMMA, thereby prompting the NASUWT to seek a meeting demanding the same.

I recall the meeting well when the very entrepreneurial Roger Ward, Director of the FE College Employers Forum, went through the motions with aplomb, which was his style. The reality was that AMMA had been recognised because it was a tame union which would give the employers few problems and provide a monopoly-breaking bolt-hole for timid or disenchanted FE lecturers to desert and embarrass NATFHE. Recognising the NASUWT in this context would have been an insult.

I felt sorry for NASUWT members in FE. They could well have done with some traditional common sense and pragmatism from the NASUWT in their dealings with government and the FE college employers.

At the 1982 Conference the NASUWT unanimously reaffirmed its party political neutrality. Subsequently a statement was issued in the Where We Stand series. By this time the first Thatcher administration had become extremely unpopular and its experiment with hard-line monetarism had produced a slump in the economy, with firms collapsing (especially in manufacturing) and unemployment rocketing. Mrs Thatcher was placing intolerable pressure on a post-Second World War consensus whereby 'hard line' partisan policies were not pursued in practice by whoever won General Elections.

In addition some social issues had forced their way on to the political agenda, notably abortion, and there were some residual issues such as unilateral nuclear disarmament and the reintroduction of capital punishment which commanded the attention of some members.

The statement declared that throughout its history the NASUWT had always kept party politics off the agenda of Conference and local association meetings: "We have quite deliberately concentrated on policies and campaigns for the improvement of the salaries, status and conditions of service of teachers. All our resources and energy are used in pursuing these objectives and protecting teachers' jobs." Among the 120,000 members were supporters of all the major parties. They saw the policy as "realistic and sensible", leaving them "free as individuals to pursue their political objectives through the political parties". "Unilateral nuclear disarmament, capital punishment and abortion are clearly important moral and political issues but the [Union] does not discuss or formulate policies on such topics."

The stance was also a reaction to the NUT, which clearly did have purely social and political issues forced on its agenda at national and local levels by militant bands of hard-left and socialist groupings. This led to a union ravaged by internal divisions and 'structural factionalism'.

Ironically, the statement was no sooner issued than it began to be eroded, but neither in divisive nor unhelpful ways. With membership of the TUC General Council and a developing involvement in teacher union international affairs, wider social and political issues did force their way on to the NASUWT's agenda. The ever-increasing size and influence of the NASUWT afforded it the time and resources to see its role in a wider context. Why should we not assist other teacher trade unionists throughout the world where rights were denied and even the subject of brutal repression? On the domestic front economic policies impacted upon the public sector which directly affected teachers' interests. The NASUWT found it was able to pursue such objectives without becoming party political although 'the left' was generally more sensitive to and aware of breaches of human and trade union rights than others.

Affiliation to the anti-apartheid movement in 1987 and to Amnesty International became possible in such a context. Abortion proved a more divisive issue with strong views held on both sides, with some based on religious beliefs. The NASUWT abstained whenever the issue arose and was forced to a vote.

The 1985 Conference had asked the Executive to reconsider the Union's bankers in the light of Barclays' persistent economic support for the apartheid regime in South Africa. After lengthy discussions with Barclays and detailed investigation of the involvement of other financial institutions in South Africa the Executive announced early in 1986 that it would transfer all its national accounts to the Co-operative Bank. On 1 September the changes were effected. The Barclays Loan Scheme for individual members was also discontinued and similar arrangements with the Co-op Bank were introduced.

Chapter 40 – The General Teaching Council

As long ago as 1924 the NAS had declared that there should be "separate unions for the various sections that make up the teaching profession, federated for common action on all questions which are purely educational, or upon which there is agreement, but each functioning separately upon questions that affect them sectionally or upon which they differ profoundly".

The NAS believed the Teachers' Registration Council already formed the basis for such a federation. Such an approach was to become typical of the NAS, being pragmatic and more conducive to better relationships between teachers' unions than those that appertained during the twentieth century.

The question of a general council resurfaced periodically. There was often much confusion between a '*teaching*' and a '*teachers*' general council. The latter was akin to a grand 'high-minded' union, looking after the interests of teachers as well as regulating the profession in the public interest. The former was outside and arguably above the 'union' or sectional interest, concerning itself with setting standards to regulate entry to the profession and the right to practice, overseeing the conduct and competence of the profession. The acronym GTC mostly relates to the former but some confusion remains.

Supporters of a GTC modelled their ambitions upon the medical profession. In 1858 a General Medical Council was established by Act of Parliament, giving doctors very real powers in the establishment of regulations for becoming qualified and for policing standards of professional performance by practitioners. Self-government of a privately available health service for the few was one thing. Self-government for a public service which was committed to providing elementary schooling to all children was something else. That was potentially too great a call upon the public purse to be left to the teachers themselves. The reality was that a GTC would at best only ever be advisory.

The earliest body having aspirations for an independent GTC was probably the College of Preceptors. It survives to the present day but is largely unknown despite being well intentioned. It tried unsuccessfully to persuade governments to establish a GTC during the second half of the nineteenth century.

A Teachers' Registration Council was finally set up in 1902 under the provisions of the 1899 Education Act. It was a messy arrangement, treating elementary and secondary teachers differently. Government through the Treasury refused to make any financial contribution. It fell apart and was abolished in 1906.

The first formal involvement of the NAS in these matters came in 1928. A new Registration Council had been established in 1912 and within ten years included a high proportion of all teachers. In December 1928 Richard Anderson, by then an Ex-President of the NAS, and Arthur Warren, GS, were elected to the Teachers' Registration Council. In 1929 those teachers on the Council were automatically transferred into membership of the Royal Society of Teachers (RST). By 1930 there were over 80,000 in membership, and the registration fee was raised from £2 to £3 one year later.

Neither the RST nor the Registration Council had any function or power beyond establishing their own existence. The Joint Four were very anxious that it should not speak for the profession. In the 1930s the world had other rather more important concerns to sort out so the RST, plagued by redundancy, was soon suffering from rampant apathy which in turn led to a largely unlamented but discreet demise by Order in Council in 1949.

If ever there had been any doubt about who was in charge it was removed by the 1944 Act, which gave the Minister of Education the function of awarding qualified teacher status.

In 1954 the NAS Executive presented a Report on Professional Status to the Annual Conference in Porthcawl. It expressed surprise that an old profession like teaching had no self-regulation. The government determined who could teach in the public sector. The private sector was unregulated with virtually anybody able to become a teacher. It was strange that the professions dealing with the body of the child – doctors, dentists, opticians and chemists – had standards and codes established by their practitioners whereas teaching, dealing with the mind, had none.

The instant conversion in 1929 of the 'list compiling' the Teachers' Registration Council into the titular RST was in the view conveyed by the Report 'nothing more than smoke and mirrors'. The NAS Report concluded with the damning judgement: "No privileges were granted to the registered and no disabilities imposed upon the unregistered."

The NAS Report contained a short appendix setting out a very brief outline of a constitution for a British Teachers' Council. The Privy Council, universities and teachers would nominate members to the Council which "alone will have the power to license teachers". Teachers would have to pay a fee for the privilege and only those registered would be recognised, able to use the official name of 'teacher' and be employed in a school.

The GS of the NUT, Sir Ronald Gould, addressing a one-day Conference of the College of Perceptors in 1957, called for a "professional Council" for teachers. In what appeared to be a set-up job the Conference unusually passed a resolution. It called for a meeting of teachers' representative organisations to explore this possibility.

With the voting arrangements the NUT had in mind it quickly became obvious, even to the Joint Four and the NAHT, that this was an attempted takeover. The NUT wished to have a 'professional council' on which it would have majority voting power to deal with conditions of entry, professional self-discipline and educational developments and research. When the Joint Four, normally if incomprehensibly the compliant partners of the NUT, insisted upon a Teacher Council based on the separate identities of organisations the initiative fell apart as it became the turn of the NUT to say 'no'.

Meanwhile the NAS had proposed a British Teachers' Council. It would license practitioners, lay down minimum requirements and have the power to debar. The NAS wrote to the Minister, Geoffrey Lloyd, in October 1958 putting forward the proposal but his Private Secretary replied dismissing the idea. There was neither need nor general demand for a Council because "the present arrangements were working well". The existence of severe overcrowding in over 70,000 classes and thousands of non-qualified teachers and untrained graduates seemed to pass the Government by.

In 1959 the NAHT took an initiative to get the teacher organisations together to promote the cause of a GTC. Everyone seemed to agree on the desired outcome; the only problem was how to get there. By May 1960 the NAHT had arranged for a few Parliamentary questions to be asked. The new Minister, Sir David Eccles, replied predictably that "this was a matter for the teachers to decide amongst themselves", which everyone knew they would not.

On 28 May 1960 the NAHT succeeded in convening a 'Main Committee' of all relevant organisations to discuss the establishment of a GTC which would have three basic functions:

1) control over entry into the profession;
2) the sole right to grant recognition of 'qualified teacher' status;
3) control over professional discipline.

In 1963 the Wheatley Report on a Scottish Teachers' Council was published and led to the GTC Scotland being established by statute in 1965. It limited itself to the core activities of registration (including decisions on granting full recognition to probationers), and dealing with disciplinary (conduct and competence) cases. Consequently it has been generally well supported by Scottish teachers.

Over the following few years the Main Committee, casting a jealous, beady eye towards Scotland, made various unsuccessful attempts to persuade Ministers to establish a GTC. Tony Crosland was quite blunt and forthright in his rejections, stating in a meeting on 31 March 1965 that he was not prepared to relinquish control over entry to the profession during a period of teacher shortage.

However, with the arrival of a new Education Secretary, former secondary headteacher Ted Short in 1968, the situation changed significantly. He favoured the establishment of a GTC. R.J. Cook, GS of the NAHT and Secretary of the Main Committee, moved quickly to check the position with Ted Short, reconvene everyone and get the LEA employers on board.

By the time of the NAS Conference, Easter 1968, Ted Short had informed GS Terry Casey that he was willing to look again at the question of a GTC. Short delegated the details of 'refining' the proposals of the Main Committee to his number three, the Parliamentary Under-Secretary, Denis Howell, in conjunction with R.J. Cook. That 'refining' work was really more fundamental, designed to retrieve crucial reserve powers to the Secretary of State. In the final analysis any GTC was only going to be advisory on crucial issues such as entry requirements, recognition of qualified status and 'right to teach'.

More formal meetings between Howell and the Main Committee and the employers followed in December 1968 and January 1969. By 10 April 1969 the DES was able to write to the teacher unions enclosing a memorandum summarising the main features of the terms of reference for a Working Party (WP). To maintain progress the DES thought it crucial to keep it small and suggested one representative per organisation, including just one from the LEAs.

A few days before the first scheduled meting of the WP (21 May) the NUT threw its customary spanner into the works demanding three representatives as the only way it could advance the interests of its claimed 230,000 members. If three places were not available on the WP it would boycott anything emanating from it.

The whole matter was referred back to Ted Short who after a two-month delay caved in to the NUT. The other unions accepted the situation, placing progress on a GTC ahead of other concerns. The principle of small but efficient and speedy which had served the Main Committee well was scrapped, with the NUT having 8 seats, NAS 3, NAHT 2 and ATCDE 2, with one each for the constituents of the Joint Four and ATTI. (Universities and employers' organisations were also represented.)

The WP's Terms of Reference revealed the Government was giving with one hand but taking back with the other. While registration with the GTC would be a condition of employment, "it would however be necessary for the Government to retain sufficient reserve powers to safeguard the supply of teachers for the public system". Standards for registration were not to be such "as to exclude categories of teachers that the government thinks are needed" or alternatively the profession would have to "accept the employment of unregistered teachers." The beloved GTC would only be advisory.

The WP met during the summer and autumn of 1969 under the chairmanship of T.R. (Toby) Weaver, a civil servant from the DES. The Weaver Report, as it came to be known, was presented to the Secretary of State on 28 January 1970 and published a little later in February. Ted Short accepted the Report, thanking everyone for their hard work. All interested parties were invited to respond to the Report.

The Easter annual union Conferences followed soon after. The NAS Conference welcomed the Report. Ted Short had addressed the opening session (thereby speaking before the Report was debated) and made a powerful speech calling for enhanced status and a better career structured salary system for teachers. Linking the two was clever politics on Short's part but it represented a tacit admission that a GTC on its own would at best only be a limited step forward.

However, over at the NUT Conference there was no such welcome for the Report. The Secretary of State waited in vain for an official NUT response. All the other teacher associations and interested parties gave support, some making points of qualification.

Time ran out unexpectedly. On 1 June 1970 the Labour Government was surprisingly defeated in the General Election. Edward Heath became PM; Margaret Thatcher Secretary of State for Education.

After allowing the Minister 'to settle in' to her new job Terry Casey approached her on several issues including the Weaver Report. The President at the time, Ron Simons, recalls a dinner at which the NAS hosted Mrs Thatcher and her Ministerial team. "Terry Casey was in one of his expansive and stimulating moods, launching into a persuasive articulation of the value of a GTC concluding that 'Weaver' should be resurrected." According to Simons, Thatcher's response was "brief but succinct": "Message received and understood."

Mrs Thatcher then canvassed all the organisations for their views. All remained in favour except, perhaps inevitably, the NUT, dissatisfied with its representation. The Weaver Report recommended a 40-seat GTC, a majority of whom, 25, would be appointed by the Secretary of State on the nomination of the teacher associations. The remaining 15 would be nominated by the Secretary of State taking other interested parties into account. The NUT was not satisfied with its allocation of 10 seats, denying it the usual overall majority. The NAS had 3, Joint Four 6, NAHT 2, ATTI 2 and ATCDE 2.

Despite the NUT having had eight seats (increased from three) on the Weaver WP as the "only way [it] could advance the interests of its members", no one had objected to the pattern of representation unanimously recommended. It had been quite consciously and deliberately decided that "the Council must not be, nor risk appearing to be, the creature of a sectional interest". Furthermore, Weaver with commendable clarity, had explicitly expressed the ultimately advisory status of the GTC: "We accept that the Secretary of State must retain reserve powers to reject or modify recommendations of the Teaching Council in part or in whole."

It appeared that the NUT Weaver WP reps could not carry the Executive. The lack of an overall NUT majority of teacher seats was undoubtedly a problem. There may have been others. The NUT Executive was known to be a divided and factionalised body with groups fighting each other for control.

By mid-August 1970 the digest of teacher association responses to Weaver had been circulated to all the parties. Terry Casey 'broke the curious silence' that had descended on the scene by writing to Mrs Thatcher on 27 August suggesting she invite members of the Weaver WP to the DES for discussions. The first indication that the GTC was now dead in the water came in the reply from one of Mrs Thatcher's civil servants, Peter Sloman. He wrote back to Terry Casey on 6 September saying that the Secretary of State was of the opinion that "the initiative should now lie with the teachers collectively and without any intervention from her".

It was clear that Mrs Thatcher was taking the easy way out. Unable or unwilling to match the candour of Tony Crosland, Mrs Thatcher batted the ball back into the teachers' court knowing what the result would be. Perhaps her civil servants, long sceptical about a rival organisation like a GTC, had talked her out of her post-prandial conviviality with the NAS Officers.

With Ted Short, the only Minister of the times who believed enough in a GTC to find a way forward, having departed the scene, the teaching profession had lost the opportunity for the best GTC that was ever going to be available. Sole responsibility lay with the NUT, honing its skills in making the wrong decision at crucial times in the history of the teaching profession.

Adding insult to injury, in December 1970 the NUT had the cheek to write to all other associations suggesting it convene a WP to discuss how agreement might be reached on the fundamental criticisms it had of the Weaver Report. Terry Casey was scathing in his reply. Needless to say no one was the least bit interested in appointing the NUT to nurse the patient it had crippled.

The issue remained dormant until 1983 when the Universities Council for the Education of Teachers (UCET) undertook the task of convening and chairing a group of 17 cross-sector associations to resurrect the possibility of a GTC. UCET was distant from the inter-union battlefield. NASUWT Conference 1983 supported the idea but the resolution betrayed some scepticism, viewing a GTC as a "valuable adjunct" to teachers' interests as opposed to the panacea it was believed to be by some enthusiasts.

As the London-based Assistant Secretary on the NASUWT staff, I drew the short straw and became the Union's representative on the 'shadow' GTC, or the GTC "in exile" as I called it. It took on the legal entity of a company limited by guarantee. The 1986 Conference at Scarborough carried another resolution which conditionally supported the establishment of a GTC subject to the "functions, composition and finances" being "acceptable". The NASUWT had to fight a rearguard battle insisting on amendments to proposals coming forward from a 'technical WP' to safeguard the distinct roles of employers and unions in determining pay and conditions of service. 'Role aggrandisement' repeatedly surfaced as a problem for the NASUWT. Other unions seemed unaware of the dangers.

However, as I describe in Chapter 66, on 30 October 1986 the Government declared its intention to abolish teachers' negotiating rights, the latest of a series of virulent anti-union measures that characterised the 1980s. Inside the GTC it became increasingly obvious that some 'enthusiasts' were pursuing their ambitions as a means of sidelining the unions as the representatives of the profession. These people recognised they needed the unions to establish a GTC but in the longer term they would be phased out as their right to nominate would be replaced by profession-wide elections. The NASUWT was sceptical of such elections. In the absence of democratic and representative organisations of some kind, be they union or other, they would invariably mean the election of the unknown and unaccountable by the largely uninformed and uninterested.

In a major Report to Conference on a GTC in 1987 the NASUWT reviewed the situation. Experience of the 1985/86 pay dispute reinforced our belief that the establishment of a genuine collegiate salary structure was far more relevant to securing real professional status for the classroom teacher. In any event a GTC could only ever be an advisory body, ultimate power over its key functions remaining with government. We said the Scottish experience of a more limited GTC model has had "no discernible influence on the professional status" of teachers, and "There must be a grave danger the Government would take proposals for a GTC and misuse them to suit its own purpose" of sidelining the unions. The concluding recommendation, "That in current circumstances the NASUWT opposes the establishment of a GTC as proposed in the report drawn up under the auspices of UCET", was carried overwhelmingly.

Consequently some inside the Executive argued we should boycott the 'shadow' GTC but the majority view was that it would continue without us and we needed to remain on the inside, minimise danger and try to keep the enthusiasts to the straight and narrow. At first it mattered little as the shadow

GTC went round in harmless circles which on behalf of the NASUWT I was content to encourage.

However, all that changed rather suddenly as the shadow GTC recruited the services of John Tomlinson as Chairman in the early 1990s. John was a former CEO and had long experience in the world of education politics, knew his way around and, as I reported to the Executive, posed a real danger of getting a GTC established! I recall one meeting when in the middle of another vigorous discussion on the role of a GTC, John let his guard slip in observing that one of the problems with the teaching profession was that it had only ever had unions speaking for it.

Soon the Shadow Education Spokesman, Jack Straw, had been persuaded to commit New Labour to introducing a GTC if elected to power. There was no problem with forward commitment, for a GTC would be extremely low cost for government, teachers being expected to cover the expenditure with a registration and annual fee. The NASUWT predicted it would be unpopular with teachers who would ask 'What for?' and receive a very unconvincing answer.

Once in power New Labour set about implementation. The Government wanted no union nominations, preferring profession-wide elections of all the teacher members of a GTC. The Government would have a substantial number of nominees but teacher members would be in majority. I had to argue long and hard with the Minister of State, Stephen Byers, for union nominations. Without them the GTC would be launched amid hostility and there would be a chronic absence of accountability. Without representative organisations supporting GTC members, meaningful consultation and feedback would be impossible; power would reside in the full-time Secretariat.

Eventually a compromise was reached. In the Teaching and Higher Education Act of 1998 setting up a GTC in England (and Wales) the 64 members of the Council would be elected or appointed as follows:

> 25 elected by the profession (11 primary, 11 secondary, 1 special, 1 primary head, 1 secondary head);
> 9 appointed by the unions (2 NUT, 2 NASUWT, 2 ATL and 1 each for SHA, NAHT and PAT);
> 17 appointed by various educational bodies;
> 13 appointed by the Secretary of State.

Wales would have its own smaller-scale GTC of 25 members constituted on the same basis. Northern Ireland would also have its own GTC a few years later.

Contrary to the advice the NASUWT had been offering over many years, the GTC was given a wide-ranging remit. Instead of concerning itself with qualifications to teach, operation of the register and discipline, the GTC was required to contribute to improving the standards of teaching and quality of learning and to do the same for standards of professional conduct amongst teachers "in the public interest". The GTC would also advise the Secretary of State (and others) on a wide range of issues, including teacher recruitment and supply, initial training, induction and professional conduct. All these involved considerable duplication of the work of other bodies.

A Secretariat was quickly established, including a Director, to get the GTC off the ground. Again on behalf of the NASUWT I had to argue in the informal consultative meetings as well as with Ministers, that the GTC should only become involved in cases of discipline (including conduct and competence) after a teacher had been sacked or resigned in circumstances which might have led to dismissal. Incredibly some in the emerging GTC wanted to deal directly with complaints against teachers by anyone, thereby cutting right across the employer's function. They seemed totally oblivious to the mountainous potential of the caseload, not to mention the minefield of employment legislation which now governed such matters. Some seemed unable to understand the appropriate GTC function was to determine suitability for teaching generally, not suitability to continue in a particular post which rightly fell to the employer. Double jeopardy for teachers seemed also to pass these people by. The NASUWT won these arguments at the time but the desire amongst some enthusiasts to build up the GTC's 'mission' remained.

Although the general view had been that a teacher should chair the GTC, for starters the Government made an interesting decision to appoint the film producer, David (Lord) Puttnam, to the position. He had been instrumental in getting the Teaching Awards off the ground and was regarded as a friend of the teaching profession. The NASUWT joined most others in welcoming his appointment.

However, no such supportive feelings greeted the news that teachers would have to pay an annual fee of £30 to the GTC to register and retain the right to teach. The resultant uproar was only relieved by the Government recommending to the School Teachers' Review Body that salaries should be increased by a sufficient amount to cover the cost, now reduced to £25 per annum in the wake of the protest.

Meanwhile the first Director of the GTC, Carole Adams, led moves on 'mission aggrandisement'. GTC promotional literature appeared, claiming it was "the voice of the profession". The claim was at best premature, certainly contentious and at worst downright confusing, ignoring as it did the supposedly vital "in the public interest" brief.

The GTC was very keen to secure publicity for its 'positive' activities, for example promoting better induction of new teachers. The NASUWT advised that this was naïve. Given the nature of the media beast, publicity would inevitably focus upon the juicy disciplinary cases. Far from promoting a better image of the teaching profession, the hearing by the GTC of disciplinary cases in public (promoted as a mark of a true profession) would only result in more adverse publicity. Previously Ministers discreetly decided such business, after interview by civil servants of 'offending teachers', all conducted in private. (Ministers retained responsibility for deciding the serious 'List 99' cases involving abuse of children, and more recently this has all been swept up in legislation dealing with various offenders' registers and the Criminal Records Bureau (CRB) checks.)

To cut a long story short, NASUWT warnings that a GTC would not attract enthusiastic support amongst teachers and that salary levels and the exercise of independent professional judgement were far more relevant to status, have proved accurate. The very low turnout in elections for the GTC, its lack of real impact and support, testify that it would serve better purpose by focussing on the basic functions of registration and discipline, avoiding 'mission aggrandisement' and unnecessarily high fees. Enthusiasts for a GTC always promised more than it could deliver and in recent times the concept itself has been seriously undermined by the failures of self-regulated professions. None the least of these was the failure of the medical profession, despite having its 'Rolls-Royce' GMC model of excellent practice (revered by GTC enthusiasts), to prevent 'mass murder' on the part of Dr Harold Shipman in Hyde, Greater Manchester in the 1990s.

It was ironic that teaching, never regarded as a true profession whilst lacking a GTC, was one of the few occupations whose practitioners genuinely put their clients ahead of their own financial interests by undertaking so many additional and voluntary tasks for their pupils without charging extra for it – a point that was well picked up by the 1993 President, John Rowlands from the Jarrow, Hebburn & Boldon Association, in his address to Conference.

Postscript

In July 2010 the new Education Secretary, Michael Gove, announced his intention to abolish the GTC.

Chapter 41 - The Durham Dispute 1969

The local aspects of the 1969 Durham Dispute provided an intriguing insight into the way some LEA employers treated teachers. On this occasion they met stern resistance from NAS members who displayed great courage, risking their jobs to be treated with some respect and dignity. Members of the fledgling UWT also joined in the protest action. I write about the national pay implications of the dispute in Chapter 26.

Problems with the NAS protest action over pay arose in areas such as Teesside, Liverpool and London, but they were soon resolved. Not so in Durham where, frankly, the Authority went over the top. Heavily influenced by members past and present of the NUM and given the history of the mining industry, the LEA seemed culturally unable to bear the thought that 'industrial action' should go unpenalised. Perhaps they believed all teachers were easily intimidated, as protest action by the NUT in Easington two years previously had been easily put down within two days, with a councillor boasting: "This is how we discipline our teachers in Durham!"

The original cause of the action, serious dissatisfaction over pay, was soon lost in the bitterness of a lengthy dispute. The issue became the right of teacher trade unionists to take official action without being disciplined. It became a fight to establish the right to fight. The NAS regarded that as crucial. If this principle were lost the ability of teachers to protect their interests would disappear for ever.

Durham schoolmasters were blessed in having one of the greatest local leaders the NAS has ever seen. Bill, some times known as Ernie, Gladstone was Chairman of the Durham NAS Representative Council but not just a 'union man'. He was a well-respected headmaster, a warden of his local church, author of several books and very knowledgeable about educational matters. He was one of several outstanding local leaders who, unfortunately from the Executive's perspective, never sought national office. However, Bill Gladstone's restrained approach was not reciprocated. On the day action commenced, 7 February, he telephoned the LEA asking if any purpose would be served by having discussions, only to be met with a sharp put-down: "None whatever"!

As the action began in Milton Hall and Acre Rigg schools the Durham Education Committee (put in day-to-day charge of dealing with the dispute) applied heavy pressure on headmasters to organise systematic scabbing. The councillors also ordered their officials to visit the schools personally to discipline NAS members.

An element of farce was introduced as the day chosen was Shrove Tuesday when the schools were closed. They tried again on 14 February and finding Milton Hall open the Deputy Director of Education personally issued letters of suspension and ordered NAS members off the premises. They could only return when prepared to resume normal duties and in the meantime no salary would be paid. Finding Acre Rigg School in Peterlee closed on 14 February for another reason (half-term) two LEA officials ascertained the addresses of NAS members and visited them at their homes. They were then suspended for their "refusal when directed by the Headmaster to undertake normal duties *today*" (while at home on half-term holiday)! The NAS advised these members to ignore such letters. They reported for work after the holiday, finally to be suspended on 19 February.

The NAS response was immediate and predictable. All Durham members, excluding probationers, were called out on a half-day strike on 20 February. GS Terry Casey addressed over 800 members at the Palladium Cinema in Durham. He then led a march to County Hall after which he kept an appointment with the Education Committee to put the NAS case. Terry Casey retired after his presentation to allow the Committee to consider their response. On being recalled Terry was somewhat surprised to be told "that was that". The councillors were not prepared to discuss the matter further.

To its credit the NAHT had issued advice to its members not to 'blackleg' the half-day strike, either by taking over the work of striking teachers themselves or encouraging others to do so. In stark contrast the Director of Education, Mr G.H. Metcalfe, wrote to all headteachers urging that no children should be sent home, but remain in school supervised by other staff.

So the tone for the dispute was set with the incitement to scab and the gratuitous snub proffered to GS Terry Casey provoking outright hostility from the NAS. Moreover such aggression raised the media profile of the dispute, from which the LEA was to suffer badly.

The Durham NAS then instructed members from 24 February to refuse to handle any school dinner money, register or forms. Despite the NAS High Court victory in the 1956 Sunderland Case securing the right of teachers to decline such voluntary 'duties', members in neighbouring Durham (as elsewhere) had continued to give goodwill and volunteer even in the absence of ancillary assistance recommended nationally. The LEA seemed blind to the need to reciprocate goodwill, so essential in the running of schools, and let the planned two-week protest pass off without unnecessary repercussions.

Once again farce and chaos entered on stage as the Director of Education and senior staff toured schools attempting to collect dinner money. Pressure was put on young clerks to assist. Once again the NAS outmanoeuvred the LEA. Now affiliated to the TUC, the NAS secured the support of other local government unions, the General and Municipal Workers Union (GMWU), NUPE and NALGO, who to their great credit told members not to take over the work left behind by those engaged in official action.

Some senior members of the Council's staff chose to ignore the advice of the NALGO Executive. Dragooned into invading schools for the purpose of collecting dinner money, they found it a largely unrewarding experience. Over 50 NAS headmasters, whilst not obstructing the hapless Council staff, left them to their own devices. However, all NAS and UWT members resolutely and correctly refused to allow their lessons to be interrupted for the purpose. Senior Council staff, including the Director himself, armed with little black bags, did their best to collect money in-between lessons. They had to rely upon the word of the children if they had paid or if they were entitled to free meals and take whatever money was offered. And at the end the NAS headmasters refused to sign off the accounts for obvious reasons. The NAS also instructed them not to record or bank any of the money.

Durham approached the RC Bishop of Hexham and Newcastle to bring ecclesiastical pressure to bear on NAS headmasters in Catholic schools. The Bishop declined to enter this "secular dispute".

Durham called for reports on all these "recalcitrant headmasters", still to no avail. On 5 March the Authority clamped down on all leave for teachers to attend in-service courses. Two days later Durham announced a determination to stand firm until there was "unconditional surrender" by the NAS. The NAS responded by including two more schools in the action, Clegwell in Hebburn and Hermitage in Chester-le-Street. The 31 NAS members involved were immediately suspended.

With the dispute over a month old the parents became very restless. They organised petitions, visited County Hall, lobbied their MPs and gave many media interviews demanding the dispute be settled. The bad news for the Durham Authority was that the parents were taking the teachers' side.

In March the LEA raised the level of intimidation on NAS headmasters as the local press ran a story that Durham had gathered a 'dossier of disruption' over dinner money collection, and those responsible would be summoned to County Hall and held to account with a view to dismissal. Bill Gladstone was personally targeted with allegations he had been absent from his school for two hours.

The LEA had earlier tried to intimidate Bill during the course of a long interview at County Hall. Having predictably failed and only further enraged NAS members, Durham tried it on another headmaster. Again the LEA had chosen the wrong man! Ralph Jackson was the sole NAS member at the small village primary school in Sherburn near the City of Durham. Not only was he a committed NAS member but a headmaster who enjoyed immense respect and loyalty amongst the parents. He also played a prominent role in the life of the village.

The LEA deliberately engineered a confrontation with Ralph Jackson. Without the customary telephone call which had marked their previous good relationship, the Divisional Education Officer (DEO) arrived at Sherburn to enforce the collection of meal money during lesson time. Ralph refused to allow lessons to be interrupted but offered to line the children up at the forthcoming morning break; but the DEO persisted.

Ralph Jackson then received a peremptory command to appear at County Hall the next day. The NAS instructed him not to appear and pointed out that the disciplinary procedures entitled teachers to seven days notice of a hearing. The NAS GS telegrammed the LEA to point out Jackson had been acting under association instructions. That did not deter the rampant Durham LEA from announcing Jackson was suspended.

However, that was one belligerent move too far for Durham's own good. The public reacted against the Authority, which appeared to be acting without any self-control in a grossly disproportionate fashion. The next day *The Newcastle Journal* ran a huge headline, "Village backs suspended headteacher". A meeting of Sherburn villagers in the local men's working club pledged to support Ralph Jackson. The local churches, parents and the Durham and District Trades Council wrote letters to the press and the LEA in strong protest, paying generous tribute to their "outstanding headmaster". On 26 March a crowded meeting of parents at Chester-le-Street, chaired by one of their own and addressed by Ned Selkirk, the local NAS Secretary and himself suspended from his school, called for the prompt reinstatement of all 'excluded' staff to enable full-time education to be resumed.

A week after Ralph Jackson's irregular suspension he appeared before the full Education Committee, accompanied by George Limburn, a very fine union activist, former member of the National Executive and now an accomplished Assistant Secretary in the employment of the NAS. It took George Limburn 20 minutes to secure assurances from the Chairman that the heckling and abuse coming from certain members of the Committee would cease. George then pointed out that Ralph Jackson had been acting on union instructions and that he had made perfectly reasonable arrangements for the collection of dinner money.

The Committee then made a statement that although Jackson had been "insubordinate", they did not wish to punish him for being loyal to his union and therefore they were "suspending his suspension". George Limburn refused to accept Ralph Jackson had been insubordinate but he was told the Committee had already passed the resolution to that effect and it could not be changed.

However, as the meeting broke up the Chairman asked George Limburn for the early commencement of talks, the first sign that the LEA was 'beginning to blink'. It was agreed there should be a meeting but it would have to await the NAS Conference taking place in Eastbourne the following week and was set for 15 April.

By this time parental anger was growing and finding public expression. The two regional newspapers based in Newcastle, *The Evening Chronicle* and *The Journal*, began to carry reports of parent groups at the four main schools affected writing strong letters of protest to the Durham LEA and demanding 'their' teachers be reinstated. In Chester-le-Street over 800 parents had signed a petition calling for the reinstatement of 12 teachers suspended from the Hermitage Secondary School. The Dawson family from Chester-le-Street became leaders overnight of the protest movement. The son, 14-year-old Bernard, led a deputation of pupils to County Hall handing in the petition. His mother, Elizabeth, publicly tore up a letter she had received from Joe Goodwin, Chairman of the Education Committee. On 8 April Mrs Dawson led a group of parents to a stormy meeting with the Education Committee. Later she threatened to withhold her son's attendance at the school if scab labour were brought in. The Peterlee and District and the Jarrow and Hebburn Trades Councils came out in support of the suspended schoolmasters.

The dispute was beginning to impact upon the preparation for public examinations, the GCE and the Northern County CSE. Around this time the Director of Education, George Metcalfe, began making pedantic distinctions between 'suspension' and 'exclusion', claiming teachers had been subjected to the latter and could return to work normally at any time. Durham had suddenly realised it had painted itself into a corner by suspending the teachers, for the relevant regulations stipulated it would either have to reinstate them and repay salary withheld or sack them.

Annual Conference 1969 in Eastbourne, with Sunderland man Joe Pretty installed as the new President, gave the traditional hero's welcome to the delegates from Durham who were in the thick of battle for the NAS cause.

After Conference the NAS prepared its negotiating position for the 15 April meeting with the Durham Authority. Several demands were drawn up including:

recognition of the right to work to rule; reinstatement of suspended members without loss of pay; no victimisation; and the Durham LEA to support the call for an independent inquiry into salary negotiations. In return the NAS would lift the ban on meals money collection.

At the meeting on 15 April Durham's first (and only) move was to collapse the talks. After listening to Bill Gladstone's presentation of the NAS case the Education Committee withdrew, only to return shortly thereafter to announce that in the absence of any compromise proposals from the NAS, a manifestly false accusation, discussion was pointless. The 'talks' collapsed before they started. As in the treatment of Terry Casey a few weeks previously, the LEA seemed incapable of negotiating.

The LEA lost again in the public relations stakes. The press reported that the LEA had rejected the NAS peace offer without discussion. Most Durham parents reacted with dismay as the disruption to their children's education entered its third month. Parents' protests grew and they called upon Education Secretary Ted Short to intervene. Other parent groups threatened legal action against the LEA for failing to discharge its duty under the 1944 Education Act. However, there were reports that some parents at the Milton Hall School were supportive of the LEA.

The NAS called an evening meeting at Dunelm House of all Durham members, so they could be kept fully informed of all the developments. The Association recognised the situation could not be allowed to remain static and decided to escalate the action. On 18 April four more secondary schools joined the action. The 32 NAS members at Murton, Whickham, Heworth and Sedgefield schools were immediately suspended.

Chairman of the Education Committee, Alderman Joseph Goodwin, announced that stronger action would be considered against NAS members. By that time 79 members were 'locked out' and some 5,000 children were having makeshift or no education at all.

After refusing to discuss the NAS's post-Conference proposals the LEA bizarrely decided on 15 April to discuss them with the NUT. The NUT had great difficulty in discerning the correct line to take and not get involved in scabbing another union's action.

The NUT had not been helped by a curious letter circulated by the Secretary of its Barnard Castle branch. The letter warned NUT members to be aware of the NAS's plan to take over the leadership of the profession and remove salary negotiations from Burnham, handing it to an independent inquiry, and lamented the success the Association had achieved in getting the media on its side. The letter went on to suggest that 'blacklegging' was justified because it would help the NUT: "Voluntary activities are voluntary and a member need not be ashamed to take over a voluntary duty from which an NAS member has withdrawn."

It was known that there were different opinions within the NUT. The NE Regional Official tried to justify scabbing when he claimed that "in a large measure, this dispute is directed against the NUT and all that it stands for. Therefore it is rather presumptuous for the NAS to take it for granted that the canons of normal industrial relations have got to be observed in this particular instance."

The NAS was not in a position to know what, if anything, had been agreed between the NUT and Durham. However, the following week's developments included teachers being approached to take 'third session' classes for examination students at 24s. 6d. per hour. Such work was advertised throughout the County, although very few teachers responded.

Four more headmasters were suspended for "obstructing staff in the collection of school meals money". The LEA then had to "suspend the suspension of the suspension" in the case of Ralph Jackson. Teachers from other unions were sent in to replace those suspended. One NAS deputy head and three NAS teachers were suspended for refusing to work with these 'blacklegs'. Durham sent an NUT member to take over the class of an NAS teacher at Chopwell School. Acting headmaster, Barry Johnson, refused to allow the teacher into the school and was immediately suspended.

The Newcastle Journal of 29 April reported that attitudes had "hardened on both sides". Durham was prepared to sack the NAS teachers; Bill Gladstone said the NAS was willing to widen the strikes to involve all 800 members.

Sixty-three of the suspended NAS members were given notice of dismissal to take effect from 6 May, unless they returned to normal work. In a surprise but very welcome development the NUT disowned its local representatives, issuing on 5 May a statement saying it would not stand idly by and see 63 teachers dismissed. In all the six schools concerned the majority of NUT members were prepared to strike, with or without official backing from their union. Some NUT members shared the concerns of the NAS about the dreadful salary position, the original cause of the dispute, as well as the overreaction of the LEA.

The NAS decided to respond to the latest challenge thrown down by the LEA by escalating the action and calling out all members in Durham on another half-day strike. Another wise decision was made to establish a Liaison Committee with the men suspended to maintain morale and channel their energies in positive ways. Spouses were included as well and invited along to meetings and social functions. A "Freedom Press" was launched giving blow-by-blow accounts of developments as they occurred. Passed to HQ, these were then sent out to Local Association Secretaries all over the country producing countless messages of sympathy, support and material help. The suspended members formed a 'Have time, will travel brigade' voyaging all over the country to bring their stories first-hand to well-attended meetings of local associations. The whole Association became involved and well briefed.

Besides the leadership of Bill Gladstone the suspended members also had unstinting support from other Officers of the NAS Durham Representative Council (DRC), notably Secretary Tom Kilkenny, together with the Chester-le-Street Secretary Ned Selkirk as well as the two National Executive Members Harry Gardner and Colin McInnes. The Bishop Auckland Secretary, Peter Matthews who went on to become NASUWT President in 1984, was one of the first group of members suspended from Milton Hall Secondary School on 14 February.

The decision of the Executive on 3 May to ask every member to pay a £2 levy for the next three months was facilitated by this unprecedented co-operative activity between many schoolmasters across the country. All the excluded men received full reimbursement of their net pay. The levy, designed to top up the Sunderland (sustentation) Fund, also sent a message to the Durham LEA that the NAS financial reserves were virtually inexhaustible for this purpose.

The success of the NAS in winning the public relations battle was again illustrated by the events in the village of Highfield. It was the home of Sydney Henderson, a suspended member and also the extremely popular headmaster of the village school. The parents called a meeting to demand his reinstatement. The village hall was packed to overflowing. Bill Gladstone and Syd addressed the meeting. Councillor Peter Hepburn, on record advocating "sacking the lot", was invited to present the LEA's case. Pandemonium broke out when he rose to speak. Despite the pleadings from Bill (and Syd) that he be heard, the meeting would have none of it and the councillor was shouted down and turfed out of the hall. The following day's *Journal* splashed the headline "Councillor howled down by parents".

On 6 May the NUT GS, Sir Ronald Gould, made the welcome statement that his union would 'black' any vacancies caused by the dismissal of NAS members.

On the same day Alderman Joseph Goodwin illustrated Durham's legal predicament when he said 'suspended' teachers would have to reapply for their jobs. He went on: "We are no longer the employers but we have not sent their cards back yet, although legally we have to. We will not as yet advertise the jobs or take steps to replace them."

On 6 May another mass meeting in the Palladium was addressed by Terry Casey. It was an angry meeting with 63 suspended members under sentence of dismissal. However, the Action Committee had only presented a motion deploring the action of the Durham LEA. The meeting demanded immediate strike action:

"In order to impress the Authority with the sense of bitterness and indignation which our members feel, NAS men in the County Service will not be in school tomorrow [7 May]."

The meeting also resolved that further escalation would follow to involve an equal additional number of members working to rule to those dismissed. It was decided to hold back publication of this information for a little while.

After the meeting Terry Casey, together with the Action Committee, visited County Hall. After some uncharacteristic warmth exchanging formalities at the beginning of the meeting, the atmosphere froze when Terry Casey informed the Chairman that strike action had been extended. The Chairman was "almost speechless with anger" according to witnesses. Furthermore Terry Casey warned the Chairman that unless talks were conducted in a realistic manner, the militant action would be further escalated.

On 7 May the five suspended headmasters and the deputy were represented by Terry Casey before the Education Committee. The 'sentences of dismissal' were deferred to allow the talks planned for 9 May to begin, another little sign that Durham was beginning to come round. When the talks began the open hostility of previous encounters had abated. The Chairman, Joseph Goodwin, was even persuaded publicly to withdraw certain press statements he had made, including the prejudicial claims (issued before the relevant disciplinary hearings) that the five headmasters would be dismissed and the 63 suspended teachers would have to reapply for any post that interested them in the future.

Progress was made on 9 May with the LEA agreeing on a provisional basis to three of the NAS's seven demands, but the key question of restitution of salary to suspended members remained unresolved. Talks resumed on 13 May but no progress was made. The regulations were on the NAS's side, clearly indicating that teachers reinstated after suspension had to receive their salaries in full. Obviously that was difficult for the LEA to swallow. Durham also felt constrained by the pending NUT Easington case in which moneys deducted were being reclaimed through the courts.

The Education Committee suggested the suspended teachers return to work normally and a court decision be obtained. That was impossible for the NAS to accept given its stand on deductions of pay for refusal to perform voluntary 'duties', not to mention that it would fly in the face of the regulations which required reinstated teachers to be paid.

A series of complicated manoeuvres then followed concerning conciliation, rejected by the LEA, to arbitration, rejected by the NAS. The latter option was rejected in light of the suggestion that Ted Short be the arbitrator.

On 14 May the AGM of the Durham Education Committee saw Councillor T.P.S. Prudham take over the chairmanship from Alderman Goodwin. The meeting decided to involve the Secretary of State and two emissaries were dispatched to London. Durham also entered correspondence with the Minister, in effect pleading for help in sorting out the mess over meals money and other matters.

At this stage the ever-active parents in Chester-le-Street wrote to the Prime Minister, Harold Wilson, asking him to intervene. There were newspaper reports at the end of May indicating that the parents were threatening to withhold the attendance of their children from school – a pupil/parent strike.

Despite the support of Ted Short for attempts to secure Department of Employment conciliation they broke down when the senior official concerned, after consulting both sides, immediately concluded he would have no choice but to uphold the clearly stated regulations.

On 30 May the NAS Officers travelled to Durham to meet with the Action Committee. In the light of the refusal over conciliation and the expressed reluctance of Ted Short to intervene 'unless the service was threatened with disruption' they decided to escalate action to bring the dispute to a speedy end with another ten schools taking the action. Over 10,000 schoolchildren would have their education seriously disrupted.

Fifty-three more schoolmasters were suspended from county schools and another 36 from RC voluntary schools, bringing the total to over 170. *The Newcastle Journal* headlined: "County Schools on brink of breakdown."

On 13 June another attempt at conciliation failed but the NAS responded positively to the Department of Employment's suggestion of a Court of Inquiry subject to the findings not being binding upon the parties.

Fearful of parental action in the courts the Durham Authority wrote to the Secretary of State to check if it had acted reasonably in not paying the teachers. Ted Short's answer was as guarded as could be, but gave the game away all the same. One of his civil servants replied on his behalf:

"He is satisfied that, in refusing to pay the teachers, the Authority have not acted in the exercise of a power conferred, or in the performance of a duty imposed, by the Education Acts."

On 17 June the Education Committee delivered an ultimatum to the NAS. Either be bound by the findings of arbitration or any inquiry established by Government or the offer of a return to employment of the suspended teachers will be withdrawn. The Association was given until 7 July to respond. The NAS

GS immediately wrote to Durham rejecting the ultimatum. Others pointed out the futility of such an ultimatum, bearing in mind no such inquiry had been established.

On 18 and 19 June after a series of meetings between the RC authorities and the LEA and also separately with the NAS, 35 members in the four voluntary RC schools recently introduced into the action were suspended. That brought the number to nearly 200, including some UWT members, although the LEA, for the well-understood reasons, deemed 41 suspended and the rest "excluded", all without pay.

On 25 June the Durham Authority retreated from its 17 June threat pending a decision by the Government on an inquiry. There were rumours that the Ministers had been angered by the LEA's ultimatum of 17 June, believing it was prejudicial to the setting up of an inquiry.

So the dispute continued into July, with just three weeks of term left. On 2 July when Terry Casey was holding a meeting of all the excluded/suspended members, he received a telephone call to hear the news that Barbara Castle and Ted Short, respectively Secretaries of State for Employment and Education, were jointly to sponsor an inquiry.

After the evening's social event, in which their spouses had joined the members concerned, Terry Casey and the Action Committee got down to hammering out a response to the day's development. They debated vigorously until well past midnight. The parents had piled on their pressure for both parties to compromise in the interests of the children.

The decision was not unanimous but a press statement was issued to welcome the independent inquiry. Furthermore, as a gesture of goodwill, the NAS Action Committee was instructing suspended members in the four primary and four voluntary secondary schools engaged in action to return to school on 8 July to resume normal working the following day.

The statement also said: "NAS was prepared to instruct its members at the 14 county secondary schools to return to duty if the LEA reinstated them without penalty of any kind." *The Journal's* Education Correspondent, David Curry, a future Conservative MP and Minister, reported that was "a clever move to pre-empt the findings of the Inquiry and if the Authority accepted it, the Inquiry would be redundant before it met".

Not surprisingly the LEA turned the NAS offer down, but the RC authorities accepted it, despite pressure from Durham to do otherwise. The return of the NAS members on 8 July to these RC schools did not unfortunately go without hitches. Most spent the day still technically suspended but making arrangements to resume normal work the following day as planned. Lines of communication had become crossed, and NAS members walked back out at one school and at another they were not allowed in! It took until 14 July to straighten matters out.

By then the Court of Inquiry was under way under the direction of Dr Bill (later Lord) McCarthy, a well-known and respected expert on industrial relations who was also trusted in union circles. The Court sat for two days taking evidence from both sides. Terry Casey spoke for the NAS; J.T. Brockbank, Clerk to Durham County Council, represented the Authority.

The McCarthy Report was published on 22 August 1969. It concluded the central nub of the dispute lay in the question of payment for the period of suspension. It was unequivocal in its judgment. The decision to suspend the teachers had been unjustified. They should be paid for the period of their exclusion. The report did not accept that the NAS action had been a work to rule as customarily understood. Both sides were criticised on other points and offered advice on how to improve relations.

Instead of using the report to move towards a settlement, the County Clerk Brockbank embarked upon a war of words in the media, claiming the NAS had been placed in a predicament and would have to admit the error of its ways before the Authority would pay any money. The Authority would pay from the day teachers returned but any retrospection would be dependent upon the NAS accepting the report.

Displaying far greater wisdom and restraint, Bill Gladstone sought to play down controversy over interpretations of the report, although he had to criticise the behaviour of Brockbank in issuing inflammatory statements. Thanks largely to Brockbank claiming 'victory' the NAS Officers, arriving in Durham on 28 August, had some difficulty persuading the Action Committee that if 'victory' were anywhere it was with the NAS. There comes a stage in disputes of this kind when bellowing "Victory!" from on high makes it more difficult to secure and retain. The report had declared the suspensions wrong and clearly recommended reinstatement with full pay. The vital principle at stake, the right to take official union action without being disciplined, had been upheld by the Inquiry.

The NAS debate went on, once again, well past midnight. The Association's representatives were due to meet the Durham Authority the following morning. Eventually it was agreed that the NAS would accept the terms of the report. A joint statement was in preparation which proposed to focus solely on the recommendations made to each party to the dispute.

The NAS accepted the Inquiry's judgment that the tactics of refusing to teach oversized classes and cover for absent staff "was not a work to rule in the customary sense"; that "such tactics are not suited to the advancement of stable joint relationships in the teaching profession" and that it would "very willingly enter into the closest consultations with the Durham Authority with a view to improving joint relationships".

The Durham Authority for its part agreed "that in the light of the acceptance of these views by the NAS" its action in 'excluding' teachers "on the grounds of alleged breach of contract was unsuitable as a means of seeking to discipline teachers" and it acknowledged that the best method for dealing with these questions was "through the provisions of the existing National Collective Agreement".

Crucially, Durham further accepted that "in the case of teachers so far 'excluded' they should be reinstated under the terms of the Agreement and paid for the period of exclusion". Durham also agreed "to take the initiative in entering into consultation with the NAS with a view to improving joint relationships".

The measure of the concession made by the LEA was the payment of £90,000 in salary restitution. The NAS's concession was not to argue the precise terms of the statement. The money was paid directly to the NAS since the members had been fully reimbursed for loss of salary from the Association's sustentation fund. The NAS used the money to purchase its first regional centre at Washington in the County of Durham. Subsequently Colin McInnes was appointed Regional Official and was based at the centre.

The Chairman of the Education Committee was later to issue a statement saying: "We have not been looking for success or defeat. We are glad it is all over. Both sides have had to make concessions and this was the only way that the decision could be reached."

The final encounter took place at 10.30 a.m. on Friday 29 August in the fine surroundings of the Durham County Hall. The place was swarming with members of the press. The atmosphere heavy with drama as the NAS representatives filed in.

The NAS was then handed a copy of the proposed Joint Statement. Apart from one very minor amendment the NAS immediately indicated acceptance. While the face of Brockbank raged with anger, the Education Committee fell into stunned silence and relief until a 'still small voice' from their number cried out:

"Is this the end? Is it finished?"

From the NAS GS Terry Casey came: "Yes".

Postscript to Durham

A journalist who rejoiced in the name of Gordon Bennett writing in *Education and Training* in October 1969, passed judgement on the NAS. I quote liberally from his article even though some of his judgements, although always interesting, were very harsh and wrong. However, warts and all, I believe it was a very perceptive evaluation of the tactics the NAS employed and an accurate assessment of Terry Casey, its GS from 1963 to 1983.

"The NAS has won a significant victory in Durham, and [its] nature demonstrates just how primitive is the state of relations between teachers and their employers. The NAS has simply taught a local authority that it cannot do just as it pleases within the formal limitations of the law but must seek some moral authority for its actions. This is a lesson [that other teachers] have notably failed to teach [other LEAs].

"Although the NAS is in some respects a political and educational monstrosity its leaders think at a level above all the other unions about the strategy and tactics of direct action and the schoolmasters have the great advantage over the NUT that they do not embark on action with many of their leaders more scared of success than failure. The recent action has the hallmark of their general secretary, Terry Casey. He is the outstanding leader produced by the teachers during the past decade and in other circumstances he would perhaps have been the natural successor to Ronald Gould as the leader of the profession.

"Casey understands two important principles of industrial strife: the necessity to hit the enemy hard where he is weak and the necessity of progressively developing strength and enthusiasm through success. He also has in abundance the one essential ingredient of leadership – the personal courage to stand alone against the howls and derision of the lesser figures who confront him.

"When the NAS launched its 'work to rule' it entertained no quibble about whether its opponents were the government, the authorities or the NUT. It selected a limited number of its strong points for action. When one authority reacted stupidly, the NAS quickly cut its losses with the others – even to the point of accepting humiliating terms of settlement – and concentrated all its power on this one authority. The assertion of power consisted not merely in bringing the whole national organisation into action in Durham, but also involving the national membership as much as possible and in raising morale and enthusiasm among its members in Durham by persuading them that they were the front line for the whole profession, with the solid support of thousands of their colleagues throughout the country. It all sounds easy enough, but it is not understood in Hamilton House [HQ of the NUT]."

Chapter 42 - Sacred Heart School – Teeside Dispute 1972-75

The Teesside County Borough (CB) came into being in 1968 when Middlesbrough CB was merged with a number of towns in north Yorkshire and Durham. Three 'waves' of secondary reorganisation in the wake of the Labour Government's Circular 10/65 on comprehensive schooling were to be implemented.

While the local NAS welcomed the educational aspects of the reorganisation serious differences soon developed over staffing matters. As a result of other disputes the previous (Labour) Government had legislated in 1968 to clarify the point that a single school undergoing reorganisation did not formally have to be closed before becoming comprehensive. Unfortunately Teesside decided against the view of the NAS, but with the apparent support of all the other unions, that every school should be closed, then immediately reopened as 'new' and all staff would have to reapply for 'their own jobs'.

On top of that, in 1969 the Teesside Education Committee adopted a policy barring non-graduates from holding head of department posts at Scale B* and above. NAS protests were overridden. (*After the arbitral award of 1971 Scale 3 replaced HoD 'B'.)

The first wave of reorganisations in the Billingham area had already exposed serious anomalies and injustice. On some occasions 'nil shortlists' of local candidates appeared and the jobs were then advertised nationally. Some 'applicants' not found worthy of interview for Scale 4 and 5 posts nevertheless secured more-senior positions in neighbouring LEAs as they scrambled to escape from trouble in Teesside.

NAS demanded 1: an end to the graduate bar; 2: an undertaking that reorganisation would not be used to demote teachers without clear evidence of incompetence; and 3: agreement on the criteria for filling posts and appointment procedures. Alas, that was all to no avail. The Teesside Schoolmasters then involved their national organisation, seeking advice and support. GS Terry Casey visited Teesside, met with the LEA and supported the demand for an end to the graduate bar and better security of tenure. Unfortunately no progress proved possible. The policies dictated by the LEA played a major role in provoking the dispute.

The Sacred Heart RC School in Teesside was reorganised on 1 September 1972 from a Group 8, 11-16 secondary modern to a Group 9, 11-16 comprehensive. No other school was involved in the reorganisation.

All staff had to reapply for their jobs. Joseph Faye, a teacher of over 20 years experience, 14 in the school, seven as deputy head, was the only senior member of staff not to be reappointed. This was despite very good testimonials, including one from the current headteacher, and having been shortlisted and interviewed albeit unsuccessfully for the then vacant headship. Joe Faye was offered a Scale 3 post and the deputy headship was advertised locally and nationally. Another NAS member, Noel Thirlaway, previously on Scale 3, was moved down to a Scale 1 post to make room for Joe Faye.

Representations were made to the governors who pleaded they had acted upon LEA advice that Joe Faye not be appointed. It appeared that Joe Faye was another victim of the graduate-only bar. In time the bar was to be revoked, but far too late to avoid this dispute developing. Chairman of Governors, Monsignor Canon O'Sullivan, said: "The NAS fight is with the LEA, not us." Terry Casey told him: "You are the employer, not the LEA. [It was a voluntary school.] Unless you keep Mr Faye as Deputy we are in dispute with you." The governors decided to stick with LEA policy.

With a strong suspicion of victimisation because of individuals' involvement in NAS and UWT action in the North East in 1969, early in October 1972 members in the school were instructed to work to contract in support of Joe Faye and Noel Thirlaway. NAS and UWT teachers were then harassed and intimidated and walked out in protest as a consequence. A UWT member and senior mistress in the school had pressure placed upon her to undertake lunchtime supervision, which was clearly voluntary. Another member had been instructed to take a class of 80 pupils.

On 6 October GS Terry Casey led another deputation to the LEA to discuss the issues of the graduate bar and security of tenure. No progress proved possible, with the LEA flatly refusing to move on both issues. Consequently all NAS and UWT members in Teesside were instructed to work to contract. Considerable disruption followed.

Discussions with the governors revealed that colleagues of Joe Faye were provoked to walk out "by the explosive situation at the school" caused by harassment. Although the governors were anxious to get the teachers back into school "without penalty of any kind" the LEA officials would not co-operate regarding loss of salary and pension rights. The NAS and UWT declared themselves in dispute with both; the dispute in the school was "indistinguishable from that with the LEA".

Despite further talks between Terry Casey, the governors and the LEA, by December the dispute was deadlocked. The NAS offered arbitration or conciliation, initially to be refused by the LEA. However, public opinion forced the LEA to conciliation. Unfortunately that led nowhere, with the LEA even refusing to meet the unions face to face unless the UWT was left outside the room. Terry Casey could hardly have suspected how understated was his prediction: "We are in for a long, hard and bitter struggle – but will win!"

In the last week of term just before the Christmas holidays, the dispute "blew its top" with an unprecedented series of wholesale suspensions and kangaroo-court sackings. The Teesside LEA brought its own education system into chaos as tens of thousands of secondary school pupils were being sent home or herded into halls without adequate supervision.

The LEA had decided to suspend 156 union members. Headteachers were called to the Education Office on Sunday 10 December to receive their orders. The head was formally to instruct a teacher to take an oversized class and in some cases to teach in underheated rooms (both the subject of union sanctions).

The NAS Teesside President, Ted Johnson, who was also deputy of a large school, was instructed by his headteacher to supervise classes refused by union members because they were overlarge. Other members were also suspended for refusing 'blacked' classes.

A special subcommittee under Chairman Peter Fulton was given plenipotentiary powers by the Authority and on 11 December decided to proceed "with the dismissal of suspended teachers". The teachers were summoned to attend star-chamber hearings before the same subcommittee which had decided to dismiss them. Each teacher was to be considered separately from the rest. Twenty-eight were called for Friday 29 December, 30 for Saturday the 30th, and the remainder equally divided between 2, 3 and 4 January. 'Justice' was not to be delayed, but at least the LEA had the decency to take New Year's Eve and Day off.

The NAS had promised every member a full defence. When the first case came, Chairman Fulton declared that Terry Casey could have no legal assistance, no transcript of the hearing and would not be allowed his own shorthand writer. Several witnesses the GS asked to call were refused by the Chairman. The Chairman did, however, slap down an elderly Conservative member on the committee who thought the GS ought not to waste time taking notes. Obviously not appreciating his legendary ability to develop a case at length, Fulton told Terry Casey: "Take all the time you want."

By 7 p.m. Terry Casey had completed his submissions on behalf of the first member, Keith Howells, who had been called. Exploiting the many and varied sources, not to mention vagueness, of the teacher's contract, Terry had taken the committee on a long tour of natural law, the elements of personal service arrangements, education statutes, statutory instruments and High Court cases, as well as national and local agreements. All 15 points of the NAS and UWT work to contract action could be justified by one or several of these sources. If the

LEA claimed the sanctions infringed the contract, it had an obligation as a statutory authority to go to the Industrial Court to seek redress.

The most eloquent counsel in the land could not have dissuaded the stony-faced subcommittee from proceeding with the LEA's declared intention to dismiss. After a short recess the committee informed Keith Howells he was sacked forthwith.

The Teesside NAS President, Ted Johnson, was one of the few who had a 'hearing'. He complained that he was embarrassed to be addressing a tribunal where one lady was manifestly in a deep sleep, one man was doing a crossword and another studying a catalogue.

At subsequent hearings members were similarly defended by AGS Bernard Wakefield and Assistant Secretary George Limburn, as well as by Terry Casey. The LEA posted no order in which the hearings were to take place each day, just expecting teachers to turn up and wait up to ten hours. Many NAS members simply had to leave the building to attend to important family and other duties as the hours rolled by. After hearings lasting five days, seven teachers had been dismissed. All the others were then dismissed without a hearing.

The scene then moved to London. Teesside LEA announced it had requested to see DES officials but was not asking for intervention. However, the following afternoon the Permanent Secretary at the DES, Sir William Pile, asked to see Terry Casey to give him the picture from the association's perspective. Terry learnt that Education Secretary Mrs Thatcher was very concerned about the dispute and the damage to pupils' education. Consequently the Secretary of State for Employment was considering setting up a Committee of Inquiry on the same lines as the one chaired by Bill McCarthy which had investigated the NAS – Durham Dispute of 1969.

Bill Pile asked Terry what terms the NAS would expect in return for a resumption of normal working pending the outcome of the proposed inquiry. Terry said the NAS would welcome an inquiry and would recommend a full return to normal working with co-operation, providing the LEA rescinded all penalties imposed on NAS and UWT members.

The next day both sides were brought back to London to the Department of Employment for attempts at conciliation which failed. The senior conciliation officer spent just one hour with the NAS but five times as long with the Teesside LEA.

The NAS position accepted a return to the 'status quo ante' which therefore had to mean no penalties on members. The LEA bizarrely insisted that those teachers still only suspended could be reinstated without penalty but those who had been dismissed (with or without a hearing) could only be re-engaged without restitution. The NAS rejected this monstrous and invidious suggestion which was also contrary to the Industrial Relations Act, which outlawed discriminatory treatment.

By January 1973 a Committee of Inquiry had been set up by the Government under the chairmanship of Professor (later Sir) John Wood of Sheffield University who was assisted by Sir Harry Page and Mr S. Hewett. It met in London for three days early in February. Its terms of reference were to inquire into the causes and circumstances surrounding the dispute. The NAS and UWT made a conciliatory move in lifting sanctions.

An initial meeting (19 January) with all the parties took place to establish arrangements to apply during the course of the Inquiry. Drawing on the precedent set by the Durham Inquiry in 1969 a draft agreement was reached which would enable all Teesside members, including those at the Sacred Heart School, to return to normal working on Monday 24 January. However, Joe Faye would proceed immediately to leave of absence. Those teachers dismissed would be paid for their period under suspension.

On 24 January 1973 Terry Casey addressed the Committee of Inquiry for over four hours, contrasting the LEAs that had carried through reorganisations smoothly with the turbulence in Teesside. Following the 1968 Act it was no longer necessary to close a single school subject to reorganisation. The 'graduates only' rule for any post above Scale 3 was bizarre, unjust and had been used to victimise local NAS leaders who had played prominent roles in militant action over pay in 1969. For example, Jim Bore, the Teesside NAS Treasurer, also head of an important department in a large secondary school, had been recommended on four occasions by his headmaster for promotion from Scale 3 to 5 but rejected by the LEA because he was not a graduate.

Terry Casey questioned the competence of the LEA in selecting its heads and teachers in the first place. Secondary reorganisation had resulted in 13 headteachers out of 37 and 18 deputies out of 36 not being re-designated in their posts after the first round of appointments. Why was this "professional massacre" necessary? asked Terry. At the same time Terry ridiculed the LEA arrangements for the dismissal hearings, which breached natural justice and every agreed procedure in sight.

Jim Bore was called as a witness and described the arrangements made by the LEA as "a prescription for a dispute". All the unions had urged the LEA to lift the graduate bar, which had already produced much bitterness in the first wave of reorganisations in the Billingham area. Twenty-three teachers in four schools had been demoted. For some posts there had been a "nil shortlist" of internal applicants.

After Joe Faye had appeared as a witness insisting he had never been informed that his work was unsatisfactory, the Chairman indicated that there was no question of him being inefficient in his old job and the Committee regarded him as a suitable candidate for the 'new' post.

Terry Casey also called Tom Smith, an NAS Past-President but also a headmaster with considerable experience of comprehensive reorganisation. Tom Smith testified that there would be no dramatic and sudden changes in organisation and educational practice which would rule out non-graduates being able to teach all relevant courses up to GCE O Level.

During the course of evidence from the LEA and Sacred Heart management personnel, the Chairman made it plain he was deeply disturbed with the dismissal hearings. The Town Clerk said the LEA had taken the power of dismissal away from the Sacred Heart governors for reasons of "consistency" but he was unable to express a view about the suspensions and had played no part in them.

The Director of Education for Teesside, Mr Mason, denied responsibility for the graduate bar. However, he had previously been Director in Middlesbrough, the only constituent of the new Teesside Authority which had such a bar applying across the profession. (Durham had such a bar only for headteacher posts.) Mr Mason claimed he had "inherited" the bar. Terry Casey retorted: "You inherited your own inheritance."

Under cross-examination by Terry Casey, the LEA Chairman, Peter Fulton, admitted that he had denied him information on who was present at the dismissal hearings. Fulton also admitted denying the right to call several witnesses. Responding to allegations from Casey that the LEA wanted to dismiss all teachers appearing before the Committee for "consistency" and to avoid looking "silly" if the hearings resulted in reinstatement, Councillor Fulton made the extraordinary claim that "they treated each case individually", even though the great majority had been dismissed without a hearing.

Terry Casey forced Fulton to admit that he had on several occasions referred to the NAS as a "disgrace to trade unionism". He had also alleged that the NAS was "leading Teesside teachers astray" and that "Terry Casey was concerned with scoring points off the NUT".

Giving his evidence, the Chairman of the Sacred Heart governors, Monsignor Canon O'Sullivan, claimed that unless the change to comprehensive was "something fundamental the public had been conned". It had to be a new school. He blamed the "very late" go-ahead from the DES on reorganisation for the 'old' staff still being in post at the date of the changeover and assuming their positions were safe. The governors then proceeded to appoint staff "in the light of the LEA's procedure document".

The Canon said he was unable to give a complete answer to the question why Joe Faye was not appointed. He denied the governors were overruled by the

LEA officers present, "but the two men gave us advice." The Canon conceded the governors "were in an awkward dilemma"; their decision would be very public and "it could look like a demotion. We did not discuss the matter at length, we took a private ballot."

The headteacher, Mr Trueman, denied all knowledge of the alleged intimidation. He acknowledged Joe Faye had his "confidence and was a fit person to join the management team". There was a conflict of evidence over the consultation that had taken place with the staff over the new structures.

Professor Wood asked Mr Trueman if he had positively recommended Joe Faye for the post in his report to the governors. Trueman said he gave "a general picture". It emerged, however, that his report was not in writing, but only oral. His written report had been sent to the LEA. One of the LEA's advisers present admitted he compiled a report from it. Professor Wood asked if he had made a positive recommendation one way or the other. The adviser replied: "It just said the Governors might like to consider the following about Mr Faye." Professor Wood said he attached "great importance to reports made by superiors being untouched by anyone else".

Trueman and the adviser, Mr Milbourne, were both asked if they gave Faye reasons why he was not appointed. Milbourne said he could not answer but he gave advice. Trueman denied that he told Faye "that it was in the field of qualifications that he fell short". Terry Casey countered: "Mr Faye states quite categorically that you did."

Two representatives from the NUT gave evidence. The NUT objected to the graduate bar but supported the LEA's procedure of 'closure' and forcing all teachers to reapply for their jobs. (On the latter point here was a sharp difference of opinion with the NAS and UWT, who believed it unnecessary to put all teachers through such agony.)

The NUT conceded that morale was very low and they had contemplated strike action after the Billingham reorganisations, adding "nowhere has there been so much trouble". The NUT believed the procedure agreement was satisfactory but that it required "goodwill and trust", which, it appeared from their comments, were absent.

The AMA gave evidence through their GS Andrew Hutchings who also spoke for the three other Associations in the Joint Four. He supported the NUT on the LEA's closure procedures. He did not state a position on the graduate bar. (AMA members were mostly graduates.)

A Mr A. Taylor appeared for the NAHT and supported the LEA's procedures. He denied Terry Casey's allegation that headteachers "were the henchmen of the authority". But asked if he was satisfied that the reports his members wrote were "being used by someone else to compile their reports", he replied: "This is a naughty one, but I can say I am not satisfied."

In their summing up Terry Casey and the LEA representatives clashed over the question of the teacher's contract. Casey claimed the NAS and UWT work to rule was not a breach of contract but if it were the Authority had recourse to the Industrial Relations Court to seek redress.

After sitting for five days the Wood Committee finished taking evidence on 29 January 1973. The Report was published later in February. Wood recommended that the governors of the Sacred Heart School should "honour their pledge" to consider Mr Faye as "a serious candidate" for the deputy headship. If they appoint him the problem will disappear but if they do not they must provide a post "of such seniority and status as to recognise and use his ability, experience and knowledge arising from his long service to the school. The post must obviously be of status near to that of deputy headmaster."

Wood also recommended that all the sackings had to be rescinded without loss of pay or service and that the teachers who walked out of the school be deemed to have been on strike. Wood recommended that the UWT be recognised for purposes of taking part in negotiations on secondary reorganisation in Teesside.

The Wood Report contained criticism of both parties to the dispute. The Committee sided with the LEA on the issue of formally closing every school being reorganised before opening the new one, citing the NAS and UWT being alone in opposition. Both sides were criticised for attitudes of "mutual suspicion and mistrust".

However, the NAS was very satisfied with the overall 'verdict' which it felt fully justified the stand it had taken on the facts of the case relevant to the individuals most affected. Furthermore the NAS felt completely vindicated on Wood's findings regarding assessment, appointment and promotion procedures, which all required urgent national attention. Teesside's assessment procedures had "several fundamental weaknesses" and were "markedly unsatisfactory". The Committee's view that the education service lacked genuine negotiating procedures was music to NAS ears.

On the vexed issue of industrial action Wood declared that whilst it raised "fundamental difficulties . . . it would be wrong to conclude that teachers do not have or do not want to have the right to take industrial action". Commenting on the unions' sanctions Wood concluded that some "have been recognised in the courts as a justifiable exercise of teachers' rights", whilst others "were they tested in a court of law would in all probability be determined to be breaches of contract".

The proof of the pudding was to be found in the eating. Over the course of the next two years the NAS and UWT were constantly to encounter almost intractable difficulties getting the LEA and the school to implement the findings of the Wood Inquiry.

It took until the end of March to secure a meeting between the NAS, UWT and the Teesside LEA. The LEA claimed it could not implement many of Wood's recommendations because they would be incompatible with their existing arrangements and other unions' views. Teesside was not prepared to grant the limited recognition recommended for the UWT without the approval of the other unions. The NAS concluded in its April 1973 Report to Schools that "it looks as if our differences have not been resolved".

Back at the Sacred Heart School, Joe Faye duly reapplied for the deputy headship. He was interviewed along with John Fullam and three other candidates, one of whom was an NAS member returning from overseas, unaware of the dispute. The two others were ineligible because they were not members of the Catholic Church. Joe Faye was not appointed. He was later offered a Scale 5 post. The governors claimed it was the post 'nearest to deputy' as recommended by Wood and they had given 'serious consideration' to Mr Faye's application.

The NAS harboured serious reservations that the governors had acted in accordance with Wood. Examination of the offer, Senior Upper School Tutor, revealed that it was in reality a dressed-up version of the same old Scale 3 post originally awarded to Joe Faye but paid at Scale 5. A Scale 3 post was nowhere "near" to the deputyship as recommended by Wood, bearing in mind the hierarchy ran from Scales 1, 2, 3, 4, 5, senior teacher, deputy, to headship. In May 1973 the NAS instructed Joe Faye not to accept the offer of Senior Upper School Tutor in the light of 'all the information' that had come to hand.

'All the information' also included dramatic if delicate material that had surfaced in the local press. It led Terry Casey to comment publicly that the man appointed as deputy was "not a fit person" for the post in an RC school. It showed the governors were determined to appoint anyone but Joe Faye. Challenged to justify that comment in a libel case, Terry Casey successfully defended his comments when the case was finally heard some seven years after the event.

At Conference in 1973 the stalwarts from Teesside were afforded a hero's welcome. The Conference unanimously carried a motion congratulating all concerned and "pledging unqualified support for any further measures the Executive might deem necessary to bring about the implementation of the recommendations of the Wood Report".

The NAS and UWT gave due and proper notice under the terms of the Industrial Relations Act that unless the findings of the Wood Inquiry were properly implemented members at the school would go on indefinite strike from the beginning of the Autumn Term.

In June 1973 the Teesside LEA Chairman and CEO met with the local UWT about the recognition recommended by Wood. Teesside provocatively suggested the NAS surrender one of its two seats on the Working Party on School Re-organisation to the UWT. Both the NAS and UWT flatly rejected such a negative and hostile proposal which was completely outwith the spirit if not the letter of the Wood Report.

The NAS AGS, Bernard Wakefield, met with the governors on 6 July to see if some accommodation could be found, but without success. At 8.45 a.m. on the first day of the Autumn Term, the recently appointed Regional Official for the North East, former NEC Member Colin McInnes, made a final but unsuccessful attempt to persuade the Chairman of Governors to agree to negotiation. The all-out strike began and continued all through the term. The NAS's offer to go to arbitration was rejected.

The TUC was requested to support and responded magnificently. The Redcar and Middlesbrough Trades Councils organised a very effective 'blockade' of the school. By October 1973 several suppliers of important services and goods, such as fuel and the post, refused to cross the NAS and UWT picket line which had been mounted day after day, night after night, at the gates of the school.

There were some bizarre incidents connected to the picket line, for which the NAS purchased a minibus to assist members and provide some protection against cold and inclement weather. One night an emergency call was made by a picket to local association leaders calling for assistance. An ambulance had appeared and been driven through the gates. It transpired that it was an elaborate plot to break the picket line and import much-needed oil and other vital supplies to keep the school running. Two prominent NAS antagonists were behind the move. On another occasion, a serious oil leak occurred. It might have been due to a lack of expertise in such 'refuelling operations'. It was later to be discovered that the headmaster himself had worked hard at personally carrying out many tasks to try to keep the school operating as normal. He was even operating the school's boilers. On several occasions the police were called to maintain the 'peace' – such as it was.

The TUC Regional Councils organised a mass march and protest in Redcar on Saturday 26 January 1974. They issued joint literature with the NAS and UWT, asking members of the public to use whatever influence they had with the governors to get them to abandon their anti-trade union attitude and agree to arbitration. The march was extremely well supported with many union members travelling far from distant parts of the country to support their colleagues in Teesside.

The National Executive Members, respectively Phil West for the NAS and Marjory Nightingale for the UWT, backed up by neighbouring comrades from surrounding districts in the persons of Harry Gardner and Peter Matthews, gave unstinted support and advice throughout this long and bitter dispute. Shortly after the General Election of February 1974, through NAS HQ they circulated every NAS and UWT representative in 21,000 schools throughout the country urging them to lobby the Prime Minister (now Harold Wilson once again), the Secretary of State for Employment, their MPs and RC authorities (especially the Bishop of Middlesbrough).

By this time some 85,000 children in the North East had the release of their CSE examination results blocked by the NAS and UWT action. Volunteer union pickets visited the Sacred Heart School from all parts of the country to provide support and relief to the beleaguered strikers.

The school governors consistently refused arbitration and any other kind of third-party involvement. They went even further, stating in a letter to the NAS in February 1974 that they "will not agree to arbitration because we are not prepared to surrender to any third party our fundamental and inalienable right to make decisions affecting the staffing, structure and conduct of the Sacred Heart School".

That was an extraordinary statement. If left unchallenged it implied that the governors of a voluntary school were asserting their right to act outwith any national and local agreements, not to mention statutes, which applied to the entire maintained sector. The statement was also totally inconsistent with the governors' previously proffered excuse of having to abide by the policy of the LEA, such as 'graduates only' for above Scale 3 posts, thereby surrendering some sovereignty – but only of course when it suited.

In the General Election of February 1974 the NAS made fair procedures for assessment, appointment and promotion, as well as individual grievance and collective disputes a key part of the briefing to be raised by members with all Parliamentary candidates. The Sacred Heart governors refused to contemplate any limit on their 'absolute autonomy'. All RC authorities throughout the country were asked to repudiate the Sacred Heart governors' blanket refusal to entertain conciliation or arbitration.

By April 1974 the NAS had extended strike action to four other schools in Teesside. The TUC publicly backed the NAS call for the dispute to go to arbitration. All Trades Councils throughout the North East joined their Redcar and Middlesbrough colleagues in providing practical support to the NAS and UWT.

Terry Casey lobbied the new Labour Secretaries of State for Education and Employment, respectively Reg Prentice and Michael Foot, to intervene. He referred the Ministers to the silly statement repeated by the governors that the strike at the Sacred Heart School had not adversely affected education, which tempted the NAS and UWT to extend the action to make it manifest that it had.

Later in April 1974 Annual Conference rose in its wrath to demand massive militant action to bring the Sacred Heart governors to Department of Employment arbitration. Delegates viewed with grave concern the intransigence of the governors, which constituted a threat to the security of all teachers, especially those serving in voluntary aided schools. Conference gave unanimous support to an urgency motion from the Teesside Association calling for militant action on a national basis so that the burden could be shared by all members rather than resting solely on the shoulders of our colleagues in the school and the LEA.

The Action Committee, recognising that widespread strike action must affect public examinations for some pupils, decided that it would be better to stop the CSE completely in the NE. (Results were still being withheld from the previous year.) That was a huge escalation. We often referred to industrial action against public examinations as our 'nuclear weapon'. One reason for the drastic action was to secure the intervention of a "responsible third party", such as the Secretary of State, to apply pressure on the governors to act reasonably.

The CSE North East Regional Examining Boards were informed of the reasons for the action and asked to apply pressure on the governors and the (newly named) Cleveland LEA to secure arbitration. All members in the North East region were instructed to take no part in the CSE examinations, inside or outside school hours as from Monday 6 May. The NAS stated that if this failed to secure arbitration, further action would follow in June to affect the GCE examinations.

That move proved to be one step too far for many NAS members, especially for those outside the immediate area of the dispute. Some said it was simply too much and the damage inflicted on the pupils too 'permanent and life affecting'. Others claimed the poorly handled publicity was to blame. Somehow the news leaked out while the Executive Members were on their way back to the North East.

To put it frankly, an uncharacteristic rebellion broke out in the ranks of the NAS. Opinions were sharply divided. A broadly acceptable compromise had to be hammered out, which resulted in a modification to the action plan. The CSE exams would go ahead with NAS members participating but the marks and grades would be withheld, as in the previous year. That would avoid permanent damage to the pupils. These sanctions were also extended to the Yorkshire and West Yorkshire Boards.

The watering down of the action involving public examinations produced favourable reactions from many MPs in the north. Although Reg Prentice expressed himself as "powerless to act", many Labour MPs pressed the Minister to intervene and called upon the governors to accept arbitration. Those included the MP for Easington, Jack Dormand, who said he expected Government action within six weeks.

Several LEAs, including Sheffield and Doncaster, now finding their areas affected by NAS action, called on the governors to accept arbitration. Back in Westminster Terry Casey addressed a meeting of the Conservative Parliamentary Education Committee who agreed to press the LEA and governors to accept arbitration. The Catholic Education Council was prevailed upon to rebut the Sacred Heart governors' claim that arbitration was incompatible with the autonomy granted to voluntary aided schools.

Monsignor Canon O'Sullivan, Chairman of Governors, remained adamant. "We stand firm against arbitration", he repeated. His solution was "for the ten teachers on strike to resign and get other jobs". The Teesside *Evening Gazette* commented: "The Monsignor puts this suggestion forward almost jokingly as if he knows the unions would never accept it." The NAS asked when would this "sick joke" end?

There were some suspicions that 'scabbing' was widespread in the school. The NUT said that its membership was larger than the combined NAS and UWT and they had been told only to do their jobs. But Monsignor O'Sullivan was able to muse publicly: "People ask how [the school] can function with 10 teachers outside the gates – the answer is that the head and senior staff are putting in a lot of extra work. We also have 30 dedicated teachers . . . who get little sympathy from the public who seem to support the 'underdogs' – the teachers outside."

There were problems with the Northern, West Yorkshire & Lindsey and Yorkshire Examination Boards, who claimed ownership of the candidates' scripts. Constructive discussions resulted in compromises involving NAS and UWT members withholding the return of scripts and the Boards the release and publication of the results.

The stalemate between the school/LEA and the NAS and UWT continued throughout the rest of 1974, although the new Conciliation and Arbitration Service (CAS – later to become ACAS) established by the Labour Government offered to intervene late in the year following an approach by the NAS in September. The governors rebuffed the approach, saying they were not prepared to alter their original offer to Joe Faye. In a meeting with the CAS Chairman, Jim Mortimer, Terry Casey said the NAS would accept the recall of the Wood Committee or conciliation/arbitration and agree to be bound by the outcome.

At the beginning of 1975 the NAS decided to try a new tack. It might originally have been viewed as a climbdown but it was to have quite dramatic and unexpected results.

With the CAS now established Terry Casey wrote to all relevant parties declaring a collective dispute with the LEA, now Cleveland in the wake of yet more local government reorganisation. Under the agreed procedures in CLEA/ST the refusal of the governors and the LEA to accept conciliation meant the dispute should now be referred to the new national conciliation body under the chairmanship of Sir Alan Bullock. Casey so informed Jim Mortimer, the Chairman of CAS, and also assured him the NAS would revert to the status quo before the dispute broke out.

Accordingly, the NAS instructed its members at the Sacred Heart School to return to work on the first day of the 1975 Spring Term so that immediate steps could be taken to process the dispute. It was not the easiest of decisions to justify to the members but the majority accepted that something different had to be tried. The dispute immediately took on a surprising and dramatic twist when, on return to work after more than two years on strike, NAS members were given no timetables, no classes to teach.

The hatred engendered in the dispute was now clouding people's judgements. Those who had arranged the scabbing were reluctant to change their habits. Perhaps the school was faced with too many 'double salaries' to be paid. By March 1975 the governors, backed by the Chairman of the Cleveland LEA, Councillor Fulton, began dismissing the NAS and UWT members. Their only 'crime' had been to support two of their colleagues who had been unfairly demoted.

The move to dismiss had not come as a surprise to the NAS in the light of the refusal to allocate timetables. The Association immediately swung into action, applying pressure on the school and the LEA through the TUC, MPs and every RC parish priest and bishop throughout the land. There was plenty of evidence to show that, during the strike, additional staff had been brought in and this was the reason for no teaching timetables being allocated to NAS members and the consequential need to sack them as a way of avoiding unsustainable and possibly unauthorised expenditure.

The irony was that the dispute had been so long and bitter that re-entry into the school was proving to be a more effective weapon than remaining outside the gates on the picket line.

On 24 March 1975 the governors considered the dismissal of the returned NAS and UWT strikers. The headmaster, Mr Trueman, made it clear that during the strike he had not included the NAS and UWT members in his timetable, thus stretching the remaining teachers to "breaking point". He said the school's survival was ensured by their extraordinary determination, loyalty and dedication. In fact the dispute had been prolonged as a result of their scabbing. According to the *Evening Gazette*, 27 March, "Mr John Alderson, Northern Regional Official for the NUT, confirmed that 14 of the 34 working teachers were members of the NUT".

NAS and UWT members in Cleveland reacted magnificently. Leaving their classes for the day on 24 March, over 1,200 marched through Redcar, mounted a vigil outside the school, handed a petition to the Chairman of Governors and attended a mass meeting addressed by the NAS Junior Vice-President, Len Cooper, and AGS, Bernard Wakefield.

In the face of so much tremendous trade union pressure and the prospect of more, the governors decided to integrate the returned strikers instead of dismissing them. Headmaster Trueman was flabbergasted and distraught. He refused to integrate the NAS and UWT members as directed by the governors. He went further, issuing a statement to the effect that the governors were incapable of running the school. He claimed that 32 of the school's 34 teachers had passed a vote of no confidence in the governors and demanded the dismissal of the returned strikers.

The governors then suspended Mr Trueman with a view to sacking him. Outside the Sacred Heart Church on Easter Sunday a few days later, a renegade NAS member, who had been promoted during the strike, handed out leaflets which stated: "He [the headmaster] has delivered food to the kitchens, personally organised oil deliveries . . . has spent countless weekends shovelling rubbish to empty the festering dustbins." There was no length to which he would not go to break the strike and "get rid" of NAS and UWT members.

The NAS, in Conference 1975 in Brighton, declared it had no locus in the dispute between Mr Trueman and the governors and had no wish to discuss the matter with other teacher associations. Conference applauded the actions of colleagues in Cleveland and declared its full support to the Executive in its efforts to get the dispute resolved.

As often occurs in such bitter disputes the main protagonists suffered. Mr Trueman, the headmaster, was sacked by the governors in the Summer Term 1975, presumably for failing to implement the decision to reinstate the NAS and UWT members. He must have felt betrayed by them after all his efforts to defeat the strike. However, on appeal to the LEA Trueman was reinstated. Relationships appeared to continue to be strained, and some five years later in

1980 the governors again suspended Trueman, reportedly for failing to obey instructions to attend a meeting. Subsequently the governors dismissed Trueman. The deputy, John Fullam, was appointed Acting Head.

Joe Faye also suffered. The strain of being the individual at the centre of such a long and bitter dispute must have been a terrible burden to carry. Unfortunately Joe ended up making some anonymous and threatening telephone calls to certain individuals. He had been charged by the police, found guilty in court and fined £120 during the course of 1974. While the NAS supported Joe in his defence, he had to pay the fine himself. My understanding is that Joe was offered early retirement which initially he declined. He continued teaching at the school on his protected deputy head's salary for some four years before accepting retirement.

The other major protagonist, the Chairman of Governors, Mgr Canon O'Sullivan, had no occupational risk to bear, although he died within a couple of years of the dispute ending. I am sure Terry Casey's health suffered, especially as the long-running and bitter Durham dispute had taken place a couple of years prior to the Sacred Heart case.

So the dispute ended in rather messy way. The NAS and UWT believed they had no respectable alternative other than to fight the dubious failure to appoint Joe Faye and the deplorable treatment of Noel Thirlaway, an entirely innocent 'bystander'. The NAS and UWT offered ways out through arbitration, which should have been accepted by responsible authorities. Whether so much 'collateral' damage was acceptable in fighting for justice for two individuals is open to debate. However, other crucial issues of principle involved in the outrageous denial of promotion above Scale 3 to non-graduate teachers who already had satisfactory records in higher-level posts and the cavalier sackings of scores of members could not be ignored.

'Pour encourager les autres' the dispute served a good purpose. For many years afterwards the mere mention of 'The Sacred Heart Teesside' when staffing problems loomed over reorganisation was enough to concentrate management minds to treat teachers fairly.

Postscript to the Sacred Heart – Teesside Dispute

The NASUWT, along with many parents of this RC school, were extremely exercised over the circumstances surrounding the candidate for deputy head preferred over Joe Faye. The successful applicant, John Fullam, was an ex-RC priest and had only been in teaching a short time. He had left the Catholic priesthood in 'difficult' circumstances which became controversial in NASUWT and indeed parental circles as the Sacred Heart dispute developed. The local press revealed he had left to marry a woman in a registry office to whom he was giving instruction in the faith as she was engaged to a Catholic man. He was a former member of the NAS. Fullam had also been a colleague of the headmaster, Mr Trueman, at their previous school in Pontefract, Yorkshire. Several NAS Representatives alleged (wrongly as it transpired) there had been collusion between the two in his appointment as deputy in place of Joe Faye.

These issues were to become the subject of libel writs, which were not heard until June/July 1980, some seven years after the events. In the main case that led to a month-long hearing before a jury at Leeds Crown Court, John Fullam failed in his case for libel and slander damages against Terry Casey, The Newcastle Journal and its reporter Susan Durkan. The last named had reported Terry Casey alleging that Fullam was not a fit person for the post of deputy in an RC school in the light of the circumstances in which he left the priesthood.

The case represented a considerable victory for the NASUWT 'legal team'. Fullam had engaged the top libel QC, Richard Hartley, to conduct his case. Mr Hartley did not hold back anything in his attack upon Terry Casey, accusing him of being "a very malicious man, wicked and evil . . . the leader of the dirty tricks brigade". The NASUWT engaged John Peppit, QC, who, despite being less renowned than his esteemed adversary, convinced the jury on a 10 to 1 vote that the defendant's comments were 'fair' and designed not to injure Mr Fullam but to show that the governors would appoint anyone apart from Joe Faye. The judge, Mr Justice Milmo, awarded all costs against Mr Fullam, which were estimated to be in the region of £100,000.

The NASUWT solicitors, Craigen Wilders & Sorrell, were represented by David Haywood, a good friend of the Union who rendered first-class service over a lifetime's work. David believes that the day on which the jury announced its verdict, 2 July 1980, was the most dramatic legal victory of his career.

It was later revealed that The Northern Echo had already paid £1,000 damages to Mr Fullam in another libel action arising from the same dispute.

Although I found no evidence that the model contract of the Catholic Education Council for teachers was raised, it is interesting to note that from time to time cases arose in which staff were dismissed from RC schools for failing to conduct themselves (including their private lives) in accordance the with teachings of the Church. The most common reasons were for 'living in sin' or marrying outside the Church. In those days 'offenders' were often dismissed, in stark contrast to the much more humane treatment afforded to Mr Fullam.

The stress of the ordeal of the 20 days of hearings on all parties prompted a spirit of compromise in the other two cases in which Trueman and Fullam claimed libel in respect of the accusations of collusion. The NASUWT apologised and withdrew the accusations and made out-of-court settlement payments to Trueman and Fullam. The Union did not pursue Fullam for its costs in defending Terry Casey in the main case.

Chapter 43 - The NAS and UWT Merge

In chapter 5 I wrote about the founding of the UWT, in Brighton in 1965, and the breakthrough it proved to be in identifying the needs of the career woman teacher. The powerful 'subtitle' of the NASUWT – "The Career Teachers' Organisation" – would not have been possible without the UWT's birth and quick development as a very significant force in education union affairs.

By January 1970 the UWT had expanded enough to appoint a full-time paid General Secretary (GS), Pennie Yaffe from Manchester. Pennie's real first name was Rosemarie but her nickname, due to her originally being a "slip of a girl" – just a 'pennyworth' – stuck. She was only the second full-time woman GS in the 140 unions then affiliated to the TUC.

Understandably Pennie Yaffe made equality for women one of the central planks of UWT policy and many of the Union's resources were devoted to that cause. Pennie was one of the guests of honour at the annual Women of the Year luncheon held at the Savoy Hotel in London in 1971. Another guest of honour was the Education Secretary, Margaret Thatcher. The UWT was very active in the Status of Women's Annual Conferences and developed close links with the Fawcett Society.

The UWT played a very prominent part in the march and rally in London on 30 June 1971, the day of an all-important Burnham arbitration which was to change the course of history in terms of the profession's salary structure.

In June 1971 a statement was issued by Terry Casey and Pennie Yaffe on behalf of the NAS and UWT respectively. It reviewed the positive developments that had taken place following the Joint Two Agreement and the potential for further advancement of the career teachers' interests. However, the statement went on to say that: "It was not the intention that a mixed organisation shall be established for if this should happen both the UWT and NAS would lose their raison d'être. The two interests, which are separate but not incompatible, can be harmonised to produce the best result for the teaching service."

In reality this statement was designed to paper over some cracks that were appearing in the relationship. The UWT was by far the smaller partner numerically and Pennie Yaffee together with supporters believed that a continuing separate UWT was essential to ensure women played an active part and were not simply dominated by men as in the NUT. Pennie accepted that men would be able to join the UWT if proposed legislation banning discrimination on grounds of sex were enacted. The 'separatists' were right to identify the problem of low female participation but their solution posed a greater risk of rivalry producing a 'Dis-Jointed Two'. The NAS viewed the statement as a holding operation to keep the Joint Two afloat.

In 1972 the UWT was very active in the Sacred Heart School – Teesside dispute. Pennie Yaffe wrote in the Union's journal about the "stimulating solidarity" and the impressive loyalty of the four UWT members who stayed the course till the end. Indeed against a background of harassment from management designed to defeat the work to rule, the immediate cause of the walkout at the Sacred Heart School that precipitated the strike was intimidation of the (UWT) Senior Mistress by a colleague who did not support the unions' case. In January of 1974 Ex-President Marie Smyth led the UWT contingent in the TUC march through Redcar in support of the striking members.

The 1972 UWT Conference held in Cambridge carried a resolution seeking recognition on the Burnham Committee in its own right. A motion on salaries called for long-service increments, reflecting the UWT's belief in the importance of the career teacher. Other motions called attention to the "pensions swindle", demanded equality of opportunity for women teachers in the promotion stakes and insisted on support for staff dealing with indiscipline and violence in schools.

A high-profile woman MP, Joan Lestor, was the guest of honour at the UWT 1972 Conference. The UWT President that year was Marie Smyth whose husband happened also to be the Honorary Treasurer of the NAS. Marie was one of the first to respond to the letter sent out by the UWT's founders, the 'Brighton Five', in 1965 seeking support for a women career teachers' union.

While the Brighton Five initiative had been completely independent, it was equally true that the NAS quickly offered practical support and advice as the UWT got off the ground in the mid-sixties. Simple things such as premises, office equipment, financial and accounting systems, and membership records as well as crucial services for members, are extremely important in establishing an organisation, and the NAS was able to be very helpful. The Joint Two Agreement reflected these arrangements.

UWT recruitment soon had the NUT seriously worried. After the NUT followed the NAS and UWT into the TUC, teachers changing their union affiliation had to abide by certain agreed procedures, including a proper resignation and settlement of any subscription owing. In its March 1972 edition of *Career Teacher* the UWT reported untold complications with the NUT who began blocking tactics which proved counterproductive, making many women teachers more determined than ever to join the union of their choice, which they believed to be more effective.

As the row over violence and indiscipline in schools raged from the union Conferences at Easter 1972, an NUT Executive Member made the mistake of affording the UWT the compliment of being important enough to attack with the sexist jibe that it was a "a motley crew of maidens".

By the time of the UWT's seventh Annual Conference in Leicester in September 1973, membership had grown to 15,000. However, tensions in the leadership over the relationship with the NAS and possible merger began to surface openly. Some UWT leaders were strongly opposed, others equally supportive of a merger.

In November 1973 Secretary of State Margaret Thatcher received an all-party deputation accompanied by UWT Officers to discuss representation on Burnham or any successor body. It was led by a Labour MP, Colonel Dick Crawshaw, and included John Pardoe from the Liberal Party and a veteran of the NAS campaign for recognition, Fergus Montgomery, from the Conservatives. Mrs Thatcher said she would consider a formal application. Once that was received she was true to her word and duly wrote to relevant parties seeking their views. Whether she would have granted recognition has to remain a matter of speculation since the Conservative Party was soon to lose power in the February 1974 General Election.

In November 1973 the UWT was very prominent in the lobby of Parliament and half-day strike that led to the reinstatement of the 6% contribution for teachers' pensions.

A visible if small manifestation of the divisions emerging over possible merger with the NAS could be found in the publication of joint 'NASUWT' Reports to Schools which were mailed out for posting up on staffroom notice boards whenever important developments took place. The practice, which had begun in January 1973, was suspended during 1974 but resumed from the beginning of 1975 when the majority view in favour of merger asserted itself.

In 1974 with membership up to 17,000 the UWT found it necessary to appoint a Deputy GS, Mary Lewis, a classroom teacher with over 26 years experience. The UWT had therefore gone from five members in 1965 to 17,000 in eight years. NAS membership exceeded 65,000 by the end of 1974, giving the Joint Two a joint total of 82,000.

Representation on local committees had been secured in a number of LEAs, including Cambridgeshire, Leicestershire, Flintshire and Belfast. UWT members pressing for representation in Derbyshire had been intrigued to discover the LEA recognised an association that was not on Burnham, the absence from which was the reason they were still being denied. It turned out to be the Community Youth Services Association, whose literature revealed that joining the organisation automatically granted full membership of the NUT. The CYSA was "a central association" of the NUT. The UWT commented that at least they stated who they were and had not resorted to wearing false beards to gain recognition!

The UWT responded vigorously to the Government's consultative document *Equal opportunities for Men and Women*, calling for a more proactive and assertive approach, particularly in the areas of pension provision and promotion. The UWT deplored the intention of the Government to exempt the education service from the provisions of its intended legislation.

The UWT 1974 Conference was due to be held in Portsmouth starting on 19 October. The second General Election of 1974 was pending for that month. The UWT duly issued two agendas. The first one, 'A', catered for a Labour victory, expected but not certain, with the Right Hon. Reg Prentice as Secretary of State for Education as guest of honour. Agenda 'B' had Margaret Thatcher, the most recent Conservative holder of that office, booked for that role! In the event Labour increased its majority and agenda 'A' was sufficient for the purpose.

The Conference agenda contained the 'usual' motions on Burnham representation, equality of pension provision, discipline, salaries (the Houghton Inquiry was current), maternity leave, a professional council, special education and the school leaving age, amongst others, all demonstrating that the UWT as it approached its tenth anniversary had accumulated a mature and wide range of policies to represent the interests of the career woman teacher.

Towards the end of 1974 the simmering row over the UWT's relationship with the NAS came to a head. The GS Pennie Yaffe was in the process of attempting to sever the link with the NAS which, amongst other things, under the Joint Two Agreement provided vital legal, professional and insurance services to UWT members. The bulk of the membership had been kept in the dark. Several members of the Executive and the Deputy GS were in support of Pennie Yaffe in calling a Special Conference in Leicester on 30 December.

When the President, Christine Skeavington, saw the agenda and realised what was happening, and having taken advice from counsel, she alerted all local associations and rallied support for the continuation of the Joint Two Agreement, which at the very least required either party to give 12 months notice of intention to terminate.

The move to end the special relationship was defeated by 146 votes to 119. Pennie Yaffe, and the Deputy GS, recently appointed Mary Lewis, together with some members of the Executive, immediately left the conference hall and convened a meeting of dissident delegates to establish a rival body to be called the Association of Career Teachers (ACT). Both the GS and Deputy resigned from the UWT. The meeting had been quite dramatic and at one stage the police had to be called.

The President then convened an emergency meeting of the Executive to carry on with essential business and to reaffirm the Joint Two Agreement, thereby assuring members they continued to be fully covered for legal and other services.

These unfortunate events took their toll on recruitment and membership. When the Transfer of Engagements took place on 1 January the following year (1976) the numbers brought to the combined association by the UWT dropped back to just over 16,000. It should have been close to 20,000 but such was the price to pay for a divided union.

It is difficult to determine exactly the motivation of those who opposed merger with the NAS. It is always easy to speculate about personality clashes or lay the blame on job and 'empire' protection in the smaller of two organisations about to merge. But some UWT members believed it was a genuine desire to keep open an avenue for women to be actively involved in a union and not dominated by men. The UWT made much of the domination of men in the NUT's democratic structures despite its heavily female membership.

Those who opposed merger were in a difficult position. Their correct course of action would have been to campaign against merger, not to try to scupper the vital Joint Two Agreement by unconstitutional means. With the impending anti-sex discrimination bill on the horizon, that would have been a hard argument to win. There was some resemblance to the events of 1919-22. Once again 'doing the right thing' cost members in the short term. In the longer term the price was well worth paying.

The President called another Special Conference in Nottingham for Saturday 22 February 1975, again acting on counsel's advice to put the future working of the UWT on to a secure basis. The Special Conference appointed a committee of ten, under the President, to lead the union. One of the dissident members brought an injunction seeking to prevent the Conference taking place on the grounds that any decisions would be invalid. Judge Blackett Orde dismissed the case and awarded costs to Christine Skeavington. The judge said the President had acted correctly in the circumstances.

The Special Conference decisively carried a motion of no confidence in the Officers, officials and Executive Members who had left the platform at Leicester after failing in their attempt to end the Joint Two Agreement. The voting was 224 in favour, 66 against. The President, Christine Skeavington, said: "The Conference decision made it clear the overwhelming majority of members wish to maintain the close relationship with the NAS. The first priority of the interim committee would be to achieve this aim." (Christine Skeavington was later to become the first woman President of the NASUWT in 1979.) NAS GS Terry Casey said he was "confident" agreement would be reached. Pennie Yaffe and Mary Lewis apparently withdrew their earlier resignations and through their solicitors accepted a financial settlement terminating their employment with the UWT.

Oddly enough the *TES*, reporting on these matters on 28 February, said: "The defecting faction inside the UWT was prepared to go it alone, form a new association, and admit men." The *TES* also correctly predicted the early demise of such an organisation. The ACT was formed but it had a hopeless task and soon faded into such obscurity that its eventual demise was scarcely noticed.

The NAS Conference of 1975 received a report on developments and discussed the possibility of further integration with the UWT. Consideration of merger was spurred on by proposed legislation which would outlaw discrimination on the grounds of sex. Thus NAS would not be able to deny full membership to a qualified woman teacher and the UWT would not be able to do likewise in respect of men.

Some delegates expressed fears that 'NASUWT' would become a mini-NUT but the majority view was that the protection and promotion of the status of the schoolmaster and his place in the education service was fully compatible with the interests of the career woman teacher. At the same time, the view in the UWT was crystallising into a strong belief that with a shared interest in the concept of the career teacher it would be better to fight within an integrated organisation rather than in two separate and possibly rival unions.

Consequently the UWT was moving towards the organisation of a ballot on integration with the NAS. Under the terms of the Trade Union Act of 1964 it appeared from advice of the Registrar of Friendly Societies that a 'Transfer of Engagements' would be the most suitable legal mechanism to effect a merger.

The immediate post-Annual Conference meeting of the NAS Executive normally dealt just with routine formal business such as establishing subcommittees. On the occasion in 1975, a historic decision was taken to convene a Special Conference in Birmingham on Saturday 12 July to consider the Transfer of Engagements with the UWT and the admission of women teachers to membership.

Meanwhile Christine Skeavington wrote on behalf of the Interim Committee to all UWT members on 24 June, advising them of "the continuous discussion with our colleagues in the NAS". The Sex Discrimination Bill would make it impossible to continue to recruit on a single-gender basis and thus inevitably rivalry would make the Joint Two Agreement impossible to operate effectively. An amendment to the Bill exempting 'women-only organisations', carried against the Government in Committee, was unlikely to survive and in any event the UWT had come to the view that "the best interests of the woman career teacher will be served by integration with the NAS".

Accordingly the Interim Committee was recommending a transfer of engagements with the NAS, in accordance with advice already received in respect of the Trade Union (Amalgamations etc.) Act, 1964.

Christine Skeavington's letter explained that the new organisation would be known as the NASUWT. Full benefits under the Joint Two Agreement would be available. Members would pay the annual subscription of £12, enjoy full voting rights and be eligible for office at local and national levels. A Special Committee of 12 women would be established to advise the Executive on the professional and educational interests of career women teachers. Until such time as the number of directly elected women members to serve on the National Executive is not less than three, arrangements would be made for the co-option of three women members to serve on the Executive.

Christine Skeavington's letter was also accompanied by a copy of the proposed Instrument of Transfer, which had been approved by the Chief Registrar of Friendly Societies, together with a ballot paper which had to be returned to the Electoral Reform Society no later than Monday 14 July 1975. A simple majority of members voting was required to pass the resolution and the result was declared on the same day. On a turnout of approximately 40% the vote in favour of the transfer of engagements was 6,402, with 305 against. That constituted a massive majority of 95% of those voting.

The NAS Special Conference on 12 July passed off very smoothly. After the usual Report from the Executive the relevant changes to the rules were moved and opened to debate. I recall only one voice in opposition. A 1950s-styled member 'of the old school' presented the case against. He was warmly and courteously received, for it was right and proper that both sides of the argument be heard. When it came to the vote the President, John Chalk, declared the motion on the Transfer of Engagements to have been "very heavily carried" by an estimated 95%.

The Special Conference also dealt with consequential rule changes, many simply adding "and schoolmistresses" to "schoolmasters". In addition the term "career teacher" found its way into the rule book. The long- standing preoccupation with "men teachers for boys" was happily amended to "boys coming under the influence of schoolmasters and girls under the influence of schoolmistresses".

On 18 June the House of Commons had overturned the amendment carried in Committee which had exempted single-gender unions and other similarly constituted organisations from the Sex Discrimination Bill proceeding through Parliament. The Special Conference also decided to permit the NAS to recruit "career woman teachers" with effect from 1 September 1975, some four months ahead of the transfer of engagements.

The Transfer of Engagements between the UWT and the NAS came into effect on 1 January 1976. The combined NASUWT, now able to recruit all teachers, men and women, boasted over 80,000 members. The stereotype misogynist schoolmaster opposed to equal pay, dating from 1919, was well and truly entombed for all except the most cantankerous of our opponents, who naturally were determined not to allow the NAS part of the combined union to forget its history.

But those who only look at history without a vision for the future quickly lose their way. The combined union was already focussed on the new agenda, the career teacher and the real needs of the practitioner in the classroom. Radical social change had taken place. Schools faced new pressures and demands. Teachers who stayed in the profession for a longer time than the two-thirds who had come and gone within five years were looking for a different kind of support from a union. That was why the UWT had been formed and expanded so quickly.

A.E. Warren, NAS's first President and General Secretary

Mavis Wright, Founding President of the UWT 1965-70

A section of the delegates at the 1922 Cardiff Conference.
A.E. Warren is seated front row third from right

Schoolmasters prepare to march from the Embankment to
Kingsway in London to protest against proposed salary cuts
(Photo: Daily Sketch, 12 September 1931)

George Cording,
photographed for the
Herald of Wales reporting
on the 1935 Conference
in Wales being held in
Swansea

The National Executive at the 1960 Hastings Conference

Back row: A.C.E. Weston, H. Stott, H.J. Weaver, A.D. Peasnell, N.J. Bowmaker,
R. Mabey, H.C. Baillie, T.A. Casey

Middle row: R.A. Simons, R. Johnson, G.F. Limburn, G.M. Civall, L.G. Harris,
B.J. Harterre, R.R. Tunstall, M.A. Langdell

Front row: B.F. Wakefield, R.M. Hall, E.W. Arnott, J.A.C. Thomson, H.J. Bell,
President A.L. Jones (Liverpool) (with presidential chain),
General Secretary E. Rushworth, Hon. Treasurer G. Lloyd Williams,
A.J. Smyth, A. Sutton, J.W. Perry

Three photographs of "The Greatest Teachers' Union Meeting of all Time", Central Hall Westminster, launching the militant campaign to secure Burnham recognition, 25 February 1961:

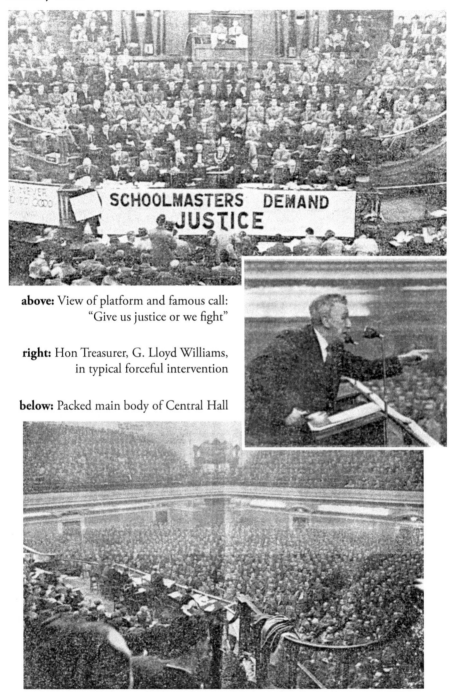

above: View of platform and famous call: "Give us justice or we fight"

right: Hon Treasurer, G. Lloyd Williams, in typical forceful intervention

below: Packed main body of Central Hall

'Schoolmasters on Strike Gather in Albert Hall' 21 September 1961. About 7,000 members of the NAS with their wives and sympathisers protested against the Government's decision to reduce the pay award.

bottom inset: President Harry Bell acknowledges the cheers that greeted his speech

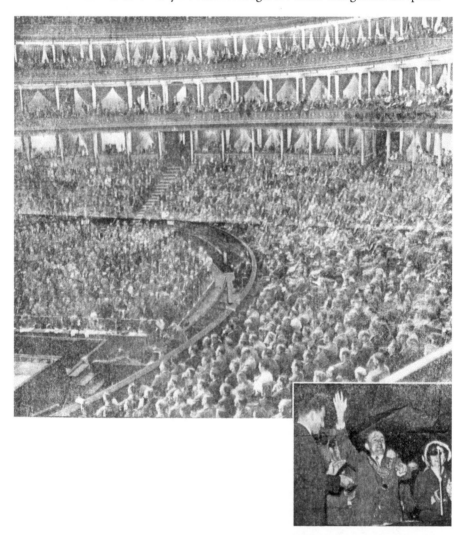

Three General Secretaries, (left to right) Dick Anderson, Terry Casey (in his presidential year) and Bert Rushworth, outside Plymouth Conference 1962. The three were collectively General Secretary for forty-two years from 1941-83

One of the entrances to the school in Brighton where the dilapidated state of the buildings prompted the founding of the UWT in 1965

Ernie 'Bill' Gladstone, Headmaster, Secretary of the Durham NAS and leader of the great Durham dispute in 1969

The interim Pay Award Campaign gets under way with a march and rally in Colchester, Essex, November 1969. Assistant Secretary George Limburn is on the left of front row

David Flood, the 50,000th NAS member receiving a presentation from President Ron Simons. General Secretary Terry Casey is in the background, January 1971

Past President (1955/56) Tom Smith addressing Conference 1971
for the last time as a practising schoolmaster

Education Secretary Margaret Thatcher addressing the NAS Conference Easter 1971 in more relaxed times before becoming a very right-wing Prime Minister. Front from left: Ray Holden Senior Vice-President, Ron Cocking President, Terry Casey General Secretary, Arthur Smyth Hon. Treasurer and Bernard Wakefield newly-appointed Assistant General Secretary

Terry Casey being interviewed for BBC TV outside the Burnham Arbitral Hearing in central London by Martin Bell, a future independent MP, 30 June 1971. A young Nigel de Gruchy is standing behind and to the left of Terry holding a placard demanding a 'London Allowance £200'

General Secretary Terry Casey and President Hywel Thomas lead the applause as Secretary of State Margaret Thatcher unveils the plaque marking the official opening of the Hillscourt Education Centre at Rednal on 3 October 1973

Pickets join Joe Faye (left) and Northern Regional Official Colin McInnes (right) outside the Sacred Heart School, November 1973

Jenifer Beeken who became the 100,000 member of the NASUWT on 4 November 1977

Christine Skeavington, President of the UWT 1978, who became the first woman President of the NASUWT in 1979, with TUC General Secretary Lionel Murray (on left) and Terry Casey

Terry Casey (with colleagues from IFFTU) meeting Senator Edward Kennedy at the
1980 Democratic Convention in New York

Conference 1985: Peter Matthews (on right), one of the heroes suspended for over six months in the 1969 Durham Dispute, hands over the Presidency to Joe Boone

NASUWT picket line outside Burnham Committee meeting, 15 May 1985.
From right: Nigel de Gruchy DGS; Fred Smithies General Secretary; Joe Boone President; Gerry Lee Past President; Peter Herbert NEM and some London members

Secretary of State for Education, Sir Keith Joseph, delivering his speech to the 1986 NASUWT Conference. Sir Keith was greeted in silence and without applause at the end

The Poundswick members outside the Scarborough Conference 1986 with front row left: President Mike Inman, School Rep Chris Elwood and Fred Smithies

Poundswick March through central Manchester to rally at Crown Square, 4 May 1986, in support of 18 members still locked out in the 'Grand Graffiti Dispute'

The National Officers and General Secretary group 1989-90.
Seated, from left: Graham Terrell, President; Dave Battye, Ex-President;
Gerry Lee, Hon. Treasurer; Fred Smithies, General Secretary.
Standing: Eamonn O'Kane, Deputy General Secretary; Nigel de Gruchy, General
Secretary Designate; Sue Rogers, Junior Vice-President; Mick Carney,
Senior Vice-President; Bill Herron, Assistant General Secretary.
Collectively they represent: 6 Presidents, 4 Treasurers and 3 General Secretaries

President Sue Rogers unveils the plaque officially opening the S.E. Regional Centre
in West Malling, Kent, one of ten centres covering the whole of the UK, in 1992
accompanied by Brian Cornish, Regional Official and Nigel de Gruchy

Nigel de Gruchy, accompanied by (left to right) Deputy General Secretary
Eamonn O'Kane, Wandsworth Secretary Mick Richardson, President
Maurice Littlewood and Hon. Treasurer Mick Carney, wheels the barrow
load of documents that made up the new National Curriculum into the
High Court in London as the Wandsworth v NASUWT case opened 31
March 1993

Nigel de Gruchy meets the media after the 'stunning' victory in the High Court, 2 April 1993. Mike Baker holds out the BBC microphone on the General Secretary's left

Arms aloft, Nigel de Gruchy emerges victorious from the Appeal Court, 23 April 1993

Nigel de Gruchy with Sir Ron (later Lord) Dearing discussing his first (Interim) report on slimming down the National Curriculum as it is about to be launched at a SCAA Press Conference on 9 May 1993

NASUWT hosts a lunch, 24 May 1994, at the Royal Horse Guards Hotel in Westminster to commemorate the twentieth anniversary of the establishment of the Houghton Committee of Enquiry into Teachers' Pay. The ageing Lord Houghton was absent through illness. Left to right: Roger Kirk, President; Baroness Blatch, Minister of State for Education; John Rowland, Ex-President; Sir John Wordie, former Chairman of Burnham Committee; Nigel de Gruchy; Lord Mark Carlisle, former Secretary of State for Education; Ken Graham, former DGS TUC; unidentified guest; and Sir John Gardiner, Chairman STRB

Sue Rogers wheels the original National Curriculum into Conference 1993 and models Sir Ron Dearing's new slim-line curriculum in its carrier bag, summer 1994

David Blunkett, then Shadow Education Secretary, addressing the 1995 Eastbourne Conference. Front row of platform, from left: Jerry Bartlett, Legal Officer; Peter Cole, Senior Vice-President; Olwyn Gunn, President, in the Chair; Nigel de Gruchy, Mick Carney, Hon. Treasurer; Roger Kirk, Ex-President; Chris Keates, Chair Equal Opportunities Committee

Hazel Spence-Young, who was the victim of an assault by a primary school pupil and who secured, with the support of the NASUWT, £82,500 compensation from her LEA in an out-of-court settlement

The customary large NASUWT contingent in the 1995 annual TUC Cheltenham March, 28 January, protesting against Margaret Thatcher's ban on union membership at the GCHQ intelligence gathering centre. Left to right: NASUWT Presidents past and future: Margaret Morgan, Olwyn Gunn and Maurice Littlewood with Nigel de Gruchy. Immediately in front of lead banner are President, Roger Kirk (wearing cap) and long serving NEM and Silver Medal holder, Dave Argent

The NASUWT delegation to TUC Congress 1994. Left to right: Peter Cole, John Petchell, Neil Fairclough, Mick Carney, Nigel de Gruchy, John Rowland, Roger Kirk (President), Margaret Morgan, Olwyn Gunn, Eamonn O'Kane

Past President and NEM Roger Kirk hands over messages of support to Jenny Fox, School Rep, and other members of the 'Manton Eight' who took strike action over attempts to reinstate a violent pupil in to the school in October 1996

Scene outside The Ridings in autumn 1996 which witnessed the most dramatic refusal to teach by the NASUWT

1998 NASUWT Equality Conference. Left to right: Nigel de Gruchy,
Patrick Roach, Chris Gaine, Jennifer Moses, President Margaret Morgan,
Graham Dawson NEM, Chair of Equal Opportunities Committee, Tony Sewell,
Olwyn Gunn Education Assistant Secretary

US President Bill Clinton addressing the 1998 EI World Congress,
Washington DC, 29 July. Nigel de Gruchy, EI Executive Board Member, is seated in
second row on right. Front row either side of Bill Clinton from left: Sandie Feldman
EI Vice President (AFT), Fred van Leeuwen EI General Secretary,
Mary Futrell EI President, Bob Chase (President NEA)

Nigel de Gruchy with Assistant Secretary Policy Co-ordination and future General Secretary Chris Keates at press coference on the NASUWT's response to the Government's Green Paper, *Teachers, meeting the challenge of change*, 15 February 1999

At the 1999 Conference, presided over by Bill Morley, the General Secretary responds with the customary 'vote of thanks' to the two opposition parties' spokespersons on education, Don Foster, Lib Dems on his immediate left, and Theresa May, Conservatives

The well-known MP Keith Vaz (centre) introducing Nigel de Gruchy to Lech Walensa, former President of Poland and Leader of Solidarity, in May 2003 at a reception in the Houses of Parliament

TUC's General Secretary Brendan Barber and President Nigel de Gruchy emerge from talks with the Prime Minister after a delegation from the TUC expressed concerns early in 2003 over plans to invade Iraq

British Prime Minister Tony Blair with TUC President Nigel de Gruchy en route to the General Council Dinner at Congress 18 September 2003 at the Grand Hotel, Brighton. Brendon Barber, Judy de Gruchy and Mary Barber follow immediately behind

TUC President Nigel de Gruchy 'getting the giggles' at 2003 Congress.
Ex-TUC President and GS TGWU Bill Morris, (on left) seems similarly amused as
Nigel introduces female TV personality about to probe Government Minister,
CBI Director and TUC GS with roving microphone

General Secretary Eamonn O'Kane signs the (January) 2004 Standards and Workload Agreement with Secretary of State for Education, Charles Clarke, keeping a watchful eye

NASUWT HQ at Rednal in the Lickey Hills south of Birmingham.
Left to right: Residential block; original House with kitchens, dining room,
lounges and bar; Executive Council /Conference Chamber;
committee/training rooms and administrative offices

Chapter 44 - The Merged NASUWT Becomes a Major Union

After Burnham recognition in 1961 the second most 'pivotal' year in the history of the NASUWT was 1976, marking the merger of its two constituent parts. It opened up the entire teaching profession 'market' to NASUWT recruitment. Many factors changed considerably as a consequence.

Membership is the most obvious point. Appendices D and E show the NAS started the sixties with an in-service membership of 21,930. The Burnham breakthrough came in October 1961. By the end of the following year membership had soared to 31,334. That represented an increase of just below 50% within the space of about 15 months, a full two point rise in 'market share' from 9.1% to 11.1%.

Membership increases remained steady through most of the 1960s but accelerated towards the end of the decade against a background of rising militancy. With the NAS and UWT opposed to another poor Burnham settlement in 1968, which led to the Interim Pay Campaign of 1969/70, members came flooding in. 1970 saw the NAS recruit its 50,000th member, the appropriately named David Flood from Cambridge who had recently returned to the UK from abroad and decided to join the NAS because of its career structured salary policy. In round figures the increases respectively for those years were from 40,000 to 45,000 to 51,000, taking market share to 14.5%.

With the campaign for career structured salaries and the (Arbitration) 'A' Day is 'D' Day march and rally on 30 June 1971, NAS membership soared further to 55,600. On 1 January 1976 the Transfer of Engagements between the NAS and UWT combined respectively 69,000 and 16,000 career teachers into one union. Within another year membership was touching 90,000 and the 100,000 mark was in sight.

On 4 November 1977 NASUWT membership soared beyond the magic 100,000 mark when "the Boeing Computer, clicking on members at a rate of knots" moved from 99,706 to 100,031 registered members. Jennifer Beeken, a young science-graduate teacher, was declared the 100,000th member.

Thus the 1960s and '70s saw the NAS and then the NASUWT membership move from 21930 to 122058 (Appendix D).

In the three decades from 1950-80 the NASUWT in-service membership rose from 13,513 to 123,896 taking its share of the market defined as England and Wales from 6.5% to 28.4% (Appendix E).

Apart from the occasional small year on year reductions and the Second World War, 1981 and 1986-88 were the only times significant membership losses were experienced. The latter two were both post-industrial action periods where battles waged had been lost. A low point was reached in 1988 of 117,610, a loss of 10,000 members over 1985, after the long and bitter strikes of the mid 1980s (Appendix D).

By 1990 the in-service paid-up membership of NASUWT was again on the increase, reaching 119,810. Total membership in that year, including the associate, retired and student categories as declared to the Certification Officer in the annual return, amounted to 168,539 at the end of 1990.

The 1990s proved to be extremely productive years for the NASUWT. The spectacular success of the 'Test Boycott' (1993) led directly to an in-service membership of 157,146 by 1995. Further action by the NASUWT in 1996 defending members against violence and disruption in four high profile cases maintained large increases in membership. The years 1992-93 to 1996-97 saw annual net increases in membership of respectively, 11,000, 8,000, 11,000, 8000 and 7,000.

By 2000 in-service membership stood at 183,681 while total membership reached 255,768, More success for the NASUWT in leading the negotiations with the New Labour Government in 2000 to secure the Threshold Payments (opposed by the NUT) led to a spectacular rise of just under 17,000 members, taking the figure beyond the magic 200,000 mark by the end of 2001.

On 22 February 2002 the NASUWT announced that Sylvia New, a young teacher at Oakfield Middle School in Lancing, West Sussex, was the 200,000th NASUWT member. Sylvia had joined the Union after being impressed with some of its publications which she had read at a training centre in Worthing. Sylvia was awarded a cheque for £2,000 as her part of the prize in a national competition to recruit the 200,000th member.

Yet another huge boost in membership in excess of 11,000 followed in 2002, the year generally marking the end of the period covered by this history. In-service membership reached 211,779. Appendix E Table 2 shows the total number of teachers in the UK to have been 505,906. On that basis the NASUWT represented 41.9% of the teacher force. Table 3 of Appendix E shows that discounting Scotland the NASUWT share of the England, Wales and Northern Ireland 'teacher market' stood at 45.5%.

For purposes of affiliation to the TUC large groups such as student teachers in training who are afforded free membership by the unions are excluded. NASUWT student membership fluctuated in line with changing numbers in teacher training. It reached a peak in excess of 40,000 in 1994.

Affiliation to the TUC is not a cheap option and for large unions the overall cost is a substantial figure. The per capita fee at that time was around £1-30. They are proably the best guide to genuine in-service/contributing members. The figures declared at Congress 2003 (based on end of previous year) were:

ATL 110,083; NUT 232,280; EIS 53,424 and NASUWT 211,779.

However, in 2001/02 NASUWT only represented about 5% of teachers in Scotland although it has strengthened its position in more recent times. Taken in the round all the above evidence points to the NASUWT having greatly increased its share of the school teaching force in England, Wales and Northern Ireland.

(On 5 December 2008 the TES reported on union memberships based strictly on serving teachers in the maintained sector in England and Wales to enable a like for like comparison to be made between the NASUWT and the NUT, the latter not organising in Scotland and Northern Ireland.   The TES reported the NASUWT to have 202,504 members; the NUT to have 190,269. This led the TES to conclude that the NASUWT had become not only the largest UK wide teachers' union, but also the largest for England and Wales.)

The NASUWT has also extended its reach outside the strict confines of the UK. The largest single group has been in the Service Childrens' Education Authority (SCEA) run by the Ministry of Defence. Over 500 members were located in Germany after the end of the Second World War to educate the children of UK military personnel. Other notable groups were in Hong Kong, Singapore and Cyprus until changes in their constitutional status came about. For many years teachers in Gibraltar had been members of UK based unions including the NASUWT. In the early 1990s, having decided they should all be in one union and having invited representatives of the major British teachers' unions over to present their cases, the overwhelming majority voted to join the NASUWT. Consequently all 300 members of the Gibraltar Teachers' Association affiliated en-bloc to the NASUWT.

The NASUWT continues to offer full support in negotiations with the relevant employing authorities to these overseas teachers which in the case of SCEA is conducted through the civil service union Prospect (formerly IPMS) as teachers are deemed to be civil servants for this purpose.

Full support has also been available nearer 'home' to members in Jersey, Guernsey and the Isle of Man. National officials from the NASUWT and other other unions have often visited these islands to assist in negotiations as they strove to ensure pay, conditions and pensions matched (and in some bases bested) the provision for England and Wales.

Most of these overseas 'local' associations were on the regular annual 'tour' of the NASUWT president. They were also very welcome to attend and participate fully in the NASUWT annual conference which many of them have continued to do on a regular basis.

The Union also represented teachers employed by the British Council all over the world. However, apart from the occasional collective approach to the British Council based in London most of the support could only amount to individual advice and casework.

The financial health of the Union fully reflected the buoyant recruitment position. In 1970, income had reached £176,000, expenditure a little more at £178,000. Presenting the Accounts to Conference in 1978 Honorary Treasurer Ron Cocking reported that the previous financial year saw subscription income rise above £1m for the first time. The assets of the Union stood at over £1m. By 1980 annual income had risen to £1.8m; expenditure stood at £1.7m, with net assets of £2.1m. At the start of the following two decades the figures were:

1990: Income £6m   Expenditure £5.4m   Net Assets £9.7m
2000: Income £16m   Expenditure £15.8m   Net Assets £19.2m

By chance these start-of-decade years were a little untypical insofar as income only slightly exceeded expenditure. The 1990s witnessed several years when income exceeded expenditure by more than £1m.

The NAS annual subscription had reached £5 by the end of the 1960s. For a brief period the Association then adopted a sliding scale of subscription depending on salary. In 1971 Conference maintained the £5 'sub' for those earning up to £1,200 per annum but raised it to £6 for those earning between £1,201 and £1,600. For members with salaries above £1,600 the sub became £7 (the new levels coming into effect in 1972).

It had been a controversial change, with many members believing the tax and social security systems should take care of such matters, not to mention the complexities of trying to ensure members paid the correct amounts! Conference soon returned to a common sub for all members, although new teachers were offered reduced rates in their first and second years on condition they paid by direct debit. Since most teachers had bank accounts the NASUWT was able to utilise direct debits as the major method of paying subs from a very early stage. We preferred that system to the debit at (salary) source, DAS, which was dependent upon the employer deducting the money and then passing it over to the union, which others chose to rely upon. The system also led naturally to the computerisation and centralisation of membership records, another area in which the NASUWT took an early lead amongst unions.

On the Transfer of Engagements taking effect 1 January 1976 the sub was increased to £12 per annum, the relatively rapid rise reflecting the high inflation of the times. High inflation persisted and by 1980 the sub had risen to £18. While the rate of inflation moderated after 1981 the massive amount of industrial action and other activity that characterised the decade led to the sub reaching £52-£80 by 1990. The 1990s were also busy times, producing a sub of £99 by 2000.

For comparison, the 2000 subs for the other mainly classroom-based unions were: NUT £101 (to which had to be added a local sub of several pounds); ATL and PAT: both £103.

In short the Union's financial state matched its political health. The development of an impressive property portfolio followed in the wake of this success, at the same time helping to ensure it continued.

The original head office of the NAS was at 59 Gordon Square, in the heart of London's Bloomsbury. The NAS had rented the premises from the University of London in 1926, Arthur Warren having spent the first four years of his period as GS working out of his home at 7 Clifford Gardens, Willesden, London, NW10. During the Second World War some records and functions were transferred to an office in Chesham, Buckinghamshire, for better safety against enemy bombardment.

By the 1960s 59 Gordon Square was becoming too small for purpose. Various attempts to find larger premises in a suitable central London location at affordable rents proved difficult. Furthermore, the University of London landlords wanted to repossess the building at the end of the lease in 1971. Accordingly, in that year the NAS moved its HQ office out to Hemel Hempstead, originally to Bank Court and then to Swan Court, with the UWT moving into the former. I recall some of the 'golden oldies' of the generation ahead of mine regretting that they had not taken the plunge and purchased a freehold property to serve as the HQ in central London.

The first freehold property the NAS ever purchased was the land for a housing project on the outskirts of Cheltenham in Gloucestershire in 1969. The Legal Aid, Benevolence and Services Committee had promoted the idea of subsidised accommodation for needy retired members and their spouses. After some financial difficulties, resolved by a direct appeal to members to make seven-year covenants, along with a substantial mortgage, enough money was raised to build 20 bungalows and 30 flats on the site. Building started in 1969 and by 1971 the first occupants were moving in. The project was named after the then recently deceased former GS, Bert Rushworth, and survives as a thriving community to the present day.

Conscious of the desirability of owning premises, in 1971 the NAS purchased the freehold of a handsome country house known as Hillscourt, on Rose Hill in Rednal, just south of Birmingham in the picturesque Lickey Hills. It had been a private preparatory school. Together with extensive grounds Hillscourt originally consisted of a large Victorian house, to which were attached a few extra buildings, including one that became the Union's social club and bar. Another one was a large prefabricated hall (the former school's gymnasium). In 1976 the National Executive relocated its meetings out of the Cora Hotel near Euston Station in London to this hall or 'hut', as those so disposed labelled the less-than-luxurious accommodation. In the late 1970s many parts of the Union's administration were relocated to Hillscourt as the Hemel Hempstead operation was scaled down.

Originally intended to serve as an education and training centre with overnight accommodation, Hillscourt was modernised and developed with the addition of substantial new offices, a new residential block and a first-class conference hall on the site of the old 'hut' which then housed the National Executive meetings in far more salubrious surroundings. During the 1990s the site was also developed as a residential and day conference centre, extensively used by the Union and also available for hire by external bodies on a commercial basis.

The NASUWT developed a tradition of securing the services of Secretaries of State to open various phases of the development at Hillscourt, starting with Margaret Thatcher who opened the refurbished 'hut' officially on 3 October 1973. Fred Mulley, Shirley Williams, Mark Carlisle and Sir Keith Joseph followed in her footsteps, all leaving plaques on various walls to commemorate their 'official opening duties'.

As relationships with Education Secretaries became too fraught in the mid-to-late 1980s during the Thatcher administrations other prominent figures were enlisted to perform opening duties. On 27 June 1986 Lord Douglas Houghton opened the new conference hall and National Executive meeting room. Fred van Leeuwen, GS of Education International, opened the new residential block in 1989. John Monks, TUC GS, opened a new office block on 29 November 1995.

As Hillscourt was developed and Hemel Hempstead scaled down the GS's office moved back to central London. Terry Casey increasingly saw the need for such a base to deal with government Ministers, civil servants, national bodies and the media, not to mention the Royal Courts of Justice. In the mid-seventies the GS's office moved to share premises with the NASUWT's solicitors, Janners, in Brook Street, London, W1 (right opposite the famous Claridge's hotel). By 1978 Janners and the GS's office had moved along the road to 22 Upper Brook Street in the upmarket heart of Mayfair. The NASUWT also purchased a 'pied-à-terre' at 48 Gladstone St, London, SE1 in 1976 to facilitate London-based activity, although this property was sold in the mid-1990s. On 31 July 1980 the NASUWT closed its Hemel Hempstead office and moved its entire administrative operation to Hillscourt in Rednal which also became the registered office of the Union.

In 1990 Janners was in the process of 'moving and merging' with other firms of lawyers when as the new GS I persuaded the Officers and Executive to purchase the freehold of 5 King Street, London, WC2, in the heart of Covent Garden. After renovation we occupied the interesting premises in May 1991. It remains the NASUWT's 'political' office housing the GS, DGS and other relevant staff such as the Press and Parliamentary Liaison Officers.

The first Regional Office was established in 1969 in the North East at Washington, County Durham, purchased with the proceeds of the reimbursed salaries handed over by the LEA after the successful conclusion of the 1969 dispute. A Regional Official was appointed to facilitate better relations with LEAs in the North East where several bitter disputes had erupted. As membership increased Field Officers and Regional Officials were appointed to help deal with casework but they had to operate from home. Faced with the challenges presented by the 1988 Education Reform Act, eight more Regional Centres in England together with three others (one each for Wales, Scotland and Northern Ireland) were purchased during the course of the 1990s mainly to house regional staff.

The Regional *Centres* (notice, not just *Offices*) were based on the 'model' pioneered by the Nottinghamshire Federation of the NASUWT under the dynamic leadership of Roy Francis, one-time negotiating secretary for the county and subsequently Regional Official for the East Midlands. Using spare accommodation at his home and then enlarging that with some financial backing from the Union, the Nottinghamshire Federation developed a system of locally elected Officers working at their centre with staff to share the many tasks to be undertaken at county and local branch levels. They focussed particularly on casework and recruitment and were soon able to claim to represent the majority of teachers in Nottinghamshire. Thus these centres were not purchased simply to accommodate regional staff but also to provide facilities for and assist elected Officers who remained employed as teachers by their LEAs. The centres became important for the local training of School Reps and health and safety representatives as well as many other functions.

With the exception of the 'Cheltenham Homes', now wholly owned by the Schoolmasters' (NAS) Benevolent Housing Association Ltd., all these properties, Hillscourt HQ, London Covent Garden and 12 regional/devolved nations' centres, were purchased with 'cash' without a penny being borrowed, reflecting the favourable financial health of the Union.

Staffing obviously had to be increased to cope with the huge rise in membership. Pre-war teacher-related staff numbers never exceeded three: the

GS Arthur Warren; an assistant, Sidney Hines, appointed in the late 1920s; and in 1937 an Organiser, Tom Smith. In addition there were two clerical staff. Records have been difficult to trace but by the mid-1960s there were between 20 and 25 staff, roughly equally divided between teacher-related and clerical. By 1980 the NASUWT employed 59 people, including staff in the regions who originally had to work from home. By 1990 101 staff were on the payroll.

During the 1990s the distinction between teacher-related and clerical began to disappear as a larger variety of skilled and professionally qualified staff were required to run a large union in an increasingly technological age. The 1990s saw another large rise in the number of employees, especially in the regions as casework exploded in the wake of non-stop fundamental reforms to the British educational systems. By 2000 the NASUWT employed 177 staff. (In 2010 the NASUWT became a medium-size employer with 291 staff.)

Reflecting more litigious and complicated times for employers and employees, the 1990s saw a dramatic expansion of the NASUWT's legal aid services under the dynamic leadership of Jerry Bartlett. A former NASUWT negotiating secretary in Hereford and Worcester and West Midlands Regional Organiser for the then National Union of Public Employees, Jerry was appointed Legal Officer in 1991 and went on to become an AGS and then DGS in 2002.

In 1990 the Association had instructed solicitors to act on behalf of members on 121 occasions and obtained £83,000 in compensation. By 1993 the respective figures had grown to 249 and over £1m. Cases varied between securing £175,000 in compensation for a member suffering from post-traumatic stress and forced into early retirement following the sinking of an educational cruise ship and another receiving £1,000 for minor injuries and damage to clothing after a theatre seat collapsed while supervising a school party.

Total annual compensation secured for members reached over £3m by 1996. That included £376,114 for a member seriously injured in a road accident whilst on a GCE A Level field study. The most common cause of injury was slipping on wet floors and amounts received were generally very modest, although one such case in 1997 received £212,538 for a very serious injury. By 2000 compensation secured was just a few pounds below £5m, half of which had been secured by Regional Officials, the other half through the national organisation.

In 2001 the total rose by almost £1m to £5.9m. Furthermore, the Union opened 1,214 legal aid files in that year. Notable outcomes were £200,000 for a work-related illness, £100,000 for sickness due to stress and two incidents of violent assault upon members by pupils, resulting in awards of £215,500 and £96,000. There were 67 applications for stress-related cases to be pursued in

2001. The £5.9m total includes £1.8m received through compromise agreements which were emerging as alternatives to the burgeoning number full Industrial Tribunal hearings.

It also became necessary regularly to engage three firms of solicitors: (1) Reynolds Porter Chamberlain (who had taken over Janners, to which David Haywood had moved from Craigen Wilders & Sorrell; (2) Thompsons, the 'trade union lawyers' who rented accommodation at the TUC HQ, Congress House; and (3) Russell, Jones and Walker (RJW) who had a very strong employment law department.

With assistance of a solicitor, Andrew Dismore from RJW who later went on to become a prominent MP and Chairman of the Parliamentary Human Rights Committee, in 1995/96 the NASUWT undertook a wholesale revision and updating of its Rules to comply with modern requirements. Sharper definitions of internal committees' powers and responsibilities, the position of the GS, categories of membership, election procedures at local and national levels, disciplinary hearings and appeals were the main features. It took two special conferences to secure the adoption of such complex and comprehensive changes. A formal Retired Members' Association (RMA) was established with limited rights to attend, speak and vote at Annual Conference. The RMA would have a formal channel of communication with the Executive through liaison with the Legal Aid, Benevolence and Services Committee.

The Benevolence Committee of the National Executive continued to carry out important work in collaboration firstly with local associations, but in later times it became the practice to encourage the formation of federations to deal with the caseload. While the business was not so much a matter of life or death as it had been in the 1920s and 1930s before the advent of the welfare state, many cases of genuine hardship were addressed. To take a random example, in 1992 the Central Benevolence Committee dealt with 218 applications for assistance (up from 124 in the previous year) and made grants worth a total of nearly £79,000 and extended interest-free loans of just over £252,000.

The NASUWT, like most other unions in the UK, provided a wide range of commercial services to members, offering favourable rates on life, car, house, property and travel insurance. Financial and investment advice, together with mortgages and loans, was also available. The insurance against malicious damage to cars while parked on school premises proved particularly 'popular' in the sense that it became increasingly needed. All such services were arranged in conjunction with external companies. The demand for trading schemes was met in the 1950s and 1960s but they tended to die away as retailing became more competitive and often offered equivalent deals directly to the public.

Prior to 1975 training had remained the province of the Recruitment Committee of the NEC. The Labour Party was restored to Government in 1974 and while enacting more union-friendly legislation also placed greater responsibility on national executives to be accountable for the activities of local and regional branches. Responding to such pressures and mindful of the inherent advantages of training local Officers the NASUWT, through the establishment in 1975 of an Executive Standing Committee for the purpose, embarked upon a massive increase in such activity. Training was originally based at Hillscourt but in time it spread out across the country, a process that was accentuated with the development of Regional Centres. By the 1990s over 1,500 training places were regularly made available every year to local Officers and grass-roots members covering a wide range of activities associated with representation, negotiation, organisation, recruitment, health and safety, IT, the media and educational reforms. Mountains of literature were produced and regularly updated, typical examples being handbooks for School Reps and Health and Safety Reps.

The NASUWT had for many years sponsored a Page Scholarship in conjunction with the English Speaking Union. Every year two members after competitive application and interview were sponsored to visit the USA for three weeks in order to study an aspect of its education system and report back. As the Union grew in size and financial resource an increasing number and variety of 'good causes' were sponsored including: school sport (rugby, football, athletics, golf and Paralympics); Voluntary Service Overseas; music including: Youth Music UK, The Riverside Band and Youth Music Theatre UK; and the Philip Lawrence Awards.

In terms of policy the most significant effect of the Transfer of Engagements between NAS and UWT was (not surprisingly) the rise to prominence of the issue of equal opportunities. Women were still treated very unequally. The Equal Pay Act 1970, the Sex Discrimination Act 1975 and the Race Relations legislation of 1965-76 were pivotal developments raising the profile of equal opportunities generally throughout society. However, the naturally cautious approach to change, coupled with the single-sex origins of the constituent bodies of the NASUWT, meant that the Union was not in the 'front line' leading the campaigns on such issues in those early days.

However, under the direct influence of an increasing number of women members the NASUWT was slowly but surely converted to the need for a more proactive approach. On the Transfer of Engagements in 1976 the ratio of men to women members was over 3:1. Year by year that differential narrowed and by the end of 1992 women outnumbered men for the first time. The annual return to the Certification Officer showed a total membership (i.e. including all categories) of 96,328 female members compared to 94,309 males. By 2003 the ratio of women to men was more than 2:1, which reflected the general composition of the teaching profession.

The NASUWT developed comprehensive policies on equal opportunities second to none and pursued cases in the courts, achieving some notable victories. Furthermore, the issue was also soon to spread beyond gender and race to encompass other areas of discrimination including religious belief, disability and sexuality.

In February 1983 the NASUWT threatened to take the Ministry of Defence (MoD) to the European Court when a member was not allowed to renew her contract because she had married when teaching abroad in the Service Children's Education Authority (SCEA). Technically such teachers were civil servants. The NASUWT and other unions partly affiliated these members to the then Institution of Professional Civil Servants (IPCS) and in the company of one of its officials conducted negotiations and consultation with the relevant officials from the MoD and SCEA. The MoD announced it had reviewed its regulations and in the future women recruited in the UK would be allowed to apply for new contracts irrespective of whether they marry or not.

Under the Transfer of Engagements the combined NASUWT established a Women's Advisory Committee (WAC) from which three members were co-opted to serve on the National Executive until such time as the number of elected women numbered no fewer than three. Significantly the moves to abolish this 'patronising and sidelining' arrangement were led by women activists and succeeded at Conference 1983 when the WAC was discontinued.

Pressure then developed inside the NASUWT to establish an Equal Opportunities Committee (EOC). It was led by a future GS, Chris Keates, then rising to prominence and influence in the NASUWT as Secretary of the Birmingham Association and (in 1986) becoming a member of the Executive. Other prominent leaders in this campaign were the late Margaret Morgan and Olwyn Gunn, both 'veterans' of the UWT and the WAC and future NASUWT Presidents, together with Sue Rogers from Sheffield, a future President and Honorary Treasurer of the Union.

The 1987 Conference established an Executive Standing Committee on Equal Opportunities (EOC). The EOC was deliberately composed of a Chairperson and a member from each of the other five Standing Committees of the Executive, namely: Education; Salaries, Pensions and Conditions of Service; Legal Aid, Services and Benevolence; Recruitment; and Training. The EOC was assisted by two Advisory Committees, on Race and Disability, both elected by the Executive on the nominations of local associations. A corresponding department was created in the administration, led eventually by an Assistant

Secretary (the third tier in the Association's staffing hierarchy) in the person of Mary Howard who later went on to become an AGS.

In 1988 'snapshot' statistics issued by the DES revealed a huge chasm between the percentage of women teachers in promoted posts compared to men. For example 1 in 30 male teachers were secondary heads compared to 1 in 125 women. There was probably no more vivid an illustration of the blatant discrimination against women than that provided by June Gill who taught in a school in Doncaster. Employed as Head of Business Studies she was appointed in 1986 on a lower scale than the other heads of departments, all of whom were men with some in charge of smaller units. Her male predecessor had also been paid at the higher scale. Three years of unsuccessful representation led June Gill with the support of the NASUWT and the Equal Opportunities Commission to pursue a 'Like Work' case at an Industrial Tribunal in 1989 which she won. The LEA appealed against the IT decision but lost. June Gill was deeply grateful for the support offered by the NASUWT and the Commission and for her male 'comparator colleagues' in the school who were unstinting in their praise for her work.

Around the same time the NASUWT supported a PE teacher, Veronica Hanlon, who had passed the relevant Football Association courses but was refused recognition as an FA coach. The FA soon relented. Both these cases signalled a very proactive approach to 'Equal Ops' by the NASUWT although it was always difficult to find volunteers willing to pursue their rights for fear of gaining a militant reputation and provoking employer hostility.

A very significant development took place at the 1992 Conference. The Objects in the Rules of the NASUWT were amended to include the promotion within the Union and employment of equal opportunities "irrespective of gender, ethnic origin, disability, sexuality and religion." In time further amendments were made to this clause, which eventually read:

"to oppose actively all forms of harassment, prejudice and unfair discrimination whether on the grounds of sex, race, ethnic or national origin, religion, class, colour, caring responsibilities, marital status, sexuality, disability, age or other status or personal characteristic."

The internal union disciplinary rules were also changed to make it an offence for one member to harass or discriminate against another on such grounds.

In time another clause was also added to the Objects of the Union under its Rules requiring it:

"to promote equal opportunities including through collective bargaining, publicity material and campaigning, representation, union organisation and structures, education and training, organising and recruitment, the provision of all other services and benefits, and all other activities."

As a consequence of this Rule change the range of Advisory Committees to the EOC was extended to include provision for lesbian, gay, bisexual and transgender members. It also became the practice to organise Annual Conferences for all of the groups referred to under the revised Rules.

An annual Equal Opportunities Conference became a regular feature in the NASUWT's calendar from 1992. The NASUWT 1993 Conference mandated that research be carried out into women teachers' career prospects. A questionnaire issued to members produced a very high response – in excess of 25,000 returns. The subsequent Report to Conference in 1995 revealed that proportionately far more men were on higher salary points and in promoted posts than women.

Many policy statements were issued throughout the 1990s for the benefit not just of minorities but also for all members, enjoining them to be proactive, confront discrimination where it occurred and support members suffering from it. Many resolutions on discrimination were put forward to Annual Conference, to the TUC Congress and to the Women's TUC.

Another measure of the Union's activity and commitment to equal opportunities can be gauged by the number of publications produced on the subject, illustrated in Appendix J.

Chapter 45 - The NASUWT Impacts on the Education Scene

Being a small union prior to the 1960s and struggling against the odds in extraordinarily difficult economic and political times, the Association naturally devoted most of its resources to the bread-and-butter issues over pay and conditions of service, not to mention important domestic concerns such as legal aid and benevolence work. Nevertheless, as the preparations for the 1944 Act revealed, the Association still managed to devote much time and effort to educational issues. The best-selling book, *Swimming in Schools*, by a National President, Walter Shimmin from Liverpool, in the 1930s provides further evidence.

By the time the 1970s arrived the NAS and UWT had begun to develop a wide range of policies which, grounded as they were on the practical considerations of the teacher in the classroom, impacted significantly upon public debate and political decision making.

If there were one person singularly responsible for putting the NASUWT firmly on the 'educational map' it must surely be Fred Smithies who joined the Association in the 1960s, later becoming an NEC Member and then Chairman of the Education Committee. He also became AGS Education in September 1976, giving up the elected office of Junior Vice-President he had won a few months previously. He succeeded Terry Casey as GS in 1983. Fred had made himself an authority on educational matters and became very strong on exposing the conditions of service implications of the many reforms which were gathering momentum at the time. The effect of Fred's leadership in putting the NASUWT on the educational map can be gleaned from the impressive list of publications in Appendix H.

Education is awash with acronyms but 'ROSLA' (raising of the school leaving age) almost became a word in its own right. It provides an excellent example of the NASUWT's educational policies reflecting the practical concerns of the teacher in the classroom.

The 1870 Act introduced the concept of compulsory education to 13, but allowed various exemptions for poor children who could secure certificates of 'educational standard'. An Act of 1880 stipulated an absolute minimum age of ten before any child could leave school. Acts of 1893 and 1899 made the minimum ages, respectively, 11 and 12.

The 'Fisher' Act of 1918 raised the leaving age to 14. Eight years later the Hadow Report of 1926 recommended 'ROSLA' to 15. A Parliamentary Bill to achieve this in 1929 was defeated by Stanley Baldwin's cost-cutting measures. The 1944 Act provided for the leaving age to be raised to 15 and it was implemented in 1947. No sooner was the leaving age 15 than calls came from various quarters to raise it to 16. Major reports on education, especially in the 1960s, supported these calls and the first Wilson Government (1964-70) pledged to raise the age to 16 in 1970.

As the sixties progressed the NAS developed an attitude of "constructive scepticism" to ROSLA. The NAS accepted the government line that success "depended upon teachers' competence and enthusiastic co-operation". But the NAS fiercely resisted the implication that no other conditions were necessary. The Association insisted on reminding government it had a duty to provide adequate resources, including accommodation, staff, equipment and a relevant curriculum.

The NAS had drawn attention to problems over resources in 1966 through the publication of a pamphlet, *Ready in Time?* Conference the same year had carried a resolution which said it all:

"This Conference urges the Government to delay the raising of the school leaving age until staffing and accommodation allow such a step to be taken without detriment to the Education Service and until there has been adequate research into devising effective means of providing worthwhile education for less able older children."

The NAS and UWT lobby proved effective and in February 1968 the Government decided to defer ROSLA. The NAS then produced another pamphlet, *Four is twice as long*, in which it urged a more realistic approach to the problem of providing resources. After more debate and delay and a change in government, implementation was finally planned to take effect in 1973.

However, as the time approached the reaction of the NAS became more "sceptical". With the Order implementing the decision to raise the age to 16 already made, NAS Conference 1971 in Torbay debated the ROSLA issue. To this day I still recall the debate as one of the finest I ever witnessed. The passion and understanding of the issues displayed on both sides of a vigorously contested debate were exhilarating to experience. Circumstances had changed from previous 'ROSLAs'. Teachers' ability to deal with indiscipline had been circumscribed with the 'Retreat from Authority'. Many NAS and UWT members, being mostly classroom teachers, feared that 'troublemakers' would resent being made to remain at school for the extra year and would increase the disruption of the education of others.

The long-standing concerns over resources remained and while developments in the curriculum were helping the motivated child, the needs of the non-academic pupil were often lost in many of the reforms taking place which ironically were intended primarily to help them.

In the event Conference "regretted the intention of the Secretary of State to raise the school leaving age to 16". Conference noted the steady increase in the number of students staying on beyond the statutory age voluntarily. Conference believed this trend should be encouraged and compulsion avoided.

Following the Conference decision the NAS published another booklet, *Raising the School Leaving Age*, later in 1971. It emphasised the need to deal with the concerns and take heed of the views of the practising teachers who would be called upon to work in the classrooms with the older pupils forced to stay on for the extra year.

To those ends the booklet called for "the democratisation of the decision making process in schools", the setting up of academic boards and representation of classroom teachers on governing bodies. The Association was very sceptical that decisions would be based on realism if the views of those burdened with the additional tasks on a day-to-day basis were ignored.

The booklet again raised the problems with the unreformed curriculum, the huge pastoral care question and the "multiplicity of overlords" with whom the classroom teacher had to contend: namely, house tutors, heads of years, departmental heads, careers advisers and counsellors – all making their own demands in addition to the normal management.

There were huge problems with space and a lack of new suitable buildings despite some 'ROSLA blocks' in all too few schools. The NAS saw a role for FE colleges in providing a wider and perhaps more relevant curriculum through link courses, but some thought we were just trying to offload 'ROSLA kids' on to them.

The Association forecast a huge increase in the need for special education and remedial studies. However, most feared was the huge increase in the number of "problem pupils" – mostly those with serious emotional and behavioural difficulties who previously would have been the 'first to leave school at the earliest opportunity'. The Association promised it would "act in members' interests, authorising appropriate action in schools where the situation has been defined as unsatisfactory".

The NAS Report to Schools in September 1971 rejected the accusation that those who highlighted the problems were "reactionary". The NAS believed that in her circular to LEAs the Secretary of State for Education, Mrs Thatcher, "glibly assumed that where head and staff were enthusiastic there would be no problems". The Association rejected this form of "blackmail which implied that any failure would be attributable to lack of enthusiasm on the part of staff" and it deeply resented the alternatives left to schools – "either cover up problems or be blamed for them".

The 1972 Conference took a different decision on ROSLA on the pragmatic ground of having to come to terms with the inevitable. A motion deploring ROSLA was lost but Conference gave a warning that members would withhold co-operation in areas where accommodation, teacher-pupil ratios or facilities were inadequate. The Chairman of the Education Committee, Fred Smithies, assured members that while it made no sense to try to turn the clock back, the Executive would give full support to members for action where LEAs failed to remedy deficiencies.

The 1972 NAS Christmas Education Conference was devoted to the theme "Unwilling to (More) School". The results of an NAS survey published in December 1972 revealed that many LEAs were seriously under-resourcing ROSLA. In 1973 several disputes in LEAs, including Bolton and Preston, led to NAS and UWT members taking action in withdrawing goodwill to protest against inadequate provision. In addition action in refusing to teach disruptive pupils escalated, with 'ROSLA youngsters' accounting for much of the increase.

By April 1974 the relentless pursuit of action in the Bolton case led to an agreement with the LEA to raise the staffing levels of their worst-affected secondary schools to address the shortages created by the additional demands of ROSLA. Agreement was also reached to create a pool of supply teachers to help cover for staff absences.

The leaving age became 16 at the end of the 1972/73 school year. Many NASUWT members believed it merely exacerbated one of the fundamental problems afflicting the UK's education systems, namely, how to develop an appropriate curriculum to motivate the lower ability ranges. It remains an issue in modern times.

Besides 1976 being a hugely significant year for the NASUWT, hindsight also reveals it was the same for the UK and the education service. The year saw PM Jim Callaghan's famous Ruskin College speech which announced that politicians would be challenging the education world, accusing it of unacceptably low standards of achievement and demanding radical reform.

The year 1976 also marked the equally famous recall of the Chancellor of the Exchequer Denis Healey en route to Heathrow Airport to deal with the crisis in public finances and negotiate the intervention of the IMF to bail out the country. It began the process of imposing huge cuts in public services and adopting the discipline of the 'free market', such as it is. The agenda was being laid for the Thatcher Governments of the 1980s and arguably for the 'Great' Education Reform Act of 1988.

After the social revolution of the 1960s, the fundamental reforms associated with comprehensive reorganisation, the abolition of the 11 plus and the widespread adoption of new teaching methods in the primary sector, the British educational systems were never to be the same again. Change and counterchange were to become the sometimes bewildering norm for the remainder of the twentieth century and beyond.

Jim Callaghan's famous Ruskin College speech, delivered on 18 October 1976, is generally taken to be the first high-level government expression of concern over standards of achievement in the education service. The PM also raised questions about teaching methods and relevance of the curriculum to the requirements of the modern British economy. The speech was delivered in the wake of the scandal of the William Tyndale Junior School in the Islington Division of the ILEA, where traditional methods had been abandoned by a group of left-wing teachers in a social experiment that ended in chaos and the eventual sacking of most of the staff concerned.

There had been one or two straws in the wind a couple of years beforehand. In 1974 the Secretary of State Reg Prentice announced at the NAS Conference that an Assessment of Performance Unit (APU) would be established. It would start with the three core subjects of English, maths and science.

The plans for the APU envisaged the monitoring by sample of pupil performance in primary school maths from September 1978 and in secondary schools by the end of the year. Existing tests of attainment would be used for maths. Test instruments in English and science were in the process of being developed. Tests would be applied in maths and English to pupils aged 10 and 15 and in science at 10 and 13. The APU tests were not intended to provide information about individual pupils, schools or LEAs. The intention was to provide reliable information on trends in the quality of pupil performance. A school could expect to be involved in one of the subjects about once every five years.

The NASUWT took a keen interest in the APU and the Head of the Unit, Mr Kay, HMI, was invited to address the NASUWT Education Conference in 1976. Many people involved in and relating to the APU believed that it operated very effectively and efficiently, but perhaps too quietly. Mrs Thatcher's Government would eventually abolish the APU. In its place came a massive testing system of the basics in the wake of the so-called 'Great' Education Reform Act (ERA) of 1988. By that time trust between the Government and the 'education establishment' had sunk to zero. Had governments listened more carefully they would have noticed that many teachers also harboured concerns, and they could have been engaged in a more consensual and constructive approach to deal with the problems.

Early in February 1977 Minister of State Margaret Jackson (later Margaret Beckett) launched the Government's Yellow Paper following up Jim Callaghan's Ruskin College speech. The NASUWT decided to consult members closely on their views to assist representatives attending a series of regional conferences organised by the DES as part of the 'Great Debate'. Many local associations and individuals responded to the request for views.

March 1977 saw the publication of the results of the NASUWT survey. It was the subject of much TV, radio and press coverage. It was a unique survey and whilst no matter in education commanded universal agreement there was a clear majority expressing concern over standards.

Later on the NASUWT decided to commission a more scientific survey going beyond its own membership to gauge the opinions of all teachers in secondary schools. The Union engaged the British Market Research Bureau to conduct the exercise. The results showed that 80% of teachers believed that pupil discipline had deteriorated and 84% defined poor motivation as a serious problem contributing to low standards of achievement. Academic standards were considered to be worse than ten years previously by 54%, and to be better by 28%. General standards of all aspects of education were believed to have deteriorated by 65%, and to have improved by 18%.

Comprehensive education was thought to have made matters worse by 58% of teachers, with 25% taking the opposite view. Women teachers were more inclined to find fault with standards and the effects of comprehensive education than men. Headteachers took different views, the majority believing standards were better.

Significantly only 25% of teachers blamed the concept of comprehensive education for falling standards. Three main factors were considered responsible: the schools were too large; inadequate resources had been committed; and teachers had not been trained or prepared for the new roles they were expected to assume.

These views fully reflected and indeed reinforced those held by the NASUWT for many years. It had repeatedly warned governments about comprehensive reorganisation proceeding on ill-prepared and inadequately resourced bases. The NASUWT had also warned against imposing methods on sceptical teachers and cited the survey which showed that only 14% supported mixed-ability teaching whereas 48% approved setting and 30% judged streaming to be beneficial. The Union formed the view that mixed-ability teaching could work in ideal conditions but in the real world it demanded a level of effort which few teachers could sustain.

In the same month the Advisory Committee on the Supply and Training of Teachers (ACSTT) recommended to the Secretary of State that all entrants to training should have two A Levels and the normal qualification should include a degree. This had long been NAS/UWT policy.

A motion was carried at Conference 1977 expressing concern over educational standards. Thanks to this conference policy and to the membership survey, NASUWT representatives to the Great Debate's regional conferences had been able to express consistent views calling, in particular, for a precise definition of standards and the need for a core national curriculum.

At the same Conference, on behalf of the NEC I moved a motion on teacher training which was critical of the over-theoretical bias of most teacher training establishments. Student teachers were unprepared for the practical problems that would confront them the moment they were left alone for the first time in front of a class of pupils. We consistently called for a more school-based approach, which admittedly was more expensive but far more relevant.

With pressure from the NASUWT governments were gradually to move towards a more practical and school-based system but, unfortunately, often with inadequate resources. Much to the NASUWT's disappointment young teachers were still complaining about the same problems when surveys were conducted in the 1990s through the Teacher Training Agency.

The NASUWT welcomed the move to an all-graduate profession with the decision to phase out the Teacher Training Certificate courses from 1979 onwards. The ACSTT also adopted the policy that all future entrants would require as a minimum passes in two A Levels and five O Levels, two of which had to be in maths and English.

As a result of this activity at Conference 1977 the Education Secretary Shirley Williams was able to welcome the NASUWT's contribution to the Great Debate, describing it as "exceptionally impressive". The Minister also expressed great interest in our proposal for School Community Councils, although nothing came of it. That had been the main plank in the NASUWT's evidence to the Taylor Committee of Enquiry into the Government and Management of Schools which was set up in 1975.

The NASUWT called for realism in its evidence to Taylor, believing most parents had neither the time nor the inclination to get involved in the running of schools, but rightly wished to have their views heard and taken into account. It was unrealistic to expect governors to be able to do justice to an executive role which some politicians and pressure groups favoured. The Union called for Community Councils to provide a voice for parents, for LEAs through their CEOs to exercise financial and administrative control and for headteachers and the staff to be responsible for professional and curriculum matters. Governors should be given statutory powers to call upon an LEA to order an inquiry into the running of a school if they believed things were going wrong.

The Taylor Committee reported in September 1977 recommending increased powers for governing bodies. The NASUWT vigorously opposed the main thrust of the report. GS Terry Casey described it as "trying to give the kiss of life to a dead duck", "a cock-eyed plan for vesting management powers in essentially lay bodies".

The Taylor Committee met in the aftermath of the Tyndale School scandal, which, amongst other things, in the view of the NASUWT brutally exposed the mismanagement of the education service occasioned by the overlapping, confusing and inadequately understood roles bestowed upon headteachers, governing bodies, LEAs and central government.

By October 1977 the NASUWT was calling for a new Education Act to be included in the forthcoming Queen's Speech. Whilst Terry Casey welcomed proposals from Shirley Williams to give parents the right to choose their own comprehensive school provided there was room, he called upon the Secretary of State for Education to go further: "Instead of tinkering with a 33-year-old banger [from the 1944 Act] Shirley should demand from Jim [Callaghan – the PM] a brand new model designed to meet the needs of the 1980s." The present Act was "in bad shape". It had been confuted in the courts and confounded by its own contradictions. Part one of the Act said the Minister should determine policy, yet Section 23 vested control of the curriculum in LEAs. Terry Casey added: "It is this conflict of responsibility which causes confusion and enabled the Tyndale case to get out of control and other disputes such as the one involving the Thameside LEA to end up in the courts." (The Thameside dispute ended with a controversial House of Lords judgment that the LEA view of 'reasonable' should prevail over the Secretary of State's even if it involved a chaotic last-minute reversion to selection for secondary schools imposed by a newly elected Conservative council.)

The NASUWT arranged a formal deputation to the Secretary of State to warn her of the consequences of taking the conduct of day-to-day affairs of schools away from teachers. In another meeting in November the NASUWT informed the Schools Minister Margaret Jackson of cases where members had been instructed by the Executive to refuse to teach pupils that governors had declined to suspend or who had been allowed to return to school without adequate consultation with staff. Government decisions to increase the powers of governing bodies would not cause the NASUWT to weaken its stand against violence and disruption in schools.

Following a seminal report on primary education by HMI in October 1978 the NASUWT developed a four-point plan in response to the criticism that bright children were not being sufficiently challenged and that standards in some specialist subjects such as science, arts, geography and history left much to be desired. On the positive side the report said that teachers were conscientious and not ignoring the basics. The NASUWT proposed: smaller class sizes for children up to the age of eight; a more subject-specialist approach for children over eight; 10% non-contact time for primary teachers; and more in-service training.

A follow-up conference in November was organised at the Rednal Centre, at which Norman Thomas, HMI Chief Inspector for Primary Schools and author of the report, elaborated on the findings. The two- day conference also heard an interesting speech from Tom Clarke, Chief Inspector for Liverpool, in which he exhorted teachers to be more critical of the 'advice' they sometimes received. Too often educationalists asked the wrong questions, concentrating on research and administration and ignoring the most important variable, the quality of the teacher. In asserting their professionalism teachers should not waste their time on non-teaching chores. People in 'administrative authority' should not be allowed to interfere with teaching. A good slogan would be: "Class in progress: Keep out."

The ideas discussed at this conference bear a remarkable affinity with the policy on collegiality the NASUWT was to develop, not to mention the Standards and Workload Agreement of 2003.

The vast expansion of comprehensive schools soon had implications for the organisation of education post-16. In November 1977 the NASUWT had issued a pamphlet on the subject warning there had to be parity of esteem between comprehensive schools. The Government could not allow some to develop sixth forms while others were denied the opportunity. Parents would assume a school without a sixth form was not capable of providing tuition to a sufficiently high level, and good graduates would shy away from them for not providing the opportunity to teach to GCE A Level.

After much speculation and many leaks the MacFarlane Report on Education for 16-19 Year Olds was finally published in February 1981. The NASUWT believed the Report skated over the problems posed by the decision to establish comprehensives, which led inevitably to 'traditional' sixth-formers being spread more thinly. The Union, aware of falling rolls in the secondary sector and the increasing cry for 'best use of resources', called upon its members to respond positively to MacFarlane's suggestions that the traditional divide between schools and FE and between academic and vocational education should be reviewed. Schools should claim their proper part in the education and training of young people.

An Interim Report by the Rampton Committee, inquiring into the education of West Indian children, was published in July 1981. Reacting to the event, Fred Smithies said the Report was long on allegations but short on evidence in its claim that an important cause of failure among such children was racism, intentional or unintentional, on the part of teachers. The NASUWT supported positive discrimination on grounds of educational need but believed it would endanger the concept of community if it were based on ethnic identity. Fred Smithies also pointed out that the success of Asian children and other minority groups destroyed the credibility of allegations that West Indian underachievement was caused by teachers' negative attitudes and racism. There was a danger that teachers, fearing such allegations, might patronise West Indian children and treat them differently from others.

In December 1981 the NASUWT produced a written response to 'Rampton', whose Committee was now presided over by Lord Swann and renamed accordingly. The response reiterated the immediate reaction given earlier in July and called for a restrained debate through which there could be intelligent and objective evaluation of complex and sensitive matters. The Union stated that important factors in the underachievement of West Indian children were cultural and language differences, which left them with an insecure base for educational development. The NASUWT rejected the allegations that racial prejudice was responsible and regretted that this charge was seized upon by many West Indian parents to explain why their children failed at school. The Union called for the extended provision of nursery education to counter disadvantage and rejected the suggestion that qualification standards should be diluted to favour ethnic minority teachers finding employment as teachers.

The final Swann Report appeared in March 1985 under the appropriately recast title: "The Education of Children from Ethnic Minority Groups". It ran to a massive 800 pages. Fred Smithies welcomed the "balanced approach to the need to ensure that all children, whatever their ethnic origins, receive the best possible education" and the refutation of the allegations in the Interim Report that racism on the part of teachers was responsible for failure amongst West Indian children. The prime concern of the NASUWT was to secure special and appropriate help for those children suffering educational disadvantage resulting in underachievement. However, Fred Smithies added: "If the recommendations are to be successfully implemented greatly increased demands will be made on teachers' time and energies and to meet these Government and LEAs had to provide additional staffing and other resources."

The increasing influence of the NASUWT over policy development was well illustrated in February 1982 with the publication of an all-party report by the Parliamentary Select Committee on Education, Science and the Arts. In a wide-ranging review of the secondary school curriculum, it criticised the DES's policy of non-intervention and expressed the view that the Secretary of State had a positive role to play in promoting education. The Committee also demanded that the Inspectorate should be completely independent of government so that it could monitor standards and report freely. The Committee even strayed into the salaries field, recommending Scale 1 should be a starter grade with competent teachers promoted to Scale 2, and expressing the view that pay and conditions of service should be negotiated together. All these recommendations largely reflected NASUWT policies.

In September 1982 the NASUWT issued another major policy statement on pupil profiles, calling for all leavers to receive a comprehensive end-of-school report not limited to academic attainment but also including information on other matters such as punctuality, reliability and initiative, which would be helpful to prospective employers. Launching the statement Fred Smithies, now GS designate, said that academic attainment applied only to a minority of pupils and any system which ignored pupils of average and below-average ability was doomed to failure. The NASUWT held that the profiles had to be nationally based and externally validated and required extra resources to guard against teacher workload increasing. Fred concluded: "Properly implemented this system would improve pupil motivation and morale. Positive statements about achievements and attributes should help to instil a sense of pride, self-confidence and self-respect among pupils for whom the present curriculum has little relevance."

HMI published a significant report in September 1983 on the impact of expenditure cuts in the education service. HMI identified major problems in staffing levels in the primary sector: "Mixed age classes and undifferentiated ability groups were more common and deficiencies were quite commonly noted in remedial teaching, mathematics, science, music and art." In middle schools "no subject was likely to be totally unscathed". There was also clear evidence that primary schools were frequently dependent upon parental contributions, not only for 'extras' but to buy books and basic materials.

In the secondary schools the cumulative effect of economies was "undermining attempts to maintain standards, particularly as falling rolls move through the sector". Staffing was the main constraint. Twelve LEAs were identified as worsening pupil-teacher ratios which were already less favourable than the national average. Shortages of specialist teachers were noted in a quarter of all returns on individual schools. There were plenty of examples of slow learners being badly provided for. Overall provision of books was judged to be satisfactory in only two-fifths of LEAs.

The Inspectors said firmly that: "There can be no question but that the right teachers in the right number (properly equipped and supported) have the first claim on educational expenditure." Fred Smithies complimented HMI on its "courage and integrity". In those days there was continuous speculation on how independent from government HMI was willing to be. HM Chief Inspector was a prestigious position to occupy but subject to fixed-term contracts. HMI reports critical of teachers and educational standards were seized upon by sections of the media eager to believe stories confirming their views. The same sections of the media were not so keen to believe the kind of report that came out in September 1983.

In October 1983 one of the more memorable 'post-Conference' deputations to the Secretary of State for Education took place. Sir Keith's inevitable response to so many of our concerns was straightforward but brutally true: "I can offer no assurances whatsoever on additional resources." When the Ex-President, Eric Powell, raised the problems of integrating handicapped pupils into mainstream schools without resources for the adaptation of buildings and criticised the Government's expenditure policies, Sir Keith interrupted him to point out that he had never pretended the money would be made available. The integration lobby would have to live with winning the argument but not the money!

Whilst the NASUWT had serious differences of opinion with Sir Keith Joseph we recognised the personal courage he sometimes displayed in making difficult decisions. In contrast to Shirley Williams and Mark Carlisle, Sir Keith bit the common examination system bullet and finally approved the merger of GCE O Levels and CSE. With comprehensive schooling widespread it was time for public examinations at 16 to reflect the new regime with a common system, the GCSE. The new examination was never to be popular with the right wing and controversy continues to the present day. The NASUWT supported the move to the GCSE.

In October 1983 the NASUWT had its first meeting with the Social Democratic Party, the breakaway group from Labour led by 'the Gang of Four'. David (later Lord) Owen appeared to be reasonably well briefed on education, argued his case well and acknowledged the NASUWT had some telling points to make on the career teacher and other issues. Once again the meeting underlined the NASUWT's non-party political stance and its readiness to meet with other groups in addition to the 'big two' of Labour and Conservative.

It is true to say that education was forced to take something of a back seat in the years between 1984 and 1988, which were dominated by the most bitter salary disputes in the history of the teaching profession. Nevertheless, in January 1985 amidst the worsening crisis over teachers' pay, the NASUWT found time to survey its members on the role of parents in schools. It was increasingly obvious to anyone who cared to look that parent volunteers were being used more and more as the 'extra body', 'helping hand', 'enthusiast', 'enhancer', 'expert', 'ancillary' or 'ear'. The NASUWT had long ago formulated a policy accepting the appropriate use of suitably trained and qualified ancillary staff in schools to assist teachers, but was deeply concerned with the completely unregulated use of volunteers.

SECTION SEVEN
BATTLING ANTISOCIAL BEHAVIOUR
IN SCHOOLS

Chapter 46 - The Retreat from Authority

The swinging, rebellious sixties might have been a wonderful time for the trendy posers in the media and other 'over-liberal' elements in society, but they produced huge problems for people inevitably placed in positions of authority, such as teachers.

Antisocial behaviour constantly reminds us that sensible discipline, while easy to mock, is essential for a good quality of life for all citizens. As a consequence the overall quality of life has not always matched the undoubted leap forward in living standards in the twentieth century. Teachers, NASUWT members included, tended to blame parents and social deprivation for the failure of some to raise their offspring to respect the rules of good behaviour in school and elsewhere in society.

A parallel problem has been the consistent poor performance of pupils from the bottom quarter of the ability range in British schools. In spite of the valiant efforts of many teachers it has proved extremely difficult to break down the anti-education and antisocial attitudes presented by some pupils and their parents. It has also proved impossible to find enough of the high-calibre people required to carry out this extremely difficult job and to do so consistently for a long period of time. And where such people have been found and recruited into teaching and headship, early burnout has often been the result.

There will be eternal debate over whether things were always thus or if a significant deterioration in standards of behaviour was occurring. Anecdotal evidence abounds on both sides of the argument. My purpose here can only be to describe the majority views that emerged from the NASUWT as expressed through the resolutions and actions of local associations, the Executive and Annual Conferences, which together constitute the channels of democracy inside the Union.

Members of the NAS had long been concerned about juvenile delinquency. The debate at the 1937 Annual Conference and the Executive Memorandum on the subject showed most of the concerns expressed related to behaviour and factors outside the school. It appeared that teachers retained sufficient authority to deal with antisocial behaviour where it occurred within the school gates; but during the 1960s this appeared to change.

The 'retreat from authority' was in the collective judgement of the Union the most significant social development of the post-Second World War period that impacted upon the professional lives of teachers. Concern over increased antisocial behaviour by some pupils in schools led the NAS in 1965 to publish another Report on Juvenile Delinquency.

NAS members believed that a sea change occurred in the 1960s when an increasing number of parents withdrew support from teachers dealing with bad behaviour. Some openly condoned bad behaviour; the worst actively encouraged their offspring to challenge teachers. Teachers understood they relied critically upon the ability to exercise authority, in the best sense of the word, to perform their duties effectively. They appreciated that where misbehaviour occurred, be it minor or major, it had to be corrected immediately. Control once lost was almost impossible to regain.

With mothers increasingly joining fathers in going out to work schools were called upon to cover for this 'parental vacuum' and assume an ever-greater social-work role. The emerging large comprehensive schools had to embrace wider pastoral care systems, inevitably accompanied by much bureaucracy. The ability to deal quickly with disciplinary problems disappeared. The pupil had to be referred to form tutors or heads of year pastoral post holders. The parent(s) had to be consulted. Social support agencies had to be involved in the more serious cases.

In short, social attitudes, school organisation and new, more informal teaching methods all combined to undermine the authority position of the teacher and aided and abetted the wayward youngster who was determined to do as he (and increasingly she) pleased. Youngsters soon learned to play the system. In a lax disciplinary context the poorly behaved and unmotivated pupils quickly realised they could get away with it. They did not want to be in school anyway. Some parents and critics of the education system blamed the problems on boring teachers whose lessons were poor.

One of the first things I noticed upon arrival on the education scene in London (in the late '60s) was the collapse of a consensus on the purpose of schooling and the standards of behaviour that were acceptable. Opinions often differed sharply amongst teachers themselves. Many tried to insist on high standards of behaviour and study, paying due attention to the basics and using reasonably reliable traditional methods. Others favoured a more relaxed approach to teaching and to standards of behaviour.

Some influential figures, such as the ILEA CEO Sir Eric Briault, argued that teachers should become 'facilitators' and abandon their traditional 'didactic authority' role. Many NAS members believed such a concept to be wrong in principle and where it was implemented in practice it lacked precision and clarity, producing confusion or something worse. As soon as teachers escaped from the classroom (the most challenging place to be in education) to become co-ordinators, advisers, lecturers, heads, inspectors, administrators or directors, they seemed seduced by idealistic theories based on the supposition that schools were populated by angels and not children.

Teachers who wanted to get on, secure promotion and earn a halfway-decent salary had to espouse the new 'progressive' philosophy. Refugees from the classroom held the power and patronage over an entirely inappropriate promotion and salary structure. Modern and 'exciting' methods triumphed over common sense and the need for good behaviour whatever educational philosophy was to be employed.

It was a culture shock for me to discover teachers in the late 1960s/early 1970s openly proclaiming that schools should be used to foster 'the revolution', whatever that meant. In those days, before becoming known as an NAS activist, I managed to infiltrate a few meetings of the Inner London NUT and witnessed at first-hand the battles between the subversive revolutionaries and the 'establishment platform'. On occasions the police had to be called to restore order.

It was not just idle talk. The scandal of the William Tyndale School affair in the Islington Division of the ILEA finally broke into the public domain in the mid-1970s, revealing serious attempts to put revolutionary principles into practice. Whilst not endemic, similar problems existed in many other schools, which should have been more generally exposed and promptly rectified.

Some staffrooms were riven with divisions between traditionalists on one side and anything ranging from 'progressives' to 'hard-left revolutionaries' on the other. As a generalisation, this was often reflected in divided union memberships. The NAS and UWT were largely identified as being on the traditionalists' side, together with a rather quiescent AMA and AAM. The NUT, populated by a silent majority of primary school members and largely run by activists from the socialist wing with a considerable admixture of hard-left revolutionary groups, was viewed as 'progressive'. The damage to good order in schools, to the education of many children and to the image of the teaching profession was severe.

One of the most disturbing aspects of the 1960s and '70s in the view of the NASUWT was the reluctance of politicians of all persuasions to accept there was a problem needing urgent attention. School management and LEA officials were often in denial or applied pressure to sweep a problem under the carpet. The teacher in the classroom could not do that. Failure to deal with it, or just hoping it would go away, quickly made teaching impossible. The lives of teachers caught up in these problems also became impossible, and the dreaded occupational disease of modern times, stress, made its unwelcome appearance.

As the 1960s passed by into the 1970s NAS members increasingly turned to their union for support in dealing with pupil indiscipline. It appeared to me indisputable from my own caseload as a young union branch secretary that whether the 'quantum' was increasing or not the support teachers should have received from those supposedly 'in authority' was disgracefully disappearing fast. Local and national representatives began to speak out publicly and in 1971 the NAS began to compile its first dossier on violence and indiscipline in schools. It was designed to ascertain the size of the problem and how indiscipline was tackled where it did occur. The NAS began to call for more support from management to back up the judgement of the teacher at the chalk face.

On 30 November 1971 *The Guardian* carried an article on violence in schools, claiming that the problem had been exaggerated in the campaign to postpone the raising of the school leaving age. A member of the NUT Executive was quoted as saying that schools were being depicted as blackboard jungles to frighten parents, local authorities and MPs.

The day before *The Daily Telegraph* had reported on the same matter but taken a somewhat different view. It said that classroom violence appeared to be on the increase and it was even suggested that some local authorities were pressing head teachers to enter into a conspiracy of silence about its extent. *The Telegraph* claimed that parents had the right to know and called for stricter discipline.

Unfortunately, in the view of the NAS, the issue of behaviour in schools became political in the sense of 'left' v 'right'. The NAS was strictly non-party political and judged matters according to the effects on its members in schools. Genuine concern recognised no party political boundaries.

The Christmas 1971 NAS Education Conference was devoted to "Management, Organisation and Discipline in Schools". The NAS was soon to be calling for teachers to have more say in decision making, not only in respect of discipline but also in relation to the curriculum and examinations. The NAS went on to produce model articles and instruments of government for schools.

The NAS Executive also decided to be proactive. In February 1972 the NAS engaged a leading educational psychologist, Dr L. F. Lowenstein, to undertake a statistical survey and study to identify specialist skills classroom teachers could develop to deal with disruptive behaviour and what practical support they should be given.

The Association also decided to sponsor outward-bound leadership courses designed to help young schoolmasters to adapt such pursuits to the needs of difficult boys in their charge. The NAS hoped that LEAs would grant paid leave for attendance at these courses.

The Spring Term of 1972 saw several newspapers highlighting violence and indiscipline in schools. Some displayed ulterior political motives, being anti-Labour and anti-comprehensive schooling. However, the schools 'exposed' as suffering from violence and indiscipline and their LEAs did themselves no favours by defensive denials that any serious problems existed.

The media latched on to cases such as one that arose in March 1972 at the Crown Court in Birmingham which proved to be a sign of the times a-coming. The NAS successfully defended a member who had been charged with assault on a 15-year-old lad who lashed out at him with his boot, only to feel the teacher's fist on his jaw. Fortunately Mr Justice Ackner took a common-sense approach to life and commented on the prosecution's case: "Have we reached the stage in schools in this country when an insolent and bolshie pupil has to be treated with all the courtesy of visiting royalty?"

The NAS Conference in April 1972 saw the issue of violence and indiscipline in schools voted top priority for debate, where it remained for the rest of the twentieth century and beyond, becoming the cornerstone of our key policy statement, "Retreat from Authority", which was published a few years later in 1976. The motion read:

"This Conference demands that the Government and Local Education Authorities provide adequate safeguards to support teachers seeking to maintain acceptable standards of discipline in their schools. Conference pledges support for the Executive in any action it authorises to maintain such standards."

The sting in the tail was the last sentence, which anticipated the policy to be formalised in *Retreat from Authority*, which became so closely associated with the NASUWT. That was to refuse to teach violent or disruptive pupils, and if instructed to do otherwise by management, to resort to strike action.

Addressing the 1972 Southport Conference Dinner, Secretary of State Mrs Thatcher signalled a departure from 'departmental policy' in announcing a fact-finding inquiry on the subject. She recognised our concern and drew strong applause when declaring she was not in favour of sweeping the problem under the carpet. Terry Casey welcomed the move but warned against a whitewash, noting that it was not an official inquiry. A recent NAS survey covering 3,000 schools would be presented to Mrs Thatcher.

The Daily Mail on 7 April 1972 reported Mrs Thatcher's decision with a page one 'splash': "Probe into Classroom 'Jungles'". Whilst acknowledging the NAS as "the professional body which has campaigned longest against indiscipline" *The Mail* claimed much of the credit for its own series of articles over the previous two months exposing incidents in some comprehensive schools.

A prominent Labour leader in the ILEA, Mrs Irene Chaplin, described Mrs Thatcher's move as a "panic measure" induced by the right-wing media. The ILEA had recently refused to conduct an inquiry into violence and indiscipline in its schools, despite protests from the LSA.

The new NUT GS, Ted Britton, delivering his 'state of the union' message to his Conference in neighbouring Blackpool, warned the Government not to cave in to the "scaremongers" and "the violence brigade" – widely interpreted as a swipe at the NAS. He also included in this impressive list of "the enemies of education" the "de-schoolers – a group of intellectual quislings", some "pseudo scientific researchers", and (amazingly) some of the union's own branches "too cowardly to fight for smaller classes in a number of areas".

In moving the main 1972 Conference motion on indiscipline the then Ex-President Ron Cocking referred to an NAS survey carried out in the West Midlands. It showed massive support among parents and teachers from all unions for the concerns we were expressing. Ron dismissed NUT President Harry Allison's "Allison-in-Wonderland" approach accusing the NAS of distortion and exaggeration.

Ron Cocking emphasised that he "was not calling for a return to barbaric methods of disciplining pupils" but, he added: "There was no reason to be blinkered against the danger signals obvious to nearly every teacher. We do not have a blackboard jungle yet but unless local authorities were willing to give proper backing to their schools it could develop into alarming proportions."

Another sharp difference of policy thus emerged between the NAS and the NUT. The NAS policy reflected the concerns of the classroom teacher. The NUT seemed more concerned to defend the 'progressive' reforms of the 1960s.

The NAS 1972 Conference was 'spot on' in being the first to identify the growing incidence of drug abuse among schoolchildren. The Conference also called for alternative special schooling for the small minority of violent and disruptive pupils who wrecked the education of the majority.

A few months later Sir Alec Clegg, a very well-known and respected chief education officer, was quoted in his local newspaper, *The Yorkshire Post*, on 10 June 1972: "Parents must take a considerable share of the blame for increased hooliganism and bad behaviour in schools. In the meantime there is no doubt that violence and aggression is on the increase but much of the evidence has been swept under the carpet."

The first recorded refusal to teach by NAS and UWT members occurred at the Pelton Roseberry Comprehensive School in Durham in 1972. Thirty-four members were so instructed by the General Secretary (GS) following a decision by the Chair of Governors (taken without consultation) to readmit a pupil suspended by the head teacher for violent and threatening behaviour towards staff. The action produced the required preconditions before members would resume teaching the pupil together with agreed procedures for dealing with such instances in the future. In the same year in Essex members refused to teach a pupil who had violently assaulted a head teacher, rendering him unconscious. The head had just suspended the boy for violent conduct. The LEA tried unsuccessfully to insist that another school admit the boy, who had four separate convictions in the magistrates' court for various offences. The action forced the LEA to establish a special unit to cater for such cases.

The 1973 Annual Report to Conference referred in the section on legal aid to "the significant increase in the number of complaints from teachers suffering physical assaults from pupils, parents and others received on a daily basis at HQ". Another case reached the National Executive when full support was offered to the headmaster and NAS members at Abergele Comprehensive School in Wales following a challenge to the suspension of two pupils.

By 1973 refusals to teach were becoming common in London, where LSA leaders blamed the teacher shortage crisis in the capital on chronically low pay and pupil behaviour problems. On 1 February 1974 the *TES* published a famous leader, "Stinking goldfish", claiming that "fact and fiction mingle so easily in the London classroom crack-up saga". The *TES* apportioned most of the blame to those whose activities were exposing the problems to public scrutiny: "Stinking fish are bad enough by themselves, without the goldfish bowl effect". The *TES* contention that solutions were more likely to be found 'on the quiet', away from the glare of publicity, was dismissed by us as naïve. Our experience proved that those 'in authority' would not move unless there was public pressure to do so.

For the General Election of February 1974 the NAS and UWT produced the customary briefing documents for members to lobby all Parliamentary candidates. Behaviour in schools featured as one of the nine main topics. Chris Price, Labour MP, Lewisham East and a prominent spokesman on education, wrote in the *TES* that he had been lobbied by all the teachers' associations and he judged the LSA Lewisham Branch deputation to have been "the most professional".

The NAS argued that the more reluctant, resistant and recalcitrant pupils who disrupt other pupils' education should be catered for outside the conventional schools in work-related schemes under firm and sympathetic guidance. The problems of behaviour and truancy were serious enough to warrant careful investigation by an independent inquiry.

The issue of school behaviour featured strongly on the agenda of the 1974 Annual Conference. In his presidential speech John Scott, from Northern Ireland, demanded that teachers should have the right to expel rebellious pupils.

He said that ROSLA had produced a new breed of reluctant pupils for whom the extra year could lead to compulsory 'miss-education'.

Conference instructed the Executive to press for amendment of the 1944 Act to allow pupils in their final statutory year to leave with the agreement of all interested parties. The NAS declared it could not stand idly by while thousands of members laboured under such difficulties, and a further motion calling for positive support for teachers facing these problems was overwhelmingly carried.

At a press conference on 31 October 1974, in response to continued membership pressure the NAS launched a report on "Discipline in Schools", which led to widespread media coverage. Evidence from a survey conducted amongst members pointed to hundreds of refusals to teach disruptive pupils whom governing bodies and LEAs had declined to expel from their schools. Practising schoolmasters spoke at the press conference giving first-hand accounts of their difficulties. One of them, Bill Meyer, said he had 30 years experience in "one of the best schools in London" but "of the 28 classes I take a week I do really effective teaching in only three. I am fed up and frustrated . . . In the corridors it is chaos. I often have to step in and stop teachers from being thumped."

The report blamed modern methods and developments and stated that teachers could no longer be "the guardians of values abandoned by the rest of society". GS Terry Casey challenged any Director of Education to suspend an NAS member rather than a violent or disruptive pupil.

I was quoted referring to the problem "moving down the age range into the primary sector" where in a Lewisham school I was supporting NAS members in refusing to teach three pupils. In another case a nine-year-old had assaulted a 60-year-old teacher, smashing his glasses and biting him. He then bit other teachers who tried to bring him under control.

The report identified 30 different causes of indiscipline in schools. They included: indiscipline within society, the weakness of parents, erosion of teachers' authority, protest as a way of life, idolising of wrongdoers, 'politicising' of attitudes and the poor quality of a minority of teachers.

Terry Casey called upon the Government to establish "minimum codes of sensible behaviour. The rot has got to be stopped if we are to save education." Chairman of the NAS Education Committee, Fred Smithies, referred to the problem of incitement, an example of which he had found outside the gates of his own school, St Mary's High, Northampton. A group of students and other adults had distributed leaflets to pupils "fomenting trouble and unrest, openly inciting them to bad behaviour. They latched on to some of the more intelligent pupils and used them as 'agents' within the school. When action was taken against the 'agents', the outsiders claimed 'victimisation and ill treatment of our comrades'." Fred Smithies demanded "to know who pays for the leaflets to be printed".

Terry Casey said there was a proliferation of such leaflets and booklets throughout the country, intended "to disrupt the good order of our schools as a prerequisite to revolution". John Izbicki, for long the renowned Education Correspondent of *The Daily Telegraph*, wrote that he had come across similar material. One leaflet marked "Top Secret" instructed pupils in low-level disruption and if "Sir doesn't notice, move on to obscenities".

Despite the intense public debate there was no change in the attitude of LEAs even though all of them received copies of the NAS report. At governmental level the Conservatives had lost power in the February General Election and the new Labour Education Secretary had no predisposition to treat the NAS concerns with sympathy as had to some extent been the case with Mrs Thatcher. The NUT remained in denial, its GS Elect, Fred Jarvis, sidestepping the issue and blandly calling for teacher unity to tackle the many challenges facing the profession, which apparently did not include this one.

Conference 1975 carried a resolution again pledging support for members who, acting on Executive instructions, refuse to teach violent and disruptive pupils. In June 1975 came the first of some cases that were to break out prominently into the public domain. Eleven members were suspended at the Sedgefield Comprehensive School in County Durham following a refusal by the entire NAS membership of 34 to teach a youngster with a long record of disruptive behaviour which included four previous assaults on teachers. The NAS insisted the boy undergo a course of rehabilitation at a nearby special unit before being considered for readmission.

The LEA had decided to close the 1,000-pupil school because one boy had been refused admission. The LEA and police had to turn away pupils arriving for school that members were willing to teach. The NAS insisted it was completely unacceptable for the LEA to override the considered judgement of so many teachers who had to deal with the boy while also ensuring the education, health, safety and welfare of all the other children in the class. An independent inquiry was subsequently agreed and it ended up recommending that although the youngster should return to normal school he should not go back to Sedgefield. The NAS accepted the recommendation, believing it vindicated the stand the members had taken.

In addition to the Durham case members at a school in Barking had received the NAS's full backing during the Spring Term in their refusal to teach violent pupils. However, in this instance the LEA had not reacted aggressively like Durham and no publicity had resulted. A similar case had occurred at Sutton Secondary Boys School in Ellesmere Port.

Launching the report by Dr Lowenstein on the results of the NAS survey concerning violent and disruptive behaviour, GS Terry Casey criticised LEAs for turning a blind eye to the manifest problems despite the evidence over the last five years. He added: "When authority abdicates the bullies take over. We are determined to back the classroom teacher who is prepared to insist that good order is a prerequisite for sound education. The only social activity they can run without discipline is a riot."

Although some schools avoided serious problems the report showed there was an alarming incidence of disruptive behaviour in every type of school of all sizes. Some 1,844 schools reported 37,470 incidents of disruptive behaviour between 14 October and 20 December 1974. Some of these incidents took place in primary schools. During the same period 6,349 incidents of violent behaviour were also reported in the same 1,844 schools.

Questionnaires had been returned by 20% of secondary schools and although a larger return would have been welcomed the evidence indicated an enormous problem demanding immediate attention.

The issue of teacher quality, frankly conceded by the NAS as a contributory but not a major factor behind pupil misbehaviour one year earlier, returned to prominence at the 1975 Annual Conference. A motion was carried to raise the minimum entry requirements for teacher training above the current 5 GCE O Levels to include 2 A Levels.

I spoke in the debate raising the problem of London's recruitment difficulties. The media picked up on my comments that "it was harder to fail than to pass teacher training courses". The failure rate was less than 1%. Referring to a recent official report which showed a sharp drop in the quality and quantity of entrants to training colleges, I observed: "Anyone can hop in and out of teaching as easily as hopping on or off a London bus. Unless the tide was turned teaching would remain the slum profession". At that time the ILEA openly acknowledged it had no choice – and some recruits were deficient in their command of English – in order, as the CEO Dr Eric Briault said, "to make sure there was at least a body in front of the class". That was just one reason why I reacted with hostility in later times when both Conservative and Labour Ministers accused teacher unions of protecting incompetent teachers.

In the same debate Fred Smithies said he was "frequently shocked by teachers who encouraged pupils who just managed to scrape together five GCE O Levels to apply for training colleges". He expected teachers "to be more sensitive about the calibre" of potential recruits. Fred believed the problems had started in the 1960s with the massive expansion of teacher numbers when "quality had been sacrificed for quantity".

The resultant headlines such as "Schoolmasters attack 'dunce' colleagues" and "Teacher, you're a dunce" did not endear us to our colleagues in other unions but it was another example of the NAS being upfront and honest in its expression of views.

Despite widespread 'official' denial of the indiscipline problem in schools, during the 1975 TUC Congress debate on violent behaviour and assaults on employees, it was impossible for the NAS and UWT speakers to get to the rostrum, which was monopolised by anxious speakers from all walks of life.

The NAS discussed the problem of discipline with the HMA and NAHT and it had informal discussions with officials of the Police Federation who, faced with a similar situation, warmly welcomed our support and co-operation. The Minister for Sport was in talks with the General Secretary and he invited the NAS and UWT to give evidence to the committee investigating trouble on the football terraces.

In the early days most cases of refusal to teach were conducted locally and with a considerable amount of success. That was my experience in authorising such refusals to teach in the Lewisham Branch and the LSA in the early to mid-1970s. I knew of similar experiences from my networking with other Local Secretaries and Executive Members around the country. Surveys conducted and reports published by local Officers of the NASUWT in Leeds, Birmingham and Cleveland revealed very similar experiences.

Local Officers of the NASUWT responded to members' requests but did not actively seek publicity for individual cases, still less naming names, for teachers did not wish unfavourable publicity to be visited upon their schools. Publicity was far more likely to occur when management resisted our refusal to teach and threatened disciplinary action. In such circumstances we deployed two countermeasures before resorting to industrial action. One was to threaten to retire to the staffroom until it was deemed safe to emerge. The second was to threaten publicity as a last resort, despite its dangers. On some occasions head teachers refused entry to external union representatives to hold meetings on the school premises. Our stock response was to threaten to organise a lunchtime meeting outside the school gates with the media invited as well. I cannot recall ever having to implement such a threat although we came very close to it one day at a school in Southwark. Such measures usually 'concentrated management minds'.

The relentless pressure from members led the now combined NASUWT to publish a seminal booklet in 1976 entitled *Retreat from Authority*. Besides once again giving an estimate of the size and gravity of the problem, the document also laid down the philosophical justification as well as the practical guidance for our policy of 'refusal to teach' violent or disruptive pupils.

While the 'political' impetus to produce *Retreat from Authority* was led by Terry Casey, most of the hard drafting had been driven by the Chairman of our Education Committee at the time, Fred Smithies, later to become GS himself. I had been elected to the National Executive in 1975 and became a member of the Working Party on Indiscipline, which under Fred's chairmanship drew up the document.

After the publication of *Retreat from Authority* in 1976 the conduct of cases was also subject to authorisation and close monitoring by the Action Committee – the National Officers advised by the GS. We realised we needed a comprehensive and coherent national policy to apply consistently across the country. Action was breaking out in many areas and procedures needed to be regularised with authority coming from the Executive. If strike action were required members would look to the National Association for support, both moral and financial if necessary. The Conservatives' 1971 Industrial Relations Act and Labour's amending 1974 Trade Union and Labour Relations Act also imposed greater responsibility on national executives for the conduct of their unions' affairs.

Retreat from Authority laid out the procedures to be followed. First, all the internal procedures of the school's behaviour policy should be followed. Only after all these procedures had been exhausted should action to refuse to teach be contemplated. Members were advised to keep accurate and full records of disruption and violence. Constant petty disruption was often more destructive of education than the less frequent dramatic confrontations. If exhausting the internal procedures failed to resolve the problem, a school union meeting should be called to consider approaching the Union at national level through their Executive Member. If intervention by these representatives failed to solve the problem then action could follow.

In addition, assaults should be reported to the police and the LEA. If both those agencies declined to prosecute, the Union would consider supporting a member taking out a private prosecution.

Retreat from Authority also examined the problem of disruption, its causes and effects. The Union conceded that teachers had a duty to understand the causes of misbehaviour. But understanding is not the same as acceptance.

As candid as ever we again conceded the problem of the poor quality of a minority of teachers. We accepted it was indefensible to condemn pupils to suffer teachers who were clearly inept. Obviously such teachers should be dismissed after due process if reasonable support had failed to produce necessary improvement. Nobody's interests were served by the tolerance of incompetence or unsuitability.

We also stated that some youngsters were determined to disrupt no matter how good the school and the teachers. The diminishing ability to deal quickly with this small minority led to the problem assuming much greater proportions.

Retreat from Authority acknowledged the need for teachers to play their part in preparing well and delivering interesting lessons. But it was not that easy given the subjects that had to be taught and the inappropriate curriculum on offer to many pupils. The poorly resourced raising of the school leaving age to 16 in 1972/73 without an appropriate curriculum on offer to motivate the eager-to-leave non-academic youngster worsened disruption in the classroom.

As a member of the National Executive as well being the London Association Secretary I was in a position to sanction action fairly quickly, as the situation in London often demanded. I recall vividly the most dramatic time being a Friday in November 1976 when, during the course of the afternoon after a hectic morning, I authorised seven refusals to teach, all in different schools. I called it "Bleak Friday".

So the pattern was set. A steady flow of cases authorising refusal to teach was reported to the Executive by the National Officers for endorsement. The Union also continued to conduct surveys, produce publications and take other proactive measures designed to help deal with the problem.

The problem of stress at work received its first significant airing in 1976. The NASUWT commissioned a survey on stress in the light of many teachers being unable to continue working until normal retirement age. Stress was at a maximum where young teachers were not properly trained to cope with modern teaching techniques, schools were badly organised, excessive noise occurred, classes were oversized, buildings were badly designed and pupils were disruptive. Experts revealed the heart rate of a teacher working with fourth-formers rose from a normal 70-80 beats a minute to 125 by 4 p.m. After 4 p.m. it dropped to around 90.

The Union published several studies on the subject, one of which, entitled *Stress in Schools,* was highly praised by members as well as outside commentators. This initiative showed once again NASUWT was first in the field in identifying and responding to new, emerging needs of teachers practising in the classroom.

In February 1978 the NASUWT published *Discipline in Schools – Supportive Roles of Psychiatric and Social Services.* The publication emphasised the NASUWT wished to work in co-operation with other professions in dealing with discipline problems, but would insist upon the need to recognise that teachers had to deal with youngsters in a group context. The behaviour of challenging pupils was often totally different in one-to-one situations from that experienced in the classroom.

In 1979 the Union produced some advice on steps members could take based on real-life case studies. The result was a booklet we published in the same year, entitled *Action on Indiscipline: A Practical Guide for Teachers*. The *Guide* was produced in conjunction with Sam Comber and Professor Richard Whitfield, both experienced and former science teachers, then currently and respectively Senior Educational Research Associate and Professor of Education at the University of Aston in Birmingham. The booklet was based upon collecting authentic incidents, judged to be critical, from a representative sample of teachers. The actions taken by the teachers in response were then categorised with discussions on other alternatives that might have been possible.

The booklet, running to about 70 pages, was widely reported on the day of publication. It was well received by members who found it very useful, but it failed to make a lasting impact beyond the immediate and interested group of our members. The theorists in the training institutions remained hostile to the NASUWT approach.

The Catch 'em Young project was another proactive initiative inspired by Terry Casey. In 1979 Terry got together a representative group of reasonably high-profile people from education, including Her Majesty's Chief Inspector of Schools Bob Bolton (in pre-Ofsted times), civil servants, LEA officials and outward-bound-focussed organisations. The idea was to identify youngsters in their primary schools showing all the signs of ending up being the subject of our refusals to teach in the secondary sector. They would then be taken out of their environments for a few weeks at a time and provided with an alternative experience, mostly of an outdoor and physically challenging nature.

The hope was that this would be a positive and socially beneficial experience which would lead the youngsters to adopt a better behaviour pattern in school. Despite much difficulty the project got off the ground and ran for three years. Terry Casey managed to persuade the hard-line 'monetarist' Education Secretary, Sir Keith Joseph, to part with around £20,000 from his Department to monitor the effectiveness of the project over three years in the early 1980s. The report of the monitoring group was very positive. But before it was published the finance had run out. North Yorkshire CC, providing the youngsters and the finance for the running costs, pulled out.

A serious dispute broke out at the Thorney Close Comprehensive School in Sunderland in 1984. A 16-year-old had assaulted an NASUWT member and had been readmitted into the school in a way which members found to be totally unacceptable. Strike action was undertaken in the school, which was backed up with a general withdrawal of goodwill by all members in the LEA. With the help of an intervention by ACAS the dispute was resolved.

The spring 1985 edition of *The Schoolmaster and Career Teacher,* mailed to all members' home addresses, contained a questionnaire on the subject of violence and serious disorder in schools to which some 4,000 members responded. Introducing the report that followed on the survey results, the new GS, Fred Smithies, observed that there was without doubt a problem which showed "no signs of diminishing".

The survey was based on experiences from September 1984 to February 1985. It showed 60% of respondents to have suffered verbal abuse on one or more occasions. A third had suffered damage to or theft of property by pupils. Twenty per cent had witnessed pupil-to-pupil violence resulting in serious injury in situations approaching open gang warfare. Almost one in four teachers had been threatened with assaults by pupils, one in ten had experienced an attempted attack and one in twenty-five had suffered actual physical violence.

We never pretended that the self-selecting respondents to the survey constituted a truly representative sample. But the results were to bear an uncanny resemblance to the more scientific study carried out (with all the resources available to the Government) by the Elton Enquiry that was established in 1988 to investigate the same subject.

Another NASUWT report in 1986, *Violence and Serious Disorder in Schools,* provided a range of examples, on an anonymous basis, of real-life incidents that had taken place. It also included for the first time examples of the emerging problem of sexual harassment of young women teachers by adolescent male pupils. There were also examples provided of the growing tendency for the problems to move down the age range into the primary sector, of the increasing use of weapons, especially knives, and of the greater involvement of girls in the disorder and violence. Another disturbing development was the hounding of teachers in their homes, not just by pupils but by angry and aggressive parents.

Two cases in 1987 broke out into the public domain as ballots were required to authorise refusals to teach two pupils, one at the Belle Vue School in Bradford and the other at Foxhills School in Scunthorpe. The calling of the ballots was sufficient to concentrate management minds and resolve the problems.

The NASUWT's 'battle to restore authority' continued in a similar vein throughout the 1980s. From time to time, cases in the courts captured the attention of the media. In 1982, in line with NASUWT policy, the ILEA successfully prosecuted a parent who had entered the school premises to protest against the disciplining of his child and then assaulted one of our members, Suzzane Puttock. In the same year, a magistrate sitting in the Highbury court was severely criticised for saying that it was an occupational hazard for teachers "to expect to be assaulted 6 to 7 times in the course of their careers." In the

1990s some dramatic cases erupted into the public domain, which I describe later in this section.

The NASUWT position on corporal punishment (CP) was often misrepresented. While undoubtedly many members believed it had a valid and useful role to play in the maintenance of good behaviour, the policy of the NASUWT was that it should be a matter for schools to determine for themselves. Decisions properly made at school level had therefore to be respected and members were advised accordingly.

The belief held by many individual members reflected the general views held amongst the population at large although many parents took a harder line. In keeping with the more relaxed approach to discipline in the 1960s, public opinion began to change. Pressure to outlaw CP grew with the UK's adherence to the European Convention on Human Rights, which, amongst other things, prohibited the use of cruel and degrading punishments. Most 'mainland European' countries had banned CP, some many years previously.

The ILEA gave the campaign led by the Society of Teachers Opposed to Physical Punishment (STOPP) to abolish CP a great impetus when it announced in the mid-1970s it would prohibit its use in primary schools. The Labour Leader of the ILEA, Sir Ashley Bramall, was a keen supporter of STOPP.

In 1979 the first case concerning the use of CP was dealt with by the European Court of Human Rights. Whilst not pronouncing on the cruel and degrading issue it upheld the right of the plaintiff parents to have their child educated "in accordance with their wishes", which meant 'no CP' in this case.

Summoned at a moment's notice to provide the NASUWT's response and giving my first national TV interview (on the early evening BBC TV News *Tonight* programme), I said that teachers "had to accept the referee's decision" but should be relaxed and simply operate on the principle that with one sanction removed the point at which the NASUWT refused to teach a disruptive pupil might arrive earlier than hitherto. Parents had to realise that asserting their rights *within* school eroded the 'in loco parentis' status of teachers, the principle underlying the heavy pastoral role traditionally accepted in British schools. I was pleased when Terry Casey complimented me the following day for taking the line I had and not attacking the judgment. No doubt ten years imbibing NASUWT culture including Terry's ways of reasoning had assisted me.

In 1981 the ILEA resolved to extend the ban to all schools. London NASUWT tried to declare a collective dispute on the ban, claiming it was a matter for each school to decide for itself. The Union nationally supported the London Branch's action and issued a pamphlet restating policy. The ILEA refused to accept the issue of CP was justiciable under the collective disputes procedure. The NASUWT took legal advice, only to be informed that CP was more likely to be considered by the courts to be a 'method working' rather than a 'condition of service' and therefore difficult to pursue as a trade dispute.

In 1982 the Derbyshire LEA announced it was banning the use of CP in its schools. There had been no consultation with the unions and the NASUWT declared a collective dispute over the issue. The LEA refused to accept it should have consulted first and that the matter was justiciable under the procedures even though Lord McCarthy, Chairman of the Central Arbitration Committee, declared to the contrary on both issues.

In September 1983 the Conservative Government announced a major consultation exercise on the steps it should take in response to various judgments of the European Court of Human Rights which effectively upheld parents' rights to object to and prohibit the use of physical punishment in respect of their own children "in accordance with their wishes". Another judgment had declared CP to be inhumane.

In a move which angered the NASUWT the Government tried to have its cake and eat it. Instead of recognising that the judgments had the effect of banning CP in British schools the Government was consulting on a system which would allow parents to opt their children out of the CP sanction. Anyone the least bit familiar with the running of a school would know the importance of equity and consistency for all in dealing with discipline. Opting individual pupils in or out of any sanction was a complete nonsense. Sir Keith Joseph, along with many Conservative Ministers, MPs and indeed voters, had proclaimed his belief in CP as a necessary sanction in maintaining discipline. This proposal, denounced by GS Fred Smithies as "impracticable and hypocritical", was the Government's way of avoiding embarrassment with their supporters.

The NASUWT also declared that there was no alternative but for the Government to provide the resources to operate more complex and sensitive discipline policies in schools once the 'cheap' and some would say 'nasty' CP sanction was no longer available. It was small comfort for the NASUWT to learn that the Government proposed to legislate for any breach of parental wishes to be justiciable as a civil rather than a criminal matter. To avoid costly compensation claims eventually the Conservative Government had to legislate to ban CP in state schools. The crucial vote passed by a majority of only one, with several prominent Ministers, including Mrs Thatcher, conveniently managing to be absent from the House at the time.

Chapter 47 - The 'Grand Grafitti Dispute'
(Poundswick School, Manchester)

The 'Grand Graffiti Dispute' in 1985 at the Poundswick School in Manchester was the first refusal-to-teach case that attracted huge media coverage nationally as well as locally. It also involved the highest number of members called upon to strike over the issue and to do so for the longest period of time. The case also contained elements of sex, yobbish behaviour and left-wing political intrigue, all of which was grist to the media mill.

The incident which provoked the dispute took place on 18 June 1985. Five boys at Poundswick High School, Wythenshawe, Manchester, scrawled foot-high, strong and explicit obscenities about individual named members of the teaching staff and their families. Painted on the outside of the school building, besides being sexually obscene, it was also racist and very personal.

The graffiti was quickly removed and every effort made to keep the precise text a closely guarded 'local' secret. However, Manchester city councillors were given "neatly typed copies of the 24 phrases" which had been daubed on the walls of the school. One councillor said: "It is not just disgusting – it is frightening to think children could do this".

Rightly the head teacher suspended the five boys. The governors reached a unanimous decision to expel them. However, on Friday 13 September the newly created South District Education Subcommittee of the Manchester City Council met to consider whether the boys' exclusions should be permanent or whether they were to be readmitted. (This was in the days before the independent appeal panels were established.)

Manchester City Council Education Committee was in the hands of some very left-wing politicians who were determined to see the number of exclusions from schools reduced. After a six-and-a-half-hour meeting and following a split vote (mostly on party lines) the Subcommittee insisted the boys be returned. A former Mayoress and a Conservative voted in favour of expulsion. The four Labour members voted to instruct the school to take back the 'Dirty Five' as the boys were beginning to be called.

The forced reinstatement represented one of the worst examples of an appalling anti-authority message being conveyed to all youngsters in Manchester and, who knows, probably to every single child in the country who read or heard about the story.

The governors reaffirmed the boys should not come back. The teachers, led by the NASUWT, declared they would refuse to have them back. The teachers were instructed by the Manchester LEA to teach the boys. When they refused they were sent home without pay. Some declared themselves to be on strike.

The NASUWT GS, Fred Smithies, visited the school very promptly and gave the 'suspended' teachers full backing. He said: "The insensitivity of the Authority beggars belief. Our members are excluded and will lose pay when it is the culprits who should be out of the school! No wonder teachers throughout the city and the rest of the community are up in arms".

Members of other teacher unions, the NUT and AMMA, joined in refusing to teach the five boys. The strong support coming from both the governing body and the head teacher played an important part in securing a unanimous staff position.

At the same time the long and bitter teachers' pay dispute of 1985-86 was well under way with widespread industrial action. Relationships with Mrs Thatcher's Government were at an all-time low, and getting worse by the day. Furthermore, redundancies loomed in the city of Liverpool, which had been plunged into financial crisis thanks to the hard-left politics of the Militant Tendency, which had taken over the local Labour Party. Widespread cutbacks also threatened the jobs of thousands of other teachers in different parts of the country. The Action Committee feared the Sunderland Reserve Fund might not be able to meet the potentially massive demands that could be made upon it in the light of these circumstances. It was 'not a good time' to have a major local dispute with many members out on an indefinite strike.

The NASUWT had 18 members out of the teaching staff of 63. With the backing of the National Executive a "Pounds for Poundswick" campaign quickly got under way to help raise the £2,500 per week required to sustain the suspended 18 members. It was organised by the two National Executive Members for the area, Ann Boone and Maurice Littlewood. Ann Boone's husband, Joe, was the NASUWT President at this very troubled time. The "Pounds for Poundswick" campaign enabled thousands of members all over the country to make direct contributions to the cause.

By October the Chairman of the Manchester Education Committee, Nick Harris, was forced onto the defensive, revealing a dogmatic opposition to expulsion almost regardless of the merits of the case. He believed the 50 or so pupils under exclusion at any one time to be "unacceptably large". He regretted the media coverage and the pressure being placed on the Dirty Five and their families, but had no words of comfort for the teachers and their families. He (rightly) claimed that the procedures used by the Subcommittee were right in line with those being proposed by the Conservative Government in its recent

White Paper, *Better Schools*. As Nick Harris observed, parents, encouraged by the Government, were increasingly "turning up and demanding their rights".

A new political agenda was emerging. In short it meant something like this: Labour committed to inclusion at all costs; the Conservatives to parental rights, even if hijacked by dysfunctional families; schools expected "to consume their own smoke" and keep disruptive children inside their gates, no matter the consequences for maintaining good standards of behaviour and effective teaching.

The politicians had not, however, reckoned with the determination of the NASUWT, and indeed the campaigning abilities of others. On 4 October a massive 'Poundswick demonstration' took place in Manchester. Hundreds of teachers and pupils streamed out of their classes as many schools were shut in a protest against the suspension of staff who had refused to teacher the Dirty Five. Traffic came to a standstill as a crowd of 2,000 massed for a rally outside the education offices and then set off for the Town Hall.

The march was led by over 60 Poundswick teachers, including the head, Keith Halstead, and 19 members of staff who had already been suspended for refusing to teach the Dirty Five. Many Poundswick parents joined their children on the march. After school hours even members of the 'pacifist' PAT, the organisation dedicated to never striking, also joined in. Many high schools were closed for the afternoon. The 'SOS' (Save Our Standards) placards made their first appearance and soon became a feature of the dispute.

When the City Council met on 8 October a very stormy exchange ensued as Liberals and Conservatives tried unsuccessfully to get the Labour majority to agree to discuss the Poundswick affair.

News also emerged that the Secondary Heads Association (SHA) in Manchester was also going to vote in favour of strike action. Subsequently they did by a 93% majority. The National Association of Head Teachers (NAHT – mostly primary school heads) soon followed suit, with 83% voting in favour of strike action. It was quite unprecedented for these exclusively head teacher organisations to take strike action.

Even *The Daily Telegraph*, not renowned as the most likely national newspaper to be first to leap to the defence of teachers taking industrial action, wrote in its editorial on 8 October: "Almost everyone will feel sympathy for the teachers at Poundswick High School . . . 47 of whom have been suspended."

Manchester City Council's Schools and Policy Subcommittee finally discussed the crisis on 10 October. Pandemonium broke out in the packed public gallery when a Liberal Party proposal to call a special session of the Education Committee to reverse the decision to reinstate the Dirty Five was defeated on a show of hands by the Labour majority. Nick Harris for Labour claimed (quite correctly from a procedural point of view) that it would make a mockery of the appeals process.

On 11 October a 90-minute meeting between councillors, education officials and union leaders failed to break the deadlock, and plans for a massive one-day strike across all Manchester schools went ahead.

Reports emerged of the police being called to investigate a stream of abusive mail and telephone calls to the four Labour councillors on the Subcommittee who had voted to reinstate the Dirty Five. They had also, apparently, been subjected to stone-throwing attacks on their homes and demonstrations by parents who supported the teachers. Needless to say, the NASUWT did not condone such tactics.

The *Times* editorial of 11 October backed the school in demanding the removal of the five boys. It argued the rights of the five boys and their parents were outweighed by those of the majority who had backed the actions of the head and governors in expelling the culprits.

On the afternoon of Monday 21 October all of Manchester's 350 schools were closed and over 75,000 children were sent home as most of the city's 5,000 teachers took strike action to protest against the Council's continued failure to back staff and the governors at Poundswick in the 'Grand Graffiti Dispute'. NASUWT members were joined by colleagues in the NUT, AMMA, SHA and NAHT, only PAT being unable to join the strike, although expressing much sympathy for the cause.

A Council meeting a few days later on 25 October, whilst reaffirming the Council's position on the return of the five boys, offered the possibility of conciliation as a means of resolving the dispute. The dispute got personal as some Tories tried to turn the heat up with accusations that at least one of the four Labour members of the Subcommittee was "a stooge of the Marxist cell at the town hall".

A meeting between the teacher unions and the Council on 30 October failed to break the deadlock. The Council insisted the five boys had to be accepted back into school before conciliation could start. For the NASUWT Ann Boone made it clear that the boys had to be dispersed to other schools elsewhere in the city and our members had to be reinstated. Nothing else would do.

In November the conciliation service, ACAS, intervened but talks broke down without progress being made. Rumours spread that the Council was considering sacking the suspended and striking teachers to get the troubled school reopened after six weeks of closure. Both the NASUWT and NUT warned this would escalate the problem to a major city-wide dispute with extended industrial action.

GS Fred Smithies repeated the determination of the NASUWT: "It is quite intolerable that an employer should expect its employees to deal with people who have insulted them. The pupils are now bragging they have kept the school closed for two months." He described the Council's suggestion that the teachers be dispersed to other schools in the city as "outrageous".

The first signs of cracks in the united teachers' position came when AMMA and NUT accepted the offer of the Dean of Manchester, the Right Reverend Robert Waddington, to act as conciliator after the ACAS initiative failed. This offer to mediate between the parents and unions was rejected by the NASUWT as being irrelevant. The mediation needed to be between the unions and the employer.

The Manchester Labour councillors tried to fight back to regain the initiative by calling upon the Poundswick governors to consider "new evidence". A 60-page dossier compiled by the Director of Education claimed that 18 teenagers had been involved. Chairman of Governors Les Roberts dismissed these claims as "ridiculous". The additional names had merely appeared in teachers' notes of interviews following the incident and showed no other involvement. The governors repeated their view that the five boys be transferred to other schools. The Council firmly rejected this.

Towards the end of November the Liberals asked the Education Secretary, Sir Keith Joseph, to intervene, using his powers under the 1944 Act. On 9 December the DES wrote to Manchester Education Department expressing concern at the failure to resolve the dispute. Sir Keith Joseph was reported to have given the Authority "one week" to sort it out.

But responding to a letter from a Manchester MP, Sir Keith Joseph said he did not believe there was a case to use his powers under the 1944 Act. Those powers did not permit him to substitute his judgement for that of the LEA except where a decision was so arbitrary or otherwise that no reasonable authority could have taken it.

Unfortunately the old problem of teacher disunity surfaced just before Christmas. Secret separate talks had been conducted by the Council with the NUT and AMMA. A deal emerged on 19 December. They would resume work on 6 January and in return the Council agreed not to discipline their members for refusing to teach the Dirty Five. But their strike would continue against the three fifth-form classes which contained the five boys. This would allow around 90% of pupils to return to school. But to our disbelief, the Dirty Five would be taught "off school premises" by a teacher from another school. Quite outrageously in the NASUWT's view, all the innocent fifth-formers would remain the only pupils without schooling.

The NASUWT rejected this shabby and outrageous deal. Besides discriminating against most of the fifth-formers it compromised the basic position on the need for expulsion. Our Manchester Secretary, Joe Lowrey, described the deal as "immoral". He added: "We have always said we are prepared to teach everyone but the five boys." National Executive Member Maurice Littlewood's comments on the deal with the other two unions were unprintable. Even *The Daily Mail* agreed with us, describing the deal as "a shabby compromise" in an editorial on 21 December: "Manchester city council has saved its face at those [fifth-formers'] expense."

Meanwhile the national pay dispute continued with Prime Minister Thatcher sending a 'Happy Christmas' message to all employers of teachers, urging them to lock out all those taking action in the national pay dispute.

So the dispute dragged on into 1986, with the NASUWT now fighting a lone battle. Eighteen members were unofficially suspended without pay, effectively on strike. On 8 January 1986 some normality returned to the school as around 400 pupils resumed lessons, their first since the previous September.

In an extraordinary statement the Manchester NUT Secretary claimed the deal was more easily reached with his union "because we withdrew our members before they could be individually victimised by the authority". With Orwellian doublespeak other defenders of the shabby deal claimed the five were not being taught at home. They were receiving 'tuition' from 'counsellors'. They were not being 'taught' but 'assessed'. The *TES* headline on 17 January had it all summed up: "Poundswick deal means tuition for 'dirty five' but not exam pupils".

The stalemate at Poundswick with the NASUWT was to continue throughout the Spring Term. Many lessons had been restored but there was still severe disruption. 'NASUWT' classes had to be sent home and most of the fifth-form ones still had to be cancelled.

The strikers' morale remained high. One of them, Mrs Vivien Sidebottom, wrote a moving article in the March edition of the union journal describing the daily activities of the strikers and the strong bonds of friendship that had developed between them all and their supporting Executive Members and local Officers. Although saddened by the loss of the other unions – blamed on the national leadership, not the members in the school – their resolve to stand firm was undiminished.

Easter arrived, the time for the teacher union Conferences, with the NASUWT gathering in Scarborough. Fifteen Poundswick members travelled over to Scarborough to join their School Rep, Mrs Christine Elwood, herself a conference delegate, for the debate on indiscipline in school, taking place on the Wednesday of Easter week.

Proposing the motion, the Bexley Secretary, Jim Hughes, pointing to the Poundswick party in the public gallery, paid tribute to their courage and determination as the entire Conference rose to give them one of the longest standing ovations in NASUWT Conference history.

Speaking in the debate Chris Elwood recounted the appalling treatment handed out to members taking official union action by their 'hard-left employer'. They had been called in one by one to be told by the Authority that they were in breach of contract; they would not be paid; a record of their action would be placed on their personal files and their right of access to the school would be withdrawn, even though they remained ready and willing to teach all their students bar the Dirty Five.

Conference gave the Executive authority to escalate the action. All schools with NASUWT members in Manchester were to be hit with selective strike action. There would be a rolling programme of single-lesson strikes by key teachers for up to three weeks, borrowing many of the tactics being used in the national pay dispute.

The NASUWT Scarborough Conference of 1985, held in the middle of that long and bitter pay dispute after years of savage cuts in public expenditure, was also the one in which the Education Secretary, Sir Keith Joseph, received the famous 'silent treatment' after his speech on the Thursday afternoon. In contrast to the 'silence' awarded to Sir Keith, the four conference delegates invited to put their questions to him were each greeted with thunderous rounds of applause. None more so than Chris Elwood, invited to put the final question: "Why had the Secretary of State not intervened to remedy the appalling situation at the Poundswick School?" There was nothing artificial about the stunned silence that greeted Sir Keith's answer. He believed the LEA "had taken all reasonable steps".

The teachers on strike, supported by local colleagues, maintained a vigil outside the school gates. The running total of lessons lost was recorded daily. On 1 May 1986 the 'blackboard' read:

Poundswick High School
Number of lessons lost since
September through City Council's obstinacy – 31,989

As announced at our Annual Conference a mass rally and march in support of the members at Poundswick was organised in Manchester for the Sunday of the bank holiday weekend on 4 May. An estimated 10,000 marchers turned out, including many parents who, remarkably perhaps, had remained very supportive of the strike. Some fifth-formers from Poundswick also marched with us that day, even though their public examination preparations were compromised by the dispute.

Among the speakers at the rally was Sheila Naybour representing the National Confederation of Parent Teacher Associations (NCPTA). As an elected parent and vice-chair of a governing body she "knew full well the heart-searching and anguish" behind a decision to expel a pupil. But "we have to judge the disruptive child against the effects on the rest of the school", she declared, to loud applause from the rally.

In their speeches to the rally, our President, Mike Inman, and GS Fred Smithies, along with Sheila Naybour, all warned the Government about its Education Bill currently going through Parliament. It purported to give LEAs the power to instruct heads and governing bodies to take back excluded pupils after three days aggregate suspension. That ended up as the infamous 1986 Education (No. 2) Act that established the independent appeal panels on permanent exclusion of pupils from school. All the speakers warned it could lead to more disputes like Poundswick. Nearly 20 years later (in 2004) it was remarkable to hear the Leader of the Conservative Opposition, Michael Howard, declare they should be abolished!

The only official exchange between the two sides from January to May 1986 was a 12-minute meeting late in February in which the NASUWT flatly refused to accept a repeat offer of the shabby deal with the other two unions. So the dispute lingered on into the Summer Term with the NASUWT spreading selective strike action to some 60 other schools in Manchester.

The 'Grand Graffiti Dispute' was suddenly ended by an abrupt and somewhat chance happening. Late in May a local journalist telephoned our London office and the call was passed to me as the Deputy GS. He reminded me that fifth-formers at Poundswick, like those in most secondary schools, were shortly to commence study leave prior to taking their public examinations, the GCEs and CSEs. Once the exams were over they effectively left school.

He reminded me that two of the five boys had left the school at Easter, as 16-year-old pupils were entitled to do in those days. The other three would soon effectively be leaving at half-term after finishing their exams. He asked me what would happen to the dispute once the Dirty Five had disappeared from the school. Almost nonchalantly, I replied that I supposed the dispute would disappear with them. Apparently my comment was carried in the local Manchester newspaper.

The Deputy Director of Education in Manchester, Mr Jobson, picked up my comment and wrote officially to GS Fred Smithies seeking clarification. The two set about negotiating, and following a series of consultations between all the parties an agreement that our members could return to work was reached.

So on Thursday 5 June 1986 our members returned to work. The Dirty Five would no longer be attending the school. Suddenly, the nine-month-long dispute was over, with just a few residual details to be resolved.

Ann Boone said the members were "glad to be back at school. It has been a very trying time for them but they have been buoyed up by the tremendous support, both moral and financial, which the whole Union has given them". GS Fred Smithies said it was "inappropriate to talk of victory in an avoidable dispute. Our members lost pay and had to endure much professional distress; the pupils lost lessons and the Council damaged its standing with teachers."

Several newspapers commented that it was too late to save public exams at Poundswick, with less than 40% of fifth-formers having turned up to take them. It fell to *The Daily Mail* to reflect the sentiments of most people in an editorial of 3 June, headed "Dirty deal":

"What kind of anarchic educational system is it, when children who besmirch authority are reprieved and teachers who struggle to maintain discipline are punished?

"When the head, staff and governors of a school are united in wanting a child kicked out, that child should stay kicked out. In an age of disorder and disrespect those at the chalk face must not be denied expulsion as their ultimate deterrent."

Fred Smithies added that we had to try to secure amendments to the Bill going through Parliament otherwise many more 'Poundswicks' would occur all over the country. The Bill was amended to extend the right to schools to appeal against LEA decisions enforcing reinstatement of expelled pupils. But it retained the clause giving the parents of expelled pupils the right to appeal to 'independent' LEA Exclusion Panels.

So there can be no excuses for the Conservatives. They passed the Education (No. 2) Act in 1986 setting up the appeal system for expelled pupils in full view of the nine months of turmoil at the Poundswick School. NASUWT warnings were ignored. Many 'independent' panels were to uphold appeals by violent or disruptive youngsters against their expulsion, in exactly the same way as the Manchester Subcommittee had done. And many more disputes did occur as we continued to refuse to teach hundreds of disruptive pupils not excluded when they should have been, be it due to lenient governing bodies, LEA review committees or independent panels with the final say.

The 'Grand Graffiti Dispute' may be viewed as a 'draw' because neither the NASUWT nor the Manchester Council gave in. It 'self-resolved' as the clock ran out. However, despite the efforts of a few – recounted elsewhere in these chapters – no other LEA or governing body again tested our resolve in the way that Manchester City Council had done. Our 'Poundswick 18' had achieved great things not just for themselves but for thousands of other teachers finding themselves in similar situations over the course of the following years.

By 2004 the tide seemed definitely to have turned with the Leader of the Opposition Michael Howard promising to restore freedom to schools, abolish appeal panels and give head teachers the right to expel violent or disruptive pupils, whilst Prime Minister Tony Blair signalled a massive drive against antisocial behaviour in schools and elsewhere. This may have been a genuine conversion or the usual search for votes, a particularly desperate one for the Conservatives after eight years in opposition. But it certainly reflected public opinion polling by both major political parties, telling them something the NASUWT had been proclaiming for over a quarter of a century.

Chapter 48 - The Elton Report

In the House of Commons on 18 March 1988, in a move rumoured to be motivated by a need to avoid being outflanked by the far right in the Conservative Party, the Education Secretary, Kenneth Baker, launched a Committee of Enquiry into Discipline in Schools, to be chaired by Lord Elton with the following terms of reference:

"In view of public concern about violence and indiscipline in schools and the problems faced by the teaching profession today, to consider what action can be taken by central Government, local authorities, voluntary bodies owning schools, governing bodies of schools, heads, teachers and parents to secure the orderly atmosphere necessary in schools for effective teaching and learning to take place."

On the day, I expressed fears that the terms of reference were too wide-ranging and diffuse, blurring the central focus which should have been: What practical measures needed to be implemented yesterday to enable the teacher in the classroom to deal effectively with serious pupil disruption? They smelled of a long 'sociological' treatise of all that was desirable at the expense of that which was possible.

Lord Elton, a man of impeccable establishment pedigree – son of a baronet, educated at Eton and Oxford, followed by the armed forces, farming and company director – was one of Mrs Thatcher's longest-serving Ministers but had recently resigned due to overwork. He did have some teaching experience, mostly in a grammar school over 20 years before.

Other members were drawn from higher education, LEA administration and business, with one secondary and one primary head. For the NASUWT I objected fiercely to the absence of a representative of the hundreds of thousands of classroom teachers, "the poor bloody infantry" most affected by the problem.

A few days later a 'token' classroom teacher was appointed. She was Colette Thomson, a former member of the England netball team and then a mathematics teacher at Alderbrook School in Solihull. While no doubt a very accomplished person of impeccable integrity, Colette Thompson had no representative status and was simply unknown to the vast majority of teachers. It was typical of the Government's approach to cut out the unions and select individuals of its own choosing, pretending they were genuinely representative.

Without a strong and experienced input from practitioners genuinely representing the voice of the teacher in the classroom, the Committee of

Enquiry was destined inevitably to have next-to-no impact upon the problem. Ken Baker knew that Fred Smithies was willing to serve on the Committee. Fred had long experience as a teacher in a comprehensive school and a representative active on this issue throughout his working life. He was also the GS of the union that had led on this issue for many years and was easily the best-qualified teacher representative for the job.

By 10 June 1988 the NASUWT had submitted a very substantial amount of evidence which included 13 publications we had produced on the subject since 1972 and reflected all the concerns we had been raising. Our evidence included the 1985 survey on indiscipline, which showed that 25% of teachers who responded reported having been threatened and 1 in 25 had been physically attacked.

The NASUWT's most important recommendations were:

more alternative forms of education for those whose antisocial behaviour was so severe they could not be contained in the mainstream classroom;

better resources to provide a more interesting and relevant curriculum;

more staff to deal with youngsters with emotional and behavioural difficulties with effective sanctions if required;

more realistic and practical teacher training;

measures to educate parents to enforce discipline in the home.

In addition the Union called for clear-cut procedures for dealing with assaults on teachers.

The unions were also invited to present oral evidence, although the arrangements proved cursory at best. Each union was allocated only 40 minutes after which the Committee was scheduled to have a ten- minute private discussion on each union's evidence. The NASUWT managed to occupy the Committee's attention for a full hour on 6 October 1988 when we presented our oral evidence and answered questions.

On that occasion the Chairman seemed excessively concerned about defining key words such as 'violence' and 'indiscipline'. It strengthened my impression that the Committee was going to be of little help to the teacher in the classroom. One did not need a dictionary to recognise a class or a pupil out of control, or violence when it smacked you between the eyes. Teachers had to make instant judgements on the spot and they needed support, not second-guessing by those distant from the classroom pondering erudite definitions safely ensconced in their comfortable offices.

The Elton Report was published on 13 March 1989. Lord Elton suggested that teacher unions had exaggerated the level of violence in schools. He was greeted by a chorus of disapproval from all the four mainly classroom-based unions and by the National Association of Head Teachers (NAHT).

"A weak and woolly whitewash" was my widely quoted sound bite summing it all up, to which I added: "The recommendations are very disappointing. They don't get to the guts of the problem, which is how teachers cope today with the minority of difficult pupils while educating the others to the high standards required."

David Hart, GS of the NAHT, also hit the nail on the head when he said the Report did not provide "nearly enough support for teachers in dealing with pupil violence and disruptive behaviour". Even the NUT, which normally favoured the 'sociological' approach to these problems, said it was "deeply disappointed" with the Report. However, the unions agreed with Lord Elton finding that "minor disruption" was a more widespread problem than the 'one off' violent incident.

It was obvious from Kenneth Baker's prompt announcement to act upon only 8 of the 173 recommendations, that he intended no serious discussion of the Report, whatever the differing views about its merits. Ken Baker was quick to point out that many of the recommendations fell to other parties to implement. He fastened upon the 'low cost' recommendations, accepting for example the proposal that initial teacher training should be more practical and focus on techniques to manage pupil behaviour. He ignored the recommendation for a specific requirement for lecturers to have recent classroom experience. Elton had recommended one term in every five years.

Another low-cost recommendation was for teachers to accept a greater burden in getting themselves trained up better to cope with poor behaviour. But Baker could only set aside an extremely modest amount of £7m in the local authority training grants scheme for this and the other recommendations, which had also to be shared with additional measures to tackle truancy.

The Elton Report urged teachers to "strike a healthy balance" between rewards and punishments, and avoid "humiliating" pupils by ridiculing them in front of others. Those were the kinds of 'motherhood and apple pie' recommendations that typified the Report. Most teachers were already well into that good practice. The support they needed centred upon how to cope when all the good practice still did not succeed with the few who wrecked the education of the many.

When it came to relatively simple, direct and effective – but potentially expensive – measures to support teachers, the Elton Committee ran a mile. It laboured the "inherent disadvantages" of off-site "sin bins" for persistently disruptive children. They were not 'disadvantageous' for the classroom teacher and the majority of well-behaved pupils!

While Lord Elton concluded that unions had exaggerated the problem of violence the survey he commissioned on behalf of the Committee painted a similar picture to that drawn by the NASUWT. The Elton survey showed that 1.7% of teachers had during the course of one week suffered "physical aggression towards you [the teacher]" and incidents "of a clearly violent nature" affected 0.5% of all the teachers questioned. If that were truly representative and capable of extrapolation it would amount overall to some 2,000 teachers. The survey insisted that "the vast majority of teachers reported that their experiences during the week [of the survey] were 'typical' or 'fairly typical'".

The NASUWT survey had shown that over a five-month period (September '84 – February '85) 4% of teachers had suffered physical assault in school. Our Cleveland local association had also conducted a survey which showed similar results, with 30 members actually attacked. (It also revealed 95% of secondary and 20% of primary teachers had suffered verbal abuse, with 20% threatened with physical violence.)

Moreover, Elton had adopted an extremely strict, arguably distorted, definition of 'violent'. Sheffield University's Educational Research Centre, conducting the survey, decided to treat aggression not involving physical contact as out-with its definition of violence. Three examples were cited: a boy who smashed a teacher's car windscreen with a pickaxe handle and threatened the head teacher, but was pacified without blows being exchanged; a girl bringing a machete into school; and a boy, totally out of control, chasing another with a hammer but being prevented from landing a blow. None was classified as 'violence' in the Elton scheme of things. They were merely examples of 'aggression'!

The Elton survey showed 15% of teachers had suffered verbal abuse or threatening remarks during the week in question. Fourteen per cent reported instances of "physical destructiveness" among pupils, such as breaking objects or damaging furniture. However, Elton did reflect the consensus view that general disruption compromising learning which affected the majority during the week of the survey was the largest problem affecting most teachers.

The Committee sidestepped the problem of how to respond to assaults, be they 'aggression' or 'violence'. Our casework indicated too many instances where the response was unsupportive of the victim, teacher or pupil. The Elton Committee seemed oblivious to simple considerations of personal safety. The NASUWT insisted that, barring truly exceptional circumstances, assaulting a teacher had to mean expulsion. Pupil victims, likewise, should not have to endure daily reminders of the trauma they have suffered. The recommendation for a national monitoring system for violent incidents was not implemented.

Elton, whilst insisting upon 'hard objective evidence' from others, was content to speculate that recent industrial action had damaged pupils' and parents' respect for teachers and so diminished their ability to maintain authority and respect. Elton overlooked the fact that increasing disruption and violence predated the mid-eighties pay disputes by at least 15 years. He also ignored other possibilities such as low pay and constant public criticism.

Elton recommended that the effects of the appeal panels on exclusions should be monitored over a five-year period but Ken Baker decided on two years. Figures were released when requested, but no evaluation was published. About a third of parental appeals succeed. The forced reinstatement of many pupils has caused great problems in the schools affected and has led to many refusals to teach by NASUWT members.

Overall I found the Elton Report suffered from a profound weakness in so rarely viewing the problem from the classroom teacher's point of view. Yet the teacher is faced with the conflicting and often impossible demands of raising standards and dealing with serious disruption without much outside support.

Elton proved strong on analysis but weak on prescription. The Committee seemed to end up making as many recommendations as they could possibly think of. The grand total was 173, comprising 138 main and 35 sub-recommendations. Many recommendations were a counsel for perfection that made no reference to the huge additional resources required to implement them.

The one solution which NASUWT members have consistently demanded is the facility to refer seriously disruptive pupils to alternative units. Elton actively argued against such units in all but exceptional circumstances on the grounds that many were badly run. The NASUWT accepted that criticism but viewed that as an argument for improvement, not abolition. (The New Labour Government was later to require LEAs to ensure education is provided to those pupils permanently excluded, and alternative units featured prominently in these arrangements.)

I observed publicly that the Elton Committee ended up "presenting a plethora of platitudinous proposals that the world be perfect". By presenting them in such volume and in such idealistic fashion, I suspect the Committee let the Government off the hook by not requiring it to focus on a few key practical measures which could have impacted quickly and significantly (albeit expensively) upon the problem. "Elton was too much advice, too little help."

On the morning after publication I was doing a radio interview (it might have been the *Jimmy Young Show*) when a school pupil came on the line and asked: "Why on earth is a pop star [presumably Elton John] writing a report on discipline in schools?" Did that say it all?

Chapter 49 - The Bishop of Llandaff School Dispute

In March 1991 a very unusual and sensitive case arose at the Bishop of Llandaff Church in Wales High School in Cardiff. The case concerned allegations of a serious sexual assault by three boys at the Bishop of Llandaff School on a girl pupil in the same class. A complaint was made to the police. Subsequently, the NASUWT understood, the girl and her family declined to offer evidence before a court and the case was dropped.

The head teacher, presumably acting on the basis that some facts had been established, suspended the three boys and recommended permanent exclusion. To everyone's consternation the governing body decided to reinstate the boys. To the best of the NASUWT's knowledge none of the boys or their families contested the facts or otherwise protested their innocence. The victim's interests appeared to have been overlooked.

The 24 members of the NASUWT at the school, about half the teaching staff, were so incensed with the decision of the governors and its implications for the maintenance of discipline and decent standards of behaviour that they demanded support for strike action from their union. National Officers and the Executive agreed. Members voted unanimously in favour of strike action in the ballot.

The strike began on Wednesday 13 March 1991. Support was widespread amongst pupils, parents and the local community. Messages of support flooded in from all over the country. By that time I had become the NASUWT GS. I called publicly upon the governors to reconsider their decision.

The strike lasted eight days. It was suspended shortly before Easter when the Chair of Governors withdrew a letter threatening disciplinary action against our members. During the strike the families of two of the three boys made very sensible decisions to move their sons on to other schools and draw a line under the unfortunate affair. That is exactly what should have happened in the first place. The one remaining boy of the three was readmitted to the head teacher's study under very stringent conditions. (Before the start of the Summer Term the family of this third boy decided he should move on.)

With the assistance of ACAS these developments were sufficient for us to suspend our strike in good time before the school was due to reopen after the Easter holidays. At the intervening NASUWT Annual Conference, Keith Morris, the NASUWT School Representative at the Bishop of Llandaff, was given a rousing standing ovation after he had spoken from the platform and thanked the Union for all the "wonderful support his members had received".

Once again firm action by the NASUWT had achieved not only a common sense outcome but also one that had considerable moral authority. The Poundswick and Llandaff cases served as excellent examples of good direct trade union action. On occasions such as the NASUWT fringe meetings at Conservative Party Conferences when the 'blue rinse brigade' and Colonel Blimps, who seemed to feature quite prominently at such events, challenged me on the morality of teachers going on strike, I simply quoted these cases and batted the question back. A curious silence would descend.

Chapter 50 – Inappropriate Inclusion

Baroness Warnock's report on special education in 1979 launched the great movement towards inclusion. A powerful lobby of the 'educational great and the good' built up and succeeded in persuading the Thatcher Government to enact many of Warnock's recommendations in the 1981 Special Education Act.

Inclusion had a dangerous allure for some politicians of all persuasions. Special education costs around three times as much per pupil as mainstream, enabling the 'progressive' and popular cause of inclusion to march hand in hand with financial savings. Virtually alone, the NASUWT raised the voice of the teacher in the classroom, insisting the problems of realism be addressed. In theory inclusion was a 'motherhood and apple pie' issue. The NASUWT agreed with the principle but had three major reservations of a practical kind.

First, mainstream schools required significant resources to provide for children with disabilities. Second, some disabilities were of such a severe kind that only special schools could meet. Third, some youngsters with extreme emotional and behavioural difficulties could not be catered for in mainstream schools, even with additional resources.

In time many parents with severely disabled children came to share our scepticism. Whilst overall the policy benefited many handicapped children, there has been a growing minority of parents who have come to see that their children would have been better served by remaining in special schools rather than being transferred to, and sometimes lost in, large comprehensives without the specialist staff and equipment.

I recall vividly a brutally frank meeting the NASUWT had with Sir Keith Joseph in 1982. He was not the normal smooth and evasive politician. Quite the contrary. He accepted the implications of his Government's hard-line monetarism and he laid it on the line to us. 'Inclusion' was not his idea. The education establishment, together with the 'inclusion lobby' led by Baroness Warnock, had campaigned successfully for the 1981 Act. They could have the Act, but there would be no additional finance.

By the same token we came away from the meeting determined more than ever before to continue with our 'refusal to teach' policy as and when requested and appropriate to do so. We believed, quite rightly as it turned out, that there would be more demand for support from members being required to teach emotionally and behaviourally disturbed youngsters who should have been placed in alternative education.

There is no better example of the lobby for inclusion triumphing over common sense and the educational needs of the majority of children in a school than that provided by the case in a West Midlands LEA of Hazel Spence-Young. Furthermore, no account of the NASUWT campaign against violence and indiscipline in schools would be complete without reference to Hazel, a woman of great courage and fortitude.

In September 1989 Hazel was teaching a class of 49 ten-year-olds, which she shared with another teacher at a junior school, when she was assaulted by one of the pupils in the class. In the altercation that took place Hazel was violently struck on the chin, damaging her spine. To this day, despite surgery, Hazel who lives in Leamington, Warwickshire, has to wear a neck brace and her right arm is partially paralysed. She is in constant pain and has to rely upon her husband to deal with the everyday necessities of living such as helping her with eating and dressing. Hazel, together with another teacher, had been trying to prevent the boy concerned ('John' – not his real name) from rushing out of school in a temper tantrum onto a nearby busy dual carriageway.

By the time Hazel's compensation case had been settled John was 16. He was asked in a newspaper interview how he felt about what he had done and, now older and possibly wiser, if he regretted the attack on Mrs Spence-Young. He replied: "Not one iota, she got what she deserved". He said that he still hated her. "She doesn't deserve a dollar, I should get the money, not her", was his concluding quote.

The newspaper report quoted John's twisted logic, saying that there were three teachers trying to hold him down. Asked why he did not accept the teachers' authority, apparently he looked astonished and said: "Nobody tells me what to do. If only she had treated me with respect none of this may have happened. I'm OK with people so long as they don't cross me".

The newspaper reporter quoted his mother at his side agreeing with him. "'So he's got a temper on him', she says, 'they knew he could fly off the handle, but they kept him at the same school. [He] is just a loveable rogue. He needed help, they didn't give him any.'"

Nothing, of course, could be further from the truth. The staff at the school had bent over backwards to try to help John from the day he joined the school in the nursery section. He came from a very deprived background, being raised apparently by a single parent on a bleak council estate in a crime-ridden area. None of his teachers had ever met his father.

From the moment he entered the nursery school, John had displayed a pattern of behaviour that was uncooperative, disruptive, unpredictable, uncontrollable, aggressive and violent towards teachers and his peers. Staff dealing with John were repeatedly astonished that he was not transferred to a special school. The only chance of containing his behaviour was to isolate him. The teaching staff was eventually denied that alternative as well. A council social worker told the teachers that it would do more harm to him than good. From that day teachers were told they had to stop isolating him.

After more violent behaviour in the Summer Term of 1989 the process of assessing John's special educational needs, known as 'statementing', had begun. All the professional staff involved recommended special education for John, with the teachers repeatedly informing the LEA of their view. Apart from a belief in 'unqualified inclusion' staff could find no explanation for the failure of the LEA to transfer John to a special school.

Yet more violent behaviour followed at the beginning of the 1989 Autumn Term. John was suspended. The acting headmistress again pleaded for help from the LEA, but it insisted that John should stay at the school pending further assessment. That proved too late. On Thursday 28 September, within days of his return from suspension, the attack on Hazel Spence-Young took place.

It had been a difficult week. The Monday saw an innocent incident during a break-time football game which led to John losing his temper and violently attacking other children. However, another boy (one of the few not intimidated) retaliated in kind, whereupon John fled out of the school, much to the consternation of the staff because of an adjacent busy dual carriageway.

The Tuesday and Wednesday were also difficult, with John's bad behaviour only partly contained with constant one-to-one attention. NASUWT members were increasingly reporting similar problems where, despite such intensive support, the retention of pupils with severe emotional and behavioural problems in mainstream schools created chaos, wrecking the education of others. This is a hugely important factor which is so often ignored by 'inclusion fanatics'.

The Thursday morning was again difficult and for numerous reasons John, along with some other pupils, had to remain in class instead of participating in the afternoon outdoor games. John refused to accept this situation and ran out of Hazel's classroom to head for the sports field. Hazel felt compelled to follow him and tried to coax him back. When he still refused Hazel gave him the option of going to sit outside the head teacher's office. She put her hand out to him, a strategy that had been successfully employed on numerous occasions in the past. But then John grabbed hold of the window fastenings in the corridor to prevent Hazel from escorting him back into the classroom. She put her hand over his but he then started hitting her hand and wrist. She caught hold of his other hand and he began kicking her.

Other teachers came to assist as the violence offered by John escalated.

Since John was kicking out violently with his feet, a male PE teacher tried to secure his legs to take him to the head's office. John continued swearing profusely, lashing out and thumping the teachers, finally twisting around to catch Hazel under the chin, causing her head to snap back and the injuries I have already described to occur.

I relate these incidents in some detail to illustrate the predicament facing teachers. With the benefit of hindsight one can see that Hazel's attempts to take John's hands to coax him back into her classroom became 'the point of no return'. Some might say that Hazel should have released John to go wherever he wished and do whatever he wanted. That could have led to even more disastrous consequences, with John out on the streets running around in a temper tantrum completely out of control. In the event of some accident or other untoward happening Hazel would have been vilified by the media. The brutal predicament confronting Hazel was that 'non-confrontation' ran up directly against pupil safety.

It was disappointing, to put it mildly, that the first official feedback Hazel received from someone in authority over the school was a call to her home on the following Sunday questioning whether she had complied with the procedures requiring staff to send for the head teacher in the event of John becoming "unreasonably uncooperative".

Following the Thursday incident the 'statementing' process in respect of John was accelerated. Within a few weeks he was transferred to a special school.

Meanwhile Hazel Spence-Young came under the care of her doctor and eventually surgeons. She approached the NASUWT for advice and support. My colleagues in the NASUWT Legal Aid Department studied her case and resolved that expert advice be obtained. The key legal question was: Could we show that the LEA had been negligent?

The NASUWT obtained expert advice from a consultant in special education. It was clear that by June 1989 the LEA was well aware of the nature and extent of John's difficulties. However, no additional support had been offered to the school to help. A hugely significant factor was the credence given to the view of John's social worker. He opposed the part internal isolation of John in the classroom. He 'insisted' John should be fully integrated into the activities of the class and not segregated when he misbehaved or was abusive. Hazel and all her colleagues who taught the boy argued strongly against this, saying it was totally impractical. They and the head (to her credit) repeatedly alerted the Authority to fears for their own safety and that of the other pupils. They continued to urge that a special school should be found for John.

The NASUWT had strongly and consistently held that in schools the views of social workers should not prevail over educational considerations, especially when the latter have been so clearly put forward by the entire teaching staff. The issue goes to the heart of one of the great problems that has affected the education service over the past 40 years. That is the elevation of the social consideration above the educational one. The NASUWT did not deny the right of social workers to put forward their views on the needs of individuals but believed strongly they should not prevail over the educational, health, safety and welfare requirements of so many others, including children and staff.

Hazel Spence-Young appeared to have had no choice but to act on the instruction of the social worker to keep John in the mainstream class without any degree of separation or isolation. As an instruction it allegedly had the force of the LEA behind it, but it was ill-conceived. The social worker was not professionally competent to give such an instruction. This might beg the question of the role those responsible for the management and governance of the schools should have played. For the classroom teacher at the bottom of the hierarchical ladder the only (relatively) safe way of resisting such an instruction would have been to seek the support of a union like the NASUWT to sanction a refusal to teach.

Apart from being told to avoid confrontation and summon the head teacher if necessary, the staff had been given no clear strategies to deal with the boy's extremely difficult behaviour in a classroom or other group situation.

The conclusion of our expert consultant on special education was that the LEA was at fault. He concluded that if the boy's special needs had been attended to earlier, the injury to Mrs Spence-Young could have been avoided. The legal advice was that, whilst there was no certainty, we had a fair chance of winning. That was good enough for the NASUWT and on 23 April 1990 our solicitors sent to the LEA the customary "letter before action" inviting the Authority to respond.

Another scandalous aspect of this, and indeed of many other similar cases, was that it took six years of legal wrangling before finally, in February 1996, the LEA agreed to an out-of-court settlement. Five days had been set aside in January 1996 for a High Court hearing. The LEA then offered £82,500 in compensation to Hazel Spence-Young, without of course admitting responsibility. The Authority added that if Hazel agreed to a no-publicity 'gagging' clause they would add another £2,500. That decision had to be left to Hazel. The NASUWT had to act one hundred per cent in the interests of the individual, although it was clear that our general cause could be well served by appropriate publicity on the out-of-court settlement.

It was a great tribute to Hazel's courage and integrity that she forsook the additional £2,500 in order to support the NASUWT's campaign against violence and indiscipline in schools. It was extremely heartening to hear her say that the Union had given her such tremendous support, she 'owed' it to us to reciprocate.

After the legal loose ends had been tied up and Hazel had received her compensation, I called a NASUWT press conference for Tuesday 19 March 1996. Unusually for teachers having suffered such trauma, Hazel had heroically agreed to appear in public. The purpose of the press conference was to alert the public to the dangers of unqualified inclusion and to pile pressure upon government and LEAs to give much better support to teachers facing these problems.

The press conference was a huge success. We could not have planned a better outcome. After my opening remarks rehearsing the well-known NASUWT policies, Hazel made a very strong and moving personal statement. The resultant publicity was instant and massive.

There could not have been a better advert for the NASUWT than the piece produced by the BBC's excellent Education Correspondent, Mike Baker, for the BBC evening news bulletins. He was very knowledgeable about education and the teacher unions and was skilled in summarising succinctly all the key issues, which came across with force and clarity. The compliments Hazel bestowed upon her union were almost embarrassing for us. We could not have written a better script for the piece ourselves. The NASUWT was sceptical of public relations officers, believing instead that doing your job effectively generated the best publicity. That was genuine, cost nothing, required no expensive PR consultants and had the maximum impact.

Hazel was much sought after on the day and beyond to give interviews to portray the 'human interest' aspect of the issue, something increasingly favoured by the media. While many teachers have been the victims of assault, few are willing to speak in public about their ordeal. Hazel continued to conduct herself over the following weeks with great courage and dignity, and as befits a teacher she came across as extremely articulate and sincere. A few weeks later as a special guest and delegate at the NASUWT Annual Conference Hazel spoke in the debate on violence and discipline and received standing ovations at the beginning and end of her speech.

Other cases showed how 'inclusion enthusiasts' cooled to the concept when they had to deal directly with the individual at the heart of the problem. At the beginning of another dispute some LEA officers, vigorously pursuing the inclusion agenda, were not very sympathetic to our members' concerns. However, we learnt on the grapevine that as they had to look after the boy and transfer him to and from the school and deal daily with the family, they became more sympathetic to our point of view.

It was no coincidence that two of the high-profile cases of the mid-1990s occurred in Nottinghamshire, which was pursuing 'unqualified inclusion'. In one case where the parent was insisting her child stay in the mainstream school, a nearby special education facility had vacant places but was being deliberately run down in accordance with the policy. Just a short time before these cases erupted, the NASUWT Conference had adopted a very critical report entitled *Unqualified Inclusivity.*

Consequently the following year the NASUWT opposed the New Labour Government's excessive reliance upon integration when it published its Green Paper on special needs, *Excellence for all Children,* in 1997. The principle of maximum integration was easy enough to support but the practice and the resources made available could not be ignored. Extra resources could usually cope with all but the severest of physical disabilities but the Union had "the gravest of reservations about the integration of pupils with severe emotional and behavioural difficulties". Such cases often failed even when one-to-one supervision and support were offered, so severe were the problems. Attempts were also being made to reintegrate some pupils into mainstream after they had been expelled from special schools which could not cope with them.

New Labour's policy was eventually modified, thanks to the pressure the NASUWT applied and of course reality finally getting through to the politicians. Once again the value of special schools and their expertise are being recognised. For a time sadly regarded as places to be avoided, they are increasingly and rightly being seen as centres of excellence with appropriate specialist provision supplied by staff qualified for the purpose.

The most painful irony was to follow in October 2004 with Baroness Warnock, the champion of inclusion, backtracking dramatically when she said: "Many children [with special needs] are simply unfit to manage in the bewildering environment of a large school. They are fragile children who above all need to know and be known by their teachers." An Ofsted report on special needs came out a few days later with the same message, that mainstream schools were often not meeting the challenge of 'inclusion'. Research commissioned by the Government and also published in October 2004 suggested that schools with 'too much inclusivity' were not performing as well as others. NASUWT members who had been around in the early 1980s must have felt like tearing their hair out. That had been the message they and their union had been conveying for years and years.

Chapter 51 - 'Lots of Advice; Little Help'
School Discipline under the Conservatives

After becoming General Secretary (GS) in 1990 I often publicly expressed surprise that teachers received little support from the Government over school discipline despite the claim of the ruling Conservatives to be the party of law and order. Sir Keith Joseph, Education Secretary from 1981 to 1986, often expressed a personal interest in the problem but little practical action followed as it seemed the departmental view prevailed that it was mostly NASUWT exaggeration. The Elton Report, encapsulating 'lots of advice but little help' typified the Government's approach. Poundswick had proved that when the crunch came, government disappeared.

I was pleasantly surprised to discover that Prime Minister John Major shared the concerns being expressed by the NASUWT. I was assisted in this discovery by none other than Chris Woodhead, from 1994 to 2000 HM Chief Inspector of Schools and teachers' pet hate figure. While we had our differences we also agreed on some issues, notably the need for good discipline in schools. During a lunchtime discussion in February 1995 Chris contradicted my (no doubt usual) complaint that Government ignored the NASUWT's concerns, assuring me that people in Downing Street were interested in my recent public comments. He offered to fix up a meeting with one of the Prime Minister's advisers. A week or so later I received a letter from a special adviser, inviting me to 10 Downing Street for a meeting. He was quite keen to hear more from me about the NASUWT's concerns on school discipline.

I learned at the first of a couple of meetings with him that John Major had noticed my quotes in *The Daily Telegraph* reacting to one of the consultative publications on school discipline emanating from the Department for Education. He had sent it back to the Secretary of State full of red crossings out and critical comments, one of which amounted to something like: 'No wonder Nigel de Gruchy was able to savage the document in *The Telegraph*!'

Those were the consultative draft circulars leading up to the publication on 27 May 1995 of a pack of six documents under the general cover "Pupils with Problems". Not for the first time were schools to be bombarded with mountains of advice, but little help, on dealing with disruption. Alas my influence lasted not a long time! When the final circulars emerged the civil servants at the Department for Education had matters back under control.

John Major's demands for common sense appeared to have been overtaken by greater concerns, none the least of which was another crisis over his stewardship, which led to him resigning as Conservative Party leader to flush out his critics. Major won the resultant contest against John Redwood but neither the real confidence of his party nor the electorate.

The 'departmental view' remained that we exaggerated the problem and money should not be wasted on unnecessary measures. The thickness of the documentation reflected the extra demands and bureaucracy inflicted upon teachers to cope with the problems. Ministerial backs were well protected against any untoward event, and material to deploy in answers to Parliamentary questions was in abundance.

The 'pack' comprised six separate circulars (numbered 8-13/94, some published in partnership with the Department of Health) which included:

Pupil Behaviour and Discipline
The Education of Children with Emotional and Behavioural Difficulties
Exclusions from School
The Education by LEAs of Children Otherwise than at School

Unusually for such a major publication it was not launched by the Secretary of State. Instead the 'number two', Minister of State Eric Forth, a right-wing hard-liner, fronted the release. The Department's press statement was disarmingly entitled "Pupils with Problems must not disrupt learning". "I want to ensure that disruption in schools is kept to a minimum and that as far as possible children are in school and learning", thundered Eric Forth like a mouse.

There was nothing new, no practical measures to help teachers. I savaged the circulars saying they "present pages and pages of pious platitudes which labour the obvious and teach grandma to suck eggs. We were promised tough measures. In practice it has been made more difficult to expel the disruptive elements. The Government exhorts the profession to raise standards but ties teachers' hands behind their backs when they try to deal with indiscipline. The Circulars are long on advice but short on help."

In December 1995 a particularly sad and dramatic murder of a London head teacher occurred. Philip Lawrence, head of St George's secondary school in Maida Vale, London, was stabbed in the heart as he went to the assistance of one of his pupils being attacked by a gang of youths just outside the school gates at the end of a Friday afternoon. Despite emergency surgery carried out on the floor of the school entrance, Philip Lawrence died from his wounds during the night. The media coverage was massive, and having a few months previously predicted it was just a question of time before a teacher was killed in the course of duty, I spent the entire Saturday morning doing TV and radio interviews.

As always the media demanded instant remedies. Although the gang involved in the attack on the St George's boy was not connected to any particular school (as far as we could tell given the reporting restrictions) the tragedy marked another significant step downhill in the slide to wanton violence amongst the dysfunctional elements of youth society.

We had received reports of knives being carried into schools and many head teachers had accumulated frightening collections of offensive weapons, having confiscated them from errant pupils. The occasional report of a gun in school was also being recorded.

Following the Philip Lawrence tragedy, the Government set up a Working Party (WP) on Security in Schools. The NASUWT warmly welcomed this development and was further pleased to note the proposed composition, which included the teacher unions as well as other 'stakeholders'.

In response to the demand for quick remedies I codified an instant NASUWT Ten Point Plan which was based on our well-known policy positions:

1 Heed the calls of classroom teachers for more support.

2 More Pupil Referral Units (PRUs) for violent or disruptive pupils.

3 Recognition of the overriding role of teachers to teach and not to patrol the neighbourhood sorting out trouble.

4 Retention, not closure, of special schools for children with emotional and behavioural difficulties.

5 Reinstatement of the sanction of indefinite exclusion.

6 Removal of the Ofsted criterion of numbers excluded in determining school failure.

7 Abolition of the Appeal Panels.

8 Risk assessments for seriously violent or disruptive pupils under Health and Safety regulations.

9 Police or security guards, to be readily available to carry out their responsibility for public order.

10 More help for schools to install closed circuit cameras, provide personal panic alarms, and introduce other security measures.

Underlining many of the points was a reminder that teachers should focus on their role in schools – teaching – and to warn them of the dangers of arrogating other social responsibilities unto themselves. Long before the fashionable phrase 'zero tolerance' hit the streets the NASUWT advocated an uncompromising policy.

Philip Lawrence's widow, Frances, with the active support of successive Home Secretaries including Michael Howard and Jack Straw, set up a trust in memory of her husband devoted to encouraging young people to set up schemes in their neighbourhoods designed to provide constructive and purposeful activities for themselves. The quiet dignity with which Frances Lawrence conducted herself impressed everyone who came into contact with her. The NASUWT supported the Philip Lawrence Annual Awards Ceremony and I made a point of attending every year. The NASUWT has continued to sponsor the Awards to the present day.

A few months after the Philip Lawrence murder, the tragedy of the Dunblane Primary School in Scotland occurred. Many children and staff were gunned down by a deranged intruder, 16 of whom were killed. The establishment of the WP on Security in Schools was given an additional, dramatic and tragic relevance.

The WP produced its first report in May 1996 and the Government accepted all the recommendations. I welcomed these developments although there was some doubt the Government would make the necessary resources available. I also suggested the WP should continue in existence, such was its importance, and was pleased the Government agreed.

The NASUWT did, however, express some reservations with the WP report, believing that a stronger line should have been taken on the establishment and maintenance of secure school boundaries. All schools should have secure entry/access points. Other unions opposed this policy, believing it was more important to keep schools open to the community. The NASUWT saw no contradiction between the two aims.

Suzy Lamplugh became a name irreversibly connected to personal security in the nation's psyche. Suzy worked as an estate agent in Fulham, West London, and disappeared in July 1986 (eventually to be presumed dead in 1994) after setting off to show a prospective buyer around a property her firm was selling for a client. Suzy's mother, Diana Lamplugh, campaigned to discover the perpetrator of the assumed murder and set up a trust in her daughter's name to promote better awareness of personal safety. Diana Lamplugh had been co-opted on to the Security in Schools WP. In October 1997 the trust produced a Report on Safety and Violence in Schools.

The Report found that:

one in six schools reported incidents of pupils assaulting staff at 'Level 1' – spitting, pushing and unwanted touching;

one in five reported 'Level 2' assaults – hitting with fist or hand, punching or kicking (the majority said these incidents had taken place at their schools more than once);

three per cent of schools reported 'Level 3' assaults – hit with weapon or other object;

ten per cent reported pupils carrying weapons onto the premises;

two per cent reported theft with threats of and actual violence;

fifty-seven per cent reported intentional and malicious damage to school property, just over half of those in turn reporting repeat incidents;

seven per cent reported arson attacks;

even more regrettable, only very few of these incidents were reported to the police.

This Report by a body entirely independent of any 'special interest group' totally vindicated the findings of similar NASUWT surveys over the years but for which the Union had been condemned by some for exaggerating the problems. It seemed to justify the strong stand taken by the NASUWT, which was to reach a climax in 1996 with unprecedented media coverage of several refusals to teach. Arguably these developments marked the start of the period when politicians at last began to take our concerns seriously.

Chapter 52 - Glaisdale Refusal to Teach Hits Headlines

Shortly after Conference 1996, quite out of the blue a routine refusal to teach case we were pursuing at the Glaisdale School in Nottingham hit the headlines. The publicity was initiated by the aggressive parents of a violent and disruptive pupil securing an interview on Central Television to air their grievance that NASUWT members were refusing to teach their son. An appeal panel had returned the boy to the school after the governing body had permanently excluded him on the head teacher's recommendation. The LEA Reviewing Officer had upheld the governors' decision. We had made no public comment whatsoever. Despite those simple facts, critics accused the NASUWT generally, and me personally as the GS, of orchestrating a media campaign.

On the scale of things the Glaisdale case was quite potent and probably one of the reasons why the publicity hit the national media and set off a chain of events that propelled the issue to great political prominence. Arguably 1996 became the year when NASUWT concerns could no longer be ignored by government and LEAs. The case highlighted the role of appeal panels in subverting the maintenance of good order in schools. The case also became a classic on how to conduct and not conduct the public relations side of things.

I first became aware of the case towards the end of March 1996, receiving a letter from John Petchell, the Executive Member on the point of retirement, outlining the history. It was an extremely serious case. The boy ('Roy' – not his real name) was already receiving support from various agencies and had been identified as in need of special education. He had inflicted serious injuries on other pupils, sometimes using weapons such as broken glass. He had brazenly assaulted a fellow pupil in front of two members of staff to whom the victim had fled in vain search of safety. Prior to January he had received fixed-term exclusions on several occasions. After continued disruptive and violent behaviour an exclusion (for five days) followed on 15 January.

Roy's mother responded in her customary fashion of threats and abuse to both teaching and secretarial staff at the school. The family did not accept the fixed-period exclusion. On the following day, Roy turned up again at school. He was asked to leave, but refused. Eventually, police had to be summoned and he was taken home. The following day, Wednesday 17 January, exactly the same happened again. On that same day the head teacher's secretary took a call from someone on the *Weekend Live* team at Central Television asking for information on the case as the family had contacted them. Wisely, the head teacher declined to take the call saying that he had no comment whatsoever to make.

Despite the double breach of the fixed-term exclusion order and the abusive behaviour of the mother, Roy was allowed back into school on 23 January. Unbelievably, but true to form, Roy became extremely disruptive and aggressive to staff and pupils within a few minutes of being readmitted, culminating with a threat to a teacher: "Come here and I'll put you in a box."

The deputy, in the head's absence, imposed a fixed-term exclusion after the boy had stormed out of the school. In the light of the history of the case the head teacher considered converting it into a permanent one but desisted on the advice of the LEA, appreciating how controversial that would appear to the family.

However, back in school Roy's outrageous behaviour continued. On 6 February he threatened to assault another teacher. Unfortunately from the boy's point of view he had chosen the wrong teacher this time. He was a member of the NASUWT. On 8 February 1996 Roy was permanently excluded. The Board of Governors backed the head teacher's decision. The Area Education Officer, called upon under the legislation to conduct a review of the case, upheld the exclusion.

Despite having had a hearing before the governors and a review by an LEA officer, the 'consumer rights' and crazy bureaucracy the Conservative Government was heaping upon the education system afforded the parents yet another opportunity to challenge the exclusion by going to the so-called 'independent' appeal panel.

The panel allowed the appeal after a hearing on 12 March. The head teacher wrote a stinging letter to the Director of Education, sending the NASUWT a copy. He said the governors and staff at the school were "incensed" that the interests of one child should so clearly outweigh the interests of the vast majority of children in the school. The youngster was being allowed to abuse and to threaten both staff and pupils "with impunity".

The head complained bitterly that "the LEA has compromised the authority of the school in being too willing to respond to the parents on their terms even when they were clearly acting illegally". Furthermore: "My governors will not easily forgive an Authority which unilaterally at the request of the parent changed the time and venue for an appeal and refused to accede to a similar request from myself and the chair of governors". The date chosen, 12 March, had proved impossible for the head and Chair of Governors but I believe they made a serious error in not sending substitutes. However, they did submit a very full dossier outlining all the history, which included over 50 serious incidents that had been logged.

The head wondered if the appeal panel, in questioning the judgement of himself, the governors and the Area Education Officer, realised the implications this had for upholding discipline in the school and he referred to the fact that three main teacher associations were being asked by their memberships in the school to proceed with refusal to teach ballots.

The teachers who saw the panel's reasoning found it unconvincing and inconsistent with the facts. The panel said they found the evidence inadequate, harboured doubts about the boy's responsibility for his actions and questioned the level of support which the boy had received.

Together with my colleague DGS Eamonn O'Kane, we reviewed the case and quickly became very confident that it was one which would receive the full support of the National Officers (our Action Committee) and, thereafter, the full National Executive, the body with the final say.

On 25 March, Eamonn wrote to all the relevant authorities in the school and the LEA, informing them of the NASUWT intention to hold a ballot for industrial action. Subject to a vote in favour, members were to refuse to teach or supervise 'a certain pupil' and to take strike action if attempts were made by management to force them to do so. The NASUWT members voted 100% in favour of action to refuse to teach the pupil concerned and if necessary to strike. The result was declared on 16 April as the Summer Term opened. With the statutory seven days notice required, the action would begin on Friday 26 April.

By this time the parents' attempts to secure an interview on TV had succeeded. The parents and the boy appeared on the *Weekend Live* programme on Central Television. It seemed to be the first time a family had deliberately allowed one of their children to be exposed to the media in this way.

The media was not slow to spot a classic confrontation developing as news of the NASUWT ballot result inevitably spread. (We were required by Thatcher's legislation of the 1980s to keep the employers fully informed of our balloting every step along the way. No longer could we quietly deploy the threat in negotiations as we had done in the early days.) The confrontation between a union taking a strong stand threatening strike action and a publicly identified and 'challenging' family over the vexed issue of discipline in school was manna from heaven for the media.

The story hit the national media 'big' on 22 April, the day on which Roy returned to the school. Roy's mother was quoted saying he did not need special education. The boy himself was quoted whining that he "would have no friends if he moved school and would be carrying a bad reputation around".

Recognising the confrontation we were now in I did not mince my words to the media. After referring to a few salient facts of the case and rejecting the "incomprehensible demand that members should put themselves and other children at risk through accepting this violent boy back into their classes," I concluded with deliberate defiance:

"With this boy we have come to the end of the road. The appeal panel sent him back. We won't have him back."

Pious and apparently oblivious to the real issues at stake, Education Secretary Gillian Shepherd said on 22 April: "It was never right for teachers to strike and harm children's education". She had not a single word to offer about the devastating "harm" the boy was literally causing to so many children and staff. But she was quick to play the party political game claiming that it was the job and duty of the Labour controlled LEA to sort out the situation and find appropriate education for the child. Outrageously that totally ignored the role of the Conservative Government in setting up the appeal panels in the first place, which cut right across sensible solutions being found.

Unfortunately, two prominent New Labour Shadow Ministers, John Prescott, a future Deputy Prime Minister, and Stephen Byers, an upcoming Secretary of State, joined in the call against strike action. It seemed that all Ministers of whatever party (some with strong union and left-wing backgrounds in their younger days) seemed fully to support the right to strike so long as you never used it.

The school was told it had no alternative but to abide by the decision of the appeal panel to readmit Roy.

While the NASUWT strike could not start before Friday 26 April, the members exercised their professional judgement and refused to teach the boy. They risked suspension in so doing but fortunately the wise head teacher kept the boy in isolation away from other pupils and, of course, NASUWT members.

In the following day's papers, 23 April, Roy and his family featured quite prominently. There were many photographs of him and his parents and sometimes the whole family. The parents objected to the treatment their son was receiving: "[He] finds it very upsetting being held in almost solitary confinement . . . he can't talk to anyone and he feels everyone is against him."

I was pleased to note strong public support for the teachers coming from the parents and the Chairman of Governors who revealed with an air of disbelief that the head teacher had spent 33 hours of the first week of the Summer Term dealing exclusively with the boy. In his 18 years as a governor he had "never known a family cause as much trouble as this one".

Informal exchanges took place between the NASUWT and the LEA during the course of 23 April but the NASUWT members were not impressed with the proposal for internal isolation and a withdrawal of the strike threat. It was quickly agreed that I would travel to Nottingham the following day personally to lead the developing negotiations and bring forward my planned visit to the members at Glaisdale.

So I travelled to Nottingham on 24 April. My first port of call, accompanied by Roger Kirk, a Past-President and once again the Executive Member for the area, was to the school to see the NASUWT teachers. It was quite deliberate and common practice for the NASUWT GS to visit members in such a dispute to show the whole National Association was right behind them. The members appreciated the support although I did not hide from them the risks involved.

After seeing the members I was in a position to say that we could not accept the proposals that had emerged the previous day. We had two serious objections. The proposed eventual reintegration into mainstream classes at Glaisdale was totally unacceptable and the plan for internal isolation within the school had serious practical problems.

Then it was on to meet with Fred Riddell, the Chairman of the Nottinghamshire Education Committee and a long-standing prominent figure in LEA circles. I had known him for a long time. He had served both on the Burnham Committee and CLEA/ST.

Negotiations were hard. For the NASUWT return to mainstream classes at the school was out of the question. Then as we discussed the 'internal isolation' proposal Roger Kirk took a call on his mobile. It was from the school. Roy had managed to cause a disturbance with another pupil on his way back from a visit to the toilet despite the one-to-one supervision. I remember well the look of pained defeat on the face of Fred Riddell as he realised he had just lost that argument as well.

We parted on good terms with Fred Riddell, keeping channels of communication open and appreciating the LEA's difficulties. The following day the story ran quite big in the national media. Obviously feeling the need to be doing something, Government Ministers began to backtrack. Education Secretary Gillian Shephard said that pupils who were excluded more than once might forfeit their rights to appeal. We were not impressed with such vague promises about the future, generated no doubt by panic over public opinion, firmly on our side.

There were more reports that Roy had threatened another pupil with a chair and he had been allowed to wander around the corridors and mix with other pupils despite his supposed 'internal isolation', taught one-to-one by a supply teacher engaged specially for the purpose. I issued another press statement: "Our members convinced us very quickly that isolation wasn't isolation, wasn't working and was most unlikely to work".

The boy's father spoke with bravado, saying the family were quite happy with the arrangement, but adding: "It is now up to the union – if it is unacceptable to them then it is tough luck". Appearing again on Central Television he attacked the teachers, dismissing our planned strike as "disgusting" and observed they "are paid to teach them, whether they are unruly or not. There are children in school with worse problems than [Roy]."

After enjoying a couple of days doing the rounds of radio and TV interviews the family began to learn the hard way that the media was a dangerous animal to deal with. Several of the tabloid press on 23 April had already carried accounts of the boy's behaviour. The media, as always in such circumstances, began 'to dig around'. They found that Roy had three brothers aged between 8 and 14. To cut a long story short, all three of them had 'distinguished' records of 'leaving' or being expelled from schools. Referring to her youngest, the mother with somewhat reckless if commendable candour said: "I don't want to talk about him because the mud would really fly." (He was attending his third primary school, having 'left' the previous two.)

Neighbours and other members of the local community began to speak out although most did so anonymously for obvious reasons. The stories were mostly about violent antisocial behaviour.

The press did not stop there. Neither the father nor the mother had a job. Apparently the father was in poor health. Where did the money come from? The right-wing tabloids enjoyed the opportunity of adding up all the social security benefits the family allegedly received. *The Daily Mail* managed to add up the sums to a figure of £50,000 per year.

And worse was to follow. The father was revealed to have a serious criminal record. The mother also had an 'interesting school record'. She had also been found guilty in court of a serious assault upon a council worker visiting her home.

The family kept walking right into the media trap. They had whole family photos taken and published. I do not wish to be unnecessarily unkind but the aggression on the faces shone through more powerfully than words could ever convey. Any competent PR person would have kept the cameras miles away.

Inside the NASUWT while obviously we were going about our business with great care, I have to admit that the publicity was not exactly our biggest problem. I could not think of a better example of giving a family enough rope to hang itself.

Faced with our rejection of the proposed agreement at the end of negotiations on 24 April, Fred Riddell or his representatives had obviously gone back to the parents to spell out the facts of life. Roy could go back to school but there would not be many teachers left to teach him or, indeed, anyone else. They seemed to have succeeded in changing the parents' minds.

By early next morning, on 25 April, we reached a deal with the strike less than 24 hours away. After consultations with the parents and their solicitor it was agreed that Roy would stay on the roll at Glaisdale School but attend a special Pupil Referral Unit (PRU) for youngsters with special needs near his home for two and a half days per week. A supply teacher would teach him at home for the other half of the school week. The members in the school were content. The retention of the boy's name on the school roll meant nothing to us if he were never to be on the premises. By mid-morning on Thursday 25 April both sides were able to announce and welcome the agreement which avoided strike action.

In a hastily convened press conference at my Covent Garden office I welcomed the agreement, stating that I was immensely proud of the NASUWT members at Glaisdale. They had made a principled stand in support of acceptable standards of behaviour. The entire nation ought to be grateful to them. I said this was trade unionism at its best, supporting teachers whilst at the same time effectively securing the best arrangements for youngsters with these problems. The boy's real needs were much more likely to be addressed as a result of the new arrangement than before. Having been fiercely critical of the parents I took the opportunity of applauding their change of mind, saying that it had been the most sensible decision they had taken for several weeks.

Pressed by the media to divulge details of the cost, Fred Riddell conceded that the supply teacher would cost around £9,000 per year but the LEA had no alternative. He asked the Secretary of State to look closely at the Government's legislation on pupil exclusions and condemned her for laying the blame for the dispute on the LEA. I had some sympathy for Fred and paid tribute to his work in finding a settlement with us although his LEA might have shared some responsibility for these problems in promoting parental rights and 'unqualified inclusion', both concepts contributing to the problems.

For her part Gillian Shephard concluded her letter to Fred Riddell in conciliatory fashion, referring to the review of the present arrangements for exclusion appeal procedures.

The case graphically illustrated the problem classroom teachers had to face and eventually confront. That would not have happened without NASUWT action. Pious pleadings from politicians to eschew industrial action serve no other purpose than to protect themselves from having to face up to the realities which cannot be avoided by those called upon daily to teach or otherwise deal with such families. Most importantly, the NASUWT had won the battle and set an important precedent.

Perhaps the most interesting postscript to the story of Glaisdale was provided by the head teacher. Within a year he had left to take up a teaching post in the Falkland Islands. Who could blame him!

Chapter 53 - Upheavel at Hebburn
The Dispute at Hebburn School, South Tyneside 1996

The second case subject to mass media coverage in 1996 took place at the Hebburn School in South Tyneside. After the dispute at Glaisdale the media wanted more. Despite pressure I declined to name any of the ongoing cases but I was already on public record admitting that between six and ten would regularly come before the National Executive every month. Most were settled quietly away from the glare of publicity, with the parent(s) concerned accepting 'internal isolation' or transfer to another school.

The problem of publicity inevitably loomed where our asserted right to take this action was challenged. As soon as our threat to refuse to teach had to be implemented, all the legalistic and bureaucratic balloting requirements laid down by the Thatcher administrations inevitably pitched the case into the public domain.

At Hebburn we were challenged by the boy's father and the LEA in May 1996. I have no evidence of any deliberate leak but an alert or lucky local journalist ran the story early in May. Then it was picked up in two national dailies, *The Guardian* and *The Telegraph*. The case had actually started in July 1995. It broke in big terms nationally on Monday 13 May 1996. If we had only been doing all this for publicity and recruitment we sure waited a long time!

The peg on which the story hung big for the national media was an anonymous announcement that on the Monday the boy ('Gregg' – not his real name) would be returned to school by his father, demanding that his son be fully reintegrated into normal classes. Gregg had been away from school for ten months after his father refused to accept the internal isolation arrangements set up after our refusal to teach following an incident in July the previous year.

The Hebburn case was a good illustration of a school taking tough decisions to maintain decent standards of discipline. The school is situated in a reasonably tough area and had recovered from a difficult period in the 1970s. The staff was well supported by a lively, competent and well-respected head teacher who took a firm and realistic attitude on the need for good behaviour. In short, the teachers were running a good tight ship and they intended to keep it that way. It was consequently a popular school with parents.

It was in such a context that Gregg got involved in an altercation with an NASUWT member and ended up physically attacking him, kicking him about the body. The incident began as a relatively trivial matter. The teacher, anxious to clear a pile of bags left dangerously close to the exit from the assembly hall, ordered pupils to hold back whilst he cleared them. Gregg ignored the order, attempted to jump over them and stumbled into the teacher. The teacher picked him up by the shoulders, whereupon Gregg lost his temper and lashed out with his fists and feet, saying "get your fucking hands off me".

The incident unfortunately deteriorated further as Gregg ignored the teacher's instructions to calm down, take a nearby seat and await his form tutor and instead ran off shouting abuse. The teacher caught up with him but slipped as he took hold of the boy's arm. As the teacher lay on the ground the boy started to kick him. The teacher regained control and took Gregg back to the assembly hall entrance area where he held him in his seat until he had calmed down. During this time Gregg continued to threaten the teacher, saying that he would get his father to break his legs.

It was a serious assault and coupled with a rather poor disciplinary record, Gregg was permanently excluded by the head teacher. The governors met on 26 September 1995 and unanimously endorsed the decision of the head.

The father decided to appeal. The panel met on 1 November 1995 and allowed the appeal. The decision was unanimous and taken after many hours of discussion because of alleged procedural flaws at the governing body hearing which did not fully explore some conflict of evidence. Apparently three statements from some pupils (belatedly submitted by the father and containing some common phrases) contradicted the other eyewitness accounts, claiming that Gregg had been pushed rather than jumped.

The appeal panel was probably right to recommend that the governors review their procedures. However, to allow the appeal was to elevate a relatively minor dispute over evidence, which overrode the most crucial issue. Even if the minority view of 'pushed' rather than 'jumped' had been correct the reaction of Gregg was still way over the top, extremely violent and totally unacceptable.

The case was already long running. The original decision on exclusion was taken by the head teacher in July 1995 but it did not come into effect until the start of the new school year in September. With reinstatement ordered for 1 November NASUWT members, who comprised a large majority of the staff, took strong objection and successfully requested the customary NASUWT support. They were balloted towards the end of the Autumn Term and came out strongly in favour of a refusal to teach.

The head teacher resolved the conflict between readmission ordered by the appeal panel and the NASUWT refusal to teach by use of the internal isolation formula, backed up with one-to-one supply teacher support for Gregg. However, Gregg's father refused to accept the arrangement and withheld his son's attendance from school.

The head teacher bravely resisted pressure from the LEA by claiming she had readmitted Gregg but once through the gates it was her responsibility to organise his education. Eventually the governors, leant on heavily by the LEA, instructed her to readmit Gregg back into full normal classes. That provoked the open and public confrontation with the NASUWT.

Soon after school returned from the Christmas holidays in January 1996 the LEA turned the pressure upon the NASUWT members to relent and take Gregg fully back into normal classes. On 26 January the Director of Education wrote to NASUWT members:

"You are advised that the action you are taking amounts in law to a breach of your contract of employment in terms of the contractual obligation to discharge your professional obligations towards the pupils of this school."

Members were given until 31 January to inform the head they would comply.

The NASUWT was not going to fall for that 'old one'! Members were acting collectively as one, under Executive instructions, and happily referred their letters to the Union. The NASUWT would respond for all. Far from objecting, members positively welcomed this approach. It afforded them more protection and was one reason why teachers joined the NASUWT.

On 23 April, local talks between all the parties failed to produce a settlement. The governors were sympathetic to the views of NASUWT members but they could not ignore the decision of the panel, the view of the LEA and the refusal of the father to accept the internal isolation arrangements.

An important principle was emerging, to be tested eventually in the High Court. Gregg's father claimed that the appeal panel had the right to stipulate precisely what should happen upon readmittance. The head teacher claimed that she had the right to make appropriate arrangements for him to be taught bearing in mind the general interests of the school.

On 10 May another similar 'heavy' letter had been distributed to staff. Again we adopted the same strategy. They were now threatened with disciplinary action, from their legal employer, the LEA, if they continued to refuse to teach the pupil. It does not get more serious or confrontational than that. We had reached the point where our refusal to teach would escalate into all-out strike action rather than have our members suspended one by one and possibly sacked. That was also the stage at which the GS would make a point of visiting the members and personally lead the conduct of the dispute to indicate the full support of the Union.

Then came the announcement in the media that the father would "march Gregg back into school" on Monday 13 May and insist upon his readmittance into all his normal classes. So over the weekend, amid growing media interest in another confrontation over discipline in schools, I arranged to travel up to the North East to visit the members and deal with any developments.

I was immediately impressed with the school. Pupils were well turned out moving between classes in a civilised fashion. The place was clean. The teachers I met all seemed of good calibre. The head teacher was open and confident despite the pressure she was under. Amongst the NASUWT members there was unanimous support for the action.

After meeting the members I returned to the head teacher's office for negotiations with representatives from the governors and the LEA, who were also in the school. I restated our refusal to teach and reinforced our determination to strike if necessary.

Gregg's father, having initially said that he would refuse to accept such arrangements, was forced to back down. However, he said he would seek legal advice on whether the LEA could be sued for its failure to integrate his son fully into the school. He was prepared to accept the compromise only in the short term.

The head teacher, Madeleine Watson, issued a very competent press statement: "As instructed by the governing body [Gregg] was readmitted this morning. Since the decision of the appeal panel, I have at no time refused admittance to the pupil. However, the NASUWT members of staff – who are those teachers responsible for the boy's class – have refused to teach him." She went on to describe the personal education programme organised for the boy which would continue and hopefully lead to a permanent solution.

That was an excellent statement from the head whose courage and support for the teacher in the classroom was much admired by the staff. The head openly supported the principle that teachers could refuse to teach violent pupils. She was bitterly critical of the Government, accusing it of speaking with a "forked tongue policy", demanding high standards in education but stopping schools taking the steps necessary to instil good behaviour.

So 13 May 1996 finished with the NASUWT having successfully stood its ground. Neither the governors nor the LEA mentioned anything further about disciplinary action. They seemed to accept that the boy could only be returned to internal isolation. This was widely seen as another victory for the NASUWT. Paying tribute to the courage shown by the members, I added that: "NASUWT had made another successful stand in the cause of discipline and good order in schools."

However, *The Sun*, in its inimitable way, headlined its leader: "Sirs win thug row".

That headline was a travesty. Gregg had proved a somewhat difficult pupil and had lost his temper on this occasion with disastrous results but he was certainly no 'thug'. Indeed he had some good points which his father raised in public. The parents seemed to be very respectable people and keen to support their son in his education. They were unlucky and genuine victims of the culture engendered by the appeal panels. They had also fallen foul of a cardinal principle held by the NASUWT: any pupil assaulting a teacher should be expelled unless there were exceptional circumstances. Such pupils deserved a second chance, but it had to be in a different school.

After the events of 13 May Gregg continued for some time in internal isolation. That seemed to take its toll and he was often absent from school. Eventually the family gave up the fight and quietly did the sensible thing and had their son transferred to another school. Gregg's father did, however, pursue the matter in the courts. In October 1997 he sought an order of mandamus requiring the respondents (the LEA and the governing body) to reinstate his son into mainstream teaching at Hebburn. With the boy now long out of the school, it was not surprising that the judge, Mr Justice Ognall (delivering his verdict on 7 November 1997), decisively refused to exercise his discretion in favour of the plaintiff and refused the application.

This second success for the NASUWT, secured against a background of a rapid rise in the number of excluded pupils, led to the issue assuming a significant political importance.

The Government was obviously concerned but did not quite know what to do next. After Hebburn I claimed that we had established a precedent whereby a pupil could be readmitted and placed in internal isolation and taught on a one-to-one basis in order for teachers to secure the conditions necessary for effective education to continue.

The NASUWT was naturally conscious of the political sensitivities, appreciating we had won through by sheer union power which had to be exercised with care. We were convinced our cause was good and knew we had public opinion on our side. The right-wing Tory Government shared our concern for law and order but hated trade unionism. The fundamental principle was unassailable: no one had the right to tell people they had to suffer assault (itself an illegal act) in the course of their duties.

The events also led to some inter-union complications. On 14 May *The Independent* used anonymous quotes to suggest that we had ulterior motives: "other teachers' unions suggested that the NASUWT's high profile anti-violence campaign is part of a membership drive. The union is trying to show its macho image."

Despising those who hid behind anonymity I responded sharply, declaring: "I had rarely witnessed such cowardice masquerading as professionalism as that displayed by the anonymous commentators." Not much of the purple prose survived the letters editors but I got it off my chest and published it in full within the Union. I referred to the NASUWT's long history supporting members on this issue and to my own personal involvement going back to my early days in Lewisham/London in the 1970s. I repeated our policy of not initiating publicity but if others did the NASUWT would respond. I quoted the many warnings given to governments over the years, especially in 1986 regarding the establishment of appeal panels in the middle of the Poundswick dispute. The NASUWT policy was firmly based upon the needs of members and nothing else.

To be fair I have also to record that we received good support from most of the media and of course the general public who sent in many unsolicited letters of support. Most teachers backed us, even those who were not in membership of the NASUWT.

The one I appreciated more than most was *The Daily Telegraph* editorial on 14 May, "Untie the teachers' hands". It began:

"It is hard to recall the last occasion on which this newspaper found itself more sympathetic to a teachers' union than to a Tory education secretary.

" . . . Mrs Shephard claims that strikes can never be justified because of the damage they cause to children's education. She is probably correct to assert this but in this instance the words would carry more conviction if she (and indeed her predecessors) had done more to give teachers the necessary disciplinary powers to handle troublesome pupils".

The editorial concluded: "Mrs Shephard should take serious note of the NASUWT proposal to leave disciplinary matters in their hands and eliminate the involvement of local education authorities and appeals panels. A few more high profile expulsions pour encourager les autres would not only do wonders for many schools . . ."

As pressure built up on the Government a consensus seemed to develop that appeal panels focussed too narrowly upon the circumstances of the individual child excluded, to the neglect of the interests of all the other pupils in the school. Mrs Shephard was reportedly considering placing an obligation on appeal panels formally to take into account the impact on the rest of the school of any decision to reinstate. It led to one of my shortest press statements ever:

"What! You mean they don't do that already!"

An important if under-debated issue in the new consumer rights philosophy being injected into the public services had been forced out into the open by the NASUWT action. Who was going to defend the collective good when it ran up against the assertion of individual rights?

To add to the pressure on the Government the NASUWT released some information about other cases on an anonymous basis where excluded pupils had recently been returned by appeal panels:

A girl in Sunderland expelled for repeated bullying and false accusations against a teacher.

A pupil in Bradford suspected of drug dealing and expelled after an assault on a teacher.

Two pupils in South Glamorgan involved in a series of violent incidents including an attack upon the head teacher.

A pupil in Rochdale excluded for knocking a woman teacher unconscious with a chair.

A 12-year-old girl in West Glamorgan expelled following incidents including violent attacks and theft.

A case in Bedford where two 15-year-olds were readmitted by a panel after being expelled for smoking cannabis on the premises. The expulsions took place in line with the anti-drugs policy adopted by the school after lengthy consultations with parents and police.

Chapter 54 – Madness at Manton
Refusal to Teach at the Manton Primary School, Worksop, Notts.

The dispute between the NASUWT and the governing body at Manton Primary School, Worksop, Nottinghamshire, in the autumn of 1996 provided another fascinating kaleidoscope of the problems affecting violent and disruptive youngsters and the mismanagement of the education service. The case involved a ten-year-old boy. I will refer to him as 'Michael', not his real name. His family revealed his identity, even arranging photo opportunities for the media.

The dispute was very different from the one at The Ridings, which took place at the same time. While less dramatic than The Ridings, with only one youngster involved, it was in other ways more complicated because of the role played by a number of key governors. Manton was unique in so far as it was the only one of the high-profile cases in 1996 where we ended up having to implement our threat of strike action.

Manton School served children on the council estate of the same name. It was a typical council estate located just outside Worksop, a town in the northern part of Nottinghamshire, close to the border with Yorkshire. The decline of the coal industry had impoverished an already poor area.

In January 1996 the seven members of the NASUWT at the school had invited the Worksop Secretary, John Peebles, to visit them to discuss their problems, which centred upon two matters. One was the uncontrollable behaviour of Michael, described as being big for his age. The other was the very poor relationships that existed between the governors and the staff. In the opinion of the teachers, governors interfered seriously in the day-to-day running of the school. The teacher governor was excluding from meetings at every conceivable opportunity. Governors bypassed the head and dealt directly with the LEA. The members were so nervous that they asked John Peebles to destroy the notes he had taken. Sensibly, John refused to do this.

The dossier on Michael's behaviour compiled by the NASUWT teachers over the previous 12 months amounted to a catalogue of violence and disruption almost on a daily basis. As well as the many acts of violence which were traumatic for pupils and teachers alike, the constant disruption was equally debilitating and destructive in its effects upon the education of the other pupils in the class and on occasions the whole school.

The dossier included many references to attacks upon other pupils (girls as well as boys), sometimes involving serious violence, using objects as weapons and often requiring the intervention of staff who were injured in the process. The boy invaded the girls' toilets and much of the violence took place in there as well as in the boys' facilities. On one occasion he managed to lock a girl in the boys' toilets. Michael frequently had temper tantrums, throwing whatever objects came to hand around the room. Defying teachers and using foul language were 'normal', almost everyday events. The boy simply had no self-control. His size meant he was a real threat to anyone, but especially to women teachers and girl pupils.

The head teacher had resorted to informal exclusions on four occasions as well as frequently calling in Michael's mother to take him home in order to diffuse difficult and dangerous situations. These common sense measures, implemented with the best of motives were, however, irregular. Michael had been placed on a special educational needs register on account of his behavioural problems, but despite support from the Emotional and Behavioural Difficulties (EBD) Team and other agencies his behaviour worsened.

The subsequent LEA inspection report referred to the dysfunctional relationship between the head teacher and some governors and appeared to apportion blame to both. The NASUWT believed a second major fault line lay in the requirement to retain a pupil like Michael in normal classes in mainstream education. No school, not even one superbly run, should be compelled against its better judgement to deal with such a difficult pupil.

On Friday 5 June, two more attacks on fellow pupils led to Michael being permanently excluded by the head teacher. Michael assaulted and terrified a girl and in a further unprovoked attack on a boy immediately afterwards, he knocked his victim to the ground and then kicked him violently in the face despite an attempt to intervene by a teacher who was pushed aside.

The Exclusions Committee of the governing body met on 17 June. Despite the mountain of evidence against Michael the Committee overturned the exclusion. It did not contend the accuracy of the facts presented but believed they did not justify permanent exclusion. However, the Chair of Governors wrote to Michael giving him a strong warning about his future conduct. The governing body met on the 28th of the same month and confirmed the decision of their Exclusions Committee, ordering reinstatement for Monday 8 July.

Inevitably, on 2 July the NASUWT informed the employer (the LEA), the Chair of Governors and the head teacher of its intention to ballot for industrial action in the event of members being directed to teach "a certain pupil". Not that further justification was needed, but during the afternoon break on 5 July

Michael appeared at the school gates behaving in a menacing fashion and wielding a baseball bat.

On his first day back Michael was found lurking around the toilets, frequently disobeying instructions to return to class. He hit another child leaving the toilets. He pushed another to the ground and spat upon him. The next day he threatened to kill another boy with whom he had frequent fights, despite a teacher intervening between the two of them. He threatened to smash the face of another child with a broken metal lid from a pencil tin. And so it continued, including threats to kill other pupils and to set fire to the school.

The deterioration in Michael's behaviour assumed a menacing significance in the light of developments taking place in relation to child protection procedures. Reports were emerging of teachers being suspended merely on the evidence of one minor making an accusation. When confronted over his behaviour, Michael began to tear his clothing in order to fake an attack by a member of staff. He fell to the ground writhing, accusing staff of having attacked him. He began to make malicious allegations and often threatened to report teaching and support staff to his mother and, more significantly, to one of the governors who was a member of the Exclusions Committee and who had befriended Michael and his family.

Activities Day on 17 July marked the final straw. More violent behaviour culminated in Michael bursting into the office threatening to break a boy's legs with a baseball bat in the presence of the head teacher. After ensuring the boy was placed elsewhere for his protection the head tried to restrain Michael from his pursuit, whereupon he slumped to the floor and accused the head of assaulting him. The head had to let Michael go and immediately summoned his mother to escort him home.

So on 17 July the head teacher again permanently excluded Michael and duly reported to the Exclusions Committee who met on the 19th and overruled the decision once again. This was despite an even fuller report being presented on Michael's behaviour and all the support he had been afforded by the school and other agencies.

There were no doubts in NASUWT members' minds that the case for permanent exclusion was overwhelming. There was also a strong suspicion that at least some of the governors were blocking Michael's permanent exclusion as a way of getting at the head to settle old scores and to bring him to heel.

Our local Officers conceded that the head could have been more diplomatic and understanding in his relationship with the governors. Equally there were some awkward and difficult governors and a number were acting very inappropriately. Indeed, the three governors on the Exclusions Committee were now frequent visitors to Michael's home, had become close friends of the family and began making public statements openly supporting the boy and his mother.

I only discovered some time later that within half an hour of the second 'permanent' exclusion the three governors concerned were at the LEA divisional offices in Worksop protesting against the head's decision. Their 'rapid response' was astonishing, revealing a position taken without hearing the evidence, which totally compromised their ability to give the matter fair and objective consideration, in flagrant breach of the principles of natural justice.

The governors ordered reinstatement for the second time to take effect on 19 July, a few days before the summer holidays commenced. We had to extend the balloting period over the holidays to comply with the bureaucratic impediments imposed by the Thatcher Government's legislation. In the event of a 'yes' vote seven days notice of action was required and it had to start within 28 days in order to retain its validity. At the same time our Nottinghamshire representatives, among the best organised in the whole Union and led by their NEM Roger Kirk, who was also a Past-President of the NASUWT and consequently very experienced in these matters, tried to keep dialogue open with the governors and the LEA.

In a move which was completely unnecessary and, apparently, undertaken upon the advice of an official from the LEA, the Chair of Governors on 18 July wrote a letter to all the parents giving some background and alerting them to the possibility of strike action in September. As the letter revealed, "the result of the ballot will not be known until 26 August. This . . . is simply to make sure you are aware of the current situation."

Local NASUWT Representatives had learnt about the draft and tried to persuade the LEA to get the chairperson to withhold the letter in order to utilise as much of the summer vacation as possible to effect a 'peaceful' solution. There was clearly no need for such advance notification (eight weeks) of what was then a hypothetical situation. But it gave us an early clue that there were some in the LEA and the governing body who thought they could turn the parents against the teachers and their union. The Chair of Governors was already on public record stating that if the teachers "go on strike I will lose what little respect I have left for the staff of Manton because we've leaned over backwards to try to help."

As a consequence of the letter and with the local media already making enquiries, I took a carefully considered decision to publish an NASUWT press statement on 24 July. We needed to have our side of the story in the public domain in what was clearly going to be an important battle for parental opinion.

I wrote to the Secretary of State for Education, Gillian Shephard, giving her the background (including the full dossier on Michael) and pointing out that I believed the decision of the governing body for a second time to refuse to uphold the head teacher's recommendation for permanent exclusion was so unreasonable as to be perverse. Were that to be the case, the Secretary of State had the power to intervene under relevant sections of the 1944 Act and order the governors to behave rationally. I formally requested the Secretary of State to consider this course of action.

I also wrote to the Chairman of the Nottinghamshire Education Committee, Fred Riddell, whose acquaintance I had so recently renewed in the negotiations over the Glaisdale case, giving him all this information and requesting him to do everything in his power to effect a settlement.

The decision of the governing body to force Michael's second reinstatement (taken on 19 July) was the final straw for the NASUWT teachers at the school. Previously, they had been nervous and hesitant, seeking the support of their union but trying to keep it quiet at the same time. Now they realised what they were up against. We explained that there was no way they could be given the union's support they desperately needed and deserved without it becoming public knowledge.

The NASUWT's detractors who accused us of publicity and recruitment motives insult the integrity and intelligence of our members who would quickly see through such a ruse and refuse to be used for such an ulterior purpose. National and local Officers appreciated all the pressure teachers come under when they take industrial action, having experienced it both as participants and leaders. There is no way the NASUWT would have survived and prospered as a union, playing such ill-conceived games.

I could hardly believe the governors, especially the three proactive members of the Exclusions Committee, realised the implications of taking on the NASUWT in a full-frontal confrontation on this issue. It was not like striking over pay. It was members risking their jobs in defence of decent behaviour essential for education to take place.

Furthermore, the NASUWT had good intelligence that Michael had a reputation in the neighbourhood and was in trouble with local residents and retail outlets. Other reports from our Worksop Branch indicated that people such as local journalists, despite their best efforts, could not find a parent outside the governing body who disagreed with the teachers at Manton.

Despite our efforts, the summer weeks proved fruitless. We replied positively to an offer from ACAS to intervene but neither the governors nor the LEA responded. So events moved towards confrontation. The NASUWT announced the result of the ballot on 27 August, with all seven members voting in favour of striking and action short of strike, the latter amounting to a refusal to teach or accept any responsibility for Michael. Notification of intention to take action was also issued at the same time. On the same day I wrote to all the Manton parents explaining the NASUWT position. The reaction we subsequently received from parents was one of overwhelming support.

The school was due to open on Monday 2 September for a staff training/planning day with the children starting on the 3rd. On 28 August interesting publicity began to appear in the national and local press. There were photos of Michael and his mother, sometimes including governors on the Exclusions Committee. They promoted the story that Michael was described by school governors as a "bright and nice boy" and by his mother as a "normal child".

In further evidence that the boy's backers were not novices when it came to publicity, *The Daily Telegraph* carried a photograph on its page 3 of Michael, all smiles, holding a baby girl in his arms. The caption below said he was described as "a bit of a monkey". One governor was quoted: "If you are looking for a fight with Michael you will find one but there are lots of kids like that. They are making him out to be Al Capone". The Chair of Governors was quoted conceding that Michael was a "challenge" but insisted he was not uniquely so. "This youngster, who should not have been named, is a bright and nice boy. He has even carried my bags for me when he has seen me in the street."

However, other newspapers gave the boy short shrift. *The Sun* proclaimed in characteristic headline: "Teachers to strike over yob"; *The Daily Mail*: "Teachers vote to walk out over boy they 'can't tame'".

Michael's mother dismissed our strike threat as "pathetic". She added: "I don't think they should be able to pick and choose who they teach just because they can't control a normal lad like Michael".

The following day, Thursday 29 August, saw the publication of another fascinating photograph of Michael and others during his visit to a Chinese healer for some rather bizarre treatment. It was not a very appropriate photograph from a number of perspectives. In the foreground was the sight of Michael lain out on the couch, clad only in his underpants and socks. Standing over Michael were his mother and a Chinese healer. But viewing the proceedings in the background just a few feet away were two of the Exclusion Panel governors.

My first letter to the Secretary of State had only attracted a formal acknowledgement (2 August) from a civil servant. On 28 August I again wrote to Mrs Shephard reminding her of the second reinstatement and bringing her up-to-date with developments, including the governors' irresponsible one-sided approach and the NASUWT ballot result. I repeated my view that the governors had acted perversely and in their public support for Michael compromised their ability to act impartially and take the interests of the whole school into account. Again, I asked her to intervene and to use her statutory powers.

That news seemed to speed up the responses from the Department. The next day, 29 August, Gillian Shephard wrote to me stating that following enquiries made by her officials of the Nottinghamshire LEA, she was not satisfied that the governors had acted unlawfully or unreasonably in reaching their decision. Mrs Shephard quoted the criteria used to define "unreasonable" by the courts in previous cases as "conduct which no sensible authority acting with due appreciation of its responsibilities would have decided to adopt". For my part I thought that to be as good a description of the governors' decision as any I had heard!

I was disappointed but hardly surprised. For all the politicians' hard 'talk' of law and order, when it came to the 'walk' they were found wanting. The Minister only risked a lost case in the courts. NASUWT members were risking their jobs in defence of decent standards of behaviour.

I wrote again saying I reached the opposite view on the same evidence and although I agreed that the precedents drew a very narrow definition of "unreasonable" I suggested they needed to be challenged for they could make Section 99 of the 1944 Act impotent.

Monday 2 September was hectic. Pursued by the media I set out on my way to The Ridings School in Halifax to deal with another refusal to teach which was due for a showdown as the mother was reportedly going to march her daughter back into the school following a successful appeal panel hearing. By the time I arrived with Ex-President Barrie Ferguson the problem had been solved by the girl's mother, shying away from the promised confrontation. That was a good, clean-cut, quick victory for the NASUWT.

After a heart-warming meeting with grateful members at The Ridings it was back to York to take the train to Newark where the National Executive member, Roger Kirk, would pick me up to take me to Worksop for talks with Fred Riddell and the Manton governing body. This part of the day was to prove far more complex and difficult than the decisive victory we had achieved at The Ridings.

Fred Riddell, as an old campaigner, was acting sensibly and wanting to do a deal, suggesting some one-to-one support in 'internal isolation' with NASUWT members neither called upon to teach nor to supervise Michael. We were prepared to talk on that basis.

The meeting with the governing body was far more strained. Fred Riddell must have previously read them the riot act, for the governors seemed to have neither the bottle nor the know-how to go against the Chairman of their LEA who did all the talking. However, I could feel the hostile electricity in the room as the governors' body language betrayed resentment at being bounced into a deal of this kind. We agreed a deal in outline which would have to be fleshed out over the next day or two in the form of an individual education plan (IEP) for Michael.

There was the immediate crisis to avoid of the mother's threat to march Michael back into school the following day, 3 September, which would provoke a strike. Somehow the mother was persuaded to keep her son at home for a few more days.

Two more days of negotiation were required, having nearly broken down over the LEA wanting the agreement to be "interim" with the "eventual aim of returning [the boy] to normal classes at Manton". That was out of the question for us and agreement only proved possible when the LEA accepted "the aim of returning [the boy] to mainstream education".

In addition the LEA would appoint a special teacher for Michael who would be kept in strict internal isolation, with absolutely no contact with staff and pupils, having different times of arrival at and departure from school as well as separate break times. Progress would be reviewed on 17 October (over half-term). All relevant parties would be involved in the review.

The NASUWT members had their doubts and remained very nervous. We convinced them it was a sensible compromise, privately assuring them that the person who would find the arrangements the most difficult to cope with would be Michael himself. Our experience in many cases around the country of 'internal isolation' had taught us that the youngsters concerned found it well-nigh intolerable. After a few weeks they and their parents invariably got the message and made the sensible decision to move on to another school.

Another tricky area, relevant to but outside the terms of Michael's IEP, was the finance. The school budget had to absorb the extra costs, the full annual amount estimated to be in the region of £13,000. A deficit from the previous financial year had already led to a reduction in staffing despite all the difficulties. Spending such a large identifiable sum on Michael proved to be an extremely unpopular measure with the parents, many of whose children were similarly disadvantaged but behaved themselves reasonably well.

Within a day or two of Michael's readmittance parents of around 50 pupils at the school began to withhold their children's attendance in protest against so much money being spent on Michael from a budget already under pressure.

I said in a press statement issued from the TUC Congress being held in Blackpool that I understood the parents' concerns, heightened as they were by the existence of several vacancies in a special school within walking distance of the boy's home but repeatedly declined by the mother. However, the extra money being spent on Michael was not a waste as it was the only way of keeping the school open.

Mindful of some criticism by Manton members that I was not pursuing a vigorous enough campaign against the governors who were extolling Michael's virtues, I was quoted in some papers on 4 September: "If they keep on saying in public he is a sweet little devil we might have to release the whole dossier although we had no desire to make his life more difficult." *The Yorkshire Post* (4 September) had the decency to admit that "out of diplomacy, it seems, the teachers held back on the full details of Michael's disturbing behaviour".

Letters to the editor of local newspapers were extremely supportive. I noted one in particular referring to the many children in families suffering from poverty and unemployment in the area in the wake of the collapse of the mining industry yet who managed to behave themselves. Others picked up on the vacancies at a nearby special school, specifically designed to tackle pupils with behavioural problems.

Equally the Nottinghamshire LEA had to share some responsibility with central government for having pursued quite unrealistic policies of inclusion with the closure of special schools against which our local representatives had fought long and hard. Michael's case illustrated that even where additional resources are provided, inclusion policies to integrate youngsters with severe emotional and behavioural problems do not necessarily work.

The success the NASUWT was achieving in defence of its members against violence and disruption in schools produced tensions with the Government, uncharacteristically wrong-footed on the crucial issue of law and order. They surfaced openly on 4 September. The Education Secretary had "lost patience" with the strike threats of the NASUWT. The unions were wrong to think they could control school discipline through confrontation, according to Gillian Shephard who also said: "What I don't want to see is the manipulation of the system by any interest group, and certainly not by teachers, because it would do the profession no good." She was not just referring to Manton but to the other disputes at Glaisdale, Hebburn and The Ridings as well.

I dismissed Shephard's comments: "She is not living in the real world. She has no idea of the sorts of problems we are facing." It was so typical for the politicians to distort our motives. We were not remotely interested in "manipulating" anything but deeply concerned for our members who were being subjected to verbal abuse and violence, with many children's education wrecked.

Scraping around for reasons Gillian Shephard accused the LEAs of lacking "focus" and avoiding confrontation with "the union". That was a travesty of the truth, an analysis that defied facts that were unpalatable to a Government that had stripped LEAs of most of their powers and backed consumer rights against the 'wicked' producer interest. Truculent and dysfunctional parents could now pursue their 'rights' to have their impossible offspring remain in the school of their choice regardless of their behaviour. This was the emerging age of consumer choice driven into the public sector by a Government determined to turn a blind eye to the more bizarre consequences of its ideology.

Gillian Shephard went on to admit: "It does seem rather a pity that it had to come to using the tactics of the NASUWT to achieve that focus." I was "astonished that such a weak statement should have come from a Government committed to law and order". I was intrigued to note "Mrs Shephard admitting solutions would not have been found but for the tactics adopted by the NASUWT which she condemns".

Mrs Shephard totally ignored my concern about the inappropriate and close personal relationships between the family and the Exclusions Panel and cloaked the Tories' pusillanimity behind a smart comment hoping that in such a fraught situation "everyone had been in close contact with everyone else".

I followed up my correspondence with the Secretary of State sending several more letters in September and October reiterating my disappointment with her decision not to intervene and pointing out the second refusal to uphold Michael's exclusion was materially different from the first. I quoted Michael's flagrant disregard of the Chair of Governor's warning on his future conduct that was attached to his first readmission, his resort to malicious allegations against staff and the continued and heightened activity of the Exclusions Panel governors, seriously compromising their responsibility to act impartially and objectively. They were not just befriending Michael and his family but publicly attacking the teachers and accusing the NASUWT of ulterior motives, saying: "This is not about Michael. He is being used by the unions because unruly pupils are big news at the moment. The unions would like to see sin-bins (units for disruptive pupils) all over the country, and this is the way of pressurising the Government to provide them".

Of course a natural by-product of our successful conduct of cases inevitably and rightly led to pressure on governments to do something. So by October 1996 Mrs Shephard was outlining some of the contents which a future Tory education bill would have in the debate on the Queen's Speech in Parliament. However, we would never be so stupid as to use individual cases as a lever for legislative change. To import extraneous matters within the gift of others into the negotiations that eventually settle such disputes would snatch failure from the jaws of success.

Mrs Shephard chose to hide behind the narrow legal definition of 'unreasonable', emphasising that whether "you or I share that reasoning is simply not relevant in a legal sense". I remained totally unconvinced but suggested as a last resort she simply wrote to the Governors reminding them of their responsibilities to the whole school. Despite having suggested appeal panels might be required to do that, Mrs Shephard could not bring herself to send such a letter.

We received reports of governors calling meetings of parents to support the sacking of teachers who went on strike and the employment of supply substitutes. I was naturally concerned but it was not just reassuring but positively heart-warming to receive reports of some extremely hostile reactions to those governors from the overwhelming majority of parents who supported us. We were sent copies of letters parents sent in protest. The governors simply did not understand the union culture that was still alive from the coal mining days. They also failed to appreciate that the majority of parents living in the vicinity knew all about the activities of Michael and their sympathies lay decisively with the teachers.

One particular meeting seems to have backfired upon the 'plotting governors', led by two members of the Exclusions Panel. It might have been the supposedly confidential meeting for a selected group of parents that was organised on 12 September at the Manton Welfare Club. The result was that at least seven of the attendees wrote variously to County Hall and the Worksop Area Education Office complaining in blunt terms that the said governors were inciting the parents to call for the sacking of the staff.

In addition on 16 September seven parents jointly signed a letter demanding an extraordinary meeting for the removal of the governors by a vote of no confidence. One letter was quite explicit in its detail:

"The governors suggested Michael should go back in his normal class this Friday morning, thereby forcing the teachers to go on strike. The governors promised that if this were to happen then supply teachers would be brought into School first thing on Monday morning, they also told us the parents that they had all the authority to dismiss the entire teaching staff if they wished. The governors were adamant that the teaching staff were telling lies about Michael . . . they just did not like him . . . they were just picking faults for no reason.

"When the meeting came to a close the governors went around individual groups of parents, emphasising the accusations against [Michael] were not true. They offered no proof to their side of the story.

"On Friday morning, the day after the meeting, the governors were waiting up at the school again trying to get parents on side."

The blatant attempts of the governors to wreck the compromise agreement with us spoke volumes. But they also illustrated a naïve and dangerous inexperience in dealing with employer-employee relations.

Other 'illuminating' complaints from parents flowed in. Perhaps the most interesting was from one who went along to find out the reasons for the "mess we find ourselves in" only to be subjected to accusations from the governors that the head and certain teachers thought "the children are thick because parents are", and "that it's not worth teaching them to a high standard as probably they won't achieve much in life".

There were many press reports on 11 and 12 September saying that over 200 parents had signed a petition criticising the decision to spend up to £13,000 for Michael's individual tuition and calling for his removal from the school. Apparently it was being organised by the local MP, Joe Ashton, who had intervened in the dispute and suggested a meeting with, and petition to, the Education Secretary would be a better way forward than withholding their children from attendance at school.

While the massive parental support was heartening and reassuring I appreciated we were taking risks. I was confirmed in my belief that many of the governors were serious in their endeavours to sack our members. However, they seemed not to appreciate that although legislation had made 'secondary' or supportive action by members in other schools unlawful, the final technical decision on sacking was for the LEA as the 'legal employer' (even if it had no option as a result of a governing body vote). That would open up the prospect of the dispute spreading across the whole of Nottinghamshire. However, I knew we were batting on a very good public relations wicket. Our financial reserves were good. We had a first-class organisation in Nottinghamshire.

Inevitably party politics intervened between Shephard and Riddell, but I was openly critical of the Secretary of State's attempts to blame the Labour-run education authority for failing to sort out the mess. While Gillian Shephard was quick to demand action from the LEA, she was reluctant to do anything herself despite my repeated requests. Her party in Government had stripped powers away from the LEAs whilst Riddell worked hard and took risks to achieve a solution. Gillian Shephard would not even agree to meet a deputation of parents led by the local MP, Joe Ashton.

John Major was also drawn into the affair at Prime Minister's questions in the House of Commons on 12 September. Like his Education Secretary he was content to pass the buck and play politics against the Labour LEA: "I'm astonished that the Nottinghamshire education authority hasn't gripped this matter a good deal earlier and taken one of the many options to deal with this particular case".

As we anticipated, the pressure of internal isolation quickly began to tell. As early as 11 September we had indications that the strict isolation conditions were beginning to be breached by Michael. Equally, the special supply teacher employed to teach and supervise him found the arrangements extremely trying.

After the second week of internal isolation Michael and mother were back in the local press: "I just want everything to go back to normal. All I want to do is play outside at break with my mates. I can't stand it when I know they're out there and I'm stuck inside. I'm fed up with it all", bewailed Michael. His mother complained he was being treated "worse than a prisoner. He spends all day cooped up. He's not even allowed to go to the toilet on his own. The way he is being treated is just downright cruel."

But Michael and mother were not the only ones complaining in the press. The same edition of the local paper reported several neighbours complaining: "It's hell living near Michael . . . they had been subjected to torrents of verbal abuse from him."

We were advised of technical legal problems over the defining date of the start of action and the 28-day rule within which it had to commence. Accordingly we decided it was necessary to ballot members again on industrial action in the event of Michael being returned to normal classes. Again there was 100% support from the membership, now increased to eight following the decision of the deputy head to join.

A couple of years later I managed to convince the new Minister for Schools, Stephen Byers, that the requirement for industrial action to commence within 28 days of the announcement of a ballot result was one of the many bureaucratic impediments placed in our path by the Thatcher administrations which the Manton case had shown to be profoundly unhelpful to everyone. Subsequently the requirements were made more flexible in the 1998 Employment Relations Act.

So the compromise hammered out at the beginning of term in September lasted a few weeks despite some difficulties. But the time soon came by mid-October when the very expensive one-to-one support for Michael was due to be reviewed by the governors.

Anticipating some problems, Fred Riddell wrote to Roger Kirk on 16 October referring to the fact that the governors were due to begin their review of Michael's situation and would meet the following Tuesday, 22 October, to take a decision. Fred Riddell helpfully suggested a meeting on the same day, to which we agreed for obvious reasons.

On 17 October, the Press Association carried comments from Michael's mother demanding that he be allowed to return to normal classes. She said: "He feels an outcast and a prisoner stuck in a room all on his own." I repeated the clear position of the NASUWT. If Michael were returned then NASUWT members would go on strike.

I continued to resist member pressure to go more on the offensive and release details of Michael's appalling behaviour record. We were under attack by the three Exclusions Panel governors and Michael's mother. I thought it wise to keep as much in reserve as possible. We still had massive support among the parents and public opinion remained on our side.

The school broke up for a week's half-term holiday on Friday 18 October, providing a bit of a breathing space. However, shortly before 3 p.m. on Tuesday 22 October we were assembled for our meeting with Fred Riddell when we received a press statement from the governing body which after the usual formalities of 'careful consideration' declared:

"The governors have decided that no further funding will be provided to enable the continuation of the current arrangements of one-to-one tuition for the individual child concerned."

Another meeting was fixed for 30 October to which the Chairman of the Education Committee and the Director of Education would be invited.

At our meeting Fred Riddell confirmed that so far £3,000 had been spent on the one-to-one support. In positive mode the NASUWT agreed that transfer to another school could be an option to give Michael a second chance subject to conditions and appropriate consultation with members in the receiving establishment. We stood ready to meet again in Worksop on Wednesday 30 October but after Fred Riddell had confirmed the governors' decision, the NASUWT restated "its adamant position that the youngster will not be accepted back into normal classes at Manton . . . If the status quo is breached, it will provoke immediate action."

In his letter (25 October) to the Chair of Governors Fred Riddell expressed surprise that the governors had unilaterally resolved to terminate the 5 September agreement. He pointed out that the review was supposed to begin on 17 October and involve all relevant parties, leading up to a decision on the 30th.

Fred Riddell observed there were only two alternatives: presentation of Michael at the school with no teachers, or transfer to another place. He pointed out that the NUT was also threatening to bring its sole member (the head) out on strike as well if he were threatened with disciplinary action over refusing to supervise Michael.

In a letter to the Chair of Governors Fred Riddell strongly suggested Michael be kept at home until after the meeting on 30 October to 'give peace a chance'. He laid his view on the line that the educational interests of Michael would be best served if his mother were to agree to a transfer to another school, hoping "that even at this eleventh hour, it will be accepted. I know that you have been visiting [the mother] at her home on a regular basis and I hope that also this is the advice you have been offering her."

The Worksop Guardian reported on Friday 25 October the opposing positions of both sides. The Chair of Governors was quoted: "If he wants to go back into class and his mother wants him to, then that's what will happen, it's his mother's decision. We will be back to square one on Monday and somebody will have to back down."

The local Labour Party was not very enamoured with things supposedly being done by representatives in its name, and some changes were afoot. Soon after the disastrous governors' meeting on 22 October, two of the Labour Party nominees were removed. One believed he had been removed for voting the 'wrong' way on the Michael question. He was right. The other declined to comment publicly. Local NASUWT colleagues, active in the Labour Party, were working behind the scenes to effect changes in the governing body.

On 28 October I wrote to the Chair of Governors reminding her of my letter of 22 October which enclosed the result of the second ballot and also gave seven days notice of strike action. I confirmed that in the light of the governors' decision NASUWT members would commence strike action on Wednesday 31 October. Again we had to state a firm decision because of the legislation. On 28 October I sent my formal letters of instruction to take strike action to each member at Manton.

Information began to leak out on the governors' 22 October meeting. The decision to withdraw the one-to-one funding was quickly given to the media. There had also been a vote of no confidence in the Chair of Governors put forward by the teacher representative. It had been ruled out of order because of insufficient notice. The meeting had lasted four hours. No governor had any details of the review of Michael's case. Furthermore, three schools had indicated their willingness to accept him. It was common practice in many LEAs for schools to co-operate in this way. Schools found it extremely helpful to arrange 'transfers' of difficult pupils in agreement with parents, on the understanding of fair give and take, one with another.

Then events took a rather dramatic and unexpected turn. On 28 October, the head teacher had accepted Michael back and supervised him personally on a one-to-one basis. He wrote to the parents at the same time, saying that this could not continue beyond the present day and would not be available tomorrow. In view of this, he could not guarantee the proper health, safety and welfare of all the children and accordingly the school would be closed the next day, 29 October.

I do not know if the head teacher's decision to close the school on the NUT's advice had anything to do with our announced strike starting on 31 October. It might appear a bit daft for us to be going on strike when the school was shut! It would have made no difference. We could not entrust the protection of our members to others who might or might not be opening or shutting the school.

I wrote to the Chair of Governors on 28 October deploring the unilateral and flagrant breach of the 5 September agreement manifested in the withdrawal of funds for Michael's education and her personal decision to accompany him into school in an attempt to force him back into his normal class.

All the parties gathered at the County Education Office in Worksop for the planned meetings on 30 October. A large gathering of parents stood in the square outside, angry at being excluded from the meetings and their opinions ignored. We had nothing new to discuss, having set the agenda, and waited for others to respond.

After some hesitation I ventured out to speak directly to the parents, being intensely interested in hearing their opinions first-hand. I quickly found that they were very supportive and indeed glad to be speaking to me face to face. No one expressed any hostility whatsoever towards me, or my local union colleagues, or the teachers. Their anger was reserved for the governing body who had sided with a violent and disruptive boy and an aggressive mother against the teachers, whom they recognised as genuine and working in difficult circumstances.

The talks dragged on for several hours before a pretty daft 'compromise' was eventually put to us. It involved a continuation of one-to-one support for Michael but with some attempts to reinstate him in the classroom from time to time. On purely tactical grounds we agreed we would not reject it out of hand, wanting to guard ourselves against predictable attacks. We noticed that the proposal would also be put to the parents the following Friday and were confident they would reject it out of hand. They did.

At the same time I insisted on our principle of absolutely nil involvement of NASUWT members in any capacity connected with the youngster. Only Fred Riddell, who desperately wanted an end to the strike, was enthusiastic, viewing the proposal as a "breakthrough".

As we were leaving the scene we were heartened to hear the reaction of the parents to an Exclusions Panel member who was reading out a statement on behalf of the governors. They shouted "No!" when they heard that one-to-one teaching would again have to come out of the school's stretched budget. I heard one parent shout out, "It's ridiculous that one boy can dictate what goes on in our school!" While we were content to leave the governor trying to placate the parents we departed into the night, thinking that we were in for a long hard slog.

I was driven off to a hotel for the night, having arranged to do BBC *Breakfast Time* TV and Radio 4 *Today* early the next morning from the Nottingham studios. Little did I realise that the following day was to be the most dramatic one in these disputes with the forced closure of The Ridings, in a state of virtual riot which I describe in the next chapter.

The meeting with parents on the Friday (1 November) proved a tempestuous affair for the governors. Overwhelmingly the parents rejected the proposal, deeply resenting the special treatment being handed out to Michael and the cost to the hard-pressed school budget.

On Monday 4 November we achieved our first real breakthrough. While visiting schools and members in Birmingham a message reached me from our Worksop Secretary reporting that three governors had resigned, including the Chair. They had 'gone quietly', without any public statement. Perhaps it was the fury of the parents that forced the three into resignation. It was very good riddance from our point of view.

Meanwhile Fred Riddell and Gillian Shephard were exchanging political blows in a flurry of letters. The Secretary of State demanded to know what steps the LEA Leader was taking to resolve the problem and set an ultimatum for the school to open by the end of the week, effectively in a couple of days time.

Fred Riddell had previously canvassed the idea with us during the Glaisdale negotiations of declaring the decision of the appeal panel to order reinstatement to be "incapable of implementation" because the resultant strike would shut the school for all pupils. He was minded to tell the school to stay open and refuse entry to the youngster at the heart of that dispute.

On Friday 8 November two dramatic developments occurred. First, Fred Riddell counter-challenged the Secretary of State to support a risky move of enforcing a compulsory transfer of Michael to another school if his mother persisted in refusing such. Riddell candidly confessed to being determined "to share the blame with you" (Gillian Shephard) if "we were successfully challenged in the courts".

In a remarkably frank letter to Gillian Shephard (faxed to her on the morning of Friday 8 November) Fred Riddell wrote that he was pleased she now accepted that the LEA had no statutory powers to take direct control of Manton School, "as distinct from your political effusions to the media". He noted her "rather graceless and inaccurate view" that he was only now "beginning" to act to resolve the dispute, whereas he had been attempting to do precisely that since the previous July.

Very helpfully from our point of view, Fred Riddell referred to Michael's behaviour and to the breakdown in relationships, observing that had they been normal "it is reasonable to assume that the Governors would have agreed to Michael being permanently excluded". He also rejected Mrs Shephard's claim "that the main responsibility for depriving pupils at Manton School of their education rests with NASUWT whose members are on strike". "I disagree", wrote Fred Riddell: "It is the defects of the badly conceived 1988 Education Act which took away so many powers of LEAs. There would have been no strike had that not occurred."

Fred Riddell emphasised that he had tried throughout to persuade Michael's mother that a transfer would be in the best interests of everyone. He would try once more today but if that failed, "Would you give me your support for my proposed course of action? If you do Manton School will open on Monday and the education of 190 pupils will be resumed. If not, what do you suggest?" he asked, throwing down the gauntlet to Gillian Shephard.

I issued a press statement "warmly welcoming this brave initiative by Councillor Riddell". If it succeeded I assured him that "NASUWT members would return to work at the earliest opportunity on Monday".

Unfortunately from the point of view of putting Gillian Shephard deservedly on the spot, my press statement only had ten minutes currency, as a second dramatic development followed. Suddenly, a few minutes after noon on 8 November the battle was over. The mother's solicitor announced that she was "battle weary" after nearly two months of dispute. She had finally given up her struggle and agreed to the transfer of Michael to another school.

I immediately issued another statement, welcoming the breakthrough and commending Michael's mother for her common sense. I said: "The move will be in the best interests of the youngster, not to mention the entire school community at Manton." I paid tribute to the "outstanding courage" of the NASUWT members who had been on strike for eight days in a good cause. They had risked their jobs in the process. "The whole country owes them a debt of gratitude." More had been achieved by NASUWT action than by all the pious pronouncements of politicians about morality and discipline, much in fashion in those days with John Major's 'back to basics' policies. I said that NASUWT members "will be delighted to return to school at the earliest opportunity, hopefully this coming Monday morning".

Fred Riddell publicly throwing all his weight behind the NASUWT demand and the resignation of the Chair of Governors (possibly jumping before being pushed) were huge blows to the mother's ambition to keep her son at Manton School. As the affair drew to a close several people were voted off the governing body, including the two other members of the Exclusions Panel. This happened thanks to an orchestrated move on the part of NASUWT teachers (not from Manton School), who were also members of the Labour Party, appalled by the unfolding events and lobbying hard for some sensible things to happen.

On Monday 11 November the eight NASUWT members returned to work and the school reopened to resume normal activities.

Chapter 55 - Riot at The Ridings
Disputes at The Ridings School, Halifax, Calderdale

The drama at The Ridings School in Halifax begins with the 'Story of Sharon'.

Sharon (not her real name), always a very difficult pupil at the best of times, arrived at school on the morning of Thursday 21 March 1996 in a foul mood. She began the day by chasing a boy into, around and then out of a science laboratory. A few minutes later, Sharon pursued the same boy down a corridor, ignoring a teacher trying to calm her down. She began to hit and kick the boy. Both pupils ended up on the floor. Requests to stop made by two teachers were ignored.

Sharon was the main aggressor, the boy mostly trying to protect himself. The pair was warned that if they did not stop the teachers would have to part them. One teacher pulled the boy away; the other took hold of Sharon's arm to extricate her from the fight. As the teacher did this, Sharon kicked out forcibly at the boy and caught him in the testicles.

Sharon remained very aggressive, trying to break away and verbally abusing both teachers. The boy, who was in considerable pain, was taken to the school office. When the teacher released Sharon's arm, he was roundly and verbally abused by her before she ran off towards the office, again in hot pursuit of the boy.

Outside the school office two more teachers became involved in this appalling incident as Sharon refused to leave the boy alone. The boy was taken inside the office for his own protection, whereupon Sharon tried to climb through the hatch to get to him. She was hysterical and had to be pulled out of the small hatch space. The boy was removed further away to a safer place.

When Sharon realised the boy had gone from the office, she rushed out of the front door to return by another entrance. She pushed past the teacher at the top of the stairs by the staffroom, shouting at the lady concerned. She eventually ran off down the corridor and out of the school building. She did not return that day.

Sharon returned the next day and was interviewed by the head teacher. That did not last long as she became very abusive to the head and rushed out once again in search of the boy. There followed a repeat of the previous day's events.

Any teacher who tried to calm her down or ask what she was doing or why she was in the wrong class was treated to a torrent of obscene abuse, or violence, or a threat to "get them done" or a combination thereof.

Pandemonium reigned and some classes were moved out of their rooms to escape the disorder which swept around the school in Sharon's wake. The two deputy heads tried in vain to restrain Sharon. Both were threatened whilst one of them, forcibly blocking her path, became the subject of a malicious accusation of assault before she finally succeeded in landing a hit by kicking him on the leg, narrowly missing her 'intended target'.

Sharon then left the school building only to reappear some 20 minutes later outside the science laboratory accompanied by a woman who turned out to be one of her aunts. They asked to speak to the teacher, who stepped outside to deal with them. The aunt's chief 'defence' of Sharon's behaviour was that the child had been acting on the instructions of her parents to kick the boy in the testicles. The police were called because there was now an intruder on the premises as well as the physical assault on a member of staff by Sharon. After a long discussion, the relative was finally prevailed upon by the head teacher to take Sharon home and keep her there at least until the end of the Easter holiday.

Despite this request, Sharon reappeared at the school gate at the end of the day, clearly waiting for the boy to come out. A rumour spread rapidly that Sharon had a knife in her possession. True or not, it illustrated how a climate of fear and chaos could be created by the outrageous behaviour of one pupil totally out of control.

The series of incidents which characterised the fracas in March 1996 were not the first time that Sharon had behaved in a violent and outrageous fashion. Sharon had a long history of such disruptive behaviour and had been previously excluded for a fixed term. It was soon discovered that Sharon had become pregnant, and presumably the boy she was seeking out to attack was denying paternity.

On Monday 25 March Sharon was permanently excluded by the head teacher. The school governing body upheld the decision. Here the 'Story of Sharon' should have finished as far as the school was concerned.

However, Sharon's mother decided to appeal to the LEA panel on exclusions. The LEA was controlled by a left-wing Labour group who had a policy of 'nil exclusions' from school. While predictable, it was nevertheless disastrous for the appeal panel on 8 May 1996 to order the reinstatement of Sharon. The governors were later to declare the decision "deplorable". The teachers at The Ridings were understandably up in arms. The overwhelming majority belonged to the NASUWT.

Even the severest critic of state education could hardly blame the school for this kind of behaviour. All the school could do was to convey a message to the other pupils that it was totally unacceptable. Expulsion was the only sensible option. But what did the system deliver? It sent Sharon back. That was thanks to the so-called 'Independent' Appeal Panels on Exclusions from School, which had been established by the Conservative Government in 1986. The teachers and the majority of well-behaved youngsters were the ones now kicked where it hurt most. Antisocial behaviour of the worst kind had been tolerated.

Tolerated by the system, yes, but thankfully not by 35 courageous and sensible teachers supported to the hilt by their union, the NASUWT. The teachers approached us for support. We quickly concluded that the case for a refusal to teach was overwhelming, and in line with our long-standing policy authorised the balloting procedures to start.

So the stage was set for another dramatic confrontation between the NASUWT and the public authorities in charge of running the country's education service.

The Summer Term 1996 at The Ridings was dominated by the controversy over the appeal panel's reinstatement of Sharon on 8 May. NASUWT members refused to have her back. Sensibly no one tried to force the issue but obviously attempts were made to persuade our members to relent. There was no chance of that happening.

Sharon's mother naturally objected. She felt that the appeal panel had vindicated her daughter and established Sharon's right to return to the school. The problem was that our members believed they had rights as well. So did the other pupils to a decent education. Attempts to find a solution continued into the summer holidays, all to no avail. NASUWT members resolutely refused to budge.

The governors said in a statement on 14 August "they deplored" the appeal panel's decision. They pointed out that the panel accepted that the pupil was responsible for the behaviour complained about. The governors felt "that this seriously undermined discipline within the school". The governors accepted the decision was legally binding from their position and therefore they had no choice but to comply.

On 22 August the Calderdale Director of Education, Ian Jennings, wrote to me warning about the likely effects of industrial action. The school was in difficulty and the dreaded Ofsted inspection was due in November. The LEA and governors pleaded with us to desist from action, citing the risk to the very future of the school. I agreed there was a big risk. But there was an even greater one in the message that would be conveyed in allowing Sharon back.

The stand-off could not continue indefinitely. The school decided to set the second day of the Autumn Term for Sharon's return. Her mother announced publicly she would march her daughter back into school, sparking off high-octane publicity. The Glaisdale and Hebburn cases had raised the issue to national prominence and now we had two more, Manton and The Ridings, breaking out, promising the media lots of copy on the 'sexy' subject of discipline in schools.

So on the day of reckoning, 2 September, I travelled from London to The Ridings in Halifax via York, having already given many media interviews to the BBC and others from early morning. I was met at York by the then NASUWT Senior Vice-President, Barrie Ferguson, a union stalwart, who helpfully hailed from that city. Barrie had been National Executive Member for the area so knew the school well. The two of us arrived at the school around 10 a.m. to be greeted by a heavy media presence outside the front gate.

From the media we learned that our refusal to teach had prevailed. Sharon and her mother had backed off and did not show up for the much-heralded confrontation. The Chairman of Governors had issued a press statement a few minutes before our arrival saying that at a meeting the parents had indicated they were withdrawing Sharon permanently from the school. This was much to our relief and satisfaction, if to the disappointment of the media.

In the sad circumstances that was a 'good', clean-cut and quick victory for the NASUWT. In my statement to the assembled media I praised the courage of our members but also complimented Sharon's parents on making a wise decision. We then met with the head teacher and the Chairman of Governors. While they were both very polite, neither one appeared at all grateful for the solution to the problem we had forced that morning.

Naturally the meeting with The Ridings' membership was much more upbeat and convivial. Of course nobody wants these kinds of problems. But given that they existed, the sense of relief and success which pervaded the gathering was palpable. The looks on members' faces revealed they were not accustomed to having their views prevail. I felt proud of the members for their achievement in having the courage to make a stand and the support the NASUWT had afforded them.

Obviously miffed at the day's developments the Chair of the Education Committee, Councillor Higgins, issued a statement which focussed first upon technical matters relating to the appeal process. It was the independent appeal panel, not the LEA, that had sent the girl back. The LEA had no legal power to meet the union's demand.

Councillor Higgins deplored the constant media pressure, unrelenting intrusion and stress which had been exerted on the family. He said it was appalling that the name of the pupil was published in the national press and disowned any responsibility for this. Mike Higgins expressed indignation against the NASUWT but had not a single word of condemnation for the outrageous behaviour that consigned the school to chaos.

Only Sharon's parents really knew why they backed down. There were press reports that Sharon's mother had only recently learnt of her daughter's condition. They might have baulked when confronted by the enormous pressure of the media and the NASUWT refusal to teach their daughter. Whatever the reasons, it was a wise decision. A Conservative councillor publicly called for the police to investigate the matter but nothing materialised.

With another decisive 'victory' for the NASUWT, media interest continued to grow. The battle line was clearly drawn between a union standing for 'discipline' against antisocial behaviour on the part of 'dysfunctional' elements in society. As the 'Sharon' and the Manton cases broke simultaneously in September 1996, inevitably the issue forced itself even more prominently on to the national political stage. It was happening too often, and as one national newspaper put it, "all the cases were being settled in the favour of the union".

The Daily Telegraph gave the 1996 disputes widespread coverage, as one might expect from a 'law and order' paper on the right. I believe it was the first major national newspaper to personalise the issues as many in the media liked to do. Early in September, as Sharon's case and the Manton dispute erupted, it featured me in very personal if favourable terms whilst also carrying comments, some attributed, others anonymous, from other union leaders offering a mixture of praise and criticism. That was the occasion when Peter Smith, GS of ATL, gave his 'memorable' quote: "The state funds schools which employ teachers to teach all children, not just those who are as good as gold". I doubt it went down well with his members. It was received with scathing comments from mine.

On the whole the NASUWT received good support from the media and the general public, from whom I received many unsolicited letters of appreciation for the stand we had taken. Some even amounted to fan mail! Most teachers were strongly in support, even those who were not in membership of the NASUWT.

The Sunday Telegraph followed up with a feature extolling the focussed approach of the NASUWT on the needs of its members. It suggested that the other teacher unions were getting rattled with the strength of our support and the efficacy with which we were implementing our policy.

The Independent on Sunday took a different angle, featuring and supporting 'the underdog' – the disadvantaged pupils at the centre of such disputes. It was also very critical of the NASUWT and me personally. However, there was no need to respond, for by quoting the disruptive pupils, in particular 'Michael' from Manton, the paper had given them enough rope to hang themselves many times over. The article referred to an earlier incident at another school when Michael, upset at being refused a second helping of stew at lunch, "gobbed" (as he delicately put it) into the saucepan. Michael was quoted boasting that his dad, summoned to see the head teacher immediately after the incident, had removed him to another school.

While the story of Sharon has its elements of tragic farce and sadness it also had its happier moments. A few weeks later, in October, Sharon by then 13 years old, gave birth to a child. A national tabloid newspaper carried pictures of Sharon and her brothers and sisters, already aunts and uncles, aged between two and nine, posing with the baby. Led by the young mother, all of them, it has to be said, were beaming with excitement and happiness in what was undoubtedly a beautiful photograph.

Thus ended the 'Story of Sharon'. But the story of The Ridings School was far from finished, as later events were to unfold with the most dramatic convulsion of a school since the William Tyndale scandal in the Inner London Education Authority in 1976.

A little later in October 1996, by sheer coincidence I was fulfilling a long-standing engagement visiting schools and members in our York Local Association, again being conducted around by my valued colleague Barrie Ferguson. By this time Barrie had just about recovered from being described as "my driver" by *The Daily Telegraph*, reporting on our arrival at The Ridings on 2 September. As a National Officer and Member of the Executive Barrie was one of my bosses!

It was the afternoon of Friday 11 October when I took a call on my mobile from Brian Garvey, one of the National Executive Members for the area. Brian told me of more incidents at The Ridings. Serious indiscipline and violence were again occurring with little or no firm response from either the head, or governors or the LEA. He asked if I could intervene to help. Given the gravity of Brian's account I had no hesitation in saying that I would be in the school at the earliest opportunity, namely the next working day, Monday 14 October, hopefully with the President as well.

So by 3.30 p.m. on that Monday afternoon the President, Peter Cole, and I arrived at the school. We issued no press statement concerning the visit. Naturally our local people had alerted the head teacher to our intended visit. The President and I wished, for obvious reasons, as well as simple courtesy, to call upon her to ascertain her perspective of the problems before meeting with our members. We were somewhat surprised on our way up to learn that the head was too busy to meet us, not even for a few minutes. Neither Peter Cole nor I was prepared to accept that situation. We could not imagine that there was anything more important than the safety and well-being of both pupils and teachers in the school. We determined that we would see her.

Will Long, our long-serving and loyal School Rep and also Local Branch Secretary, greeted us upon arrival, impressed that "two such high-ranking union officers had arrived so promptly" but a bit concerned about our determination to meet the head.

The head teacher could hardly prevent us opening her office door and walking straight in, although we did afford her the courtesy of knocking first. She was obviously not overjoyed to see us. I enquired solicitously about her busy day. We were astonished by her reply that she was tied up with a problem concerning the paperwork required for the looming Ofsted inspection, not knowing the exact number of pupils on roll; was it 603 or 605?

While that provided an illuminating reflection upon the all-pervading influence of the Ofsted inspection system, it was enough to convince us that the head would not be able to offer much assistance. Mutual eye contact between Peter and me quickly established an understanding that it was time to leave to go and talk to the members. As we left the head's office I asked if she realised that we had some 35 members upstairs waiting to meet us, tearing their hair out and demanding action be taken on the chaotic disciplinary situation at the school. She did not respond, appearing not to appreciate the gravity of the situation.

Our local Officers had also arranged for us to meet with representatives of the LEA and the governing body. We were due to meet them after allowing about half an hour for our discussions with the membership.

So profound and dramatic were the problems raised by our members that our discussions with them lasted a long time. My notes of the meeting showed that one member after another related accounts of serious incidents taking place with little or no response from the school management. Several violent attacks had taken place upon fellow pupils and one upon a teacher. The pupils had only been sent home to return the next day. Twice the police had been involved and took statements but nothing further happened. On another occasion a firework had been set off in class, which was to lead to the member of staff concerned to be off school with stress for over four months.

Not only was there a state of indiscipline but it was positively dangerous as well. Staff feared for the safety of the Ofsted inspectors due at the end of November. Another said he had never known a school to be so unsafe in ten years of teaching. Some teachers said that as many as 30 pupils were totally out of control.

The disciplinary system was totally inadequate. Problems were identified but nothing was done about them. There was an isolation room but it was inadequately staffed. The LEA had promised but never delivered on additional resources, particularly the in-school referral unit.

Another teacher complained that every single lesson was seriously disrupted. The senior management team was inconsistent and ineffective. The head teacher appeared to be reluctant to exclude pupils.

Some believed that the inability to tackle the hard cases was leading to other pupils emulating the disruptive behaviour. Other pupils felt unsafe and some good youngsters were leaving the school as a consequence. There had been much vandalism to staff cars. There was a problem of security around the site. Books had been thrown at teachers. One woman teacher had been touched sexually by a male pupil.

Another member with an uncanny anticipation of future events suggested the school should be closed to enable the staff to take stock. Support and advice were desperately needed. The LEA support was weak. Another said that she had never experienced anything like the last few weeks in her 25 years of teaching experience. Three weeks ago she had to protect a girl who was being stoned by ten other boys.

I was anxious for everyone to have their full say. But we were already running half an hour late, so I suggested that they continue their deliberations while the President and I went on to meet the governing body and LEA representatives. Before leaving I delivered my usual 'pep talk' to members in these situations. Whilst I assured them of full NASUWT support, I also emphasised the risks involved. Bearing in mind all the recent cases, I said that there was bound to be a huge amount of publicity. As well as the forthcoming Ofsted inspection the media would find a way of investigating all aspects of the school's life. Some teachers would be exposed as weak. I warned that when we threw 'our book' at the system it would respond by subjecting us to close and critical scrutiny. Criticism there would be, for nobody is perfect. Some could easily end up losing their jobs.

To their great credit members said they were prepared to take the risks. Several were remarkably candid, conceding they had weaknesses and might well end up losing their jobs. But they were prepared to go on strike and risk closing the school down permanently rather than continue as they were.

I also emphasised, even for those who survived, that the pressures could be enormous. In disputes which lasted any length of time members came under intense pressure and stress, with most of them having to visit their doctors. They appreciated my realism and straightforward honesty but they were insistent upon going ahead. I was taken aback by their courage and honesty.

We left our members drawing up a list of violent and seriously disruptive youngsters whom we should be refusing to teach. I suggested that it might add to the drama of the occasion, not to the mention the psychological pressure I was intending to apply, if during the meeting the School Rep were to join us and bring the list of pupils we were going to refuse to teach. This interesting suggestion of mine turned out to have much more dramatic effects than even I had intended.

After a short time into the meeting with the Calderdale Director of Education, Ian Jennings, and his personnel officer, together with the head teacher and the Chair of Governors, we soon appreciated that they were not truly apprised of the serious nature of the situation and our intent to do something about it.

I was soon explaining to them that they had 28 days to sort matters out otherwise the NASUWT would be taking action. I said 28 because that was the approximate time which it took us to ballot members on action and comply with all the bureaucratic requirements of the law. Building on the drama I said that any minute now the School Rep would enter the room and provide the list of those pupils we would be refusing to teach, and, if instructed otherwise by anyone in authority, then proceed to take strike action.

Will Long seemed to be taking a long time but we kept the exchanges going without much difficulty. I had anticipated a list of around 15, which was roughly the numbers canvassed at the start of the earlier discussion with our members, although one had said 30 pupils were out of control.

Little did we realise that the discussion had continued and with it the list had lengthened accordingly. Eventually Will Long caught up with us, entered the room and passed me the list of names that were to be the subject of our action. I glanced down the page, a typical one torn from a school exercise book. I noticed every line was covered, from top to bottom. That was 30. I turned overleaf just to check and was rather stunned to find the other side was full of names as well.

I had to make a quick decision. I could see that all eyes were upon the paper and many had seen both sides covered from top to bottom. Pretending to be cool and calm I confidently said that the number appeared to be somewhere in the region of 60. This was the origin of our famous refusal to teach 61 pupils.

In fact we never did take a formal decision to refuse to teach all the 61. The media insisted on interpreting matters in this way. I admit I did not lean over backwards to explain 'pedantic details' which, in the unlikely event of being believed, would only have detracted from the gravity of the situation and our determination to get something done about it.

Our normal procedures would have involved us studying the case history of each and every pupil concerned. I realised the risk but there was no going back. In any event I was confident that the situation was serious enough in the school and that significant numbers of pupils were involved. Whether it had been 20, 40 or 60, in terms of justifying the NASUWT ballot for action, the decision would have been the same.

I observed the problem seemed worse than I had anticipated, but all the more reason for taking urgent and serious action. My interesting observations did not appear to be of much comfort to the distraught faces across the table that appeared stunned.

Some of the more 'liberal' press and opinion criticised us for going over the top in respect of the sheer numbers involved, some 10% of the total number of pupils. Countering those arguments I referred to the high percentage of pupils who had been sent to The Ridings after being expelled from other schools.

I also referred to other precedents where 'failing' schools had been turned round with new head teachers arriving on the scene and beginning with large numbers of exclusions. The whole country held in awe the heroic efforts of the murdered head teacher, Philip Lawrence of the St George's RC School in Maida Vale, London. He had been stabbed to death in December 1995 outside the school as he tried to defend a pupil who was being attacked by a gang of youths not connected with St George's. Yet he had found it necessary to exclude some 60 youngsters during his first year at the school, admittedly, however, not all at the same time.

The NASUWT had reached another crunch moment in the battle to restore sensible authority in schools. The fundamental point had to be grasped. If schools tolerated unacceptable behaviour it would spread. The message had to be conveyed that serious antisocial behaviour led to exclusion. Once that message was understood behaviour could improve. Teachers understood that, and being a union ultimately run by those still practising in the classroom, the NASUWT acted accordingly.

Having demanded action to deal with the problems it was only fair to give the school management and the LEA a chance to respond. I said that we would not issue any press statement or otherwise comment publicly. But I had to emphasise our determination. The bureaucratic burdens associated with balloting meant we had to begin the process immediately. Immediately meant at 8.30 a.m. the next day, when our HQ office opened. The Director of Education, Ian Jennings, promised to write to me within two to three days.

Our members did not lack deadly determination. Although the requisite paperwork could be done by fax the next day, the members left nothing to chance. Later that night the Calderdale Secretary, Colin Grunstein, brought a written notification of our intention to commence balloting, to the school. He was assisted over the locked gate by two NASUWT activists to deliver the notice by hand through the school letterbox!

Ian Jennings did write to me after three days, confessing he had been unable to find another head teacher to assist but would keep trying. I appreciated that he had at least got the basic message that the management of the school desperately needed to be strengthened.

The following week, on the Thursday and Friday, I was again visiting schools and members, this time in North Wales. Some local journalists, believing there was another 'case', took a keen interest in my movements. They did not believe my perfectly innocent but true explanations that I was simply visiting schools and members as I was always keen to do. However, as the Executive Member for North Wales, Vernon Rowlands, can confirm, I took a call whilst in his car on that Friday afternoon. It was from the NASUWT Press Officer, Graham Terrell, at our London office to report that a story was running that we were refusing to teach 61 pupils at The Ridings School in Halifax.

I authorised Graham Terrell to issue a short statement confirming that a meeting had been held on 14 October between the authorities and the NASUWT to discuss the situation at the school. Beyond that it was "No comment".

Several subsequent telephone calls on my mobile from a variety of journalists pointed towards the leak having a local origin. Indeed three local journalists confirmed to me personally that the story had come from the Town Hall although of course they would not divulge more detail. That was how the story broke. My 'no comment' order to my colleagues was the last and a predictably forlorn attempt to hold back the tide of publicity that I knew would engulf the school. I just hoped that the story might blow over quickly.

I laid low over the weekend. But by the Monday the story was running big and by the following day, Tuesday 22 October, I recorded in my diary "saturation media coverage Ridings and Manton".

The Chairman of The Ridings' governors issued a statement on 22 October complaining about the distorted picture of the school painted by the press. He criticised the NASUWT decision to ballot for action, claiming we were fully aware of the LEA's package of measures designed to support the school from the start of the term. We were of course aware of the promises, just as we were of the failures to deliver in the past.

The Chairman of Governors looked forward to the appointment of a new head teacher for the following term in the wake of the incumbent's resignation. The Ridings' governing body had met in special session on Saturday 12 October and accepted the honourable decision of the head to resign at the end of term. To her credit she had also courteously and confidentially informed our School Rep Will Long of her decision. As things turned out her departure came much more quickly as the crisis erupted.

The Chairman of Governors claimed that the way forward for the school did "not lie in mass exclusions but in sweeping changes". However, the entire NASUWT membership at the school firmly believed both were needed. He said he would write individually to all union members, asking them to consider their decision very carefully in the ballot.

The meagre package of half measures offered by the LEA was simply no match to the size of the school's problems. Four neighbouring schools were creaming off the higher-ability children. There were two church schools, Halifax Catholic High and Holy Trinity High Church of England. In addition there were two grant maintained schools, North Halifax School and Crossley Heath High School.

Many teachers had little confidence in the Calderdale LEA. They regarded it as still in the "Dark Ages", way behind other LEAs. It had never achieved a true comprehensive system and eventually there was such a lack of confidence that several schools within Calderdale chose to 'opt out' and become grant maintained, in line with the Conservative Government's intentions.

The Ridings had been formed on 1 January 1995 as a result of a merger between Ovenden and Holmfield, effectively two secondary modern schools located in two distinct and rival council estates. Many of the teachers attended the three public meetings prior to the decision to amalgamate the two schools, vociferously criticising the planned merger as a potential disaster on account of the bitter rivalries between the two estates. The merger had taken place to reduce surplus places. The capacity of The Ridings was 750, but only around 600 pupils were enrolled.

Some 20 pupils had been expelled from, or had their arms twisted to leave, other schools and had entered The Ridings, which was forced to take these pupils because it had surplus places. The LEA had complained bitterly about the inordinate delay in the Secretary of State reaching a decision to establish the new school. The Ridings had only existed for 20 months and was competing with two grammar schools and a number of well-established 11-18 comprehensive schools.

The area reflected the social divisions of the country. There were some very poor parts in and around the old industrial towns such as Halifax. There were some very wealthy areas in the suburbs and the countryside. Thus the Calderdale Authority had vacillated between Labour and Conservative control over many years.

The establishment of grant maintained and the retention of grammar schools undoubtedly led to the more affluent families making sure their youngsters accessed the better establishments. Thus Ovenden, Holmfield and eventually The Ridings were left to pick up the pieces and operated as secondary moderns. Over 50% of the pupils were entitled to free school meals, with 45% on the special needs register for learning and behaviour difficulties.

The LEA denied having a total opposition to permanent exclusions, pleading an expenditure of "some half a million pounds a year providing education for pupils with emotional and behavioural difficulties (EBD) in special schools outside the LEA". That was true but it could not hide the fact that pressure was placed upon head teachers and governors to avoid permanent exclusions. The complete absence of specialist EBD schools in Calderdale spoke volumes.

It took the NASUWT threat of action at The Ridings finally to secure a slice of the £4.3m that had been promised but not delivered for the school several years before. At last £1m was to be spent building the promised sports hall. However, the LEA's support for The Ridings was too little too late.

On Thursday 24 October the Secretary of State, Gillian Shephard, had called a press conference at her Department and announced a special inspection of The Ridings, in effect bringing forward the 'normal' Ofsted one due later that term. Again it was a day of saturation media coverage.

I quickly arranged a press conference of my own – hiring a room at Church House, Westminster, the HQ of the Anglican faith, right opposite the Department for Education – to follow Gillian Shephard's. The journalists were very grateful for the convenient arrangements. For my part I was not going to let Mrs Shephard create the impression that the Government was the only one stressing the need for urgent action over the state of affairs at The Ridings.

I surprised many journalists by warmly welcoming the Secretary of State's initiative. I believed, quite correctly as it turned out, that at last someone in a position of authority was beginning to take the matter seriously and instituting action which could lead to a resolution of the problems.

A meeting took place on Wednesday 29 October between local representatives of the NASUWT and the LEA Director, Ian Jennings, to explain our position in more detail in respect of the action required over a number of the most troublesome pupils. We were able to convey our more considered position that 15 had to be permanently excluded immediately whilst another 30 needed serious remedial measures including fixed-term suspensions.

Ian Jennings outlined the timetable of events envisaged by the LEA: the HMI inspection, the announcement of the temporary headteacher, Peter Clark, and later the appointment of an associate head.

On 30 October I received a log of serious pupil misbehaviour compiled as arranged by the members. It was difficult to comprehend the full magnitude of the chaotic disciplinary situation at the school. The log related mainly to the last five weeks and concerned pupils from Years Seven, Eight and Nine. Logs for Years Ten and Eleven were expected but were overtaken by events and they never reached me.

The Ridings School Behaviour Log
Five weeks during Autumn Term 1996
Years Seven, Eight and Nine

	Year Seven	Year Eight	Year Nine
Threats/assaults			
on staff	11	5	15
on pupils	19	14	49
Offensive language			
to staff	33	11	28
to pupils	11	21	64
Internal truancy	4	29	72
Classroom disruption	48	25	75
Open defiance	51	31	0
Throwing objects	0	3	2
Spitting	2	1	1
Smoking	1	3	11

Year Seven   Based on *12 Reports* on 7 pupils
Year Eight   Based on *31 Reports* on 5 pupils
Year Nine   Based on *86 Reports* on 10 pupils

Let me give a slight flavour behind the statistics:

one of the spitting incidents was into a teacher's cup of tea;

one of the offensive remarks was: "I want to go to the loo Miss, open your mouth";

one threat to a male teacher was that a pupil's dad would "fucking kick your head in";

one of the throwing incidents related to a pupil running amok in a classroom throwing textbooks about, kicking open an emergency door and throwing them outside into the mud;

another offensive-language-to-staff incident concerned a refusal to allow a pupil to visit the toilet, the pupil responding: "Shall I piss all over your floor"?

one of the smoking incidents related to a pupil lighting up a cigarette in class.

Having welcomed Gillian Shepherd's initiative I hoped that the presence of inspectors at The Ridings would lead to a few days of significantly better behaviour. Alas the very opposite turned out to be the case.

A shorter 'HMI' rather than a full Ofsted inspection was planned. A team of seven was assembled, led by the then Director of Inspection, Mike Tomlinson, who later assumed the office of Chief Inspector in the wake of the sudden resignation of Chris Woodhead in November 2000. Mike Tomlinson was a tall, imposing figure and had apparently good previous experience as a teacher. I thought if anyone could impose good order in a school it would be someone like Mike Tomlinson.

On Monday 28 October the inspectors arrived at the school in the company of a full media circus. Unfortunately behaviour deteriorated even further. It would be entirely wrong to blame the inspectors. Some pupils were determined to misbehave to exploit the situation. The combination of the TV cameras and the inspection sent the school from admitted chaos into freefall.

That was the day on which a girl pupil gave the famous 'V' sign behind the back of the head teacher as they walked up the school steps. There was widespread TV coverage of such a 'perfect picture' summing up the state of discipline in the school. The girl who gave the 'V' sign was a long way from being the worst in the school. The head was a kindly person trying against the odds to handle an immensely challenging job, who had with commendable integrity resigned. However, according to teachers at the school, the girl who made the 'V' sign later admitted that she had been paid money by a member of the press to do so.

The media were having a field day. Various vantage points were set up and cameras zoomed in to the school and playground. A 'cherry picker' was elevated on a road just above the school in full view of pupils on the playground and in some classes. This was a gross intrusion and against the media code that photographing of children in school should only be undertaken by agreement with the relevant authority. Some pupils duly availed themselves of the opportunity of becoming famous for 15 minutes and their behaviour descended deeper into the abyss.

There were some reports of money being offered in return for interviews. Some parents and pupils could not resist the opportunity. One or two of these were among the most serious problem pupils who would also feature prominently amongst those soon to be permanently excluded. I am informed that two such boys, together with their parents, were paid a fee of £250 each, with all expenses met, to be interviewed on one of the TV channels.

As the rumours spread along the grapevine, a number of youngsters who had been permanently excluded in previous years (without appealing) returned to the school to participate in the 'fun'. But for all the rough justice undoubtedly suffered by some who deserved no such fate, at least the problems were being exposed. It was the lamentable failure of the authorities to take our concerns seriously that had really led to the media 'taking over'.

There is some evidence that the presence of the inspectors made the situation worse. They certainly found life difficult. Given the problems, that was no bad thing. The NASUWT has long advocated that they should regularly return to the classroom as full-time teachers so they can be reminded first-hand of the pressures of the job they are inspecting.

The inspectors struggled on a little longer than planned until Thursday 31 October, a day etched in my memory as the most hectic in my 33 years as a teacher union representative. While all this was going on I was up and down to the Manton School in Nottinghamshire dealing with the escalating crisis, which led to an eight-day strike. With two major high-profile disputes raging I had to react instantaneously to a seemingly endless series of media interviews. On 31 October they began early in the morning with BBC TV *Breakfast Time* and the Radio 4 *Today* programme and ended up on *Newsnight*, finishing just before midnight. I started in the BBC Nottingham studios, having spent the night in that city after the negotiations in Worksop over the Manton School, with the strike already started.

On *Today* I had a vigorous exchange with the renowned John Humphrys, fast becoming the most feared scourge of politicians in the land. But much to my disgust the BBC, possibly influenced by a couple of Labour MPs, was trying to turn the issue into an inter-union dispute with the NUT. I suggested to John Humphrys that he had been badly briefed and the BBC ought to be ashamed of itself for seeking to trivialise this matter. I wondered why he was not asking me about the state of violence and indiscipline in schools, a matter of grave concern to teachers, pupils and parents, a major deterrent to teacher recruitment and probably the single biggest factor behind standards not being as high as they might otherwise be.

Unfortunately the BBC was becoming more 'tabloid', putting controversy, however trivial, ahead of more serious issues. The priority seemed to be ego building for the interviewer by embarrassing the interviewee. The BBC took the same angle the following day on the one o'clock radio news.

Just before my interview with John Humphrys I discovered that two prominent Labour members of the Parliamentary Education Select Committee were attacking the NASUWT and me personally. Margaret Hodge said of the industrial action: "I don't think it is appropriate for a professional group of teachers to take industrial action in these circumstances". Perhaps it was not deliberate, but I found the implicit assumption that 'professional' people did not participate in union action to reflect a snobbish attitude.

The other MP, former teacher David Jamieson, said: "There was some unhappiness among his parliamentary colleagues at the extreme views expressed by Mr de Gruchy". He told *Today*: "It does look as if the NASUWT is making some hay out of this. I believe they are on some sort of recruitment drive."

I responded that it was desperately sad to see MPs engaged in cheap point scoring, fitting facts to their preconceptions, in total ignorance of the pressure teachers were under and the crisis hitting the schools. Later on that day, after the crisis had reached its climax, I received an interesting call from the PA to the then Shadow Education Secretary, David Blunkett, dissociating himself and the Labour Party from Hodge's and Jamieson's attacks.

The rest of Thursday morning was taken up travelling back from Nottingham to London. During the course of the train journey I learnt that ITN wanted me live on their 12.30 news bulletin. During this time the situation at The Ridings was deteriorating even more, with the school in freefall, with a virtual riot taking place. As I was soon to discover, three more assaults on NASUWT members had taken place. One woman teacher had her breasts fondled in the classroom.

While waiting to be interviewed I took a call from a member, Steve Kellett, at The Ridings School. (I had left all the members with my mobile number in case of emergency.) He related more serious incidents of assault including a sexual one that had just taken place that morning. Furthermore nothing had been done about it. I told him I would get right back the minute I had done my interview, to which I was with some panic being summoned by the ITN studio staff.

As soon as the interview was over I got back to Steve Kellett and told him to contact Will Long who should then gather together all the members in the staffroom and tell the head that they were refusing to come out unless and until their safety could be guaranteed and order restored. I then telephoned my colleague, the Deputy GS, Eamonn O'Kane, who was in our London Covent Garden office, asking him to contact the LEA Director, Ian Jennings, to tell him what we were doing. ITN staff listened with some incredulity to my conversation.

It was my intervention, 'instructing' members to retire to the staffroom that forced the Authority to close the school. Despite all that had happened in the weeks before, on the previous day and in the morning, there was still no decisive intervention from anyone in authority. Even the inspectors, who admittedly were not there to deal with disciplinary problems directly, seemed unable or unwilling to take control.

After my instruction to members to retire to the staffroom went around the school Will Long tells me he witnessed from his classroom the inspectors making 'panic' calls on their cellphones, huddled in a group outside the English block. In one sense I felt sorry for them. In another, given that such awful events do occur in schools, it was good for them to witness them at first-hand. Some had stones thrown at them by the pupils during the morning break.

Another inspector had been to told "to fuck off" by a Year 10 student as he left a classroom following a period of observation.

Within two hours the school was closed and pupils sent home. The closure dominated the day's news and the following morning's headlines. Despite all that had gone on, despite the ongoing emergency inspection, chaos still reigned. It took decisive NASUWT action to force meaningful intervention by those in authority. I could not have authorised immediate strike action without exposing the Union to risk. But something had to be done immediately and I used an old tactic that I had learnt when I had been Secretary of our London Association many years before.

Neither the LEA nor the Secretary of State for Education referred to the NASUWT retirement to the staffroom when explaining the decision to close the school. They tried to claim some credit for 'their' decisive intervention. Politicians rarely tell lies, being too clever for that. But they have a canny knack of selective presentation of the facts. They lacked the courage to take decisive action early enough, only taking risks if they had no alternative.

But on the positive side, at long last decisive action had been taken. The school was closed. A breathing space had been created. The school could now take stock and begin the attempt at recovery. This would not have happened but for action by the NASUWT.

After leaving the ITN building I returned to my London office to hold a press conference at 3.00 p.m. to release the result of the NASUWT ballot for action. As expected all 35 members had voted unanimously 'yes' on the two questions, namely to refuse to teach certain pupils and, second, to take strike action if instructed otherwise by management.

By this time juicy details of the inspectors' findings that some lessons were unsatisfactory were being leaked by sources, presumably from Ofsted or the Department for Education. Some controversy appeared in the following day's papers. Participants at a conference of business people addressed by the Chief Inspector were reported as saying he had made such comments. Chris Woodhead strongly denied he had said anything about the school. He said he had spoken in general terms about incompetent teaching leading to poor behaviour. Chris had made himself controversial by asserting there were 16,000 incompetent teachers in England's schools. The evidence for that assertion was not so clear-cut as the figure was precise.

Some journalists were keen to exploit the incompetent teachers' angle but I rehearsed all the points I had been through with the members at the meeting on 14 October. Members had been candid and straightforward, acknowledging some of them were not coping. That was why they had asked the union to intervene to support them. I was not going to criticise people for failing in such a challenging situation. I was pleased to learn a few weeks later when speaking to the new temporary and very able head teacher, Peter Clark (seconded from a neighbouring grant maintained school), that he thought most of the teachers were good. He had known many for a long time. He said the biggest gap was that so many had not had their skills updated.

It was to their credit that the teachers, some of whom had been rendered less effective by the appalling disciplinary situation, were prepared to be honest and to admit their limitations but also to demand that the issues be tackled. When the inspectors officially released their preliminary findings, the readiness to be honest had spread to others, including the LEA and the governors. I was pleased that national newspaper editorials recognised this and complimented all those who had admitted some share of responsibility for the state into which the school had slumped. That included me, speaking on behalf of the teachers.

It was hugely significant that the only 'partner' in the education service that refused to accept any responsibility was the Government. As I describe elsewhere in these chapters there were many aspects of the Conservative Government's policies which had contributed significantly to The Ridings' problems. Having said all that, no one should forget that the main reason for the antisocial behaviour stemmed from the youngsters and often the families they came from.

There was some irony in that on the day we chose to announce the result of the ballot for industrial action, by the time my press conference commenced we had forced the closure of the school by other means. The retirement to the staffroom might be regarded as a form of withdrawal of labour, but equally it could be regarded as refusing to accept intolerable conditions which made teaching impossible.

I expressed the hope that matters would soon be resolved and the school reopened under new management. At the same time I insisted that a certain number of pupils had to be moved on in one way or another.

On 5 November I returned to Halifax for more negotiations with the LEA and the new head teacher over future arrangements in The Ridings. Our ballot result was still current but inactive. Following further consultation the NASUWT came to the conclusion that some 15 pupils needed to be expelled urgently and immediately. A further 30 required serious attention, such as temporary removal to facilitate remedial measures. The escalation of the number to 61 illustrated the problem of 'imitation' when serious problems are not dealt with and dogma such as 'nil exclusions' is elevated above common sense.

After more hectic work the 'remedial' measures for the relevant pupils had been identified and all informed of the co-operation required before the school could reopen. That seemed to proceed remarkably smoothly, proving once again that authority can be restored if those responsible choose to exercise it. Much media attention focussed of course on the precise numbers. The NASUWT was very pleased with the result of our discussions with the LEA. Again we undertook to keep matters confidential. Twelve pupils were identified for 'straightforward' immediate permanent exclusion. A further 23 were to be removed in one way or another from the school to alternative provision. Consultations with our membership and local Officers soon indicated that this was an acceptable start to resolving the school's problems. There would now be no need to implement the industrial action authorised by the ballot.

On my way out of the town I was soon telephoned by various media channels in full possession of all the information about the numbers involved. I knew that no national representative of the NASUWT had leaked the figure, for we had been together for the whole time. I could neither prove it was not a local union source nor establish it was an LEA one. Realising the usual 'angles' to the story would now run, I claimed victories for common sense and praised the courage and integrity of the NASUWT members who had forced those in positions of authority to face up to their responsibilities. Recovery could now be attempted.

The full inspectors' report, as opposed to the selective leaks, was published on 6 November. Armed with the report, Gillian Shephard set about making as much political capital out of the affair as she could. At the same time she took perfectly justified and responsible action on the education front. She welcomed the appointment of Peter Clark as a temporary head and praised his decision to suspend a number of pupils. I was left wondering why the NASUWT had been so severely criticised for demanding similar action a few weeks previously.

Whilst the media played a few of its dirty tricks in the story of The Ridings' collapse, undoubtedly inflicting serious injustices on some people, overall it played a positive role. Looking at the big picture, violence and indiscipline in schools had been under-reported rather than over-sensationalised.

Without the NASUWT action there would have been no media involvement. Both were necessary to prompt the Secretary of State to intervene to start the recovery process. After all, the NASUWT had told Minister after Minister of this kind of situation only to be accused of exaggeration. Our motives were easily traduced, fitting nicely into accusations of publicity seeking and recruitment rather than responding to members' rightful demands for support. Such accusations insulted the intelligence and integrity of our members in implying they would fall for such deception and not crucify their union leaders for attempting it.

The BBC TV *Panorama* programme on The Ridings, broadcast on 4 November 1996, was probably the most comprehensive media analysis of the school's collapse. Despite its distorting preview publicity: "Former head tells of staffroom conflict at The Ridings – reveals *Panorama*", it played an immensely valuable role in airing the issues in a very compelling way. It rightly reflected the whole range of contributory factors: the poor state of buildings, the £4.8m promised but never delivered by the LEA, the appalling behaviour of many pupils, the vandalism, the demoralised and cynical staff (acknowledged by the CEO) that did indeed contain some divisions and produced some poor teaching, management's failure to implement an effective behaviour policy, the bitter rivalries between the two 'constituent' council estates, and the existence of selection in the area, to name but a few.

Having failed to engage the head in discussion I was pleased to be able to listen to her comments on the programme. She said that the problems started before the school had even been opened. Staffs from the two schools were effectively competing for each others' jobs and inevitably there were winners and losers, and a lot more of the latter than the former. She conceded there had been two nervous breakdowns before the school opened. There was a high level of illness and stress among the staff right at the outset: "As the staff came under pressure as a result of the disappointments, the increasing disruption, the failure of the system that we have to cope with and the apparent lack of support we have had, people under pressure have parted and have developed into separate camps".

The head described how the teachers were given just four days in which to meet and bond with each other but most of that time had to be spent working as removal men to set up the school. She said: "The staff were manual labourers for most of those four days. We did manage a full school staff meeting but by that stage people were absolutely exhausted, physically exhausted." This was astonishing. What kind of management and LEA would ever allow such an outrageous waste of professionally qualified people's time?

The head went on to admit that within four days of the school opening she was forced to exclude 13 pupils for two days each for fighting on school premises. In her view the reason behind the fighting was simply "to establish the pecking order of pupils". The two schools had previously been rivals and they had to sort out who was going to be the boss. How can teachers be blamed for that!

The head conceded that teachers' ability to deliver good education had been affected by all the pressures. She said she had no misgivings about the staff as regards their personalities but was worried about their ability to cope with the number of disruptive pupils. She felt contempt for those involved in the dispute who appeared to be passing the buck, but to her great credit and pointing out she had resigned, she accepted responsibility for her own mistakes. Issues like these were not brought out in the inspectors' report.

After watching the programme I felt a sense of frustration and sadness that such honest, open assessment had not been possible before. It also heightened my disappointment that the BBC *Panorama* team had chosen to lead with 'a divided staff' in its pre-broadcast press release flagging up the programme. It was neither justified by its own comprehensive and fair reporting nor by the facts, but was typical tabloid journalism, unbecoming of the BBC.

By Friday 8 November the Manton dispute was resolved by the mother withdrawing the youngster concerned. I had no idea 1996 would turn out as it did but I look back upon the time with great pride. The NASUWT fought the good fight like never before. Of course nobody in their right mind wants these kinds of problems; but given they exist I was immensely proud that the NASUWT had proved up to the challenge. I believe 1996 was a turning point. As a result of the stand by the NASUWT and the high-profile accompanying the cases, Government Ministers and politicians ceased accusing the NASUWT of exaggeration and began to take the issue more seriously, although it took several more years for real support to come through. Other unions also changed their attitudes.

Postscript to The Ridings

Those who were eager to lay the major blame upon poor teaching might reflect carefully on experience since 1996. Many so-called failing schools have been turned round. Indeed the New Labour Government quite rightly claimed credit for overseeing the recovery of nearly 800 schools previously judged by the Ofsted inspectors to be failing during its first administration, 1997-2001.

The quality of teaching is but one of many factors that have to be addressed in raising standards in 'challenging' schools. Many schools have seen significant staff changes as a consequence. Good younger teachers have tended to replace older 'burnt out' ones. Yet many problems remain. Lifting a school out of the 'failing' category is difficult enough. But even more difficult is maintaining improvement into the long term.

The Ridings has been no exception. Despite the heroic efforts of many good teachers, including excellent heads and deputies, problems remained. Several years after the traumatic events of 1996 I again had to visit the school. Yes, the reader has probably guessed it in one! There was a serious difference of opinion over one particularly ill-behaved pupil. In the view of most classroom teachers that pupil needed to be permanently excluded. I understand that my visit, undertaken quietly without any publicity, was helpful in securing the desired outcome from the classroom teachers' point of view.

I say my visit was "without any publicity". That was true at the time. However, a week or two later a journalist at the *TES* telephoned to ask if it were true that I had recently visited The Ridings. I had no idea where the journalist had secured the information and I harboured no expectation that sources would be divulged. I answered truthfully, "Yes". Was it to deal with more disruption? "No", I answered untruthfully, in a good example of a little white lie for the greater good. "Just routine follow-up to see how they were getting on," I said.

I felt more than justified in telling this white lie because the atmosphere I found in the school was a complete transformation from my earlier visits in the autumn of 1996. There were many new faces (mostly younger) on the staff. All appeared to me in conversation to be very impressive individuals. The new head, Anna White, was open, very helpful and communicative, exuding confidence in doing her job. She obviously carried respect from everyone. Yet despite this, there were still problems, for which no one blamed the teachers. On the contrary, I was pleased to observe that they were admitted and tackled seriously, as best they could be. That was the difference from 1996.

More recently (2008) a decision was taken to close The Ridings School. Problems had persisted and standards attained at GCSE and in the national tests were judged too low. There was, however, no criticism of staff, who were considered to have tried everything reasonably possible. Those who proclaimed incompetent teachers were solely or largely to blame for failing schools had at least in this famous case been proved wrong.

Chapter 56 - New Labour – Old Problems

New Labour, coming to power in 1997, initially made the problem worse for teachers, but eventually came to realise that disruptive behaviour was one of the chief reasons behind so-called 'failing' schools and as such a major impediment to raising standards of achievement. Attitudes of those 'in authority' were in the process of changing, prompted by the resolute action taken by the NASUWT.

The controversy over the appeal panels continued. DfEE Circular 10/99 placed even more bureaucratic hurdles in the path of schools wishing to expel violent or disruptive pupils. The number of permanent exclusions had risen dramatically from 1,300 in 1992 to 3,500 in 1993. The Tories then ceased the collection of the figures but later had to reinstate them, accused of a scandalous attempt to conceal the truth.

In November 1997 the DfEE reported a 13% rise in the number of permanent exclusions from schools for the year 1995/96. The number increased from 11,100 the previous year to reach 12,500. In the primary sector the number rose from 1,400 to 1,600. Secondary school permanent exclusions rose from 9,200 to 10,300. Nearly three-quarters of all secondaries reported at least one permanent exclusion. Those in special schools rose to 500, with 25% reporting at least one.

New Labour set targets for the reduction in the number of pupils permanently excluded by a third, to around 8,200 by 2000. Naturally I was severely critical of the use of targets for this purpose, knowing how they corrupted the process.

In my press statement I blamed three factors for the increase: the 'integration' of EBD youngsters into mainstream schools in line with the misguided policy of 'unqualified inclusivity'; the market pressures generated by the publication of league tables; and the deteriorating standards of behaviour amongst pupils. I was "saddened but not surprised" by the news.

Other details showed that 83% of exclusions were of boys and 67% were of pupils between the ages of 13 and 15. The overall exclusion rate of the school population was 0.19%. However, the rate for black pupils was 0.66%. Immediately some blamed racism, intentional or otherwise, on the part of teachers, but the rate for pupils of Asian descent was 0.11%. The relevant figure for white pupils was 0.18%.

The NASUWT organised a special one-day conference in London in March 1998 entitled "Drawing the Line" to promote solutions. I was intrigued to hear a well-known and respected figure in the world of education, Heather du Quesnay, openly acknowledge the problem of indiscipline in schools. As a teacher, deputy head and a Director of Education in some tough areas such as Lambeth in Inner London, she had accumulated wide experience and later became the first Director of the new National College for School Leadership in 2000. At our conference she admitted to having experienced disciplinary problems as a teacher. She conceded that the NASUWT was absolutely right to raise the issue although she sometimes disagreed with the action we took. People who 'got on' in the education service rarely said such things.

By January 2000 the situation was deteriorating so badly that I wrote to David Blunkett warning him of "the rising tide of complaints from members that schools were being unreasonably pressurised to cope with and tolerate serious misbehaviour". The problem lay in DfEE Circular 10/99, *Social Inclusion: Pupil Support*, promoting national targets for the reduction of exclusions, which militated against judging cases on their merits. Financial penalties were imposed on schools permanently excluding offenders and Ofsted began monitoring their number as one criterion for judging a school to be failing. In my letter I was as blunt as ever: "NASUWT will not stand idly by while members have to pick up the pieces of the Government's impractical ideologies."

On the very day I wrote to Blunkett the Union was conducting seven ballots for industrial action on the issue. The situation was getting so out of hand that other organisations were rethinking their attitudes to the problem. The previous September the SHA joined with the NASUWT in issuing a statement on common principles on behaviour management. The SHA GS John Dunford also wrote to David Blunkett echoing the NASUWT's concerns and stating that Circular 10/99's unintended side effects were making it difficult for school leaders to maintain good discipline. In a press statement he reminded the Government that: "Exclusion can be an expression of a headteacher's determination to uphold standards in the school."

The Government immediately made some concessions. It issued guidance that minor breaches of procedure should not of themselves allow appeals to succeed and that a permanent exclusion could be imposed for a first offence. The NASUWT welcomed these two positive steps in the right direction.

Conference 2000 at Llandudno, North Wales again saw much debate about antisocial behaviour. In my Monday evening GS address I rebutted the allegation that the NASUWT was interested merely in kicking out disruptive pupils onto the streets. That was a "monstrous misrepresentation for we had constantly argued for suitable alternative provision". However, "if a hard choice has to be made it is better for a violent and disruptive youngster to receive only two hours of home tuition a week than to wreck the 27 hours of education for everyone else in the class".

In his speech to Conference David Blunkett said: "Parents carried a prime responsibility for the behaviour of their children. You will get my backing in tackling unacceptable conduct head on. By the year 2002 there will be 1,000 learning and support units in both secondary and primary schools." Responding, I welcomed the extra support but warned that the crunch question remained: What does a school do when all alternative in-house support measures have been tried but failed? Persistent and serious antisocial behaviour had to result in exclusion; offenders could not just be sent across the playground or down the corridor.

On 10 August 2000 came more news that New Labour was (wisely) backtracking further on Circular 10/99 and 'excessive inclusion'. 'Juicy details' of a Ministerial speech later in the day (to the PAT Annual Conference) were deliberately 'leaked' through the usual channel of the *Today* programme on BBC Radio 4. "Give Heads Power to Bar Violent Pupils: [says] Minister" ran the headlines. The Minister, Jacqui Smith, said: "Heads must have the power to bar violent pupils and local appeal panels should only overturn their decisions in exceptional circumstances". This all seemed a huge step towards NASUWT policy.

Forgetting their own past, the Tories were on the attack, accusing the Government of doing a U-turn. Even the Chief Inspector, our erstwhile friend Chris Woodhead, was reported to be backing Tory calls for more power for head teachers.

Jacqui Smith announced new guidelines stating that appeal panels should not normally reinstate a pupil expelled for:

> serious, actual or threatened violence against another pupil or staff member;
>
> sexual abuse;
>
> drug dealing;
>
> persistent and malicious disruptive behaviour, including refusal to follow school policies on discipline and uniform.

Jacqui Smith added for good measure: "That means that heads must be able to get disruptive pupils out of the classroom quickly, using on-site units where appropriate". That statement could have been lifted from any number of my press statements or NASUWT publications on the subject over many years.

But I was still wary the Government wanted to have its cake and eat it. Despite the trenchant headlines, in the small print Jacqui Smith still insisted: "It is right that parents have some recourse to appeal where their child is excluded but it is equally important that the needs of all other children at the school are met".

Conference 2001, presided over by Tony Hardman from Liverpool (a rare but welcome example of a secondary head who stayed loyal to his Union), was held in Jersey, the island where I was born and brought up. It was addressed by Estelle Morris, then Minister of State at Education but soon to succeed David Blunkett in the top job. Estelle was forced on to the defensive, claiming it was an "absolute myth that Government was concerned to keep violent youngsters in mainstream schools".

Tory Education Opposition spokeswoman, Theresa May, gave two pledges to the 2001 Conference. The first was to preserve the anonymity of teachers accused of child abuse until a case is heard in court. The second was to abolish independent appeal panels for excluded youngsters. Whilst thanking her for these two very helpful developments, I had to remind her that it was a Conservative Government that had introduced the appeal panels in 1986 against the strong advice of the NASUWT and in the middle of the Poundswick strike in Manchester about this very issue.

A motion from Sandwell on malicious allegations was carried, setting out a six-point policy which the Union was to pursue to good effect over the coming years:

1 Teachers to be informed of the nature of the allegations against them.
2 Cases to be investigated quickly.
3 Accused teachers to be allowed to continue working.
4 Anonymity for accused teachers to be guaranteed.
5 Teachers to be treated as innocent until proven guilty.
6 Wrongly accused teachers to be compensated.

The incoming President in 2002, my last Conference as GS, was Peter Butler who had been elected JVP two years earlier without having served on the National Executive. Policy on exclusion was further developed with a commitment to campaign for:

government funding for special schools and Pupil Referral Units (PRUs);
ending financial penalties on excluding schools;
needs assessments and appropriate placements for excluded pupils; high-quality off-site provision for excluded pupils;
consultation and resourcing on the admission of an excluded pupil to a new school.

In the 2002 debate on discipline in schools a Croydon delegate and incoming NEC member, Anne Marie Flavin-Lees, accurately articulated teachers' concerns about antisocial behaviour when she said: "It is the level of contempt, rudeness and crudity that we often have to contend with, that would shock most people in the real world. Indiscipline has also increased since Social Inclusion was introduced into an under-resourced system."

Another manifestation of intolerable pupil misbehaviour was the growing number of false and malicious allegations of physical or sexual abuse against teachers. The entirely understandable developments to improve child protection had one unfortunate side effect in allowing some 'streetwise' children to ruin a teacher's life and career simply by making accusations, no matter how false they might be. The NASUWT was concerned that teachers could be suspended on the say-so of one child without any corroborating evidence. While not wanting for one minute to defend the indefensible or to protect the guilty, the NASUWT argued for natural justice to prevail. While appropriate investigation had to take place, the Union argued that suspension should not be automatic if based solely on 'one word against another'. If it were considered necessary anonymity should be afforded to the teacher unless and until a court found the accused guilty. The Union was also concerned at how easily some cases got into the press, undoubtedly facilitated by leaks from people on the inside.

The NASUWT was already aware through casework that suspension itself was enough to make it impossible for a teacher to return to school even if the accused were found to be completely innocent. The teacher's family life was also ruined, their children suffering as well. We became aware of some very sad cases of breakdown and threatened suicide, and in the course of time some accused teachers did take their own lives.

The NASUWT records showed that the number of accusations made against members per year rose from 71 in 1991 to 158 in 1993 before dipping and rising again to 154 in 1998. The overall total for the period was 974, of which 109 went to court and 46 ended in convictions.

The NASUWT used this information to campaign for various reforms including anonymity until a guilty verdict was reached in court. We, lobbied Education and Home Office Ministers, as well as Opposition spokespersons and many other MPs. In 1999 a Private Member's Bill put forward by Crispin Blunt, a Conservative MP, to secure anonymity, was strongly supported by the NASUWT but did not receive the support of the Government and fell.

Only government has access to the large-scale resources required to experiment with and develop alternative education to cope with the problems of antisocial behaviour in schools. But whenever we could help we did so. The NASUWT did much to spread the good practice exemplified by the Zacchaeus Centre, formerly run by a member, Moira Healey.

The Zacchaeus Centre was formed by a consortium of Catholic schools in Birmingham. It takes in pupils identified as being at risk of permanent exclusion and seeks to modify their behaviour with a range of measures not available in mainstream schools. It has proved very successful, so much so that Moira was engaged to work for the Department for Education and Employment.

Moira provided much material, including a video, for the course offered by the NASUWT to young members beginning their teaching careers on dealing with behavioural problems. This section of the course, originally delivered by Moira, has consistently proved to be the most popular part according to the feedback from participants.

The confidence we have in local government to play a relevant part was not enhanced when the Birmingham LEA cut the grant the Zacchaeus Centre needed to continue its excellent work. The NASUWT lobbied hard and to her immense credit the Secretary of State at the time, Estelle Morris (a Birmingham MP), agreed to give the Centre a government grant to ensure its survival.

The NASUWT experience in this area led it to doubt the relevance of initial teacher training, which was genuinely disappointing, for there had been many good reforms of the system aimed at rectifying this deficiency.

By the time of my retirement in 2002 the problems of violence and indiscipline were being openly acknowledged by Ministers and others alike. More alternative forms of education were being considered and changes were made to the appeal panel system for excluded pupils. More support and in-service training was being offered to teachers to help them deal with poor behaviour.

The negative effect on the attractiveness of teaching to young, well-educated people of the disciplinary problems were also being openly acknowledged by an increasing range of opinion inside education as well as in government circles. For example, the Teacher Training Agency, established in 1994 to assume overall control of the system, published the results of a survey of sixth-formers (conducted ironically in collaboration with the NUT) which showed that two-thirds declined even to consider teaching as a career due to the challenging behaviour they would face.

The Conservative Shadow Education spokesperson, Tim Collins, launching a policy statement 'U' Turn Around Schools, in blissful ignorance blamed the Labour Government's Education Act of 1998 for the appeal panels. While the 1998 Act had indeed perpetuated the panels, they were originally introduced by the Conservative Government in 1986 (the Education (No. 2) Act).

At the same time it was heartening to hear the Education Secretary, Ruth Kelly, despite her young age of 36 for such a job, identifying the corrosive effects of constant "low-level disruption" on the quality of education. Much of her statement on Labour Government policy on 1 February 2005 could have been lifted from NAS and UWT publications of the 1960s and '70s.

The NAS report in 1971, "Management Organisation and Discipline", had concluded with the words:

"The achievers in a well-motivated school have as much right or more to education as have the disturbed youngsters whose purpose appears to be to disturb and disrupt others. If we are dedicated to the cause of education we must maintain the subtlety of authority. If we wish peace to reign we must have discipline. For discipline, like peace, is indivisible. Above all, we must have the courage of our convictions."

That kind of philosophy was ridiculed and belittled by many people who did not have to cope with the problems themselves. Unfortunately these included many politicians in government and opposition as well as others in leadership positions in education administration, training and inspection.

The policy of 'refusal to teach' started in the early 1970s, continued for the rest of the twentieth century and is still in operation today (2008). In the huge majority of cases success was achieved with little or no publicity. On occasions cases became public and hit the headlines, notably Poundswick in 1985/86 and those in 1996 culminating in the strike at Manton and the dramatic convulsion at The Ridings. While uncomfortable in some respects, they played a huge role in forcing politicians to take note. By the time of the 2005 General Election campaign the two main protagonists, Prime Minister Tony Blair and Leader of the Opposition Michael Howard, were battling it out to be seen as the champion of good order in schools and chief scourge of antisocial behaviour in society. The accusations of exaggeration against the NASUWT and officialdom's complacency were finally things of the past.

Society has discovered that good behaviour, like justice, is indivisible. You cannot tolerate antisocial behaviour in schools without it spreading elsewhere. A nation cannot beat the 'retreat from authority' in one area and maintain it in others.

Chapter 57 - Refusal to Teach Challenged in the Courts

One of the unintended consequences of the (Conservatives') Education (No. 2) Act of 1986 was to offer remedies at law to families who wantonly broke it themselves. Parents of violent and disruptive pupils excluded from school, despite already having the right to a hearing before a governing body, were given additional recourse to independent appeal panels.

Thatcher's employment legislation of the 1980s made it virtually impossible for unions safely to take industrial action for reasons other than those "wholly or mainly connected to terms and conditions of employment". Taking action solely to ensure the safety of children, however worthy, would expose unions to injunctions and possibly huge fines and sequestration of assets.

It was always easy for critics to portray our action refusing to teach disorderly pupils reinstated under statutory appeal panels to be a direct challenge to the supposed 'rule of law'. The loaded, political and emotional charge was only one rhetorical question away: "Who runs our schools: the legitimate authorities or the unions?"

My only surprise was that it took so long for the expected challenges to emerge and take us all the way to the House of Lords. But we had prepared ourselves, studying the issues in depth and taking much legal advice. We approached each case with great caution. There were obvious legal as well as 'political' advantages in ensuring that if we were going to have to go 'all the way' with a case it had better be a strong one.

We were also very careful to accept compromises whenever possible that met our minimum demands. Those were normally that our members had neither to teach nor accept supervisory responsibility for the disruptive pupils in question, a strike-saving formula that came to be known as 'internal isolation'. Transfer to a different school was another option.

Such compromises were important in demonstrating to the courts that we were genuinely concerned to ensure our action met the criteria of a trade dispute, namely that it related to teachers' abilities to do their jobs under reasonable, safe and healthy conditions. We were neither in the business of denying education to the youngsters nor thwarting the decisions of the appeal panels. If that happened it was an unintended side effect, not the objective of the dispute. No matter how strong we felt our case to be, it was always important to act reasonably from a common sense and public relations point of view.

We drew a careful distinction between the exercise of 'professional' judgement and industrial action. Under their contracts teachers are required to carry out "reasonable" instructions from their head teachers. Our members were entitled to argue that a requirement to teach certain pupils was unreasonable and to put that view to the test. However, once a head, or governing body or LEA, had delivered a clear ruling, any defiance of such clearly became a possible breach of contract. The only (relatively) safe way for an employee to breach contract is to do so under the protection of properly balloted, lawful industrial action organised by a trade union.

The ballot papers had to be carefully drafted and the definition of the dispute firmly linked to teachers' contracts. The process of balloting took time and had been made deliberately complicated by the Thatcher Governments to ensnare unions.

In the Bishop of Llandaff High School, Cardiff case we took a calculated risk knowing it would take a very brave person to challenge us on such high moral ground. There was a legitimate ground of maintaining good order, but there was no doubt that 'moral outrage' and a deep concern for the position of the victim, presumably simply expected to return to the same classroom as her alleged violators, had entered the equation. A skilled lawyer could have argued that the strike action was not motivated "wholly or mainly" by a trade dispute, as required by the law, but it was in large part occasioned by other morally worthy but legally unsound factors. Tellingly, unions could retain immunity from injunctions and damages when striking over pay but not when protecting a young girl from having to suffer the humiliation of renewed and constant daily contact with her alleged violators.

To the best of our knowledge the first case challenging these issues in the courts arose in Birmingham in 1993 at the city's Westminster Junior School. A ten-year-old pupil (I will call him 'Ian') had been expelled from the school but returned by the LEA's exclusions committee reviewing the case after the governing body had upheld the head teacher's decision. The governors then took their case to an LEA appeal panel but lost.

The boy had an appalling record of serious misbehaviour and violence against fellow pupils and staff. He had already been in four other schools before his mother moved him to Westminster Junior. At Westminster Ian had been excluded on two occasions for fixed terms during 1992. On 26 January the following year he had been involved in a fight and torn his clothing. The head issued an indefinite exclusion upon the boy, a penalty allowable at the time but later removed by government in favour of fixed-term suspensions.

Defying that exclusion, Ian's mother brought him to the school the next day and argued aggressively with the head that one of the teachers, who had her skin cut by Ian's 'deliberate' digging of his fingernails into her hand as she attempted to end the fight, had assaulted her son. A confrontation followed which ended with the police having to be called.

The mother was totally uncooperative, refusing to sign contracts for good behaviour and declining all offers of support. The head concluded he had to exclude Ian permanently. That was eventually overturned as described above and reinstatement ordered for 10 May by the appeal panel at its hearing on 23 April. The head teacher soon had to take extended sick leave, suffering from all the stress involved in dealing with the case.

The case was given publicity when a pirate radio station broadcast calls for demonstrations outside the school in support of the boy. The governors closed the school for a week on 20 May 1993 to allow for a cooling-off period.

NASUWT members refused to teach the boy, and the 'internal isolation' formula with one-to-one teaching with two supply teachers specially engaged for the purpose (at a cost of £125 per day) was employed to avoid strike action. The then Secretary of our Birmingham Association and National Executive Member, Chris Keates, was widely quoted in some national newspapers on 25 May 1993. She said: "We will neither teach nor supervise [Ian]. If any attempt is made to pressurise our members into teaching him we will ballot for strike action."

Ian's mother was not content with these arrangements and wasted no time in formulating claims. In a letter dated 27 May she claimed £7,683 against Birmingham City Council for damage to clothing, strain, hardship, stress, anxiety, disruption to education, racial discrimination and loss of education. On the same day she sought an ex parte interim injunction before a district judge against the governors and the teachers to declare the 'internal isolation' arrangements unlawful. That was refused.

On 11 June lawyers for Ian's mother pursued matters in the county court without serving notice to the defendants. That was adjourned to 18 June when the case came before His Honour Judge Wilson-Mellor sitting in the same court and highly critical of the previous failure to serve notice of action upon the defendants by the plaintiff's counsel.

Plaintiff's counsel argued that the internal isolation arrangements were contrary to the decision of the appeal panel to order reinstatement. Reinstatement had to be to the full position that had operated prior to the exclusion, i.e. the pupil taught in his normal class and participation with other children in playtimes, lunch and other activities. This was to turn out to be one of the main principles tested eventually in the House of Lords.

Judge Wilson-Mellor gave the plaintiff very short shrift. Having reviewed all relevant matters, he rejected all the plaintiff's claims. He stated the head teacher had a duty to secure good order in the school and could not be dictated to by an appeal panel on this day-to-day duty. The judge also firmly rejected claims of racial discrimination, encountering no evidence to that effect.

Undeterred and legally aided Ian's mother still pursued her case. On 6 January 1994 she applied for a judicial review. On this occasion only two respondents were named, the governors and the headmaster. Once again the application failed.

The next move in the courts came as expected from the father of the boy involved in the Hebburn dispute in South Tyneside in 1996. Early in November the following year, 1997, he sought an order of mandamus in the High Court requiring the two respondents, South Tyneside LEA and the governors of Hebburn, to reinstate his son into mainstream teaching in the school.

The case was heard by Mr Justice Ognall who gave judgment on Friday 7 November 1997. He began by saying, "This is an unusual, unhappy and troublesome matter", but concluded that even if he conceded all the plaintiff's grievances and the apparent prima facie breach of statutory duty by both respondents (the governors and the LEA) he would not exercise his discretion and grant the order. He said it would be unnecessarily disruptive and incapable of practical fulfilment.

On a lighter note Justice Ognall observed that the refusal of the Secretary of State to intervene in 1996 had been conveyed on her departmental letterhead with the "entirely apposite address – Sanctuary House". Noting the "difficulty had been imposed squarely on [his] shoulders", he was not anxious to tread where others had feared to go! Justice Ognall also refused an application to appeal.

We continued with our refusals to teach as the problems remained. In a typical year we had around 50 cases that could not be resolved locally, but hundreds were settled in the knowledge that the NASUWT was serious in its threat to act in defence of its members.

Developments across the Channel in Europe, both in respect of EU legislation and directives as well as the Court of Human Rights, were prompting lawyers to challenge us more and more. The 1998 Human Rights Act incorporated the European Convention of the same name in UK domestic law.

However, the new emphasis on individual and 'consumer' parental choice rights without parallel legislation stipulating responsibilities, inevitably set up situations in which rights and statutes clashed. Strident criticism of public services, alleged 'failing' schools, incompetent teachers and the 'wicked producer interests' all added to the pressure, exposing our refusal to teach action to challenge in the courts.

The case of pupil 'H' versus the governors of William Edwards School and the Thurrock LEA flared up in November 1999. 'H' had already left one secondary school 'under a cloud' and arrived at William Edwards midway through Year 7 in February 1998. As Justice Blofeld, who presided over the case in the High Court in July 2000, diplomatically recorded, "he was by no means a model pupil". He could not control his temper, demanded much attention and resorted to antisocial methods when he did not receive it. There were violent confrontations with pupils and staff. The final straw leading to permanent exclusion was an assault upon another pupil in the dinner queue followed by abuse to the teacher who dealt with the situation, those events taking place on 15 November 1999.

The governors supported the head teacher's decision on permanent exclusion in December. The mother appealed to the panel and won, with reinstatement ordered for 31 January 2000. The main reason given by the panel was uncertainty over the exact nature of 'H's involvement in the incident on 15 November.

'H' came to school with his mother on 31 January to discover that NASUWT members were refusing to teach him. Temporary arrangements were made with a Pupil Referral Unit (PRU). 'H' had been formally assessed as in need of special education. However, his mother remained dissatisfied with the PRU arrangement as a permanent solution. She therefore sought a judicial review in the High Court, which was heard in July 2000.

Ms C. Hamilton, QC, for the applicant, argued the precedential case of *Meade v Haringey*. However, Meade won against Haringey because the LEA 'semi-supported' a strike by its caretakers and did not do everything reasonably possible to meet its statutory duty to keep its schools open. There was no parallel with 'internal isolation', which was a formula specifically intended to maintain as much education for as many pupils as possible. Thurrock had provided education at the PRU fully in accordance with the requirements of the national curriculum.

Ms Hamilton suggested the NASUWT strike was only a threat and our bluff should have been called. She asked if there were any record of strike action having been taken in such circumstances. At lunchtime on that day I received an urgent call from the school's solicitors, desperately seeking a definitive answer for the judge that same afternoon. I was able to reassure the caller that the NASUWT had taken strike action, the most recent being Manton in 1996, as well as hundreds of refusals to teach over many years.

Again the judge reminded the court that the requested judicial review was not a question of law but a matter for his discretion. He was entitled to take into account all relevant considerations. He noted that 'H' had already been out of the school since the previous November. It was now July. He had a better chance of receiving an education elsewhere than in an uncertain return to his former school, which would provoke a refusal to teach him.

Justice Blofeld accepted the contention of the governors that the threat of strike action was a "real possibility", indeed a "probability", which would deal "a savage blow to the morale of everyone at the school". Justice Blofeld seemed very critical of us although he conceded that he had heard no representations from either the NASUWT or NUT. "In those circumstances I go no further than to say, on the face it, their actions appear to be unlawful. I dislike the idea that Parliament sets up detailed procedures for dealing with unruly children and yet in specific circumstances, teachers, through their unions, are able to circumvent the law."

The judge said he did not accept that the Ognall judgment in 'G' versus South Tyneside set a precedent on the question of the lawfulness of our action. He believed that "it seemed unattractive that teachers at this school were not prepared to teach 'H' but viewed with equanimity him being placed in another mainstream school where other union teachers will have to deal with his behaviour". Justice Blofeld, through no fault of his own, did not understand our position. There was no inconsistency. We certainly did not 'view with equanimity' other colleagues having unruly pupils 'dumped' on them. We insisted on prior consultation with the receiving school's members and a contract for good behaviour, the breaching of which could lead immediately to permanent exclusion. We also believed in giving such youngsters a second chance while at the same time making sure the right message got through to all the other pupils.

Nevertheless Justice Blofeld concluded that, weighing up all the factors, he could quote the words of Justice Ognall in reaching a similar decision, although with some reluctance: "A proper use of my discretion leads me compellingly to the conclusion that the relief sought should be refused". Justice Blofeld did not share Justice Ognall's confidence; although it seemed to him "to be the better of two options . . . I do not find either really satisfactory." Justice Blofeld also refused leave to appeal.

When the judgment was given on 31 July I welcomed the common sense decision of Justice Blofeld. However, I rejected his criticism of the NASUWT, claiming that teachers and pupils had the right to work in a safe environment free from threats and violence. We had balloted for lawful industrial action. 'Appeal panels' were not the only 'law'; there were others as well.

When in January 2001 we learned that 'H' had secured leave to appeal by direct application to the court, our lawyers advised us we should give serious thought to demanding to be included as a respondent, or at least apply to be heard by the court of appeal in order for our case not to go by default. The arguments were finely balanced as we did not wish to put ourselves in the firing line unnecessarily. Our conundrum was solved by 'H' withdrawing his appeal.

In February 2000 another case, pupil 'W' versus school 'B', had arisen. A Year 10 (age 15) female pupil with a long history of disruptive behaviour was involved in an incident in the school where, along with friends recruited from elsewhere, other pupils were attacked. Her permanent exclusion was overturned by an appeal panel, with reinstatement ordered. The NASUWT implemented a refusal to teach, unusually in this case joined by NUT and ATL colleagues whose leadership had previously been very critical of our approach. A compromise 'internal isolation' was reached which avoided strike action, using supply teachers operating by the head's office in the mornings and an external pupil support centre in the afternoons.

On 21 November 2000 Richard McManus, QC, appearing for the family, applied to the High Court for a judicial review, claiming that the school governors were unlawfully refusing to comply fully with the appeal panel's ruling. He argued reinstatement had to be full restoration of the 'status quo ante' as the Latin phrase goes, meaning the situation completely as it previously existed.

But Mr Justice Richards, hearing the case, disagreed. Reinstatement did not necessarily entail full reintegration into the normal classroom as before. The governing body had discretion to make other arrangements to facilitate the end of the exclusion and balance other conflicting demands. Justice Richards helped our case enormously by explicitly rejecting the family's claim that the school had no right to take into account the supposedly "irrelevant consideration" of the threatened industrial action.

By 2001 more and more challenges to our standard response were coming in. Not all reached the courts. Some LEAs and governors 'tried it on' but we responded vigorously, citing the judgments given in the courts so far. But still the NASUWT had not been challenged directly on the big issue: was our action a legitimate trade dispute under Section 244 of the Trade Union and Labour Relations (Consolidation) Act of 1992?

Sandwell Metropolitan and Hertfordshire County Councils sent us threatening letters on behalf of two of their schools in February 2001. They argued that our members were in breach of their contracts and the NASUWT was guilty of an 'industrial tort'. Sandwell also argued that by insisting upon the 'internal isolation' formula we were denying the pupil education to which he was entitled under the Human Rights Act.

While we rejected all their arguments there were new angles of attack emerging. The human rights legislation, recently enacted, was an area of uncertainty. But we concluded we would have to take that risk and argue our case wherever and whenever required.

Early in 2001 the first of the two cases that went through all the legal stages up to the House of Lords erupted. Reporting restrictions were imposed by the judges and the case could only be referred to as (pupil) 'L' versus (school) 'J', which was in the county of Hertfordshire.

The NASUWT was never enjoined in the case, again somewhat to our surprise. The relevant incident took place on 22 January 2001 when a gang of boys attacked another pupil in the toilets and administered a severe beating and kicking. The victim was hospitalised. The head teacher permanently excluded six boys. The governors supported the head. Three of the boys appealed to the panel who surprisingly reinstated all of them at hearings early in March.

The head in conducting his investigations had been hampered by a lack of co-operation and some confusing and contradictory statements. He became convinced from the pupils' statements (or reluctance to make them), his knowledge of the boys and their demeanour during the interviews, that intimidation was holding back some from telling all that they knew.

Unfortunately the head either got some facts wrong or was unable to prove everything he strongly suspected. In the case of 'L', he had been accused of kicking the victim and this allegation featured in the letter the head sent home to his parents explaining the reasons for exclusion. 'L' admitted being present and aiming a kick. But the chief point in his defence was that he had missed. Therefore he should not have been excluded. The appeal panel concluded that the 'technical' facts on which he had been excluded were wrong and together with other reasons ordered reinstatement.

The head and staff were appalled with the reinstatements but accepted that in respect of two of the boys, despite the gravity of the assault, they could resume teaching them, for there had been little history of previous problems. But in respect of 'L' the staff had other concerns which the NASUWT understood were not presented in evidence to the appeal panel.

The other problem we faced as a union was that all these matters had proceeded without us being informed or involved. The school reps of the three main classroom teacher unions, the NASUWT, NUT and ATL, only involved their national organisations after they had 'accepted', albeit very reluctantly, two of the boys back into their classes but wished to refuse to teach the third, namely pupil 'L'.

We were in a quandary. Had we been involved earlier we would most likely have proceeded on the basis of refusing to teach all three who had been reinstated by the appeal panel. We believed strongly that the assault had been so bad that all involved in it should be permanently excluded on the merits of the case.

We certainly understood the reasons given by the panel and the legal technicalities but we attached much more importance to the merits of the case from the point of view of upholding good standards of behaviour and the ability of teachers to do their job. Once again the authority of teachers, heads and governors was being fatally compromised by the importation of legalistic procedures into the day-to-day life of schools. We appreciated the potential inconsistencies of 'only' refusing to teach one, as opposed to all three, of the returned pupils. The issue was not so clear-cut as we normally demanded but we decided to ballot in the usual way for a refusal to teach and strike action if required.

There were exchanges towards the end of March between the head and 'L's parents, during which the former did not disguise his belief that the boy should not have been reinstated. Nevertheless the head made clear his plans for the reintegration based on a very strict pattern of 'internal isolation' which he had developed in discussion with the unions and the Chair of Governors. 'L's parents complained bitterly that the internal isolation was another way of enforcing the overturned exclusion. They believed their son should be 'properly' reintegrated into all the normal classes and activities and he should not be treated differently from the other two. He had won his case after being expelled on 'false pretences'. The head insisted 'L' had been reinstated but he had to balance that with the responsibility to ensure all the other pupils continued to receive an education in the light of our refusal to teach and threatened strike.

'L' returned to school on Monday 26 March, to internal isolation. He was to be supervised in the parlour at the reception area by a supply teacher, who had recently retired from the school and had 27 years experience. He was a maths specialist so could provide active tuition in that important subject. There would be nil contact with other members of the school community but work would be set and marked by his 'normal' teachers. The school broke up for the Easter holidays on 6 April. On return (23 April) Year 11 GCSE pupils were to attend normally until 18 May. After that they would be on study leave, only attending school to take their exams as necessary.

Ironically, 'L's teachers considered that he worked better under the isolation arrangements than he had done at any time during his GCSE courses. The head stated that any problems with progress stemmed from his poor behaviour and lack of commitment before his exclusion.

Lawyers acting for 'L's parents secured an expedited hearing in the High Court in April seeking a ruling that their son be fully reintegrated. The case was heard by Mr Justice Henriques, who delivered his judgment on 26 April.

Justice Henriques ruled decisively in favour of the head and governors. They were entitled to make arrangements as they thought appropriate to teach the boy in isolation if that were necessary to safeguard the education of all the pupils against our threats of strike action. The judge also ruled that 'L's right to an education was not being denied.

I made my usual trenchant comments to the press on common sense and the rights of teachers and pupils, appealing yet again to the Government to rid schools of all these legalistic procedures. But I also 'turned up the volume' on the general issue saying: "Something is rotten in the state of the UK when youngsters can kick a fellow pupil senseless and then have their permanent exclusions overturned by these ridiculous appeal panels. Then they claim that any resultant isolation in the school amounts to 'inhuman treatment' and a breach of their 'human rights'. The sickening hypocrisy with which these families assert their human rights while victims have to be kept at home or moved to other schools in order to guarantee their safety, has now reached such depths of staggering stupidity that law-abiding citizens can only view with total incredulity."

In 2001 two cases reached the appeal court. Justice Richards, whilst dismissing the case of pupil 'W' versus school 'B' (2 November 2000), had nevertheless granted leave to appeal. In pupil 'L' versus school 'J' (Mr Justice Henriques' judgment given 26 April 2001) leave to appeal had been refused, but permission was subsequently secured directly from the court. Since they raised the same issues they were heard together in the appeal court in July 2001 before Lord Justices Thorpe, Clarke and Laws, with the last named giving the Leading Judgment, with which the other two concurred on the 24th of the same month.

While these matters were winding their way through the courts another case had been taken out, and on this occasion the NASUWT was finally challenged directly and named as the respondent. The most important question was being put to the test: was our action within the legal definition of a trade dispute? We were also challenged on a technical matter concerned with the conduct of the ballot. In addition the right to an education was raised under the recent Act and the European Convention.

This was the (pupil) 'P' versus NASUWT case which began in the High Court on 4 April 2001. It ended up going all the way through the judicial system up to the House of Lords, which it reached in 2003. I shall refer to this case later. I mention it at this stage because, as we defeated our challengers in the High Court, the precedent was quoted in the two other cases I have just referred to, proceeding concurrently through the appeal court.

The 'W' versus 'B' and 'L' versus 'J' appeals were heard during the course of the Summer Term with judgment delivered on 24 July 2001. Although not named as a respondent, the NASUWT was obviously an 'interested party'. At the time I was in Thailand attending the Triennial Congress of the worldwide organisation of teacher unions, Education International, upon whose Executive Board I sat. Keeping in close contact with my office I was delighted to receive the news that both appeals had been dismissed.

In the 'W' case Lord Justice Laws concluded that the initial reinstatement was in compliance with the relevant provisions of the 1998 School Standards and Framework Act. In both cases Lord Justice Laws agreed with Richards' and Henriques' High Court rulings that reinstatement did not have to amount to the same conditions that applied before the exclusion.

Laws also agreed that the governors had been entitled to exercise their discretion in endorsing the arrangements made by the head teachers to take account of the threat of industrial action and so balance the interests and educational needs of all the pupils in the school. They had not acted out of an improper motive to defeat the appeal panels' decisions.

Counsel for pupil 'L' argued that the governors had a duty to conduct a searching inquiry into whether the unions' threatened action was lawful and within the definition of a trade dispute. Counsel for school 'J' was able to quote the 'P' versus NASUWT case, which had then been heard in the High Court and established clearly that the action was a genuine trade dispute.

Laws quoted circumstances where a head teacher might have taken the internal isolation measures rather than exclude a pupil, possibly in response to union pressure. In so doing the head and governors were merely exercising their normal discretion to conduct the affairs of the school as they deemed appropriate.

Justice Laws helpfully concluded that not merely was the threat of action with all its consequences a relevant consideration to be taken into account, but "in a reasonable world, [it was] a mandatory one". This was the case even if the union's attitude were "wholly intransigent". The head and governors had to act proportionately and not out of a motive to thwart the appeal panel.

Nigel Giffin, counsel for school 'B', had pertinently pointed out that the respondents, the governing bodies, were not the ones withholding the services; those were the union members. Lord Justice Laws took up the point of the union's involvement without having been heard or represented in these hearings. He said that in the light of the decisions in the 'P' versus NASUWT case there was no merit whatsoever in arguing the point further on the trade dispute and immunity from damages. But he went on: "All that said the position of the unions in this case troubles me. But for their stance, I am sure these proceedings would have been unnecessary and uncontemplated. I mean no levity, therefore, when I say that their absence makes the case look like Hamlet without the Prince. I make it plain there is no conceivable blame to be attached to them; they were obviously not obliged to seek to intervene."

However, Lord Justice Laws expressed "scant regard" for the head teacher of school 'J' for his "personal protestations that the appeal panel got it wrong, and even less regard for his having told 'L' as much". But Justice Laws still believed the head did his best to reintegrate the boy as much as possible, bearing in mind all the difficulties posed by the unions. With that he dismissed the appeals. Lord Justices Clarke and Thorpe concurred.

Chapter 58 – The Big One – 'P' versus NASUWT

While pupil 'P' had a long history of problems in the schools he attended, the facts which concerned the courts began to occur during the Summer Term 2000 at 'P's secondary school. 'P' was excluded on 6 June 2000 for violent behaviour.

The discipline committee of the governing body did not, however, support the head's decision and ordered reinstatement on 30 June. The committee felt there was a conflict of evidence. It certainly did not exonerate 'P', concluding that his "tendency to confront teachers is viewed even more seriously. The evidence on this is completely clear and the committee want you to know that such behaviour cannot be tolerated". The committee believed that permanent exclusion was the wrong penalty and ordered reintegration with appropriate arrangements.

It was only with extreme reluctance that NASUWT members accepted the situation. They believed the governors, contrary to their declaration, were 'tolerating such behaviour'. Refusal to teach was actively considered but not adopted at the time.

Effectively 'P' returned to normal classes in September 2000, the last part of the Summer Term having been taken up with work experience for students in his year group. There was no change in 'P's behaviour. In the view of staff he continued to be aggressive and bullying towards other pupils, disruptive in the classroom, abusive to teachers and violent on several occasions. In October he was excluded for two days following an altercation outside a classroom in which he beat up a fellow student. The incident which led NASUWT members to request authorisation to refuse to teach and ballot for industrial action occurred at the beginning of November. 'P' ended up pushing a teacher through a French window.

Sworn statements by NASUWT members presented in evidence to the courts included the following complaints:

> 'P' mocking an Indian accent and Hinduism to embarrass a Sri Lankan pupil and employing the term "fucking Pakis";
> making "loud and vulgar remarks about menstruation in a mixed geography class";
> implied male teachers were homosexual (by corrupting one teacher's name to "Bendover" and by saying to another: "I'm not like all of your other bumchums";
> making comments of a sexual nature to a female teacher;

repeated refusals to accept teachers' reasonable instructions – refused to do any work during the lesson . . . he said "go and do some more training"; has blatantly refused to leave the classroom;

countless complaints of him being "rude and aggressive";

threatening others to fear for their physical safety – "We should take this out onto the streets to see who is in control";

threatening language, including saying "he would knock me [a teacher] down";

(to a teacher) "You are all mouth and no action . . . Do you want to sort it out?";

"for the first time in four years of teaching [I] began to worry about my personal safety";

making physical contact with teachers by deliberately tripping a teacher who was going into the classroom and pushing another through a French window;

he has behaved strangely, e.g. by bringing screwdrivers into school, entering the girls' toilets and pouring glue over the teacher's bench;

he disrupts classes and tends to influence others to behave badly;

"this is ['P's] first day back after exclusion [for two days]. I have had two days of perfect lessons without him – first day back problems".

The last-mentioned complaint surely summed it all up and reflected the damage inflicted on other pupils' education.

'P's mother and counsel were later to argue that his behaviour improved significantly after reinstatement in September 2000. That was hotly disputed by NASUWT teachers. They had been advised to avoid confrontation and saw little point in going to all the trouble to record incidents and stick to the behaviour policy if the governors were not ultimately to support them.

Even after our members had begun to refuse to teach 'P' he throttled another pupil in February 2001. In March he declared in a class he was attending: "This lesson is shit". Around the same time he bragged to another teacher: "I banged your niece over the weekend."

Finally, I quote a threat which has to be taken seriously these days: "His remark that he wishes he could kill all of the teachers with one bullet" – taken from one of our member's witness statements laid before the courts.

After the 'French window' incident in October our members finally concluded there was no solution to the problem likely to come from within the school's management and governance. They resolved to call in the NASUWT once again and to request the usual support. On seeing the evidence we had no hesitation in offering it. The balloting procedures were commenced in November.

Responding to the pressure the head offered alternative 'solutions' – including one-to-one supply teacher support to accompany 'P' into every class subject, to our action being suspended – but we considered all these to be either impractical or undesirable.

Members of the NASUWT numbered 32 of the 40 teaching staff. There were, as always, complications with the accuracy of the membership list, which I shall return to in due course as, despite being irrelevant to the outcome of the vote, they featured prominently in the courts. Of the 26 who returned ballot papers all voted in favour of a refusal to teach while 25 to 1 voted in support of strike action if required. The action commenced on 1 December. Internal isolation was arranged in the now customary way of avoiding all-out strike action. 'P' was supervised (mainly) by two supply teachers whilst his 'usual subject teachers' set and marked his work. All direct contact with NASUWT members was cut.

Before reaching the High Court, lawyers acting for 'P' had tried unsuccessfully to secure a judicial review against the head teacher. The judge considering their claim was none other than Mr Justice Richards who had already ruled on these matters in the 'W' versus 'B' case. He duly refused leave in a letter dated 1 March 2001.

On 16 March 2001 the NASUWT solicitors, Russell Jones & Walker, received notification from 'P's lawyers that they were taking action against us in the High Court. They were seeking an order to require the NASUWT to cease: the industrial action; inducing a breach of the statutory duties owed to their client under the 1998 Human Rights Act; and intentionally causing harm to him by unlawful means.

Because of the "urgency", despite the refusal to teach being three and a half months old, Ashok Patel & Co., 'P's solicitors, said they intended to apply to the court for interim relief within the week on Friday 23 March. They believed "the balance of convenience" lay with their client's return to the classroom.

Through our lawyers we argued against an interim hearing, declaring we were prepared even at short notice to go for a full expedited one. We had done the same in the Wandsworth case in 1993 raising parallel issues concerning the definition of a legitimate trade dispute. We had already prepared a defence; all we needed to do now was to relate it to the facts of this case and gather witness statements from our members at the school.

'P's representatives in his Particulars of Claim argued that he was in effect excluded from school, that his quality of education was suffering and that the NASUWT was inducing torts by causing a breach of the governors' (or LEA's) statutory duty and getting teaching staff to break their contracts of employment. They claimed our action demanded that 'P' be permanently excluded from the school or deprived of normal classroom teaching. It was therefore outwith the legal definition of a trade dispute, having nothing to do with the teachers' "terms and conditions of employment".

The Claim also stated that 'P's right to education under the Human Rights Act 1998, which incorporated the European Convention of the same name into UK law, was being breached in a number of ways. He also claimed breach of rights under Article 3, i.e. "no one shall be subjected to torture or to inhuman or degrading treatment or punishment", in the light of his internal isolation at the school.

Claims were also raised against us that we had breached the (very complicated) requirements of the balloting procedures under the 1992 Act. We had, allegedly, given insufficient information on the number, identities and subject specialisms of the teachers concerned and had unlawfully excluded some of our members from the ballot.

These balloting issues were later to occupy an enormous amount of time in the courts. Apart from trying to trip us up on technical grounds, they had no merit in terms of common sense whatsoever.

On 26 March an order was secured by Mr Justice Bell for an expedited full trial. So the need for an application for interim relief was avoided. All parties agreed the facts of the case, save (very significantly) in respect of 'P's behaviour, but there would be no cross-examination of witnesses. Argument would focus on the law. I detected in these arrangements and subsequently in the court proceedings a marked reluctance on the part of representatives of the claimant for the disputed facts to be tested.

As soon as the expedited trial was ordered, press reports emerged. The *London Evening Standard* (26 March) and *The Times* (28 March) were the first two to carry them, pointing out that it would be the first time a union had been the subject of such action. We had made no public statements.

However, on 3 April (the day before the court case opened) the spokesman for a self-styled 'Race Equality Council' issued a very aggressive and contentious press statement accusing the NASUWT of racial discrimination and singing the praises of the saintly student 'P'. The press statement climaxed with a right-wing rhetorical flourish: "Are we now saying schools are run by Unions and not Head Teachers and Governors?" 'P's supporters were obviously keen to turn the case into one of racial discrimination, but no evidence to that effect had been presented in the court papers in our possession.

In my statement to the media on entering the Royal Courts of Justice I said: "This will be a defining moment in the history of the education service. NASUWT is defending the right of teachers to refuse to teach seriously disruptive and/or violent pupils. NASUWT declares loud and clear that a union has the right to take lawfully balloted industrial action to protect its members from such danger."

Later in court the judge, Mr Justice Morrison, went to great pains to clarify whether a case alleging racial discrimination was being pursued. 'P's counsel confirmed "definitely not". As he did this there was a commotion in the area occupied by 'P's representatives and supporters. I turned around and saw a woman being assisted out of the room in a state of semi-collapse.

Not only was evidence of racial discrimination lacking, but the sworn statements from NASUWT members raised some delicate matters which suggested, amongst other things, that 'P's interests were not best served by raising such issues.

'P's counsel, Nigel Giffin, QC, whose acquaintance we had made during his appearance as the junior counsel for Wandsworth in the 1993 'Test Boycott' case, had a very difficult brief to argue. All the precedents had gone against him. Not surprisingly he quoted from the judges' adverse comments about the unions and played the 'rule of law' card, declaring: "Whatever the claimant may or may not have done, it's not for teachers to usurp the role which Parliament has given to the head and governing body or an independent appeal tribunal".

When it came to the most fundamental issue – was our 'refusal to teach' action "wholly or mainly" related to teachers' "terms and conditions of employment" – Mr Giffin had to make the unreal argument that employees could only have disputes about the written clauses of a contract, not their application to a given set of circumstances. We could have a legitimate trade dispute if employers declined to insert a clause into the contract giving the right to refuse to teach disruptive pupils, but we could not have one about a real live case. This interpretation defied common sense, missed the importance of the inclusion of both "terms and *conditions*" in the statute and had never been intended by Parliament in the legislation.

Nigel Giffin alleged a breach of statutory duty to provide education and denial of human rights to 'P' by the head, governors and LEA, into which they had been forced by the NASUWT action. NASUWT counsel David Bean denied both, pointing out that 'P' was still receiving an education. There was no right to a particular kind of education at any one specific school. In any event, even if there were such a breach, the union enjoyed protection from claims for damages by virtue of the fact that it was a genuine trade dispute supported by a legitimate ballot.

It was in the area of the statutory provisions for balloting on industrial action that the law was made to live up to its sometimes popular perception of being an ass. To cut a long story short, counsel for 'P' argued that the legislation stated that union immunity against damages was lost if one or more members included in the action had not been balloted. A literal reading of the relevant part of the 1999 Employment Relations Act supported this conclusion, but the same section made cross-references to other paragraphs, which made no sense whatsoever.

The implication, as our counsel David Bean quickly pointed out, was that in a national dispute involving all the members of the largest union in the country with around a million members, a failure to ballot one or two would lead to a massive 99% 'yes' vote being invalid and subsequent industrial action not enjoying the relevant immunities.

That was plainly absurd. Examination of the legislation in detail revealed that New Labour's 1999 Act, in seeking to simplify some of the worst bureaucratic requirements of Thatcher's legislation, had produced confusion over the sections on "small accidental errors" in the balloting procedures. Amusingly, the error stemmed from Sections 232A and 230(2A), which could be mistaken for each other. When read together, with their cross-references, they did not make any sense whatsoever. They were gobbledegook! Everyone, including the judge and counsel for the claimant, agreed that Parliament could not have intended to create this situation.

There were many other attempts by counsel for 'P' to trip us up on all kinds of technical matters concerning the incredibly complicated provisions for balloting.

The High Court hearings lasted three days, 4-6 April. The reserved judgment was delivered by Mr Justice Morrison on 9 April. He began by saying there were difficult questions of law and that no evidence had been heard and tested regarding 'P's conduct. The initiative for 'P's removal from the classroom came from the teachers, clearly outside of any statutory process. Superficially, the union might be accused of taking the law into its own hands. But on the other hand, teachers had a difficult job and deserved support. Justice Morrison: "Disruptive pupils are a menace and quite apart from the direct effect upon teachers, they damage the educational interests of the other children in the class."

Justice Morrison emphasised it would be superficial for the court to pass any judgment on these general matters since no evidence had been tested. He respectfully suggested others, including the media, ought to show similar restraint. He would simply have to consider the questions of law without any assumptions as to general merits.

The reluctance of the claimants to submit to cross-examination seemed to tell when Justice Morrison said he was not "prepared to assume or infer that 'P' is educationally worse off under the present regime than he would have been had he remained in class". He did not seem "to thrive in the classroom". He had lost all confidence in and respect for his teachers. They regarded him as "unteachable".

But coming to the crunch of his judgment, Justice Morrison said the order requested required the NASUWT to cease its action and any resultant claims for damages depended upon whether it was a trade dispute and whether the ballot had been properly carried out. The claim under the Human Rights Act was self-standing.

Mr Justice Morrison declared that despite not having heard oral evidence, "I am of the view that there was a trade dispute as to the teachers' terms and conditions of employment in the sense that there was a dispute as to the entitlement of the head teacher to give an instruction to the teachers of 'P' to teach him in the classroom. There is sufficient evidence of such a dispute; in particular the reference by the Union to the unreasonableness of the instruction". Any claim for damages thereby fell.

We were entitled to feel that our meticulous attention to detail over the years had paid off. We had spent many hours discussing in meetings of staff, National Officers and the Executive how we should phrase such matters. In our ballot material, communications to employers and action authorisation to members, we were very careful to spell out the basis of our dispute in precise terms, namely, the unreasonableness of the head's instructions given under Regulations drawn up pursuant to the terms of the Teachers' Pay and Conditions Act.

On the balloting issues and the complications of the inconsistent sections, Justice Morrison was extremely critical of the legislators, stating, "it is intolerable that these questions should arise. It is the duty of Parliament to enact legislation which has some reasonable degree of clarity." But in any case, he took the view "that there was no breach" on these matters. And for good measure he added: "But if I were wrong, and there were a breach then I take the view that any such failure was accidental and without affect on the result. It seems to me that Parliament has made an obvious mistake which the courts are entitled to correct."

Under the Human Rights Act 'P' also lost heavily. Justice Morrison declared unequivocally: "Mr Giffin has completely failed to persuade me that it is arguable let alone correct that 'P' has a claim against the Union or the teachers. 'P' has not been denied an education . . . It may be that he is better off with the education he is now receiving . . . One of the reasons why the School obviously has power to educate 'P' as they are doing is because the rights which 'P' asserts are rights which other pupils in the class may also assert. It is at least possible that their rights have been better respected by moving 'P' out of the class room."

With that, the case was dismissed, with Mr Justice Morrison once again declaring that "it is a tragedy that the difficulties in 'P's schooling should have reached the courts". The judge had also refused to grant leave to appeal on the grounds that although there were arguable points of law, 'P' wanted to be "put back in the classroom and no court order is likely to achieve that result".

Emerging from the court I said: "While undoubtedly the judgment represents another landmark legal victory for the NASUWT, I feel a profound sense of relief rather than elation. The NASUWT has secured another great victory for civilised standards of behaviour. We had defended the rights of teachers exercised for over 25 years to resist unreasonable instructions and refuse to accept or risk physical assault and abuse in the course of their duties."

Once again members, led by their School Rep Dave Carver, had displayed great courage in risking their jobs in support of decent standards of behaviour. Dave Carver was given a standing ovation when he spoke at the NASUWT Conference which followed a few days later in Jersey.

The very relaxed afternoon following the judgment was made even better when we saw over the wires: "NUT welcomes outcome of NASUWT court case". Even our erstwhile colleague Doug McAvoy, GS of the NUT, had approved our victory!

The newspaper headlines the following morning were by and large reasonable and responsible. "Judge backs right of teachers to bar violent pupils" (*The Independent*) was typical of the broadsheets. Even the normally sensational *Sun* was reasonably restrained, headlining: "'Violent' lad loses battle for lesson" along with *The Mail*: "Teachers win right to root out class thugs". *The Mail's* earlier headline after the first day in court, "'Lout' sues his teachers", possibly represented the kind of premature comment on untested evidence which the judge had criticised.

Within a few days, however, by 12 April, we received a letter from our solicitors, Russell Jones & Walker, informing us that Ashok Patel, acting for 'P', were applying directly to the court for permission to appeal, Mr Justice Morrison having refused.

On 19 April 2001 Mr Justice May gave permission to 'P' to appeal Morrison's judgment on the trade dispute issue. The other grounds on which permission to appeal were being requested, namely the ballot and human rights, would have to be considered by the appeal court itself.

P's lawyers secured the appeal hearing for 3 May. A week before, we learnt that they were strengthening their team by employing the top counsel in this area of law, namely Mr Eldred Tabachnik, QC, with Nigel Giffin relegated to the number two slot.

Viewing the appellant's 'skeleton argument' (a very helpful practice whereby all sides exchange their cases in outline in advance) and listening to the presentation in the appeal court, it seemed to us that there was not much new except perhaps the point that union action of the kind complained about was becoming increasingly commonplace. P's counsel played up the 'rule of law' issue, finding a few more emotive expressions: "The truth is that, if an organised boycott of the present kind is lawful, the statutory procedures and the ministerial guidance are not worth the paper they are written on. The unions and their members would enjoy an effective veto . . . the child's individual rights and interests are worth nothing."

Counsel said (correctly) that it was well known that the NASUWT dislikes the system of appeal panels and wishes to see it abolished. But he went on to accuse us of using such cases as 'P' as a means of campaigning to achieve our policy end, which he said was political and not a trade dispute. Once again we had to point out that we would never be so stupid as to base our action on a political objective rather than the demands of each and every case judged on merit and very much driven by the needs of our members in the specific circumstances.

Our counsel, David Bean, rejected these claims as "heavy with political argument about the rule of law and criticism of the union" in which the court had no place. Quoting a precedent from Lord Diplock, "Immunity under [the relevant law] is not forfeited by being stubborn or pig headed", David Bean added quickly that of course he did not accept that our actions could be "so characterised"!

Mr Tabachnik had another go at the argument that a trade dispute could only be about the terms and conditions of employment as general rules and not in their application in practice. I must confess I thought his junior colleague, Nigel Giffin, had made a much better fist of this admittedly difficult task in the High Court.

David Bean also turned the *BBC v Hearn* precedent (when unions pulled the plug on the transmission of the 1977 Cup Final to South Africa) against the claimant, by quoting from Lord Denning's leading judgment: "Terms and conditions of employment may include not only the contractual terms and conditions but those terms which are understood and applied by the parties in practice, or habitually, or by common consent, without ever having been incorporated into the contract".

Eldred Tabachnik repeated the claim that unions were only protected from tort for a breach of contract, not for inducing a breach of statutory duty. David Bean countered by arguing that would rule out any industrial action in the public sector, since there was always some statute behind a state service. Had there been such a suggestion at the time of the legislation, there would have been an outcry in Parliament and amongst the general public,

At the beginning of this court hearing, 'P' had secured permission to appeal on the balloting issue. But on the question of human rights the judges made clear that would have to entail a longer hearing with cross-examination. I suspected the other side was nervous of cross-examination. The prospect of success in any event was low and 'P' agreed to drop that part of the appeal.

Much of the second day of the appeal hearing was taken up with the vexed issue of the balloting arrangements and the incredibly complicated parts of the legislation. It is impossible to explain the complexities without quoting, sometimes verbatim, huge chunks of the relevant sections of the 1992 Act as amended in 1999. As I struggled to understand the complexities I thought how ridiculous it was that teachers' last line of defence against the outrageous behaviour of some violent pupils should be at the mercy of this morass of legalistic debate. The nation's top judges and QCs were obviously struggling to understand it as well.

And then a mistake within a mistake was discovered. The numbering of the Sections 230(2A) and 232A and surrounding paragraphs had indeed been bungled by the Parliamentary draughtspersons, but not in the way our counsel had suggested in the High Court.

The appeal judges were also disturbed that Justice Morrison had decided for himself that Parliament had made an error. The court resolved that the question of what Parliament intended should at least be asked of the Attorney General. Accordingly in rather dramatic fashion their Lordships demanded the immediate attendance in the court of someone called 'the Master'. This turned out to be Master Venn, who appeared somewhat breathless if not a trifle distraught. He was despatched post-haste to raise the relevant questions with the Attorney General over in Westminster.

The next day counsel for the Attorney General, a Mr William Hoskins (engagingly described in the official papers of the case as 'Amicus Curiae') duly appeared to "explain" the situation. There had indeed been an error but not the one originally identified in the lower court.

However, Mr Justice Waller was later to say in his judgment that our counsel, Mr Bean, had subsequently been able to put forward "a powerful case" to the effect that the provisions safeguarding the validity of ballots notwithstanding, "small accidental errors" had not been lost by the complicated changes to the 1992 Act, which went through the Lords and Commons 'on the nod' in 1998, leading to the amended legislation the following year.

The hearing finished on 4 May with judgment reserved. That was delivered on 9 May, another of the many 'crunch days' in the NASUWT's battles to retain the right to take action against serious antisocial behaviour in schools. Mr Justice Waller gave the leading judgment, summarising all the relevant facts with great precision and clarity, as top judges tend to do. He agreed with Mr Justice Morrison in the High Court that without a full examination no assessment could be made as to the justification for the teachers' fears or the reasonableness of the head's direction to teach 'P' in his 'normal' class. He agreed with the key question: Was it a genuine trade dispute under Section 244 of the Act?

Mr Justice Waller declared it was an obvious fact that the dispute was about the direction to teach 'P' in the classroom. Whether the teachers' view was justified or not was irrelevant. The teacher's contract clearly specified a duty to carry out the reasonable instructions of the headteacher. The union admitted it induced a breach of contract and accordingly balloted to secure immunity from being sued for damages.

Concluding his verdict on the first point of appeal, Justice Waller declared his firm agreement with Morrison's view: "I agree with his view that the reality is that 'the working conditions of teachers were in dispute as were the instructions they were given' and that thus the dispute related to the terms and conditions of employment of the teachers."

The second half of the 24-page judgment was devoted to the complicated ballot issue. To cut a very long story short, Justice Waller dismissed that point of the appeal as well. Lady Justice Hale and Sir Philip Otton added their own extremely brief and identical comments: "I agree."

We were granted our costs, to be paid by the Legal Aid Commission. The judges refused leave to appeal to the House of Lords.

The only problem remaining for me was to find fresh words for the same message. I headlined our press statement: "NASUWT strikes another blow to uphold decent standards of behaviour in schools" and went on: "Once again, all teachers, right minded pupils and parents can breathe a sigh of relief at the success of the NASUWT in beating off yet another challenge to good order and common sense in schools."

Press coverage the next day was low key since the NASUWT had won and it was a repeat of the High Court victory. Had the NASUWT lost, it would have been a huge story.

Chapter 59 - High Noon in the House of Lords

A reminder that 'P' was not going to go away arrived in the form of a letter from his solicitors dated 6 June 2001 complaining about the conditions under which he was having to take his GCSE exams. Our lawyers advised us it might be a prelude to claims for damages based on the contention that our ballot did not relate to the conditions under which 'P' took his public examinations. On 18 June, Russell Jones & Walker informed us that 'P's solicitors were applying for public funding to seek leave to appeal to the House of Lords. Estimates for the appeal hearing costs were in the region of £75,000, not to mention the High Court.

Our lawyers informed us on 10 October that the Legal Services Commission had agreed in principle to fund 'P' to petition the House of Lords. A final decision was expected soon. A judicial committee of the House of Lords would decide whether leave to appeal were to be granted. The NASUWT had the right to make submissions in writing.

The petition was based on the same old grounds heard in the appeal court, namely the trade dispute and the balloting issues. Even the issue that had been battered to death – the dispute could only be about the rules themselves, not their application – was given a premature resurrection from the grave.

In the petition 'P' conceded that the injunction to stop our action was now academic as he had left school after taking his GCSE exams in the summer. But there was still the possibility of damages and he believed his results had suffered because of our action.

The matter raised an important point of law which could affect a very large number of industrial disputes in all sectors, not just schools, which would also influence governing bodies in their reactions to reinstatements. 'Refusals to teach' were becoming increasingly common. In short, a decision was required from the highest court in the land. The petition rehearsed all the salient facts and quoted the cases that had already been before the courts.

'P' also asked that his case be heard together with the 'L' versus governors of school 'J' and the 'W' versus 'B' school. In 'L' v 'J' the appeal court judge, Justice Laws, had expressed regret that the issues had to be decided without having the unions in court, his noteworthy remark about "Hamlet without the Prince".

Our lawyers did their best to oppose acceptance of the petition. The points were moot, the claim academic and the damages 'unparticularised', theoretical and unrealistic. The only valid point was that it raised an issue of general importance. The NASWUWT argued that the case was not started as a test case to decide a matter of general importance and it neither involved a public authority nor public law. It was a dispute between two private parties.

With time having moved on to early January 2002, the NASUWT was able to quote the changed Guidance from the Department for Education and Employment to appeal panels. This stated that panels should not normally reinstate in cases of violence, sexual abuse, drug pushing and persistent and malicious disruptive behaviour. If this were followed such cases would no longer arise. We questioned whether such a poor case justified yet more public expenditure and pointed out that the petition raised no new arguments from the appeal court.

Despite NASUWT arguments leave to appeal to the House of Lords was granted (around January/February 2002). One of the two other cases suggested by 'P' to be taken together, 'W' v 'B', had been resolved by negotiation. So the two cases were 'P' v NASUWT and (pupil) 'L' v (school) 'J'.

It took until November 2002 for the cases to be heard in the Lords. By that time I had retired as GS of the NASUWT (at the Easter Conference). Despite having become President of the TUC those duties were not so onerous as to impede my attendance at the Lords' hearings in a matter of great interest to me.

The five law lords hearing the case were: Lord Bingham of Cornhill (presiding), Lord Hoffmann, Lord Hobhouse of Woodborough (who died in March 2004 as I drafted this chapter), Lord Scott of Foscote and Lord Walker of Gestingthorpe. Our lawyers told us this was an impressive array of top law lords, reflecting the importance of the case being heard. The hearings lasted over four working days, starting on 18 November.

The NASUWT was not directly enjoined in the (pupil) 'L' v (school) 'J' case. The governors were the defendants. Cherie Booth, QC was the boy's counsel. It was deplorable that some tabloid newspapers used her appearance for the boy as a means of political attack as her husband happened to be the Prime Minister. "Cherie's legal battle for thug" and "Cherie defends thug pupils" were two grossly unfair and inappropriately personalised headlines.

As the petition on behalf of 'P' seeking leave to appeal had hinted, there was nothing new of significance in the arguments on all sides. It proved to be a refresher course, albeit an interesting one in the rarefied atmosphere of the Lords' chambers in the Houses of Parliament.

Judgment day was a long time coming, arriving finally on 27 February 2003. Although Lord Hoffmann had done most of the drafting, some of the other law lords chipped in with additional comments of their own.

The presiding judge, Lord Bingham, referring to the 'rules' v 'application of the rules' issue under the trade dispute question, began by saying: "I was for a time attracted by this argument, which was skilfully deployed and appeared to reflect the language of the statute. But I am persuaded that such a construction would be too narrow and deny protection to genuine, employment-related disputes . . . It is plain that the dispute between the teaching staff and the governing body as their employers related directly to the job the teachers were required to do and were unwilling to do, which was to teach 'P'."

Lord Bingham also took a strong, common-sense view on the ballot question. He said: "It would be absurd if an immaterial and accidental failure to send a ballot paper to a single member were to invalidate the ballot and so deprive the union of immunity. It was inconceivable that Parliament intended the 1999 amendments to the 1992 Act to have that result". Lord Bingham hoped for "remedial legislative action".

Lord Hoffmann, who summarised most of the relevant facts of the case, agreed strongly with Lord Bingham, saying: "I do not believe that Parliament could have intended the immunities conferred upon trade unions in industrial disputes to turn upon such fine distinctions. In my opinion it is impossible in this context to formulate a coherent distinction between a rule and the application of the rule to particular cases."

Lords Hobhouse and Scott followed suit, dismissing the appeal in brief words expressing support for the views of their "noble and learned friends".

The 5:0 rout was completed when Lord Walker also dismissed the appeal, taking the opportunity of rehearsing the long history of the definition of a trade dispute, going back to the 1906 Act because of its "importance and interest". The first definition in the 1906 Trade Disputes Act had referred to any dispute between employers and workmen "which is connected with the employment, or non-employment or terms . . . " The Tory Industrial Relations Act of 1971 had disturbed that formula by imposing the more demanding test that the dispute should "relate wholly or mainly" to the subject matter. That important amendment had been reversed by the 1974 Act under a Labour Government but restored under Section 18 of the 1982 Employment Act, introduced by the Thatcher administration.

Eamonn O'Kane as the new GS maintained the fine NASUWT tradition of trenchant comment, saying:

"This landmark victory will give heart to every teacher in the country. It constitutes a total vindication of the stand consistently taken by the NASUWT over the years giving total support to members when faced with violent and/or disruptive behaviour.

"The union has done this often in the face of hostile opposition which has accused us of exaggerating the problem. As a result we have been dragged through the courts because of our determination not to yield on this vital matter.

"We have had to fight against the tight legal restrictions placed upon union action by the previous Conservative administration. In winning this case by a unanimous vote today, the NASUWT has struck a blow for trade union freedom against the anti-union legislation of the 1980s and 1990s".

Eamonn concluded his remarks by calling for more support for teachers. He welcomed the recent moves by the new Education Secretary, Charles Clarke, amending the guidance given to appeal panels. Much more remained to be done to rid schools of the antisocial behaviour that had prompted our action. As anticipated, the media coverage was not very extensive since the NASUWT had won.

The (pupil) 'L' v (school) 'J' case from Hertfordshire turned out to be a close call, with a split decision. It was delivered after the verdict in 'P' v NASUWT.

The NASUWT was not enjoined in the action. The claim was against the school governing body. By the time the case reached the House of Lords the youngster, 'L', was 18 years old and had left the school. He had been one of the gang of boys who badly beat up another pupil in the toilets. The victim ended up in hospital. The NASUWT deeply regretted the fact that the police were not involved and that appropriate public prosecutions did not follow in the youth courts.

Although not silver tongued, succinct and incisive as some QCs I have listened to in my many visits to courts, 'L's QC Cherie Booth presented a very detailed and technically well-argued case. She contended that 'L' had not been properly reinstated and that the conditions he was subjected to amounted to humiliating and degrading punishment.

'L's conditions of 'internal isolation' were undoubtedly strict. By letter dated 23 March 2001 the head wrote to 'L's parents stating that he had a duty to the health and safety of all the children and that provision had been made with the LEA for 'L's transport to and from the school by taxi. It went on: "['L'] will be provided with work and a teacher in a room isolated from the mainstream of the school. He will not return to the classroom but will be taught privately. He will not be allowed to circulate with other pupils at any stage in the school day". 'L' had to report to the reception area first thing every morning.

On 'L's return to the school on 26 March 2001, he was given a document signed by the head spelling out the arrangements in even more detail, culminating with a stern warning: "Failure to keep to any of these requirements will be considered a serious breach of school discipline and will result in permanent exclusion". Some of the law lords commented that these conditions were severe, perhaps unjustified, but not illegal.

Some of the law lords were sympathetic to 'L' on the 'reinstatement conditions' but they dismissed almost in peremptory fashion his claims to have been denied an education under the Human Rights Act. The 'big issue' became the definition of reinstatement.

Cherie Booth described the internal isolation as 'inhuman and degrading', which did not amount to a genuine reinstatement. She said it amounted to a punishment. It was designed to thwart the appeal panel's decision.

The presiding Lord (Bingham of Cornhill) agreed with Cherie Booth, in effect arguing against the five judges who had previously declared on the issue of reinstatement in the lower courts. Quoting the *Oxford English Dictionary* and employment law precedents, Lord Bingham said that to reinstate is to restore the status quo ante. "He [pupil 'L'] must (subject to some qualification) be put back in substantially the same position as he was in before he was excluded. Nothing less will deliver what the statute promises and requires".

Lord Bingham's view represented a much tighter definition of reinstatement than that which had prevailed in the lower courts. "'L' was either reinstated or he was not. There is no room for a conclusion that he was reinstated to the greatest extent possible in the circumstances." He believed the question of whether the union's action was "actionable", while now resolved in the 'P' v NASUWT case, was not relevant to the reinstatement issue.

Lord Bingham dismissed 'L's claim under the European Convention that he had been denied education. 'L' had been treated differently from others because of the teachers' refusal to teach him, but he had not been denied education. I thought that accurate observation tended to undermine his reasoning on the reinstatement issue.

Lord Bingham's final point was to note that 'L' was now 18 and had left school, so there could be no question of "effective reinstatement". "But", he continued, "I would for my part make a declaration that the arrangements . . . did not amount to reinstatement of 'L' as a pupil at the school in accordance with the decision of the appeal panel . . . "

Lord Hoffmann said he agreed with Bingham and would allow the appeal. He noted the obvious contradiction, the "uneasy co-existence", between the statutory powers bestowed on appeal panels (now under the 1998 Education Act) and the right of teachers to take industrial action, as declared in their decision just a few moments before in 'P' v NASUWT. Lord Hoffmann observed "the majority decision achieves this result (squaring the contradiction) by deeming the pupil to have been reinstated even though he remains entirely excluded from the school community". This was the first formal indication that despite two judges supporting the appeal, the governors of 'J' were to win a 3:2 decision.

Hoffmann conceded that the relevant parts of the 1998 Act (Section 67) did not define reinstatement. The only power apart from saying 'yes' or 'no' given to the appeal panels was to stipulate a time, i.e. immediately or at a later date. The judges were well into the area where they made law by whatever definition they gave to reinstatement.

Hoffmann believed reinstatement required at least substantial restoration of the status quo ante but he also recognised the resultant contradictions: "It is not for your Lordships in your judicial capacity to express any views about what might be done to resolve the present conflict that exists between the scheme of the 1998 Act and the right of teachers to take industrial action. But conflict there is; and I do not think it is helpful to wish it away by an interpretation of 'reinstatement' which nearly empties that notion of practical content."

Lord Hoffmann had been very searching in the questions he put to 'L's counsel, Cherie Booth, on the human rights of one pupil being exercised at the expense of others. I attach no blame to Cherie Booth for floundering around in a desperate search for a decent answer. There is no sensible reply available.

The NASUWT believed the contradictions referred to by Lord Hoffmann fully supported its contention that school discipline should be a predominantly professional, as opposed to a legal, matter with full rights of hearing (before governing bodies) granted to parents in a context which guaranteed education of some kind to every child.

The more 'academic' approach of Bingham and Hoffmann was counterbalanced by the refreshingly practical considerations (fully reflecting NASUWT philosophy) which influenced (the now late) Lord Hobhouse. He noted the statute did not define reinstatement and turned to the facts, 'the other half of the law': "It is a practical problem which needs to be put in its context. The teaching of the pupils has to be a collective activity in which the teachers and pupils interact successfully and individual pupils do not obstruct or imperil the education of others. Each pupil has the right to a safe environment. The assertion of a liberty by one or more pupils to . . . inflict violence on or to victimise or bully another will involve a denial of the rights of that other. The responsibility of teachers and the head are owed to the body of pupils as a whole not merely to an individual pupil in isolation."

Hobhouse said the real complaint of 'L' was a failure, as his counsel had argued "to reintegrate him fully into the social life of the school". It was a complaint about the quality of the education 'L' was receiving, and not one about reinstatement.

Lord Hobhouse recalled the events of 21 January 2001. "'L' was part of a group of boys who took part in a concerted and vicious attack upon another boy from the same school year. It took place when they cornered him in the lavatories. Besides being very severely frightened, 'A' was repeatedly stamped on and kicked and suffered substantial injuries." The extreme seriousness of the incident was never in dispute, but the precise role played by 'L' was.

Hobhouse held that an appeal panel had no powers beyond reinstatement: "To require the school to treat the incident as if it had never happened and to treat the pupil as if he had never offended is not merely wholly impractical but gives the decision of the independent panel content beyond that authorised by the statute."

Hobhouse found the special regime was a matter of educational and managerial choices lying "wholly outside the jurisdiction of the independent panel. If the head teacher had imposed the special regime from the outset would that have constituted exclusion? . . . Obviously not," concluded Lord Hobhouse. "Accordingly I would dismiss this appeal."

Lord Scott believed the appeal panel had no power to impose conditions upon reinstatement, apart from the one of timing. The word 'reinstated' had no statutory meaning. It was an ordinary word in the English language capable of various nuances of meaning. The two "extremes" were full restoration of the status quo ante in all respects and a mere formal acceptance amounting only to restoration of a name on the school roll. Scott rejected both. Formal reacceptance had to be accompanied "by treatment of the pupil that was consistent with his or her status as a pupil in the school. Comprehensive restoration of the status quo ante overlooked the nature of a school." It was not like restoring the head knocked off of a statue (as had recently happened to one of Mrs Thatcher in the Palace of Westminster). A school is an organic structure with individual staff and pupils and a body 'whole'.

Lord Scott observed the denial of social contact (in any event short-lived) had also to be measured against the possible disruption to the teaching of all the other pupils in the school and particularly those, like 'L', approaching public exams – not to mention the need to protect the victim from further social contact with him.

Lord Scott said that although Lord Bingham may not have considered the head's response "the best practical solution", it was a permissible response to the problem and consistent with treating 'L' as a pupil at the school. Like Lord Hobhouse he believed that had the head imposed the special regime from the outset it could not have been successfully challenged as a lawful decision.

Lord Scott's concluding sentence, "For these reasons, and those contained in the opinion of my noble and learned friends, Lord Hobhouse . . . and Lord

Walker . . . I would dismiss the appeal", confirmed the decision was going to be 3:2 in favour of the school, 'J'.

Lord Walker also agreed that reinstatement was not a mere formality but also led to other consequences, reintroducing all the statutory and common law obligations owed by a school to its pupils. Like all his "noble and learned friends" he noted the significant fact that appeal panels could not attach any conditions (apart from timing) to reinstatement.

Very perceptively Lord Walker picked up on a Government circular drawn up under the 1998 Act and issued in 2000 giving guidance on the use of sanctions. He quoted some in full:

"Removal from the group (in class);

Withdrawal of break or lunchtime privileges;

Detention;

Withholding participation in any school trips or sports events that are not an essential part of the curriculum;

Withdrawal from, for example, a particular lesson or peer group."

The same circular made clear that learning support units could be used for pupils at risk of exclusion, helping them remain at school while minimising disruption in class. A case study quoted even referred to an "in-school exclusion centre", making clear that such a regime, far from being regarded as exclusion, was a means of avoiding it.

Lord Walker said that any judgment as to the lawfulness of the conditions had to take account of the teachers' "clear threat" of industrial action, backed up by all the balloting arrangements. It was common ground that but for the teachers' threat 'L' would have been fully reintegrated into ordinary classroom life. He went on: "Your Lordships have to accept this agreed fact at face value, but I have to say that I find it surprising and rather disturbing . . . [The] pressing need to protect the victim against further stress (while he prepared for his GCSE exams), would have necessitated some restrictions on the appellant's freedom of association during the short final period of his career at the school."

Lord Walker asked if the strict regime would have been unlawful in the absence of the threat from the teachers. He thought it was "undoubtedly severe, and for my part I think its severity was ill-advised". But Lord Walker rejected Miss Booth's claim that it was humiliating and degrading. Some non-union teachers visited him so his isolation, while severe, was not total. Only 30 school days were involved before all GCSE students went on study leave. The separate travel arrangements were justified by the need to protect the victim.

Lord Walker concluded that "the arrangements in total were not so extreme or disproportionate as to go beyond the limits of [the school's] managerial and pastoral discretion. I would take that view even if teachers had not made their threat of industrial action." Walker said that the threat of action was relevant but he thought it was "a most regrettable event . . . The teachers' reaction was irresponsible and unprofessional, however exasperated they were at the turn of events." Their Lordships had accepted it was a genuine trade dispute and the ballot had been conducted properly: "The teachers' action was deplorable but it cannot to my mind detract from the lawfulness of the governors' decision."

Lord Walker recognised that the teachers owed loyalties in many directions but "by putting pressure on the governors and the head the teachers sought to interfere in the statutory arrangements for the governance of the school in a way that threatened to frustrate the decision of the appeal panel. Nevertheless their action was in itself lawful."

Walker speculated that the action may have come close to putting the governors and head in breach of their statutory duties and he wondered what might have happened if no suitable teacher had come forward to supervise 'L': "It was a risky and irresponsible course. But in the event it did not, in my view, lead to unlawful action by the governors or head teacher." Lord Walker then dismissed the appeal.

The NASUWT had won 5:0 over the challenge from 'P' on our claim that our action was in pursuit of a lawful trade dispute. School 'J' had won 3:2 on the issue of 'internal isolation' following reinstatement. Because we had won, the publicity was low key. I was pleasantly surprised the journalists from the usual suspect papers failed to pick up on the criticisms made by Lord Walker.

I left the House of Lords that day with a profound sense of relief but satisfaction that the NASUWT had once again won a historic and crucial battle for teachers.

SECTION EIGHT
THE DESCENT INTO DEBACLE
Teachers' Negotiations 1977-87

Chapter 60 - Houghton Surrendered 1977-79

The latter years of the 1970s proved to be a sobering reminder to the trade union movement that wider 'Social Contract' measures were necessary to maintain the value of increases in 'money wages' and the comparative position of employees (such as nurses and teachers) who did not carry much industrial clout.

By 1977 severe inflation, peaking at nearly 30%, had virtually wiped out the Houghton uplift. Whilst the minimum of Scale 1 had only lost 3% compared to the average national earnings rise of 67%, teachers at the maximum had lost 21%, those at the Scale 2 equivalent 23%.

Recognising the need for a Social Contract the NASUWT had accepted the flat rate £6 per week pay policy ordained by the Labour Government for 1976 despite its adverse effect upon career structured salary scales. After the drama of the Houghton Award, which dominated the 1974-75 pay rounds, the £6 per week at least made Burnham 1976 an uncharacteristically simple and straightforward affair.

The NASUWT argued inside the TUC-Government talks over the next phase of the social contract for percentage increases after the flat-rate award of 1976. The 1977 teachers' settlement, whilst not completely flat rate, did represent some further erosion of differentials with varying increases around 5%.

In November 1977 the NASUWT won a significant legal victory against the Welsh LEA, Dyfed. The LEA had submitted a list of schools for designation as social priority schools (SPS) following the scheme agreed in Burnham in 1974. Burnham had designated 22 in accordance with the agreed criteria. Dyfed (and Gwynedd) subsequently tried to withdraw from the scheme when they learned they would have to pay a share of the costs themselves. The NASUWT through the person of Peter Lewis, our courageous Dyfed Negotiating Secretary, took out an action against the LEA. In the High Court Mr Justice O'Connor ruled the designation valid and legally binding. Peter Lewis and his fellow teachers were owed £928 each plus interest. Payment was delayed while Dyfed tried other legal moves which also failed.

By 1978 the NUT was feeling the pressure generated by the NASUWT's continued rise in membership (now surpassing the magic 100,000 mark) by dropping its flat-rate policy in favour of a common percentage increase for all teachers.

However, Management's judgement seemed to desert them, for in February 1978 instead of offering the full 10% allowed under the Social Contract they decided on 9%, arguing the 1% (£23m) 'cut' was to allow for incremental drift. The NASUWT argued fiercely that the incremental scale represented delayed payment of the full rate for the job in recognition that experience generally generated greater competence. The deduction of the £23m was "daylight robbery".

It was a silly decision, the potential savings heavily outweighed by the dramatic loss of goodwill. However, Management stuck at 9% and made matters worse by refusing to support the aim of restoring Houghton levels because employers "were no longer short of teachers".

The NASUWT Action Committee decided on a withdrawal of goodwill to commence on 13 March. All voluntary activities were banned. The action was well supported by the membership. Before the end of the month the Management Panel was in disarray, the Leader, Sir Ashley Bramall from the ILEA, courageously repudiating the "skinflint offer".

Faced with rising anger and the Easter teacher unions' Conference season the Management finally saw sense and offered the full 10%. Management also conceded a historic "commitment to a phased restoration of Houghton" which was to have huge repercussions for the conduct of negotiations over the coming years. Agreements were also soon reached to establish working parties to consider salary structure and pay data.

The controversy over the 'commitment' to Houghton restoration began the moment it was born. The Minute of the Agreement reached in Burnham on 22 March 1978 records:

"The Management Panel confirms its wholehearted commitment to the principles enunciated in the Houghton report and shares the view of the teachers that the report accurately reflects a proper assessment of the value and role of teachers in our society. The maintenance of that assessment remains their objective, as it is the teachers', but the speed with which they move in any particular year must depend upon the economic situation at the time."

Ominously the DES representatives formally recorded a statement of reservation to avoid any future commitment:

"The Government does not repudiate the Houghton report relativities but their implementation must be subject to pay policy and the economic situation at the relevant time."

Conference 1978 commended the Executive for its "swift and decisive imposition of sanctions" but also carried another resolution calling upon all members to refuse voluntary activities unless and until their LEA gave a categorical assurance they were non-contractual. Action on the contract was to break out again soon after the start of the Summer Term. Addressing the Conference, Shirley Williams repeated Government's reservation on Houghton restoration.

In October 1978 the Secretary of State finally conceded part of the NASUWT's case for Burnham reform. NASUWT representation was doubled following its increase in membership to 110,000. The NUT retained its overall majority with a disproportionate 16 seats for its claimed 220,000 membership. Membership of the Teachers' Panel became: NUT 16, NASUWT 6, AMMA 4, NAHT 2, SHA 1 and NATFHE 1.

By October the Management was awaiting 'fuller information' over 'Houghton Relativities'. Terry Casey accused Management of procrastination, observing "that when he was out of his depth he did not want someone to measure the depth of the water in feet and inches before throwing him a lifeline". The basic facts were already well known:

Since 24 May 1974 (the operative date for the Houghton award):

RPI had increased by 81%;

Index of Average National Earnings by 86%;

basic wage rates by 96%;

teachers' pay (England and Wales) by 51%.

Out of the blue in January 1979 the NUT launched a salary claim of 35%, torpedoing the previous 22 March agreement that the shared objective of Houghton restoration had to be phased. The NASUWT dissociated itself from the "unrealistic" NUT claim, stating that it "imperilled the teachers' case". Examination of the NUT claim quickly revealed it seriously distorted the Houghton internal relativities, once again favouring the young entrant on Scale 1. Government Ministers went on to the offensive against the NUT's absurd claim.

At the Burnham meeting of 7 March the Management only offered 8% and, more significantly, took the opportunity of the NUT's breach of faith by backsliding on Houghton restoration, suggesting the matter be referred to the Standing Commission on Pay Comparabilities. The NUT quickly dropped its 35% claim, abandoning its brief but reckless 'Houghton restoration in one go' stance and expressed interest in going to the Standing Commission, being established the same day, which would require agreement on the terms of reference.

Sensing the obvious danger that terms of reference for the Commission could jeopardise the Houghton criteria, the NASUWT suggested that Management's good faith should be put to the test through a joint employer/union approach to the Commission in order to seek its assistance in securing Houghton restoration. The NUT-dominated Panel blocked the NASUWT motion and left it "lying on the table" with the excuse that more information was needed on the Commission. The 8% offer was rejected, with the possibility of reference to the Commission left for further consideration.

GS Terry Casey's 'state of the union' address to Conference delegates was a sombre affair. Terry outlined the huge significance of the breakthrough in 1974 and the danger posed by the weak and vacillating leadership of the NUT which was about to surrender the gains of "the Houghton hill". The nation had just come through the 'Winter of Discontent' with widespread industrial action. In the Burnham Management Panel, Conservative Party hawks had taken over and were reneging on the 'commitment', seeking to establish a lower baseline for teachers' pay through the Commission. The only way out was arbitration. Terry Casey concluded: "If we went to the Commission we could kiss Houghton goodbye for ever."

The main salary motion of the week was a lively affair with the employers condemned for reneging on Houghton and for refusing to negotiate or submit to arbitration. The motion also "empowered the Executive to instruct all members to work only the prescribed five hours per day specified in the statutory Burnham Report". The action would start on 8 May.

Despite NASUWT members demonstrating outside the Burnham meeting, held at Church House, Westminster, 24 April (in Terry Casey's words): "Amid an Orwellian welter of double-think and double-talk the Teachers' Panel surrendered to Management pressure and agreed to go to the Commission on terms of reference which had been rejected before Easter."

The NUT rejected the NASUWT's preferred option of arbitration. GS Fred Jarvis openly conceded that its much-vaunted 35% claim was "in no fit state to go to arbitration". The Chairman of Burnham, Sir John Wordie, had warned that despite the weeks of endless debate over terms of reference, they remained in the gift of the Secretary of State who would alter them if the Government so wished.

The six NASUWT Representatives walked out of the Burnham meeting in protest. Having joined the staff the previous November as an Assistant Secretary whose job included covering national negotiations, my first 'Burnham round' saw me left inside alone to take notes and report back. The NUT tried to get me to speak to prove the NASUWT had not walked out. I had to smile and remain uncharacteristically silent.

The war of words between the two main unions became ferocious. The NASUWT said everyone knew what was going on. Even *The Teacher*, the NUT's own newspaper, had previously described the Management's "manoeuvre" as cynical, "a transparent ploy" and "a squalid breach of faith". Terry also debunked Jarvis' pleasure at securing the deletion of conditions of service from the terms of reference, by pointing out that the Commission's own 'constitution' required it " . . . to examine the terms and conditions of service of particular groups referred to it by the Government . . . " Predictably, just before the General Election of May 1979 the Education Secretary Shirley Williams duly vetoed such terms of reference, provoking a "futile fury" from the NUT.

Faced with this war of words, the NUT published a hard-hitting, indeed savage, attack upon the Union, entitled "NASUWT's Diary of Shame", in *The Teacher*, 27 April. The NASUWT dismissed the allegations, at best a series of half-truths; at worst plain "distasteful".

On 3 May 1979 an event of huge importance occurred with the General Election victory of Mrs Thatcher's Conservative Party. Labour was to be out of power for 18 years and the forces of economic liberalisation given free rein. The public sector was to be exposed to market forces through privatisation and competitive tendering. Severe restraints were to be placed on public expenditure, including education and teachers' pay. The NASUWT declared its 'Five Hour Day' action would continue unless arbitration was conceded.

Burnham effectively remained suspended whilst the new Government decided the future of the Standing Commission. In the event, having made commitments to honour the award during the General Election campaign the Conservatives retained the Commission to complete its work on teachers' pay. The Commission did not survive long afterwards.

At the 18 May meeting of Burnham, the NUT-led Teachers' Panel finally and formally accepted the reference to the Commission. The NASUWT report No. 8 for 1979 was headlined: "Houghton is Lost", quoting the words of the Teachers' Panel Leader, Fred Jarvis, declaring: "We want to go to the Commission." Terry Casey wrote: "In the most abject capitulation since Burnham volunteered a 10% salary cut in 1931, the Teachers' Panel supinely accepted Management's terms for reference to the Commission." Teachers settled for £1.38 per week (£72 a year), which would be clawed back with the first instalment from the Commission due on 1 January 1980, with the second coming in September.

Terry Casey, who had fought for over 15 years to secure an independent inquiry into teachers' pay in 1974, predicted: "Teachers will rue the day when

Houghton was surrendered." Recognising that "when teachers betray teachers one cannot blame the employers", the following day, 22 May, the Executive suspended the controversial Five Hour Day action.

Interestingly Management stated that Appendix IV of the Burnham document (the five-hour day salary calculation) had to be changed so that it no longer related to full-time teachers. The NASUWT took that to constitute further justification for the nature of its protest action.

Predictably the Chairman of the Standing Commission, Professor Hugh Clegg from Warwick University, decided not to follow Houghton in a straightforward link with civil servants' pay. Instead a job evaluation exercise would be conducted by a firm of management consultants with the apt name of Inbucon.

The NASUWT quickly decided to engage its own management consultants to advise on job evaluation. It soon became apparent that job evaluation was a massive pseudoscientific exercise in which teaching and comparator jobs were broken down into different components – skills and knowledge required, responsibility carried, amidst others – each of which was weighed against every other in thousands of subjective judgements, establishing a pecking order of difficulty-cum-importance. Membership of the steering group was crucial since it set all the rules and made the outcome-determining decisions, including the selection of the comparator jobs and the final link of the results to salary levels.

True to form the NUT kept every other union off the steering group, except its allies – the NATFHE for the FE exercise and the EIS for the one in Scotland. All unions could, however, serve on the judging panels to carry out the donkey work of the thousands of 'factorial comparisons'. Denied membership of the steering group, the NASUWT decided to boycott the exercise.

The NUT kept the Burnham Teachers' Panel in the dark but the NASUWT gleaned crucial information via the Scottish Teachers' equivalent, to which the EIS reported. The NASUWT was alarmed to discover the list of 50 outside jobs in the exercise for Scotland revealed few of any status whatsoever, the better ones appearing to be computer operator, statistician and merchant navy officer. The NASUWT learned later that stress had been omitted from the factorial comparisons because it rarely existed in the outside comparator jobs.

Terry Casey wrote another of his famous leaders in the *Schoolmaster and Career Teacher* (in the words of Fred Jarvis) "racily entitled" "INBUCONNED", which also appeared as a pamphlet in October 1979. Terry Casey concluded his piece: "When some of these sobering facts begin to sink in, many outside our ranks may come to regret we didn't get the salary issue settled by arbitration. Down the years teachers have almost invited management to trick and cheat them. But being 'INBUCONNED' is something new."

In the light of looming threats over pay and jobs the NASUWT called a Special Conference for 17 November. The Executive sought endorsement for the action taken over Inbucon, a commitment to sanctions should Clegg lower Houghton levels and 'no cover action' and a 'refusal to work unacceptable timetables' in the event of staffing reductions not justified by falling rolls.

The Special Conference in Birmingham duly supported the Executive. Feelings ran even higher than expected with the publication of Government and employers' evidence to the Clegg Commission. Government made it clear that Clegg had to abandon Houghton and make a modest award. Management was again "ratting on Houghton" and demanding contractual concessions, including dinner supervision, compulsory out-of-school activities and in-service training in school holidays. Headteachers were alarmed to see the employers' views of their real management responsibilities – "very limited".

The teacher organisations jointly met with the Clegg Commission on 7 December 1979. Terry Casey emphasised our "gravest misgivings about the conduct of the job evaluation exercise".

The NASUWT called for an immediate 10% increase 'on account', which was surprisingly agreed by the Teachers' Panel. The Union rejected accusations by the NUT that it was "completely misinforming teachers" and "scaremongering from the sidelines". We stood by everything we said, all of which was based on the documents available.

Come January 1980, events began to prove the NASUWT concerns were well justified. With Clegg not meeting the January 1980 deadline, the Management did, however, offer teachers 7.5% 'on account', unwilling to offer more in case it compromised the eventual 'Clegg settlement'. The NASUWT described the offer as "pitiful" but the rest of the Teachers' Panel accepted it.

The end of January brought dramatic leaks in some of the press that the Clegg job evaluation exercise was on the brink of collapse. There was to be "a last ditch attempt to salvage results". Despite attempts by some to cover up, by March further leaks revealed it was a fiasco, a massive time-waster and statistically worthless. The *TES*, via an inside source, reported: "The raw material, if used by the Clegg Commission, would give rises to some teachers and cuts to others. The margin of error is as high as 45%." Peter Dawson, NATFHE GS, who had earlier complained about Management "block voting" and said his union had reached "the limit in its efforts to participate constructively", added: "If the Commission came within a million miles of using the data there would be complete chaos in FE."

The *TES* continued: "The confusion of the second stages comes only a few weeks after the first stage flopped. Quite simply, results of various statistical comparisons between teachers and other employees have varied wildly. Rises or cuts are put forward, depending on which comparability survey is used. There are six to choose from."

The NASUWT strongly recommended that Clegg had "better stick to the sound statistics of the Houghton Relativities WP rather than the fanciful figures produced by Inbucon."

The NASUWT rejected demands from the AMA employers that a simultaneous and parallel agreement on conditions of service be concluded before the employers paid out a penny on 'Clegg'. The NASUWT would continue to boycott 'COSWOP' (the WP of CLEA/ST) since the employers had no money to buy concessions from teachers on the contract. The local authority journal, *Education*, conceded that the NASUWT was the most formidable obstacle standing in the employers' way.

On 10 March paramedical staff in the NHS complained bitterly that their Clegg Commission award of 15% failed miserably to restore the 55% erosion in comparative earnings. They walked out of their pay talks complaining that the methods used by the Commission to evaluate the jobs of paramedics were "subjective and irrelevant". On the same day a meeting between the teacher unions and the Clegg Commission revealed the *TES* reports were accurate. We were later to learn in an official government report by Sir Alan Marre into an error made by the Standing Commission, that it had met in private (excluding its OME officials) on 6 March to ditch the Inbucon report and revert to a graduate comparability exercise.

Conference 1980 was a baleful time. It was small comfort for the Union to have been proved right. In his Monday evening GS address to the delegates Terry Casey reminded everyone present that "there was not a single aspect of the Clegg fiasco that we had not predicted". Subsequently the Conference unanimously supported the stand taken by the Executive on Clegg and the contract, declaring its determination "to resist with all the power at its disposal" any worsening of conditions of service.

Conference also adopted a Report on Salaries and Promotion based on an earlier consultative document, *Pointing the Way*, both of which may be seen as steps on the way to the NASUWT's unique policy on collegiality. Mark Carlisle, the first Education Secretary in Mrs Thatcher's 11 years of office, addressed Conference and seemed in some discomfort explaining the planned cuts in expenditure.

The Clegg Report (No. 7 of the Standing Commission) was finally published in the week following the union Easter Conferences. It recommended rises averaging 18% to be implemented in the two stages, 1 January and 1 September 1980.

Point 10 on Scale 1 (generally taken to be close to the average pay for teachers), £4,590 as at 1 April 1979, rose to £4,980 w.e.f. 1 January and to £5,370 w.e.f. 1 September 1980. (The 7.5% on account payment was subsumed in the former.) The NASUWT declared that it fell short of Houghton restoration by at least 10%.

The Clegg Report rejected the Management's 'claim' that salaries should be adjusted to take account of conditions of service such as holidays. On the comparability study the Clegg Report declared: "We had no alternative but to abandon the idea of basing our recommendations on the consultants' [Inbucon] study. We therefore set about constructing an alternative approach."

Clegg was very critical of the promotion and pupil points score system, commenting: "There are no job descriptions or precise criteria for promotion from one scale to another. Headteachers have wide discretion. Nor are we satisfied that the system can be accepted as fair and effective."

Burnham met on 18 April and agreed to the Clegg recommendations. However, a couple of weeks later an alleged 4% error was spotted. Abandoning the Inbucon exercise, Clegg had apparently resorted to a fairly simple 'quick fix', establishing a key point of parity to ensure that no trained good honours degree graduate *three years** into teaching would be paid less than the average figure received by private sector graduates three years into their careers. All the recommended salary levels were related to this key point. However, the complex arrangements for granting different numbers of increments to various kinds of teacher graduates (not to mention others) resulted in incorrect information being supplied to the Clegg Commission, which overestimated the required 'catch-up' by 4% at every point of the scale. Professor Clegg confirmed these facts in a letter, 16 May 1980, to Prime Minister Thatcher.

*(The choice of 'three years' was extremely significant and gives credence to sceptics who believe enquiries start with conclusions and work backwards to justification. Comparative graduate teacher salaries erode far more seriously after five years into careers.)

"Clegg Clanger" tolled the media, blaming an unnamed civil servant. All of a sudden the practical priority for the teacher unions was to defend Clegg rather than demand Houghton! Government and Management sought to have Burnham reopen the question of the 18% agreement. Terry Casey referred to "an explosive situation", with members sending in messages demanding the GCE O and A Level exams be targeted if the Clegg award were reopened. The Teachers' Panel stood firm in refusing to reopen the agreement.

Despite having received a full and frank explanation in Professor Clegg's 16 May letter, six days later Prime Minister Thatcher set up an inquiry under Sir Alan Marre to find out how the £130m error had occurred. The DES and LEAs considered the possibility that the error rendered the subsequent Burnham agreement invalid. Rumours of 'claw back' abounded.

On 23 May a leader in the *TES* seemed to sum it all up:

"Somehow it all brings the pay comparability saga to a fitting conclusion in a mixture of farce and tragedy. People whose common sense told them that what was going on was nonsense, were caught up in the process to the extent that they resented outsiders learning about the bizarre activities in which they engaged. And to what purpose? The purpose was not to undertake scientific research, but to establish new salary scales somewhere near revalued Houghton levels. A 'quick and dirty' arbitration could have done this in six weeks, but six weeks would have been inconveniently quick."

As events turned out the 'Clegg award' Burnham settlement was allowed to stand. However, it was inevitable that Government and Management would never really forget it. The strong suspicion entertained by teachers that the Clegg error would be somehow clawed back was quickly justified.

Chapter 61 - The Storms before the Tempest

The pay awards from 1980 to 1984 were characterised by a steep erosion of teachers' salaries. Each award fell below the RPI and average earnings, reflecting the harsh anti-public sector philosophy of the Thatcher Government. They played a crucial role in building up a depth of anger which had perhaps only one precedent – the schoolmasters in the 1930s. The scene was being set for unprecedented and widespread industrial action by teachers, which lasted from 1985 to 1987.

Having just got 1979 and 'Clegg' out of the way, the impasse quickly reached in May 1980 was, unlike the previous year, promptly referred to arbitration. The employers tried to reduce their 13% offer to 9% in the light of the 'Clegg Clanger', but thanks to an NASUWT intervention the Chairman ruled that the former had to stand for purposes of arbitration. To the astonishment and chagrin of the NASUWT the Teachers' Panel in submissions to the arbitral body refused to take advantage of the favourable ruling by the Chairman. The NUT-dominated Panel insisted on responding to the reduced 9.3% offer, effectively worsening the arbitral terms of reference to a judgment between 9.3% and 21.2% (the Teachers' claim) instead of one between 13% and 21.2%.

Despite inflation running at 20% the arbitral panel awarded all teachers 12% w.e.f. 1 April 1980 and further variable amounts up to 4% depending on the detailed levels awarded by Clegg. One could obviously read into the award some adjustments for the Clegg error.

By November 1980, with inflation still high, the Government announced a 6% cash limit for public sector pay for 1980/81. The Government was also keen to undermine effective trade unionism and quickly recognised a small new organisation, the Professional Association of Teachers, giving it a seat on Burnham. PAT was formed for teachers who were pledged never to take industrial action whatever the circumstances.

The NASUWT quickly reminded Mark Carlisle of his pledge to review the composition of the Teachers' Panel and that his decision to recognise PAT ahead of this exercise smacked of prejudgement. The Minister quickly took the point but also went ahead with other reforms. He granted an extra seat to the NASUWT (giving it seven representatives), although the NUT retained an overall majority. In January 1981 Mark Carlisle changed the rules over arbitration. Instead of the Chairman deciding the issue if deadlock had been reached, both sides would have to agree. The NASUWT criticised the decision, stating it was biased, short-sighted and likely to cause more militant action.

The Secretary of State also announced his intention to combine pay and conditions in new unified negotiating machinery. Whilst supporting radical but fair reform, the NASUWT objected fiercely to the ridiculously short period allowed for consultation – a mere two weeks – and the blatantly pro-employer proposals which made a mockery of consultation. The *TES* supported the NASUWT position, adding that "this further open attack on the teachers' negotiating position will lead to a deteriorating atmosphere in the education service".

In February 1981 the Teachers' Panel agreed with the NASUWT on a 15% claim with only PAT dissenting. However, by March the NUT, openly admitting their members had no stomach for a fight, forced through a majority decision to accept 7½%. The media described the teachers' settlement as "boosting Thatcher's hopes of limiting increases in the public sector", "a shot in the arm for Government pay policy" and "strengthening the Government's resolve to defeat civil servants after set backs with the miners and water workers".

With the pay issue resolved albeit unsatisfactorily if uncharacteristically 'on time', Conference 1981 concentrated on the threats posed by the Conditions of Service WP (COSWOP) which the NASUWT had boycotted to prevent another sell-out.

After several weeks of intensive lobbying of MPs by NASUWT activists, in July 1981 Mark Carlisle decided to postpone his plans to force pay and conditions together in Burnham, incurring the wrath of *The Daily Telegraph* for caving in to union pressure. The employers expressed strong disappointment, also blaming the Government's failure on the NASUWT boycott of COSWOP. The NASUWT reiterated its support for radical reform but remained adamant not to accept a joint pay and conditions machine modelled on Burnham.

Despite inflation running at 12% the Government had decided to pin public sector employees down to 4% increases for the 1982 pay round. The NASUWT supported the TUC's efforts (which unfortunately came to nothing) to secure a co-ordinated approach based on claims for 12% to protect living standards and avoid groups being picked off one by one as happened the previous year. Civil servants, an important comparator group for teachers, were also suffering as the Government repudiated the PRU (Pay Research Unit) findings upon which civil service pay had long been based. The pay settlement of the manual workers (in October 1981) would essentially set the norm for teachers, nurses, and town hall workers.

In November Terry Casey picked up reports of secret DES and local government discussions aimed at reducing the teaching force by 43,000 over the next two to three years. Over 10,000 teachers could suffer compulsory redundancy. The NASUWT had taken the lead in negotiating the early retirement scheme which had provided 12,000 teachers with a way out. The Union also argued for the huge surplus in the Teachers' Pension Fund to cover the costs of early retirement rather than the LEAs being left to shoulder the burden.

Matters took a sharp turn for the worse when at the delayed Burnham meeting in February 1982 Management made an offer of only 3.4% in response to the Teachers' 12% claim. The civil service had been offered rises between 0% and 5% with a right to go to arbitration. Local government manual workers had received 7%. Scottish teachers received a significantly better offer of 6%. 1 April would see sharp rises in National Insurance contributions, wiping out between 1% and 2% of any pay increase.

The NASUWT warned ominously that "The Crunch is Coming". Teachers' living standards had been depressed for several years. The Government was intent on pursuing its disastrous experiment with monetarism, which was savaging swathes of industry, depressing the economy and imposing exorbitant rates of interest on mortgage payers and firms.

A totally obdurate Management refused to budge from its 3.4% offer, provoking the entire Teachers' Panel to "frustration and fury". After two long meetings the NASUWT proposed arbitration and the Teachers' Panel agreed. However, now armed with Mark Carlisle's change to the arbitration procedures, Management was able to block the issue being decided by the Chairman and curtly retorted: "We will not go to arbitration."

Ironically the London Allowances were referred to arbitration, making the Management's stance on the main salary issue even more indefensible. The employers had only offered 7.5%, with a take-it-or-leave-it attitude despite the official indices dating from the Pay Board Report of 1974 showing an increase of 13.6% to be required.

Terry Casey's comments carried historic significance: "When there is so much condemnation of irresponsible industrial action, what are we to say to Management's arrogant and contemptuous refusal to follow a procedure allowed for by Act of Parliament? Even the most timid teacher must now admit that when all procedures have been exhausted, we must either lie down like a doormat or show a righteous indignation in the face of blatant injustice."

By 11 March the NASUWT Executive had instructed all members "to withdraw completely from mid-day supervision and staff/parent meetings outside school hours". On this occasion sports and social activities were not banned, being left to personal decision. With overwhelming membership support, action began to bite immediately. Many schools had to close at lunchtime and tens of thousands of pupils went home because there was no teacher supervision.

Attempts via the TUC to secure co-ordinated action by the two main unions proved problematic at first, with the NUT anxious to exempt employers who had declared for arbitration. The NASUWT pointed out that the AMA had voted with their ACC colleagues to stick to 3.4% and refuse arbitration. Many LEAs had budgeted for a 7% increase. Scottish teachers had achieved arbitration.

Uncharacteristically some sections of the media sympathised with the teachers. *The Guardian*, 9 March, said teachers' fury was "understandable". They were offered even less than the Government's 4% norm. The policemen had received 13%, water workers 9% and manual workers 7%. Teachers, like nurses, were obviously being penalised through their reluctance to strike. The escape route of arbitration had been closed. Eventually parity for teachers would have to be restored. *The Guardian* concluded: "Such short term cynicism seems a particularly dotty way to run a public sector pay policy."

The NASUWT preferred the nil cost ban on voluntary activities; strikes saved government and LEAs money. Nevertheless, in a spirit of compromise and to maintain unity the NASUWT agreed with the NUT to a series of strikes and joint rallies in 44 different LEAs if deadlock persisted at the Burnham meeting planned for 18 March.

However, on 18 March the NUT immediately showed signs of weakness in wanting to 'go behind the chair' with Management to explore a conditional offer instead of insisting upon an open one in full Burnham as promised. There was a lack of support locally in the NUT for the planned strikes. In the event, embarrassment was saved by arbitration finally being agreed after meetings on 18 and 25 March.

Addressing Conference delegates in his traditional GS Easter Monday evening address Terry Casey reflected ruefully on the difficulties of joint action with the NUT: "An alliance becomes difficult when your ally is anxious to quit the field before the battle begins". He praised the leadership of local NASUWT activists.

In his final involvement in salary negotiations before retirement Terry Casey struck a historically significant note when he warned delegates that more battles lay ahead in the future: "If the mass of teachers ever forget that it is action in the schools rather than empty phrases in Burnham that secures results they will deserve shabby treatment." Terry was given a standing ovation.

The new Secretary of State for Education, Sir Keith Joseph, addressed Conference. He steered well clear of reference to pay although as the leading intellectual architect of monetarism and advocate of public expenditure cuts he was the chief villain behind the problems.

Conference 1982 was marred by the personal tragedy of the Honorary Treasurer and a Past-President, Ron Cocking, who collapsed and died from a heart attack on the platform during the Tuesday afternoon private session. Although he received immediate treatment from first aid staff and was quickly taken to hospital he was pronounced dead upon arrival. The tragedy occurred just a few minutes before Fred Smithies was due to be ratified as the GS designate to take over from Terry Casey the following year. Ron had been an applicant for the post. Conference immediately adjourned and the following day the President, Eric Powell, paid warm tributes to Ron for his outstanding contribution to the Union. Conference then stood in silent tribute to him. Ex-President Alan Poole was appointed by the Executive to fulfil the duties of Acting Treasurer. In accordance with precedent, Harry Gardner, as the senior member of the floor of Executive who had indicated he would not be seeking election as JVP, became the Appointed Officer to serve out the time as the fifth member of the National Officers' Committee until the by-election for the new Treasurer had been completed.

The report of the arbitral body was published in June. It awarded a "mere 6%", matching the award in Scotland. The belated increase still left teachers poorer in real terms. Full restoration of Houghton would have required 27½%. The NASUWT concluded that without arbitration we would have fared even worse but no teacher could feel satisfied with the outcome.

Prospects had not improved for 1983. Management began by refusing to negotiate unless the Teachers' agreed to parallel meetings of CLEA/ST to deal with conditions of service. Government stipulated a maximum of 3½% for pay settlements despite Department of Employment statistics indicating that average earnings had risen by 8½% over the previous 12 months. After several abortive attempts at negotiations in March Management forced the Teachers' to quantify their claim which they did at 15% to cover inflation – a small element of catching up. The employers feigned outrage before deciding to offer the expected 3½%, which was rejected.

In Burnham on 25 March deadlock seemed inevitable and another round of action beckoned. However, after some Management 'verbal belligerence' the NUT weakened and soon indicated a willingness to come off the 15% claim "for something lower". Arbitration was also being abandoned as a consequence. The NASUWT smelt sell-out in the air as the Management suggested an adjournment, promising to make a revised offer.

Easter and the Conference season intervened. The 1983 Conference was a very significant one for NASUWT, marking the retirement of GS Terry Casey.

Under Terry's indomitable and charismatic leadership from 1963 to 1983 the Union's membership had risen from under 30,000 to over 120,000. He was by far the most outstanding teachers' leader of his time. In his last GS Monday evening address to delegates he reviewed the battles to secure Burnham recognition, then an independent inquiry – Houghton – achieved in 1974, only to be followed by more struggle "to recapture the Houghton hill". He also reviewed some of the battles in the North East, and the campaigns over pensions, dinner duties, salary safeguarding and more latterly the contract. "Every fight the NASUWT engaged in was worth it. It has been a marvellous experience and I could not have asked for anything more", were his last words as he sat down to a rapturous standing ovation together with musical honours which lasted several minutes.

A similar speech followed on the Friday morning's special session to mark the retirement of Terry as GS. Terry had some fine words of thanks to the many members, Officers and staff throughout the NASUWT for their support and camaraderie "who had done so much to make it all worthwhile". As I recorded in the Conference Report to Schools which I drafted in those days: "A few minutes before 1 p.m. on 8 April an era in the history of the Union drew to a close."

On 15 April the Teachers' Panel capitulated. After several hours of secret talks 'behind the chair', unions fell over themselves rushing to second the NUT proposal to accept the conditional offer of 4.98%. Newly installed GS Fred Smithies described the events as a "double betrayal of teachers' interests", for the settlement failed to match inflation at 5.3% and average earnings at 7.9%. For the third successive year teachers had fallen behind.

In September the NASUWT went in delegation to Sir Keith Joseph to warn him of the inevitable backlash against the continued depression of teachers' pay. Since 1974 teachers' pay had lost ground to the tune of 16.8% against the cost of living and by a massive 35.7% compared with increases in average earnings. Blunt exchanges characterised the meeting, with an unyielding Sir Keith stating "the era of comparability is at an end".

The NASUWT was pleased the Teachers' Panel agreed the long-term strategy "to shelter from extinction the flickering flame of Houghton" and press for a minimum 'average earnings' increase for 1984. Despite the unpropitious background the Joint WP on Salary Structure (JWPSS) held an intensive three-day meeting at the Midland Hotel, Manchester from 13 to 15 December (1983).

The NASUWT knew it was largely on its own amongst the unions in openly favouring reform of the salary structure along collegiate lines. We welcomed the expressed belief of the employers in "the central importance of the teacher in the classroom" with a new main professional grade (MPG). We recognised the promotion bottleneck. Some 63% of teachers were on Scales 1 and 2 and a further 90,000 were trapped at the top of their scales with no hope of further promotion. We recognised a new contract would be required for an MPG teacher and were prepared to negotiate one that established fair limits. Last, and by no means least, the Government would have to put up enough money through the Revenue Support Grant to facilitate such reforms. The NASUWT was working on a major policy document to present to Conference 1984. In private social exchanges with some Management reps we learned they considered the NASUWT the only union really prepared for the talks and the only one from which they received consistent answers.

At the end of 1983 GS Fred Smithies warned members of the "unparalleled threats" to teachers and education. After ten years of increasingly savage cuts in expenditure it was no good members "burying their heads in the sand". If "constitutional means failed to turn the tide they would have to employ less palatable means". The Teachers' Panel seemed not to appreciate the gravity of the situation and the Management delayed responding to the 'average earnings plus a step towards restoration' claim (submitted by the unions in November) until 29 February. Even the normally calm Chairman, Sir John Wordie, was exasperated with the Management's delaying antics.

The sense of crisis over salaries spread to all areas of the Union's activities. Following up on a Report to Conference in 1982, "A Strategy for the Eighties", the Executive prepared another, entitled "All our Future", in 1984. The Report focussed on all the fundamental challenges posed to the survival of the NASUWT in the context of the right-wing Government's policies and the decline in pupil numbers. Recommendations were adopted to concentrate on the fundamentals of recruitment, communication, services to members, internal organisation and policy development/implementation in a fast-changing context. The continued expansion of the NASUWT in such difficult times seemed to indicate that we 'got it right'.

In February 1984 a NASUWT Executive meeting approved a Report on Salary Structure to be presented to Conference at Easter. The report built on three predecessor documents: "Pointing the Way", 1979; "Salaries and Promotion", 1980; and "Flesh on the Bones", 1982. The concepts embraced by the Report included:

> a main professional grade (MPG) which recognised the central importance of the teacher in the classroom;
> acceptance that teaching is a collegiate profession;
> movement to the MPG based on fair and open assessment;
> negotiation of a fair contract with a second contract for those teachers willing to volunteer for lunchtime supervision;

a relatively small superstructure of posts carrying additional allowances.

The employers' derisory offer of 3% was rejected out of hand by the Teachers' Panel. At further meetings in March, despite having settled with their manual workers at 4½%, Management claimed they were being generous in offering "the full 3%" bearing in mind the additional 1.05% they had been forced to make on pension contributions. That cut little ice with the NASUWT, given its consistent criticism of the notorious Notional Fund. Recent Government Actuary's figures showed a surplus of contributions over benefits paid out for 1981-82 of £720m.

Management Leader Phillip Merridale had not helped matters when under pressure of arguments about fairness and justice he retorted: "Justice and injustice, morality and lack of morality, are neither here not there." The NASUWT referred to the moralising rebukes heaped upon teachers when they took industrial action against poor pay. The NASUWT prepared for the inevitable calling upon members "to be ready to respond to the call for action".

The deadlock persisted. Come 3 April, and despite nine hours of mostly secret talks behind the chair, Management stood rigidly by Sir Keith Joseph's 3% even though Scottish Teachers had received an offer of 4.5%. Once again Burnham was deadlocked, with Management able to block a reference to arbitration. Fred Smithies declared: "The whole Association is united by a sense of dismay and outrage that teachers should be so blatantly set up as targets for transparent exploitation."

The Special NASUWT Executive on 5 April duly initiated industrial action, instructing members to withdraw goodwill with immediate effect by refusing midday supervision and participating in staff, parents' and departmental meetings during the lunch break and outside normal school hours. In addition members were instructed to take a half-day national strike on 11 April. Support for the strike was overwhelming and set the tone for more action to follow.

The willingness to escalate to strike action, despite the saving it presented to the employers, was significant. Members were simply too angry and insisted on stronger protest. Also extremely significant was the participation of the NUT who on this occasion showed much more determination than in previous years.

Conference 1984, dominated by the pay dispute, insisted that there must be access to arbitration in default of an acceptable salary offer. It gave unanimous support to the Executive's action, which included a carefully drafted sentence which read: "Public examinations are not a target of NASUWT action but the Association cannot guarantee that industrial action during the Summer Term will not have some adverse effect on the examination system."

The plan of action included selective strike action, mass rallies and picketing of LEAs, no-cover action, and the lobbying of parents, local councils and Parliament as well as continuing the sanctions approved before Easter.

The selective strike action was highly significant. This was a tactic that had been developed by the Durham NASUWT Council under the leadership of its Secretary and National Executive Member, Mick Carney, during the long and bitter dispute with the LEA over deductions of pay for refusing to cover in protest against worsened staffing standards in 1983. Mick was destined to become National President and thereafter served as Honorary Treasurer for ten years. It involved a highly sophisticated system examining members' timetables and then bringing them out on strike for a few periods at a time in order to create maximum impact. It was very cost-effective and could be targeted at the constituencies of Government Ministers and key Management figures.

On 30 April Management finally made an open offer in full Burnham of 4½%. This time the Teachers' Panel stood firm and rejected the offer unanimously. The employers were rumoured to be divided, with the largely Labour-controlled AMA together with London favouring arbitration but overruled by the mostly Conservative ACC and of course the weighted 15 votes deployed by the two DES representatives.

The following day in the House of Commons Sir Keith Joseph repeatedly told MPs that it was "the trade union leaders who were fomenting unrest among teachers". He was horribly wrong. Indeed the NASUWT leadership was forced on 2 May by popular demand to involve more members in the action and to organise a national stoppage of one hour on 24 May, the tenth anniversary of the establishment of the Houghton Committee in 1974. The focus on 24 May with its mass meetings provided a series of unifying and rallying events with other teachers as well.

Meticulously prepared selective strike action started in May, focussing on Cambridgeshire, Cheshire, Hampshire, the Isle of Wight, Leeds and South Glamorgan. In Sir Keith Joseph's Leeds constituency 452 teacher half-day strikes had resulted in 25,000 children having to be sent home. Members were keen for their own schools to be included, and disappointed if they were not. With the withdrawal of goodwill and refusal to cover involving all NASUWT members, the action was proving very effective.

By June the selective strikes had spread, with 11 LEAs being targeted and more than 100,000 pupils per day having to stay away from school. In those LEAs that declared for arbitration the strike action was suspended and moved to other areas. NUT strikes were also proving effective and even the AMMA was providing modest supportive action in some places. The NAHT, in

Conference over the summer half-term break, took the unprecedented step of expressing solidarity with their mainly classroom-based colleagues taking action.

Despite all the aggravation over the 1984 pay claim the JWPSS held another weekend residential gathering in Plymouth, 3-5 June. Management Leader Phillip Merridale had often proclaimed in the Burnham dispute that teachers could solve their salary grievances through the WP. The NASUWT said it was high time Management showed the colour of their money, especially for the MGP maximum, but the meeting was 'all talk and no walk'.

Management finally conceded arbitration at the Burnham meeting on 22 June. In an uncharacteristically short meeting Management openly conceded that the pressure of the unions' action had forced arbitration on them. In welcoming the breakthrough the NASUWT said Sir Keith Joseph bore a heavy responsibility for the obvious "malign influence" he had exerted over the employers. All action was immediately brought to an end.

Arbitration finally took place in the last of July and lasted an unprecedented nine hours. The arbiters reported in September recommending an increase of 5.1%. Significantly, the arbitral report was signed only by the Chairman, indicating that the body was split and his vote had decided matters. Although 0.6% better than Management's final offer, Fred Smithies described the award as "disastrous. It just covers us for inflation but leaves us further down the average earnings league and will result in further demoralisation of teachers." Point 10 of the new Common Spine was set at £7,734.

Management denied that the award was a victory for them, citing many LEAs that had only budgeted for 3%. Ominously Fred Smithies concluded: "It can only result in the resumption of the pay struggle for the 1985 pay round, which will have to commence soon!"

Chapter 62 - The Great Disaster of 1985

The challenge facing the teachers' unions as 1985 approached was to devise a strategy to secure some restoration of comparative and absolute salary levels which were being so seriously eroded by the monetarist and anti-public sector policies of the Thatcher Government. The NASUWT believed that it was essential to embrace restructuring of the salary system as well as facing up to the problems over the teacher's contract. Merely making traditional demands of government and employers, even if supported by industrial action, would not be sufficient. The miners' year-long bitter strike (1983-84), which inflicted an estimated £8 billion worth of damage on the UK economy, had ended in defeat for the NUM. Where such a powerful union had failed, the teachers were the least likely to succeed.

To meet the huge challenge facing teachers, in September 1984 the Union published its policy on collegiality, emphasising the "central importance of the teacher in the classroom", which was the culmination of many years of radical thought and several reports presented to Annual Conferences over the years.

The collegiate approach advocated higher salaries for good classroom teaching and greater participation by teachers in the running of schools. There would be less need for the complicated and unnecessarily hierarchical superstructure of promoted posts, which had diminished the status of the most important job in schools – teaching in the classroom.

The NASUWT also realistically acknowledged that if teachers were to be properly remunerated for good teaching in its own right, management would want to ensure high quality was being delivered in the classroom. That could only be done by a process of assessment which we insisted had to be based on correct criteria and carried out in a fair and transparent way. Indeed we saw great benefits for classroom teachers in this collegiate approach over the old, discredited and increasingly threatened promotion system, heavily corrupted as it was by patronage and inconsistency.

The detail of the salary reform we advocated focussed on a two-year entry grade of £7,100 rising to £7,250 giving way to a main professional grade (MPG) from £8,000 to £16,500, achieved through ten annual increments of £850.

The NASUWT had also adopted a pragmatic and sensible approach to the contract, which did not ignore the concerns of the employers and indeed the Government. We recognised the need for clearer definition but insisted on satisfactory safeguards and protection against future erosion of pay. We also believed it was sensible to discuss pay and conditions together; indeed teachers' best interests were served by doing so, but it had to be done in a forum that was fit for purpose.

The NASUWT recognised that the Burnham structure WP (JWPSS) was the only channel through which teachers' unions could sensibly pursue such desirable reforms. The Union wished to work collaboratively with other unions and proposed an interim claim for 1985 if the restructuring talks could not be completed in time for 1 April. Such an interim claim should be the percentage increase in average non-manual earnings plus £500. That was deliberately constructed to cater for the career teacher but also appeal to the NUT through the element of £500 'flat rate'.

By October 1984 Fred Smithies was able to report and welcome the fact that the NASUWT and NUT, with the assistance of the TUC acting as honest broker, had decided to put their differences to one side and work together on the 1985 claim. At the Teachers' Panel meeting on 11 October agreement was reached in principle on the 1985 claim:

1 Reform of the present salary structure based on a professional scale for all teachers.

2 Reform of the promotion system.

3 Punctual payment in April of a staged payment such that no teacher received less than £1,200 increase.

While there was some historical significance in this claim as it was the first time the NUT had not forced through its own policy, it did not require a genius to spot that beneath this 'unity' lay several huge differences over how items 1 and 2 of the claim could be achieved. Nevertheless, the claim was immediately submitted to the Management to facilitate a prompt start to negotiations.

In Burnham on 1 November discussions began in a positive spirit as the Management acknowledged the increased demands on teachers and the structural problems. Management looked forward to the JWPSS meeting on 15 November to set out its thinking in greater detail. When the day came Management duly presented its document "A New Remuneration Structure for Teachers". The 'shape' of the structure certainly reflected NASUWT policy but the money was insufficient, particularly the maximum of the MPG set at only £11,800. The contractual strings were too onerous and the proposal to reintroduce compulsory midday supervision was out of the question. The NASUT recognised this was the 'first throw of the dice' and that much more discussion would be required. The NASUWT's initial conclusions were: "Too little money. Too many strings."

However, the NUT ran scared from the Management's proposals and then took a disastrous decision which was to have historic implications for all concerned. The NUT decided to walk out of the WP. I was substituting for Fred Smithies who was on vacation. Aware of the gravity of the NUT's decision and having witnessed at first-hand the filibuster over three years, I pleaded with the employers to continue with discussions, but they did not have the bottle to continue without the NUT.

Inter-union relations were not helped when we discovered that the NUT had made a prior decision to make its walkout permanent. No mention had been made of its plans despite a bilateral NASUWT–NUT meeting on 27 November. The following day the NUT confirmed in a press conference that its walkout was permanent and it intended to collapse the JWPSS. The next day it forced its position through the Teachers' Panel and informed the Management in full Burnham. Fred Smithies was flabbergasted to read NUT literature accusing the NASUWT of "completely abandoning the principles of Houghton" but decided with infinite statesmanship and patience not to respond publicly. On 5 December with one of its own in the Chair the NUT closed down the JWPSS refusing to allow further discussion despite numerous requests to speak from representatives of both sides.

Early in the new year the Government published its White Paper on public expenditure from 1985 to 1988, openly declaring it would continue to depress public sector pay. While the Government's exact position on finance for reform of teachers' pay and conditions remained uncertain, Sir Keith Joseph and the employers had made it crystal clear that new money was totally dependent on restructuring. By refusing to discuss these aspects of pay and conditions the NUT was sending the 1985 negotiations up a cul-de-sac.

In bilateral discussion with the NUT the NASUWT had been free and frank in laying out its strategy. We anticipated another difficult year and said we believed 1985 was not the year to make 'the big push' on Houghton restoration. Short sharp action similar to the previous year would likely be needed to get a settlement of some kind which should at least mark a small step forward. The 'big push', which would have to include restructuring, should await times closer to the next General Election, likely to take place in 1987.

Despite repeated requests to state their views the NUT remained uncharacteristically silent. I noticed they looked furtively at one another. One did not have to be an expert in body language to suspect something was up. It was obvious the NUT had different plans, if any, but was divulging nothing.

Immediately the structure talks were torpedoed by the NUT, the Management reverted to type. Delay and procrastination were back. The next meeting could not be arranged until 28 January, when the Management offered 4%. That was rejected. Management then offered to go to arbitration. This time it was the Teachers' turn to reject arbitration. That turned out to be the last chance to avoid disaster. Deadlock was back; industrial action inevitable.

More efforts were made during the course of February, mostly prompted by the Chairman of Burnham and the NASUWT, to explore ways in which restructuring could be reopened and additional government money found. The NUT repeatedly blocked the NASUWT efforts, insisting that pay and conditions of service had to be discussed separately.

With offers in excess of 4% already made to other local government workers and with teachers' relative pay down 35% since Houghton, the NASUWT declared the Burnham meeting on 25 February to be the make- or-break day. The Union's objectives for 1985 were a salary increase in excess of 7.5% (the movement in average earnings) and the resumption of the restructuring talks. Therein lay the contradiction vis-à-vis the NUT. We were supposed to be in joint action but there was a fundamental difference in respect of the two unions' tactics and objectives.

The plans for joint action then came under strain as the NUT jumped the gun, pre-empting intended discussions on co-ordination, and unilaterally announced plans for action. We were concerned and somewhat angry but maintained a public silence, not wishing to jeopardise the possibility of a joint campaign.

In another attempt to please others, this time keeping in step with TUC policy of opposing the industrial relations reforms of the Conservative Government, the Executive decided to continue to rely upon its traditional informal channels of communication with members rather than the prescribed pre-industrial action balloting required by the new legislation to retain union immunity from damages. Solihull LEA soon forced us to conduct a formal ballot on their patch. Later, in a different action, we were challenged after the event by Hereford and Worcester and following a court judgment in February 1988 settled the matter, paying £30,000 damages. We then adopted the required balloting practices despite all their anti-union bias and bureaucracy-laden procedures.

Deadlock persisted and on 26 February 1985 the NASUWT, beginning with a half-day national strike, embarked with the NUT on a course of action that was to have the most profound implications for the future of teacher trade unionism. Members were also instructed to withdraw goodwill by banning all management-initiated activities outside normal school sessions and to withdraw from supervision during the lunch break. Selective strike action, the highly cost-effective and extremely disruptive sanction which must have enraged Government and employers, was planned to start on 4 March.

Naturally a public and bitter debate broke out at the same time between union leaders, the employers and Government. The main Government spokesman was the Education Secretary, Sir Keith Joseph, the man with the huge intellect and the chief architect of the disastrous experiment with hard-line monetarism. While he never disguised his policies and was prepared to debate them openly in front of friend or foe, he came across as unyielding and unsympathetic and aroused an intense level of personal hatred from a huge section of the teaching profession.

Many employers sent threatening letters to individual teachers, claiming every aspect of their jobs was contractual. That served only to heighten tension and increase bitterness in the parallel 'dispute' that was ongoing in CLEA/ST over the teacher's contract. In an understatement of historic proportions the NASUWT declared that: "The lines are being drawn for what could be a long and bitter dispute."

During the remainder of the Spring Term selective strike action escalated to affect 28 LEAs. More confusion reigned following statements made by Sir Keith Joseph in Parliament and in the media debating with union leaders, including Fred Smithies, on the amount of new money available for restructuring. Action was also continuing in Scotland, although the NASUWT could not understand why the majority union, the EIS, was still refusing to quantify its claim for 1985.

Naturally the dispute dominated the proceedings at Conference. A motion from the Executive to continue and escalate the action was overwhelmingly carried. The mover of the motion, Honorary Treasurer Len Cooper from Yorkshire, delivered his finest speech in a long and distinguished career of service to the Union, using the format of an open letter to Sir Keith, inviting him to come into his classroom to witness the challenging job of teaching first-hand.

There was an impassioned debate on whether public examinations should be targeted. Whilst it was agreed to ban developmental work connected with the new GCSE, Conference backed the now standard formula that 'public exams were not a target . . . but no guarantees could be given'. An amendment "to use external examinations as a legitimate target" was lost on a counted vote of 576 against, 374 in favour.

Selective strikes were extended into 16 new areas whilst some took a break from the action. At any one time the practice became to ensure that it was ongoing in some 30 LEAs. In addition, after Conference all teacher-initiated activity outside normal school hours was also banned with effect from 28 April.

The NASUWT published a 20-page booklet entitled (and charting) *The Decline in Teachers' Pay*. It was very well received and sent to every MP. The stark, striking design on the front cover enabled me to be 'studying' it hard on several occasions as the TV cameras came into Burnham meetings to get background footage. Close-ups of the booklet featured strongly in the news bulletins, getting across the NASUWT message at peak viewing times much more cost-effectively than extremely expensive advertising advocated by some. The fundamental statistic showed that as a percentage of average non-manual salaries teachers' pay had declined from 137.2% in May 1974 to 108.3% in April 1984.

The action was placing the LEAs under severe pressure although Sir Keith Joseph appeared immune. After the unions' Easter Conferences the LEAs suggested 'talks about talks' on how both sides might jointly approach Government for additional cash. That was the first of several initiatives taken during the course of the Summer Term to make progress, all of which were vetoed by the NUT.

During the month of April in traditional fashion the NUT conspired to meet separately with one section of the Burnham Management Panel, namely the AMA employers, to cobble together a move which would result in an improved offer (4% 'plus') with no strings regarding restructuring. The forthcoming local government elections were expected to deliver a Labour majority on the Management Panel. The meeting might have been another example of the 'blurred lines' between the NUT leadership and the Labour Party.

At the resulting Teachers' Panel meeting on 29 April, the NASUWT stated it had no objection to the move but insisted such an offer had to be satisfactory, i.e. improve teachers' relative position, and had to be followed immediately by restructuring talks. All the other unions supported this position except inevitably the NUT who duly voted down the NASUWT proposal and forced through its own position. Meanwhile informal union–employer exchanges failed to set up a joint approach to the Government although the Management met separately with Sir Keith Joseph.

The ensuing Burnham meeting on 15 May marked another 'first'. The NUT permitted all unions to be included in the behind-the-chair talks which occupied most of the time. We soon discovered why. As Management pressed on how the Teachers would respond to 'say' 5% and then 6% as an interim measure with a clear recognition of the need to address restructuring, the NUT remained silent and it fell to Fred Smithies to say 'not enough'. The meeting ended inconclusively.

A resumed meeting on 23 May did produce an improved offer of 5% which was rejected along with a subsequent proposal to go to arbitration. Management was split three ways: the DES wanted to stick at 4%; the ACC would go to 5%; AMA beyond 5%. The stumbling block was always the NUT refusal to contemplate restructuring.

The NUT seemed impervious to any appeal to rationality, even apparently ignoring the announcement on 2 May by Sir Keith Joseph that he would be reviewing representation on the Teachers' Panel. Another offer of arbitration was also rejected by the Teachers', despite some reservations inside the NASUWT group. Fred Smithies also emphasised that teachers were still being paid on 1984 rates and the operative date for a new settlement, 1 April 1985, had come and gone. Furthermore the RPI had risen from 4.6% to 6.9%.

On 22 May Sir Keith Joseph finally clarified the Government's position, stating in a letter to LEAs that extra money could only be available for teachers' pay in 1986/87 subject to agreement on a restructuring package.

The local government elections in May had resulted in the Conservatives losing seats and in due course their majority on the Management Panel of Burnham. The new Leader was Nicky Harrison, a Labour councillor from Haringey representing the AMA. At the 3 July meeting most of the time was spent trying to agree a joint employer-union approach to Government. That left the two DES representatives with their weighted 15 votes under the 1965 concordat with a conflict of interest and they were soon to become 'semi-detached' members of the Management Panel.

Burnham on 3 July ended rather inconclusively. The summer vacation beckoned and the NASUWT Executive on 5/6 July set down plans to escalate the action in September. The ban on teacher-initiated activities would be suspended and replaced by selective strike action by all members, who would be expected to bear the loss of a half-day's salary themselves. Sensitive Parliamentary constituencies would be specially targeted.

In July, three significant events occurred. The LEAs repudiated the 1965 concordat with Government and the 15 votes it gave Sir Keith Joseph. This was to give the LEAs more freedom on manoeuvre in negotiations (if not in finance). The NALGO local government workers settled for 5.6% in one day. Burnham FE met on 15 July and the NATFHE settled for 5.8%, including some structural reform merging lecturer scales 1 and 2.

There was movement in Burnham on 16 July with an informal offer of 6% in return for a reduced Teachers' claim, but ultimately a very long day ended unproductively in the early hours of the following morning.

The NASUWT pressed for a meeting of Burnham to be requisitioned to take advantage of several developments including the 'Top People's' Review Body making generous awards. However, on 23 July the NUT quashed the idea and insisted instead on elevating the fourth principle of the Teachers' claim, a commitment to full Houghton in the future, as an absolute precondition for the 1985 settlement. (The three other well-known principles related to RPI, average earnings and an element of restoration.) No one else could understand the

NUT's insistence, for in the words of the new leader of the Management: "You could have those words tomorrow but they wouldn't be worth the paper they were written on" (as they had been in 1979). The NASUWT abstained in the vote. The full significance of the NUT move became apparent later.

Not content to let matters rest Fred Smithies sought a meeting with Sir Keith Joseph. The Minister agreed, subject to a curious stipulation that a classroom teacher should accompany the President, Joe Boone, and Fred. Not to allow relatively small representational matters to hinder more important things, Fred found a willing volunteer in Janet Maggs, a prominent London Association member, and the three went along to meet Sir Keith on 29 July. It was hard going and when Sir Keith repeated his offer of more money subject to restructuring he was told bluntly it was pointless to continue uttering an empty formula; figures were required upfront. The NASUWT left empty-handed – at least for a few days.

In rather dramatic circumstances the teachers' unions were telephoned on 5 August and urged to attend a meeting at the DES that very night to hear a very important statement from Sir Keith. Apparently responding to the NASUWT demand for figures, the Secretary of State called for an end to disruption. In return he would find money for teachers' pay but a package agreement had to be reached by October. The money would be additional to what would normally have been provided, amounting to an extra £200m in 1986/87, rising in broadly equal steps to a maximum of £480m in 1989/90. LEAs would have to bear their share of these costs.

There was undoubtedly movement but far too little. After the sums had been done Fred Smithies rejected the deal. Teachers would have to accept another pay cut in 1985 and wait until 1990 for a salary still some 25% short of the Houghton standard. The NUT also rejected the proposal.

Around the same time some private unofficial activity had also taken place. Two prominent members of the Executive, recently elected Junior Vice-President Eamonn O'Kane and one of the Inner London Representatives, Brian Jones, on their own initiative had a private meeting with Sir Keith Joseph and his special adviser, Stuart Sexton, briefing them on all the intricacies of union membership figures. Soon afterwards Sir Keith announced he would be reviewing the membership of the Burnham Committee. There was open speculation the NUT would lose its overall majority.

These events may have played a part in the extraordinary antics of the NUT in the Autumn Term of 1985. The NUT could see the other unions, led by the NASUWT, effectively taking over the responsibility for negotiations but not yet having the power to conclude agreements before the changes to Burnham were implemented. (They had to go through statutory procedures.)

By the Autumn Term 1985 the NASUWT had been forced into a re-evaluation of strategy, which was disclosed in a very long letter marked "Private and Confidential" to NASUWT School Reps from GS Fred Smithies. It referred to the divisions with the NUT sharpening; the need for a phased strategy with restructuring to apply maximum pressure at the right time (the run-up to a General Election); and to the "sheer madness in allowing 1985 to run into 1986 with teachers still paid on 1984 rates".

"We now find ourselves pursuing a strategy quite different from, and arguably in conflict with, that of the NUT," the letter continued. The difficult question asked by the media at the start of 1985 – how teachers could possibly succeed where the NUM had failed – had been resurrected with a vengeance following the NUT's futile precondition of 23 July.

The NASUWT now realised that its attempts to keep restructuring to the forefront of the 1985 dispute had been overtaken by the immediacy of the minimum £1,200 pay claim for the year and the unprecedented level of teachers' anger. In not stipulating that joint action would only be possible if the NUT returned to the JWPSS, the NASUWT had unwittingly ditched its restructuring ambitions but fully supported the NUT's side of the 'bargain' – the campaign for a minimum £1,200 for all for 1985. The reason for the NUT's reticence to share its strategy with us in our bilateral meetings back in January and February became apparent.

Effectively the NASUWT joined the NUT in its disastrous turn up the cul-de-sac created by its collapse of the JWPSS. The joint campaign with the NUT was about to end in tears and bitter recrimination as the NASUWT could no longer ignore the reality that restructuring had to be imported back onto the agenda for progress to be made.

The NASUWT leadership was soon to experience the worst time it ever had in terms of its relationship with grass roots members. As the inevitable unfolded, the NASUWT wanting a settlement, the NUT opposing everything no matter how irrational, some sections of our rank and file rebelled, joining in the NUT's accusation of sell-out.

Such was the deep anger felt by so many teachers against the Government that the NUT leadership simply indulged their members. The media were quick to point out the leaders were now having to ride their tigers, out of control. The NASUWT leadership determined to "tame the [NUT] tiger we now found ourselves riding". It caused us temporary embarrassment, but as soon as we faced the music in some stormy meetings around the country we convinced the overwhelming majority of our members that our approach was realistic and right and the NUT's bound to end in grief.

Many had simply not understood that the NASUWT and NUT had fundamental differences. The NASUWT leadership reflected ruefully that was the price of a spurious unity with the NUT. Irony of ironies, having tried to persuade the NUT to fight more militantly over many years, they were now going over the top, completely oblivious to where they were heading – towards self-destruction. I said at the time, "the NUT is giving industrial action a bad name".

Some in the NUT openly boasted they were giving the NASUWT 'the Terry Casey treatment'. Terry was sometimes accused of opposing everything just to attack the NUT. That analysis was simply wrong. On several occasions Terry had advocated arbitration as the only way out and had also supported moves for speedy settlements when more difficult conditions loomed around the corner. One or two wiser NUT people counselled their colleagues not to miss this opportunity to work with the NASUWT and seek to build a real unity. But the temptations were too great for some. However, as the wiser ones appreciated, their enjoyment could not last for ever and reality would eventually reassert itself.

Burnham resumed on 12 September with Management backsliding somewhat on previous 'hints behind the chair' but eventually asking whether 6.9% could get things moving again. This floundered when the employers insisted it be linked to restructuring courting the inevitable NUT veto.

The NASUWT put forward a constructive proposal for an increase of at least 6.9% for 1985 with endloading to achieve salary levels by March 1986 which exceeded the average earnings index for the period April 1984 to March 1985 and for discussions about restructuring without preconditions by either side with the intention of achieving Houghton restoration. The NUT vetoed the proposal and insisted on taking the Panel backwards. In addition to the veto on restructuring, the NUT was insisting on a further futile and 'impossible' precondition – the full Houghton commitment within the 1985 settlement.

Once again Burnham had reached an impasse. The NASUWT reissued its instructions for action and continued with selective strikes based on every member losing a half-day's salary during the two months of October and November.

Following the September breakdown, the Management Leader Nicki Harrison, a colourful character and risk taker, took an enterprising initiative and using her casting vote committed Management to offering "a straight – no strings attached" pay deal for 1985. The two DES reps took the unprecedented step of issuing a statement dissociating the Government from the decision. In effect Nicki Harrison was tearing up the 'concordat', overriding the Secretary of State's veto and weighted 15 votes. The Minister was then forced to return to the pre-1965 realities by exercising the Government veto from the outside. Once again Burnham was exposed as a sham negotiating machine.

Nicki Harrison then took another unprecedented step, publicly requesting more cash from Sir Keith, only to be bluntly refused. The NASUWT organised a protest rally outside the Conservative Party Conference being held in Blackpool shortly afterwards. Over 1,000 Lancashire members attended a rally and march addressed by Honorary Treasurer Len Cooper.

In October NASUWT escalated its action in respect of the planned new examination, the GCSE. Members were instructed to refuse: 1) to cover for teachers absent from school or class on work connected with the GCSE; 2) to participate in GCSE work outside normal school hours; and 3) to take part in phases 2 and 3 of the cascade in-service training due to begin in January 1986.

Burnham was not to meet again for over two months. The Teachers' Panel met on 16 October to consider an interesting 'no strings' offer of 6.9% rising to 7.5% by March 1986 from the employers, which, after being forced through on the casting vote of the Chair, AMA's Nicky Harrison, was communicated by post. While the NASUWT supported the rejection of the offer we proposed that negotiations be reopened in recognition of movement by the Management. True to form, all the other unions supported this proposal but the NUT voted it down, insisting on its futile precondition once again.

Fred Smithies accused the NUT of "playing politics with teachers' money". The NUT had conceded that the LEAs could not find anything beyond the 6.9% (7.5% endloaded) offer but still insisted on a 'Houghton restoration commitment' from the Management, which Nicki Harrison had already declared "would not be worth the paper it is written on".

Autumn 1985 also saw the crisis develop in Liverpool over the city's finances under the control of Militant Tendency members. Furthermore NASUWT members at the Poundswick School in Manchester were two weeks into a strike that was to last many months over the forced reinstatement of five pupils who had been expelled by the governors for painting disgraceful and obscene graffiti against named teachers on the walls of their school. The pressure on the NASUWT leadership, especially GS Fred Smithies, was enormous.

By October the futility of the NUT's approach plumbed new depths as it put out propaganda that its insistence on the 'commitment' proved it was the sole defender of 'Houghton'. The NASUWT reminded teachers that the NUT had opposed the establishment of Houghton in 1974 and constantly undermined it in every Burnham agreement it had reached thereafter.

With speculation in the media about an imminent removal of the NUT's overall majority, Fred Smithies warned against an assumption that the change would produce an early settlement. The requirements for RPI and no further erosion vis-à-vis average earnings would still be insisted upon by the NASUWT.

A historic day arrived on Friday 1 November 1985. The Secretary of State announced that membership of the Burnham Teachers' Panel would be changed. The new pattern of seats would be: the NUT 13, NASUWT 7, AMMA 4, NAHT 2, SHA 1 and PAT 1. NATFHE would lose its one remaining seat. The overall balance would be the NUT 13, others 15. The 67-year hegemony of the NUT over teachers' pay negotiations, set up with the establishment of the Burnham Committee in 1918, was at an end.

The routine November NASUWT Executive meeting also took place on this historic day in teacher union affairs. I delayed my attendance to stay in London to do a series of media interviews in which I welcomed the historic development which "would result in an outbreak of common sense in the Teachers' Panel".

The NASUWT Executive decided to go for a negotiated settlement of 1985, to put any agreement out to a ballot of the membership and begin immediately to lay plans for the next (1986) phase of the campaign for restoration. Following requests from a number of local associations, the Executive also agreed to hold a Special Salary Conference on 18 January 1986.

The NASUWT then masterminded plans for the internal reforms on the Teachers' Panel. There would be two spokesmen, one each from the NASUWT and NUT. All unions would be represented behind the chair. All organisations could speak in Burnham if the circumstances so justified. A Working Party would be established to consider arrangements for an Independent Secretariat. The new Chairman would be Geoff Beynon of AMMA, and the new Honorary Secretary David Hart of NAHT.

A few days before the Teachers' Panel meeting scheduled for 11 November the NASUWT and NUT met at the latter's HQ, Hamilton House, near Euston Station. The NASUWT discussed its plans for revised arrangements inside the Teachers' Panel with positions and jobs shared equitably. Despite being post-prandial the meeting was far from convivial as foul-tempered NUT representatives accused us of doing dirty deals with non-TUC unions and entering "unholy alliances". Fred Smithies dismissed and regretted these "unnecessary and insulting public slanders", insisting the NASUWT would continue to judge issues on their merits and negotiate sensibly in the best interests of teachers. In a prophetic mode Fred predicted that if Burnham "fails to improve its track record in the very near future it will have to be abolished".

The meeting of the Teachers' Panel on 11 November was a historic occasion, with the NUT for the first time not in overall majority. The NASUWT proposed reopening negotiations, noting the offer of 14 October (6.9% endloaded to 7.5%) while improved was still unacceptable. Two matters conspired to allow the NUT to maintain the status quo and frustrate the will of the new majority. While the reduction in the NUT representation had taken effect on 1 November, the removal of the NATFHE did not operate until 2 December. Then PAT, in an extraordinary move, decided to abstain on the NASUWT's proposal. The NUT openly prodded the NATFHE, who rightly wished to abstain, into voting against the motion. The motion was tied 14-14. The newly elected Chairman, AMMA's GS Geoff Beynon, declared the motion "not carried", declining with characteristic impartiality to exercise a casting vote in such controversial circumstances with uncertain standing orders. Long accustomed to the NUT overall majority, the Teachers' Panel standing orders had never entertained anything like a tied vote!

Fred Smithies condemned PAT, which by its inexplicable abstention would maintain the industrial action it so piously deplored. Fred found it "even more galling" that NATFHE (with no members in schools), who settled for a much lower pay rise in the FE sector, should use its disappearing vote to hinder negotiations for primary and secondary teachers. Fred Smithies concluded by observing that "the Panel has been blown open by a healthy blast of democracy", and he was "confident that once NATFHE loses its vote sensible progress will be made". The NUT escalated its attacks on the NASUWT, accusing us of preparing a sell-out and abandoning 'Houghton'.

The Teachers' Panel met on 5 December. The NASUWT motion which had been stymied on 11 November was reintroduced and this time carried by 15 votes to (the NUT's) 13. Fred Smithies observed that the NUT's preoccupation with words and preconditions had proved "sterile and unproductive" in wasting opportunities and preventing any resumption since Management made its improved offer of '6.9%-endloaded-7.5%' on 14 October. The NASUWT would not be stampeded into poor agreements; the RPI/average earnings/element of restoration criteria remained essential.

By December 1985 NASUWT membership had reached a record 127,203, up from 126,435 over the previous year. That was a very commendable achievement bearing in mind the difficulties and pressures often generated upon individuals by management during times of industrial action.

With a more balanced representation of the teaching profession things immediately began to move more constructively. A 'behind-the-chair' Burnham meeting was arranged for 17 December, with all the unions represented. The teachers agreed to act on the basis that the 6.9-7.5% offer was still on the table. After cagey opening exchanges Nicky Harrison said 6.9% was fixed; the endloaded figure depended entirely upon Government assistance. Management pressed the Teachers' to stipulate what figure they had in mind for the endloaded element. The Teachers' withdrew.

By this time there was open discussion of Government intervention in Burnham, possibly imposing its own settlement, even abolishing the Committee. Fred Smithies asked Fred Jarvis what the NUT had in mind and how it intended to deal with the Government threats. Jarvis was uncommunicative and evasive. Fred Smithies took the initiative, proposing the Teachers' stipulate 9.9% for the endloaded element. Did anyone object? No.

Back in joint session Management said 8% was the maximum on which they (hopefully jointly with the Teachers') would approach the Government. Other alternatives, including arbitration, an independent inquiry (also favoured by the Labour Party) and a reference to ACAS, were discussed. The talks ended without agreement but with a much improved atmosphere between the two sides. Both sides agreed to meet early in January.

On 19 December the NASUWT and NUT met at the TUC under the chairmanship of its GS, Norman Willis, since a reference to ACAS had emerged as the favoured alternative. A statement was agreed and issued saying that "both unions intended to work as closely as possible . . . and will consider a positive response to the invitation from ACAS that both sides of Burnham should meet with ACAS for informal exploratory talks".

Chapter 63 – Burnham begins to Topple

The year 1986 got off to a difficult start with the NUT resiling from the TUC statement and insisting it would only deal with ACAS separately. Pleas to reconsider and practise some 'unity' fell on deaf ears. In a bad-tempered Teachers' meeting the following day (7 January) belligerent NUT members objected to the floating of 9.9% behind the chair as the endloaded figure despite its GS having been present and not objecting even when invited to do so.

Despite fierce opposition from the NUT the NASUWT proposal to accept the invitation from ACAS "in order to explore the present position and any possible avenues for the resolution of the dispute" was carried on the now customary 15:13 majority.

The Teachers' Panel minus the NUT met with ACAS that same afternoon. Fred Smithies outlined the history of the dispute. Sir Pat Lowry, Chairman of ACAS, stressed the independence of his organisation, its flexible procedures and neutrality between the two sides. ACAS had "no money of its own" but it could persuade others to find some and had done so in the past. ACAS would listen to all points of view before deciding whether it could assist.

As we were departing we discovered Fred Jarvis holding forth in the press room ignoring Sir Pat Lowry's plea for a cessation of public hostilities and announcing the NUT would boycott the ACAS talks. And so another huge row broke out between the unions in full view of the media gathered in numbers at the impressive ACAS building in London's St James's Square. The NASUWT said it would hand a massive propaganda victory to the Government if the unions refused ACAS's offer of help. It was "sheer stupidity" to allow the 1985 dispute to run into 1986. Better to pocket '85, get on with '86 and resume action if necessary. ACAS could provide us with a more sensible forum to achieve this, unlike the collapsing Burnham machinery. ACAS soon announced it would be holding conciliation meetings with both sides on 14 January.

The NUT threatened to continue action if the Teachers' Panel reached a negotiated settlement. We reminded the NUT that the NASUWT had consistently respected majority decisions, lifting action when agreements had been reached even if we did not like them. We looked to the NUT to respect the same democratic principles. Pending agreement with the help of ACAS on the 1985 claim, the NASUWT would continue with action and issued further instructions for selective strikes for the months of February and March on the basis of each member sacrificing half-a-day's pay.

In February, notwithstanding all the disunity over ACAS, the two TUC unions managed a joint statement on action relating to the planned new GCSE examination. The points of action were not identical but very similar. The statement opened with a frank admission of other differences. However, there was "total agreement in rejecting the sheer effrontery of the Secretary of State's expectation that teachers will undertake the massive amount of additional work required to prepare for and implement the new GCSE examinations whilst their salaries remain so deplorably low".

On 14 January a series of encounters took place with ACAS meeting the two Panels separately, with one 'plenary' session involving all the parties. The NUT boycotted the Teachers' meetings but attended the joint session with Management and ACAS.

The Teachers' Panel had to disabuse Sir Pat on his apparent belief that Sir Keith Joseph was prepared to make an extra £1.25 billion available for restructuring. That figure was simply a cumulative amount over four years. The real final annual additional sum was £450m. Sir Pat, for his part, wanted to know if the Teachers' could conclude an agreement without the NUT. 'Yes' was the resounding answer that came forth.

Most of the afternoon was spent by the Management in session with Sir Pat, whilst we ate our ACAS sandwiches and went for walks! Just after 5 p.m. Sir Pat was able to report to the Teachers' that Management would drop some strings but still showed no sign of improving their latest informal offer. A resumption of structure talks would obviously help. The Management was adamant on two points for an agreement. All industrial action would have to cease (including the NUT's) and the details worked out beforehand so Burnham would simply be a formality.

The day ended shortly afterwards with the NASUWT reasonably content without being overly optimistic. Fred Smithies said he had picked up an unmistakeable message – that if we could not find a way around the constitutional problem the Secretary of State would drastically reform Burnham.

I kept an eye on the press room situated just inside the entrance on the ground floor. Despite Sir Pat's repeated pleas to refrain from unhelpful comment to the press I saw and heard Fred Jarvis holding forth on "the NUT's determination not to betray their members".

The pace ACAS set was refreshing after the tortuous machinations of Burnham. We were all back at ACAS the very next day. Sir Pat Lowry and Denis Boyd, ACAS Chief Conciliator, came to the Teachers' Panel shortly after 11 a.m. to outline areas of 'agreed concern' and map out some possible ways forward. They identified the need to restructure, the recognition of inadequate pay levels and the need to settle 1985 quickly and separately. Sir Pat was encouraged by what he had read about the JWPSS believing there was much in common. He acknowledged the problem of funding and floated the idea of a new deal for teachers with problems identified and agreed principles to solve them.

Sir Pat suggested an independent presence, neither arbitrator nor mediator, who would "advise, assist and counsel", set targets and report back to ACAS, Burnham and Government. ACAS might arbitrate on issues as developments unfolded. He said that if 1985 were settled and if restructuring were to stand a chance, a period of peace in the schools would be essential.

The Teachers' (minus the NUT) withdrew to consider the proposals. By mid-afternoon a consensus in favour of ACAS producing a draft preamble was reached. Receiving the news Sir Pat confided to us that his ideas had gone down "like a lead balloon" with the NUT. He said he had again pleaded with the NUT to rejoin the Panel. The NUT was placing ACAS in a very difficult position and Management was deterred from improving its offer in the light of the NUT boycott and threat to continue action regardless. The Management had received his ideas as "interesting and constructive" and would probably request an adjournment to consult more widely. Significantly, he had persuaded Management to consider improving their offer to the Teachers'.

Sir Pat returned later in the afternoon to ask us if we were still prepared to proceed without the NUT. 'Yes' was the answer. Management, as expected, then requested an adjournment until the following week, which was agreed. Despite ACAS's request for confidentiality to give the talks a chance to get off the ground, I was telephoned later in the evening at home by a journalist checking out Sir Pat's ideas in every detail. Malicious and false rumours were already spreading that the NASUWT had agreed to call off its industrial action.

A few days later on Saturday 18 January at Warwick University the NASUWT held a Special Salaries Conference. The Executive's policy and conduct of the dispute was overwhelmingly supported. In particular the Conference approved the leadership's moves to seek an interim settlement for the 1985 dispute with the help of ACAS and to allow "a period of peace" to allow restructuring and restoration talks to get under way and succeed. The Union's claim for 1986 put forward by the Executive and emphasising the collegiate philosophy in the running of schools was also approved. At the same time provision was made for industrial action if the talks failed, which would see selective strike action on a larger scale than before as well as the customary withdrawal of goodwill and ban on cover. However, an amendment from the floor to regard examinations as a legitimate target for action was narrowly defeated on a card vote by 59,538 to 55,130.

Everyone reconvened at ACAS on 21 January with the 'semi-detached' NUT on standby at their Hamilton House HQ, in case of developments. Sir Pat Lowry announced ACAS would table a document separately in each Panel.

Sir Pat introduced his document to the Panels separately before laying copies around each table. It was quite promising from the Teachers' viewpoint. The preamble declared the two basic aims: settling 1985, and charting a way forward for the future. There followed three appendices. The 'beef' was in Appendix B, which set out objectives and principles for the future. It described three main problems: inadequate salary levels, outdated structure and lack of agreement on the contract. As objectives it highlighted the need: to attract and retain sufficient people of the right quality, to improve the status of the classroom teacher, to establish fair comparisons with salaries available elsewhere in education and the professions, to make arrangements for appraisal and training and clearly to define teachers' duties and responsibilities.

Individual unions separated for their own discussions. The NASUWT quickly decided the order was important and it had to be 1985 first. The Union's Reps were also pleased with Section B, seeing that it contained much of our collegiate philosophy, recognising the central importance of the teacher in the classroom. It even made reference to Fred Smithies' point about FE lecturers having a minimum expectation of £13,000 salary p.a.

There was a crucial omission in the need for overall limits if duties and responsibilities were to be defined more clearly in a new contract. The 'period of peace and calm' was another problem, but it could be facilitated by a payment on account for 1986. The NASUWT decided its timetable would be: 1985 agreement, followed by ballot on acceptance of NASUWT membership which if positive would lead to cessation of industrial action one day before formal rubber-stamping in Burnham.

The Teachers' Panel reconvened at the end of the morning to discover a remarkable degree of consensus along the lines I have already described in respect of the NASUWT 'caucus'. Frank Mills for the NAHT was gracious enough to pay tribute to Fred Smithies' statesmanship and the NASUWT's positive policies despite the "high risks" associated with the NUT's propaganda and recruitment drive. The NAHT and AMMA also wished to raise particular points of concern they had and there was no 'one voice' preoccupation to prevent them.

The Teachers' Panel was ready within the hour to invite Sir Pat and Denis Boyd back to hear their response. Speaking for the Teachers', Fred Smithies said they were prepared to enter broad discussions on a without-prejudice basis, subject to some amendments which he then outlined.

The exchanges were very positive, ACAS agreeing that it might be better to delete formal naming of the negotiating machines to help everyone. Sir Pat observed that in all his considerable experience he had never before come across the separation of pay and conditions as exemplified in Burnham and CLEA/ST. Despite NUT protest, Denis Boyd said that to avoid premature press comment ACAS would not pass the document to that union. The NUT was free to rejoin the discussions, whereupon it would of course have access to the document.

The NAHT raised some objections to some aspects of lunchtime supervision whilst AMMA was extremely concerned about differentials in some of the restructuring proposals. The Teachers' set up a small group to draft suggested amendments.

Shortly after 7 p.m. Sir Pat returned to tell us that Management had also submitted amendments – and the gulf was widening! ACAS would formally withdraw its document and reconsider matters in the light of developments. He said it would require a few days adjournment.

On 24 January the Teachers' Panel reconvened, to be greeted by a letter threatening court action by the NUT. The NUT demanded a copy of the ACAS document tabled on 21 January. Irony of ironies, the NUT quoted the court case in which PAT had successfully established the right of all organisations to receive relevant Burnham documentation which the NUT had had denied it! The Panel "noted" the NUT's request, believing the document was the property of ACAS, which had now withdrawn it.

Addressing a plenary session Sir Pat said he had become quite pessimistic at the end of the previous Tuesday with all the 'opposing' amendments pushing the two sides further apart. However, on reflection he had recognised there was agreement on the procedure for the future, which needed to be retained. He suggested the contentious areas of Appendix B be substantially amended. The document in its new form constituted a draft agreement. Then came the blunt message. Both sides could resume 'competitive amending' and drift further apart to inevitable breakdown. All the agreed areas of Tuesday would then be lost. Sir Pat's message was simple. It was this draft or nothing. The choice was ours!

The Teachers' Panel met immediately after the plenary session. Fred Smithies was blunt. First, any organisation not taking industrial action had no option but to accept the new draft. Fred said the redraft did far more damage to the Management's position than to the Teachers'. The timetable previously agreed had to be maintained and Fred anticipated one or two dummy offers from the Management for 1985 before a final one would be unveiled.

The unions then separated. Inside the NASUWT there was quick consensus on Fred Smithies' analysis. The draft Memorandum of Agreement retained all the 'good beef' of the first draft including 'take account of responsibilities and salaries elsewhere' (a softer euphemism for pay comparability) and 'defined limitations' on the contract. It committed everyone to negotiate constructively and expeditiously to achieve such ends.

On future procedures, ACAS would establish an impartial panel to guide and assist and to control the programme and procedure of negotiations, with a view to early resolution of differences. ACAS would provide the Secretariat. After a period of six months the panel would review its work in a final report to both sides and ACAS on any outstanding key issues with formal recommendations on how such problems should be resolved.

On industrial action the unions would undertake "immediate steps with a view to cessation and a return to full normal duties". The parties to this agreement would take it to their constituents for ratification as appropriate and then to adopt it in Burnham and CLEA/ST. The section on the settlement for 1985 was, naturally at this stage, devoid of figures.

The NASUWT delegation appreciated how much of the 'career teacher-collegiate approach' was reflected in the draft agreement.

Back in the Teachers' Panel, minus of course the NUT – still refusing almost daily pleadings to return – there was quick agreement on the same lines as the NASUWT had reached. Shortly after midday Fred Smithies was able to inform Sir Pat that subject to a satisfactory improved offer from Management on 1985, the Teachers' Panel would accept the ACAS Memorandum of Agreement.

At the start of the afternoon the three Teachers' Panel Officers, Fred Smithies, Geoff Beynon and David Hart, began informal talks with Sir Pat over a 1985 settlement. Reporting back soon afterwards Fred said Sir Pat had floated the idea of 7% for 1985 and a 3% payment on account from 1 April 1986. We did not know if Management or Sir Pat had floated the idea, but it was rejected and the Panel endorsed the decision.

We got an indication that 'things were happening' when the NUT (still boycotting despite repeated requests to relent) was asked to put someone on standby to be briefed. Sir Pat said he would be writing officially to the TUC to assist. It was quite unprecedented for the Chairman of ACAS to act in this way. The TUC was a member of ACAS.

By teatime Management made another offer informally 'behind the chair' through Sir Pat that would produce 6.9% for the year and an endloaded base up by 8% to start in 1986. Sir Pat added the offer had been made with "serious anxiety", "heavy heart" and "worried to death about the cost consequences".

That was quickly rejected by the Panel, standing firm on the absolute necessity of ensuring all teachers received a significant rise above the average earnings of 7.5%. Management had to drop the flat-rate element (perhaps put there to entice the NUT back). Management moved a little but not enough. A long night loomed as Fred Smithies reported back on informal talks with the Management. He had threatened collapse of the talks unless Management could meet the cardinal principle of 8.5% endloaded for all.

Soon after 8 p.m. Sir Pat returned to ask, beaming all over his face, "How does 6.9% from 1 April 1985 and 1.6% from 31 March 1986 [added to the 31 March 1985 scales and attaining the 8.5% endloaded figure] strike you?"

All teachers' organisations present immediately indicated agreement. Sir Pat and Denis Boyd left to draft the final agreement for the plenary session with the Management. The Teachers' thanked Fred Smithies for his negotiating skills and determination.

By 9.30 p.m. the final plenary session was under way and agreement quickly registered. Everyone thanked everyone else. Sir Pat, Nicky Harrison and Fred Smithies moved downstairs to front the press conference announcing the agreement.

As the press conference was well under way a familiar but forlorn figure appeared. Straining his neck around the crowd at the back of the room, striving to see what was going on was Fred Jarvis of the NUT. I wished I had carried a camera to record the scene. It encapsulated the demise of the NUT as the majority teachers' union better than any words could have done.

The ACAS Memorandum of Agreement effectively re-established the business of the JWPSS. The rigidities of Burnham were cast to one side. The 1985 dispute could be drawn to a close. The NUT had been outflanked. Instead of relentless industrial action the teaching profession was presented with the prospect of positive progress.

The NASUWT was quick to point out it was the first pay settlement for over a decade which had actually improved teachers' relative position to average earnings. It had improved on the employers' "absolutely final offer" (6.9%) and was the best settlement across the entire local authority sector. NASUWT members were to be balloted on acceptance of the deal.

As expected the NUT propaganda headed "Bleak Friday" went overboard, suffused as it was with the words "shoddy surrender", "sell-out" and "capitulation", all of which could have well described the majority of the agreements it had negotiated over so many years, the proof of which lay in the massive salary erosion about which it had complained so violently but mostly done so little. NUT complaints about the absence of comparability principles, a no-strike deal and 'worsened conditions of service' suggested they had not read the Memorandum of Agreement, or if they had, something worse. The NUT announced it would ballot its members on continuing action in the event of the agreement being ratified. Fred Smithies deplored such an anti-democratic intention to defy the majority vote on the Teachers' Side.

The NASUWT naturally put out reports – "Getting the facts straight" – and challenged the NUT to say what it would do if this opportunity were rejected. The NUT had no alternative but indefinite industrial action in 1986 and beyond, with teachers still paid at 1984 rates.

The NASUWT Executive unanimously endorsed the actions of its representatives at the earliest opportunity (Monday 27 January) and strongly recommended the membership to vote 'yes' in the ballot on the ACAS Memorandum of Agreement. It met the RPI, average earnings and step towards restoration criteria, putting over £300m into teachers' pockets and presaging a brighter future with restructuring back on the agenda.

Conversely a negative vote would mean resorting to indefinite industrial action against LEAs with no more money, as the NUT conceded, whilst the Government remained totally hostile, determined to release no money without restructuring. We would expend yet more militancy chasing the difference between 8.5% in the bag and the 1985 claim of 12%, which was itself incapable of resolving the Houghton erosion. We would be handicapping ourselves fighting two claims at the same time (1985 and 1986). We would be jeopardising teacher trade unionism and inflicting yet more 'collateral' damage on the education service.

Despite all the anger still felt in the teaching profession, the arguments in favour of the deal were overwhelming and got through to the majority of teachers. NASUWT members voted by a majority of two to one in favour: 43,899 (69%) 'yes' and 20,407 (31%) 'no'. Turnout was 58% of those eligible to vote. (The Electoral Reform Society informed the Union that over 11,000 ballot papers had been received after 21 February despite having postmarks significantly prior to that closing date. While the percentages in favour and against would not have been altered, the turnout figure would have been considerably improved.)

Fred Smithies described the result as a "convincing endorsement of the National Leadership's strategy over the past 12 months, a period fraught with Government obstinacy, financial impotence on the Employers' Side and, latterly, irresponsible and negative behaviour from the NUT".

A meeting of Burnham was set for 28 February to ratify Section 2 of the ACAS Agreement (the part dealing with the pay settlement for 1985). Prior to the Teachers' Panel the NASUWT met to hear a report from Fred Smithies that he had been busy until 3 a.m. the previous night at ACAS dealing with serious Management concerns with continuing no-cover action and bitter disputes over letters threatening pay deductions involving all three classroom-based unions. The NUT court case further complicated the situation. Management was taken aback by the ferocious tone of the NASUWT local Officers demanding the withdrawal of the letters. AMMA members were trying to get away with one-day cover, the position established de facto during the industrial action, in which they had not officially participated. The LEAs were so upset as to threaten the non-ratification of the ACAS deal in Burnham.

Fred had checked the NASUWT position on the full "return to normal duties" and Sir Pat Lowry believed the Union had met its obligations in withdrawing all the instructions for action. Voluntary duties remained as such, as they were before the dispute. The crisis was resolved by publishing a statement from the signatory unions confirming that all instructions and advice issued in connection with the 1985 pay dispute had been or would be withdrawn forthwith so that the position reverted to that in force before the dispute began.

Our hopes for a speedy despatch of business to clear the way for 1986 and restructuring were distracted as the Teachers' Panel began the stormiest meeting it was ever to have. While everyone had expected some form of protest from the NUT, none of us had appreciated the depths of rancour and sheer ineptitude to which the NUT was determined to stoop. For the whole of the morning the NUT pursued wrecking tactics, raising petty points about the order of the agenda, the accuracy of minutes of meetings they had boycotted and the procedural decisions of the Chairman, Geoff Beynon of AMMA, a real gentleman of the old school who was scrupulously fair to friend and foe alike. The proceedings made Prime Minister's question time in the House of Commons look like the proverbial vicar's tea party. Every time, the NUT was voted down by 14:13 majority, the Chairman, scrupulously impartial as ever, abstaining.

It was gone midday before we were finally able to get down to the business of the day, ratification of the 1985 pay deal in Burnham. Fred Smithies moved the Teachers' agreed to a settlement of the 1985 pay claim on the basis set out in Section 2 of the ACAS Memorandum of Agreement. Fred referred briefly to the main arguments, all of which had been batted to death across the media. He challenged anyone present to refer to a better negotiated settlement in Burnham over the past 20 years.

The NUT belligerently asked lots of questions about other unions' positions, totally ignoring how more pertinent they were to their own. The most notable was how were we going to extract more than the £450m per annum additional money Sir Keith Joseph had offered, a rich question to ask when the NUT's refusal to discuss restructuring made it 'more impossible'! Perhaps the only realistic NUT contribution to the debate came from Peter Griffin, who conceded that for many years Burnham had betrayed the interests of teachers but disclaimed sole NUT responsibility, alleging we all shared it. Towards the end of the debate Joe Boone, President of the NASUWT, reminded everyone that the Panel's claim for 1985 had amounted to 12%, a long way from full restoration of Houghton which mysteriously had in the process become the NUT's position.

With lunchtime already upon us a closure motion had to be moved to clear the way for a vote. Amid more acrimony that was carried by 15:13 as was the motion to accept the 1985 pay settlement as outlined in the ACAS Agreement. The Teachers' Panel then adjourned for lunch and its own badly needed "period of peace and calm".

Hostilities resumed immediately upon resumption after Joe Boone for the NASUWT moved the second motion required for the day: "This Panel recommends the adoption by the Burnham Committee of the Memorandum of Agreement reached in ACAS, the Parties to the Agreement having already ratified it."

That was the cue for more NUT challenges claiming the motion to be 'ultra vires' Burnham because it dealt with conditions of service. That required an adjournment to consult the Chairman, Sir John Wordie, who duly ruled the matter under consideration dealt solely with pay.

The time was well past 6 p.m. when Joe Boone, as the mover of the motion several hours before for anyone with a good memory, replied to the debate in the briefest possible way, not wanting to aid and abet the filibuster. The motion requesting Burnham to adopt the ACAS pay deal was duly carried 15:13.

Shortly afterwards Sir John Wordie appeared in the shadows of the entrance to the room, wanting a word with the Panel Officers. One hour later we learnt that Sir John was 'adjourning' the Burnham meeting (it had never started) until 3 March for two reasons. Management leaders had still not sold the '3 a.m.' statement to their Panel, and the threat of injunction loomed from the NUT. The ACAS Agreement was in double jeopardy.

I recorded in my final paragraph reporting on the day's extraordinary events to NASUWT Executive Members and Local Secretaries that the alternatives to ACAS openly speculated upon by many people present were intervention by the Secretary of State to impose conditions of service on Burnham or to abolish "the whole darn Committee, lock, stock and barrel".

With Burnham due to meet in the afternoon, the NASUWT spent the morning of 3 March in a special meeting with Management Leader and Deputy, Nicky Harrison and John Pearman. The purpose of the meeting was stark and simple – to save the ACAS Agreement. We were told they had failed to sell the 3 a.m. statement. Many LEAs remained deeply unhappy with the situation on the ground. Fred Smithies repeated the NASUWT's refusal to tell members to carry out voluntary duties.

After several withdrawals by both sides a text was agreed which committed everyone to advising their constituents to minimise the difficulties and not to take any action which would exacerbate the problems so long as the ACAS talks continued. It was clear that without a solution there would be no pay deal for 1985. The whole ACAS initiative would collapse.

The Burnham meeting scheduled to start at 2 p.m. was delayed for four hours as both Panels sorted out problems with the amended 3 a.m. statement, some more soothing if largely uncontroversial words finally doing the trick. That was except for the NUT who announced they would be boycotting further discussions in the Teachers' Panel.

Shortly before 6 p.m. Burnham finally met! Chairman Sir John Wordie recorded the changed composition of the Teachers' Panel, the reduction in NUT seats to 13 and the dismissal of NATFHE. Fred Jarvis registered the NUT's objections, saying that the Secretary of State "had abused his powers and reached partisan decisions". Sir John graciously thanked the outgoing NUT team of Leader, Chairman and Secretariat and welcomed the new one. Nicky Harrison and Fred Smithies associated themselves with the Chairman's comments. Fred Jarvis thanked people for their comments and concluded in prophetic mode: "The NUT is still alive and kicking and who knows what the future holds?"

By 6 p.m. Nicky Harrison was at long last able formally to offer the Teachers' the 'ACAS' increase for 1985. She hoped the ACAS talks would start that Friday, 7 March, and that CLEA/ST would adopt the Agreement when it met the day before.

Fred Smithies indicated the Teachers' acceptance, referring briefly to some of the most promising aspects of the ACAS talks, highlighting the "central importance of the teacher in the classroom". Fred paid tribute to the work of Sir Pat Lowry and his ACAS colleagues and reminded everyone of the sobering thought that the 1986 pay round was only four weeks away!

Fred Smithies concluded his remarks by indicating that another union, the NUT, wished to present its view and referred to the generosity of the new Teachers' Panel in granting this right to those that had for years denied it to others. Fred Jarvis tested the spirit of generosity to (and many would say beyond) the limit, going on for nearly one hour rehearsing all the NUT grievances which had already been considered at length and rejected by democratic majority.

On several occasions the Chairman interrupted Jarvis, making quite pertinent and blunt comment in a way I had never seen him do to anyone in Burnham before. The most patient and likeable of chairpersons I experienced in all my years in the business had clearly had enough of pointless point making. He contradicted Jarvis, saying the wording of the Agreement was correct, referring as it did to the majority of teachers' organisations. Although Jarvis had cited the reference to the Clegg Commission in 1979 in support of the NUT's grievances, Sir John thought the involvement of ACAS was similar. There had been no decisions on conditions of service here in Burnham. Sir John concluded: "In my view ACAS is the only avenue forward."

Jarvis attempted to resume his speech. Sir John interrupted and spoke over him, asking if all the parties to the Agreement had ratified it. "Yes" came from both the Panels. Had both Panels adopted the Burnham Agreement? "Yes" again. Were both Panels agreeable to him transmitting Section 2 to the Secretary of State? Again came the answers "Yes".

Despite Sir John's intervention Jarvis persisted. Surprisingly he conceded that the settlement represented "a modest improvement in teachers' pay" thereby contradicting his own union's propaganda. When Jarvis claimed that comparability had been abandoned Sir John referred him to the words of the ACAS Agreement "taking account of salaries elsewhere". "What is that if it is not comparability?" asked Sir John in exasperation.

By the time Jarvis finished his speech he was being received with a mixture of disdain and derision from all sides, save of course the NUT contingent. The Chairman quickly brought proceedings to an end, quoting from the prophet Isaiah on teachers, adversity and a democratic society! Sir John wished all those who were to participate in the ACAS talks "the best of luck". Shortly after 7.15 p.m. on 3 March 1986, Burnham 1985 came to an end.

The NASUWT immediately withdrew all instructions for action connected to the pay dispute. Instructions for action in respect of the GCSE remained in force as they concerned the Government in a different dispute.

Chapter 64 - Restructuring Resurrected

At a meeting on 4 March the Teachers' Side of CLEA/ST split into two over serious disagreements on representation and rights to the offices of Chair and Secretary. The ACAS signatory unions decided to withdraw with the exception of AMMA.

Thus there were two 'teachers' side' pre-meetings called for CLEA/ST on 6 March, one by the majority of unions, another by the NUT trying to insist on its traditional role. The NUT claimed an overall majority despite such matters never having been agreed and the recent Burnham representation changes which were the only available and credible adjudication which carried some objectivity. After its little 'wobble' AMMA decided to stay with the ACAS signatory unions. Each organisation would indicate its assent to the Agreement, thereby committing the majority of unions to discuss conditions of service in the ACAS exercise.

The joint meeting began with the Management withdrawing to allow the Teachers' Side to settle an internal dispute over the presence of PAT. The Chair, Bob Richardson of NUT (and controversially in that position) was rather foolishly trying to maintain the exclusion of PAT. A compromise was reached and Management returned to hear Peter Dawson, GS of PAT, make a short statement before withdrawing, cleverly indicating during the course of it that he wished to indicate PAT's desire to adopt the ACAS Memorandum of Agreement in CLEA/ST and to have this recorded in the minutes. That was all most of us were there for!

So we moved on to the crunch issue of the day, the adoption of the ACAS Agreement in CLEA/ST. There followed the most bizarre 'no you can't, yes we can' episode. The NUT proclaimed 'no' because it had the overall majority on the Teachers' Side. Management proclaimed it hereby endorsed the Agreement in CLEA/ST as did all the signatory unions. The 'highlight' of the debate was an emotional tirade from the Management's Deputy Leader, John Pearman, appealing to his NUT "brothers and sisters in the TUC and Labour movement", asking how they could possibly "place themselves outside the circle where everyone else firmly believed it was sensible to negotiate pay and conditions together".

The greatest irony was that ultimately it would not matter. The 'signatories' were going to get on with it and if the NUT did manage to block the business the Government would intervene and legislate for Burnham to encompass both pay and conditions, or do something even worse. The surprisingly early end to the meeting was explained by the NUT contingent having to return to HQ for a meeting of their National Executive at 5 p.m.

On 7 March ACAS had called a small 'behind the chair' group to meet with the Independent Panel. For the Teachers' Side it was intended to be the Officers and one per union, with a facility for the two largest to have one adviser/reporter also present. To our astonishment we arrived to find five NUT people present.

Sir Pat Lowry introduced the three-member Independent Panel. The Chairman was Sir John Wood, Professor of Industrial Relations, Sheffield University (and well known to the NASUWT, arbitrating on disputes). He would be accompanied by Bill Kendall, former GS, Council of Civil Service Unions, and Tony Peers, Personnel Director, Babcock and Wilcox (a large engineering firm).

Speaking over belligerent NUT interventions Sir Pat stressed the Independent Panel was neither arbitration, nor inquiry, nor anything of that kind, but simply a team of experts to help the parties reach provisional agreement on matters of great concern to the future of the teaching profession. Sir Pat said this was the end of the conciliation stage; ACAS would now withdraw to let the parties get on with it with Sir John Wood in the Chair.

Sir John's desperate attempts to close the meeting quickly were thwarted by Nicky Harrison for the Management, after a short withdrawal, insisting that the NUT had to signify assent to the Memorandum of Agreement before being able to participate in the ACAS talks. More verbal fireworks erupted as Sir John attempted to push the problem to one side, hoping it would be resolved at a forthcoming special meeting between the NUT and ACAS. Just before 5 p.m. Sir John succeeded in closing the meeting down with an appeal to avoid another public row across the media. Fat chance of that happening as the NUT held forth that while it would attend the meeting with ACAS it was adamant there would be no change of mind on industrial action or accepting the Memorandum of Agreement.

The NASUWT described the ACAS-assisted 1986 negotiations as "getting off to a shaky start" thanks to the spoiling negative tactics of the NUT. The NASUWT was also critical of the large Scottish union, the EIS. In 1984 the EIS had hindered teachers south of the border by accepting 4.5%. Now the EIS was accepting a Government-inspired inquiry into their pay and conditions which was announced on 6 March 1986 along with a 5.5% settlement for 1985. The terms of reference were "horrific" in the view of the NASUWT, dominated as they were by "affordability" and "the need to observe continuing public expenditure restraint" as well as issues surrounding the contract and negotiating machinery. NASUWT Scotland voted against the settlements, which it regarded as scant reward for some 19 months of strike action.

The inquiry (subsequently to be chaired by Sir Peter Main) had obviously been established to pre-empt the ACAS exercise, which had vastly more favourable terms of reference. Furthermore, the Government would not be bound by the findings despite dictating the terms of reference. 'Heads I win; tails you lose!'

The 1986 NASUWT Conference took place during Easter week from 31 March to 4 April. Besides 'ACAS' the Conference dealt with other important issues hitting the headlines, including the long ongoing strike at the Poundswick School in Manchester and Militant Tendency-run Liverpool Council's budget crisis threatening thousands of teachers' jobs, to name but two.

The atmosphere was extremely tense when the leading 'teacher hate figure' of the year, Sir Keith Joseph, addressed the Conference at Scarborough. The Government's handling of the teachers' dispute, against the background of anti-union legislation, the defeat of the miners, the creation of millions of unemployed through the experiment with 'mad monetarism', together with its anti-public sector pro-free market policies, drove teachers to unparalleled degrees of personal hatred towards the Prime Minister and her Education Secretary.

Whatever views one had about Sir Keith and his monetarist convictions he could never be accused of lacking moral courage in agreeing to debate in public with opponents, notwithstanding his obvious lack of finesse in public relations. The Secretary of State's speech was received in a stony silence which continued as he sat down. In contrast, thunderous applause greeted each one of four hostile questions put to him by delegates, provoking the Minister to comment with irony that he was glad we had not completely lost our ability to applaud.

Fred Smithies' 'vote of thanks' to Sir Keith was so brutal that the Minister demanded the right of reply. The encounter got a lot of emotion off our collective chests but relationships with Government, already at rock bottom, sank ever further. Eventually Mrs Thatcher was forced to drop Sir Keith, who also seemed to start suffering from poor health. The Prime Minister was believed to be extremely upset with the treatment Sir Keith received at the hands of teachers. It was to be another eight years before a Conservative Minister agreed to address our Annual Conference.

Despite all the difficulties over pay and the contract the NASUWT published a major report, "Education in Crisis", in time for the Annual Conference. Besides the effects of the dispute, it also highlighted the effects of the cuts in public expenditure on the education service. A couple of months later in May HMI published its own report which was also very critical of the Government.

After the Easter Annual Conferences the unions returned to the negotiating business with the first full working meeting between all the parties under the ACAS Panel chaired by Sir John Wood on 14 April. It proved to be another extraordinary day in the 'soap opera' that teachers' negotiations had become.

The day started for the NASUWT in its own pre-meeting at 10 a.m. to receive news from Fred Smithies that Management was objecting strongly to the NUT's presence. The NUT-ACAS meeting on 11 April had failed to make any progress.

On the brighter side the NASUWT delegation was pleased to note the Management's paper on salary structure had moved away from the DES insistence on traditional hierarchy (low basic scale and complex promotion allowances), to the more collegiate approach favoured by us. Perhaps because of that the DES had submitted its own paper on the subject. However, on the negative side the Management's proposals on the contract were largely unacceptable, extending working time with no clear limits suggested.

Instead of a prompt start we kicked our heels in the Teachers' Side. It was gone 11.30 when the NUT contingent was called out to meet Sir John Wood who was desperate to keep the obvious problem outside the plenary group. Around midday the door opened and instead of the NUT returning we saw Sir John Wood, accompanied by one of ACAS's able lieutenants, Richard Harrison.

Sir John reported Management was still most unhappy with the NUT. He said Management's reasons "were soundly based" but he hoped for a resolution all the same. It seemed the Management had shown some flexibility by relaxing its original demands that the NUT both sign the ACAS Agreement and cease all industrial action, simply insisting the NUT indicate a measure of acceptance of the spirit of the Agreement by returning to some normality in schools. The NUT was refusing even to do that. Sir John had declined to open the meeting without the NUT present despite pressure from the Management to do so.

Sir John was obviously prepared, if not desperate, to keep the NUT in the talks whatever the price. So another day of toings and froings got under way with the fundamental business relegated to second place.

Despite several helpful compromises put forward the NUT would not budge. Sir John Wood became increasingly irritated and suggested the signatory unions take a walk and a long lunch break. Whilst aware of the difficulties of proceeding without the NUT, Fred Smithies reminded Sir John of the inevitable consequences for the NASUWT delivering the 'period of peace' if the NUT were allowed into the talks and permitted to continue industrial action with impunity. Sir John would have nothing of that and after lunch bravely declared that the ACAS exercise would have to ride whatever action continued on the ground. He said the plenary session would start at 3 p.m.

Three o'clock came and went. More toings and froings soon revealed Sir John had underestimated the Management's determination.

Meanwhile the NUT had suddenly and surprisingly left their own room to join us in the Teachers' Side chamber. But when Fred Smithies returned from some more exchanges with an important question to put to the ACAS signatory unions, the NUT, plumbing new depths, refused to budge and we were forced to have a meeting in the corridor outside. We soon learned the reason behind the NUT's childish discourtesy. Management wanted to know if the five of us would proceed without the NUT if necessary. The NASUWT was adamant: we could not allow the NUT to repeat its disastrous veto over restructuring talks of November 1984. The others quickly agreed.

Faced with such intransigence the Management had insisted the NUT could not participate. If the Chairman ruled they could, Management would pull out. Sir John, despite enjoying the support of Sir Pat Lowry for his position, was forced to choose between the Management and the NUT. He chose the Management, as he had to. The NUT was excluded from the talks.

The ACAS plenary group finally was able to get down to its real business a few minutes before 7 p.m., a delay of eight hours. Sir John Wood regretted the decision of the employers to insist on conditions which excluded the NUT, notwithstanding the behaviour of that union. His long experience in industrial relations was the basis of his view. Sir John's propensity to express his opinions so openly had not endeared him to the employers, who had come close to suggesting a different Chairman might be required.

Sir John proposed four Working Parties (WPs) be set up to deal with:

1 Pay structure
2 Duties
3 Appraisal and training
4 Negotiating machinery.

Questions of money should await developments in the WPs. Sir John also suggested a small plenary group for negotiating purposes. He set a tight timetable for the WPs of between four and six weeks. The size of WPs should be between ten and 12 and they would meet in private but representatives would report back to their organisations.

Fred Smithies demanded to know where pay fitted in. It was quite unacceptable to leave it to one side. While it would be premature to talk in cash terms some markers (such as Houghton and the Pay Data WP Report) and general principles needed to be discussed. How could duties be discussed without reference to pay?

Sir John said this was the second of the two rocks he had expected today! He said Management could not stipulate cash levels for a structure about to be abolished. We needed to decide first if we wanted a 'professional' or a 'contract' system. Fred Smithies observed, in that case, duties could be left until later. Sir John thought end-on WPs would lead to delay. Fred Smithies suggested therefore that pay levels could have its own WP. Management was worried about WPs becoming negotiating groups and also thought the plenary body needed to be larger.

Questioned on the pay settlement for 1986 Sir John said that was a matter for Burnham. Fred Smithies and Nicky Harrison both disagreed with that. While reference to Burnham would be required at some stage the real work would be better done here under ACAS. After Sir John had been referred to the terms of the Memorandum of Agreement he accepted the point.

The NASUWT continued to press the case for a pay WP, adding that the shape of the structure and contract could not be divorced from salary levels. The NASUWT eventually won the point when Sir John "ruled" that the first WP would deal with structure, principles and levels of pay. However, the WP would not negotiate for the 1 April 1986 settlement.

The plenary meeting finished a few minutes before 8 p.m. after another trying, if not exhausting, day in the life of those involved in teacher negotiations.

The Teachers' Panel of Burnham met on 16 April. It was in every way business as before. On the ACAS signatories' side there was much consultation and collaboration about the future. From the NUT came repeated attempts to turn the clock back. The NASUWT had taken advantage of the long delays at the ACAS meeting two days before to draft the opening statement for the Teachers' claim for 1986, and AMMA had indicated its desire to second such a proposal.

The claim would refer to the findings of the Pay Data WP and then propose that the 1986 negotiations must aim to resolve the total pay problem involving levels and a collegiate structure. The negotiations had to agree pay levels and determine the specific phases by which they would be reached, including the 1 April 1986 increase. The proposals represented a good albeit rather generalised consensus among the ACAS signatory unions' policies.

The NUT proposed various amendments aimed against restructuring by deleting reference to an MPG and inserting 'basic scale', maintaining the present promotion system and submitting a claim for 1986 based on its Conference policy of a flat-rate £800 for all.

The NUT amendments would stymie restructuring, close down ACAS and return to the Burnham-CLEA/ST set-up. These might also conveniently resolve the NUT's problems over its self-isolating boycott but they would push 1986 up the same disastrous 1985 cul-de-sac. The NASUWT would have none of it. We had learnt our lesson. This time NASUWT speakers made fun of the NUT's swift but staggering conversion to the need to put money into teachers' pockets. The NASUWT supported a payment on account but believed to put it upfront immediately would condemn the ACAS exercise to early breakdown. Eventually the NUT motions were defeated, 15:13.

The last item of Panel business was poignant. Fred Jarvis reported the death of Sir Ronald Gould, the last of the 'great' General Secretaries of the NUT. As a mark of respect the Panel stood in silence in tribute to him. I remember thinking we were also marking the end of another aspect of the NUT's historical dominance of the teaching profession.

The next twist in this extraordinary saga came on 23 April. The NUT served papers on the new Teachers' Panel Secretary, David Hart (NAHT), indicating its intention to apply for a judicial review of the decision by the Management and Teachers' Sides and Sir John Wood to exclude the union from the ACAS talks. The NUT was also seeking an injunction to prevent "any meeting" between the Management and Teachers' from proceeding.

The NASUWT viewed the intended ACAS-wrecking action as logically incomprehensible. No union had taken such a decision. On the contrary, unions had pleaded with the NUT to accept the majority decision and participate. Strictly speaking, neither had Management taken a decision to exclude the NUT. Management had simply stated it would withdraw if the NUT were present and continued with industrial action.

Late on Wednesday 23 April, together with David Hart, I briefed leading counsel David Pannick. The following day we were in the High Court before Mr Justice Kennedy. James Goudie, QC for the NUT, based his case on the proposition that the ACAS talks were an integral part of the Burnham Committee. He pleaded the McPherson Judgment as a precedent, which was rich in irony as that had been won by PAT against the NUT, successfully establishing the right of all organisations in membership of Burnham to be represented on its subcommittees. This uncomfortable fact was not to pass unnoticed by the judge.

After taking us through the recent history (which we needed as badly as a hole in the head) Mr Goudie was interrupted by the judge asking some hostile questions. He pressed Mr Goudie hard: Would the NUT sign the Agreement? After equivocating Mr Goudie was forced to answer: "No".

Mr Jones for the Management relied heavily upon the NUT's refusal to sign and cease industrial action to justify his client's position. Mr Pannick emphasised the Teachers' Panel had taken no decision to exclude the NUT. ACAS was not Burnham. The five signatory unions attended as individual organisations.

Justice Kennedy took no time in arriving at his decision. He would grant neither the leave to seek judicial review nor the injunction to prevent unions and Management meeting. The fault lay entirely with the NUT in refusing to accept the entirely reasonable framework adopted by everyone else in the ACAS Memorandum of Agreement. The hearing was over by 11.35 a.m.

The NUT's appetite for the absurd was still not satiated. Within a couple of minutes Mr Goudie came over to us to announce the NUT would be lodging an appeal, hoping to have it heard this afternoon or tomorrow. At two in the afternoon we were back, this time inside the appeal court. The appeal was presided over by Lord Justice Lawton, sitting with Lord Justices Stephen Brown and Sir George Waller.

Mr Goudie embarked upon an afternoon that was to prove extremely difficult for him and his client. Within a few minutes of opening his case he mentioned the McPherson Judgment. That was it! Lord Justice Lawton pounced. His voice croaking with fearsome authority he turned upon the hapless NUT counsel: "Yes, Mr Goudie, I remember that and you were here arguing the contrary. How come the NUT has donned the whitened sheet and come along here today?" That was the end of the McPherson precedent for this case!

Lord Justice Lawton dismissed more arguments by the NUT's counsel with increasing disdain, even impatience. Soon he could contain himself no longer. In voice of imposing gravitas he went on: "Let's get to the nitty gritty of all this Mr Goudie. The NUT objects to being excluded from the talks at ACAS. Things might go on, which if successful, will affect teachers' pay and terms of employment. The NUT won't sign the Agreement because it wants to continue with industrial action. The Employers refuse to talk with the NUT so long as the industrial action continues. The NUT now wants this Court to solve its problems. That's what it's all about, isn't it Mr Goudie?"

Justice Lawton then examined the precise wording of the NUT case for an injunction. It sought to prevent "*any* meeting between Management and Teachers". It was badly worded.

The judges withdrew at 4.40 p.m. and returned within two minutes to deliver their verdict. Lord Justice Lawton summarised the relevant facts of the case with piercing clarity and concluded he could see no basis in law to stop ACAS from proceeding; it was entirely outside Burnham.

In further scathing remarks Lord Justice Lawton observed that the NUT, by attacking the Agreement, boycotting talks and refusing to call off industrial action, "while taking the money" had "absolutely nothing to complain about being excluded". He accepted David Pannick's point about an injunction serving no useful purpose as individual organisations could still meet with whomsoever they wished. The other Lord Justices quickly concurred with Lawton. Costs of the appeal were awarded against the NUT.

The shattering NUT defeat in the courts probably served a purpose. Together with unofficial reports of poor ballot returns for the NUT's planned industrial action it led to a fundamental change in approach. The NUT began to sue for 'peace'.

There were signs of discreet lobbying behind the scenes. The NASUWT had reason over the years to believe a close relationship existed between many NUT leaders and the Labour Party that sometimes led to 'confusion' over whose interests were being represented. The issue resurfaced openly when NASUWT President Joe Boone was invited to a meeting of Labour Party members of Burnham Management and the NUT. Joe very wisely drew the attention of his invitation to the NASUWT delegation. After a long discussion it was decided that Joe should not attend for fear of compromising our non-party political stance and clear-cut role of representing teachers' interests and no one else's.

It soon became obvious the NUT had returned to its old habits of unilateral approaches to the employers. The NUT still had enough seats to requisition a meeting of the Burnham Committee, which it did for 9 May. Inside the Teachers' pre-meeting the NUT spoke of "firm evidence" of Management's willingness to make a payment on account so long as a claim came from the whole Panel, and "if we could bring peace and harmony to the schools the NUT would be delighted".

As unions broke away for separate consideration of this intriguing change of mood from the NUT, we noticed that the Labour Group on the Management Side was also meeting in caucus. The NASUWT delegation was sceptical but recognising the NUT's obvious desire to get off the hook and the agreed Panel policy to pursue an interim claim at the right moment we decided to probe a little further.

Substituting for Fred Smithies and admittedly a little tongue in cheek I invited the NUT to be more specific on the "firm evidence". The new salaries spokesman for the NUT, Peter Griffin (another sign of change) said the NUT "had received signals" (possibly a set-up job) that if the interim claim were supported by the whole Panel the employers would respond positively and added: "The NUT cannot succeed, but the Panel can". On behalf of the NASUWT I probed further on the question of distribution (flat rate or straight percentage) and whether an interim claim was to be a basis for negotiation or a bone of contention leading to industrial action. Peter Griffin responded 'constructively' stating that an interim payment would reduce tensions in schools and enable a satisfactory conclusion to be reached in 1986 "hopefully with an NUT presence". The NASUWT and AMMA ensured these sentiments were translated into firm Panel positions although the NUT abstained in the formal voting.

The Burnham Committee convened in the afternoon. After formalities as Fred Smithies' substitute I spoke briefly about the need for an interim payment to clear the decks for the all-important restructuring and long- term revaluation of salaries in accordance with Houghton standards. Fred Jarvis' rehearsal of recent history was helpfully curtailed by Nicky Harrison interrupting to ask him to refer to the interim claim, which she obviously knew all about, so she could withdraw her Panel to consider it! Responding, Fred Jarvis was far more 'Panel' than simply NUT orientated, referring as he did to different views on how the claim might be distributed. Chairman Sir John Wordie was quick to see the potential breakthrough and sought clarification that the £800 claim might be flat rate, straight percentage or a combination of the two. Jarvis' answer of 'yes' marked another significant change in the conduct of teachers' pay negotiations.

Around teatime following a short Management withdrawal, a long series of behind-the-chair discussions began which were to last until 8.30. The presence of all unions behind the chair proved extremely productive, greatly assisting a collaborative approach. It was my first direct experience of them. There was nothing special about the process. People got straight down to the real business of mentioning figures and reacting. Exchanges moved swiftly on without the need for long speeches or grandstanding. It was not rocket science, just fairly straightforward, even sometimes common sense!

Predictably Management insisted on several conditions including that: "The entire Teachers' Panel assures us that there will be a return to peace and calm immediately in our schools and will support the ACAS talks and co-operate in every respect. Furthermore a payment from 1 April 1986 would be without prejudice to any subsequent considerations in Burnham and in 'ACAS'".

After report back to the Teachers' Panel, unions separated to consider their positions. It did not take long for the NASUWT to reach unanimous agreement to the conditions, in fact only ten minutes. Understandably it took the NUT longer, only returning to the full Panel one hour later. There was general agreement to accept but the NUT still harboured some reservations over distribution.

A succession of further behind-the-chair talks ensued. It soon emerged that Management would not make a flat-rate offer but had voiced no objections to a mixed one. After some toings and froings tinkering with the Management's first offer, a revised figure of £520 or 5.5%, whichever was the greater for the individual teacher (equating to 5.73% overall), was informally agreed. In addition the Management offered to increase the London Allowances (unchanged since 1985) by 7%. The figures applied to the current scales from 1 April 1986.

By 8.30 p.m. Management was ready to make the offer formally in full Burnham. Nicky Harrison was careful to read the three conditions into the verbatim record. Fred Jarvis indicated acceptance. On behalf of the NASUWT and the other unions I sought clarification that the term 'without prejudice' clearly allowed for a further pay increase for 1986. Management replied 'yes'. The agreement of both Panels was then registered. Shortly after 9 p.m. Sir John Wordie was able to close the meeting with the uncharacteristic but extremely welcome words: "Well done!"

As expected there was a rush to claim the credit for the breakthrough, the like of which had but a few weeks before been savagely labelled "sell-out". The NASUWT Report to Schools drew the lessons: "There is a time for industrial action. There is a time for constructive negotiation. The NASUWT knows when!" The Union claimed six major achievements, often secured against "fierce opposition":

1 Ended the 1985/86 dispute.
2 Produced pay scales 8.5% higher.
3 Reopened structure talks – the only route to Houghton restoration.
4 Led to the 5.7% payment on account.
5 Led to teachers now receiving 15% more on 1984 scales.
6 Changed the whole atmosphere from endless confrontation to one of constructive co-operation.

The NUT had with much-belated common sense performed a major U-turn, accepting the need to close down 1985 and enter the ACAS talks on restructuring. While the NASUWT officially welcomed the NUT into the ACAS talks, on a personal note, to be frank, I was not pleased to have them back. I preferred the recent experience of the NASUWT being the effective leader of the Teachers' Panel even with the NUT outside shouting "sell-out". Now we would have to share the leadership with the NUT.

On 23 May the NUT suffered another humiliating defeat in the High Court. The NUT had ignored warnings not to pursue restoration of 'no cover' deductions of pay in the courts but to fight the issue by traditional union action as the NASUWT had successfully done in some cases. The NUT took four test cases on behalf of members in Rotherham, Solihull, Doncaster and Croydon. Mr Justice Scott not only ruled that teachers could be contractually required to cover for absent colleagues, but went further, adding that they had a "professional obligation" which was tantamount to a "contractual requirement" to do so. That principle extended throughout: "In my judgment, teachers have a contractual obligation under their contracts to discharge their professional obligations as teachers towards their pupils and their schools."

Referring to the timetable and administrative arrangements Justice Scott held that any non-teaching periods mentioned in the timetable actually meant "free unless required for cover." And if that was not enough, Justice Scott went even further, saying that "teachers' duties are not confined to their obligations to be on the school premises during school hours and to work during those hours."

Fred Smithies predicted the judgment would be "an albatross around our necks for a long time to come". Not only did the judgment seriously compromise the teachers' bargaining position on cover and the contract but the disaster did not end there. Justice Scott ruled that LEAs were entitled to make pay deductions by way of damages "through equitable set off". The TUC was moved to comment that this was the first time the doctrine of equitable set off had been applied to wages under contracts of employment. Hitherto, it had been assumed employers would have to sue for breach of contract if they wised to recover damages for imperfect delivery of duties under action short of strikes such as a work to rule.

In contrast, after the signing of the ACAS Memorandum of Agreement and the establishment of a period of 'peace and calm', the NASUWT pursued 15 different LEAs for unjustified deductions of pay in respect of various sanctions, including selective strike action, ban on voluntary duties and no cover. We did not always succeed but in most cases we secured the repayment of moneys. In others the LEA issued suitably amended letters to the 'hard line' ones they had sent out after action began in 1985. These included Croydon, Doncaster and Rotherham – three of the four against whom the NUT had launched its court case. The only exception was the fourth, Solihull, who refused repayment and to amend its letter and against whom the NASUWT took some protest action.

Meanwhile the work of the four ACAS Working Groups (WGs) continued apace. They managed to keep to the timetables in the sense that by 9 July Sir John Wood was able to chair a plenary meeting between all the parties to receive reports. However, it had been 'all talk and no walk'. All the issues had been rehearsed but no attempts made to move forward to a consensus. Perhaps the stipulation not to engage in negotiation made this inevitable.

The WG on Salary Structure, Principles and Levels made no progress in choosing between the NASUWT collegiate approach, also favoured by the employers, and the traditional hierarchical structure supported by the NUT, AMMA and the DES. Eamonn O'Kane, the NASUWT Rep on the WG, noticed that the report had wrongly attributed to himself the potentially significant 'independent' view expressed by the Chairman, Tony Peers, a leading industrialist, that the head of a typical size group 10 secondary school should have a salary differential in the range of 1.7-1.9% with the maximum of the MPG.

Everyone agreed that pay levels "had to be sufficient to recruit, retain and motivate" but no attempt to apply that worthy principle in practice had been made. Fred Smithies also deplored the lack of reference to salary levels.

In the Duties and Responsibilities WG report no progress whatsoever had been made between the 'professional' and 'contract of employment' approaches. Management and some unions had opposed limitations by hours, which the NASUWT supported.

In the Appraisal and Training WG fundamental differences remained between and within the DES, employers and unions on the uses appraisal should be put to: 'supportive' or 'judgemental'. The NASUWT believed they were not mutually exclusive.

The report on the Future Negotiating Machinery WG revealed six meetings "full of disagreement" within and between the Sides. I was the NASUWT Rep on this group and had put forward a compromise of a modified National Joint Council based on the FE model but no one had supported my move. The DES/Government paper hopelessly confused acceptable outcomes (such as agreements without industrial action) with the kind of machinery most likely to achieve such.

Tony Peers emphasised that the process had to change at the meeting planned for Coventry in a few weeks time. We had to avoid circular discussions and get down to negotiations. That said it all. Sir John Woods wanted to ditch Future Negotiating Machinery and Appraisal to concentrate on Pay and Duties but John Pearman said Management had different ideas for Coventry and would produce a paper covering all the areas.

Chapter 65 – Collapse at Coventry

And so to Coventry, a city which forever in the minds of NASUWT activists at the time will be regarded with a mixture of sadness and bewilderment.

The whole operation had been planned by Sir John Wood to be on the basis of a small group. He was in my opinion impartial but determined to preside over an agreement. A larger gathering might not have reached an agreement. There were only ten representatives from each side with the three-man ACAS Panel, some with Secretariat support. Teachers' Side representation was the NUT, 3; NASUWT, 2; and AMMA, 2, with one apiece for the NAHT, SHA and PAT. The promised paper from the Management arrived on 23 July, a couple of days ahead of the start of the Coventry meeting.

After opening formalities Sir John Wood invited John Pearman to introduce the employers' paper. Pearman emphasised the paper was a catalyst for discussion, a package embracing all four areas represented by the Working Groups. The employers' aim was to agree a package to be put jointly to Government to seek release of resources. He said "the stakes were high" and we had to protect an agreement from the "cold winds" blowing from elsewhere. The Government through the DES had submitted a position paper to the Employers' Side, which took a very different and threatening line.

Examining the employers' paper the NASUWT Representatives were bitterly disappointed. Despite all the fine talk of salaries "to recruit, retain and motivate sufficient teachers of the right calibre" the employers' cash 'offer' was woefully inadequate and way short of Houghton restoration. The key point for the NASUWT was the maximum of the Main Professional Grade (MPG). The paper suggested only £14,000 p.a. and it would take 12 years to reach (after three on the entry grade). The MPG would run from £9,600 to £14,400 by 12 annual increments of £400. The assimilation arrangements from the current to the proposed structure were very poor.

The contractual aspects were equally disappointing. Maximum working time available for direction by the headteacher was increased (from the NASUWT-established 'status quo' of 1,040) to 1,300 hours per year spread over 195 days, which implied the loss of one week's holiday for most teachers. In addition to the 1,300 hours, the job descriptions should be constructed "in a way which allowed the 'professionalism inherent' in teaching to find voluntary expression beyond the confines of the contract". In other words schools would still have to rely upon voluntary activities for which teachers would remain under enormous pressure and moral blackmail to perform.

Maximum class contact time was suggested to be 25 hours per week, worsening the practice of most schools. Non-contact time amounting to two periods per week was offered only to secondary teachers, again worsening established practice in most schools. These proposals were hedged around with so many caveats as to be completely devoid of any practical significance. There was scant mention of employers' responsibilities to provide the necessary resources.

The shape of the salary structure was the only redeeming feature of the employers' paper. It proposed four grades in addition to head and deputy: Entry grade, MPG and two levels of principal teacher, the last named being one more than the NASUWT thought necessary. It was an improvement over the existing multi-scale hierarchy and represented a decisive step towards the collegiate approach.

The full annual additional cost after five years would amount to £581m, compared to Sir Keith Joseph's £450m (which he double counted to produce a figure of £1.25 billion over four years).

Shortly before midday on Friday 25 July the Teachers' Side withdrew to consider the employers' paper. It was not long before Fred Smithies was declaring that £14,000 was far too low for the maximum of the MPG. If the employers were not shifting on that we might as well end now. Initially all the unions agreed the MPG was too low and the length of the scale too long.

Discussions continued late into Friday night with no one on the Teachers' Side contradicting Fred Smithies' overall view. Indeed there was deep disappointment over the contract proposals in particular. After an early resumption 'behind the chair' on the Saturday morning Fred Smithies reported back that there was no movement from the employers on the big issues of the MPG maximum and the contract.

By this time the two NASUWT reps, GS Fred Smithies and President Mike Inman, had called upon the 'back-up team' "tending the gardens" at our nearby HQ, Hillscourt in the Lickey Hills just south of Birmingham, to come along to Coventry for a meeting over lunch. Fred and Mike had reached the point of declaring breakdown from the NASUWT point of view and wanted to check out their judgement. The back-up team was any National Officer or member of the ACAS Group who was not away on holiday.

It was in the Saturday Teachers' Side session that the first discordant debate ensued. The NUT began the process by indicating the maximum of the MPG was not necessarily a "break point". For example, if the percentage of promoted posts were increased . . ! The march away from the collegiate approach back towards the proliferation of hierarchies was already under way. Other unions indicated likewise. It always struck the NASUWT how 'conservative' (with a small 'c') the so-called 'progressive' NUT really was. The collegiate approach bestowed salary, status and influence upon the classroom teacher who formed the overwhelming majority of the profession. It was radical but democratic and offered the primary teacher, in particular, unrivalled opportunity.

Other dramatic developments were also taking place. Late in the morning the DES civil servant, Ian Langtry, informed the employers of a statement he was making on behalf of his Minister. He had also released it to the press. John Pearman had already responded. The Teachers' Side was given this information at 1 o'clock. The statement from Ian Langtry was cold, stark and ominous. There was "no question of the Government releasing the resources" (Sir Keith Joseph's double counted figure of £1.25 billion over four years) for the employers' proposals. "So I say to you frankly that you must regard yourselves as under notice that you should assume that the Government will not underwrite a package in the area now under examination. In my view, you have chosen not to take cognisance of the Government position on resources. I believe that you should do so with your eyes open."

John Pearman had responded by recognising the significance of the points being made, regretting the "unhelpful language in which the message was conveyed" but insisting it was the employers' view that "the best interests of the education service will be met by securing a joint agreement on such fundamental matters".

Sir John Wood declared it was imperative to avoid breakdown. The NASUWT disagreed profoundly. Over lunch the extended NASUWT group confirmed the judgement of Fred Smithies and Mike Inman.

To the enormous frustration of the NASUWT the other unions then began a long series of discussions over details, totally losing sight of the main points that the 'offer' was nowhere near Houghton restoration and the contractual aspects were deplorable. It was a sure sign that the Teachers' were sliding into acceptance of a dismal deal. Ironically, it would have been better for the NUT to have remained 'outside the tent' screaming "sell out" for whatever was agreed. Now it was inside, leading a real sell out.

The SHA and NAHT were keen to discuss the question of heads' and deputies' differentials as much as salary levels. Behind the chair the employers had suggested that the percentage of staff on the principal teacher grade might be increased and the upper tier differential improved. In historical terms, once again the employers' ploy of avoiding an expensive main grade by dangling a few extra promoted posts whilst also beefing up the first few steps was well in evidence. The employers began to throw a few sweeteners to the other unions to keep them going in the right direction.

Towards the end of Saturday afternoon PAT and the SHA were indicating they could accept the offer. Even more significantly, Doug McAvoy for the NUT, whilst feigning some concern over the MPG, said the starting salaries were acceptable and the NUT wished to withdraw for a separate meeting.

Sir John Wood and his ACAS colleagues often joined the Teachers' Side, pressing them to continue 'negotiating' and avoid breakdown. Bill Kendal revealed that Pearman had been "put on the rack by his own group" for not clearing some improvements to their 'offer'. Apparently the total cost accumulating through five years had risen way beyond the employers' original offer of £2.3 billion and the Government's £1.25 billion over four years. By 10 p.m. Sir John Wood was informing the Teachers' Side of "implacable hostility" from the employers; "the figures were mind-boggling"; when money was put on the structure "things got out of hand"; "they wanted to go back to their original offer" as described in the paper they had prepared for the meeting and "start again from a monetarily aware base".

One of the 'improvements' had been to raise the MPG maximum to £14,500. Further discussion revealed many on the Teachers' Side were curious about the employers' sums. A relatively small increase in the MPG seemed to have escalated the costs dramatically. Bill Kendal shared the Teachers' confusion. Were the costings correct? The employers could not provide a proper response due to the absence of computer facilities at the hotel, revealing a major fault in the planning of the whole weekend.

By midnight on the Saturday Fred Smithies suggested 'Coventry' was at an end. Talks should be adjourned until September. John Wood outlined three alternatives: secure a heads of agreement, adjourn or break down. The NUT jumped in quickly to insist "we must stop the impasse". The NUT had resumed its familiar historical role: secure an agreement at any price and restore its position as leader in teachers' pay negotiations.

Around 1 a.m. (Sunday) Sir John Wood adjourned the talks until 9 a.m. Most of the Sunday was again spent in 'behind the chair' and different side meetings. When Fred Smithies pressed on the MPG issue, John Pearman asked for unions to keep to "united views and priorities". The significance of this remark might have indicated that the NUT view that "the maximum of the MPG was not a break point" was now well understood by the employers. There may have been many 'side meetings' of different kinds. In response to a question from Fred Smithies Pearman said the conditions of service elements were over and above any figure quoted thus far, including the "mind-boggling" £4.3 billion.

Most of the unions spent the whole day trying to adjust details while ignoring the main defects. The NASUWT tried to raise the fundamentals of Houghton restoration and the maximum of the MPG together with the contract, but everyone could see the Teachers' Side had no serious intention of standing firm.

One of the few 'lighter' moments of the day came when the NUT's Peter Griffin said: "There comes a time when you must recognise you cannot have it all" – a rich volte-face when measured against the NUT's vitriolic condemnation of the NASUWT for securing the ACAS Memorandum of Agreement.

By teatime on the Sunday the revised 'offer' from the employers totalled £2.57 billion, again raising questions of reliable costings. An extra £400 had been added to the MPG. A one-off payment of £500 for all teachers was also offered which obviously appealed to the NUT's flat-rate philosophy. Sir John visited the Teachers' Side to indicate the time was nigh to get into genuine negotiations.

Shortly after 4 p.m. the Teachers' considered their response. Fred Smithies immediately declared he was "appalled. It's not worth discussing." AMMA said on balance they accepted the deal. PAT also indicated acceptance. The NUT was moving close to acceptance, suggesting one last attempt to raise the MPG to £14,800. The SHA supported the NUT position.

Fred Smithies said he wished to be courteous but could not help observing that in opposite circumstances the NUT would launch a tirade against the NASUWT (as it had done over the settlement for 1985). He reminded the group that they were only here thanks to the efforts of all the NASUWT, some NUT and a few AMMA members. They were now only discussing hollow gestures.

Doug McAvoy claimed the deal was only about pay and structure; it was not a package. Fred Smithies immediately questioned if the NUT would then repudiate the proposals on 195 working days, 1,300 hours annual directed time and 25 hours weekly contact time. Doug McAvoy still insisted it was only about pay. At this point Fred Smithies indicated that the NASUWT could no longer act as one of the spokesmen for the Teachers' Side.

Around 10 p.m. after some more improvements to the details (such as raising the MPG to £14,500 after two years, and increasing the number of principal posts), the dissenting position of the NASUWT emerged loud and clear. During the next hour Fred Smithies and Mike Inman came under enormous pressure from the three-man ACAS Panel, the other unions and the employers, but refused to budge. "We cannot and will not move and in any event the Government will denounce any settlement and we cannot sign," insisted Fred Smithies.

Sir John was about to declare breakdown. However, he was reminded that in January only five of the six unions had signed the ACAS Agreement. He asked what the NASUWT would do. Fred Smithies replied the Union would stay in and keep fighting for its policies but would not take action against a democratic majority decision on the Teachers' Side as the NUT had previously done. That seemed to change Sir John's mood. He paid handsome tributes to the work of NASUWT reps in the ACAS exercise, "who alone knew what they wanted, had pursued consistent policies and contributed greatly to the collegiate reforms" (he might have added: 'such as they had become'). Despite the late hour Fred alerted the NASUWT 'gardening group' at Hillscourt HQ to the situation.

Sir John then took the Teachers' Side through the Heads of Agreement the employers were busy drafting. The money (with an eventual £14,500 MPG maximum) was meant to secure all the contractual concessions; appraisal; job specifications and descriptions with a 'professional' role over and above the 'contract'; and unspecified new negotiating machinery. The 'goodies' on maximum class sizes and non-contact time were referred for "further study" with no commitment.

Doug McAvoy seemed taken aback and challenged the employers' assumption that agreement had been reached on the contract. Sir John overruled him, insisting that the package had been laid out from the start. It was obvious the Teachers' Side was being bounced into an agreement. The Teachers' Side, with only the NASUWT dissenting, had made the cardinal mistake of indicating acceptance of the money before dealing with the contract. It was incompetent and inept, a stark reminder of the danger of pretending that pay and conditions could be kept separate. Sir John gave the Teachers' the choice of spending Monday looking over the draft or adjourning to meet later in the week in London. Notwithstanding the mess the Teachers' were now in, Doug McAvoy revealingly said the business should be done here in Coventry. The unseemly haste was to avoid problems (presumably of others on the NUT Executive taking a different view).

The talks adjourned shortly after 1 a.m. Fred Smithies and Mike Inman journeyed to our Rednal HQ for a middle-of-the-night consultation with the NASUWT ACAS Group. They received endorsement for the crucial decision taken earlier not to accept the Heads of Agreement. At this stage Fred Smithies dropped out of 'Coventry' and Eamonn O'Kane as Senior Vice-President joined Mike Inman with a 'watching brief'.

On resumption on Monday morning the NUT soon withdrew from the Teachers' Side for their own discussions which were to last a long time. The NUT still seemed 'shell-shocked' at the employers' (and the Chairman's) hard line on the contract. But having decided they had to have an agreement, the NUT was being forced to swallow the contract. There had in fact been precious little negotiation about it. The NUT was also desperate to have an agreement on cover following the disaster over the Scott Judgment, and the employers were coming under pressure from district auditors to stop wasting public expenditure in paying unnecessarily for teachers to cover absences.

By Monday morning Mike Inman had had enough of 'Coventry' (as well as a teaching job to attend to) and he was replaced by Joe Boone. It proved to be another frustrating day with much time spent extracting a minor concession from the employers on the contract. By this time many of the ACC employers had left for another meeting, making negotiations almost impossible. It took until 10 p.m. for the plenary session to be resumed. Eventually the employers agreed to defer the 1,300 hours and "to negotiate the maximum number of hours in the next five months" but the 195 days would stay in.

It was on that basis that the Coventry Heads of Agreement was signed by the LEA employers and five unions – the NUT, AMMA, PAT, SHA and NAHT – at 12.30 in the morning on Tuesday 29 July 1986, witnessed by Sir John Wood.

So ended the Coventry negotiations. The NASUWT, which had undoubtedly done the most of all the unions to bring them about, was unable to sign, believing passionately that far too much had been conceded for far too little. As Sir John had openly acknowledged, the NASUWT was the only union which had a comprehensive and coherent set of policies covering all the areas. All were necessary to reform the profession in the interests of the whole education service. The Employers proved unreliable. They ended up betraying their belief in the need for reform, preferring the familiar and cheaper option of buying off a weak NUT, with the AMMA reverting to type, preoccupied with petty hierarchies and status and returning to the NUT fold.

After all the insults and propaganda thrown at the NASUWT over the settlement of the 1985 dispute and the reference to ACAS, the NUT caved in and reached an agreement miles below the Houghton standard on pay and disastrous on conditions of service. The NUT had squandered a year of industrial action pursuing the limited 12% claim to exhaustion. Thereby it fatally compromised its ability to retain enough in reserve to fight the key battle on restructuring, which was the only chance of getting anywhere near the Houghton standard. An NASUWT-led Teachers' Side would not have accepted 'Coventry'. The return of the NUT was history repeating itself in shabby deals for teachers.

There was naturally a battle of words and statistics between the unions when teachers returned from their summer vacation for the Autumn Term 1986. The NASUWT had posted a summary of the Coventry Agreement to all members at their home addresses. While teachers needed rises of at least 30% to secure restoration of Houghton standards, in round figures the overall increase of 'Coventry' amounted for most teachers to 2% on top of the 5.7% payment on account. The lump sum one-off payment of up to £700 for teachers, a highly unusual device, was obviously the spoonful of sugar to make the Coventry potion palatable. The NASUWT regarded it as a cheap bribe, inimical to the career teachers' long-term interests.

The NUT post-Coventry booklet *A New Deal for Teachers* highlighted "cash increases" and subtly could convey the false impression to all but the most careful reader that the one-off 'soon to disappear' cash payments varying between £600 and £700 for most teachers were permanent. Even that exercise only produced 'Houghton-style' figures in the region of 22% for the teachers on the first five steps of Scale 1. For the overwhelming majority the exercise, flawed as it was, produced figures of between 14% and 16%, at best around half the amount required to achieve 'Houghton standards'.

The NUT's newspaper, *The Teacher*, 1 September 1986, resorted to comparing the double-counted cost of Coventry, £2.9 billion, with the real annual additional cost of Sir Keith Joseph's £450m after four years, claiming the former to be six times greater than the latter.

By the start of the Autumn Term there was much evidence of a backlash against the leaders of those unions who had signed the Coventry Agreement. The first signs surfaced in mid-August when the employers and teachers met in London to consider how to take forward the outstanding issues left in the wake of Coventry.

The NUT wanted an agreement on cover to disguise its defeat in the Courts, and Pearman was happy to oblige to keep them on board regarding 'Coventry', gaining more unpopularity by the day. A wordy but worthless agreement on cover was duly reached with only the NASUWT dissenting at a meeting which had to be slightly delayed until 1 September to ensure it took place after the NUT Executive had gathered over the bank holiday weekend to ratify 'Coventry'. I was the unlucky NASUWT staffer designated to represent the NASUWT in this cosmetic exercise, made worse by lasting the whole night, only finishing at 5 a.m.

As a series of meetings of the ACAS Working Groups called to deal with the Heads of Agreement resumed in the autumn term, 'the march away from Coventry' gathered momentum as representatives of signatory unions felt the backlash of discontent and criticism coming from their members.

The Working Group on Future Negotiating Machinery resumed discussions. The NUT and AMMA reasserted their traditional objections to negotiating pay and conditions together, which prompted the NASUWT to enquire why they had signed on at Coventry, which did precisely that. Ironically, the only teacher union representative who spoke up in favour of new machinery was me for the NASUWT that had refused to sign 'Coventry'! John Pearman for the employers repeated his view in favour of an NJC but recognised agreement was nowhere in sight.

The Conditions of Service WG met on 29 September amidst further disarray, with the employers Leader disowning an article in the weekly publication *Education* (generally regarded as the LEAs' voice) reporting that a "historic offer" on class sizes was imminent. John Pearman explained that "management was still getting its act together". He wanted to end the ritualistic exchanges in WGs and get down to the business of fleshing out the Heads of Agreement quickly. The employers would invite the unions to another residential weekend 'somewhere in the Midlands on 8/9 November'. The NASUWT along with most of the other unions were horrified at the prospect, realising how underprepared they were, except the NUT who favoured the employers' proposal. McAvoy spoke about the 'package' he had previously believed did not include conditions of service requiring a unified approach, and the days of separate WGs were coming to an end. The NUT was keen to claim we were now working under the CLEA/ST umbrella, as opposed to the 'ACAS machinery'.

Back inside the joint meeting Pearman, on hearing the Teachers' reactions, could not resist asking us "if we were serious". With so many issues outstanding from Coventry, unions were going to get the invitation to the weekend whether they wanted it or not. Displaying signs of its age-old predilection to stitch things up with the employers before the official joint meetings, the NUT supported Pearman's proposal. The meeting was over by lunchtime, having had no discussions on the details behind the conditions of service in the Coventry Heads of Agreement. It was becoming apparent that the NUT wanted to have a quick 'get-it-all-over fix' for there were no resources allocated to the conditions of service 'head' of 'Coventry' whereas the principle of agreement having to be reached had been conceded. From the NASUWT's perspective the Coventry Agreement was descending further into disaster and disarray.

The NASUWT Executive meeting 3/4 October took a momentous decision. Noting that a substantial revolt had grown in the NUT with many of its local associations and divisions rejecting 'Coventry', that the SHA and NAHT had expressed so many reservations that their members must be wondering why they signed the Agreement, and that a national meeting of AMMA Secretaries had severely criticised their negotiators, the Executive decided to apply as much pressure as possible in the lead-up to the residential weekend now planned for Nottingham, 8/9 November. The Executive decided to call more strikes in the week beginning 3 November and a march and mass rally on the Saturday morning in Nottingham. The announcement of the action would be delayed for a few days whilst detailed pans were finalised. The NASUWT even decided to produce a video on the Coventry Agreement which proved very popular and effective when distributed to local associations.

The move to re-institute strike action was to prove a fateful decision which the Government would exploit to the full. However, the Executive believed that a show of strength at Nottingham was the last chance to rescue teachers from disaster. Fred Smithies met with Ken Baker on 5 October to emphasise that the Coventry Agreement would not solve the problems of teachers' pay. The Minister remained unconvinced and unyielding but at this stage revealed nothing of his intentions, although much could be gleaned from the Government's acceptance of the Sir Peter Main Report for Scotland which had recommended an average increase of 16.4% over two years from 1 October 1986 (the day it was published). The Government also indicated that from April 1988 an independent Scottish review body might take over and replace negotiations between unions and employers.

To help retrieve the situation the NASUWT suggested a meeting of the Teachers' ACAS Group for 7 October. All attended except the NUT who boycotted it unilaterally, claiming that ACAS was now in abeyance and we could only be operating under CLEA/ST, the arrangements for which on the Teachers' Side were in its (self-proclaimed) gift.

Fred Smithies said the Teachers' Side was in total disarray on fundamentals and strategy and that it would be suicide to enter further negotiations on 8/9 November as there was insufficient time to prepare. Fred reported hearing on good authority that Pearman was going about proclaiming that "Coventry had killed Houghton for good" after more reports of an NUT-employers' meeting at the Labour Party Conference in Blackpool. The employers insisted on a package in respect of pay and conditions, but were content to ignore it for Appraisal and Future Negotiating Machinery, which were empty shells in the Coventry Heads of Agreement.

The very articulate Peter Smith for AMMA took us through an elaborate overview with great verbal dexterity (as was his custom), skilfully massaging into obscurity anything which might lay claim to be a conclusion. 'Smithy' could not see a fence without rushing to sit on it! However, with characteristic verbal aplomb but uncharacteristic clarity he declared he did not want a repeat of the "Coventry dawn-chorus Agreement".

SHA and NAHT joined in the 'retreat from Coventry', although David Hart was the only one from the signatory unions who openly admitted so. The NASUWT remarked that if so many issues were going to be reopened, why not include the maximum of the MPG.

The NASUWT suggested that a larger representation should be present at Nottingham and that organisations should be more cautious about what they agree to, especially bearing in mind the employers' reborn habit of dealing bilaterally with the NUT and then expecting at least one or two other organisations to fall into line and deliver the majority required.

The day of 9 October saw another extraordinary meeting of the Teachers' Side of the ACAS Group on Salaries called supposedly to discuss outstanding issues from Coventry. Mick Carney for the NASUWT had prophetically asked (tongue in cheek) if we were here to deal with outstanding issues or renegotiation. Chairman Geoff Beynon from AMMA said that was a very good question. However, nobody answered it. But the resultant three-and-a-half-hour discussion left NASUWT Reps in no doubt that all the Coventry signatory organisations wanted renegotiation. They had got their fingers burned! The "forces of conservatism" were back in control of the Teachers' Side. Collegiality – "the central importance of the teacher in the classroom" through a high MPG maximum – was dead in the water. The NUT, AMMA, SHA and NAHT wanted all the old hierarchical allowances reintroduced, as one put it, "no matter how high the MPG". PAT's Brian Round tellingly observed that the only organisation (apart presumably from his own) who understood the Coventry Agreement was the one who had refused to sign it!

The Special Schools Allowance was a genuine matter left over from Coventry and there was general agreement to retain it over and above other payments.

It was soon back to reality at the joint meeting of the Salary WG at ACAS on 16 October. First, John Pearman referred to press speculation about the Secretary of State's intentions. Rumours were circulating that Government was losing patience with the LEAs and teacher unions. Pearman and his deputy, Josie Farringdon, were seeking a meeting with Ken Baker. Undeterred Peter Griffin then presented the Teachers' claim for 'improvements', making a couple of Freudian slips along the way such as "moving away from Coventry" and "developing Coventry".

John Pearman exploded. He was bitterly disappointed and alarmed at what was going on. The extra costs were huge and they still excluded the elements for conditions of service. The teachers could not just cherry-pick the good parts of Main. Did the teachers want the Scottish primary-secondary differential, with the lower equivalents of the MPG (£12,500 and £12,900 respectively)? He could not find words to respond to the claim for unlimited safeguarding. He hoped the Employers' Side meeting on 24 October would be on the ground floor, "otherwise his colleagues would sustain grave injuries when they threw themselves out of the windows"! The employers stood by the Heads of Agreement and he was "extremely depressed and frightened" by the Teachers' new claims. He did not want "to rubbish anything the teachers had said" (although he had!) "but our joint collective credibility was on the line".

Peter Griffin replied there was no point in reaching agreement just for its own sake. Throwing credibility to the winds, Griffin claimed that the unions intended "to adhere to Coventry but had to consider the 400,000 teachers outside". In my notes I recorded: "That surely said it all!"

Pearman then revealed all his people had cleared their diaries for the next two weeks up to the planned residential weekend in Nottingham 8/9 November in order to make it a success. Pearman spoke of having taken great risks with his side. He saw the present talks as a unique opportunity, as opposed to the "sterile Burnham exchanges". 'Coventry' still represented "a great stride forward".

The Teachers' Side retired at the end of the afternoon to consider its position. The NUT, AMMA, SHA and NAHT spoke of the gravity of the situation. Nevertheless they insisted that unless significant improvements were made no agreement would be possible. PAT was the only signatory who said they should stand by the Coventry Heads of Agreement.

However, on return to the joint meeting, Peter Griffin, leading for the Teachers' Side, adopted a completely different tone. Instead of stating 'no improvements, no agreement' as per the talk, he simply spoke about how seriously the teachers viewed the situation. The lie to the real position was more than given away by the desperate search for dates for meetings of the Salaries and the Joint Secretarial Groups to examine details. The NUT was in a quandary over Coventry but still desperate for a final agreement at Nottingham.

Chapter 66 – Government passes the Death Sentence

Before the Nottingham weekend two significant developments took place. First, on 27 October the NASUWT announced its plans for action. The Report to Schools headlined "Once More Unto the Breach" declared that a critical point had been reached. 'Nottingham' would set the standard for teachers' pay for the foreseeable future. It was the last chance for decent pay. We had to show our determination that "peace and calm" could only be restored when teachers were given proper professional Houghton standard salaries.

The Report (No. 25 for the year) continued: The deal cobbled together at Coventry had been rejected by the vast majority of teachers. The NASUWT stood by its objectives of a high MPG, a collegiate structure, a just and comprehensive contract and fair and open appraisal. Accordingly all members were instructed to take half-day strike action in the week commencing 3 November as directed by local associations. Members were urged to attend regional rallies. In addition a national march and mass rally would take place in Nottingham on the Saturday morning, 8 November.

However, the second development was even more dramatic and far reaching. On 30 October the Secretary of State, Kenneth Baker, made a relatively short but blunt statement to the House of Commons. He began by referring to the previous two years of disruption in schools and extremely limited progress in negotiations despite the assistance of ACAS. "Now, scandalously, further disruption is threatened" and with the meeting planned for Nottingham "I must make the Government's position clear", continued Ken Baker. The Government regarded the Main Committee findings for Scotland (including the salary structure and teachers' duties) to be "well judged" and, subject to some differences in practice, eminently suitable for England and Wales.

Baker would write to the Management laying out the additional resources the Government was prepared to make available, together with two very important conditions for releasing them. First, there must be a pay structure with differentials which reflected the varying responsibilities of teachers and the need to recruit, retain and motivate staff throughout their careers. In Baker's view the structure envisaged at Coventry did not meet this condition. A structure more in line with 'Main' was necessary. All teachers would receive higher pay with more than half of them on promoted posts.

Second, teachers' duties had to be more sharply defined and clarified, leaving no room for ambiguity, and carried through into enforceable contracts of employment. The 19 points under discussion at Coventry had to be incorporated into the contracts. In particular, school teachers should be under an express obligation to cover for absent colleagues and be available to work at the discretion of the headteacher for 1,300 hours over 195 days each year.

In return for delivering these conditions teachers would receive two pay rises, each of 8.2%, the first on 1 January 1987, the second on 1 October the same year. That would mean teachers' pay increasing by 25% over the two years to October 1987. Baker emphasised, "if and only if these conditions are met is the Government prepared to add £118m in 1986-87 and £490m in 1987-88 to planned educational expenditure".

Baker expected the employers and unions to accept the Government's position as outlined at Nottingham "quickly and positively". "I must make it clear that the matter must now be resolved on all the terms and conditions I have set out." The Government would not countenance any amendments.

Turning to the future, Baker's statement became even more draconian. He believed "it had become widely accepted that the present negotiating machinery should be replaced". The Government therefore intended to repeal the 1965 Remuneration of Teachers Act, thereby abolishing the Burnham Committee, and "bring forward proposals for new machinery which will involve an interim committee to advise the Secretary of State on pay and conditions within the resources available at the appropriate time".

A copy of Baker's letter to Pearman, together with an appendix which amounted to the details of the pay scales and conditions of service (including the list of 19 duties for teachers) which had to be 'agreed', was placed in the Vote Office on the same day. The letter made it plain the employers and unions had to reach this 'agreement' in Nottingham. And afterwards the Burnham Committee would be abolished anyway and the Government would openly seize direct control of teachers' pay and conditions of service. Teachers' negotiating rights were to be abolished; the LEA employers were to be sidelined. Baker had in effect passed the death sentence on our activities.

Despite its laudable intentions to rescue teachers' pay from the disastrous fiasco of Coventry, the NASUWT had played right into the hands of the Government with its announcement of more strikes. It was the moment Ken Baker had been waiting for. The NASUWT Executive expected to be accused of breaking the agreement on "peace and calm" but we thought we had no alternative if the Houghton aspiration were to be kept alive and a decent contract negotiated. Unfortunately everything was irretrievably lost at Coventry.

The NASUWT belief in the value of working together with the NUT was misplaced. Against NASUWT advice the NUT had pursued 1985 to the point of exhaustion, squandering massive amounts of militancy. The NUT had no credible policies on the key elements of salary structure, the contract and future negotiating machinery. We tried checking these matters out way back in January 1985 but the NUT had remained suspiciously silent. We gambled on persuading the NUT as we went along. The gamble failed. Time and time again in the NASUWT Executive, Fred Smithies referred to the enormously high stakes that were involved. Somehow we did not heed our own warnings. The NUT had given up and entered the ACAS talks and surrendered at Coventry, probably doing so in return for regaining the upper hand on the Teachers' Side in dealings with the LEA employers. There would have been no agreement at Coventry with the NASUWT leading the Teachers' Side.

The LEA employers abandoned its commitment to restructuring as soon as it smelled a cheap deal, pandering to the "forces of conservatism" in the NUT and AMMA, except of course in respect of tying teachers down to a tight contract. AMMA realigned itself with the NUT, ensuring that once again 'timid acquiescence', as opposed to 'backbone', reasserted itself as the 'natural majority' on the Teachers' Side.

After Baker's House of Commons statement the Nottingham meeting became completely academic. But that did not stop all the parties pretending otherwise. John Pearman's statement that "the stakes were high" was gloriously irrelevant. They were neither high nor low but simply non-existent. Unions and employers could either agree to implement Baker's plans themselves and thereafter have the negotiating machine abolished or reach their own agreement only to find the Secretary of State legislating to close down the Burnham Committee and imposing his own 'solution'.

The NASUWT, while deploring the abolition of negotiating rights, pointed out that Baker's statement proved that more money was available than was offered at Coventry.

The NASUWT produced figures to show that even with the 'Baker' increases, and with average earnings currently rising at 9% and expected to continue at least at 7.5% in the medium term, the Houghton shortfall would widen from 34% in March 1986 to 45% at March 1988. This included an element required to compensate for the 20% increase in working time demanded by Baker. Fred Smithies expressed despair, asking: "When will they ever learn?" The NASUWT determined to proceed with its plans for action.

In an air of unreality another meeting of the ACAS Group on Salaries went ahead on 3 November. Not only were many people determined not even to mention the word 'Baker' but they obviously had either not read or understood the employers' paper which had been circulated and would constitute the starting point for discussions at Nottingham. It was a 'hard' paper, adhering to the salary levels agreed at Coventry and imposing a very tight contract immediately, with the 'benefits' for teachers, such as limits on class sizes, subject to much qualification and conditionality in the future.

The same old arguments took place with the NASUWT pointing out the anomalies that arose as other unions pursued their 'hierarchical' amendments to Coventry which were totally inconsistent with the MPG/collegiate approach, such as it was in that agreement.

The joint meeting was no better. John Pearman read out his bold reply to Baker, of which he was obviously quite proud. However, appeals based on morality, responsibility and democracy were no match for the brutal determination of the Thatcher Government. Management had yet to put the finishing touches to their proposals for Nottingham and all approaches from the Teachers' Side were met with the stock response: "We will discuss that at Nottingham".

The only realistic, if doom-laden, contribution to the meeting came from the DES civil servant, Ian Langtry. He reminded everyone present of the Secretary of State's statement to the House on 30 October. His 'master' expected co-operation with his approach, failing which there would be an imposed settlement.

Chapter 67 – Nottingham in November

THE NASUWT series of half-day strikes during the course of the working week (3-7 November) leading up to Nottingham went off well in terms of support and turnout for the mass rallies, of which there were 30 in different cities all over England, Wales and Northern Ireland. The ones held at Salford University (over 2,000 members) and Birmingham (over 4,000) were particularly well attended. The week's activities culminated in a march of nearly 3,000 NASUWT members starting at the Forest Recreation Ground and ending with a rally in the Nottingham Market Square in the morning ahead of the talks due to begin in the afternoon at the Strathdon Thistle Hotel on Saturday 8 November.

Over the course of the following week a hectic series of interlocking meetings took place which did not finish until the early hours of Saturday 15 November, by which time the action had moved back to the ACAS offices in St James's Square, central London.

The NASUWT had decided to participate actively to take every opportunity to minimise the damage if the situation could not be pulled back to 'pre-Coventry'. We could just as well have pulled out completely and blamed the fiasco on those who had surrendered so much at Coventry the previous July. It was completely unreal, with virtually everyone acting as if Baker's statement of 30 October had not been made or was subject to negotiation. The week's discussions did, however, reveal some interesting matters.

Saturday and Sunday were taken up with talks in the Contract WP, with the NUT still complaining there had been no formal agreement but nevertheless swallowing it all the same. Only after the event did Baker realise that he had no need to impose his contract, for the majority of unions had accepted one that was just as draconian. It was gone 1.30 a.m. on the Monday morning before a brief plenary session took place. Before that could start Sir John Wood finally lost his patience with the media circus who had spent the whole day hanging around and most of the night intrusively filming non-events. They were expelled from the hotel premises and banished to the pavement outside, from where they soon disappeared.

As the plenary group resumed on the Monday morning the Teachers' march away from 'Coventry' was so blatant that Pearman eventually put them on the spot. He demanded to know which salary structure they wanted: Baker or Coventry? The NUT and AMMA said they wanted 'Coventry' but pursued more and more principal teacher (PT) promoted posts, effectively Baker's structure.

Meanwhile Fred Smithies' attempts to resurrect the issue of the MPG maximum got no further than the Teachers' Side, with the NUT as anxious as Pearman and Sir John to get it all over as soon as possible. Later on the Monday afternoon we learned some more interesting facts. Charles Nolda for the employers presented 'the real sums' and revealed that the cost of 'Coventry' was only 7.9% over two years. This confirmed NASUWT suspicions over the quoted Coventry costings, especially bearing in mind the one-off payment of around £700 for 1986-87 and the convoluted double-counting exercise.

Despite repeated reminders from the DES civil servants that their Minister would reject all that was being proposed, both the NUT and Pearman for the Employers' Side continued to promote the entirely naïve belief that a negotiated settlement would be difficult for the Secretary of State to reject.

By the Monday evening Sir John was again running short on patience, expressing concern that the Teachers were still considering scores of minor improvements to the contract, all of which were destined for instant rejection from Management. His deadline of midnight was reached with fully six minutes to spare as the Teachers' Side response was handed over to the Management for consideration overnight.

Everyone bar the lead speakers and the ACAS Panel had then to be transported to another hotel, the Post House, on the outskirts of Nottingham as accommodation had been taken up by another booking. The domestic arrangements descended further into farce as the Teachers' Side spent all of Tuesday morning kicking their heels as Management considered their response, only to learn that the negotiations would have to decamp to ACAS HQ in London, owing to no more rooms being available for meeting at the hotel in Nottingham after midday.

The business resumed shortly after 9 a.m. on the Wednesday (12 November) at the ACAS HQ in St James's Square in the West End of London. The Teachers' Side continued to seek changes to the list of duties in the contract, all to no avail. Indeed the only movement from Management came on salary structure with an offer to increase the percentage of promoted posts to 23, further undermining the collegiate approach.

By the end of the afternoon the salary arrangements had been finalised and the time arrived for the Chairman, Geoff Beynon, to conduct a formal vote. The NUT said 'yes', it would accept the salary arrangements reluctantly. PAT gave no definitive reply, apparently swayed by the NASUWT's call to see the conditions of service matters first. The SHA said 'no'. The NAHT said 'no' unless various improvements were made including another tier of PT allowance for primary schools. AMMA said 'yes', subject to conditions of service. The vote was then taken along Burnham lines:

For: NUT 13, AMMA 4.

Against: NASUWT 7, NAHT 2, SHA 1, PAT 1.

The resolution to accept the salary arrangements was carried by 17 votes to 11.

The NASUWT came under great pressure to relent and agree to what was emerging to ward off the Government's 'takeover'. Pearman had appealed to the NASUWT, claiming that the future of local government was at stake. Why Pearman should have thought the NASUWT would put the interests of local government ahead of those of its members who had suffered for years under the sham negotiations run by the LEA employers in Burnham was beyond understanding.

In a final attempt to avert disaster the NASUWT offered support if the deal could be treated as a normal annual settlement with an improved MPG and a total withdrawal of all contract matters. Not unexpectedly Pearman responded: "absolutely impossible".

Throughout the Wednesday evening into the early hours of the following morning, the NASUWT insisted on a line-by-line examination of a revised and hardened version of the contract from the employers. Sharp words were exchanged with the NUT, the employers and Sir John Wood who all demanded near-instant assent to such a massive change to the teacher's contract. The NASUWT felt disgusted with the situation and refused to be browbeaten and managed around 1.30 a.m. to secure an adjournment of the Teachers' Side.

Somehow we all managed to struggle back bleary-eyed and bombed out by 8 a.m. for the Teachers' Side meeting. We then resumed the previous night's activities with the NASUWT constantly being voted down. By the end of the (Thursday) morning it was all over on the main contractual issues 'lost for a second time' although many details remained to be filled in.

Then the NUT quickly ditched its admittedly unsustainable position on negotiating machinery, accepting the employers' proposal for an NJC bringing pay and conditions together. The rest of a relatively short day, ending 'early' at 8 p.m., was spent in a morass of detail on the contract, with the NAHT legitimately complaining that business was ending with no details on the contracts for heads and deputies. John Pearman said the Management would work through the night to produce a final paper.

By 9 a.m. on the Friday (14 November) the Teachers' Side was in session again for what was to prove a truly historic if desperately sad day for the profession. The NASUWT noticed that the paragraph in 'Coventry' exempting teachers from lunchtime supervision was missing in the document from Management and managed to secure its reinstatement.

During the morning Pearman, Farringdon and Nolda, together with the ACAS Panel, arrived to deliver the Management's final offer. It was not unanimous, but majority Employer support came from across the political divide. Inside the NASUWT group a quick reading soon revealed that matters could hardly be worse. If anything the language was harsher than previous versions. There was no concession on any significant matter raised over the week-long talks. I wrote in my report: "In short, disaster was descending into abyss."

Within half an hour the NASUWT delegation had "unanimously and emphatically" rejected the offer. Over ACAS sandwiches at lunchtime we speculated on the horror the document would produce in the staffrooms up and down the country, bearing in mind the revolt against the Coventry Agreement. It was agreed to call National Officers to a meeting on Monday and the Executive to one on Thursday of the following week.

Unbelievably the other unions insisted on trying again to wring concessions, all of which had been rejected. As afternoon turned into evening NASUWT Reps immediately concluded we were in for another night and off people went to reserve hotel rooms and purchase items of clothing in the interests of minimum standards of health and sociability.

Around 7 p.m. Sir John began interviewing each union to twist arms. The NASUWT 'interview' was over quickly and we adjourned to the Italian restaurant next door which was making a fortune out of the negotiations. Over dinner we observed that Baker had no need to intervene when the majority of teacher unions had given the Government everything it wanted bar a small dose of the collegiate approach.

Around 10 p.m. the interviews with individual unions were finished and the Teachers' Side resumed consideration of heads' and deputies' duties and then the contract. People were exhausted. Concentration was difficult, sometimes impossible. Representatives took their turns to leave the room and get a breath of the (relatively) fresh London air in the damp but balmy evening outside.

Around 2 a.m. Sir John made one last attempt to get the NASUWT on board. He asked Fred Smithies if he wished to carry the responsibility for Baker intervening. Fred Smithies was not falling for that one. Sir John asked again about industrial action. Fred said he could give no guarantees.

The final plenary session took place from 2.10 to 2.20 on the Saturday morning (15 November). Fred Smithies could not bring himself to witness the final surrender and the demise of the great effort he personally and the NASUWT generally had undertaken to secure Houghton restoration for teachers. As the Deputy GS I was despatched into the final plenary session to register the NASUWT's vote against the Agreement. The Management formally made its offer on pay and conditions in a 21-page document:

For acceptance: NUT, AMMA, SHA and PAT.

Against acceptance: NASUWT and NAHT.

I stayed around for all the press conferences. John Pearman flourished his rhetoric about "landmarks", "historical decisions", "freedom" and "local democracy", naïvely claiming it would be difficult for the Government to reject this agreement with four unions when Ken Baker had well signalled his intention to do precisely that even if there were six.

Peter Smith, AMMA DGS, significantly claimed with some justification that his organisation had played a vital role in securing majority acceptance on the Teachers' Side. The NUT's Doug McAvoy claimed the Agreement was different from and better than 'Baker's deal' and echoed Pearman's view that it would be difficult for Government to overturn. In the view of the NASUWT that was a difference without a difference. There was only a small element of collegiality left in the ACAS Agreement. The conditions of service 'concessions' at best offered jam tomorrow subject to numerous escape clauses, not to mention the possibility of worsening existing majority practice.

I was one of the last to leave the ACAS HQ building on that Saturday morning, detained by a request by the BBC TV news team for one last interview: Would the NASUWT fight on? I could give no clear indication either way, saying we had ruled nothing in or out. Taking action against a democratic majority agreement is one thing; accepting an imposition is another.

Chapter 68 – The Execution

Following the "historic agreement" (born to be strangled) reached at ACAS in the early hours of Saturday 15 November 1986, a series of meetings involving ACAS, the employers, teachers' unions and then Burnham and CLEA/ST took place to tidy up dozens of matters left in the rush on that fateful night. I surmised that we had done enough negotiating over the past few months to last ten years, a thought that was to be realised in practice.

Looking back I still find it astonishing that we sailed merrily on in our negotiating ship, holed below the waterline by Secretary of State Ken Baker's blunt but crystal clear statement of 30 October, slowly but surely sinking. We carried on for yet another month in this way, fighting and re-fighting the same old issues either by way of redrafting sentences and paragraphs or, if the opportunity arose, resurrecting fundamental principles. Some issues left outstanding were quite substantial, for example many important points concerning heads' and deputies' salaries and duties. Another example was the need, as the NASUWT saw it, for a 'no detriment' clause to prevent existing practice being worsened.

At the meeting with ACAS on 19 November Sir John Wood came hotfoot from an encounter with Kenneth Baker. The Minister's clear message had been that he could possibly live with the 'non-pay' elements of the ACAS Agreement (proof enough of the abject surrender of the Teachers' Side on the contract) but the salary structure was completely out of the question. Sir John dropped a very heavy hint that the signatories to the Agreement might like to reconsider the matter.

The 'final final' meeting with ACAS took place on 21 November for the formal signing ceremony. The changed room allocations placing the NASUWT at some distance from 'the action' did not prevent us from noticing the many comings and goings as Sir John consulted the signatories on ditching the last remnants of collegiality to satisfy Ken Baker and save the ACAS Agreement. Having got themselves into an impossible position the answers had to be 'no'. The choice was absurd: accept Baker 'voluntarily', so destroying your credibility in condemning his intervention and imposition, or fight on to certain defeat. The only 'real' option left to the signatories was to ignore 'reality', plough on and hope for the best.

After more interminable attempts to draft and redraft to gain an inch or two of ground after losing miles, the Teachers' Side finally reached the end of the road. Around 5.30 p.m. the document was in a state to be signed and all parties were summoned to the 'final final' plenary session. Fred Smithies had departed downstairs to get his retaliation in first with the media, so I was dispatched to the plenary business.

In solemn succession Sir John asked each of the unions in descending order of size to indicate agreement or otherwise. The NUT was first, with Doug McAvoy saying "yes", for it was the "best possible agreement in the circumstances". For the NASUWT I said "no, for reasons which have been rehearsed many times over the past few weeks and need no repeating at this stage", the brevity of my statement calling forth a grateful "thank you" from Sir John. AMMA, PAT and SHA said "yes"; the NAHT declared "no". The cameras and press were called in to record the signing ceremony.

A meeting between the employers and teacher unions on 2 December cleared up the "misunderstanding" about possible exclusion from further discussions of the NASUWT and NAHT for having voted against the Agreement, for which John Pearman eventually apologised. My 'sophisticated' arguments denying the parallel with the NUT who continued industrial action against a formal (albeit majority) agreement probably counted for less weight than Joe Boone's substantial frame and booming voice declaring: "They'll have to get some big buggers to shift us!"

Pearman said the employers had met with Ken Baker who refused to budge on the ACAS Agreement. He revealed Ken Baker had been unaware that the 23% of PT posts was a national minimum. The employers would do nothing to destabilise various union ballots on the Agreement.

To their credit the employers had produced a very succinct and eloquent defence of the collegiate philosophy (known as the 'Pink Paper', after the colour on which it was printed) for presentation to the Secretary of State. The Pink Paper acknowledged that pay and the Burnham points (promotion) system were inadequate. As a result management structures in schools had become "fossilised" with "artificial responsibilities invented to justify promotion". The centrepiece of any teaching structure had to be the classroom teacher. Hence the MPG was proposed "to extend the basic grade teachers' horizons beyond their own classrooms", giving them a "corporate role which contributes to the management of schools". As it was, the ACAS Agreement provided for four different levels of 'management', a third of all posts were 'promoted', and schools had substantial backup from LEAs' advisory and administrative staff. The Government's suggestion that this level of managerial provision was inadequate was "extremely puzzling and not supported by evidence based on commercial or international comparisons". Only a few schools had more than

100 teachers, with over 80% having 15 or fewer. Baker's structure would produce as many "chiefs as Indians"!

The Government's own key White Paper, *Better Schools,* stated (paragraph 152): "Teachers need time away from their classes to plan . . . prepare . . . assist colleagues . . . " (in short to do all the things listed in the MPG teacher's duties and responsibilities). And paragraph 143 stated: "The professionalism of the teacher involves playing a part in the corporate development of the school. HMI reports frequently refer to the importance of professional team work . . . "

Pearman hoped the NASUWT would not mind being quoted in support. I said we did not but were dumbfounded the employers should produce such a fine rationale for the collegiate philosophy which they had so cynically all but abandoned.

The signatory unions' strategy of accepting the Pearman package for fear of something worse (Baker) was quickly blown apart. Ken Baker moved swiftly after the formal signing of the ACAS Agreement, the following week announcing his Teachers' Pay and Conditions Bill, implementing the measures promised in his letter of 30 October. The 1965 RTA was to be repealed. It was the end of Burnham's 69-year existence. Baker intended to appoint an Interim Advisory Committee which would consult with employers and unions on terms of reference set by him. The Committee would then make recommendations to the Minister which could be accepted, amended or rejected.

The meeting between unions and employers on 2 December ended with unanimous agreement to conduct a vigorous campaign against the 'Baker Bill' abolishing negotiations, with its second reading planned for 8 December. Most unions briefed their members and urged them to lobby their MPs. Four unions, the NASUWT, NUT, AMMA and SHA, sent a joint letter to the Minister indicating total opposition to the Bill, which PAT and the NAHT declined to sign. NASUWT GS Fred Smithies wrote to every MP and member of the House of Lords on 3 December.

At the same time despite Ken Baker's determination to crush the ACAS Agreement and impose his own will by legislation, the unions and employers continued to meet to hammer out residual issues such as joint guidance and to line up the official meetings of Burnham and CLEA/ST, necessary to adopt the otherwise 'unofficial' Agreement reached at ACAS. The NASUWT continued patiently to participate to limit the damage as, when and if possible.

It emerged that the SHA and PAT, despite their leaders having signed the ACAS Agreement, had declined to ratify it. They protested that they had neither agreed to ratify nor refused to do so. The SHA claimed it was still in the business of "negotiating". PAT's relationship and dealings with Ken Baker were the subject of some speculation. Our suspicions were aroused when, in other discussions, Ken Baker claimed he was responding to representations from unions when he defended his decision to intervene and overturn the ACAS Agreement. He declined to divulge further details.

Several unions balloted their members on the ACAS Agreement. The NASUWT decided to include both the ACAS and the Baker packages in its ballot. Announcing the ballot Fred Smithies said he anticipated much anger against a "shabby deal" and the "wilful squandering" of the negotiating opportunity created by the NASUWT. President Mike Inman predicted: "The clank of the contractual chains will resound down the years." The only way the ACAS deal could now be defeated was for members of the NASUWT, NUT and AMMA to reject it in their ballots.

The NASUWT results announced in mid-December showed massive rejections of both the 'Baker' and ACAS deals. However, NUT and AMMA members voted by clear majorities in favour of the ACAS package. Overall, the number of teachers rejecting the ACAS deal was in a small majority:

ACAS	Yes	%	No	%
AMMA	32,871	66	16,747	34
NUT	60,912	58	44,216	42
NASUWT	5,178	11	41,994	89
Totals	98,961		102,957	

Baker	Yes	%	No	%
NASUWT	2,403	5	44,691	95

The NASUWT turnout was surprisingly down to 42%. The AMMA and NUT turnouts were considerably higher at, respectively, 57% and 55.5%.

While we did not conduct any systematic investigation my informal contacts led me to believe members, aware that the ballots were academic in the light of Baker's clearly signalled intentions, had become so angry and disillusioned with the whole process that many could not be bothered to register their votes.

Despite Baker's Bill, discussions progressed with relative speed on the details to implement the ACAS Agreement on a new NJC to provide an alternative. There was even agreement amongst the teacher unions on a more balanced and rational distribution of seats, with the NUT 6, the NASUWT 4, AMMA 3, with one each for the NAHT, PAT and SHA. Having argued the case for such sensible changes for so long the NASUWT could take no pleasure with this 'deathbed victory'. It was "too little too late". Nothing was going to stop Baker.

A remarkable little series of interconnected meetings of Burnham and CLEA/ST took place on 7 January 1987 at the Mount Royal Hotel in London's

West End. The same groups of people moved seamlessly between side and plenary meetings of the two bodies to ratify their respective parts of the ACAS Agreement, with the NUT-AMMA axis ensuring majorities. Fred Smithies asked if the signatories to the Agreement understood and still believed in what they had signed. It was supposed to be an interdependent package but Section 7 (on Future Negotiating Machinery) could no longer stand, thanks to Baker's Bill.

Burnham Chairman Sir John Wordie threw his own legal spanner into the works by hesitating to transmit the Agreement to the Secretary of State because it was conditional upon the Government releasing the funds, and the 30 October letter from Baker was pretty explicit. The signatories were driven to distraction and eventually decided to ratify the relevant (pay) parts of the ACAS Agreement "conditionally", "in order to show the machinery worked"!

Another long day in the terminally ill Burnham Committee came to an end shortly before 10 p.m. on 7 January.

The NASUWT met with the Secretary of State on 12 January when all the arguments over salary and structure, the contract and negotiating machinery were rehashed, but to no avail. Ken Baker claimed the employers had ditched the concordat and that the amounts of money were "enormous and affected the whole economy". He insisted on his "tiered structure" and rejected the collegiate approach for its 'egalitarian philosophy'. Not for the first time in the history of teachers' pay negotiations central government was intervening not just on the global sum but also on the question of distribution.

In the House of Lords the Government spokesman Lord Belstead conceded that the Bill would have been introduced "regardless of whatever package was agreed at ACAS", reflecting the contents of Baker's letter of 30 October.

The NASUWT sought the assistance of the TUC and the International Federation of Free Teachers' Unions (IFFTU), to which it was also affiliated, in tackling the Government over breaches of the International Labour Organisation (ILO) Conventions 98 and 151 which were supposed to ensure free collective bargaining in signatory countries of which the UK was one. Formal objections were lodged with the ILO, which is a constituent body of the United Nations. While the NASUWT worked through its national and international affiliations the NUT chose to approach the ILO directly, as it was entitled to do, although complications were to follow.

On 2 February Burnham reconvened to hear formal confirmation that the Secretary of State had rejected the request for funding attached to the conditional agreement of 7 January. The Teachers' Panel tried to find solutions to deal with the impossible situation. There was none. Inside Burnham John Pearman launched into an emotional tirade against those who had aided and abetted Baker's abolition of our "civil liberties and negotiating machinery", predicting "chaos, confusion and bitterness" ahead. Pearman's suggestion of a joint approach to Baker to raise the issues of funding and the "horrendous implications of imposition" came to nothing after another of those surreal debates in the Teachers' Panel with the NUT chopping and changing its view and only the NASUWT and PAT finally voting in favour. Not that it mattered anyway, for nothing would have shifted Baker.

Back in plenary session, an item of 'real' business was concluded with an agreement to raise the London Allowances by approximately 7% (endloaded to 9.5%) with a new review period of 1 July to 30 June. That produced an Inner London Tier of £1,215, Outer £795 and Fringe £309.

In the final session, the speeches took on a distinct flavour of valediction. Controversially Pearman blamed the imposition on teacher disunity, conveniently ignoring the dysfunctional relationship between central and local government. Pearman's real concern was to protect the LEA 'empire', now crumbling before his eyes. Like the unions, he had gambled and lost. Fred Jarvis also lay the blame on teacher disunity, conveniently ignoring the NUT's refusal to practise what it preached. With one foot in the grave the Burnham Committee had a relatively early night, finishing shortly before 8 p.m. on 2 February, the occasion of its penultimate meeting.

The two TUC-affiliated schoolteacher unions, the NASUWT and NUT, held a meeting on 10 February to co-ordinate responses to the Baker Bill. It was agreed to organise a joint representative lobby of Parliament on the day the Bill returned to the Commons; to conduct simultaneous ballots on strike action, closing on 5 March with public announcements the following day; and a rolling series of half-day strikes.

In subsequent discussions with AMMA and the SHA over possible support, Geoff Beynon argued that having voted to accept the ACAS version it would be difficult to take action against 'Baker's contract', which he revealingly thought was virtually the same. AMMA and the SHA would, however, support the joint lobby of Parliament.

On 24 February a TUC-led delegation, including the NASUWT and NUT, met with Kenneth Baker to discuss the abolition of negotiating rights. No progress was made, which was not surprising as the Minister was not being serious, citing as he did the NAHT minority demand for separate negotiating rights for headteachers to justify his disregard of majority views. However, Ken Baker did make one telling observation to the effect that the remit to be set for the Interim Advisory Committee was simply an explicit expression of what had previously operated as the concordat.

On 16 February the Bill passed its final stages in the House of Lords. A representative lobby of Parliament supported by four unions took place on 26

February when the Bill returned to the Commons for its final stage. The lobby was never going to change the Government's mind, and the Secretary of State secured "tyrannical and unprecedented powers" over pay and conditions as Fred Smithies described the Teachers' Pay and Conditions (TPC) Act 1987.

This historic day in teacher union affairs was also marked by an event of great poignancy for the NASUWT and for me personally. On the same evening, I attended a mass and ceremony at Westminster Cathedral to witness the award of a papal knighthood to Terry Casey, who was by that time terminally ill. In the post-ceremony reception, Terry scarcely had the breath left in him to respond to his toast. It was to be the last time I saw and spoke to him, for he died a few weeks later on 18 March.

Meanwhile the NASUWT and NUT ballots on industrial action went ahead over the last week of February/first week of March.

The last meeting of the Burnham Committee took place at the AMMA HQ in Northumberland Street near Trafalgar Square on Friday 27 February. It was a very low key affair with just two representatives from each organisation. The morning's proceedings started at 10 o'clock as we met in session as the Burnham Reference Committee dealing with three individual cases requiring interpretation under the rules laid down in the statutory document that always followed an agreement. That business was completed by 12.25 and the gathering immediately reconstituted itself as the Burnham Committee. The business was to receive and approve the report from the Reference Committee and to approve the attendant draft Statutory Order and another one implementing the increases in the London Allowances. In keeping with the statutory requirements the verbatim recorders were brought in at considerable public expense to record the proceedings. The agreements were registered and conveyed to the Secretary of State through the person of the DES official present.

On the previous occasion Burnham had met, I counted 88 people present in the room. This occasion seemed overwhelmingly anticlimactic, the dying patient having shrivelled up with illness. In the Chair was Sir John Wordie, the affable barrister who had presided for many years over huge gatherings surrounded often by intensive media coverage. I proposed a vote of thanks to him, saying whatever weakness Burnham had suffered from was no fault of his. Indeed his benign and impartial chairmanship had often saved the Committee from "internal combustion". The Management spokesman, Charles Nolda, associated his side with my comments. Sir John replied graciously, saying that despite everything he had enjoyed it! He expressed the hope that everybody would use the intended three-year period of the Interim Advisory Committee to work towards a good negotiating forum, one that was "practical and sensible".

At 12.35 p.m. on 27 February 1987 the Burnham Committee passed away, aged 69 years. A few days later Burnham was buried as the TPC Act duly received royal assent on Monday 2 March. On the same day Baker moved quickly to impose his 'solution'. He made a statement and issued a letter to all teachers setting out his intentions. It was a replica of the measures outlined in his letter of 30 October last. At the same time he published a draft Statutory Order for consultation which would lead to formal implementation of the new measures.

An NASUWT Report to Schools summarised the main points:

a 13-point contract (embracing all the list of 19 duties) almost identical to the one agreed by the NUT and AMMA at ACAS would come into force on 1 August 1987 which included:

> a teacher would have "to work as directed by the head for 1,265 hours per year" but also "in addition teachers shall perform such other duties as may reasonably be required by the head . . . to discharge professional duties including marking and preparation" – the infamous clause that was numbered 36 1 (f) in the 1987 pay and conditions document;
>
> cover would be provided for absent colleagues normally for not more than three days but indefinitely if supply teachers are not available;
>
> from 1 January 1987 salaries would be increased by 8.4%. For example, Scale 1 would run from £7,011 to £11,193; Senior Teacher from £14,424 to £16,416;
>
> from 1 October 1987 a further 8% rise would be awarded on a slightly modified structure merging Scales 1 and 2 to a basic or main scale of £7,600 to £13,300. Former Scale 3 teachers would receive an allowance of £1,000, former Scale 4 an allowance of £3,000 and former senior teachers an allowance of £4,200.

The structure for the future would then become a main scale with five incentive allowances, of £500, £1,000, £2,000, £3,000 and £4,200. Baker was imposing his petty hierarchical structure, even adding the lower-level £500 allowance, presumably to please those who had argued against the necessity for yet another PT tier. It was the same old structure with a new label which even in the view of the employers administering it had become "fossilised" and inappropriate.

Two days later on 4 March the Secretary of State placed whole-page adverts in the national press outlining his intentions.

Far from promoting peace in schools, Fred Smithies declared Baker's imposition would achieve the opposite. Worst of all in the view of the NASUWT, the overall increase of 16.4% still left teachers 25% down on the Houghton standard which related teachers' pay to the average non-manual index based on 1974. And that took no account of the seriously worsened contract. At the same time the relentless increase in demands on teachers was well under way. Huge changes were approaching with the move to the GCSE which had massive workload implications for teachers. Other pressures were soon to follow in 1988 with the Education Reform Act which were to lead to more disputes in the 1990s.

The following day, 5 March, the NASUWT Executive met in emergency session and after receiving news of the ballot results decided on action.

The following day the ballot results were declared at a joint NASUWT-NUT press conference held at Congress House, HQ of the TUC. Both unions' members voted to take action against the imposition. The NASUWT voting figures showed:

Total poll	64,266	57.8%
Voting 'yes'	54,462	84.8%
Voting 'no'	9,319	14.5%
Spoilt papers	485	0.7%

NASUWT members were then instructed to take half-day strike action in the weeks commencing 9 and 16 March 1987. Mass rallies with the NUT were planned and members exhorted to attend. The two unions established a joint Action Committee.

National leaders of the NASUWT addressed the rallies and having gained first-hand evidence of the strong support convinced the Executive meeting on 13 March to begin the series of rolling selective strikes in ten LEAs from Sunderland to Surrey starting on 23 March.

Baker was unable or unwilling to assure the NASUWT, NUT and AMMA that negotiating rights would be restored and that the £608m global sum for the April 1988 pay increase was subject to genuine consultation. Again he pleaded "the concerns put to me by teacher unions" as an excuse for the imposition. It was again difficult to take Baker seriously as he pleaded minority opinion as justification to deny majority views, not to mention those of the employers.

In the week commencing 30 March NASUWT and NUT selective strike action spread to ten more areas including Birmingham and Belfast. The action was having a definite effect but it was always doubtful that it would succeed against the Thatcher Government. However, a *TES* survey of parental opinion in March showed that whilst the majority condemned the resumption of industrial action it blamed Ken Baker for being responsible for it.

Uncharacteristically Ken Baker found it necessary one weekend in March 1987 to appeal to teachers through *The Observer*, a Sunday newspaper normally opposed to the Conservative Party. While commending PAT and AMMA for declining "the call for action" Baker went overboard in singling out the

NASUWT for special condemnation. Somewhat on the defensive, he claimed his pay proposals were generous and "took serious account of the views expressed by the unions". Baker claimed the imposed conditions did "little more than set out clearly what most teachers have done for years". The discussions on IAC reports would "inevitably have something of the character of negotiations". He understood concerns about negotiating rights. "The Act was a temporary measure introduced to escape from a negotiating cul-de-sac."

In April the NASUWT and NUT jointly produced Guidelines for School Representatives on the Operation of the Government's Imposed Conditions of Employment. The detailed three-page document drew attention to the provisions for directed time, planned activities and job descriptions. It pointed out that the only protection for teachers lay in the interpretation of what was "reasonable". If approaches to the headteacher failed to produce agreement on what was "reasonable" the grievance procedure should be used. Appropriate action in certain circumstances was not ruled out by either union.

The NASUWT Conference 1987 authorised further action against Baker's imposition. During the course of April and May another 38 LEAs were targeted for selective strike action. With the General Election looming the following month (on 11 June) the NASUWT and NUT offered to meet the Prime Minister to discuss the restoration of negotiating rights in time for the 1988 round. Mrs Thatcher peremptorily rejected the offer.

In May the NASUWT and NUT jointly produced another pamphlet, entitled *Teachers' Rights, Children's Gains,* and exhorted members to make the fundamental right to negotiate one's pay and conditions an issue in the General Election campaign through public meetings and lobbying candidates.

In May Ken Baker wrote another letter to all heads, requesting although not requiring them to make copies available to their staffs, informing them of the implementation of the TPC Act. Once again the NASUWT and NUT issued another joint 'flyer' accusing Baker of being "economical with the truth". The following month the joint NASUWT-NUT Action Committee agreed unanimously to continue with action in 52 LEAs in the run-up to the General Election on 11 June. More action was planned post the election.

The General Election on 11 June 1987 returned Margaret Thatcher to power for a third successive term. The hope that the NASUWT had harboured of using an impending election to put Government under pressure to restore teachers' pay to Houghton standards had been dashed. Instead we were fighting a rearguard action to restore negotiating rights with diminishing prospects of success.

Even though trying to negotiate alongside the NUT had proved so difficult the NASUWT continued to focus on the need to secure the restoration of such a right. The day after the election the NASUWT and NUT announced a suspension of action to facilitate constructive exchanges with the Government, and a letter from 'the two Freds' – Smithies and Jarvis – was sent to the Prime Minister by hand. Mrs Thatcher referred the matter to Ken Baker, unfortunately reappointed as Secretary of State for Education.

At the meeting on 2 July Baker refused to budge one inch. He even refused to commit himself to the principle of normal negotiating rights for teachers. He admitted Parliamentary time was available but would not revise the arrangements for 1988.

On 3 July the NASUWT Executive met and decided to resume selective strike action immediately in view of "Mr Baker's provocative and entirely negative response". A meeting of the joint Action Committee followed on 6 July. The NUT decided it would wait until next term to resume action. The NASUWT went ahead with more selective strike action for the rest of the Summer Term, involving about a quarter of all LEAs.

On 1 June a meeting took place between unions and employers when another attempt was made to breathe life into the NJC corpse but it was a lost cause. Large parts of the Burgundy Book summarising the collective agreements on conditions of service in CLEA/ST had been rendered redundant by the overriding statutory provisions of the 1987 TPC Act. CLEA/ST was left with only a few significant areas of responsibility such as entitlement to sick pay, rights to time off for public duties, maternity leave and notice periods.

Before the end of the Summer Term 1987 other issues began to rise in importance for the NASUWT. Education itself began to take centre stage with talk of a 'Great Education Reform Bill' in the autumn. The GCSE was coming on stream and, following much pressure to postpone its introduction due to inadequate resources, the Government had finally taken some measures. Kenneth Baker wrote to the NASUWT on 8 July assuring us that the Government intended to keep improving staffing standards with GCSE in mind and HMI had been in contact with LEAs to that effect. Three additional in-service training days had been granted and other resources made available. Consequently the NASUWT withdrew the instruction to members issued in the wake of the Baker imposition which related to all additional administrative and assessment work for GCSE having to be carried out in session time. However, the NASUWT continued to press the Examination Boards' Joint Council to improve the payments made to teachers for carrying out work on behalf of the Boards.

There was no mistaking what had happened. The NASUWT had exhausted itself fighting to the bitter end, but the battle over negotiating rights was lost. However, there were other battles to be fought and the NASUWT would rise from the ashes of 1985/86 – one of the longest and most bitter disputes in UK industrial relations history.

SECTION NINE
THE NEW ERA

National Curriculum
The Great 'Test Boycott'
The New Pay Regime

Chapter 69 - The Education Reform Act 1988

The Education Reform Act (ERA) 1988 was the most fundamental reform of the education system in England and Wales since the 1944 statute. It also had direct repercussions in Northern Ireland where parallel reforms were implemented. In stark contrast to the 1944 Act, built on consensus, the 1988 ERA was based on contention and contempt for any opposing view. Many observers believed it was 'Thatcher's revenge' for the industrial action of the 1980s coupled with the suspicion that the Labour-led LEAs had been too 'tolerant' of the highly effective selective strike action as a way of embarrassing the Conservative Government.

The Act was designed to 'incentivise' the education service by exposing it to the equivalent of competitive free market pressures, outright privatisation being regarded as impractical. The established 'producers' – the LEAs – were to be sidelined, reduced to minor or unpopular roles nobody else wanted or could possibly perform. Unions had already been 'taken care of' by the 1987 Teachers' Pay and Conditions Act.

Sailing under a false flag of 'freedom', the 1988 ERA transferred power and control massively to Westminster. In the early stages the NASUWT counted 140 significant powers to be transferred to the Secretary of State. Later estimates by others such as the LEAs put the number at over 200. Those LEA roles not 'nationalised' were in large number delegated to schools which had to carry them out in a straightjacket imposed by central government. Ken Baker wheeled out an analogy, describing the thrust of the ERA as transferring power "from the hub to the rim". He might have added the LEAs were the ones with a spoke put into their wheels. That was the rhetoric. In reality, roles not powers were delegated to schools.

The four fundamental areas of reform were:

1 National curriculum (NC), testing and assessment;
2 Local management of schools (LMS), also known as devolved financial management, under nationally imposed formulae (largely per capita) funding;
3 Opting out of LEA control by grant maintained (GM) schools;
4 Increased parental choice through more open enrolment.

The Government launched a so-called consultative document outlining its plans in July 1987 which proved to be a cynical sham. Some 21,000 responses were to be received from organisations and individuals. Literally no more than a handful favoured the proposals. A massive and overwhelming majority opposed the plans in strong terms. Even where there was agreement in principle in some areas, such as a core NC, huge opposition remained against the proposed practice. Yet the consultation exercise produced very few changes, the only significant one being special education which, incredibly, had been entirely absent from the consultation document, revealing much about the authors. Ken Baker's attitude to opposing opinions was one of sublime arrogance: such people would soon change their minds. It was difficult to take the debate seriously.

The NC laid down the subjects children from 5 to 16 had to be taught. The core subjects were maths, English and science. The foundation subjects were history, geography, technology, music, art and PE and (in the secondary sector) a modern foreign language. Religious education remained compulsory as it had been under the 1944 Act.

The NASUWT along with countless others criticised the assumption of central control over the curriculum. It was 'out-Frenching the French' where Education Ministers could boast they knew what was being taught in the nation's classrooms by glancing at their watches. The Act was another and probably decisive assault on the tradition of protecting educational practice from direct interference by politicians.

The NASUWT also criticised the ERA for overloading the curriculum, driving out 'minority subjects' such as extra modern languages, classics and economics. It also further sidelined vocational elements where funds specially provided in recent years to make secondary education more relevant to working life were already being sharply reduced.

The proposed NC was at odds with the Government's 1985 policy document *Better Schools,* which argued the need for all pupils to have access to a broad, balanced, relevant and differentiated curriculum. Teachers would be left with little opportunity to tailor the curriculum to the needs of individual pupils.

The NASUWT emphasised its long-standing policy in favour of a core NC: maths, English and science, with the emerging importance of IT as another possible element. The rest of the curriculum should be left to schools' discretion. In the House during adjournments of the standing committee considering the Bill I tried personally to get Ken Baker to limit the statutory NC to the core subjects and thereby gain the support of the profession, including a majority of the unions. He was simply not open to any ideas other than his own.

The NASUWT raised questions about finance and staffing. There were already severe shortages of maths, science and technology teachers. Primary school teachers were generalists and in a short space of time would have to become quite specialist in a number of subjects without any help retraining and in-service education. In secondary schools many 'shortage subjects', such as maths, IT, the sciences and modern foreign languages, were already taught in over 25% of cases by teachers who had neither university degree nor A Level qualifications in them. No audit had been undertaken to identify the staffing required for effective implementation of the NC. The Government blandly expected the NC to be implemented "broadly within the planned level of resources".

The NASUWT argued that the requirements of very young children, those with special needs, the multicultural aspects and the interests of the non-academic pupils had all been seriously underestimated, indeed in some cases entirely neglected in the Government's Bill. The NASUWT warned that disruptive behaviour would worsen with many bored and truculent youngsters having a curriculum they regarded as irrelevant rammed down their throats in greater doses than ever. The Technical and Vocational Educational Initiative (TVEI), which had started life as a promising and well-resourced pilot, would be left to flounder without adequate resources.

The ERA enabled the Government to prescribe detailed programmes of study in each subject, together with specified levels of attainment. National testing was introduced at the ages of 7, 11, 14 and 16. Besides the monumental demands being made on teachers' time the NASUWT warned that excessive testing was dangerous on educational grounds. The externally set tests, also to be made the subject of national league tables, would "assume excessive importance in the eyes of pupils, teachers and the public. Teachers will be strongly tempted to teach to the test knowing full well they would be judged by the results."

LMS in schools with more than 200 pupils was another subterfuge, sold under the wrapping of freedom. In practice LEAs were tied to central government formulae, insisting that at least 85% of their relevant schools spending had to be delegated to governing bodies on a simplistic per capita formula. The figure of 85% was soon raised to 90% and thereafter to 95%. In practice it meant money followed 'bums on seats', the nearest one could get to vouchers without mentioning the dreaded word. It prevented LEAs from discriminating in favour of disadvantaged schools.

The NASUWT argued that LMS was illusory, for minimum staffing levels, consuming at least 80% of a school's budget, were essential to deliver the planned NC. Far from demolishing bureaucracy in the town and county halls, LMS was simply redistributing and amplifying administration to numerous different points in schools, distracting heads and others from their core responsibility for education. Many schools began to employ bursars to enable heads to retain their main focus on educational issues.

Enhanced provision including insurance for cover and emergencies such as fire and flood were required. Provision to honour national and local agreements on conditions of service could be compromised by unexpected demands such as sickness absence falling upon individual schools. Responsibility for health and safety, another huge and sometimes quite complicated subject, involving potentially enormous risk, was delegated to schools. The NASUWT, already extremely active in this area, stepped up its training courses on health and safety.

Given the same level of resources overall, any new system was bound to produce winners and losers. The problem was exacerbated by the Government insisting upon a formula that devolved funds on the basis of the average and not the actual costs of teachers' salaries. Thus schools with better retention rates of staff (inevitably higher up the incremental scales) were penalised. When LMS came to Scotland the NASUWT lobbied successfully for it to be based on actual staff costs. The sceptre of teacher redundancy loomed in some schools alongside serious staff shortages in others. The NASUWT worked hard at LEA level seeking to engage as many schools as possible in voluntary redeployment schemes to avoid compulsory redundancy.

Over the years the NASUWT monitored the unspent balances kept by schools, which mounted consistently. Many heads and governors believed they needed to build up reserves for the rainy day, each one acting as its own insurance company, a function previously and more cost-effectively carried out by the LEA. Some schools began to save revenue expenditure moneys to provide for capital projects which properly fell to be financed through other channels, effectively charging the present generation for future developments.

The NASUWT was strongly critical of the opting out proposals. Schools with more than 300 pupils would be encouraged to become 'grant maintained' (GM) and opt out of their LEA. The LEA would have to continue funding such schools but the money would be channelled to them through central government, resembling the former direct grant establishments. Local responsibility for providing education for all pupils was retained (as under the 1944 Act) but the ability to plan sensibly circumscribed to the extent that schools became GM. Ministerial promises that GM schools would not be more favourably financed than their LEA counterparts were soon brazenly broken as fewer opted out than the Government desired.

The arrangements for opting out were bizarre. Twenty per cent of parents could trigger a ballot. A simple majority of those voting would suffice. The 'constituency' consisted of the parents at the time. Thus parents of pupils leaving at the end of the year had a vote whilst those with children aspiring to enter in the future would be disenfranchised. A decision to opt out would be irreversible.

The NASUWT believed GM schools would be afforded a special status. In a context of increased parental choice GM schools would 'capture' the market and end up being able to select pupils. Indeed they would be under great pressure to prove their worth and even if selection by ability were circumscribed, it could easily be achieved by social background. In a press statement I described the aim to be the creation of 'social grammar schools'.

The NASUWT feared that LEA-teacher union agreements on staffing levels, premature retirement, time off for public and union duties, redeployment and promotion procedures would no longer apply in the GM sector. Job security would be diminished.

Open enrolment and parental choice would be enhanced by creating a 'standard number' based on 1979 (a peak year) pupil numbers. Only when and if the standard number were exceeded would a school be able to turn pupils away. The NASUWT along with many others issued clear warnings that the most popular schools would end up choosing their pupils, not parents choosing their schools. Less popular schools, already having more than their fair share of problems, would suffer even more.

Figures recording parental satisfaction over school choice have shown a consistent decline in the post-1988 era.

Besides the imposition of a totally controlled NC the Government also took powers to determine the content of courses leading to public examinations. The public examinations themselves, largely GCSE and GCE A Levels, had all to conform to requirements laid down by the School Examination and Assessment Council (SEAC) to the satisfaction of the Secretary of State. Controversy raged over politically sensitive subjects, such as history and English language and literature. The right-wing press campaigned to have '1066', grammar, spelling and Shakespeare made mandatory in these subjects.

With our Parliamentary Adviser Ken Weetch, a former MP, one-time member of the NAS Executive and a lifelong supporter of the Union, we had many meetings drafting over 140 amendments to the Bill which were then fed through to Labour and Liberal Democratic MPs serving on the standing committee considering the proposed legislation line by line. Absolutely none was ever accepted by the Conservative majority on the standing committee. The NASUWT also joined with the Parents Initiative, a wide body representing teachers and parents, in lobbying for many amendments to the Bill. The AMA and ACC were also part of this ad hoc group that met on a regular basis with Labour and Liberal Democrat MPs, suggesting amendments to put forward in committee.

The Conservative-controlled ACC estimated that implementing the ER Bill would cost an extra £800m at least. It condemned the Government for expecting LEAs to finance such upheaval within existing resources. The ACC expressed major criticisms of the Bill, believing it left LEAs with responsibilities but few powers for providing school places, parental choice and sufficient staff. The Secretary of State would take 200 new powers, exercised through civil servants, thereby creating a whole new Government-directed machine for education. The NASUWT also feared the new financial system of LMS could destabilise LEA planning and expose some schools to new problems.

After the ERA was enacted the NASUWT published a stream of booklets briefing local Officers and giving advice to members on the implications of the legislation as part of a campaign on "Action for Equality". (See Appendix J.) Schools were not well placed to take on board responsibility for employment and equality rights.

In November 1990 John MacGregor (who had succeeded Ken Baker in July 1989) was replaced by Ken Clarke as Secretary of State for Education. John MacGregor was reported "to have gone native" – in other words to have recognised there were genuine problems raised by teachers and others.

By 1991 teachers of pupils at Key Stage 1 (7-year-olds) were being confronted with the horrific bureaucracy and workload associated with assessment and testing. A NASUWT survey showed teachers working an average of 51 hours per week. In January 1991 the 'Six Teacher Organisations' reached agreement on advice to be issued to their members on the workload problem, with copies also sent to all LEAs and the Government.

Basically the advice followed the principles set out in the NASUWT's workload strategy. Teachers had to combine and argue the case of 'reasonableness' with their 'line managers'. Unreasonable responses would then be tackled on a case-by-case basis. The NASUWT warmly welcomed the development, saying "it could prove to be a significant breakthrough" with wide implications. Given the differences between the unions there was less agreement on resorting to industrial action to deal with unreasonable management, which each union had to decide for itself.

Conference 1991 also identified excessive workload as the biggest problem facing the entire profession. It was to dominate my 12 years as GS. In my Monday evening address to delegates I said that: "Too many teachers were prepared to make the unworkable system work by putting their health and well-being at risk. Teachers must learn to say 'no'. All the unions have now agreed to this strategy in respect of pupil assessment and it is a small step to apply this to all aspects of the problem."

The Conference took up the theme with vigour. Conscious of the fact that most teachers in the country were reeling under excessive and unnecessary workloads, Conference called upon all members to participate in the campaign and congratulated those who were already doing so. A limit on working time needed to be restored to classroom teaching for the benefit of pupils and staff. More time was being spent on mind-boggling systems of assessment than on teaching. Conference committed the NASUWT to give "full support, which may include strike action, to members faced with opposition" to the implementation of the strategy.

In September 1991 the NASUWT released the results of another survey on workload which confirmed the problem was worsening. The results were written up to form part of the evidence to be presented to the School Teachers' Review Body (STRB), which had recently been established and would operate for the first time in respect of pay and conditions w.e.f. 1 April 1992.

Two major reports on schools were adopted at the 1991 Conference, one on staffing, the other on physical conditions. The staffing report revealed that, thanks to formula funding under LMS, schools were receiving insufficient cash to pay for teachers, with the result that redundancies were increasing, the curriculum was being squeezed, and pupils and staff were suffering increased stress. The report called for staffing of schools to be based on the needs of the curriculum and not on a crudely calculated cash level which ignored real needs.

The "Physical Survey of Schools" was the product of a nationwide survey which revealed some schools were getting dirtier and more unhealthy and were dangerous places to work in. The survey suggested well over half of Britain's 25,000 schools had a problem such as: repairs not carried out, equipment not properly maintained or replaced, toilets left uncleaned, or cockroach and vermin infestation.

The NASUWT issued a report, *Testing Time for Schools,* in December 1991. The report claimed the Government's aims of a broad, balanced and relevant curriculum were being subverted by violent policy changes and an obsession with testing. In my accompanying press statement I warned that "if the pencil and paper tests planned for 7-year-olds the next summer spread throughout the system, schools will be turned into little more than exam factories".

In April 1992, following advice from the NASUWT, many schools and departments decided to withdraw from the Key Stage 3 (14-year-olds) pilot tests. Teachers were beginning to see the tests could consume between 15 and 30 hours per class and that did not include internal moderation and external audit. Far from being 'simple pencil and paper' tests as reportedly desired by the Prime Minister at the time (Margaret Thatcher), they had somehow been transformed into complicated and bureaucratic Standard Assessment Tasks (SATs). There were rumours abroad that the tests would have to be modified for their introduction intended the following year and so there was little point in participating in a pilot that was born redundant.

At the same time, Secretary of State Ken Clarke announced an inquiry into primary school teaching methods by the 'three wise men' who included Chris Woodhead, then Chief Executive of the National Curriculum Council (NCC). It was an important step for Chris Woodhead, a self-confessed "progressive teacher" in his early days in the classroom, on his way to becoming HM Chief Inspector of Schools. The other two members were Jim Rose, Chief Inspector of Primary Education, and Robin Alexander, Professor of Education, Leeds University.

Teaching methods were firmly plunged into the political arena with an orchestrated right-wing backlash against so-called progressive philosophies, viewed by some as a major cause behind allegedly low standards. The teaching of reading was at the heart of the controversy, with the two camps broadly divided between 'phonics' (the traditional) and 'look say' (the modern progressive) methods, representing respectively the right and the left. The NASUWT had never taken a view favouring one side or the other, reflecting the diversity of opinion within its own ranks.

The 'three wise men' produced their report at staggering speed – within seven weeks – prompting speculation from critics that they had started with their conclusions. The report criticised schools for being under the influence of "highly questionable methods". Those included: fragmentary and superficial teaching characterised by much topic work; resistance to single subject teaching; a belief that children only 'learn by doing' and thus cannot be told things; and neglect of the most able children through fear of elitism and a reluctance to correct mistakes "because it discourages the learning process". However, a little 'progressive' balance was restored by finding that attractively displayed work in a classroom is indicative of purposeful education.

Much of the philosophy of the report was to be echoed in the future pronouncements of Chris Woodhead when he became HM Chief Inspector of

Schools. That did not mean that the report's findings were necessarily wrong. Much teacher opinion was also critical of so-called progressive teaching. The general consensus was that a combination of teaching methods, old and new, progressive and traditional, was probably the best.

Mindful that in 1979 the NASUWT had developed a policy advocating a more subject specialist approach, particularly in the upper forms of primary schools, in my press statement reacting to the report I said that: "In many ways the recommendations were knocking on open doors, confirming the views of many teachers that undue emphasis should not be placed on any single method and that a balanced approach was best." The reference to dogma was "surprising, Government being as guilty of that sin as anyone". Furthermore the report did not take up many of the 'dogmas' favoured by the right and widely predicted to feature in it.

The NASUWT was also able to welcome the report's conclusions that significant changes were required to the funding arrangements under LMS and that in-service training was essential for a more specialist approach. Unfortunately in-service raining was fast disappearing, "dare I say it, because of Government's dogmatic approach to formula funding under LMS". The NASUWT believed the majority of teachers would be willing to respond positively to the report if matters were handled sensibly with time, resources and space provided.

In January 1992 Ken Clarke announced consultation over plans to reduce college involvement in teacher training to 20% of the process. Since the mid-'70s the NASUWT had been calling for a more school-based approach. However, I observed that Ken Clarke "risked ruining a good idea by pushing it to extremes". A more school-based approach had been proceeding steadily down the tracks but Ken Clarke's politically motivated intervention, inspired by a right-wing 'think tank', the Policy Studies Institute, could derail the process. Huge problems over workload, training teacher mentors and costs remained completely unaddressed.

The new Secretary of State, John Patten who had replaced Ken Clarke (moving on to Chancellor of the Exchequer) in April 1992, seemed to bow to the latest breeze blowing from his right wing. In the customary late-summer controversy – that accompanied the publication of the GCSE and A Level results – over declining standards, John Patten seemed to be associating himself with the right wing in rubbishing the improved GCSE results. He announced he would be calling the Examination Boards to account. The immediate pretext for this initiative was a forthcoming HMI report which had been selectively leaked. The full report did not support the conclusions reached by the tabloids.

More turbulence in Government education policy followed in September 1992. The NCC announced an inquiry into the teaching of English, the subject taught by Chris Woodhead when he was a teacher. The press seemed to know the findings the 'impartial' inquiry would reach. Banner headlines ran: "Back to Basics" and "Progressive Teaching Abandoned". In my public comments I observed that "the teaching of English has become a political football being booted up and down the right wing of the Conservative Party". I added: "Teachers are entirely justified in complaining bitterly about the ceaseless change in the nature of the Government's reforms, zig-zagging from one view to another." In such a context action from the NASUWT became both inevitable and desirable.

Chapter 70 – The New Pay Regime

When schools returned for the Autumn Term 1987 the dispute over negotiating rights fizzled out. The NUT had decided not to restart action which it had suspended around the time of the June General Election. The NASUWT decided there was little purpose to be served in continuing industrial action on its own. I was pleased personally for I saw no merit in the NASUWT fighting to restore negotiating rights which others would only squander with customary pusillanimity.

The NASUWT Report to Schools starting the new academic year 1987/88 moved members in the direction of taking stock and regrouping for the times ahead. The Union reminded teachers that Ken Baker imposed a draconian contract which had already been conceded by those who signed the Coventry Agreement. But Baker rejected the MPG/collegiate approach which would have benefited the classroom teacher. He was able to do that with a considerable amount of collusion from at least one other union, and possibly more. Many head teachers wished to retain the patronage of promoted posts, seemingly oblivious to the enforceability of the wide-ranging collegiate contract to ensure all relevant duties and responsibilities were met and that appraisal ensured access to the MPG was not just automatic. AMMA was preoccupied with promoted posts, reflecting an infuriating tendency amongst many teachers (and probably people generally) to be more interested in 'status', in earning a little more than their colleagues, rather than securing higher salaries for all.

The NASUWT advised members to act together at school level to ensure heads did not exceed their admittedly considerable powers under the new contract. Members were urged to persuade other colleagues to support our approach, to regroup and be ready for another opportunity which would surely present itself to campaign for decent professional salaries and conditions for teachers.

Fred Smithies, in a letter to all School Reps at the same time, pointed out that Government needed the co-operation of teachers for the education service to succeed. The NASUWT should be prepared to engage in "short, sharp bursts of industrial action" to prove they were still determined to secure justice. In addition we had to cultivate parental and public support and prepare for the forthcoming Education Bill which promised so many fundamental reforms which deliberately contained provisions to weaken the unions, thereby exposing teachers to 'more work and less pay'.

The NASUWT also warned around the same time that Thatcher's proposal (in a new Social Security Act) to allow employees to opt out of compulsory occupational pension schemes was a dangerous 'freedom' to sacrifice long-term benefit for short-term cash.

On 27 October 1987 Baker published his Green Paper on future negotiating machinery. At the same time he also published terms of reference for the Interim Advisory Committee (IAC) to consider the pay award for teachers in 1988. With the crisis on the stock exchange it was a 'good day on which to publish bad news'.

The Green Paper proposed a 'Teachers' Negotiating Group' (TNG) to deal with pay and conditions. The preamble rehearsed the well-known conundrum referring to the need to "recruit, retain and motivate sufficient teachers of the right quality" but only against a background which "ensures that settlements have due regard to affordability and to the needs of the national economy". The NASUWT believed most government decisions on the second of the two principles destroyed the first.

The proposed TNG would:

provide the Government with a majority of votes on the Management Side;

cede power to the Government to intervene and impose a settlement if negotiations continued beyond the end of the month of January in each year;

restore to Government the authority to determine the composition of the Teachers' Side by statute;

deny unions the right of unilateral access to arbitration;

enable the Secretary of State for Employment to appoint arbitrators;

set up separate arrangements for heads and deputies.

Despite being a supposed 'Green Paper' the alternatives of a National Joint Council (NJC) or a Pay Review Body were pre-emptively rejected. The NASUWT had always kept open the option of a review body, having historically called for independent third-party involvement as the only way of circumventing the fundamental weakness of the Burnham machinery and giving teachers a chance of fairer treatment.

The terms of reference set for the IAC for 1988/89 were delivered in a letter from Baker to the Chairman, Lord Chilver. The key criterion set down: "The recommendations of the Committee should be such that they do not cost more than an additional £300m in the 1988/89 financial year or in later years", implying that teachers' pay would rise by no more than 4.5%. Inflation was likely to be above that figure; average earnings almost certainly to be so.

Membership of the IAC was determined by Government. Industry, business, employers and management were always to be well represented. Only one person with a background representing employees, a retired TUC Deputy GS, Ken Graham, was ever appointed, and he only for a short term.

The NASUWT concluded that teachers' relative pay erosion was set to continue. It amounted to "professional serfdom" in the words of Fred Smithies. The intentions of the Government were clear: depress teachers' salaries, cut spending on education and dodge responsibilities through 'reforms'. It was "Education on the Cheap" and in the view of the NASUWT would jeopardise quality.

By January 1988 the NASUWT had settled down to deal with the new situation on the annual pay round. Gone were the days of endless meetings of the Teachers' Panel and the Burnham Committee. Instead the NASUWT developed policy statements and met to compare notes with other unions to see if joint submissions could be made to the IAC. With no formal forum and no union in overall majority, the need for co-operation and compromise came to the forefront and, perhaps surprisingly for some, the unions worked better together in the new situation compared with the traditional 'free collective bargaining' arena.

On 14 January 1988 the first of a novel but interesting series of encounters took place in which unions each met in turn with the IAC to present oral evidence and answer questions.

The NASUWT soon discerned that despite the outrageous abolition of negotiating rights the new pay determination machinery was not all negative. It had the distinct advantage of placing the Government in the front line, for the Secretary of State's letter set the IAC's remit for the year and revealed the global sum from the outset. There could be no more hiding behind the LEAs and the 'stock departmental Pontius Pilate reply' to any question on teachers' pay being "a matter for the Burnham Committee".

The second positive factor was that the process was streamlined and infinitely faster than the interminable machinations of Burnham. Pay increases, whilst still far from adequate, arrived on time. And thirdly, the resultant pay rises, taken in the round despite a poor start, were to prove no worse than those achieved under Burnham agreements and were in some respects better in so far as they often exceeded other local government settlements. Put another way, Government imposition was not necessarily worse than LEA/NUT-led negotiations in Burnham and arguably somewhat better.

At the NASUWT meeting with the IAC, GS Fred Smithies deplored the inadequate global sum of £300m (4½%), both below the inflation rate and the increase in average earnings – the two most important yardsticks governing our salary claims. (DES figures published a little later on 18 February revealed average earnings increasing at the rate of 8.5%.) Fred Smithies ridiculed Ken Baker's latest proposal on 'incentive' allowances, especially the lowest tier, which equated to £1.60 per day or around 25p per "excellent lesson" it was supposed to induce and reward. On conditions of service the NASUWT deplored the lack of planning assumptions made by LEAs about the number of teachers required to deliver the ever-expanding programmes and reforms of the education service.

The 'united' stance of the NASUWT and NUT over boycotting the National Steering Group on Appraisal collapsed in January 1988. Without a word to the NASUWT, the NUT announced it would return to the Group. There had been no change whatsoever to the four factors which led to the boycott, the main one being the Government's torpedoing of the ACAS Agreement, in which appraisal was originally intended to be part of the package.

On the first anniversary of the abolition of negotiating rights, 2 March 1988, protest meetings were organised across the country. In London NASUWT representatives accompanied by national Officers and officials stood across the road from the DES building (an awful steel and glass tower located alongside and overlooking Waterloo Station), handing out leaflets protesting against such "dictatorial power" to thousands of commuters in the morning rush hour.

In March 1988 as the first pay award under the new arrangements approached, more figures appeared showing the private sector pulling further away from teachers. Workers at Ford secured a 14% increase over two years. NHS workers and nurses in particular were gaining much public support for their campaign over pay and placing the Government under pressure. Meanwhile DES statistics were published showing that between 1981/82 and 1985/86 the proportion of GDP spent on education fell by 12.7%.

The first report of the IAC, together with the Secretary of State's reaction to it, was published on 14 April. The IAC adhered strictly to the £300m cash limit set by the Government. In the curious and incestuous 'logic' of the 'game', Ken Baker accepted the 'recommendations' of the report, most of which had been predetermined by his remit to the IAC. The pay rise would be 4.25% for all teachers. The IAC did, however, reject regional and subject specialist pay and it recommended LEAs should consider "carefully where, why and how cover is being provided".

The new main scale (inappropriately named MPG) would run from £7,921 by ten increments to £13,682. The new incentive allowances would be A £800, B £1,200, C £2,400, D £3,200 and E £4,400. London Allowances would be increased by 7.5%.

The recommendations in the report did not reflect the commentary it made. Comments (following visits to schools by the Committee) included:

"Our first conclusion was that teachers' morale is low.

"We found the financial constraint of £300m to be limiting.

"There are already signs that recruitment is becoming more difficult.

"From what we saw and heard, we believe that the great majority of teachers are dedicated to their work and put their children's education above all else.

"Even with implementation of our recommendations there is still some doubt that teachers' motivation will be assured.

"The Secretary of State should consider how much he is prepared to make available to secure the willing co-operation of teachers."

The award of 4.25% compared badly with others. The average increase for white-collar workers was 8.5% and even Scottish teachers were receiving 6%. Nurses received 15.3%, doctors 7.9%, the armed forces 6.4% (all three being covered by pay review bodies). Baker described the award as "fair", arguing that it followed the "substantial" increase of the previous year. That was a red rag to a bull for the NASUWT since the 1987 award was supposed to represent some restoration of previous ground lost, not to mention the worsened contract.

Baker also referred to many teachers receiving increments, but those were supposed to reflect deferred 'rates for the job' as experience generally improved performance. In any event over 150,000 teachers would not receive an increment. Once again history was repeating itself 'with a few waves of restoration coming ashore while the tide of teachers' salaries remained eternally on the ebb'.

The IAC had commissioned research on 'career earnings comparability' which it duly reported but then ignored. It showed that after five years, comparable occupations saw a 70% increase in salary, after ten years 110% and at the height of their careers 150%. The figures for teachers were respectively 40%, 56% and 80%.

Fred Smithies dismissed the award as "contemptuous" and "exploitative". He believed the NASUWT had no choice "but to make a tangible response to this insult". On Friday 6 May the NASUWT Executive decided to ballot members on a half-day protest strike action. Papers had to be returned by 9 June. In addition to the need for protest, the action was also designed to leave the Government in no doubt about teachers' anger, to act as a warning for 1989 and to make sure the general public was not lulled into thinking that the problem of teachers' pay had been solved.

In May 1988 the ILO finally ruled on the complaint submitted by the NASUWT through the TUC and by the NUT unilaterally that the UK Government was in breach of Convention 98 (Article 4), which stated that measures "shall be taken . . . to promote voluntary negotiation between employers and workers organisations" for "the regulation of terms and conditions of employment by means of collective agreements". The Government claim that consultations in relation to the IAC "inevitably took on something of the character of negotiations" was specifically rejected as not "constituting true freedom of negotiation". However, there was no measure that could be taken through the courts to enforce the ruling. The UK had signed the ILO Convention but it had never been formally incorporated into domestic legislation.

On Friday 13 May the NASUWT held its first formal consultation with the Secretary of State on the IAC report. We decided at our pre-meeting to focus on simple, direct questions which stemmed from critical observations in the report. For example, would the Government increase the global sum of £300m which the IAC found "limiting" and would he act on the IAC's recommendation for comparability with graduates to be taken into account?

Ken Baker replied 'no' to these and all other questions. In reply to Baker's request for the NASUWT to call off our ballot on action (accusing us of "not having the interests of the children at heart") Fred Smithies replied 'no'.

The complete lack of any element of genuine consultation in the exercise served only to increase the justification to vote 'yes' in the ballot for action. Although there was a large majority in favour of action, the turnout was rather modest, and being left on our own the Executive decided there was little point in proceeding. Teachers' capacity for industrial action had been well and truly exhausted.

The pattern set by the 1988 IAC report was largely to be replicated over its four-year lifetime except in one important aspect. It gradually departed from the strict 'cash limits' set by the Government although not by huge amounts. Furthermore, the IAC did not always agree with some government proposals, for example on performance related pay.

The 1989 pay round began in September of 1988 with clear indications of a crisis in teacher supply partly at least caused by the profession's decline in relative and real pay levels. Despite the difficulties and against all the odds, the introduction of the GCSE had been declared a success, Baker himself paying tribute to the teachers. Yet his 1989 cash limit was £385m (equivalent to 5.1%), implying increases would again be below the rate of inflation and average earnings.

The NASUWT focussed upon the unpromoted teacher at the top of the main scale who post the Houghton award of 1974 earned 152.8% (£3,474) of average non-manual earnings. That would fall to 106.4% (£14,750) in the projected figure for 1989. There had been a decrease of 8% in the number of applicants for secondary training. Primary rolls were rising, following a 9%

increase in the birth rate during the period 1982-87. Of those who entered training only 62% took up a teaching post.

The more consensual approach induced by the new system between the three mainly classroom-based unions, the NASUWT, NUT and AMMA, resulted in a joint submission highlighting the IAC's own research on career earnings for graduates and the Department of Employment's New Earnings survey showing teachers slipping badly behind.

In presenting oral evidence to the IAC on 2 November 1988 the NASUWT also highlighted the massive increase in workload and the 'burgeoning bureaucracy' associated with the educational reforms. Opposing the proposals for differential increases for head teachers, the NASUWT argued strongly that the educational reforms in the 1988 Act impacted as severely upon classroom teachers as financial delegation did upon heads. Indeed classroom teaching was a far more demanding occupation than balancing school budgets.

Another feature which characterised many of these oral exchanges with the IAC from 1988 to 1991 was the bee-in-the-bonnet issues raised by Committee members. Thus performance related pay (PRP), shortage subject specialist premium payments (especially for maths and science teachers), regional pay, incompetent 'unsackable' teachers, academic qualifications versus teaching ability (as if they were mutually exclusive), long holidays and short working days became "hardy annuals" as we called them. Although a little repetitive the 'bee in the bonnet' questions served a useful purpose in challenging our basic assumptions and forcing us to justify long-established policies and practices.

The bee in the bonnet for 1989 was the Government's suggestion of PRP. We argued with vigour that our collegiate salary policy was a more professional, comprehensive and effective approach. Higher standards of entry to teacher training, coupled with the Entry Grade arrangements, were designed to weed out incompetent or unfit persons before fully qualified status was granted. Access to the Main Professional Grade was dependent upon passing appraisal. A good 'blast' of the NASUWT's collegiate philosophy was usually enough to silence the 'PRP bee-in-the-bonnet people'.

December 1988 saw the NASUWT pressing Baker to honour the ILO judgement and restore negotiating rights. The Minister pleaded lack of Parliamentary time. In the same correspondence Fred Smithies urged the Secretary of State to raise the £385m (5.1%) limit set for the IAC. Inflation was well above 6%. Non-manual earnings were still rising above 9%.

The high levels of stress in teaching, already identified by the Union in the 1970s as largely occasioned by poor pupil behaviour, assumed a much higher profile as escalating workloads and ill-resourced reforms exacerbated the problem. The NASUWT commissioned two important studies on the subject.

The National Foundation for Educational Research was engaged to survey relevant literature on the subject and interview teachers in a number of schools. A second empirical study would be carried out by Professor Cary Cooper of Manchester University, an acknowledged expert in the field, in which over 1,000 teachers would be interviewed and a number asked to co-operate with medical studies to establish the nature of reactions during periods of stress.

The IAC's 1989 report, together with the Government's response, was published on 16 February. Classroom teachers were limited to 6% but heads and deputies awarded 7.5% in recognition of additional burdens. Pay review bodies' reports for others were also published on the same day. Doctors and dentists received 8.2%, nurses 6.8%, the armed forces 6.8% and judges and 'top people' 6.5%. Classroom teachers were again at the bottom but not so badly discriminated against as in some previous years. The IAC had in fact edged beyond Baker's strict cash limit of 5.1%, although LEAs would have to meet the entire additional cost themselves with no extra RSG moneys. Point 10 of the main scale became £13,923.

LEA discretions over pay and conditions were to be transferred to school governors under local management of schools (LMS). Discretion was granted to accelerate a teacher's progression to the top of the main scale.

I said in my press statement that once again teachers had "won the arguments but not the money" and quoted from the report: "Our considered assessment is that the position this year is even more serious . . . by the end of March 1990 some teachers' living standards will have fallen still further." (The RPI figure for the end of January was published the day after the IAC report. It stood at 7.5%.)

I quoted further from the IAC report: " . . . If an occupational group's pay increases begin to fall significantly below the rate of inflation and, without evidence of justification, increases awarded to other groups seen as comparable, then lower morale – with potential damage to motivation – is the probable result."

Rejecting criticism of the profession, the IAC members "continue to be impressed by teachers' commitment and their high professional standards; but morale appears to be as low as we judged it to be last year. We believe pay to be a critical factor in morale, and therefore in motivation." The IAC complimented classroom teachers who "were often working well in excess of the minimum prescribed working year in order to achieve the high standards they had set themselves".

The IAC picked up on an important part of the NASUWT evidence, calling into question the mounting administrative workload on teachers. The IAC recommended "relatively modest increases in expenditure on specialist administrative and technical support" for a "more effective deployment of teachers" which could "raise [their] morale".

With 55 LEA schemes for LMS closely examined, the NASUWT published its findings that some 10,000 teacher jobs could be at risk. Given the context of a tight overall education budget, the new method of devolving money to schools from LEAs inevitably meant creating winners and losers. If schools with enhanced budgets did not take on teachers displaced by 'deficit' schools as they were unlikely to do in the absence of enforceable redeployment agreements, redundancies on the scale identified by the NASUWT were possible.

In the fraught and uncertain times of the late 1980s the NASUWT conducted a vote on the establishment of a political fund. The Tory Government, in a brazen attempt to make life difficult for trade unions and the Labour Party, passed legislation to require donations and other payments to political parties to be authorised by membership-wide ballots. Whilst the NASUWT had always guarded its political neutrality and was not affiliated to any party, payments of various kinds were made to run stalls and meetings at all the major Conferences. The Union also made small donations to the campaigns of its members from UK-wide parties who stood as Parliamentary candidates.

The ballot was conducted during the course of the 1988 Summer Term and produced a 90% vote in favour (44,652 for, 4,759 against) of the near-50,000 turnout from an eligible membership of 140,988.

On 24 July 1989 Ken Baker was appointed Home Secretary and John MacGregor became Secretary of State for Education. He appeared to the NASUWT to be a more 'listening' and reasonable person, more concerned with doing a competent job than pursuing personal ambition. He inherited Baker's decision made in the last couple of weeks of his 'reign' at the DES to continue with the IAC for another year. The NASUWT regretted the decision, but now that it was a 'fait accompli' proposed that the IAC should at the very least be given a genuinely independent remit for 1990 and not be pre-empted yet again by a preordained cash limit.

On 1 September 1989 I became GS designate, to succeed Fred Smithies on his retirement at the end of Conference at Easter 1990. Unfortunately the NASUWT was forced to conduct a membership-wide ballot for the post of GS under Mrs Thatcher's anti-union legislation in the wake of the Cardiff Association nominating one of its members, Brian Williams.

We had hoped to be able to continue to do things 'our' way under the democratically established rules of an open organisation which no one was compelled to join. That was to appoint a new GS by open advertisement, shortlisting, interview and appointment by the full National Executive, subject to ratification by the Annual Conference. The NASUWT believed this was the correct procedure for appointing a chief executive who, as a member of staff contractually required to carry out the decisions of the Executive and Conference, did not exercise a vote. Brian Williams had not applied for the 'post' under the long-established procedures which now had to be amended to constitute 'the Executive nomination for'. Others had applied in the traditional way and in addition to myself three had been interviewed by the full Executive. They were Eamonn O'Kane, President 1987-88 and Chairman of the Salaries Committee; Bill Herron, AGS and a former Regional Official, Northern Ireland; and Dave Battye, the renowned 'Conference debater' from Sheffield, President 1988-89 and a future Honorary Treasurer. They were all high-calibre people with extremely strong credentials who had honourably accepted the outcome in spite of having the legal right to seek nomination through Thatcher's destabilising alternative route.

The Thatcher legislation set up potentially conflicting channels of democracy: the elected National Executive subject to the sovereignty of Conference on one side; an elected GS able to pursue a personal mandate despite a contract to implement the decisions of the Executive and Conference on the other.

In the event, I won the election on a 2:1 majority, 27,092 (67.8%) against Brian Williams' 12,856 (32.2%). Under the legislation an election has to be called every five years and early in 1995 the majority wish to abide by our own rules was upheld and I was returned unopposed upon the nomination of the Executive and 70 local associations.

To return to 1990 . . . I was very keen to make progress on pay determination machinery and suggested the NASUWT take an initiative and invite the other unions to a meeting on 12 September to discuss three principles which should govern any machinery which might eventually replace the IAC:

1 No party to have the right to impose preconditions or to exercise a veto ahead of the process taking place.

2 Teachers to be accorded genuine participation in the determination of their pay and conditions.

3 New arrangements to remain national.

Responses to the latest proposals on new machinery put forward by the Government had to be lodged before the end of September, and the six unions were able to unite behind the three principles the NASUWT had put forward. The Government's proposals were similar to earlier ones which would recreate and worsen the features of Burnham.

The appeal of the NASUWT for an independent remit for the IAC fell on deaf Government ears. The invitation to 'getting to know you' drinks from the new Secretary of State to union leaders and others on 14 September, while mildly encouraging, did not herald a significant change in Government policy.

On 26 September John MacGregor announced the remit for the IAC 1990 round. The cash limit was set at a £600m increase in the global sum, amounting to 7.5% of the pay bill.

The remit also called for increases in the number and value of the incentive allowances, measures to recruit teachers in areas of high vacancy rates, additional rises for heads and deputies for extra work and shortage subject premium payments.

The below-inflation (then at 8.3%) remit produced a significant degree of anger from members, conveyed through the usual channels of branch meetings, correspondence and telephone calls. Responding, the Executive decided to mount an escalating campaign on pay and workload "in the belief that industrial action may be necessary to secure much needed improvement in teachers' pay and conditions of service".

John MacGregor did show he could respond positively to genuine concerns when in October he decided to suspend plans for appraisal. In an unusual concession from Government he acknowledged that schools were being overwhelmed with a flood of reforms.

The NASUWT meeting with the IAC for the 1990 pay award witnessed another intensive discussion on our collegiate approach. We always thought we won the argument but not the day. The DES again submitted recommendations for changes to the structure, all of them variations of the hierarchical approach which diminished the "central importance of the teacher in the classroom". The NASUWT quoted the successful introduction of the GCSE, which reflected a very collaborative approach by teachers and was a vital feature of collegiality.

Another (later) example amongst many was the introduction of 'accelerated progression', enabling teachers to receive more than one increment in a year. The NASUWT pointed out that the incentive allowances were supposed to cater for this apparent 'need'. The IAC (and its successor body) often acceded to the Ministerial promptings on structural matters. However, they never seemed to realise that the constant tinkering raised the fundamental question: had they got the structure right in the first place?

The NASUWT took the initiative and secured the support of all the other teacher unions to unite on a common platform to lobby Parliament on 5 December 1989, the occasion on which the Government laid a Draft Order in the Commons to extend the life of the IAC for a further year. The lobby was well supported by local Officers and activists and addressed by a good range of MPs from all parties. As well as negotiating rights the straightjacket of the preordained cash limit of 7.5% (once again behind inflation and average earnings) was given a good airing.

Later in the evening when the Order was debated, many speakers from all sides of the House, including the Conservatives, were very critical of the Government's failure to honour its undertaking to restore negotiating rights. When the vote came shortly after midnight the Government's majority was reduced to 40 despite a three-line whip. The 'ayes' supporting the Order numbered 221, the 'noes' amounting to 181. The decision to lobby had been well judged and some pressure was placed on the normally unmoveable Thatcher Government.

As 1990 got under way the NASUWT Executive focussed on the Pay Review Body alternative, which had long been an option for the NASUWT and which had my strong personal support. Whilst no one had any objections in principle to free collective bargaining, between 1970 and its abolition in 1987 Burnham had only delivered three agreed settlements. Teachers secured better awards when third parties intervened, the best example being Houghton in 1974. Arbitral bodies secured more than 'normal' negotiations in Burnham. Even Clegg, which deliberately undercut the Houghton standard, nevertheless yielded more than the employers wished to concede. ACAS 1986 was another example.

Baker's consultations on his Green Paper of the previous year indicated that restored negotiations would be a sham, even worse than the old Burnham Committee. We noticed how several unions, including the NUT, had nevertheless reacted favourably to the Green Paper, obviously desperate to retrieve some semblance of negotiations, however flawed. Given our recent experience of negotiations we came to the view that a Pay Review Body which worked well for other occupations would be far preferable. By January 1990 the Executive had approved a policy paper calling for an independent review body to replace the IAC.

The IAC, reporting at the end of January 1990, redeemed some of its tarnished reputation as a Government 'poodle'. It recommended overall an increase in the pay bill of 9.3%, significantly above the Government's £600m (7.5%) 'limit' at £733m. Whilst still below average earnings, around 10%, it was above the RPI, at 7.7%.

However, the 'heads I win, tails you lose' Government philosophy underpinning the IAC then swung into action. John MacGregor announced the Government would not accept the IAC recommendations in full but would phase the award with most of it paid on 1 April, the remainder on 1 January 1991. The effect of this phasing would reduce the 1990-91 award overall to 7.9% (£622m). The award was also differentiated, with heads averaging just over 10%. The pay improvements for classroom teachers ranged from 6.4% to 11.2%. Point 10 on the main scale would move from £13,923 to £14,898 on 1 April and to £15,000 on 1 January 1991. Soon afterwards teachers in Scotland were awarded an increase of 9%, which was not phased.

The NASUWT condemned the staged pay increase as an "insult and a provocation" made worse by the IAC admitting that their recommendations only addressed the two problems of low pay and morale "to a small extent". The NASUWT believed the Government was overplaying its already strong hand in pay determination, being prosecutor, judge and jury in the process, reflecting "a touch of the banana republic about it" as I publicly observed. However, such powers had long been exercised behind the scenes in Burnham whereas now they had been forced into the open, exposing government to political pressure.

At its February 1990 meeting the Executive called a Special Salaries Conference on the 24th of the month to discuss the holding of a ballot of all members with a "view to instituting appropriate protest action". Much literature was circulated explaining the award in full, one broadsheet quoting from the IAC report itself:

"Any profession would be justifiably proud of the level of commitment on the part of teachers we have met during our school visits in all three years.

"Throughout our three years, pay has been a major cause of low morale.

" . . . We fear that commitment is closer to breaking point this year

" . . . Even if inflation falls back to 7.5% at the end of the financial year, the majority of teachers will be worse off than a year previously, whatever then happens during 1990-91."

The broadsheet concluded with a challenge to members: "What are you going to do about it?"

At the same time the setting of poll tax levels posed threats to the funding of education and the employment of teachers. The Labour Opposition projected the possibility of 78,000 teacher redundancies in England and Wales. Some LEAs were threatened with poll tax capping, making the dire situation worse. In a letter responding to Fred Smithies, John MacGregor still prevaricated on the restoration of negotiating rights. Members were enjoined to vote 'yes' in the ballot on action and a strike was provisionally being arranged for 4 April in conjunction with a national rally in London.

Early in March in a Report to Schools members were informed of a new strategy on workload being prepared by me as the incoming GS. Members would be encouraged to define 'reasonable workload' in their own terms and apply it in practice. If challenged by the head teacher or governors a dispute would be declared and industrial action taken if possible and appropriate under Executive control. It was the only strategy available short of full-scale national industrial action. It required strong leadership from NASUWT School Reps backed up by a sizeable membership in a school to operate effectively. I knew it was not perfect, but it was a start and someone somewhere had to do something to address this massive problem.

A NASUWT deputation met the Secretary of State on 19 March for the consultation required by statute over the IAC report. Stepping into Fred Smithies' shoes as the incoming GS I concentrated on two simple questions to John MacGregor: one, did he think it fair to impose yet another cut in teachers' living standards; and two, was it right to do this against the unprecedented additional demands being made upon them?

The deputation formed the impression that MacGregor was uncomfortable 'defending the indefensible' for he seemed to be a basically fair-minded person. However, this was no time for sentiment and in the subsequent Report to Schools I wrote that MacGregor's fine words in his recent letter to head teachers – "I believe that the teaching profession deserve gratitude, recognition and respect for their professionalism and the commitment they show to their pupils" – were "hollow and hypocritical". The NASUWT concluded that the encounter with the Secretary of State proved that rational argument and all other 'peaceful' measures had been exhausted. The time for action had arrived.

The result of the NASUWT ballot was announced on 26 March (1990). On a turnout of 59% of eligible voters 35,450 (62%) had voted 'yes'; 21,949 (38%) 'no'. It was not the largest majority the NASUWT had secured for action but it was decisive and clear-cut and the Executive decided to proceed with the planned strike on 4 April. Members were instructed in the usual way by the GS acting under the Executive's authority and also exhorted to travel to London on the day to participate in the mass rally in Hyde Park.

The action on 4 April was well supported and thousands attended an impressive rally in Hyde Park. For Fred Smithies it was his last day of strike action and the final rally he addressed as the retiring GS. He concentrated on the huge injustices over salary and the withdrawal of negotiating rights. My speech to the rally was devoted to the equally important issue of excessive workload, plugging the strategy I had outlined to NASUWT negotiating secretaries at our HQ just a couple of weeks previously.

Conference 1990 was dominated by the crucial issues of pay, job security and workload. An emergency motion empowering the Executive to take whatever steps were necessary, including strike action, to defend jobs was taken and carried, largely as a response to the Nottinghamshire LEA issuing redundancy notices to 188 teachers as a result of the introduction of LMS.

The Executive was also authorised to continue the campaigns to secure just salaries and limits on teachers' workloads. A recent survey had shown teachers to be working in excess of 50 hours per week, much of it on paperwork surrounding Government reforms.

Fred Smithies was given rousing standing ovations for his work as GS. He had been GS for seven gruelling years in the middle of the Thatcher premiership with unions under constant attack by the Government. Just to have survived as a union was no mean feat, let alone wage the courageous battles that Fred had led in the teaching profession. As had become the custom Fred and I shared the 'Monday evening state of the nation GS slot'. I emphasised the need to keep genuine trade unionism alive as the only protection for teachers. On the issue of 'professional unity' I said it was more important to put genuine trade unionism into all teachers than all teachers into one union.

The year 1990 was also the year in which Mick Carney became President. He was to assume a very influential role in NASUWT affairs over the course of the following decade, becoming Honorary Treasurer after his four years going through the offices of the presidency. In his presidential speech he brought a sharp classroom-teacher focus to our deliberations and was on that account extremely critical of the Government's reforms for failing to take account of the views of those who had to implement them in everyday practice.

Shortly following Conference and after four years of imposition the Government released proposals for the future determination of teachers' pay and conditions. There would be no Government presence at the negotiating table with employers and unions but it would retain massive reserve powers, making the exercise completely bogus. I immediately dismissed the proposals as "a recipe for disaster. The Government was restoring negotiations with one hand and taking them back with the other."

The reserve powers included a requirement upon employers to negotiate within Government decisions about standard local authority spending (the old preordained global sum repackaged). In addition the Secretary of State could: (1) refer back for further consideration any agreement of which he disapproved; (2) override a negotiated settlement, imposing his own views; and (3) if the negotiating body failed to reach an agreement within an imposed timetable, intervene and set up his own committee, similar to the existing IAC arrangements. Furthermore, LEAs and GM schools' governing bodies could, with the approval of the Secretary of State, opt out of national negotiations and engage in local or school-based negotiations.

I was genuinely surprised that even the Thatcher Government could propose such an outrageous sham and devise a machine that was worse than Burnham. Even more alarming was the NUT reacting favourably despite the three principles all six unions had recently agreed.

That settled our determination more than ever to campaign hard for a Pay Review Body although we believed conditions of service were not best served by such machinery. Independent bodies could examine pay data, make comparisons and arrive at reasonable conclusions, but conditions of service were best dealt with by people with hands-on experience of how schools worked. Our policy in favour of a Pay Review Body included the provision for a 'side committee' to run parallel to it and determine conditions of service in tandem with it.

In a deputation to John MacGregor on 15 May we rehearsed all these arguments and also emphasised the positive advantages of a Pay Review Body. It could raise morale, giving teachers confidence that their voice was being heard and heeded. It could take pay out of the arena of endless conflict between government, employers and unions. However, the Government would have to be flexible and surrender its right to determine everything in advance. MacGregor graciously conceded that the NASUWT had argued "a cogent and consistent case". We formed the impression that he did not believe strongly in the case he had to argue. The proposals had a touch of the authoritarian and facetious about them, typical of a Government that had just won a third successive term.

The Parliamentary Education Select Committee published a report on teacher supply for the 1990s. Despite a Conservative majority, it was extremely critical of the treatment teachers had received, stating that the IAC award should be paid in full, not phased, and that negotiating rights should be restored as soon as possible.

Around the same time the Government announced an advertising campaign to be run by Saatchi and Saatchi at a cost of £2m. I said it was no good conning people into teaching through slick PR. If it worked it would only do so for a short time. Reality would quickly destroy the glossy image. My press statement concluded: "The teaching profession needs salary and salary, not Saatchi and Saatchi!"

In September the Government published the Parliamentary Bill it intended to introduce on teachers' pay and conditions machinery. It contained all the objectionable provisions the NASUWT had denounced when the proposals first emerged in the consultative Green Paper. The Government retained powers to intervene, override and impose its own views. The deadline set for agreement before the Government would take over and re-establish the IAC arrangements was set very early – 31 January each year. The employers would have no reason to negotiate. I denounced the Bill as a "monstrous charade, a hundred times worse than the discredited Burnham Committee. Teachers would be negotiating with their hands tied behind their backs, their feet bound and a gun held to their heads!"

Meanwhile there was no stopping the agony piled on by the Thatcher Government. In September MacGregor announced yet again a below-inflation cash limit for teachers' pay in 1991, months before the IAC was to get down to considering the evidence. The limit was set at 8% and on the same day the RPI was published, showing a rate of 10.6% and expected to rise even higher. Taken with the absurd proposals on negotiating machinery, I greeted these successive cuts in teachers' standard of living as a "calculated insult".

In October the NASUWT submitted its 'claim' for 1 April 1991 in the now customary form of evidence to the IAC. It called for a 15% increase, a genuine collegiate salary structure, a 35-hour contractual week and an independent inquiry into teachers' pay.

The arguments were familiar; only the detailed figures changed, such as the inflation rate then running at 11%. The NASUWT highlighted the need for a reasonable limit to working hours. The infamous 36 (1) (f) clause in the imposed contract (the open-ended "In addition (to the 1,325 hours) teachers shall perform such other duties as may reasonably be required ... ") was the conduit through which crippling and bureaucratic workload had been imposed, seriously hindering effective classroom teaching.

The NASUWT also demanded the abolition of the five in-service days (or 'Baker Days'), which were widely regarded with cynicism since they were often an excuse for more futile and time-wasting meetings. Many of these measures would cost nothing but would dramatically improve the efficiency and morale of the teaching force.

In November John MacGregor was axed as Education Secretary. There was much speculation that he had 'gone native', which was 'Thatcher-speak' for believing opposing views might have some validity. He probably sealed his fate when he spiritedly rejected internal Conservative Party criticism that the pace of reform had slowed, on the common-sense basis of ensuring one fundamental change is successfully introduced before proceeding to the next.

In MacGregor's place came the urbane figure of Kenneth Clarke. He was not to stay very long in Education before moving on to greater things as Chancellor of the Exchequer. Clarke was more like MacGregor than Baker in having his feet firmly on the ground, and his more common-sense approach was possibly assisted by the internal party 'coup' which was soon to oust the seemingly invincible Mrs Thatcher.

Margaret Thatcher's difficulties had continued, with several senior Ministers and ex-Ministers plotting against her, and a formal leadership challenge mounted. Although Thatcher gained more votes than any other candidate in the first round of voting she was a little short of the overall enhanced majority the Party rules required. Despite determining famously "to fight on" in an impromptu press conference outside an EEC meeting in Paris, a majority of her Cabinet convinced her she was irreparably damaged, and on Thursday 22 November 1990 Margaret Thatcher resigned as Prime Minister.

In December 1990 the Teachers' Pay and Conditions (TPC) Bill had its second reading in the House of Commons. It was widely condemned from every side, but the Government, despite the change in Prime Minister, seemed determined to proceed as before. The NASUWT encouraged its members to lobby their MPs and many did so, both in their constituencies as well as at Westminster. The ILO indicated it believed the Bill was in breach of Convention 98. The proposed negotiations would not be free and independent but always subject to massive reserve powers of the Secretary of State.

The new Secretary of State for Education reminded the IAC that the pay rise for teachers should be between 8% and 10% despite the fact that inflation was still running at 11%. The NASUWT calculated that teachers' pay was now 40% below the Houghton standard of 1974. In December Ken Clarke reversed the decision of his predecessor and announced he would make appraisal of teachers compulsory.

The Government decision to go over union leaders' heads and communicate directly with teachers through bulletins distributed to all schools backfired badly in December when it made extravagant claims on restoring negotiating rights in its TPC Bill in an attempt "to set the record straight". It was met by a torrent of criticism from teachers who clearly agreed with the NASUWT's view.

As part of our lobby against the TPC Bill our Parliamentary Adviser Ken Weetch set up a meeting with Sir Malcolm Thornton, a Conservative MP who was also Chairman of the Parliamentary Select Committee on Education. I had known Malcolm when he was on the Management Panel of Burnham. He was a one-nation Tory, a rare breed after the ravages of Thatcherism, having grown up on Merseyside and been a pilot on the river before becoming an MP. He was one of the few Conservative MPs I had managed to maintain a dialogue with notwithstanding the bitter strikes of the mid-1980s.

Ken Weetch, DGS Eamonn O'Kane and I met with Sir Malcolm and we managed to convince him with our arguments for a Pay Review Body. We focussed upon the case for taking more of the cost of teachers' salaries off the highly unpopular poll tax (and whatever its successor was to be), which had replaced the local rates and contributed in no small measure to Mrs Thatcher's downfall. If Government assumed responsibility for centrally funding a higher proportion of the total teacher salary bill, it could justifiably introduce a review body system under which it would assume a much greater direct role, admittedly diminishing still further the functions of LEAs, already weakened in the wake of the legislation of 1987 and '88.

Michael Heseltine, having "wielded the knife" against Thatcher, did not "gain the crown". However, he was appointed Deputy PM by the newly installed Premier, John Major. As one of the fiercest critics of the poll tax he was charged with finding a replacement and making sure that in turn it did not become too burdensome a local levy. Sir Malcolm suggested we put our ideas on one side of A4 – no more he insisted; Heseltine did not read anything longer! Malcolm promised to "walk the paper straight into Heseltine's hands", bypassing the civil servants who might lose it in the system. We had found a little bit of magic – a rare confluence of interests between the NASUWT and Government. Malcolm recommended we be discreet to enhance the chances of success. No press statements please! I was happy to oblige. Within 24 hours Sir Malcolm had our one side of A4 in his possession.

During the month of January 1991 we were uncertain about the fate of our paper as the Government pushed ahead with the Parliamentary process. All we could do was to continue lobbying vigorously against the TPC Bill.

The IAC report was published on 31 January. It was "Another raw deal", as I headlined my press statement. The below-inflation award, which was differentially structured in favour of heads and deputies, was phased by the Government. Classroom teachers received 7.5% from 1 April and another 2% from 1 December. Heads and deputies received the same amount on 1 January but 5.25% extra on 1 December. The outmoded Incentive Allowances were increased by the staggering amount of 30%, more a sign of their failure than of anyone's generosity. The London Allowances were increased by 9.38%. The maximum of the Main Scale became £17,208 on 1 April and £17,522 on 1 December.

Despite the classroom teacher's increase for the year overall being 8.17% against inflation at 9.3%, Ken Clarke managed to claim it would "restore the status and esteem of teachers". When we met Clarke on 28 February for the statutory consultation, in response to our complaints about the "double disadvantage" of the cash limit and phasing he revealingly said if the IAC report had arrived on his desk as a negotiated agreement he would have sent it back. We immediately asked how that squared with his claim the Government was restoring negotiating rights in the TPC Bill! For a moment or two Ken Clarke was uncharacteristically flummoxed.

On 13 March I had another meeting with Sir Malcolm Thornton. The 'lobby' was quite promising but not yet conclusive. A decision had been taken to withdraw the TPC Bill from the legislative timetable because of the review of the poll tax and the readjustment of the financial relationship between central and local government. However, the argument over a Pay Review Body for teachers was gaining ground but not yet won. I learned that there had been considerable support even inside Mrs Thatcher's Cabinet for a review body to replace the IAC but 'the majority of one' – 'the boss herself' – had ruled it out.

As a consequence of this intelligence I encouraged members and local Officers to step up the NASUWT lobby, for "the Bill was delayed but not dead". At the same time I was able to steer the emphasis towards highlighting the potential of an independent review body to take the confrontational element out of teachers' pay determination every year.

We had already noted the growing tendency of the IAC, for all its limitations, nevertheless to exceed the tight financial remit by small but increasing amounts year by year, so much so that we now had to face the problem of Government phasing the awards. I described that as "a good problem to have". There was never a 'need' to phase Burnham agreements! A third party of this kind could often exert greater pressure on the Government to increase the global sum.

Conference 1991 opened as usual on Easter Monday, 1 April. Using the 'state of the union' GS address to delegates on the Monday evening I reported that a Pay Review Body was definitely "on the agenda". We had managed to get through to some "influential MPs" and "it may not be too long before some serious proposals are advanced".

Conference 1991 also saw the installation as President of another colourful and dynamic leader in the person of Sue Rogers from Sheffield. Sue was destined to go on to become Honorary Treasurer and a great ambassador for the NASUWT in TUC and international labour circles. In her presidential speech Sue criticised the Government for its "divisive and discriminatory educational policy". An overall reduction of resources combined with LMS and opting out "had put education at the mercy of market forces in which there were few winners and lots of losers. Schools were strapped for cash and had been reduced to begging bowl status while Government wastes public money on expensive city technology colleges for the favoured few."

Conference decisions reflected the emergence of excessive workload as the major problem facing teachers, with the imminent arrival of SATs making it even more urgent. Conference declared unequivocally that strike action would be available to members implementing the workload strategy but meeting with unreasonable responses from management. The Conference also adopted two major reports on Staffing of Schools (based on the clearly defined needs of the national curriculum) and a Physical Survey of Schools (revealing a massive backlog of badly needed repairs).

Chapter 71 - A Pay Review Body for Teachers

On 16 April 1991, the day after returning from an NASUWT educational visit to the USA hosted by our 'partner union', the American Federation of Teachers, I found myself engaged in detailed consultation with a senior civil servant, Nick Sanders, Head of Teachers' Branch at the DES. He was keen to get me on board for a major statement from Ken Clarke on a review body for teachers to be announced the following day. It was not everything we wanted. There would be some 'guidance' on the global sum but the review body would be free to make independent recommendations which the Government would undertake to implement "unless there were compelling reasons to the contrary". Clarke would also refer to an expectation of no industrial action. I was able to respond positively.

In the House of Commons the next day, 17 April, Ken Clarke took just ten minutes to announce plans to establish the Teachers' Pay Review Body. He ditched the TPC 1991 (No. 1) Bill and replaced it with another of the same name, No.2. Reacting publicly I "warmly welcomed the decision to ditch the disastrous No. 1 Bill" and described the establishment of the School Teachers' Review Body (STRB) as "a major breakthrough for the NASUWT". All the other unions also welcomed the proposals except the NUT who strongly objected. Traditionally 'the left' inside the trade union and labour movement had opposed review bodies, favouring 'free collective bargaining'. However, the NUT was on weak ground in having supported the No. 1 Bill, which suffered even more acutely from the weaknesses it attributed to the review body system.

On the delicate issue of industrial action to which Ken Clarke had indeed referred, I made it plain the NASUWT could only ever *consider* a no-strike agreement if the Government were prepared to bind itself in advance to review body reports (knowing full well that would never happen). Instead of making "impossible demands upon each other" I suggested, "Let's suck it and see". That indeed happened, arguably with a lot more success than the old-style Burnham negotiations.

Ken Clarke also confirmed the arrangements for 'guidance', as opposed to rigid cash limits and other important aspects Nick Sanders had discussed with me over the phone. I paid tribute to the effective lobbying of MPs by thousands of NASUWT members and pointed out the long-term strategic advantage in placing schoolteachers in the company of doctors, dentists, nurses, the armed forces, senior civil servants, the judiciary and other 'top people' who all enjoyed 'review body status' and showed no signs of wanting to embrace or revert to 'traditional style' negotiations. However, on the downside the membership of the review body was to reflect the IAC with 'management and business' well to the fore with not a single classroom teacher or union representative in sight.

Unfortunately within a week Ken Clarke had lost much of the positive gain of the STRB announcement. In aggressive mood, he issued draft regulations on appraisal which departed radically from the National Steering Group (NSG) model. The Government failed to distinguish the different procedures required for promotion, the exercise of pay discretion, discipline and dismissal in allowing "relevant information from appraisal records to be taken into account" by management. In October 1991 the final regulations were duly promulgated requiring employers to appraise half of all teachers by the end of the 1992-93 school year and the remainder by August 1995. Schemes had at least to be established in consultation with teachers. The NASUWT issued advice to members not to participate in schemes which had not been properly constructed by the employers.

In October 1991 the NASUWT submitted its first claim to the STRB. Against the background of the decline in pay, the crushing workload and the speed of educational change, the NASUWT made its customary call for a collegiate salary structure and a new management philosophy. PRP was rejected by the NASUWT as an excuse to pay a few teachers decent salaries instead of ensuring that all were of a high calibre and suitably rewarded. Specifically the NASUWT evidence called for an overall 15.43% increase, to include an element of catch-up, and for a maximum 35-hour working week. The latest NASUWT survey on workload revealed that more time was taken up with meetings and form-filling administration than was spent teaching in the classroom.

A furious row between Westminster and local government broke out in December 1991 over the global sum for the next teachers' pay increase. LEAs claimed 3.7% was all they had. The Government's guidance to the STRB "to have regard to" was emerging at just over 7%. It was an interesting development vis-à-vis the debate over Burnham-style negotiations and the review body process. I said "7% was nowhere near enough but 3.7% would be a disaster." The LEAs claimed anything over 3.7% would place jobs in jeopardy, a very familiar threat over the previous 20 years in my experience.

The STRB with (later Sir) John Gardiner as its Chairman, delivered its first report on Monday 10 February 1992. Overall it recommended an increase of 7.8% against the Government's 'guidance' of 7.1%. The award was 7.5% across the board and an extra 26,000 incentive allowances. In my press statement I described the award as "a small step forward". It was twice the rate of inflation, slightly above the estimated current level of average earnings and "definitely much better that the 3.8% the LEA employers would have offered under traditional-style negotiations". The (Main) now called Standard Scale would run from £11,184 by ten increments to £18,837. Average pay for the classroom teacher now stood at £18,200 p.a.

The Review Body had also rejected the Prime Minister's approach to PRP. It suggested a different system based on whole-school evaluation be considered for the following year and it recognised that formula funding would have to be altered to accommodate PRP. The STRB announced its future intention to simplify the pay structure, an interesting development for the NASUWT, bearing in mind our collegiate philosophy. Conditions of service were left unchanged.

Meanwhile the Conservative Government had continued to suffer in the opinion polls and PM John Major was going the full length of five years before having to call the next General Election at the latest in April 1992.

The NASUWT engaged Gallup to undertake some polling of teacher voting intentions and opinions on other matters. The results showed 48% of teachers would vote Labour, 22% Liberal Democrat and 17% Conservative if an election were called 'tomorrow'. A *TES* survey in 1979 had shown 55% of teachers voting Conservative. The 'Thatcher' years had taken their toll on teacher support for the Tories. Only 8% believed the Conservatives had the best policies for education. During the 1980s, when many believed the Labour Party was unelectable, the teacher vote had swung significantly to the Lib Dems, but now it was flowing back to Labour with its Leader Neil Kinnock having fought a brave and largely successful battle to rescue the Party from the hard left.

The NASUWT leadership was pleased to note the support amongst the profession for the establishment of the review body, with 87% in favour. Broken down by union membership the support was 86% amongst NASUWT members, 84% amongst the NUT and 90% amongst AMMA. The leadership was reassured to note that 84% of teachers believed that unions still had an effective role to play. Indeed 64% of those not in unions believed that to be the case as well.

With the 1992 General Election announced for 9 April the NASUWT issued its customary briefing material, advising members of the key issues to raise with as many Parliamentary candidates as possible.

The *TES* conducted its customary pre-election survey of teacher opinion. It confirmed the NASUWT findings although it seemed to show a continued swing to Labour. It reported 51% intending to vote Labour, 24% Lib Dem and 20% Conservative. The *TES* also endorsed my publicly stated view that teachers "could have a significant bearing on the outcome in key marginal constituencies".

The media onslaught against the personal aptitude of the Labour Leader Neil Kinnock to be Prime Minister, perhaps coupled with some premature victory 'celebrations', may have been the decisive factors turning an expected hung result into a modestly comfortable 30-seat majority for John Major's Conservative Party (although much reduced from the 100-plus seat margin in 1987).

Most members were devastated by the result. In my GS 'state of the union' address to Conference I tried to lift morale by encouraging delegates to take comfort from the fact that we had survived 13 years of rampant Thatcherism, the Tory majority was much reduced, we had increased membership and we had won a Pay Review Body which had just produced the best pay award for many years.

By December 1992, however, it was back to the familiar business of pay restraint with a Government policy discriminating viciously against the public sector, stipulating that pay rises for 1993 would be limited to 1.5%.

On 12 February the STRB Report for 1993 was published. The recommendations duly followed the Government's prescriptive 1.5% maximum for the public sector. I condemned the award for the usual reasons, adding that "no one had any right to expect teachers to shoulder the massive increase in workload following all the reforms". I predicted a greater majority of members would vote in support of the boycott of excessive workload associated with the new national testing and assessment regime which was under way.

Amidst all the gloom there were, however, some promising signs. The Review Body again sidelined the Government's proposals on PRP. There was also an interesting change to the salary structure, merging the former 'main scale' with the incentive allowances and other discretionary payments into a new Common Spine running to 17 points (£11,244 to £30,441) with the unpromoted maximum at point 10, £20,244. The details applying to the Common Spine were complex, with assimilation to and progress up the Common Spine dependent upon various factors such as qualifications, experience, defined responsibilities, recruitment and retention, special needs and, most interesting from the NASUWT's 'collegiate point of view', good-quality teaching in the classroom. Despite serious reservations about some aspects, the NASUWT saw the potential to open up progress beyond point 10 for good classroom teachers judged against fair and open appraisal procedures in line with our policy of collegiality.

The remainder of 1993 was dominated by the extremely successful NASUWT-led and inspired 'Test Boycott' and its aftermath.

Chapter 72 - The Great 'Test Boycott'

The great 'Test Boycott' of 1993 was "the mother of all victories" for its creator, the NASUWT. It was the only time a trade union forced   government into retreat during the 18 years of 'torrid Tory rule' from 1979 to 1997. It was a brilliant example of combining industrial action with professionalism, for the boycott served the interests of pupils and teachers alike. Initially condemned by the usual suspects including Government Ministers and the media, it was not long before such pundits were applauding the 'slim down' of the inflated monster that the national curriculum (NC) had become. A distinguished public servant, Sir Ron (later Lord) Dearing, was appointed to review the reforms following the pressure generated by the boycott.

Popularly, if somewhat inaccurately, labelled the 'Test Boycott', its true purpose was to protest against all the excessive and unnecessary workload occasioned by the NC reforms. This distinction was not mere pedantry but a vital legal ingredient revealing the action to be a genuine trade dispute related wholly or mainly to terms and conditions of employment. Mrs Thatcher's employment legislation of the 1980s had greatly restricted the scope of a trade dispute, exposing action based on other grounds, such as philosophical, political or educational, to challenge in the courts and union liability for damages.

A purely test boycott could well have been adjudged illegal in the courts. As events turned out, against all the predictions except our own, the NASUWT won spectacular battles in the courts against the Government's 'surrogate litigant', the London Borough of Wandsworth. The hapless Secretary of State for Education at the time, John Patten, was eventually dropped from the Cabinet after returning to work following a prolonged period of absence through illness.

The origins of the boycott lay in the 1988 Education Reform Act, which spawned a massive NC, assessment and testing regime in all state schools in England and Wales. It also applied to Northern Ireland, where it was known as the common curriculum. No one appears fully to understand how and why Mrs Thatcher's original idea of "simple pencil and paper tests in maths, English and science" developed into this "Byzantine monster" – so described by none other than a prominent Government adviser and Conservative peer, Lord Skidelsky.

It later became apparent that Ken Baker had effectively ignored his Prime Minister's 'simple pencil and paper' ambitions and striven instead to create a grandiose NC of great depth and breadth as he implemented his 1988 ERA. The establishment via Baker's patronage of unrepresentative subject committees to lay down detailed programmes of study, attainment targets and much else for each of the ten NC subjects resulted in the competitive development of 'empires' by teams of enthusiasts. With each group acting independently, no one spotted the "bureaucratic nightmare" of over 8,000 pages of detailed instructions they were collectively constructing. The planters could not see the wood for the trees.

The separation of curriculum from examinations following the establishment of two government 'quangos', respectively the National Curriculum Council (NCC) and the School Examinations and Assessment Council (SEAC), may have been another cause leading to the "Byzantine monster".

Workload had already been massively increased by the negotiation-abolishing 1987 Teachers' Pay and Conditions Act. Banking successfully on the NASUWT and NUT having exhausted themselves with three years of industrial action over pay, the Government imposed a draconian new contract upon teachers detailing a long list of duties and responsibilities without any limits of time save what might be judged "reasonable". That set up the contractual conduit through which the NC juggernaut began to roll in the early 1990s.

On what proved to be the last day of national strike action over pay and conditions for 18 years, 4 April 1990, the outgoing GS Fred Smithies addressed the massed ranks of the NASUWT on the issue of salaries at the rally in London's Hyde Park. As the incoming GS I devoted my speech to launching the Campaign on Workload. The first stage was to encourage members to act collectively and apply the test of "reasonableness" to what they were being required to do. Not surprisingly that was only effective in schools with large and active NASUWT memberships and even then provided inadequate protection against the juggernaut.

Primary school teachers were the first to be hit by the juggernaut with big changes to the curriculum and the development of tests (Standard Attainment Tasks – SATs) at Key Stages 1 and 2, respectively for the 7- and 11-year-olds. The SATs were incredibly complicated and required massive amounts of recording and assessing. In June 1991 a well-attended seminar for primary teacher members was held at our Rednal HQ. After listening to the tales of woe, on behalf of the Executive (and in line with the promulgated views of the Six Teachers Organisations) I reminded the members of the full support available to start refusing to carry out the worst absurdities. However, the members present seemed reluctant to contemplate action of this kind.

With the domestically unpopular Mrs Thatcher deposed (in 1990) by an internal Party coup, the Conservatives managed to win the 1992 General Election on 9 April. The opinion polls had indicated a possible hung Parliament.

Teachers were in the most depressed mood I was ever to experience. I recall my GS address to Conference at Easter just 11 days after the election, to be the most difficult one to deliver in my lifetime. What on earth could I say to lift members' spirits? After reminding delegates of our successes, such as securing a Pay Review Body, I fell back on a very simple, apparently naïve, seemingly implausible but intriguing notion all the same – open rebellion! If all teachers simply rebelled and refused to implement the nonsense that was developing there would be nothing Government could do about it. We had to develop new and more subtle tactics, traditional strike action still being in need of rest and recuperation. Little did I realise it at the time but within a year the NASUWT was to be at the heart of organising such a rebellion.

By the Summer Term of 1992 the juggernaut was rolling into the secondary sector, where NASUWT had much greater strength of membership. On 8 June the first pilot for Key Stage 3 (14-year-olds) tests began. They were in science and, having in the preceding few weeks consulted closely with members teaching that subject, I issued a press statement on the day saying that the pilot tests "had been a catalogue of woe". The science curriculum had been changed eight times, with important information arriving late in schools, in some cases just a couple of weeks before the tests. Totally unrealistic allowances were made for marking time, for example bands 5 to 8 which contained 91 pages of questions, assumed 13 minutes for the purpose. Teachers said at least two full days would be required for each class. The amount of recording was enormous. Many schools experienced serious logistical problems as the time of year coincided with the major public examinations at 16 and 18, GCSE and A Levels.

Wisely, many schools that had volunteered for the pilot withdrew as they saw the volume and complexity of paperwork tumbling through the post. In short I concluded that "set against the disruption and enormous increase in workload the value of the tests is brought seriously into question". Science was not alone. In the other subjects coming on stream, notably English and technology, similar problems were presenting themselves.

The politicisation of the issue was well illustrated a few weeks later on 23 June. The Daily Mail, a right-wing anti-union tabloid and self-appointed guardian of moral and middle-class values, ran a front page story under the obligatory banner headline: "School Tests Win Top Marks". The 'evidence' put forward was a confidential inspectors' report which claimed children enjoyed taking the tests. Two pupils from a grant maintained school were quoted in support. Mr Patten was "delighted" and believed the union criticisms "blown out of the water". Strange that such a 'wonderful' report was not immediately published!

I spent much of the 1992 Autumn Term trying to convince members to put the NASUWT Workload Strategy into practice but it was only 'taking off' in a limited number of schools. In November the National Association for the Teaching of English (NATE), supported strongly by its London Branch, began calling for a refusal to implement the Key Stage 3 tests on philosophical and educational grounds. Feelings were running high, with NATE members objecting fiercely to reductions in the teacher assessment elements in public exams, the soul-destroying rigidities of the curriculum and the crude national tests being devised for their subject. There was also much controversy over a bungled pilot test for Key Stage 3 English when it emerged through leaks to the press that the Government planned to use the same questions for the 'real thing' in the summer.

While applauding NATE's fighting spirit I wrote to all branch Secretaries in January 1993 reasserting full NASUWT support to members facing unreasonable demands but warning them against unofficial action along the lines proposed by NATE. In the light of the circumstances, I wrote, "I believe it would be possible to declare a legitimate trade dispute with the relevant Minister of the Crown and to ballot members accordingly".

The NASUWT had checked the 1992 Trade Union and Labour Relations (Consolidation) Act and found that the Minister of the Crown was treated as an employer if (among other things) the matters in dispute could not be settled without him exercising a power conferred on him by or under an enactment. We engaged one of our firms of lawyers specialising in trade union matters, Robin Thompson & Partners, who also supported the Union on casework all over the country. The solicitor assigned to us, Simon Walton, was a real gem, a fighter who would concede nothing. He confirmed our view about the 1992 Act and agreed that workload was at the heart of terms and conditions of employment, thereby justiciable as a trade dispute.

The NASUWT was also concerned that the media was vigorously promoting the view that trade union immunity against damages was lost if there were a statutory duty to perform the work involved. Simon Walton claimed it was not. Furthermore, there was a clause in the controversial 1987 Teachers' Pay and Conditions Act and maintained in its successor of 1991 stating that teachers' duties and responsibilities were to be drawn up by Orders made under the statute but they were applied by way of a contract. Thus the legislation itself stipulated teachers had contractual but not statutory duties. We knew a boycott would breach contractual duty; that was why we had to ballot (and comply with many other requirements) to secure immunity from action for damages. Simon Walton was adamant that any action taken by teachers was bound to affect a statutory duty laid upon someone, e.g. the requirement to provide education itself. If the 'popular' view prevailed it implied no one in the public sector could take industrial action. The House of Lords had decided in the 1989 dock workers' case that contractual duties could not be regarded as statutory ones.

Furthermore the wide-ranging Education Reform Act of 1988 set up a new flood of statutory Orders and regulations implementing (inter alia) the NC, which had direct and indeed massive implications for teachers' duties and workloads. Clearly, changes to both the 1988 and 1991 Acts, together with Orders and regulations made thereunder, could only be effected by the Minister exercising powers bestowed by these enactments.

Fortified by this legal advice the NASUWT called for a meeting of teacher organisations which assembled on 12 January. We shared all our legal advice and analysis with the other five unions. Our legal view was not disputed, but only one person, David Hart from the NAHT, a qualified lawyer himself, said "no doubt Nigel's analysis is right".

However, all the other unions agreed with the NUT that any boycott should be limited to English at Key Stage 3 because there was total unity on that issue. The NASUWT strongly disagreed. Workload had to be the basis of the dispute and that issue affected everyone. A boycott aimed solely at English would betray other non-workload motives and risk losing immunity, exposing unions to damages. Indeed NATE was making matters worse by openly calling for more workload-heavy teacher assessment in SATs and other public examinations.

The meeting ended up in some disagreement, with the NASUWT declaring it would likely ballot its entire membership on the workload issue concerning the national curriculum, assessment and testing. However, there was a considerable degree of consensus building up on the need to take some appropriate action, and NATE's activities, while in one crucial aspect unsound, had undoubtedly played an important part.

The NASUWT Executive meeting on 15 January 1993 resolved to remind primary school members that the pilot Key Stage 2 (11-year-olds) tests in English, maths and science planned for the summer were voluntary. Members would be fully supported in declining to volunteer.

The same Executive meeting came to a very firm view that the problems were not just limited to Key Stage 3 English but they affected all teachers. The National Officers were mandated to explore the possibility of formulating a ballot question to be put to all members affected by "the enormous workload and sheer unreasonableness" that was being imposed on teachers. Following more consultation with Simon Walton I was able to recommend to the National Officers' meeting on 28 January that we go ahead. The Officers agreed and so did the Executive on 5 February.

Whilst other organisations were considering their positions, the NASUWT moved swiftly ahead. A NASUWT Report to Schools was immediately issued conveying the news that the Executive had resolved to ballot all members on a boycott: "The point is being reached where there is more testing and bureaucracy than teaching. A beneficial side effect of a boycott would be to restore teaching to the classrooms. Far from disrupting pupils' education this would be of great value to the children."

The Report emphasised there was no proposal for strike action. The ballot question would be:

"In order to protest against excessive workload and unreasonable imposition made upon teachers, as a consequence of National Curriculum Assessment and Testing: Are you willing to take action, short of strike action?"

Balloting would commence in the last week of February with the result announced early in March.

We then moved rapidly into our top gear. Unprecedented amounts of literature were circulated. As the GS I wrote to all members individually and many Reports to Schools were circulated. Local Secretaries received briefing notes. More literature accompanied the ballot papers, which had by law to be sent to members' home addresses.

Although we had all been teachers at some stage in our careers, neither I nor any of my senior colleagues on the staff had hands-on experience of the NC. We relied heavily upon being briefed by Executive Members and local activists whose teaching was caught up in all the changes. Without that input we would not have got it right.

Thus our literature, whilst emphasising the workload basis for the proposed action, was also able to identify the beneficial 'professional' side effects. A vote in favour of the action meant members would *not undertake:*

statutory assessments, preparing pupils for SATs, setting SATs, marking SATs, recording attainments in ways demanded by the Government or reporting to parents in ways newly required.

However, they would on the positive side *continue to:*

teach the NC, assess pupils using their professional judgement on methods and report to parents appropriately.

In every statement to the media I emphasised that "no single child would lose one second of education. On the contrary education would be enhanced as teachers were liberated from a bureaucratic nightmare."

Another meeting of the six unions on 9 February resulted in a joint letter (rather mild in the view of the NASUWT) to the Secretary of State outlining four areas of concern: the tests were an unreasonable imposition; the trialling had been unsatisfactory; there had been excessive haste and continually changing advice from SEAC; and the proposed tests conflicted with good practice.

Late on 10 February journalists informed me that Mr Patten had agreed to meet the five other unions, but was ostentatiously excluding the NASUWT unless we called off our ballot. I condemned him for "prating on piously about professionalism while lacking the basic courtesy to ensure I received his letter before it was faxed with such frenetic activity to every education journalist in the land". 'My' letter arrived two days later.

"Prissy Patten Boycotts NASUWT" ran the headline on the next Report to Schools in mid-February. That was our 'punishment' for going ahead with the ballot. Far from 'punishment' it was a relief to be kept out of the meeting which Patten had in the same breath pre-empted by declaring that the KS3 English tests "must go ahead".

The NASUWT was far more concerned with the reaction of the five unions to the "minor change in the reporting arrangements" which Patten offered them at the famous 'NASUWT-less' meeting on 19 February. The Minister declared: "I recognise the feelings . . . and have therefore decided that in future test results will be included in performance tables from the second year of their introduction nationally." I rubbished "Patten's Palliative" as nothing more than a crumb of a concession, which "did absolutely nothing to address workload and the inherent nonsense of the tests". The SHA "congratulated Mr Patten on acting quickly to ensure the education of young people would not be disrupted" and they looked forward "to a continuation of this growing constructive dialogue with him". The NAHT said the concession met its major objection to the tests. The ATL GS, Peter Smith, fawned over "the statesman-like decision". At least the NUT retained credibility in saying the Minister's announcement "did nothing to address the four areas of concern" contained in the joint union letter of 9 February. The NASUWT concluded that the Secretary of State had "failed lamentably even to begin to address our concerns"; our ballot would continue and, indeed with the refusal to meet us, there was an even stronger reason for members to vote 'yes' for action.

During the course of February the NUT announced the results of a consultative ballot amongst its members who taught Key Stage 3 English. They revealed deep hostility to the tests and an expressed willingness of 90% of the respondents to boycott. The NASUWT was concerned that of the nine questions asked in the survey only one mentioned workload. The NUT was clearly embarking on action to limit a boycott only to the English tests and to do so mainly on educational grounds.

The NASUWT activity continued apace, with scores of meetings and briefings to support the Executive's strong recommendation to vote 'yes' in the ballot. More literature was distributed to members at their home addresses, and detailed briefings on every angle we could conceive of supplied to local Secretaries and School Reps. We took care to emphasise all the positive aspects of a boycott and encouraged our members to engage with parents, school governors, MPs and local councillors. We emphasised that the NASUWT had long supported a core national curriculum and believed in sensible testing of pupils and reporting to parents but not in the bureaucratic nightmare being imposed by the Government. We knew we had an important battle to win on public opinion.

We also expected to be challenged on the legal issues. We supplied all our local representatives with chapter and verse about the legal arguments. Indeed, in Campaign Bulletin (No. 2) to School Reps, issued late in February, I predicted "the anti-union press will seek to stir up people to question the legality of our ballot and will encourage employers and perhaps others to challenge us".

While the ballot was taking place the 1993 teachers' pay award was announced. I described the 1.5% award as "appalling and abysmal" while also observing that the award "will certainly increase the 'yes' vote in the ballot on boycott; while we might not be able to shift the Government on pay we could on workload".

The ballot result was announced on Tuesday 9 March in a well-attended press conference at Congress House, HQ of the TUC. The 'yes' vote was overwhelming, 88% in favour.

The official return from the Electoral Reform Society was:

Total number of votes cast:	59,647
Those voting YES:	52,493
Those voting NO:	7,154
Percentage voting YES:	88%
Percentage voting NO:	12%
Percentage turnout:	57%

The news was well covered in the media. The NASUWT press statement described the result as "a devastating vote of no confidence in the Government; a stunning indictment of its policies on testing and assessment". I added that the action should not accurately be described as 'militant', for members would continue to operate their full timetables but do so much more effectively, banishing mindless bureaucracy and restoring teaching to the classrooms. No child, no parent would be disadvantaged: "Somebody somewhere has to call a halt to the Government's testing and assessment juggernaut which is careering out of control, wrecking teachers' lives and doing great damage to children's education".

The press statement referred to the NC reforms at that stage not even being half introduced and speculated: "What it would be like fully implemented does not bear thinking about." The final decision on implementing action would rest with the National Executive a few days later on Friday 12 March.

That same Tuesday evening (9 March) I had an evening commitment to address the AGM of the Somerset Federation of the NASUWT. I had been so busy with running the ballot that I had thought little about the 'afterwards'. Within seconds of arriving at the meeting in Taunton I knew the NASUWT had done the best thing for years. Cheers greeted me as I walked into the meeting. The change in 'teacher mood' was instantaneous and palpable. In one day spirits which had been depressed for years were uplifted. At last someone was doing something to alleviate the ridiculous burden being placed on teachers.

The Executive duly directed me to issue the well-signalled instructions for action to all members in first, primary, middle, secondary and special schools in England, Wales and Northern Ireland. All work in connection with SATs was banned as was all the unreasonable and unnecessary elements of (1) assessment connected with the NC and (2) the new system for reporting to parents. The very bureaucratic quality audit procedures and timetable alterations designed to defeat the boycott were also banned.

The letter containing the instructions which had already been drafted in anticipation of the Executive decision was issued on the same day. My letter also emphasised that members had to continue their normal teaching, assess pupils and report to parents appropriately. It pointed out there would be the need for much discretion and flexibility over interpretation in schools and emphasised there was no intention to affect public examinations such as GCSE. Where Key Stage 4 (16-year-olds) was effectively the same as GCSE no action should occur. Special advice would be issued to deputy and head teacher members.

The NASUWT also issued letters to every LEA Chief Education Officer and to the head teachers and Chairs of Governors of all schools. Local Officers and School Reps were encouraged to meet with those people to explain our action and urge them to adopt a "measured approach". (They had their own responsibilities and could not be openly supporting or encouraging our action without some risk to themselves.) Where such a reasonable response was forthcoming there would be no disruption to children's education. Where it was not, members were advised to contact their National Executive Member for further advice. That was well understood code for strike action. Privately, we were prepared to fight 'disciplinary' responses with strike action. Apart from token deductions nor were we going to tolerate loss of pay since our members were delivering a full week's work.

HQ printing and distribution staff worked all through the Friday night and most of Saturday to ensure material arrived in schools on the following Monday morning. My letter made it clear the boycott should commence with immediate effect upon receipt of the instructions.

Report (No. 8) to Schools issued the following week reinforced all these messages. It also picked up on over 2,000 late votes which had arrived after the official close of the ballot (8 March). They pushed the majority in favour of action to 51.5% of all those entitled to vote. Some politicians predictably criticised our 'low' turnout of 57%. I quickly reminded the Government it had been elected in 1992 with the support of only 43% of those voting and 34% of those entitled to vote. Our figures of 88% and 51.5% compared extremely well! A parental school ballot to go grant maintained (GM) under the Government's pet project would have succeeded with plenty to spare on a similar result.

The NASUWT also made a point of writing to all Members of Parliament (about 630) in a letter dated 16 March explaining our action and summarising the reasons for it.

We met with parent organisations, governors, LEA employers, and representatives of the GM and independent sectors at national level to explain the NASUWT action. We found they agreed completely with the NASUWT on the excesses of the national curriculum regime but had reservations about industrial action. We assuaged many of their fears explaining our "pupil friendly" action would enhance teaching and diminish bureaucracy.

Predictable events then began to develop. The Campaign for Real Education, which never seemed able to field more than a couple of activists, began to encourage parents to sue the NASUWT. As well as being based on dubious legal merits it was highly irresponsible in that, if followed, it could expose parents to substantial costs. The advice also seemed to correlate closely to the legal views being circulated by the ATL. I wrote to the ATL's GS, Peter Smith, seeking clarification, but no response was forthcoming.

The press devoted a lot of space to questioning our right to boycott and many newspapers openly called on Government, LEAs and parents to challenge us in the courts. To counteract this view of teachers' statutory duty and the legitimacy of our claimed trade dispute I called a press briefing to share our legal reasoning with journalists. Only a handful attended but they expressed surprise at the cogency of our case. I recall Paul Marston of *The Telegraph*, who I much respected for his fair and balanced reporting, confessing he was pleasantly surprised by the strength of our case, adding he would advise his leader writers accordingly.

Two editorials stand out in my memory. The first was *The Times* leader on 13 March which fuelled my suspicion that editorials were as much about telling the readers what they wanted to hear as anything else. *The Times*, supposedly a quality newspaper, accused us of merely wanting "to embarrass John Patten". In keeping with the NASUWT tradition, I was never afraid of genuine debate based on a different evaluation of facts. But I objected fiercely to those who claimed to speak with authority but were simply in the business of smearing, being culpably ignorant or perversely wrong.

It took a long time (until 29 March) and several telephone calls to the letters editor for my 'blistering' reply (toned down) to be published. I regretted "the intemperate terms" in which the NASUWT had been attacked and how *The Times* had ignored the mountain of evidence on workload we had presented which was widely supported throughout the education service, including the independent schools.

The second editorial was in the *TES*, 12 March, "Waiting for a test case", in which it argued we should be pressing for incremental improvements in the tests year by year to avoid alienating parental and public opinion. The *TES* "heaved a weary sigh at the news that the NASUWT has voted to boycott all the tests. Even with the Government as weak as it is, there is no chance that the union can win; that *all* tests should be scrapped and rewritten at this juncture is, frankly, unthinkable. It is hard to imagine the union will muster much outside support for such a root-and-branch rethink, in spite of the real concerns shared by parents and the public."

Accusing the NASUWT of "creating a climate of confrontation" the *TES* editorial went on: "By going for broke in this way the union is setting off on a rocky road without any idea of where it will lead. How long before a parent, a governor, a local authority or even John Patten himself issues an injunction designed to force NASUWT members to carry out their statutory duty?"

How utterly wrong the poor *TES* was to be proved. But its editorial gave some idea of what we were up against and the nerve and courage required to stand by our beliefs.

The *TES* published an article in reply from me on 26 March to which it had appended its own headline, "Hellbent on a rocky road to salvation". I wrote that "whilst the *TES* might heave a weary sigh at the boycott", NASUWT members in their thousands were "heaving a sigh of relief that someone was at last doing something about their crippling workload". Far from the NASUWT wanting to "create a climate of confrontation with the Government", it had been the Prime Minister himself who had boasted to his Party Conference in the autumn that "he looked forward to a row with the educational establishment". After explaining the legal arguments in our favour I stressed the NASUWT's support for a core NC but our opposition to the "juggernaut careering out of control". I regretted others seemed not to have the courage to join us on the "rocky road".

Reaction from members in schools was overwhelmingly positive and positively brilliant! Letters of appreciation began flowing into HQ. The only significant criticism was why had we not done this earlier! The instructions were being sensibly interpreted on the ground. Our detailed planning and consultation were paying dividends. The flexibility was proving crucial. Members appreciated the restoration of their own professional judgement inherent in the instructions.

Whatever some editorials promulgated it soon became evident that parents, the general public and even LEAs and school governors were very supportive. Again our efforts to consult and explain to everyone outside the Union were paying handsome dividends. It seemed only Mr Patten, backed up by the cranky Campaign for Real Education, and some newspaper editorial writers, were upset.

The most welcome, if surprising, 'support' (intended or otherwise) came from a very unusual quarter. On 17 March a right-wing think tank, the Centre for Policy Studies (CPS), which had been established by Margaret Thatcher, held a seminar with Mr Patten as the principal speaker. According to Ray Massey, Education Correspondent of *The Mail* who seemed the only journalist invited, Patten "railed against militant teachers planning a boycott of the summer's tests". However, Massey went on to report that "Mr Patten looked uncomfortable as he listened to a blistering attack on the curriculum which was likened to a juggernaut careering towards disaster".

Leading that attack was none other than Lord Skidelsky, Professor of Government at Warwick University but also a member of SEAC. He blamed teachers and Government for creating this "monster". The tests were "bewildering and bamboozling, the product of loose thinking, hair-raising methods and insane proliferation of unnecessary detail". Massey reports that he was backed by speakers from "the Who's Who of the Tory educational right". These included Dr John Marks, another member of SEAC, who said: "The way the ten point NC scale had been drawn up is highly questionable and unnecessarily complicated." Another critic was Donald Naismith, who was (wait for it) Director of Education for the London Borough of Wandsworth, soon to be our hostile litigants, describing the whole business as "over-bureaucratic and unworkable. The sooner it is buried the better."

However, another influential member of the Tory right wing coming from the same CPS stable, Lord Griffiths of Fforestfach who was Chairman of SEAC, seemed out of step having previously defended the tests at a conference in Birmingham on 19 January claiming they were "reliable, accurate and manageable".

The press cuttings that morning of 18 March made interesting reading, to put it mildly. Back in London on the same day, the NASUWT had a meeting with Mr Patten but it was only due to the statutory requirement for him to consult unions over the Pay Review Body award. A civil servant had telephoned my office the previous day to relay the Minister's insistence that no mention be made of the boycott. When we came to complain about the Review Body and the Minister failing to recognise our case on excessive workload Mr Patten began responding, until he realised he was trespassing upon his own forbidden territory! Suddenly he stopped, almost in mid-sentence. It was amusing, but incredibly childish all the same.

The next day in Glasgow on a visit to NASUWT Scotland I took a call from my London office to learn that the expected threat of an injunction against our boycott had arrived. However, it had not come from the Government but from its favourite cost-cutting London borough, Wandsworth. I was initially depressed; the boycott had been going so well and now it might all have to stop – but my spirits revived when I saw the details and considered our defence.

With the letter faxed through I saw that Wandsworth claimed our boycott was unlawful; it was not in dispute with its employees and unless the NASUWT undertook "by return" to withdraw the instructions to boycott the borough's solicitor would seek an application for an interlocutory injunction against us. I decided not to make public comment to avoid provocation. I sent a holding reply. It was Friday and we needed time to consider our response and consult our lawyers.

Before we sent a reply the news of the threatened writ was leaked to *The Daily Mail* on Wednesday, 24 March. The story was, however, overshadowed by a sensational allegation of rape by a pupil on a teacher in a school in south-east London.

On 25 March we received a writ from Wandsworth seeking to secure an injunction to stop our boycott. We were well prepared, although little did we realise how urgent and dramatic our work was soon to become. We had already asked Simon Walton to brief counsel and he engaged David Bean on our behalf. David Bean turned out to be an excellent choice. Then a junior counsel, he was soon to become a QC and was then elevated to Sir David and a High Court judge. We met that same afternoon in a case conference. David recommended we apply immediately to the court the following day for an expedited full hearing the next week. He advised it was the best way to counteract Wandsworth's request for an interim injunction stopping the boycott as that was likely to be decided on the balance of inconvenience, not on the merits of the case, which would be determined later.

On the Friday morning (26 March) we were before Mr Justice Stephen Sedley, in chambers, requesting the expedited full hearing. Full of confidence, Wandsworth readily agreed. The judge set the case down to be heard starting on the following Wednesday. It was also agreed that the case would be 'heard' by statement only; there would be no cross-examination of witnesses. That was a little disappointing, for whatever the legal technicalities I was confident we had a strong 'moral' case and was rather looking forward to defending and promoting the NASUWT cause in such an 'upmarket theatre' as the High Court.

That Friday afternoon was hectic. We had to get our defence ready by Monday, to be submitted to the court for the hearing on the Wednesday. Our lawyers told us this was the second-fastest hearing ever to be set for a High Court case. Luckily several key staff were in our Covent Garden office that day. Our HQ in Rednal was also turned upside down drawing out all the relevant files. Simon Walton told us we needed documentary evidence that we had long been concerned with excessive workload, had put forward such claims in the relevant quarters and had approached employers and Ministers on the issue. We would also need all our literature and public statements issued over the boycott. The plan was to meet Saturday to draft my affidavit and compile our 'bundle' of evidence, consult with our QC, Jeffrey Burke, on Sunday and submit our defence to the court on Monday.

Most of Friday afternoon seemed to be nothing but daunting chaos but by the end things were coming together. We had more than we needed. Indeed evidence of our long-standing concern over workload was in such abundance that we had an embarrassment of choice.

Besides all the documentation from ACAS 1986 and the controversy over the 1987 Act, we had submitted claims to the IAC and then the STRB for a 35-hour limit to the contractual week as the only effective means of curtailing excessive workload. In 1991 we had conducted a survey which showed that teachers' working hours had increased to nearly 53 hours a week, which equated to working Monday-Saturday eight hours per day with five hours worked on Sunday.

On the NC, I asked our education department based at our HQ in Rednal to check all the material we had received on the subject. It amounted to 26 ring binders containing 2,560 pages, 30 proposals/consultation documents (3,300 pages), SATs assessment folders (500 pages), and statutory guidance documents (1,725 pages), giving a grand total of 8,085 pages.

We also included in our bundle of evidence the Parliamentary Written Answer given by the Minister of State, Tim Eggar, to Jack Straw, Labour Education Shadow Secretary, on 13 December 1991 listing the national curriculum publications to date that had emanated since 1987 from the DES, NCC and SEAC. The list, in very small print, ran to five columns in *Hansard*.

We had dozens of statements to the press as well as in our own publications complaining about the mountainous workload added by the NC reforms, not to mention correspondence with four Secretaries of State for Education raising the very same issues. Furthermore, the ballot question, over which we had pored for hours, was watertight, stipulating workload as the core of the dispute.

Amidst the apparent chaos, we enjoyed some good moments. I was indebted to Joe Boone, President of the Union in 1985-86 and now an Assistant Secretary for Conditions of Service, for perhaps the 'juiciest' piece of evidence. Joe recalled the quotes from Donald Naismith in *The Daily Mail* report of the CPS seminar a few weeks previously and located a copy. We licked our lips at the prospect of hearing the Wandsworth Director of Education's words describing the NC as "unworkable and the sooner it is buried the better" read out in open court!

The Saturday was a hard grind. Eamonn O'Kane, Mick Richardson, our Wandsworth Branch Secretary, and myself met with Simon Walton to draft our affidavit and attach the supporting documentary evidence. It took all day but was very productive and Simon had the draft typed up for us to take copies home. (Mick deserves a special mention for displaying the degree of commitment that characterises so many NASUWT activists. He was supposed to be moving house that day!)

By Sunday evening Simon was in touch with me to report that Jeffrey Burke thought the affidavit was excellent. However, he wished to know if I could sign off the affidavit with a concluding and 'clinching' paragraph which recognised the widely held professional objections to the assessment and tests but emphasised they were *not* the subject of the dispute. If they were made professionally acceptable but contained the same workload we would still be recommending industrial action. Conversely, if the tests remained as they were but the extra workload were to be balanced by a corresponding reduction in our members' other duties, we would *not* be recommending industrial action. I indicated immediately that I could with total conviction sign such a statement.

On Wednesday 31 March the case of Wandsworth v NASUWT opened. It was to become precedent setting in industrial relations case history. We decided to begin by making our case available to the public. Having obviously alerted the media to the event, we were filmed leaving our nearby Covent Garden office and then arriving at the Royal Courts of Justice pushing a wheelbarrow load of all the documents and publications that together constituted the national curriculum, testing and assessment regime.

Inside the courtroom, Wandsworth's QC, Patrick Elias, a leading expert in this field and someone we came to respect and even like as the proceedings went on, opened the case in which his client was seeking an injunction to restrain the NASUWT from instructing its members to carry out the boycott. He argued there was no trade dispute; it was not about terms and conditions but based upon objections to the content of the NC regime.

When Mr Elias went on to argue that in any event the statutory duty laid upon teachers under the 1988 Act overrode any claim to trade union immunity, the judge, Mr Justice Mantell, lost no time in interrupting him. "You know the business Mr Elias", said the judge, "take me to the clause in the 1988 Act which lays down the statutory duty for teachers". Mr Justice Mantell must have known what he was doing. Mr Elias could not find any, for no such clause existed. Instead he quoted the many Orders implementing the new NC regime made by the Minister under the Act. However, Mr Mantell declared that if Parliament had intended to impose a statutory duty on teachers it would have been in the primary legislation. In the judge's eloquent, if sharp, words, "Parliament would not have slipped a knife between the ribs of teachers" by placing such an important and new burden in subsidiary orders.

Mr Elias found himself relying on political and emotional charges such as Wandsworth children being "caught in the crossfire of guerrilla warfare conducted by the NASUWT".

Presenting the NASUWT case, Jeffrey Burke's eloquence was rarely interrupted by the judge seeking clarification, or indeed asking any questions which might be described as 'hostile'. Our case certainly seemed more logical and related to the real world of education, and we had a mountain of evidence, not one piece of which was ever directly contradicted by Mr Elias.

Mr Naismith's affidavit on behalf of Wandsworth seemed to be somewhat sloppy in its research. It contained serious factual errors such as alleging the NASUWT was opposed to all testing and assessment when we had repeatedly instructed our members to continue with appropriate elements thereof in the new arrangements. Obviously the claim that the NC testing and assessment were essential for the education of Wandsworth children was seriously compromised by Donald Naismith's recent quotes in *The Mail* ("the sooner it is buried the better"). When Jeffrey Burke came to these quotes in my affidavit, I looked up at the judge to see if he reacted and noticed a little wry smile on his face as he looked down towards our 'friend' who stared straight ahead, emotionless!

The hearing lasted two days. On the Thursday night I stayed in our Covent Garden office flat as there was a train strike planned for the next day, when Justice Mantell was due to deliver his judgment. I recall attending Robin Thompson & Partners' reception that evening and mixing with hundreds of lawyers. There was much talk that the NASUWT had done well in the hearing. All the speculation about statutory duty bringing us down, vigorously promoted by the media, seemed to have evaporated.

Judgment came at 2 p.m. on Friday 2 April. Mr Justice Mantell declared: "In my judgement the dispute is about workload, working hours and terms and conditions of employment" and was a legitimate trade dispute involving the Minister. Mantell also found that teachers had no statutory duties to administer the NC, testing and assessment. The NASUWT victory was comprehensive and complete.

On emerging from the Royal Courts of Justice to greet the media massed outside I declared: "This is a stunning victory. It is a great day for teachers and pupils. It enables the NASUWT to continue its action to protect teachers against excessive workload." It was a defining day in the history of the NASUWT and for me personally a great moment, probably the highlight of my teacher trade union career.

Wandsworth was ordered to pay our costs, estimated to be around £30,000. The Leader of Wandsworth Council, Edward Lister, said: "This ruling is an obvious disappointment. It puts all LEAs in a difficult situation. The union now has legal support to continue its boycott, but we have a legal duty . . . to implement the national curriculum introduced by Parliament." Lister added that Wandsworth would be seeking urgent advice on whether to appeal.

The reactions of other teacher unions was somewhat 'mixed'. The NAHT GS, David Hart, welcomed the decision, despite declaring that this was "irrespective of one's view about whether action should be taken" – a fine fence to sit on since without our boycott there would have been no court case and no judgment! The GS most renowned for 'fence sitting', Peter Smith of the ATL, was in his characteristic ambivalent mode, declaring that: "Wandsworth's failure to achieve an injunction cannot really be described as a victory for anyone." In the same breath he asserted: "If pressure for a boycott is to be avoided Mr Patten must announce measures to ease workload." The ATL Executive had advised against a boycott despite growing pressure to the contrary from its members.

To his credit the NUT GS, Doug McAvoy, very magnanimously wrote me a letter of congratulations and welcomed the judgment as it reinforced his union's decision to ballot on a boycott of English tests. However, he remained cautious about extending the boycott to other subjects because "there is a danger that if you widen the focus you blunt the instrument". The real problem here might have been Doug's fear that his primary school-dominated membership might not vote in favour of a comprehensive boycott.

The press speculated that the NUT and ATL would face pressure from members at their upcoming Easter Conferences to join the NASUWT boycott.

Returning to my Covent Garden office after giving more media interviews I was astonished to find scores of messages of thanks and congratulations pouring in from all over the country. It was only then that the enormity of what we had achieved began to sink in. We had stopped the Conservative Government, which had been 'hell-bent' on destroying all trade unionism, in its tracks. It would have to deal with us now.

I wrote immediately to John Patten offering to meet with him to begin addressing the problems, which had to start with a massive slim down of the national curriculum (NC) arrangements. I reiterated that the NASUWT favoured a core NC backed up with sensible testing and assessment. Mr Patten did not reply but, in his hole, he kept on digging. He was due to speak at the ATL Conference the following week and would continue trying to dissuade teachers from boycotting. "The tests must go ahead", defiantly declared Mr Patten.

I also despatched a letter to Peter Smith, to his Cardiff hotel at the ATL Conference, advising him that the NASUWT had won on every legal point. The main reason why the ATL had been advising its members to steer clear of the NASUWT boycott, the 'certainty' we would be 'injuncted out', was no longer valid. The ATL could now join the NASUWT in its boycott and indeed a growing body of opinion throughout the educational world.

Although our action was about much else in addition to the tests (due to take place in May/June) they were to be the most visible manifestation of the boycott. Most of the boycott was invisible to the outside world but, as we had predicted, it was already banishing bureaucracy, enhancing professionalism and raising the morale of our members. However, it did not match the media stereotype for teachers' industrial action of "chaos in the classroom". The tests themselves would be the arena where the media had decided the next battle of the boycott would be fought and the winner declared.

The NASUWT had to be careful about being too triumphalist since Wandsworth had openly stated it would consider an appeal. Everyone knew Wandsworth was the Government's "surrogate litigant" as I described the LEA. In the lead-up to the court case a prominent former Education Minister, Dr Rhodes Boyson, always a man to call a spade a spade, had written publicly and let slip " . . . if the Government loses its case . . . " Later on I was personally informed by a highly placed source in the GM sector that Mr Patten had approached him "expecting" one of their schools to volunteer for the task. The Minister had been rather surprised, even offended, to be rebuffed, told in no uncertain terms that GM schools "were not in the business of taking their teachers to court". Eventually, the London Borough of Wandsworth (LBW, to draw on the cricketing acronym which I was not slow to exploit) had bravely come in to bat.

We had been much heartened with a little piece of overheard conversation gleaned by our Junior Vice-President, OIwyn Gunn, who had come down to the High Court for the judgment on the Friday. Olwyn found herself seated near the Wandsworth people as there were no spare seats left on 'our side' of the courtroom. Emerging from the court immediately after the judgment had been announced she overheard the Wandsworth QC briefing his clients that the NASUWT "had been very clever in the way they had mounted their boycott". Mr Elias appeared to be advising his clients there was not much point in appealing. Whatever Wandsworth decided, we were prepared to go all the way to the House of Lords and had set aside £200,000 in case we lost.

The High Court judgment in our favour could not have come at a better time for us. The following week was the start of the unions' annual Easter Conferences. The ATL kicked off on Monday 5 April, the NUT on 8 April and the NASUWT on Easter Monday, the 12th.

Encouraged by Peter Smith's ambivalence, John Patten attempted to garner support and turn teachers, governors and parents against the NASUWT. In contrived and craven comments carried in some tabloids, John Patten praised the "professional teachers" he would soon be addressing, i.e. the members of the ATL, contrasting them with the NASUWT – the 'boycotters'. He would not be addressing the NASUWT and NUT Conferences. Although Peter Smith declared the ATL Conference vote "to be on a knife edge" and while it afforded Mr Patten a polite but cool reception, it promptly voted by a massive majority to follow the NASUWT and ballot its members for a boycott. Mr Patten was further humiliated and badly wounded once again. He was utterly out of touch with teachers.

A few days later at the NUT Conference, its leaders came in for criticism from its left-wing activists for letting the NASUWT make all the running. In the end they voted to ballot on a comprehensive boycott, not one limited to Key Stage 3 English tests. By our action and victory in the High Court we had forced the two other major classroom teacher-based unions to follow in our footsteps.

The atmosphere at the NASUWT Conference was jubilant. Morale had been miraculously lifted. The leadership had done everything right. I had a very easy, indeed enjoyable time, greeted with standing ovations before and after the traditional Monday 'state of the union' GS address to delegates.

Throughout the week several large banners hung above the platform. They were the famous NC quotes from the CPS seminar including the Wandsworth Director's: "What we have now is not what was intended. Chickens are coming home to roost. The Government will have to re-think it on original lines. It is over-bureaucratic and unworkable. The sooner it is buried the better."

The main (Wednesday morning) debate of the week was a highly charged affair as it focussed on our great victory and reiterated our demands for sanity. The motion also kept a positive focus on the future, repeating our policy in favour of a core national curriculum backed up with sensible testing and a willingness to meet the Minister to move forward.

The Honorary Treasurer Mick Carney moving the motion, in his search for suitable words to capture our achievement, quoted Yeats: "All has changed, changed utterly; a terrible beauty is born." This time it was Past-President Sue Rogers' turn to steer the wheelbarrow load of 8,085 pages of print that constituted the NC into the auditorium and up to the podium to a boisterous reception. Speaker after speaker told of the misery that the NC had become and of the joy of liberation brought by our boycott and court victory.

Ex-President Maurice Littlewood read out a letter from Tom Smith, President 1955-56. Tom had written to me expressing his pride and congratulations on the NASUWT legal success, recalling how it had reminded him of his similar exit from the same Royal Courts of Justice on the occasion of the victory over Sunderland in the school meals case way back in 1956.

Soon after the conference season ended Wandsworth announced it would appeal. It was a poor decision. The London borough would have been better employed piling the pressure back on to the hapless Mr Patten to start listening to the voice of the profession, united as never before in demanding sensible change.

Patten had already begun to lose support in his own party. The concerns originally expressed by Mrs Thatcher herself back in 1988 had resurfaced. The stark question "Where had it all gone wrong?" was well answered by Lord Skidelsky's exposé from the inside as a prominent member of SEAC in a penetrating article written for *The Daily Telegraph* on 20 March, the day after we received the first notice of writ from Wandsworth. While he was no natural ally of the NASUWT, I found his writings on this subject to be sharp and often accurate.

In his article, following up the CPS seminar and the famous quotes in *The Daily Mail*, Skidelsky began by recognising the obvious – national testing was in trouble. He acknowledged the NASUWT boycott, stating that we complained about "intolerable bureaucratic burdens and professionally unacceptable practices". He went on candidly: "I agree with them." But he said teachers had to share the blame for what had happened. The NC only started because of the widespread public distrust of teachers and educators and the perception of falling standards. Teachers professed to believe in "assessment" but in many primary schools all testing had come to a complete halt. Such views were controversial, but I believed he had some evidence to support his case even if it did not apply to the majority of schools.

However, Skidelsky's views on how the tests became unmanageable resonated with the NASUWT. He started from the position of not understanding how standard tests for 7-year-olds in English, maths and science could take 40 hours to do, half a term to administer, and require four booklets of test materials totalling 224 pages! He believed the paper mountain was the product of conflicting views on testing. The educationalist saw 'testing' as a continuous process of assessment for diagnostic and formative purposes. The Government, sharing the general public perception of testing, saw it as 'summative' – measuring in quantitative terms how effective teaching had been. Mrs Thatcher intended the 'simple pencil and paper tests' to be the latter. But the 'educational establishment' had wormed its way into the Government quangos set up to introduce and run the NC and tried to reconcile the two different philosophies, producing a bureaucratic nightmare.

Skidelsky claimed the main progenitors of the "Byzantine monster" to be the Task Group on Assessment and Testing (TGAT), chaired by Paul Black, Professor of Science Education at King's College London. TGAT tried the impossible of squaring the circle of diagnostic and summative testing. It set learning targets of ascending difficulty in each subject on a 10-point scale with explicit "performance criteria" for each level. But "this attempt to produce 10 distinguishable levels in the numerous aspects of all subjects led to an insane multiplication of criteria arranged hierarchically over the levels. The hierarchies were highly questionable and the attempt to award the same levels of achievement to different content made no sense." The statements of attainment, akin to performance criteria, "almost defy belief in their mechanistic simplicity. The stories of how some of the empty boxes of the TGAT report were filled up with subject specific performance are hair-raising."

Naturally such comments featured prominently in the NASUWT evidence presented in the High Court.

(Later on Professor Black defended the TGAT report, claiming that simple tests did not provide reliable information for any purpose. Furthermore, being simple, they would inevitably restrict the curriculum as teachers increasingly taught to the tests upon which they and their schools would be judged.)

Skidelsky's explanation perfectly matched the horror stories being relayed to the Union's leadership by members who were faced with having to tick literally thousands of boxes in this nightmare of assessing their pupils' progress.

This "insane system" was accepted by Kenneth Baker in 1988 as he drove his Education Reform Act through Parliament. Come implementation he was gone, promoted to Home Secretary and destined to emulate his previous record with the 'Mad Dogs' Act. His successor, John MacGregor, tried to make it work, got distracted from other aspects of the educational reforms, protested he could only implement one fundamental change at a time and consequently found himself sacked as Secretary of State, accused of 'going native' with the 'educational establishment'. The next Education Secretary, Kenneth Clarke, summed up his view of SATs in one word – "madness" – and could not get out of the Department quickly enough – but not before he had decided that Ofsted reports and league-table test results would be published, thereby heralding the 'management by public humiliation' era. Then poor John Patten came along to reap the bitter harvest, making himself extremely unpopular, many teachers rightly or wrongly regarding his personal style as aloof.

The NASUWT's "stunning victory" in the High Court back-footed the Government and soon led to open divisions as the prospect for a widespread and effective boycott of the tests loomed large. Despite Patten defiantly declaring "the tests must go on", wiser people, I believe operating through No. 10, where the beleaguered John Major was trying to run the country, began to plan some sensible changes. Recognising the mistake of separating the curriculum from examinations, on 19 April 1993 Sir Ron Dearing, the former Post Office boss, was brought in to run the show as Chairman of both NCC and SEAC with the two bodies to merge as the School Curriculum and Assessment Authority (SCAA) planned for October.

David Pascall, a man with strong religious convictions and Chairman of NCC, had been the favourite for the new job but was unceremoniously and, from his own viewpoint, unfairly dumped amidst internal wrangling inside the Tory Party. Lord Griffiths, Chairman of SEAC and another of the Tory right who seemed well represented in these quangos, was also dropped despite being one of the 'plotters' behind Mrs Thatcher's letter to Kenneth Baker in 1988 enquiring what was going on with all these "elaborate and complex tests". Within a short space of time several more jumped before possibly being pushed.

Meanwhile the obdurate ignorance of some people continued to surprise us. The editorials in *The Times*, "Class War" on 12 April and "Classroom Discipline" on the 15th, continued to take a hostile line against the NASUWT and in tandem with John Patten wrongly claimed statutory duty would be decided by the court of appeal. *The Times* published my reply on 20 April reminding their readers that Wandsworth had dropped the claim that teachers had statutory duties from its appeal.

On 20 April we were back in the Royal Courts of Justice for the appeal by Wandsworth. Three days had been set aside for the hearing before Lord Justices Neill (presiding), Steyn and Rose.

The NASUWT simply stood by the affidavit I had signed together with the supporting evidence. Wandsworth changed tack. As it had indicated in submitting the appeal, the LEA no longer contested teachers had statutory duties. Instead QC Patrick Elias claimed that we were educationally and politically opposed to the content of the NC and the tests. Workload was only a minor element. Therefore our action was not "wholly or mainly about terms and conditions" and so outside the definition of a trade dispute and susceptible to injunction and liable for damages. It was a weak ground on which to appeal. There was our mountain of unchallenged evidence pointing in precisely the opposite direction as did the ballot question itself.

Indeed, the NASUWT case presented by Jeffrey Burke was so overwhelming that during the afternoon session on the second day he was uncharacteristically interrupted by Lord Justice Neill. After briefly consulting with his fellow justices the presiding judge informed Jeffrey Burke, who was by then barely halfway through his presentation, that he could continue if he wished but there was no need to do so. Our QC readily took the hint and concluded his remarks. Seated in front of our counsel, I turned around to check I had heard correctly. I will always remember the immensely satisfied smile on his face and his words: "It is obvious we have won".

By 3 p.m. on Wednesday 21 April "it was all over". Lord Justice Neill informed the court that judgment would be delivered on Friday the 23rd. Obviously we could not openly celebrate as we emerged from the Royal Courts of Justice that afternoon and we tried our best to keep a straight face. Our only comment could be that judgment was due on Friday.

However, the disgraceful behaviour of the Government was far from over. No doubt having received reports of how the appeal court hearing had gone, someone connected to or in the Government leaked a copy of a letter Gillian Shephard, then Employment Secretary, had written (26 February) to John Patten who ironically she was destined to succeed as Secretary of State for Education. *The Telegraph* reported simply that the Government "published" the letter. Rather cleverly it was 'published' or leaked firstly to the NUT as it focussed on the specific threat to boycott the English tests alone. However, the timing suggested it represented a warning to any union taking action "designed to frustrate the carrying out of specific statutory duty". A suitable clause could easily be attached to the Trade Union Reform and Employment Rights Bill proceeding through Parliament at this time.

The headlines on 23 April duly picked up the intended message – *The Guardian:* "Millions face strike curb"; *The Times:* "Right to strike may be curbed in battle over school tests". Never one to miss out on such an opportunity *The Mail* also weighed in: "Teachers in front line of clampdown on militants." Despite *The Guardian*'s sensational headline, its leader, "The right to boycott", rubbished the proposal, concluding "it will only take a competent industrial lawyer a few minutes to deconstruct the false construction."

Doug McAvoy, GS NUT, described the letter as a "sinister Government plot". I said it would "probably provoke open rebellion" if it were enacted. The TUC called it "offensive and heavy handed". However, when I eventually had full sight of the letter (one often had to comment semi-blind when stories were spun late in the evening) the 'threat' was exposed as a sham. Mrs Shephard conceded the Government could, but should not, go so far as "to withdraw immunity from any action which interfered with the performance of statutory duties [as we] would be attacked for removing the right to strike from public sector employees". Mrs Shephard was consulting on a "specific ban" aimed at cases such as "the threatened teachers' boycott of English tests" (i.e. the NUT line). In the same letter she had to concede that teachers' action designed to secure additional payment for administering the tests would be legal.

It was nonsense. In our view it would have made no difference to the High Court decision. But it showed the Government keen to use any threat it could think of to defeat the unions rather than address genuine problems.

The controversy over Shephard's leaked letter lasted but a few hours as by 11 a.m. on Friday 23 April we were assembled to hear the appeal court verdict. Lord Justice Neill's delivery of the judgment dismissing the appeal provided an extremely satisfying hour for all NASUWT Officers and staff present. In particular we were extremely pleased to hear Lord Justice Neill declare the issue to be decided was a matter of fact rather than law. Our long-running concern over workload, well documented in the 'bundle' of evidence supporting my affidavit, established the facts. We were equally pleased to note the judges "attached particular importance to the ballot question", over which we had deliberated for hours, and the concluding paragraph of my affidavit which Jeffrey Burke considered to be a 'clincher'. Leave to appeal to the House of Lords was refused and our Honorary Treasurer, Mick Carney, was doubly pleased to hear that Wandsworth was ordered to pay all the costs, estimated to be around £100,000.

Inside the courtroom I was able to hand out my prepared 'victory' press statement to the journalists, leaving my alternative version (dealing with a defeat) safely in my briefcase, which I was intrigued to rediscover on researching this chapter. This time I proclaimed a "scorching victory for the NASUWT". I went on: "It is also a victory for all teachers, pupils, parents and education over mindless Government-imposed bureaucracy. The law is stacked against unions. To have won through the Courts in the face of everything the Government and its surrogate litigant could throw at us is an outstanding achievement without parallel in modern times."

The NASUWT had also established several important legal precedents: a union could have a legitimate trade dispute with a Minister of the Crown who was not an employer of teachers; that the boycott was a genuine trade dispute; and that teachers had no statutory duties.

The judges had decisively rejected the accusations widely levelled against us that our boycott was politically motivated. Again I offered constructive talks with Mr Patten on how we could establish a sensible NC. How could Mr Patten continue to shun us? It would be humbug for him to persist in preaching professionalism while rejecting the verdicts of the Courts.

As the NASUWT contingent emerged from the Royal Courts of Justice to face the massed ranks of the media I could not resist raising my arms in a victory salute.

After loads of interviews and a live feed to one of the lunchtime TV news bulletins I caught up with my colleagues back in our Covent Garden office to join them in a few glasses of champagne. With the news during the lunch hour having spread rapidly around the staffrooms of the nation's schools our HQ and London offices were again flooded with the most heartening messages of congratulations. Initially disappointed to receive the news of the writ in Glasgow I was now grateful to the London Borough of Wandsworth for presenting the NASUWT with not just one great victory but with a repeat in the appeal court.

The great day for the NASUWT was by the same token the bleakest for John Patten. On the day, he was in Southport due to speak to the SHA Annual Conference in the afternoon. At lunchtime the news of the appeal court verdict reached him. Malcolm Hewitt, Vice-President, began by 'taking the mickey' out of the hapless Minister by presenting him with a large SHA golf umbrella to protect him from "the gathering storm". Uncharacteristically blunt, the SHA VP told Mr Patten: "You should know that . . . our sympathies are with the teachers."

Mr Patten plunged into a state of denial. He declared with fatuous irrelevance that the court had neither ruled on the "merits of the tests" nor on the "desirability of industrial action". It had simply declared the union had a valid trade dispute – *"nothing more"* (my emphasis).

In a hole but still digging, Mr Patten remained adamant the tests would go ahead because "that is Parliament's will". He appealed to NUT and ATL members not to vote for a boycott which would harm pupils, cause bewilderment to parents and "do terrible damage to your profession. Industrial action is as undesirable in the classroom as it is on the railways." Patten told the heads the court decision did not affect their statutory duty to set the tests. (In fact Mr Justice Mantell in the High Court had observed that it was not certain that head teachers had statutory duties.) Mr Patten went on to issue a thinly veiled threat: without the results of the tests he would have difficulty persuading the Treasury to increase spending on education.

Press reports told of Mr Patten being "visibly shaken by the hostile reception" he received from the normally compliant heads. "The Minister's appeals had brought, successively, laughter, jeers and groans."

The press immediately concluded that the NUT and ATL members would vote heavily in favour of boycott. NUT GS Doug McAvoy said: "Teachers will be delighted at the court's decision." Peter Smith, the ATL GS, (at last) magnanimously conceded: "We must congratulate the NASUWT." The exclusively head teachers' organisations, the SHA and NAHT, said they would advise their members not to ask other staff to take over the work of those engaged in the boycott. David Hart, NAHT, added that if, as expected, the NUT and ATL joined the boycott, "Mr Patten will not have a leg to stand on". The journal *Education* awarded me the 'quote of the week' on 30 April: "The NASUWT took on the rest of the world and won." In short, the whole educational world was rising up in rebellion against the Government.

Most of the editorials conceded, albeit some through gritted teeth, that we had a legitimate grievance with the overloaded NC. But most could not concede that 'industrial action' had produced a sensible development. Some called on Mr Patten to tough it out with the teacher unions. But the NASUWT, through the sheer logic of its case and the trouble taken to explain it to so many organisations and people, had won the public relations battle. Furthermore, despite the usual merchants of "classroom chaos" peddling their predictable prejudice in the tabloids, led by *The Sun*'s "Schools face a long hot summer of strife after teachers won a legal victory", the parents could see for themselves that, as we had predicted, "not one single child will lose one second of education".

In his interview on the Brian Walden ITV programme the following Sunday, John Patten seemed preoccupied with me, "punching the air . . . proclaiming a scorching victory . . . and then seen on TV drinking champagne", all of which he deplored as unprofessional. I was as much surprised as amused, for instead of dealing with his biggest problem – what he was going to do about the situation – Patten trapped himself in trivia, stubbornly refusing to acknowledge the boycott and its likely effects. He was brought down to earth with a savage interruption by Brian Walden, telling him with devastating bluntness: "If I take you at face value, you don't seem to know what's going on. Your chances of persuading them are absolutely zilch."

I was equally amused to read a 'sour grapes' right-wing columnist in *The Evening Standard* likening my exit from the Royal Courts of Justice to a "released IRA convict"!

During the course of April Sir Ron Dearing got on with his job, doing the rounds, consulting everyone concerned and making a good impression as a fair and open-minded person. He, rather than a Tory right-winger, had surprisingly been given the job of reviewing the NC. I first met Sir Ron in my Covent Garden office on 26 April. The fact that he came to everyone rather than everyone going to him was good psychology on his part. I liked the man and was to have many meetings with him, some at very short notice. I was often to use his good offices to put right problems which arose in some LEAs and schools where the message of 'slim down' had not been well understood, deliberately or otherwise. Sir Ron had insisted on his independence, revealing he had never had any political affiliation and declaring publicly on his appointment on 18 April that he was "not just accountable to Parliament but also to parents and very much to teachers".

Late in April Patten fastened on to a recent Ofsted report on the NC regime thus far. The Minister's press release proclaimed: "Tests prove vital to improving educational standards." He wrote a snotty letter to all school governors reminding them of their statutory duty to ensure the NC and tests were delivered. There was a heavy hint that governors should discipline teachers who engaged in any boycott. Governors were not impressed. Mr Patten was not just digging while still in a hole; he was excavating. Governors refused to be bullied and reminded Patten sharply that they were volunteers to help run schools and who had no intention of doing the dirty work of a Government refusing to heed the legitimate concerns of teachers. The National Association of Governors and Managers (NAGM) spokesman (Walter Ulrich, a former DES civil servant) said governors would resign en masse if the Government persisted in its threats. The parents' organisation, the National Confederation of Parent Teacher Associations (NCPTA), called for the tests to be abandoned. Parents, alarmed that their children might be judged on the basis of flawed tests, sided with teachers. In Scotland a coalition of parents and teachers forced the Scottish Office to make similar tests voluntary.

The NASUWT piled in and wrote to all school governors on 30 April restating our case and pointing out that Patten's very selective letter seriously distorted the Ofsted report. Ofsted's own press release was headed: "Mixed progress in the National Curriculum and Assessment." The report acknowledged the "considerable burden on teachers, which is growing as new subjects are introduced" and observed that "the benefits and the costs . . . are finely balanced". Furthermore, as the tests took place the other children in the class are "often set work of a limited value . . . and are supervised by a non-teaching assistant or parent or left to work alone."

Other events kept the boycott in the news. On 26 April the Government announced a £700,000 advertising campaign promoting the value of the tests. Not only was it to prove to be a serious waste of public expenditure but the contentious claims the adverts made on the value of the tests provided more ammunition for the teachers who were winning the PR battle hands down with the parents.

On 28 April *The Independent* reported that, the day before, heads representing leading fee-paying schools had backed their colleagues in the state sector and had urged Ministers to abandon plans for nationally administered testing. Around this time the cross-party Parliamentary Select Committee on Education, led by its Chairman Sir Malcolm Thornton MP, unanimously came out in support of the teachers.

Wandsworth announced it was importing "supply teams" to carry out the tests, to which I responded, "fine, that would protect members from the additional workload although the educational merit of the initiative is doubtful".

The six teacher unions sent another letter to Patten asking for the testing and assessment arrangements to be suspended pending the outcome of the Dearing Inquiry.

On 30 April the ATL held a press conference to announce the results of its ballot. Although Peter Smith was hedging his bets, saying a few days beforehand that the vote was "in the balance", the result was heavily in favour of joining the boycott. Misinformed by a journalist on the time of the ATL's embargo I unwittingly broke it, issuing my welcome of the result somewhat prematurely. I declared it to be another damning indictment of Mr Patten who had succeeded in galvanising the normally placid ATL membership into action.

On 3 May came the first hints of high-level resignations from SEAC. Lord Skidelsky had again written several very perceptive newspaper articles explaining why the SAT tests had become such a "bureaucratic nightmare" and was complaining about Mr Patten's failure to introduce radical changes to the tests as well as to the history syllabuses.

The next day Lord Skidelsky resigned from SEAC. He was followed one day later by another 'prominent right-wing academic' on SEAC, Dr John Marenbon, Director of Studies at Trinity College, Cambridge. He shared Skidelsky's scepticism that the Dearing review would neither be independent of Ministers and their civil servants nor thorough enough to resolve the fundamental problems of the entire structure of the NC and testing. Marenbon also complained about advice he had drafted not even being placed on the agenda of the NCC.

Speaking more freely Skidelsky revealed how he had pleaded in vain with Mr Patten around the time of the court case: "For goodness sake act now before it explodes." Patten dismissed his fears, claiming that the trouble was just with the English tests, which he had dealt with. Skidelsky told Patten: "The tests will be a complete washout." I commented that this second high-level resignation within two days was further proof that the "whole exercise is in complete disarray".

On 6 May the six teacher unions despatched a nine-page document to the Secretary of State detailing how the prescribed NC and the amount of time spent testing could be sensibly reduced. This impressive display of unity was further enhanced by the document being endorsed by five representative bodies of the independent sector, including the Headmasters' Conference, the Girls' Schools Association and the Independent Schools Association Incorporated. Sir Ron Dearing quickly welcomed the document.

On 10 May came more bad news for the Government. A Gallup opinion poll showed conclusively that we had won the PR battle. Sixty-two per cent of all voters sympathised with the teachers' concerns. Detailed results showed:

Percentage sympathising with:	All voters	Con	Lab	LibDem
Teachers	62	37	79	59
Government	20	40	8	16
Both equally	9	15	5	12

(The remainder were 'neithers' and 'don't knows'.)

Of the 62% who sympathised with the teachers 83% said they believed teachers were justified in boycotting. Only 28% believed that teacher unions were playing at politics.

Other results showed that only 58% supported the NC. And yet more bad news for Mr Patten: only 50% were in favour of testing at 7, 11 and 14 years of age.

The Daily Telegraph who had commissioned the poll, surveyed the dismal scene in a revealing editorial. The Secretary of State had alienated the entire education world, including the Conservative's beloved independent sector. The tests had to be simplified and accountability preserved. Still *The Telegraph* believed the militants had to be faced down although it conceded that Mr Patten had lost so much credibility "it is now most uncertain whether he can retrieve himself" – a call to resign without mentioning the word.

It appeared there was nothing I could say to allay the obdurate prejudice of the right wing despite my oft-repeated reminder that the leading 'militants' in the boycott, the NASUWT, had long ago come out in favour of a national curriculum and actually preferred workload-light testing over bureaucratic assessment. The right wing could not accept the verdict of four leading judges that we had a legitimate dispute over workload and that we were not in the business of destroying the principles of testing and accountability.

The same *Telegraph* editorial in prejudgemental mode asked what was to happen *when* (notice not *if*) the Dearing review comes up with answers that "fail as they must to meet the profession's overheated expectations". The answers were sooner in the coming than expected. And when they came the NASUWT welcomed them with open arms.

A later opinion poll conducted by NOP for *The Independent* newspaper revealed that 62% of those polled believed this year's test should be dropped;

64% said 7-year-olds should not be tested; over 50% said they supported the teachers' boycott; 70% believed league tables would be misleading; 44% thought tests should be limited to core subjects; and barely half (49%) wanted all ten subjects tested.

On 10 May a meeting of Tory Party leaders took place. The Conservatives had fared disastrously in the Newbury by-election, losing a safe seat to the Liberal Democrats. The local government elections were also a huge setback, with the Conservatives retaining overall control in only one council, Buckinghamshire. The Government's economic policy was still in disarray after the collapse of Britain's participation in the European Exchange Rate Mechanism, the pound sterling was weak and the Chancellor, Norman Lamont, under continuous pressure to resign. There had been a major backbench revolt over the imposition of VAT on domestic fuel and power, almost defeating the Government. PM John Major was warned by the 'men in grey suits', led by Party Chairman Norman Fowler, that he would come under pressure to resign himself if he did not take drastic action to improve the Government's waning popularity. Its own opinion polls showed (remarkably, from a historical perspective) that the storm over testing was as big a vote loser as the economy. The Party leaders delivered a telling two-point message: first, stop losing the 'Battle of the Boycott'; second, Lamont and Patten had to go. The Government had to change direction and do it quickly, in fact right now! Major decided immediately to change tack on testing.

Selective briefing of the media was conducted overnight. Early in the morning of Tuesday 11 May the headlines appeared. *The Times*: "Major calls for rethink over testing schools"; *The Telegraph*: "Major orders retreat over school tests". They both predicted a huge slimming down of the NC and testing.

Meanwhile other less-favoured newspapers carried more defiant comments from Mr Patten: The tests must go on; it would be "a tragedy if the whole process was brought to a shuddering halt". In *The Guardian* I was quoted (unwittingly prophetic) comparing Mr Patten to a tired old boxer who refuses to fall over. "If referee John Major had any sense he would step in and stop the fight." *The Financial Times* had picked up hints that Mr Major was considering a compromise but the Department for Education late into the evening on 10 May said that was not an option.

Number 10 announced the Education Secretary would be making a statement in the Commons later in the day. The Education Department at first reacted with surprise, press officers in effect saying this was the first they had heard about it. In the early morning John Patten protested to 'No. 10' – the apparent source of the leak. Patten was told in no uncertain terms that if he did not make the statement, his successor would! Patten decided he had no choice and his department fell into line with the Prime Minister's commands.

I had been woken up early by BBC TV's *Breakfast Time* to go on the programme. On learning the news I immediately issued a press statement pointing out that the announcement totally pre-empted the Dearing review but did so in a very helpful way. Later in the day Sir Ron Dearing, diplomatic as ever, said he was comfortable with the Minister's statement, which reflected his thinking.

I was invited to ITN to be live on its lunchtime bulletin and to be filmed watching Patten's House of Commons statement on its Westminster feed. On his feet John Patten was shouting and speaking very quickly, sure signs of nerves. He was possibly distraught. He pleaded a convenient and plausible line: the Government was just anticipating the expected conclusions of Sir Ron Dearing's review, an interim version of which was due in the summer.

John Patten announced a 70% suspension of the NC testing and assessment programme and a streamlining of the core subjects. From 1994 the tests for 7- and 14-year-olds would be limited to the core of English, maths and science. Testing itself would be severely streamlined. Testing at 11 would be limited to the core subjects, start with a pilot next year and become mandatory in 1995. Dearing would also consider the merits of external marking for the tests at 11 and 14. Tests in history and geography for 14-year-olds, due in 1994, would be postponed pending Dearing's review.

As I listened to John Patten I could hardly believe my ears. His statement was one concession to the NASUWT after another. After he had finished, my only problem was to find another adjective to describe yet another victory. The next NASUWT Report to Schools was headed: "Another Glorious Victory".

However, having travelled (or perhaps been transported) so far Patten failed to go the extra mile and do the obvious thing which the logic of his new position screamed to be done – scrap the tests for the summer. Everything, curriculum and tests, was subject to radical revision. Patten's obdurate refusal to do this meant that the flawed and now redundant tests had to proceed while Dearing wielded his sharp knife. Patten's position thereby moved from the untenable to the incomprehensible. I could only respond to the journalists' questions about the future of the NASUWT action by saying that if the SATs had to stay for this year so did the boycott. This silly attempt to save face robbed Patten of substantial credit he could have salvaged by doing the sensible thing.

The headlines on 12 May spoke for themselves, resplendent as they were with words like "Climbdown", "Retreat" and "Patten fails test". *The Times* was more colourful, with: "The ink of panic". The prize for the 'best' headline inevitably went to *The Sun*: "Patten joins Lamont on Death Row".

On 21 May the NASUWT wrote to all its School Reps recording all the great workload-reducing potential of Patten's 11 May statement, congratulated members on having shifted the Government so far but called for one further push to secure such advances immediately through the scrapping of the arrangements that year. Members were exhorted to swamp their MPs and Ministers with letters demanding the obvious, which would enable the boycott to come to a natural end.

A second letter sent at the same time was confidential. It referred to recent statements from the NUT which envisaged a continuation of the boycott on educational grounds. The NUT had been alone in reacting negatively to Patten's massive U-turn on 11 May. The NASUWT warned of the danger of the NUT "snatching defeat from the jaws of victory" by breaking faith with ballot questions and inviting retaliation from the Government. The NASUWT insisted that once the workload issue was resolved the boycott would end. Opposition to the current testing regime on professional and educational grounds would continue by other means. The NUT complained to the TUC but the NASUWT refused to apologise, insisting the NUT had to appreciate its actions had implications for all unions in the public sector.

Support for the boycott was massive when the crunch time came early in June. National tests were due to be conducted for Key Stage 3 (14-year-old) pupils in four subjects, English, maths, science and technology. Only a handful of schools conducted the national tests.

The 5 July meeting of the National Executive resolved to continue the boycott, for the SATs regime was still in place and the promised slim down not yet implemented on the ground. The instructions of 12 March were repeated. The boycott would continue into the new academic year in September.

The Executive also approved a written submission to the Dearing review. Our policy statement focussed first and foremost upon workload. In addition we called for the NC at Key Stages 1 and 2 to be limited to the core subjects, English, maths and science. Key Stage 3 (14-year-olds) should include all the present arrangements but only English, maths and science should be the subject of national testing. Key Stage 4 (age 16) should be constituted by the present GCSE.

The Union conceded that simple 'pencil and paper tests' had serious limitations and that traditional teacher assessment had an important role to play. However, moderated teacher assessment, used to determine in part final grades in SATs and public examinations, remained extremely problematic in terms of its own feasibility, not to mention the excessive workload it generated.

Nevertheless, insistence upon simple pencil and paper tests in the context of the results forming the basis for the publication of school league tables would inevitably result in 'teaching to the test'.

Sir Ron Dearing published his Interim Report on 2 August. He had adopted nearly all the NASUWT recommendations. The report acknowledged the excessive workload, over-prescription and poor administration and recommended:

the slimming down of the statutory NC;

that only the core subjects should be nationally tested;

the duration of national tests in the core subjects be reduced by roughly 50%;

the number of statements of attainment be greatly reduced;

research into developing ways of measuring value added by schools.

In a press statement welcoming the report and the Government's quick acceptance of it, I said it "represents another successful landmark in the NASUWT-led campaign to reduce excessive workload. Furthermore, despite early 'macho-management' threats back in February '93, only a handful of teachers in a couple of schools have been subject to pay deductions for implementing the boycott. Governors and employers can only agree with our criticisms of the 'bureaucratic nightmare'. However, until the promised reduction is delivered on the ground the boycott will remain." The NASUWT advised teachers "to keep a vigilant eye on the methods of assessment which will be afforded equal status with the test results. 'Enthusiasts' must not be allowed to invent complicated systems which even if desirable on educational grounds are not commensurate with the resources available to schools".

Chapter 73 - War Against Workload Continues

There was no doubt that the school-teaching profession, led by the NASUWT, had won the Battle of the Boycott. Sadly, however, the war against workload had to continue. The SATs regime was still in place, and excessive workload burgeoning from other quarters required the boycott to remain in place. Pleas from John Patten and his 'number two', Minister of State Baroness Blatch, to end the boycott at a meeting on 27 September called to discuss Dearing's Interim Report had to be declined.

The main culprit appeared to be the new Ofsted inspection regime, introduced under the 1992 Act. Ofsted's Framework for Inspection was heavily prescriptive, almost totalitarian, in the requirements it placed on teachers, especially in respect of lesson planning, recording and reporting. Ofsted was laying down similar prescriptive requirements for head teachers on how schools had to be managed. Since Ofsted reports were to be published heads and teachers felt under enormous pressure and were even browbeaten into maintaining many of the detailed NC requirements which Patten and Dearing had already announced were to be reformed or abolished.

Similar pressure came from examination groups, LEA inspectors, advisers and consultants, to name but a few. Instead of resisting, many head teachers cascaded the stress and strain down to the 'poor bloody infantry' in the classroom. Some NASUWT members believed heads were content to keep the discredited system in place as a management tool. Many in management also wished to continue with moderated teacher assessment as a bulwark against any testing system however much slimmed down.

At his Party's Conference in Blackpool in October John Patten reverted to type and paid me the compliment of a strong personal attack in his keynote speech on education. Patten scraped the bottom of the barrel, claiming that I sent my son Paul to a GM school. It only went GM (against my expressed wishes and vote) five years after he had started there.

In a Report to Schools (No. 14) in October 1993, appropriately entitled "Operation Slim Down", the NASUWT raised some key questions for School Reps to consider. It appeared that many head teachers were not acting on recommendations from Sir Ron Dearing's Interim Report. Dearing had written a letter in August 1993 to all heads, followed up with a pamphlet, *Assessment arrangements for 1994*. In these documents Dearing recognised the huge administrative burden of assessment, blaming much of it on a false view "that it was necessary to have detailed tick lists covering pupils' progress against every single statement of attainment". Dearing explicitly stated: "There is absolutely no requirement to keep records at this level of detail. Nor is there a requirement to keep substantial quantities of pupils' work as evidence of the assessment made." Dearing issued similar messages in respect of record keeping and reporting to parents.

In November 1993 a joint letter from SCAA, Ofsted and the Welsh Chief Inspector was sent to all schools repeating the same message.

Membership pressure to maintain the boycott was considerable. Report 14 concluded that non-government sources of excessive workload, principally Ofsted, exam/assessment moderators and head teachers, must not be allowed to thwart the 'Dearing slim-down'. The boycott would remain in place.

As 1993 came to an end the NASUWT submitted further evidence to Dearing, highlighting the need to dispense with assessment playing any role in the determination of levels of achievement at Key Stages 1, 2 and 3. "Assessment linked to examination results requires moderation. Moderation multiplies meetings, burgeons bureaucracy and wreaks havoc with workload. 'Normal assessment', long used by teachers for their own purposes and for reporting to parents, should continue", was the strong message sent by the NASUWT. To these ends the Union strongly favoured external marking for the national tests.

The NUT was lobbying strongly for more teacher assessment. It was solely due to the pressure exerted by the NASUWT, including some of my 'early morning meetings' with Sir Ron Dearing, that he decided "to park" the issue of teacher assessment despite his support in principle for it.

On 6 January 1994 Sir Ron Dearing published his final report. He identified four major aims: to cut the curriculum back to a manageable size, to focus on the core subjects (English, maths and science), to restore the scope for teacher initiative and to reduce workload in administration and assessment.

I identified 12 specific and "dramatic" achievements of the NASUWT-led boycott secured with the publication of the latest Dearing Report:

1 National tests abolished for history, geography, technology and other subjects at all Key Stages (with science tests at Key Stage 1 dropped for 1994).

2 Only maths, English and science to be nationally tested.

3 The length of tests cut by a half.

4 The English Anthology at Key Stage 3 (much criticised) dropped.

5 Non-core subjects halved in their statutory content.

6 Attainment targets halved.

7 Statements of attainment halved.

8 The 10-level scale simplified.

9 Much assessment "parked" and subject to further consideration.

10 Reporting requirements slashed.

11 The proposed school league tables at Key Stages 1 and 3 abolished.

12 No more change for at least five years after establishment of the new system.

In giving a preliminary NASUWT reaction I welcomed the Report, observing at the same time that our boycott had achieved much but that more needed to be done to curb excessive workload in the system. I suggested a complete lifting of our boycott was unlikely. All would depend upon the impact on the ground of Dearing's recommendations.

The National Executive meeting on 14 January decided to lift the boycott in respect of the national tests but retain it for all other aspects, which would be kept under constant review. Thus members would now prepare pupils for the SATs and engage in the setting, invigilation, marking and reporting of them.

The NASUWT informed its members that further workload-saving measures had been lost through the failure of other unions to support the demand for external markers for the tests, the end of moderated teacher assessment and the abolition of the 10-level scale. Thus the boycott in respect of assessment had to be maintained.

I went on to state that "It would be political suicide for teacher unions not to respond positively to the massive concessions made, through Sir Ron Dearing, by the Government. It would surrender the high moral ground to the Government and invite further repressive anti-union legislation. The NASUWT was not in the business of snatching defeat from the jaws of victory." All the other unions agreed except the NUT, which did not welcome the Dearing Report and declared it would continue with the ban on the national tests, the hot political potato at the heart of the dispute.

At the same time (January 1994) I was greatly heartened to notice an article in *The Times* by Professor Michael Barber of Keele University. On 10 January he wrote: "Teachers have won far more than anyone might have dreamt a year ago. For unions, the most difficult decision always is when to settle. Courageous leadership is required. Continuing the action is often the easier option. Genius is knowing when to stop. A boycott in 1994 would be strategically disastrous." *The Guardian* had recently dilated on the same issue in an editorial aptly entitled "The Thorny Task of Admitting Victory".

Michael Barber had recently (November '93) left his job at the NUT as a very effective head of its Education Department where he gained the respect of NASUWT representatives. He went on to become a very influential adviser to David Blunkett, Education Secretary, and thereafter to Prime Minister Tony

Blair. In his article he went on to refer to the "crushing" defeat of the teacher unions by the Conservative Government in 1987, after the long pay dispute. The unions had found themselves "in an unpleasant grimy pit beyond the margins of the policy process". However, to their credit, they had climbed out of it and "the Dearing settlement represented the greatest achievement since the war. A 1994 boycott of the tests would lead straight back to the pit. The teacher unions must choose between responsibility and oblivion."

Unfortunately it was to take Michael Barber's former colleagues in the NUT a further year to get his message. As soon as the NASUWT Executive lifted the boycott in respect of the tests, the NUT went on a recruitment drive aimed at the potentially lucrative market of teachers seriously opposed on educational grounds to the SATs. In so doing it openly contradicted the workload basis of the boycott which had been the foundation of our success. Fortunately for the NUT its inability to deliver its 'revised' boycott on the ground saved it from serious trouble.

The antics of the NUT naturally caused us some problems as mini-rebellions broke out in some areas against our amended boycott. We did our usual thing in circulating detailed briefings to all members at their home addresses and engaging fully with those who opposed. Few if any problems persisted and Conference 1994 overwhelmingly approved the Executive decision. Our task was made easier by the continued success we were having in persuading Sir Ron Dearing to do the right thing and the hostility of the NUT towards external markers for the tests, which belied its true motives.

The huge cost of the introduction of the NC was another point of pressure on the Government. In a written Parliamentary answer on 19 January 1994 Mr Patten revealed that the costs amounted to £469m. In addition the flawed and aborted national tests had cost an extra £35m.

NASUWT Conference 1994 in Blackpool proved to be a landmark, being addressed by an Education Minister for the first time since 1986 when Sir Keith Joseph had received the 'silent treatment' from the delegates. Baroness Blatch, who had effectively become acting Education Secretary, substituting for the indisposed John Patten, hit the right note with Conference delegates with some humorous remarks about the accusations from the NUT GS Doug McAvoy that she and I were "snuggling up". Turning to me the Baroness said: "Whatever they might be doing to your reputation they were certainly ruining mine!"

I was very grateful to Doug, for he enabled me to respond, accusing him of being "puerile and petty". All unions had complained bitterly since 1979 that Government ignored us. But thanks to the successful boycott and the mostly positive response to the huge Government concessions, we had prised open the door to meaningful consultation which the NUT would have us kick shut.

In my Monday evening address to Conference delegates I stated my belief that the best approach was to build on the "stunning" and "scorching victories" of the 1993 boycott. There was more to be achieved in influencing the Dearing exercise than by continuing with a boycott against all the tests. That kept faith with our ballot question, guarded us from legal challenge, protected against political retaliation from the Government and retained parental and public support. In contrast the NUT alternative involved never-ending industrial action despite the bitter lessons of recent history, great political and possibly legal risks, and, ironically, landing teachers with even greater burdens by favouring workload-heavy assessment over slimmed-down tests.

Furthermore, the opening of a genuine dialogue with Baroness Blatch was quickly leading to further progress, no better exemplified than by the Minister's announcement in her address to our Conference that the Government was considering the introduction of external markers for the tests.

More progress came on 9 May when, in a joint Government/SCAA press conference, John Patten and Sir Ron Dearing announced another consultation exercise over further slimming down of the NC. A good example lay in the replacement of 966 detailed statements of achievement by 200 level descriptions to summarise pupils' progress. In stark contrast to previous practice, union officials were invited to attend the press conference and I enjoyed the event enormously.

The NUT's intransigence afforded some limited opportunities for John Patten, restored to good health, to regain some credibility, but not enough to save him in Prime Minister John Major's Cabinet reshuffle that was to follow in a couple of months time.

The next breakthrough for the NASUWT came on 1 July 1994 with the Government's announcement conceding external markers for the tests at Key Stages 2 and 3, costing an estimated £12m per annum. Supply teachers would be provided for Key Stage 1 to cover teachers marking those tests. The NASUWT Report to Schools described this as "Another Storming Victory". External markers had been secured despite the opposition of all the other teacher unions.

On the same day the Government also announced key concessions to the NASUWT over moderated teacher assessment. At Key Stage 1 the mandatory external audit of teachers' own assessments was dropped. Only the marking of the English and maths tests would be audited. At Key Stage 2 there would be no external audit of teachers' assessments. At Key Stage 3 external auditing, currently suspended, would be permanently abolished. The reporting of pupils' progress in the core subjects would be a matter for teachers' own professional judgement. There would be no requirements governing the collection of supporting evidence or the keeping of records.

The Government also confirmed its decision to abolish league tables for 7- and 14-year-olds and they would only be introduced at Key Stage 2 (11-year-olds) when the tests were successfully established. (They would remain for GCSE and A Levels.)

I concluded my press statement on 1 July: "If snuggling up to the Government produces such reduction in workload, if it strips away the bureaucracy inherent in moderated teacher assessment, if it restores professional independence, then let's snuggle up some more!"

John Patten's letter to me of 1 July was particularly satisfying when it stated that his "proposals have evolved in part as a result of constructive discussions my Ministers and officials have had with you and your Association". John Patten highlighted the decision on external markers. We had good reason to believe that the clinching moment had come in a recent meeting with Baroness Blatch when the NASUWT pointed out to her that employing external markers directly would give the Government much control over the conduct of the tests. Her eyes had suddenly lit up!

The NASUWT Executive would consider the future of the ballot at its September meeting. However, before the month of July was out John Patten had been sacked and Gillian Shephard appointed Secretary of State for Education. Mrs Shephard immediately adopted a conciliatory and consultative style deliberately designed to emphasise the difference from her immediate predecessor. That was just a little unfair on John Patten who had tried his best to be a reformed character since his return from illness; but, unfortunately for him, his earlier reputation was not easily dispelled.

The NASUWT held an important meeting with Gillian Shephard on 28 July. We reviewed the progress made so far but explained why we could not bring the boycott to a complete end. We were still receiving many complaints from members that head teachers, LEAs and Ofsted inspectors continued to expect delivery of the curriculum and assessment according to the 'old system' which was in the process of supposed serious slim down. We had also picked up signals that some LEAs were loath to pay their share of the supply cover costs for the tests at Key Stage 1. We suggested a repeat version of the 4 November 1993 joint letter signed by Sir Ron Dearing and the English and Welsh Chief Inspectors, this time with the DFE adding its weighty signature.

The NASUWT was also experiencing 'difficult discussions' in SCAA where supporters of moderated teacher assessment were active. For some that meant 'the profession' would be more in control but, in the view of the NASUWT, not those in the classroom. The excessive workload and bureaucracy would be borne by the 'poor bloody infantry in the classroom'. The NASUWT was also very conscious that while teachers of English, as represented by NATE, remained hostile to the tests, our members who taught maths and science were largely content with the much reformed and slimmed-down equivalents in their subjects.

On 5 September Gillian Shephard had confirmed the Government's decisions to use external markers, provide additional supply cover and eliminate the audit moderation of teacher assessment. However, the Minister also referred to continuing reviews of these new arrangements, including the cost-effectiveness of the external markers.

In another meeting with the new Secretary of State the NASUWT also repeated its strong dissatisfaction with the open-ended nature of the teacher's contract, exemplified in the infamous paragraph 36 (1) (f) in the Pay and Conditions Document (which had become 38.6 through other additions). Effectively, with minimum contractual hours defined, but no maximum, unlimited demands could be placed upon teachers from the ever-increasing multiplicity of sources. We warned Gillian Shephard of the danger of another formal dispute in the future and I took the precaution of summarising our concerns formally in a follow-up letter to her on 26 September.

In the Secretary of State's reply, 11 October, she was very supportive generally but left several specific issues of concern to the NASUWT open for further consideration in the light of all the views being put forward. The NASUWT began to sense that the new Education Secretary was less sympathetic to our concerns over workload and moderated teacher assessment.

In October 1994 the Executive agreed to circulate a very positive pamphlet entitled *The Continuing Campaign on Workload* to all members at their home addresses, summarising the many gains achieved, congratulating them on the disciplined and effective way they had conducted themselves and consulting them on the alternatives for the future. Those envisaged an end to the boycott at some stage subject to certain conditions which were not yet satisfied.

We were soon into 1995, with the boycott nearly two years old. The year 1994 had been another extremely successful one for the Union, with a net increase in paid-up in-service members of over 8,000 to 146,266, thereby approaching another landmark – 150,000. Membership had risen from 127,000 in 1990.

The NASUWT was not able to lift the boycott completely for another eight months as battles broke out largely behind the scenes over the role that assessment would play from 1 September 1995 as the new Subject Orders came into effect. There were moves to resurrect moderated teacher assessment and more reviews of the NC in breach of the five-year moratorium agreed as part of the 'Dearing' settlement.

The NUT continued to lobby hard for moderated teacher assessment to sideline the SAT tests and external markers, finding an apparently willing ally in Gillian Shephard. The Minister failed to provide the NASUWT with clear assurances that such bureaucracy-laden measures would not be reimported to replace the slimmed-down, workload-friendly, externally marked tests. The NASUWT warned of a full-scale reimposition of the boycott.

The NUT had a meeting with Gillian Shephard on 15 December. Around that time the NUT decided to ballot its members to lift its boycott, perhaps to avoid having to deliver it a few months later and possibly as part of a deal with the Minister for "a fundamental review of testing and assessment" it claimed in January to have secured. As the NUT launched its ballot in breath-taking defiance of reality it accused "the other teacher organisation" of "capitulating to John Patten" whereas in stark contrast it had secured a host of significant breakthroughs with Gillian Shephard. I dismissed the NUT attack as "far-fetched and farcical" since all the claimed 'breakthroughs' had been achieved months ago by the NASUWT and other unions in discussions with Patten, Blatch and Dearing.

With rich irony the NUT Executive repeated the NASUWT rationale for amending the boycott to justify lifting its own and for which we had been condemned for "capitulation"! The NUT literature described the changes to workload as "inadequate", making its recommendation to end the boycott even more puzzling. It all pointed to a vintage NUT performance, getting itself off the boycott hook in return for advancing its favoured assessment agenda and co-operating with Gillian Shephard in a shift of direction.

We could have taken all this nonsense in a 'statesman-like stride' had it not been for the serious matter of moderated teacher assessment. The NASUWT fears, first stirred by Shephard's ambivalence, were dramatically realised a few months later when we saw draft advice SCAA was proposing to send out heralding a return to moderated teacher assessment. I wrote immediately to Shephard, Dearing and the Chief Inspector of Ofsted spelling out the consequences.

Matters came to a head in March 1995 despite efforts by SCAA to consult the unions only on the basis of confidentiality. The NASUWT had already pointed out that 'advice' from SCAA would become 'mandatory', especially if further supported by elements within Ofsted and the Teacher Training Agency, not to mention panicky head teachers scared to death by school league tables based on pupil test results.

Ironically, the unpopular head of Ofsted, Chief Inspector Chris Woodhead, had made many anti-bureaucracy statements which the NASUWT supported. But Ofsted's own Framework for Inspection replicated the tendency in several other education quangos to produce bulky documents full of repetitious detail, piling mountains of frustrating paperwork on teachers which imperilled their efforts to focus upon teaching in the classroom, their most important role.

A meeting between the unions and SCAA convened by its Director, Nick Tate, on 27 March revealed that the NASUWT was the only union resisting the reintroduction "through the local back door" of bureaucratic systems of assessment. The SHA and NAHT indicated agreement with the draft despite the admitted workload problems that would arise. The NAHT reiterated its opposition to external marking of the tests, cloaking head teachers' fears over league tables with claims that assessment would be "more professional". The ATL sat on its usual fence, conceded the workload problem which on its own admission could lead to industrial action (inevitably someone else's), but supported the document. PAT acknowledged the problems but appeared ambivalent on the assessment issues raised. However, the NUT 'position' 'took the biscuit'. The NUT was represented only by a junior official in its Education Department. That might have been deliberate, for he confessed to feeling "more and more uncomfortable in the meeting" and did not want to express his union's view "for fear of Nigel de Gruchy misquoting me"! The NUT would convey its view in writing.

The inevitable happened as the discussions were leaked to the education press. I immediately secured another of my 'early morning' meetings with Sir Ron Dearing. When I arrived I found him accompanied by the SCAA Director, Nicholas Tate, who had left the classroom many years ago. They both sought to reassure me but I would have none of it. I restated the NASUWT's firm belief, gained from experience, that 'advice' from such authority would effectively be mandatory. Whatever the so-called 'educational' arguments, the workload issue overruled everything. I made it absolutely clear that if the current draft went out the NASUWT would be back in action.

The result was a compromise, with SCAA issuing a Guidance Document "Consistency in Teacher Assessment" in the Summer Term ahead of the new Subject Orders coming into effect 1 September. It was accompanied by a strong letter from Sir Ron Dearing and Chris Woodhead, stating:

"We must emphasise that this document is intended to provide a basis for discussion. Schools are not required to adopt any of the procedures in this document, nor will it be used by Ofsted as part of the criteria for inspection. Schools will develop effective practices for assessment, reporting and recording in different ways. Whatever system is developed, however, must be manageable and realistic. As we have said before, there is no need for elaborate systems or tick lists to record every detail of each pupil's progress."

The NASUWT Executive finally decided to lift the remainder of the boycott at its meeting in July 1995. It would end with effect 31 August. The new Subject Orders confirming all the slim down were to operate from 1 September and the issue of unreasonable assessment would now become a local one given the clear statement from Dearing and Woodhead on behalf of SCAA and Ofsted. We could hardly be in dispute with the Government nationally in the light of such statements. The NASUWT emphasised its willingness to offer full support, including authority for action, in schools which defied the criteria of "manageable and realistic".

Thus the boycott which had started in March 1993 was finally terminated at the end of August 1995. There is no doubt who won 'The Battle of the Boycott'. Sadly, however, the war against bureaucracy and excessive workload had to continue. More battles were to follow. The NASUWT could see huge workload implications for teachers as New Labour under the leadership of Tony Blair was promising mountains of reforms under his three top priorities of "education, education, education".

The old problems were soon to return. Tackling workload seemed to be like squeezing a balloon. The 'Master of Bureaucracy', David Blunkett, was to become Education Secretary (and thereafter Home Secretary), leaving mountains of paperwork in his trail. One shudders to think how bad the situation for teachers would be without the constant struggle by the NASUWT. The struggle continues to the present day although the 2004 Standards and Workload Agreement, achieved through Social Partnership between government and staff unions (the teacher ones led by the NASUWT with the NUT self-excluded), has provided a boost in the right direction.

Chapter 74 - Pay – Normal Service Resumed

Against the hectic 'Battle of the Boycott', salaries did not return to the forefront until the Government announced the second phase of its public sector pay policy. Pay was to be frozen, with increases only related to those linked to improved performance. The announcement on 23 December 1993 of a 15% pay increase for MPs did not go down well with teachers, and millions of other employees.

The STRB reported on 3 February 1994 and recommended rises of 2.9% for teachers. I commented that it was "no freeze, but cold comfort" but "just about enough to maintain the uneasy truce over pay levels". The Government refused to fund its share of the increase, again illustrating its deplorable 'heads I win, tails you lose' attitude. It expected teachers to accept the Review Body reports but failed to do so itself.

On the positive side 2.9% was better than the results of traditional collective bargaining and once again the Review Body effectively sidelined PRP for at least another year. Common Spine point 10 moved to £20,832 and the maximum point 17 to £31,323. Unions and the Review Body could claim some credit for having moved the Government away from a total freeze. Nurses and other NHS staff had done slightly better at 3%; top civil servants and judges a little worse at 2.75%.

Unfortunately, in the NASUWT view, the STRB had made no recommendations for improvements in conditions of service despite the context of the massively popular 'Test Boycott'. However, it had decided to undertake a survey of teachers' workloads.

On 19 July 1994 John Patten was finally dropped from the Cabinet in a reshuffle which saw the Employment Secretary, Gillian Shephard, moved to education. She set out on a 'charm offensive' to illustrate the differences from her predecessor. The NASUWT had its first meeting with the new Education Secretary on 28 July when we were able to welcome some recent developments, such as external markers for the tests, but deplore the failure of the STRB and the Government to provide a more secure and permanent solution to excessive workload through reform of the contract. The STRB survey showed teachers working 49 hours a week on average, with one in ten exceeding 60. The proportion of working time spent on teaching had fallen to 40%.

Following the 1992 FHE Act, sixth-form colleges were removed from the schools' sector and the control of LEAs, incorporated as separate institutions (along with their FE counterparts) and placed under the ambit of the FE Funding Council (and later the Learning and Skills Council). No longer subject to the STRB, in 1994 an NJC for Sixth Form Colleges was established to determine pay and conditions of service. The NASUWT, NUT and ATL, representing the overwhelming majority of teachers in the sector, were recognised by the college employers for negotiating purposes. With each union having equal representation we collaborated well and succeeded by and large (sometimes belatedly) in maintaining parity with school teachers under the STRB, although some problems remain and may become more difficult. Helpfully, all the employers agreed to opt in to these national negotiations, although in the early stages Huddersfield College declined to do so. Strike action brought Huddersfield into line. A new contract for sixth-form college teachers was agreed.

The year 1995 opened up with NASUWT in-service membership approaching another landmark, 150,000. On 1 January it stood at just over 146,000. With student membership at 40,000 and 27,000 associate members, overall membership topped 213,000. The successful campaigns of the NASUWT over the previous two years were paying handsome dividends.

Press speculation about Government reluctance to fund Pay Review Body reports surfaced a few days before the STRB reported on teachers' pay on 9 February. Our fears were realised with another modest increase of only 2.7% (across all the scales and allowances) which was to be entirely unfunded by the Government, leaving LEAs to pick up the bill alone.

I observed the award was so "modest it did not need phasing". The award was typical of its time – barely compensating for inflation, below the average earnings increase, but better than traditional bargaining as illustrated by the Scottish teachers' 2% settlement. Other review bodies awarded GPs 3%; judges 2.6%; armed forces between 2.5% and 3.8%; dentists and hospital doctors 2.5%; and nurses doing unusually poorly in relative terms, with only 1% basic but higher rises for some.

However, the NASUWT could not ignore indefinitely the ever-tightening financial squeeze imposed by the Government while at the same time being expected to implement the mountain of fundamental reforms recently legislated. Plans were afoot for the Executive to make recommendations at the Easter Annual Conference for industrial action aimed mainly at tackling the inevitable increases in class sizes.

The NASUWT also highlighted the disadvantage of LMS, which produced large, unspent balances in school budgets, mostly as a result of head teachers and governors believing they had to put money aside for the 'rainy day'. Under the old system contingencies would have been more cost-effectively covered by the LEA. The average level of unspent balances varied between 4.3% and 7.3% of annual budgets. In 1992/93 29% of secondary schools had unspent balances exceeding £100,000, with 7% of primaries over £50,000. Total unspent balances had risen from £420m in 1990/91 to £812m in 1993/94. Average unspent balances for 1993/94 were £72,900 (4.5% of total budget) for secondary schools and £22,138 (8% of total budget) for primaries. The NASUWT survey results were based on over 13,000 schools.

These unspent balances partly explained the Government's reluctance fully to fund recent pay increases. The NASUWT asserted that schools had the money and would not tolerate redundancies attributed to unfunded pay awards. The NASUWT accepted that some balances were required and supported the Government's guidance that 2% of budget was sufficient, barring exceptional circumstances.

Conference 1995 duly carried a comprehensive motion criticising the Government's funding policies and setting out a comprehensive campaign for action against oversized classes. The emphasis was on responsible action. Pupil-teacher ratios had improved from 1974 to 1990 but worsened in the nineties. In 1994 over 1 million children had been taught in classes exceeding 32.

Confidence in the NASUWT was high. The Union seemed to have survived the worst of the 16 years of Conservative Government since 1979. In my GS 'state of the union' session on the Monday evening I reminded delegates of recent successes – the great 'Test Boycott' of 1993, external markers for the tests, and persuading the Government to abolish the over-bureaucratic workload-heavy teacher assessment regime. Secretary of State Gillian Shephard addressed Conference in a very conciliatory mood, speaking about her desire to raise the morale and status of teachers. She received a polite if sceptical reception.

That was in stark contrast to the reception given by some NUT activists to the new Shadow Education Secretary, David Blunkett. Arriving at the NUT conference hall he was subjected to some intimidation by a group of NUT delegates. Together with his guide dog (he was born blind), David had to seek temporary refuge in a small room. Naturally the media made a meal of the event, 'antisocial behaviour' by NUT conference delegates being a 'hardy annual' which the press relied upon heavily in most years to fill the news void created by the absence of politicians and journalists on their Easter vacations.

Never an organisation to forget about its internal affairs, we conducted a survey of members' opinions and experiences of their union to assist in the production of a Report to Conference 1996 on the Structure and Organisation of the NASUWT. We were pleasantly surprised with the very positive feedback we received. A high percentage, usually between 70% and 80%, were aware of our activities and publications, with over half indicating they regularly read at least part of them. Furthermore a good majority were aware of their School Reps and felt the Union to be active and effective at grass-roots level. Local Officers were strongly in favour of more full-time regional staff to support them – a view towards which the Executive was very sympathetic. More staff would be appointed and training to deal with representation and negotiation at school and local levels extended.

David Blunkett had lobbied me hard to secure an invitation to address the NASUWT Conference. Our tradition had been only to invite the Secretary of State, no matter which party held power. After much discussion the Executive agreed, stipulating that in the interests of political neutrality the official education spokespersons for all the three main UK-wide parties should be invited. David Blunkett spoke well and received a standing ovation, promising as he did that a future Labour Government would fully fund Review Body awards.

By 1995, with the untimely and sudden death a year earlier of John Smith, Leader of the Opposition, Tony Blair had been elected as his successor and 'New Labour' had been born. An indication that there would be 'two education departments' in a New Labour Government came soon afterwards. He 'gate crashed' a routine Party press conference on education and sidelined the official spokesperson, Ann Taylor, announcing that New Labour would preserve many of the Tories' controversial reforms. Another came in the run-up to the 1997 General Election. Against strong lobbying by many teacher unions and others not to reappoint the HMI Chief Inspector and head of OFSTED, Tony Blair committed himself in a TV interview to keeping Chris Woodhead. Blair was determined not to be seen in hock to any unions and was keen to cultivate the right who viewed Chris Woodhead as the last surviving guardian of traditional teaching and values, somewhat surprising given his own admission of having been a 'trendy 1960s teacher' in his younger days. The NASUWT kept out of it, fearing such public pressure was bound to be counterproductive. By October the following year (1998) rumours were rife that Chris Woodhead was reappointed to another (four-year) term of office "against the wishes of everyone at the DfEE".

In office (from 2 May 1997 onwards) David Blunkett was to become more controversial as New Labour retained many of the unpopular Tory reforms, noticeably the national tests and league tables, Ofsted, and (during the first two years in power) the Conservatives' spending plans. Within a couple of years David Blunkett had lost his appetite to address NASUWT Conferences and excuses for absence replaced his earlier hard lobbying for invitations to attend.

The NASUWT went ahead with its consultative ballot on action against oversized classes. Not surprisingly, 99.6% of the 47,247 members who cast their votes believed oversized classes led to additional and unreasonable workload. Ninety-five per cent were prepared to take action short of strike but only 49% strike action itself. The Executive was nevertheless comfortable with the result, the lower turnout perhaps due to the greater predominance of the problem in the primary sector.

During the course of the ballot a timely study of 7,100 children in Tennessee, USA named 'STAR' (Student Teacher Achievement Ratios) had produced strong evidence that education cuts and increased class sizes produced lower standards of achievement. Tennessee had been so impressed with the results as to legislate for a maximum class size of 25 to be reduced to 20 by the year 2000.

The campaign on class sizes and funding run by the NASUWT produced considerable pressure on the Government, now suffering from poor showings in the opinion polls and serious divisions in its own ranks. Amidst rumours that the Chancellor would refuse to fund the 1996 pay rise for teachers and insist "efficiency savings" met the bill, Gillian Shephard was forced to deny ownership of a leaked Government document which stated that "insufficient resources threatened the provision of education in the state sector".

The more sensible Review Body arrangements were again in evidence during the Autumn Term 1995 as the four mainly classroom-based teacher unions, the NASUWT, NUT, ATL and PAT, submitted a joint pay and conditions claim to the STRB. The principles underlying the joint claim were a simplified salary structure, a substantial increase in all salary levels and sensible limits to be placed on the teacher's contract.

In autumn the setting of a tight STRB remit by the Government followed the familiar pattern. The STRB published its report for 1996 on 8 February. This time the Government decided to fund its share of the cost but phase the award in two stages. The STRB recommended increases across the board of 3.75%. The Government resolved that only 2.75% would be paid on 1 April, a further 1% coming on 1 December. The overall effect was to reduce the value of the award for the 1996/97 year to 3.1%, which was slightly below the rate of inflation at 3.2%. Again the award was well below the average earnings movement. Point 10 on the Common Spine moved to £21,981 on 1 April and to £22,194 on 1 December. However, the award appeared better when viewed against the local government workers' negotiations which were deadlocked at 2.5%.

I dismissed the phasing as "disgraceful". The previous November the Chancellor Kenneth Clarke had dished out significant tax concessions. I said: "Today we are told the Government cannot afford to pay its salary bill on time. Phasing in such a modest award could lead to teachers phasing out their enthusiasm and accelerating demands for a 'response' after a third successive low award."

Disappointingly the Review Body recommended a reversal of the structural changes of recent years by introducing half-increments as suggested by the DES and inevitably 'accepted' by the Government in this incestuous arrangement. These half-increments could be awarded for any aspect of a teacher's professional duties, including work outside the classroom. The Secretary of State specifically mentioned sports activities, possibly at the instigation of her boss, Prime Minister John Major, who was an avid cricket fan and no doubt much depressed by the dismal performance of the English national team. That was blamed, at least in part, on teachers who had abandoned after-school sport in large numbers in the wake of all the discontent, disagreements and disputes of recent times.

In the statutory consultation the NASUWT continued the fight, arguing strongly in the meeting with Gillian Shephard against the structural change to half-increments. Again doing a little simple arithmetic we worked out that 'rewarding' "excellence in the classroom" with half-increments added between 20p and 75p per lesson subject to tax; some reward!

We also followed up another important detail, namely the change to allow teachers moving school or returning after a break in service voluntarily to surrender discretionary points for non-teaching experience. This was in danger of breaching equal opportunities legislation, discriminating overwhelmingly against women who took career breaks for the well-known reasons.

In a surprise move Gillian Shephard announced she would reconsider such matters. This was the first time under the STRB system that a Secretary of State had engaged in genuine consultation and indicated some flexibility. I publicly welcomed "the rethink on the half-baked half-point scheme". This good news was, however, tempered by the Minister's decision to retain the phasing, no doubt dictated by the Chancellor of the Exchequer.

The 1996 Annual Conference was held in Glasgow, emphasising the UK coverage of the NASUWT. In my Monday evening address I was able to report the "astonishing progress of the Union". We had not only surpassed another landmark in reaching over 150,000 in-service members, but we had assumed the leadership of the teaching profession in our successful campaigns over workload and the excesses of the national curriculum, testing and assessment.

The Wednesday morning 'urgency' motion, traditionally reserved for pay and conditions, dealt with the fundamental issues facing the NASUWT in the long term. I had devoted my GS article "Facing the Future" in the Spring Term edition of *Teaching Today* to raising the question of a Social Partnership with government. I had been much impressed with the experience of unions in

Australia and Ireland where considerable mutual benefits had been secured through Social Partnership. Both those countries for obvious historical reasons had inherited the British confrontational approach to industrial relations. After much discussion in the months leading up to Conference, the Executive decided that the NASUWT should position itself to offer a genuine Social Partnership to the incoming government due at the latest in about one year's time after the next General Election. A very carefully drafted motion for Conference began by reviewing the pros and cons of the Review Body and the Government's reactions to it and went on to list the six most important problems confronting the teaching profession:

> the exploitative contract, particularly the open-ended clause (now renumbered 40.7 from its infamous 36 (1) (f) beginning);
>
> excessive and unnecessary workload;
>
> serious lack of resources;
>
> funding crises;
>
> redundancies and insecurity of employment;
>
> increases in class sizes.

The motion went on to say that addressing these problems will require substantial resources over a long period of time, which only a successful economy and a socially enlightened government could provide. Conference supported the National Executive, endorsing measures to 'spread the gospel of partnership' in all relevant quarters.

Arguing for Social Partnership was not an easy matter for a trade union. Many trade unionists were opposed to it as a matter of principle, believing that it was not the job of unions to solve management's problems. However, a clear majority of the NASUWT had taken the view that management's problems are also employees' problems and vice versa. At the September 1996 TUC Congress the NASUWT successfully moved a motion calling for Social Partnership which was seconded by the large GMB union. (The NASUWT had successfully proposed a similar motion at the 1985 Congress.) The NASUWT published a booklet on the subject. As it was, events beyond our control conspired to put Social Partnership on to the back-burner. The year 1996 turned out to be the one in which our long-standing policy of refusing to teach violent or disruptive pupils reached a climax. Four high-profile cases hit the headlines, culminating in the dramatic collapse of The Ridings School in Halifax in November.

Nor was the cause of Social Partnership with New Labour, expected to win the upcoming General Election, much helped by the controversial policies the Party adopted in the field of education. Holding tight to the Tory spending plans for the first two years might have been more readily accepted by unions if future intentions to invest more in public services when the economy allowed had been revealed. While we appreciated the financial constraints that would face a new government, the biggest concern of teachers was excessive and unnecessary workload caused mainly by mountains of paperwork and endless meetings. That could all be stripped away at nil cost to the Exchequer and to the great benefit of teachers and pupils.

In September 1996 the STRB published the results of its survey on teachers' working time. The findings confirmed those of the NASUWT. Primary teachers' working hours had risen from a weekly average of 48.8 in 1994 to 50.4 in 1996. Those for secondary teachers had risen from 48.9 to 50.3. Primary heads turned in 55.7 hours and those in secondary 61.7 in 1996. In many ways the worst aspect of this problem was the proportion of time devoted to teaching. Only around 20 of the 50-plus hours being worked were spent teaching, representing some 40% of the total. Around 30% was spent on marking and preparation. Much work was also being carried out in the evenings and at weekends.

Confirming the long-expressed fears of the NASUWT, the evidence pointed to excessive workload producing huge amounts of stress, causing many to suffer from burn-out and seek early ill-health retirement. The NASUWT repeated its demand for a fair contract, setting a limit of 35 hours per week. The STRB had it within its power to recommend limits.

In October 1996 another crisis blew up over teachers' pensions, their increased cost and the numbers seeking early retirement. Once again the NASUWT led a rearguard action which had some success but did not prevent the loss of benefits to teachers taking early retirement. I describe the events in section 5, Teachers' Pensions.

On 6 February 1997 the STRB published its report following another tight remit set by the Government the previous November. Government expected recommendations on pay to be "considerably lower" than the increase in education Standard Spending Assessments of 3.4%. The STRB recommended increases of 3.3%. Once again the Government decided to phase the award with 2% conceded for 1 April and 1.3% on 1 December, effectively reducing its value to 2.43% for the 1997/98 year. The RPI stood at 2.5% but average earnings were at 4%. Once again teaching was being made a comparatively less attractive profession. Point 10 of the Common Spine rose to £22,638 on 1 April and to £22,926 on 1 December. To save a little money the Government again aroused much anger in teachers. On the same day, as had become the custom, the awards of the other review bodies were also announced. Judges received 7%, nurses 3.3%, the armed forces 3.3%, doctors 3.4% and senior civil servants 2.75%.

I wrote a strong letter of protest to the PM, John Major, asking: "How can the Government have the audacity to ask Parliament to phase modest pay awards for public servants after having voted hefty (26%) increases for themselves following the free-ranging remit you gave to the Senior Salaries Review Body to investigate MPs' pay?" The Secretary of State replied for the PM, saying the Government had merely implemented the recommendations of the report on MPs' pay, totally ignoring the key difference that it had given a free-ranging remit to its Review Body, with no guidance on affordability.

However, the most depressing aspect of the 1997 award was the behaviour of Gordon Brown, then Shadow Chancellor. Early in the morning of 6 February, obviously with some foreknowledge of the announcement due later in the day, Gordon Brown had "beaten the Government in the rush to call for the phasing of the Teachers' award", as I put it. I wrote a furious letter to Gordon Brown, faxing it immediately to his office, pointing out: "While the majority of teachers loathe the treatment they have received from the Conservative Government over the last 18 years, they are feeling a deep sense of despair with New Labour 'out-Torying the Tories'."

Later in the day I encountered Gordon Brown as we both entered the BBC Westminster studios on Millbank to give interviews. I attempted to engage Gordon in conversation, only to be met by him refusing to look me straight in the face but declaring "I have read your letter" as he continued on his way protected by a wall of American football-style linebackers.

The Easter Annual Conference season arrived in-between the Review Body reports and the General Election. The NASUWT condemned the phasing of the pay award by the Government as well as the STRB's failure to recommend much-needed improvements in conditions of service.

The incoming President in 1997 was Barrie Ferguson from York. He was a self-made expert in health and safety and used his presidential address to highlight his pride in trade unions' efforts in this field where thousands of activists gave up their time to help their colleagues in the workplace. But the facts spoke for themselves. Over 6,000 teachers had their health destroyed at work and over 12,000 sought early retirement every year thanks to overload and stress.

Mindful of all the ambitious plans New Labour had for education, I observed in my 'state of the union' GS address to Conference that pressure on teachers would not recede if Tony Blair won power. We remained keen to enter constructive Social Partnership with any incoming government but not to the extent of neglecting our basic duty to look after teachers. We appreciated the financial realities of life but again I emphasised 'until I was blue in the face' that workload could be reduced at nil cost to the taxpayer. I warned that if a new Government failed to resolve these problems we would simply have to tackle them ourselves.

Reflecting on other long-term issues at Conference 1997 I responded to those who argued that the three largely 'classroom based' teacher unions should merge. I drew on our experiences in 1996 fighting the good fight over violent and disruptive pupils at Glaisdale, Hebburn, Manton and The Ridings schools. There was widespread support from the public and grass-roots teachers for our courageous stand. Ironically our two biggest critics were the leaderships of the two other unions with whom some would have us merge.

The NASUWT commissioned its own survey into teachers' voting intentions. The results matched an NOP poll carried out a few weeks before the General Election which showed voting intentions amongst teachers to be: 52% Labour; 27% Liberal Democrat; and 17% Conservative.

Leading politicians from the three main parties addressed Conference, including Secretary of State Gillian Shephard. She received a polite but mixed reception, some hisses of disbelief after her claiming Government credit for improving education, but applause for complimenting the NASUWT for its stand on good discipline in schools. Mrs Shephard concluded her speech by defiantly promising, General MacArthur-style, that (despite the opinion polls!) "I shall return". In my 'vote of thanks' to her I expressed confidence that she would, "albeit as a shadow of her former self".

Chapter 75 – Life under New Labour

The first of May 1997 was truly a historic day for the UK. Eighteen years of "torrid Tory rule", as most trade unionists viewed it, came to an end and New Labour under Tony Blair was elected to power with an overall majority of 179 in the House of Commons.

Education got off to a "roller-coaster start" in respect of union-Government relations. On 20 May the New Labour Government took an initiative which threatened to wreck any chance of a constructive relationship being established with the teacher unions. The Minister of State Stephen Byers published a list of 18 "failing schools" and threatened them with closure if they did not reform and do so quickly.

I immediately condemned this "naming and shaming" and "management by public humiliation", a practice which would be shunned by any organisation in the much-vaunted private sector. I also made immediate contact with some of the schools mentioned. One in Birmingham had an NASUWT member as head who, as a very successful leader, had been persuaded by the LEA to leave a good school and take over the challenge of the very difficult one now "named and shamed". The exam results had immediately improved. The head had also suffered a heart attack due in his opinion to the intense pressure generated by the job. I visited the school a few days later and saw for myself the challenges the school faced and the enormous effort and vitality the head and other members of staff put into their work, which had yielded positive results. They were all, naturally, furious and pointed to neighbouring 'unnamed' schools that had inferior examination results, as those appeared to be the criteria used by the Government in its exposé. I left the school fearing for the health of the head teacher. I was not surprised to learn that he died a couple of years later, although he had by then moved to the USA having given up on New Labour.

However, the following day (21 May) the new Secretary of State, David Blunkett, accompanied by his two Ministerial colleagues, Steven Byers and Estelle Morris, met with the six teacher union GSs. David Blunkett offered "a fresh start and a new partnership" to build a better education service. His first proposal under the new partnership was to establish a working group of departmental and union representatives, together with LEAs and business people, to slim down the bureaucracy and paperwork which had swamped teachers in recent years.

None of my fellow GS colleagues seemed to have prepared a definitive statement of their unions' priorities, preferring instead to pick up on the latest relatively minor spat with Chris Woodhead and Ofsted. I took along one sheet of paper with six main points in bold print which I was happy to lay on the table in such a way as to make sure the three Ministers could read them. They were workload/bureaucracy, pupil behaviour, pay, incessant reform, Social Partnership and collegiality. I moved briskly through them, obviously giving a warm welcome to the working group. David Blunkett responded positively.

However, when I raised, as I had to, the question of the "naming and shaming" I was greeted by a wall of embarrassed silence from all three Ministers. This uncharacteristic Ministerial silence fed my suspicion that the naming and shaming initiative had come from the 'other Education Department' – the one at 10 Downing Street.

(Stephen Byers was rather apologetic about it when I tackled him later in private. There appeared to be no clear criteria for inclusion in the infamous list but the new Government had to take an initiative of this kind in order to send out 'the right message'.)

Towards the end of the meeting, which I regarded as highly important, all three Ministers emphasised the determination of the new Government to consult closely over its forthcoming White Paper on education. They were anxious to avoid the mistakes of their immediate predecessors.

Afterwards I described the meeting as a breakthrough for the NASUWT. We had been the only union to make Social Partnership and a resolution of the workload problem the two top priorities at our Annual Conference. A recent NASUWT-sponsored NOP opinion poll had confirmed that excessive workload was the major grievance felt by 93% of teachers. The joint working group provided a real opportunity to solve the problem. Despite the naming and shaming we had to give partnership a try and we were able to point to positive progress in Northern Ireland where an NASUWT deputation to the new Minister, Tony Worthington, had led to the Government agreeing to restore some of the cuts made to education to finance the additional costs of security in the wake of the breakdown of the peace process.

On 7 July 1997 the Government published its White Paper *Excellence in Schools*, which was later to form the basis of its first major piece of education legislation. There were some laudable proposals the NASUWT could support but the workload implications for teachers were alarming. It marked the beginning of a tendency which continued throughout New Labour's administration that while Ministers talked about reducing bureaucracy and workload they took initiatives which piled on the agony.

By September 1997 we were back in familiar if unfortunate territory on salaries. Leaks were coming of the Government's apparent intention to freeze the public sector pay bill (for the fifth consecutive year). I predicted publicly that "sooner or later there is bound to be an explosion of anger amongst teachers" with some form of industrial action 'inevitable'.

Stephen Byers accused the NASUWT of fomenting immediate strike action, which was nonsense. I wrote to Stephen asking how, in the light of the Treasury spokesman's expressed determination to maintain the freeze on the pay bill, the Government was going to pay for its declared intention to employ extra staff to reduce class sizes and reward the newly announced Advanced Skills Teachers.

Meanwhile the Working Group (WG) on Reducing the Bureaucratic Burden on Teachers had quickly got down to business after the meeting between the Ministers and the six GSs on 21 May. We held many meetings but by November, the time intended for an interim report, the WG was running into serious difficulties.

The NASUWT had been concerned from the outset when the (now newly renamed) Department for Education and Employment (DfEE) decided to commission the management consultants Coopers & Lybrand to produce a report. The Union argued we all knew the problems; we needed solutions, not regurgitation – however sophisticated – at considerable cost which no one would disclose on the dubious grounds of commercial confidentiality.

Unfortunately the DfEE tried to insist the WG had to limit itself to identifying ways of reducing the bureaucratic burden on teachers "within the existing statutory framework". The NASUWT took an entirely opposite view and argued strongly, alas with only PAT supporting, that unless the statutory requirements were examined a resolution was impossible. They were a major source of the problem.

Coopers & Lybrand had been asked to conduct in-depth investigations in 13 schools and worked expeditiously to produce a draft report. This first draft raised two fundamental issues. First, was there simply enough time for teachers to cope with all the demands? Coopers & Lybrand observed that despite the many new demands, teachers had the same contact ratios as in the 1970s. Second, the report raised major questions about the quality of the management and organisation of schools. It stated with commendable if uncharacteristic candour and clarity that much of the problem lay in the nervous overreaction of heads to all the demands placed upon schools, particularly those generated by Government, legislation and the Ofsted inspection system. Naturally the draft report generated a lively discussion and the exclusively head teacher organisations were on the defensive, especially the NAHT with its predominance in the primary sector, which seemed to feel the pressure most.

At the next meeting of the WG we found the amended draft of the Coopers & Lybrand report had been edited to exclude these and other important findings. It was intended for publication as an annexe to an interim report from the WG. We were deeply unhappy with the changes and could only speculate that a combination of head teacher association and departmental pressures were behind the 'doctoring'.

The NASUWT was also angry that the 30 recommendations contained in the interim report only skirted round and failed miserably to get to the heart of the problem, namely the massive statutory framework and how that was interpreted and managed at school level. Accordingly I brought along an NASUWT Minority Report and commented that we were deeply saddened by the 'cover-up', believing that classroom teachers suffered from the same problem as the heads – of 'nervous overreaction' to the demands made upon them. Unless such issues were honestly and openly recognised no solution would be forthcoming.

The Coopers & Lybrand findings were supposed to be published in the week beginning 3 November together with an interim report from the WG. The NASUWT was raising so much hell about the inadequacies of both that Estelle Morris, who had been given Ministerial responsibility for the WG, was forced to postpone publication and call another meeting to discuss the NASUWT concerns. A special meeting of the WG was called for 17 November.

Meanwhile the publication of the New Labour Government's first piece of education legislation, the massive School Standards and Framework Bill, posed yet another threat to the continuation of a national system for teachers' pay and conditions. In the proposed Education Action Zones (EAZs), clusters of schools could be brought under the control of groups of parents and business and community leaders where they were deemed to be failing. The EAZs would be given extra resources and allowed to opt out of the national curriculum if they wished and to disapply the Teachers' Pay and Conditions Document, the means by which the statutory national arrangements were delivered.

The Government seemed keen to pre-empt the Parliamentary procedures, not to mention the Review Body. Education Ministers spoke publicly of establishing EAZs with five already "in mind", and were openly discussing appointing Advanced Skills Teachers (ASTs) in them. The Government had only recently asked the STRB to consider how its proposals for ASTs might be piloted in a last-minute submission before the closing date for evidence to be presented for 1 April 1998.

Alone amongst the unions, the NASUWT declared the principle of an AST had potential for good but the Government's ideas for implementation were ill thought out. If the collegiate approach were adopted, the sound principle of recognising and rewarding good classroom practice inherent in the AST could provide a long-overdue alternative for teachers to seek 'promotion' through excellence in the classroom rather than administrative duties.

In keeping with its collegiate approach to salaries and the running of schools, in December 1997 the NASUWT restated its policy calling for a Social Partnership with Government in a pamphlet entitled *New Deal: New Future*.

In the same month, the NASUWT published the results of a survey of nearly 1,500 members showing that 80% believed the primary national curriculum to be unmanageable and in desperate need of slimming down. Other major findings revealed 91% in favour of more focus on literacy and numeracy and a reduction in depth of the non-core subjects. Most called for more time for the exercise of professional judgement. David Blunkett accepted many of these points and agreed that the Subject Orders would be suspended for two years from September 1999 pending the review of the national curriculum to take place for the year 2000.

Chapter 76 - "Let Teachers Teach"

In January 1998 the NASUWT launched its "Let Teachers Teach" campaign. Although the Government had just announced significant slimming down of the statutory requirements of the national curriculum in the primary sector, the problem of excessive workload had grown and grown under New Labour's ambitious programmes of reform. Ofsted and the examination system were also piling on the pressure and the Dearing reforms earlier in the 1990s were being overtaken and submerged by such developments.

The NASUWT Executive had concluded that a more vigorous approach was needed. The WG on Reducing the Bureaucratic Burden on Teachers had reported together with the parallel study by Coopers & Lybrand and both were widely acclaimed. Minister of State Estelle Morris proclaimed: "Teachers should be free to teach, not slaves to paperwork."

The NASUWT found the analysis good but the prescription on remedies was weak. In a nutshell, the remedy proposed lay in general exhortation to slim down, which even if successful in the short term would quickly be swamped by new initiatives such as benchmarking and target setting, already heralding a new flood.

Direct action might be required. It was no good relying upon school managements to sort things out; Coopers & Lybrand had identified them to be part of the problem. The most recent survey the NASUWT had undertaken showed 93% of teachers regarding excessive bureaucracy as the major problem. Everyone, including the DfEE, LEAs, QCA, Ofsted and the TTA, agreed that bureaucracy was a serious problem compromising teachers' abilities to raise standards and meet the ambitious targets the New Labour Government had set. The Office of Manpower Economics (OME)/STRB report had shown only 40% of teachers' time was spent teaching. The average working week exceeded 50 hours for teachers.

In short, the direct action being contemplated would amount to instructions from the Executive to members to implement the recommendations of the Bureaucracy WG and Coopers & Lybrand reports. There was no question of strike action. Action would simply be to implement recommendations emanating from Government and employers.

In practice, the action would aim to cut out the bureaucratic overload exemplified by excessive and unnecessarily complicated: documentation; lesson plans; assessing, recording and reporting arrangements; action and development plans; target setting at too frequent intervals; behaviour management policies; and numerous and unnecessary meetings.

The sources for this overload were many and various. They included the mind-boggling demands of moderated assessment which had survived the Dearing 'cull' and impacted particularly on post-16 and GNVQ courses; Ofsted demands for detailed lesson plans and schemes of work and for written evidence of what is taught rather than what is learnt; reports to parents, records of achievement; portfolios of work; LEA demands for school development plans; the special educational needs (SEN) code of practice, especially for individual education plans (IEPs); and the information required for benchmarking.

The Conservative Government had been bad enough, but now New Labour was outdoing its predecessor in addiction to micro-management of schools. Summarising the likely effects of our action I said: "The campaign is in the interests of both teachers and pupils. Reducing bureaucracy will not cost a penny but will boost teaching. It will be teacher liberating, pupil friendly and standards enhancing." In short it would be "Industrial action with a halo" – one of my favourite sound bites, for it conveyed the NASUWT message in five simple words.

On 29 January 1998 the STRB published its report recommending a 3.8% increase across the board. In familiar fashion it just covered teachers for inflation, running at 3.6%, but made teaching relatively less attractive once again since average earnings were rising at 4.7%.

To the dismay of teachers the New Labour Government decided to phase the award, paying only 2% from 1 April and the remaining 1.8% from 1 December, reducing its value to 2.6% in the full year. Point 10 of the salary spine for teachers rose to £23,385 on 1 April and to £23,796 on 1 December.

The STRB had specifically recommended paying the award in full:

"Our recommendations represent our considered judgement of all the factors involved and, with the prospect of improved funding, we hope that they will in future be implemented in full from the due date.

"Staging is strongly resented by teachers and permanently affects the pensions of those who retire before the salary award is fully in payment."

In my public reaction I condemned the staging of "a modest award" as "outrageous. It is not justified by the healthy state of the public finances. Labour used to condemn the Conservatives for doing this. The anger it will generate is out of all proportion to the small savings achieved." I also deplored the failure of the STRB to make recommendations to improve conditions of service, adding: "This can only heighten the probability that the NASUWT will have to take direct action to lighten the ludicrous bureaucratic burden which all the reforms of the last ten years have imposed upon the teaching profession."

The fact that other Review Body awards were also staged was little comfort. Other awards were the armed forces 4.2%, doctors 4.2%, nurses 3.8%, senior civil servants 3.5% and judges 3.5%. Once again the close proximity of the figures one to another suggested a certain amount of 'collusion' between review bodies, possibly with someone from the OME, who provided the Secretariats, engaging in some 'appropriate liaison' with Government departments including of course the Treasury.

Within days of claiming that the country could not afford to pay the modest 3.8% in full the Chancellor of the Exchequer found the resources to repay £10.4 billion of public debt. There was a £1.5 billion underspend on current Government programmes. An additional £250m was allocated to education.

Later several Ministers admitted privately to me that the staging had been done to impress the financial markets at home and abroad, demonstrating that New Labour was not in hock to the unions and could be relied upon to pursue "prudent spending policies". A decade later the world's financiers' strictures on 'prudence' were to resemble the Devil's sermons on sin.

It was not surprising that on 6 February the National Executive decided to proceed with a formal ballot in support of the "Let Teachers Teach" campaign. The ballot question was: "Are you willing to take action short of strike action to secure changes in your conditions of employment in order to ensure practical implementation of the principles and recommendations enshrined in the Report of the Working Group on Reducing the Bureaucratic Burden on Teachers, published by the Government on 16 January 1998?"

As always the ballot question (unavoidably 'wordy and bureaucratic') had been very carefully drafted to protect against challenge in the courts. The NASUWT also allowed a generous timetable to prepare the membership, facilitate voting and give the Government plenty of time to respond positively if it wished. One month would be used for preparation; the next for balloting, allowing the result to be announced one week ahead of Conference opening on 13 April, with the action planned to commence at the beginning of the Summer Term.

Stephen Byers, the Minister of State, expressed concern that our action would be the first of any union under New Labour and he expected the media to react negatively against the Government. I told him there would be the usual "chaos in the classroom" predictions of the press to feed the stereotypical preconceptions their readers apparently demanded. However, after the initial publicity it would all go quiet because the effects of our action would be invisible to the outside world as it would be the very opposite of 'chaos producing'. That is precisely what happened.

The campaign and ballot were extremely well received by members and indeed by others. The NUT requested a meeting under the auspices of the TUC to which the NASUWT agreed. The NUT expressed some concerns but had much sympathy for our proposed action and would consider adopting similar measures. We had a very constructive meeting with the NAHT, who while very sympathetic to our objectives hesitated before taking action themselves. I wrote to every organisation I could think of as relevant, offering to meet and explain our action.

As part of the supporting literature in the campaign, the NASUWT supplied examples of the type of instruction to members that would follow a positive ballot result:

Limit documents to 400 words maximum.

Limit attendance at meetings after school hours to one per week.

Implement the Government's decision to abolish detailed programmes of study.

Boycott pre-Ofsted inspections at the expressed wish of Chief Inspector Chris Woodhead.

Operate one single streamlined system for assessing and recording pupil achievement.

Limit length of pupil reports, participation in benchmarking and target setting.

Use their own professional judgement to employ ready-made lesson plans (available through the National Learning Grid) if deemed appropriate.

Boycott administrative tasks such as collecting money, copy typing, copying out lists.

It was made clear that the instructions would apply to the annual 1,265 directed hours as well as to the 'open-ended' time specified (now in paragraph 40.7) in the Teachers' Pay and Conditions Document.

The NASUWT met with David Blunkett on `11 March. The talking was blunt but the atmosphere remained positive. During the discussion the idea of a DfEE circular promoting the bureaucracy-reducing measures advocated by the NASUWT campaign arose and we said we would gladly consider such a development although we harboured more ambitious plans for a change to the contract.

Meanwhile I got on with the business of meeting as many 'partner' organisations in the education service as I could, including Ofsted and the SHA, to explain our "Let Teachers Teach" campaign.

The NASUWT had its formal statutory consultation meeting with the Government on the STRB report on 19 March. Stephen Byers said the Government would not change its mind on phasing. That was predictable but disappointing, bearing in mind the improved public finances, which blew the case for phasing to pieces.

The NASUWT called a press conference on 6 April to announce the result of the ballot to "Let Teachers Teach" and bust bureaucracy. I described the 93% vote in favour to be "a thumping majority". Of the 45,719 votes cast 42,407 were in favour and only 3,282 against (with 30 spoiled papers). The turnout was seriously affected by unofficial action being taken by Post Office workers but nevertheless the Electoral Reform Society declared the result could stand, given the massive majority in favour. The action was set to start on 27 April after the Easter break. I emphasised again the benign effects of the campaign – the "industrial action with a halo."

After almost one year of New Labour it was, alas, 'old problems' that dominated Conference 1998. Incoming President (the sadly now late) Margaret Morgan, from Devon and a very popular veteran from the fledgling days of the UWT, echoed the moral force behind the "Let Teachers Teach" campaign. She emphasised in her speech how she loved "the feeling of being in school and the interaction with pupils. I get a real buzz out of seeing the young people I teach achieve and progress. All I ask is to be allowed to get on with the job I love and for which I was trained."

In my GS Monday evening 'state of the union' address I found myself dealing with the old problems of pay, bureaucracy/workload and disruptive/violent pupils, together with the new 'naming and shaming' or 'management by public humiliation' as I labelled the new Government's approach to the education service. I emphasised that the "Let Teachers Teach" action was a perfect marriage between the 'trade union' and the 'professional'. It would restore teachers' professional judgement and independence, enhancing the education provided to the nation's children.

David Blunkett addressed the 1998 NASUWT Conference for the first time as Secretary of State for Education. His address, the questions posed by members of Conference and my reply as the GS were lively affairs with robust but constructive exchanges in the finest traditions of NASUWT plain speaking and common sense. The phasing of the pay award featured strongly. In an attempt to head off the likelihood of action over bureaucracy and workload, the Minister announced he was reconvening the WG.

Two more meetings of the WG on Bureaucracy took place on 22 and 23 April, both going on late into the night. The NASUWT appreciated the progress made in discussing a draft circular but there had been no clear-cut breakthrough to justify calling off the action due to start in a few days time (27 April). The three senior Labour Education Ministers, together with the other unions and top-ranking civil servants and advisers, had all been present but the fundamental problem of the open-ended contract remained completely unresolved. We feared the solutions offered in the draft circular would only last a year or two, if that, as had the previous 'operation slim down' by Lord Dearing in the period 1993-95.

In the draft circular itself, sticking points remained over the frequency of meetings and the length of written reports, areas in which the support the NASUWT had received from other unions had been disappointing, to put it mildly. Nevertheless the draft circular could provide a basis for some immediate tackling of the workload problem. There would be a special meeting of the NASUWT Executive on 1 May to consider the draft circular.

I emphasised that were it not for the oppressive anti-union legislation of the 1980s, which required action to commence within 28 days of a ballot, the NASUWT could suspend the instructions pending consideration of the draft departmental circular. We could not risk having to re-ballot, with all that entailed in terms of time, feasibility and expense. I know that Stephen Byers took this point well and it was later to find expression in some of the reforms New Labour brought to Mrs Thatcher's employment legislation.

The Executive duly met on 1 May but declined to accept the provisional circular. Progress was acknowledged on the frequency of pupil reports, the exercise of professional judgement, pupil assessment, lesson plans, pre-Ofsted inspections and target setting. However, serious weaknesses persisted in the number of meetings after school hours, the length of documents, a no-detriment clause in relation to existing practice and an effective mechanism for ensuring the guidelines were delivered given no suitable change in the open-ended clause in the teacher's contract.

Executive members fully reflected the messages we were receiving at HQ that the action was extremely popular with members and non-members alike. Indeed many head teachers, particularly in the secondary sector, were supportive. A sense of liberation had come over the profession, rediscovering some independence and professional judgement, not to mention family and social life. As with the 1993 boycott, not a single child was losing a single second of education.

Some of the letters we received from members were positively heart-warming:

"Thank God it is being recognised by somebody that something has to be done to make teaching central to the lives of teachers."

"I am in complete agreement . . . The points which you highlight are absolutely spot on and exactly the thoughts I have been having myself."

"Thank you for your letter re 'Let Teachers Teach'. This is the best letter I have ever received from the NASUWT . . . Well done!"

" . . . to wish you all success with this fight against paperwork and meetings, the twin worst blights that disfigure education in 1998."

An interesting division of opinion sprung up between the SHA and NAHT (the latter representing mostly primary heads). Many SHA members found one staff meeting a week to be adequate; the NAHT apparently did not. Given the difference in size of establishment in which the respective memberships mostly worked, that was a revealing divergence of view.

The inability of the NUT to mount a convincing action of this kind was again exposed. Faced immediately with difficulties of delivery on the ground, the NUT quickly called off such action as there was when the talks started on the proposed circular. The NASUWT would have understood that and remained diplomatically silent had it not been for an attack by the NUT accusing us of a lack of leadership, continuing the action merely because it was popular. The NASUWT felt compelled to set the record straight on who had made all the running. We were not inclined to take lectures in leadership from the NUT!

The NUT was also causing problems in the parallel exercise in Wales, now required under devolution. Assistant GS Jerry Bartlett, leading these negotiations for the NASUWT, reported that the NUT was actively opposing our proposals for a limit to one staff meeting per week of one hour's duration. However, good progress was being made on the 'purely Welsh' dimensions of the bureaucracy problems.

NASUWT action continued into May and the publication of the circular was delayed. Reactions from grass-roots members and indeed other teachers were still extremely gratifying:

Yorkshire:

"The best thing we ever did."

"It has opened people's eyes to accept our professional judgement. No longer having to justify in writing, everything has increased people's self-esteem."

"It was interesting to see for the first time a well-organised staff meeting and the head getting agitated with the deputy for wasting time."

West Midlands:

"Members want a lasting culture change."

"The action is going exceptionally well, much better than anticipated. Comments from members have been extremely complimentary, particularly about the clarity of the instructions, especially popular the one meeting a week."

"The action has put a smile on teachers' faces."

Inner London:

"We are on a roll! Younger members involved – membership feeling its strength."

North Midlands:

"We, the 65 members at the school, have indeed been liberated by the action."

East Midlands:

"All contacts so far suggest that the action is being positively welcomed by members and supported by most heads."

By this time bilateral as well as multilateral exchanges were taking place, rather than full meetings of the WG. It appeared than only the SHA and NASUWT were insisting on improvements to the draft text, setting out as it did the Government's now 'informed' view of how the teacher's contract should be implemented in schools. In exchanges with Stephen Byers I insisted on 'one meeting a week', word limits on reports and documents and a no-detriment clause to guard against schools already operating efficiently within the new guidelines worsening practice.

Stephen Byers informed me the Government accepted the case for one meeting per week subject to some flexibility. To our astonishment the NUT GS Doug McAvoy issued a statement rejecting the Government's position. I can only surmise it was because the NUT had accepted the earlier inferior version and possibly took umbrage at not being party to the improvement: "Doug in the Manger", as I headlined a Report to Schools. Other unions, led by the NAHT, also rejected the proposal, although the SHA, in its wisdom, supported it.

David Blunkett then lost patience and understandably but unwisely decided to issue the circular with no references at all to a limit on the number of meetings (neither two nor one) and to do so during the course of the upcoming half-term holiday.

The NUT, in a hole, kept digging, putting out a press statement attacking the NASUWT and developing the extraordinary argument that a change from two to one would "worsen teachers' conditions of service". In various Reports to Schools I did not mince my words, describing the NUT's claims as a "deliberate distortion designed to disguise its disgracefully weak and shambolic on/off, on/off action". The NUT's involvement had been "an unmitigated disaster".

A Special Meeting of the NASUWT Executive on 22 May decided to postpone a decision on the "Let Teachers Teach" action until June. Pressure had to be kept up on the Government to change its mind on the 'unilateral' issuing of the departmental circular. I still acknowledged the circular retained "enormous benefit for teachers, but the shine would be lost if it is issued without the full agreement of all."

Circular 2/98 on Reducing the Bureaucratic Burden on Teachers was duly published on 3 June without a specified limit on meetings although reference was made to curtailing them. It was accompanied by a very helpful letter from the Secretary of State which included a clearly expressed 'no detriment' clause for which the NASUWT had argued so strongly.

With some reluctance the National Executive on 5 June decided to lift the instructions for action issued on 6 April but to do so with effect on 29 June. It was felt desirable to allow adequate time for local representatives to be fully briefed on how to maximise the potential of the circular at school level before lifting the action.

The key factor in deciding to lift the action was the fact that we now had an official Government circular as a means of pursuing our workload-reducing agenda. That was not perfect but preferable to indefinite industrial action and formal dispute with the Government and perhaps others. In lifting the action the Executive also committed itself fully to support members in schools where the circular was not properly implemented.

The following Report to Schools was entitled "Sustaining Success". The "Let Teachers Teach" campaign could now move seamlessly on from 29 June as industrial action moved into implementation of Circular 2/98. Soon popularly referred to as simply '2/98' it offered reductions in:

the number of meetings after school hours and their duration;
the length of documents;
the frequency of reports;
assessment;
individual education plans under special needs;
preparation and submission of lesson plans and schemes of work;
preparation for Ofsted inspections;
target setting.

The Report concluded: "The Circular could also enhance the exercise of professional judgement by individual teachers. The achievements embodied in 2/98 are considerable and offer a constructive and safe way forward for all teachers."

The very title of our campaign, "Let Teachers Teach" (which I dreamt up after a minute's reflection without any assistance from expensive PR 'experts'), had a resonance which endured and was frequently to be taken up by politicians, including Conservative Party education spokespeople.

Nevertheless the NASUWT kept a wary eye on developments. The Literacy Hour was a good example. Michael Barber, as Director of the Standards and Effectiveness Unit (SEU), another bureaucracy-spawning creature grafted on to the DfEE, had commendably 'done the rounds', consulting with all the unions on the Government's proposed Literacy Hour. Michael carried some credibility in so far as he had been a very effective and collaborative Assistant Secretary (Education) for the NUT. While the Literacy Hour was over-detailed and potentially prescriptive, its central endeavour – to ensure all pupils could read and write – and its advocacy of a 'proven' method of teaching reading sat quite comfortably in NASUWT circles.

However, contradictory messages were coming from Ministers and others as to whether the Literacy Hour was compulsory. Some claimed it was not, but if schools were failing to meet their literacy targets they would have difficulty ignoring it. LEA and Ofsted inspectors would effectively be the 'enforcers'. Reports from NASUWT members were already flooding in complaining about the workload involved in implementing the Literacy Hour. Teachers in successful schools already meeting or exceeding the official targets but not employing every aspect of the Literacy Hour felt particularly aggrieved to find themselves under instructions to change their lesson plans and methods in order simply to comply for its own sake.

A few months later (in January 1999) a letter from Michael Barber to CEOs revealed that the Literacy Hour was compulsory. I wrote immediately to David Blunkett seeking clarification, which was not forthcoming. The whole business soon proved to be another example of the Government cutting back on bureaucracy in some areas but forging ahead in others. It also revealed that the Government, despite paying lip service to the contrary, did not trust the professional judgement of teachers, even where they were succeeding.

New Labour's first piece of education legislation, the School Standards and Framework Act, began life as the White Paper *Excellence in Schools* published in July 1997, just two months after its General Election victory.

Describing "the white heat of the white paper" as "the most ambitious programme for education I have witnessed in my lifetime", I stressed that "the NASUWT [was] keen to play a positive role but will continue to judge issues on their merits".

The NASUWT was able to support proposals such as:

the abolition of vouchers and the extension of nursery education;

the reduction in class sizes for 6- and 7-year-olds;

improvements in the Ofsted process;

national training and pre-appointment qualifications for head teachers;

more relevant teacher training focussing upon the 'realities of the classroom';

abolition of GM status and a new framework of foundation, community and aided schools;

fair and transparent systems for calculating school budgets.

Proposals "causing concern" were:

stipulating an hour a day for literacy and numeracy for all pupils;

dictating teaching methods to the profession;

prescribing minimum time for homework;

imposing bureaucratic home-school contracts for every child;

too much target setting threatening a mountain of paperwork;

the time and resources being proposed for the massive in-service training programme required;

the "unrelenting pressure" David Blunkett intended to maintain upon teachers.

I concluded my press statement: "Everyone of goodwill supports the Government's aims but monumental problems will surround the practicalities and resources required. Can the patient survive another massive dose of medicine? I fear it can not if the excessive workload problem remains."

Towards the end of 1997 the Government introduced its massive School Standards and Framework Bill, which received its second reading in the House of Commons on 22 December. The Government intended the Bill to complete all its Parliamentary stages within six weeks.

Many of the proposals from *Excellence in Schools* naturally figured prominently in the Bill. However, there was a major new element in the proposed Education Action Zones (EAZs), which would cluster schools that were underperforming in a given area and place them under the control of groups of parents and business and community leaders. The EAZs would be given extra resources and allowed to opt out of the national curriculum and disapply the Teachers' Pay and Conditions Document.

It was another example of the 'second education department', a collection of special advisers to the Prime Minister, amongst whom Andrew (later Lord) Adonis was prominent. Labour candidates may have been elected to Parliament, but Adonis, a recent convert from the Liberal Democrats, had been selected as a special adviser. Parliament was relegated to the sidelines. While the proposal was still subject to discussion and decision at committee stage in Parliament (January 1998), the Government announced plans relating to five EAZs it had in mind for September. Whilst the Government had requested the STRB to consider the principle of Advanced Skills Teachers (ASTs), it was publicising plans to appoint them in EAZs. The Government's pre-emptive approach made constructive co-operation difficult. The NASUWT had reacted as positively as possible to ASTs, believing they had value in recognising and rewarding good classroom practice, but they could only succeed in the context of a truly collegiate system operating in schools.

The NASUWT was publicly critical of the element of bribery inherent in the offer of additional resources for EAZs, suggesting that the proposal could not stand on its own merits. The freedom to disapply the NC surely undermined its fundamental principle – offering a minimum entitlement for all pupils, the bedrock of the great reforms Tony Blair had declared himself determined to maintain despite their Conservative origins.

The value of a national system for teachers' pay and conditions which already incorporated many local flexibilities was similarly undermined by the EAZ facility to opt out. The NASUWT believed the ability of groups of parents and business and community leaders to run schools was completely unknown. In one of my public statements I predicted that EAZs would fade away into the obscurity they deserved.

The Bill contained some welcome measures previewed in the White Paper on abolishing GM status for schools, reverting many back to voluntary aided, whilst introducing a new category of foundation. Head teachers would be able to exclude disruptive pupils permanently or for up to 45 days (as opposed to three periods of 15 days each) although the appeal panels would be retained. Infant class sizes would be limited to 30. There would be safeguards on the continuity of employment for teachers in the event of a change of employer, effectively restoring some of the rights abolished by the Conservatives' 1988 ERA. Some flexibility was also to be introduced for the Annual Meetings of Parents, mandated under the 1988 ERA.

Whilst supporting the selective use of home-school contracts the NASUWT was sceptical of the scattergun approach applying then universally to the entire pupil population of over six million. The 13 million pieces of paper would soon have the value of Monopoly money and inevitably fall into disregard and then disuse.

The lack of confidence in LEAs implied by the EAZ proposal sat ill with the requirement for all of them to draw up Education Development Plans. They would certainly add to the paper mountain, while their impact on practice was anybody's guess.

The NASUWT shared the Government's ambition to raise levels of achievement but doubted it would be best achieved by more structural reform. The NASUWT believed the focus needed to be more sharply on helping teachers perform well in the classroom.

Chapter 77 - The Green Light for the Green Paper
Including "Time for a Limit"

The first 'green shoots' of a more enlightened approach to teachers sprung up suddenly one Friday (24 July 1998) with an intriguing piece by David Blunkett published in the *TES*. In an article I described as "unprecedented" David Blunkett presaged a new future for the profession in a Green Paper to be published before the end of the year. His central point was that "high quality teaching is not rewarded". He was writing against a background of a dramatic decline in the profession's popularity as illustrated in applications for teacher training. The Government had instigated its much-vaunted advertising campaign based on the slogan "Nobody forgets a good teacher", which apparently I ruined by immediately responding: "They just forget to pay them!"

The article seemed to indicate that the Government might be coming round to the NASUWT's collegiate policy, which emphasised the central importance of the teacher in the classroom. I recalled having bent David Blunkett's ear at the previous year's TUC General Council dinner on the subject, emphasising how I could not understand minister after minister and review body after review body rejecting our "win-win" policy. I probably ruined his supper with what turned out to be mostly a monologue on my part, to which his monosyllabic mumbles indicated either disinterest or disagreement or distaste for detail.

I contrasted David's article with the evidence the DfEE had recently presented to the STRB, warning the Government that its 'standards agenda' would crumble unless teachers were treated properly as true professionals. I resurrected all the old arguments about collegiality from the mid 1980s. I concluded that the Green Paper might be the last chance for the Government to get it right. If the Green Paper gave the green light to collegiality the entire profession could look forward to a better future.

These developments continued in positive mode at the Labour Party Conference a few weeks later. In his keynote address in the education debate David Blunkett made in my view "the most supportive speech for teachers by a Minister for years". Reminding the Conference of the promised Green Paper before Christmas, the Secretary of State said there could be better rewards for good teaching and more special units for disruptive pupils. He went on: "I want to celebrate success by rewarding success. Teachers are our most precious asset. Up and down this country teachers are doing a first rate job. In the past they were doing it against the odds, in the future they will do it with our support."

The positive atmosphere was further enhanced at the NASUWT fringe meeting at the Labour Party Conference. Speaking alongside the Secretary of State I reminded him that the NASUWT remained firmly opposed to individual performance related pay (PRP) but our collegiate policy accepted, indeed required, a fair and sensible system of appraisal to be established to enable good teaching to be identified and then appropriately rewarded.

Nothing in education ran completely smoothly and despite New Labour's claim to "joined-up government", a few days later the PM, Tony Blair, speaking in New York, claimed "having to confront vested interests such as teachers for the greater good of society". I immediately wrote to Tony Blair asking him how his comments squared with David Blunkett's, and how they were going to put teachers into a positive frame of mind to respond to the Green Paper.

The Green Paper, entitled *Teachers – Meeting the Challenge of Change,* was duly published on 3 December 1998. In his foreword to the document the Prime Minister described it as "the most fundamental reform of the teaching profession since State Education began".

The NASUWT gave the Green Paper a "guarded welcome". There was great potential in the proposal to enable classroom teachers to break through the current maximum of £23,000 and secure an increase of up to 10% subject to appraisal. However, there were difficulties over the contract and as always the detail required careful consideration. A further, more detailed 'Technical Paper' was promised for early next year.

The Green Paper also proposed tests in English and maths (as well as ICT) for new teachers, which caused the NASUWT to express surprise, given that entry to training already required passes in those two basic subjects at GCSE. Was this an expression of no confidence in the GCSE examination by the Government?

The NASUWT also welcomed the Government's commitment to genuine consultation, but only time would tell. The Green Paper related solely to England but the NASUWT expected a document promised for Wales in the new year to be very similar. The Union called upon the Northern Ireland Office to do likewise.

The NASUWT Executive's routine December meeting took place the following day. In introducing the Green Paper before the Executive debate I suggested there was more potential for good than bad and that the Union should therefore respond positively: "We should work hard to make it work".

The Executive agreed and, while making no immediate formal or final decisions, identified several key strands of NASUWT policy running through the Green Paper:

1 The extended pay scale for classroom teachers, adding £2,000 to the current maximum (taking it to £25,000) for those crossing the 'threshold' and opening up movement to even higher salaries up to £35,000 p.a.

2 The heartening statement that: "the Government would expect the majority of teachers to be of the standard which would allow them to cross the 'threshold' if they wished".

3 The three-tiered approach to appraisal, involving head teachers, line managers and external assessors.

4 The rejection of crude links between teacher performance and pupil outcomes.

Major difficulties were:

1 The reliance upon governing bodies exercising discretion.

2 Provision for individual pay ranges within the upper scales.

3 The extension of working time for certain groups of teachers.

The Executive also identified some serious deficiencies in the area of equality. Analysis of the implications for race, gender and disability indicated the proposals had considerable potential for direct and indirect discrimination. The NASUWT response would have to take up such issues.

Despite David Blunkett's soothing noises of the autumn, when it came to the traditional pay round it was unfortunately all very much business as usual. Late in 1998 the Secretary of State gave his remit to the STRB, the burden of which was to imply that a low award should be given to teachers to avoid the need for phasing. I wrote to the Chairman of the STRB and stated publicly that was tantamount "to inviting him to do the Government's dirty work to save it embarrassment". The case for staging in 1998 had been proved demonstrably phoney at the time and now we had the proud boast of Government that it was investing £19 billion of new money over three years, making it positively absurd.

The different arrangements emerging for the governments of Wales and Scotland and the separate needs of Northern Ireland produced problems of their own, sometimes exacerbated by the development of more devolution. In January 1999 the Scottish Office took a major initiative in target setting without much consultation. There was no statutory basis for target setting in Scotland and the workload implications for teachers were massive. Scottish teachers regarded target setting as diametrically opposed to the whole ethos of assessment of pupils aged 5-14.

At the same time Northern Ireland 'caught up' with the DfEE Circular 2/98. DENI Circular 1998/33, "Reducing the Bureaucratic Burden on Schools", was published and the NASUWT responded by withdrawing the "Let Teachers Teach" instructions w.e.f. 11 January 1999 on the same basis that had applied for England.

The STRB still applied to Wales but other aspects of education, some having a direct bearing on teachers' conditions of service, had become devolved. The NASUWT was sceptical about devolution in Wales, fearing the longer-term danger of a 'regional rate' for teachers in the Principality. On 29 January (two months later) the Welsh equivalent of the Green Paper was published under the differentiated title of *The Best for Teaching and Learning*. Much of the basic content was the same but a significant difference of practice later emerged with the funding for 'crossing the Threshold' channelled through the Welsh Assembly with the risk of virement elsewhere, as opposed to earmarked moneys directly paid to schools in England. The GTC for Wales would also have a role to play.

The positive attitude the NASUWT was taking towards the Green Paper received a severe jolt with the publication of the STRB report on Monday 1 February 1999. On the same day came more bad news with the release of the Technical Paper.

The overall pay award for teachers was 4% but classroom teachers were limited to 3.5%. Overall, head teachers received 6%, with some in primaries gaining 6.5% and others in very small schools 9.5%. The rationale for the differential payments lay in recruitment difficulties. However, as the NASUWT together with the SHA and NAHT (to their credit) had also pointed out in evidence to the STRB, shortages went all the way through the system.

I was blistering in my criticism, accusing the Government of "making a 'pig's ear' of teachers' pay". The previous year we had staging; now we had discrimination. This was all the more deplorable bearing in mind that over 70% of heads had gained discretionary enhancements, in stark and shocking contrast to only 2% of classroom teachers. It was obvious that heads had stitched up cosy deals with Chairs of Governors, often without other teachers knowing anything about it. I concluded that "an opportunity to improve the atmosphere had been squandered with the inferior treatment of the classroom teacher souring the discussions on the Green Paper".

Point 10 of the pay spine rose to £24,630. The spine for heads and deputies went from £27,258 to £61,665. Despite all this the STRB's decision had still resulted in a 4% overall increase in the pay bill, as opposed to the LEAs insisting that 3% was already over the top and unaffordable.

It took us a day or two more to digest the Technical Paper and our first impressions were confirmed. The National Executive meeting a few days later on 5 February gave a decisive "thumbs down" to the Technical Paper. The major disappointments were:

1 Teachers passing through the threshold would have to sign a new contract involving additional "responsibilities and commitments", such as teacher training.

2 The appraisal and performance management systems proposed were burgeoning with bureaucracy and completely unmanageable.

3 Contrary to earlier indications, performance pay was too 'crude' and closely linked to pupil results.

4 Funding arrangements remained unchanged, running the risk of budget-determined outcomes.

5 Governors were given completely inappropriate responsibilities in determining teachers' pay and appraising heads.

I was very critical once again in my public comments. "The Technical Paper is a misnomer. It is 'non-technical' for a start. It is simply Green Paper Part 2 – the Difficult Bits. Government is reneging on its publicly stated commitment to reward good classroom teaching for its own sake."

The Government pressed ahead with its own consultation. It organised an unprecedented series of regional conferences and "road shows" involving individual heads, teachers, governors, LEA people and others all over the country, no doubt hoping to get a 'better' and different reaction than that coming from the unions. A major question was emerging: Was the consultation genuine or simply a way of the Government saying, Can you suggest a better way of implementing our ideas?

There were huge implications for teacher workload. The Government's proposals would impose a workload-heavy bureaucracy-ridden annual appraisal regime from 1 September the same year. The new performance management system would have to be completed by September 2000. The Literacy Hour and target setting were adding massively to workload at a time when Circular 2/98, "Reducing the Bureaucratic Burden on Teachers", was supposed to be in the process of implementation. The Numeracy Hour was just around the corner. I warned: "The NASUWT can not just stand idly by as members are swamped."

Despite all the odds the NASUWT kept on battling to amend the Government's plans, based on our simple message: "We agree with your principle – identify and reward good classroom teaching. But we seriously disagree over the proposed practice which would destroy the very principle you purport to be promoting." The NASUWT would engage in consultation but at the same time prudently prepare plans to defend teachers against totally unmanageable impositions: "If that can only be achieved by direct action, then so be it."

The NASUWT commissioned NOP to conduct a survey of over 1,000 teachers on PRP. The Union was pleased to note the results showing 57% agreed with the collegiate approach of linking pay to appraisal based on teacher input, not on pupil output or results. Relating pay simply to pupil progress was opposed by 73%. Giving discretion to governors was also opposed.

Before Conference the NASUWT had again to dispose of one aspect of Thatcher's legacy to trade unions, namely, conducting another of the five-yearly requirement to conduct a ballot of all members on the continuation of the political fund. The low turnout was further proof that having repeatedly to re-ballot was a turn-off. A total of 29,234 voted in favour, 6,868 against, producing an 81% majority.

Out of the blue I received an invitation to tea on 2 March 1998 with David Puttnam in the House of Lords. The famous film producer, now ennobled, had taken his seat on the Labour benches in the Lords. It transpired that he wished to establish an annual 'Oscar'-style teaching awards to help raise the status of the profession. He needed the support and material assistance of the teacher unions. I said I had no hang-ups on such things but views varied and many teachers found them capricious and elitist. I reported back to the Executive and after some discussion the NASUWT decided to back the project.

Teacher union input was very important for getting members involved in persuading schools to make nominations, in running regional qualifying 'rounds' leading up to the national event and for drawing up the all-important criteria against which teachers would be judged. Several GSs, including myself, agreed to serve on the Board of Trustees set up to oversee the project and raise the necessary sponsorship. It was deemed important for the project not to be seen to be a Government initiative.

By 1999 the Teaching Awards were established. Lord Puttnam was invited to address the 2000 NASUWT Conference and he went down very well, coming over as a genuine friend of the teaching profession.

There can be little doubt that the project has been a roaring success and the annual televised Teaching Awards ceremony is a moving event and a great advert for the profession. The articulate speeches delivered by winning teachers contrast vividly with the emotional incoherence which characterises the words of the famous and fabulously rich film stars receiving their Oscars! My only regret is that the contribution of the unions has been pushed further and further into the background to the point that it is now no longer even acknowledged 'on the big night'.

"Teachers – Meeting the Challenge of Change" duly dominated the 1999 NASUWT Conference. The incoming President, Bill Morley, used his speech to call for a salary structure to enable the vast majority of teachers to secure decent pay in a way that was "open, fair, based on recognised criteria and consistent from school to school. It is difficult to see how this could be achieved if too much flexibility is given to head teachers and governors."

In my 'state of the union' address I suggested five crucial changes which Government had to make to keep the NASUWT on board and away from contemplating action:

1 Withdraw the payment-by-results elements.

2 Drop requirements for additional commitments and responsibilities – the teacher's contract needed to be improved, not worsened.

3 Simplify appraisal, postpone the September start.

4 Construct a clear post-Threshold scale; remove the confusing and complicated governors' discretion.

5 Fund the new structure properly.

In the Wednesday morning urgency motion the Executive sought endorsement of its response to the Green and Technical Papers. Moving the motion, Honorary Treasurer Mick Carney pointed out the nonsense in the present system of 158 different ways of paying a classroom teacher. He said the Government's commitment to education would be judged by the degree to which it demonstrated an understanding of the structural problems and the necessity of reform to reflect the central importance of the teacher in the classroom.

Conference gave a massive endorsement to the motion, calling on the Secretary of State to act on the widespread criticism and authorising the Executive to exhaust the consultative process in seeking agreement and to conduct action ballots in the event of the Government imposing unacceptable measures.

Addressing the 1999 Conference the Minister of State, Estelle Morris, acknowledged the NASUWT had made a very positive response to the Green Paper and thanked us for it. She announced an important concession – that the first year should be spent "getting it right", and postponed the introduction of appraisal until September 2000. Estelle Morris appeared to show flexibility by denying her Government had any plans to introduce a 'simplistic formula for payment by results'. She was also anxious to allay our fears over extended contractual requirements for teachers passing the 'Threshold', saying "we are seeking to reward those who go the extra mile and are not asking for additional commitment".

In my reply I welcomed Estelle Morris' response to our concerns and called upon her to drop the link to pupil results completely, adding "that would transform the atmosphere and open up a constructive debate on the many other issues that need to be resolved".

The NASUWT had tackled the problem of teacher appraisal head-on. Some believed it should only be used for 'professional and supportive' purposes. We said that was naïve. Information gleaned would inevitably be used in other areas such as promotion, competency and possibly disciplinary procedures. It was crucial to define and differentiate clearly between the various procedures and to ensure they were transparent, fair and appropriate.

The NASUWT had proposed ten criteria to the Government which could form the basis of an acceptable system of appraisal. They were:

1 Lesson planning and preparation.

2 Subject knowledge.

3 Teaching methods.

4 Communication and motivational skills.

5 Discipline.

6 Marking, assessment and monitoring of pupils' work and progress.

7 Effective use of homework.

8 Classroom organisation.

9 Implementation of school policies.

10 Management skills where applicable.

We accepted the logic of our own policy. If you wanted to reward good classroom teaching for its own sake there was no other way of doing it properly without a system for appraisal. Judging teachers through their *input* into their work was acceptable; judging them by *output* such as the results of national tests and public examinations was not, since these depended upon too many variable factors outside the control of teachers.

The passage of the consultative process on the Green Paper continued on its bumpy ride. The positive developments around Conference seemed to be reversed when in June the DfEE issued a letter on appraisal to schools. It encouraged schools to anticipate events by developing their own systems of appraisal and made highly contentious and false statements on the NASUWT attitude to PRP. It claimed the opinion poll we had commissioned showed teachers in favour.

I had complimented the education journalists at one of my Conference lunchtime press sessions on their achievement in getting into print the vital distinction between the appraisal 'input' and exam results 'output' factors, no mean feat in modern media terms. That was all the more reason for me to write to Ministers strongly critical of the misrepresentation of the NASUWT position and the undermining of the consultative process.

The Government remained silent after the end of the formal consultation period (31 March). In the meantime the NASUWT Executive advised members to refuse to have anything to do with schools or LEAs devising new or revised schemes of appraisal pending the Government's response.

Meanwhile a repeat crisis was rapidly building up in the area of excessive workload. New Government initiatives were emanating almost on a weekly basis, swamping the anti-bureaucracy Circular 2/98, issued a year previously. Pressure was growing for the introduction of a five-year term, which would inevitably impact on the overall length of working time. Yet another review of the national curriculum was taking place, threatening further increases in the demands on teachers, with citizenship being added as 'voluntary' in primary schools but mandatory in secondary.

The Secretary of State was openly considering compulsory increases in the number of hours of teaching. In the view of the NASUWT the hopelessly open-ended contract was the conduit through which workload spiralled out of control. We had made another strong case for this issue to be addressed in our response to the Green Paper. The Executive would consider another boycott at its June meeting. The deficiencies in the contract had to be addressed. It was 'time for a limit'.

The National Executive duly decided at its June 1999 meeting to launch a new campaign on the contract – "Time for a Limit" – to start the following September. If progress were not made members would be balloted with a view to another boycott.

The NASUWT issued publicity material under the slogan "All work and no play makes Jackie a dull teacher". Many teachers were working between 60 and 70 hours per week. The workload and stress had contributed to an exodus from the profession through premature retirement accompanied by a high rate of sickness absence and a recruitment crisis. The NASUWT claimed that the lack of a limit on working time bred inefficiency, produced bad time management and enabled management to escape responsibility for establishing sensible priorities. Endless meetings and unnecessary paperwork hindered effective teaching. Agreeing a limit would cost the Government nothing but would make an immediate and beneficial impact upon recruitment, retention and morale.

The NASUWT produced a very effective poster quoting several Ministers, including Tony Blair advocating "family friendly" policies around the time of May 1998.

Prime Minister:

"We want to encourage more family friendly employment so that parents can spend more time with their children."

Stephen Byers, Secretary of State for Trade and Industry:

"Why should a woman have to choose between her love for her family and her ambitions at work? Why should a man have to decide between spending time with his growing family and his desire for promotion?"

"We are tackling the culture of excessively long hours with the implementation of the (EU) Working Time Directive."

Margaret Hodge, Junior Education and Employment Minister:

"Time to get rid of the long hours work ethic."

Almost in desperation for some kind of limit for teachers, I had asked David Blunkett and Stephen Byers why at the very least the EU 48 hours could not be stated in the Teachers' Pay and Conditions Document. I reminded them that 48 hours per week was the equivalent of working 9 to 6 (one hour off for lunch) for six days. Did they expect teachers to work on Sundays as well? The unstated answer was 'yes' as they piled more bureaucratic demands on teachers.

The Education Secretary finally published the Government's response to the Green Paper consultations on 8 July, more than three months late. In my initial reaction I described it as a "poor progress report", adding that "it is difficult to understand why it has taken so long to leave so many questions unanswered".

On the positive side the dropping of a new contract for teachers crossing the Threshold represented real and significant progress. Confirmation that assessment for the Threshold would be kept voluntary with the present scales remaining and subject to annual review by the STRB was also welcome. However, the NASUWT criticised the report for failing to address the serious concern about payment by results; the level of Threshold salary boost which remained modest when compared to the amount of change demanded and the burdensome and bureaucratic performance management process.

The Department claimed a generally favourable response based on 41,000 responses from organisations and individuals. The DfEE summary was at odds with other surveys. The NASUWT's own surveys showed 61% supported rewarding good performance by teachers through appraisal and 66% opposed the Government's way of achieving this through pupil outcomes. The respective figures in the NASUWT-commissioned NOP survey had been 57% and 73%.

Despite the Department's gloss on the consultation findings, it could not conceal the simple facts that even on its evidence well over 60% were opposed to the performance pay system, 68% were against the School Performance Award and 76% objected to the 'fast tracking' proposals. The NASUWT remained convinced it had a much better 'win-win constructive alternative'. We also believed the bureaucratic system of performance management still 'on the table' provided further justification for the "Time for a Limit" campaign.

Despite the difficulties, we noticed a very positive development taking place at this time. We were spending a lot of time with civil servants, and sometimes with Ministers, going through all the proposals and consistently putting forward our constructive alternatives. I never bothered to enquire of other unions, except I knew from contact with John Dunford, GS of the SHA, that his organisation was similarly involved. The degree of almost daily involvement was significantly more than I had ever known. I was convinced that our 'constructive alternatives' played a large part in maintaining the dialogue.

I was greatly helped by National Officers and some staff colleagues. Eamonn O'Kane, the Deputy GS, and Chris Keates, a recent recruit to the NASUWT staff and previously the NEC Member and Secretary of the Birmingham Association, who had been appointed Assistant Secretary, Policy Co-Ordination, attended many of these 'back-room' meetings, taking much of the daily pressure off me. The National Officers and Executive were also very supportive, their monthly meetings a vital check that we were on the right track. We did not realise it at the time but it was Social Partnership in the making. I recall that at the TUC Executive and General Council I found myself alone in reporting much better communication and involvement with Ministers than ever before. Other unions, even those affiliated to the Labour Party, were still deeply disgruntled with the relationship with 'their' Government.

In September 1999 the Government published revised proposals. Much more progress had been made although some problems remained. The most notable 'fly in the ointment' was the link to "pupil outcomes" which the Government insisted on retaining. I said if only we could crack that issue it would be possible to reach agreement with the Government.

The revised proposals reflected the gathering influence of the NASUWT. The new advances principally made by the NASUWT were:

the proposed performance management framework was a vast improvement over the original draft and in the light of this development the duplicating appraisal regulations would be dropped;

the burden would remain on management to demonstrate poor performance to withhold an increment from teachers on the pre-Threshold points of the salary spine;

there would be a new system for financing the Threshold and other new payments by direct billing of the LEA with no quota or prior financial constraint on the number of teachers passing through the Threshold;

the external assessor could overrule the head teacher.

The NASUWT now had to tread a careful line, welcoming some vital breakthroughs on pay but still having to object to the link to pupil outcomes. In addition the workload problem remained unresolved. We did not want to throw out the baby with the bath water and therefore refrained from threats of industrial action against an improved pay system which, while suffering one serious flaw, remained voluntary and offered the possibility of much needed pay rises for classroom teachers. However, the "Time for a Limit" campaign had to go on and the possibility of balloting for action remained. Indeed one of the rarely mentioned advantages of the review body system (for obvious reasons) was we could pick and choose which parts to accept, including some pay rises, but still take action on other issues if we wished to do so.

Developments were not going too well in Scotland. The meeting of the reformed Scottish Joint Negotiating Committee on 8 October produced no offer from the local authority employers. Following devolution and the establishment of the Scottish Parliament, the Education Minister, Sam Galbraith, was proving to be a very confrontational figure. The McCrone Committee had been set up to inquire into Scottish teachers' pay and conditions under an unfavourable remit in the view of NASUWT Scotland. It amounted to the Scottish equivalent of the Green Paper exercise south of the border. The NASUWT commended a review body system to Scottish teachers to deal with pay, with a parallel committee acting in conjunction to determine conditions of service.

A UK national/Scottish delegation from the NASUWT met with Sam Galbraith on 20 October to raise concerns over the pay situation, the SJNC negotiating machinery, the composition of the McCrone inquiry and the timescale for consultation on improving the Scottish Education Bill. The exchanges were surprisingly positive, with Mr Galbraith accepting many of our points, especially in relation to a review body. The Minister assured us the McCrone Committee's composition was entirely independent.

On 26 October the majority union, the EIS, accepted an effective imposition of a 3.6% salary increase, a fraction above the amount for England and Wales, in recognition of previous comparative 'slippage'.

On 21 October I attended a special gathering of some 500 newly appointed head teachers at the QE II Centre in Westminster who had been invited to hear an address by the Prime Minister. It appeared to have been organised as a morale-boosting event for the heads and an opportunity for Tony Blair to promote his policies. The big development announced was the establishment of the National College of School Leadership.

I challenged the Prime Minister on his recent remarks about "the culture of excuses which still infests the teaching profession" and the allegation that we were amongst those constituting "the dark forces of conservatism". I reminded him of the NASUWT policy on collegiality, which was more modern and enlightened than his performance related pay proposals. I suggested he needed to take his own advice on "modernising". The media relished the 'head to head' aspect of the encounter, which was not on the PM's PR agenda for the day; but it was the only opportunity I had to press the issue with one of the people most likely to have been behind the insistence that the link to 'pupil results' had to be retained.

On the afternoon of the same day, I joined NASUWT colleagues to meet the STRB to present our oral evidence for the 1 April 2000 award. On pay we pressed for a substantial rise to reward the significant increase in productivity already achieved. We argued for a limit on teachers' working hours and for the ever-increasing bureaucratic burden to be addressed. Naturally we also continued to press our policies in respect of the Green Paper issues which formed part of the STRB's remit.

The NASUWT held a Special Conference at the QE II Centre to endorse the attitude taken by the Executive to the Green and Technical Papers. It was another very successful day for the NASUWT. Debate was honest and realistic and the Executive accepted some amendments from branches, such as Leicester, Brent and Cardiff, seeking some changes to policy positions.

In my GS report to the Conference I forecasted that we were approaching another "defining moment in the history of the teaching profession". Reflecting the emerging influence of the NASUWT behind the scenes in discussions with Government I advised delegates that while all-out opposition and boycott were simpler and sometimes necessary, constructive engagement was potentially more productive, despite its difficulties. I appealed to the assembled representatives to endorse the recommendations of the Executive and "continue to send a clear message to Government that if it wants our support then changes must be made".

Honorary Treasurer Mick Carney proposed the main motion seeking endorsement, saying: "The present system allows the exploitation of teachers, the exercise of patronage and management by whim. We must not stand and defend the palpably unfair structure but take the opportunity to advance our key policy of collegiality."

The Special Conference gave its near-unanimous support to the Executive, endorsing the 'input' appraisal-related-pay approach to crossing the Threshold, seeking contractual limits and accepting performance management so long as it was used constructively and not as a method of punitive control of teachers. The "Time for a Limit" campaign was also endorsed, together with the commitment to ballot for action in the event of failure to secure protection on teachers' working time, the principle of which was enshrined in the relevant EU Directive.

In January 2000 we learned that the consultants HayMcBer's initial proposals on the criteria for Threshold assessment had been rejected by the DfEE. As usual I condemned the unnecessary and expensive use of consultants when there was more knowledge and understanding of the ingredients of good teaching freely available from within the profession. Indeed the exorbitant fees charged by consultants seemed to dictate a need to produce long-winded repetitive descriptions of well-known practice disguised as 'innovative' through new 'sophisticated' ways of describing old truths. The NASUWT for one had long ago produced short and incisive criteria for judging good practice.

My request to see the HayMcBer document was declined. I had good reason to believe, but I could not prove the point, that the DfEE had rejected the proposals knowing what the reaction of the NASUWT would have been.

On 18 January 2000 an unusual meeting took place. All three mainly classroom-based teacher unions were now affiliated to the TUC, with the ATL having joined after (and some might say in the light of) the election of the New Labour Government in 1997. The ATL had been steered to that wise decision under the leadership of its GS, Peter Smith, a closet member of the Labour Party. The exclusively 'Welsh' union, UCAC, was also involved. Together we requested John Monks, TUC GS, to lead a deputation to the Secretary of State for Education on the Green Paper. John Monks was very happy to oblige and David Blunkett agreed to the meeting.

The unions identified two crucial issues to focus upon: firstly, the proposed link of pay with exam and test results and the framework for performance management; secondly, funding arrangements for 'post- Threshold' career progression. Estelle Morris stated the Government's major concern was to reflect in salary terms the "truth" that good teachers made a difference to pupil performance, as in the past too much of the pay bill had been devoted to administration and management. Estelle claimed the Government was not looking for crude payment by results.

I was tempted to make several observations, none the least of which was to compliment the Government on recognising the deficiency of the promotion structure and ask why it continued to present evidence to the STRB to the contrary. It was also tempting to challenge the claimed "truth", for it was not "the whole truth" that good teachers made a difference to pupil performance. The NASUWT believed the "whole truth" was they could, depending upon other factors as well.

I resisted temptation and simply replied that the NASUWT 'input appraisal' approach offered the Government the best means of achieving its objective through agreement, which was far preferable to imposition. The ATL had indicated a willingness to take matters forward constructively. More to the point, the hitherto hostile NUT had found a way around its problem through a Coopers & Lybrand report it had commissioned suggesting a link between the "acquisition of competencies" and salary advances – which was a more acceptable 'getting off the hook' expression for appraisal related pay.

Helpfully Doug McAvoy requested the Government to remove the examples in the draft performance management framework stipulating teachers would be judged on national test and public examination results. Doug emphasised that if those examples were dropped it would be possible to reach agreement on other aspects and then there could be a link between pay and this form of acceptable appraisal.

I thought to myself, surely this should get David Blunkett seriously interested in our point. Instead of enthusiastically welcoming Doug's indication of a very significant change of direction by the NUT, Blunkett remained 'deadpan', saying the Government had tried to balance input and output factors and despite differences on details he wanted to see a general measure of agreement. However, he concluded with nothing more than a Delphic promise to produce a note of the Government's position to help progress the matter.

John Monks was right in his concluding remarks to observe the differences between the Government and the unions were "not unbridgeable". The crucial issue was left hanging in the air. Time would tell.

Meanwhile the NASUWT strongly advised members to have nothing to do with heads, LEAs and commercial interests flogging their own performance management schemes ahead of the Government's final decision. Early sight of unofficial drafts of HayMcBer's second attempt to define criteria for national standards for teacher assessment typically revealed much dependence on paperwork and little focus on classroom teaching. The standards could lead to subjective and potentially discriminatory judgements. The NASUWT assured members their representatives would continue to press for significant changes.

On 1 February 2000 the STRB published its report. It recommended pay rises of 3.3% on all scales and allowances w.e.f. 1 April. It also recommended adoption of a new salary structure to facilitate, amongst other things, the proposed Threshold and Upper Pay Range, to operate from 1 September. Other proposals included the replacement of the existing responsibility points with management allowances and a Leadership Tier catering for heads, deputies and senior teachers.

The effect was to raise the maximum of the unpromoted classroom teacher by over £2,000 by 1 September. Furthermore it opened up a new Upper Pay Range along which the classroom teacher could progress to a maximum of just over £30,000. Progression would be on the basis of "substantial and sustained performance and contribution to the school as a teacher with each point awarded normally after at least two years have elapsed".

It represented a significant breakthrough, raising the 'career' maximum potential of the unpromoted classroom teacher from slightly under £23,200 (September '99) to just over £30,000. True, it was subject to a performance check but teachers were far more likely to access such salary levels through this system than the only other genuine alternative of squeezing more money out of government by militant action.

Advanced Skills Teachers (ASTs) were also introduced, with a salary range of £26,943 to £42,981, salaries which were impressive in their own right but of very limited availability and subject to other conditions.

The new Management Allowances ran from £1,485 to £7,092, heads' salaries would run from £32,184 to £75,972, deputies from £28,158 to £46,320, all w.e.f. 1 September. London Allowances went to £2,316 (Inner), £1,524 (Outer) and £591 (Fringe).

I found myself making similar comments to previous years in respect of the 1 April increase of 3.3% – beating inflation but falling below "Mr and Mrs Average". However, the award was above the Government's recommended 2.2% 'affordability' criteria which would probably have applied if bargaining as in Burnham had still been in existence.

There was a certain 'pig in a poke' element in the STRB recommending salary levels for the Threshold and Upper Pay Range in advance of the determination of the criteria for teachers accessing them. Controversy still raged behind the scenes in the DfEE, with the NASUWT and others contesting the HayMcBer criteria, which still retained the unpopular payment by 'results' – or 'pupil outcomes', the preferred Ministerial euphemism.

In addition, and in the view of the NASUWT "incomprehensibly", the HayMcBer criteria remained insufficiently focussed on the classroom and geared too much to building up a mountain of "bureaucratic bull" as I frankly put it, mindful as always of this tendency among consultants.

Yet again, despite acknowledging the considerable concerns widely expressed about workload, the Review Body had lamentably failed to tackle the appalling problem. It specifically rejected the suggestion of the NASUWT of closing down the open-ended element of the contract, the conduit through which excessive workload flowed. To the amazed anger of the NASUWT the STRB prayed in aid of its decision the evidence from another union: "The NUT said in its evidence that it did not think it tenable professionally for a ceiling to be placed on teachers' overall hours of work." Whilst in keeping with positions taken by the NUT in a longer-term historical perspective, it ran against positions taken on some recent occasions in the 1980s and 1990s.

By March 2000 the DfEE had published its considered proposals for assessment at the Threshold for a final round of consultation. Teachers on point 9 of the salary scale (or above) as at 1 September 1999 would be eligible to apply for assessment to cross the Threshold and receive an extra £2,000 w.e.f. 1 September 2000 and be placed on the new Upper Pay Range.

Assessment would be against five national standards:

1 Professional knowledge and understanding
2 Teaching and assessment

3 Pupil progress

4 Wider professional effectiveness

5 Professional characteristics.

Heads could use their 'wider knowledge' of the applicant to inform their final recommendation. All standards had to be met to pass. External assessors would receive all applications, review a random sample and report back to heads and governors. The review might involve classroom teachers. School budgetary and financial considerations would play no part in the assessment. Funding would come directly from the DfEE.

In my press statement I welcomed the substantial improvements secured but said that teachers would still be "daunted by the complexity and detail of the DfEE proposals". Unnecessarily complex hurdles had been set which could lead to very few crossing the Threshold "as opposed to the majority trumpeted by the Secretary of State".

The NASUWT counter-proposed six key requirements to make the Threshold work:

1 A dramatic reduction in the evidence collection to avoid excessive bureaucracy.

2 Increased emphasis on assessment of the standards through classroom observation.

3 Withdrawal of the Pupil Progress standard.

4 Amendment and clarification of the Wider Professional and Effectiveness standard.

5 Removal of reference to voluntary activities and the elimination of subjective information provided by school managers.

6 The procedures had to meet the test of fairness and equity and be consistent with equality legislation.

Pressing for classroom observation, which often put teachers under pressure, might appear unusual. However, being observed was something younger teachers were becoming more accustomed to. It was crucial for avoiding bureaucracy and for ensuring teachers were judged on their abilities 'doing the real job' as opposed to their skills in hyping up their performance on paper, a process that seemed so attractive to management and consultants. Once again the NASUWT pledged itself "to work hard to make it work" and we engaged in almost daily meetings with civil servants amending the proposals line by line. Significant progress was made on all the points except Pupil Progress, although that was later 'softened'.

The NASUWT advised its members not to rush to complete the Threshold application form (deadline 15 June), which was in the process of being distributed to schools. We soon got rid of the requirement to collect a huge amount of evidence or compile a portfolio to support applications. Teachers would only be required to verify the sources of the information eventually used on the application forms.

Members were strongly advised to be in contact with the Union, to attend regional briefings, read *Teaching Today* and await the publication by the NASUWT of an important advice document, *Crossing the Threshold*.

Conference 2000 was an opportunity to review progress on the Green Paper. Reflecting on the issue in my 'state of the union' address I reminded delegates that one year ago we had taken a conscious decision to be as positive as possible since there was much potential for good, indeed the best for years. Day in, day out, week after week, month after month in detailed discussion with Ministers and civil servants, arguing issues and fighting every line, we sought to make the Green Paper as acceptable as possible. Being positive and constructive, I predicted that our media profile would diminish and be taken up by the NUT who despite a brief interlude of serious engagement (with the TUC-led delegation) had reverted to type and become extremely hostile and negative. I reminded delegates we were in business to promote the interests of our members and not to achieve publicity for its own sake.

Conference endorsed the line taken by the Executive, reiterated support for the elements of collegiality in the Green Paper, acknowledged the flexibility shown by the Government, but registered deep disappointment that the Pupil Progress criterion had been retained. Nevertheless, while being unable to register an 'agreement', Conference instructed the Executive to give full support and advice to members volunteering to apply to cross the Threshold, monitoring the process and advising those unreasonably denied entry to the post-Threshold pay range.

At the same time, with the workload problem completely unresolved, indeed getting worse almost by the day, Conference instructed the Executive to ballot for action to implement the "Time for a Limit" campaign. The highly successful "Let Teachers Teach" campaign and Circular 2/98 had been entirely swamped by a flood of Government initiatives. I stressed there was no proposal for strike action. Indeed the action was very much in the interests of the pupils as well as the teachers; it was "Industrial action with a halo" – a sound bite headlined by none other than the *Financial Times*.

The usual arrangements went ahead and the ballot result announced on 22 June. Of the 47,910 votes cast, 45,175 were in favour, 2,735 against. The majority in favour of action was 94.3%, the only area of concern being the relatively low turnout, which had dipped below one-third of those entitled to vote. Action was based on instructions to implement the terms of Circular 2/98 and other more recent workload/bureaucracy-reducing measures announced by the Government. Action would start on 30 June.

The NUT approached the NASUWT, seeking a joint campaign. We reacted cautiously, with memories of the debacle over the Circular 2/98 negotiations still fresh in our minds. The fact that the NUT was now supporting our positions on the 'one meeting per week' maximum and an overall limit on contractual hours served more to heighten our feelings of frustration than entice us into joint action.

Chapter 78 - Crossing the Threshold

Meanwhile the proof of the 'Threshold pudding' proved to be in the eating. By June the NASUWT advice document *Crossing the Threshold* had been circulated to all members at their home addresses and further copies made available to staffrooms up and down the country. It has to be a candidate for the most popular and helpful document ever produced by a union for its members and indeed others. In essence, it listed all the points a teacher could think about putting down against all the criteria relating to the Threshold. There were versions for secondary, primary, special and centrally attached or 'other' teachers. All teachers had to do was to select the half-dozen or so that best reflected their greatest strengths and have the evidence on hand if requested.

Credit for the initial idea has to be awarded to Chris Keates, who co-ordinated input from staff and Executive Members. My contribution to the effort was very limited, just giving Chris the 'yes, go right ahead – very good idea' response to her suggestion that such a document should be produced.

By July we knew we had 'got it right' as a Report to Schools was headlined. Over 197,000 teachers had applied to cross the Threshold. We felt totally justified in the stance we had taken and our *Crossing the Threshold* was widely acclaimed as easily being the best means of doing so.

Moving briskly on we declared our next task was to ensure the applications were properly assessed and any members experiencing difficulties supported and advised. We continued pressing to have the criterion of Pupil Progress removed. We also wanted less bureaucracy. To this end we agreed a Best Practice Model Performance Management Policy with the SHA. Together with the SHA we secured the endorsement of the DfEE who declared in a letter to us on 19 June 2000 that "the basic structure and key points are in accord" and "it is certainly compatible with the Regulations [on Performance Management] for teachers to have just three objectives". Members were strongly advised to participate in performance management only to the extent permitted by the joint NASUWT/SHA policy.

Further illustrating our willingness to embrace Social Partnership we were soon to extend our collaboration with the SHA in the production of a joint 'model' Individual Education Plans (IEP) for children with special needs and Behaviour Management Plans for schools. They facilitated better relationships at school level and cut down on bureaucracy and workload. These developments led in turn to joint stands and fringe meetings at the major UK-wide party political conferences in the autumn season. The collegiate style of the SHA GS at the time, John Dunford, who had a good track record as the head teacher of a very successful secondary school in Durham, helped to facilitate these developments.

These arrangements proved extremely helpful in dealing with casework, where the most common problem was heads demanding observation after the deadline to verify the content of applications. The collation of evidence, copying of application forms to senior members of staff and interviews of individual teachers by the head were other common problems.

The NASUWT had concluded that applications using the *Crossing the Threshold* document should take no longer than two hours. Many teachers took a lot longer, some saying it took them many hours over one or two days. We said that even if it took two days, at £2,000 extra each year it was still well worth it and way beyond teachers' normal daily rates of remuneration!

In teacher union affairs nothing, not even success itself, is allowed to succeed without some interference. Sure enough the NUT again obliged. I have already referred to the Government's extensive, indeed unprecedented, degree of consultation with the NASUWT, SHA and perhaps other unions. At times it amounted to something close to negotiation. The problem lay in that all the consultation had been informal and not put through the statutory STRB machinery. I had warned Government about the problem, indeed writing six letters to Ministers on the subject during the relevant period. I was not trying to be obstructive, but simply protecting the position in the future. Whilst we found the informal arrangements more helpful and appropriate than the statutory consultation inherent in the Review Body process, we still harboured ambitions to have a 'proper and permanent' parallel body on conditions of service to operate alongside the STRB.

When the NUT announced it was considering application for an injunction or a judicial review to halt the Government in its tracks and process the Threshold assessment and other arrangements through the STRB, we knew there was a strong 'technical' case. Our lawyers confirmed our view and that the most likely outcome would be delay whilst the Government was redirected through the full STRB statutory procedures. The biggest losers would be the teachers through delayed pay rises!

However, faced with the threat of legal action from the NUT, the Government, realising it was on weak ground despite having used common sense, compounded its problem by deciding to use a fast-track procedure available under the legislation but which was intended for other purposes.

The NUT leadership, being hostile to the whole business, decided to proceed with action in the High Court and duly won a "great victory", upholding in the view of its Deputy GS, Steve Sinnott, "the supremacy of the law". My public response was to say, "if this were a victory Heaven save us from defeat!" The irony was heightened by the fact that the NUT was still completely opposed to the STRB and here it was winning a "great victory", enhancing its role even more.

The High Court ruling came on 14 July. On the day, the NASUWT telephone lines at HQ and in Regional Centres were inundated by angry teachers demanding to know what was happening; had they wasted their time? would they have to reapply? would they lose the £2,000? I understand the NUT experienced a similar reaction.

The Government announced its policy remained unchanged and it was taking advice on its options. It soon came to the conclusion it would have to comply with the ruling and process everything through the STRB, which would obviously take time. The NASUWT observed how ironic it was that at a time when together with the NUT it was fighting against bureaucracy, all this legal business could mean teachers having to repeat their applications, which had already consumed many hours of their time.

The delays were serious. First, the Government had to give the STRB a remit. The STRB had to consult with interested parties. A report had to be written to the Government. The Government had to consult with the unions and employers over its response to the report. The Government then had to draft Parliamentary Regulations implementing its decisions and consult over those. All this demonstrated that the STRB was not a suitable body for dealing with conditions of service, further justifying the NASUWT policy in favour of a parallel body to deal with such matters.

The STRB had already awarded pay levels for the Threshold and Upper Pay Ranges and common sense dictated that the detailed implementation of the new system was best worked out by Government, employers and unions with the necessary statutory orders being drafted as and when required. Relying on common sense had left the NUT out of the equation.

Meanwhile in Northern Ireland NASUWT members were catching up with their English and Welsh colleagues in balloting for "Time for a Limit" action to combat excessive workload and burgeoning bureaucracy. Total votes cast were 3,196, with 3,042 in favour, representing a majority of over 95%. Action would start on 4 September.

On pay Northern Ireland employers had established working groups to examine Threshold assessment, management of performance and the pay scales for principals and vice-principals. The NASUWT considered parity with England and Wales to be absolutely essential in the changed context of the eventual establishment of the Northern Ireland Assembly following the long-awaited implementation of the Good Friday Agreement. In July the Chancellor of the Exchequer had announced an additional £1 billion allocated to Northern Ireland to be spent on public services over the next three years. The NASUWT wrote to Martin McGuinness, now Education Minister in the Northern Ireland Executive, urging him to ensure his department secured its fair share.

Two months after the launch of the "Time for a Limit" action in Northern Ireland the Department of Education issued Circular 2000/13 to help teachers and combat bureaucracy. The circular advised teachers to stop doing things that were not essential; to say 'no' to unjustified requests for information; and to limit the frequency of regular tasks, e.g. writing reports and holding staff meetings. While welcoming these steps the NASUWT did not consider them sufficient to call off the action.

There was better news around the same time when Martin McGuinness announced consultations on whether to scrap school league tables in Northern Ireland. The NASUWT responded positively, indicating that the provision of information to parents was important but no justification for league tables.

In September 2000 the Office for Manpower Economics (OME) issued a report which had been commissioned by the STRB on teachers' workloads. It confirmed what we all knew: that teachers had a longer, more intensive working day, with 25% of their work being undertaken in the evenings and at weekends. Average number of hours worked per term-time week had risen from 50.3 in 1996 to 51.8 for secondary teachers and 50.8 to 52.8 in the primary sector. The OME, following in-depth interviews with staff, identified six main reasons:

> burdensome and labour-intensive lesson planning;
> updating schemes of work;
> pre-Ofsted inspection preparation;
> Government initiatives;
> administrative tasks such as photocopying, form filling and creating display work;
> external demands from LEAs and the DfEE.

The NASUWT said the findings totally vindicated the "Time for a Limit" action, which had picked up on every factor identified by the report.

By September the Government had set up the remit for the STRB to consult over the Threshold. The NASUWT, in its evidence, proposed that all the arrangements for the Threshold remain the same for that year, including even the Pupil Progress, for fear of having to cause applications to be repeated. The Union repeated its call for Pupil Progress to be dropped for the following year. We drew attention to the McCrone report in Scotland on teachers' conditions of service, which rejected reliance on pupil results in reviewing teachers' performance.

In October further threats from the NUT came against the Threshold proposals. Astonishingly, the NUT threatened more action in the courts, opposing the involvement of the third-party external assessor being granted the power to overturn a recommendation from the head. The NASUWT took entirely the opposite view, believing the involvement of a third party focussed minds on ensuring justice, fairness and consistency across schools, minimising the risk of personal bias and other inappropriate considerations being brought to bear. Furthermore, the NASUWT believed problems were best resolved through mutual discussions rather than in the courts.

On 20 October the STRB published its report on the Threshold payments. It recommended the status quo on all the main standards and procedures. It specifically rejected the NUT's main demand to reopen the deadline for applications. Many NUT members had fallen for their union's advice to boycott the Threshold. All but a minority of diehards were now regretting their decisions.

The STRB did recommend the right to a review mechanism being set up. Again ironically, although it fell short of the full-scale right to appeal requested by the NASUWT, progress on the issue was being made prior to the NUT court action, which itself had not made the point in its challenge. The NASUWT declared the Threshold "back on track", despite the strong likelihood that delay would stretch beyond Christmas, denying teachers a much needed boost in income at such a time.

Divisions between the NUT and the rest in England and Wales were exported to Northern Ireland where the 'sectarian'-based unions UTU and INTO used the opportunity provided by the court action to oppose the Threshold payments on grounds they represented 'payment by results'. The positions adopted by those two unions ignored all the amendments the NASUWT had secured but more dangerously threatened pay parity between the Province and England and Wales. The employers in Northern Ireland had taken advantage of the NUT court challenge to delay making an offer which should have been effective from 1 September. The NASUWT and ATL in Northern Ireland warned their colleagues of the long-term dangers of losing parity, which the purely 'local' unions appeared content to risk in support of other objectives.

On 22 November the Regulations and Supplementary Guidance on the Threshold were finally issued, enabling the process to resume. Cambridge Education Associates was put in charge of externally verifying the process. Whilst all payments were to be backdated to 1 September 2000, no money was likely to be received before spring 2001. Furthermore, the delay knocked on to those who became eligible to apply from 1 September 2000, whose deadline would now be 29 October 2001.

Just before Christmas the NUT managed to distinguish itself once again. With the relevant Order (No. 4) (implementing the 'Threshold arrangements') laid before Parliament, the NUT GS, Doug McAvoy, wrote to all MPs requesting them to support a prayer of annulment against the said Order. When the draft Order was produced the NUT had proclaimed a victory in light of the changes it claimed to have secured. Now the NUT was lobbying against its 'victory'! In my public statement I could only express my disbelief: "You cannot be serious!"

The NUT may privately have been 'praying' that its efforts would come to nothing, for if successful there would surely have been an unprecedented backlash from grass-roots members, whose pay increases had been seriously delayed by their leaders' tactics which at best could only postpone the inevitable.

In stark contrast the NASUWT continued to focus on improving matters for the classroom teacher by issuing instructions under "Time for a Limit" to members to participate in performance management subject to certain conditions, namely:

> only three objectives for each teacher;
>
> a maximum of three hours classroom observation per year for all purposes;
>
> no grading of teachers on classroom observation other than satisfactory or not;
>
> allocation of team leader role to those with paid line-management responsibilities;
>
> no other in-year review meetings;
>
> no self-review/evaluation schemes.

As soon as the Threshold was operational the NJC for Sixth Form Colleges set about the customary 'keeping up with the [school] Joneses'. After much patience and hard work an equivalent scheme was introduced under the banner of 'Professional Standards'. The tradition of collaborative working between the unions was maintained and the NUT did not engage in oppositional tactics in this case.

There were also many reports coming in from schools recording advances made in working practices as a result of the "Time for a Limit" action. Numbers of meetings had been reduced, parental consultation meetings were being rationalised, interim reports and reviews were being cut and pre-Ofsted reviews were being boycotted.

As the late-autumn edition of Union's monthly newspaper, *The Career Teacher*, recorded in its headline, the NASUWT had spent "A Good Year Getting it Right".

Chapter 79 – Cover to Contract

The December 2000 meeting of the Executive decided to implement with immediate effect a ban on cover for absent teachers to supplement the "Time for a Limit" action. One of the Executive Members for the North East, Hans Ruyssenaars, suddenly moved an amendment to the Officers' Report to this effect. There was a growing problem of shortages of teachers, particularly in high-cost-of-living areas. This was adding to the workload problem, already grave enough.

On this occasion we did not allow the usual time for the Government and employers to be advised of our intentions, not to mention the customary preparation of the membership.

With little of the normal time allowed for preparation, staff and Executive Members had to work extra hard to get the action off the ground. Several ballots were authorised in various parts of the country, including London and the South East. The effect of the mere threat of action, with one or two instances of refusal to cover starting, was once again out of all proportion to the impact it would have on the ground. The Government reacted as if we were about to bring the state education service to its knees. David Blunkett threatened a heavy-handed "robust response", as did national spokesmen for LEAs. I commented that instead of issuing threats and blaming union leaders, the Government should pay attention to the problems over working conditions which lay at the heart of the recruitment crisis and the escalating difficulties of finding supply teachers to cover for absent staff.

The action was quite modest and reflected the spirit, if not the letter, of the teacher's contract. Teachers were only supposed to cover for vacancies and absences known in advance in "exceptional circumstances" where the employer could not find a supply teacher. The problem was that the 'exceptional' had now become the norm. Members would therefore refuse to cover for vacancies and for any absence known in advance to last longer than three days. Members would continue to cover for up to three days for unforeseen absences. It was a very restrained and moderate response to a serious problem. Consequently we named the action "Cover to Contract". By February the NUT was joining in and the two unions were co-ordinating their actions.

Meanwhile in Scotland the McCrone Implementation Group issued its report on pay and conditions of service, *A Teaching Profession for the 21st Century*. The key provisions were:

an overall limit on working time of 35 hours per week;

no increase in the length of the working year;

maximum class contact hours per week reducing to 22.5 for all by 2006;

pay to increase by 10% w.e.f. April 2001 plus annual increments, 4% in April 2002, 3.5% in January 2003 and 4% in August 2003.

The Main Grade would rise over that time to a maximum of £28,200, Chartered Teacher grade to £34,850 and Principal Teacher to £40,303. Pupil Progress as a measure by which to judge and assess teacher performance was rejected.

A new Scottish Negotiating Committee for Teachers (SNCT) would be established to include representatives from the recently established Scottish Executive, employers and teacher unions, including NASUWT Scotland. The NASUWT National and the Scottish Executives recommended acceptance to the membership and a ballot to determine the issue was organised, resulting, as expected, in an overwhelming 'yes' vote.

The STRB published its report for 2001 on 2 February. It recommended rises of 3.7% across the board. However, in spite of the overwhelming evidence of excessive working hours, the STRB made no proposals to establish an overall limit. It simply recommended that the DfEE should take the lead in organising an urgent and independently run programme to identify, clarify and tackle the problems of workload.

I described the report as the most disappointing for many years. It all added up "to nothing more than a pathetic patchwork of piecemeal measures which lamentably fail to tackle the fundamental problem of making teaching an attractive career." I also observed that the award left teachers in England and Wales with significantly inferior conditions. The failure to improve the contract was a "major flaw", again contrasting sharply with the Scottish limit of 35 hours per week together with maximum contact time.

In the short term Scottish teachers' pay seemed to be above the English and Welsh in so far as the equivalent of the starting point for the 'Threshold' at £28,200 and the maximum of £38,450 were higher. However, the settlement was to cover a longer period of time and (as subsequent experience proved) access to the higher pay levels was severely restricted.

By March 2001, with a General Election likely in a few months time, the NASUWT-led campaign on workload was making good progress. In addition to the useful precedent set by 'McCrone' in Scotland, the four TUC-affiliated unions, the NASUWT, NUT, ATL and the (Welsh) UCAC, announced agreement to debate an identical motion at their Annual Conferences. The planned motion condemned the STRB and Government for their repeated failure to take effective action to remove excessive workload. The motion also called for an independent inquiry into workload as well as pay levels and salary structure. The motion concluded by declaring that in the event of Government failure to take appropriate measures, action would be taken to limit teachers' working time to no more than 35 hours per week.

Writing in *The Daily Mail* on 12 March, Secretary of State David Blunkett made bolshie and hostile comments about the NASUWT's "Cover to Contract" action. David had made (hopefully) jocular comments about wanting to "break [my] legs" as he 'welcomed' a deputation from the NASUWT into his office. Perhaps that was another example of many a true word spoken in jest. Scrapping around for 'things to be seen doing', the Government had announced measures to import teachers from abroad and to entice early retirees back into the classroom. I had no trouble rubbishing such short-term "panic palliatives", asking: "What is the point of enticing early retirees back if nothing is done to deal with the conditions that drove them out of teaching in the first place?"

Soon afterwards the Chairman of the Local Government Association's Education Committee, Graham Lane, played the 'hard man soft man' role. First he threatened teachers with punitive deductions of salary for refusing to cover but then offered the unions talks with employers on cover and the contract. The NASUWT Action Committee responded promptly and offered to suspend the action in return for talks on the contract. There had been no national talks on the contract for 16 years (since the mid-1980s).

David Blunkett then moved, possibly concerned about the LEAs taking the initiative, and changed his mind about the STRB's recommendation for an independent study into teachers' workload, which he had originally rejected. I immediately welcomed "this far more positive response" which was "a vast improvement of his previous vicious anti-trade union stance, reminiscent of the worst days of Tory rule, when he incited employers to make excessive pay deductions against teachers and sue them for damages".

The NASUWT emphasised its offer to suspend action related to "Cover to Contract". The "Time for a Limit" action would continue. Despite the offers of talks no formal measures were taken and by April the NASUWT Action Committee decided to press on with both actions. NASUWT members in 40 LEAs and 256 individual schools continued to "Cover to Contract". Thirteen more ballots were planned as LEAs claimed to be preparing "groundbreaking proposals" on the contract but dismissing prematurely any possibility of a 35-hour limit to the working week.

Conference intervened, this time being held in my native island of Jersey. The Conference duly carried the 'four union' joint motion on workload, pay levels and salary structure. In my 'state of the union' address to members I summed up the workload problem saying it stemmed "from the sheer weight of all that has been imposed in recent years: the detailed statutory prescription of the national curriculum; the constant changes; the complex public examinations system; the wide-ranging national tests; the miserable mismanagement by many heads requiring mind-boggling amounts of planning, lesson preparation, recording, reporting, target-setting, evaluating – sometimes on a daily basis; the literacy and numeracy strategies; and the unending supply of new initiatives. All this adds up to a monstrous and suffocating system of over-accountability."

Minister of State Estelle Morris addressed the Jersey Conference. She conceded the pressure on teachers was unprecedented but claimed our demand for a 35-hour week was "unprofessional" since "most professions do not count their hours". The NASUWT had never accepted such an assertion. Many other professions did charge according to the time spent on clients' work, lawyers being a notable example. I asked the Minister in my 'vote of thanks' if she was condemning 70,000 Scottish teachers as unprofessional for accepting a new contract stipulating a 35-hour working week.

Anxious to avoid militant action during a General Election campaign, as polling day beckoned (scheduled for 7 June) the Government offered talks. A rather large meeting of Ministers and union and employer representatives was called for 1 May.

Meeting under the auspices of the TUC on 23 April, the NASUWT and NUT issued a joint statement welcoming this development and suspending their "Cover to Contract" action. The NASUWT also emphasised its "Time for a Limit" action continued. I commented publicly that the "Cover to Contract" action had been "an enormous success in securing immediate improvements on the ground and kicking open the door on talks on our contract which had been slammed shut since the Baker imposition of 1987".

The talks got off to a faltering start on the evening of 1 May. It was to be the last meeting we had with David Blunkett as Secretary of State for Education. Inside the teachers' pre-meeting the mood and the talk had been quite militant, somewhat to my pleasant surprise, with much reference to the joint 'identical' motions put to union Conferences over the Easter period. The four TUC-affiliated unions had also met separately beforehand and had adopted a very critical position over the recently circulated DfEE paper on a proposed study on workload. We all considered that to be a totally inadequate response to the problem and to the demands set out in the Conferences' joint resolution. We suspected it would be merely a repeat of Circular 2/98 and previous STRB surveys.

However, once inside the plenary meeting, the militant mood dissipated. My colleague General Secretaries seemed to fall over themselves rushing to accept with grateful thanks the offer from David Blunkett. The 'spin' had been real talks on the contract. The reality was a proposal to have further talks in a Steering Group with civil servants over an 'independent review' into the problems, subject to the "Cover to Contract" action being withdrawn rather than just 'suspended'. The 'independent review' would be conducted by PriceWaterhouseCoopers (PWC), another firm of Government's beloved management consultants.

David Blunkett must have read my body language, for he chose to get reactions to his proposal 'going round the table' starting with the union on my left and proceeding in (his) clockwise direction, which ensured my contribution would be the last.

The employers were very happy with the proposal, for they were already in their usual state of panic over being in the front line dealing with day-to-day problems of action in the schools. Rather to my surprise all the other union representatives quickly supported the 'offer', the like of which in my view we had rejected just a matter of minutes beforehand. All the militancy seemed to evaporate in the face-to-face encounter with the Ministers.

The NASUWT proved to be the fly in the ointment, with me being the only one distinctly unimpressed by such a modest proposal, dripping as it appeared to be with 'let's get through the General Election period' procrastination. I rubbished the proposal for a so-called independent review into the problem which had plagued teachers for years, already investigated to exhaustion and the subject of the supposedly 'bureaucracy busting' Circular 2/98. I demanded the contract be openly on the agenda for discussion. Responding to my lonely dissent David Blunkett waffled.

I interrupted him saying, "David you are dissembling. Why can't you say the contract will be on the agenda?" I added that it did not commit the Government to any changes, but simply to talk. David said he did not want the papers to be reporting tomorrow morning that the Government had caved in to teacher union demands on the contract.

I reminded David of the time, already approaching 8 p.m. I could hardly see the front pages being held for the 'shattering' development that the Government would be prepared to talk to teachers' representatives about their contract, when everyone now accepted there were problems over excessive workload which had to be addressed.

Attempting to placate me, David said that "nothing is ruled in, nothing ruled out". I said I had heard that one many times before! I insisted the contract had to be openly on the agenda. David Blunkett finally agreed, saying, "Yes, it could be". I welcomed this clarification, which was "just about enough to keep NASUWT involved in the process".

In the event, media coverage was limited and rather low key. Government sources (probably David Blunkett's spin doctor Conor Ryan) talked up the harmonious nature of the meeting and condemned my expressed view of "getting there after a struggle" to be in a minority of one. I readily confessed to being that minority, determined to get the contract on to the agenda, saying "we should not underestimate the huge difficulties ahead. The reluctance of David Blunkett to let the word 'contract' slip from his lips through fear of headlines in the media said it all."

Chapter 80 – Social Partnership is Born

The concession dragged out of David Blunkett to discuss the contract openly might have been a huge turning point. The National Steering Group set up to oversee the PWC exercise led directly to the National Remodelling Group. That in turn spawned a whole series of meetings and reports leading up some two years later to the National Agreement on Standards and Workload, which proved to be the birth of the Social Partnership between the Government and (most of) the teacher unions. True to form the NUT stood outside this great breakthrough in relationships between Government and the unions.

On 8 May (2001) progress was made in talks with the employers to maintain and enhance the improvements made for cover arrangements during the course of the action. The employers also agreed that the contract had to be on the agenda, albeit a little further down the road. They appeared to be impressed with the procedures used to implement the McCrone recommendations in Scotland.

On 20 June a firm agreement between the six teachers' unions and the employers' organisation NEOST was concluded. Amongst other improvements provision was made that in the event of teachers being requested to cover beyond the requirements of the Pay and Conditions Document the time involved would be 'banked' and repaid within a month. The agreement even conceded that as a last resort the school day could be changed, with "pupils attending school for shorter periods of time".

On 12 November unions and employers were given sight of the PWC study into teacher workload. It consisted of 100 pages of detail accompanied by a thick technical annexe. It was a perfect example of management consultants producing mountains of detail to justify their charges. The details obfuscated the main issue. Plant enough trees and you won't be able to see the wood, I thought to myself as I read the turgid document.

PWC relied heavily upon guidance on good practice being delivered by head teachers, the very people previously identified as part of the problem. Nevertheless, sifting through the 100 pages of text it was possible to identify the following proposals of reasonably clarity if limited efficacy:

> spreading good practice on planning, recording and reporting;
> transferring routine administrative tasks away from teachers;
> redesigning some aspects of schoolwork;
> adopting more flexible approaches to staffing;
> better use of ICT.

As expected PWC claimed "in terms of other contractual measures there was little support for a limit to the working week". They obviously spoke to different teachers from NASUWT members, not to mention the four unions' 'joint Conference motions' and the 70,000 teachers in Scotland. However, there were two additional and potentially promising 'contractual spots' buried in the text, with the possibilities raised of overtime payments for a range of activities and guaranteed non-contact time.

Assuming normal practice with reports and inquiries of this kind, there would have been some 'liaison' with 'the department'. It was probably not just coincidence that on the same day the PWC report was published, Estelle Morris, now Secretary of State for Education in the second Blair administration, addressed a seminar organised by the Social Market Foundation and published a pamphlet entitled *Professionalism and Trust* which raised controversial issues over the use of support staff in schools. I attended the seminar.

Controversial for some, but less so for the NASUWT who had on several occasions in the past raised such issues in a very constructive way. The NASUWT had a very open mind on the use of support staff to assist teachers, which was in stark contrast to other more 'conservative'-inclined unions.

Ironically that was the occasion on which I made my 'infamous' remarks allegedly likening support staff to "pig ignorant peasants". The story took five days to take off for neither the Secretary of State nor any of the many education correspondents present in the room interpreted my remarks in that way. Responding to Estelle Morris' speech I actually welcomed the potentially good ideas being put forward while warning her that schools needed appropriately qualified staff for whatever roles were envisaged because there was no point in employing "pig ignorant peasants". A few days later the *TES* telephoned me to check I made that remark and the following Friday ran a story with the twisted line that I had "appeared to equate support staff with pig ignorant peasants". One of the Government's spin doctors, in a revealing insight into their role, spotted the potential for a story and then persuaded the media to develop it.

To return to the PWC report, I called for direct talks with Ministers to rescue the exercise and do something of immediate relevance to help teachers. I was glad to note in their public comments that many other unions shared my analysis that the PWC report "was good on description but weak on remedies".

As the Steering Group met on 5 December some improvements were noted in the final PWC report. Although we could have got on with the job months ago without the PWC report, Ministers seemed to need it for various reasons, and given that they seemed to be showing a greater sense of urgency the NASUWT accepted their proposals to identify solutions immediately. Civil servants then presented a skeletal plan to take issues forward including references to changing the contract, which was the key to getting the NASUWT fully on board and not 'carping on' too much about PWC. The Government indicated some progress was possible in the short term but other more costly proposals would have to await the outcome of the Comprehensive Spending Review due by July of the next year.

The NASUWT, ATL, NUT and UCAC agreed to exercise patience and through the TUC asked Estelle Morris to do the same and stay her hand in sending the STRB its remit for the supplementary report due on workload pending discussions over the contract. The four unions were pleased to note the SHA and NAHT associated themselves with the TUC initiative.

The constructive developments at the Steering Group meeting were followed up on 17 December in a meeting between the Secretary of State, employers and unions. Estelle Morris spoke openly about making changes to the contract. Agreement was reached to establish a Remodelling Working Party to examine the future structure of the teaching profession. In addition, the STRB would be asked to produce as quickly as possible a supplementary report to consider the implications of the recent PWC study into workload.

On behalf of the NASUWT I welcomed these developments, publicly indicating that we had "a completely open mind and are willing to examine and if necessary redefine the roles of teachers and support staff. The potential for workload reduction is enormous." I also welcomed the consultation over the preparation of the Secretary of State's remit letter to the STRB.

The year 2001 ended on an optimistic and constructive note. I commended everyone concerned for the greater readiness to address the workload issues and to discuss the contract openly without the earlier pre-General Election hang-ups. If the unions responded positively to Estelle Morris' speech to the Social Market Foundation we might be able to achieve a better and more professional definition of the teacher's role and couple that with reduced workload and enhanced salaries: "All round, a more consultative approach [is] being taken by Government towards the teaching unions and could lead to a much improved atmosphere between us".

The more positive atmosphere at the start of 2002 was suitably reflected in another milestone reached by the NASUWT in having recruited its 200,000th member, Sylvia New. I have already referred (in chapter 44) to Sylvia being impressed with NASUWT literature but the particular publication that persuaded her to join was *Crossing the Threshold*.

Even the STRB award for 1 April 2002 was slightly better than 'usual'. The report was published on 23 January and represented a "modest basic increase of 3.5% with a 5% overall rise in earnings". The award was above the inflation rate but failed to match the average increase in white-collar earnings. The context was also helped by the £2,000 Threshold payments having at last arrived in teachers' pockets, some 200,000 having qualified.

The award also shortened the Main Scale from nine to six points, leaving the maximum for the unpromoted and 'un-thresholded' teacher on an annual salary of £25,746 w.e.f. 1 April 2002 but also allowing earlier access to the Threshold. The Threshold uplift became £2,148. The maximum of the Upper Pay Spine (point 5) rose to £32,250.

The NASUWT strongly challenged the Government over its decision to leave progress along the Upper Pay Spine dependent upon local financial discretion. The Report to Schools in February was headlined: "Pay Up Government – it was your idea!" The six teacher unions held a special joint meeting with the Minister of State, Steven Timms, to press the case for progress along the Upper Spine to be based entirely and openly on merit. The special Government grant to LEAs implied at most only half the eligible teachers could progress and as such was a hopeless if revealing prejudgement paralleling the most common fault with PRP schemes.

The position in Wales was complicated by the absence of performance management, which under the somewhat curious arrangements for devolved government was a matter for the Welsh Assembly and had not been introduced at this stage.

In my parting Report to Schools in March 2002 with my retirement as GS due at the end of Conference on 5 April, I chose the old saying "Teacher, teach thyself" as my theme. Estelle Morris had just sent out a letter and poster to all schools setting out with "commendable clarity" the many measures teachers could take to reduce their workload. The poster spelt out that teachers should:

> implement the proposals in the anti-bureaucracy Circular (2/98) issued nearly four years before;
>
> put the "Reducing Bureaucracy Toolkit" into practice;
>
> use the DfEE work/life balance website to "help strike a balance between work and other areas of life".

The poster dramatically listed 25 common tasks which did not need teachers to be carried out and which should be transferred to support staff or ICT as soon as practicable. They ranged from collecting money, chasing absences and bulk copying, to managing and inputting pupils' data. Estelle Morris referred to the PWC study showing that "some 20% of teachers' time is spent on tasks not directly related to classroom teaching". The Minister had asked the STRB to report, amongst other things, on:

> "whether a meaningful guarantee of professional time for teachers and managers" could be implemented; and

"whether it is possible to moderate the impact of paragraph 59.8 in the Pay and Conditions Document which is open-ended and can lead to high demands on teachers."

"What are we waiting for?" I asked. "Estelle Morris is effectively recommending the entire profession implement many of the provisions of the NASUWT's action 'Time for a Limit', issued in June 2000. While obviously we need the contract change to guarantee progress for the future, there are scores of measures teachers could take from today to help themselves. Go to it, Teacher, teach thyself."

That having been said I remained sceptical about the willingness of the Government to take the step really needed – amend the relevant and infamous paragraph now numbered 59.8, originally 36 (1) (f) in Ken Baker's imposition of 1987. Estelle Morris' remit to the STRB referred to its "open-ended" nature, the very criticism the NASUWT had voiced about it from the beginning. When I asked Estelle Morris why the Government would not introduce some overall hours limit even at the 'high end', she replied: "such a decision would not be for me". I could only conclude that PM Tony Blair would not permit such a 'concession' to the trade unions.

Many of the discussions-cum-negotiations that were to follow and lead to the complex Standards and Workload Agreement of 2003, whilst very good in themselves and an excellent example of the benefits of Social Partnership, were made unnecessarily complicated by the refusal to contemplate a simple overall hours limit. If target setting were so popular, why not set one to reduce working time? If workload reduction did not mean fewer hours being worked what did it mean? I suspected that problem would remain and I am intrigued to hear NASUWT leaders voicing the same concerns in 2008.

Conference 2002 duly supported the Executive's policy of working through the TUC with other unions to press the Government to release funding necessary to implement the outcome of the workload review and to redefine the roles and responsibilities of teachers and support staff. It adopted a report on "The Changing Role of the Teacher", emphasising that high standards of academic and pedagogic achievement should continue to inform qualified teacher status (QTS); the work of teaching assistants must always be carried out under the supervision and management of teachers; and defined teaching duties must only be performed by those with QTS.

Conference also endorsed the Executive's strategy on the Upper Pay Spine (UPS) to put the performance management system to the test but to take action should eligible teachers be denied progress. The incoming GS, Eamonn O'Kane, warned the Government that while the NASUWT would continue to engage in constructive talks the growing anger and impatience of teachers should not be underestimated.

The eagerly awaited STRB report on workload was published on 8 May '02. Reacting to it Eamonn O'Kane said he was "underwhelmed". The main recommendations covered areas including guaranteed planning time, reductions in average weekly term-time hours from 52 to 48 and thereafter to 45, limits on cover, work/life balance, professional development, additional support staff and statutory guidance for implementation.

Eamonn O'Kane argued that some recommendations were helpful, some not; others were vague and the means of implementation less than convincing. He added much would depend upon the Government's willingness to enter genuine dialogue on significant changes to the contract.

On 3 July on the initiative of the NASUWT, the TUC coordinated a joint lobby of Parliament by the four affiliated unions to press for an agreed ten-point "Charter for Change – Reduce Workload, Raise Standards". The Charter sharpened up many of the STRB recommendations, for example calling for the transfer to support staff from September '02 of the 25 administrative tasks already identified as unnecessary for a teacher to perform. The Charter also called for a weekly overall hours limit of 35 to be phased in from September '03 (thereby again openly contradicting PWC claims that the NASUWT was on its own on this issue); a clear, guaranteed limit on cover; and guaranteed preparation and marking time, as well as other changes.

Later in July the Government announced details of its Comprehensive Spending Review. The Secretary of State for (the once again renamed) the Department for Education and Skills (DfES) announced an intention to seek a national agreement with teacher unions on 'Investment for Reform'. A series of meetings took place between the Government, employers, and teacher and support staff unions which was chaired by David Miliband, the impressive and up-and-coming Minister of State. David brought a fresh and confident approach to the work of the DfES, including willingness to debate openly with everyone. He seemed to grasp the details of his brief quickly, a quality no doubt lending strength to his confidence in debate.

The NASUWT, NUT and ATL submitted a joint motion to the TUC Congress in September '02 highlighting the need for action to tackle excessive workload. In October '02 the four TUC-affiliated unions were joined by PAT in submitting joint evidence to the STRB for the award to operate from 1 April '03. The evidence called for a substantial pay increase, improved working conditions and enhanced salary and career progression. The five unions highlighted the significant differences that could open up between salaries in Scotland and those in England and Wales. Eamonn O'Kane commented that "a defining moment" was arriving for teachers' pay, adding that: "Failure to deliver on David Blunkett's promise that the vast majority of teachers could access salaries over £30,000 will seriously jeopardise the future of the current structure."

The five unions opposed the Secretary of State's letter of remit suggesting that progression along the Main Scale should be performance related and that along the Upper Pay Spine be based on "progressively more challenging standards".

The Government also floated the idea of multi-year awards. In separate supplementary evidence to the STRB, the NASUWT reacted cautiously to the idea, insisting such an arrangement had to be by agreement and as part of a package substantially improving pay and conditions along the lines of McCrone in Scotland.

By October the Government was planning for consultation on its formal response to the STRB report on workload, its proposals on the role and responsibilities of support staff and draft regulations and guidance to support the provisions of the 2002 Education Act on the role of the teacher.

Welcoming these developments, Eamonn O'Kane spoke of the "unrelenting pressure from the NASUWT" over many years leading to the Government accepting 'something had to be done'. He anticipated teachers would not want to waste the first opportunity in 15 years to improve their conditions, but they expected genuine change including a reduction in overall working hours.

On 22 October the pack of documents was duly published for consultation under the title *Time for Standards: Reforming the School Workforce*. The NASUWT identified eight major gains including:

> a commitment to reduce overall working hours and restore work/life balance;
>
> the introduction of guaranteed planning, preparation and assessment (PPA) time;
>
> a limit on the amount of cover a teacher could be required to undertake;
>
> transfer of agreed administrative tasks to other appropriate staff.

Eamonn O'Kane observed, "the progress made should not be underestimated"; however, there was still much "devil in the detail", particularly in respect of the definition of roles and responsibilities of staff to safeguard the pedagogic role of teachers and the precise limit on cover (the DfES was suggesting 38 hours per year). More discussion was needed "but genuine improvements were within teachers' grasp", concluded Eamonn.

The following day, 23 October 2002, Estelle Morris suddenly resigned as Secretary of State for Education. Her decision was never fully explained, but one factor appeared to be some self doubt in her ability to do the job. Charles Clarke was appointed as her successor.

Meanwhile the NASUWT and NUT acted jointly in stepping up the campaign for increases in the London Allowances. The capital was experiencing serious teacher shortages once again. A joint rally and march were organised for 26 November in central London. The unions highlighted the difference between the allowances for the police and those for teachers. Police received allowances up to £6,111 together with housing and free transport. Teachers received only £3,105 (Inner), £2,043 (Outer) and £792 (Fringe).

After the publication of the *Time for Standards: Reforming the School Workforce* documents, another intensive series of meetings took place between the parties. By early December the NASUWT was reporting progress on some issues and difficulties on others. On cover the NASUWT believed the 38 hours requirement was excessive and counter-proposed that in return for accepting the principle of 'cover supervisors' teachers on the establishment of a school should not be required to cover at all. The NASUWT supported the continued use of supply teachers for the purpose.

Developing the role of support staff was perhaps one of the most difficult areas, with the unions insisting that the pedagogic role of fully qualified teachers must not be compromised. Unambiguous safeguards were needed to clarify the role of the higher-level teaching assistants. It was to prove a breaking point for the NUT.

There appeared to be only limited progress on paragraph 58.9 of the teacher's contract, with the DfES offering to amend the wording to require LEAs, heads and governors to have regard to the work/life balance in the expectations they place upon staff. Notice: the DfES did not include the Government on the list!

Progress was being made on the less controversial items, such as the transfer of administrative tasks, cover and rigorous monitoring and timescales to ensure implementation of an agreement.

The consultation period was extended to 6 December. As schools broke up for the Christmas holidays the NASUWT reported the workload agreement was "on track". Minister of State David Miliband made a helpful statement, saying that "teachers have everything to gain and nothing to fear. New regulations and guidance will make it clear that high-level teaching assistants and qualified teachers are not interchangeable. The agreement will regulate what is now unregulated. Teacher numbers will continue to rise with at least 10,000 more [in the lifetime of the current Parliament]." Eamonn O'Kane welcomed David Miliband's statement emphasising "the paramount importance of the pedagogic role of the qualified teacher".

Early in January 2003 a draft agreement was reached between all the parties except the NUT. The emerging National Agreement on Raising Standards and Tackling Workload envisaged eight key principles being implemented:

> guaranteed time for marking, preparation and planning for all teachers;
>
> reduction in working hours;
>
> the objective that teachers should rarely cover;
>
> timetabled time for teachers with management responsibilities, including special needs co-ordinators;
>
> amendment to the contract to ensure work/life balance;
>
> introduction of regulations to protect the role and status of qualified teachers;
>
> transfer of administrative staff and clerical tasks from teachers to support staff;
>
> concerted attack on bureaucratic burdens.

At its 10 January meeting the NASUWT Executive unanimously approved the Agreement. The usual procedures were then put in place to provide members with all the relevant information, sent to their home addresses together with regional briefings so that every member who was interested could participate fully in the ratification process. Welcoming "good news at last for teachers", GS Eamonn O'Kane described the Agreement as a "real and sustainable improvement in working conditions", secured mainly through the unrelenting pressure exerted by the NASUWT over many years.

Despite the assurances over use of ancillary staff with an unequivocal statement as part of the Agreement that teachers and teaching assistants were not interchangeable the NUT decided to oppose it. The NUT soon launched a belligerent and hostile attack upon the NASUWT and others who were supporting the Agreement. The NUT placed weekly adverts in the *TES*, vilifying and grossly misrepresenting the position of the signatory unions – which included three of the largest affiliates to the TUC who represented non-teaching staff in schools.

The NASUWT emphasised that the Agreement marked the 'formal' start of a Social Partnership between Government, employers and unions. It was far from the end but merely the beginning of a process of developing and implementing the Agreement in concert with all the partners. Various groups were established to implement and monitor the Agreement in detail, the most prominent of which rejoiced in the acronym WAMG – Workload and Management Group.

The Agreement was formally signed by the Secretary of State, the employers' representatives and all the teacher and support staff unions with the exception of the NUT on 15 January 2003.

The STRB produced its Twelfth Report on 7 February 2003. The NASUWT described it as "a bitter disappointment". Increases at 2.9% for most teachers were below the rate of inflation. The overall rise in the pay bill was 3.25% as relatively significant rises were awarded to Inner London teachers in the form of a new scale to replace the former allowance. Eamonn O'Kane said the award "would do nothing for the recruitment and retention of teachers". The STRB had broken with its recent pattern of awarding above-inflation rises.

Nevertheless, there were some positive developments, with the Review Body rejecting the Government's proposal that progression on the Upper Pay Spine should be made increasingly more difficult. The STRB also rejected the suggestion of multi (three) year pay deals. The NUT had put out propaganda that the Standards and Workload Agreement was tied to a three-year pay freeze.

Pay for the teacher crossing the Threshold rose to £28,688, with the possibility of attaining a maximum further four steps leading to £33,150. The new Inner London Scale equivalents were £34,002 and £39,093. The effective Inner London 'allowance' thereby became £5,334 and £5,943, up significantly from its previous level of £3,105 but still hopelessly inadequate in terms of allowing career teachers to purchase homes in reasonably attractive parts of the capital. The 'other' London allowances rose very modestly to £2,247 (Outer) and £870 (Fringe). Advanced Skills Teachers could earn between £35,700 and £53,412.

The NASUWT strategy on both the Threshold and Upper Pay Spine was soon to be fully vindicated. Approximately 95% of applicants (over 200,000 teachers) successfully crossed the Threshold in the first year of its operation. In respect of movement to point 2 on the Upper Spine, 90% of eligible teachers progressed at the first opportunity.

The Easter Annual Conference held at Bournemouth overwhelmingly endorsed the Agreement. The TUC Congress held in September also endorsed the Agreement on a proposal by the NASUWT, seconded by UNISON and supported by the ATL, T&G and GMB. Moving the motion for NASUWT, Eamonn O'Kane made what proved to be his last public speech before tragically succumbing to a recurrence of cancer the following spring. Sitting as I was a few feet away and chairing Congress as the TUC President for the year, I was acutely aware that Eamonn should have been back in London in hospital (having defied doctor's orders by delaying his return). But as courageous as ever he was on his feet defending the Agreement he had done so much to achieve.

Eamonn's courage was sadly in stark contrast to the behaviour of the NUT. Despite continuing to wage a vitriolic public campaign against the Agreement the NUT failed to deliver a speaker to the Congress rostrum to oppose the motion.

Eamonn had also displayed a remarkable degree of restraint over the NUT's vitriolic attacks upon the NASUWT for signing the National Agreement. Eamonn's patience was finally broken and he responded in kind to the NUT. The brutality of Eamonn's put-down of the NUT was all the more impressive for his earlier restraint. Eamonn dismissed the NUT as a paper tiger, a faction-ridden union, bereft of positive ideas without the guts to stand up and defend its position at the TUC Congress, which endorsed the Standards and Workload Agreement. The whole episode did, however, shake the confidence Eamonn had previously displayed in the value of one teachers' union through a merger of the NASUWT, ATL and AMMA although the NASUWT Conference in 2002 had decisively declined to entertain such a proposal.

Business began early for the 1 April 2004 award. In September the NASUWT combined with the ATL to submit joint evidence to the STRB. The claim called for a real-terms salary increase, the rejection of artificial quotas for progress up the Upper Pay Spine and the continuation of national – and rejection of regional – scales, and asserted that multi-year pay awards must be the subject of mutual agreement, not imposed.

The two unions also gave joint oral evidence to the Review Body in October. The opportunity was taken to challenge the Government's estimate of future inflation. The Government was also in the process of moving over to a new system, based on the different Consumer Price Index, dropping the more established RPI as the official measure of inflation for wage determination in the public sector. That remains controversial to the present day (2008). Eamonn O'Kane complimented the STRB on playing a pivotal role in addressing workload issues by setting unions and government on the road to agreement and Social Partnership. He urged the Review Body to adopt a similar approach on pay, calling for dialogue and agreement rather than imposition.

The unions argued for the retention of the external assessors for the Threshold as well as supporting the proposals put forward in their written evidence.

The STRB, as anticipated, published its Thirteenth Report on 10 November 2003. This time the Review Body accepted the Government's call for a multi-year award and recommended rises of 2.5% from 1 April 2004; 3.25% from April 2005 to run until 31 August 2006. Thereafter the 'pay' would run in tandem with the school year and operate from 1 September to 31 August. The STRB also recommended a reopener clause in the event of inflation exceeding an average of 3.25% over a 12- month period.

Most unhelpfully the Government decided to phase part of the award. The 2.5% from 1 April '04 would be paid in full. However, the 3.25% from 1 April '05 would be phased with 2.5% paid from the start and the additional 0.75%

topped up on 1 September. The next increase would operate from September '06.

The advent of genuine partnership did not extend to the area of the annual pay rise. Once again the meagre financial savings made by the Treasury from phasing was out of all proportion to the massive loss of goodwill. While the NASUWT had no objection in principle to multi-year pay deals, everything depended upon the levels of salary that applied. It should not become a device to depress pay in the long term. The NASUWT was also conscious of the age-old problem of some restoration (the higher increases generated by the Threshold and Upper Spine) being immediately clawed back by a succession of miserly annual awards.

The NASUWT welcomed the reopener clause, without which there could have been serious problems, but expressed concern that it was triggered at a level of inflation that was too high.

The NASUWT detected a move towards regional pay scales with the introduction of separate scales for the Outer London and Fringe areas, mirroring the arrangements made the previous year for Inner London. The Recruitment and Retention allowances, controversially introduced a few years previously, were recommended for abolition, with the Government agreeing to consult further on the proposal. The NASUWT had never believed they were effective for the purposes implied and resolved to argue that the money so saved should be retained for other elements in the pay package.

The STRB recommended urgent consultation between the 'pay partners' to be completed by 4 January '04 on a new framework for progression beyond point 3 on the Upper Pay Spine (UPS). The NASUWT welcomed the recommendations for a system of external assessment using the Threshold model to apply for the Upper Spine and for there to be no freeze on progression, with a discrete grant for the finance required coming from Westminster.

The other side of the UPS coin was of course the management allowances. They had to be replaced by 2005 with the new system, which remunerated only specific additional and weighty responsibilities linked firmly to teaching and learning. The STRB had recommended uprating for 2004, with temporary allowances awarded in the interim period. The Government rejected any increase and insisted on immediate freezing. The STRB recommended a maximum level of payment under the new system of £11,000.

The NASUWT decided to enter the proposed discussions between the parties in constructive mode but determined to ensure that teachers, especially those already two-thirds of the way through their two-year performance cycle, should be able to progress 'normally' and not be subject to new criteria designed to limit their opportunities.

Eamonn O'Kane described the overall multi-year package as "deeply disappointing" and condemned the decision to phase part of the award as "without any credible justification". Nevertheless, there was still much to play for and an opportunity to end once and for all the now annual argument over UPS progression. The NASUWT strategy had been immensely successful in ensuring that in respect of eligible teachers 97% had crossed the Threshold and 95% had progressed along the UPS.

Intensive discussions got under way under the title "Rewards and Incentives", which gave its name to a more formal and permanent group, soon to be known as RIG, to operate alongside WAMG in the new Social Partnership. As the business dealt with pay under the statutory STRB arrangements, the NUT (as well as the Welsh UCAC) had been specifically invited to attend. Both declined, the NUT presumably deciding it was so opposed to the Standards and Workload Agreement that boycott of any consequential proceedings was the only logical option available.

By early January the parties – Government and representatives of employers and the five unions – had reached a draft agreement subject to ratification by their respective organisations. The main provisions were:

> no new criteria for UPS progression;
>
> no quota on the number of teachers who can progress on the UPS;
>
> recognition of UPS3 as the salary to which all good classroom teachers can aspire (£31,602 in September '04 and £32,628 by September '05 outside London);
>
> (consequent of the above) removal of UPS4 and 5;
>
> a new excellent teachers' scheme;
>
> light touch external validation of schools' performance management systems;
>
> resources for schools to implement the draft agreement identified, making it affordable within the framework for school funding for 2004/05;
>
> regular meetings throughout 2004 and beyond to monitor implementation of the agreement and for further discussion on pay issues.

A remarkable development occurred, with agreement between the parties that subject to ratification they would jointly present written and oral evidence to the Review Body. The prospect of Government, employers and unions doing this together was nothing short of revolutionary. The 1991 Act still required the STRB processes to be followed on teachers' pay and conditions. In one way it was quirky for Government to join with employers and unions in seeking to persuade a third party (the STRB) to make recommendations for it (the

Government) to consider! The effect was a de facto quasi-restoration of negotiations between the three parties in attempts to reach consensus on issues for presentation to the STRB. The NUT, for so long hostile to the Review Body and in favour of restoration of negotiations, had excluded itself from the process.

For the NASUWT the draft agreement, which was ratified by all concerned, represented a significant victory. Whilst not perfect, the agreement, taken with the Threshold and other developments, represented the establishment of the collegiate approach. Emphasis was placed on the classroom teacher being better rewarded for the core task of teaching. Promotion was to become firmly tied to significant additional responsibilities linked not to administration and extraneous matters but to teaching and learning.

The agreement to continue with such 'talks-cum-negotiations' and the establishment of RIG, with a view to joint evidence being presented to the STRB, represented another breakthrough for the NASUWT. It was very similar to the kind of 'parallel body' the Union advocated should be established to operate alongside the Review Body. It could better deal with details where pay and conditions inevitably came together and which were best settled by representatives active in and knowledgeable about the day-to-day running of schools, something which members of review bodies were unlikely to be.

Eamonn O'Kane and I thought we had convinced the Minister of State, Stephen Byers, in 1997 of the good sense of such a parallel body. Unfortunately when the written reply came to the short paper we had submitted at his request the answer was in the negative. We believed that one of Stephen's 'bosses' – possibly David Blunkett or even Tony Blair himself – would not allow it.

The NUT determined to rubbish everything in sight. It focussed upon the loss of the old allowances and now the abolition of UPS4 and 5. Acting against the interests of the thousands of classroom teachers the NUT purported to represent, it ignored the injustices of the old promotion system and the opening up of opportunities for salary advancement represented by the Threshold and the ability to progress along the UPS. The NUT wantonly ignored the fact that very few teachers managed to secure the former management allowances of 4 and 5. That now stood in stark contrast to the vastly increased number of teachers who could access the Threshold and points 2 and 3 of the UPS, not to mention the new teaching and learning responsibility payments. And in any event the 'excellent' and 'advanced skills' teachers' (AST) schemes were capable of collecting up as many as those who secured by fair means or foul management allowances 4 and 5.

On 16 March the STRB published Part 2 of its Thirteenth Report dealing with the issues that had been the subject of the draft agreement between the parties. The Review Body endorsed all the key provisions with some variations on other matters. Most importantly the agreement on UPS progression was maintained. Without this the NASUWT believed the Review Body would have followed its initial inclination towards ranking and grading of teachers, with restricted access to the higher salaries.

The NASUWT would have preferred the continuation of external assessors for the Threshold. However, the establishment of an independent element in a new appeal process went a long way to meeting NASUWT concerns. The Union determined to press in ongoing discussions for this appeal process to be available for other pay-related decisions.

It was poignant that the breakthrough National Agreement on Standards and Workload was secured under the general secretaryship of Eamonn O'Kane. Whilst the collegiate philosophy had deep roots in the Union's history, Eamonn was its leading advocate of the modern era and his articulation of the case through the turbulent times of the 1980s was inspirational. With the National Agreement the collegiate approach figured prominently in the salary structure for England and Wales. Ironically it is proving somewhat difficult to secure full implementation in Northern Ireland, from where Eamonn hailed, thanks to some resistance from other unions more interested in maintaining a degree of separation from the UK for its own sake even if it costs their members money.

Conference 2004 endorsed the positions taken by the Executive in all the lengthy and complicated negotiations. Conference reaffirmed opposition to the phasing of the 2004-06 award and the flawed inflation review mechanism. It resolved to resist additional obstacles to progression on the Main Scale, to secure a new framework for management allowances, to ensure consistency, transparency and fairness in performance management and to press for further improvements in the salary structure and oppose any moves to undermine national pay determination.

Eamonn O'Kane lived long enough to receive reports of another productive and successful NASUWT Annual Conference but sadly he died in May 2004. He deserved to live much longer if for no other reason than to see his lifelong aspiration for a collegiate salary structure firmly on the road to fruition.

The Standards and Workload Agreement together with the establishment of WAMG and RIG as the instruments of Social Partnership were historic in terms of industrial relations in the field of education. The TUC had played an important role in bringing all the different unions together to negotiate the Agreement. The NUT was perfectly entitled to vote against the Agreement (which like most had its compromises), but the savage attacks it launched against so many fellow TUC-affiliated unions might have commanded a little credibility if its own record in negotiations had not been so dismal.

The NUT seemed to have forgotten the lesson of the 1980s that it could no longer exercise a veto. Once again Government, through the persons of both Secretary of State Charles Clarke and Minister of State David Miliband, was prepared to proceed apace without the NUT. The NUT refused to accept the majority decision and so was excluded from the WAMG and other groups forming the new Social Partnership in education.

The social partnership approach, better reflected in a review body system, has proved more effective in keeping teachers better paid in absolute as well as comparative terms. The government is exposed as the major player and placed under more subtle pressure to concede fairer pay levels.

The total salary bills for teachers in England and Wales had risen from £9790 millions in 1992 (the first year of the STRB) to £14905 millions by 2002 (in cash prices for the stated years). While inflation for this period totalled 26.4% the increase in the salary bill was 52.2% for a very similar number of teachers, see Appendices E, G and F. (Note also that the employers' on costs are included in the total salary bill.)

According to the ONS 2007 Annual Survey of Hours and Earnings, by April 2008 median annual salaries were £35,300 for secondary and £33,400 for primary teachers. For professional occupations the figure was £35,400 and for all employees £24,900 That compares favourably with many periods in the past when teachers' lost purchasing power.

Furthermore, there had been no national industrial action over pay for 18 years until 2008 when the NUT took a one-day strike protesting against a settlement falling below the RPI. That alone says a lot. The struggle for decent pay itself is perhaps never-ending. It is more likely to be achieved through genuine Social Partnership when that is possible. And, as the NASUWT has shown in many recent disputes with individual schools refusing to abide by the national agreements, resort to militant action remains an option if teachers are not treated fairly.

SECTION TEN

Chapter 81 - Conclusion

In his famous 1944 report commissioned by the Government, Arnold McNair, Vice-Chancellor of Liverpool University, confirmed the state education service had an air of cheapness about it from its foundation in 1870. Poor pay for teachers was endemic from the outset. That was the context in which the NAS, aware of the growing campaign for equal pay (EP) in a low-paid profession where women would be in large majority, harboured fears that schoolmasters' salaries would be seriously depressed.

The NAS's attempts to secure official recognition to put the schoolmaster's case was denied by successive governments for nearly 40 years, aided and abetted as they were by the veto willingly granted to the NUT. The long denial of elementary justice to the thousands of schoolmasters in the NAS undoubtedly had long-term costs. Principal amongst those 'costs' was the firm belief that militant action was both necessary and justified if justice were to be secured. I freely admit to having inherited that culture myself and preaching it accordingly. Unknowingly at the time I was reflecting the words of our founding General Secretary, Arthur Warren: "These are days when to right the wrong you are compelled to adopt measures which may be distasteful to you."

The only way of avoiding this belief, deep inside the culture of NAS for many years, would have been a greater sense of fair play on the part of politicians of both the major parties who formed governments in those times. Instead they chose the easier path of expediency. In my view they had no case to complain about NAS militancy which inevitably grew. It is hypocrisy to demand high principles and 'professional ethics' from those to whom you deny elementary justice.

The treatment of teachers in the recession-ridden years of the 1920s and '30s got no better. They were singled out for particularly severe cutbacks on salaries and pensions, which were not applied generally in the public sector. That pattern continued into the Second World War years, with 'bonuses' effectively denied to many schoolmasters and at other times depressed to facilitate back-door steps to EP. Schoolmasters' patriotism, freely given in wartime, was exploited in attempts to entrap them in permanent and inappropriate contractual concessions regarding meals duties and 'holiday' work.

The late 1940s and 1950s saw one low-pay award after another as well as 'The Calamity of 1956' – the double blow of an unwarranted pension contribution increase and another lost salary opportunity. The successful case against Sunderland, establishing the right of teachers to decline voluntary activities, proved a pivotal point in the development of the NAS, bolstering membership and influence as it geared up to take action over the continuing denial of recognition on Burnham.

Some believe the NAS's Achilles heel was its opposition to EP, which many MPs pressed the Association to drop. Perhaps the NAS might have been recognised earlier if it had complied. I doubt it. The NAS had been excluded for a variety of reasons, EP only being quoted after 1956 when the Government conceded the principle for civil servants and teachers.

It was obvious that by the end of the 1950s the NAS was indicating an acceptance of reality regarding EP even if wise political heads like Bert Rushworth and Terry Casey were letting it wither on the vine rather than stirring up a hornets' nest by seeking a formal policy decision at Conference. Despite giving assurances not to use EP as an excuse for wrecking tactics, the NAS was still denied representation. Recognition only came to the NAS in 1961 when the balance of inconvenience shifted. The NAS would cause more trouble if it were denied recognition (which it did) than the NUT would if it were granted (which it did not). Who could blame Terry Casey for expounding the 'doctrine' that the only way to fight injustice "was to make a thundering nuisance of yourselves"!

With NAS recognition secured in 1961 the era of supine capitulation by the NUT-dominated Teachers' Panel of the Burnham Committee began to crumble. The NAS injected a rightful sense of angst and anger into the business of teachers' pay negotiations, beginning by busting open the unbelievable secrecy in which Burnham had operated.

As the 1960s progressed the NAS focussed its increasing strength and membership on a number of interrelated policies. Whilst accepting the reality of EP the NAS was not prepared to accept the inevitable consequences of depressing men's salaries even further. The Association always said it was not opposed to genuine EP at the men's rate. The NAS believed the structure of the salary system was wrong. Higher pay was needed for the classroom practitioner and the longer-serving 'career teacher'. The Burnham Committee was a fundamentally flawed negotiating machine in that the major paymaster was not at the table but pulled all the important strings. The Association repeated its earlier call for a Royal Commission to examine teachers' pay and make recommendations.

The same period saw the rise to prominence of the 'career teacher', a term cleverly coined by the NAS which also featured on all its publications and official headed paper. The concept of the 'career teacher' had played a crucial role in the birth of the UWT, which soon adopted the term as the title for its journal. Concern with having to tolerate low pay, indiscipline and poor buildings for the rest of their working lives motivated a small group of women teachers in Brighton in 1965 to think about their 'union' needs. Their meeting bore some parallels with the group of men teachers in Cardiff (1913) and others elsewhere leading up to the 'Men of Cheltenham Meeting' at the NUT Conference in 1919.

The result was the establishment of the UWT in 1965 which in turn was to lead to merger with the NAS ten years later to produce a forceful organisation to pursue the interests of long-serving staff. The career teacher was crucial to the development of a first-class education service which would otherwise be difficult to build on the shifting sands of high staff turnover. The development of the career structured salary philosophy by the NAS and UWT in the 1960s was a neat, timely and apposite policy to apply to the seemingly eternal problem of low pay.

In the early days of 1919 and the twenties 'career teachers' would have probably implied men and spinsters. By the sixties social patterns were changing and more and more women were becoming career professionals, returning to work after raising their children. The NAS and UWT were alarmed that the NUT continued to promote the interests of the short-term teachers at the expense of those making a lifelong career commitment to the profession. Irritated by the NAS and UWT purloining the concept of the 'career teacher', the NUT challenged Terry Casey to define it. Terry responded there was no need to; teachers defined it for themselves and then joined us!

With recognition achieved in 1961 the NAS brought rationality as well as backbone into the pay negotiating set-up. The improvements of 1965 – arbitration, retrospection and the more explicit (although still inadequate) acknowledgement of the central government's role – were wholly driven by the NAS. The first significant step towards career structure was achieved by the 1971 arbitration, accompanied by a huge NAS and UWT demonstration.

The best thing that ever happened to teachers' pay, the Houghton Inquiry in 1974, was welcomed by the NAS and UWT as the achievement of a long campaign, but opposed by the NUT still anxious to keep the sinking Burnham ship afloat. My analogy of the "few waves of restoration coming ashore but the tide of teachers' salaries being eternally on the ebb" proved unfortunately apposite as the reference to the Clegg Commission was achieved against NASUWT opposition as a deliberate act to march away from the Houghton standard. That set the scene for the calamitous 1980s and the disastrous and unnecessarily long strike of 1985 which led directly to the abolition of Burnham as well as to the demise of the NUT's overall majority.

The abolition of teachers' negotiating rights was to prove to be a case of 'things having to get worse before getting better' as the Interim Advisory Committee, established in 1987, gave way to the School Teachers' Review Body in 1992. At last in the STRB, a development skilfully lobbied for by the NASUWT, we had a machine that was far more sensible and infinitely more efficient than the protracted Burnham negotiations. Whilst pay awards remained modest they usually exceeded those achieved by comparator groups through traditional collective bargaining. After constant tinkering with Ken Baker's wholly inappropriate 'incentive allowance' system imposed in 1987, the salary structure eventually moved decisively under New Labour in the collegiate direction. It seemed that as the pay determination machinery became more appropriate so did the salary levels and structure.

Teachers carried the huge handicap of being a large occupational group where even small percentage pay rises proved immensely expensive for the public purse. Instead of guile and hard-nosed reality, teachers had the NUT, deeply committed to principles such as the 'primacy of the basic scale' with scant regard for the practical consequences. Sir Ronald Gould's famous dictum – 'either everybody or nobody gets it' – invariably ended up with the latter.

Undoubtedly some NUT members were prepared to fight for a better salary, but there was little appetite for direct action from the majority. 'Militant' motions could be carried at Conferences, but rarely survived the admittedly rigorous and complicated rules governing NUT action. Ironically when the NUT did finally display some real determination in the great strikes of the mid-1980s, possibly under the influence of the steadily expanding NASUWT, it went overboard, "giving industrial action a bad name", as I was quoted saying at the time.

It would be idle to pretend that every NASUWT member was prepared to take militant action. On some occasions most were but there were others when feelings were mixed. The crucial difference was that the Union's leadership recognised this difficulty and worked around it. The NASUWT never had complicated rules which effectively stifled those who were prepared to take action. Schools were selected carefully, particularly in the early days of direct action. However, there had to be general support and a good rational cause to secure majorities in the Executive and at Conference.

In contrast the NUT tied itself up in knots with complicated balloting requirements at school, LEA and national levels, making militant action difficult if not impossible even when some members wished to take it. Not even Margaret Thatcher in her vicious anti-trade union legislation of the 1980s imposed such impediments on unions taking action as the NUT laid upon itself. Other teacher organisations generally considered industrial action beneath their dignity, something reserved for 'blue-collar workers', many of whom as a consequence earned higher pay.

After the social revolution of the 1960s, the fundamental reforms to secondary schooling and widespread adoption of new teaching methods in the primary sector, the British educational systems were never to be the same again. Change and counterchange were to become the sometimes bewildering norm for the remainder of the twentieth century and beyond.

With the Labour Party firmly committed to comprehensive schools and the Conservatives opposed, the politicisation of the education service had well and truly begun. The great reforming Act of 1944 was built carefully upon consensus. The 1960s heralded a more widespread and party political controversy not just on the general character of the education system but also on the internal organisation, management and governance of schools, including teaching methods themselves.

Teachers in the primary sector were liberated by the abolition of the 11 plus. The development of many new ideas for the curriculum and teaching methods gave teachers more professional autonomy even if university GCE examination boards retained much power in determining the curricula to be followed in the secondary schools. In the newer areas such as the CSE teachers exercised more influence over curricular matters as well as the examinations. Whilst most teachers exercised their professional autonomy responsibly, a minority did not. Unfortunately the political agenda was set by those reacting to the minority, conveniently alleged by some to be ever-increasing in size. The traditionalists were fed with plenty of propaganda for their cause. The scandal of the William Tyndale School broke out in 1974, providing the perfect backdrop for Prime Minister James Callaghan's Ruskin College speech in 1976 questioning whether education had lost its way.

NASUWT members, like most people, always acknowledged the personally self-fulfilling aspects of education for its own sake but never neglected the importance of qualifications and the requirements of the world of work. The basics of literacy and numeracy had to be taught. I formed the view from my own first-hand evidence in the ILEA that these sensible requirements were simply not being fulfilled in too many schools.

Classroom career teachers, in particular, became exasperated with problems over pupil behaviour, which in itself was another major reason why sensible things were not always happening. Viewing such problems in the round, the Union argued that a more relevant curriculum was required to engage the interest of the non-academic adolescent and so help motivation and reduce bad pupil behaviour.

During the course of the sixties the NAS and UWT expressed more and more concern over the issue of antisocial behaviour by some pupils in schools. At first governments, LEAs and indeed other teacher unions tried to downplay the significance of the ever-increasing problem. The Union was accused of sensationalism and worse.

The NASUWT refused to be cowed into silence and spoke up when others tried to deny the existence of the problem that was to blight the lives of so many teachers and disrupt, in some cases destroy, the educational opportunities of thousands of pupils for many years to come. In close touch with grass-roots classroom teachers, we knew we were reflecting their concerns. Alone, we took action when others and those in authority tried to insist we should tolerate such behaviour, masking their own pusillanimity, if not cowardice, in allegations that we had ulterior motives of recruitment and publicity.

The problems and the disputes were set to increase. On occasions strong disagreements emerged between the NASUWT and some head teachers, governing bodies and LEAs. Members stood their ground, refusing to teach certain pupils, taking strike action when necessary. While the issue was hotly debated in the media, few cases in relation to the size of the problem broke into the public domain with individuals and schools exposed.

All that changed dramatically in 1996 when four cases 'went public', assuming a very high media profile. That was caused by a seriously dysfunctional family publicly challenging the right of NASUWT members to refuse to teach one of their offspring. The year 1996 marked the time when officialdom, including national and local government – not to mention others – under intense pressure from the massive publicity, had at last to concede there was a problem in urgent need of attention.

Not everyone in education liked the way the NASUWT and I personally handled the cases but we knew from experience and our mailbag that parent, public and indeed teacher opinion were firmly on our side. It was no coincidence that by the time of the 2005 General Election Prime Minister Tony Blair and Leader of the Opposition Michael Howard were vying with one another to be seen as the champion of good order in schools and scourge of antisocial behaviour in society. Their successors, Prime Minister Gordon Brown and Opposition Leader David Cameron, continue the battle to the present day (2008). Whilst problems remain they are being tackled in a far more consensual way between teachers and those in authority, including national government.

The cautious NASUWT approach to comprehensive reorganisation seems today to have been well justified. It was all too often implemented on the cheap, with huge split-site institutions created almost overnight with heads and teachers ill-prepared for the management and pedagogic challenges that inevitably emerged. Both Conservative and Labour Governments have searched desperately for alternatives to the 'bog-standard comprehensive' (as graphically if unfairly labelled by Tony Blair's leading spin doctor, Alistair Campbell) without mentioning the dreaded 'S' word – selection.

The NASUWT's courageous stand on the obvious need for good discipline in schools combined well with its common-sense approach to educational reform based on experience and the 'pragmatic principle' of that which works best in practice. These features were accompanied by enlightened salary policies, notably career structured scales and collegiality, which emphasised 'the central importance of the teacher in the classroom'.

Undoubtedly we made some mistakes along the way but the sensible policies promoted by the NASUWT were backed up by an open acknowledgement that we were a union and proud of it. The unique feature of a union that separates it from all other forms of organisation is the willingness to defy employers (including government for this purpose) and breach contract by taking direct action against blatant injustice and totally unreasonable demands. Such exercise of raw muscle has to be conducted with care, for it is pitched against the greater power typically at the disposal of governments and employers. 'Guts and guile' are the ingredients of successful action.

I believe the history of the NASUWT over its first 80 years shows a consistent willingness to fight the good fight and to refuse to go away until some justice is secured. How else can one explain the quite remarkable ability of a breakaway union against all the odds and the precedents of history not just to survive but positively to prosper?

The first two years of New Labour were difficult as the Government insisted on following its predecessor's public expenditure plans. The skies brightened with a new Green Paper on the future of the teaching profession at the end of 1998 which eventually resulted in the Threshold Payments in 2002 specifically rewarding good classroom teaching, the bedrock of the NASUWT's favoured collegiate salary philosophy. Although we did not realise it at the time these were the first steps towards Social Partnership, another long-standing policy of the NASUWT.

Building on the Threshold Pay improvements the National Agreement on Standards and Workload was secured in 2003/04 under the leadership of the NASUWT and against the bitter and almost hysterical hostility of the NUT sniping from the sidelines in its self-imposed exclusion. It marked the formal establishment of a Social Partnership between the Government and school staff unions.

By this time the NASUWT with over 200,000 in-service members was the equal of the NUT in terms of size and just a few years away from 2008 when it was able to claim to be not just the largest teachers' union covering all parts of the UK but also the biggest in England and Wales. Assuming the leadership of the profession, it marked the end of the era of the NASUWT as 'a battling minority'. Accordingly, it also marks the end of this book.

Appendix A - Presidents of NAS, UWT and NASUWT

Past Presidents and Local Association	Year of Office and Conference Venue
NAS	
A.E. WARREN (Willesden)	1920-1921 Margate
S.H. HOULDSWORTH (Manchester)	1921-1922 Cardiff
G.E. CORDING (Cardiff)	1922-1923 Liverpool
W. WOODWARD (London)	1923-1924 London
F.C. GREAVES (Leeds)	1924-1925 Leeds
W.H. YOUNG BA (Liverpool)	1925-1926 Nottingham
J.A. RICE (Hull)	1926-1927 Hull
R. ANDERSON BA (London)	1927-1928 Bristol
C.C. CARTER BA (Liverpool)	1928-1929 Newcastle-upon-Tyne
C.B. DODD BA (London)	1929-1930 Leicester
W.R. SHIMMIN (Liverpool)	1930-1931 Manchester
A.L. SHIRES (Leeds)	1931-1932 Birmingham
W.E. CRAY (London)	1932-1933 Sunderland
A.H. RUSSELL BA (Bristol)	1933-1934 Southampton
H. GORDON (London)	1934-1935 Southport
F.C. ARKLESS (Sunderland)	1935-1936 Swansea
P.E. AGAR BA (Leicester)	1936-1937 Sheffield
W.L. MARSLAND (Manchester)	1937-1938 Stoke-on-Trent
A.E. EVANS MA (Liverpool)	1938-1939 Coventry
W. BARFORD (Leeds)	1939-1943 Nottingham
E.C. MARTIN (Nottingham)	1943-1944 London
E. RUSHWORTH (Calder & Ryburn)	1944-1945 Blackpool
J. MASON (Nottingham)	1945-1946 Blackpool

G.H. SNOW (Liverpool)	1946-1947 Blackpool
F.A. GIBBS (London)	1947-1948 Southend-on-Sea
B. MORTON DPA (Sheffield)	1948-1949 Scarborough
H. MEIGH BSc (London)	1949-1950 Bournemouth
G.B. BELL MC BSc (Newcastle)	1950-1951 Morecambe
W.A. TAYLOR BSc (Hull)	1951-1952 Weston-super-Mare
G. LLOYD WILLIAMS (Newport)	1952-1953 Harrogate
J.J. THOMAS (Liverpool)	1953-1954 Margate
R.I. RAND (Sunderland)	1954-1955 Porthcawl
T. SMITH BSc (London)	1955-1956 Buxton
D.I. DAVIES (Walthamstow)	1956-1957 Southsea
J.E. JENKINS (Cardiff)	1957-1958 Edinburgh
E.W. ARNOTT (Leeds)	1958-1959 Brighton
J.A.C. THOMSON MA (Scotland)	1959-1960 Llandudno
A.L. JONES (Liverpool)	1960-1961 Hastings
H.J. BELL (Croydon)	1961-1962 Blackpool
T.A. CASEY (London)	1962-1963 Plymouth
R.M. HALL BEM BCom (Newcastle-upon-Tyne)	1963-1964 Southport
A.J. SMYTH (Liverpool)	1964-1965 Folkestone
L.G. HARRIS (Bristol)	1965-1966 Edinburgh
R.R. TUNSTALL (St Helens)	1966-1967 Douglas
M.A. LANGDELL BSc ARCM (Haringey)	1967-1968 Torquay
B.F. WAKEFIELD (Southend)	1968-1969 Llandudno
E.J. PRETTY MA (Sunderland)	1969-1970 Eastbourne
R.A. SIMONS BSc (London)	1970-1971 Scarborough
R.B. COCKING (Birmingham)	1971-1972 Torbay
E.R. HOLDEN (Stretford)	1972-1973 Southport
H.H. THOMAS (Caernarvonshire)	1973-1974 Eastbourne
J.A. SCOTT (Derry County & Antrim)	1974-1975 Harrogate

UWT

M. WRIGHT	1965-1970 London
S. MORTEN	1971 Birmingham
M. BUGG	1972 Cambridge
M. SMYTH	1973 Liverpool
C. SKEAVINGTON	1974 Portsmouth

NASUWT

J. CHALK (London)	1975-1976 Brighton
L. COOPER BSc (Barkston Ash)	1976-1977 Blackpool
B. FARRELL (Halton)	1977-1978 Torbay
C.S. JONES (Basildon & Brentwood)	1978-1979 Harrogate
C. SKEAVINGTON MEd FRSA (Jersey)	1979-1980 Eastbourne
C.F. ABRAHAM (Devon East)	1980-1981 Harrogate
A.M.S. POOLE (Merton)	1981-1982 Brighton
E.E. POWELL BA FRGS (South Glamorgan)	1982-1983 Blackpool
G.W. LEE JP (London)	1983-1984 Eastbourne
P. MATTHEWS (Sedgefield)	1984-1985 Llandudno
J. BOONE (Bolton)	1985-1986 Torquay
J.M. INMAN BA NDA Dip REd (Leek)	1986-1987 Scarborough
E.R. O'KANE MA Dip Ed (Belfast)	1987-1988 Bournemouth
D. BATTYE MSc (Sheffield)	1988-1989 Blackpool
G. TERRELL BA (Oxon) Dip Ed JP (Merton)	1989-1990 Eastbourne
M. CARNEY (Peterlee)	1990-1991 Scarborough
S. ROGERS BA (Sheffield)	1991-1992 Bournemouth
M. LITTLEWOOD FRSA (Middleton)	1992-1993 Scarborough
J. ROWLAND BA (Jarrow, Hebburn & Boldon)	1993-1994 Bournemouth
R. KIRK (Newark)	1994-1995 Blackpool

O. GUNN (Aycliffe)	1995 Eastbourne
P. COLE (Sandwell)	1995-1997 Glasgow
B. FERGUSON (York)	1997-1998 Bournemouth
M. MORGAN (Devon)	1998-1999 Scarborough
W. MORLEY (Sefton)	1999-2000 Eastbourne
M. JOHNSON (Lewisham)	2000-2001 Llandudno
T. HARDMAN (Liverpool)	2001-2002 Jersey
P. BUTLER (Bedfordshire)	2002-2003 Scarborough
T. BLADEN (Darlington)	2003-2004 Bournemouth
P. LEREW (NE Hampshire)	2004-2005 Llandudno
P. McLOUGHLIN (Stockport)	2005-2006 Brighton
B. GARVEY (Wakefield)	2006-2007 Birmingham
J. MAYES (Knowsley)	2007-2008 Belfast
A. HAEHNER (Croydon)	2008-2009 Birmingham
J. CHAPMAN (Cheltenham Cotswold)	2009-2010 Bournemouth
C. LINES (West Suffolk)	2010-2011 Birmingham
J. RIMMER (Warrington)	2011-2012 Glasgow

Appendix B - Honorary Treasurers

NASUWT

F.G. Reynolds	1920-1923
W.H. Thoday	1923-1926
W. Woodward	1926-1929
R. Anderson	1929-1941
C.C. Carter	1941-1946
H. Gordon	1946-1951
E. Rushworth	1951-1956
G. Lloyd Williams	1956-1965
A.L. Jones	1965-1969
B.F. Wakefield	1969-1970
A.J. Smyth	1970-1975
R.B. Cocking	1975-1982
L. Cooper	1982-1987
G.W. Lee	1987-1990
D. Battye	1990-1992
M. Carney	1992-2002
S. Rogers	2002-2009
B. Cookson	2009-

Appendix C - General Secretaries

NAS

A.E. WARREN	1923-41
R. ANDERSON	1941-56
E. RUSHWORTH	1956-63
T.A. CASEY	1963-75

UWT

S. ROGERS	1965-67
B. GANDY	1967-69
G. JONES	1969-70
P. YAFFE	1970-75

NASUWT

T.A. CASEY	1976-83
F.A. SMITHIES	1983-90
N.R.A. de GRUCHY	1990-2002
E.R. O'KANE	2002-04
C. KEATES	2004-

Appendix D - NASUWT Membership 1923- 2008

Year	Membership	Year	Membership
1923	5113	1966	38095
1924	5813	1967	39256
1925	5169	1968	39967
1926	6173	1969	44945
1927	6561	1970	50654
1928	6812	1971	55646
1929	7024	1972	57603
1930	7610	1973	61810
1931	8595	1974	65030
1932	7911	1975	est. 69000
1933	8241	1976	89305
1934	8882	1977	102031
1935	9328	1978	111566
1936	9507	1979	122058
1937	9672	1980	123896
1938	10923	1981	119545
1939	10103	1982	120241
1940	9602	1983	119668
1941	9353	1984	126453
1942	no record	1985	127612
1943	9359	1986	123945
1944	8801	1987	120544
1945	8888	1988	117610
1946	8786	1989	118230
1947	10305	1990	119810
1948	11148	1991	121142
1949	12420	1992	127365
1950	13513	1993	13 8381
1951	13199	1994	146266
1952	13714	1995	157146
1953	14478	1996	165501
1954	15114	1997	172852
1955	16679	1998	178518
1956	17484	1999	180652
1957	18268	2000	183681
1958	19045	2001	200257
1959	21930	2002	211779
1960	23623	2003	223486
1961	31344	2004	236005
1962	31887	2005	248479
1963	33252	2006	251763
1964	35457	2007	265202
1965	37558	2008	274911

Appendix E - NASUWT Membership
'Market Share'(i)

The calculation of teacher numbers and union memberships are subject to many complications including differences in methods of compilation, regions covered and definitional issues. The following information is therefore approximate but an accurate indication of trends.

Table 1 England & Wales

Year	Total Teacher Numbers	NASUWT In-service Members	Share of 'Market'
1923	182085	5113	2.8%
1938	191739	10923	5.7%
1950	207500	13513	6.5%
1960	260900	23623	9.1%
1961	283000	31344	11.1%
1969	347,000	44945	13.0%
1970	349600	50654	14.5%
1974	413300	65030	15.7%
1976	434000	89305	20.6%
1980	436700	123896	28.4%

Table 2 UK

1985	505000	127612	25.3%
1988	491200	117610	23.9%
1990	497500	119810	24.1%
1995	497487	157146	31.6%
2000	497533	183681	36.9%
2002	505906	211779	41.9%

Table 3 England, Wales, Northern Ireland

2002	455932	209279	45.9%

Appendix F - Inflation

Composite Price Index: annual percentage change
1900-2003 (ii)

Year	%				
1900	5.1	1935	0.7	1970	6.4
1901	0.5	1936	0.7	1971	9.4
1902	----	1937	3.4	1972	7.1
1903	0.4	1938	1.6	1973	9.2
1904	- 0.2	1939	2.8	1974	16.0
1905	0.4	1940	16.8	1975	24.2
1906	----	1941	10.8	1976	16.5
1907	1.2	1942	7.1	1977	15.8
1908	0.5	1943	3.4	1978	8.3
1909	0.5	1944	2.7	1979	13.4
1910	0.9	1945	2.8	1980	18.0
1911	0.1	1946	3.1	1981	11.9
1912	3.0	1947	7.0	1982	8.6
1913	- 0.4	1948	7.7	1983	4.6
1914	- 0.3	1949	2.8	1984	5.0
1915	12.5	1950	3.1	1985	6.1
1916	18.1	1951	9.1	1986	3.4
1917	25.2	1952	9.2	1987	4.2
1918	22.0	1953	3.1	1988	4.9
1919	10.1	1954	1.8	1989	7.8
1920	15.4	1955	4.5	1990	9.5
1921	- 8.6	1956	4.9	1991	5.9
1922	-14.0	1957	3.7	1992	3.7
1923	- 6.0	1958	3.0	1993	1.6
1924	- 0.7	1959	0.6	1994	2.4
1925	0.3	1960	1.0	1995	3.5
1926	- 0.8	1961	3.4	1996	2.4
1927	- 2.4	1962	4.3	1997	3.1
1928	- 0.3	1963	2.0	1998	3.4
1929	- 0.9	1964	3.3	1999	1.5
1930	- 2.8	1965	4.8	2000	3.0
1931	- 4.3	1966	3.9	2001	1.8
1932	- 2.6	1967	2.5	2002	1.7
1933	- 2.1	1968	4.7	2003	2.9
1934	----	1969	5.4		

Appendix G - Average Salaries
England & Wales

Full-time qualified teachers in maintained nursery, primary and secondary schools sector
1974- 2007   31 March each year

Year	Cash prices			March 2007 prices*		
	Nursery/ primary	Secondary	All	Nursery/ primary	Secondary	All
1974	2120	2390	2260	16660	18780	17760
1975	3220	3550	3390	20890	23030	21990
1976	3790	4110	3960	20290	22010	21200
1977	4180	4460	4330	19170	20460	19860
1978	4410	4680	4560	18540	19680	19170
1979	4900	5180	5060	18760	19830	19370
1980	5920	6220	6090	18930	19890	19470
1981	7430	7790	7640	21100	22120	21690
1982	8090	8460	8300	20820	21770	21360
1983	8670	9050	8890	21320	22260	21860
1984	9160	9580	9400	21400	22380	21960
1985	9660	10160	9950	21280	22380	21920
1986	10490	11120	10850	22170	23500	22930
1987	11970	12740	12410	24320	25890	25210
1988	12920	13780	13400	25370	27060	26310
1989	13850	14830	14380	25210	26990	26170
1990	14500	16020	15520	24410	26970	26130
1991	16490	17720	17140	25650	27560	26660
1992	18450	19950	19230	27590	29830	28750
1993	19970	21470	20750	29300	31500	30450
1994	20280	21630	20970	29090	31030	30080
1995	20860	22200	21550	28910	30760	29860
1996	21370	22730	22060	28830	30670	29760
1997	22080	23480	22790	29040	30880	29980
1998	22700	24130	23430	28850	30670	29780
1999	23570	25060	24340	29360	31210	30320

2000	24550	25980	25280	29800	31530	30680
2001	26210	27980	27120	31110	33210	32190
2002	27590	29500	28580	32320	34550	33480
2003	29290	31300	30340	33280	35560	34470
2004	30540	32510	31580	33820	36000	34970
2005	31700	33750	32760	34010	36210	35150
2006	32800	34720	34000	34380	36390	35640
2007	33800	35700	34810	33800	35700	34810

*Figures are adjusted using the all-times RPI

Sources: School Workforce in England (including LA level figures Jan 2008 (Revised) DCSF

DCSF time series – teachers' pay; ONS –CSDB database series CHAW

Appendix H - Educational Policy Publications 1980s

1 Pupil Profiles
2 Curriculum Related Staffing Levels
3 Middle Schools
4 Community Education
5 Nursery Education
6 Initial Teacher Training
7 The Staffing of Primary Schools
8 In-Service Training of Teachers
9 Raising Educational Standards: The Need for Good Order
10 Headteacher Selection and Training
11 HMI Inspections and Publication of HMI Reports
12 LEA Provision for 1-19 Year Olds and Post-Statutory Education and
   Training
13 'Education for All' – The Swann Report
14 The Development of Higher Education into the 1990s
15 Music from 5-16
16 Role of LEA Advisory Services
17 Home Economics from 5-16
18 Schoolteachers Numbers in the Longer Term
19 Review of Vocational Qualifications in England and Wales
20 New In-Service Training Grants Scheme 1987-88
21 Special Educational Needs in Mainstream Education
22 Young People at Risk
23 Micro-Electronics in Education
33 Teacher Involvement in Examinations and the Case for Remuneration
34 'A' Levels
35 Admission of Pupils to Maintained Schools
36 Charges for School Activities
37 Community Education
38 Education and Training 14-19
39 Educational Visits and Journeys
40 English Language (Kingman Committee)
41 Ethnically Based Statistics on Pupils and on School Teachers
42 Foreign Languages in the School Curriculum
43 Geography from 5-16

44 Grant Maintained Schools

45 Grant Related In-Service Training

46 National Curriculum 5-16

47 Post Statutory Education and Training

48 Records of Achievement

49 Educational Provision for the Under Fives

50 Report on Primary Education

51 Review of Vocational Educations

52 Schoolteacher Numbers and Deployment

53 Section 11 Provision for Ethnic Minorities

54 Sex Education at School

55 Special Educational Needs in Mainstream Education

56 TVEI Extension

57 Teacher Supply in Mathematics, Physics and Technology

58 The ERA 1988: Special Educational Needs

59 The Modular Curriculum

60 The Role of LEA Advisory Services

61 The Teacher Governor

62 Discipline in Schools

63 Discipline or Disorder in Schools: A Disturbing Choice

64 The Supply and Employment of Teachers

65 Induction Year and In-Service Training

66 Education: Policies – Resources – Standards

67 A New Training Initiative

Appendix J - Equality Publications Post 1988 Education Reform Act

'Action for Equality'
1 ERA and Equal Opportunities for the Teacher – A Practical Guide Series:
(1) Adotion Leave
(2) Advice on Pay and Conditions
(3) Appointment Procedures
(4   Appraisal
(5) Career Breaks
(6) Compassionate Leave
(7) Disciplinary/Competence Agreements
(8) Employment Policy for Disabled Persons
(9) Equal Opportunities: A Code of Practice
(10) Facilities for Union representatives
(11) Governors' Guide
(12) Grievance Procedure
(13) Health Screening for Employees
(14) Health and Safety
(15) Job Descriptions
(16) Job Sharing Agreements
(17) Leave of Absence
(18) Local Management of Schools
(19) Maternity Leave
(20) Medical Leave/Occupational Health
(21) Parental Leave
(22) Paternity Leave
(23) Redeployment
(24) Retirement and Early retirement
(25) Safety Policy
(26) Sexual Harrassment
(27) Time Off Agreement
(28) Racial Harrassment
(29) Wage and Salary Grading

2 Improving the Health of Women at Work
3 A School Equal Opportunity Policy
4 Childcare and After Hours Use of School Premises
5 Developing a School/College Based Policy on Racist Behaviour
6 Part Time Teachers
7 Report to Conference: Black Teachers and Employment
8 The Education of Travellers
9 Strategies for the Elimination of Bias in Appraisal

Notes to Appendices

(i) Appendix E

In Table 1 I have taken B.R. Mitchell's (British Historical Statistics 1988) compilation from official sources of numbers of teachers in state schools in England and Wales from 1923-1980 which is based on full time equivalents (FTEs) including part-timers.

Teacher numbers for Table 2 are based on FTEs as published by the DfE (Form 618G) for England & Wales, together with figures published by the ONS for the UK based in part on figures sourced from DENI (Northern Ireland) and the Scottish Executive. However, the DENI and Scottish figures relate only to full-time teachers. I have therefore adjusted the DENI and Scottish figures to include part-timers on a FTE basis, increasing them by 7%. In Table 3 I have discounted Scotland in respect of teacher numbers and NASUWT membership.

Post Second World War until 1990 figures were rounded to the nearest 100.

In Table 2 I quote the NASUWT market share based on the whole of the UK. This is in recognition of the emphasis the NASUWT began to place upon its unique 'whole UK' coverage during the 1980s. The systems of education particularly in respect of Scotland and Northern Ireland are quite different from England and Wales. Furthermore, by the end of the 1970s the NASUWT was becoming a significant player in Northern Ireland.

Table 3 shows the effect of discounting Scotland both in respect of NASUWT membership and overall teacher numbers. The evidence points to the NASUWT securing a remarkable increase in the share of the teacher market in England, Wales and Northern Ireland.

England and Wales remained the main recruiting regions for all the school based unions apart from the Welsh UCAC and the EIS who had obviously self-defining areas. In addition to the NASUWT the ATL also recruited in Northern Ireland. The NUT restricted itself to England and Wales. However all the unions had other additional groups of members to England and Wales state maintained schools. The ATL was prominent in the private sector. The NUT had affiliations from other groups such as the Association of Domestic Science

Teachers and the Youth and Community Workers. The NASUWT was prominent in Jersey, Guernsey, the Isle of Man, Gibraltar and the Service Children's Schools and also recruited qualified instructors.

Overall union memberships inevitably exceeded total teacher numbers. Supply and part-time teachers (not to mention the category described as 'Others'), who must number at least 50,000, count as full members of unions even if paying reduced subscriptions. Where they are included in official statistics it is normally on the basis of FTEs.

(ii) Appendix F

Source: Office for National Statistics, Economic Trends 604, published March 2004, Composite Price Index: annual percentage change: 1751 to 2003.

The index is based on both official and unofficial sources covering the period from 1750 to 2003 to present a composite price index facilitating analysis over a long period of time during which the annual RPI has been rebased on several occasions and the basket of goods and services upon which it is calculated updated to take account of different spending patterns.

At least from 1949 onwards the results of the above table equate to the annual movements in the Retail Price Index (all items) based on 1987=100.

Between 1750 and 1938 prices rose by a little over three times.
Between 1750 and 2003 prices rose by approximately 140 times.
Most of the inflation has taken place post 1938 with prices rising more than forty fold.

Index

11 plus 52, 89, 97, 343, 346, 348, 350, 454, 851

AAM (Association of Assistant Mistresses) 44, 45, 97, 98, 116, 117, 119, 465

Aberfan 355

ACAS (Advisory, Conciliation and Arbitration Service) 638–40, 641–49, 653–57, 661–62, 670–71, 673, 677–78, 679, 684

ACAS Memorandum Agreement 642–43, 644–49, 650–51, 653, 654–57, 667–71, 683, 684–89, 709

ACC (Association of County Councils) 273–74, 361, 364, 617, 622, 629, 669, 701

accelerated progression 713, 716

ACSTT (Advisory Committee on the Supply and Training of Teachers) 331, 455–56

ACT (Association of Career Teachers) 432–33, 434

Action on Indiscipline: A Practical Guide for Teachers (NASUWT, 1979) 476

Adams, Fred (NAS) 6

Advanced Skills Teachers *see* ASTs

Advisory Committee on the Supply and Training of Teachers *see* ACSTT

Advisory, Conciliation and Arbitration Service *see* ACAS

AEC (Association of Education Committees) 133, 190, 235–36, 247, 273–74, 294, 352

AHM (Association of Head Mistresses) 44, 45

Alexander, Sir William 151, 155, 172, 174, 222–23, 224, 235–36, 243, 244–45, 247, 256, 259, 271–72, 274, 346–47

AMA (Assistant Masters' Association) 8, 45, 417, 465

AMA (Association of Metropolitan Authorities) 271, 273–74, 361, 611, 617, 622, 629, 630, 701

AMMA (Assistant Masters and Mistresses Association) 45, 176, 363, 381, 385, 606, 622, 635, 655, 658, 661, 670, 692, 706, 712, 728, 841

  ACAS Memorandum Agreement 641, 642, 646, 650, 685, 687, 688, 689

  Coventry Agreement 663, 667, 669, 671, 672, 673, 674, 679

  Grand Graffiti Dispute 481, 483, 484

Northern Ireland 335

Nottingham Agreement 677, 680, 681, 683

TPC Act 686, 689

Ancillary Assistance in Schools (NAS) 327–28

ancillary staff 120, 329, 331, 462, 839

Anderson, Richard (Dick) (NAS) 27, 33, 50, 52, 55–56, 63, 64, 65, 69, 78, 79, 81, 225, 388

anti-apartheid movement 386

antisocial behaviour 2, 463–72, 473–79, 489, 504–5, 507–8, 565–69, 570–71, 851–52

Elton Report 477, 490–94, 504

appeal panels 478, 494, 522–23, 565, 568, 570, 572, 596, 600, 601

Glaisdale School 509, 510–11, 512, 540

Hebburn School 518, 519

Ridings School 543–44

Westminster Junior School 573, 574

APU (Assessment Performance Unit) 454

ASCL (Association of School and College Leaders) 45

Assistant Masters and Mistresses Association *see* AMMA

Assistant Masters' Association *see* AMA

Association of Assistant Mistresses *see* AAM

Association of Career Teachers *see* ACT

Association of County Councils *see* ACC

Association of Education Committees *see* AEC

Association of Head Mistresses *see* AHM

Association of Metropolitan Authorities *see* AMA

Association of School and College Leaders *see* ASCL

Association of Teachers and Lecturers *see* ATL

Association of Teachers in Technical Institutions *see* ATTI

ASTs (Advanced Skills Teachers) 644, 785, 786–87, 798, 815, 840

ATL (Association of Teachers and Lecturers) 61, 376, 394, 439, 441, 546, 774, 787, 813

Northern Ireland 335, 823

STRB 777, 841

'Test Boycott' 739, 746, 747, 748, 754, 755, 757

workloads 826, 833, 836

ATTI (Association of Teachers in Technical Institutions) 116, 119, 122, 167, 168, 171, 177, 210, 260, 303, 306, 383, 384

Baker, Ken 692–93, 694, 706, 709, 710, 711, 712, 730–31, 750

ACAS Memorandum Agreement 684, 685–87, 688–89

Coventry Agreement 672, 675, 676

Elton Report 490, 491, 492, 494

Nottingham Agreement 675–76, 677, 679

TNG 707, 717

TPC Act 686, 688, 689–90, 691

Ballymoney Castle High School, Northern Ireland 336

Barber, Michael 765–66, 796, 797

Barford, William (Leo) (NAS) 24, 67, 77, 78, 79

Benevolent Fund (NAS) 48, 62, 63, 445

Bennett, Gordon 409–10

Beveridge Plan 95, 105

Bishop of Llandaff High School, Cardiff (1991) 495–96, 573

'Black Papers' (1969) 347

Blair, Tony (New Lab) 111, 380, 489, 571, 772, 776, 781, 783, 799, 811, 852

Blunkett, David (New Lab) 321, 772, 775, 776, 783–84, 787, 791, 792, 795, 800, 802

'Cover to Contract' 825, 827, 828–29

Manton Primary School 558

Teachers-Meeting the Challenge of Change 800, 801–2, 809, 813, 814

Boyle, Sir Edward 119, 166–67, 170, 241–42, 328

Breakaway Unions (Lerner, 1961) 2

British Teachers' Council 357, 388, 389

Britton, Sir Edward (Ted) (NUT) 152–53, 254, 255, 259, 278, 306, 468

Brown, Gordon (New Lab) 781, 852

Bullock Inquiry (1972) 331–32

Burgundy Book 360–61, 694

Burnham Committee 17, 89–90, 112, 115, 118–19, 157, 165–66, 167–71, 174–75, 183–84, 188, 361–62, 690–91

1919 pay negotiations 18–19, 183–84

1920s pay negotiations 20, 25, 184, 186, 187

1930s pay negotiations 194, 198

1940s pay negotiations 199–200, 202–3, 206–7

1950s pay negotiations 208, 209, 215, 227–30, 235–36, 237

1960s pay negotiations 149, 150–51, 174–75, 176, 239–40, 241, 242, 243, 245–46, 248, 249–50, 253

1970s pay negotiations 253, 255, 257–60, 263–66, 271–73, 276–78, 279, 283–85, 286–87

ACAS Memorandum Agreement 645–49, 658–60

Education Act (1944) 116, 117, 118, 119, 158, 165, 202

JWPSS 365–67, 619–20, 623, 625–26, 632, 644

NAS representation 3, 112–14, 119–21, 124–26, 135–42, 143, 156–64, 847, 848, 849

Provisional Minimum Scale 15, 183–84, 185

Butler, R.A. (Rab)(Con) 81, 88, 114, 115, 201, 210

Byers, Stephen (New Lab) 394, 512, 536, 783, 784, 785, 790, 791–92, 793, 795, 844

Callaghan, James (Lab) 377, 453, 454, 851

Campaign on Workload (NASUWT) 731, 732, 733–42, 769, 826–27

Wandsworth v NASUWT case 586, 730, 742–48, 749, 751–52, 753–54

Cardiff Schoolmasters' Association 10–11

career teachers 2, 122, 180, 234, 246, 249, 279–80, 849

structured salary scales 43, 158, 178, 206, 241, 253, 256, 260–61, 265, 268, 271

UWT 429, 430, 432, 434, 435–36

Carlisle, Mark (Con) 363, 364, 383, 442, 611, 614–15

Carney, Mick (NASUWT) 622, 673, 720, 749, 753, 806

Casey, Terry (NAS/NASUWT) 64, 88, 131, 152–53, 335, 375, 381, 457, 618–19, 690, 848, 849

antisocial behaviour 470, 471

Burnham Committee 138–39, 171, 172, 245–46

Catch 'em Young project 476

Durham Dispute 398, 405, 407

extraneous duties 361, 364

Northern Ireland 338–39

pensions 296, 298, 303, 305–6, 311

Sacred Heart RC School Dispute 411, 412, 413, 414, 415, 416, 418, 419, 424, 427

Castle, Barbara (Lab) 376–77, 407

Catch 'em Young project (NAS) 476

Cazalet, Thelma (Con) 116–17, 201

Certificate of Secondary Education see CSE

'Charter for Change - Reduce Workload, Raise Standards' (2002) 836

Children and their Primary School (Plowden, 1966) 327, 328–30

church schools 44, 90–91

Churchill, Winston (Con) 116–17, 174, 187, 212, 216

Circular 10/65 (1965) 246, 343–46, 411

Circular 10/70 (1970) 346

Circular 10/99 (1999) 565, 566, 567

Circular 1350 52

Circular 1596 (1942) 75–76

Circular 16/68 (1968) 108–10

Circular 2/98 (1998) 791, 792–96, 804, 807–8, 817–18, 829

Circular 5/63 (1963) 106, 107, 108, 354

Circular 6/59 (1959) 99

Circulars 8-13/94 (1994) 504, 505

Clarke, Ken 701, 703, 704, 722, 723, 724, 726, 727, 750–51

class sizes 94–95, 97, 247, 373, 775, 776–77, 799

CLEA/ST (Council of LEAs/School Teachers' Committee) 341, 354, 358–59, 424, 694

  ACAS Memorandum Agreement 648, 650, 686, 687–88

  Burgundy Book 360–61, 694

  conditions of service 360–61, 362–64, 694

  COSWOP 362–63, 611

HASAWA 356

Clegg Commission 287, 316–17, 362, 609, 610–12, 849

Clegg, Hugh 287, 609

Clegg Report 611–12, 613, 614, 717

Cleveland LEA (formerly Teesside LEA)

  Sacred Heart RC School 422, 423, 424

Cobb, Cyril 16, 18

Cocking, Ron (NAS) 43, 264, 357–58, 439, 468, 618

collective bargaining 165, 688, 717

collegiate approach 178, 349, 624, 664–65, 712, 786–87, 800, 801, 845, 850, 853

comprehensive schools 89, 97, 98, 343–46, 347–48, 349–53, 458, 464, 852–53

  Sacred Heart RC School 230, 352–53, 411–18, 419–26, 430

conditions of service 1, 2, 360–61, 362–63, 365–67, 611, 615, 694

Conditions of Service WP *see* COSWOP

Coopers and Lybrand report 785–86, 788, 813

Cording, George (NUT/NAMT/NAS) 9–11, 12, 13, 31, 32, 34, 341

corporal punishment 478–79

COSWOP (Conditions of Service WP) 362, 363, 364, 611, 615

Council of LEAs/School Teachers' Committee *see* CLEA/ST

Coventry Agreement 663–70, 671–72, 673–74, 675–76, 679

'Cover to Contract' (NASUWT) 825, 827–28

Crosland, Anthony (Lab) 174, 343, 389–90

Crossing the Threshold (NASUWT) 819, 820

CSE (Certificate of Secondary Education) 97, 461, 851

de Gruchy, Nigel (NASUWT) 521, 714–15, 718–19, 720, 775, 781, 783–84, 811–12, 833, 834, 844, 853

   Campaign on Workload 731, 732, 733–38

   Elton Report 494

   Glaisdale School 509, 511–13, 515

   Grand Graffiti Dispute 487

   Hebburn School 517, 520

   'Let Teachers Teach' 792, 795, 796

   Pay Review Body 725, 726–27

   Ridings School 530, 539, 544, 545, 547–51, 554–55, 560–61, 563–64

   Social Partnership 778–79

   Teachers-Meeting the Challenge of Change 373, 800

   Wandsworth v NASUWT case 744–48, 753–54

Dearing Interim Report 758, 761, 762, 763

Dearing Report 764–65

Dearing, Sir Ron 730, 751, 755–56, 760, 762, 763–64, 766, 767, 771

'Discipline in Schools' (NAS, 1974) 470, 472

Down County Secondary Schools (Bexhill-on-Sea, 1967) 246, 351–52

Dunblane Primary School, Scotland (1996) 507

Durham Dispute (1969) 246, 247–48, 397–409, 410

Durham LEA 96, 230, 352, 369

   Durham Dispute 247–48, 397–401, 402–3, 404, 405–8, 409, 410

   Pelton Roseberry School 468–69

   Sedgefield School 471

Dyfed LEA 604–5

EAZs (Education Action Zones) 786, 798–99

Eccles, Sir David (Con) 98, 106, 130, 156–58, 165, 166, 215–17, 220, 227–28, 389

   NAS representation 121, 124, 125, 128, 159, 160, 161, 163–64

   Superannuation Bill 218, 220, 223, 224, 226, 228

Economist Intelligence Unit *see* EIU

Education: A Framework for Expansion (1972) 331

Education Act (1902) 181

Education Act (1918) 16, 48, 50, 102, 181, 450

Education Act (1944) 4, 52, 82, 88, 89–92, 94, 104, 105, 220, 225, 357, 388, 851

   Burnham Committee 116, 117, 118, 119, 158, 165, 202

   class sizes 247

   equal pay 116–17, 201

   ROSLA 451, 470

   salaries 85, 89–90, 181

Education and Standards Framework Act (1998) 91

Education International *see* EI

Education (No. 2) Act (1986) 487, 488, 570, 572

Education of the Adolescent (Hadow, 1926) 51, 52, 54–55, 61, 94, 450–51

Education (Provision of Meals) Act (1906) 102, 104

Education Reform Act (ERA, 1988) 90, 91, 369, 370, 454, 692, 696–701, 706, 730–31, 734, 750, 799

Educational Institute of Scotland *see* EIS

Educational Reconstruction (1943) 82, 84–85, 201

EEC (European Economic Community) 273, 311, 380

EI (Education International) 3, 382

EIS (Educational Institute of Scotland) 68–69, 139, 381, 439, 609, 628, 651, 811

EIU (Economist Intelligence Unit) 246, 249, 256, 282

elementary schools 67, 73, 85–86, 115, 387

Elementary Teachers' (Superannuation) Act (1898) 290

Elton, Lord 490, 491, 493–94

Elton Report (1989) 477, 490–94, 504

Emergency Training Scheme (1945) 87–88, 95

Emmott Committee (1922) 28, 51, 289, 290, 291

English 705, 733, 734, 736, 760, 761

equal opportunities 446–49

equal pay 1, 2, 4–8, 9, 120, 178, 183, 200, 201, 206, 209, 210–11, 216, 229–30, 236

   Education Act (1944) 116–17, 201

   NAS 5, 6, 8, 40, 121–22, 123–24, 130–31, 160–61, 240, 847, 848

   NUT 5, 6, 11, 13, 18, 46, 65, 98, 201

   NUWT 10, 44, 115–16

Equal Pay (LSA, 1921) 7

ERA (1988) *see* Education Reform Act

ETTUC (European Teachers' Trade Union Committee) 380, 381

ETUCE (European Trade Union Committee for Education) 381, 382

European Economic Community *see* EEC

extraneous duties 75–76, 84, 86–87, 103–4, 108–10, 192, 327, 361, 362–63

    school meals 104–6, 107, 108, 109, 110, 224–25

    Sunderland Case 212, 225–27, 232, 848

Fairness at Work (1998) 379–80

Faye, Joseph (Sacred Heart RC School) 412, 415–16, 417, 418, 419, 426

FE (Further Education) 116, 167, 282, 299, 383–85, 452, 609, 630, 636, 641

Ferguson, Barrie (NASUWT) 356, 530, 545, 547, 781

FHE Act (1992) 773–74

First World War 4, 11, 101, 102

'Fisher' Education Act (1918) 16, 48, 50, 102, 181

Fisher, H.A.L. (Lib) 8, 16–17, 25, 26, 27, 29, 112, 180, 183, 186, 189

    Teachers' Superannuation Act 16–17, 27, 28, 290

Fletcher-Cooke, Charles (Con) 129–30

Friern (mixed) School, London (1931) 56

Fullam, John (Sacred Heart RC School) 419, 426–28

Fulton, Peter (Teesside LEA) 413, 416, 424

GA (Government Actuary)

    Notional Fund 307, 308, 310, 317, 318–19, 320, 321

    TSS 212–13, 217, 292, 312, 317

Galbraith, Sam 811

Gardner, Harry (NAS) 93, 421, 618

GCE (General Certificate of Education) 97, 416, 458, 461, 700, 851

GCHQ dispute 379

GCSE (General Certificate of Secondary Education) 461, 692, 694, 700, 704, 711, 716

Geddes Axe (1922) 6, 26, 27–28, 180, 185, 186, 290

Geddes, Sir Eric 25–26, 52, 66, 185

General Certificate of Education *see* GCE

General Certificate of Secondary Education *see* GCSE

Gibbs, Frank (LSA) 59, 74, 78, 79, 80, 190–91, 192, 193, 194, 197

Gibraltar (NASUWT) 439

Gilling-Smith, Dryden 257, 289, 296, 297, 298–99, 300, 302, 303, 308, 313

Given, Bruce (LSA) 6, 132, 139–40, 142, 144, 145–46

Gladstone, Bill (NAS) 117, 397, 399–400, 402, 403, 404, 408

Glaisdale School, Nottingham (1996) 509–16, 540

global sum 151, 158–59, 166, 167, 168, 169, 176, 237, 708, 725

GM (grant maintained) schools 679, 699–700, 720, 799

Gordon, Harold (NAS) 58, 69, 79, 96

Gould, Sir Ronald (NUT) 96, 151–52, 153–54, 168, 174, 222, 245, 254–55, 270, 388, 404, 656, 850

   Interim Pay Campaign 251–52, 253

Government Actuary *see* GA

grammar schools 73–74, 85, 89, 97, 102, 204, 343–44, 346

Grand Graffiti Dispute, Manchester (1985) 480–89

'Gregg' (Hebburn School) 517–19, 520–21, 575

Groves, Paul (Lancastrian Secondary Boys School, Chichester) 147–48

GTC (General Teaching Council) 326, 387, 389–96

Hadow Report (1926) 51, 52, 54–55, 61, 94, 450–51

Hailsham, Lord 118–19, 120

Half our Future (Newsom, 1963) 327, 328

Hannington, Ray (NAS) 230, 231

Harris, Henry Bolton (LSA) 22–23, 25

HASAWA (Health and Safety and Welfare at Work Act, 1974) 356

Hatton, Derek (Liverpool LEA) 370

HayMcBer report (2000) 812, 813, 814, 815

headships 54–55, 56, 58, 59, 60, 265

Healey, Dennis (Lab) 368, 453

Health and Safety and Welfare at Work Act (1974) *see* HASAWA

health and safety issues 355, 356, 699

Heath, Edward (Con) 42, 258, 266, 274, 345–46, 377, 391

Heath Government (1970-74) 258, 266, 274, 345–46, 377, 391

Hebburn School, South Tyneside (1996) 517–21, 575

Henderson, Sydney (NAS) 404

Heseltine, Michael (Con) 368, 723–24

Higher Education (Robbins, 1960) 327

HMA (Head Masters' Association) 45, 119, 473

HMI (Her Majesty's Inspector) 49, 460–61

Holden, Ray (NAS) 367, 378, 383, 384

Horsburgh, Florence (Con) 117, 212, 213, 214, 215, 345

Houghton Committee (1974) 276, 277, 278–79, 280–86, 287, 361, 362, 604, 605–7, 717, 849

IAC (Interim Advisory Committee) 693, 707–10, 711, 712, 713–14, 715–18, 721–22, 723, 724–25, 743

'Ian' (Westminster Junior School) 573–75

ICTU (Irish Congress of Trade Unions) 380

IEP (Individual Education Plans) 789, 819

IFFTU (International Federation of Free Teachers' Unions) 380, 381–82, 688

ILEA (Inner London Education Authority) 272, 275, 277, 365, 468, 472, 477, 478–79

William Tyndale Junior School 454, 457, 465, 851

ILO (International Labour Organisation) 173, 688, 710–11, 712, 723

indiscipline 466–69, 474, 475, 476–78, 504–5

Elton Report 477, 490–94, 504

Individual Education Plans see IEP

industrial relations 63, 376–78, 572

Wandsworth v NASUWT case 586, 730, 742–48, 749, 751–52, 753–54

Industrial Relations Act (1971) 355, 377, 474, 597

Inner London Education Authority see ILEA

Interim Pay Campaign (1969/70) 40–41, 251–52, 253–61, 267, 437

International Federation of Free Teachers' Unions see IFFTU

International Labour Organisation see ILO

INTO (Irish National Teachers Organisation) 334–35, 339, 340, 381, 823

Iraq invasion 380

Irish Congress of Trade Unions see ICTU

Jackson, Margaret (Lab) 455, 457

Jackson, Ralph (NAS) 400–401, 403

James Report (1972) 330–31

'John' (Spence-Young case) 498–500, 501

Joint Four 44, 97, 112, 115, 116, 171, 204, 250, 263, 268, 389 see also AAM; AHM; AMA; HMA

Joint Two Agreement (NAS/UWT) 39–40, 41, 264, 429, 430, 432, 433–35

Joint Working Party on Salary Structure *see* JWPSS

Jones, Arthur L. (NAS) 128, 132, 136

Joseph, Sir Keith 370, 461, 476, 479, 497, 504, 617–18, 619, 628, 630, 631, 652

Grand Graffiti Dispute 484, 486

juvenile delinquency 71–72, 463–64

JWPSS (Joint Working Party on Salary Structure) 365–67, 619–20, 623, 625–26, 632, 644

Key Stage testing 701, 702–3, 732, 733, 734, 736, 738, 761–62, 767–68

Kinnock, Neil (Lab) 728, 729

Labour Relations Agency, Northern Ireland *see* LRA

Lamplugh, Suzy 507

Lancastrian Secondary Boys School, Chichester (1961) 147–48

LAS (Liverpool Association of Schoolmasters) 21, 67, 103, 118

Lawrence, Philip (St George's RC School, London) 505–7, 551

Layfield Inquiry (1974) 235, 332

LCC (London County Council) 8, 16, 20, 25, 56, 59, 77, 146, 181, 184, 194, 197, 344, 345

William Penn School 6, 106, 132–33, 144–46

leaving age *see* ROSLA

Legal Aid Fund (NAS) 34, 49, 51, 62, 63, 444–45

'Let Teachers Teach' (NASUWT) 788–89, 790–91, 792–96, 802

Lewis, Mary (UWT) 43, 431, 432, 434

Literacy Hour 796–97, 804

Littlewood, Maurice (NAS) 378, 481, 485

Liverpool Association of Schoolmasters *see* LAS

Lloyd George, David (Lib) 16, 26, 29, 185

Lloyd Williams, George (NAS) 39, 132, 140, 163, 207, 239–40, 341

LMS (Local Management of Schools) 370, 371, 372, 697, 698–99, 701, 702, 704, 713, 714, 719, 774–75

Lomas, Harold (NAS) 57–58

London Allowances 203, 209, 211, 264, 265, 268, 272–73, 616, 659, 689, 709, 724, 815, 838, 840

London County Council *see* LCC

Lowry, Sir Pat (ACAS) 463, 638, 639–40, 641–42, 644, 646, 651

LRA (Labour Relations Agency, Northern Ireland) 337

LSA (London Schoolmasters' Association) 7, 22–23, 27, 56, 59, 61, 80, 190–91, 192, 193–96, 209, 264, 276–77, 344–45

MacFarlane Report (1981) 458

MacGregor, John (Con) 701, 714, 715–16, 717–18, 719, 721–22, 750

main professional grade *see* MPG

Major, John (Con) 371, 372, 504–5, 535, 728, 729, 751, 759

Manchester LEA, Grand Graffiti Dispute 480–89

Manton Primary School, Worksop (1996) 524–32, 533–41, 546–47, 557, 558, 563

Martin, Ernest (NAS) 82, 84, 91

May Report (1931) 6, 66, 67, 68, 182, 188–89

May, Teresa (Con) 568

McAvoy, Doug (NUT) 363, 591, 666, 667, 668, 671, 683, 746, 795, 813–14, 824

McCarthy Report (1969) 408

McCrone Report (2000) 811, 822, 825–26, 831

McNair Report (1944) 86, 115, 180, 181, 201, 204, 206, 241, 267, 847

Meigh, Harry (NAS) 27, 183, 185, 186, 198, 203

Memorandum on Juvenile Delinquency (1938) 71–72

'Michael' (Manton Primary School) 524–29, 530, 531–32, 533, 534, 535–39, 540, 541, 546–47, 563

Miliband, David (New Lab) 836, 838, 846

Morris, Estelle (New Lab) 568, 570, 783, 786, 806, 813, 828, 832, 833, 834–35, 837

Morton, Bernard (NAS) 78–80, 94

MPG (main professional grade) 366, 619–20, 624, 625, 655, 663, 664, 666, 667, 685, 706

NAHT (National Association of Head Teachers) 8, 13, 44, 107, 115, 158, 268, 389

   ACAS Memorandum Agreement 685, 686

   Coventry Agreement 665, 669, 671, 672

   Elton Report 491, 492

   Grand Graffiti Dispute 482, 483

   'Let Teachers Teach' 791, 794

   Nottingham Agreement 680, 681

   Sacred Heart RC School 417, 423

NAMT (National Association of Men Teachers) 11–14, 19, 20, 21, 23, 25

NAS (National Association of Schoolmasters) 1–2, 9, 10, 14–16, 22–25, 29–34, 46, 48–53, 61–66, 68, 69–72, 74–80, 81–83, 86–88, 441–42

Ancillary Assistance in Schools 327–28

antisocial behaviour 465, 466–67, 469–70

Burnham Committee 165, 166, 167, 169–72, 174–75

Burnham representation 3, 112–14, 119–21, 124–26, 135–42, 143, 156–64, 847, 848, 849

Catch 'em Young project 476

Down County Secondary Schools 246, 351–52

Durham Dispute 246, 247–48, 397–409, 410

Educational Reconstruction 82, 84–85, 201

equal pay 5, 6, 8, 40, 121–22, 123–24, 130–31, 160–61, 240, 847, 848

Lancastrian Secondary Boys School 147–48

Lomas case 57–58

membership 61, 72, 93, 100, 112–13, 114, 119, 264, 437

Northern Ireland 334, 335–41

pensions 294, 295, 296, 297, 301, 307, 313

ROSLA 451–53

Safety and Health in Schools 356

Special Committee 'K' 126, 131, 142, 143, 144, 146, 149–50, 160, 162, 163–64

Staffing of Schools 329

Sunderland Case (1956) 98, 212, 225–27, 230–32, 848

Teacher Aides - Help or Substitutes 329

Transfer of Engagements 1, 43, 54, 70, 342, 433, 434–36, 437, 440, 446, 447

TSS 212–13, 217

TUC 374–76, 383–84

Wales 341–42

William Penn School 6, 106, 132–33, 144–46

NASUWT (National Association of Schoolmasters Union of Women Teachers) 1, 2, 3, 46, 179, 230, 270, 385–86, 441–49, 450, 575, 775–76

ACAS Memorandum Agreement 642–43, 644–47, 649, 654–55, 667–68

Action on Indiscipline 476

antisocial behaviour 566–69, 851–52

Burnham Committee 176–77, 360

Campaign on Workload 731, 732, 733–42, 769, 826–27

corporal punishment 478–79

Coventry Agreement 663–64, 665, 666–68, 669–70, 671–73, 674, 676–78

'Cover to Contract' 825, 827–28

Crossing the Threshold 819, 820

equal opportunities 446–49

extraneous duties 110, 362–64

Glaisdale School 509–16, 540

Grand Graffiti Dispute 480–89

Hebburn School 517–21

'Let Teachers Teach' 788–89, 790–91, 792–96, 802

Manton Primary School 524–32, 533–41, 546–47, 557, 558, 563

membership 3, 437–40, 774, 854, 861, 862

Northern Ireland 334, 335, 341

Nottingham Agreement 677, 679, 680–81

pensions 316–17, 319–22

pupil 'H' versus William Edwards School 575–78

pupil 'L' versus school 'J' 579–81, 582, 583, 595, 596, 598–603

pupil 'P' versus NASUWT 581, 582, 584–94, 595–98, 599, 603

pupil 'W' in school 'B' 578, 581, 582

refusal to teach 468–69, 470, 471, 473, 477, 571, 572–73

'Retreat from Authority' 326, 349, 464, 467, 541

Ridings School 524, 530, 539, 542–46, 547–51, 552–53, 554–57, 558–64, 779

Sacred Heart RC School 230, 352–53, 411–18, 419–26, 430

SCEA 439, 447

Scotland 342, 378, 439, 652

teacher training 456, 472–73

'Time for a Limit' 808–9, 810, 812, 817–18, 821, 822, 824, 826–27

Time for Standards 837, 838

Transfer of Engagements 1, 43, 54, 70, 342, 433, 434–36, 437, 440, 446, 447

Violence and Serious Disorder 477

Wales 342, 378

Wandsworth v NASUWT case 586, 730, 742–48, 749, 751–52, 753–54

Westminster Junior School 573–75

NAT (National Arbitration Tribunal) 75

NATE (National Association for the Teaching of English) 733, 734, 768–69

National Agreement on Raising Standards and Tackling Workload (2003/04) 329, 458, 772, 831, 835, 839, 840–41, 845, 853

National Association of Head Teachers see NAHT

National Association of Men Teachers see NAMT

National Association of Schoolmasters see NAS

National Association of Schoolmasters Union of Women Teachers *see* NASUWT

National Curriculum *see* NC

National Curriculum Council *see* NCC

National Economy Bill (1931) 189, 190

National Federation of Professional Workers *see* NFPW

National Foundation on Educational Research *see* NFER

National Provisional Minimum Scale 15, 183–84, 185

National Steering Group *see* NSG

National Union of Miners *see* NUM

National Union of Students *see* NUS

National Union of Teachers *see* NUT

National Union of Women Teachers *see* NUWT

NC (National Curriculum) 697–98, 699, 730–31, 734, 747, 748–49, 755–56, 757–58, 761, 766, 767, 798–99

NCC (National Curriculum Council) 705, 731, 751

negotiating rights 177, 393, 676, 677, 689, 693–94, 716–17, 718, 850

New Labour Government 565, 776, 779–80, 781, 783–84, 789–90

Fairness at Work 379–80

School Standards and Framework Bill 786, 797, 798–99

Social Partnership 3, 321–22, 772, 831, 839, 843–44, 845–46

Teachers-Meeting the Challenge of Change 800, 801–2, 803–4, 805–6, 817, 853

Newsom Report (1963) 327, 328

NFER (National Foundation on Educational Research) 347

NFPW (National Federation of Professional Workers) 374

Northern Ireland 281, 334–41, 380, 394, 696, 730, 784, 802, 821–22, 823

Houghton Committee 278, 281

INTO 334–35, 339, 340, 381, 823

'Let Teachers Teach' 802

'Time for a Limit' 821, 822

UTU 335, 340–41, 381, 823

Notional Fund 213–14, 258, 289, 291–92, 295, 298, 300–302, 306–9, 310, 313, 316–17, 318–19, 320–21, 621

Nottingham Agreement 675–76, 677–78, 679–83

NSG (National Steering Group) 609, 709, 727, 829, 831–33

NUM (National Union of Miners) 2, 96, 274, 378, 397, 624

NUS (National Union of Students) 382–83

NUT (National Union of Teachers) 1, 3, 5, 9–10, 29, 44, 46–47, 115, 820–21, 844, 845–46, 849, 850–51

    ACAS Memorandum Agreement 646, 650–51, 653, 654, 657–58, 660

    Burnham Committee 150–52, 167, 168, 169, 206–11, 250, 255, 260, 263

    Coventry Agreement 664–65, 666–67, 668–69, 670, 673, 674, 676–78, 679, 683

    Durham Dispute 402–3, 404

    equal pay 5, 6, 11, 13, 18, 65, 98, 123–24, 201

    Grand Graffiti Dispute 481, 483, 484, 485

    'Let Teachers Teach' 791, 794, 795

    membership 97–98, 119

    Nottingham Agreement 680–81

    Sacred Heart RC School 417

    'Test Boycott' 748, 755

    'Time for a Limit' 818

NUWT (National Union of Women Teachers) 7, 10, 44, 56, 76, 115–16, 122–23

Oath of Allegiance, Ireland 339–40

Office for Manpower Economics *see* OME

Ofsted (Office for Standards in Education) 503, 566, 756, 763, 770–71

O'Kane, Eamonn (NASUWT) 335, 715, 835–37, 839, 840, 841, 843, 844, 845

    Glaisdale School 511

    pupil 'P' versus NASUWT 597–98

O'Malley, Brian (Lab) 309–10

OME (Office for Manpower Economics) 788, 822

Operation Motorman, Ireland 340

Ordish, Frank (NAMT/NAS) 11–12, 13, 22, 31, 49

O'Sullivan, Monsignor Canon (Sacred Heart RC School) 416–17, 423, 426

PAT (Professional Association of Teachers) 46, 323, 441, 614, 771, 777, 785, 836

    ACAS Memorandum Agreement 650, 656, 663, 666, 667, 669, 674, 680, 686

    Burnham Committee 46, 614, 615, 635, 636, 642

    Grand Graffiti Dispute 482, 483

Patten, John (Con) 704, 730, 736, 741–42, 747, 748, 749, 751, 754, 755, 756, 759–61, 763, 766, 767, 768

pay negotiations *see* ACAS
Memorandum Agreement; Burnham
Committee; Coventry Agreement;
IAC; Nottingham Agreement; STRB

Pay Review Body 159, 707, 717,
720–21, 723, 724–25 *see also* STRB

Pearman, John 647, 663, 665, 666,
670–71, 673, 674, 678, 679, 680,
681, 683, 685, 688–89

Pelton Roseberry Comprehansive
School, Durham (1972) 468–69

pensions 1, 27, 28–29, 294–315, 316–
22, 373, 707, 780, 847–48

Notional Fund 213–14, 258, 289,
291–92, 295, 298, 300–302, 306–
9, 310, 313, 316–17, 318–19,
320–21, 621

superannuation contributions 98,
185, 186, 187, 193, 197, 212,
217, 218, 219–20, 221

TSS 197–98, 212–14, 216, 217,
218, 219, 289–93, 295–96, 305,
312, 315, 317, 322

Pensions (Increase) Act (1947) 213

Pensions (Increase) Act (1956) 295

Pensions (Increase) Act (1971) 301

performance related pay *see* PRP

Philip Lawrence Awards 506–7

'Physical Survey of Schools' (1991)
702, 725

Pile, Sir William (Con) 311, 414

Plowden, Lady Bridget Horatia 328

Plowden Report (1966) 327, 328–30

poll tax 370–71, 718, 723

Poole, Alan (NASUWT) 368–69, 618

Poundswick School, Manchester
(Grand Graffiti Dispute, 1985) 480–
89

PRC (premature retirement
compensation) 316, 318, 319–20

Prentice, Reg (Lab) 176, 274, 275,
276, 285, 384, 454

Sacred Heart RC School 422, 423

primary education 328–29, 348, 457–
58, 460, 711–12, 731, 734, 780, 851

Professional Association of Teachers
see PAT

Provisional Minimum Scale 15, 183–
84, 185

PRP (performance related pay) 712,
727, 728, 729, 773, 801, 804, 807,
809, 834

pupil behaviour *see* antisocial
behaviour; indiscipline; violence

pupil 'H' versus William Edwards
School (1999) 575–78

pupil 'L' versus school 'J' (2001) 579–
81, 582, 583, 595, 596, 598–603

pupil 'P' versus NASUWT (2001)
581, 582, 584–94, 595–98, 599, 603

pupil 'W' versus school 'B' (2000)
578, 581, 582

Puttnam, David 395, 805

Raising of the School Leaving Age (NAS, 1971) 452

Rampton Interim Report (1981) 459

reading 703, 796–97, 804

refusal to teach 468–69, 470, 471, 473, 477, 571, 572–73

    Glaisdale School 509–16, 540

    Grand Graffiti Dispute 480–89

    Hebburn School 517–21, 575

    Manton Primary School 524–32, 533–41, 546–47, 557, 558, 563

    pupil 'H' versus William Edwards School 575–78

    pupil 'L' versus school 'J' 579–81, 582, 583, 595, 596, 598–603

    pupil 'P' versus NASUWT 581, 582, 584–94, 595–98, 599, 603

    pupil 'W' in school 'B' 578, 581, 582

    Ridings School 524, 530, 539, 542–46, 547–51, 552–53, 554–57, 558–64, 779

    Westminster Junior School 573–75

religious education 90, 91, 697

religious schools 44, 90–91

Remuneration of Teachers Act *see* RTA

'Retreat from Authority' (NASUWT) 326, 349, 464, 467, 541 *see also* refusal to teach

Retreat from Authority (NASUWT, 1976) 467, 473–75

Revenue Support Grant *see* RSG

Rewards and Incentives *see* RIG

Rice, Jim (NAS) 24, 78, 79–80

Riddell, Fred (Nottinghamshire LEA) 513

    Glaisdale School 513, 514, 515, 540

    Manton Primary School 528, 530–31, 535, 536, 537, 539, 540–41

The Ridings School, Halifax (1996) 524, 530, 539, 542–46, 547–51, 552–53, 554–57, 558–64, 779

RIG (Rewards and Incentives) 843, 844, 845

Robbins Report (1960) 327

Robens Report (1972) 356

Rogers, Sue (NASUWT) 371–72, 447, 725, 749

Roman Catholic VA schools 91

ROSLA (Raising of the School Leaving Age) 41–42, 52, 61, 68, 94, 97, 328, 450–53, 470

'Roy' (Glaisdale School) 509–12, 513–14, 515

Royle, Peter (NASUWT) 369

RSG (Revenue Support Grant) 367, 368, 620

RST (Royal Society of Teachers) 388

RTA (Remuneration of Teachers Act, 1965) 166, 168, 176, 242, 243, 363, 364, 676, 686

Rushworth, Bert (NAS) 104, 106, 132, 137–38, 153, 158

   Burnham Committee 123, 126, 134, 136–37, 159–60, 163, 164, 239

   equal pay 121–22, 123, 125, 848

   Sunderland Case 232

Ruskin College speech (Callaghan, 1976) 453, 454, 851

Russell, A.H. (NAS) 54, 69

Sacred Heart RC School Dispute, Teesside (1972-75) 230, 352–53, 411–18, 419–26, 430

Safety and Health in Schools (NAS, 1969) 356

salaries *see* Burnham Committee; Education Act (1944); equal pay; Houghton Committee; IAC; London Allowances; STRB; structured salary scales

SATs (Standard Attainment Tasks) 703, 725, 731, 732, 733, 734, 735–36, 741, 749–51, 756–62, 765

   boycott 438, 734, 735–41, 744–49, 753–55, 756–58, 759–61

   Key Stage testing 701, 702–3, 732, 733, 734, 736, 738, 761–62, 767–68

SCAA (Schools Curriculum and Assessment Authority) 751, 764, 767, 768, 770, 771–72

SCEA (Service Childrens' Education Authority) 439, 447

School Examinations and Assessment Council *see* SEAC

school meals 101, 102–4, 105–6, 107–11, 225, 226, 354

   Sunderland Case 98, 212, 225–27, 230–32, 848

School Meals Agreement (1968) 110, 233, 337, 354

School Standards and Framework Bill (1997) 786, 797, 798–99

Schoolmaster in the EEC, The (FOBAS) 273, 279

Schools Council (1963) 332–33

Schools Curriculum and Assessment Authority *see* SCAA

Scotland 139, 237, 389, 609, 672, 675, 699, 802, 811

   Dunblane Primary School 507

   EIS 139, 381, 439, 609, 628, 651, 811

   Houghton Committee 281

   McCrone Report 822, 825–26

   NASUWT 342, 378, 439, 652

   SSA 68, 68–69, 172–73, 301, 307, 342

   UWT 40

Scott Inquiry 316–17

Scott, John (NAS) 93, 281, 335, 336, 338, 339, 341, 469–70

Scottish Negotiating Committee for Teachers *see* SNCT

SEAC (School Examinations and Assessment Council) 700, 731, 741, 749–50, 751, 757

Second World War 73–78, 86, 102

secondary education 52–53, 94, 98, 112, 459–60, 780, 851

Secondary Heads Association *see* SHA

Security in Schools Working Party 506, 507–8

Sedgefield Comprehansive School, Durham (1975) 471

Service Childrens' Education Authority *see* SCEA

SHA (Secondary Heads Association) 45, 566, 754, 755, 819–20

    ACAS Memorandum Agreement 686, 687, 689

    Coventry Agreement 665, 666, 667, 669, 671, 672, 673

    Grand Graffiti Dispute 482, 483

    'Let Teachers Teach' 794, 795

    Nottingham Agreement 680

'Sharon' (The Ridings School) 542–43, 544, 545, 546, 547

Shephard, Gillian (Con) 320, 373, 752, 752–53, 768, 769, 770, 773, 775, 777, 778, 782

    Glaisdale School 512, 513, 515

    Manton Primary School 527–28, 529–30, 532–34, 535, 540–41

    Ridings School 554, 561

Short, Ted (Lab) 94–95, 252, 253, 306, 324–26, 390, 391, 392

    Durham Dispute 402, 406, 407

Simons, Ron (NAS) 54–55, 57, 63, 65, 74, 131, 132–33, 299–300

Sixth Form Colleges 774, 824

Skeavington, Christine (UWT) 432, 433–34, 435

Skidelsky, Lord 730, 741, 749–50, 757

Smith, Jacqui (New Lab) 567–68

Smith, Tom (NAS) 5, 61–62, 72, 132, 416

Smithies, Fred (NASUWT) 378, 381, 450, 459, 460, 470–71, 491, 677, 680, 706, 719, 720

    ACAS Memorandum Agreement 645, 646, 648, 688

    Grand Graffiti Dispute 481, 484, 487, 488

Smyth, Arthur (NAS) 261–62, 302

SNCT (Scottish Negotiating Committee for Teachers) 826

Social Contract 284, 285, 287–88, 604, 605

Social Partnership 3, 242, 321–22, 772, 778–80, 781, 819–20, 831, 835, 839, 843–44, 845–46, 853

Social Security Act (1987) 318

South Tyneside LEA (Hebburn School, 1996) 517, 519, 520, 521, 575

Special Committee 'K' (NAS) 126, 131, 142, 143, 144, 146, 149–50, 160, 162, 163–64

Special Education Act (1981) 497

Spence-Young, Hazel 498, 499–500, 501–2

SPS (social priority schools) 604–5

SSA (Scottish Schoolmasters Association) 68–69, 172–73, 301, 307, 342

St Mary's High, Northampton 470–71

Staffing of Schools, The (NAS, 1974) 329

Standard Attainment Tasks *see* SATs

Standards and Workload Agreement (2003) 835, 839, 840, 843

Standards for School Premises Regulations (1959) 355

STAR (Student Teacher Achievement Ratios) 777

Stewart, Michael (Lab) 169–70, 171, 172–73, 174, 224

Stott, Harry (NAS/NASUWT) 352, 377, 383–84

STRB (School Teachers' Review Body) 702, 726–28, 729, 773–74, 777–78, 780, 789, 802–3, 814–15, 820–21, 833–35, 840, 841–42, 843–45, 850

structured salary scales 43, 158, 178, 206, 241, 253, 256, 260–61, 265, 268, 271

student teachers 66, 68, 382–83, 438

substitute teachers 329, 839

Sunderland Case (1956) 98, 212, 225–27, 230–32, 848

Sunderland LEA (Sunderland Case, 1956) 98, 212, 225–27, 230–32, 848

Superannuation Bill (1956) 218, 220, 223, 224, 226, 228

superannuation contributions 98, 185, 186, 187, 193, 197, 212, 217, 218, 219–20, 221

Superannuation Working Party 214, 215, 216–17

support staff 832, 838

Swann Report (1985) 459

Task Group on Assessment and Testing *see* TGAT

Taylor Committee (1977) 456–57

Teacher Aides - Help or Substitutes (NAS) 329

teacher assessment 806–7, 815–17

teacher contracts 286, 354–64, 366, 573, 663–64, 675–76, 731, 773–74, 809, 828–30, 838

'Time for a Limit' 808–9, 810, 812, 817–18, 821, 822, 824, 826–27

teacher training 81, 84, 95, 97, 99, 327, 330–31, 455–56, 472–73, 570, 704

Teachers - Meeting the Challenge of Change (1998) 373, 800, 801–2, 803–4, 805–6, 817, 853

Teachers' Negotiating Group *see* TNG

Teachers' Pay and Conditions Acts *see* TPC Act

Teachers' Registration Council 387–88

Teachers' Superannuation Act (1918) 16–17, 27, 28, 290

Teachers' Superannuation Act (1922) 27, 28, 290

Teachers' Superannuation Act (1924) 291

Teachers' Superannuation Act (1925) 291

Teachers' Superannuation Scheme *see* TSS

Teachers' Superannuation Working Party *see* TSWP

Teaching and Higher Education Act (1998) 394

Teaching Awards 805

Teesside LEA (renamed Cleveland LEA)

Sacred Heart RC School 230, 352–53, 411–15, 416, 417–18, 419

'Test Boycott' (NASUWT) 438, 730–31, 744–49, 753–55, 756–58, 759–61

TGAT (Task Group on Assessment and Testing) 750

Thatcher Government 254, 318, 364, 385, 497, 572, 624, 720–22, 730

Thatcher, Margaret 110, 310, 311, 314, 345–46, 391, 392, 722, 750

Thompson, J.A.C. (NAS) 236, 237, 342

Thornton, Malcolm (Con) 723, 724, 757

Threshold payments 284, 809, 812, 815–17, 819–20, 822–24, 834, 840, 844, 845, 853

'Time for a Limit' (NASUWT) 808–9, 810, 812, 817–18, 821, 822, 824, 826–27

Time for Standards: Reforming the School Workforce (NASUWT, 2002) 837, 838

TNG (Teachers' Negotiating Group) 707

Tomlinson, George (Lab) 117

Tomlinson, John 394

Tomlinson, Mike (HMI) 555–56

'Tottenham Case' (1931) 56

TPC Act (Teachers' Pay and Conditions, 1987) 689–90, 691, 693, 694, 733

TPC Act (Teachers' Pay and Conditions, 1991) 723, 724–25, 726, 733

Trade Union and Labour Relations Act *see* TULRA

Trade Union Congress *see* TUC

Transfer of Engagements 1, 43, 54, 70, 342, 433, 434–36, 437, 440, 446, 447

Trueman, Mr (Sacred Heart RC School) 417, 425–26, 427–28

TSS (Teachers' Superannuation Scheme) 197–98, 212–14, 216, 217, 218, 219, 289–93, 295–96, 305, 312, 315, 317, 322

TSWP (Teachers' Superannuation Working Party) 297, 299, 300–302, 303–4, 305–6, 307, 312–13, 317

TUC (Trade Union Congress) 3, 374–76, 377, 378–79, 380, 383–84, 420–21, 439

TULRA (Trade Union and Labour Relations Act, 1974) 355, 359, 474, 597

Upper Pay Spine 815, 835, 840, 842, 844

UTU (Ulster Teachers' Union) 335, 340–41, 381, 823

UWT (Union of Women Teachers) 1, 2, 35–36, 37–43, 46, 262, 264, 288, 324, 332, 367, 429–36, 849, 852

career teachers 429, 430, 432, 434, 435–36

Durham Dispute 399, 407

Northern Ireland 40, 340

pensions 306, 307, 309, 313, 314, 315

ROSLA 451, 453

Sacred Heart RC School 412, 413, 414, 415, 418, 419, 420, 421, 423, 425, 426, 430

Transfer of Engagements 1, 43, 54, 70, 342, 433, 434–36, 437, 440, 446, 447

VA (voluntary aided) schools 90, 91, 423

Van Straubenzee, William (Con) 306

violence 466, 467–69, 474, 476–78, 504–5, 507–8

Elton Report 477, 490–94, 504

Violence and Serious Disorder (NASUWT, 1986) 477

voluntary duties *see* extraneous duties

Wakefield, Bernard (NAS) 326, 420

Wales 341–42, 378, 394, 794, 803, 834

Walton, Simon 733–34, 742, 743, 744

WAMG (Workload and Management Group) 839, 843, 845, 846

Wandsworth v NASUWT case (1993) 586, 730, 742–48, 749, 751–52, 753–54

war bonuses 80, 183, 199, 200

Warren, Arthur E. (NAS) 15–16, 49, 50, 63, 64, 72, 77–78, 388

WCOTP (World Confederation of Organisations of the Teaching Profession) 381–82

Weaver Report (1970) 391–92

West Ham Men Teachers 19–20

Westminster Junior School, Birmingham (1993) 573–75

Weston, A.C.E. 'Tubby' (NAS) 325

William Edwards School (1999) 575–78

William Penn School, Dulwich (1961) 6, 106, 132–33, 144–46

William Tyndale Junior School, Islington (1974) 454, 457, 465, 851

Williams, Brian (NASUWT) 714, 715

Williams, Shirley (Lab) 362, 368, 456, 457, 606, 608

Wilson Government (1964-70) 249, 258, 391, 451

'Winter of Discontent' 368

Wood Report (1973) 415–20

Wood, Sir John 651, 653–55, 663, 665, 666, 669, 679, 681, 684, 685

Woodhead, Chris (HMI) 504, 559, 567, 703–4, 770, 771–72, 776

Wordie, Sir John 176, 272, 607, 620, 647, 648, 659, 688, 690

Workload and Management Group see WAMG

workloads 773, 780, 784, 788–89, 807–8, 822, 826–28, 831–33, 836–37, 838–39

World Confederation of Organisations of the Teaching Profession see WCOTP

Wright, Mavis (UWT) 36, 37, 40–41

Yaffe, Pennie (UWT) 43, 264, 429–30, 432–33, 434

Zacchaeus Centre 569–70

Nigel de Gruchy,
NASUWT General Secretary 1990-2002

Nigel de Gruchy was born in 1943 in the Channel Island of Jersey under the Occupation by Nazi Germany. He was educated at the De La Salle College and went up to Reading University, graduating in Economics and Philosophy in 1965. He then spent three years working in Spain and France where living in the Latin Quarter in Paris he witnessed the Student Riots and General Strike of 1968 and met his American wife Judy. They came to London in 1969 when he began a ten year period teaching economics at St. Joseph's Academy, an ILEA grammar school that became a comprehensive in the mid-1970s. He became "hooked" on teacher trade union affairs, rising rapidly through the ranks of the NASUWT to become general secretary from 1990-2002, having been appointed the deputy in 1983. He served on the TUC General Council for 13 years, becoming its President for 2002-03.

Lightning Source UK Ltd.
Milton Keynes UK
UKHW020646190722
406066UK00005B/527